2021
Guidebook to
NEW YORK
TAXES

Wolters Kluwer Editorial Staff Publication

Editors . . . . Brian Nudelman and Brian Plunkett

Production Coordinator . . . . Govardhan L

Production Editors . . . . Darshan. C and Latha. L

This publication is designed to provide accurate and authoritative information in regard to the subject matter covered. It is sold with the understanding that the publisher is not engaged in rendering legal, accounting or other professional service. If legal advice or other expert assistance is required, the services of a competent professional person should be sought. All views expressed in this publication are those of the author and not necessarily those of the publisher or any other person.

ISBN: 978-0-8080-5511-2

2700 Lake Cook Road
Riverwoods, IL 60015
800 344 3734
CCHCPELink.com

No claim is made to original government works; however, within this publication, the following are subject to CCH Incorporated's copyright: (1) the gathering, compilation, and arrangement of such government materials; (2) the magnetic translation and digital conversion of data, if applicable; (3) the historical, statutory and other notes and references; and (4) the commentary and other materials.

Do not send returns to the above address. If for any reason you are not satisfied with your book purchase, it can easily be returned within 30 days of shipment. Please go to *support.cch.com/returns* to initiate your return. If you require further assistance with your return, please call: (800) 344-3734 M-F, 8 a.m. – 6 p.m. CT.

Printed in the United States of America

FSC
www.fsc.org

MIX
From responsible
sources
FSC® C099992

PREFACE

This *Guidebook* gives a general picture of the taxes imposed by the state of New York and the general property tax levied by the local governments. All 2020 legislative amendments received as of press time are reflected, and references to New York and federal laws are to the laws as of the date of publication of this book.

The emphasis is on the law applicable to the filing of income tax returns in 2021 for the 2020 tax year. However, if legislation has made changes effective after 2020, we have tried to note this also, with an indication of the effective date to avoid confusion.

The taxes of major interest—income and sales and use—are discussed in detail. Other New York taxes are summarized, with particular emphasis on application, exemptions, returns, and payment.

Throughout the *Guidebook,* tax tips are highlighted to help practitioners avoid pitfalls and use the tax laws to their best advantage.

The *Guidebook* is designed as a quick reference work, describing the general provisions of the various tax laws, regulations, and administrative practices. It is useful to tax practitioners, businesspersons, and others who prepare or file New York returns or who are required to deal with New York taxes.

The *Guidebook* is not designed to eliminate the necessity of referring to the law and regulations for answers to complicated problems, nor is it intended to take the place of detailed reference works such as the CCH NEW YORK TAX REPORTS. With this in mind, specific references to the publisher's New York and federal tax products are inserted in some paragraphs. By assuming some knowledge of federal taxes, the *Guidebook* is able to provide a concise, readable treatment of New York taxes that will supply a complete answer to most questions and will serve as a time-saving aid where it does not provide the complete answer.

SCOPE OF THE BOOK

This *Guidebook* is designed to do three things:

1. Give a general picture of the impact and pattern of all taxes levied by the state of New York and the general property tax levied by local governmental units.

2. Provide a readable quick-reference work for the personal income tax and the tax on corporate income. As such, it explains briefly what the New York law provides and indicates whether the New York provision is the same as federal law.

3. Analyze and explain the differences, in most cases, between New York and federal law.

HIGHLIGHTS OF 2020 NEW YORK TAX CHANGES

The most important 2020 New York tax changes received by press time are noted in the "Highlights of 2020 New York Tax Changes" section of the *Guidebook*. This useful reference gives the practitioner up-to-the-minute information on changes in tax legislation.

LOCAL TAXES

The *Guidebook* also features a chapter on New York City taxes. Included in this chapter are the principal features of the New York City personal income tax on residents. Persons subject to tax, computation, basis of tax, and rate of tax are covered.

FINDERS

The practitioner may find the information wanted by consulting the general Table of Contents at the beginning of the *Guidebook*.

November 2020

CONTENTS

Paragraph   **Page**

       Highlights of 2020 New York Tax Changes 11

CORPORATE INCOME

10-050	Federal/Multistate Issues	21
10-200	Business Entities	30
10-325	Regulated Industries	51
10-375	Rates	52
10-500	Taxable Income Computation	56
11-500	Allocation and Apportionment	74
12-000	Credits.	98

PERSONAL INCOME

15-050	Federal/Multistate Issues	103
15-100	Taxpayers	106
15-150	Special Taxpayers	117
15-200	Estates and Trusts	124
15-250	Filing Thresholds	130
15-300	Filing Status.	131
15-350	Rates	131
15-500	Taxable Income Computation	133
16-000	Taxable Income Computation—Additions	140
16-200	Taxable Income Computation—Subtractions	146
16-500	Sourcing Rules	159
16-600	Withholding	177
16-800	Credits.	188

PROPERTY

20-100	Taxability of Property and Persons	191
20-400	Rates	228
20-500	Exemptions	229
20-600	Valuation, Assessment, and Equalization	230
20-750	Payment, Collection of Taxes	233
20-800	Credits, Abatements, Refunds, Incentives	237
20-900	Taxpayer Rights and Remedies	239

MISCELLANEOUS TAXES AND FEES

32-220	Unrelated Business Income Tax—Organizations Subject to Tax	249
32-230	Unrelated Business Income Tax--Exemptions	249
32-240	Unrelated Business Income Tax--Basis of Tax	250
32-250	Unrelated Business Income Tax--Allocation and Apportionment.	251

Paragraph   **Page**

32-260   Unrelated Business Income Tax--Rate of Tax   252
35-000   Health Facility Tax   253
35-050   Taxicab Trip Tax   254
35-100   Waterfront Commission Gross Payroll Tax   256
35-150   Yonkers Income Tax Surcharge on Residents   257
35-200   Yonkers Earnings Tax on Nonresidents   258
35-250   Medical Marijuana Tax   259
35-275   Opioid Excise Tax   259
35-300   Gaming and Wagering Taxes   261
35-325   Congestion Surcharge   263
35-350   Transportation Network Company Services
          Assessment   266
37-000   Alcoholic Beverages   267
37-050   Document Recording Tax   268
37-100   Motor Vehicles   332
37-150   Environmental Taxes and Fees   332

UNCLAIMED PROPERTY

37-350   Unclaimed Property   337

MOTOR FUELS

40-000   Motor Fuels   341

CIGARETTES, TOBACCO PRODUCTS

55-000   Cigarettes, Tobacco Products   367

SALES AND USE

60-000   Introduction   389
60-100   Rates   404
60-200   Taxability of Persons and Transactions   406
61-000   Exemptions   575
61-100   Basis of Tax   583
61-200   Returns, Payments, and Records   585
61-600   Taxpayer Remedies   612
61-700   Local Taxes   616

TRANSPORTATION AND TRANSMISSION COMPANIES

80-000   Transportation and Transmission Companies   625

TAX ON FURNISHING OF UTILITY SERVICES

80-200   Tax on Furnishing of Utility Services   635

TELECOMMUNICATION SERVICES PROVIDERS

80-400   Telecommunication Services Providers   639

LOCAL UTILITY TAXES

80-500   Local Utility Taxes   649

Paragraph   **Page**

INSURANCE

88-000   Insurance   651

PRACTICE AND PROCEDURE

89-100   Returns Filing and Payment of Tax   669
89-130   Audits   694
89-160   Collection of Tax   698
89-200   Interest and Penalties   710
89-220   Taxpayer Rights and Remedies   725

NEW YORK CITY CORPORATE INCOME

505-200   NYC Corporate Income Taxpayers and Rates   751
505-400   NYC Corporate Income Computation of Tax   756
506-500   NYC Allocation and Apportionment   783
507-000   NYC Credits   795

NEW YORK CITY BANKS

510-200   NYC Banks Income Taxpayers and Rates   807
510-400   NYC Banks Computation of Income   810
510-600   NYC Allocation and Apportionment   819
510-800   NYC Credits   823

NEW YORK CITY PERSONAL INCOME TAX ON RESIDENTS

515-000   NYC Personal Income Tax on Residents   829
515-200   NYC Taxpayers and Rates   829
515-400   NYC Personal Income Tax Computation   839
516-400   NYC Credits Against Tax   840
516-600   NYC Personal Income Tax Withholding   843

NEW YORK CITY UNINCORPORATED BUSINESS TAX

519-001   NYC Unincorporated Business Tax   845
519-100   NYC Unincorporated Business Taxpayers and Rates   845
519-200   NYC Unincorporated Business Tax Computation of
           Income   849
519-300   NYC Unincorporated Business Tax Exemptions   860
519-350   NYC Unincorporated Business Tax Allocation and
           Apportionment   862
519-400   NYC Unincorporated Business Tax Credits   867

NEW YORK CITY PROPERTY

520-000   NYC Introduction   869
520-100   NYC Taxability of Property and Persons   870
520-400   NYC Rates   902
520-600   NYC Valuation, Assessment, and Equalization   903
520-750   NYC Payment, Collection of Taxes   905

Paragraph   **Page**

NEW YORK CITY HOTEL OCCUPANCY TAX

531-001   NYC Hotel Occupancy Tax   911
531-010   NYC Hotel Occupancy Tax Exemptions   915
531-020   NYC Hotel Occupancy Tax Basis   917
531-030   NYC Hotel Occupancy Tax Rate   920
531-040   NYC Hotel Occupancy Tax License   922
531-050   NYC Hotel Occupancy Tax Reports   923
531-060   NYC Hotel Occupancy Tax Collection   926
531-080   NYC Hotel Occupancy Taxpayer Remedies   927

NEW YORK CITY COMMERCIAL RENT OR OCCUPANCY TAX

532-100   NYC Commercial Rent or Occupancy Tax   929
532-200   NYC Commercial Rent or Occupancy Tax--
            Exemptions   931
532-300   NYC Commercial Rent or Occupancy Tax
            Computation   935
532-400   NYC Commercial Rent or Occupancy Tax Credits . .   943
532-500   NYC Commercial Rent or Occupancy Tax Returns,
            Records and Payments   943

NEW YORK CITY ALCOHOLIC BEVERAGE TAXES

535-100   NYC Alcoholic Beverage Taxes   947

NEW YORK CITY TAXICAB LICENSE TRANSFER TAX

536-001   NYC Taxicab License Transfer Tax   949
536-100   NYC Taxicab License Transfer Tax Exemption   949
536-200   NYC Taxicab License Transfer Tax Rate and Basis .   949
536-300   NYC Taxicab License Transfer Tax Returns   950
536-400   NYC Taxicab License Transfer Tax Collection   950

NEW YORK CITY MOTOR VEHICLES

550-001   NYC Motor Vehicles.   951

NEW YORK CITY TOBACCO

555-100   NYC Tobacco Tax Rates and Products Subject to Tax   959
555-200   NYC Tobacco Tax Exemptions   962
555-500   NYC Tobacco Tax License   963
555-600   NYC Tobacco Tax Returns   964
555-800   NYC Tobacco Tax Collection   966
555-810   NYC Tobacco Tax Penalties   969

NEW YORK CITY REAL PROPERTY TRANSFER TAX

556-100   NYC Persons And Conveyances--Subject to Tax . . .   971
556-200   NYC Real Property Transfer Tax--Exemptions   974
556-300   NYC Real Property Transfer Tax--Rate and Basis . .   979
556-400   NYC Real Property Transfer Tax--Returns   982

Paragraph   **Page**

556-600   NYC Real Property Transfer Tax--Collection   984

NEW YORK CITY MORTGAGE RECORDING TAX

557-001   NYC Mortgage Recording Tax   987
557-100   NYC Taxpayer and Rates   987
557-150   Mortgage Recording Tax Computation   988

NEW YORK CITY SALES AND USE

560-000   NYC Sales and Use Taxes...................   989
560-040   NYC Sales and Use Taxes Penalties   998

NEW YORK CITY UTILITIES

580-100   Utilities Subject to Tax   999
580-200   NYC Utilities Tax Exemptions................   1000
580-300   NYC Utilities Tax Rate and Basis   1000
580-500   NYC Utilities Tax Credits   1004

NEW YORK CITY INSURANCE

585-100   NYC Insurance Taxpayers and Rates...........   1005
585-200   NYC Insurance Tax Computation   1005

NEW YORK CITY PRACTICE AND PROCEDURE

589-050   NYC Administration of Taxes   1007
589-100   NYC Return Filing and Payment of Tax   1010
589-130   NYC Audits   1017
589-160   NYC Collection of Tax   1019
589-200   NYC Interest and Penalties   1025
589-220   NYC Taxpayer Rights and Remedies   1033

Topical Index   1043

HIGHLIGHTS OF 2020 NEW YORK TAX CHANGES

The most important late 2019 and 2020 tax changes received by press time are noted below.

Multiple Taxes
(See also specific tax headings below)

• *Enacted Budget Extends and Revises Credits, Makes Other Changes*

Enacted as part of New York's 2020-21 budget package, S.B. 7509 contains a variety of personal income, corporate franchise, property, and other tax changes, including those detailed below. (S.B. 7509, Laws 2020, delivered to governor April 3, 2020, effective on signature or as noted; *Memorandum in Support,* New York Division of the Budget)

Debt collection. The law extends for five years, until April 1, 2025, the tax commissioner's authority to (1) use the financial institution data match system for collection of fixed and final tax debts, and (2) serve income executions (wage garnishments) on individual tax debtors and, if necessary, on their employers, without the necessity of filing a warrant.

Hire-A-Veteran Credit. The law extends the credit received for hiring a veteran for an additional year, through tax years beginning before 2022.

Oil and Gas Fee. The law extends the expiration date of the property tax schedule of fees to recover the cost of setting unit of production values for the gas and oil industry to March 31, 2024.

Long-Term Care Insurance Credit. The law amends the long-term care insurance credit under the personal income tax to cap the credit amount at $1,500 and to limit eligibility to taxpayers with New York adjusted gross income of less than $250,000. The amendments apply to taxable years beginning on or after January 1, 2020.

Earned Income Credit and Standard Deduction. The law requires the tax department to (1) compute and issue an earned income credit when it discovers a taxpayer is eligible for the credit but did not claim it, and (2) apply the standard deduction instead of the itemized deduction elected by the taxpayer when the standard deduction is greater than the allowable itemized deductions.

Tobacco Products Tax. The law clarifies that the "wholesale price" for tobacco products tax purposes is the actual amount paid by the distributor, whether paid to a manufacturer or some other entity, effective October 1, 2020.

Cigarette Tax Enforcement. The law enhances cigarette tax enforcement and licensing penalties against retail dealers and affiliated persons who sell unstamped or unlawfully stamped cigarettes, effective September 1, 2020. The law also authorizes the Department of Taxation and Finance to suspend or revoke a retail dealer's and affiliated person's sales tax certificate of authority when its registration to sell cigarettes has been suspended or revoked, effective September 1, 2020.

Alcoholic Beverage Tax. The law eliminates the current alcoholic beverage tax rate of 1 cent per liter tax on liquor containing less than 2% of alcohol by volume, effective June 1, 2020.

Excelsior Jobs Credit and Green Projects. The law amends excelsior jobs program provisions to add statutory caps for the years 2025 through 2029, set at $200 million per year. No tax credits may be allowed for taxable years beginning on or after January 1, 2040 (previously, 2030).

In addition, the credit is enhanced for green projects. The existing jobs credit is increased from up to 6.85% for traditional projects to up to 7.5% for green projects. The excelsior investment tax credit is increased from 2% of the cost of the qualified investment for traditional projects to 5% if the participant is engaging in a green project. The excelsior research and development credit cap is increased from 6% to 8% of the research and development expenditures attributable to activities conducted in New York if the project is a green project.

Film Tax Credits. Film credits are extended for one year, through 2025, and various revisions are made. The amount of the empire state film production credit is reduced from 30% to 25%. The law also reduces the post production credit from 30% to 25% for qualified films produced at qualified post production facilities located within the Metropolitan Commuter Transportation District and from 35% to 30% for qualified films produced at qualified post production facilities located elsewhere in the state.

In addition, the law excludes from the term "qualified film" an episode of a television series. It also requires, for the film production credit, that a qualified film, other than a television pilot, must have a minimum budget of $1 million if the majority of principal photography shooting days for the qualified film are shot in the counties of Westchester, Rockland, Nassau, or Suffolk, or the five New York City boroughs, and have a minimum budget of $250,000 if the majority of principal photography shooting days are shot in other counties of the state. Finally, variety entertainment, variety sketch, and variety talk programs, other than relocated television productions, are excluded from the definition of a "qualified film." Series that were conditionally eligible prior to April 1, 2020, continue to be eligible, provided that they remain in continuous production and continually apply for each season.

STAR. The law allows an extension of the enrollment period for the STAR income verification program (IVP). It also allows checks to be sent to qualified late enrollees in an amount equal to the difference between the school tax bill that the property owner actually received and the school tax bill that the property owner would have received had the enrollment been timely.

• *Enacted Budget Extends Various Tax Authorizations and Provisions for Three Years*

Enacted as part of New York's 2020-21 budget package, S.B. 7508 extends various sales and use, mortgage recording, real estate transfer, and property tax authorizations and provisions for three years. (Ch. 58 (S.B. 7508), Laws 2020, effective April 3, 2020, except as noted)

Authorizations To Impose Additional Local Sales And Use Taxes. Authorizations for the following counties to impose additional local sales and use taxes at the indicated rates have been extended for three years until November 30, 2023: Albany (1%); Allegany (1.5%); Broome (1%); Cattaraugus (1%); Cayuga (1%); Chautauqua (1%); Chemung (1%); Chenango (1%); Clinton (1%); Columbia (1%); Cortland (1%); Delaware (1%); Dutchess (0.75%); Erie (1% and 0.75%); Essex (1%); Franklin (1%); Fulton (1%); Genesee (1%); Greene (1%); Hamilton (1%); Herkimer (1% and 0.25%); Jefferson (1%); Lewis (1%); Livingston (1%); Madison (1%); Monroe (1%); Montgomery (1%); Nassau (0.75% and 0.5%); Niagara (1%); Oneida (1% and 0.75%); Onondaga (1%); Ontario (0.125% and 0.375%); Orange (0.75%); Orleans (1%); Oswego (1%); Otsego (1%); Putnam (1%); Rensselaer (1%); Rockland (0.625% and 0.375%); St. Lawrence (1%); Schenectady (0.5%); Schoharie (1%); Schuyler (1%); Seneca (1%); Steuben (1%); Suffolk (1%); Sullivan (0.5% and 0.5%); Tioga (1%); Tompkins (0.5%); Ulster (1%); Wayne (1%); Westchester (1%); Wyoming (1%); and Yates (1%).

In addition, authorizations for the following cities to impose additional local sales and use taxes at the indicated rates have been extended until November 30, 2023: New Rochelle (1%); Oswego (1%); and Yonkers (0.5%).

Authorizations To Impose Local Occupancy Taxes. Authorizations for the following counties to impose local occupancy taxes have been extended until December 31, 2023: Albany; Nassau; and Suffolk. In addition, authorization for Chautauqua County to impose a local occupancy tax has been extended until November 30, 2023.

Exemptions For Certain Purchases Related To New Commercial Office Space. The sales and use tax exemptions for certain purchases of tangible personal property and services related to new commercial office space leases (as opposed to ground leases) of 10 years or more have been extended for three years.

Authorizations To Impose Local Mortgage Recording Taxes. Authorizations for the following counties to impose local mortgage recording taxes have been extended until the indicated dates: Albany (December 1, 2023); Cortland (December 1, 2023); Fulton (November 30, 2023); Genesee (November 1, 2023); Greene (December 1, 2023); Hamilton (December 1, 2023); Herkimer (December 1, 2023); Schoharie (December 1, 2023); Steuben (December 1, 2023); Warren (December 1, 2023); and Yates (December 1, 2023).

In addition, authorization for the city of Yonkers to impose a local mortgage recording tax is extended until August 31, 2023.

Authorization To Impose Local Real Estate Transfer Tax. Authorization for Columbia County to impose a local real estate transfer tax is extended until December 31, 2023.

Property Tax Abatement For Solar Electric Generating Systems And Electric Energy Storage. The property tax abatements for the construction of solar electric generating systems and electric energy storage in certain buildings in New York City are extended until January 1, 2024.

Expiration Date Of New York City Sales and Use Tax On Certain Services. The expiration date of the New York City 4.5% sales and use tax imposed on credit rating and credit reporting services and certain personal services, such as beauty, barbering, hair restoring, manicuring, pedicuring, electrolysis, massage, and health salon services, is extended through November 30, 2023.

• *ECET Election Revocation Allowed, Certain Property Tax Exemptions and Abatements Amended*

New York has amended the employer compensation expense tax provisions to allow for revocation of the employer election. Specifically, if an employer determines that the election was in error and the employer does not wish to participate in the program for the calendar year and has taken no action to comply, the employer may revoke the election to participate in the program. For calendar year 2020, revocation of the employer election may be made on or before April 15, 2020. For calendar years beginning 2021 and later, revocation of the employer election must be made no later than January 15th of the immediately succeeding calendar year after the employer election was made.

A property owner whose primary residence is subject to past-due property taxes will not be allowed to receive a STAR credit or STAR exemption unless the past-due property taxes are paid in full on or before a specified date.

In addition, no property tax abatement benefits can be granted for construction work on real property where any portion of such property is to be used as a self-storage facility. This applies to projects for which the first building permit is issued after July 1, 2020, or if no permit is required, for which construction commences after July 1, 2020. (Ch. 56 (S.B. 7506), Laws 2020, effective April 3, 2020, applicable as noted)

- *Tax Preparers Allowed to File Clients' Returns With Electronic Signatures*

New York law now provides that if a tax document is authorized to be filed electronically, then any associated e-file authorization may be signed using an electronic signature. An e-file authorization signed electronically will have the same force and effect as a handwritten signature and may be provided to a tax preparer by electronic means. (Ch. 167 (S.B. 8832), Laws 2020, effective August 24, 2020)

- *State Decouples From Certain CARES Act Provisions*

Enacted as part of New York's 2020-21 budget package, S.B. 7508 decouples the state from certain federal income tax changes. Under the corporate franchise tax, an addition modification is required for the amount of the increase in the federal interest deduction allowed under IRC Sec. 163(j)(10)(A)(i). This relates to the federal CARES Act amendment increasing the cap of the business interest expense limitation. The modification is required for taxable years beginning in 2019 and 2020. In addition, the tax law is amended to provide that, for taxable years beginning before January 1, 2022, any amendments made to the Internal Revenue Code after March 1, 2020, do not apply to the New York personal income tax. (Ch. 58 (S.B. 7508), Laws 2020, effective April 3, 2020, applicable as noted)

- *Television Diversity Tax Credit Enacted*

New York enacted a television writers' and directors' fees and salaries credit available against the corporate franchise and personal income taxes. The credit applies to fees and salaries paid to writers and directors who are women or minority group members. Press reports indicated that the governor reached an agreement with the legislature to conduct a study first, in order to demonstrate the underutilization of minority and women directors and screenwriters, and to require a minimum number of days of work to be done in the state. The credit equals 30% of qualified salaries and fees paid, but it cannot exceed $150,000 for fees and salaries claimed for any one specific writer or director. The credit is also capped at $50,000 for fees and salaries claimed per specific writer or director for the production of a single television pilot or a single episode of a television series. The maximum aggregate amount of tax credits allowed under the program in any calendar year is $5 million. (Ch. 683 (S.B. 5864), Laws 2019, effective December 18, 2019, applicable to taxable years beginning on or after January 1, 2020)

- *Television Diversity Credit and Research Tobacco Product Provisions Amended*

New York amended its recently enacted television writers' and directors' fees and salaries credit available against the corporate franchise and personal income taxes. Among other revisions, the amendments modify various definitions and make salaries or fees paid to a non-credited writer ineligible. Although no longer required to be a New York resident, a director must meet the minimum criteria for work on qualified productions in the state, as established by the Commissioner of Economic Development by regulation. The amendments also provide for a disparity report to determine whether there is a statistically valid underutilization of women and minority screenwriters and directors. The credit program will not be implemented until the disparity study is completed. The amendments are effective December 18, 2019.

Research Tobacco Products. The definition of "research tobacco product" is amended. Specifically, it means a tobacco product or cigarette that is labeled as a research tobacco product, manufactured for use in research for health, scientific, or similar experimental purposes, is exclusively used for such purposes by an accredited college, university or hospital, or a researcher affiliated with an accredited college, university or hospital, and is not offered for sale or sold to consumers for any purpose. Also, every accredited college, university or hospital that receives research tobacco products must, in good faith, file an annual information return on or before the last day of January reporting all research tobacco products received by such college, university or hospital or its affiliated researcher within the preceding calendar year. Any person required to file an information return who willfully fails to timely file such return or willfully fails to provide any material information required to be reported on such return may be subject to a penalty of up to $1,000. The amendments are effective December 20, 2019. (Ch 55 (S.B. 7505), Laws 2020, effective as noted)

• *LGBT Veterans Given Access to Veterans Benefits*

The New York State Legislature recently approved legislation that amends the New York state tax law and the real property tax law in relation to veterans with qualifying conditions and discharged Lesbian, Gay, Bisexual and Transgender (LGBT) veterans. The amendment adds veterans who have qualifying conditions or who are discharged as an LGBT veteran to provisions that apply to veterans who have been honorably discharged or released from military service. The amendment provides that no veteran with a qualifying condition will be denied eligibility for any program, service, benefit, or activity of departments, divisions, boards, bureaus, commissions or agencies of the state, or of any political subdivision of the state, that provides services or facilities to veterans for which they would otherwise be eligible, solely on the basis of the veteran's status as a discharged LGBT veteran. (Ch. 490 (S.B. 45), Laws 2019, effective November 12, 2020)

Corporate Franchise Tax
(See also "Multiple Taxes," above)

• *MTA Surcharge Rate Increased for 2020*

The New York corporate franchise tax MTA surcharge rate increased from 28.9% to 29.4% for tax year 2020 and will remain the same in later tax years unless the Commissioner of Taxation and Finance establishes a new rate. (Reg. Sec. 9-1.2(f))

Personal Income Tax
(See also "Multiple Taxes," above)

• *COVID-19 Telecommuting Addressed*

New York announced that for a nonresident whose primary office is in the state, days telecommuting during the pandemic are considered days worked in New York, unless the employer has established a bona fide employer office at the employee's telecommuting location. Generally, unless the employer specifically acted to establish a bona fide employer office at the telecommuting location, the nonresident employee will continue to owe New York income tax on income earned while telecommuting. (Telecommuting FAQ, New York Department of Taxation and Finance, October 19, 2020)

Sales and Use Taxes
(See also "Multiple Taxes," above)

• *Number and Size of Beer Tastings Qualifying for Exemption Changed*

Enacted legislation changes the number and size of beer tastings that qualify for the New York sales and use tax exemption for alcoholic beverage tastings. In order to qualify for the exemption for beer tastings conducted by a licensed brewery or farm brewery, the beer sample size cannot be more than four samples, not exceeding four fluid ounces each (previously, no more than five samples, not exceeding five fluid ounces). Also, each sample must be a different beer than the other samples. Only a customer's first purchase during each calendar day at each licensed brewery would be exempt under this provision. (Ch. 7 (A.B. 8956), Laws 2020, effective December 20, 2019)

• *Certain Beer Tastings No Longer Subject to Tax*

New York enacted legislation that exempts certain beer tastings from retail sales and use taxes. (Ch. 722 (A.B. 7947), Laws 2019, effective December 20, 2019)

• *Onondaga County Imposes Local Tax on Residential Energy Sources and Services*

Beginning September 1, 2020, Onondaga County imposes a temporary 4% local sales and use tax on receipts from the retail sale of residential energy sources and services. The term residential energy sources and services means the following tangible personal property and services used for residential purposes: natural gas; propane sold in containers of 100 pounds or more; electricity; steam; gas, electric, and steam services; fuel oil (except highway diesel motor fuel); coal; and wood (for heating purposes only). Sales of consumer utilities are subject to sales tax at the rate in effect at the time of delivery to the customer, even if the sales were contracted for before this change, except as described in Tax Bulletin Transitional Provisions for Sales Tax Rate Changes (TB-ST-895). This local tax will expire on November 30, 2022. (*ST-20-1*, New York Department of Taxation and Finance, August 13, 2020; *Publication 718-R and Publication 718-PPA*, New York Department of Taxation and Finance, August 2020)

• *Sullivan County Imposes Local Tax on Residential Energy Sources and Services*

Beginning September 1, 2020, Sullivan County imposes a temporary 4% local sales and use tax on receipts from the retail sale of residential energy sources and services. The term residential energy sources and services means the following tangible personal property and services used for residential purposes: natural gas; propane sold in containers of 100 pounds or more; electricity; steam; gas, electric, and steam services; fuel oil (except highway diesel motor fuel); coal; and wood (for heating purposes only). Sales of consumer utilities are subject to sales tax at the rate in effect at the time of delivery to the customer, even if the sales were contracted for before this change, except as described in Tax Bulletin Transitional Provisions for Sales Tax Rate Changes (TB-ST-895). This local tax will expire on February 28, 2023. (*ST-20-2*, New York Department of Taxation and Finance, August 13, 2020; *Publication 718-R and Publication 718-PPA*, New York Department of Taxation and Finance, August 2020)

• *Prepaid tax rate on cigarettes increased*

New York announces that for the period September 1, 2019, through August 31, 2020, the amount of the prepaid sales tax on cigarettes is as follows: 88 cents (previously, 86 cents) on packages of 20 cigarettes, and $1.10 (previously, $1.08) on packages of 25 cigarettes. The sales tax prepayment rates are determined using the following base retail sales prices: $11.040 for a pack of 20 cigarettes, and $2.757 for each additional five cigarettes. (*Important Notice N-19-5*, New York Department of Taxation and Finance, August 2019, ¶ 409-524)

For the period September 1, 2020, through August 31, 2021, the amount of the prepaid sales tax on cigarettes is as follows: 91 cents (previously, 88 cents) on packages of 20 cigarettes, and $1.13 (previously, $1.10) on packages of 25 cigarettes. The sales tax prepayment rates are determined using the following base retail sales prices: $11.327 for a pack of 20 cigarettes, and $2.829 for each additional five cigarettes. (*Important Notice N-20-11*, New York Department of Taxation and Finance, July 23, 2020, ¶ 409-708)

• *Wayne County No Longer Provides Clothing and Footwear Exemption*

New York has revised a publication listing local sales and use tax rates on clothing and footwear, effective March 1, 2020. Clothing and footwear worn by humans and costing less than $110 per item are exempt from the state sales and use tax. This exemption does not apply to any locally imposed sales and use tax, unless the county or city elects to provide for it. The publication identifies the jurisdictions that have adopted the local exemption and provides the rates of tax on sales of eligible clothing and footwear in localities that have not adopted the exemption. Effective March 1, 2020, Wayne County will no longer provide for this exemption and will impose local tax on eligible clothing and footwear at the rate of 4%. (*Publication 718-C*, New York Department of Taxation and Finance, February 2020)

• *Cap Amount for Electronic News Services Exemption Increases*

The cap amount for the New York sales and use tax exemption for sales and uses of electronic news services that occur from June 1, 2020, to May 31, 2021, is set at $3,502. The new cap amount is an increase from last year's amount of $3,441. (*Important Notice N-20-4*, New York Department of Taxation and Finance, May 14, 2020, ¶ 409-657)

Property Tax
(See also "Multiple Taxes," above)

• *Municipalities Authorized to Extend Deadline for Filing Property Tax Abatements and Exemptions*

New York allows municipalities to extend the deadline for the filing of applications and renewal applications for real property tax abatement or exemption programs to July 15, 2020. The governing body of such municipality must adopt a local law, ordinance, or resolution to extend the deadline. (Ch. 92 (S.B. 8122), Laws 2020, effective June 8, 2020, applicable as noted)

• *Redemption Period of Abandoned Property Subject to Delinquent Tax Lien Reduced; Other Changes Made*

Enacted New York legislation amends the real property tax law to lower the tax redemption period for abandoned buildings from two years to one year for properties that have been certified as vacant and abandoned, provided the property is placed on a vacant and abandoned roll, registry, or list prior to the date on which the taxes became delinquent. The legislation also provides for expedited foreclosure process for vacant and abandoned residential real property and clarifies when a residential real property will not be deemed vacant or abandoned. (Ch. 704 (S.B. 1864), Laws 2019, effective January 1, 2020)

• *Exemption for Improvements to Property of Severely Injured Members of Armed Forces*

New York has amended its real property law in relation to establishing a tax exemption for improvements to the property of service members of the armed forces of the United States who have a service-connected disability due to combat and who are found fit to serve by the physical evaluation board of such service member's branch of service. The amendment provides that an existing property used solely for residential purposes by a service member altered, installed or improved for the purposes of removal of architectural barriers that challenge his mobility is exempt from taxation and special ad valorem taxes. However, there will be no exemption for alterations, installations, or improvements unless such alterations, installations, or improvements were commenced after the date of the member's disability due to combat and subsequent to the effective date of the local law or resolution adopted to grant the exemption. Further, the exemption will not apply to any portion of the property that is not used exclusively as the applicant's primary residence. Furthermore, the terms alteration, installation and improvement do not include ordinary maintenance and repair. (Ch. 479 (A.B. 7289), Laws 2019, January 2, 2020, applicable as noted)

• *Assessment Changes for Businesses Making Payments in Lieu of Taxes Established*

Enacted New York legislation amends the real property tax law to establish changes in assessment for businesses that make payments in lieu of property taxes.

Any property with a payment in lieu of taxes agreement with an assessment challenge through the grievance process is permitted reductions in the payments made in lieu of taxes to a school district resulting from the challenges, but the reductions will not take effect until the following taxable status year. (Ch. 421 (S.B. 3972), Laws 2019, effective December 28, 2019)

Miscellaneous Taxes
(See also "Multiple Taxes," above)

- *Petroleum Business Tax Rates Decreased for 2020*

New York revised a publication that lists the decreased aggregate petroleum business tax (Article 13-A) rates, effective January 1, 2020. The publication also lists the rates for previous years. (*Publication 908*, New York Department of Taxation and Finance, December 2019)

Motor Fuel. The rate for motor fuel decreases 17.7¢ to 17.4¢ per gallon.

Aviation Gasoline. The rates for aviation gasoline decrease as follows: aviation gasoline—from 17.7¢ to 17.4¢ per gallon; and retail sellers of aviation gasoline—from 7.1¢ to 7.0¢ per gallon.

Kero-Jet Fuel. The rate for kero-jet fuel decreases from 7.1¢ to 7.0¢ per gallon.

Highway Diesel Motor Fuel. The rates for highway diesel motor fuel decrease as follows: highway diesel motor fuel—from 15.95¢ to 15.65¢ per gallon; and highway B20—from 12.76¢ to 12.52¢ per gallon.

Non-Highway Diesel Motor Fuel. The rates for non-highway diesel motor fuel decrease as follows: commercial gallonage—from 9.7¢ to 9.5¢ per gallon; B20 (commercial gallonage)—from 7.7¢ to 7.6¢ per gallon; nonresidential heating—from 5.2¢ to 5.1¢ per gallon; B20 (nonresidential heating)—from 4.1¢ to 4.0¢ per gallon; railroad diesel—from 9.3¢ to 9.1¢ per gallon; B20 (railroad diesel)—from 7.4¢ to 7.2¢ per gallon; electric corporation (without a direct pay permit)—from 16.8¢ to 16.5¢ per gallon; and commercial vessels (sales to commercial vessels)—from 16.8¢ to 16.5¢ per gallon.

Residual Petroleum Product. The rates for residual petroleum products decrease as follows: commercial gallonage—from 7.4¢ to 7.3¢ per gallon; nonresidential heating—from 4.0¢ to 3.9¢ per gallon; and electric corporation (without a direct pay permit)—from 14.5¢ to 14.3¢ per gallon.

Credits/Reimbursements. The rates for electric utility credit/reimbursement decrease as follows: non-highway diesel motor fuel—from 6.50¢ to 6.38¢ per gallon; and residual petroleum product—from 6.47¢ to 6.35¢ per gallon. The rate for commercial gallonage reimbursement decreases from 7.1¢ to 7.0¢ per gallon. The rate for aviation gasoline credit/refund/reimbursement decreases from 10.6¢ to 10.4¢ per gallon.

- *Tax-Exempt Cigarette Annual Amounts Announced*

New York has determined the annual amount of stamped tax-exempt packs of cigarettes for each of the Indian nations or tribes for the 12-month period beginning September 1, 2020 and ending August 31, 2021. (*Important Notice N-20-10*, New York Department of Taxation and Finance, July 1, 2020, ¶409-699)

- *Madison County Increases Wireless Communications Surcharge Rates*

Beginning September 1, 2020, Madison County increases its New York state and local surcharge rates on wireless communications services. (*WCS-20-1*, New York Department of Taxation and Finance, August 19, 2020, ¶409-721)

Postpaid: WCS-1, Postpaid Wireless Communications Surcharge Return. The combined state and local surcharge rate will increase from $1.50 to $2.15. When using

Web File, use the Madison County $2.15 entry line to report the surcharge on all devices in service during any part of a month for every customer whose place of primary use is in Madison County.

Prepaid: WCS-2-PRE, Prepaid Wireless Communications Surcharge Return. The combined state and local surcharge rate will increase from $1.20 to $1.85. When using Web File, use the Madison County $1.85 entry line to report retail sales of prepaid wireless communications services in Madison County.

Expiration Date. Each increase of $0.65 will expire on November 30, 2029.

• *Tax-Exempt Cigarette Annual Amounts Announced*

New York has determined the annual amount of stamped tax-exempt packs of cigarettes for each of the Indian nations or tribes for the 12-month period beginning September 1, 2020 and ending August 31, 2021. (*Important Notice N-20-10*, New York Department of Taxation and Finance, July 1, 2020, ¶409-699)

• *Madison County Imposes Additional Mortgage Recording Tax*

Effective February 1, 2020, Madison County, New York, imposes an additional county mortgage recording tax of 25 cents for each $100.00 secured by a mortgage. Currently, mortgages in Madison County are subject to the basic and special additional mortgage recording taxes at the combined rate of 75 cents for each $100 secured by a mortgage. Thus, effective February 1, 2020, the total combined rate of mortgage recording taxes imposed on the recording of mortgages on real property located in Madison County will be $1.00 for each $100.00 secured by the mortgage. (*MT-20-1*, New York Department of Taxation and Finance, January 2020, ¶409-615)

• *Washington County Imposes Additional Mortgage Recording Tax*

Effective April 1, 2020, Washington County, New York, imposes an additional county mortgage recording tax of 25 cents for each $100 secured by a mortgage. Currently, mortgages in Washington County are subject to the basic and special additional mortgage recording taxes at the combined rate of $1 for each $100 secured by a mortgage. Thus, effective April 1, 2020, the total combined rate of mortgage recording taxes imposed on the recording of mortgages on real property located in Madison County will be $1.25 for each $100 secured by the mortgage. (*MT-20-2*, New York Department of Taxation and Finance, March 2020, ¶409-645)

New York City Taxes
(See also "Multiple Taxes," "Property Taxes," and "Sales and Use Taxes," above)

• *Expiration Date of Sales and Use Tax on Certain Services Extended*

(The expiration date of the New York City 4.5% sales and use tax imposed on credit rating and credit reporting services and certain personal services, such as beauty, barbering, hair restoring, manicuring, pedicuring, electrolysis, massage, and health salon services, is extended through November 30, 2023. Previously, the tax could only be imposed through November 30, 2020. (Ch. 58 (S.B. 7508), Laws 2020, effective April 3, 2020, except as noted)

• *Property Tax Rates for Tax Year 2021 Announced*

The New York City Department of Finance has released the following property tax rates for tax year 2021: Class 1 - 21.045%; Class 2 -12.267%; Class 3 - 12.826%; and Class 4 - 10.694%. The property tax rates for tax year 2020 are: Class 1 - 21.167%; Class 2 - 12.473%; Class 3 - 12.536%; and Class 4 - 10.537%. (*Notice*, New York City Department of Finance, July 2020)

• *Property Tax Exemption for Alterations and Improvements to Substandard Multiple Dwellings Amended*

Enacted legislation amends the New York City property tax exemption and abatement program for alterations and improvements to substandard multiple dwellings (J-51 program) by: extending the program from June 30, 2019, through June 30, 2020; and increasing the assessed value limitation from $35,000 to $40,000. (NYC L.L. 023 (Intro. No. 1710-A), Laws 2020, effective January 19, 2020)

• *Various Tax Rates Extended*

The New York City general corporation tax rates currently imposed under Administrative Code Sec. 11-604(1)(E) are extended for three years, through 2023. The transition to New York City personal income tax rates imposed under Tax Law Sec. 1304(b) is delayed until tax years beginning after 2023. The additional personal income tax surcharge, imposed at the rate of 14%, is also extended through taxable years beginning before 2024. Previously, the additional tax surcharge was authorized only for taxable years beginning before 2021. (Ch. 58 (S.B. 7508), Laws 2020, effective April 3, 2020)

• *Relocation and Employment Assistance Credits Extended*

New York City relocation and employment assistance credit provisions are amended to state that, unless certain requirements are met, no certification of eligibility will be issued on or after July 1, 2025 (previously, July 1, 2020). In addition, for the duration of the benefit period, the recipient of benefits is required to file an annual statement of the average wage and benefits offered to the applicable relocated employees. (Ch. 56 (S.B. 7506), Laws 2020, effective April 3, 2020)

• *City Decoupled From Certain CARES Act Provisions*

A New York law has decoupled the New York City business corporation tax, general corporation tax, banking corporation tax, and unincorporated business tax from certain federal income tax changes contained in the CARES Act.

Business interest expense limitation. For all four taxes, an addition modification is required for the amount of the increase in the federal interest deduction allowed under IRC Sec. 163(j)(10). This relates to the federal CARES Act amendment increasing the cap of the business interest expense limitation and allowing an election to use 2019 adjusted taxable income for 2020. The modification is required for taxable years beginning in 2019 and 2020.

Net operating loss deduction. For the general corporation tax, banking corporation tax, and unincorporated business tax, the law provides that for taxable years beginning before 2021, any amendment to IRC Sec. 172 made after March 1, 2020, does not apply.

Excess business loss limitation. For the unincorporated business tax, for taxable years beginning before 2021, an addition modification is required for the amount of increase in the federal deduction allowed under any amendment to IRC Sec. 461(l) made after March 1, 2020. This relates to the federal suspension of the excess business loss limitation. (Ch. 121 (S.B. 8411), Laws 2020, effective June 17, 2020, applicable as noted)

CORPORATE INCOME

[¶10-050]

FEDERAL/MULTISTATE ISSUES

[¶10-055] Comparison of Federal/State Key Features

The following is a comparison of key features of federal income tax laws that have been enacted as of March 27, 2020, and the New York corporation franchise tax laws. The starting point for computing New York business income is federal taxable income before the net operating loss and special deductions (see ¶10-510). State modifications to federal taxable income required by law differences are listed at ¶10-600 for additions and ¶10-800 for subtractions.

• *Foreign Tax Credit (IRC Sec. 27)*

New York has no equivalent to the federal foreign tax credit (IRC Sec. 27).

• *Alcohol Fuels Credit (IRC Sec. 40)*

New York has no direct equivalent to the federal alcohol fuels credit (IRC Sec. 40). However, New York does provide a biofuel production credit (see ¶12-001).

• *Incremental Research Expenditures Credit (IRC Sec. 41)*

New York has no direct equivalent to the federal incremental research expenditures credit (IRC Sec. 41). However, New York allows a subtraction from federal taxable income for the portion of wages and salaries not allowed as a business expense deduction for federal purposes under IRC Sec. 280C because a federal credit was taken (see ¶10-855). In addition, New York does provide a credit for investment in research and development property and an Excelsior Jobs Program credit that includes a research and development credit component (see ¶12-001).

• *Low-Income Housing Credit (IRC Sec. 42)*

New York provides a low-income housing credit that coordinates with the federal low-income housing credit under IRC Sec. 42 (see ¶12-001).

• *Disabled Access Credit (IRC Sec. 44)*

New York has no equivalent to the federal disabled access credit (IRC Sec. 44).

• *Indian Employment Credit (IRC Sec. 45A)*

New York has no equivalent to the federal Indian employment credit (IRC Sec. 45A). However, New York allows a subtraction from federal taxable income for the portion of wages and salaries not allowed as a business expense deduction for federal purposes under IRC Sec. 280C because the Indian employment credit was taken (see ¶10-855).

• *Employer Social Security Credit (IRC Sec. 45B)*

New York has no equivalent to the federal employer social security credit (IRC Sec. 45B).

• *Orphan Drug Credit (IRC Sec. 45C)*

New York has no equivalent to the federal orphan drug credit (IRC Sec. 45C). However, New York allows a subtraction from federal taxable income for the portion of wages and salaries not allowed as a business expense deduction for federal purposes under IRC Sec. 280C because a federal credit was taken (see ¶ 10-855).

• *New Markets Credit (IRC Sec. 45D)*

New York has no equivalent to the federal new markets credit (IRC Sec. 45D).

• *Small Business Pension Start-Up Costs Credit (IRC Sec. 45E)*

New York has no equivalent to the federal small business pension start-up costs credit (IRC Sec. 45E).

• *Employer-Provided Child Care Credit (IRC Sec. 45F)*

New York allows an employer-provided child care credit, based on the federal credit (IRC Sec. 45F), beginning in 2020 (see ¶ 12-001).

• *Fuel from Nonconventional Source Credit (IRC Sec. 45K)*

New York has no equivalent to the federal fuel from nonconventional source credit (IRC Sec. 45K).

• *New Energy Efficient Homes Credit (IRC Sec. 45L)*

New York has no equivalent to the federal new energy efficient homes credit (IRC Sec. 45L).

• *Energy Efficient Appliance Credit (IRC Sec. 45M)*

New York has no equivalent to the federal energy efficient appliance credit (IRC Sec. 45M).

• *Investment Credit (Former Law) (IRC Sec. 46 — IRC Sec. 49)*

With respect to the former federal investment credit (repealed effective for property placed in service after 1985), New York allows a comparable investment credit (see ¶ 12-001). New York does not have an equivalent to the current federal investment credits (IRC Sec. 47, IRC Sec. 48, IRC Sec. 48A, IRC Sec. 48B, and IRC Sec. 48C). In addition, New York allows a biofuel production credit and an Excelsior Jobs Program credit that includes jobs tax credit and investment tax credit components. A credit for historic property rehabilitation is also available (see ¶ 12-001).

• *Wage Credits (IRC Secs. 51 — 52 and IRC Sec. 1396)*

Although New York has no direct equivalent to the federal work opportunity credit (IRC Sec. 51—IRC Sec. 52) or the empowerment zone employment credit (IRC Sec. 1396), New York allows a subtraction from federal taxable income for the portion of wages and salaries not allowed as a business expense deduction for federal purposes under IRC Sec. 280C because a federal credit was taken (see ¶ 10-855). New York provides credits for employing disabled persons and for employment in an emerging technology company. In addition, the Excelsior Jobs Program includes a jobs tax credit (see ¶ 12-001).

• *Alternative Minimum Tax (IRC Sec. 55 — IRC Sec. 59)*

New York has no equivalent to the federal alternative minimum tax on tax preference items (IRC Sec. 55—IRC Sec. 59). New York's tax on a corporation's minimum taxable income base was repealed for tax years beginning after 2014 (see ¶ 10-530).

• *Base Erosion and Anti-Abuse Tax (IRC Sec. 59A)*

New York has no equivalent to the base erosion and anti-abuse tax (IRC Sec. 59A).

• *Deemed Dividends (IRC Sec. 78)*

Amounts of foreign dividend gross-up under IRC Sec. 78 are subtracted from federal taxable income for New York purposes, to the extent the dividends are not deducted under IRC Sec. 250. (see ¶10-810).

• *Interest on Federal Obligations*

Any interest received on federal obligations that was exempt from federal taxation is added back for New York corporation franchise tax purposes (see ¶10-610).

• *Interest on State Obligations (IRC Sec. 103)*

Interest income received on state or local obligations, including those of New York and its political subdivisions, must be added back to federal taxable income (see ¶10-610).

• *Discharge of Indebtedness (IRC Sec. 108)*

The same as federal (IRC Sec. 108) because the starting point for New York business income is federal taxable income before the net operating loss and special deductions (see ¶10-510).

• *Contributions to the Capital of a Corporation (IRC Sec. 118)*

Generally the same as federal (IRC Sec. 118) because the starting point for New York business income is federal taxable income before the net operating loss and special deductions (see ¶10-510). However, New York decoupled from the TCJA amendment that removed certain contributions from the exclusion, and therefore a subtraction is allowed.

• *Certain Excessive Employee Remuneration (IRC Sec. 162(m))*

The same as federal (IRC Sec. 162(m)) because the starting point for New York business income is federal taxable income before the net operating loss and special deductions (see ¶10-510).

• *Interest on Indebtedness (IRC Sec. 163)*

Generally, the same as federal (IRC Sec. 163) because the starting point for New York business income is federal taxable income before the net operating loss and special deductions (see ¶10-510). However, for the IRC Sec. 163(j) limit, for tax years 2019 and 2020, the state does not conform to the federal amendment increasing the adjusted taxable income limit from 30% to 50%, and an addition modification is required accordingly (see ¶10-645).

• *Income and Franchise Tax Deductions (IRC Sec. 164)*

Income taxes paid to states (including New York) and local governments that were deducted from federal taxable income are added back for New York purposes (see ¶10-615).

• *Losses (IRC Sec. 165)*

Generally, the same as federal (IRC Sec. 165) because the starting point for computing New York business income is federal taxable income (see ¶10-510).

• *Bad Debts (IRC Sec. 166)*

The same as federal (IRC Sec. 166) because the starting point for computing New York business income is federal taxable income (see ¶10-510).

- *Depreciation (IRC Secs. 167, 168, and 1400N)*

Generally the same as federal (IRC Sec. 167, IRC Sec. 168, and IRC Sec. 1400N) because the starting point for computing New York business income is federal taxable income (see ¶10-510). However, for taxable years beginning after 2002, and applicable to property placed in service on or after June 1, 2003, New York is decoupled from federal bonus depreciation under IRC Sec. 168(k), except with respect to qualified Resurgence Zone property and qualified New York Liberty Zone property. In addition, adjustments may be required for property placed in service in taxable years beginning before 1994 (see ¶10-670).

- *Safe Harbor Leasing (Pre-1984 Leases) (IRC Sec. 168(f))*

New York does not follow federal treatment of safe harbor leases under former IRC Sec. 168(f)(8); adjustments to federal taxable income are required (see ¶10-670, ¶10-900).

- *Pollution Control Facilities Amortization (IRC Sec. 169)*

The same as federal (IRC Sec. 169) because the starting point for computing New York business income is federal taxable income (see ¶10-510).

- *Charitable Contributions (IRC Sec. 170)*

The same as federal because the starting point for computing New York business income is federal taxable income (see ¶10-510).

- *Amortizable Bond Premium (IRC Sec. 171)*

The same as federal (IRC Sec. 171) because the starting point for computing New York business income is federal taxable income (see ¶10-510).

- *Net Operating Loss (IRC Secs. 172 and 1400N)*

Separate from the federal computation (IRC Sec. 172), New York law provides for a prior NOL conversion subtraction and a deduction for NOLs generated in taxable years beginning after 2014. For NOLs incurred after 2014, a 3-year carryback is allowed, but no NOL can be carried back to a tax year beginning before 2015. As before, a 20-year carryforward is allowed (see ¶10-805).

- *Research and Experimental Expenditures (IRC Sec. 174)*

The same as federal (IRC Sec. 174) because the starting point for computing New York business income is federal taxable income (see ¶10-510).

- *Asset Expense Election (IRC Sec. 179)*

Generally the same as federal because the starting point for computing New York business income is federal taxable income (see ¶10-510). An addition is required, however, with respect to the expensing of certain sport utility vehicles (see ¶10-670).

- *Energy Efficient Commercial Buildings Deduction (IRC Sec. 179D)*

The same as federal (IRC Sec. 179D) because the starting point for computing New York business income is federal taxable income (see ¶10-510).

- *Deduction for Barriers Removal (IRC Sec. 190)*

The same as federal (IRC Sec. 190) because the starting point for computing New York business income is federal taxable income (see ¶10-510).

- *Start-Up Expenditures (IRC Sec. 195)*

The same as federal (IRC Sec. 195) because the starting point for computing New York business income is federal taxable income (see ¶ 10-510).

- *Amortization of Intangibles (IRC Sec. 197)*

The same as federal (IRC Sec. 197) because the starting point for computing New York business income is federal taxable income (see ¶ 10-510).

- *Domestic Production Activities (IRC Sec. 199)*

New York requires an addition modification for amounts deducted under IRC Sec. 199 (see ¶ 10-660).

- *Reporting for the Qualified Business Income Deduction (Pass-Through Deduction) (IRC Sec. 199A)*

New York has not adopted the pass-through deduction (IRC Sec. 199A).

- *Dividends Received Deduction (IRC Sec. 243 — IRC Sec. 245)*

The federal deduction for dividends received (IRC Sec. 243—IRC Sec. 245) is not allowed for New York corporation franchise tax purposes. However, New York allows a subtraction for investment income and other exempt income, including exempt CFC income and exempt unitary corporation dividends (see ¶ 10-810).

- *Participation Dividends Received Deduction (IRC Sec. 245A)*

Regarding the participation dividends received deduction (IRC Sec. 245A), New York treats the dividend and Subpart F income as other exempt income or investment income that is not taxable.

- *Organizational Expenditures (IRC Sec. 248)*

The same as federal (IRC Sec. 248) because the starting point for computing New York business income is federal taxable income (see ¶ 10-510).

- *Foreign-Derived Intangible Income and Global Intangible Low-Taxed Income (IRC Sec. 250)*

New York requires an addback for the deduction allowed in computing foreign-derived intangible income (FDII) (IRC Sec. 250) and, for tax years beginning after 2018, the deduction allowed under IRC Sec. 250(a)(1)(B)(i) in computing global intangible low-taxed income (GILTI) (see ¶ 10-695).

- *Corporate Distributions and Adjustments (IRC Sec. 301 — IRC Sec. 385)*

The same as federal (IRC Sec. 301—IRC Sec. 385) because the starting point for computing New York business income is federal taxable income (see ¶ 10-510).

- *Accounting Periods and Methods (IRC Sec. 441 — IRC Sec. 483)*

Generally, the same as federal (IRC Sec. 441—IRC Sec. 483) (see ¶ 10-510). New York has a provision similar to IRC Sec. 482 that authorizes the Tax Commissioner to allocate income and deductions to clearly reflect income.

- *Exempt Organizations (IRC Sec. 501 — IRC Sec. 530)*

An organization that is exempt from federal income taxation pursuant to IRC Sec. 501(a), will be presumed to be exempt from the New York corporation franchise tax (see ¶ 10-245). Exempt organizations are subject to the unrelated business income tax, which generally conforms to federal law (see ¶ 32-225).

• *Corporations Used to Avoid Shareholder Taxation (IRC Sec. 531 — IRC Sec. 547)*

New York has no provisions regarding corporations used to avoid shareholder taxation (IRC Sec. 531—IRC Sec. 547); New York does not impose a tax on accumulated earnings or an additional tax on the undistributed income of personal holding companies (IRC Sec. 541).

• *Banking Institutions (IRC Sec. 581 — IRC Sec. 597)*

New York has no provisions comparable to the federal provisions regarding banking institutions (IRC Sec. 581—IRC Sec. 597). For tax years beginning after 2014, the Article 32 bank franchise tax is repealed, and banks are merged into the Article 9-A corporate franchise tax (see ¶ 10-245).

• *Natural Resources (IRC Sec. 611 — IRC Sec. 638)*

The same as federal (IRC Sec. 611—IRC Sec. 638) because the starting point for computing New York business income is federal taxable income (see ¶ 10-510).

• *Insurance Companies (IRC Sec. 801 — IRC Sec. 848)*

There is no equivalent to the federal provisions relating to insurance companies (IRC Sec. 801—IRC Sec. 848). Insurance companies are exempt from the corporation franchise tax, but are subject to the franchise tax on insurance companies (see ¶ 10-245, ¶ 88-010).

• *RICs, REITs, REMICs, and FASITs (IRC Sec. 851 — IRC Sec. 860L)*

RICs are subject to tax to the same extent as under federal law; REITs are also subject to the corporation franchise tax; REMICs are exempt; New York has no provisions regarding former FASITs (IRC Sec. 851—IRC Sec. 860L). Special combined reporting provisions apply to captive RICs and captive REITs.

• *Foreign Source Income (IRC Sec. 861 — IRC Sec. 865)*

New York does not follow the federal foreign sourcing rules (IRC Sec. 861—IRC Sec. 865). Multistate and international businesses that conduct business both inside and outside New York use the state's allocation rules (see ¶ 11-515) for determining whether income is attributable to state sources.

• *Foreign Tax Credit (IRC Sec. 901 — IRC Sec. 908)*

New York has no provisions comparable to those relating to the foreign tax credit (IRC Sec. 901—IRC Sec. 908).

• *Global Intangible Low-Taxed Income (GILTI) (IRC Sec. 951A)*

For taxable years beginning after 2018, New York allows a 95% exemption for global intangible low-taxed income (GILTI) required to be included in the taxpayer's federal gross income under IRC Sec. 951A, without regard to the IRC Sec. 250 deduction, received from a corporation that is not part of the taxpayer's combined report (see ¶ 10-810).

• *Transition (Repatriation) Tax (IRC Sec. 965)*

New York allows a subtraction for all of Subpart F income, including IRC Sec. 965 repatriated income, that is included in federal taxable income (see ¶ 10-810). However, the state does require an addition adjustment for the federal deduction allowed under IRC Sec. 965(c).

• *Gain or Loss on Disposition of Property (IRC Sec. 1001 — IRC Sec. 1092)*

Generally, the same as federal (IRC Sec. 1001—IRC Sec. 1092), but the amount of the special additional mortgage recording tax that was paid and that is reflected in the computation of the basis of the property must be added back to federal taxable income (see ¶ 10-640).

¶10-055

- *Alternative Capital Gains Tax (IRC Sec. 1201)*

New York does not provide for an alternative tax rate on capital gains (IRC Sec. 1201).

- *Capital Losses (IRC Secs. 1211 and 1212)*

Generally, the same as federal (IRC Sec. 1211 and IRC Sec. 1212) (see ¶10-635).

- *Determining Capital Gains and Losses (IRC Sec. 1221 — IRC Sec. 1260)*

The same as federal (IRC Sec. 1221—IRC Sec. 1260) because the starting point for computing New York business income is federal taxable income (see ¶10-510).

- *S Corporations (IRC Sec. 1361 — IRC Sec. 1379)*

New York S corporations are subject to a corporate-level franchise tax (i.e., fixed dollar minimum tax amounts, based on the level of New York receipts). In addition to the corporate level tax, New York S corporation shareholders are liable for personal income tax on their shares of pass-through S corporation income and losses (see ¶10-215).

- *Empowerment Zones and Renewal Communities (IRC Secs. 1391 — 1397F and IRC Secs. 1400E — 1400J)*

The same as federal (IRC Sec. 1391—IRC Sec. 1397F and IRC Sec. 1400E—IRC Sec. 1400J) because the starting point for computing New York business income is federal taxable income (see ¶10-510). Taxpayers may deduct expenses for which a federal empowerment zone employment credit was claimed (see ¶10-855).

- *Consolidated Returns (IRC Sec. 1501 — IRC Sec. 1504)*

New York does not allow the filing of a consolidated return (IRC Sec. 1501—IRC Sec. 1504) except by all corporate stockholders in a tax-exempt DISC (see ¶11-545 and ¶89-102). New York has adopted unitary water's-edge combined reporting with an ownership requirement of more than 50% (see ¶11-550).

[¶10-075] Nexus--P.L. 86-272--Doing Business in State

What is the New York nexus standard?

New York has an economic presence nexus standard. Physical presence is not required to create nexus.

A taxpayer has nexus if it is (Sec. 209(1), Tax Law; Reg. Sec. 1-3.2(a)(1)):

— doing business in New York;

— employing capital in New York;

— owning or leasing property in New York;

— maintaining an office in New York; or

— deriving receipts from activity in New York.

If a partnership does any of those things, then any corporate partner in the partnership will be subject to tax. (Sec. 209(1)(f), Tax Law)

Doing business. The facts in each case will determine if a corporation is doing business in New York, and these factors will be considered (Reg. Sec. 1-3.2(b)):

— the nature, continuity, frequency, and regularity of the corporation's activities in New York;

— the reason why the corporation was organized;

— the location of the corporation's offices and other places of business;

— the employment of agents, officers, and employees in New York; and

— the location of the actual seat of management or control of the corporation.

Employing capital. There are many ways of employing capital that may overlap with other activities and can create nexus. In general, the use of assets in maintaining or aiding the corporate enterprise or activity in New York will make the corporation subject to tax. Employing capital includes activities like maintaining stockpiles of raw materials and inventories, or owning materials and equipment assembled for construction. (Reg. Sec. 1-3.2(c))

Owning or leasing property. Property owned by or held for the taxpayer in New York, whether or not it is used in the taxpayer's business, is sufficient to create nexus. Property held, stored, or warehoused in New York also creates nexus. Property held as a nominee for the benefit of others creates nexus. Consigning property to New York may also create nexus, if the consignor retains title to the consigned property. (Reg. Sec. 1-3.2(d))

Maintaining an office. A corporation has nexus if it maintains an office in New York. An office is any area, enclosure, or facility used in the regular course of the corporate business. A salesperson's home, a hotel room, or a trailer used on a construction job site can be considered an office. (Reg. Sec. 1-3.2(e))

Deriving receipts. A corporation has nexus if it has receipts in New York (i.e., receipts included in the numerator of the apportionment factor) of $1 million or more in the taxable year. (Sec. 209(1)(b), Tax Law)

A corporation is also subject to tax if:

— it has issued credit cards to 1,000 or more customers with New York mailing addresses;

— it has merchant customer contracts covering at least 1,000 locations in New York (to which the corporation remitted payments for credit card transactions during the taxable year); or

— the sum of the number of customers plus the number of locations covered by its contracts equals 1,000 or more.

A corporation with between $10,000 and $1 million of receipts in New York in a taxable year, and that is part of a combined reporting group, is deriving receipts from activity in the state if the New York receipts of the group members (those having at least $10,000 of receipts in New York) meet the $1 million threshold combined. (Sec. 209(1)(d), Tax Law)

A corporation that does not meet any of the credit card thresholds, but has at least 10 New York customers and/or locations and is part of a combined reporting group, is doing business in the state if the number of New York customers and/or locations of the group members (those having at least 10 customers and/or locations within New York) meet any of the credit card thresholds when combined. (Sec. 209(1)(d), Tax Law)

The receipt thresholds are subject to adjustment, based on changes in the consumer price index. (Sec. 209(1)(e), Tax Law) As of tax year 2020, the thresholds have not yet been adjusted. (TSB-M-19(6)C)

In the case of a corporate partner, when applying the $1 million receipts test, the general partner's receipts in New York are combined with the partnership's receipts in New York. (Corporate Tax Reform FAQs, New York Department of Taxation and Finance)

Activities not creating nexus. The following activities are insufficient on their own to establish nexus with New York (Sec. 209(2), Tax Law; Reg. Sec. 1-3.3):

— maintaining cash balances with banks or trust companies in New York;

— owning stock or securities kept in New York in a safe deposit box, safe, vault or other rented receptacle rented for the purpose, or if pledged as collateral security, or if deposited with one or more banks or trust companies, or brokers who are members of a recognized security exchange, in safekeeping or custody accounts;

— banks, trust companies or brokers taking any action that is incidental to the rendering of safekeeping or custodian service to a corporation;

— maintaining an office in New York by one or more officers or directors of a corporation who are not employees of the corporation, if the corporation otherwise is not doing business in New York and does not employ capital or own or lease property in New York;

— keeping books or records of a corporation in New York if the books or records are not kept by employees of the corporation and the corporation does not otherwise do business, employ capital, own or lease property or maintain an office in New York;

— participating in trade shows in New York for 14 days or less during a corporation's tax year;

— storing advertising on a server or other computer equipment, not owned or leased by the taxpayer, located in New York, or disseminating or displaying advertising on the Internet (Sec. 12(b), Tax Law; TSB-M-97(1.1)C); or

— trading stocks, securities, or commodities by a corporation for its own account.

P.L. 86-272—Soliciting orders. P.L. 86-272, the federal Interstate Income Act, prohibits any state from imposing a net income tax on income derived in that state from interstate commerce, if the only business activity in the state is soliciting orders for tangible personal property, provided that the orders are approved and filled outside the state. (Reg. Sec. 1-3.2(a)(3))

Soliciting orders includes offering tangible personal property for sale, pursuing offers for the purchase of tangible personal property, and ancillary activities, other than maintaining an office, that serve no independent business function aside from their connection to soliciting orders. (Reg. Sec. 1-3.4(b)(9)(iv))

Solicitation activities do not include activities that the corporation would have reason to engage in, aside from soliciting orders, but chooses to assign to its New York sales force. (Reg. Sec. 1-3.4(b)(9)(v))

Examples of activities that are entirely ancillary to soliciting orders and exempt from state taxation under P.L. 86-272, include (Reg. Sec. 1-3.4(b)(9)(iv)):

— using free samples and other promotional materials in connection with the solicitation of orders;

— passing product inquiries and complaints to the corporation's home office;

— using automobiles furnished by the corporation;

— advising customers on the display of the corporation's products, and furnishing and setting up display racks;

— recruiting, training, and evaluating sales representatives;

— using hotels and homes for sales-related meetings;

— intervening in credit disputes;

— using space at the salesperson's home solely for the salesperson's convenience; and

— participating in trade shows for not more than 14 days during the corporation's tax year.

Examples of activities that go beyond soliciting orders and create nexus, include (Reg. Sec. 1-3.4(b)(9)(v)):

— making repairs to or installing the corporation's products;

— making credit investigations;

— collecting delinquent accounts;

— taking inventory of the corporation's products for customers or prospective customers;

— replacing the corporation's stale or damaged products; and

— giving technical advice on the use of the corporation's products after the products have been delivered to the customer.

Activities in New York that go beyond soliciting orders will create nexus, unless they are minimal or "de minimis." However, activities will not be considered minimal if they establish a nontrivial additional connection with New York. (Reg. Sec. 1-3.4(b)(9)(v))

> *EXAMPLE:* An out-of-state corporation sends an employee to New York once every three years to repair its product for a customer in the state. The repair work only takes a few hours, so the employee is in New York each time for only one day. The corporation is not subject to the New York corporate franchise tax, because its activities in the state are minimal. (TSB-A-05(17)C).

A corporation is not engaging in business activities in New York just because of sales, or solicitation of sales orders, made on its behalf by independent contractors. Similarly, a corporation is not considered to be engaging in business activities in New York based on an office maintained by independent contractors, whose activities for the corporation are limited to sales or soliciting orders of tangible personal property. (Reg. Sec. 1-3.4(b)(9)(ii) and (iii))

[¶10-200]

BUSINESS ENTITIES

[¶10-210] C Corporations

Corporations are subject to Subchapter C of Chapter 1 of Subtitle A of the Internal Revenue Code relating to corporate distributions and adjustments, which is comprised of IRC Sec. 301—IRC Sec. 385. New York's treatment of C corporations is generally the same as federal because the starting point for computing New York net income is federal taxable income (See ¶ 10-510 Starting Point for Computation).

•*Interaction of federal and state provisions*

All domestic corporations and foreign corporations doing business, employing capital, owning or leasing property, or maintaining an office in New York are subject to the corporation franchise tax unless specifically exempted from the tax or subject to other New York franchise taxes (see ¶ 10-075 Nexus—P.L. 86-272—Doing Business in State and ¶ 10-245 Exempt Organizations). (Sec. 209, Tax Law)

A New York C corporation is a corporation subject to tax under Article 9-A of the Tax Law that is not a New York S corporation. (Sec. 208(1-A), Tax Law) (See ¶ 10-215 S Corporations)

Domestic corporation.—A domestic corporation is subject to the tax by reason of its possession of the privilege to exercise its corporate franchise. Consequently, the tax is imposed on a domestic corporation for every fiscal or calendar year, or other period of its existence, whether or not it does business, employs capital, owns or leases any property, maintains any office or engages in any activity, within or without New York. For the same reason, a domestic corporation must pay the tax even though it carries on its business entirely outside New York. (Sec. 209(1), Tax Law; Reg. Sec. 1-3.1)

An exemption from the fixed dollar minimum tax is available to certain domestic business corporations that have filed final returns (Sec. 209(8), Tax Law); see ¶ 10-245 for a complete discussion.

Foreign corporations.—A foreign corporation is subject to New York corporate franchise (income) tax if it is engaged in one or more of the following activities:

(1) doing business in New York,

(2) employing capital in New York,

(3) owning or leasing property in New York, or

(4) maintaining an office in New York. (Sec. 209(1), Tax Law; Reg. Sec. 1-3.2(1)) A foreign corporation engaging in any of these activities in New York is subject to tax even though its activities are wholly or partly in interstate or foreign commerce. (Reg. Sec. 1-3.2(2))

Certain incidental activities are specifically excluded, however, and do not, by themselves, result in liability. For a complete discussion of these activities and whether a foreign corporation is subject to tax, see ¶ 10-075 Nexus—P.L. 86-272—Doing Business in State.

Corporate distributions, reorganizations, and liquidation.—Because the New York taxable income computation starting point is federal taxable income (Sec. 208(9), Tax Law), New York generally follows the federal income tax treatment with respect to corporate distributions, reorganizations, and liquidations (See ¶ 10-510 Starting Point for Computation). For a discussion of prior years, see ¶ 10-540 Corporate Distributions, Reorganizations, and Liquidations.

Entities not organized as corporations.—The tax also applies to various business entities not organized as corporations (see the definition of "corporation" below). There are also special provisions applicable to real estate investment trusts (REITs), regulated investment companies (RICs), and domestic international sales corporations (DISCs).

Corporation defined.—The term "corporation" means an entity created as such under the laws of the United States, any state, territory or possession thereof, the District of Columbia, or any foreign country, or any political subdivision of any of the foregoing, which provides a medium for the conducting of business and the sharing of its gains. (Reg. Sec. 1-2.3) The term "corporation" includes an association (as defined under IRC Sec. 7701, including a limited liability company), a joint-stock company or association, a publicly traded partnership (treated as a corporation for purposes of IRC Sec. 7704), and any business conducted by a trustee or trustees wherein interest or ownership is evidenced by certificate or other written instrument. The term also includes a domestic international sales corporation (DISC). (Reg. Sec. 1-2.3)

The expansion of the definition of a corporation to include associations, as defined under IRC Sec. 7701, and publicly traded partnerships, treated as corporations for purposes of IRC Sec. 7704, applies to tax years which begin on or after January 1, 1989, and which end after April 19, 1989. (Sec. 208(1), Tax Law)

A New York C corporation is a corporation subject to tax under Article 9-A of the Tax Law that is not a New York S corporation. (Sec. 208(1-A), Tax Law) (See ¶ 10-215 S Corporations)

The following are examples of organizations that are subject to tax: (TSB-M-89(12)C)

(1) An association formed to operate an oil and gas management, for security from termination of the enterprise by death of any beneficial owner, for transfer of beneficial interest without affecting the continuance of the enterprise, and for limitation by contractual agreement with creditors of the members' personal liability.

(2) A fund established and funded by franchised dealers, administered by the manufacturer of the product in which the dealers deal. The accumulated funds are spent exclusively on national advertising of the manufacturer's product for the dealers' benefits.

(3) A business arrangement involving the investment by some 70 individuals in oil and gas leases, the development activities being conducted by a management team operating under powers of attorney.

(4) A group of 25 persons form an organization for the purpose of engaging in real estate investment activities. Under their agreement, the organization is to have a life of 20 years, and under local law, no member has the power to dissolve the organization prior to the expiration of that period. The management of the organization is vested exclusively in an executive committee of five members elected by all the members, and no one acting without the authority of this committee has the power to bind the organization by his acts. Each member is personally liable for the obligations of the organization, but that member must first advise the organization of the proposed transfer and give it the opportunity on a vote of the majority to purchase the interest at its fair market value. The organization has associates and an objective to carry on business and divide the gains therefrom. While the organization does not have the corporate characteristic of limited liability, it does have continuity of life, centralized management, and a modified form of free transferability of interests.

Dissolved corporations.—A dissolved corporation which continues to conduct business is subject to the corporation franchise tax. However, a dissolved corporation, the activities of which are limited to the liquidation of its business and affairs, the disposition of its assets (other than in the regular course of business), and the distribution of the proceeds, is not subject to tax. (Reg. Sec. 1-2.2)

¶10-210

Bankruptcy and receivership.—Receivers, referees, trustees in bankruptcy and assignees conducting the business of a corporation are subject to the corporation franchise tax in the same manner and to the same extent as if the business were conducted by the agents or officers of the corporation. (Sec. 209(3), Tax Law)

Fiduciaries and assignees.—Any receiver, referee, trustee, assignee or other fiduciary, or any officer or agent appointed by any court, who conducts the business of any corporation, will be subject to the corporation franchise tax in the same manner and to the same extent as if the business were conducted by the agents or officers of the corporation. (Sec. 209(3), Tax Law)

Aviation.—Taxpayers principally engaged in the conduct of aviation (other than air freight forwarders acting as principal and like indirect air carriers) are subject to the corporate income tax. (See ¶11-540 Apportionment Factors for Specific Industries)

Omnibus and taxicab corporations.—Omnibus and taxicab corporations are subject to the tax during any period in which the New York motor fuel tax exceeds 2¢ per gallon. (Sec. 183(1)(c), Tax Law) The tax rate is presently more than 2¢; see ¶40-001.

Railroad and trucking companies.—Businesses formed for or principally engaged in the conduct of a railroad, palace car, sleeping car or trucking business or formed for or principally engaged in the conduct of two or more of such businesses are subject to Art. 9-A corporation franchise tax or Art. 32 bank franchise tax, rather than Art. 9 taxes on transmission and transportation companies, *unless* they elect to continue to be subject to Article 9 tax. (Secs. 183(1)(b) and 183(10), Tax Law)

Time limitations for electing to remain subject to Art. 9.—Railroad and trucking companies subject to Sec. 183 and 184 tax for the 1997 tax year must make their election on or before March 15, 1998. Once made, the election will apply to the 1998 and succeeding tax years, until revoked.

Railroad and trucking companies that are *not* subject to Art. 9 transportation and transmission franchise taxes for the 1997 tax year, but thereafter would be subject to Article 9-A or 32 taxes if the election were not made, must make their election by the first day on which they would be required to file a return or report (without regard to extensions). An election, once made, will continue in effect until revoked by the taxpayer.

Revocation of election: A revocation of the election will be irrevocable. The election, and a revocation thereof, must be made in the manner prescribed by the Commissioner of Taxation and Finance, and will apply as of the following January 1.

Cable television companies.—In *Capitol Cablevision Systems* the New York Tax Appeals Tribunal held that cable television companies were subject to Article 9-A corporate franchise taxes, rather than Article 9 taxes imposed on transportation and transmission companies. In making this determination, the Tribunal noted that cable television companies are primarily engaged in the business of selling television entertainment to subscribers by packaging television signals that, in their judgment, represent the best blend of channels and subject matter to achieve their goal of attracting and keeping subscribers; transmission is merely the means by which the companies convey their product to customers, not their primary business.

In *NewChannels Corp.* the Tribunal addressed the issue of whether its holding in *Capitol Cablevision Systems* should be applied prospectively or retroactively. Noting that the proper filing status of cable television companies was one of first impression for the Tax Appeals Tribunal and that the holding effectively overruled a long-standing policy of the Department of Taxation and Finance, the Tribunal held that *Capitol Cablevision Systems* could only be applied prospectively.

However, in a separate, later decision (see *NewChannels Corp. et al. v. TAT*, No. 86041, January 11, 2001), the Supreme Court, Appellate Division, Third Department, found that certain taxpayers providing cable services should actually be subject to the Article 9 franchise tax imposed on transmission companies under Sec. 183 and Sec. 184, Tax Law, rather than the Article 9-A tax on general business corporations. Noting that the taxpayers had no control over the content of the signals received and that the taxpayers' largest capital investments were their cable plants, together with the cables, amplifiers, and other equipment necessary to receive and transmit signals, the court held that the taxpayers' provision of entertainment was merely incidental to their demonstrated function as cable operators engaged in the transmission of clear and viewable signals.

[¶10-215] S Corporations

After an examination of the New York state tax provisions relative to an S corporation, a review of the applicable federal income tax statutes is also provided below.

• *Interaction of federal and state provisions*

New York S corporations are subject to a corporate-level tax. (Sec. 210(1)(g), Tax Law) For tax years beginning after 2002, the law with respect to New York S corporations has been amended to eliminate the tax on the entire net income base and to impose only the fixed dollar minimum tax (see *TSB-M-03(5)C*, and *Important Notice N-07-1*). Rate information is discussed in detail at ¶10-380.

For prior tax years, the tax was equal to the higher of the following: (1) the entire net income base (see ¶10-510), or (2) the fixed dollar minimum tax, reduced by the "Article 22 (personal income tax) equivalent." (Sec. 210(1)(g), Tax Law) New York S corporation treatment is afforded only to general business corporations (Article 9-A corporations), and Article 32 banking corporations. It is not afforded to special corporations that are taxable under Articles 9 or 33 of the Tax Law. (See Publication 35, New York Treatment of S Corporations and their Shareholders)

S corporation election.—New York S corporation treatment is generally elective, not automatic. Shareholders must make a separate New York S election to be taxed as a New York S corporation. If this separate election is not made, the corporation is treated as a C corporation for New York tax purposes (see ¶10-210 C Corporations). (TSB-M-98(4)C; Publication 35)

A corporation may elect to be a New York S corporation only if it meets all of the following qualifications.

— the corporation is already a federal S corporation, or the corporation is making a federal S election at the same time it is making its New York S election;

— the corporation is an eligible corporation; and

— all the corporation's shareholders agree to make the New York S election.

(TSB-M-98(4)C; Publication 35)

The election must be made at any time during the preceding tax year, or on or before the 15th day of the third month of the tax year to which the election will apply. For taxable years of two and one-half months or less, an election made not later than two months and 15 days after the first day of the taxable year will be treated as timely filed for that year. (TSB-M-98(4)C; Publication 35)

The election will be effective for the entire year for which it is made and for all succeeding years until the election is terminated.

Late and invalid S elections.—If an election is made by an eligible S corporation for any taxable year after the election filing deadline for that taxable year, or if no election is made at all, and it is determined by the Commissioner that there was a reasonable cause for the failure to make a timely election, the Commissioner may treat that election as timely filed for that taxable year. (TSB-M-98(4)C; Publication 35)

Inadvertent invalid elections.—If an election by an eligible S corporation was not valid because the corporation failed to obtain the consent of all the shareholders, and within a reasonable amount of time after discovering the failure, the corporation took steps to acquire the necessary consents, the Commissioner may determine that the omission was inadvertent, and may retroactively validate the election. A retroactive validation requires both the shareholders and the corporation to recognize the tax consequences of the election for the retroactive period.

Validated federal elections.—When an S election is retroactively validated for federal purposes, pursuant to IRC Sec. 1362(f), then the Commissioner may retroactively validate the New York election. The validation will apply for any taxable years occurring within the period validated by the Internal Revenue Service. As above, any retroactive validations require both the shareholders and the corporation to recognize the tax consequences of the election for the retroactive period. (TSB-M-98(4)C; Publication 35)

Mandated election.—Under the 2007 budget legislation, for taxable years beginning after 2006, if an entity is an eligible S corporation for federal tax purposes and has not made the election to be a New York S corporation, it will be deemed a New York S corporation if the corporation's investment income for the current taxable year is more than 50% of its federal gross income for the year. This does not apply to S corporations that are subject to the bank franchise tax. (Sec. 660(i), Tax Law)

Authority to disregard.—For taxable years beginning after 2006, the Commissioner of Taxation and Finance is authorized to disregard personal service corporations or S corporations formed or availed of primarily to avoid or evade New York income tax. (Sec. 632-a, Tax Law)

Amount of corporate level tax.—New York S corporations are subject to the fixed dollar minimum tax, based on New York receipts, from a minimum of $25 to a maximum of $4,500 (Sec. 210(1)(g), Tax Law).

For additional discussion, see ¶ 10-380 Rates of Tax.

Shareholder level.—At the shareholder level, S corporation treatment (pass-through of income) applies if the New York S election is made. (Publication 35)

Under certain circumstances, New York S corporations that have income derived from New York sources are required to make estimated tax payments on behalf of nonresident shareholders. (Sec. 658(c)(4), Tax Law) Such nonresident withholding is discussed further at ¶ 89-104. See also Important Notice N-03-30.

C corporation treatment (non-pass through of income, but inclusion of distributions) applies to residents if the New York S election is not made (see ¶ 10-210 C Corporations). Nonresident shareholders are not subject to tax. If the corporation is an ineligible S corporation, resident shareholders are subject to S corporation treatment through conformity with the federal election, even though New York S corporation treatment is not available at the corporate level. (Publication 35)

Note.—New York City does not recognize S election status for purposes of its general corporation tax. Therefore, a federal S corporation that makes the S election for New York State purposes would still be a C corporation for New York City general corporation tax. (Publication 35)

Tax-exempt organizations that are shareholders of a federal S corporation and are subject to the New York tax on unrelated business income (see ¶ 32-225) may elect New York S corporation status with respect to the corporation. (Sec. 660(a), Tax Law) (TSB-M-98(2)C)

Terminating a New York S election.—An election to be a New York S corporation will terminate (1) on the day the election to be a federal S corporation terminates under IRC Sec. 1362(d), or (2) on the day a person becomes a new shareholder of the corporation and that person affirmatively refuses to consent to the New York S election. (Publication 35)

Revoking a New York S election.—An election to be a New York S corporation may be revoked only if shareholders who collectively own more than 50% of the outstanding shares of stock of the corporation consent to the revocation. The revoking shareholders must hold their stock on the day that the revocation is filed. (Publication 35)

A revocation is effective:

— on the first day of the corporation's tax year, if the revocation is made on or before the 15th day of the third month of the tax year;

— on the first day of the following tax year of the corporation if the revocation is made after the 15th day of the third month of the tax year; or

— on the date specified, if the revocation specifies a date on or after the date of revocation.

(Publication 35)

Re-electing to be a New York S corporation.—A termination or revocation of the New York S election does not bar a corporation that continues to be a federal S corporation from making another New York S election for a succeeding tax year. There is no five year disqualification period, as applies for federal tax purposes. However, the corporation must meet the qualifications to make the New York S election. (Publication 35)

Credits.—A New York S corporation may claim the credit for the special additional mortgage recording tax, except for the fixed dollar minimum. (Sec. 210(21), Tax Law) Any unused credit can be refunded or carried forward. The carryover of the credit is determined without regard to whether the credit is carried from a New York C year to a New York S year or vice versa. (Publication 35)

Other Article 9-A credits are not allowed against the New York S corporation tax. Rather, the corporation credits for which there are comparable credits under the personal income tax are allowed to the corporation's shareholders on their personal income tax returns (see ¶ 12-001 Overview of Credits). (Publication 35)

Credits allowable in a New York C year may not be carried over to a New York S year. (Sec. 210(21), Tax Law) No credit allowable in a New York S year, or carryover, may be deducted from the franchise tax. (Publication 35) The tax replaces the former $325 S corporation filing fee. (Sec. 210(1)(g), Tax Law)

Metropolitan Transportation Business Tax Surcharge.—A New York S corporation is not subject to the Metropolitan Transportation Business Tax surcharge under Article 9-A. (Publication 35)

Qualified subchapter S subsidiaries.—In most instances, New York will follow the federal qualified subchapter S subsidiaries (QSSS) treatment in the Article 9-A taxes. QSSS are not subject to the corporate net income tax, provided certain conditions are met. (Sec. 208(1-B), Tax Law) If the QSSS is exempt, the assets, liabilities, income, deductions, property, payroll, receipts, capital, credits, and all other tax attributes and elements of economic activity of the QSSS are considered to be those of the parent corporation. The parent company may be either a C corporation or an S corporation (see ¶ 10-210 C Corporations).

The term "qualified subchapter S subsidiary" has the same meaning as under IRC Sec. 1361(b)(3)(B). (Sec. 208(1-B), Tax Law) An exempt QSSS refers to a nonexcluded New York QSSS that is owned by a parent that is either a New York S corporation or a New York C corporation that is subject to tax under Article 9-A. If the QSSS is not a taxpayer, a New York C corporation that the owns a QSSS must make an election to include the QSSS' tax attributes in the calculation of its own net income or the C corporation company will be taxed as if the federal QSSS election had not been made. Upon election by the parent, all assets, liabilities, income, deductions, property, payroll, receipts, capital, credits, and all other tax attributes and elements of economic activity of the QSSS are considered to be those of the parent corporation. A non-New York subchapter S corporation that is not a taxpayer under Article 9-A and owns a QSSS that, but for the new qualified subchapter S subsidiary provisions would have been subject to tax under article 9-A, may make an election to be taxed as New York S corporation. For any taxable that such an election is not in effect, the QSSS will be taxed as a New York C corporation, and its entire net income must be determined as if the federal QSSS election had not been made.

Enactment of the tax-equalization measure in 1990 did not, however, change the basic structure of S corporation election, in which the majority of the tax liability is passed through, along with net income and tax attributes, to the shareholders. Shareholder liability under the personal income tax is discussed at ¶ 15-185.

• *Federal income tax provisions*

An S corporation is a small business corporation that satisfies the requirements of Subchapter S of the tax code and has elected to be taxed under those rules. In order to qualify as a small business corporation, the corporation must be a domestic corporation and is restricted on the number and types of shareholders it can have and on the type of stock that it can issue.

The difference between an S corporation and a regular corporation is that the S corporation has elected to be taxed similarly to a partnership for federal tax purposes. After making the S election, the income, losses, tax credits, and other tax items of the corporation flow through the corporation to the shareholders. Thus, income is only taxed once, at the shareholder level. However, an S corporation that was formerly a C corporation may be subject to taxes at the corporate level for LIFO recapture, excessive net passive income, and built-in gains.

[¶ 10-220] General Partnerships

New York generally follows IRC Sec. 701—IRC Sec. 761, the federal income tax provisions addressing partners and their partnerships, because the starting point for New York entire net income is federal taxable income before the net operating loss and special deductions (see ¶ 10-510). (Sec. 208(1), Tax Law) Since New York follows the federal income tax treatment of a partnership and its partners, income and losses, including net operating losses (NOLs) of the partnership flow to its partners. (Sec. 601(f), Tax Law) After an examination of the state provisions, an overview of the applicable federal income tax law is provided.

• *Interaction of federal and state law*

Aside from limited liability partnerships (LLPs) classified as associations for federal income tax purposes (¶10-225), partnerships are not subject to the general corporate franchise (income) tax under Article 9-A. However, a corporate partner of a partnership is subject to the Article 9-A corporate franchise (income) tax.

The term "partnership" has the same meaning as set forth in IRC Sec. 761(a) and 26 CFR § 1.761-1(a) whether or not the election provided for therein has been made. (Reg. Sec. 1-2.6) In addition, the term "partnership" does not include a corporation as defined in Reg. Sec. 1-2.5(b). (Reg. Sec. 1-2.6)

A partnership may be either a general partnership or a limited partnership (see ¶10-225 Limited Partnerships; Limited Liability Partnerships). In a general partnership, all partners share in the partnership's income and liabilities and all partners have, as a matter of law, a right to participate in the partnership management. However, the general partners can agree to turn management of the partnership over to one or more managing partners.

Filing fee.—Under the 2009 budget legislation, applicable to tax years beginning on or after January 1, 2009, partnerships are subject to the annual filing fee previously applicable only to LLCs and LLPs (see ¶10-225). However, partnerships (other than LLPs under Article 8-B of the Partnership Law and foreign LLPs) with less than $1 million in New York source gross income are exempt from the filing fee. (Sec. 658(c)(3), Tax Law)

Source and character of corporate partner partnership income.—For corporate partners, the law generally provides for use of the aggregate method to compute tax. (Sec. 210(3), Tax Law)

The Department of Taxation and Finance has adopted various regulation amendments relating to the taxation of corporate partners. The amendments were adopted to provide comprehensive guidance on the computation of tax for corporations that are partners in partnerships or that are members of limited liability companies (LLCs) treated as partnerships (TSB-M-07(2)C). As amended, the regulations provide that, except for certain foreign corporate limited partners, a taxpayer that is a partner in a partnership must compute its tax with respect to its interest in the partnership under either the aggregate or entity method. The regulations discuss each method and set forth the determination of the applicable methodology. Under the aggregate method, a corporate partner takes into account its distributive share of receipts, income, gain, loss, or deduction and its proportionate part of assets, liabilities, and transactions from the partnership. Under the entity method, a corporate partner is treated as owning an interest in a partnership entity, and the interest is considered an intangible asset that constitutes business capital. The regulations make it clear that the aggregate method, which was required under the previous regulations, is the preferred method.

The regulations specifically cover the following:

— general information (Reg. Sec. 3-13.1);

— determination of applicable methodolgy (Reg. Sec. 3-13.2);

— computation under the aggregate method (Reg. Sec. 3-13.3);

— computation under the entity method (Reg. Sec. 3-13.4);

— election by foreign corporate limited partner (Reg. Sec. 3-13.5);

— tiered partnerships (Reg. Sec. 3-13.6); and

— gain or loss on the sale of a partnership interest (Reg. Sec. 3-13.7).

For additional information regarding the amendments discussed above, see TSB-M-07(2)C. (*Note:* Among other provisions discussed in the memorandum are clarifying amendments related to the definition of investment capital and a change in the treatment of stock of a corporation owned by a partnership.)

• *Federal income tax provisions*

A partnership is a pass-through entity that does not pay tax on its income. Instead, the partnership passes along its income or loss, gains, deductions, and credits to the partners. Each partner reports a percentage of the partnership income and other items on the partner's own tax return.

A partnership does not pay tax, but it does compute income, deductions and credits on an annual basis. Information about the business is reported to the IRS on Form 1065 and to the individual partners on separate Schedules K-1. The partners report the partnership income on their own returns and pay any taxes due based on their own tax rates.

[¶10-225] Limited Partnerships; Limited Liability Partnerships

New York generally follows IRC Sec. 701—IRC Sec. 761, the federal income tax provisions addressing partners and their limited partnerships, because the starting point for computing New York entire net income is federal taxable income (see ¶10-510 Starting Point for Computation and ¶10-515 Federal Conformity). (Sec. 208(1), Tax Law) Since New York follows the federal income tax treatment of limited partnerships (LPs) and limited liability partnerships (LLPs) and their limited partners, income and losses, including net operating losses (NOLs) of the LP and LLP flow to their partners. (Sec. 601(f), Tax Law)

After an examination of the state provisions related to the taxation of LPs, LLPs, and their general and limited partners, a summary of the related federal income tax laws is provided.

• *Interaction of federal and state law*

New York law allows for the formation of LLPs in New York State, LLPs formed under the laws of other states, and for registration of general partnerships providing professional services as registered limited liability companies (RLLPs).

Classification.—Since New York is a federal conformity state, it follows the IRS classification of an LLP as a partnership or a corporation for federal income tax purposes.

The New York corporate franchise (income) tax provisions classify LLPs in accordance with the federal "check-the box" regulations. (Reg. Sec. 301.7701-1 et seq.) Therefore, an LLP that is treated as a partnership for federal income tax purposes will be treated as a partnership for New York corporate franchise (income) tax purposes. Likewise, an LLP that is treated as a corporation for federal tax purposes is treated as a corporation for New York corporate franchise (income) tax purposes. (Publication 16, New York Tax Status of Limited Liability Companies and Limited Liability Partnerships) The term corporation includes an association within the meaning of IRC Sec. 7701(a)(3). (Sec. 208(1), Tax Law)

Limited liability partnerships (LLPs) are general partnerships (see ¶10-220) that have registered as LLPs. An LLP has one or more general partners and one or more limited partners. The limited partners are not responsible for partnership liabilities beyond the agreed amount of their investments.

Formation and registration.—The formation of a domestic LLP is governed by Article 8-B of the New York Partnership Law. Domestic LLPs are required to register with the New York Department of State. Foreign LLPs that wish to carry on or conduct business or activities in New York State must also register with the Department of State. The Department of Taxation and Finance does not administer the formation and registration process. (Publication 16)

Filing fees.—Every partnership having any income derived from New York sources is subject to an annual filing fee. For taxable years beginning before 2009, this requirement applied only to LLPs. Sec. 631 of the Tax Law provides that items of income, gain, loss, or deduction from New York sources include those items attributable to (a) the ownership of any interest in real or tangible personal property located in the state or (b) a business, trade, profession, or occupation carried on in the state. The filing fee applies to each taxable year of the entity. For purposes of the filing fee, the New York taxable year of the entity is always the same as its taxable year for federal income tax purposes. (Sec. 658(c)(3), Tax Law) (Publication 16)

Partnerships (other than LLPs under Article 8-B of the Partnership Law and foreign LLPs) with less than $1 million in New York source gross income are exempt from the filing fee. (Sec. 658(c)(3), Tax Law)

Amount of filing fee.—The fee is based on the New York source gross income of the partnership for the immediately preceding taxable year, as follows:

— $25 (if New York source gross income is not more than $100,000)
— $50 (if $100,001 -- $250,000)
— $175 (if $250,001 -- $500,000)
— $500 (if $500,001 -- $1,000,000)
— $1,500 (if $1,000,001 -- $5,000,000)
— $3,000 (if $5,000,001 -- $25,000,000)
— $4,500 (if more than $25,000,000)

New York source gross income is the sum of the partners' shares of federal gross income from the partnership derived from or connected with New York sources, determined in accordance with the provisions of Sec. 631, Tax Law, as if those provisions and any related provisions expressly referred to a computation of federal gross income from New York sources. For this purpose, federal gross income is computed without any allowance or deduction for cost of goods sold. No credits provided by Article 22 of the Tax Law may be taken against the fee. (Sec. 658(c)(3), Tax Law)

Prior to 2008, the filing fee was $50 multiplied by the total number of partners in the LLP as of the last day of the taxable year. (Sec. 658(c)(3), Tax Law) However, the fee could not be less than $325 nor more than $10,000 annually. (Sec. 208(1), Tax Law) There is no proration of the filing fee if the LLP has a short taxable year for federal income tax purposes.

Increased fees were previously effective from 2003 through 2006 ($100 per member, with a minimum of $500 and a maximum of $25,000).

Any fee not timely paid must be paid upon notice and demand, and is subject to assessment, collection, and payment in the same manner as taxes. (Sec. 658(c)(3), Tax Law)

A domestic or foreign LLP that does not have any income, gain, loss, or deduction from New York sources, but is required to file a New York State partnership return because it has a partner who is a New York State resident, is not subject to the filing fee. (TSB-M-94(6)I, (8)C, (7)M, (7)S, (6)R) Similarly, domestic LLPs with no New York source income as not subject to filing fees solely because they were formed under the laws of New York. Also, dormant LLPs with no items of income, gain or loss, or deduction are not subject to the fee. (Publication 16, New York Tax Status of Limited Liability Companies and Limited Liability Partnerships) Furthermore, an LLP that elects to be treated as a corporation for federal income tax purposes is not subject to the fee.

Payment of the filing fee.—The fee must be paid using Form IT-204-LL on or before the 15th day of the third month following the close of the taxable year.

Foreign limited partnerships.—A foreign corporate limited partner that does not file on a combined basis and is subject to corporation franchise tax solely because of the application of Reg. Sec. 1-3.2(a)(6) may elect to compute its tax bases by taking into account only its distributive share of each partnership item of receipts, income, gain, loss and deduction (including any modifications relating thereto) and its proportionate part of each partnership asset and liability, and each partnership activity, of each such limited partnership that is doing business, employing capital, owning or leasing property, or maintaining an office in New York, regardless of whether that share is actually distributed. (Reg. Sec. 3-13.5) The election may not be claimed if the limited partnership and corporate group are engaged in a unitary business, wherever conducted, and there are substantial inter-entity transactions between the limited partnership and the corporate group.

In determining whether there are substantial inter-entity transactions, the Commissioner will consider transactions directly connected with the business conducted by the limited partnership and the corporate group, such as the following:

— the manufacturing or acquiring of goods or property or the performing of services by the limited partnership for the corporate group, or by the corporate group for the limited partnership;

— the selling of goods acquired by the limited partnership from the corporate group, or by the corporate group from the limited partnership;

— the financing of sales of the corporate group by the limited partnership, or of the limited partnership by the corporate group; or

— the performing of related customer services using common facilities and employees.

(Reg. Sec. 3-13.5)

Service functions (such as accounting, legal, and personnel services) will not be considered when they are incidental to the business of the limited partnership or the corporate group providing the service. (Reg. Sec. 3-13.5) The substantial inter-entity transactions requirement is met if (1) at least 50% of the limited partnership's receipts or expenses are from engaging in one or more qualified activities described above with the corporate group, or (2) at least 50% of the corporate group's receipts or expenses are from engaging in one or more qualified activities described above with the limited partnership.

EXAMPLE: Limited partnership Z sells 30% of its product to limited partner X corporation and 40% of its product to Y corporation, a wholly owned subsidiary of X corporation. Corporations X and Y constitute a corporate group. There are substantial inter-entity transactions between Z and the corporate group because 70% of Z's sales are to the group.

EXAMPLE: X corporation is a limited partner in limited partnership Z. If 60% of X's expenses arise from its purchases of products from Z, there are substantial inter-entity transactions between X and Z.

EXAMPLE: X corporation is a limited partner in limited partnership Z. Y corporation is a wholly owned subsidiary of X. X and Y constitute a corporate group. 95% of X's receipts are from sales of products to Z. 10% of Y's receipts are from sales of products to Z. However, in the aggregate only 40% of the receipts of the corporate group consisting of X and Y are from sales of products to Z. There are not substantial inter-entity transactions between Z and the corporate group.

The election is made at the time of filing the report and, once made, may not be revoked by filing an amended report. The election is binding with respect to that partnership interest for all future taxable years.

A corporation that makes an election with respect to one or more partnerships ("election partnerships"), but not with respect to other such partnerships ("non-election partnerships"), must compute its tax bases with respect to nonelection partnerships by reducing its deductions and liabilities by the amounts which are directly and indirectly attributable to such election partnerships.

Registered limited liability partnerships.—New York permits the creation of registered limited liability partnerships (RLLPs). This allows a general partnership providing professional services to register as an LLP, which secures for partners the same liability protection received by professionals operating as a professional corporation under the Business Corporation Law.

A filing fee of $200 must accompany the registration of LLP documents.

• *Federal income tax provisions*

The state laws regulating limited liability partnerships (LLPs) vary widely. Accordingly, it is difficult to generalize about the requirements and state law consequences of obtaining LLP status.

LLPs are general partnerships in which each individual partner is liable for the partnership's general contractual obligations, his or her own individual business liability, and the tort liabilities deriving from the acts of those over whom the partner had supervisory duties. By complying with a prescribed registration requirement, the partner is otherwise insulated from the malpractice, negligence and similar liabilities of the other partners in excess of the value of the partner's interest in the partnership. The classification and tax treatment of LLPs is not affected by the check-the-box entity selection rules. The federal income tax status of an LLP depends on the provisions of the state law under which the partnership is formed.

[¶10-240] Limited Liability Companies (LLCs)

New York generally adopts the federal income tax treatment of a limited liability company (LLC) as set out in the federal "check-the-box" regulations. Like the federal check-the-box regulations (*i.e.*, Treas. Reg. Secs. 301.7701-1 through 301.7701-3, which are addressed more fully below at *Federal income tax provisions*), the applicable New York provisions permit an LLC to elect classification as either a corporation, partnership, or "disregarded entity", unless the entity meets certain specifications requiring classification as a corporation. Note that classification of an LLC for New York corporate franchise (income) tax purposes is dependent upon the LLC's federal income tax classification as either a corporation, partnership, or disregarded entity. The classification elected for federal tax purposes is the same for New York tax purposes.

LLCs classified as partnerships for federal purposes are not subject to New York income tax. (Sec. 601(f), Tax Law) Since New York follows the federal income tax treatment of an LLC and its members, income and losses, including net operating losses (NOLs) of the LLC flow to its members. See also ¶ 10-220 General Partnerships.

• *Interaction of federal and state provisions*

The New York Limited Liability Company (LLC) Law allows the formation of LLCs. The New York corporate franchise (income) tax conforms with the federal income tax classification of LLCs. Therefore, an LLC that is treated as a partnership for federal income tax purposes will be treated as a partnership for New York corporate franchise (income) tax purposes. An LLC that is treated as a corporation for federal income tax purposes will be treated as a corporation for New York tax purposes. (Publication 16, New York Tax Status of Limited Liability Companies and Limited Liability Partnerships)

LLCs are business entities that share characteristics of both partnerships and corporations. Like partnerships, properly configured LLCs are pass-through entities in those states in which they are not specifically subject to corporate tax. Instead, each member must report on a separate return his or her, or its, distributive share of income, gain, loss, deductions, and credits of the LLC.

Unlike other choices of business organizations, LLCs offer owners corporate-like limited liability along with pass-through partnership taxation treatment. Unlike general partnerships (see ¶ 10-220), all members (shareholders) of an LLC can be protected from personal liability for the debts and other obligations of the LLC. Unlike limited partnerships (see ¶ 10-225), LLC members can actively participate in management without sacrificing their limited liability. Unlike C corporations (see ¶ 10-210), the LLC, if properly structured, will not be taxed at the entity level on its income. Unlike S corporations (see ¶ 10-215), LLCs are not subject to the many restrictions placed on S corporations, such as the limitations on the number and types of shareholders, the allowable classes of stock, and the flowthrough of losses (discussed below).

An LLC is more flexible and has certain advantages compared to a limited partnership (see ¶ 10-225) or an S corporation (see ¶ 10-215). For example, an S corporation may have only one class of stock and may have no more than 75 shareholders. While a limited partnership is not subject to the qualification restrictions of an S corporation, a limited partnership must have at least one general partner who is liable for the debts of the partnership. In contrast, all of the members of an LLC may be protected from such liability. Moreover, the participation of limited partners in the management of a limited partnership can result in the loss of limited liability protection. Participation by members in the management of an LLC will not have such an effect.

See ¶ 10-225 Limited Partnerships; Limited Liability Partnerships and ¶ 10-215 S Corporations.

Annual filing fee.—LLCs are subject to an annual filing fee. For taxable years beginning on or after January 1, 2008, the fee is based on the New York source gross income of the LLC for the immediately preceding taxable year, as follows:

— $25 (if New York source gross income is not more than $100,000)

— $50 (if $100,001 -- $250,000)

— $175 (if $250,001 -- $500,000)

— $500 (if $500,001 -- $1,000,000)

— $1,500 (if $1,000,001 -- $5,000,000)

— $3,000 (if $5,000,001 -- $25,000,000)

— $4,500 (if more than $25,000,000)

¶10-240

New York source gross income is the sum of the members' shares of federal gross income from the LLC derived from or connected with New York sources, determined in accordance with the provisions of Sec. 631, Tax Law, as if those provisions and any related provisions expressly referred to a computation of federal gross income from New York sources. For this purpose, federal gross income is computed without any allowance or deduction for cost of goods sold. No credits provided by Article 22 of the Tax Law may be taken against the fee. (Sec. 658(c)(3), Tax Law)

Single member LLCs, which are disregarded entities for federal income tax purposes, are required to remit a filing fee of $25 beginning in 2008. (Sec. 658(c)(3), Tax Law) See also Important Notice N-08-16.

Prior to 2008, the filing fee was $50 multiplied by the total number of members in the LLC as of the last day of the taxable year. (Sec. 658(c)(3), Tax Law) However, the fee could not be less than $325 nor more than $10,000 annually.

Increased fees were previously effective from 2003 through 2006 ($100 per member, with a minimum of $500 and a maximum of $25,000). During that period, single member LLCs were required to pay $100 annually.

Payment of the filing fee.—The fee must be paid using Form IT-204-LL on or before the 15th day of the third month following the close of the taxable year.

New York LLC law flexible rather than bulletproof.—The New York Limited Liability Company Law is a flexible, rather than a bulletproof, statute. Under bulletproof statutes, an LLC can be organized and structured only according to the terms of the statute. The advantage of this form of legislation is that once the statute is blessed by the Internal Revenue Service, the entity can be assured of pass-through taxation. Under flexible statutes such as New York's, however, the members of an LLC may agree in the articles of organization or the operating agreement to deviate from the statute in structuring the governance and operation of the LLC. This affords LLC organizers broad flexibility in structuring the LLC, but the trade-off for this flexibility is that if the LLC deviates from the default rules concerning transferability of interests, centralized management and continuity of life, it runs the risk that it will not be structured as a partnership from a federal tax standpoint.

LLC suitability checklist.—The following is a general checklist that is useful in determining the suitability of an LLC.

Question 1: Will all states in which the enterprise is operated recognize LLC status?

Comment: Operating an LLC in a state that does not recognize limited liability companies creates uncertainty as to state tax treatment and the extent of a member's personal liability for business debts, business acts or omissions and acts or omission of other members. The loss of LLC status could subject the company to another state's corporate income tax or pierce the corporate veil to impose personal liability for the company's debts on New York LLC members.

Question 2: Will the enterprise have only one member?

Comment: New York allows the formation of an LLC with only one member, therefore a single-member LLC may, if allowed under the law of the foreign jurisdiction, operate as an LLC in states that grant LLC status to registered foreign LLCs (i.e., an LLC that is duly formed and authorized by another jurisdiction) even though that state may not allow formation of a domestic LLC with only one member. For example, under New Jersey law, a duly registered foreign LLC will be taxed in New Jersey as a partnership unless classified otherwise for federal income tax purposes. (Sec. 42.2B-59, N.J.S.A.)

¶10-240

Question 3: Will any investors be partnerships, corporations, trusts foreign entities or nonresident aliens?

Comment: Under state and federal tax provisions, such investors (with the exception of certain qualified trusts) may not own shares in an S corporation. However, the New York LLC Act (except for the Professional LLCs provisions) does not limit the type of "person" that may be a member of an LLC.

Question 4: Do all participants in the enterprise desire the combination of limited liability, the ability to participate in management, and federal pass-through tax treatment?

Comment: A New York LLC provides all three of these characteristics. An S corporation also provides all three characteristics, but imposes restrictions on the type of permissible investors, allowable percentage of passive investment income, and does not allow the same pass-through of certain tax benefits available to an LLC. Limited partnerships and Limited Liability Limited Partnerships severely restrict a limited partner's right to participate in management of the enterprise and the general partner continues to be liable for partnership debts. LLPs provide limited partners and general partners with protection against liabilities that are attributable to the negligent or wrongful acts of another partner, provided that the partnership maintains liability insurance in the amount required by statute.

Question 5: Are significant tax losses anticipated at any time during the life of the enterprise?

Comment: LLC members, (like general or limited partners), are allowed to increase the basis in their ownership interests by the amount of their shares of entity-level debt. By application of IRC partnership debt allocation rules to LLCs (Treas. Reg. Secs. 1.752-1—1.752-5), it appears that LLC-level debt, even if secured by business assets, is non-recourse liability and is allocated among the members according to their shares, as provided in the operating agreement. Therefore, except for enterprises engaged in certain real estate investment activities, the "at risk" limitations of IRC Sec. 465 might prevent an LLC member from realizing that portion of a loss attributable to an increase in basis from LLC-level liabilities because members are not "at risk" for LLC debt in excess of a member's capital contributions (i.e. LLC-level debt is "non-recourse debt" with respect to a member because the member cannot be ultimately liable for the obligation). A partnership may treat debt that is secured by the partnership assets as "recourse" debt, but the increase in a partner's basis for the liabilities is generally allocated to general partnership who have ultimate responsibility for repayment.

Question 6: Do the enterprise participants need to structure variable forms of ownership, such as preferred stock, preferred returns, guaranteed payments, indemnification or special allocations of tax losses?

Comment: S corporations may only have a single class of stock, thereby preventing allocation of specific items or otherwise accommodating divergent ownership interests. New York LLCs may designate in the operating agreement that members have differing rights, powers and duties (including differing voting rights with respect to any specified matter), different classes of members, or provide for guaranteed payments.

Formation and operation generally.—An LLC may be formed in New York to carry on any lawful business purpose except one for which another statute requires some other form of business entity. (Sec. 201, Limited Liability Company Law) LLCs may, like other business entities, own property, sue and be sued, enter into contracts, etc. (Sec. 202, Limited Liability Company Law)

Formation.—An LLC is formed by the preparation and filing of articles of organization with the Department of State. For the law, see Sec. 203, Limited Liability Company Law; Sec. 204, Limited Liability Company Law; and Sec. 205, Limited Liability Company Law

Membership requirements.—An LLC, unlike a partnership, can be formed in New York with a single member (Sec. 203, Limited Liability Company Law), although a one-person LLC will not be viewed as a partnership by the Internal Revenue Service (IRS).

CCH CAUTION: One-person LLCs.—Since a one-person LLC cannot logically be categorized as a partnership, it could be considered by the IRS as either a sole proprietorship or an association treated for tax purposes as a corporation. Arguably, the presence or absence of corporate characteristics should determine the tax treatment of the single-member LLC, but the IRS has not yet established a position on this issue. Until this uncertainty is resolved, there are risks in carrying on a business as an LLC with only a single member. In many circumstances, this risk can be avoided by providing for a second member of the LLC without undermining other planning goals.

Articles of organization.—For the law outlining the requirements for the articles of organization, see Sec. 203, Limited Liability Company Law.

Membership interests.—Membership interests in LLCs are personal property. A member has no interest in specific property of the LLC. (Sec. 601, Limited Liability Company Law)

Personal liability of members.—Members and managers of an LLC are not liable for any debts, obligations or liabilities of the LLC solely by reason of being a member, manager or agent or participating in the conduct of the business. This is true whether the debt arises in contract, tort or any other manner. (Sec. 609, Limited Liability Company Law)

Fees.—For a list of fees imposed in connection with the formation or maintenance of an LLC, see ¶1-610 in the "Initial Taxes—Doing Business" division.

Annual fees.—For a discussion of annual filing fees on LLCs classified as partnerships for federal income tax purposes, limited liability partnerships (LLPs) and foreign limited liability partnerships with New York source income, see ¶1-510 in the "Initial Taxes—Doing Business" division.

Contributions and distributions.—As under the Partnership Law, member contributions to an LLC may be in the form of cash, property or services rendered or an obligation to contribute any of these. (Sec. 501, Limited Liability Company Law) For further information, see Sec. 501, Limited Liability Company Law; Sec. 502, Limited Liability Company Law; and Sec. 503, Limited Liability Company Law.

Transfers of LLC interests.—An LLC interest is a capital asset whose sale results in a capital gain or loss to the selling member (IRC Sec. 741). However, receipts from the sale of an LLC interest are treated as ordinary income to the extent they are attributable to unrealized receivables of the LLC or inventory items of the LLC that have appreciated substantially in value (IRC Sec. 751). Exchanges of LLC interests in different LLCs do not qualify for nonrecognition treatment under IRC Section 1031 (IRC Sec. 1031(a)). Gain and loss during the year of sale must be allocated between the transferring member and the transferee, and special rules prevent retroactive allocations of tax benefits to members entering late in the year (IRC Sec. 706(d)).

If an interest in an LLC with appreciated assets is sold, exchanged or passed by inheritance, an IRC Section 754 election gives the transferee a positive basis adjustment in the LLC's appreciated assets (IRC Sec. 743(b)). This prevents an incoming member from recognizing taxable gains due to appreciation that occurred before the interest was acquired. A similar adjustment to inside basis is allowable if a member recognizes gain from a distribution.

The sale or exchange within a 12-month period of 50% or more of the total interest in LLC capital and profits results in a termination of the LLC for tax purposes, even if, for all other purposes, the LLC continues to operate as it had before the transaction or transactions giving rise to the termination (IRC Sec. 708(b)). The practical effect of the termination is to close the books of the LLC as of the date on which the sale or exchange occurs, and open the books on what is for tax purposes a new LLC immediately thereafter.

Annual reporting.—New York does not specifically require annual meetings of members or annual reporting.

Dissolution.—LLC dissolution and winding-up provisions closely track those of the Partnership Law.

Winding up.—In the event of a dissolution, except with respect to a judicial dissolution, the members may wind up the LLC's affairs. (Sec. 703, Limited Liability Company Law)

Articles of dissolution; no members.—Within 90 days following the commencement of winding up, articles of dissolution must be filed with the Department of State setting forth certain basic information regarding the LLC and its dissolution. The filing of articles of dissolution serves to cancel the articles of organization of the LLC. (Sec. 705, Limited Liability Company Law)

When an LLC has no members, it will not be dissolved if the legal representative of the last remaining member agrees in writing to continue the LLC within 180 days (or another time period as provided in the operating agreement) after the event that terminated the last remaining membership. However, if the time period expires with no such agreement by the legal representative, articles of dissolution must be filed.

Foreign limited liability companies.—Foreign LLCs may apply for authority to do business in New York, subject to provisions analogous to those found in the New York Partnership Law. (Sec. 801, Limited Liability Company Law)

Powers of foreign LLC.—A foreign LLC authorized to do business in New York will have the same powers to conduct business in New York as it has in its home state, but can not have greater powers than those of a domestic LLC. A foreign LLC may not engage in any profession in New York, although this rule does not apply to foreign registered limited liability partnerships. (Sec. 805, Limited Liability Company Law)

Professional service limited liability companies.—Article XII of the New York Limited Liability Company Law authorizes the establishment of professional service LLCs and imposes additional requirements on such entities. These requirements parallel those contained in the Business Corporation Law for professional service corporations. (Sec. 1205, Limited Liability Company Law)

Foreign professional limited liability companies.—Article XIII of the New York Limited Liability Company Law authorizes foreign professional service LLCs to register in New York. (Sec. 1301, Limited Liability Company Law) These professional service LLCs may only provide services through individuals authorized to render such services in New York. (Sec. 1302, Limited Liability Company Law)

• *Federal income tax provisions*

A limited liability company (LLC) is a business entity created under state law. Every state and the District of Columbia have LLC statutes that govern the formation and operation of LLCs. An LLC has the characteristics of both a corporation and a partnership. Like a corporation, the owners (referred to as members) are usually not personally liable for the debts and other obligations of the LLC. Like a partnership or sole proprietorship, an LLC has great flexibility in the way it operates and does not need to follow corporate formalities, such as holding special and annual meetings with shareholders and directors.

An LLC has the flexibility to decide whether to be taxed as a partnership, an S corporation, or a C corporation. A single-member LLC is a disregarded entity, unless it elects to be taxed as a corporation for federal tax purposes. If an LLC chooses to be taxed as a partnership or an S corporation, or if a single-member LLC is disregarded as an entity, the LLC profits and losses are reported on the member's personal federal income tax return. Special check-the-box election timing requirements apply to LLCs.

[¶10-245] Exempt Organizations

Organizations seeking exemption from federal taxation are governed by Subchapter F (Exempt Organizations) of the Internal Revenue Code. New York's corporation franchise tax provisions regarding exempt organizations are generally similar to the federal income tax provisions, IRC Sec. 501—IRC Sec. 530. A discussion of the applicable federal income tax provisions follows the discussion of the state provisions.

• *Interaction of federal and state provisions*

As stated above, the New York corporate franchise tax provisions applicable to exempt organizations generally follow IRC Sec. 501—IRC Sec. 530. For instance, an organization that is exempt from federal income taxation pursuant to IRC Sec. 501(a), will be presumed to be exempt from the New York corporate franchise tax. Exempt organizations are subject to the unrelated business income tax, which conforms to federal law. In addition, corporations subject to other franchise taxes and certain other specified corporations are exempt from the corporate franchise tax.

Unrelated business income.—The New York tax on unrelated business income (UBI) conforms to the comparable federal income tax on the UBI of exempt organizations. The tax is reported on Form CT-13 (Instructions, Form CT-13). For a complete discussion of the tax, see ¶32-225. Returns are discussed at ¶89-102.

Corporations subject to other franchise taxes.—The following are exempt from the corporation franchise tax because they are subject to other New York franchise taxes:

—Cooperative farmers', fruit growers' and other like agricultural corporations (subject to Sec. 185 of Article 9, Tax Law); *Note:* Although the Sec. 185 tax is repealed for tax years beginning after 2017, the exemption continues to apply under Sec. 209(12) (TSB-M-15(1)C);

—Transportation and transmission corporations (corporations that remain subject to Secs. 183 and 184 of Article 9 of the Tax Law; see ¶80-010, ¶80-030, and ¶80-035) (see also discussion below under "Railroad and trucking companies");

—Insurance companies (subject to Article 33, Tax Law; see ¶10-335 Insurance Companies);

¶10-245

—For tax years beginning before 2015, banks, trust companies, savings and loan associations and other financial corporations (subject to Article 32, Tax Law; see ¶ 10-340 Banks—Financial Corporations); and

—For tax years beginning before 2015, bank holding companies filing combined returns with affiliated corporations (under Sec. 1462(f) of Article 32, Tax Law). (Sec. 209(4), Tax Law) (See also ¶ 10-340 Banks—Financial Corporations)

When a corporation's activities change, so that it becomes exempt from the corporation franchise tax, and subject to tax under another article of the Tax Law, the date of the change of classification will be determined by specific facts. If the change occurs during the corporation's taxable year, it will be treated for franchise tax purposes in the same way as a corporation which dissolved or otherwise ceased to be taxable during the year. In the opposite situation, when a corporation becomes subject to franchise tax because of a change of classification, it will be treated the same as a corporation which first becomes liable during a taxable year. (Reg. Sec. 1-3.5)

Other exempt corporations.—In addition to those corporations that are exempt from the corporation franchise tax because they are subject to other franchise taxes (discussed above), the following corporations are exempt from the corporation franchise tax:

—Nonstock corporations organized and operated exclusively for nonprofit purposes (Reg. Sec. 1-3.4);

—Any domestic corporation exclusively engaged in the operation of vessels in foreign commerce (Sec. 3, Tax Law);

—Any trust company organized under New York law, all of the stock of which is owned by not less than 20 New York savings banks (Sec. 209(4), Tax Law);

—Limited-dividend housing companies (Sec. 93, Private Housing Finance Law);

—Limited-profit housing companies (Sec. 209(4), Tax Law);

—Redevelopment companies operating pursuant to Article 5 of the private housing finance law;

—Housing development fund companies organized pursuant to Article 11 of the private housing finance law (Sec. 209(4), Tax Law);

—An organization organized exclusively for the purpose of holding title to property under federal law (26 U.S.C. § 501(2), (25)), and which turns over the net income so derived to an exempt organization (Sec. 209(9), Tax Law); and

—Certain domestic international sales corporations (DISCs) (See ¶ 10-255).

—Qualified settlements received by victims of Nazi persecution or their successors are exempt from state and local income taxes, regardless of whether this income is subject to federal income tax. Similarly, qualified settlement funds or grantor trusts established to settle claims arising the Holocaust, are exempt from state and local income taxes. (Sec. 13, Tax Law) (TSB-M-99(3)C)

Fixed dollar minimum tax exemption.—An exemption from the fixed dollar minimum tax is available to certain domestic business corporations. Specifically, the exemption applies to a domestic corporation that is no longer doing business, employing capital, owning or leasing property, or deriving receipts from activity in New York, provided that the corporation has no outstanding Article 9-A franchise taxes for its final tax year, or any prior tax year, and has filed an Article 9-A franchise tax return (original or amended) that has the "final return" box checked. (Sec. 209(8), Tax Law; TSB-M-06(5)C)

A domestic corporation that meets all of these criteria will no longer need to file any additional franchise tax returns for taxable years or periods occurring after the period covered by the final return. After filing its final return, the domestic corporation can seek consent to be dissolved. A qualifying domestic corporation that does not voluntarily dissolve will be subject to dissolution by proclamation after it has not filed franchise tax returns for at least two years. (TSB-M-06(5)C)

A domestic corporation that ceases to do business, employ capital, and own or lease property in New York but wishes to retain its certificate of incorporation must continue to file Article 9-A franchise tax returns and pay the applicable tax. (TSB-M-06(5)C)

The Department of Taxation and Finance has issued a memorandum that provides a number of examples illustrating the application of the exemption. (TSB-M-06(5)C)

New York State Urban Development Corporation.—The New York State Urban Development Corporation is exempt from corporate franchise (income) tax. (Sec. 4, S.B. 7803, Laws 2004)

Terrorist organizations.—Effective September 7, 2004, the law includes a provision that revokes the New York tax-exempt status of terrorist organizations whose federal tax-exempt status has been revoked by the IRS. For personal income and corporate franchise (income) tax purposes, the revocation applies with respect to the entire taxable year in which the date of revocation occurs and to subsequent taxable years. If an organization makes a sale of property or services on or after the date of revocation, the sale is taxable. An organization whose tax-exempt status is restored by the IRS is required to submit a new application and be approved before tax-exempt status is restored with respect to any tax or fee administered by the New York Commissioner of Taxation and Finance. (Sec. 27, Tax Law)

Cooperative corporations.—Until January 1, 2020, certain cooperative corporations that were organized without capital stock and were exempt from federal tax pursuant to IRC Sec. 501(c)(12) were required to pay the New York Commissioner of Taxation and Finance a $10 annual fee in lieu of franchise, license or corporation taxes. (Sec. 77, Cooperative Corporations Law) The fee was eliminated by the 2019 budget legislation. Cooperative corporations previously subject to the fee remain exempt from the franchise, license or corporation taxes. (Sec. 77, Cooperative Corporations Law; TSB-M-19(3)C)

Railroad and trucking companies.—Businesses formed for or principally engaged in the conduct of a railroad, palace car, sleeping car or trucking business, or formed for or principally engaged in the conduct of two or more of such businesses are excluded from Art. 9 franchise taxes on transportation and transmission companies, unless those corporations elect to continue to be subject to Art. 9 taxes. Accordingly, where the election to remain subject to Art. 9 tax is *not* made, railroad and trucking companies will be subject to Art. 9-A business corporation franchise tax (or, if applicable, Art. 32 bank franchise taxes). (Secs. 183(1)(b) and 183(10), Tax Law)

Time limitations for electing to remain subject to Art. 9.—Railroad and trucking companies subject to Sec. 183 and Sec. 184 of the Tax Law for the 1997 tax year must make their election on or before March 15, 1998. Once made, the election will apply to the 1998 and succeeding tax years, until revoked.

Railroad and trucking companies that are *not* subject to Art. 9 transportation and transmission franchise taxes for the 1997 tax year, but thereafter would be subject to Article 9-A or 32 taxes if the election were not made, must make their election by the first day on which they would be required to file a return or report (without regard to extensions). An election, once made, will continue in effect until revoked by the taxpayer.

Revocation of election.—A revocation of the election will be irrevocable. The election, and a revocation thereof, must be made in the manner prescribed by the Commissioner of Taxation and Finance, and will apply as of the following January 1.

• *Federal income tax provisions*

Organizations may qualify for tax-exempt status if they are organized and operated exclusively for religious, charitable, scientific, testing for public safety, literary, or educational purposes, promotion of amateur sports, or the prevention of cruelty to animals or children (Section 501(c)(3) organizations). Any corporation, community chest, fund, trust, or foundation may qualify for this exemption. Private foundations and organizations that are not public charities are exempt from tax if they are not organized for profit and their earnings do not benefit any individual. Each type of organization must meet specific requirements for exemption. Organizations that are granted exemption will still be taxed on their unrelated business income. In general, an organization must apply for exemption.

[¶10-325]

REGULATED INDUSTRIES

[¶10-335] Insurance Companies

Since New York does not subject insurance companies doing business in the state to its Article 9-A corporation franchise (income) tax, there is nothing comparable in state corporation franchise (income) tax law to IRC Sec. 801—IRC Sec. 848, the federal income tax provisions addressing the treatment of insurance companies. Instead, insurance companies are subject to the insurance franchise (income) tax under Article 33 of the Tax Law. (Sec. 209(4), Tax Law; Reg. Sec. 1-3.4)

Franchise tax.—Every domestic insurance corporation and every foreign or alien insurance corporation is required to pay a franchise tax annually for the following (except for certain exempt corporations):

—the privilege of exercising its corporate franchise;

—doing business in New York;

—employing capital in New York;

—owning or leasing property in New York in a corporate or organized capacity; or

—maintaining an office in New York.

Generally, the insurance franchise (income) tax on insurance corporations is based on premiums or, for life insurance corporations, measured by allocated entire net income (or one of three alternative bases) plus subsidiary capital. The tax is similar to the corporation franchise (income) tax.

Note.—The term "doing business" is not defined under Article 33 of the Tax Law. Historically, the New York Department of Taxation and Finance has looked to whether a company must be licensed by the Superintendent of Insurance to determine if it is doing an insurance business.

Additional franchise tax.—For life insurance companies, an additional franchise tax based on gross premiums less certain deductions also is imposed by Article 33. Prior to 2003, the additional franchise tax was levied at differing rates for nonlife and life insurance companies.

For a detailed discussion of the insurance franchise (income) tax imposed by Article 33 of the Tax Law, see ¶ 88-010 and following.

• *Federal income tax provisions*

Insurance companies are generally subject to income tax computed at the normal corporate tax rates. However, the taxable income of insurance companies is determined under special rules. A company qualifies as an insurance company if more than half of its business during the tax year is the issuing of insurance or annuity contracts, or the reinsuring of risks underwritten by insurance companies. If an insurance company's net written premiums or direct written premiums (whichever is greater) for the tax year do not exceed a specified amount, the company may elect to be taxed only on its taxable investment income. Very small property and casualty (non-life) insurance companies may be exempt from tax if they meet certain requirements.

[¶ 10-340] Banks--Financial Corporations

Note: For tax years beginning after 2014, the Article 32 bank franchise tax is repealed, and banks are merged into the Article 9-A corporate franchise tax. The change is the result of corporate tax reform enacted by the 2014 budget bill.

For special taxable income computation modifications applicable to financial corporations, see ¶ 10-525.

[¶ 10-375]

RATES

[¶ 10-380] Rates of Tax

What is the New York corporate income tax rate?

The New York corporate income tax rates are different for each tax base. The tax is the highest of the amounts computed under the business income base, the capital base, or the fixed dollar minimum base.

Business income base. The applicable rates are (Sec. 210, Tax Law):

— for qualified New York manufacturers: 0%

— for qualified emerging technology companies (QETCs): 5.7% (2015), 5.5% (2016 and 2017), 4.875% (2018 and later years)

— for small businesses: 6.5% (prior to 2016, graduated rates applied)

— for other taxpayers: 7.1% (2015), 6.5% (2016 and later years)

For a discussion of the requirements to be a qualified New York manufacturer, see *TSB-M-19(5)C.*

Capital base. For qualified New York manufacturers and QETCs, the rates are: 0.132% (2015), 0.106% (2016), 0.085% (2017), 0.056% (2018), 0.038% (2019), 0.019% (2020), and 0% (2021 and later years).

For cooperative housing corporations, the rates are: 0.04% (through 2019), 0.025% (2020), and 0% (2021 and later years).

For other taxpayers, the rates are: 0.15% (2015), 0.125% (2016), 0.1% (2017), 0.075% (2018), 0.05% (2019), 0.025% (2020), and 0% (2021 and later years).

For tax years beginning on or after January 1, 2015, a tax cap applies, set at $350,000 for qualified New York manufacturers and QETCs and $5 million for all other taxpayers.

Small business taxpayers are exempt from the capital base tax in their first two years. (Sec. 210(1-c), Tax Law)

Fixed dollar minimum. For tax years after 2014, the fixed dollar minimum generally ranges from $25 (if New York receipts are not more than $100,000) to $200,000 (if New York receipts are over $1 billion).

A separate table applies to S corporations (see below).

For qualified New York manufacturer C corporations and QETCs, the amounts decrease over time. The amounts range from $22 to $4,385 (depending on New York receipts) for tax year 2015; from $21 to $4,230 for tax years 2016 and 2017; and from $19 to $3,750 for tax year 2018 and later years.

Under the 2017 budget legislation, applicable to taxable years beginning on or after January 1, 2016, special fixed dollar minimum tax amounts apply to a REIT or RIC that is not a captive REIT or a captive RIC. The tax amount depends on the amount of New York receipts, as follows: $25 if not more than $100,000; $75 if more than $100,000 but not over $250,000; $175 if more than $250,000 but not over $500,000; and $500 if more than $500,000. (Sec. 210(1)(d)(1)(D-1), Tax Law)

For a qualified entity that is located in an innovation hot spot, only the fixed dollar minimum tax applies. (Sec. 209(11), Tax Law; TSB-M-13(6)C; TSB-M-14(1)C)

S corporations. For S corporations (other than qualified New York manufacturers or QETCs), the fixed dollar minimum tax amounts are:

New York receipts	Fixed dollar minimum
not more than $100,000	$25
$100,001 to $250,000	$ 50
$250,001 to $500,000	$ 175
$500,001 to $1,000,000	$300
$1,000,001 to $5,000,000	$ 1,000
$5,000,001 to $25,000,000	$ 3,000
over $25,000,000	$ 4,500

For S corporations that are qualified New York manufacturers and QETCs, the amounts decrease over time. The amounts range from $22 to $3,947 (depending on New York receipts) for tax year 2015; from $21 to $3,807 for tax years 2016 and 2017; and from $19 to $3,375 for tax year 2018 and later years.

Former AMT and tax on subsidiary capital. The corporate tax reform legislation enacted in 2014 eliminated the minimum taxable income base (alternative minimum tax) and the additional tax on subsidiary capital for tax years beginning on or after January 1, 2015. (Sec. 210, Tax Law)

Metropolitan Commuter Transportation District surcharge. The 2014 budget legislation made the Metropolitan Commuter Transportation District surcharge, also known as the MTA surcharge, permanent and increased the rate from 17% to 25.6% for tax year 2015. The rate is 28% for tax year 2016, 28.3% for tax year 2017, 28.6% for tax year 2018, 28.9% for tax year 2019, and 29.4% for tax year 2020. The rate will remain the same in later tax years, unless the Commissioner of Taxation and Finance determines a new rate. (Reg. Sec. 9-1.2; TSB-M-16(1)C; TSB-M-17(1)C; TSB-M-17(4)C; TSB-M-18(5)C; TSB-M-19(6)C)

The base of the MTA surcharge is New York state tax before credits for the current year.

An economic nexus standard applies to the MTA surcharge; the *de minimis* MTA receipts threshold is $1 million. There will be an annual review of the thresholds at which a corporation is deemed to be deriving receipts from activity in the Metropolitan Commuter Transportation District, and the thresholds will be adjusted if the cumulative percentage change in the Consumer Price Index since January 1, 2015, or since the thresholds were last adjusted, is 10% or more. Newly adjusted receipts thresholds will be published on the department's website. (Reg. Sec. 9-1.1)

For tax years 2016, 2017, 2018, 2019, and 2020, the "deriving receipts" thresholds are unchanged and remain the same as set forth in Tax Law Sec. 209-B(1). (TSB-M-16(1)C; TSB-M-17(1)C; TSB-M-17(4)C; TSB-M-18(5)C; TSB-M-19(6)C)

MTA payroll tax. The Metropolitan Commuter Transportation Mobility Tax, also known as the MCTMT or the MTA payroll tax, applies to employers and self-employed individuals engaging in business in the Metropolitan Commuter Transportation District (MCTD). Specifically, the tax applies to (1) employers required to withhold New York state income tax from employee wages and whose payroll expense exceeds $312,500 in any calendar quarter, and (2) individuals with net earnings from self-employment allocated to the MCTD that exceed $50,000 for the tax year. (Sec. 800, Tax Law; Sec. 801, Tax Law; TSB-M-12(1)MCTMT; Publication 420)

The tax rate is 0.11% for employers with payroll expense over $312,500 but not over $375,000 in any calendar quarter; 0.23% for employers with payroll expense over $375,000 but not over $437,500 in any calendar quarter; and 0.34% for employers with payroll expense exceeding $437,500 in any calendar quarter. (Sec. 801, Tax Law; TSB-M-12(1)MCTMT)

For individuals, the tax rate is 0.34% of net earnings from self-employment allocated to the MCTD during the tax year. (Sec. 801, Tax Law)

Professional employer organizations. A professional employer organization (PEO) determines its MCTMT liability, if any, for a calendar quarter using the following method: (1) determine a separate quarterly payroll expense for each client and for itself; (2) multiply each payroll expense determined in step 1 by the applicable MCTMT rate for that expense amount; and (3) add together the MCTMT amounts computed in step 2 to determine the total MCTMT liability for the calendar quarter. (Sec. 801(a), Tax Law; TSB-M-12(2)MCTMT)

START-UP NY program. The START-UP NY program provides an exemption from the MCTMT. (Sec. 39(d), Tax Law; Sec. 803(b), Tax Law; TSB-M-13(1)MCTMT)

Opt-in payroll tax—ECET. The 2018 budget legislation created an optional employer compensation expense program (ECEP), under which affected employers are subject to an employer compensation expense tax (ECET) on annual payroll expenses exceeding $40,000 per employee. For employers opting in, the tax is phased in over three years, with a rate of 1.5% in 2019, 3% in 2020, and 5% beginning in 2021. (Sec. 852, Tax Law; *TSB-M-18(1)ECEP*)

The department has provided a web-based registration system for the employer election. (*TSB-M-18(1)ECEP*)

Revocation of election: The law has been amended to allow for revocation of the employer election. Specifically, if an employer determines that the election was in error and the employer does not wish to participate in the program for the calendar year and has taken no action to comply, the employer may revoke the election to participate in the program. For calendar year 2020, revocation of the employer election had to be made on or before April 15, 2020. For calendar years beginning

2021 and later, revocation of the employer election must be made no later than January 15th of the immediately succeeding calendar year after the employer election was made. (Sec. 851, Tax Law)

Covered employees: The tax applies to the employer's payroll expense over $40,000 for the year paid to each employee subject to New York withholding.

An employee is considered to be employed in New York if one of the following tests is met. (*TSB-M-18(1)ECEP*)

— **Localization.** An employee works in New York if he or she performs services (1) entirely within the state, or (2) partially in the state, if the out-of-state services are incidental to the in-state services.

— **Base of Operations.** An employee works in New York if his or her base of operations is in the state.

— **Place of Direction and Control.** An employee works in New York if (1) the employer's place of direction and control is in the state, and (2) the employee performs some services in the state.

Part-year employment in New York: For a part-year employee, the tax applies only when the wages and compensation paid for employment in New York exceed $40,000. The department has provided examples illustrating how tax is calculated for part-year employment in New York (see *TSB-M-18(1)ECEP*).

Payments and returns: Electing employers must pay the tax electronically on the same dates applicable to the employer's withholding payments. Employers must file quarterly returns by the same due dates applicable to withholding returns. (*TSB-M-18(1)ECEP*)

Withholding: New York will make no change to the withholding tables for electing employers.

But the state will update the 2019 Form IT-2104 to allow employees with wages subject to the new tax to adjust their income tax withholding accordingly.

Employers may not deduct or withhold any portion of the tax from an employee's wages. (*TSB-M-18(1)ECEP*)

Tax years beginning before 2015. The New York corporation franchise tax was the largest of the four amounts under A, plus the amount computed under B. (Sec. 210(1), Tax Law)

A

— 7.1% on allocated entire net income (Sec. 210(1)(a), Tax Law) (special rules applied for manufacturers, QETCs, and small business taxpayers); *or*

— 0.15% (0.136% for qualified New York manufacturers and QETCs for 2014) for each dollar of allocated business and investment capital (0.04% in the case of cooperative housing corporations), not to exceed $350,000 for qualified New York manufacturers and QETCs or $1 million for all other taxpayers (Sec. 210(1)(b), Tax Law); *or*

— 1.5% of the taxpayer's minimum taxable income base (Sec. 210(1)(c), Tax Law) (special rules applied for manufacturers and QETCs); *or*

— a fixed dollar minimum tax, based on New York receipts (Sec. 210(1)(d)(4), Tax Law; TSB-M-08(12)C; Instructions, Form CT-3)

Plus B

0.9 mill for each dollar of allocated subsidiary capital. (Sec. 210(1)(e), Tax Law)

[¶10-500]
TAXABLE INCOME COMPUTATION

[¶10-505] Overview of Taxable Income Computation

As the result of corporate tax reforms enacted by recent budget legislation, significant changes to the corporate franchise tax bases and rates became effective for tax years beginning after 2014. The 2015 and 2016 budget bills contained technical and clarifying amendments to the corporate tax reform statute enacted in 2014. These technical and clarifying amendments are also effective for tax years beginning after 2014. For example, the minimum taxable income base (alternative minimum tax) is eliminated for tax years beginning on or after January 1, 2015, as is the additional tax on subsidiary capital. Accordingly, the tax is generally the highest of the amounts under the entire net income (ENI)/business income base, the capital base, or the fixed dollar minimum. However, the capital base tax is phased out over six years, beginning in 2016. See ¶10-380 for additional details about the rate changes. For a discussion regarding the entire net income base for tax years beginning before 2015, see ¶10-510.

Tax years beginning after 2014.—A corporate tax reform outline issued by the Department of Taxation and Finance provides the following information.

The starting point for the business income base is federal taxable income (FTI) for U.S corporations and effectively connected income (ECI) for alien corporations not deemed domestic under the IRC. Taxpayers are required to add back treaty benefits to ECI (Sec. 208(9)(b)(1), Tax Law), consistent with the existing treatment of alien banks under Article 32. The requirement that taxpayers add back the amount of foreign taxes paid is eliminated. Most of the other existing 9-A modifications are continued. (Sec. 208, Tax Law; Corporate Tax Reform, New York Department of Taxation and Finance)

The exemptions for income from subsidiary capital and 50% of dividends from non-subsidiaries are eliminated. Income is reclassified as investment income, other exempt income, or business income.

Business income equals entire net income (ENI) minus investment income and other exempt income.

Discrete components of business income are not articulated, but business income includes the following:

— interest income and gains and losses from debt instruments or other obligations, unless the income cannot be included in apportionable business income under the U.S. Constitution;

— gains and losses from stock of a unitary corporation;

— dividends and gains and losses from stock held in a non-unitary corporation for 6 months or less; and

— cash.

To prevent the overcapitalization of non-life insurance corporations, the Commissioner is provided with discretionary powers to make a deemed distribution of non-premium income from overcapitalized Article 33 corporations to the affiliated Article 9-A corporations to properly reflect the activities of the unitary business. (Sec. 211.5, Tax Law)

The existing approach to partnership items of receipts, income, gain, loss, and deduction that flow through a partnership to a corporate partner, as well as gains or losses from the sale of a partnership interest itself (i.e., under the existing regulations), is retained. (Sec. 209.1(f), Tax Law; Sec. 210.3, Tax Law)

Allocated business income is the amount subject to tax. (Sec. 210.1(a), Tax Law; Corporate Tax Reform, New York Department of Taxation and Finance)

Investment income: The Article 9-A definition of investment income is amended to include income, including capital gains in excess of capital losses, from investment capital, less any interest deductions directly or indirectly attributable to investment capital or income. Additionally, investment income may not exceed entire net income (ENI and any excess amounts of interest deductions over investment must be added back to ENI). Finally, investment income, determined without regard to interest deductions, cannot exceed 8% of the taxpayer's ENI. (Sec. 208, Tax Law; Corporate Tax Reform, New York Department of Taxation and Finance)

Solely for purposes of determining whether that stock should be classified as investment capital after it is acquired, if a taxpayer acquires stock that is a capital asset under IRC Sec. 1221 during the taxable year and owns that stock on the last day of the taxable year, it will be presumed that the taxpayer held that stock for more than one year. (Sec. 208, Tax Law)

However, if the taxpayer does not own that stock at the time it actually files its original report for the taxable year in which it acquired the stock, then the above presumption does not apply and the actual period of time during which the taxpayer owned the stock will be used to determine whether the stock should be classified as investment capital after it is acquired. (Sec. 208, Tax Law)

If the taxpayer relies on the presumption that the taxpayer held the stock for more than one year, but does not own the stock for more than one year, the taxpayer must increase its total business capital in the immediately succeeding taxable year by the amount included in investment capital for that stock, net of any liabilities attributable to that stock computed and must increase its business income in the immediately succeeding taxable year by the amount of income and net gains (but not less than zero) from that stock included in investment income, less any interest deductions directly or indirectly attributable to that stock. (Sec. 208, Tax Law)

The election to reduce investment income and other exempt income by 40%, in lieu of attribution of interest expenses, is revocable. (Sec. 208, Tax Law)

Other exempt income: The new "other exempt income" category of income is defined as the sum of exempt CFC income and exempt unitary dividends. "Exempt CFC income" is (1) income received from a controlled foreign corporation that is conducting a unitary business with the taxpayer but is not included in the combined group (this includes Subpart F income and § 956 dividends); (2) (for taxable years beginning on or after January 1, 2017) repatriated income received from a corporation not included in a combined report with the taxpayer; and (3) in the Commissioner's discretion, any interest deductions attributable to such income. "Exempt unitary dividends" are dividends from unitary corporations not in the combined group because they are: (1) taxable under another tax article; (2) alien corporations not deemed domestic with no ECI; or (3) less than 50% directly or indirectly owned. (Sec. 208, Tax Law; Corporate Tax Reform, New York Department of Taxation and Finance)

Attribution of expenses: Investment income and other exempt income are not taxable, and the deductions for interest expenses attributable to such income are disallowed.

If actual expense attribution exceeds income, the excess expenses are required to be added back to income.

In lieu of computing actual interest expenses disallowed, taxpayers generally can elect to reduce investment and other exempt income by 40%. If the election is made, it covers both other exempt income and investment income. Taxpayers receiving dividends from unitary affiliates subject to tax under Article 9 or Article 33 are precluded from making the 40% election for those dividends and must perform actual expense attribution.

The actual attribution methodology for taxpayers not making the 40% election will be based on existing rules and detailed in revised guidance issued by the Department. (Sec. 208, Tax Law; Corporate Tax Reform, New York Department of Taxation and Finance)

The computation of expense attribution for a combined group is done on a "one company" basis. If the taxpayer chooses the 40% election, it applies to both the investment income and other exempt income of all members of the combined group. (Sec. 210-C, Tax Law; Corporate Tax Reform, New York Department of Taxation and Finance)

• *Tax years beginning before 2015*

The New York corporate franchise tax has several possible bases. Primarily, the tax is measured by entire net income. Alternatively, if a higher payment will result, the taxpayer will be subject to a tax on business and investment capital (see ¶ 10-535 Non-Income Tax Base Computation), a tax on minimum taxable income (see ¶ 10-530 Alternate Taxable Income Computation Methods), or a fixed dollar minimum tax (see ¶ 10-380 Rates of Tax).

Any tax base (except the fixed dollar minimum) may be subject to allocation procedures in order to determine the actual amount subject to tax (see ¶ 11-505 Allocation and Apportionment).

Entire net income is equal to federal taxable income (¶ 10-510), with certain additions (¶ 10-600) and subtractions (¶ 10-800).

New York's conformity to the Internal Revenue Code is discussed at ¶ 10-515.

[¶ 10-510] Starting Point for Computation

What is the starting point for computation of the New York corporate income tax?

The starting point for computation of the New York corporate franchise tax on the business income base is the taxpayer's federal taxable income reported on line 28 of its federal income tax return. This amount reflects federal taxable income before federal net operating loss and special deductions. (Sec. 208(9), Tax Law; Instructions, Form CT-3)

Consolidated federal return. A taxpayer that is a member of a federal affiliated group filing a consolidated return must complete a *pro forma* Form 1120 reporting the federal taxable income it would have been required to report on a separate federal tax return. The taxpayer must also attach a copy of the federal consolidating workpaper indicating its separate taxable income before any elimination of intercorporate transactions included in the federal consolidated return. (Instructions, Form CT-3)

[¶ 10-515] Federal Conformity

New York does not conform to the IRC through the specific adoption of IRC provisions. However, New York uses federal taxable income as the starting point for determining entire net income. (Instructions, Form CT-3, New York General Business Corporation Franchise Tax Return). Accordingly, New York generally follows the federal treatment of items of income and deduction.

See ¶ 10-505 for an overview of New York's taxable income computation.

[¶10-525] Special Industries or Entities

Note: As the result of corporate tax reforms enacted by recent budget legislation, significant changes to the corporate franchise tax bases and rates became effective for tax years beginning after 2014. See ¶10-380 and ¶10-505 for details.

New York has special computation provisions for certain entities and industries.

• *S corporations*

New York S corporations are subject only to the fixed dollar minimum tax. (Sec. 210(1)(g), Tax Law) For further discussion, see ¶10-215 S Corporations, and ¶10-380, Rates.

• *Regulated investment companies*

For a regulated investment company (RIC), the base is "investment company taxable income," as defined in IRC Sec. 852(b)(2) (but before the deduction for dividends paid and the deductions for tax imposed under IRC Secs. 851(d)(2) and 851(i)), as modified by IRC Sec. 855, plus the amount taxable under IRC Sec. 852(b)(3). (Sec. 209(7), Tax Law; Instructions, Form CT-3)

• *Real estate investment trusts*

For a real estate investment trust (REIT), "entire net income" means "real estate investment trust taxable income," as defined in IRC Sec. 857(b)(2), as modified by IRC Sec. 858. (Sec. 209(5), Tax Law; Instructions, Form CT-3)

• *Insurance companies*

Insurance companies are subject to a separate insurance franchise tax. See ¶10-335 Insurance Companies.

• *Financial corporations*

For tax years beginning before 2015, financial corporations were subject to a separate bank franchise tax. See ¶10-340 Banks—Financial Corporations.

For tax years beginning after 2014, they are subject to the Article 9-A corporate franchise tax. For certain thrifts and qualified community banks, subtractions are allowed for:

(1) holding a qualified residential loan portfolio (Sec. 208(9)(r), Tax Law);

(2) holding a significant amount of New York small business loans and New York residential mortgages (Sec. 208(9)(s), Tax Law); or

(3) maintaining a captive REIT on April 1, 2014 (Sec. 208(9)(t), Tax Law).

The law provides that total assets include leased real property that is not properly reflected on a balance sheet, for purposes of the asset tests under subtractions (1) and (2) above. Leased real property that is not properly reflected on the balance sheet is valued at the annual lease payment multiplied by eight. (TSB-M-16(3)C)

• *Utilities, power producers, and pipelines—Transition adjustments*

For purposes of computing entire net income, certain transition adjustments are provided for qualified public utilities and power producers that were subject to Sec. 186, Tax Law, in 1999. With respect to transition property, for example, the deduction for federal income tax purposes for depreciation will not be allowed. Other adjustments are set forth in the statute. (Sec. 208(9)(c-2), Tax Law; Sec. 208(9)(c-3), Tax Law)

Similar adjustments are provided for pipeline companies that were subject to Sec. 183 and Sec. 184, Tax Law, in 1999. (Sec. 208(9)(c-3), Tax Law)

Qualified gas transportation contracts (Prior law).—For taxable years commencing after 1999, any corporate franchise tax paid under Tax Law Article 9-A allocable to receipts attributable to a qualified gas transportation contract will be deemed to have been paid under Article 9, provided that all of the following conditions are met: (1) for periods ending prior to 2000, the taxpayer paid the Article 9 utility tax due under Tax Law Sec. 184; (2) for the taxable year, all of the receipts from the pipeline transportation of natural gas attributable to the taxpayer and included in the taxpayer's entire net income are solely from the transportation of natural gas for wholesale customers and commercial retail customers; (3) the taxpayer's corporate franchise tax liability for the taxable year is determined under Tax Law Sec. 210(1)(a), and that liability is greater than the liability the taxpayer would have incurred under Tax Law Secs. 183 and 184, as they existed on December 31, 1999, based on the same taxable period; and (4) the taxpayer is a party to a qualified gas transportation contract. These provisions are deemed repealed for taxable years commencing after 2014. (Sec. 208(9)(n), Tax Law; *TSB-M-02(5)C*)

The above provision permits gas pipeline companies with contracts in effect when New York's energy taxes were restructured and reduced to continue to recover tax costs as those contracts intended. (*Summary of Tax Provisions in SFY 2002-03 Budget,* Office of Tax Policy Analysis, New York Department of Taxation and Finance, June 26, 2002)

See ¶ 10-505 for an overview of New York's taxable income computation.

[¶ 10-530] Alternate Taxable Income Computation Methods

For tax years beginning before 2015, although the tax is primarily measured by entire net income (see ¶ 10-510 Starting Point for Computation), if a higher payment will result, one of the following alternatives will apply: (1) business and investment capita; (2) minimum taxable income (see below); or (3) fixed dollar minimum (see ¶ 10-380 Rates of Tax).

Under the 2014 budget legislation, the minimum taxable income base is eliminated for tax years beginning on or after January 1, 2015. In addition, the capital base tax is phased out over six years beginning in 2016 (see ¶ 10-380).

For an overview of the New York taxable income computation, see ¶ 10-505.

• *Minimum taxable income (tax years beginning before 2015)*

All taxpayers must determine a minimum taxable income base and tax, regardless of whether they file federal Form 4626 (Alternative Minimum Tax–Corporations). (Sec. 210(1)(c), Tax Law; Reg. Sec. 3-4.1; Instructions, Form CT-3, New York General Business Corporation Franchise Tax Return)

Minimum taxable income defined.—The term "minimum taxable income" is defined as the entire net income of the taxpayer for the taxable year modified as follows (Sec. 208(8-B), Tax Law; Reg. Sec. 3-4.2; TSB-M-90(13)C):

(1) An addition is made of the IRC Sec. 57 tax preference items, which are modified by deducting "tax-exempt interest" and "accelerated depreciation or amortization on certain property placed in service before January 1, 1987," as determined under IRC Sec. 57(a)(5) and (7).

(2) Entire net income is modified to reflect the following federal adjustments, which have the same meaning and are computed in the same manner as under IRC Secs. 56 and 58:

(a) depreciation under IRC Sec. 56(a)(1), except that this item excludes amounts attributable to property on which New York has disallowed ACRS;

(b) IRC Sec. 56(a)(2) mining exploration and development costs;

(c) IRC Sec. 56(a)(3) treatment of certain long-term contracts;

(d) IRC Sec. 56(a)(6) installment sales of certain property;

(e) IRC Sec. 56(b)(2)(C) circulation expenditures of personal holding companies;

(f) IRC Sec. 56(c)(2) merchant marine capital construction funds;

(g) IRC Sec. 58(b) disallowance of passive activity loss; and

(h) "adjusted basis," as that term appears in IRC Sec. 56(a)(7) (but without that section's reference to the "pollution control facilities" preference item at IRC Sec. 56(a)(5)).

(3) An addition equal to the amount of the New York net operating loss (NOL) deduction otherwise allowed under Tax Law Sec. 208(9)(f) is made.

(4) A subtraction is made for the alternative net operating loss deduction (ANOLD), as defined in Tax Law Sec. 208(8-B)(d); the ANOLD is discussed in detail in TSB-M-94(5)C.

Allocation.—Minimum taxable income is allocated by the use of an alternative business allocation percentage and the regular investment allocation percentage. (Sec. 210(3-a), Tax Law; TSB-M-90(13)C; Instructions, Form CT-3, New York General Business Corporation Franchise Tax Return) See ¶11-505 for a discussion of New York allocation provisions.

[¶10-600] Additions to Taxable Income Base

For computation of the entire net income base, New York requires certain additions to the federal taxable income starting point amount (see ¶10-510 Starting Point for Computation). The respective additions are discussed at the paragraphs listed below.

— Bonus depreciation . . . . ¶10-670

— Deferred gain from sale of qualified emerging technology investment . . . . ¶10-640

— Depreciation . . . . ¶10-670

— Gain on sale of property when special additional mortgage recording tax credit claimed . . . . ¶10-640

— Interest from federal, state and municipal obligations . . . . ¶10-610

— Interest paid to corporate parent . . . . ¶10-645

— Qualified production activities deduction . . . . ¶10-660

— Royalty and interest expense addbacks . . . . ¶10-620

— Safe harbor leases . . . . ¶10-670

— SUV expensing under IRC Sec. 179 . . . . ¶10-670

— Taxes . . . . ¶10-615

Additions to income are reported on Form CT-3 and Form CT-225. (Instructions, Form CT-225)

Subtractions from the taxable income base are discussed beginning at ¶10-800 Subtractions from Taxable Income, and an overview of the taxable income computation is provided at ¶10-505 Overview of Taxable Income Computation.

[¶ 10-610] Additions--Federally Exempt Interest

All interest received or accrued from federal, state, municipal, and other obligations that was exempt from federal income tax must be added back in computing New York entire net income. (Sec. 208(9)(b)(2), Tax Law; Reg. Sec. 3-2.3; Instructions, Form CT-3, New York General Business Corporation Franchise Tax Return)

Taxpayers may deduct from the add-back amount any expenses that are attributable to the interest but that were denied deductibility for federal purposes under IRC Sec. 265 (concerning expenses and interest relating to tax-exempt income). (Reg. Sec. 3-2.3; Instructions, Form CT-3, New York General Business Corporation Franchise Tax Return)

Other additions to the taxable income base are listed at ¶ 10-600.

[¶ 10-615] Additions--Taxes

To the extent that the following taxes were deducted or excluded from income for federal purposes, they are added back to federal taxable income in computing New York entire net income:

(1) Taxes payable to the United States, or its possessions, territories, or commonwealths, if imposed on or measured by income or profits, or regularly imposed in lieu of such taxes (*Note:* Foreign income taxes were included in the addback for tax years beginning before 2015). (Sec. 208(9)(b)(3), Tax Law; Reg. Sec. 3-2.3; Instructions, Form CT-225)

(2) Taxes on or measured by profits or income, or which include profits or income as a measure, paid to any other state of the United States, or any political subdivision thereof, or to the District of Columbia. (Sec. 208(9)(b)(3-a), Tax Law; Reg. Sec. 3-2.3; Instructions, Form CT-225)

(3) The New York Article 9-A corporation franchise tax, the former Article 32 franchise tax on banking corporations, and the Article 9 franchise taxes on transportation and transmission corporations and associations. The Metropolitan Transportation Authority (MTA) surcharge is included. However, taxpayers should not include New York City taxes. (Sec. 208(9)(b)(4), Tax Law; Reg. Sec. 3-2.3; Instructions, Form CT-225)

(4) The MTA payroll tax (also known as the MCTMT or Metropolitan Commuter Transportation Mobility Tax) imposed under Article 23. (Sec. 208(9)(b)(20), Tax Law; TSB-M-09(1)MCTMT)

• *Taxes for which New York credits are provided*

Real property taxes paid on qualified agricultural property and deducted in determining a taxpayer's federal taxable income must be added back to the entire net income tax base to the extent of the amount of the agricultural property tax credit allowed under Sec. 210(22), Tax Law. (Sec. 208(9)(b)(15), Tax Law; Instructions, Form CT-225)

A similar requirement applies with respect to (Instructions, Form CT-225):

— the credit for special additional mortgage recording tax (Sec. 208(9)(b)(4a), Tax Law; Reg. Sec. 3-2.3);

— the START-UP NY telecommunication services excise tax credit (Sec. 208(9)(b)(20-a), Tax Law); and

— the manufacturer's real property tax credit (Sec. 208(9)(b)(21), Tax Law).

Other additions to the taxable income base are listed at ¶ 10-600.

[¶10-620] Additions--Corporate Transactions

The following provisions concerning royalty expense addbacks were enacted by A.B. 2106, Laws 2003, and amended by S.B. 5725, Laws 2003. The 2013 budget legislation further revised them; among other changes, the income exclusion provision was eliminated.

• *Addback of related member expenses*

For the purpose of computing a taxpayer's entire net income or other applicable taxable basis, royalty payments made by the taxpayer to a related member during the taxable year must be added back, to the extent deductible in calculating the taxpayer's federal taxable income. (Sec. 208(9)(o), Tax Law)

There is an exception from the addback requirement for any taxpayer included in a combined return with a related member under Sec. 211(4). (Sec. 208(9)(o)(2)(A), Tax Law)

In addition, for taxable years beginning on or after January 1, 2013, the addback is not required if (Sec. 208(9)(o)(2)(B), Tax Law; Summary, New York Department of Taxation and Finance):

— the amount was included in the related member's tax base, the related member paid all or part of the amount to an unrelated party, and the transaction between the taxpayer and the related member had a valid business purpose;

— the related member paid significant taxes on the amount;

— the related member was organized in a foreign country, the income from the transaction was subject to a comprehensive income tax treaty, the related member was taxed by the foreign country at a rate at least equal to New York's rate, and the amount was paid in a transaction with a valid business purpose and arm's-length terms; or

— the taxpayer and the Department agree to alternative adjustments.

For taxable years beginning before 2013, the addback of royalty payments was not required to the extent that such payments met either of the following conditions:

—the related member during the same taxable year directly or indirectly paid or incurred the amount to a person or entity that was not a related member, and such transaction was done for a valid business purpose and the payments were made at arm's length; or

—the royalty payments were paid or incurred to a related member organized under the laws of a country other than the United States, were subject to a comprehensive income tax treaty between such country and the United States, and were taxed in such country at a tax rate at least equal to that imposed by New York. (Sec. 208(9)(o)(2)(B), Tax Law)

A "valid business purpose" is one or more business purposes, other than the avoidance or reduction of taxation, which alone or in combination constitute the primary motivation for some business activity or transaction, which activity or transaction changes in a meaningful way, apart from tax effects, the economic position of the taxpayer. The economic position of the taxpayer includes an increase in the market share of the taxpayer, or the entry by the taxpayer into new business markets. (Sec. 208(9)(o)(1)(D), Tax Law)

For purposes of these provisions, "royalty payments" are defined as payments directly connected to the acquisition, use, maintenance or management, ownership, sale, exchange, or any other disposition of licenses, trademarks, copyrights, trade names, trade dress, service marks, mask works, trade secrets, patents and any other similar types of intangible assets as determined by the Commissioner. The definition includes amounts allowable as interest deductions under IRC Sec. 163 to the extent such amounts are directly or indirectly for, related to or in connection with the acquisition, use, maintenance or management, ownership, sale, exchange or disposition of such intangible assets. (Sec. 208(9)(o)(1)(C), Tax Law)

"Related member" means a related person as defined in IRC § 465(b)(3)(c), except that "50%" is substituted for "10%." (Sec. 208(9)(o)(1), Tax Law)

For a discussion of passive investment companies, see ¶ 10-212.

Other additions to the taxable income base are listed at ¶ 10-600.

[¶10-630] Additions--Dividends

The federal deduction for dividends received is not allowed for New York purposes. (Sec. 208(9)(b)(2), Tax Law) However, because computation of entire net income begins with federal taxable income before the special (dividends) deduction (see ¶ 10-510), no addback is required.

Subtractions for dividends are discussed at ¶ 10-810.

Other additions to the taxable income base are listed at ¶ 10-600.

[¶10-635] Additions--Losses

Note: As the result of corporate tax reforms enacted by recent budget legislation, significant changes to the corporate franchise tax bases and rates became effective for tax years beginning after 2014. See ¶ 10-380 and ¶ 10-505 for details.

• *Capital losses*

By adopting federal taxable income as a starting point (see ¶ 10-510), the New York corporation franchise tax law generally adopts the federal income tax treatment of items of gross income and deductions. Capital loss carryovers, permitted to the same extent as under federal law, are discussed below.

Capital losses may be carried back for three years and the excess carried over five years. The amount is carried back or forward to the same years as under federal law, and the amount deducted in any year may not exceed the amount allowed federally, or, in the case of an S corporation, the amount that would have been allowed federally had the taxpayer not been an S corporation. (Reg. Sec. 3-7.1)

If a taxpayer has a capital loss carryback or carryforward, federal taxable income and entire net income must be recomputed. In recomputing entire net income, any loss from subsidiary capital included in the capital loss carryback or carryforward must be added to recomputed federal taxable income. (Reg. Sec. 3-7.2)

Other additions to the taxable income base are listed at ¶ 10-600.

[¶10-640] Additions--Gains

If the taxpayer elected to defer the gain from the sale of qualified emerging technology investments (see ¶ 10-845 Subtractions—Targeted Business Activity or Zones), then the amount deferred must be added back to federal taxable income when the taxpayer sells the New York qualified emerging technology company reinvestment that qualified the taxpayer for the deferral. (Sec. 208(9)(a)(m), Tax Law; Instructions, Form CT-3, New York General Business Corporation Franchise Tax Return)

The gain on the sale of real property on which the special additional mortgage recording tax credit was claimed must be increased when all or any part of the credit was also used in the basis for computing the federal gain. (Sec. 208(9)(b)(4-a), Tax Law; Reg. Sec. 3-2.3(13); Instructions, Form CT-3, New York General Business Corporation Franchise Tax Return)

Other additions to the taxable income base are listed at ¶ 10-600.

[¶10-645] Additions--Expense Items

An addition modification is required for the amount of the increase in the federal interest deduction allowed under IRC Sec. 163(j)(10)(A)(i). This relates to the federal CARES Act amendment increasing the cap of the business interest expense limitation. The modification is required for taxable years beginning in 2019 and 2020. (Sec. 208(9)(b)(26), Tax Law)

Corporate tax reform.—For details on corporate tax reform legislation that made significant changes to the corporate franchise tax bases and rates for tax years beginning after 2014, see ¶ 10-380 and ¶ 10-505.

Pre-2015.—For tax years before 2015, because corporations were exempt from tax on income received from subsidiaries (Sec. 208(9)(a)(1), Tax Law), an addback was generally required for any expenses directly or indirectly attributable to subsidiary capital or to income, gains, or losses from subsidiary capital. (Sec. 208(9)(b)(6), Tax Law; Instructions, Form CT-3, New York General Business Corporation Franchise Tax Return) However, the addback might not be required, at the discretion of the Tax Commissioner. (Reg. Sec. 3-2.3)

For details on the attribution of interest expenses, see TSB-M-88(5)C. For the attribution of noninterest expenses, see TSB-M-95(2)C.

[¶10-660] Additions--Items Related to Federal Deductions or Credits

New York requires an addition modification for the IRC § 199 domestic production activities deduction. (Sec. 208(9)(b)(19), Tax Law)

Note: As a result of the Tax Cuts and Jobs Act, the federal domestic production activities deduction (DPAD) under IRC § 199 is repealed for tax years beginning after 2017.

Other additions to the taxable income base are listed at ¶ 10-600.

[¶10-670] Additions--Depreciation

Does New York require an addback of federal bonus depreciation deductions?

Yes, New York generally requires an addback of federal bonus depreciation deductions.

The addback applies to taxable years beginning after 2002 for property placed in service on or after June 1, 2003.

However, the addback does not apply to qualified Resurgence Zone property or qualified New York Liberty Zone property. (Sec. 208(9)(b)(17), Tax Law; Sec. 208(9)(n-1), Tax Law; Sec. 208(9)(q), Tax Law; Instructions, Form CT-225; Instructions, Form CT-399)

Does New York require an addback of federal deductions taken for depreciation other than bonus depreciation?

New York generally does not require an addback of federal deductions taken for depreciation other than bonus depreciation. However, taxpayers may need to add back certain amounts related to safe harbor leases or property placed in service before 1994.

Safe harbor leases. A corporation having a safe harbor lease must add back (Instructions, Form CT-225):

— any amount claimed as a deduction in computing federal taxable income solely as a result of an election made under IRC § 168(f)(8) as it was in effect on December 31, 1983 (Sec. 208(9)(b)(8), Tax Law; Reg. Sec. 3-2.3(a)(15); Instructions, Form CT-225); and

— any amount the taxpayer would have been required to include in the computation of its federal taxable income had it not made the election permitted under IRC § 168(f)(8) as it was in effect on December 31, 1983 (Sec. 208(9)(b)(9), Tax Law; Reg. Sec. 3-2.3(a)(16); Instructions, Form CT-225).

Property placed in service before 1985. For property placed in service after 1980 in tax years beginning before 1985, New York requires an addback of federal accelerated cost recovery system/modified accelerated cost recovery system (ACRS/MACRS) deductions. (Sec. 208(9)(b)(10), Tax Law; Instructions, Form CT-225)

Property placed in service outside New York in 1985-1993. For property placed in service outside New York in tax years beginning in 1985 through 1993, New York requires an addback of ACRS/MACRS deductions if the taxpayer elected to continue using the IRC § 167 depreciation deduction. (Sec. 208(9)(b)(10), Tax Law; Instructions, Form CT-225)

The election for property placed in service outside the state from 1985-1993 resulted from a court decision that invalidated New York City's provision disallowing the IRC § 168 depreciation deduction (ACRS method) for property placed in service outside the state. (*R.J. Reynolds Tobacco Co. v. City of New York Department of Finance*) After the decision, the state Department of Taxation and Finance announced that it would allow taxpayers the option of switching to the IRC § 168 depreciation deduction or continuing to use the IRC § 167 depreciation deduction. (TSB-M-99(1)C)

Does New York require an addback of Sec. 179 asset expense deduction amounts?

No, New York generally does not require an addback of IRC § 179 asset expense deduction amounts.

However, taxpayers who are not eligible farmers must add back the amount deducted under IRC § 179 for a sport utility vehicle with a vehicle weight over 6,000 pounds. (Sec. 208(9)(b)(16), Tax Law; Instructions, Form CT-225)

[¶ 10-695] Additions--Foreign Source Income

New York has various modifications related to foreign source income.

Repatriated income deduction.—Under the 2018 budget legislation, an addback is required for the amount of the federal deduction allowed under IRC § 965(c). This provision applies to taxable years beginning on or after January 1, 2017. (Sec. 208(9)(b)(23), Tax Law)

Important Notices explain how IRC § 965 amounts should be reflected on 2017 returns; see N-18-7 (for C corporations, insurance corporations, and exempt organizations), and N-18-8 (for pass-through entities).

See also TSB-M-19(1)C.

GILTI.—An addition modification is required for the amount of any federal deduction allowed under IRC Sec. 250(a)(1)(B)(i), applicable to taxable years beginning after 2018. (Sec. 208(9)(b)(25), Tax Law)

Foreign-derived intangible income (FDII).—An addback is also required for the amount of the federal deduction allowed under IRC § 250(a)(1)(A). (Sec. 208(9)(b)(24), Tax Law; TSB-M-19(1)C)

Foreign airlines.—Foreign airlines that have a foreign air carrier permit under § 402 of the Federal Aviation Act of 1958 can exclude from entire net income all income from international operations effectively connected to the United States, foreign passive income, and income earned from overseas operations, as long as the foreign country where the airline is based has a similar exemption from tax with respect to U.S. airlines. (Sec. 208(9)(c-1), Tax Law; Instructions, Form CT-3)

In addition, when computing the tax on capital, foreign airlines can also exclude from business capital those assets used to generate the income that was excluded based on the paragraph above (to the extent the assets were employed in generating that income). (Sec. 208(7)(b), Tax Law; Instructions, Form CT-3)

However, if the country where the foreign airline is based does not provide a similar exemption from tax with respect to U.S. airlines, the foreign airline is not entitled to the exclusions from income and capital described above. (Instructions, Form CT-3)

[¶10-701] Additions--Items Related to New York Credits

An addition modification is required for environmental remediation insurance premiums that were deducted in determining federal taxable income, to the extent of the amount of the environmental remediation insurance credit allowed under Tax Law Secs. 23 and 210(35). (Sec. 208(9)(b)(18), Tax Law; TSB-M-03(8)C)

Farm donations to food pantries.—An addition modification is required for the amount of any deduction for charitable contributions allowed under IRC § 170 to the extent that the contributions are used as the basis of calculation for the farm donations to food pantries credit. (Sec. 208(9)(b)(22), Tax Law)

Other additions to the taxable income base are listed at ¶ 10-600.

[¶10-800] Subtractions from Taxable Income Base

For computation of the entire net income base, New York allows certain subtractions from the federal taxable income starting point amount (see ¶ 10-510 Starting Point for Computation). The respective subtractions are discussed at the paragraphs listed below.

- Bonus depreciation decoupling . . . . ¶ 10-900
- Credit or refund of certain New York taxes . . . . ¶ 10-840
- Depreciation . . . . ¶ 10-900
- Dividends . . . . ¶ 10-810
- Foreign dividend gross-up under IRC Sec. 78 . . . . ¶ 10-810
- Innovation hot spots . . . . ¶ 10-845
- Net operating loss . . . . ¶ 10-805
- Qualified emerging technology investment–gain deferral . . . . . . ¶ 10-845
- Safe harbor leases . . . . ¶ 10-900
- School bus income . . . . ¶ 10-845

    — SUV expensing recapture . . . . ¶ 10-900

    — Wages disallowed under IRC Sec. 280C because federal credit claimed . . .
. . . . ¶ 10-855

Subtractions from income are reported on Form CT-3 and Form CT-225. (Instructions, Form CT-225)

Additions to the taxable income base are discussed beginning at ¶ 10-600 Additions to Taxable Income, and an overview of the taxable income computation is provided at ¶ 10-505 Overview of Taxable Income Computation.

[¶ 10-805] Subtractions--Net Operating Loss

Does New York allow a net operating loss (NOL) deduction?

New York allows taxpayers to take both a prior NOL conversion subtraction and an NOL deduction. (Sec. 210.1(a)(viii), Tax Law)

Taxpayers use Form CT-3.3 to compute the prior NOL conversion subtraction and Form CT-3.4 to compute the NOL deduction. (Instructions, Form CT-3.3; Instructions, Form CT-3.4)

Taxpayers apply the NOL deduction against apportioned business income, after applying the prior NOL conversion subtraction. (Sec. 210.1(a)(viii), Tax Law; Instructions, Form CT-3.4)

"NOL" defined. An NOL is the business loss amount incurred in a particular tax year, multiplied by the apportionment factor for that year, as determined under Tax Law Sec. 210-A. (Sec. 210.1(a)(ix), Tax Law; Instructions, Form CT-3.4)

Effect of federal deduction amount. New York does not limit the NOL deduction to the amount allowed under IRC § 172 or the amount that would have been allowed if the taxpayer had not made a federal S election. (Sec. 210.1(a)(ix)(1), Tax Law; Instructions, Form CT-3.4)

NOL deduction limitations. New York limits the NOL deduction in any tax year to the amount required to reduce the tax on the apportioned business income base to the higher of the capital base tax or the fixed dollar minimum tax. (Sec. 210.1(a)(ix), Tax Law; Instructions, Form CT-3.4)

The deduction does not include NOLs incurred in a tax year beginning before January 1, 2015, or in any tax year when the taxpayer was not subject to tax under Article 9-A. (Sec. 210.1(a)(ix)(2), Tax Law; Instructions, Form CT-3.4)

IRC Sec. 382. The Department of Taxation and Finance has advised that it believes the IRC Sec. 382 limitations will apply to New York State net operating losses incurred in tax periods beginning on and after January 1, 2015. However, the department is currently in the process of drafting the net operating loss (NOL) regulations, so that position could change. (*Response*, New York Department of Taxation and Finance, January 22, 2019)

S corporations. The NOL deduction does not include any NOL incurred during a New York S year (i.e., a tax year for which a valid New York S election is in effect). (Sec. 210.1(a)(ix)(5), Tax Law; Instructions, Form CT-3.4)

Annual filing requirement. Taxpayers must file Form CT-3.4 for every tax year, even when they are not using an NOL deduction to reduce business income. Failure to file the form each tax year may cause a delay in receiving NOL deduction benefits. (Instructions, Form CT-3.4)

Prior NOL conversion subtraction. New York's corporate tax reform law provides for converting unabsorbed NOLs incurred in tax years beginning before January 1, 2015, to a prior NOL conversion subtraction pool, which a taxpayer applies, with certain limitations, as a prior NOL conversion subtraction against the apportioned business income base. (Sec. 210.1(a)(viii)(B), Tax Law; Instructions, Form CT-3.3)

Limitation. New York limits the prior NOL conversion subtraction in any tax year to the amount required to reduce the tax on the apportioned business income base to the higher of the capital base tax or the fixed dollar minimum tax. (Sec. 210.1(a)(viii)(B)(4), Tax Law; Instructions, Form CT-3.3)

Using the subtraction. Taxpayers may claim 1/10 of the pool, plus the amount of any prior tax period's unused allotments, in each of the first 10 tax periods following the base year. After that, taxpayers may continue to claim any unused amount for up to 20 tax periods following the base year. Alternatively, taxpayers may elect to use up to 1/2 of the pool in each of the tax years beginning on or after January 1, 2015, and before January 1, 2017. A taxpayer that has not exhausted the pool at the end of that period forfeits the remainder of the pool. Small businesses may use 100% of the prior NOL conversion subtraction pool in the first year succeeding the base year, and they can carry forward any unused amount for up to 20 tax periods following the base year. (Sec. 210.1(a)(viii)(B)(2), Tax Law; Instructions, Form CT-3.3)

Annual filing requirement. Taxpayers must file Form CT-3.3, with all schedules completed, for every tax year that they carry a prior NOL conversion subtraction balance, even if they cannot apply the subtraction, so that they will properly account for carryforward amounts. Failure to file Form CT-3.3 for any tax year when carrying a prior NOL conversion subtraction balance may cause a delay in receiving the benefits. (Instructions, Form CT-3.3)

Does New York allow NOL carryback and/or carryforward adjustments?

New York allows a 3-year carryback and a 20-year carryforward. (Sec. 210.1(a)(ix)(4), Tax Law; Instructions, Form CT-3.4)

Carrybacks. Taxpayers can carry back an NOL to three tax years preceding the tax year of the loss. However, taxpayers may not carry back a loss to a tax year beginning before January 1, 2015. Taxpayers must first carry the loss to the earliest of the three tax years. If the taxpayer does not entirely use the loss in that year, the taxpayer carries the remainder to the second tax year preceding the loss year. The taxpayer carries any remaining amount to the tax year immediately preceding the loss year. (Sec. 210.1(a)(ix)(4), Tax Law; Instructions, Form CT-3.4)

Carryforwards. The taxpayer may carry forward any remaining unused loss amount for up to 20 tax years following the loss year. (Sec. 210.1(a)(ix)(4), Tax Law; Instructions, Form CT-3.4)

Carryback waiver. Taxpayers may elect to waive the entire NOL carryback period. Taxpayers must make the election on their original timely filed return (including valid extensions). Once the taxpayer makes the election, it is irrevocable for that tax year. Taxpayers must make a separate election for each loss year. (Sec. 210.1(a)(ix)(7), Tax Law; Instructions, Form CT-3.4)

Amended returns. Taxpayers filing an amended return to claim an NOL carryback must file Form CT-3.4 with the amended return. (Instructions, Form CT-3.4)

Multiple NOLs. If a taxpayer is carrying back or forward two or more apportioned NOLs to be deducted from apportioned business income in one tax year, the taxpayer must first apply the earliest apportioned loss incurred. (Sec. 210.1(a)(ix)(6), Tax Law; Instructions, Form CT-3.4)

S years. Although the NOL deduction does not include any NOL incurred during a New York S year, New York S years count as tax years when determining the number of tax years to which an NOL may be carried forward. (Sec. 210.1(a)(ix)(5), Tax Law; Instructions, Form CT-3.4)

[¶10-810] Subtractions--Dividends

A subtraction from federal taxable income is allowed for amounts of foreign dividend gross-up under IRC §78, to the extent the dividends are not deducted under IRC §250. (Sec. 208(9)(a)(6), Tax Law; Reg. Sec. 3-2.4(a)(6))

Under the 2014 budget legislation, for tax years beginning after 2014, the specific exclusions for income from subsidiary capital and 50% of dividends from non-subsidiaries were repealed (see "Pre-2015 provisions" discussed below).

However, subtractions are allowed for investment income and "other exempt income," which is defined as the sum of exempt CFC income and exempt unitary corporation dividends. (Sec. 208, Tax Law) For further details on the corporate tax reform changes that became effective after 2014, see ¶10-505.

Subpart F income and dividends from foreign affiliates.—The Department of Taxation and Finance has advised that Subpart F income (including IRC §965 repatriated income) and dividends paid by foreign affiliates to U.S. corporations are generally not taxed in New York. Subpart F income is designated by statute as other exempt income, by reference to IRC §951, and dividends from affiliates with no ECI also qualify as other exempt income. (Sec. 208(6-a), Tax Law; *Preliminary Report on TCJA*, January 2018)

Form CT-3.1 is used to compute other exempt income. (Instructions, Form CT-3.1)

Under the 2018 budget legislation, the definition of "exempt CFC income" is expanded to encompass repatriated income received from a corporation not included in a combined report with the taxpayer. However, an addback is required for the amount of the federal deduction allowed under IRC §965(c) (see also ¶10-695). These provisions apply to taxable years beginning on or after January 1, 2017.

Important Notices explain how IRC §965 amounts should be reflected on 2017 returns; see N-18-7 (for C corporations, insurance corporations, and exempt organizations), and N-18-8 (for pass-through entities).

See also TSB-M-19(1)C.

Global Intangible Low-Taxed Income. New York has created a 95% exemption for global intangible low-taxed income, applicable to taxable years beginning after 2018. Specifically, the state expanded the definition of "exempt CFC income" to encompass 95% of the income required to be included in the taxpayer's federal gross income under IRC Sec. 951A(a), without regard to the IRC Sec. 250 deduction, received from a corporation that is not part of the taxpayer's combined report. (Sec. 208(6-a)(b), Tax Law)

Before 2019: For C corporations, net GILTI income, which is the GILTI recognized under IRC Sec. 951A less the allowable IRC Sec. 250(a)(1)(B)(i) deduction, is included in entire net income. IRC §78 dividends attributable to GILTI are not included in entire net income. For more details on the treatment of GILTI for C corporations and other types of entities, see TSB-M-19(1)C.

• *Pre-2015 provisions*

Subtractions from federal taxable income are provided for the following dividends:

(1) For tax years beginning before 2015, dividends from subsidiaries. (Sec. 208(9)(a)(1), Tax Law; Reg. Sec. 3-2.4(a)(1)); and

(2) For tax years beginning before 2015, 50% of other dividends on shares of stock conforming to the holding requirements of IRC Sec. 246(c). (Sec. 208(9)(a)(2), Tax Law; Reg. Sec. 3-2.4(a)(2))

The pre-2015 50% dividend exclusion does not apply to real estate investment trusts (Sec. 209(5), Tax Law; Reg. Sec. 3-11.1(b)) or to regulated investment companies. (Sec. 209(7), Tax Law; Reg. Sec. 3-12.1(b))

Other subtractions from the taxable income base are listed at ¶10-800.

[¶10-815] Subtractions--Interest

For tax years beginning before 2015, income, gains, and losses from subsidiary capital were excluded from federal taxable income in computing New York entire net income. Accordingly, interest from subsidiary capital could be subtracted. (Sec. 208(9)(a)(1), Tax Law; Reg. Sec. 3-2.4(a)(1))

Other subtractions from the taxable income base are listed at ¶10-800.

[¶10-825] Subtractions--Gains

For tax years beginning before 2015, gains from subsidiary capital could be subtracted because they were specifically excluded from federal taxable income in computing New York entire net income. (Sec. 208(9)(a)(1), Tax Law; Reg. Sec. 3-2.4(a)(1))

Other subtractions from the taxable income base are listed at ¶10-800.

[¶10-835] Subtractions--Corporate Transactions

For taxable years beginning after 2002 and before 2013, a taxpayer was allowed to deduct royalty payments received from a related member during the taxable year, to the extent included in the taxpayer's federal taxable income, unless the royalty payments were not required to be added back under the expense disallowance provisions discussed at ¶10-620 or other similar provisions of the Tax Law. (Sec. 208(9)(o)(3), Tax Law)

The royalty income exclusion described above was eliminated by the 2013 budget legislation. (Summary, New York Department of Taxation and Finance)

[¶10-840] Subtractions--Taxes

A subtraction modification is allowed for any refund or credit of the New York Article 9-A corporation franchise tax or the Article 32 franchise tax on banking corporations, for which no exclusion or deduction was allowed in determining the taxpayer's entire net income for any prior year, and also for any refund or credit of a tax imposed under Article 9, Sec. 183, Sec. 183-a, Sec. 184, or Sec. 184-a (franchise taxes and surcharges on transportation and transmission corporations and associations). (Sec. 208(9)(a)(5), Tax Law; Reg. Sec. 3-2.4(a)(4); Instructions, Form CT-3, New York General Business Corporation Franchise Tax Return)

In the subtraction amount, taxpayers should not include any refund or credit of tax that was used to offset an addition with respect to taxes deducted on the federal return (see ¶ 10-615 Additions—Taxes). Also, taxpayers should not include any refund or credit of New York City taxes. (Instructions, Form CT-3, New York General Business Corporation Franchise Tax Return)

Other subtractions from the taxable income base are listed at ¶ 10-800.

[¶ 10-845] Subtractions--Targeted Business Activity or Zones

To the extent that the items discussed below were included in determining federal taxable income, they are subtracted from the federal base in computing New York entire net income.

• *Innovation hot spots*

Under the New York State Business Incubator and Innovation Hot Spot Support Act, Empire State Development (ESD) is authorized to issue an annual request for proposals for grants and assistance based on available appropriations and to designate qualified applicants as New York State incubators. In addition, in each of state fiscal years 2013 and 2014, ESD is authorized to designate five qualified New York State incubators as New York State innovation hot spots. These innovation hot spots can certify certain clients as a qualified entity eligible for tax benefits under Tax Law § 38. (Sec. 38, Tax Law; Sec. 208(9)(a)(18), Tax Law; Sec. 209(11), Tax Law; TSB-M-13(6)C; TSB-M-14(1)C)

The tax benefits available to a qualified entity subject to tax under Article 9-A are described below (these tax benefits are allowed for five tax years beginning with the first tax year a qualified entity becomes a tenant in, or is part of, a New York State innovation hot spot):

— A qualified entity that is located within the innovation hot spot will only be subject to the fixed dollar minimum tax under Article 9-A.

— An entity that is (1) a corporate partner of a qualified entity, or (2) a qualified entity that is located both within and outside an innovation hot spot is allowed only a deduction (in the form of a subtraction modification) for the amount of income or gain included in its federal taxable income that is attributable to operations at or as part of the innovation hot spot.

A taxpayer that claims any of the tax benefits described above (or related sales tax benefits) is no longer eligible for any other New York State exemption, deduction, credit, or refund to the extent attributable to the business operations of a qualified entity at (or as part of) a New York State innovation hot spot. The election to claim any of the tax benefits described above is not revocable.

• *School bus income*

A subtraction modification is allowed for receipts from school districts and from nonprofit religious, charitable or educational organizations for the operation of school buses. (Sec. 208(9)(a)(4), Tax Law) The subtraction applies only to receipts from transportation for school activities, and it must reflect the elimination of any related deductions allowed for federal purposes. (Reg. Sec. 3-2.4)

• *Qualified emerging technology investments (QETI)—Gain deferral*

The gain from the sale of any emerging technology investment sold on or after March 12, 1998, and held for more than 36 months will be recognized for New York State corporate franchise tax purposes only to the extent that the gain realized exceeds the cost of any qualified emerging technology investment purchased by the taxpayer within 365 days from the date of the sale. (Sec. 208(9)(l), Tax Law) The amount deferred will be added to federal taxable income when the reinvestment is sold (see ¶ 10-640 Additions—Gains).

If the purchase of the reinvestment within the 365-day period occurs in the same tax year as the sale of the original investment, or in the following tax year and before the date on which the corporation's franchise tax return is filed, then the taxpayer should take the deduction on that return. However, if the purchase of the reinvestment within the 365-day period occurs in the following tax year on or after the date when the corporation's franchise tax return is filed, then the taxpayer must file an amended return to claim the deduction. (Instructions, Form CT-3, New York General Business Corporation Franchise Tax Return)

Other subtractions from the taxable income base are listed at ¶ 10-800.

[¶ 10-855] Subtractions--Items Related to Federal Deductions or Credits

A subtraction is provided for the amount of wages disallowed under IRC Sec. 280C for federal purposes because the taxpayer claimed a federal credit. (Sec. 208(9)(a)(7), Tax Law; Reg. Sec. 3-2.4(a)(7)) A copy of the appropriate federal credit form must be attached to the New York return. (Instructions, Form CT-3, New York General Business Corporation Franchise Tax Return)

Other subtractions from the taxable income base are listed at ¶ 10-800.

[¶ 10-900] Subtractions--Depreciation

New York law provides for several depreciation modifications, as set forth below.

• *Bonus depreciation*

For taxable years beginning after 2002, and applicable to property placed in service on or after June 1, 2003, the New York corporate franchise tax is decoupled from federal accelerated depreciation under IRC Sec. 168(k), except with respect to qualified Resurgence Zone property and qualified New York Liberty Zone property. Accordingly, for affected property, New York permits the depreciation deduction allowable under IRC Sec. 167 as it would have applied to the property had it been acquired by the taxpayer on September 10, 2001. (Sec. 208(9)(b)(17), (o), (p), and (q), Tax Law)

Prior to the enactment of the above provisions under A.B. 2106, Laws 2003, New York had conformed to the federal bonus depreciation provisions (see TSB-M-02(2)C).

• *IRC Sec. 179 expense election—Decoupling for SUVs*

With respect to the addition modification discussed at ¶ 10-670, which is required for the amount deducted by a taxpayer (except an eligible farmer) under IRC Sec. 179 for certain sport utility vehicles, a subtraction modification was also enacted under A.B. 2106, Laws 2003, for any recapture amount included in federal adjusted gross income attributable to such deduction. (Sec. 208(9)(a)(16), Tax Law)

• *Safe harbor leases*

For corporations having a safe harbor lease, a subtraction is allowed for the following: (1) any amount included in federal taxable income solely as a result of an election made under IRC Sec. 168(f)(8) as it was in effect on December 31, 1983; (2) any amount the taxpayer could have excluded from federal taxable income had it not made the election provided for in IRC Sec. 168(f)(8) as it was in effect on December 31, 1983. (Sec. 208(9)(a)(9) and (a)(10), Tax Law; Reg. Sec. 3-2.4(a)(9) and (10); Instructions, Form CT-3, New York General Business Corporation Franchise Tax Return)

• *Property placed in service before 1994*

Adjustments made to the federal base as the result of differing federal/state treatment of depreciable property placed into service outside New York state or prior to 1985 may be additions or subtractions depending upon the depreciation method chosen. The manner of applying adjustments is discussed at ¶ 10-670.

Other subtractions from the taxable income base are listed at ¶ 10-800.

[¶ 10-911] Subtractions--Contributions to Capital

New York is decoupled from the federal Tax Cuts and Jobs Act provision that limited the exemption for contributions to the capital of a corporation. Thus, for taxable years beginning on or after January 1, 2018, New York allows an exclusion from entire net income for contributions to the capital of a corporation by a governmental entity or civic group. (Sec. 208(9)(a)(20), Tax Law)

See also *TSB-M-19(3)C.*

Other subtractions from the taxable income base are listed at ¶ 10-800.

[¶ 11-500]

ALLOCATION AND APPORTIONMENT

[¶ 11-505] Allocation and Apportionment

Note: For a discussion of apportionment provisions enacted by the 2014 budget legislation, and applicable to taxable years beginning after 2014, see ¶ 11-525. Provisions in effect prior to the those changes are discussed below.

The tax liability of multistate and multinational corporations doing business in more than one state or country is problematic. For such corporations, it is difficult to determine with precision the amount of income that is properly taxable in a state because corporate activities both inside the taxing state and elsewhere may contribute to the production of total income.

Assigning the income of a multijurisdictional taxpayer among various taxing states is generally accomplished by a process known as allocation and apportionment. In New York, the pattern for assigning income and capital to different states is based on apportionment principles (see ¶ 11-520 Apportionment). Although New York's statutory pattern is based on apportionment concepts, since New York does not assign income on the basis of its source under nonbusiness rules, the laws and regulations do not make the distinction between "allocation" and "apportionment" (they have the same meaning), and generally use the term "allocation" (see ¶ 11-515 Allocation).

Most states that impose franchise and/or corporation income taxes have adopted the Uniform Division of Income for Tax Purposes Act (UDITPA) or have enacted legislation substantially similar to UDITPA. A number of states have also signed the Multistate Tax Compact. These enactments specify how income of a corporation doing business in, and deriving income from, more than one state or country is divided and assigned to a state for tax purposes.

New York has not adopted the Multistate Tax Compact, the Uniform Division of Income for Tax Purposes Act (UDITPA), or the allocation and apportionment regulations issued by the Multistate Tax Commission (discussed after New York's allocation provisions). Instead, taxpayers computing New York corporate franchise tax liability under alternative tax bases (see ¶10-505 Overview of Taxable Income Computation) must determine the appropriate tax base components and allocate income and capital to New York by applying allocation percentages as follows:

— business income and business capital are multiplied by a business allocation percentage;

— investment capital and investment income are multiplied by an investment allocation percentage; and

— subsidiary capital is multiplied by a subsidiary allocation percentage. See ¶11-510 Income Subject to Allocation and Apportionment and ¶11-515 Allocation.

In New York, all of the corporate franchise tax bases (except for the fixed dollar minimum) are subject to allocation (see ¶11-505 Income Subject to Allocation and Apportionment). The Tax Law does not divide a taxpayer's income into business and nonbusiness income. (Sec. 210, Tax Law; Reg. Sec. 4-1.1)

Under federal constitutional principles, a corporation's income is not subject to allocation or apportionment unless the corporation engages in an income-producing activity that has a relationship ("nexus") with the taxing state. A corporation is subject to corporate franchise (income) tax in New York if it is "doing business" in the state. (See ¶10-075 Nexus—P.L. 86-272—Doing Business in State)

Discretion of the Commissioner.—The Commissioner may adjust the business allocation percentage or the investment allocation percentage to properly reflect the activity, business, income, or capital of a taxpayer within New York. The Commissioner may also eliminate assets in computing any allocation percentage, provided the income therefrom is also excluded from entire net income or minimum taxable income (see ¶11-515 Allocation).

• *Business allocation percentage*

Single sales factor.—Although New York previously had a three-factor formula with a double-weighted receipts factor, the computation of the business allocation percentage has been amended by Ch. 61 (S.B. 3671), Laws 2005, and Ch. 60 (S.B. 2110), Laws 2007, to phase in a single receipts factor. Specifically, the receipts factor constitutes 60% of the business allocation percentage for taxable years beginning on or after January 1, 2006, and 100% for taxable years beginning on or after January 1, 2007. The property and payroll factors have each be reduced from 25% of the percentage to 20% in 2006 and 0% in 2007. Under the 2005 budget bill, the phase-in was originally scheduled over a three-year period, but full implementation was moved up one year by the 2007 budget bill. (Sec. 210(3)(a)(10), Tax Law)

Prior to the phase-in of the single receipts factor, the business allocation percentage was computed as described below, using a three-factor formula—property (¶11-530), receipts (¶11-525), and payroll (¶11-535). For taxpayers (other than S corporations) computing corporate franchise tax liability on the basis of entire net income or business and investment capital, the receipts factor is double-weighted and the sum of the factors is divided by four. If either the property or payroll factor is missing, the other factors are added and the sum is divided by three. (Reg. Sec. 4-2.2) If both the property and payroll factors are missing, the receipts factor alone is used. If a taxpayer's property is limited to office equipment, a business expense factor may be substituted for the property factor. (Reg. Sec. 4-6.2) (See ¶ 11-515 Allocation)

For a discussion of pass-through entity apportionment, see ¶ 11-515 Allocation.

Property factor.—The property factor is a ratio equal to the "average value" of the taxpayer's real and tangible personal property owned or rented in New York over the average value of the taxpayer's real and tangible personal property everywhere. (Sec. 210(3)(a)(1), Tax Law; Reg. Sec. 4-3.1)

For a detailed discussion of the property factor, see ¶ 11-530.

Payroll factor.—The payroll factor is a ratio equal to the total wages, salaries and other personal service compensation paid to employees within the state over the taxpayer's total wages, salaries and other compensation paid by the taxpayer everywhere for the taxable period. (Sec. 210(3)(a)(3), Tax Law; Reg. Sec. 4-5.1)

For a detailed discussion of the payroll factor, see ¶ 11-535.

Receipts factor.—The *receipts factor* is a ratio equal to the receipts from sales of tangible personal property, services, rentals, royalties and other business receipts attributable to New York over such receipts from all business transactions. (Secs. 210(3)(a)(2) and (6), Tax Law; Reg. Sec. 4-4.1)

For a detailed discussion of the receipts factor, see ¶ 11-525.

• *Investment allocation percentage*

A taxpayer allocates its investment income, alternative investment income, and investment capital within and without New York State by the investment allocation percentage. (Sec. 210(3)(b), Tax Law; Reg. Sec. 4-7.1(a)) If a taxpayer's investment allocation percentage is zero, interest received on bank accounts is multiplied by the taxpayer's business allocation percentage. (Sec. 210(3)(b), Tax Law; Reg. Sec. 4-7.1(b)) (See ¶ 11-515 Allocation)

Computation of investment allocation percentage.—The investment allocation percentage is determined by:

— multiplying the amount of a company's investment capital invested in securities (other than government securities) during the reporting period by the issuer's or obligor's allocation percentage;

— adding together the amounts so obtained; and

— dividing the result by the total of the company's investment capital that was invested during the period in stock, bonds and other securities, including government securities.

(Sec. 210(3)(b), Tax Law; Reg. Sec. 4-7.2(a)) (See ¶ 11-515 Allocation)

The issuer's allocation percentage is the percentage of the appropriate measure required to be allocated to New York on the issuer's or obligor's report for the preceding year (see ¶ 11-515 Allocation).

• *Subsidiary allocation percentage*

The subsidiary allocation percentage is determined by the amount of capital employed in New York by the taxpayer's subsidiaries. (See ¶ 11-515 Allocation) In the case of combined reports, allocation is made on the basis of the combined accounts from which intercorporate items are eliminated (see ¶ 11-550 Combined Reports).

• *Special industries*

Special rules apply to the apportionment of income by the following industries and activities: newspaper and periodical publishers; printers; investment companies; indirect air carriage and freight forwarders acting as principals; securities and commodities brokers; television and radio broadcasting companies; owners of cable television and closed-circuit transmission rights; omnibus companies; telephone and telegraph companies; and government contractors. For a complete discussion of these special industries, see ¶ 11-540 Apportionment Factors for Specific Industries.

• *Consolidated returns*

New York does not follow the federal provisions (IRC Sec. 1501—IRC Sec. 1504) allowing affiliated corporations to file consolidated returns.

• *Combined reports*

Corporations meeting unitary business and common capital stock ownership requirements may be permitted or required to file combined reports. If a combined report is filed, attribution of income is made on the basis of combined accounts from which intercorporate items are eliminated. (Reg. Sec. 4-1.2) The receipts factor is computed as though all corporations included in the report were one corporation. (Reg. Sec. 4-4.8) Intercorporate business receipts are eliminated in computing the receipts factor. Corporations filing combined reports will not be permitted to use only the business allocation percentage or the investment allocation percentage to attribute income.

For a detailed discussion of combined reports, see ¶ 11-550.

• *Comparison of New York, UDITPA, and MTC regulations*

Even though New York has not adopted the Uniform Division of Income for Tax Purposes Act (UDITPA) nor the Multistate Tax Compact (MTC), the discussion below is informative.

Under UDITPA and the MTC, allocation refers to directly assigning certain types of income, which are usually designated nonbusiness income, to a state on the basis of rules varying according to the type of property that gave rise to the income. Rental income from real property, for instance, is commonly assigned to the state in which the property is located. Allocation rules purport to assign income to the state that is its source. However, when the source of the income is intangible property, e.g., patents or investments, the location of which may be difficult to ascertain, allocation rules may adopt an objective criterion for assignment, such as the taxpayer's commercial domicile.

New York has not adopted the MTC, UDITPA, or the allocation and apportionment regulations issued by the Multistate Tax Commission. Business income of a multistate taxpayer is attributed to New York by a single receipts factor (see ¶ 11-515 Allocation). In addition, New York has not adopted the UDITPA and MTC concept of nonbusiness income discussed above (the New York Tax Law does not divide a taxpayer's income into business and nonbusiness). For New York franchise tax purposes, the term "business income" means entire net income minus investment income. (Sec. 208(8), Tax Law) Because New York does not assign income on the basis of its source under the nonbusiness rules discussed above, the language of the statutes does not make the distinction noted above between "allocation" and "apportionment," but generally uses the term "allocation."

Uniform Division of Income for Tax Purposes Act (UDITPA).—The Uniform Division of Income for Tax Purposes Act (UDITPA) is a model act for the allocation and apportionment of income among states. UDITPA was drafted to remedy the diversity that existed among the states for determining their respective shares of a corporation's income. UDITPA divides income into business income, which is apportioned by means of a three-factor formula, and nonbusiness income, which is allocated according to the type of income and the type of property giving rise to the income.

Although the majority of states have adopted UDITPA, in whole or in part, New York has not adopted the act. Some New York allocation and apportionment provisions are similar to those in UDITPA, but the basic pattern of the New York law is not similar enough to UDITPA to afford meaningful comparison and contrast.

Multistate Tax Commission regulations.—Although New York has not adopted the Multistate Tax Commission (MTC) regulations, several New York corporation franchise tax regulations are comparable. However, New York has also adopted many regulations without MTC counterparts. These include: allocation regulations concerning computation of the investment allocation percentage; allocation of the net operating loss deduction; allocation of business, investment, and subsidiary capital; and regulations on combined reports.

Primary MTC regulations, with New York counterparts where appropriate, are noted in the following table:

MTC Reg. No. & Title	New York Reg. Sec. & Subject:
IV.1.(a) Business and nonbusiness income defined:	4-8.2, 4-8.3 defines "business income" as entire net income minus investment income, and "investment income" as income from "investment capital."
IV.1.(b) Two or more businesses of a single taxpayer	
IV.1.(c) Business and nonbusiness income: application of definitions	
IV.1.(d) Proration of deductions	
IV.2.(a) Definitions	
IV.2.(b)(1) Application Article IV: apportionment	
IV.2.(b)(2) Application of Article IV: combined report	6-2.1—6-2.7 gives the Tax Commission discretion to permit or require a group of corporations to file a combined report.
IV.2.(b)(3) Application of Article IV: allocation	
IV.2.(c) Consistency and uniformity in reporting	
IV.3.(a) Taxable in another state: in general	
IV.3.(b) Taxable in another state: when a corporation is "subject to" a tax under Article IV.3.(1)	
IV.3.(c) Taxable in another state: when a state has jurisdiction to subject a taxpayer to a net income tax	
IV.9. Apportionment formula	4-2.2 provides for the computation of the business allocation percentage on the basis of a three-factor formula with a double-weighted "receipts" factor, in lieu of the UDITPA sales factor.
IV.10.(a) Property factor: in general	
IV.10.(b) Property factor: property used for the production of business income	
IV.10.(c) Property factor: consistency in reporting	
IV.10.(d) Property factor: numerator	4-3.1 allocates income from omnibuses and other rolling equipment to New York on either a time or mileage ratio; the N.Y. regulation also includes a definition for the term "tangible property."
IV.11.(a) Property factor: valuation of owned property	4-3.1(b) provides for the valuation of owned property at its average fair market value.
IV.11.(b) Property factor: valuation of rented property	4-3.2 substitutes the term "gross rents" for the MTC term "annual rent"; there is a special N.Y. rule for allocation of leasehold improvements.
IV.12. Property factor: averaging property values	3-3.5 and 3-3.6 defines "fair market value" and "average value".
IV.13.(a) Payroll factor: in general	4-5.1 provides for the inclusion of compensation paid in the connection with the production of nonbusiness income in the N.Y. factor; compensation paid to executive officers is excluded for New York purposes.
IV.13.(b) Payroll factor: denominator	4-5.1 provides for the inclusion of all compensation paid to all of the taxpayer's employees in the denominator of the payroll factor.

MTC Reg. No. & Title	New York Reg. Sec. & Subject:
IV.13.(c) Payroll factor: numerator	4-5.1
IV.14. Payroll factor: compensation paid in this state	4-5.1(d) provides for the inclusion of all employees regularly connected with or working out of an office in the state.
IV.15.(a) Sales factor: in general	4-4.1 replaces the MTC sales factor with a receipts factor.
IV.15.(b) Sales factor: denominator	4-4.1
IV.15.(c) Sales factor: numerator	4-4.1
IV.16.(a) Sales factor: sales of tangible personal property in this state	4-4.2
IV.16.(b) Sales factor: sales of tangible personal property to United States government in this state	
IV.17. Sales factor: sales other than sales of tangible personal property in this state	4-4.3—4-4.6 specifies the following to be allocable to N.Y.: all services performed in the state, receipts from rentals of real and personal property situated in N.Y., royalties for the use in N.Y. of patents or copyrights, receipts from an investment company arising from the sale of management, administration, or distribution services to such investment company, and all "other business receipts." Under the MTC Reg., sales are allocable to the state where the income-producing activity giving rise to the receipts took place.
IV.18.(a) Special rules: in general	4-6.1
IV.18.(b) Special rules: property factor	
IV.18.(c) Special rules: sales factor	
IV.18.(d) Special regulation: construction contractors	
IV.18.(e) Special rules: airlines	
IV.18.(f) Special rules: railroads	
IV.18.(g) Special rules: trucking companies	
IV.18.(h) Special rules: TV and radio broadcasting	4-4.3(f)
IV.18.(i) Special rules: financial institutions	No regulation, but Sec. 1454, Tax Law, provides a three-factor formula consisting of a payroll factor, a double-weighted receipts factor, and a double-weighted deposits factor, with a denominator of five.

IV.18.(j) Special rules: publishers

The following New York corporation franchise tax allocation and apportionment regulations have no counterpart in the MTC regulations:

Reg. Sec. 4-1.1, which provides general rules for the allocation of business income, business capital, investment income, investment capital, alternative business income, alternative investment income, and subsidiary capital;

Reg. Sec. 4-1.2, which provides rules for allocating items on combined reports;

Reg. Sec. 4-2.1, which details instances in which a business allocation percentage must be used;

Reg. Sec. 4-2.2, which provides rules for computation of the business allocation percentage;

Reg. Sec. 4-4.8, which provides rules for computation of the receipts factor in combined reports;

Reg. Sec. 4-5.2, which provides a definition for the term "employee";

Reg. Sec. 4-5.3, which defines the term "general elected officers";

Reg. Sec. 4-6.2, which permits certain taxpayers to eliminate the property factor and/or substitute an expense factor;

Reg. Sec. 4-6.3, which provides rules for government contractors;

Reg. Sec. 4-6.4, which provides for proration of the allocated income of taxpayers subject to the corporation franchise tax for a period less than their federal taxable year;

Reg. Sec. 4-6.5, which provides rules relating to allocation and apportionment of partnership or joint venture income to a corporate partner;

Reg. Sec. 4-7.1, which provides instances in which a taxpayer must use an investment allocation percentage;

Reg. Sec. 4-7.2, which provides rules for computation of the investment allocation percentage;

Reg. Sec. 4-7.3, which provides a definition for the term "government securities";

Reg. Sec. 4-7.4, which provides for an adjustment of the investment allocation percentage at the discretion of the Tax Commission;

Reg. Sec. 4-8.1, which provides general rules for the allocation of entire net income;

Reg. Sec. 4-8.4, which provides for a deduction of expenses related to investment income;

Reg. Sec. 4-8.5, which provides rules for the apportionment of the net operating loss deduction;

Reg. Secs. 4-9.1, 4-9.2, and 4-9.3, which provide rules for the computation of allocable business capital and investment capital;

Reg. Sec. 4-10.1, which provides rules for the allocation of subsidiary capital; and

Reg. Secs. 41.1 through 41.6, which provide rules for the allocation and apportionment of the income of telephone and telegraph companies;

Multistate Tax Compact.—The Multistate Tax Compact is a document to which states may subscribe in the interest of uniform taxation of multistate taxpayer income. The Compact created the Multistate Tax Commission and established for member states a joint audit program for multistate taxpayers. The Compact adopts UDITPA as an optional method of apportionment in member states. New York has not become a member.

[¶11-510] Income Subject to Allocation and Apportionment

Note: For a discussion of apportionment provisions enacted by the 2014 budget legislation, and applicable to taxable years beginning after 2014, see ¶11-525, "Sales Factor." Provisions in effect prior to the those changes are discussed below.

Hedge fund deferred compensation.—For corporations taxable under Article 9-A (including New York S corporations), nonqualified deferred compensation, including any appreciation and earnings related to such deferrals, that is includible in federal taxable income in accordance with P.L. 110-343, Div. C, §801(d)(2), is considered business income under Article 9-A and is included in the apportionment factor under the rules in Tax Law §210-A and the applicable regulations. (TSB-M-18(2)C, (3)I)

Pre-2015 provisions.—In New York, all of the corporate franchise tax bases (except for the fixed dollar minimum) are subject to allocation so that corporations doing business in other states in addition to New York are subject to New York corporate franchise (income) tax only on the portion of their income and capital attributable to New York. Therefore, taxpayers must separately allocate business income and business capital, and investment income and investment capital. The Tax Law does not divide a taxpayer's income into business and nonbusiness income. (Sec. 210, Tax Law; Reg. Sec. 4-1.1) (See ¶11-505 Allocation and Apportionment)

After calculating the entire net income base, the primary base of the general corporation franchise tax, taxpayers must divide their entire net income into two components: (1) business income and business capital, and (2) investment income and investment capital, each of which is subject to tax under a separate formula (See ¶11-515 Allocation).

• *Business income and business capital*

Business income defined.—The term "business income" means entire net income minus investment income. (Sec. 208(8), Tax Law) Business income includes deemed DISC distributions taxed federally as dividends (Sec. 208(8-A)(b), Tax Law), gains recognized federally on sales of DISC or former DISC stock (Sec. 208(8-A)(c), Tax Law), and actual DISC distributions unless treated as made out of "other earnings and profits" (Sec. 208(8-A)(d), Tax Law) under federal law. (IRC Sec. 996)

Business capital defined.—The term "business capital" means the total average value of all the taxpayer's assets (whether or not shown on its balance sheet), exclusive of stock issued by the taxpayer (treasury stock) or assets constituting subsidiary capital or investment capital, less the average value of liabilities not deducted in computing subsidiary capital or investment capital. (Sec. 208(7), Tax Law; Reg. Sec. 3-3.3(a))

Business allocation percentage.—Under the 2005 and 2007 budget bills, a single sales factor has been phased in, beginning in 2006 (with full implementation in 2007) (see ¶11-505). Prior to the phase-in, business income and business capital were allocated by a business allocation percentage derived from a three-factor formula based on property, payroll, and receipts. (Sec. 210(3), Tax Law) (See ¶11-515 Allocation) The percentage was determined by a formula that compared the in-state amounts of property value, receipts (double-weighted), and compensation to the taxpayer's total amounts of such items. (Sec. 210, Tax Law; Reg. Sec. 4-1.1; Reg. Sec. 4-2.2)

For purposes of allocating minimum taxable income, the business allocation percentage is computed differently than for purposes of allocating entire net income. (See ¶11-525 Sales Factor)

• *Investment income and investment capital*

Investment income defined.—"Investment income," broadly defined, is income that is derived from investment capital less, at the discretion of the Commissioner, deductions allowable in computing entire net income that are directly or indirectly related to the investment capital or investment income and less a portion of the net operating loss equal to the ratio of investment income to entire net income. (Sec. 208(6), Tax Law) Deductions that are directly and indirectly attributed to investment income are briefly described at ¶10-530 and more thoroughly explained in a Technical Services Bureau memorandum. (TSB-M-88(5)C)

Investment income includes capital gains in excess of capital losses from investment capital. It also included (for taxable years beginning before 1997) income derived from subsidiary capital that has been disqualified as subsidiary stock because of premature dispositions of target stock or target assets as described at ¶10-535 Non-Income Tax Base Computation.

Investment income may not exceed entire net income.

Investment capital defined.—Investment capital is that capital invested in corporate securities other than those of the investing corporation.

Investment allocation percentage.—Investment income and investment capital are allocated by an investment allocation percentage. The percentage is computed by dividing an allocated portion of the investment in corporate securities by the total investment in includable securities. (Sec. 210(3)(b), Tax Law; Reg. Sec. 4-7.2(a))

See ¶11-515 Allocation.

¶11-510

• *Subsidiary capital*

Subsidiary capital is allocated by using the subsidiary allocation percentage, which is determined by the amount of capital employed in New York by the taxpayer's subsidiaries in connection with Tax Law or Insurance Law reports filed by them in the preceding year (See ¶11-515 Allocation). (Reg. Sec. 4-10.1) In the case of combined reports, allocation is made on the basis of the combined accounts from which intercorporate items are eliminated. (See ¶11-550 Combined Reports)

• *Specific types of income or activities*

Distributive partnership income.—With respect to partnerships, the business income determination is made at the partner level. (Reg. Sec. 3-13.3) Apportionment for pass-through entities is discussed at ¶11-515.

[¶11-515] Allocation

Note: For a discussion of apportionment provisions enacted by the 2014 budget legislation for corporate taxpayers, and applicable to taxable years beginning after 2014, see ¶11-525. Provisions in effect prior to those changes are discussed below.

Provisions applicable to pass-through entities are also discussed below.

Pre-2015.—After the taxpayer's entire net income was ascertained (¶10-510 and following), the portion allocated to New York and subject to the franchise tax was determined by:

— multiplying business income and business capital by a business allocation percentage (Sec. 210(3)(a), Tax Law);

— multiplying investment income and investment capital by an investment allocation percentage (Sec. 210(3)(b), Tax Law); and

— adding the two products. (Sec. 210(3)(c), Tax Law)

Subsidiary capital was allocated by using the subsidiary allocation percentage. For a discussion of the income subject to allocation and apportionment, see ¶11-510.

Special rules relating to the apportionment factors of specific industries are discussed at ¶11-540.

• *Pass-through entity apportionment*

S corporations use a single-factor receipts formula. (Sec. 210-A, Tax Law; Instructions, Form CT-3-S, New York S Corporation Franchise Tax Return) For details, see ¶11-525.

For partnerships, LLCs, and LLPs, if books and records do not reflect income earned in New York, then an evenly weighted three-factor formula is used. (Reg. Sec. 132.15; Instructions, Form IT-204, Partnership Return) The factors are property, payroll, and gross income.

Sourcing of receipts.—S corporations use the same market-based sourcing rules applicable to C corporations; see ¶11-525.

Partnerships use an origin method, based on the location of the office where a receipt is generated. (Reg. Sec. 132.15) Specifically, the amount sourced to New York is the part of total gross sales or charges representing sales made or services performed by or through an agency in New York. This includes sales made or services performed by employees, agents, agencies, or independent contractors situated at, connected with, or sent out from offices of the partnership (or its agencies) located in New York. For example, if a salesperson working out of a New York office covers the states of New York, New Jersey, and Pennsylvania, all sales made by him or her are allocated to New York. (Instructions, Form IT-204)

Nonresident individual owners.—For nonresident individual owners, apportionment of distributive income is determined by applying the entity's apportionment factors. (Sec. 631, Tax Law; Sec. 632, Tax Law)

Corporate owners.—Requirements for allocation by a corporate partner are set forth in Reg. Sec. 4-6.5. See also TSB-M-07(2)C.

In the case of a unitary business, the corporate partner's factors are combined with the distributive share of the partnership's factors. (Reg. Sec. 4-6.5; TSB-M-07(2)C)

Tiered partnerships.—Where a taxpayer is a partner in a partnership and is using the aggregate method pursuant to Reg. Sec. 3-13.3 or is a foreign corporate limited partner that has made an election with respect to such partnership pursuant to the provisions of Reg. Sec. 3-13.5, and such partnership (the upper tier partnership) is a partner in another partnership (the lower tier partnership), the source and character of such taxpayer's distributive share or proportionate part, as the case may be, of each partnership item of receipts, income, gain, loss, deduction, asset, liability, and activity of the upper tier partnership that is attributable to the lower tier partnership retains the source and character determined at the level of the lower tier partnership. Such source and character are not changed by reason of the fact that the item flows through the upper tier partnership to such partner. (Reg. Sec. 3-13.6)

- *Business allocation percentage*

Single sales factor.—Although New York previously had a three-factor formula with a double-weighted receipts factor, the computation of the business allocation percentage has been amended by Ch. 61 (S.B. 3671), Laws 2005, and Ch. 60 (S.B. 2110), Laws 2007, to phase in a single receipts factor. Specifically, the receipts factor constitutes 60% of the business allocation percentage for taxable years beginning on or after January 1, 2006, and 100% for taxable years beginning on or after January 1, 2007. The property and payroll factors have each be reduced from 25% of the percentage to 20% in 2006 and 0% in 2007. Under the 2005 budget bill, the phase-in was originally scheduled over a three-year period, but full implementation was moved up one year by the 2007 budget bill. (Sec. 210(3)(a)(10), Tax Law)

The business allocation percentage is a formula used for the allocation of income of corporations doing business within and without New York. Prior to the phase-in of the single receipts factor, the formula was based on property (¶11-530), receipts (¶11-525), and payroll (¶11-535).

Computation of business allocation percentage.—Prior to the phase-in of the single receipts factor, as described above, the business allocation percentage was computed by adding together the percentages of the property factor (¶11-530), the receipts factor weighted doubly (¶11-525) and the payroll factor (¶11-535), and dividing the total by four. (Sec. 210(3)(a), Tax Law). Special provisions relating to pass-through entities are discussed below.

Special provisions relating to apportionment factors for specific industries are discussed at ¶11-540.

Business income defined.—The term "business income" means entire net income minus investment income. (Sec. 208(8), Tax Law) (See ¶11-510) Income Subject to Allocation and Apportionment.

Allocated incomes.—Ordinarily, the allocated business income and allocated investment income are added to find the total allocated income subject to tax, but in some cases only one allocation percentage applies. Except for corporations principally engaged in the conduct of aviation or in the conduct of a railroad or trucking business, the business allocation percentage cannot be used if a taxpayer has only investment income, or if there is investment income and a business loss. (Reg. Sec. 4-8.1)

• *Investment allocation percentage—Pre-2015*

A taxpayer allocated its investment income and investment capital within and without New York by the investment allocation percentage.

The investment allocation percentage was determined by:

— multiplying the amount of a company's investment capital invested in each stock, bond, or other security (other than governmental securities) during the period covered by its report by the allocation percentage of the issuer or obligor, as explained later in this section;

— adding together the sums obtained; and

— dividing the result by the total of the company's investment capital that was invested during the period in stocks, bonds and other securities, including government securities.

(Sec. 210(3)(b), Tax Law) (TSB-M-86(6)C)

For rules relating to computing the investment allocation percentage for corporate partners of a partnership or joint venture, see Reg. Sec. 4-6.5.

Investment income defined.—"Investment income," broadly defined, is income that is derived from investment capital less, at the discretion of the Commissioner, deductions allowable in computing entire net income that are directly or indirectly related to the investment capital or investment income and less a portion of the net operating loss equal to the ratio of investment income to entire net income. (Sec. 208(6), Tax Law) Deductions that are directly and indirectly attributed to investment income are briefly described at ¶10-530 and more thoroughly explained in a Technical Services Bureau memorandum. (TSB-M-88(5)C)

Investment income includes capital gains in excess of capital losses from investment capital. It also includes (for taxable years beginning before 1997) income derived from subsidiary capital that has been disqualified as subsidiary stock because of premature dispositions of target stock or target assets as described at ¶10-535 Non-Income Tax Base Computation.

Investment income may not exceed entire net income.

Investment capital defined.—Investment capital is that capital invested in corporate securities other than those of the investing corporation.

Issuers allocation percentages.—The New York State Department of Taxation and Finance provides lists of issuers allocation percentages for the purpose of allocating investment income. (*Note:* Subscribers can find the latest percentages, as well as percentages for prior years, by using the lookup tool located in the New York Smart Charts and Tools under the New York State Tax Reporter.) The allocable investment in each corporate security is determined by applying the allocation percentage shown by the issuing corporation in any return for New York Tax Law or Insurance Law purposes for the preceding tax year. (Reg. Sec. 4-7.2)

For issuers or obligors subject to franchise tax on transportation and transmission companies or franchise tax on farmers, fruit growers, and other cooperative agricultural corporations, the appropriate measure is issued capital stock; for businesses subject to Article 9-A business corporation franchise tax, the appropriate measure is entire net capital; and, for insurance companies subject to Article 33 franchise taxes, the appropriate measure is gross direct premiums. Special rules also apply for determining the issuer's allocation percentage of banks subject to taxation under Article 32.

Investments held for only a portion of the taxable period are prorated in determining the amount of investment capital attributable to such investments. Professional service corporations must use an investment allocation percentage of 100%. (Reg. Sec. 4-7.1)

Determination of issuer's allocation percentage.—For purposes of the calculation discussed earlier in this section, the allocation percentage of each issuer or obligor is determined in the following manner. The issuer's allocation percentage is the percentage of the appropriate measure that is required to be allocated to New York State on the report required under the Tax Law for the preceding year. (Reg. Sec. 4-7.2)

(1) For issuers subject to the franchise tax on transportation and transmission corporations and associations (Sec. 183, Tax Law) and for those subject to the franchise tax on farmers, fruit growers and other cooperative agricultural corporations (Sec. 185, Tax Law) the appropriate measure is capital stock.

(2) For those subject to the tax on business corporations (Article 9-A), the appropriate measure is entire net capital.

(3) For those subject to the franchise tax on insurance companies, except for savings and insurance banks and domestic insurance companies (Article 33), the appropriate measure is gross direct premiums.

(4) In the case of an issuer or obligor subject to the banking corporation tax (Article 32), the issuer's allocation percentage is the alternative entire net income allocation percentage determined under Sec. 1454(c), Tax Law, for the preceding taxable year. When the banking corporation's alternative entire net income for the preceding year is derived exclusively from business carried on within New York State, the issuer's allocation percentage is 100%.

A corporation or association which is organized under the laws of a foreign country to do a banking business determines its issuer's allocation percentage by dividing the (1) loans (including a taxpayer's portion of a participation in a loan) and financing leases within New York State, and all other business receipts earned within New York with respect to the issuer or obligor from all sources within and without the United States, by (2) the gross income of the issuer or obligor from all sources within and without the United States, for the preceding year, whether or not included in alternative entire net income for the year.

In the case of an issuer or obligor either (1) subject to Article 3-A, (2) registered under the Federal Bank Holding Company Act of 1956, or (3) registered as a savings and loan holding company, the allocation percentage is determined by dividing the portion of the entire capital allocable to New York State for the preceding year by the entire capital, wherever located, of the issuer or obligor for the preceding year.

If a report for the preceding year is not filed, or, if filed, does not contain adequate information to determine the issuer's allocation percentage, then the percentage to be used is, at the discretion of the Commissioner, either the issuer's allocation percentage derived from its most recently filed report or a percentage calculated by the Commissioner to indicate the issuer or obligor's degree of economic presence in New York State during the preceding year.

If a taxpayer's investment allocation percentage is zero, interest received on bank accounts will be multiplied by the taxpayer's business allocation percentage. (Sec. 210(3)(b), Tax Law; Reg. Sec. 4-7.1) (TSB-M-86(6)C)

Except for corporations principally engaged in the conduct of aviation or in the conduct of a railroad or trucking business, the investment allocation percentage is not used if a taxpayer has only business income, or has business income and an investment loss. (Reg. Sec. 4-8.1)

The Commissioner may adjust any investment allocation percentage that does not properly reflect the investment activity, business, income or capital of the taxpayer in New York.

Professional service corporations.—Professional service corporations must use an investment allocation percentage of 100%. (Reg. Sec. 4-7.1)

Reinsurance allocation percentages.—The current list of reinsurance allocation percentages, issued annually by the Department of Taxation and Finance.

• *Discretionary allocation by Commissioner*

The Commissioner is authorized to adjust the apportionment fraction if it does not properly reflect the business income or capital of a taxpayer within New York. (Sec. 210-A(11), Tax Law; Reg. Sec. 4-6.1)

[¶11-520] Apportionment

What is the standard New York apportionment formula?

For apportioning business income to the state, New York uses a single receipts factor. (Sec. 210-A, Tax Law; Instructions, Form CT-3)

The business apportionment factor is computed on Part 6 of Form CT-3.

S corporations. S corporations use a single receipts factor. (Sec. 210-A, Tax Law; Instructions, Form CT-3-S)

An S corporation is required to complete the "Computation of Business Apportionment Factor" section of the return, even if its business allocation percentage is 100% to report the computation of New York state receipts used to determine the fixed dollar minimum tax. Nonresident shareholders of a New York S corporation need the business apportionment factor to determine their New York state source income under Tax Law Sec. 632(a)(2). (Instructions, Form CT-3-S)

Partnerships. For partnerships, LLCs, and LLPs, if books and records do not reflect income earned in New York, then an evenly weighted three-factor formula (property, payroll, and gross income) is used. (Reg. Sec. 132.15; Instructions, Form IT-204)

If formula apportionment is required, it is computed on Part 2 of Section 10 of Form IT-204.

Nonresident individual owners. For nonresident individual owners, apportionment of distributive income is determined by applying the entity's apportionment factors. (Sec. 631, Tax Law; Sec. 632, Tax Law)

Corporate partners. For corporate partners computing tax under the aggregate method, the partner's factors are combined with the distributive share of the partnership's factors. (Reg. Sec. 4-6.5; TSB-M-07(2)C; Instructions, Form CT-3)

Does New York allow alternative apportionment methods?

If it appears that the apportionment fraction determined under Tax Law Sec. 210-A does not properly reflect the taxpayer's business income or capital in New York, the Commissioner of Taxation and Finance is authorized to make a discretionary adjustment. In addition, taxpayers can request an adjustment. (Sec. 210-A(11), Tax Law; Reg. Sec. 4-6.1; Instructions, Form CT-3)

Adjustments are done by excluding or including items, or by using any other method calculated to effect a fair apportionment of the taxpayer's business income and capital reasonably attributed to the state. (Sec. 210-A(11), Tax Law; Reg. Sec. 4-6.1; Instructions, Form CT-3)

Burden of proof. The one seeking the adjustment has the burden of proof to show that the apportionment fraction determined according to Tax Law Sec. 210-A does not result in a proper reflection of the taxpayer's business income or capital in New York and that the proposed adjustment is appropriate. (Sec. 210-A(11), Tax Law; Instructions, Form CT-3)

Reporting the adjustment. If a taxpayer has received approval from the Commissioner to make an adjustment, it should be reported on the appropriate line of Part 6 of Form CT-3. If the taxpayer has not received the Commissioner's approval before filing the return, then the taxpayer is required to file using the statutory rules for apportionment. The taxpayer may file an amended return after receiving approval. (Instructions, Form CT-3)

[¶11-525] Sales Factor

The discussion below applies to corporate taxpayers.

For partnerships, a three-factor apportionment formula applies, and receipts are sourced using an origin-based method rather than market-based; see ¶11-515 for details.

What is the New York sales factor?

The New York sales factor is a fraction, with the numerator including the taxpayer's total receipts in New York during the tax period and the denominator including the taxpayer's total receipts everywhere during the tax period. (Sec. 210-A, Tax Law)

The sales factor is computed on Part 6 of Form CT-3.

What are the New York sourcing rules for sales of tangible property?

Receipts from sales of tangible personal property are sourced to New York if the shipment is made to a point in the state. (Sec. 210-A(2)(a), Tax Law)

Real property. Net gains from sales of real property are sourced to the location of the property. (Sec. 210-A(2)(d), Tax Law)

What are the sourcing rules in New York for sales of other than tangible personal property?

Business receipts not otherwise addressed in Sec. 210-A are sourced to New York based on the following hierarchy of methods (Sec. 210-A(10), Tax Law):

— first, where the benefit is received;

— second, the delivery destination;

— third, except for the first tax period beginning on or after January 1, 2015, the apportionment fraction determined for the preceding taxable year for the receipts (Instructions, Form CT-3); or

— finally, the fraction in the current taxable year for those receipts that can be sourced, using the first two methods above.

The taxpayer must use due diligence under each method before rejecting it and moving on to the next method in the hierarchy. The determination has to be based on information the taxpayer knows (or information that the taxpayer would know after a reasonable inquiry). (Sec. 210-A(10), Tax Law)

Electricity. Receipts from sales of electricity are sourced to the delivery location. (Sec. 210-A(2)(b), Tax Law)

Digital products. Receipts from sales of digital products are sourced to New York based on the following hierarchy of methods (Sec. 210-A(4), Tax Law):

— first, the customer's primary use location of the digital product;

— second, the location where the digital product is received;

— third, except for the first tax period beginning on or after January 1, 2015, the apportionment fraction determined for the preceding taxable year for that digital product (Instructions, Form CT-3); or

— finally, the fraction in the current taxable year for those digital products that can be sourced, using the first two methods above.

The taxpayer must use due diligence under each method before rejecting it and moving on to the next method in the hierarchy. The determination has to be based on information the taxpayer knows (or information that the taxpayer would know after a reasonable inquiry). If a digital product receipt reflects a combination of property and services, it cannot be divided into separate components and is considered to be one receipt, regardless of whether it is separately stated for billing purposes. The entire receipt has to be allocated by the hierarchy. (Sec. 210-A(4), Tax Law)

GILTI. For New York S corporations, global intangible low-taxed income is included in the denominator of the apportionment fraction, but not in the numerator. For C corporations, applicable to taxable years beginning after 2018, global intangible low-taxed income is not included in the numerator, and 5% global intangible low-taxed income is included in the denominator. (Sec. 210-A(5-a), Tax Law)

For tax years beginning before 2019, the law provided that net global intangible low-taxed income is included in the denominator of the apportionment fraction, but not in the numerator. (Sec. 210-A(5-a), Tax Law)

When filing the return, taxpayers must attach a statement indicating the amount of GILTI included in the "Everywhere" column. (Instructions, Form CT-3; *TSB-M-19(1)C*)

What are the New York sourcing rules for the rental, leasing, or licensing of property?

Receipts from rentals of real and tangible personal property are sourced to New York if the property is located in the state. (Sec. 210-A(3)(a), Tax Law)

Intangibles. Royalties from the use of patents, copyrights, trademarks, and similar intangibles are sourced to New York if the intangibles are used in the state. (Sec. 210-A(3)(b), Tax Law)

Digital products. Receipts from the licence to use (or granting remote access to) digital products are sourced to New York based on the following hierarchy of methods (Sec. 210-A(4), Tax Law):

— first, the customer's primary use location of the digital product;

— second, the location where the digital product is received;

— third, except for the first tax period beginning on or after January 1, 2015, the apportionment fraction determined for the preceding taxable year for that digital product (Instructions, Form CT-3); or

— finally, the fraction in the current taxable year for those digital products that can be sourced, using the first two methods above.

The taxpayer must use due diligence under each method before rejecting it and moving on to the next method in the hierarchy. The determination has to be based on information the taxpayer knows (or information that the taxpayer would know after a reasonable inquiry). If a digital product receipt reflects a combination of property and services, it cannot be divided into separate components and is considered to be one receipt, regardless of whether it is separately stated for billing purposes. The entire receipt has to be allocated by the hierarchy. (Sec. 210-A(4), Tax Law)

What are the New York sourcing rules for services?

Receipts from services are sourced to New York based on the following hierarchy of methods (Sec. 210-A(10), Tax Law):

— first, where the benefit is received;

— second, the delivery destination;

— third, except for the first tax period beginning on or after January 1, 2015, the apportionment fraction determined for the preceding taxable year for the receipts (Instructions, Form CT-3); or

— finally, the fraction in the current taxable year for those receipts that can be sourced, using the first two methods above.

The taxpayer must use due diligence under each method before rejecting it and moving on to the next method in the hierarchy. The determination has to be based on information the taxpayer knows (or information that the taxpayer would know after a reasonable inquiry). (Sec. 210-A(10), Tax Law)

Does New York have a throwback or throwout rule?

New York does not apply a throwback or throwout rule.

[¶11-530] Property Factor

Under the 2005 and 2007 budget bills, a single sales factor has been phased in for corporate taxpayers (see ¶11-505).

For partnerships, a property factor still applies; see ¶11-515.

The property factor of the business allocation percentage is the following fraction: (Sec. 210(3)(a)(1), Tax Law)

$$\frac{\text{Average Value of Real and Tangible Personal Property in New York}}{\text{Average Value of Real and Tangible Personal Property Everywhere}}$$

The property factor is computed on Form CT-3, General Business Corporation Franchise Tax Return.

• *Factor determination*

The property factor of the business allocation percentage is determined by ascertaining the percentage that the average value of the taxpayer's real and tangible personal property, owned or rented, within New York during the period covered by its report bears to the average value of all the taxpayer's real and tangible personal property during the period. (Sec. 210(3)(a)(1), Tax Law)

Average value defined.—"Average value" is computed on a quarterly basis if the taxpayer's usual accounting permits, or more frequently at the option of the Commissioner or the taxpayer. (Reg. Sec. 4-3.1)

"Value of all of the taxpayer's real and tangible personal property" defined.— The term "value of all of the taxpayer's real and tangible personal property" generally means the adjusted bases of the properties for federal income tax purposes. The value of rented property is determined by multiplying gross rents payable for the rental of the property during the taxable year by eight. (Sec. 210(3)(a)(1), Tax Law)

Fair market value election.—A taxpayer may make a one-time revocable election to use fair market value as the value of all of its real and tangible personal property. Such an election must be made for the taxpayer's first taxable year beginning after January 1, 1987. In addition, the election does not apply to any taxable year in which the taxpayer is included on a combined report unless each of the taxpayers included in the report has made such an election, which remains in effect for the year. (Sec. 210(3)(a)(1), Tax Law)

Metropolitan Commuter Transportation District.—The property factor is similarly determined in the Metropolitan Commuter Transportation District to calculate the portion of the taxpayer's business activity occurring in the district for purposes of levying the surcharge. (Sec. 209-B, Tax Law) See ¶ 10-380 Rates of Tax.

Elimination of property factor.—For circumstances in which the property factor may be eliminated, see ¶ 11-515 Allocation.

• *Tangible personal property*

The property factor includes the average value of all of the taxpayer's real and tangible personal property, whether owned or rented to it (for tax years beginning prior to 1987, the property factor included rented real property, but not rented tangible personal property). The value of tangible personal property rented to the taxpayer is determined by multiplying the "gross rents" payable during the taxable period by eight. However, a corporation could make a one-time election by the extended due date for filing its 1987 return to phase in leased tangible personal property over a five-year period. If such an election was made, the following percentages of the value of leased tangible personal property were included in the value of tangible personal property. (Sec. 210(3)(a)(1), Tax Law; Reg. Sec. 4-3.2)

For taxable years commencing in	The percentage will be
1987	20
1988	40
1989	60
1990	80
1991 and thereafter	100

Tangible personal property defined.—The term "tangible personal property" means corporeal personal property, such as machinery, tools, implements, goods, wares and merchandise, but not money, deposits in banks, shares of stock, bonds, notes, credits or evidences of an interest in property or evidences of debt. Tangible personal property is considered to be in New York if it is physically in the state, even if it is in a bonded warehouse or held by an agent, consignee or factor. Property in transit is generally considered to be located at its destination. Omnibuses and other

¶11-530

rolling equipment may be allocated by mileage or by time operated within and without New York, or by any other approved method. (Sec. 208(11), Tax Law; Reg. Sec. 4-3.1)

Gross rents defined.—"Gross rents" are any amount payable for the use or possession of the tangible personal property, including amounts designated as a fixed sum or as a percentage of sales, profits, or otherwise. Gross rents also include a proportionate part of the cost of improvements to tangible personal property made by or on behalf of a taxpayer if the improvements revert to the owner or lessor upon termination of the lease or other arrangement. (Reg. Sec. 4-3.2)

• *Real property*

The value of real property rented to the taxpayer is determined by multiplying the "gross rents" payable during the taxable period by eight. "Gross rents" means the actual sum of money or other consideration payable directly or indirectly by the taxpayer or for its benefit for the use or possession of property. Gross rents include amounts designated as a fixed sum or as a percentage of sales, profits, or other income and any amounts payable as additional rent or in lieu of rent, such as interest, insurance, repairs, or any other amount required to be paid by the terms of the lease or other arrangement. (Reg. Sec. 4-3.2)

Gross rents also include a proportionate part of the cost of improvements to real property (other than a building on leased land) made by or on behalf of a taxpayer if the improvements revert to the owner or lessor upon termination of the lease or other arrangement. The cost of the improvement is included in gross rents proportionately over the unexpired term of the lease commencing with the date the improvement is completed or over the life of the improvement if its life expectancy is less than the unexpired term of the lease. (Reg. Sec. 4-3.2)

If a building is erected on leased land by or on behalf of the taxpayer, the value of the land is determined by multiplying the gross rent by eight, and the value of the building is determined in the same manner as if owned by the taxpayer.

The term "gross rents" does **NOT** include (1) intercorporate rents if both the lessor and lessee are taxed on a combined basis (See ¶ 11-550 Combined Reports), (2) amounts payable as separate charges for water and electric service furnished by the lessor, (3) amounts payable for storage, provided such amounts are payable for space not designated and not under the control of the taxpayer, or (4) the portion of rental payment applicable to a space subleased from the taxpayer and not used by it.

Real property and related equipment, except inventoriable goods, that is under construction and is not occupied and used during the construction is excluded from both the numerator and the denominator of the property factor. (TSB-M-82(3)C, ¶ 9-897)

• *Metropolitan Commuter Transportation District*

A property factor is similarly calculated in the Metropolitan Commuter Transportation District to determine the portion of the taxpayer's New York business activity occurring in the district for purposes of levying the surcharge imposed in taxable years ending before December 31, 2009. (Sec. 209-B, Tax Law) See ¶ 10-380 Rates of Tax.

[¶ 11-535] Payroll Factor

Under the 2005 and 2007 budget bills, a single sales factor has been phased in for corporate taxpayers (see ¶ 11-505).

For partnerships, a payroll factor still applies; see ¶ 11-515.

The payroll factor of the business allocation percentage is the following fraction: (Sec. 210(3)(a)(3), Tax Law)

$$\frac{\text{Wages, Salaries and Other Personal Service Compensation of Employees Within New York}}{\text{Wages, Salaries and Other Personal Service Compensation Everywhere}}$$

The payroll factor is computed on Form CT-3, General Business Corporation Franchise Tax Return.

Wages, salaries, and other compensation are computed on the cash or accrual basis in accordance with the taxpayer's regular method of accounting (See ¶ 10-520 Accounting Methods and Periods). (Reg. Sec. 4-5.1)

Officer compensation.—Compensation paid to general executive officers of a corporation (chairman, president, vice-president, etc.) is excluded from both the denominator and the numerator of the payroll factor. (Reg. Sec. 4-5.3) In order to be considered a general executive officer, the officer must have company-wide authority or have responsibility for an entire division. (Sec. 210(3)(a)(3), Tax Law; Reg. Sec. 4-5.3)

Generally, if an employee is regularly connected with, or working out of, an office or place of business in New York, the compensation will be allocated to New York regardless of where the employee's service is performed. However, if the taxpayer can establish that a substantial part of its payroll is paid to employees attached to a New York office who perform substantial services elsewhere, and that the general rule would not properly reflect the amount of business done in the state by the employees, the taxpayer may be permitted to compute the payroll factor on the basis of services performed in the state. (Reg. Sec. 4-5.1)

An individual is considered to be an employee if the taxpayer has the right to control and direct the individual as to both the result to be accomplished by the individual and the means by which it is to be accomplished. (4-5.2)

Earnings included in a qualified cash or deferred arrangement under IRC Sec. 401(k), which are excluded from federal taxable income, are included in the payroll factor (*Answer to CCH Questionnaire*, New York Department of Taxation and Finance, April 23, 1986).

• *Metropolitan Commuter Transportation District*

A payroll factor is calculated in the Metropolitan Commuter Transportation District to determine the portion of the taxpayer's New York business activity occurring in the district for purposes of levying the surcharge imposed in taxable years ending before December 31, 2018. (Sec. 209-B, Tax Law)

See ¶ 10-380 Rates of Tax.

[¶ 11-540] Apportionment Factors for Specific Industries

What special industry apportionment formulas does New York use?

Under New York's corporate tax reform legislation, effective for tax years beginning after 2014, taxpayers generally apportion business income based on a single receipts factor using customer sourcing rules. (Sec. 210-A, Tax Law; Instructions, Form CT-3)

Taxpayers compute the business apportionment factor on Part 6 of Form CT-3.

New York has special receipts factor sourcing provisions for the following industries.

Advertising. In the case of taxpayers engaged in the business of publishing newspapers or periodicals, the law assigns advertising receipts to New York based on the ratio of New York circulation, compared to total circulation for the publication. (Sec. 210-A(8)(a), Tax Law; Reg. Sec. 4-4.3)

For receipts from sales of television or radio advertising, taxpayers multiply the receipts by a fraction, with the numerator equal to the number of viewers or listeners in the state and the denominator equal to the number of viewers or listeners everywhere. (Sec. 210-A(8)(b), Tax Law)

For sales of other advertising, which is furnished, provided, or delivered to or accessed by the viewer or listener through the use of wire, cable, fiber-optic, laser, microwave, radio wave, satellite or similar successor media, taxpayers multiply the receipts by a fraction, with the numerator equal to the number of viewers or listeners in the state and the denominator equal to the number of viewers or listeners everywhere. (Sec. 210-A(8)(c), Tax Law)

Financial transactions. The following sourcing rules apply for apportioning income from financial instruments. (Sec. 210-A(5)(a), Tax Law; *Corporate Tax Reform Outline*)

Taxpayers can use one of two sourcing methods for qualified financial instruments (QFIs):

— use customer-based sourcing for each income stream that does not constitute tax exempt income; or

— treat all income from QFIs as taxable business income and apportion 8% of the net income (dividend income, interest income, and net gains), not less than zero, from QFIs to New York.

Taxpayers make the 8% QFI election on an annual basis. The election is irrevocable and, in the case of a combined group, applies to all QFI income of all group members.

Customer-based sourcing applies to income from non-qualified financial instruments (non-QFIs).

For sourcing purposes, an individual is located in New York if his or her billing address is in the state. A business entity is located in New York if its commercial domicile is in the state.

Taxpayers use the following hierarchy to determine a business entity's commercial domicile (Sec. 210-A(5)(e), Tax Law):

(1) the entity's seat of management and control; or

(2) the entity's billing address in the taxpayer's records.

Taxpayers must exercise due diligence before rejecting the first method and using the second method.

For receipts constituting the primary spread of selling concession from underwritten securities, taxpayers source the receipts to the customer's location. (Sec. 210-A(5)(b)(3)(B), Tax Law)

Credit cards. Service charges, fees, and interest are earned in New York if the card holder has a New York mailing address. (Sec. 210-A(5)(c), Tax Law)

Receipts from merchant discounts are generated in New York if the merchant is located in New York.

¶11-540

Taxpayers source receipts from credit card authorization processing, as well as clearing and settling processing, to the location where the credit card processor's customer accesses the processor's network.

Taxpayers source all other credit card processing receipts to New York using the average of 8% and the percentage of New York access points.

Software and digital service providers. Taxpayers generally source receipts from digital products to the customer's primary use location of the product. (Sec. 210-A(4), Tax Law)

Management services for RICs. For services provided to regulated investment companies (mutual funds) (RICs), taxpayers apportion receipts based on the domicile of the mutual fund's shareholders.

Taxpayers determine the New York percentage of shareholders by averaging monthly percentages reflecting the number of shares held by New York domiciliaries compared to the total number of shares. (Sec. 210-A(5)(d), Tax Law; Reg. Sec. 4-4.3) (TSB-M-88(9)C)

For example, a mutual fund management corporation with receipts of $1 million from services to a RIC apportions the receipts by first determining its monthly percentage, as follows:

$$\frac{\text{Number of shares owned by shareholders domiciled in New York State on the last day of the month}}{\text{Total number of shares owned by shareholders in the investment company on the last day of the month}} = \text{monthly percentage}$$

In January there were no outstanding shares. For the remaining months in the taxable period the monthly percentages were 47%, 51%, 46%, 45%, 48%, 50%, 49%, 47%, 50%, 49%, and 46% respectively.

528%	Sum of monthly percentages	
11	Number of monthly percentages	= 48% allocation percentage
$1,000,000	Receipts of the management corporation	
× 48%	Allocation percentage	
480,000	Receipts of the management corporation allocated to New York State and included in the receipts factor of Business Allocation Percentage	

Railroad and trucking companies. Corporations principally engaged in the conduct of trucking or railroad businesses use a mileage percentage to source income to New York. Taxpayers determine the percentage by dividing their mileage in New York for the period covered by the return by the mileage both in and outside the state. (Sec. 210-A(6), Tax Law)

Aviation. For receipts from air freight forwarding acting as principal and similar indirect air carrier receipts from that activity, taxpayers source 100% of the receipts to New York if both the pick up and delivery associated with the receipts are made in the state, and 50% of the receipts if either the pick up or delivery associated with the receipts is made in the state. (Sec. 210-A(7)(a), Tax Law)

For other aviation service providers (including a "qualified air freight forwarder"), the receipts factor uses arrivals and departures, revenue tons, and originating revenue. A corporation is a qualified air freight forwarder for another corporation if (1) it owns or controls all of the other corporation's capital stock; or if all of its capital stock is owned or controlled by the other corporation; or if all of the capital stock of both corporations is owned or controlled by the same interests; (2) it is principally engaged in the business of air freight forwarding; and (3) its air freight forwarding business is carried on principally with airlines operated by the other corporation. (Sec. 210-A(7)(b), Tax Law; Instructions, Form CT-3)

Pre-2015. For tax years before 2015, air freight forwarders and foreign airlines used a formula with a double-weighted receipts factor and special rules for computing the factors. Other taxpayers engaged in aviation activities used a three-factor formula with special rules for computing each factor. (Former Sec. 210(3)(a)(7), Tax Law)

Security and commodity brokers. Except for receipts from financial instruments, taxpayers apportion receipts from broker or dealer activities under Tax Law Sec. 210-A(5)(b).

For brokerage commissions (Sec. 210-A(5)(b)(1)), margin interest (Sec. 210-A(5)(b)(2)), fees related to underwriting (Sec. 210-A(5)(b)(3)(A)), account maintenance fees (Sec. 210-A(5)(b)(4)), and management or advisory service fees (Sec. 210-A(5)(b)(5)), taxpayers source receipts based on the customer's location (generally, the customer's mailing address).

If, for purposes of (b)(1), (b)(2), (b)(3)(A), (b)(4), or (b)(5), the taxpayer is unable to determine the customer's mailing address from its records, then the taxpayer must include 8% of the receipts in the apportionment fraction numerator. (Sec. 210-A(5)(b)(8), Tax Law)

For receipts constituting the primary spread of selling concession from underwritten securities, taxpayers source the receipts to New York if the customer is located in the state. (Sec. 210-A(5)(b)(3)(B), Tax Law)

For receipts constituting interest earned by a taxpayer on loans and advances made to an affiliated corporation, but with which the taxpayer is not permitted or required to file a combined report, the law deems the receipts to arise from services performed at the affiliated corporation's principal place of business. (Sec. 210-A(5)(b)(6), Tax Law)

Sellers of closed-circuit and cable TV transmission rights. For the sale of rights for closed-circuit and cable television transmission of an event (other than events occurring on a regularly scheduled basis) taking place in the state as a result of services rendered by a corporation's employees as athletes, entertainers, or performing artists, the corporation includes the receipts in the receipts factor numerator to the extent that they are attributable to transmissions received or exhibited in New York. (Sec. 210-A(3)(c), Tax Law)

Pipeline companies. For the transportation or transmission of gas through pipes, taxpayers source the receipts to New York based on the transportation units in New York, compared to the taxpayer's transportation units everywhere. (Sec. 210-A(9), Tax Law)

Vessels. For receipts from the operation of vessels, taxpayers source the receipts to New York using a fraction, with the numerator equal to the aggregate number of working days of the vessels owned or leased by the taxpayer in New York territorial waters during the period covered by the taxpayer's report. The denominator is equal to the aggregate number of working days of all vessels owned or leased by the taxpayer during the period. (Sec. 210-A(6-a), Tax Law)

[¶11-550] Combined Reports

Does New York allow elective combined reporting?

New York does not allow elective combined reporting. (Sec. 210-C, Tax Law)

Does New York require combined reporting for unitary business groups?

Water's edge combined reporting is required for corporations that meet a more-than-50% stock ownership test and are engaged in a unitary business. (Sec. 210-C, Tax Law)

Combined groups use Form CT-3-A to file their return. In addition, each group member, except for the designated agent, has to file Form CT-3-A/BC. (Instructions, Form CT-3-A)

Form CT-3-A/BC is used to report each corporation's business capital and business apportionment details, which are then included on Form CT-3-A, column B. Each corporation in the combined group, other than the designated agent, also computes its fixed dollar minimum tax on Form CT-3-A/BC. (Instructions, Form CT-3-A)

Corporations required to file combined returns. A corporation is required to file a combined return if it is engaged in a unitary business and it meets the more-than-50% stock ownership test, based on voting power (i.e., one corporation directly or indirectly owns the other, or the corporations are controlled by a common interest). (Sec. 210-C.2(a), Tax Law; Instructions, Form CT-3-A)

Corporations required to file combined returns include (Sec. 210-C.2(b), Tax Law; Instructions, Form CT-3-A):

— captive real estate investment trusts (REITs) or captive regulated investment companies (RICs) that are not required to be included in a combined return under the Article 33 insurance franchise tax;

— combinable captive insurance companies; and

— a non-U.S. corporation that meets the stock ownership and unitary business tests, if the corporation is treated as a domestic corporation under the IRC or has effectively connected income under Tax Law Sec. 208.9(iv).

If the capital stock requirement is met for only part of a tax year, then the combined report will include the unitary corporations' activities conducted during the portion of the tax year when the capital stock requirement is met. (Corporate Tax Reform FAQs, New York Department of Taxation and Finance)

Excluded corporations. The following corporations are not required or permitted to file a combined return (Sec. 210-C.2(c), Tax Law; Instructions, Form CT-3-A):

— corporations that are taxable under the Article 9 or Article 33 franchise tax;

— REITs and RICs that are not captive;

— New York S corporations; and

— non-U.S. corporations that the IRC does not treat as domestic corporations and have no effectively connected income under Tax Law Sec. 208.9(iv).

In addition, if a corporation is subject to the Article 9-A general business corporation franchise tax just because it has a limited partner interest in an entity that is doing business, employing capital, owning or leasing property, maintaining an office, or deriving receipts from activity in New York, and none of the corporation's related corporations are subject to tax under Article 9-A, then the corporation will not be required or permitted to file a combined return with the related corporations. (Sec. 210-C.2(c), Tax Law; Instructions, Form CT-3-A)

Computation of tax. The combined group's tax is the sum of (1) the tax on combined business income, the tax on combined business capital, or the designated agent's fixed dollar minimum tax, whichever is highest, plus (2) the fixed dollar minimum tax for every other taxpayer member of the group. Combined income is generally computed using the federal intercorporate deferral rules. Credits, prior net operating loss (NOL) conversion subtractions, and NOL deductions can be used by the group, not just the corporation that generated the item. (Sec. 210-C.4, Tax Law; *Corporate Tax Reform Outline*, New York Department of Taxation and Finance, April 2014)

The tax on the combined business income base is computed on Part 3 of Form CT-3-A. (Instructions, Form CT-3-A)

The tax on the combined business capital base is computed on Part 4 of Form CT-3-A. (Instructions, Form CT-3-A)

The capital of a captive REIT, captive RIC, or combinable captive insurance company is included in the computation of a combined group's capital base. (Corporate Tax Reform FAQs, New York Department of Taxation and Finance)

Designated agents. Every combined group is required to have one designated agent that will act on the group's behalf for all matters related to the combined return. (Sec. 210-C.7, Tax Law; Instructions, Form CT-3-A)

Group members' liability. Every combined group member that is subject to tax under Article 9-A is jointly and severally liable for the tax due on the combined return. (Sec. 210-C.6, Tax Law; Instructions, Form CT-3-A)

Different tax years. Both fiscal year and calendar year filers can be included in a combined report. The Department of Taxation and Finance has posted an FAQ explaining the process when the designated agent is a calendar-year filer and the member is a fiscal-year filer, and vice versa. (Corporate Tax Reform FAQs, New York Department of Taxation and Finance)

Does New York authorize or require affiliated group combined reporting?

Combined reporting is not required for affiliated groups that are not engaged in a unitary business. (Sec. 210-C, Tax Law)

Corporations are allowed to make an election, called the "commonly owned group election," that will treat all corporations meeting the stock ownership test as a combined group, even if they are not engaged in a unitary business. (Sec. 210-C.3, Tax Law; Instructions, Form CT-3-A)

The election is made on the combined group's original return that is timely filed, including valid extensions of time for filing. (Sec. 210-C.3, Tax Law; Instructions, Form CT-3-A; Corporate Tax Reform FAQs, New York Department of Taxation and Finance)

Any corporation entering a commonly owned group after the election year will be included in the combined group. (Sec. 210-C.3, Tax Law; Instructions, Form CT-3-A)

The election is irrevocable and is binding for the applicable tax year, plus the next six tax years (not including short tax years). The election will be automatically renewed for another seven tax years, unless it is revoked by the designated agent. (Sec. 210-C.3, Tax Law; Instructions, Form CT-3-A)

Limited time withdrawal procedure (until June 1, 2018): For a limited time, certain New York taxpayers can withdraw the commonly owned group election made on a 2015 or 2016 combined return. For the withdrawal to be allowed, all corporations in the original combined group must follow all of the required procedures by June 1, 2018. For details, see TSB-M-18(1)C.

[¶12-000]

CREDITS

[¶12-001] Overview of Credits

New York allows credits against corporate franchise (income) tax (Article 9-A) for the following purchases, activities, and practices. Credits are claimed on Form CT-3, General Business Corporation Franchise Tax Return.

Recodification of credits after 2014: As the result of corporate tax reform enacted by the 2014 budget legislation, New York's corporate franchise tax credits are moved from Tax Law § 210 to new § 210-B, effective for tax years beginning after 2014.

The Department of Taxation and Finance has advised that amounts of credit carryforwards that existed in pre-reform years are preserved, with the exception of the alternative minimum tax credit. (Corporate Tax Reform, New York Department of Taxation and Finance)

• *Business tax credit deferral*

For tax years 2010, 2011, and 2012, taxpayers with more than $2 million in aggregated business tax credits are required to defer the amounts above $2 million until 2013. The total amount of credits deferred will be paid back to taxpayers over tax years 2013, 2014, and 2015. (Sec 33.1 Tax Law; Sec 34.1 Tax Law)

Specifically, only credit that would otherwise have been used or refunded are deferred; credits earned but not used or refunded because of statutory limitations or insufficient liability are subject to their normal rules. Credit amounts deferred are accumulated in one of two new credits - temporary deferral nonrefundable payout credit and temporary deferral refundable payout credit. The amounts of these credits will either remain the same or grow until tax year 2013. (Sec 33.1 Tax Law; Sec 34.1 Tax Law)

Taxpayers can begin to use the nonrefundable payout credit on their 2013 tax returns. Any amounts not used can be carried forward indefinitely. Taxpayers can use and refund 50% of the refundable payout credit on their 2013 tax return. They can use and refund 75% of the remaining credit on their 2014 tax return, and the entire remainder on their 2015 tax return. (Sec 34.2 Tax Law)

Finally, taxpayers are required to make any mandatory first installment or estimated tax payments due after August 11, 2010 as if the credit deferral were in effect for the periods upon which the payments are based. (Sec 33.2 Tax Law)

See also, TSB-M-10(5)C,(11)I, September 13, 2010.

• *Investment credits*

Investment tax credit (ITC)

• *Enterprise zone credits*

Empire zone (EZ) investment tax credit

¶12-000

Empire zone (EZ) employment incentive tax credit

Empire zone (EZ) capital tax credit

Empire zone (EZ) wage tax credit

- *Economic zone equivalent area (ZEA) credits*

Economic zone equivalent area (ZEA) wage tax credit

- *Qualified empire zone enterprise (QEZE) credits*

Qualified empire zone enterprise (QEZE) credit for real property tax paid

Qualified empire zone enterprise (QEZE) tax reduction credit

- *Research credits*

Life sciences research and development credit

- *Job creation/hiring credits*

Employment incentive tax credit (EIC)

Employing qualified disabled persons

Excelsior Jobs Program

Economic Transformation and Facility Redevelopment Program

Empire State Jobs Retention Program

Hire a Veteran Credit

Minimum Wage Reimbursement Credit

Farm Workforce Retention Credit

- *Worker training/basic skills credits*

E-TIP credit

Empire State Apprenticeship Tax Credit

- *Environmental credits*

Investment in alternative-fuel vehicle property (see ¶ 12-080)

Green buildings credit

Brownfield credits

Biofuel production credit

Clean heating fuel credit

- *Economic development credits*

Empire state film production credit

Qualified emerging technology company (QETC) employment credit

Qualified emerging technology company (QETC) capital tax credit

Qualified emerging technology company (QETC) facilities, operations, and training credit

Empire state commercial production credit

START-UP NY

- *Historic property credits*

Historic barn renovation credit

Historic property rehabilitation credit

- *Housing credits*

    Low-income housing credit

- *Family credits*

    Employer-provided child care credit

- *Health credits*

    Automated external defibrillator credit

    Long-term care insurance credit

    Recovery tax credit

- *Youth credits*

    New York Youth Jobs Program

- *Other credits*

    Special additional mortgage recording tax credit

    Credit for servicing SONYMA mortgages

    Minimum tax credit

    Agricultural property tax credit

    Annual maintenance fee credit

    Industrial and manufacturing businesses (IMB) credit for energy taxes

    Security training tax credit

    Conservation easement tax credit

    Handicapped accessible vehicle credit

    Alcoholic beverage producer credit

    Real property tax credit for manufacturers

    Musical and theatrical production credit

    Farm donations to food pantries credit

- *Estimated tax*

    All payments made as estimated tax are applied as a credit toward the tax due. (Sec. 213-a(b), Tax Law; Reg. Sec. 7-2.3)

- *Overpayment of taxes*

    The Commissioner of Taxation and Finance, within the applicable period of limitations, may credit an overpayment of tax against any liability in respect of any tax imposed by the Tax Law on the taxpayer who made the overpayment. (Sec. 1086, Tax Law)

- *Credit carryforward*

    With limited exceptions, credits not used in one year may be carried forward to subsequent years. Any specific carryforward provisions are provided for in each particular credit.

¶12-001

• *Limitations*

Corporate franchise tax credits may not reduce a taxpayer's tax liability below the fixed dollar minimum.

• *Recapture*

Recapture rules may apply if property ceases to remain in qualified use. Any recapture provisions are provided for in each credit.

• *Disregarded SMLLCs*

The law has been amended to clarify that a single member limited liability company (SMLLC) that is disregarded as an entity separate from its single member or owner for federal income tax purposes must be treated as a disregarded SMLLC for purposes of determining whether its owner is eligible to claim any New York tax credit allowed under Article 9, 9-A, 22, 32 (prior to its repeal) or 33 of the Tax Law. (Sec. 43, Tax Law)

•*Repealed and expired credits*

New York has several credits that have expired or have been repealed, and for which the carryforward periods have ended.

PERSONAL INCOME

[¶15-050]

FEDERAL/MULTISTATE ISSUES

[¶15-055] Comparison of Federal/State Key Features

The following is a comparison of key features of federal income tax laws that have been enacted as of March 27, 2020, and New York personal income tax laws. New York taxable income is based on federal adjusted gross income (AGI) (see ¶15-505). State modifications to federal adjusted gross income required by law differences are discussed beginning at ¶16-005 for additions and ¶16-205 for subtractions.

Nonresidents and part-year residents.—Nonresidents and part-year residents are subject to New York income tax only on income derived from New York sources (see ¶15-105).

• *Alternative Minimum Tax (IRC Sec. 55 — IRC Sec. 59)*

For tax years beginning after 2013, New York no longer imposes a minimum income tax on certain tax preference items.

• *Asset Expense Election (IRC Sec. 179)*

Generally, the same as federal (IRC Sec. 179) because the starting point for New York taxable income is federal adjusted gross income (see ¶15-510). However, an addition is required with respect to the expensing of certain sport utility vehicles (see ¶16-040).

• *Bad Debts (IRC Sec. 166)*

The same as federal (IRC Sec. 166) because the starting point for New York taxable income is federal adjusted gross income (see ¶15-510).

• *Capital Gains and Capital Losses (IRC Secs. 1(h), 1202, 1211, 1212, and 1221)*

New York does not have a special tax rate for capital gains. Capital gains and losses are determined in the same manner as under federal law (IRC Sec. 1(h), IRC Sec. 1202, IRC Sec. 1211, IRC Sec. 1212, and IRC Sec. 1221) because the starting point for New York taxable income is federal adjusted gross income (see ¶15-510).

• *Charitable Contributions (IRC Sec. 170)*

New York generally follows the federal treatment (IRC Sec. 170) of charitable contributions, although deductions are limited for certain high-income taxpayers (see ¶15-545). In addition, New York provides a credit for certain charitable contributions, beginning in 2019. However, New York does not follow federal amendments made by the CARES Act, such as an above-the-line deduction of up to $300 allowed for tax years beginning in 2020 for an individual who does not itemize deductions for charitable contributions made to churches, nonprofit schools, nonprofit medical institutions, and other organizations (see ¶15-515).

• *Child Care Credit (IRC Sec. 45F)*

New York allows an employer-provided child care credit, based on the federal credit (IRC Sec. 45F), beginning in 2020. In addition, New York provides a credit for child and dependent care expenses.

- *Civil Rights Deductions (IRC Sec. 62)*

The same as federal (IRC Sec. 62) because the starting point for New York taxable income is federal adjusted gross income (see ¶ 15-510).

- *Dependents (IRC Sec. 152)*

New York provides its own dependent exemption, with state law referring to the federal definition of an eligible dependent (IRC Sec. 152) (see ¶ 15-535).

- *Depreciation (IRC Secs. 167, 168, and 1400N)*

Generally, the same as federal (IRC Sec. 167 and IRC Sec. 168) because because the starting point for New York taxable income is federal adjusted gross income (see ¶ 15-510). However, except with respect to certain property, New York is decoupled from bonus depreciation provisions under IRC Sec. 168(k); accordingly, amounts claimed as bonus depreciation on the federal return generally must be added back (see ¶ 16-040). Other modifications are required with respect to safe harbor leases and certain property placed in service before 1994 (see ¶ 16-040 and ¶ 16-245).

- *Earned Income Credit (IRC Sec. 32)*

New York has an earned income credit that is a percentage of the federal credit (IRC Sec. 32), and an enhanced EIC is also available for noncustodial parents.

- *Educational Benefits and Deductions (IRC Secs. 62(a)(2)(D), 127, 221, 222, and 529)*

Generally the same as federal (IRC Sec. 62(a)(2)(D), IRC Sec. 127, IRC Sec. 221, IRC Sec. 222, IRC Sec. 529) because the starting point for New York taxable income is federal adjusted gross income (see ¶ 15-510 and ¶ 15-685). In addition, New York provides a college tuition credit or deduction (see ¶ 15-545). However, New York does not conform to federal changes exempting certain 529 withdrawals used to pay for K-12 tuition, or to federal provisions effective after December 31, 2018, allowing distributions from 529 plans to be excluded from gross income of the designated beneficiary if used to cover: 1) up to $10,000 of student loan payments, or 2) the costs associated with registered apprenticeship programs. New York also does not follow the federal CARES Act amendment allowing payments made before January 1, 2021, by an employer to either an employee or a lender to be applied toward an employee's student loans to be excluded from the employee's income (see ¶ 15-515).

- *Excess Business Loss Limitation (IRC Sec. 461(l))*

New York follows the federal excess business loss limitation (IRC Sec. 461(l)), but does not conform to the federal suspension of the limitation for tax years beginning in 2018, 2019, and 2020 (see ¶ 15-515).

- *Foreign Earned Income (IRC Sec. 911 — IRC Sec. 912)*

The same as federal (IRC Sec. 911—IRC Sec. 912) because the starting point for New York taxable income is federal adjusted gross income (see ¶ 15-510).

- *Health Insurance and Health Savings Accounts (HSAs) (IRC Secs. 105(b), 106(e), 139D, 162(l), and 223)*

Generally, the same as federal (IRC Sec. 105(b), IRC Sec. 106(e), IRC Sec. 139D, IRC Sec. 162(l), IRC Sec. 223) because the starting point for New York taxable income is federal adjusted gross income (see ¶ 15-510). For taxable years beginning before 2022, New York does not follow federal amendments made by the CARES Act (see ¶ 15-515).

¶ 15-055

- *Indebtedness (IRC Secs. 108 and 163)*

Generally, the same as federal (IRC Sec. 108 and IRC Sec. 163) because the starting point for New York taxable income is federal adjusted gross income (see ¶ 15-510). However, under New York's expense disallowance provisions, an addition may be required for certain interest payments made to a related member. See also ¶ 16-075 regarding an addback for interest on loans to buy tax-exempt securities.

- *Interest on Federal Obligations (IRC Sec. 61)*

Interest income on obligations of the U.S. and its possessions may be subtracted from federal AGI in computing New York adjusted gross income (see ¶ 16-280).

- *Interest on State and Local Obligations (IRC Sec. 103)*

New York requires an addback for interest income on state and local bonds and obligations, but not those of New York State or its local governments (see ¶ 16-075).

- *Losses Not Otherwise Compensated (IRC Sec. 165)*

New York generally follows the federal treatment, including the pre-TCJA itemized deduction treatment for personal casualty losses (IRC Sec. 165) (see ¶ 15-510 and ¶ 15-545).

- *Net Operating Loss (IRC Secs. 172 and 1400N)*

New York generally follows the federal treatment of net operating losses (IRC Sec. 172). If state NOL deduction is limited to federal taxable income (computed without NOL deduction), then state NOL addition modification must be computed. New York does not conform to federal CARES Act amendments, including (1) a five-year carryback period for NOLs arising in tax years beginning in 2018, 2019, and 2020, and (2) suspension of the 80% of taxable income limitation for those years (see ¶ 15-515).

- *Pass-Through Deduction (IRC Sec. 199A)*

New York has not adopted the federal provisions regarding the pass-through deduction (IRC Sec. 199A). New York uses federal adjusted gross income as its starting point. Because this is a deduction from adjusted gross income to arrive at taxable income (a below-the-line deduction), no adjustment is required for individual taxpayers. However, an addback is required for estates and trusts filing fiduciary returns (see ¶ 15-215).

- *Personal Residence (IRC Secs. 121, 132(n), 163(h)(3), and 1033)*

Generally the same as federal (IRC Sec. 121, IRC Sec. 132(n), IRC Sec. 163(h)(3), and IRC Sec. 1033) because the starting point for New York taxable income is federal adjusted gross income (see ¶ 15-510). However, New York allows the itemized deduction for home mortgage interest as it existed before the TCJA (see ¶ 15-545).

- *Retirement Plans (IRC Secs. 401 — 424 and IRC Sec. 1400Q)*

New York generally conforms to federal provisions regarding retirement plans. (IRC Sec. 401—IRC Sec. 424 and IRC Sec. 1400Q) However, an addition to federal adjusted gross income is required for certain public employee retirement contributions (see ¶ 16-135), and employees are allowed subtractions for certain pension and annuity income, government pensions, railroad retirement income, and social security benefits (see ¶ 16-345). For taxable years beginning before 2022, New York does not follow federal amendments made by the CARES Act (see ¶ 15-515).

- *Start-Up Expenses (IRC Sec. 195)*

The same as federal (IRC Sec. 195) because the starting point for New York taxable income is federal adjusted gross income (see ¶15-510).

- *Taxes Paid (IRC Sec. 63(c)(1), IRC Sec. 164)*

New York's itemized deduction computation begins with a base amount that includes all state and local taxes claimed as federal itemized deductions, as those deduction existed before the TCJA. However, state, local, and foreign income taxes deducted federally must be added back for New York purposes (see ¶16-145). In addition, New York does not allow a deduction for state and local sales tax in computing the New York itemized deduction (see ¶15-545). New York allows a subtraction for state and local income tax refunds included in federal adjusted gross income (see ¶16-360), and a credit is provided for income taxes paid to other states.

- *Unemployment Compensation (IRC Sec. 85)*

The same as federal (IRC Sec. 85) because the starting point for New York taxable income is federal adjusted gross income (see ¶15-510).

[¶15-100]

TAXPAYERS

[¶15-105] Taxation of Part-Year Residents and Nonresidents

Nonresidents and part-year residents are liable for tax on New York source income (see ¶16-505). (Sec. 631(a), Tax Law)

Both nonresidents and part-year residents must use Form IT-203, *Nonresident and Part-Year Resident Income Tax Return.* (Instructions, Form IT-201, Resident Income Tax Return)

Taxpayers are subject to tax on income received from New York sources while a nonresident and on all income received while a New York State resident. The tax is computed in the following manner (Instructions, Form IT-203):

(1) Compute a base tax as if the taxpayer were a resident for the entire year, including items of income, gain, loss, and deduction from all sources.

(2) Divide New York source amount of New York adjusted gross income by federal amount of New York adjusted gross income, to determine an income percentage.

(3) The base tax is multiplied by the income percentage to arrive at the amount of tax apportioned to New York based on New York source income.

See also *TSB-M-87(13)I.*

Married taxpayers filing a joint return, in the case of one spouse having no income from New York State sources, are required to enter in the Federal Amount column the combined return of each item of income that the taxpayers included in their joint federal return. (Instructions to Form IT-203) The taxpayer's federal adjusted gross income is entered on Form IT-203 (Nonresident and Part-Year Resident Income Tax Return). The New York modifications are applied to the taxpayers' federal adjusted gross income to yield their New York adjusted gross income. The New York adjusted gross income is reduced by the taxpayers' itemized or standard deduction and dependent exemptions to yield New York taxable income to which the tax is applied. Any applicable credits (such as the child and dependent care credit and the household credit) are subtracted from the tax and any additional New York

State taxes (such as the separate tax on lump-sum distributions and the minimum income tax) are added to the tax to yield the base tax. Finally, the income percentage is applied to the base tax to yield the allocated New York State tax.

Residency and domicile are discussed in detail at ¶ 15-110.

• *Income and deductions partly from New York sources*

If a business, trade, profession or occupation is carried on partly within and partly without New York, the items of income, gain, loss and deduction derived from or connected with New York sources will be determined by allocation and apportionment. (Sec. 631(c), Tax Law) For a discussion of allocation and apportionment, see ¶ 16-505.

• *New York deductions and exemptions*

Nonresidents are allowed the same standard deduction, itemized deductions, and New York exemptions as resident individuals. (TSB-M-87(11)I)

[¶ 15-110] Residents

New York residents are taxed on income from all sources.

For information on the treatment of nonresidents and part-year residents, see ¶ 15-105.

• *Resident individual*

A "resident individual" is defined as:

(1) Any person domiciled in New York (subject to the exceptions listed below); or

(2) Any individual (other than an individual in active service in the U.S. Armed Forces) who maintains a permanent place of abode in New York and spends in the aggregate more than 183 days of the taxable year in New York, whether or not domiciled in New York for any portion of the taxable year. (Sec. 605(b)(1), Tax Law)

CCH COMMENT: *Burden of proving nonpresence in New York.*—The taxpayer has the burden of proving nonpresence in New York. Thus, where the auditor estimated the taxpayer's days in New York during one year as 173 days, which is less than 184 days, this did not preclude the conclusion that the taxpayers failed to establish that they were in New York for no more than 183 days. Since the estimate was close to 183 days, the Division of Taxation was justified in requiring the taxpayers to prove how many days they were present in New York. (*Hellman*)

Exceptions for domiciliaries.—In the case of domiciliaries, there are two exceptions. The first is for an individual who during the tax year:

(1) maintains no permanent place of abode in New York;

(2) maintains a permanent place of abode outside New York; and

(3) is present no more than 30 days of the taxable year in New York.

EXAMPLE: A, a calendar-year taxpayer, sells his New York residence in December 1969 and leaves for England on January 6, 1970, for an assignment at his employer's London office. He purchased a home in England in the fall of 1969. His family, however, remains in New York. On January 20, 1970, he returns to the state to pick up his wife and daughter, and they live in a hotel in New York from January 28 through 30. If A cannot prove that he changed his domicile from New York to England in 1970, he is taxable as a resident for 1970 because he did not maintain a permanent place of abode outside New York for the entire year.

EXAMPLE: A nondomiciliary who spends 200 days in New York during the tax year and maintains an abode in New York for the second half of the year is not a New Yor resident for tax purposes.

EXAMPLE: New York residency was established where rent was paid for a New York City apartment, the taxpayer's child attended a Queens, New York, school and the taxpayers listed their address and telephone number in a Queens directory.

The second exception to being a resident individual for personal income tax purposes applies to a domiciliary individual who meets the following requirements:

(1) the taxpayer is present in one or more foreign countries for at least 450 of 548 consecutive days; and

(2) during the period of 548 consecutive days, the taxpayer, the taxpayer's spouse (unless legally separated), and the taxpayer's minor children are not present in New York for more than 90 days. (Sec. 605(b)(1), Tax Law)

Where the 548-day period contains a status period of less than one calendar year, the 90-day period is prorated.

EXAMPLE: A calendar-year taxpayer is assigned by his employer to a location outside the United States on September 30. From October 1 to December 31 (a period of 92 days), the taxpayer will be taxed as a nonresident even if he keeps his New York home or apartment, but only if, during the three-month period, he, his spouse or minor children spend less than 16 days there (92 ÷ 548 × 90). Nonresident status during this short period, however, depends on continued presence in a foreign country for at least 450 out of 458 days and meeting the less-than-90-day requirement for the full period.

Estoppel.—A determination of nonresident status does not preclude the state from a finding of resident status in a later year. (*Marx v. Goodrich,* (1955, NY SCt, AppDiv), 286 AppDiv 913, 142 NYS2d 28)

CCH COMMENT: The burden is on the taxpayer to prove the number of days spent inside and outside New York. If, during the year, the taxpayer is likely to travel to New York on a regular and frequent basis, it is a good idea for him to maintain a diary that clearly indicates the days on which he was in New York solely for travel purposes, and to maintain supporting records, such as transportation tickets and receipts. The diary will be an invaluable aid on audit. Furthermore, it may be very useful for year-end tax planning if the individual is able to structure his affairs so as not to be present in New York for the number of days in any tax period that could change his residency status. A diary may help determine tax residence for New York City and Yonkers as well. However, calendar notations are not sufficient to establish the taxpayer's whereabouts without evidence that the notations were made contemporaneously.

Domicile.—A domicile is the place which an individual intends to be such individual's permanent home—the place to which such individual intends to return whenever such individual may be absent. (Reg. Sec. 105.20)

Domicile is discussed in more detail below.

Permanent place of abode.—A "permanent place of abode" is a dwelling place suitable for year-round use, containing ordinary dwelling facilities for cooking, bathing, etc., that the taxpayer maintains but need not own. The term usually includes a dwelling owned or leased by the taxpayer's spouse.

The term does not include camps or cottages that are suitable and used only for vacations, nor barracks or other construction that do not contain facilities ordinarily found in a dwelling.

CCH COMMENT: A summer home is not a permanent residence unless it is suitable for year-round habitation. Therefore, out-of-state taxpayers who own New York summer homes that are not winterized with sufficient heat or cold-weather plumbing and water lines should not seek unwittingly to make improvements without first checking whether they might thereby acquire tax residence under the 183-day rule or as a domiciliary.

Substantial part of year.—New York regulations provide that a New York nondomiciliary must maintain a permanent place of abode for substantially all of the tax year to be taxed as a statutory resident, and the Department of Taxation and Finance interprets that to mean a period exceeding 11 months. (Reg. Sec. 105.20)

EXAMPLE: An individual who acquires a permanent place of abode on March 15 would not be a statutory resident, since the permanent place of abode was not maintained for substantially the entire year. Similarly, if an individual maintains a permanent place of abode at the beginning of the year but disposes of it on October 30 of the tax year, he would not be a statutory resident.

EXAMPLE: Two aspects of the definition of a "permanent place of abode" were examined by the Tax Appeals Tribunal in *Matter of Evans*:

"Given the various meanings of the word 'maintains' and the lack of definitional specificity on the part of the Legislature, we presume that the Legislature intended, with this principle in mind, to use the word in a practical way that did not limit its meaning to a particular usage so that the provision might apply to the 'variety of circumstances' inherent to this subject matter. In our view, one maintains a place of abode by doing whatever is necessary to continue one's living arrangements in a particular dwelling place. This would include making contributions to the household, in money or otherwise."

"We reject the petitioner's assertion that since he did not pay for many of the operating expenses of the dwelling (such as the utilities or major repairs, or any costs of ownership such as mortgage payments), he was not 'maintaining' the living quarters as required by the statute. We find no support for the conclusion that the Legislature intended to define a resident individual solely by the types of expenses incurred by the individual and to limit the definition only to individuals who incur the types of expenses suggested by the petitioner. As there can be many financial or other arrangements that determine how the costs of a dwelling are paid for (such as where expenses are shared or provided by another, or where an individual's contribution to the household is not in the form of money), the nature of the expenses incurred in and of themselves cannot determine whether an individual is maintaining a place of abode in the city."

"With regard to whether a place of abode is 'permanent' within the meaning of the statute, we do not agree with petitioner that the statute requires that the place of abode be owned, leased, or otherwise based upon some legal right in order for it to be permanent. . . . In our view, the permanence of a dwelling place for purpose of the personal income tax can depend on a variety of factors and cannot be limited to circumstances which establish a property right in the dwelling place. Permanence, in this context, must encompass the physical aspects of the dwelling place as well as the individual's relationship to the place. For example, it seems clear that an apartment leased by one individual and shared with other unrelated individuals may be the permanent place of abode of those who are not named on the lease, given other appropriate facts."

In affirming the decision of the Tax Appeals Tribunal, the New York Supreme Court, Appellate Division, stated:

"the permanence of a dwelling place [. . .] cannot be limited to circumstances which establish a property right in the dwelling place."

Temporary lodgings (Prior law).—For taxable years ending before December 31, 2008, Reg. Sec. 105.20(e) stated that a place of abode, whether in New York or elsewhere, was not deemed permanent if it was maintained only during a temporary stay for the accomplishment of a particular purpose. (For a discussion of the amendment removing that language, see TSB-M-09(2)I.)

Military personnel.—Barracks, bachelor officers' quarters, quarters assigned on vessels, and related lodgings generally do not qualify as permanent places of abode maintained by an individual in the Armed Forces of the United States. Further, the maintenance of a place of abode by an individual in the Armed Forces of the United States outside New York State will not be considered permanent if it is maintained only during a duty assignment of a limited or temporary nature.

Days spent within and outside New York.—In counting the number of days spent within and without New York State, presence within New York State for any part of a calendar day constitutes a day spent within New York State. However, such presence within New York State may be disregarded if it is solely for the purpose of boarding a plane, ship, train or bus for travel to a destination outside New York State, or while traveling by motor, plane or train through New York State to a destination outside New York State.

Extended presence in foreign countries.—The term "resident individual" does not include a New York domiciliary who meets each of the following conditions:

(1) within any 548-day consecutive period, the individual is present in a foreign country or countries for at least 450 days;

(2) during such 548-day period, the individual, the individual's spouse (unless legally separated), and the individual's minor children are not present in New York for more than 90 days; and

(3) during the nonresident portion of the taxable year within which the 548-day period begins and the nonresident portion of the taxable year with or within which such period ends, the individual is not present within New York for a number of days that exceeds the amount that bears the same ratio to 90 as the number of days contained in such portion of the taxable year bears to 548. (Sec. 605(b)(1), Tax Law)

Provided each of the above conditions is met, the domiciliary will be considered a nonresident of New York for personal income tax purposes. The burden is upon the individual to show that he or she satisfied each of the requirements noted above.

EXAMPLE: B, a single individual, is domiciled in New York State. During the period July 2, 1991 through December 31, 1992 (a period of 548 consecutive days), B was present in a foreign country 463 days.

During the above period, B was present in New York State a total of 50 days, 15 days during the period July 2, 1991, through December 31, 1992, and 35 days during 1992. Since B was present in a foreign country 463 days, B satisfies the requirements of subparagraph (1).

B also meets the requirements of subparagraph (2) because the total of 50 days B was present in New York during this 548 consecutive day period is less than the maximum of 90 days allowed.

To ascertain whether B meets the requirements of subparagraph (3), B must determine if the number of days present in New York State during the period July 2, 1991, through December 31, 1991, exceeds the maximum allowed for the nonresident portion of the taxable year within which the 548 consecutive day period began. The maximum number of days B may be present in New York State during the period July 2, 1991, through December 31, 1991, is 30, determined by making the following computation:

183 (number of days in/548 × 90 = 30 (maximum number
the nonresident portion of the taxable   of days B may spend in New York State
year)   during the period July 2, 1991 through
                                                 December 31, 1991)

Since B was present in New York State 15 days during the period July 2, 1991, through December 31, 1991, B did not exceed the maximum of 30 days allowed for this period. Therefore, B meets the requirements of subparagraph (3).

Based on the information contained in this example, B would be considered a nonresident of New York State for income tax purposes during the period July 2, 1991, through December 31, 1992. Therefore, B would be required to file as a part-year resident of New York State for the 1991 taxable year and as a nonresident of New York State for the 1992 taxable year.

Medical recuperation.—Time spent by a nondomiciliary in a New York medical facility being treated for a serious illness does not count toward the 183 days required to establish residency for personal income tax purposes.

CCH CAUTION: However, this exception applies only when the taxpayer is in a medical facility for the treatment of an illness. Thus, days spent seeing a doctor or receiving outpatient treatment do not qualify for the exception and are counted as New York days.

CCH COMMENT: The Department's residency audit guidelines take a narrow view of the medical emergency exception. They state that days spent in the state for medical treatment should not be counted only in those instances where the presence is totally involuntary. This would include situations where an incompetent person is placed in a facility in New York or where an individual suffers a medical emergency while present in the state for other purposes and cannot realistically be removed from the state.

Estates and trusts.—An estate is a New York resident if the decedent was domiciled in New York at the date of death, and a trust is a resident if the grantor was a New York resident when the trust received the property or if certain other tests are met.

EXAMPLE: Taxpayer A who is domiciled in New York State and taxpayer B who is domiciled in New Jersey together create an irrevocable trust. The portion of such trust attributable to property transferred by A is a New York State resident trust and the portion of such trust attributable to property transferred by B is a New York State nonresident trust. (Reg. Sec. 105.23)

EXAMPLE: Taxpayer C creates an irrevocable trust while such taxpayer is a domiciliary of New York State. Subsequent to the creation of such trust, C moves and becomes a domiciliary of California and transfers additional property to such irrevocable trust. The portion of such trust attributable to property transferred while C was a domiciliary of New York State is a New York State resident trust and the portion of such trust attributable to property transferred while C was a domiciliary of California is a New York State nonresident trust. (Reg. Sec. 105.23)

EXAMPLE: D, who is domiciled in Canada, creates an irrevocable trust with the X Trust Company in New York City as trustee. The entire corpus of the trust consists of securities of American corporations, which are actively traded by the trustee on the New York Stock Exchange. The beneficiaries of the trust are all New York State residents. Regardless of whether the trust is held to be a resident of the United States for federal income tax purposes; it is, for New York State income tax purposes, a nonresident trust. (Reg. Sec. 105.23)

• *Domicile*

Domicile, in general, is the place that an individual intends to be his or her permanent home—the place to which he or she intends to return whenever absent. (Reg. Sec. 105.20)

Citizenship.—Domicile is not dependent on citizenship; that is, an immigrant who has permanently established his or her home in New York is domiciled in New York regardless of whether he or she has become a U.S. citizen or has applied for citizenship. (Reg. Sec. 105.20) However, a U.S. citizen will not ordinarily be deemed to have changed domicile by going to a foreign country unless it is clearly shown that the citizen intends to remain there permanently.

Example: A U.S. citizen domiciled in New York, who goes abroad because of an assignment by his employer or for study, research or recreation, does not lose his New York domicile unless it is clearly shown that he intends to remain abroad permanently and not return.

Multiple home.—A person can have only one domicile (Reg. Sec. 105.20) If a person has two or more homes, such person's domicile is the one which such person regards and uses as such person's permanent home. In determining such person's intentions in this matter, the length of time customarily spent at each location is important but not necessarily conclusive.

≫→*CCH Comment:* A person who maintains a permanent place of abode for substantially all of the taxable year in New York and spends more than 183 days of the taxable year in New York is taxable as a resident even though such person may be domiciled elsewhere.

• *Charitable contributions*

Charitable contributions, gifts, bequests, donations, pledges, loans, volunteering, and other activities covered in this act, made in taxable years beginning on or after January 1, 1994, may not be used in determining where an individual is domiciled. (Sec. 605(c), Tax Law)

• *Husband and wife*

Generally, the domicile of a husband and wife are the same. (Reg. Sec. 105.20) However, if they are separated in fact they may each, under some circumstances, acquire their own separate domiciles, even though there is no judgment or decree of separation. (Reg. Sec. 105.20)

⮞⮞⮞→*Example:* A taxpayer who separated from his wife and moved to New Jersey was found to have established a change of domicile even though the separation was not pursuant to a written agreement and the couple later reconciled and the taxpayer moved back to New York. (*Matter of Angelico*)

It should be noted that even a husband and wife who are living together may have separate domiciles.

⮞⮞⮞→*Example:* Where a couple had moved from New York to Florida and the wife testified that she intended to make Florida her permanent home while the husband indicated that he still considered himself to be a New Yorker, it was held that the wife had established a change of domicile.

Children.—A child's domicile ordinarily follows that of the child's parents, until the child reaches the age of self-support and actually establishes his or her own separate domicile. Where the mother and father have separate domiciles, the domicile of the child is generally the domicile of the parent with whom the child lives for the major portion of the year. The domicile of a child for whom a guardian has been appointed is not necessarily determined by the domicile of the guardian.

• *Military personnel*

Federal law provides that, for purposes of taxation, military and naval personnel are not deemed to have lost their residence or domicile in any state solely by reason of being absent from the state in compliance with military or naval orders. (Reg. Sec. 105.20) Thus, federal law insures that personnel who are domiciled in New York State will not be deemed domiciliaries for income tax purposes in other states in which they are stationed.

On the other hand, an individual who is domiciled in another state and stationed in New York State will not be deemed a domiciliary, for tax purposes, of New York.

The rule is, generally, that the domicile of a person is in no way affected by service in the armed forces of his or her country. A change of domicile has to be shown by facts that objectively manifest a voluntary intention to make the new location a domicile.

CCH COMMENT: Although it is possible for a military or naval person to change domicile, the requisite intent is difficult to prove.

• *Change of domicile*

A domicile, once established, continues until the person moves to a new location with a *bona fide* intention of making the new location his or her fixed and permanent home. (Reg. Sec. 105.20)

Intent.—Intention is thus the decisive factor in determining whether a particular residence occupied by a person qualifies as his or her domicile; no change of domicile results from a removal to a new location if the intention is to remain there only for a limited time. In determining intent, all surrounding circumstances are considered, but no one (i.e. voting, or selling one's residence and moving away) is dispositive. (Reg. Sec. 105.20)

Burden of proof.—There is a legal presumption against a change in domicile from one location to another. Accordingly, the burden of proof is on the party claiming a change in domicile to establish, by clear and convincing evidence, both a change in residence and the intention to effect a change in domicile. While a taxpayer's declarations of domiciliary intent are considered, they are subject to comparison with his conduct. (Reg. Sec. 105.20)

Review.—The Appellate Division's review of Division of Tax Appeals determinations is limited to deciding whether there are any facts or reasonable inferences from the evidence of record to support the determination of change of domicile. If there are, the determination must be confirmed. Thus, if there is evidence to sustain a finding either for or against the taxpayer, an adverse determination will be confirmed.

> **CCH COMMENT:** If taxpayers are to have assurance that an attempted change of domicile will be respected by the Division of Taxation, the severance of ties with New York must be complete and any remaining ties must be trivial and incidental, of such a nature as to be consistent with nondomiciliary status.

> **EXAMPLE:** The following are examples of failure to establish a change in domicile:

—New York domiciliaries wintered in Florida solely for health reasons. (see *Feldman*)

—New York domiciliaries lived out of state while renovating a New York City apartment that became a primary residence. (*Roth*)

—A New York domiciliary resided primarily in other states for ten years but never intended to establish a permanent place of abode in any other state. (*Simon*)

—New York domicile is not abandoned despite documentary efforts to do so. (*Zapka*)

—New York domiciliaries spent winters in Florida or retired to Florida but retained their New York residence. (*Gellerstein*)

—New York domiciliaries moved to Florida to pursue a temporary work assignment. (*Haney*)

—A New York domiciliary maintained strong ties to family in New York and continued business and social activity in the state. (*Buzzard*)

• *New York State District Office Audit Manual guidelines*

The Department of Taxation and Finance has provided "primary" and "other" factors for auditors to consider in determining whether nonresidents are domiciliaries of New York for state personal income tax purposes. (Department of Taxation and Finance, Income Tax, District Office Audit Manual)

Documentation related to the "primary" factors (home, active business involvement, time, items "near and dear" and family connection) is considered first during the audit process.

Information concerning the "other" (i.e. secondary and tertiary) factors will only be requested when a basis for New York domicile, using the primary factors, is found to exist or where the primary factors are approximately equal between New York and another state.

"Primary factors.—"Primary factors evidencing a change in domicile include:

(1) The individual's use and maintenance of a New York "residence," compared to the nature and use patterns of a non-New York residence (i.e. whether the taxpayer disposed of his New York residence and acquired a new residence in a new state);

> **CCH COMMENT:** The situation that has arisen most frequently is that in which the taxpayer acquired a new home in Florida while still maintaining his New York home. Taxpayers have argued that their purchase of a new home in

Florida proves that they have changed their domicile in Florida, but in most cases, the Florida homes has been viewed as a vacation home only and the taxpayer has been held to remain a New York domiciliary.

Even where the taxpayer has been able to point to other factors indicating a change of domicile, the fact that the taxpayer retained his New York homes has often been cited as a critical factor leading to a finding that the taxpayer failed to prove a change of domicile.

EXAMPLE: A married couple moved to Louisiana because of an employment transfer, leased an apartment while looking for a home, obtained a driver's license and registration, voted, and joined various clubs. They did not sell their New York home until they returned to New York due to illness, however, and it was held that they had not changed their domicile.

EXAMPLE: The taxpayer left New York for Florida and married a Florida domiciliary, but maintained a home in New York. The taxpayer claimed a change of residence by filing a declaration of Florida domicile, registering his motor vehicles in Florida, registered to vote in Florida, opening a safe-deposit box and checking and savings accounts in Florida, purchasing two condominiums in Florida, and quitting New York organizations while joining Florida organizations. The taxpayer remained a New York domiciliary primarily because he did not abandon his New York home and spent considerable time there (more time there than at his Florida residence) as a director of two banks.

(2) The individual's pattern of employment, as it relates to compensation derived by the taxpayer in the particular year being reviewed;

(3) The retention of business connections in New York, including active participation in a New York trade, business occupation or profession and/or substantial investment in, and management of, any New York closely-held business such as a sole proprietorship, partnership or limited liability company;

EXAMPLE: The taxpayer acquired a Florida residence and performed certain formalities such as filing Florida residence declarations, registering to vote in Florida, and putting their Florida address on their wills, licenses, etc. Nevertheless, the husband's active involvement in his New York engineering business contradicted these declarations and led to a finding that the taxpayers had not changed their domicile to Florida. (*Kartiganer*)

However, taxpayers who have shown a reduced level of involvement in New York business after moving to another state have been more successful in showing an intent to change domicile.

EXAMPLE: A taxpayer who sold his New York business prevailed even though he continued to work as a consultant in New York during part of the tax year. (*Scheman*)

EXAMPLE: Similarly, a taxpayer proved that he had changed his domicile from New York City to Shelter Island by showing a reduction in the number of days he worked in New York City. (*Doman*)

(4) An analysis of where the individual spends time during the year. Neither occasional visits to New York nor repeated or extended visits to New York will prevent a finding that the taxpayer has abandoned his New York domicile;

CCH COMMENT: However, the more time spent in New York, the more likely it is that the taxpayer will be found to remain a New York domiciliary.

⫸→*Example:* Taxpayers who acquired a Florida residence but maintained their home in New York admitted that they never intended to live in Florida year-round because the husband could not bear the heat and humidity of Florida summers. Nevertheless, the taxpayers prevailed by showing that the center of their lives had moved to Florida. (*Stevens*)

⫸→*Example:* The taxpayers' accountant prepared an analysis of the taxpayers' whereabouts using credit card statements, checking account statements for New York and Florida accounts, canceled checks and utility bills, which demonstrated that the taxpayers had spent less than 183 days in New York. (*Golub*)

(5) The location of items that the individual holds "near and dear" to his or her heart, or those items that have significant sentimental value, such as family heirlooms, works of art, collections of books, stamps and coins, and those personal items that enhance the quality of lifestyle;

CCH COMMENT: Under the Department of Taxation and Finance residency audit guidelines, the auditor is instructed to review insurance policies, which may disclose the actual location of such items. The auditor is also admonished that reason must prevail, and some items may need to be excluded from consideration just as a matter of practicality.

⫸→*Example:* A taxpayer claiming a new permanent place of abode in a warm climate would not be expected to move a mink coat from the New York location to the newly claimed residence.

(6) An analysis of the taxpayer's family connections both within and without New York; and

⫸→*Example:* The fact that minor children of the taxpayer attend a nonboarding school within reasonable commuting distance from the taxpayer's residence may indicate that the taxpayer intends this residence to be his domicile.

CCH COMMENT: *Severed New York social ties.*—The fact that a taxpayer has generally severed his New York social ties, such as religious or club membership, and established new ties at his new residence is a strong indication that the taxpayer has abandoned his New York domicile.

No single primary factor listed above is determinative. The auditor's decision must be based upon an objective review of the "primary" factors affecting domicile.

"Other Factors".—Where the primary factors indicate a New York domicile, "other" factors will be reviewed. These "other" factors are all relevant, but are not considered to carry the weight and significance of the primary factors. Thus, the Department of Taxation and Finance residency audit guidelines label such other factors as "secondary" and "tertiary" factors.

In an audit, these factors are relevant only if one or more of the primary factors are present, and if no primary factors are present, the Division will not contest the issue of domicile, regardless of the number of secondary or tertiary factors present. However, if one or more primary factors are present, the auditor is instructed to analyze the secondary and tertiary factors to make the domicile determination.

CCH COMMENT: Importance of "other factors".—These factors are not as important in determining domicile as the primary factors because the taxpayer has the ability to control and regulate these factors. For example, a taxpayer, because of varying residency rules, may be able to change his voter registration, auto registration, or driver's license to another state for convenience purposes while never intending to change domicile.

Secondary factors include.—

(1) The address at which bank statements, bills' financial data and correspondence concerning other family business is primarily received;

(2) The physical location of the safe deposit boxes used for family records and valuables;

(3) Location of auto, boat, and airplane registrations as well as the individual's personal driver's or operator's license;

(4) Indication as to where the taxpayer is registered to vote and an analysis of the exercise of said privilege;

CCH CAUTION: All elections considered.—Auditors will not limit the review to the general elections in November, but will also question the taxpayer's participation in primary or other off-season elections, including school board and budget elections. The auditor will also want to know how and where the taxpayer voted (in person or mail-in).

(5) The frequency and nature of business conducted within New York State for legal, medical and other professional services in relationship to the services performed at other locations;

(6) Possession of a New York City Parking Tax exemption; and

(7) An analysis of telephone services at each residence including the nature of the listing, the type of service features, and the activity at the location.

Tertiary factors.—Tertiary factors, which are below secondary and far below primary in importance, include:

(1) The place of internment;

(2) The location where the taxpayer's will is executed and probated;

(3) Passive interest in partnerships or small corporations;

(4) The mere location of bank accounts in contrast to the activity of the account;

(5) Passive, honorary, lifetime or casual membership in clubs and organizations, including religious or cultural affiliations, where active participation is not required or demonstrated;

(6) Contributions made to political candidates or causes; and

(7) The location where the taxpayer's individual income tax returns are prepared and filed.

[¶15-150]
SPECIAL TAXPAYERS

[¶15-175] Military Personnel

Any member of the Armed Forces who was *domiciled* in New York State at the time of entrance into military service continues to be a New York domiciliary, regardless of where he or she may be assigned to duty or how long. Military assignments do not affect domicile. (*Publication 361*) Consequently, such an individual will continue to be taxed as a New York resident unless, during the taxable year, he or she satisfied *all three* of the conditions in either Group A or Group B:

• *Group A*

(1) the taxpayer maintained no permanent place of abode in New York during the taxable year;

(2) the taxpayer maintained a permanent place of abode outside New York during the entire taxable year; and

(3) the taxpayer did not spend more than 30 days in New York during the taxable year. (*Publication 361*)

CCH COMMENT: If you meet all three conditions in Group A for qualifying as a New York State nonresident for a full tax year, and you want a refund of any New York State income tax withheld from your pay, file Form IT-203, *Nonresidents and Part-Year Resident Income Tax Return*, with the Tax Department, and attach an explanation that contains the following:

---

(1) A statement that you did not have a permanent place of abode in New York during the tax year; and

(2) The location and a brief description of the permanent place of abode you maintained outside New York, including the beginning and ending dates of your stay there; and

(3) The exact number of days you were in New York during the tax year.

• *Group B*

(1) the taxpayer was present in a foreign country or countries for at least 450 days within any period of 548 consecutive days;

(2) during the period of 548 consecutive days, the taxpayer, the taxpayer's spouse (unless legally separated), and the taxpayer's minor children were not present in New York for more than 90 days; and

(3) during any period of less than one year within the 548 day period, which would be treated as a separate taxable period if the individual changed his or her resident status during the year, the individual was present in New York for no more than the number of days bearing the same ratio to 90 as the number of days in the less-than-one-year period bears to 548. (*Publication 361*)

A member of the Armed Forces who was *not domiciled* in New York State at the time he entered the Armed Forces will not be considered a New York resident during the individual's period of service even though he or she may be assigned to duty in New York State for more than 183 days in the taxable year and establish a permanent place of abode in New York. (Sec. 605(b), Tax Law)

CCH COMMENT: If you meet all three conditions in Group B for qualifying as a nonresident for a full tax year, and you want a refund of any New York State income tax withheld from your pay, file Form IT-203, *Nonresidents and Part-Year Resident Income Tax Return*, and attach a statement explaining how you met all three conditions.

CCH COMMENT: If you meet all three of the Group B conditions, you must file Form IT-203, *Nonresidents and Part-Year Resident Income Tax Return*, for the tax year in which the 548-day period began. For the part-year resident period, include any items of income, gain, loss, or deduction received or accrued up to the time of change of residence. For the nonresident period, include any items of income, gain, loss, or deduction derived from or connected with New York State sources. In the year you return to New York, you may also be required to file Form IT-203.

Military pay.—Military pay received by a nonresident member of the Armed Forces does not constitute income derived from New York sources. (Reg. Sec. 132.11)

• *Spouses*

Applicable to state or local income tax returns for tax years beginning after 2008, the Military Residency Relief Act of 2009 (P.L. 111-97) amended the Servicemembers Civil Relief Act (P.L. 108-189) to prohibit a servicemember's spouse from either losing or acquiring a residence or domicile for purposes of taxation because he or she is absent or present in any U.S. tax jurisdiction solely to be with the servicemember in compliance with the servicemember's military orders, if the residence or domicile is the same for the servicemember and the spouse. P.L. 111-97 also prohibits a spouse's income from being considered income earned in a tax jurisdiction if the spouse is not a resident or domiciliary of such jurisdiction when the spouse is in that jurisdiction solely to be with a servicemember serving under military orders.

The New York State Department of Taxation and Finance issued a memorandum explaining the application of the Military Residency Relief Act of 2009 to state and local personal income tax as well as to the Metropolitan Commuter Transportation Mobility tax. (*TSB-M-10(1)I, TSB-M-10(1)MCTMT,* New York State Department of Taxation and Finance, January 11, 2009)

2018 Amendment.—On December 31, 2018, the Servicemembers Civil Relief Act was amended by the Veterans Benefits and Transitions Act (P.L. 115-407) so that a spouse can now elect to have the same residence for state and local tax purposes as the servicemember. This applies beginning with tax year 2018.

For New York guidance on making the election, see *TSB-M-19(3)I.*

• *Relief provisions*

A subtraction from federal adjusted gross income is allowed for certain New York state militia pay (Instructions, Form IT-201, Resident Income Tax Return); see ¶ 16-308.

Extensions of time for filing returns, payment of tax, etc., are provided for members of the Armed Forces, or those individuals serving in support of such Armed Forces, serving in areas designated as "combat zones" by the President of the United States, or hospitalized inside or outside the state due to injuries sustained as a result of such service. (Sec. 696(a), Tax Law)

The same benefits apply to individuals performing services in Afghanistan, including the airspace above it (*Important Notice N-02-5*), the Persian Gulf Desert Shield area (Sec. 696(e), Tax Law), those individuals considered under hostile fire (Sec. 696(f), Tax Law), and personnel serving in a qualified hazardous duty area (i.e. Kosovo) as part of Operation Allied Force. (Sec 1., S.B. 5000, Laws 1999; *Important Notice N-99-9*)

Effective September 7, 2004, the extension provisions are expanded to include personnel serving outside the United States in a contingency operation. (Sec. 696(a), Tax Law)

The period of service in such an area or operation, plus the period of continuous hospitalization attributable to injury sustained while serving, plus the next 180 days thereafter are disregarded in determining whether any of the following acts was performed in the time prescribed therefore, as pertaining to the income tax liability of the individual:

(1) filing a return of income tax (except withholding tax);

(2) payment of income tax (except withholding) or any liability to the state in respect thereof;

(3) filing a petition or application;

(4) allowance of credit or refund of income tax;

(5) filing claim for credit or refund;

(6) assessment of income tax;

(7) giving or making notice or demand for payment of tax or liability to the state with respect thereto;

(8) collection of any liability in respect of income tax (*Note:* However, under a 2016 amendment, the collection period after an assessment will not be extended due to a hospitalization; specifically, the amendment states that, with respect to any period of continuous hospitalization described in § 696(a), and the next 180 days thereafter, the provision does not apply to the collection of personal income tax liabilities);

(9) bringing of suit by or on behalf of the state in respect of any income tax liability; or

(10) any other act required or permitted by Article 22 or specified in regulations prescribed under Sec. 696.

Additionally, the above-described period is disregarded in determining the amount of any credit or refund (including interest).

Collection.—The assessment or collection of tax or liability owed the state in respect of income tax, or any action proceeding by or on behalf of the state may be initiated in accordance with the law without regard to the above provisions unless it was previously ascertained that the individual is entitled to such benefits. (Sec. 696(c), Tax Law)

Deaths.—In the case of the death of a member of the Armed Services while in active service in a combat zone as described above, or as a result of injuries sustained while so serving, the personal income tax will not apply for the tax year in which the date of death falls, or for a prior tax year ending on or after the first day served in the combat zone. No returns will be required on behalf of the individual or the individual's estate for such year, and the unpaid tax for that year, if any, will not be assessed for that year. Also, any assessment will be abated and any collected tax refunded. (Sec. 696(d), Tax Law)

Iraq.—Service members directly supporting operations in Iraq from other locations, who are receiving imminent danger pay or hostile fire pay, are deemed to be serving in a combat zone. The relief described in *Important Notice N-03-07* also covers individuals serving in any other designated combat zone or qualified hazardous duty area that remains in effect, such as Afghanistan (discussed below). Spouses of those qualifying are also entitled to this relief. The available relief includes:

(1) an extension of time to file their New York personal income tax returns until at least 180 days after departure from the combat zone, with no penalty or interests

charges. The deadline for payment of taxes, including any installment of estimated tax, is similarly extended. These extensions of time do not apply to withholding taxes and returns;

(2) a suspension from all New York personal income tax return examinations and collections for the same period of time;

(3) exemption from New York personal income tax for military pay received while serving in the combat zone to the extent that military pay is exempt from federal income tax; and

(4) interest on overpayments of personal income tax from the original due date of the return if the return is filed by the extended due date. (*Important Notice N-03-07*)

The same relief provisions apply to those hospitalized as a result of injury sustained while serving in the combat zone. The extension of time for those hospitalized will be until at least 180 days after the later of the date of discharge from the hospital or the date of departure from the combat zone. (*Important Notice N-03-07*) In addition, if a member of the Armed Forces or support personnel dies as a result of serving in the combat zone, New York state personal income tax will not be imposed for any tax year during which the decedent served in the zone. Any unpaid personal income tax for years prior to service in the combat zone will be waived. Further, New York estate tax will be forgiven.

Taxpayers who are eligible for the above mentioned tax relief should write **COMBAT ZONE** at the top of their 2002 tax return.

Using discretionary power, the Tax Department is granting members of the Armed Forces and support personnel impacted by the military action in Iraq, who are not otherwise eligible for the combat zone tax relief, a six-month extension of time to file their 2002 New York state personal income tax return and to pay any tax due. However, interest will be due on any unpaid tax from the original due date of the return. Taxpayers who qualify for this relief should write **COMBAT ZONE-ASSIST** at the top of their 2002 tax return.

Other benefits.—In addition to the various combat zone relief provisions, the members of the Armed Forces or support personnel may be entitled to other relief provisions described in Publication 361, *New York State Income Tax Information for Military Personnel and Veterans. (Publication 361)*

Afghanistan.—Effective retroactively to September 19, 2001, Afghanistan, including the airspace above it, is designated as a combat zone. As a result, individuals serving in the Armed Forces, or serving in support of the Armed Forces, in the combat zone will receive New York state tax relief. Service members directly supporting operations in Afghanistan from other locations, who are receiving imminent danger pay or hostile fire pay, are deemed to be serving in the combat zone. The main tax relief available are the same as those available for military personnel in Iraq, discussed above. (*Important Notice N-02-5*)

In addition, members of the Armed Forces, Reserve Forces, and National Guard may qualify for the relief available under the New York State Soldiers' and Sailors' Civil Relief Act.

Deferral of the collection of back income taxes.—Regular members of the Armed Forces, Reserve Forces, and National Guard who have been called to active duty and owe back New York personal income taxes are reminded that they may qualify for a deferral of the collection of the back income taxes owed under the New York State Soldiers' and Sailors' Civil Relief Act if they can show that their ability to pay the taxes is impaired because of their military service. (*Important Notice N-02-3*)

The deferral only applies to income taxes that became due before or during the military service, and extends the payment deadline to six months after active military service ends. No interest or penalty will accrue during the deferral period. To take advantage of the deferral, a taxpayer must show both an inability to pay the tax and that this inability resulted from military service. A taxpayer must have received a notice of tax due, or be on an installment agreement with the state before applying for the deferral. (*Important Notice N-02-3*)

Interest rate benefits.—Active members of the U.S. military who have a New York tax liability for any New York taxes owed and whose military service has materially affected their ability to pay the liability may be eligible for an interest rate benefit under the Federal Soldiers' and Sailors' Civil Relief Act. (*Important Notice N-02-4*)

Persian Gulf.—Pursuant to an executive order signed by President Bush, certain contiguous areas in the Persian Gulf region have been designated active combat zones, effective January 17, 1991.

[¶15-185] Owners of Pass-Through Entities

New York generally follows the federal income tax treatment of pass-through entity owners. Accordingly, the income of the entity is passed through to the owners, and each owner's distributive or proportionate share is subject to tax.

Resident individual owners of pass-through entities report their personal income on Form IT-201, Resident Income Tax Return.

A partnership as such is not subject to New York personal income taxes. (Sec. 601(f), Tax Law) However, persons carrying on business as partners are liable for personal income tax in their separate or individual capacities.

In determining the New York adjusted gross income and the New York taxable income of a resident partner or resident shareholder, any modification which relates to an item of partnership income, gain, loss or deduction will be made in accordance with the partner's distributive share, for federal income tax purposes, of the item to which the modification relates. (Sec. 617(a), Tax Law) Where a partner's distributive share of any such item is not required to be taken into account separately for federal income tax purposes, the partner's or shareholder's share of the item will be determined in accordance with the partner's share, for federal income tax purposes, of partnership or S corporation taxable income or loss generally.

Each item of partnership income, gain, loss or deduction will have the same character for a partner for New York personal income tax purposes as for federal income tax purposes. (Sec. 617(b), Tax Law) Where an item is not characterized for federal income tax purposes, it will have the same character for a partner as if realized directly from the source from which realized by the partnership.

Where a partner's distributive share of an item of partnership income, gain, loss or deduction is determined for federal income tax purposes by special provision in the partnership agreement with respect to the item, and where the principal purpose of the provision is the avoidance or evasion of New York income tax, the partner's distributive share of the item, and any modification required with respect thereto, will be determined as if the partnership agreement made no special provision with respect to the item. (Sec. 617(c), Tax Law)

For additional information regarding New York's treatment of partnerships, see ¶ 10-220.

• *New York treatment of LLCs*

New York substantially conforms to federal law. A properly structured LLC that is classified as a partnership for federal income tax purposes will be treated as a partnership for New York State personal income tax purposes, City of New York and City of Yonkers purposes. (Sec. 601(f), Tax Law) Accordingly, to the extent that an LLC is doing business in New York or is otherwise generating state income, both resident and nonresident members of the LLC must file New York (plus, if applicable, New York City and City of Yonkers) income tax returns and pay tax on their shares of New York source income in the same manner as partners of a partnership doing business in New York. An LLC that is not classified as a partnership for federal income tax purposes is classified as a corporation for New York corporate franchise tax purposes and is required to file a New York corporation franchise tax return.

For additional information regarding New York's treatment of LLCs, see ¶ 10-240.

• *S Corporation shareholders*

Certain additions (see ¶ 16-113) and subtractions (see ¶ 16-317) are provided for use by S corporation shareholders in determining New York adjusted gross income.

If a corporation which is an S corporation for federal income tax purposes is subject to the New York tax on business corporations, the shareholders of the corporation may elect to take into account the S corporation items of income, loss, deduction and reductions for taxes described in paragraphs two and three of subsection (f) of IRC Sec. 1366, which are taken into account for federal income tax purposes for the taxable year. (Sec. 660(a),(b)(1), Tax Law)

This election is made by filing Form CT-6, and to be valid all of the shareholders must consent. Generally, for an election to be valid for a taxable year, it must be made during the previous taxable year or on or before the fifteenth day of the third month of the tax year to which the election will apply. The election will be effective for the entire year for which it is made and for all succeeding years until the election is terminated. (*TSB-M-98(4)C; TSB-M-98(2)I*)

The Commissioner of Taxation may treat a corporation as having filed a timely election if an election is made after the filing deadline for that taxable year, or, if no election is made at all, where he determines that there was reasonable cause for the failure to timely file the election. (Sec. 660(b)(5), Tax Law; TSB-M-98(4)C; TSB-M-98(2)I) If an election was not valid because the corporation failed to obtain the consent of all shareholders, and within a reasonable period the consents have been obtained, the Commissioner may determine that the omission was inadvertent, and may retroactively validate the election. If an S election has been retroactively validated for federal purposes under IRC Sec. 1362(f), the Commissioner may retroactively validate the New York State election. Any retroactive validation requires both shareholders and corporation to recognize the tax consequences of the election for the retroactive period. (TSB-M-98(4)C; TSB-M-98(2)I)

For additional information regarding New York's treatment of S corporations, see ¶ 10-215.

Mandated election.—Under the 2007 budget legislation, for taxable years beginning after 2006, if an entity is an eligible S corporation for federal tax purposes and has not made the election to be a New York S corporation, it will be deemed a New York S corporation if the corporation's investment income for the current taxable year is more than 50% of its federal gross income for the year. This does not apply to S corporations that are subject to the bank franchise tax. (Sec. 660(i), Tax Law)

Authority to disregard.—For taxable years beginning after 2006, the Commissioner of Taxation and Finance is authorized to disregard personal service corporations or S corporations formed or availed of primarily to avoid or evade New York income tax. (Sec. 632-a, Tax Law)

• *Character of items*

In determining the New York adjusted gross income and the New York taxable income of a resident shareholder of an S corporation, any modification which relates to an item of S corporation income, gain, loss or deduction will be made in accordance with the shareholder's pro rata share, for federal income tax purposes, of an item to which the modification relates. (Sec. 617(a), Tax Law) Where a shareholder's pro rata share of any such item is not required to be taken into account separately for federal income tax purposes, the shareholder's share of the item will be determined in accordance with his share, for federal income tax purposes, of S corporation taxable income or loss generally.

Each item of S corporation income, gain, loss or deduction will have the same character for a shareholder for New York personal income tax purposes as for federal income tax purposes (Sec. 617(b), Tax Law) Where an item is not characterized for federal income tax purposes, it will have the same character for a shareholder as if realized directly from the source from which realized by the S corporation or incurred in the same manner as incurred by the S corporation.

• *Short taxable year*

Due to conformity with federal income tax provisions, a shareholder's income from the short period year is spread over four consecutive years beginning with tax year 1987 when the S corporation changed from a fiscal year to a calendar year. (*Letter to CCH,* from New York State Department of Taxation and Finance, April 28, 1988)

• *S termination year adjustments*

During an S termination year, S corporation items of income, loss and deduction included in a shareholder's federal adjusted gross income or allowed as a reduction for tax must be pro-rated and assigned to each day of the S corporation's federal taxable year. (Sec. 612(s), Tax Law) Items that fall within the S short year must be treated as items of a New York S corporation; items that fall within the C short year must be treated as items of an S corporation that is a New York C corporation. Normal tax accounting rules will be used to allocate items between S and C short years only if all shareholders (determined as of the first day of the C short year) consent, or there is a sale or exchange of 50% or more of the stock in such corporation during the New York S termination year.

[¶15-200]

ESTATES AND TRUSTS

[¶15-205] Estates and Trusts--Residency

New York distinguishes between resident and nonresident estates and trusts in determining what income is taxable for New York purposes. A resident estate or trust is taxable on entire net income as modified for New York purposes. A nonresident estate or trust is also taxable on entire net income, but only pays tax allocable to New York.

• *Resident estate or trust*

Sec. 605(b)(3), Tax Law, defines a "resident estate or trust" as:

(1) The estate of a decedent who at the time of his death was domiciled in New York;

(2) A trust, or portion of a trust, consisting of property transferred by will of a decedent who at his death was domiciled in New York; or

(3) A trust, or portion of a trust, consisting of the property of:

(a) a person domiciled in New York at the time the property was transferred to the trust, if the trust or portion of a trust was then irrevocable, or if it was then revocable and has not subsequently become irrevocable; or

(b) a person domiciled in New York at the time the trust, or portion of a trust, became irrevocable, if it was revocable when the property was transferred to the trust but has subsequently become irrevocable. (Sec. 605(b)(3), Tax Law)

If property is transferred to a trust at differing times, the portion that meets the preceding requirements is treated as a resident trust. The balance is treated as a nonresident trust. A trust may be a resident during part of the year and a nonresident during the remainder of the year. (Sec. 605(b)(3), Tax Law; Reg. Sec. 105.23)

≫≫→ CCH Caution: The mere fact that a trust is considered to be a "resident" for New York personal income tax purposes does not automatically mean that it is subject to tax. In *Mercantile-Safe Deposit and Trust Company v. Murphy et al.* (1964, NY SCt AppDiv), 19 AD2d 765, 243 NYS2d 26; aff'd 15 NY2d 579, 255 NYS2d 96, 203 NE2d 490 (1964), the New York Supreme Court, Appellate Division, held that New York lacked jurisdiction to tax income accumulated in a trust established by a New York resident where the trust was administered, the corpus was located, and the trustee was domiciled in Maryland. As the Court noted:

Although this trust must be deemed a resident trust by statutory definition (Tax Law, Sec. 350, subd. 7; Sec. 605, subd. [c], par. [3]) the related statutes which impose a tax upon its accrued income (Tax Law, Sec. 351, Sec. 365, subd. [1], par. [c]) undertake in the circumstances disclosed here to extend the taxing power of the State to property wholly beyond its jurisdiction and thus conflict with the due process clause of the Fourteenth Amendment of the Federal Constitution. (*Safe Deposit & Trust Co. of Baltimore, Md. v. Commonwealth of Virginia*, 280 U.S. 83.)

Following *Mercantile-Safe,* New York amended its regulations to clarify that the determination of whether a trust is a resident trust is not dependent on the location of the trustee or the corpus of the trust or the source of income. (Reg. Sec. 105.23) However, no state personal income tax will be imposed on a resident trust if all of the following conditions are met:

(1) all the trustees are domiciled in a state other than New York;

(2) the entire corpus of the trust, including real and tangible property is located outside of New York; and

(3) all income and gains of the trust are derived or connected from sources outside of New York state, determined as if the trust were a nonresident. (Sec. 605(b)(3), Tax Law; Reg. Sec. 105.23)

A banking corporation located outside New York state continues to be a nonresident corporate trustee even if it later becomes an office or branch of a corporate trustee domiciled in New York state. (Sec. 605(b)(3), Tax Law)

Situs of intangible assets.—The situs of intangible assets of a trust is deemed to be at the domicile of the trustee. (Sec. 605(b)(3), Tax Law; *Moss, Jr., (Advisory Opinion),* Commissioner of Taxation and Finance, TSB-A-94(7)I)

CCH CAUTION: In TSB-M-10(5)I, the Department of Taxation and Finance revoked the policy set forth in TSB-M-96(1)I, below, effective January 1, 2010. At that point, trusts that meet the above conditions will be required to file a New York fiduciary income tax return.

CCH CAUTION: In TSB-M-96(1)I, (Revoked by TSB-M-10(5)I, effective January 1, 2010) the Department of Taxation and Finance noted that, where the above conditions are met, and New York State personal income tax cannot be imposed, the filing of a New York fiduciary income tax return will not be required. (TSB-M-96(1)I) In such instances, and where it is anticipated that the trust will continue to meet the conditions for income tax exemption, the Department recommended that the trustee file a final return on Form IT-205, Fiduciary Income Tax Return, check the "Final return" box at the top of the Form, and attach a statement indicating that the trust is a trust meeting the conditions for exemption under Reg. Sec. 105.23(c).

CCH CAUTION: In TSB-A-96(4)I, the Department of Taxation and Finance determined that tax did not apply to a resident trust for years in which:

(1) the trustees were domiciled outside New York,

(2) the corpus of the trust consisted of intangible assets that were deemed to be located at the domicile of the trustee, and

(3) none of the assets of the trust were employed in a business carried on in New York and all income and gains of the trust were derived from sources outside New York. (TSB-A-96(4)I)

Revocable/Irrevocable trust.—A trust or portion of a trust is deemed revocable if it is subject to a power, exercisable immediately or any future time, to revest title in the person whose property constitutes the trust or portion of a trust. A trust or portion of a trust becomes irrevocable when the possibility that such power may be exercised has been terminated.

• *Nonresident estate or trust*

An estate or trust that is not a New York resident for any part of the tax year is a nonresident estate or trust. (Sec. 605(b)(4), Tax Law) A nonresident estate or trust is taxable only on its New York source income as modified for New York purposes. (Sec. 601(e), Tax Law)

• *Part-year resident trust*

A part-year resident trust is a trust which is not a resident or nonresident for the entire taxable year. (Sec. 605(b)(6), Tax Law) A part-year resident trust is required to allocate its income between the resident portion and the nonresident portion of the tax year. (Sec. 638(b), Tax Law)

• *Taxation of estates and trusts*

For a discussion of the taxation of resident and nonresident estates and trusts, see discussion at ¶ 15-215.

• *Examples*

The following are examples that illustrate these provisions (Reg. Sec. 105.23):

EXAMPLE: Taxpayer A who is domiciled in New York and taxpayer B who is domiciled in New Jersey together create an irrevocable trust. The portion of such trust attributable to property transferred by A is a New York resident trust and the portion of such trust attributable to property transferred by B is a New York nonresident trust.

EXAMPLE: Taxpayer C creates an irrevocable trust while such taxpayer is a domiciliary of New York. Subsequent to the creation of such trust, C moves and becomes a domiciliary of California and transfers additional property to such irrevocable trust. The portion of such trust attributable to property transferred while C was a domiciliary of New York is a New York resident trust and the portion of such trust attributable to property transferred while C was a domiciliary of California is a New York nonresident trust.

EXAMPLE: D, who is domiciled in Canada, creates an irrevocable trust with the X Trust Company in New York City as trustee. The entire corpus of the trust consists of securities of American corporations, which are actively traded by the trustee on the New York Stock Exchange. The beneficiaries of the trust are all New York residents. Regardless of whether the trust is held to be a resident of the United States for federal income tax purposes; it is, for New York State income tax purposes, a nonresident trust.

[¶15-215] Estates and Trusts--Computation of Income

The New York taxable income of a resident estate or trust means its federal taxable income with the following modifications (Sec. 618, Tax Law):

(1) With respect to gains from the sale or other disposition of property, excluded from federal distributable net income, subtractions from federal taxable income are made for the following: (a) the portion of any gain, from the sale or other disposition of property having a higher adjusted basis for New York income tax purposes than for federal income tax purposes on December 31, 1959 (or on the last day of a 1959—1960 fiscal year). that does not exceed such difference in basis; and (b) the amount of any gain from the sale or other disposition of property which had been previously reported under Article 16 by the estate or trust or by a decedent as a result of whose death the estate or trust acquired the right to the gain. (Sec. 618(2), Tax Law)

(2) The share of the estate or trust in the "fiduciary adjustment" (see below) must be added to or subtracted from its federal taxable income. (Sec. 618(3), Tax Law)

(3) The amounts specified in the following provisions must be added to federal taxable income: (a) Sec. 612(b)(10), amounts deducted on the federal return as an allowance for percentage depletion; (b) Sec. 612(b)(17), amounts required to be added in the case of a sale or other disposition of property acquired from a decedent where no federal estate tax return was required; (c) Secs. 612(b)(18)—612(b)(20), certain amounts required to be added by shareholders of a federal S corporation where an election to be treated as a New York S corporation shareholder has not been made or where such election terminates on a day other than the first day of a taxable year of a corporation (see ¶16-113); (d) Sec. 612(b)(21), amounts required to be added because of adjustments to the basis of stock in federal S corporations for taxable years in which the election to be treated as a New York S corporation shareholder was not made (see ¶16-113); Sec. 612(b)(22), new business investment deferral; (f) Secs. 612(b)(23)—612(b)(25) and Sec. 612(b)(27), additions relating to safe harbor leases and ACRS deductions (see ¶16-040); and (g) Sec. 612(b)(29), basis adjustment relating to former credit for solar and wind energy systems. (Sec. 618(4), Tax Law) In addition, in the case of a transfer to a trust at less than fair market value, the amount of any includable gain, reduced by any deductions properly allocable thereto, upon which tax is imposed for the taxable year pursuant to IRC Sec. 644 must be added to federal

taxable income. (Sec. 618(5), Tax Law) [The Taxpayer Relief Act of 1997 (P.L. 105-34) amended IRC Sec. 644, which dealt with gains on property transfers to trusts at less than fair market value, by striking it and redesignating IRC Sec. 645, which concerned taxable years of trusts, as IRC Sec. 644. The above amendment applies to sales or exchanges after August 5, 1997.—CCH.]

Changes made by 2014-15 Budget Bills-- The budget legislation closed the so-called "resident trust loophole" by treating resident trusts as grantor trusts for the purposes of calculating New York income tax. This change is effective for income earned **after June 1, 2014**. The change in tax treatment of these trusts causes the trust income to be included in the grantor's taxable income, for purposes of New York personal income computation. (Sec. 612(b)(40); *TSB-M-14(3)I*, May 16, 2014)

The **2014-2015 budget legislation** also addresses Incomplete Gift Non-grantor Trusts ("ING trusts") which were reputed to be "tax avoidance vehicles." The budget legislation states that the "ING trusts" must be treated as grantor trusts, for New York personal income tax computation purposes. Therefore, the "ING trust" settlor must pay New York personal income tax on the income of the "ING trust." This particular change applies to taxable years beginning on or after January 1, 2014, but does not apply to income from a "ING trust" liquidated before June 1, 2014. (Sec. 612(b)(41); *TSB-M-14(3)I*, May 16, 2014)

(4) The amounts specified in the following provisions may be subtracted from federal taxable income: (a) Sec. 612(c)(13), the New York depletion allowanc; (b) Sec. 612(c)(15), that portion of wages and salaries paid or incurred for the taxable year for which a deduction is not allowed pursuant to IRC Sec. 280C; (c) Sec. 612(c)(19), amounts which may be subtracted in the case of a sale or other disposition of property acquired from a decedent where no federal estate tax return was required; (d) Secs. 612(c)(20) and 612(c)(23), a percentage of gains from new business investments (see ¶16-270); (e) Sec. 612(c)(21), amounts which may be subtracted because of adjustments to the basis of stock in federal S corporations for taxable years for which the election to be treated as a New York S corporation shareholder was not made (see ¶16-317); (f) Sec. 612(c)(22), amounts which may be subtracted by shareholders of a federal S corporation where an election to be treated as a New York S corporation shareholder has not been made (see ¶16-317); and (g) Secs. 612(c)(24)—612(c)(26) and 612(c)(28), subtractions relating to safe harbor leases and ACRS deductions. (Sec. 618(4), Tax Law)

• *New York fiduciary adjustment*

A resident estate or trust may realize items of income or gain or incur items of loss or deduction which, if received or incurred by an individual taxpayer, would give rise to one or more modifications. (Reg. Sec. 119.1) In the case of a resident estate or trust, all such modifications are combined in the New York fiduciary adjustment, which must be allocated among the estate or trust and its beneficiaries. The net amount of modifications comprising the fiduciary adjustment will not include any modification with respect to any amount which, pursuant to the items of the governing instrument, is paid or permanently set aside for a charitable purpose during the taxable year and any modification with respect to gains from the sale or other disposition of property, to the extent excluded from federal distributable net income. (Sec. 619(b), Tax Law)

The respective shares of an estate or trust and its beneficiaries in the New York fiduciary adjustment are in proportion to their respective shares of federal distributable net income of the estate or trust. (Sec. 619(c), Tax Law) If the estate or trust has no federal distributable net income for the taxable year, the share of each beneficiary in the New York fiduciary adjustment is in proportion to the beneficiary's share of the estate or trust income for the year, under local law or the governing instrument, which is required to be distributed currently, and any other amounts of such income distributed during the taxable year. Any balance of the New York fiduciary adjustment will be allocated to the estate or trust.

The Commissioner may, by regulation, establish such other method or methods of determining to whom the items comprising the fiduciary adjustment will be attributed as may be appropriate and equitable. (Sec. 619(d), Tax Law) Such method may be used by the fiduciary in his or her discretion whenever the allocation of the fiduciary adjustment set forth in the statute would result in an inequity which is substantial both in amount and in relation to the amount of the fiduciary adjustment.

TCJA Adjustments. In response to the federal Tax Cuts and Jobs Act, New York's 2019-20 budget legislation amended the Tax Law to add the following estate and trust modifications (Sec. 619(e), Tax Law; TSB-M-19(4)I):

- a subtraction for certain taxes not deducted at the federal level because of limitation under IRC Sec. 164(b)(6)(B) or denial under IRC Sec. 164(b)(6)(A);

- a subtraction for certain miscellaneous itemized deductions; and

- an addition for the amount of any deduction allowed under IRC Sec. 199A.

New York has issued updated instructions for Forms IT-205, Fiduciary Income Tax Return, and IT-225, New York State Modifications, in order to clarify how taxpayers should report the new modifications.

Specifically, the updated instructions apply to fiduciary return filers having any of these deductions:

- IRC Sec. 199A deduction;

- deduction for foreign real property taxes;

- deduction for taxes under IRC Sec. 164 that was limited to $10,000; or

- miscellaneous itemized deductions disallowed under IRC Sec. 67(g).

• *Nonresident estates and trusts*

The New York source income of a nonresident estate or trust is determined as follows (Sec. 633(a), Tax Law):

(1) The estate's or trust's share of income, gain, loss and deductions from New York sources included in federal distributable net income is determined (Sec. 633(a)(1), Tax Law); and

(2) The amount derived from or connected with New York sources of any income, gain, loss and deduction which would be included in the determination of federal adjusted gross income if the estate or trust were an individual and which is recognized for federal income tax purposes but excluded from the definition of federal distributable net income of the estate or trust is added or subtracted, as the case may be. (Sec. 633(a)(2), Tax Law) For transfers in trust, the amount of any includable gain, reduced by any deductions properly allocable thereto, upon which tax is imposed for the taxable year pursuant to IRC Sec. 644 is added. (Sec. 618(5), Tax Law) [The Taxpayer Relief Act of 1997 (P.L. 105-34) amended IRC Sec. 644, which dealt with gains on property transfers to trusts at less than fair market value, by striking it and redesignating IRC Sec. 645, which concerned taxable years of trusts, as IRC Sec. 644. The above amendment applies to sales or exchanges after August 5, 1997.—CCH.]

Deductions with respect to capital losses, passive activity losses and net operating losses are based solely on income, gains, losses and deductions derived from or connected with New York sources, but otherwise determined in the same manner as the corresponding federal deductions. (Sec. 633(b), Tax Law)

•*Determination of share in income from New York sources*

The share of a nonresident estate or trust, and the share of a nonresident beneficiary of any estate or trust, in estate or trust income, gain, loss and deduction from New York sources is determined as follows (Sec. 634(a), Tax Law):

(1) A determination is made of the items of gain, loss, and deduction, derived from or connected with New York sources, which would be included in the determination of federal adjusted gross income if the estate or trust were an individual, and which enter into the definition of federal distributable net income of the estate or trust for the taxable year (Sec. 634(a)(1), Tax Law); and

(2) The amounts determined above are allocated among the estate or trust and its beneficiaries in proportion to their respective shares of federal distributable net income. (Sec. 634(a)(2), Tax Law) The amount so calculated will have the same character for New York personal income tax purposes as for federal income tax purposes. Where an item entering into the computation of such amounts is not characterized for federal income tax purposes, it will have the same character as if realized directly from the source from which realized by the estate or trust, or incurred in the same manner as incurred by the estate or trust.

If the estate or trust has no distributable net income for the taxable year, each beneficiary's share will be in proportion to his or her share of the estate or trust income for such year, under local law or the governing instrument, which is required to be distributed currently, and any other amounts of such income distributed in such year. (Sec. 634(b)(1), Tax Law) Any balance will be allocated to the estate or trust.

The Commissioner may, by regulation, establish such other method or methods of determining the respective shares of the beneficiaries and of the estate or trust in its income derived from New York sources as may be appropriate and equitable. (Sec. 634(b)(2), Tax Law) Such method may be used by the fiduciary in his discretion whenever the allocation of such respective shares under the statutory method would result in an inequity which is substantial in amount. See Reg. Sec. 119.3.

[¶ 15-250]

FILING THRESHOLDS

[¶ 15-260] Filing Thresholds--Residents

An income tax return must be filed for every resident individual:

— Required to file a federal income tax return for the taxable year;

— Having federal adjusted gross income for the taxable year, increased by the amounts required to be added to federal adjusted gross income in determining New York adjusted gross income, in excess of $4,000, or in excess of the individual's New York standard deduction, if lower (see ¶ 15-540); or

— Having received during the taxable year a lump sum distribution any portion of which is subject to the separate tax on the ordinary income portion of a lump sum distribution.

(Sec. 651(a)(1), Tax Law)

[¶15-265] Filing Thresholds--Nonresidents and Part-Year Residents

A return must be filed by every nonresident or part-year resident individual:

— Having New York source income for the taxable year, and having New York adjusted gross income in excess of the individual's standard deduction (see ¶15-540);

— Having received during the taxable year a lump sum distribution any portion of which is subject to the separate tax on the ordinary income portion of a lump sum distribution; or

— Incurring a net operating loss for New York purposes without incurring a similar net operating loss for federal income tax purposes.

(Sec. 651(a)(3), Tax Law)

[¶15-300]
FILING STATUS

[¶15-305] Filing Status

In almost all cases, a taxpayer must use the same filing status that was used on the federal return (i.e., single, married filing joint return, married filing separate return, head of household, or qualifying widow(er) with dependent child). A taxpayer who did not have to file a federal return should use the same filing status that he or she would have used for federal income tax purposes. (Instructions, Form IT-201, Resident Income Tax Return)

The only exceptions apply to married individuals who file a joint federal return and:

— one spouse is a New York State resident but the other is a nonresident or part-year resident (in this case, the taxpayers must either file separate New York returns or file jointly, as if they were both New York State residents); or

— are unable to file a joint New York return because the address or whereabouts of one spouse is unknown, or one spouse refuses to sign a joint New York return (in this case, the taxpayer may file a separate New York return, provided that reasonable efforts have been made and certain other conditions are satisfied).

[¶15-350]
RATES

[¶15-355] Rates of Tax

New York personal income tax rates vary by filing status. The rates and brackets for 2020 are noted below.

Single, Married Filing Separately:

$0 - 8,500 x 4.000% minus $0

$8,501 - 11,700 x 4.500% minus $42.50

$11,701 - 13,900 x 5.250% minus $130.25

$13,901 - 21,400 x 5.900% minus $220.60

$21,401 - 80,650 x 6.090% minus $261.26

$80,651 - 215,400 x 6.410% minus $519.33

$215,401 - 1,077,550 x 6.850% minus $1,467.09

$1,077,551 and over x 8.820% minus $22,694.82

Married Filing Jointly, Qualifying Widow(er):

$0 - 17,150 x 4.000% minus $0

$17,151 - 23,600 x 4.500% minus $85.75

$23,601 - 27,900 x 5.250% minus $262.75

$27,901 - 43,000 x 5.900% minus $444.10

$43,001 - 161,550 x 6.090% minus $525.80

$161,551 - 323,200 x 6.410% minus $1,042.75

$323,201 - 2,155,350 x 6.850% minus $2,464.83

$2,155,351 and over x 8.820% minus $44,925.22

Head of Household:

$0 - 12,800 x 4.000% minus $0

$12,801 - 17,650 x 4.500% minus $64.00

$17,651 - 20,900 x 5.250% minus $196.37

$20,901 - 32,200 x 5.900% minus $332.22

$32,201 - 107,650 x 6.090% minus $393.40

$107,651 - 269,300 x 6.410% minus $737.87

$269,301 - 1,616,450 x 6.850% minus $1,922.79

$1,616,451 and over x 8.820% minus $33,766.85

A separate tax computation applicable to nonresidents and part-year residents is also discussed at ¶ 15-365.

• *Minimum income tax*

Prior to taxable years beginning on or after January 1, 2014, The New York minimum income tax rate was 6%. (Sec. 602(b), Tax Law)

• *Supplemental tax*

The New York personal income tax law contains certain tax table benefit recapture provisions. (Sec. 601(d-1), Tax Law)

The tax benefit recapture provisions are discussed in TSB-M-14(2)I, and in the Department's 2016 Budget Summary.

• *Separate tax on ordinary income portion of lump sum distribution*

A separate tax is imposed for each taxable year on the ordinary income portion of a lump sum distribution of every individual, estate and trust which has made an election of lump sum treatment under IRC Sec. 402(e). (Sec. 603(a), Tax Law) The amount of tax is equal to five times the New York personal income tax which would be imposed under the schedules applicable to unmarried individuals, married individuals filing separate returns and resident estates and trusts if the New York taxable income were an amount equal to one-fifth of the excess of the total taxable amount of the lump sum distribution for the taxable year over the minimum distribution allowance. (Sec. 624(a), Tax Law)

¶15-355

Minimum distribution allowance.—The minimum distribution allowance is that which is calculated according to IRC Sec. 402(e)(1)(C) (Sec. 624(b), Tax Law), which provides that the "minimum distribution allowance" will be equal to (1) the lesser of $10,000 or one-half of the total taxable amount of the lump sum distribution for the taxable year, reduced (but not below zero) by (2) 20% of the amount (if any) by which such total taxable amount exceeds $20,000.

The federal rules concerning multiple distributions and distributions of annuity contracts are applicable. (Sec. 624(c), Tax Law) Also applicable are the definitions and special rules as specified in IRC Sec. 402(e)(4) and the special rules relating to individuals who were 50 years old by January 1, 1986. (Sec. 624(d), Tax Law) The special rules for capital gains under the following sections of the federal Tax Reform Act of 1986 are also adopted: (1) Sec. 1122(h)(3), allowing individuals who have attained age 50 by January 1, 1986, to elect capital gains treatment with respect to a lump sum distribution; (2) Sec. 1122(h)(4), regarding the five-year phase out of capital gains treatment; (3) Sec. 1122(h)(5), regarding election of ten-year averaging; and (4) Sec. 1122(h)(6), regarding existing capital gains treatment under the 1954 code. With respect to the ten-year averaging provisions only, the amount of tax will be equal to ten (rather than five) times the New York personal income tax which would be imposed if the New York taxable income were an amount equal to one-tenth (rather than one-fifth) of the excess of the total taxable amount of the lump sum distribution over the minimum distributable allowance.

Credits against tax.—No credits are allowed against the separate tax except for the household and dependent care credit, the earned income credit, the real property tax circuit breaker credit, the credit for taxes withheld, and the credit for income taxes paid to another state. (Sec. 603(a), Tax Law; Sec. 620-A, Tax Law)

Nonresidents.—With respect to the ordinary income portion of a lump sum distribution received by a nonresident or part-year resident, the tax will be applicable to the ordinary income portion of a lump sum distribution wholly or partly derived from or connected with New York sources. (Sec. 637(a), Tax Law) If the lump sum distribution was partly derived from or connected with New York sources, the total taxable amount and the ordinary income portion of the lump sum distribution will be determined by apportion and allocation, pursuant to regulations.

If the status of a taxpayer changes during the taxable year from resident to nonresident, or from nonresident to resident, the taxpayer must, regardless of the taxpayer's method of accounting, accrue for the portion of the taxable year prior to the change of status the total taxable amount of a lump sum distribution accruing prior to the change of status, if the ordinary income portion of the distribution is not otherwise subject to tax for such portion of the taxable year or for a prior taxable year. (Sec. 637(b), Tax Law) No ordinary income portion of a lump sum distribution, the total amount of which is accrued, will be subject to tax for any subsequent taxable period.

[¶15-500]

TAXABLE INCOME COMPUTATION

[¶15-505] Determination of Income

New York adjusted gross income is federal adjusted gross income with certain modifications. (Sec. 612(a), Tax Law) These modifications (also designated "NY Adjustments" or "New York Additions and Subtractions" on Form IT-201, Resident Income Tax Return) represent items whose New York treatment differs from their federal treatment.

For a discussion of the required additions, see ¶ 16-005.

For the subtractions, see ¶ 16-205.

> **EXAMPLE:** *Deduction of IRA contributions.*—A taxpayer deducts IRA contributions for federal but not New York income tax purposes. The taxpayer cannot exclude a premature IRA distribution from his New York income because it is included in his federal adjusted gross income, and no express modification exists for his failure to take the New York deduction. (*Matter of Mulvey*)

> **EXAMPLE:** *Contributions to Keogh plan.*—A taxpayer pays a tax in Massachusetts on contributions to a Keogh plan. The Keogh distributions are taxable in New York because New York conforms with federal tax treatment, which includes distributions rather than contributions in adjusted gross income. (*Matter of Clapsaddle*)

Specific items of adjusted gross income are discussed in the following paragraphs.

• *Married taxpayers*

If married individuals determine their federal income tax on a joint return but are required to determine their New York income taxes separately, they must determine their New York adjusted gross incomes separately as if their federal adjusted gross incomes had been determined separately. (Sec. 612(f), Tax Law)

• *Holders of interests in REMICS*

Holders of interests in Real Estate Mortgage Investment Conduits (REMICS) who are New York State residents will include in their New York taxable income the same amount included in their federal taxable income. (TSB-M-87(22)I)

• *Paid Family Leave*

The New York Department of Taxation and Finance has issued a notice discussing the tax implications of the state's Paid Family Leave program. The notice provides the following specific guidance (*Important Notice N-17-12*, August 2017):

> — benefits paid to employees will be taxable non-wage income that must be included in federal gross income;

> — taxes will not automatically be withheld from benefits, but employees can request voluntary tax withholding;

> — premiums will be deducted from employees' after-tax wages;

> — employers should report employee contributions on Form W-2 using Box 14—State disability insurance taxes withheld; and

> — benefits should be reported by the State Insurance Fund on Form 1099-G and by all other payers on Form 1099-MISC.

[¶15-510] Starting Point for Computation

New York adopts federal adjusted gross income for individuals, federal taxable income for resident estates and trusts, and federal distributable net income in the case of a nonresident estate and trust as the starting points for the determination of New York taxable income. (Sec. 612, Tax Law; Sec. 618, Tax Law; Sec. 634(a)(1), Tax Law)

[¶ 15-515] Federal Conformity

Although New York does not conform to the IRC through the specific adoption of IRC provisions, the state uses federal adjusted gross income as the starting point for determining taxable income. For further discussion regarding the New York computation, see ¶ 15-505.

However, for taxable years beginning before January 1, 2022, any amendments made to the Internal Revenue Code after March 1, 2020, do not apply to the New York personal income tax. (Sec. 607(a), Tax Law)

[¶ 15-535] Personal Exemptions

A resident individual is allowed a New York exemption of $1,000 for each exemption for which he or she is entitled to a deduction for the taxable year under IRC Sec. 151(c) (exemption for dependents). (Sec. 616(a), Tax Law) The personal exemption is no longer allowed for the taxpayer and spouse. (TSB-M-87(11)I)

Dependent exemptions are claimed on line 36 of Form IT-201, Resident Income Tax Return.

• *Husband and wife*

If the New York income taxes of a husband and wife are required to be separately determined, but their federal income tax is determined on a joint return, each of them will be separately entitled to a New York exemption for each federal exemption to which he or she would be separately entitled for the taxable year if their federal income taxes had been determined on separate returns. (Sec. 616(b), Tax Law)

[¶ 15-540] Standard Deduction

The standard deduction amounts are set forth below.

Note: For tax years 2013 through 2017, the New York standard deduction of a resident individual provided for in Tax Law Sec. 614 was indexed by a cost of living percentage adjustment, if applicable, computed under Sec. 601-a. For tax years 2018 and after, the standard deduction is fixed at the amount allowable for tax year 2017. (TSB-M-12(3)I; Summary, New York Department of Taxation and Finance)

• *Unmarried individuals*

The New York standard deduction of a resident individual who was neither married, the head of a household, a surviving spouse, nor an individual who was claimed as a dependent by another New York state taxpayer (prior to tax year 2018, an individual whose federal exemption amount was zero) is:

For tax year 2020, the standard deduction is $8,000. (Instructions, Form IT-2105)

For tax year 2019, the standard deduction is $8,000. (Instructions, Form IT-2105)

For tax year 2018, the standard deduction is $8,000. (Instructions, Form IT-2105)

For tax year 2017, the standard deduction is $8,000. (Instructions, Form IT-2105)

For tax year 2016, the standard deduction is $7,950. (Instructions, Form IT-2105)

For tax year 2015, the standard deduction is $7,900. (Instructions, Form IT-2105)

For tax year 2014, the standard deduction is $7,800. (Instructions, Form IT-2105)

For tax year 2013, the standard deduction is $7,700. (Instructions, Form IT-2105)

Previously, the New York standard deduction of a resident individual who was neither married, the head of a household, a surviving spouse, nor an individual whose federal exemption amount was zero was $7,500 for taxable years beginning after 1996; $7,400 for taxable years beginning in 1996, and $6,600 for taxable years beginning in 1995. (Sec. 614(a), Tax Law) For taxable years beginning after 1989 and before 1995, an unmarried individual was entitled to a standard deduction of $6,000.

• *Married filing jointly and surviving spouse*

For tax year 2020, the standard deduction is $16,050. (Instructions, Form IT-2105)

For tax year 2019, the standard deduction is $16,050. (Instructions, Form IT-2105)

For tax year 2018, the standard deduction is $16,050. (Instructions, Form IT-2105)

For tax year 2017, the standard deduction is $16,050. (Instructions, Form IT-2105)

For tax year 2016, the standard deduction is $15,950. (Instructions, Form IT-2105)

For tax year 2015, the standard deduction is $15,850. (Instructions, Form IT-2105)

For tax year 2014, the standard deduction is $15,650. (Instructions, Form IT-2105)

For tax year 2013, the standard deduction is $15,400. (Instructions, Form IT-2105)

Previously, under the 2006 budget legislation, in an effort to eliminate the marriage penalty, the standard deduction was increased. Accordingly, a husband and wife whose New York taxable income was determined jointly and a surviving spouse were entitled to a New York standard deduction of $15,000 for taxable years beginning after 2005. The standard deduction was $14,600 for taxable years beginning after 2002 and before 2006; $14,200 for taxable years beginning in 2002; $13,400 for taxable years beginning in 2001; and $13,000 for taxable years beginning after 1996 and before 2001. (Sec. 614(b), Tax Law)

Pre-1997.—For taxable years beginning after 1989 and before 1995, a husband and wife filing jointly and a surviving spouse are entitled to a standard deduction of $9,500; for taxable years beginning in 1995, the standard deduction is $10,000; and for taxable years beginning in 1996, the standard deduction is $12,350. (Sec. 614(b), Tax Law)

• *Head of household*

For tax year 2020, the standard deduction is $11,200. (Instructions, Form IT-2105)

For tax year 2019, the standard deduction is $11,200. (Instructions, Form IT-2105)

For tax year 2018, the standard deduction is $11,200. (Instructions, Form IT-2105)

For tax year 2017, the standard deduction is $11,200. (Instructions, Form IT-2105)

For tax year 2016, the standard deduction is $11,150. (Instructions, Form IT-2105)

For tax year 2015, the standard deduction is $11,100. (Instructions, Form IT-2105)

For tax year 2014, the standard deduction is $10,950. (Instructions, Form IT-2105)

For tax year 2013, the standard deduction is $10,800. (Instructions, Form IT-2105)

Previously, the New York standard deduction of an individual who was a head of household was $10,500 for taxable years beginning after 1996; $10,000 for taxable years beginning in 1996; and $8,150 for taxable years beginning in 1995. (Sec. 614(c), Tax Law) For taxable years beginning after 1989 and before 1995, a head of household was entitled to a standard deduction of $7,000.

• *Married individuals filing separately*

For tax year 2020, the standard deduction is $8,000. (Instructions, Form IT-2105)

For tax year 2019, the standard deduction is $8,000. (Instructions, Form IT-2105)

For tax year 2018, the standard deduction is $8,000. (Instructions, Form IT-2105)

For tax year 2017, the standard deduction is $8,000. (Instructions, Form IT-2105)

For tax year 2016, the standard deduction is $7,950. (Instructions, Form IT-2105)

For tax year 2015, the standard deduction is $7,900. (Instructions, Form IT-2105)

For tax year 2014, the standard deduction is $7,800. (Instructions, Form IT-2105)

For tax year 2013, the standard deduction is $7,700. (Instructions, Form IT-2105)

Previously, for married individuals filing separately, the New York standard deduction was $7,500 for taxable years beginning after 2005; $6,500 for taxable years beginning after 1996; $6,175 for taxable years beginning in 1996; and $5,400 for taxable years beginning in 1995. (Sec. 614(d), Tax Law) For taxable years beginning after 1989 and before 1995, a married individual filing separately was entitled to a standard deduction of $4,750.

• *Dependent individuals*

For tax year 2020, the standard deduction is $3,100. (Instructions, Form IT-2105)

For tax year 2019, the standard deduction is $3,100. (Instructions, Form IT-2105)

For tax year 2018, the standard deduction is $3,100. (Instructions, Form IT-2105)

For tax year 2017, the standard deduction is $3,100. (Instructions, Form IT-2105)

For tax year 2016, the standard deduction is $3,100. (Instructions, Form IT-2105)

For tax year 2015, the standard deduction is $3,100. (Instructions, Form IT-2105)

For tax year 2014, the standard deduction is $3,100. (Instructions, Form IT-2105)

For tax year 2013, the standard deduction is $3,050. (Instructions, Form IT-2105)

Previously, for a resident individual whose federal exemption amount was zero (a dependent individual), the New York standard deduction was $3,000 for taxable years beginning after 1996. (Sec. 614(e), Tax Law) For taxable years beginning in 1996, the standard deduction was $2,900, and for taxable years beginning after 1989 and before 1996, the deduction was $2,800.

• *Nonresidents*

Nonresident individuals are allowed the same standard deduction as resident individuals, as outlined above. (TSB-M-87(11)I)

[¶15-545] Itemized Deductions

The 2018 budget legislation contains a number of significant provisions related to New York itemized deductions. First, the legislation eliminates the restriction that allowed taxpayers to itemize on their New York return only if they itemized on their federal return. In addition, the New York itemized deduction provision is amended to refer to federal deductions as they existed immediately prior to the enactment of the TCJA. These amendments apply to taxable years beginning on or after January 1, 2018.

The legislation also creates state-operated charitable contribution funds to accept donations, which can be claimed as itemized deductions. Further, taxpayers making a donation are allowed a state tax credit.

If the federal taxable income of a resident individual is determined by itemizing deductions or claiming the federal standard deduction from his or her federal adjusted gross income, the individual may elect to deduct the New York itemized deduction or claim the New York standard deduction. (Sec. 615(a), Tax Law) The

New York itemized deduction of a resident individual is equal to the total amount of his or her deductions from federal adjusted gross income allowed, other than federal deductions for personal exemptions, as provided in the laws of the United States for the taxable year, as those deductions existed immediately prior to the enactment of the TCJA (P.L. 115-97), with certain modifications. (Sec. 615(a), Tax Law)

Itemized deductions may be claimed on Form IT-201, Resident Income Tax Return.

• *Husband and wife*

A husband and wife, both of whom are required to file New York personal income tax returns, will be allowed New York itemized deductions only if both elect to take New York itemized deductions. (Sec. 615(b), Tax Law) The total of the New York itemized deductions of a husband and wife whose federal taxable income is determined on a joint return, but whose New York incomes are required to be determined separately, will be divided between them as if their federal taxable incomes had been separately determined.

• *Modifications reducing federal itemized deductions*

The total amount of deductions from federal adjusted gross income is reduced by the amount of the federal deductions for:

(1) income taxes imposed by New York or any other taxing jurisdiction, or (for tax years beginning on or after January 1, 2010) state and local general sales taxes included in federal itemized deductions (Sec. 615(c)(1), Tax Law; Reg. Sec. 115.2; TSB-M-10(8)I);

(2) interest on indebtedness incurred or continued to purchase or carry obligations or securities the interest on which is exempt from New York personal income taxes (Sec. 615(c)(2), Tax Law);

(3) ordinary and necessary expenses paid or incurred during the taxable year for (a) the production or collection of income which is exempt from New York personal income tax, or (b) the management, conservation or maintenance of property held for the production of income which is exempt from New York personal income tax, and the amortizable bond premium for the taxable year on any bond the interest on which is exempt from New York personal income tax, to the extent that such expenses and premiums are deductible in determining federal taxable income (Sec. 615(c)(3), Tax Law); However, the modification for amortizable bond premiums is subject to the investment interest itemized deduction limitation imposed for federal purposes for bonds acquired after October 22, 1986 and before January 1, 1988 (in the case of a taxpayer who does not elect offset treatment for federal purposes). (Reg. Sec. 115.2) Also, the modifications for expenses incurred for the production of income and amortizable bond premiums is subject to the federal 2% floor on miscellaneous itemized deductions pursuant to IRC Sec. 67;

(4) premiums paid for long-term care insurance to the extent that they are deductible in determining federal taxable income (Sec. 615(c)(4), Tax Law);

(5) real property taxes imposed on renters on or after the April 1st occurring more than six months after an Internal Revenue ruling to the effect that renters may deduct the taxes for federal income tax purposes, pursuant to Sec. 926a, Real Property Tax Law. (Sec. 615(c)(5), Tax Law; Reg. Sec. 115.2) Since the Commissioner of Internal Revenue has not ruled on this issue, this section has never gone into effect (*Letter from Department of Taxation and Finance to CCH*, March 8, 1990);

(6) in the case of a shareholder of a federal S corporation, (a) where the election to be treated as a New York S corporation has not been made, S corporation items of

deduction included in federal itemized deductions, and (b) in the case of a New York S termination year, the portion of such items assigned to the period beginning on the day the election ceases to be effective (Sec. 615(c)(6), Tax Law; Reg. Sec. 115.2); and

(7) (for taxable years beginning before 1997) 5% of acquisition-related interest (to the extent deducted in the computation of New York itemized deductions), in the event of a stock or asset acquisition during the taxable year or within the three immediately preceding taxable years. (Sec. 615(c)(7), Tax Law; Reg. Sec. 115.2)

Note that the modifications reducing federal itemized deductions will be limited in the case of a resident individual subject to the federal overall limitation on itemized deductions imposed pursuant to IRC Sec. 68. In such a case, the modifications referred to above may not exceed the federal tax benefit of the itemized deductions subject to the modifications. (Reg. Sec. 115.2)

• *Modifications increasing federal itemized deductions*

The total amount of deductions from federal adjusted gross income is increased by:

(1) interest on indebtedness incurred or continued to purchase or carry obligations or securities the income from which is subject to New York personal income tax but exempt from federal income tax, to the extent that such interest is not deductible for federal income tax purposes and has not been subtracted from federal adjusted gross income pursuant to Sec. 612(c)(9), Tax Law (see ¶16-280) (Sec. 615(d)(2), Tax Law);

(2) ordinary and necessary expenses paid or incurred during the taxable year for (a) the production or collection of income which is subject to New York personal income tax but exempt from federal tax, or (b) the management, conservation or maintenance of property held for the production of income which is subject to New York personal income tax but exempt from federal tax, and the amortizable bond premium for the taxable year on any bond the interest on which is subject to New York personal income tax but exempt from federal income tax, to the extent that such expenses and premiums are not deductible in determining federal adjusted gross income and are not subtracted from federal adjusted gross income pursuant to Sec. 612(c)(10), Tax Law (Sec. 615(d)(3), Tax Law); and

(3) college tuition expenses, up to $10,000 annually, multiplied by the applicable phase-in percentage:

—in 2001, 25%

—in 2002, 50%

—in 2003, 75%

—after 2003, 100%

However, if the taxpayer chooses in the alternative to take the college tuition credit, then no deduction is allowed under this provision. (Sec. 615(d)(4), Tax Law; TSB-M-00(4)I)

• *Itemized deduction adjustment; limit for high-income taxpayers*

Higher-income New York taxpayers are allowed only a portion of their total federal itemized deductions. (Sec. 615(f) and (g), Tax Law) The percentage varies according to the taxpayer's New York adjusted gross income and filing status. (Reg. Sec. 115.5)

AGI over $1 million.—Under the 2009 budget legislation, for taxable years beginning after 2008, new provisions reduce by an additional 50% the amount of itemized deductions, except charitable contributions, that can be claimed by individuals having New York State or New York City adjusted gross income exceeding $1 million. Accordingly, for such taxpayers, the New York itemized deduction is limited to 50% of the federal itemized deduction for charitable contributions. No other federal itemized deductions of the taxpayer will be allowed for New York purposes. (TSB-M-09(11)I)

AGI over $10 million.—Under the 2010 budget legislation (as extended by the 2013, 2015, 2017, and 2019 budget bills), for tax years 2010 through 2024, provisions limit the amount of the New York itemized deduction allowed for an individual whose New York adjusted gross income exceeds $10 million to 25% of the individual's federal itemized deduction for charitable contributions. No other federal itemized deductions of the individual will be allowed for New York purposes. (Sec. 615(g)(2), Tax Law; TSB-M-10(8)I; TSB-M-19(4)I)

[¶16-000]

TAXABLE INCOME COMPUTATION--ADDITIONS

[¶16-005] Additions to Taxable Income Base

New York requires the following additions to federal adjusted gross income:

— Agricultural property tax credit ¶16-090
— Alimony ¶16-012
— Basis reduction attributable to credit for solar and wind energy systems ¶16-090
— Bonus depreciation ¶16-040
— Depletion ¶16-037
— Employee/member retirement system or pension fund contributions paid by the employer ¶16-135
— Environmental remediation insurance premiums ¶16-090
— Excess distributions from family tuition account ¶16-050
— Expenses for the production of exempt income ¶16-080
— Flexible benefit program contributions ¶16-065
— Interest on loans to buy or carry exempt securities ¶16-075
— Interest on obligations of other states and their political subdivisions ¶16-075
— Interest on obligations or securities of certain federal authorities ¶16-075
— Net operating losses ¶16-105
— Qualified production activities deduction ¶16-085
— Related member expenses ¶16-125
— S corporation additions ¶16-113
— SUV expensing ¶16-040
— Safe harbor leases and ACRS deductions ¶16-040
— Taxes ¶16-145

Additions to income are reported on Form IT-201, Resident Income Tax Return.

Subtractions are discussed at ¶16-205.

¶16-000

[¶16-012] Additions--Alimony

For taxable years beginning on or after January 1, 2018, an addition to federal adjusted gross income is required for any applicable alimony or separate maintenance payments received by the taxpayer during the taxable year. (Sec. 612(w)(1)(B), Tax Law)

"Alimony or separate maintenance payments" means payments as defined under IRC § 71 in effect immediately prior to the enactment of the TCJA (P.L. 115-97). (Sec. 612(w)(2)(A), Tax Law)

The term "applicable alimony or separate maintenance payments" means payments made under an alimony or separation instrument (as defined in IRC § 71 in effect immediately prior to the enactment of P.L. 115-97) that was executed after December 31, 2018, and any divorce or separation instrument executed on or before that date and modified after that date if the modification expressly provides that the relevant amendments apply to the modification. (Sec. 612(w)(2)(B), Tax Law)

[¶16-037] Additions--Depletion

Amounts deducted on the federal return as an allowance for percentage depletion must be added to federal adjusted gross income in determining New York adjusted gross income. (Sec. 612(b)(10), Tax Law)

[¶16-040] Additions--Depreciation

Under the 2003 budget bill, for taxable years beginning after 2002, and applicable to property placed in service on or after June 1, 2003, the New York personal income tax is decoupled from federal accelerated depreciation provisions under IRC Sec. 168(k), except with respect to qualified Resurgence Zone property and qualified New York Liberty Zone property. (Sec. 612(b)(8), (c)(16), (k), (l), and (m), Tax Law; TSB-M-04(1)I)

• *Sport utility vehicle expensing*

Under the 2003 budget bill, applicable to taxable years beginning after 2002, an addition modification is required for the amount deducted by a taxpayer (except an eligible farmer) under IRC Sec. 179 for a sport utility vehicle (SUV) with a vehicle weight over 6,000 pounds. A subtraction modification is enacted for any recapture amount included in federal adjusted gross income attributable to such deduction. (Sec. 612(b)(36), (c)(37), Tax Law; TSB-M-04(1)I)

A sport utility vehicle means any four wheeled passenger vehicle that is manufactured primarily for use on public streets, roads, and highways. However, the term does not include:

— any ambulance, hearse or combination ambulance-hearse used by the taxpayer directly in a trade or business;

— any vehicle used by a taxpayer directly in the trade or business of transporting persons or property for compensation or hire; or

— any truck, van, or motor home.

(TSB-M-04(1)I)

For further discussion of the modification for sport utility vehicles, see TSB-M-04(1)I.

• *Safe harbor leases*

The amount claimed as a deduction in computing federal adjusted gross income (except for qualified mass commuting vehicles) solely as a result of a safe harbor lease election under IRC Sec. 168(f)(8), as it was in effect for agreements entered into prior to 1984, must be added to federal adjusted gross income in computing New York adjusted gross income. (Sec. 612(b)(23), Tax Law)

The amount which the taxpayer would have been required to include in the computation of its federal adjusted income (except for qualified mass commuting vehicles) had the safe harbor lease election under IRC Sec. 168(f)(8), as it was in effect for agreements entered into prior to 1984, not been made must be added to federal adjusted gross income in computing New York adjusted gross income. (Sec. 612(b)(24), Tax Law)

• *ACRS deductions*

In the case of property placed in service in taxable years beginning before 1994, the amount allowable as an accelerated cost recovery system deduction under IRC Sec. 168 must be added to federal adjusted gross income in determining New York adjusted gross income. (Sec. 612(b)(25), Tax Law) This requirement does not apply to property subject to IRC Sec. 280-F (relating to luxury automobiles) and property subject to the provisions of IRC Sec. 168 that was placed in service in New York in taxable years beginning after December 31, 1984. With regard to property placed in service outside New York State in tax years 1985—1993, taxpayers may elect to use either the IRC Sec. 167 or 168 depreciation deduction. (TSB-M-99(1)I and (1)C)

Upon the disposition of property which is subject to IRC Sec. 168 other than luxury automobiles and property placed in service in New York State for taxable years beginning after 1984, the amount, if any, by which the depreciation deduction under IRC Sec. 167 exceeds the accelerated cost recovery system deduction under IRC Sec. 168 must be added to federal adjusted gross income in determining New York adjusted gross income. (Sec. 612(b)(27), Tax Law)

[¶16-050] Additions--Education Expenses

An addition is required for excess distributions received during the taxable year by a distributee of a family tuition account established under the New York state college choice tuition savings program, to the extent that the excess distributions are attributable to deductible contributions under Tax Law Sec. 612(c)(32). Excess distributions are deemed to be attributable to deductible contributions to the extent that the amount of any such excess distribution, when added to all previous excess distributions from the account, exceeds the aggregate of all nondeductible contributions to the account. (Sec. 612(b)(34), Tax Law)

[¶16-065] Additions--Fringe Benefits

Amounts deducted or deferred from an employee's salary under a flexible benefits program established under Sec. 23, General Municipal Law, or Sec. 1210-a, Public Authorities Law, must be added to federal adjusted gross income in determining New York adjusted gross income. (Sec. 612(b)(31), Tax Law)

"Flexible benefit programs" defined.—"Flexible benefit programs" include qualified cafeteria and similar benefit plans provided as part of an employee benefits program administered by the Commissioner of Labor Relations (on behalf of New York City, the City University of New York, the New York City Health and Hospitals Corporation, the New York City Transit Authority, the New York City Housing Authority, the New York City Off-Track Betting Corporation, the New York City Rehabilitation Mortgage Insurance Corporation, the New York City Board of Educa-

tion, or the New York City School Construction Authority), the New York City Transit Authority, the Manhattan and Bronx Surface Transit Operating Authority, or the Staten Island Rapid Transit Operating Authority. (Sec. 23, General Municipal Law; Sec. 1210-a, Public Authorities Law)

For the manner of declaring flexible benefit program contributions on New York State tax returns, see Important Notice N-91-62.

• *Fractional plan members of NYCERS and BERS*

The amount by which an employee's salary is reduced for health insurance and welfare benefits pursuant to Sec. 12-126.1(d), New York City Administrative Code, must be added to federal adjusted gross income when determining the New York adjusted gross income of a resident individual. (Sec. 612(b)(32), Tax Law)

[¶16-075] Additions--Interest

Interest on obligations of other states and their political subdivisions must be added to federal adjusted gross income in determining New York adjusted gross income. (Sec. 612(b)(1), Tax Law)

> *EXAMPLE:* Interest received by a resident individual on bonds of the State of California must be added to his federal adjusted gross income in arriving at his New York adjusted gross income, because this interest is subject to the New York State personal income tax but not to federal income tax. (Reg. Sec. 112.2(a))

For additional details, see discussion at ¶15-720.

Interest on obligations or securities of federal authorities, commissions or instrumentalities that are exempt from federal income tax but not from state income tax must be added to federal adjusted gross income in determining New York adjusted gross income. (Sec. 612(b)(2), Tax Law)

Interest, deducted in determining federal adjusted gross income, on loans incurred to buy or carry securities, the income from which is exempt for New York State income tax purposes, must be added to federal adjusted gross income in determining New York adjusted gross income. (Sec. 612(b)(4), Tax Law)

> *EXAMPLE:* A dealer in U.S. securities borrowed $100,000 from his bank to purchase a new issue of U.S. Treasury certificates for ultimate sale to his customers. In computing his federal adjusted gross income, he includes the interest received on these certificates and deducts as a business expense the interest payable on the loan. However, the interest received on the certificates is not subject to New York personal income tax and is subtracted from federal adjusted gross income in computing his New York adjusted gross income. (see ¶16-280) Conversely, the interest incurred on the bank loan used to purchase these certificates is not deductible for purposes of the New York personal income tax and must be added to federal adjusted gross income in computing New York adjusted gross income. (Reg. Sec. 112.2(d))

[¶16-080] Additions--Investment Expenses

Expenses paid or incurred for the production of income, which is exempt in New York but taxable for federal purposes, for the management, conservation or maintenance of property producing such income, and amortizable premiums on bonds, the income from which is exempt from New York but not federal tax, must be added to federal adjusted gross income in determining New York adjusted gross income, to the extent deducted in determining federal adjusted gross income. (Sec. 612(b)(5), Tax Law)

Expenses, otherwise allowable, which are directly attributable to any class of income (either taxable or exempt for New York State personal income tax purposes) must be allocated to the class to which they relate. (Reg. Sec. 112.2) If an item of expense is attributable to both taxable and exempt income, a reasonable proportion of the expense, determined in the light of all facts and circumstances, must be allocated to each class.

[¶16-085] Additions--Items Related to Federal Deductions or Credits

Under the 2008 budget legislation, applicable to taxable years beginning after 2007, an addition modification is required for the IRC §199 qualified production activities deduction. (Sec. 612(b)(38), Tax Law)

Other additions to the taxable income base are listed at ¶16-005.

[¶16-090] Additions--Items Related to State Credits

Applicable to taxable years beginning on or after April 1, 2005, an addition modification is required for environmental remediation insurance premiums that were deducted in determining federal taxable income, to the extent of the amount of the environmental remediation insurance credit allowed under Tax Law Secs. 23 and 606(ff). (Sec. 612(b)(37), Tax Law).

Real property taxes paid on qualified agricultural property and deducted in determining federal adjusted gross income must be added back to fedreal adjusted gross income to the extent of the amount of any agricultural property tax credit allowed under Sec. 606(n) or (i), Tax Law. (Sec. 612(b)(33), Tax Law)

The amount of the pre-1988 new business investment deferral must be added to federal adjusted gross income when the reinvestment in the New York new business which qualified the taxpayer for the deferral is sold. (Sec. 612(q), Tax Law)

When gain from the sale or other disposition of property is included in federal gross income, the amount of reduction in the basis of the property attributable to the pre-1987 credit for solar and wind energy must be added to federal adjusted gross income in determining New York adjusted gross income. (Sec. 612(b)(29), Tax Law)

[¶16-105] Additions--Net Operating Losses

The tax law has been amended to provide that, for taxable years beginning before January 1, 2022, any amendments made to the Internal Revenue Code after March 1, 2020, do not apply to the New York personal income tax (Sec. 607(a), Tax Law). Therefore, for example, New York does not conform to federal CARES Act amendments, including (1) a five-year carryback period for NOLs arising in tax years beginning in 2018, 2019, and 2020, and (2) suspension of the 80% of taxable income limitation for those years. Adjustments are required accordingly (*Important Notice N-20-7*).

Prior to the amendment noted above, New York provided that, for any carryback or carryforward year where the amount of NOL deduction allowed for New York purposes is limited, the difference between the NOL deduction allowed on the federal income tax return and the NOL deduction allowed for New York state income tax purposes must be accounted for. Beginning with New York state income tax returns for tax years 2013 and after, the difference must be accounted for by using a New York addition modification to federal adjusted gross income (individuals) or federal taxable income (estates and trusts). (Publication 145)

[¶16-113] Additions--Pass-Through Entity Adjustments

The law provides for various additions to be made by S Corporation shareholders in determining New York adjusted gross income.

• *Reductions for taxes*

In determining New York adjusted gross income, a New York S Corporation shareholder must add to federal adjusted gross income an amount equal to his pro rata share of the corporation's reductions for taxes described in IRC Secs. 1366(f)(2) (tax on built-in gains) and 1366(f)(3) (tax on excess net passive income). (Sec. 612(b)(18), Tax Law)

• *Items of loss and deductions*

In the case of a shareholder of a federal S Corporation, where the election to be treated as a New York S corporation has not been made, any item of loss or deduction of the corporation included in federal gross income must be added to federal adjusted gross income in determining New York adjusted gross income. (Sec. 612(b)(19), Tax Law)

• *Distributions*

A New York S corporation shareholder must add to federal adjusted gross income S corporation distributions to the extent not included in federal gross income for the taxable year because of the application of IRC Secs. 1368, 1371(e) or 1379(c), which represent income not previously subject to New York personal income tax because New York S Corporation status had not been elected. (Sec. 612(b)(20), Tax Law)

• *Disposition of stock or indebtedness*

Where gain or loss is recognized for federal income tax purposes upon the disposition of stock or indebtedness of an S Corporation, an addition to federal adjusted gross income is required equal to the amount of increase in basis with respect to the stock or indebtedness pursuant to IRC Sec. 1376 (passive investment income), as in effect for taxable years beginning before 1983, and IRC Sec. 1367(a)(A) and (B) for each taxable year of the corporation beginning after 1980 for which an election to be treated as a New York S corporation was not in effect. (Secs. 612(b)(21), 612(n), Tax Law)

• *S termination year adjustments*

For adjustments to S corporation items of income, loss and deduction included in a shareholder's federal adjusted gross income or allowed as a reduction for tax during a S termination year, see ¶15-185.

[¶16-125] Additions--Related Party Transactions

New York requires an addition for certain royalty payments made to a related member. (Sec. 612(r), Tax Law)

However, the addback is not required if (Sec. 612(r), Tax Law; Summary, New York Department of Taxation and Finance):

— the amount was included in the related member's tax base, the related member paid all or part of the amount to an unrelated party, and the transaction between the taxpayer and the related member had a valid business purpose;

— the related member paid significant taxes on the amount;

— the related member was organized in a foreign country, the income from the transaction was subject to a comprehensive income tax treaty, the related member was taxed by the foreign country at a rate at least equal to New York's rate, and the amount was paid in a transaction with a valid business purpose and arm's-length terms; or

— the taxpayer and the Department agree to alternative adjustments.

These personal income tax provisions are similar to the corporate franchise tax provisions; see the detailed discussion at ¶10-620.

[¶16-135] Additions--Retirement Plans and Retirement Benefits

The amount of member or employee contributions to a retirement system or pension fund picked up or paid by the employer pursuant to the state Retirement and Social Security Law or Education Law or the Administrative Code of the City of New York must be added to federal adjusted gross income in determining New York adjusted gross income. (Secs. 612(b)(26), 612(b)(26-a), Tax Law)

[¶16-145] Additions--Taxes

Income taxes imposed by New York or any other taxing jurisdiction must be added to federal adjusted gross income in determining New York adjusted gross income, to the extent deductible in determining federal adjusted gross income and not credited against federal income tax. (Sec. 612(b)(3), Tax Law)

A specific addback requirement also applies to any deduction permitted for federal income tax purposes for the MCTMT. (Sec. 612(b)(39), Tax Law; TSB-M-09(1)MCTMT)

For a discussion of adjustments required in computing the New York itemized deduction, see ¶15-545.

[¶16-200]

TAXABLE INCOME COMPUTATION--SUBTRACTIONS

[¶16-205] Subtractions from Taxable Income Base

New York allows the following subtractions from federal adjusted gross income:

— Accelerated life insurance benefit payments . . . . ¶16-240
— Alimony . . . . ¶16-207
— Basis adjustment . . . . ¶16-215
— College savings plan contributions . . . . ¶16-255
— Depletion . . . . ¶16-243
— Disability income . . . . ¶16-247
— Executive mansion trust fund contributions . . . . ¶16-220
— Expenses for production of taxable income . . . . ¶16-285
— Gains from emerging technology investments . . . . ¶16-270
— Gains from new business investments . . . . ¶16-270
— Income tax refund or credit . . . . ¶16-360
— Income taxed under former personal income tax law . . . . ¶16-320
— Innovation hot spots . . . . ¶16-350
— Interest on federal obligations . . . . ¶16-280

— Interest on loans to buy taxable securities . . . . ¶16-280

— Interest on obligations of certain federal authorities . . . . ¶16-280

— Interest or dividend income on exempt obligations or securities . ¶16-280

— Long-term care health insurance premiums . . . . ¶16-307

— Militia active duty service pay. . . . . ¶16-308

— Nazi victims . . . . ¶16-335

— Organ donor expenses. . . . . ¶16-307

— Pensions and annuities, 59$^{1}/_{2}$ years or older . . . . ¶16-345

— Pensions, federal and New York state . . . . ¶16-345

— Restoration of amount held under claim of right . . . . ¶16-225

— S corporation subtractions . . . . ¶16-317

— Safe harbor leases and ACRS deductions . . . . ¶16-245

— Small business income subtraction . . . . ¶16-350

— Social security benefits . . . . ¶16-345

— START-UP NY. . . . . ¶16-350

— Wages and salaries not allowed as business expense deductions . ¶16-290

Subtractions from income are reported on Form IT-201, Resident Income Tax Return.

Additions are discussed at ¶16-005.

[¶16-207] Subtractions--Alimony

For taxable years beginning on or after January 1, 2018, a subtraction from federal adjusted gross income is allowed for any applicable alimony or separate maintenance payments made by the taxpayer during the taxable year. (Sec. 612(w)(1)(A), Tax Law)

"Alimony or separate maintenance payments" means payments as defined under IRC § 71 in effect immediately prior to the enactment of the TCJA (P.L. 115-97). (Sec. 612(w)(2)(A), Tax Law)

The term "applicable alimony or separate maintenance payments" means payments made under an alimony or separation instrument (as defined in IRC § 71 in effect immediately prior to the enactment of P.L. 115-97) that was executed after December 31, 2018, and any divorce or separation instrument executed on or before that date and modified after that date if the modification expressly provides that the relevant amendments apply to the modification. (Sec. 612(w)(2)(B), Tax Law)

[¶16-215] Subtractions--Basis Adjustments

A deduction from federal adjusted gross income is allowed for the portion of any gain, from the sale or other disposition of property having a higher adjusted basis for New York income tax purposes than for federal income tax purposes on December 31, 1959 (or on thee last day of a 1959-1960 fiscal year), that does not exceed such difference in basis. (Sec. 612(c)(4), Tax Law)

[¶16-220] Subtractions--Charitable Contributions

Contributions made to the Executive Mansion Trust Fund, whether by gift, devise or bequest, qualify as deductions in computing the net taxable income of the donor for purposes of any income tax imposed by New York or any political subdivision thereof. (Sec. 54.15, Arts and Cultural Affairs Law)

[¶16-225] Subtractions--Claim of Right Adjustment

If a taxpayer includes an amount in New York adjusted gross income in a prior taxable year because it appeared that the taxpayer had an unrestricted claim of right to the amount in that year and then the taxpayer repays the amount because it is discovered he or she did not have a right to the amount, the amount previously included is deductible and the tax imposed for the year of repayment is the tax for that year minus the decrease in tax for the prior year of inclusion which would result solely from the exclusion of the amount. If the decrease in tax due to the repayment exceeds the tax due for the year of the adjustment, the excess is credited or refunded in the same manner as an overpayment. For nonresidents and part-year residents, the repayment of an item previously included in New York adjusted gross income will also be reflected in the New York source fraction. (Sec. 662, Tax Law)

[¶16-240] Subtractions--Death Benefits

Amounts received by any person as an accelerated payment or payments of part or all of the death payment or special surrender value under a life insurance policy pursuant to Sec. 1113(a)(A) or (B), Insurance Law, may be deducted from federal adjusted gross income in determining New York adjusted gross, to the extent properly included for federal income tax purposes. (Sec. 612(c)(30), Tax Law)

• *Accelerated insurance payments*

Secs. 1113(a)(A) and (B), Insurance Law, permit accelerated payments of part or all of the death benefit or a special surrender value of a life insurance policy upon diagnosis of a terminal illness (defined as a life expectancy of 12 months or less) or of a medical condition requiring extraordinary medical care or treatment regardless of life expectancy.

[¶16-243] Subtractions--Depletion

With respect to the property as to which the taxpayer has used percentage depletion for federal income tax purposes and has been required to add to federal adjusted gross income the amount of the allowance for percentage depletion (see ¶16-037), an allowance for depletion may be subtracted from federal adjusted gross income in the amount that would have been deductible under IRC Sec. 611 if percentage depletion had not been used (cost depletion). (Sec. 612(i), Tax Law)

[¶16-245] Subtractions--Depreciation

The following amounts may be subtracted from federal adjusted gross income in computing New York adjusted gross income:

(1) The amount which is included in federal adjusted gross income (except for qualified mass commuting vehicles) solely as a result of the safe harbor lease election under IRC Sec. 168(f)(8) as it was in effect for agreements entered into prior to January 1, 1984 (Sec. 612(c)(24), Tax Law);

(2) The amount which could have been excluded from federal adjusted gross income had the taxpayer not made the safe harbor lease election under IRC Sec. 168(f)(8) as it was in effect for agreements entered into prior to January 1, 1984 (Sec. 612(c)(25), Tax Law);

(3) The amount with respect to property which is subject to the provisions of IRC Sec. 167 as that section would have been applied to property placed in service on

December 31, 1980. (Sec. 612(c)(26), Tax Law) However, this deduction does not apply with respect to property subject to the provisions of IRC Sec. 280-F (relating to luxury automobiles) or to property subject to the provisions of IRC Sec. 168 which is placed in service in New York State in taxable years beginning after December 31, 1984. With regard to property placed in service outside New York State in tax years 1985—1993, taxpayers may elect to use either the IRC Sec. 167 or 168 depreciation deduction (TSB-M-99(1)I); and

(4) Upon the disposition of property (except for property subject to the provisions of IRC Sec. 168 which is placed in service in New York State for taxable years beginning after 1984 and property subject to IRC Sec. 280-F, concerning luxury automobiles), the amount, if any, by which the aggregate of the accelerated cost recovery system deduction under IRC Sec. 168 exceeds the aggregate of the depreciation deduction under IRC Sec. 167. (Sec. 612(c)(28), Tax Law)

For a discussion regarding bonus depreciation, and other addition modifications related to depreciation, see ¶16-040.

[¶16-247] Subtractions--Disability Income

Disability income included in federal gross income may be subtracted from federal adjusted gross income in computing New York adjusted gross income to the extent that the disability income would have been excluded from federal gross income pursuant to the provisions of IRC Sec. 105(d) had such provisions continued in effect for taxable years beginning after 1983. (Sec. 612(c)(3-b), Tax Law) The sum of disability income excluded under this provision and pension and annuity income excluded under the provision relating to pensions and annuities received by individuals who have attained the age of $59^1/_2$ (see ¶16-345) may not exceed $20,000.

If a husband and wife determine their federal income tax on a joint return but are required to determine their New York income taxes separately, the amounts of disability income which may be excluded will be determined in the same joint manner as such amounts would have been determined under IRC Sec. 105(d)(5), but will be attributed for New York income tax purposes to the spouse who would have been required to report any such amount as income if the spouses had determined their federal income taxes separately.

Where a husband and wife file a joint state income tax return, the $20,000 limitation will be applied as if they were filing separate income tax returns.

Volunteer firefighter enhanced cancer disability benefits.—Effective January 1, 2019, New York will allow eligible taxpayers to take a subtraction from federal adjusted gross income for insurance payments they receive for volunteer firefighter enhanced cancer disability benefits under General Municipal Law §205-cc. The subtraction will apply to the extent that the payments are includable in gross income for federal income tax purposes. (Sec. 612(c)(42), Tax Law)

[¶16-250] Subtractions--Dividends

Interest or dividend income on obligations or securities of any authority, commission or instrumentality of the U.S. may be deducted from federal adjusted income in computing New York adjusted gross income, to the extent that the interest or dividend income is includable in gross income for federal income tax purposes but exempt from state income taxes under the laws of the U.S. (Sec. 612(c)(2), Tax Law)

Interest or dividend income on obligations or securities that are exempt from income tax under the laws of New York authorizing the issuance of the obligations or securities but includable in gross income for federal income tax purposes may be subtracted from federal adjusted gross income in computing New York adjusted gross income. (Sec. 612(c)(6), Tax Law)

Other subtractions from the taxable income base are listed at ¶ 16-205.

[¶ 16-255] Subtractions--Education Expenses

New York resident taxpayers can deduct contributions to one or more family tuition accounts established through the New York's College Savings Program of up to $5,000 per year ($10,000 for a husband and wife filing jointly) from the account owner's New York taxable income. (Sec. 612(c)(32), Tax Law) The contributions are subtracted from the taxpayer's federal adjusted gross income (to the extent not deductible or eligible for credit for federal income tax purposes) as a modification in deriving New York adjusted gross income. (Sec. 612(c)(32), Tax Law)

A subtraction is also allowed for distributions from a family tuition account established under the New York state college choice tuition savings program, to the extent includible in gross income for federal income tax purposes. (Sec. 612(c)(33), Tax Law)

The addition for excess distributions is discussed at ¶ 16-050.

For a detailed discussion of IRC Sec. 529 State College Savings Plans, see ¶ 15-685.

Deduction for certain student loan interest: Interest paid on an education loan made under the New York Higher Education Loan Program will be allowed as a subtraction modification for purposes of computing an individual's New York adjusted gross income. This provision applies to interest paid on or after July 1, 2009. (Sec. 694-a(3), Education Law; TSB-M-09(11)I)

[¶ 16-270] Subtractions--Gains

Specific modifications are provided for the gains described below.

Gains from emerging technology investments.—The gain from the sale of any emerging technology investment acquired on or after March 12, 1998, and held for more than 36 months will be recognized for New York State personal income (as well as corporate franchise, bank franchise, and insurance company franchise) tax purposes only to the extent that the gain realized exceeds the cost of any qualified emerging technology investment purchased by the taxpayer within 365 days from the date of the sale. (Sec. 612(u), Tax Law; Ch. 56 (S.B. 6094-B), Laws 1998) The amount deferred will be added to federal adjusted gross income (federal taxable income in the case of corporations, banks, and insurance companies) when the reinvestment is sold. (Sec. 612(v), Tax Law; Ch. 56 (S.B. 6094-B), Laws 1998)

Gains from new business investments.—A taxpayer may subtract from federal adjusted gross income a portion of an amount constituting new business investment gain as follows: (1) if the new business investment is held for at least four years but less than five years, 25% of the gain; (2) if the new business investment is held for at least five years but less than six years, 50% of the gain; and (3) if the new business investment is held for at least six years, 100% of the gain. (Sec. 612(o), Tax Law)

If the modification for a new business investment gain is less than 100% of the portion of the gain includable in federal adjusted gross income, and, within six months of the realization of the gain, the taxpayer purchases a new business investment which is then held for a period of at least six months, the taxpayer may subtract from federal adjusted gross income 10% of the amount of the gain where the purchase price of the new business investment is equal to or greater than the proceeds of the sale giving rise to the gain. However, the taxpayer may not subtract an amount that will reduce the portion of the gain included in New York income below zero. If the purchase price of the new business investment is less than an amount equal to the proceeds of the sale giving rise to the gain, the modification will be equal to 10% of an amount equal to the product of the amount of the gain and a fraction the numerator of which is the purchase price of the new investment and the denominator of which is an amount equal to the proceeds of the sale.

In order to be eligible for the modification, the new business must have adopted a plan on or after July 1, 1981, and before January 1, 1988, to conduct a new business and to issue new business investments, at least 90% of the assets (valued at original cost) of the new business must be located and employed in New York, and 80% of the employees must be principally employed in New York during each taxable period. The taxpayer must have been subject to tax on the date of the adoption of the new business plan or within one year thereafter.

The term "new business investment" refers to the following investments issued before January 1, 1988, by a new business, on or before the expiration of the third taxable year of the new business or 42 months from the adoption of the plan, whichever is sooner: (1) original issuance capital stock as part of a new issue; (2) other original issuance securities of a new issue of a like nature as stocks which are designed as a means of investment and issued for the purpose of financing corporate enterprises and providing for a distribution of rights in such enterprises; (3) debt obligations such as bonds and debentures for a term of at least one year; and (4) certificates and other instruments representing proprietary interests in, and assumption of general liabilities of, a partnership enterprise.

For special rules applicable to new businesses, see Sec. 612(o)(1)(B)(v).

[¶16-280] Subtractions--Interest

Interest income on obligations of the U.S. and its possessions may be subtracted from federal adjusted gross income in computing New York adjusted gross income. (Sec. 612(c)(1), Tax Law)

Such interest income includes the amount received as dividends from a regulated investment company which has been designated as interest income in a written notice to shareholders not later than 60 days (45 days, for taxable years of regulated investment companies ending prior to July 31, 1992) following the close of its taxable year, provided that, at the close of each quarter of the regulated investment company's taxable year, at least 50% of the total assets of the company consists of obligations of the United States and its possessions.

The aggregated amount so designated by the regulated investment company for the taxable year may not exceed the amount determined by multiplying the total distributions paid by the company to its shareholders with respect to that taxable year (attributable to income earned in that year), including any such distributions paid after the close of the taxable year, by the ratio that the interest income received in that taxable year on obligations of the U.S. and its possessions, after reduction for the deductions and expenses directly or indirectly attributable thereto, bears to the investment company taxable income of the regulated investment company for the taxable year.

Interest or dividend income on obligations or securities of any authority, commission or instrumentality of the U.S. may be deducted from federal adjusted income in computing New York adjusted gross income, to the extent that the interest or dividend income is includable in gross income for federal income tax purposes but exempt from state income taxes under the laws of the U.S. (Sec. 612(c)(2), Tax Law)

Interest or dividend income on obligations or securities that are exempt from income tax under the laws of New York authorizing the issuance of the obligations or securities but includable in gross income for federal income tax purposes may be subtracted from federal adjusted gross income in computing New York adjusted gross income. (Sec. 612(c)(6), Tax Law)

Interest on indebtedness incurred or continued to purchase or carry obligations or securities the income from which is subject to New York income tax but exempt from federal income tax may be deducted from federal adjusted gross income in computing New York adjusted gross income, to the extent that the interest is not deductible in determining federal adjusted gross income and is attributable to a trade or business carried on by the taxpayer. (Sec. 612(c)(9), Tax Law)

• *Build America Bonds*

Generally, interest received on any bond or other obligation issued by a state or local government is not taxable for federal purposes and is not included in the computation of a taxpayer's federal adjusted gross income. However, a Build America Bond pays interest that is taxable for federal purposes. For state income tax purposes, interest income from Build America Bonds will be treated the same as if the interest was from any other tax exempt obligation issued by a state or local government. Therefore, interest income from Build America Bonds issued by New York or its local governments is not subject to tax, but interest income from Build America Bonds issued by other states and their local governments is subject to tax. For tax years after 2009, taxpayers should refer to the instructions for the income tax return they are filing to make the required modification for BAB interest income. For tax year 2009, see the special instructions in TSB-M-10(4)I. The special instructions describe how to reflect a subtraction for interest income attributable to Build America Bonds issued by New York or its local governments and how to recompute federal adjusted gross income for purposes of determining eligibility and/or the credit amount allowed for certain credits.

[¶16-285] Subtractions--Investment Expenses

In computing New York adjusted gross income, a deduction from federal adjusted gross income is allowed for ordinary and necessary expenses paid or incurred during the taxable year for (1) the production or collection of income which is subject to New York State income tax but exempt from federal income tax or (2) the management, conservation or maintenance of property held for the production of such income, and the amortizable bond premium for the taxable year on any bond the interest on which is subject to New York State income tax but exempt from federal income tax, to the extent that the expenses and premiums are not deductible in determining federal adjusted gross income and are attributable to a trade or business carried on by the taxpayer. (Sec. 612(c)(10), Tax Law)

> *EXAMPLE:* An individual engaged in business as a building contractor owns state and local bonds (other than New York municipalities) which he posts as security in lieu of performance bonds to guarantee completion of contracts entered into in the course of his business operations. Where such bonds are purchased at a premium, the taxpayer is required to amortize the premium under the Internal Revenue Code even though no deduction for the amortized premium is allowed in determining federal adjusted gross income. Since the bonds are used in the taxpayer's contracting activities, the premium which is amortized is attributable to a trade or business carried on by him, and the amount allocable to the taxable year, computed in accordance with the federal rules regarding amortization of bond premiums, is to be deducted from federal adjusted gross income in computing New York adjusted gross income. (Reg. Sec. 112.3(j), Tax Law)

[¶16-290] Subtractions--Items Related to Federal Credits or Deductions

In computing New York adjusted gross income, a deduction from federal adjusted gross income is allowed for that portion of wages and salaries paid or incurred for the taxable year for which a deduction is not allowed pursuant to IRC Sec. 280C as a result of the taxpayer having claimed employment credits for federal income tax purposes. (Sec. 612(c)(15), Tax Law)

[¶16-307] Subtractions--Medical Expenses and Savings Accounts

Organ donors are allowed to take a subtraction of up to $10,000 from federal adjusted gross income, applicable to taxable years beginning after 2006. The subtraction modification may be claimed for unreimbursed travel expenses, lodging expenses, and lost wages incurred by the taxpayer with respect to his or her organ donation. The taxpayer must claim the modification in the taxable year in which the human organ transplantation occurs. "Human organ" means all or part of a liver, pancreas, kidney, intestine, lung, or bone marrow. (Sec. 612(c)(38), Tax Law)

The modification may be claimed by a taxpayer only once, and it is not available to nonresidents or part-year residents. (Sec. 612(c)(38), Tax Law)

Long-term care insurance (Prior law).—For tax years beginning after 1995 and before 2002, a taxpayer could subtract from federal adjusted gross income, in computing New York adjusted gross income, premiums paid for certain long-term care health insurance policies that covered the taxpayer. (Sec. 612(c)(31), Tax Law) Qualifying premiums could be subtracted to the extent that they did not exceed the limitations set forth under Section 213(d)(10) of the Internal Revenue Code (IRC).

This subtraction modification was repealed on January 1, 2002, when the credit discussed at ¶16-920 became effective. (TSB-M-00(4)I)

[¶16-308] Subtractions--Military Pay

A subtraction from federal adjusted gross income is allowed for income received by a member of the New York state organized militia as compensation for performing active service within New York. The subtraction applies to taxable years beginning on or after January 1, 2004. (Sec. 612(c)(8-b), Tax Law)

Applicable retroactively to such taxable years, the 2006 budget legislation expanded the subtraction modification so it is also available with respect to active service of the *United States* pursuant to *federal* active duty orders, for service other than training, issued under Title 10 of the United States Code. Before the amendment, the modification was allowed only with respect to state active duty orders issued under New York Military Law Sec. 6(1).

For taxpayers who included such income on a 2004 or 2005 return and did not make the subtraction modification, a refund may be claimed by filing an amended return. (*Important Notice N-06-9*, August 2006)

Applicable to taxable years commencing after December 31, 2007, compensation received by military personnel serving in a combat zone is exempt from New York personal income tax. (Sec. 612(c)(8-c), Tax Law)

Compensation and bonuses received for active service in the armed forces of the U.S. while a prisoner of war or missing in action during the hostilities in Vietnam may be deducted from federal adjusted gross income in computing New York adjusted gross income, to the extent includable in gross income for federal income tax purposes. (Sec. 612(c)(8-a), Tax Law)

[¶16-317] Subtractions--Pass-Through Entity Adjustments

The law provides for the following subtractions to be made by S corporation shareholders in determining New York adjusted gross income.

• *Items of income*

A shareholder of a federal S corporation which has not elected S corporation status for New York personal income tax purposes may deduct from federal adjusted gross income any item of income of the corporation included in federal gross income pursuant to IRC Sec. 1366. (Sec. 612(c)(22), Tax Law)

• *Disposition of stock or indebtedness*

Where gain or loss is recognized for federal income tax purposes upon the disposition of stock or indebtedness of an S corporation, a subtraction is allowed from federal adjusted gross income for the amount of the reduction in basis with respect to the stock or indebtedness pursuant to IRC Sec. 1376 (passive investment income), as in effect for taxable years beginning before 1983, and IRC Sec. 1367(a)(2)(B) and (C) for each taxable year of the corporation beginning after 1980 for which an election to be treated as a New York S corporation was not in effect. (Secs. 612(c)(21), 612(n), Tax Law)

[¶16-320] Subtractions--Previously Taxed Income

The amount necessary to prevent the taxation of any amount of annuity, other income or gain properly reported and taxed under the former personal income tax law (Article 16) to the taxpayer, or to a decedent by reason of whose death the taxpayer acquired the right to receive the income or gain, or to a trust or estate from which the taxpayer received the income or gain, may be subtracted from federal adjusted gross income in computing New York adjusted gross income. (Sec. 612(c)(5), Tax Law)

[¶16-330] Subtractions--Related Party Transactions

For taxable years beginning after 2002 and before 2013, in computing New York adjusted gross income, taxpayers could subtract from federal adjusted gross income royalty payments received, either directly or indirectly, by the taxpayer during the tax year from a related member or members, to the extent such payments were included in calculating the taxpayer's federal taxable income, and the payments were required to be added to federal adjusted gross income by the related member (see ¶16-125 for a discussion of the addback provisions). (Sec. 612(r), Tax Law)

The royalty income exclusion described above was eliminated by the 2013 budget legislation. (Summary, New York Department of Taxation and Finance)

[¶16-335] Subtractions--Reparation Payments

Effective May 21, 2002, no state or local taxation of any kind, including income taxation, may be imposed on any payment from the September 11th Victim Compensation Fund of 2001 established under Title IV of the federal Air Transportation Safety and System Stabilization Act, P.L. 107-42, as amended. (Sec. 7, S.B. 7356, Laws 2002)

Applicable to taxable years beginning after 1994, victims of Nazi persecution (as identified under federal law) who receive federally taxable compensation due to their status, as well as their spouses and qualified dependents, may subtract such compensation from their federal adjusted gross income for New York State and New York City personal income tax purposes. A subtraction modification also applies to items of income (such as interest on insurance proceeds) attributable to assets stolen from, hidden from, or otherwise lost by the victim immediately prior to, during, or immediately after World War II. This subtraction modification will not apply, however, with respect to assets acquired with such stolen, lost, or hidden assets or with the proceeds acquired from the sale of those assets. Finally, the subtraction modification only applies to the first recipient of the assets who is a victim or the spouse or qualified descendant of that victim. (Sec. 612(c)(35), Tax Law; Sec. 612(c)(36), Tax Law)

Qualified settlements received by victims of Nazi persecution or their descendants are exempt from state and local income taxes. Similarly, qualified settlement funds or grantor trusts established to settle claims arising from the Holocaust, World War II, or Nazi persecution are exempt from state and local income taxes.

Other subtractions from the taxable income base are listed at ¶ 16-205.

[¶ 16-345] Subtractions--Retirement Plans and Benefits

A number of subtractions are allowed, as described below.

• *Social security benefits*

Social security benefits may be deducted from federal adjusted gross income in computing New York adjusted gross income to the extent includable in gross income for federal income tax purposes pursuant to IRC Sec. 86. (Sec. 612(c)(3-c), Tax Law)

• *Certain pensions and annuities*

Pensions and annuities received by an individual who has attained the age of 591/2, not otherwise excluded as a pension paid to an officer or employee of the federal or state government, may be subtracted from federal adjusted gross income in computing New York adjusted gross income. (Sec. 612(c)(3-a), Tax Law) The amount excluded may not exceed $20,000. In order to come within this provision, the pensions and annuities must be periodic payments attributable to personal services performed by the individual prior to his retirement from employment, which arise (1) from an employer-employee relationship or (2) from contributions to a retirement plan that are deductible for federal income tax purposes.

Effective for tax years beginning on or after January 1, 2002, distributions from government IRC Sec. 457 deferred compensation plans will qualify for this exclusion, provided the individual is age 591/2 or older at the time the distribution was received, and the distributions from the plan are being made in period payments. (TSB-M-02(9)I) If an individual, estate, or trust received pension and annuity income of a decedent, they may also qualify for the up to $20,000 exclusion if the decedent would have been entitled to it, had the decedent continued to live, regardless of the age of the beneficiary. (TSB-M-02(9)I)

For a complete discussion of the New York tax treatment of distributions and rollovers relating to government IRC Sec, 457 deferred compensation plans, see TSB-M-02(9)I.

The term "pensions and annuities" includes distributions received from an individual retirement account or an individual retirement annuity, as defined in IRC Sec. 408, and distributions from self-employed individual and owner-employee retirement plans which qualify under IRC Sec. 401, whether or not the payments are periodic in nature.

For purposes of the exclusion, lump-sum distributions, as defined in IRC Sec. 402, are not included within the term "pensions and annuities."

Where a husband and wife file a joint state personal income tax return, the modification will be computed as if they were filing separate personal income tax returns.

Where a payment would otherwise qualify for the exclusion except that the individual is deceased, the payment will, nevertheless, be treated as a pension or annuity for purposes of the exclusion if the payment is received by the individual's beneficiary.

- *Pensions of officers and employees of New York*

Pensions of officers and employees of New York, its subdivisions and agencies may be subtracted from federal adjusted gross income in computing New York adjusted gross income, to the extent includable in gross income for federal income tax purposes. (Sec. 612(c)(3), Tax Law)

> *CCH EXAMPLE 1:* A retired employee of New York State receives a pension which is taxed under the Internal Revenue Code as annuity income. Since the pension of a retired New York employee is exempt under New York State law, the amount included in federal adjusted gross income on account of this pension is subtracted in computing the taxpayer's New York adjusted gross income. (Reg. Sec. 112.3(c))

> *CCH EXAMPLE 2:* A New York State employee resigns and withdraws from the New York State Employees' Retirement System the amount of the employee's contributions, plus the interest accumulated thereon. The Retirement and Social Security Law provides that all rights in this retirement system are exempt from New York State personal income tax. Accordingly, the amount of the interest by the withdrawing employee, if included in the employee's federal adjusted gross income, is subtracted in determining New York adjusted gross income.

- *Pensions of officers and employees of the federal government*

Pensions of officers and employees of the U.S., any territory or possession or political subdivision of such territory or possession, the District of Columbia, or any agency or instrumentality of any one of the foregoing, may be subtracted from federal adjusted gross income in computing New York adjusted gross income, to the extent includable in federal gross income for federal income tax purposes. (Sec. 612(c)(3), Tax Law) In the event the Federal Public Salary Act of 1939 or federal law (decisional or legislative) no longer requires federal and state pension benefits to be treated equally for state and city personal income tax purposes, the exemption for pensions of officers and employees of the federal government will no longer be in effect, except as pertaining to federal pension benefits received in taxable years ending before the effective date of the change in federal law.

> *CCH CAUTION:* For taxable years beginning after 1995, federal law (P.L. 104-95) curtails states' rights to subject retirement income of former residents to state income taxation. (P.L. 104-95, 104th Cong, 1st Sess.) The statute protects from source taxation all pension income or other retirement distributions received from IRC Sec. 401(a) trusts exempt from taxation under IRC Sec. 501(a), simplified IRC Sec. 408(k) plans, IRC Sec. 403(a) annuity plans, IRC Sec. 403(b) annuity contracts, IRC Sec. 7701(a)(37) individual retirement plans, IRC Sec. 457

deferred compensation plans, IRC Sec. 414(d) government plans and IRC Sec. 501(c)(18) trusts. Also included are prohibitions on out-of-state taxation of distributions from three non-qualified plans. First, plans described in IRC Sec. 312(v)(2)(C) are protected if payments are made at least annually and spread over the actual life expectancy of the beneficiaries. Second, the same plans are protected if payments are spread over at least a ten-year period. Third, in instances where plans are trusts under IRC Sec. 401(a), but exceed limitations set forth in IRC Secs. 401(a)(17) and 415, the pensions are exempted from out-of-state taxation.

• *Distributions and Rollovers—Government IRC Sec. 457 Deferred Compensation Plans*

Federal legislation amended IRC Secs. 457 and 3401 to change the characterization of distributions from government Sec. 457 deferred compensation plans, applicable to tax years beginning on or after January 1, 2002. The legislation does not affect the characterization of distributions from the plans of any other exempt organizations. The federal law provides that distributions from these plans will be characterized as pension or annuity payments (under prior law, these distributions were characterized as wages). In addition, the new law allows for tax-free transfers, via a trustee-to-trustee transfer, between government Sec. 457 deferred compensation plans and other qualified retirement plans and traditional individual retirement accounts (IRAs). These changes affect the New York personal income tax treatment of distributions from government Sec. 457 plans, effective for tax years beginning on or after January 1, 2002. Distributions from the Sec. 457 deferred compensation plans of any other tax exempt organizations are addressed in Publication 36, *General Information for Senior Citizens and Retired Persons—For Tax Year 2007.*

For a complete discussion of the personal income tax treatment, see TSB-M-02(9)I.

• *MTA Police 20-Year Retirement Program*

Members of the Metropolitan Transportation Authority's (MTA) Police 20-Year Retirement Program can subtract their pension distributions in determining New York adjusted gross income to the extent that the distributions are included in the member's federal adjusted gross income. For a complete discussion, see TSB-M-04(4)I.

• *Distributions used for flood repairs*

A New York personal income tax subtraction from federal adjusted gross income has been enacted for certain distributions from an eligible retirement plan made on or after April 1, 2017, and before April 2, 2022. The subtraction will apply only if: (1) the taxpayer's primary residence was located in the area affected by the disaster declared under the governor's Executive Order 165 of 2017, declaring a state of emergency, dated May 3, 2017; (2) the residence incurred damage due to coastal flooding, widespread erosion, and water damage caused by the disaster; (3) the damage qualifies for the casualty deduction under IRC § 165 (determined without regard to whether the loss exceeds 10% of adjusted gross income); and (4) during the taxable year, the taxpayer uses the entire amount of the distribution to pay for repairs needed as a result of the damage. The amount of the distribution that otherwise may be subtracted must be reduced by any deduction claimed by the taxpayer for the damage under IRC § 165. In addition, the taxpayer cannot claim a subtraction modification (for certain pensions and annuities) under Tax Law § 612(c)(3-a) for the distribution. The subtraction applies to taxable years beginning on or after January 1, 2017. (Sec. 612(c)(42), Tax Law)

For additional information, see TSB-M-17(2)I.

[¶16-350] Subtractions--Targeted Business Activity or Zones

Small businesses.—For a small business having business income and/or farm income, a subtraction is allowed equal to 3% of the net items of income, gain, loss, and deduction attributable to such business or farm entering into federal adjusted gross income, but not less than zero, for taxable years beginning after 2013. The amount increases to 3.75% for taxable years beginning after 2014 and to 5% for taxable years beginning after 2015. The term "small business" means a sole proprietor or a farm business that employs one or more persons during the taxable year and that has net business income or net farm income of less than $250,000. (Sec. 612(c)(39), Tax Law)

The Department of Taxation and Finance has issued a memorandum that discusses the subtraction modification in detail; see *TSB-M-14(3)C, (5)I.*

Innovation hot spots.—Under the New York State Business Incubator and Innovation Hot Spot Support Act, Empire State Development (ESD) is authorized to issue an annual request for proposals for grants and assistance based on available appropriations and to designate qualified applicants as New York State incubators. In addition, in each of state fiscal years 2013 and 2014, ESD is authorized to designate five qualified New York State incubators as New York State innovation hot spots. These innovation hot spots can certify certain clients as a qualified entity eligible for tax benefits under Tax Law §38. (Sec. 38, Tax Law; Sec. 612(c)(39), Tax Law; TSB-M-13(4)I; TSB-M-14(1)I)

The tax benefits available to a taxpayer subject to tax under Article 22 are described below (these tax benefits are allowed for five tax years beginning with the first tax year a qualified entity becomes a tenant in, or is part of, a New York State innovation hot spot):

— An individual who is the sole proprietor of a qualified entity will be allowed a deduction (in the form of a subtraction modification) for the amount of income or gain included in his or her federal adjusted gross income (FAGI), to the extent that the income or gain is attributable to the operations of the qualified entity at (or as part of) an innovation hot spot.

— A member of a limited liability company (LLC) treated as a partnership, a partner in a partnership, or a shareholder in a New York S corporation (where the LLC, partnership, or New York S corporation is a qualified entity), will be allowed a deduction (in the form of a subtraction modification) for the amount of income or gain included in his or her FAGI to the extent that the income or gain is attributable to the operations of the qualified entity at (or as part of) an innovation hot spot.

A taxpayer that claims any of the tax benefits described above (or related sales tax benefits) is no longer eligible for any other New York State exemption, deduction, credit, or refund to the extent attributable to the business operations of a qualified entity at (or as part of) a New York State innovation hot spot. The election to claim any of the tax benefits described above is not revocable.

START-UP NY.—Employees working at a business under the START-UP NY program (see ¶16-893 for details) are authorized to claim a personal income tax deduction equal to the wages earned from the business in the tax-free area. The deduction will apply to all wages and salaries in the first five years of tax benefits. In the remaining five years, for single individuals, heads of households, and married couples, the deduction will apply to the first $200,000, $250,000, and $300,000 of wages, respectively. The total number of new employees eligible for the deduction will be capped at 10,000 per year. (Sec. 39(e), Tax Law; Sec. 612(c)(40), Tax Law; TSB-M-13(6)I)

The START-UP NY tax benefits apply to taxable years beginning on or after January 1, 2014.

[¶16-360] Subtractions--Taxes

The amount of any refund or credit for overpayment of income taxes imposed by New York, or any other taxing jurisdiction, may be deducted from federal adjusted gross income in computing New York adjusted gross income, to the extent properly included for federal income tax purposes. (Sec. 612(c)(7), Tax Law)

[¶16-500]

SOURCING RULES

[¶16-505] Income Attributable to State Sources

Nonresidents and part-year residents are liable for tax on taxable income derived from sources within New York. The New York source income of a nonresident individual is the sum of: (1) the net amount of items of income, gain, loss and deduction entering into the individual's federal adjusted gross income, derived from or connected with New York sources, including (a) the individual's distributive share of partnership income, gain, loss or deduction, (b) pro rata share of New York S corporation income, loss and deduction, increased by reductions for taxes described in IRC Sec. 1366(F)(2) (tax on built-in gains) and IRC Sec. 1366(F)(3) (tax on excess and passive income) and (c) share of estate or trust income, gain, loss or deduction, and (2) the portion of the modifications to federal adjusted gross income described in Sec. 612(b) (see discussion beginning at ¶16-005) and Sec. 612(c), Tax Law (see discussion beginning at ¶16-205), that relate to income derived from New York sources (including modifications attributable to the individual as a partner or shareholder of a New York S corporation). (Sec. 631(a), Tax Law)

The New York source income of a part-year resident individual is the sum of the following: (1) federal adjusted gross income for the period of residence, computed as if the individual's taxable year for federal income tax purposes were limited to the period of residence; (2) New York source income for the period of nonresidence determined as if the individual's taxable year for federal income tax purposes were limited to the period of nonresidence; and certain special accruals. (Sec. 638(a), Tax Law)

Income from pass-through entities.—See ¶16-565.

• *Income and deductions from New York sources*

Items of income, gain, loss and deduction derived from or connected with New York sources are those items attributable to (1) the ownership of any interest in real or tangible personal property in New York; (2) a business, trade, profession or occupation carried on in New York; (3) the ownership of shares issued by an electing shareholder of an S corporation; (4) winnings from a wager placed in a lottery conducted by the Division of the Lottery if the proceeds from the wager exceed $5,000; (5) (for taxable years beginning on or after January 1, 2019—see TSB-M-19(4)I) gambling winnings over $5,000 from wagering transactions within New York; (6) gains from the sale, conveyance, or other disposition of shares of stock in a cooperative housing corporation in connection with the grant or transfer of a proprietary leasehold by the owner, and subject to the provisions of Tax Law Article 31 (i.e., the New York real estate transfer tax), whether such shares are held by a partnership, trust, or otherwise; (7) for shareholders of certain S corporations, income from an installment sale contract (see ¶16-565); or (8) (applicable to taxable years beginning on or after January 1, 2010) income received by nonresidents related to a business, trade, profession, or occupation previously carried on in New York, whether or not as an employee, including but not limited to covenants not to compete and termination agreements. (Sec. 631(b)(1), Tax Law)

The Department of Taxation and Finance has issued a tax bulletin that provides a list of the items of income, gain, loss, and deduction that are included in New York source income, as well as a list of those items that are not included; see TB-IT-615.

Regarding nonresidents' sales of coop shares, see also *Important Notice N-04-15* and TSB-M-04(5)I.

A nonresident, other than a dealer holding property primarily for sale to customers in the ordinary course of trade or business, is not deemed to carry on a business, trade or occupation in New York solely by reason of the purchase and sale of property or the purchase, sale or writing of stock option contracts, or both, for his own account. (Sec. 631(d), Tax Law)

Income from intangible personal property, including annuities, dividends, interest and gains from the disposition of intangible personal property, constitute income derived from New York sources only to the extent that such income is from (1) property employed in a business, trade, profession or occupation carried on in New York or (2) winnings after September 30, 2000, from a wager placed in a lottery conducted by the Division of the Lottery if the proceeds from the wager exceed $5000. (Sec. 631(b)(2), Tax Law)

In addition, applicable to taxable years beginning on or after January 1, 2004, income from the disposition of intangible personal property constitutes income derived from New York sources to the extent that such gains are from the sale, conveyance, or other disposition of shares of stock in a cooperative housing corporation in connection with the grant or transfer of a proprietary leasehold by the owner, and subject to the provisions of Tax Law Article 31 (i.e., the New York real estate transfer tax), whether such shares are held by a partnership, trust, or otherwise. (Sec. 631(b)(2), Tax Law)

Income directly or indirectly derived by an athlete, entertainer, or performing artist from closed-circuit and cable television transmissions of an event (other than events occurring on a regularly scheduled basis) taking place within the state as a result of the rendition of services by such athlete, entertainer or performing artist constitutes income derived from New York sources only to the extent that such transmissions were received or exhibited within the state. (Sec. 631(b)(3), Tax Law)

Deductions with respect to capital losses, passive activity losses and net operating losses are based solely on items of income, gain, loss and deduction derived from or connected with New York sources, but otherwise are determined in the same manner as the corresponding resident deductions. (Sec. 631(b)(4), Tax Law)

In the case of a nonresident individual or partner of a partnership doing an insurance business as a member of the New York Insurance Exchange, any item of income, gain, loss or deduction of the business which is the individual's distributive or pro rata share for federal income tax purposes or which the individual is required to take into account separately for federal income tax purposes does not constitute income, gain, loss or deduction derived from New York sources. (Sec. 631(b)(5), Tax Law)

The deduction allowed by IRC Sec. 215, relating to alimony, does not constitute a deduction derived from New York sources.

¶16-505

• *Business previously carried on in New York*

The 2010 budget legislation amended the definition of "New York source income" of a nonresident individual by adding a new provision under which income, gain, loss, and deduction from New York sources includes income that is includable in federal adjusted gross income and that is related to a business, trade, profession, or occupation previously carried on within the state, whether or not as an employee. This income includes, but is not limited to, income related to covenants not to compete and income related to termination agreements. The new provision applies to income received in tax years beginning on or after January 1, 2010, even if the income is attributable to a contract or other agreement entered into before 2010. (Sec. 631(b)(1)(F), Tax Law)

The Department of Taxation and Finance has issued a memorandum explaining how to compute the amount to be included in New York source income. If the nonresident's business, trade, profession, or occupation was carried on partly within and partly outside the state, the amount of income to be included is determined using the rules described in the memorandum for employees or for businesses, as applicable. (TSB-M-10(9)I)

• *Members of Armed Forces*

Compensation paid by the U.S. for active service in the U.S. Armed Forces, performed by an individual not domiciled in New York, does not constitute income derived from New York sources. (Sec. 631(e), Tax Law)

• *Holders of interests in REMICS*

Nonresidents, in determining New York source income, include only the income received from their interests in Real Estate Mortgage Investment Conduits (REMICS) where such interests are employed in a trade, business, profession or occupation carried on in New York State. (TSB-M-87(22)I)

• *Stock options, stock appreciation rights, and restricted stock*

The New York Department of Taxation and Finance has adopted amendments to the personal income tax regulations to provide allocation rules for certain nonresidents and part-year residents receiving compensation income from stock options, stock appreciation rights, or restricted stock. The amendments apply to taxable years beginning on or after January 1, 2006. The amended regulations provide for a grant-to-vest allocation period for statutory stock options, nonstatutory stock options without a readily ascertainable fair market value at the time of grant, and stock appreciation rights. However, because taxpayers may have relied on TSB-M-95(3)I (see discussion below) to compute their estimated tax and/or withholding requirements for 2006, taxpayers are allowed an election for 2006 to use either the new method or the method outlined in TSB-M-95(3)I. (Reg. Sec. 132.24; Reg. Sec. 154.6) The material below also includes a discussion of the *Michaelson* and *Stuckless* decisions.

Taxable year beginning in 2006.—For a taxable year beginning in 2006 only, nonresident individuals have the option of using a different allocation period when determining New York source income from compensation relating to statutory stock options, restricted stock, and stock appreciation rights for nonresidents. In each instance, nonresident individuals could elect to use the period of time from the date the option was granted to the earliest of: (1) the date that the option was exercised; (2) the date that the individual's services terminated; or (3) the date that the compensation was recognized for federal income tax purposes. TSB-M-07(7)I.

Michaelson, TSB-M-95(3)I, and Stuckless.—In (*Michaelson v. The New York State Tax Commission*, 67 N.Y. 2d 579), the New York Court of Appeals held that a nonresident individual employed in New York who received an incentive stock option, exercised the option and subsequently sold the stock at a gain, was subject to New York State personal income tax only on the portion of the gain that represented the difference between the option price and the fair market value of the stock at the time the option was exercised. The Court held that this difference constituted compensation for services performed in New York. Any further appreciation in the value of the stock after the exercise date was investment income not taxable to a nonresident.

The Court further held that, although the compensation element of an incentive stock option is realized on the date the option is exercised, the compensation amount is not taxable for New York State purposes until the income or gain is recognized for federal income tax purposes upon the sale of the stock. If the stock has been held for the required holding period to qualify as a long-term capital gain, the entire gain (both the gain related to the exercise of the option and the gain attributable to the appreciation in the value of the stock after the date of exercise) is treated as capital gain for federal and state income tax purposes.

However, the Court also stated that this capital gain treatment does not mean that the employee did not realize compensation at the time of exercise, but merely that the compensation, when later recognized, is recognized as capital gain. Accordingly, the amount of capital gain that represents the compensation element is considered gain derived from New York State sources and is subject to New York State tax when recognized for federal income tax purposes.

Although *Michaelson* resolved the issue concerning the total compensation that may be includable in the New York source income of a nonresident, the Court did not address how the total amount should be allocated for New York purposes if the employee performs (or performed) services both inside and outside New York. Since the court determined that compensation constitutes the appreciation in the value of the stock from the date of grant to the date of exercise, that period is considered the period over which the employee's performance of services will be measured (compensable period).

In a Technical Services Bureau Memorandum, the Department stated that any allocation had to be based on the allocation applicable to regular (non-option) compensation received by the employee during the compensable period. (TSB-M-95(3)I)

In *Stuckless*, the New York Tax Appeals Tribunal (TAT) canceled a personal income tax deficiency asserted against a taxpayer who, while he was a nonresident, exercised stock options that had been granted when he was working and residing in New York. The TAT rejected the Division of Taxation's position, as set forth in TSB-M-95(3)I, that a nonresident's stock option income had to be allocated to New York based upon a date-of-grant to date-of-exercise allocation period rule. Reg. Sec. 132.18(a) provided for an allocation of income based on days worked in New York, but Reg. Sec. 132.18(b) then provided that there would be no such allocation when there were no New York work days in a period. The taxpayer successfully argued that Reg. Sec. 132.18(b) was the governing provision in this case because the compensation at issue was received in a period in which no New York work was performed. The only situation for which the regulations provided a multiple year allocation method was the receipt of certain retirement payments, under Reg. Sec. 132.20. The rules and examples set out in Reg. Sec. 132.18 generally provided for an allocation based on work days within the taxable year in which the income was realized. If the Division wished to create a separate set of new rules for identified special circumstances, such a change should have been effected through legislation or adopted in regulations, as was done with Reg. Sec. 132.20 in the case of retirement payments.

¶16-505

The TAT concluded that TSB-M-95(3)I was not entitled to deference. Further, the TAT rejected the Division's argument that the issuance of TSB-M-95(3)I constituted the adoption of an alternative method of apportionment and allocation, as authorized by the regulations.

• *Hedge fund deferred compensation*

A New York memorandum discusses the treatment of nonqualified deferred compensation to which IRC Sec. 457A does not apply because the amount deferred is attributable to services performed before 2009. P.L. 110-343, Div. C, § 801(d)(2) requires those deferrals to be included in gross income for federal tax purposes in the later of (1) the last tax year beginning before January 1, 2018, or (2) the tax year when there is no substantial risk of forfeiture of the rights to the compensation. The memorandum explains how to determine the amount of such nonqualified deferred compensation that must be included in a nonresident's New York source income. (TSB-M-18(2)C, (3)I)

The memorandum also discusses the treatment for: resident individuals; sole proprietorships; partnerships; estates and trusts; and corporations. (TSB-M-18(2)C, (3)I)

• *Nonresident professional athletes*

For taxable years beginning on or after January 1, 1995, the New York source income of nonresident members of professional athletic teams includes their total compensation for services rendered as team members during the taxable year, multiplied by a fraction, the numerator of which is the number of "duty days" spent within New York State rendering services for the team in any manner during the taxable year, and the denominator of which is the total number of duty days spent both within and without New York State during the taxable year. (Reg. Sec. 132.22)

"Duty days".—"Duty days" include:

(1) all days during the taxable year from the beginning of the professional athletic team's official pre-season training period through the last game in which the team competes or is scheduled to compete;

(2) days that do not fall within (1), above, on which the team member renders services for a team (e.g., participation in instructional leagues, the "Pro Bowl" or promotional "caravans"). "Renders services" includes conducting training and reha-bilitation activities, but only if conducted at the facilities of the team; and

(3) game days, practice days, days spent at team meetings, promotional caravans and preseason training camps, and days served with the team through all post-season games in which the team competes or is scheduled to compete.

Example: Player A, a member of a professional athletic team, is a nonresident of New York State. Player A's contract for such team requires A to report to such team's training camp and to participate in all exhibition, regular season, and playoff games. Player A has a contract which covers seasons that occur during yr.1/yr.2 and yr.2/yr.3. Player A's contract provides that A receive $500,000 for the yr.1/yr.2 season and $600,000 for the yr.2/yr.3 season. Assuming player A receives $550,000 from such contract during taxable year 2 ($250,000 for one-half the yr.1/yr.2 season and $300,000 for one-half the yr.2/yr.3 season), the portion of such compensation received by player A for taxable year 2, attributable to New York State, is determined by multiplying the compensation player A receives during the taxable year ($550,000) by a fraction, the numerator of which is the total number of duty days player A spends rendering services for the team in New York State during taxable year 2 (attributable to both the yr.1/yr.2 season and the yr.2/yr.3 season) and the denominator of which is the total number of player A's duty days spent both within and without New York State for the entire taxable year.

Example: Player D, a member of a professional athletic team, is a nonresident of New York State. During the season, D travels to New York State to participate in the annual all-star game as a representative of D's team. The number of days D spends in New York State for practice, the game, meetings, etc., shall be considered to be duty days spent in New York State for player D for that taxable year, as well as included within total duty days spent both within and without New York State.

Travel days that do not involve a game, practice, team meeting, promotional caravan or other similar team event are not considered duty days spent in New York State, but are included in the total duty days spent both within and without New York State.

Example: Assume the same facts as given in the prior example, except that player D is not participating in the all-star game and is not rendering services for D's team in any manner. Player D is instead travelling to and attending such game solely as a spectator. The number of days player D spends in New York State for such game shall not be considered to be duty days spent in New York State. However, such days are considered to be included within total duty days spent both within and without New York State.

Duty days for a person who joins a team between the beginning of the team's official pre-season training period and the last game in which the team competes, or is scheduled to compete, begin on the day that he or she joins the team. Duty days for a person who leaves a team during the same period end on the day that he or she leaves the team. Separate duty day calculation must be made if a person switches teams during the taxable year.

Days on which a team member is not compensated and does not render services for the team in any manner (for example, days during which a team member is suspended without pay and prohibited from performing team services) are not treated as duty days.

Days during which a team member is on the disabled list, and does not (a) conduct rehabilitation activities at facilities of the team or (b) otherwise render services for the team in New York State, are not considered duty days spent in New York State. However, days on the disability list are included in total duty days spent both within and without New York State.

EXAMPLE: Player B, a member of a professional athletic team, is a nonresident of New York State. During the season, B is injured and is unable to render services for B's team. While B is undergoing medical treatment at a clinic, which is not a facility of the team, but is located in New York State, B's team travels to New York State for a game. The number of days B's team spends in New York State for practice, games, meetings, etc., while B is present at such clinic, shall not be considered duty days spent in New York State for player B for that taxable year, but such days are considered to be included within total duty days spent both within and without New York State.

EXAMPLE: Player C, a member of a professional athletic team, is a nonresident of New York State. During the season, C is injured and is unable to render services for C's team. C performs rehabilitation exercises at the facilities of C's team in New York State as well as at personal facilities in New York State. The days C performs rehabilitation exercises in the facilities of C's team are considered duty days spent in New York State for player C for that taxable year. However, days player C spends at personal facilities in New York State shall not be considered duty days spent in New York State for player C for that taxable year, but such days are considered to be included within total duty days spent both within and without New York State.

"Member of a professional athletic team" defined: A member of a professional athletic team includes employees who are active players, players on the disabled list and any other persons required to travel and who travel with and perform services on behalf of the team on a regular basis (e.g., coaches, managers, trainers, etc.).

"Total compensation" defined: The term "total compensation for services rendered as a member of a professional athletic team" means the total compensation received during the taxable year for services rendered (a) from the beginning of the official pre-season training period through the last game in which the team competes or is scheduled to compete during the taxable year and (b) during the taxable year on a date which does not fall within the aforementioned period (e.g., participation in instructional leagues, the "Pro Bowl" or promotional "caravans"). Compensation includes salaries, wages, and bonuses for services performed during the year, but does not include strike benefits, severance pay, termination pay, contract or option year buy-out payments, expansion or relocation payments, or any other payments not related to services rendered for the team.

The term "bonuses" includes performance bonuses received during the season, including bonuses paid for championship, playoff or "bowl" games played by a team, or for selection to all-star league or other honorary positions, and signing bonuses, unless: (1) the payment of the signing bonus is not conditional upon the signee playing any games for the team, or performing any subsequent services for the team, or even making the team; (2) the signing bonus is payable separately from the salary and any other compensation; and (3) the signing bonus is nonrefundable.

[¶16-515] Sourcing of Business Income

If a nonresident individual, or a partnership of which a nonresident individual is a member, carries on a business, trade, profession or occupation both within and outside New York State, the items of income, gain, loss and deduction attributable to the business, trade, profession or occupation must be apportioned and allocated to New York State on a fair and equitable basis in accordance with approved methods of accounting. (Reg. Sec. 132.15)

If the books and records of the business do not disclose, to the satisfaction of the Commissioner, the proportion of the net amount of the items of income, gain, loss and deduction attributable to the activities of the business carried on in New York State, the proportion will be determined by multiplying (1) the net amount of the items of gain, loss and deduction of the business by (2) the averages of the property, payroll, and gross income percentages.

Business previously carried on in New York: For provisions regarding income received by a nonresident related to a business, trade, profession, or occupation previously carried on within New York, see ¶16-505.

• *Property percentage*

The property percentage is computed by dividing (1) the average of the values, at the beginning and end of the taxable year, of real and tangible personal property that is owned by or rented to the taxpayer and is connected with the business and located within New York State, by (2) the average of the values, at the beginning and end of the taxable year, of all real and tangible personal property that is owned by or rented to the taxpayer and is connected with the business and located both within and outside New York State. (Reg. Sec. 132.15) The fair market value of real and tangible personal property, both within and outside New York State, that is rented to the taxpayer is determined by multiplying the gross rents payable during the taxable year by eight.

• *Payroll percentage*

The payroll percentage is computed by dividing (1) the total wages, salaries and other personal service compensation paid or incurred during the taxable year to employees in connection with business carried on within New York State, by (2) the total of all wages, salaries and other personal service compensation paid or incurred during the taxable year to employees in connection with the business carried on both within and without New York State. (Reg. Sec. 132.15)

• *Gross income percentage*

The gross income percentage is computed by dividing (1) the gross sales or charges for services performed by or through an office, branch or agency of the business located within New York State, by (2) the total of all gross sales or charges for services performed within and without New York State. (Reg. Sec. 132.15) The sales or charges to be allocated to New York State include all sales negotiated or consummated, and charges for services performed, by an employee, agent, agency or independent contractor chiefly situated at, connected by contract or otherwise connected with, or sent out from, offices, branches of the business, or other agencies, situated within New York State.

• *Security and commodity brokers*

Special rules apply to the allocation of receipts of security and commodity brokers. (Reg. Sec. 132.21)

• *Source income formula for part-year residents*

For purposes of New York State, New York City, and Yonkers personal income tax, pursuant to *Matter of Greig*, New York Tax Appeals Tribunal, No. 815529, September 16, 1999, the amount of an individual's distributive or pro rata share of items of partnership income, gain, loss, and deduction to be included in New York source income is computed using the following formula, effective for tax years beginning in 1999 and thereafter and also applicable to any prior tax year for which the statute of limitations is still open (*Memorandum TSB-M-00(1)I*, New York Department of Taxation and Finance, February 23, 2000):

Step 1: Multiply the individual's distributive or pro rata share of income, gain, loss, and deduction for federal income tax purposes for the tax year by a fraction, the numerator of which is the number of days in the individual's tax year that the individual was a resident of New York State and the denominator of which is the total number of days in the individual's tax year.

Step 2: Multiply the individual's federal distributive or pro rata share of income, gain, loss, and deduction for federal income tax purposes for the tax year by a fraction, the numerator of which is the number of days in the individual's tax year that the individual was a nonresident of New York State and the denominator of which is the total number of days in the individual's tax year. This result is then multiplied by the partnership's New York allocation percentage for the year.

Step 3: Add the amounts computed in Step 1 and Step 2. This is the amount includable in New York source income. The same steps are used to determine the amount of the distributive or pro rata share of New York addition and subtraction modifications from the partnership to be included in New York source income. In addition, if an individual is a partner of more than one partnership, these steps must be repeated for each partnership.

¶16-515

Part-year New York State resident trusts: A part-year resident trust computes its New York State tax in the same manner as a part-year resident individual.

Part-year New York City residents.—A New York City part-year resident individual or trust is subject to New York City personal income tax for the period of residence and, if applicable, New York City nonresident earnings tax for the period of nonresidence. For a part-year resident, New York City personal income tax is computed based upon all income, gain, loss, and deduction for the period of residence, and the nonresident earnings tax, if applicable, is based upon wages or net earnings from self-employment derived from New York City sources for the period of nonresidence.

For New York City part-year resident individuals and trusts, Step 1 of the shareholder formula, using New York City days, is used to determine the amount of partnership income, gain, loss, and deduction subject to personal income tax for the resident period. Due to the partial repeal of the nonresident earnings tax on June 30, 1999, if a partnership has income from New York City sources, partnership income included in the nonresident earnings tax computation is determined using the formula set forth under the caption "Part-year New York City residents," in Memorandum TSB-M-99(6.1)I.

Part-year Yonkers residents.—A part-year Yonkers resident individual or trust is subject to the Yonkers income tax surcharge for the period of residence and, if applicable, the Yonkers nonresident earnings tax for the period of nonresidence. The Yonkers income tax surcharge is equal to the allocated net New York State tax multiplied by the Yonkers income tax surcharge rate (10% for 1999, 5% for 2000). The allocated net New York State tax for the resident period is equal to the net New York State tax for the entire year (the sum of all state taxes imposed by Article 22 of the Tax Law on the individual or trust, reduced by any allowable state credits) multiplied by a fraction. The numerator of the fraction is the individual's or trust's New York adjusted gross income for the period of residence. The denominator of the fraction is the individual's or trust's New York adjusted gross income for the entire year. The nonresident earnings tax, if applicable, is based upon wages or net earnings from self-employment derived from Yonkers sources for the period of nonresidence.

For part-year Yonkers resident individuals and trusts, Step 1 of the formula is used to determine the amount of partnership income, gain, loss, and deduction to be included in the numerator of the fraction used to compute the allocated net New York State taxes. If applicable, Step 2 of the partner/shareholder formula is used to determine the amount of net earnings from self-employment from a partnership subject to Yonkers nonresident earnings tax during the nonresident period, except that net earnings from self-employment and the Yonkers allocation percentage are used in the computation. In addition, in using Steps 1 and 2, Yonkers days are used instead of New York State days.

Minimum income tax.—New York State minimum personal income tax for a part-year resident is imposed on federal items of tax preference, with any New York modifications, for the period of residence and federal items of tax preference, with any New York modifications, that are derived from New York sources for the period of nonresidence. If a part-year resident individual or trust has federal items of tax preference from a partnership, the formula is used to determine the amount of tax preference items, and any New York modifications, reportable in the resident and nonresident periods.

New York City minimum personal income tax for a part-year resident is imposed on federal items of tax preference, and any New York City modifications, for the resident period only. Accordingly, only Step 1 of the formula is used to determine the amount of federal items of tax preference and modifications subject to New York City minimum income tax. In using Step 1, New York City days must be substituted for New York State days.

[¶16-530] Sourcing of Income from Intangibles

Income from intangible personal property, including annuities, dividends, interest and gains from the disposition of intangible personal property, constitute income derived from New York sources only to the extent that such income is from (1) property employed in a business, trade, profession or occupation carried on in New York or (2) winnings after September 30, 2000, from a wager placed in a lottery conducted by the Division of the Lottery if the proceeds from the wager exceed $5000. (Sec. 631(b)(2), Tax Law)

In addition, applicable to taxable years beginning on or after January 1, 2004, income from the disposition of intangible personal property constitutes income derived from New York sources to the extent that such gains are from the sale, conveyance, or other disposition of shares of stock in a cooperative housing corporation in connection with the grant or transfer of a proprietary leasehold by the owner, and subject to the provisions of Tax Law Article 31 (i.e., the New York real estate transfer tax), whether such shares are held by a partnership, trust, or otherwise. (Sec. 631(b)(2), Tax Law)

For further discussion, including provisions regarding stock options, stock appreciation rights, and restricted stock, see ¶16-505.

[¶16-545] Sourcing of Retirement Income

Sourcing in general is discussed at ¶16-505.

[¶16-555] Sourcing of Gains and Losses

Deductions with respect to capital losses, passive activity losses and net operating losses are based solely on items of income, gain, loss and deduction derived from or connected with New York sources, but otherwise are determined in the same manner as the corresponding resident deductions. (Sec. 631(b)(4), Tax Law)

For further discussion, see ¶16-505.

[¶16-565] Sourcing of Pass-Through Entity Income and Deductions

Provisions concerning pass-through entity income are discussed below.

• *Nonresident partners*

For a nonresident partner of any partnership, New York source income includes only the portion derived from or connected with New York sources of the partner's distributive share of items of partnership income, gain, loss or deduction entering into the partner's federal adjusted gross income. If a nonresident is a partner in a partnership where a sale or transfer of the membership interest of the partner is subject to the provisions of IRC § 1060, then any gain recognized on the sale or transfer for federal income tax purposes will be treated as New York source income allocated in a manner consistent with the applicable methods and rules for allocation in the year that the assets were sold or transferred. (Sec. 632(a), Tax Law)

In determining the New York sources of a nonresident partner's income, no effect will be given to a provision in the partnership agreement which (1) characterizes payments to the partner as being for services or for the use of capital, (2) allocates to the partner, as income or gain from sources outside New York, a greater proportion of the partner's distributive share of partnership income or gain from sources outside New York to partnership income or gain from all sources, except as specifically authorized by the Commissioner, or (3) allocates to the partner a greater proportion of a partnership item of loss or deduction connected with New York sources than his proportionate share, for federal income tax purposes, of partnership loss or deduction generally, except as authorized by the Commissioner. (Sec. 632(b), Tax Law)

The Commissioner may, on application, authorize the use of such other methods of determining a resident partner's portion of partnership items derived from or connected with New York sources, and the modifications related thereto, as may be appropriate and equitable, on such terms and conditions as it may require. (Sec. 632(c), Tax Law)

• *Sale of entity interest*

Generally, the gain or loss on the sale of a partnership interest in a New York partnership does not constitute gain or loss from New York sources and is not taxable to a nonresident. (TSB-M-92(2)I; *Loehr*, DTA No. 807015)

For additional information, see the discussion beginning on page 39 of the 2013 Nonresident Allocation Guidelines issued by the New York Department of Taxation and Finance.

However, a nonresident who employs a partnership interest as an asset in a New York trade or business will be subject to tax on the gain or loss from the sale of the interest.

In addition, under the 2009 and 2017 budget bills, gains from the sale of interests in certain partnerships and other entities are included in nonresidents' New York source income, to the extent attributable to ownership of New York real property. Specifically, the law was amended to provide that "real property located in this state" includes an interest in a partnership, LLC, S corporation, or non-publicly traded C corporation with 100 or fewer shareholders that owns real property located in New York or owns shares of stock in a cooperative housing corporation where the cooperative units relating to the shares are located in New York, provided that the sum of the fair market values of the real property, cooperative shares, and related cooperative units equals or exceeds 50% of all of the entity's assets on the date of the sale or exchange of the taxpayer's interest in the entity. (Sec. 631(b)(1)(A)(1), Tax Law)

Only those assets that the entity owned for at least two years before the date of the sale or exchange are to be used in determining the fair market value of all of the entity's assets on that date. The gain or loss derived from New York sources from the taxpayer's sale or exchange of an interest in such an entity is the total gain or loss for federal income tax purposes from that sale or exchange, multiplied by a fraction. The numerator of the fraction is the fair market value of the real property, and the cooperative housing corporation stock and related cooperative units, located in New York on the date of the sale or exchange, and the denominator is the fair market value of all of the entity's assets on that date.

For additional information, see TSB-M-09(5)I.

• *Source income formula for part-year residents—Partners*

For purposes of New York State, New York City, and Yonkers personal income tax, pursuant to *Matter of Greig*, New York Tax Appeals Tribunal, No. 815529, September 16, 1999, the amount of an individual's distributive or pro rata share of items of partnership income, gain, loss, and deduction to be included in New York source income is computed using the following formula, effective for tax years beginning in 1999 and thereafter and also applicable to any prior tax year for which the statute of limitations is still open (*Memorandum TSB-M-00(1)I*, New York Department of Taxation and Finance, February 23, 2000):

Step 1: Multiply the individual's distributive or pro rata share of income, gain, loss, and deduction for federal income tax purposes for the tax year by a fraction, the numerator of which is the number of days in the individual's tax year that the individual was a resident of New York State and the denominator of which is the total number of days in the individual's tax year.

Step 2: Multiply the individual's federal distributive or pro rata share of income, gain, loss, and deduction for federal income tax purposes for the tax year by a fraction, the numerator of which is the number of days in the individual's tax year that the individual was a nonresident of New York State and the denominator of which is the total number of days in the individual's tax year. This result is then multiplied by the partnership's New York allocation percentage for the year.

Step 3: Add the amounts computed in Step 1 and Step 2. This is the amount includable in New York source income. The same steps are used to determine the amount of the distributive or pro rata share of New York addition and subtraction modifications from the partnership to be included in New York source income. In addition, if an individual is a partner of more than one partnership, these steps must be repeated for each partnership.

Part-year New York State resident trusts.—A part-year resident trust computes its New York State tax in the same manner as a part-year resident individual.

Part-year New York City residents.—A New York City part-year resident individual or trust is subject to New York City personal income tax for the period of residence and, if applicable, New York City nonresident earnings tax for the period of nonresidence. For a part-year resident, New York City personal income tax is computed based upon all income, gain, loss, and deduction for the period of residence, and the nonresident earnings tax, if applicable, is based upon wages or net earnings from self-employment derived from New York City sources for the period of nonresidence.

For New York City part-year resident individuals and trusts, Step 1 of the shareholder formula, using New York City days, is used to determine the amount of partnership income, gain, loss, and deduction subject to personal income tax for the resident period. Due to the partial repeal of the nonresident earnings tax on June 30, 1999, if a partnership has income from New York City sources, partnership income included in the nonresident earnings tax computation is determined using the formula set forth under the caption "Part-year New York City residents," in Memorandum TSB-M-99(6.1)I.

Part-year Yonkers residents.—A part-year Yonkers resident individual or trust is subject to the Yonkers income tax surcharge for the period of residence and, if applicable, the Yonkers nonresident earnings tax for the period of nonresidence. The Yonkers income tax surcharge is equal to the allocated net New York State tax multiplied by the Yonkers income tax surcharge rate (10% for 1999, 5% for 2000). The allocated net New York State tax for the resident period is equal to the net New York State tax for the entire year (the sum of all state taxes imposed by Article 22 of the Tax Law on the individual or trust, reduced by any allowable state credits) multiplied by a fraction. The numerator of the fraction is the individual's or trust's New York adjusted gross income for the period of residence. The denominator of the fraction is the individual's or trust's New York adjusted gross income for the entire year. The nonresident earnings tax, if applicable, is based upon wages or net earnings from self-employment derived from Yonkers sources for the period of nonresidence.

For part-year Yonkers resident individuals and trusts, Step 1 of the formula is used to determine the amount of partnership income, gain, loss, and deduction to be included in the numerator of the fraction used to compute the allocated net New York State taxes. If applicable, Step 2 of the partner/shareholder formula is used to determine the amount of net earnings from self-employment from a partnership subject to Yonkers nonresident earnings tax during the nonresident period, except that net earnings from self-employment and the Yonkers allocation percentage are used in the computation. In addition, in using Steps 1 and 2, Yonkers days are used instead of New York State days.

Minimum income tax.—New York State minimum personal income tax for a part-year resident is imposed on federal items of tax preference, with any New York modifications, for the period of residence and federal items of tax preference, with any New York modifications, that are derived from New York sources for the period of nonresidence. If a part-year resident individual or trust has federal items of tax preference from a partnership, the formula is used to determine the amount of tax preference items, and any New York modifications, reportable in the resident and nonresident periods.

New York City minimum personal income tax for a part-year resident is imposed on federal items of tax preference, and any New York City modifications, for the resident period only. Accordingly, only Step 1 of the formula is used to determine the amount of federal items of tax preference and modifications subject to New York City minimum income tax. In using Step 1, New York City days must be substituted for New York State days.

• *S corporation shareholders—Tax years beginning after 2014*

The Department of Taxation and Finance has issued TSB-M-15(7)C, (6)I to explain how the state's corporate tax reform legislation affects the determination of New York source income for nonresident and part-year resident shareholders of New York S corporations. For tax years beginning on or after January 1, 2015, the business apportionment factor reflects a corporation's New York market-based receipts. To calculate amounts derived from New York sources, nonresident shareholders apply the S corporation's business apportionment factor to all New York S corporation items of income, gain, loss, and deduction (and any related Tax Law § 612 modifications) that are included in New York adjusted gross income. For part-year resident shareholders, the allocation applies only to the New York S corporation items received during the nonresident period (and any related § 612 modifications).

The memorandum emphasizes that, for tax years beginning on or after January 1, 2015, **all** New York S corporation items entering into a nonresident shareholder's federal adjusted gross income must be allocated to New York using the business apportionment factor, even if there are amounts that would have qualified as exempt investment income or other exempt income for a New York C corporation filer under Article 9-A. There is no statutory provision in Article 22 to exempt those amounts from personal income tax, or to modify federal adjusted gross income to remove those amounts. The memorandum provides an example to illustrate the application of these provisions. (Sec. 631, Tax Law; Sec. 632(a)(2), Tax Law; *TSB-M-15(7)C, (6)I*)

• *Source income formula for part-year residents—S corporation shareholders*

For purposes of New York State, New York City, and Yonkers personal income tax, pursuant to *Matter of Greig*, New York Tax Appeals Tribunal, No. 815529, September 16, 1999, the amount of an individual's distributive or pro rata share of items of New York S corporation income, gain, loss, and deduction to be included in New York source income is computed using the following formula, effective for tax years beginning in 1999 and thereafter and also applicable to any prior tax year for which the statute of limitations is still open (*Memorandum TSB-M-00(1)I*, New York Department of Taxation and Finance, February 23, 2000) (TSB-A-03(1)I):

Step 1: Multiply the individual's distributive or pro rata share of income, gain, loss, and deduction for federal income tax purposes for the tax year by a fraction, the numerator of which is the number of days in the individual's tax year that the individual was a resident of New York State and the denominator of which is the total number of days in the individual's tax year.

Step 2: Multiply the individual's federal distributive or pro rata share of income, gain, loss, and deduction for federal income tax purposes for the tax year by a fraction, the numerator of which is the number of days in the individual's tax year that the individual was a nonresident of New York State and the denominator of which is the total number of days in the individual's tax year. This result is then multiplied by the S corporation's New York allocation percentage for the year.

Step 3: Add the amounts computed in Step 1 and Step 2. This is the amount includable in New York source income. The same steps are used to determine the amount of the distributive or pro rata share of New York addition and subtraction modifications from the S corporation to be included in New York source income. In addition, if an individual is a shareholder of more than one New York S corporation, these steps must be repeated for each New York S corporation.

Part-year New York State resident trusts.—A part-year resident trust computes its New York State tax in the same manner as a part-year resident individual.

Part-year New York City residents.—A New York City part-year resident individual or trust is subject to New York City personal income tax for the period of residence and, if applicable, New York City nonresident earnings tax for the period of nonresidence. For a part-year resident, New York City personal income tax is computed based upon all income, gain, loss, and deduction for the period of residence, and the nonresident earnings tax, if applicable, is based upon wages or net earnings from self-employment derived from New York City sources for the period of nonresidence.

For New York City part-year resident individuals and trusts, Step 1 of the formula, using New York City days, is used to determine the amount of New York S corporation income, gain, loss, and deduction subject to personal income tax for the resident period.

Part-year Yonkers residents.—A part-year Yonkers resident individual or trust is subject to the Yonkers income tax surcharge for the period of residence and, if applicable, the Yonkers nonresident earnings tax for the period of nonresidence. The Yonkers income tax surcharge is equal to the allocated net New York State tax multiplied by the Yonkers income tax surcharge rate (10% for 1999, 5% for 2000). The allocated net New York State tax for the resident period is equal to the net New York State tax for the entire year (the sum of all state taxes imposed by Article 22 of Tax Law on the individual or trust, reduced by any allowable state credits) multiplied by a fraction. The numerator of the fraction is the individual's or trust's New York adjusted gross income for the period of residence. The denominator of the fraction is the individual's or trust's New York adjusted gross income for the entire year. The nonresident earnings tax, if applicable, is based upon wages or net earnings from self-employment derived from Yonkers sources for the period of nonresidence.

For part-year Yonkers resident individuals and trusts, Step 1 of the formula is used to determine the amount of New York S corporation income, gain, loss, and deduction to be included in the numerator of the fraction used to compute the allocated net New York State taxes. In addition, Yonkers days are used instead of New York State days.

Minimum income tax.—New York State minimum personal income tax for a part-year resident is imposed on federal items of tax preference, with any New York modifications, for the period of residence and federal items of tax preference, with any New York modifications, that are derived from New York sources for the period of nonresidence. If a part-year resident individual or trust has federal items of tax preference from a New York S corporation, the formula is used to determine the amount of tax preference items, and any New York modifications, reportable in the resident and nonresident periods.

New York City minimum personal income tax for a part-year resident is imposed on federal items of tax preference, and any New York City modifications, for the resident period only. Accordingly, only Step 1 of the formula is used to determine the amount of federal items of tax preference and modifications subject to New York City minimum income tax. In using Step 1, New York City days must be substituted for New York State days.

Shareholders of ineligible corporations.—An ineligible corporation is a federal S corporation that cannot make the New York S election because it is not subject to New York corporate franchise (income) tax. The shareholders of an ineligible corporation are treated for New York purposes as shareholders of a New York S corporation. Accordingly, a part-year resident individual or trust shareholder of an ineligible corporation also uses the partner/shareholder formula to prorate the amount of S corporation income, gain, loss, and deduction between the resident and nonresident periods. The amount prorated to the resident period is includable in New York source income. The amount prorated to the nonresident period should not be included in New York source income unless the stock of the S corporation is employed in another business carried on by the shareholder in New York State.

Shareholders of New York C corporations.—A New York C corporation is a federal S corporation that is eligible to make the New York S corporation election but does not make the election for the taxable year. A part-year resident shareholder of a New York C corporation does not have to make the prorations required of other S corporation shareholders.

- *Electing Nonresident Shareholders of S Corporations*

In determining the New York source income of an electing nonresident shareholder of an S corporation, there will be included only the portion of the shareholder's pro rata share of items of S corporation income, loss and deduction entering into his federal adjusted gross income, increased by reductions for taxes described in IRC Sec. 1366. (Sec. 632(a), Tax Law)

In *Matter of Reiner* (DTA No. 820266, July 13, 2006), an administrative law judge held that the Division of Taxation was estopped from applying the proration rule against S corporation shareholders who demonstrated their reliance on the former year-end rule.

- *S Corp shareholders—Installment obligations; IRC § 338(h)(10); installment sale contracts*

Note: The Court of Appeals found that the retroactive application of the installment obligation sourcing provision discussed below was permissible with respect to certain taxpayers; see *Caprio v. New York Department of Taxation and Finance*, July 1, 2015.

If a nonresident is a shareholder in an S corporation that has made the election to be a New York S corporation, and the S corporation has distributed an installment obligation under IRC § 453(h)(1)(A) to the shareholders, any gain recognized on the receipt of payments from the installment obligation for federal income tax purposes will be treated as New York source income. The amount of the gain to be included in

New York source income is determined using the applicable allocation percentage under the corporate franchise tax or bank franchise tax in effect for the year when the assets were sold. (Sec. 632(a)(2), Tax Law)

If a nonresident is a shareholder in an S corporation that has made the election to be a New York S corporation, and the S corporation has made an election under IRC § 338(h)(10), then any gain recognized on the deemed asset sale for federal income tax purposes will be treated as New York source income. The amount of the gain to be included in New York source income is determined using the applicable allocation percentage under the corporate franchise tax or bank franchise tax in effect for the year that the § 338(h)(10) election was made. (Sec. 632(a)(2), Tax Law)

In addition, when a nonresident shareholder exchanges his or her S corporation stock as part of the deemed liquidation, the law provides that any gain or loss recognized on the stock sale for federal income purposes will be treated as the disposition of an intangible asset for New York purposes and will not increase or offset any gain recognized on the deemed asset sale as a result of the § 338(h)(10) election. Therefore, the gain or loss from the deemed liquidation of S corporation stock is not included in New York source income. (Sec. 632(a)(2), Tax Law)

Generally, the above provisions apply to taxable years beginning on or after January 1, 2007. However, they will also apply to any other taxable years where the statute of limitations for issuing an assessment remains open because the taxpayer, for that year, did any of the following:

— failed to file a return;

— failed to report federal changes;

— filed a false or fraudulent return with the intent to evade tax; or

— substantially omitted income under Tax Law § 683(d).

In addition, the provision related to IRC § 453(h)(1)(A) applies to installment payments received in any tax year described above even if the payments are attributable to an installment obligation entered into prior to that year.

A taxpayer who is affected by these amendments for any prior year described above must file an amended return for any of the years affected if a return was previously filed for that year, or must file an original return if no return was filed for the prior year. Taxpayers amending returns or filing original returns will not be assessed penalties for any underpayment of tax attributable to these amendments. (TSB-M-10(10)I)

Installment sale contracts.—If a nonresident is a shareholder in an S corporation that has made the election to be a New York S corporation, and that S corporation terminates its taxable status in New York, any income or gain recognized on the receipt of payments from an installment sale contract entered into when the S corporation was subject to tax in New York will be treated as New York source income. The amount of the income or gain to be included in New York source income is determined using the applicable allocation percentage under the corporate franchise tax or bank franchise tax in effect for the year that the S corporation sold the assets that gave rise to the installment sale contract. This amendment is applicable to installment payments received in taxable years beginning on or after January 1, 2010, even if the payments are attributable to an installment sale contract entered into prior to 2010. (Sec. 631(b)(1)(E-1), Tax Law; TSB-M-10(10)I)

[¶ 16-570] Sourcing of Compensation for Personal Services

If a nonresident employee (including corporate officers but excluding salespeople whose compensation depends on the volume of business transacted) performs services for an employer both within and outside New York State, his or her income derived from New York sources includes that proportion of the total compensation for services rendered as an employee which the total of number of working days employed within New York State bears to the total number of working days employed within and outside New York State. (Reg. Sec. 132.18) The items of gain, loss and deduction of the employee attributable to his or her employment, derived from or connected with New York sources, are similarly determined. Any allowance claimed for days worked outside New York State must be based upon performance of services which, of necessity, as distinguished from convenience, obligate the employee to out-of-state duties in the service of the employer. In making the allocation, no account is taken of non-working days, including Saturdays, Sundays, holidays, days of absence because of illness or personal injury, vacation, or leave with or without pay.

Telecommuting employees and COVID-19. New York announced that for a nonresident whose primary office is in the state, days telecommuting during the pandemic are considered days worked in New York, unless the employer has established a bona fide employer office at the employee's telecommuting location. Generally, unless the employer specifically acted to establish a bona fide employer office at the telecommuting location, the nonresident employee will continue to owe New York income tax on income earned while telecommuting. (*Telecommuting FAQ,* October 19, 2020)

• *Revised application of "convenience" test*

The New York Department of Taxation and Finance has released a memorandum explaining its revised position concerning the application of the convenience of the employer test. The memorandum addresses situations in which an employee whose assigned or primary work location is in New York performs services for an employer at that location and at a home office located outside New York. (*TSB-M-06(5)I,* May 15, 2006)

For tax years beginning on or after January 1, 2006, in the case of a taxpayer whose assigned or primary office is in New York, any normal work day spent at the home office will be treated as a day worked outside New York if the taxpayer's home office is a bona fide employer office. A normal work day means any day when the taxpayer performs the usual duties of his or her job. For this purpose, responding to occasional phone calls or e-mails, reading professional journals, or being available if needed does not constitute performing the usual duties of his or her job. Any day spent at the home office that is not a normal work day will be considered a nonworking day.

Bonafide employer office.—Employees should use the factors set forth below to assist them in determining whether a home office constitutes a bona fide employer office. In order to be considered a bona fide employer office, the home office must either (1) meet the primary factor or (2) meet at least four of the secondary factors and three of the other factors.

Primary factor.—The home office contains or is near specialized facilities. If the employee's duties require the use of special facilities that cannot be made available at the employer's place of business, but those facilities are available at or near the employee's home, then the home office will meet this factor.

Secondary factors.—The secondary factors are as follows:

— the home office is a requirement or condition of employment;

— the employer has a bona fide business purpose for the employee's home office location;

— the employee performs some of the core duties of his or her employment at the home office;

— the employee meets or deals with clients, patients, or customers on a regular and continuous basis at the home office;

— the employer does not provide the employee with designated office space or other regular work accommodations at one of its regular places of business;

— the employer provides reimbursement for substantially all expenses related to the home office.

Other factors.—The other factors are as follows:

— the employer maintains a separate telephone line and listing for the home office;

— the employee's home office address and phone number are listed on the employer's business letterhead and/or business cards;

— the employee uses a specific area of the home, separate from the living area, exclusively to conduct the employer's business;

— the employer's business is selling products at wholesale or retail and the employee keeps an inventory of the products or product samples in the home office for use in the employer's business;

— business records of the employer are stored at the employee's home office;

— the home office location has a sign indicating a place of business of the employer;

— advertising for the employer shows the employee's home office as one of the employer's places of business;

— the home office is covered by a business insurance policy or by a business rider to the employee's homeowner insurance policy;

— the employee is entitled to and actually claims a deduction for home office expenses for federal income tax purposes;

— the employee is not an officer of the company.

The memorandum also discusses part-year resident individuals and the Yonkers nonresident earnings tax. (*TSB-M-06(5)I,* May 15, 2006)

• *Salespeople*

If the commission for sales made or other compensation for services performed by a nonresident traveling salesman, agent or other employee depends directly upon the volume of business which he transacts, his items of income, gain, loss and deduction derived from or connected with New York sources include that proportion of the net amount of such items attributable to such business which the volume of business which he transacts within New York State bears to the total volume of business which he transacts within and without New York State. (Reg. Sec. 132.17)

• *Telecommuting*

CCH COMMENT: *Sourcing of wages for telecommuting employees.*—As more employers utilize employees who telecommute from their homes in another state, either on a full-time or part-time basis, issues relating to which state may tax what portion of these employees' wages become more prevalent. Absent a compact between states regarding the sourcing of wages of each other's residents, the states use one of two tests to source wages of telecommuting employees: the physical presence test or the convenience/necessity test.

Under the physical presence test, employee income is allocated to the employee's location at the time the work was performed. For example, an employee who works from his home in State A two days a week, and from his employer's office in State B three days a week, would have 40% of his income sourced to State A and 60% of his income sourced to State B.

Under the convenience/necessity test, all employee income is allocated to the employer's location unless the employee is able to prove that she performed her work away from the employer's location due to employer necessity, rather than employee convenience.

Only four states (New York, New Jersey, Nebraska, and Pennsylvania) utilize the convenience/necessity test. (Reg. Sec. 132.17)

Note: As discussed above, the Department of Taxation and Finance has revised its application of the convenience of the employer test for tax years beginning on or after January 1, 2006. See also *TSB-M-06(5)I*, May 15, 2006.

[¶16-600]

WITHHOLDING

[¶16-605] Withholding Introduction

New York provides for the withholding of the New York personal income tax from wages of all resident employees for services performed either within or outside New York and from wages of nonresidents for services performed within the state. (Reg. Sec. 171.5; Reg. Sec. 171.6)

In general, the New York withholding provisions parallel the federal. The New York law specifically adopts the federal terms (such as "wages," "employer," "employee," "payroll period," and "withholding exemptions"). (Reg. Sec. 171.1)

Payments of withheld tax are credited against any tax liability. (Sec. 673, Tax Law)

Withholding tables and instructions issued by the state are discussed at ¶16-620. For an additional discussion of employer requirements concerning the reporting of New York state, New York City, and Yonkers wages beginning with tax year 2003, see TSB-M-02(3)I.

For a general discussion of New York City withholding, see ¶516-605. New York City Withholding tables are discussed at ¶516-610.

• *Supplemental wages*

The treatment of supplemental wages is set forth in Reg. Sec. 171.4(b). For New York City, see Reg. Sec. 291.1(b).

• *Reporting of newly hired employees*

Employers, as defined under Sec. 3401(d) of the Internal Revenue Code, are required to report the following information to the Department of Taxation and Finance regarding their newly hired employees who will be employed in the state:

Employee Name;

Employee Address;

Employee Social Security Number;

Employer Name;

Employer Address; and

Employer Identification Number. (Sec. 171-h, Tax Law)

Employers must report the above information within 20 calendar days from the hiring date. Beginning July 1, 2005, the hiring date is considered to be the first day on which compensated services are performed by the employee (i.e., the first day when any services are performed for which the employee will be paid wages or other compensation, or the first day when an employee working for commissions is eligible to earn commissions). Previously, an employee's "hiring date" could be any of the following: the day that the employee signed the Internal Revenue Service Form W-4, "Employee's Withholding Allowance Certificate;" the date the employee was appointed to a position; the first day of work; or the date of first payment for service, which was the latest acceptable date for reporting. (Sec. 171-h, Tax Law; TSB-M-05(3)I)

Employers who file by magnetic media must report the same information as above using bi-monthly submissions made 12 to 16 days apart. Employers who have employees working in more than one state and file by magnetic media need only designate one of the states to report any newly hired employees. (Sec. 171-h, Tax Law)

Previously issued guidance no longer current.—The Department previously issued TSB-M-98(3)I, which superseded, summarized, and supplemented Important Notices N-96-2, N-96-2-A and N-97-10. However, because of various refinements made to the new hire reporting program since 1998, the Department has advised that TSB-M-98(3)I is no longer current and should not be relied upon. (TSB-M-98(3.1)I)

• *Returns and remittances after the making of any payroll where cumulative aggregate amount of withholdings not paid over during calendar quarter is $700 or more*

Employers who were required to remit a cumulative aggregate amount of at least $15,000 in withholding tax during the calendar year preceding the previous calendar year must make a withholding tax return and remittance after any payroll as specified above within 3 business days of such payroll. If the cumulative aggregate withholding tax amount was less than $15,000 during the calendar year preceding the previous calendar year the withholding tax return and remittance must be made within 5 business days following such payroll. (Sec. 674(a)(1), Tax Law)

Educational organizations and health care providers are required to make the return and remittance within 5 business days following such payroll, without regard to the amount of cumulative aggregate withholding tax during the calendar year preceding the previous calendar year.

All employers described in ¶16-615 must file a quarterly combined withholding, wage reporting, and unemployment insurance return detailing the withholding tax transactions, wage reporting information, and (for calendar quarters beginning after 2018) withholding reconciliation information of the preceding calendar quarter (Form NYS-45, Quarterly Combined Withholding, Wage Reporting and Unemployment Insurance Return). (For calendar quarters beginning before 2019, the return covering the last calendar quarter was required to include an annual withholding reconciliation.) The quarterly combined return is due no later than the last day of the month following the last day of each calendar quarter. (Sec. 674(a)(4), Tax Law)

Employers previously required to file quarterly combined withholding and wage reporting returns and employers liable for unemployment insurance contributions, or for payments in lieu of such contributions, must file quarterly combined withholding, wage reporting, and unemployment insurance returns. The returns must be filed no later than the last day of the month following the last day of each calendar quarter. When filing a combined quarterly return, the employer must pay, in a single remittance, the unemployment insurance contributions and aggregate withholding taxes required to be paid over with the return. Any overpayment of unemployment insurance contributions or aggregate withholding taxes made by an employer with the quarterly combined return may be credited only against the employer's liability for such contributions or taxes, respectively. (Sec. 674(a)(4), Tax Law)

Seasonal employers.—An employer who, due to the seasonal nature of its business, does not make payment of wages that are subject to both federal and New York income tax withholding to any employee during a calendar quarter, is not required to file either Part A or Part B of the quarterly combined withholding and wage reporting return for the calendar quarter. However, such employers must, on or before the due date for filing the quarterly combined withholding and wage reporting return covering the last calendar quarter of the year, file the annual employee specific withholding reconciliation portion of Part B of the return. (Reg. Sec. 174.2)

If a seasonal employer discontinues business or permanently ceases to pay wages during the calendar year, the annual employee specific withholding reconciliation information must be furnished on the employer's final quarterly combined withholding and wage reporting return.

Electronic fund transfers.—Except as noted below, every taxpayer required to deduct and withhold $35,000 or more of tax for either of the semi-annual periods ending June 30 or December 31 must pay tax through electronic fund transfers (EFT) or certified checks. Where applicable, EFT transfers will serve as a substitute for the filing of a paper New York State employer's return of tax withheld (Form WT-1). Paper returns are required, however, for taxpayers that elect to pay over withheld tax by certified check. (Sec. 9(b), Tax Law; Reg. Sec. 2396.3; Reg. Sec. 2396.6; Reg. Sec. 2396.7)

For purposes of determining whether the $35,000 threshold has been met, New York State, New York City and City of Yonkers withholding taxes will be aggregated. (Reg. Sec. 2396.3) Taxpayers identified by separate federal or New York State employer identification numbers will be treated as separate withholding taxpayers.

> *EXAMPLE:* Corporation Y is a subsidiary of Corporation X. Both corporations possess their own federal employer identification numbers; neither possesses its own special New York State employer identification number. During each of the periods January 1 through June 30, 1991, and July 1 through December 31, 1991, Corporation X deducts and withholds $30,000 of New York State, City of New York and City of Yonkers taxes, and Corporation Y deducts and withholds $20,000 of such taxes during each of such periods. Neither Corporation X nor Corporation Y is required to participate in the Program.

> *EXAMPLE:* Corporation A has two branch offices, one located in New York State and one located in New Jersey. Each branch office prepares its own payroll. Corporation A possesses its own Federal employer identification number. In addition, Corporation A has obtained a New York State employer identification number covering its New York branch office and another New York State employer identification number covering its New Jersey branch office. The branch office in New York has deducted and withheld $25,000 of New York State, City of New York and City of Yonkers taxes during each of the periods January 1 through June 30, 1991, and July 1 through December 31, 1991. The branch office in New Jersey has deducted $20,000 of such taxes for each of the periods January 1 through June 30, 1991 and July 1 through December 31, 1991. Both branch offices of Corporation A are exempt.

Exemptions,—Taxpayers required to make electronic fund/certified check payments are generally exempt from such requirements if the aggregate tax withheld by the taxpayer under the most recent annual reconciliation of withholding required to be filed is less than $100,000, beginning with the July 1, 2002 program period. (Sec. 9(d), Tax Law; Reg. Sec. 2396.3)

Health care providers are exempt from electronic fund payment provisions unless an application is made for voluntarily participation in the program. Other taxpayers that do not meet the dollar thresholds noted above may also apply for participation on a voluntary basis. Applications for voluntary participation will be granted unless the Commissioner of Taxation and Finance determines that the administrative costs associated with accepting new enrollees outweigh the revenue and tax administration benefits associated with payment by EFT or certified check.

For special rules applicable to educational organizations, see Reg. Sec. 2396.9.

• *Returns and remittances on a quarterly basis (due one month after last day of calendar quarter)*

An employer who has deducted and withheld, but not paid over, a cumulative aggregate amount of less than $700 of withholding tax at the close of a calendar quarter must remit the tax with the quarterly combined withholding and wage reporting tax return as described above. (Sec. 674(a)(2), Tax Law) Effective January 1, 1999, this provision is amended to reflect the new requirement that employers file quarterly combined withholding, wage reporting, and unemployment insurance returns.

Employers making more than one payroll per week.—In determining the applicability of the above filing and payment provisions, employers making more than one payroll per week generally must consider the last payroll made within the week. (Sec. 674(a)(3), Tax Law) However, if the end of the calendar quarter occurs between the making of payrolls, any tax required to be deducted and withheld in those payrolls prior to the end of the quarter must be paid over with the quarterly combined return (if the criteria for returns and remittances on a quarterly basis are met) or on or before the 3rd or 5th business day following the date of the last payroll in the quarter (depending upon the amount of the employer's required cumulative aggregate withholding during the calendar year preceding the previous calendar year—see above).

[¶16-615] Withholding on Wages

Every employer maintaining an office or transacting business within New York and making payment of any taxable wages to a resident or nonresident individual must deduct and withhold from such wages for each payroll period a tax computed in such a manner as to result, as far as practicable, in withholding from the employee's wages during each calendar year an amount substantially equivalent to the personal income tax reasonably estimated to be due resulting from the inclusion in the employee's adjusted gross income or New York source income of his wages received during each calendar year. (Sec. 671(a)(1), Tax Law)

The Commissioner may provide, by regulation, for withholding from the following sources: (1) remuneration for services performed by an employee for his employer which does not constitute wages; or (2) any other type of payment, with respect to which the Commissioner finds that withholding would be appropriate if the person making and the person receiving the payment agree to the withholding. (Sec. 671(a)(2), Tax Law)

See Reg. Sec. 171.4 for withholding provisions on supplemental wages and vacation allowances.

The Commissioner is required to provide, by regulation, for an exemption from withholding for: (1) employees under 18 years of age; (2) employees under 25 years of age who are full-time students; and (3) employees over 65 years of age, provided such employees had no income tax liability in the prior year and can reasonably anticipate none in the current year. (Sec. 671(a)(3), Tax Law)

> **CCH CAUTION:** For New York state withholding tax purposes, the provisions of the Internal Revenue Code and applicable regulations regarding the deducting and withholding of federal income tax by employers from wages generally apply. (Reg. Sec. 171.1)

• *Same-sex married employees*

As of September 2013, the department has advised that employers and same-sex married employees should follow the general withholding tax rules for married employees. (Notice, New York Department of Taxation and Finance, September 2013)

For additional information concerning the personal income tax treatment of same-sex married couples, see ¶ 15-125.

Prior to September 13, 2013, the department had issued the information set forth below.

Information applicable prior to September 2013.—Following the enactment of New York's Marriage Equality Act, the Department of Taxation and Finance provided the following instructions to employers (Notice, New York Department of Taxation and Finance, February 2012):

— Do not withhold New York tax on certain benefits provided to a same-sex married employee. You do not need to withhold tax for New York State, New York City, or Yonkers income tax purposes on the value of certain benefits (e.g. health benefits that are treated as domestic partner health benefits for federal tax purposes), even though it is subject to federal withholding. This applies if the employee's federal taxable wages subject to withholding include the value of the benefits, and the value of these benefits would not be included in taxable wages if provided to a different-sex married spouse.

— When reporting the annual wage totals on Form NYS-45, *Quarterly Combined Withholding, Wage Reporting, and Unemployment Insurance Return*, Part C, column d, report the federal wages minus any amount of benefits discussed above that you do not withhold on for New York purposes (plus any amount of any taxable 414(h) retirement contributions and any IRC § 125 amounts from a New York City flexible benefits program for governmental employees).

— Continue to use the rules described in NYS-50, *Employer's Guide to Unemployment Insurance, Wage Reporting, and Withholding Tax,* for reporting State and local wages on federal Form W-2, *Wage and Tax Statement.*

In addition, the Department provided the following guidance to same-sex married employees (Notice, New York Department of Taxation and Finance, February 2012):

— You may want to file a new Form IT-2104, *Employee's Withholding Allowances Certificate*, with your employer because you will file a New York return using a married status beginning in tax year 2011.

— Provide proof that you are legally married to have your employer stop withholding New York tax on the value of certain benefits (e.g. health benefits that are treated as domestic partner health benefits for federal tax purposes). This applies if your federal taxable wages subject to withholding include the value of the benefits, and the value of these benefits would not be included in taxable wages if provided to a different-sex married spouse.

• *Nonresident employees*

Generally, an employer must deduct the New York income tax on all wages paid to a nonresident employee for services performed in New York. (Reg. Sec. 171.6; Publication NYS-50) Wages paid to a nonresident employee for services rendered entirely outside New York are not subject to withholding. If the services of a nonresident employee are performed entirely in New York, the employer must deduct and withhold New York personal income tax from all wages paid to the employee.

If a nonresident employee performs services partly within and partly outside New York, the employee should file Form IT-2104.1, Certificate of Nonresidence and Allocation of Withholding Tax, showing the employee's estimate of the percentage of services to be performed in New York State, and therefore subject to withholding. An employer is required to withhold tax from all wages paid to a nonresident employee who works partly within and partly outside New York unless the employee files Form IT-2104.1, or unless the employer keeps adequate current records to determine the amount of wages from New York sources.

However, the mere filing of Form IT-2104.1 does not relieve the employer from the duty to withhold the proper amount of New York personal income tax from wages paid to an employee. Form IT-2104.1 must be retained by the employer and must be available for inspection. (Reg. Sec. 171.6(b)(5))

Wages allocable to New York.—The amount of wages allocable to New York is generally based on the proportion of days worked in New York compared to the total number of days worked both in and out of New York, exclusive of nonworking days (i.e., Saturdays, Sundays, holidays, and days of absence because of illness, personal injury, vacation or leave with or without pay). However, for traveling salespeople and other employees whose compensation depends entirely on the volume of business transacted by them, the amount allocable to New York is based on the volume of business transacted in New York compared to the total volume of business transacted both in and out of New York. (Reg. Sec. 171.6(b)(2); Publication NYS-50)

Based on preceding year.—The portion of wages allocable to New York may be determined by the employer on the basis of the preceding year's experience, except that the employer must make any necessary adjustments during the year to insure that the required New York personal income tax is withheld for the current year. (Reg. Sec. 171.6(b)(3); Publication NYS-50)

If the employee reasonably expects that the preceding year's experience will not be applicable to the current year, he or she may furnish a certificate on Form IT-2104.1 estimating the proportion of wages allocable to New York, or the employer may make such an estimate and withhold on that basis; in either case, the employer is required to make the necessary adjustments during the year so that the proper amount of New York personal income tax is withheld from the employee's salary for the current year. (Reg. Sec. 171.6(b)(3); Publication NYS-50)

14-day rule.—An employer will not be penalized for failing to withhold New York state tax on wages paid to a nonresident employee who performs services both within and outside of New York if all of the following conditions are met (TSB-M-12(5)I):

    — the employee is assigned to a primary work location outside of New York state;

    — the employer reasonably expects that the employee will work in New York state for 14 days or fewer in the calendar year;

— the employee does not work in New York state for more than 14 days (see "Special rules" below); and

— the employee's compensation does not fall under the list of exceptions below.

If the employer reasonably expects that an employee will be required to work in New York state for more than 14 days in the calendar year, then the 14-day rule cannot be applied and the employer must withhold on all New York state wages paid to that employee. (TSB-M-12(5)I)

When applying the 14-day rule, any part of a day spent working in New York counts as a full day. However, an employer should not count any day spent in New York state for the sole purpose of job-related training, such as in-house training courses, trade association conferences or symposia, or professional development workshops, seminars, or conventions. (TSB-M-12(5)I)

Special rules: If a nonresident employee was not initially expected to work more than 14 days in New York state during the calendar year, but does in fact work more than 14 days in New York, the employer is required to withhold on all New York state wages paid after the 14th day. (TSB-M-12(5)I)

If, during the calendar year, a nonresident employee is reassigned to a primary work location in New York state or to a different position that will result in the employee working more than 14 days in New York state, the employer is required to withhold on New York state wages paid on and after the date of the change. (TSB-M-12(5)I)

Exceptions to the 14-day rule: The 14-day rule does not apply to the following types of compensation (TSB-M-12(5)I):

— compensation paid to nonresident traveling salespersons or other employees when the compensation depends entirely on the volume of business transacted by them;

— compensation paid in one year that is related to services performed in a prior year (for example, deferred compensation and compensation from nonstatutory stock options);

— compensation paid to nonresident public speakers performing services in New York state (this includes, but is not limited to, services in the form of a speech, presentation, or personal appearance);

— compensation paid to nonresident athletes performing services in New York state (this includes, but is not limited to, wrestlers, boxers, golfers, hockey players, basketball players, football players, tennis players, baseball players, and other athletes, as well as referees, coaches, and trainers);

— compensation paid to nonresident entertainers performing services in New York state (this includes, but is not limited to, actors, singers, musicians, dancers, circus performers, writers, directors, producers, set designers, any other person appearing on television, radio, the stage, in a night club performance or hotel show, and compensation to any person whose performance in New York state is recorded or filmed).

Information is available in the Department of Taxation and Finance's April 5, 2005 Withholding Tax Field Audit Guidelines, which provide additional details regarding the 14-day rule, including numerous illustrative examples (see pages 14 through 26 of the Guidelines).

For the Multistate Tax Commission's uniformity project concerning mobile workforce withholding, see http://www.mtc.gov/Uniformity.aspx?id=4622.

Personal exemption threshold.—Where a nonresident employee will work only a short period of time within New York and it is reasonably expected that the total wages of the employee for services rendered within New York will not exceed the amount of the employee's personal exemptions, the employer need not withhold or deduct any amount of New York personal income tax from the employee's wages until the aggregate amount paid exceeds the amount of the employee's personal exemptions. (Reg. Sec. 171.6(b)(4))

• *Existence of employer-employee relationship*

The issue of whether an employer is required to withhold and pay over tax is dependent upon whether an employer-employee relationship exists. Although the existence of such a relationship is dependent upon the applicable facts, the Internal Revenue Service has developed a list of 20 factors as an aid in determining such a relationship. (Rev. Rul. 87-41) These factors include:

1. *Instructions.* If the individual is required to comply with instructions about when, where and how the work is to be performed, it indicates that he or she is an employee.

2. *Training.* If a worker is trained by being required to work with an experienced employee, to work with others, to attend meetings or to use specified work methods, this indicates an employment relationship.

3. *Integration.* Integration of the worker's services into the business operation generally shows that the worker is subject to direction and control.

4. *Rendering Services Personally.* If the services must be rendered personally, it indicates the existence of an employment relationship.

5. *Hiring, Supervising and Paying Assistants.* If the person for whom the service is performed hires, supervises and pays assistants, such action shows control over the workers on the job.

6. *A Continuing Relationship.* A continuing relationship performed at frequently recurring though irregular intervals is indicative of an employment relationship.

7. *Set Hours of Work.* The establishment of set hours of work by the person(s) for whom the services are performed is a factor indicating control.

8. *Full Time Required.* If the worker must devote substantially full time to the business, control exists over the amount of time the worker spends working and is indicative of an employment relationship.

9. *Doing Work on Employer's Premises.* The fact that the work is performed on the premises of the person(s) for whom the services are performed suggests control over the worker, especially if the work could be done elsewhere.

10. *Setting Order or Sequence.* If the services must be performed in an order or sequence set by the person(s) for whom the services are being performed, it shows that the worker is not free to follow his or her own pattern of work.

11. *Oral or Written Reports.* The requirement that the worker submit regular oral or written reports indicates control by the person(s) for whom the services are being performed.

12. *Payment at Regular Intervals.* Payment by the hour, week or month indicates an employment relationship, provided that it is not simply a way to pay a lump sum set forth in an agreement.

¶16-615

13. *Payment of Business and/or Travel Expenses.* Payment of the worker's business and/or traveling expenses by the person(s) for whom the services are being performed indicates an employment relationship.

14. *Furnishing Tools and Material.* The fact that the person(s) for whom the services are being performed furnishes tools, materials and other equipment tends to show the existence of an employer-employee relationship.

15. *Significant Investment.* Investment by the worker in significant facilities used in performing services and not typically maintained by employees tends to indicate that the worker is an independent contractor.

16. *Realization of Profit or Loss.* A worker who can realize a profit or suffer a loss as a result of services provided (in addition to the profit or loss ordinarily realized by an employee) is generally an independent contractor.

17. *Working for More Than One Firm at a Time.* If a worker performs more than de minimus services for a number of unrelated firms or persons at the same time, it generally indicates that the worker is an independent contractor.

18. *Making Service Available to the General Public.* The fact that a worker makes his or her services available to the general public on a regular basis indicates an independent contractor relationship.

19. *Right to Discharge.* The right to discharge a worker indicates that the worker is an employee.

20. *Right to Terminate.* An employer-employee relationship is indicated if a worker has the right to end the relationship at any time he or she wishes without incurring liability.

• *Interstate carriers*

Compensation paid by a rail, rail-water, express, pipeline, motor carrier or private motor carrier to an employee who regularly provides duties in more than one state is subject to the income tax laws of the state (or subdivision of the state) that is the employee's residence. (49 U.S.C. 11504(a) and (b))

• *Resident employees of employer required to withhold other state or local income taxes*

An employer required to deduct and withhold income taxes of other states or their political subdivisions or of the District of Columbia from wages paid to a New York resident is required to deduct and withhold from those wages the amount of New York income tax determined according to withholding tables or other method provided by regulation *less* the amount required to be deducted and withheld for the other jurisdiction. (Reg. Sec. 171.5)

• *Cancellation of employment*

Amounts an employer pays to an employee for cancellation of an employment contract and relinquishment of contract rights are wages subject to income tax withholding. Employers who maintain an office or transact business in New York State who make these types of payments subject to New York State, New York City, or Yonkers income tax withholding must withhold the tax and comply with New York State withholding requirements for employers. (TSB-M-10(9)I)

• *Third parties' liability under withholding provisions*

If a fiduciary, agent, or other person has the control, receipt, custody, or disposal of, or pays the wages of, an employee or group of employees, the Commissioner is authorized to designate the fiduciary, agent, or other person to perform such acts as are required of employers under the personal income tax law. (Sec. 677, Tax Law)

In addition, if a lender, surety or other person, who is not an employer with respect to an employee or group of employees, pays wages directly to the employee or group of employees, or to an agent on behalf of the employee or employees, the lender, surety or other person will be liable for the amount of taxes (plus interest) required to be deducted and withheld from such wages by the employer. (Sec. 678(a), Tax Law) Further, if a lender, surety or other person supplies funds to or for the account of an employer for the specific purpose of paying wages of its employees, with actual notice or knowledge that the employer does not intend to or will not be able to make timely payment or deposit of the amounts of tax required by the personal income tax law to be deducted and withheld by the employer from such wages, the lender, surety or other person will be liable for the amount of the taxes (plus interest) which are not paid over by the employer with respect to such wages. (Sec. 678(b), Tax Law)

Any amounts paid under the provision relating to lenders, sureties or other persons paying wages directly to employees will be credited against the liability of the employer. (Sec. 678(c), Tax Law)

• *Information statement for employee*

Every employer required to deduct and withhold personal income tax from the wages of an employee, or who would have been required to deduct and withhold tax if the employee had claimed no more than one withholding exemption, must furnish to each employee, in respect of the wages paid by the employer to the employee during the calendar year, a written statement showing the amount of wages paid by the employer to the employee, the amount deducted and withheld as tax, and such other information as the Commissioner may prescribe. (Sec. 672, Tax Law) The statement must be filed on or before February 15 of the succeeding year. If the employee's employment is terminated before the close of the calendar year, the statement must be furnished to the employee within 30 days from the date on which the last payment of wages is made.

[¶16-620] Withholding Tables and Schedules

Form NYS-50, Employer's Guide to Unemployment Insurance, Wage Reporting, and Withholding Tax, provides information on the following:

— employer rights, responsibilities, and filing requirements;

— New York unemployment insurance;

— New York wage reporting;

— state, New York City, and Yonkers income tax withholding; and

— reporting new or rehired employees.

The Department has issued NYS-50-T-NYS containing the state withholding tax tables and methods.

New York City withholding tables and methods are discussed at ¶516-610

The City of Yonkers withholding tables and methods are discussed at ¶35-151 (personal income tax surcharge on residents) and at ¶35-201 (earnings tax on nonresidents).

[¶16-655] Withholding at Source from Nonwage Income

For purposes of withholding, the following payments are treated as if they were payments of wages by an employer to an employee:

¶16-620

(1) Any supplemental unemployment compensation benefit paid to an individual to the extent includible in the individual's New York adjusted gross income or New York source income;

(2) Any member or employee contributions to a retirement system or pension fund picked up by the employer pursuant to the state Retirement and Social Security Law, Education Law or the Administrative Code of the City of New York;

(3) Any payment of an annuity to an individual to the extent includible in the individual's New York adjusted gross income or New York source income, if at the time the payment is made a request that the annuity be subject to withholding is in effect;

(4) Any payment of winnings from a wager placed in a lottery conducted by the Division of the Lottery, if the proceeds from the wager exceed $5,000. For prizes won before October 1, 2000, this provision applies only if the proceeds are payable pursuant to a prize claim made by an individual who was a New York State resident at the time of the selection of the prize winning lottery ticket;

(5) (for taxable years beginning on or after January 1, 2019—see TSB-M-19(4)I) Any gambling winnings from a wagering transaction within New York, if the proceeds are subject to withholding under IRC Sec. 3402;

(6) Any amount deducted or deferred from an employee's salary under a flexible benefits program established under Sec. 23, General Municipal Law, or Sec. 1210-a, Public Authorities Law, (see ¶ 16-065); and

(7) The amount by which an employee's salary is reduced for health insurance and welfare benefits pursuant to Sec. 12-126.1(d), New York City Administrative Code. (Sec. 671(b), Tax Law)

In addition, amounts that an employer pays to an employee for cancellation of an employment contract and relinquishment of contract rights are wages subject to income tax withholding. (TSB-M-10(9)I)

[¶16-660] Withholding Exemptions

The number of New York withholding exemptions which an employee receiving taxable wages may claim may not exceed the number of New York exemptions to which the employee is entitled, whether the employee is a resident or nonresident, and such additional New York withholding exemptions as may be prescribed by regulations or instructions of the Commissioner of Taxation and Finance, taking into account the applicable standard deduction and such other factors as he finds appropriate. (Sec. 671(c), Tax Law) The amount of each New York withholding exemption is the amount of New York exemption to which the employee is entitled, whether the individual is a resident or a nonresident.

Wages due or accruing to a master or seaman on a vessel in the foreign, coastwise, intercoastal, interstate or noncontiguous trade or an individual employed on a fishing vessel or any fish processing vessel may not be withheld under the tax laws of a state or a political subdivision of a state. (46 U.S.C. Sec. 11108) However, the withholding of wages of a seaman on a vessel in the coastwise trade between ports in the same state is not prohibited if the withholding is under a voluntary agreement between the seaman and the employer of the seaman.

[¶16-800]
CREDITS

[¶16-805] Credits Against Tax

The following credits are allowed against the New York personal income tax:

— Agricultural property tax credit;
— Alcoholic beverage production credit;
— Automated external defibrillator credit;
— Biofuel production credit;
— Brownfield credits;
— Central Business District Toll Credit;
— Child and dependent care expenses;
— Clean heating fuel credit;
— College tuition credit;
— Conservation easement tax credit;
— Contributions to charitable funds;
— Earned income credit;
— Economic Transformation and Facility Redevelopment Program;
— Emerging technology credits;
— Empire state child credit;
— Empire state commercial production credit;
— Empire state film production credit;
— Empire state jobs retention program;
— Empire zones;
— Employee training incentive program (E-TIP) credit;
— Employer compensation expense tax credit;
— Employer-provided child care credit;
— Employing qualified disabled persons;
— Excelsior Jobs Program;
— Excess deductions credit;
— Family tax relief credit;
— Farm workforce retention credit;
— Fuel cell electric generating equipment credit;
— Green buildings credit;
— Handicapped accessible vehicles credit;
— Historic barn renovation credit;
— Historic property rehabilitation credit;
— Home heating system credit;
— Household credit;
— Income taxes paid by residents to other states or a province of Canada;

Personal Income

189

— Investment in alternative-fuel vehicle property;

— Investment tax credit;

— Long-term care insurance credit;

— Low-income housing;

— New York Youth Jobs Program;

— Nursing home assessment credit;

— Property tax relief credit;

— Real estate circuit breaker credit for resident individuals;

— Recovery tax credit;

— Research and development tax credit;

— Residential fuel oil storage tank credit;

— School district property tax credit;

— Security training tax credit;

— Separate tax on lump sum distributions for taxes paid by residents to other states or a province of Canad;

— Shareholders of S corporations;

— Solar energy;

— Special additional mortgage recording tax;

— STAR credit;

— START-UP NY;

— Trust beneficiaries receiving accumulation distributions; and

— Volunteer firefighters and ambulance workers credit.

In addition, a credit against tax is allowed for amounts of taxes withheld from wages. (Sec. 673, Tax Law)

Credit is also allowed for estimated tax payments made for the taxable year, any amount of overpayment from the prior year that was applied to estimated tax, and any amount paid with an extension application. (Instructions, Form IT-201)

Credits may be claimed on Form IT-201, Resident Income Tax Return.

New York City: New York City credits are discussed at ¶516-405.

Disregarded SMLLCs.—The law has been amended to clarify that a single member limited liability company (SMLLC) that is disregarded as an entity separate from its single member or owner for federal income tax purposes must be treated as a disregarded SMLLC for purposes of determining whether its owner is eligible to claim any New York tax credit allowed under Article 9, 9-A, 22, 32 (prior to its repeal) or 33 of the Tax Law. (Sec. 43, Tax Law)

¶16-805

PROPERTY

[¶20-100]

TAXABILITY OF PROPERTY AND PERSONS

[¶20-105] Classification of Property

Property is generally characterized in the same broad categories by most states, although the states differ in which of these categories they choose to tax. New York does not require taxing jurisdictions to classify property except in New York City and Nassau County, as discussed below. However, jurisdictions that have undertaken a general revaluation of property may classify property as homestead or nonhomestead property and tax the classes at different rates to maintain the relative share of the tax burden at levels that preceded the revaluation. (Sec. 1903, Real Property Tax Law)

• *Classification in New York*

Homestead class.—The "homestead class" consists of the following real properties: (Sec. 1901, Real Property Tax Law)

• all one-, two- or three-family dwelling residential property, including dwellings used primarily for residential purposes but also used, in part, for nonresidential purposes;

• residential real property of more than three dwelling units used as condominiums, provided they have not previously been assessed as dwellings other than condominiums;

• all vacant land parcels located in assessing units which have zoning laws or ordinances in effect, provided that the parcel does not exceed 10 acres and is located in a zone that only permits specific residential use; and

• eligible land used for agricultural production (see ¶20-115 Agriculture), including farm buildings and structures essential to the operation of agricultural or horticultural lands.

For a discussion of homesteads, see ¶20-205.

Nonhomestead class.—The nonhomestead class consists of all real property not included in the homestead class.

Real or personal property.—An area of ambiguity in classifying property as real or personal is determining whether an item is permanently affixed to the land. Calling the property a "fixture" is not helpful, as a fixture could be either real or personal property. The importance of the distinction derives from differences in the tax rates. (see ¶20-405 Rates of Tax) Items commonly questioned include machines, equipment, towers, tanks, antennas, and silos. The common law provides the following three-prong test to classify this type of property:

• actual annexation (the manner in which an item is affixed to realty);

• appropriation or adaptation (the manner in which the item is used); and

• intention (whether the property is intended to be permanently or temporarily affixed to the realty).

Real property is taxed in all the states, although frequently the tax is imposed by local jurisdictions, rather than by the state, as is the case in New York. Personal property is taxed in a number of states, but not in New York (see ¶20-295 Personal Property).

Intangible personal property.—Intangible personal property, not taxed in New York, is property that has no value in itself, but rather represents value. Items classified as intangibles include stocks, bonds, patents, royalties, and goodwill (see ¶ 20-230 Intangible Property).

• *Classification of property in Nassau County and New York City*

Assessing units with a population of 1 million or more (New York City and Nassau County) must classify property as follows: (Sec. 1802(1), Real Property Tax Law)

Class one property.—Class 1 property consists of:

• all one-, two- and three-family residential real property, other than property held in cooperative or condominium form of ownership, with the exception of condominiums of no more than three dwellings units that were included in Class 1 on a previous assessment roll and bungalow colonies in existence prior to 1940 located on land held in cooperative ownership for the sole purpose of maintaining one-family residences for its members own use;

• residential condominiums of no more than three stories in height, no dwelling unit of which was previously on an assessment roll as a dwelling unit in other than condominium form of ownership;

• mobile homes or trailers that are owner-occupied and separately assessed;

• vacant land other than land in the borough of Manhattan south of or adjacent to the south side of 110th St., provided the land is zoned residential, or is immediately adjacent to property improved with a residential structure and has been owned by the same owner as the adjacent residential property since January 1, 1989, and has a total area of 10,000 square feet or less; and

• vacant land located within a special assessing unit that is not a city, provided that the vacant land that is not zoned residential must be situated immediately adjacent to real property as defined above and be owned by the same person who owns the real property immediately prior to and since January 1, 2003.

Class two property.—Class 2 property consists of all residential real property that is not designated as Class 1, except hotels and motels and other commercial properties. Class 3 consists of utility real property. Class 4 consists of all property not classified as Class 1, 2, or 3.

[¶20-115] Agriculture

Land used in agricultural production may be assessed at its agricultural value upon application of the owner, provided the land meets the following requirements:

(1) the land is located within an agricultural district; (Sec. 305, Agriculture and Markets Law) or

(2) the owner commits the land exclusively to agricultural uses for a period of eight years (the owner may withhold any portion of a parcel from agricultural commitment, in which case only the portion for which a commitment is filed is exempt). (Sec. 306, Agriculture and Markets Law)

(Sec. 481, Real Property Tax Law)

Applications for agricultural assessment must be filed annually with the local assessor before the tax status date. (Sec. 481, Real Property Tax Law) A landowner will be required to certify that the landowner continues to meet the eligibility requirements for receiving an agricultural assessment for the same acreage that initially received an agricultural assessment by filing a form prescribed by the Tax Commissioner. (Sec. 305, Agriculture and Markets Law)

The landowner must maintain records documenting the property's eligibility and is required to apply for agricultural assessment for any change in acreage, regardless of whether land is added or removed, after the initial grant of agricultural assessment. A new owner of the land who wishes to receive an agricultural assessment must make an initial application for the assessment. (Sec. 305, Agriculture and Markets Law)

If the land is eligible for agricultural assessment, the portion of the value of the land in excess of its agricultural assessment value is exempt. (Sec. 305, Agriculture and Markets Law) The State Board of Equalization and Assessment determines agricultural assessment values, based on soil productivity and capability. (Sec. 304-a, Agriculture and Markets Law)

Farm operation.—The definition of "farm operation" means the land and on-farm buildings, equipment, manure processing and handling facilities, and practices which contribute to the production, preparation and marketing of crops, livestock and livestock products as a commercial enterprise, including a commercial horse boarding operation and timber processing. It also includes the production, management and harvesting of farm woodland. (Sec. 301(11), Agriculture and Markets Law)

A farm operation also includes a commercial equine operation, which means an agricultural enterprise consisting of at least seven acres and stabling at least 10 horses, regardless of ownership, that receives $10,000 or more in annual gross receipts from fees generated through the provision of commercial equine activities. Those activities include, but are not limited to: riding lessons; trail-riding activities; the training of horses; the production for sale of crops, livestock, and livestock products or both the provision of such commercial equine activities and such production. A commercial equine operation does not include operations whose primary on-site function is horse racing. (Sec. 301(11) and (17), Agriculture and Markets Law)

Corn, hay bale mazes.—A farm operation includes land that is used for agricultural amusements that are produced from crops grown or produced on the farm. The crops must be harvested and marketed in the same manner as other crops produced on a qualifying farm. Agricultural amusements include, but are not limited to, corn mazes and hay bale mazes. (Sec. 301(4)(c), Agriculture and Markets Law)

New farms.—The definition of "land used in agricultural production" includes land of at least seven acres used as a single operation for the production for sale of orchard or vineyard crops, provided that the land is used solely for the purpose of planting a new orchard or vineyard. In addition, the land must be owned or rented by a newly established farm operation in its first, second, third, or fourth year of agricultural production. Further, "land used in agricultural production" includes land of not less than seven acres used as a single operation for the production for sale of hops when such land is used solely for the purpose of planting a new hopyard, and when such land is also owned or rented by a newly established farm operation in the first, second, third or fourth year of agricultural production. (Sec. 301(4)(i), Agriculture and Markets Law)

• *Commercial horse boarding operations*

Land used in agricultural production includes land used to support a commercial horse boarding operation. (Sec. 301(4), Agriculture and Markets Law) "Commercial horse boarding operation" means an agricultural enterprise that boards at least 10 horses and that receives at least $10,000 in gross receipts annually from fees generated either through the boarding of horses or through the production for sale of crops, livestock, and live stock products or through both activities. (Sec. 301(13), Agriculture and Markets Law) See also "Improvements," below.

Creation of agricultural districts.—Agricultural districts are created in two ways. The owners of land may submit a proposal for the creation of an agricultural district, provided the total amount of their land comprises at least 500 acres or at least 10% of the land proposed to be included within the agricultural district. Proposals are made to the county legislative body, which refers them to the county planning board and the agricultural districting advisory committee for hearings, examination and reporting. The proposal must then be certified by the State Commissioner of Agriculture and Markets. The proposed district becomes effective 30 days after certification, or if the county legislative body conducts a public hearing following certification, 30 days after the hearing. (Sec. 303, Agriculture and Markets Law)

In addition, the Commissioner of Environmental Conservation may create agricultural districts not districted as a result of a landowner proposal if the proposed area is of at least 2,000 acres and:

- the land within the district is predominantly unique and irreplaceable agricultural land;

- the Commissioner of Environmental Conservation has determined that the district would further state environmental plans, policies, and objectives;

- the Secretary of State has determined that the proposed district would be consistent with state comprehensive plans, policies and objectives; and

- the Director of the Division of the Budget has given approval of the establishment of the district.

(Sec. 304, Agriculture and Markets Law)

• *District data collection for agriculture district administration*

In order to evaluate the environmental and economic effects of the agricultural district program, the Commissioner of Agriculture and Markets must develop and maintain information on agricultural districts and lands. Owners and operators of land used for agricultural production in agricultural districts must provide the county with information about their property including total acreage, number of acres of cropland, number of acres by land classification, principal products, and approximate annual sales. (Sec. 304-b, Agriculture and Markets Law)

• *Roll-back taxes*

Parcels of land converted from agricultural to nonagricultural use are subject to payments equalling five times the taxes saved in the last year in which the land benefited from an agricultural assessment, plus interest of 6% per year, compounded annually for each year in which an agricultural assessment was granted, not exceeding five years. (Sec. 305, Agriculture and Markets Law)

If land committed to agricultural use is converted to a nonagricultural use, the conversion constitutes a breach of commitment. Therefore, to compensate for the benefits received through an agricultural assessment, the land is subject to payments equalling five times the taxes saved in the last year in which the land benefited from agricultural assessment, plus interest of 6% per year, compounded annually for each year in which an agricultural assessment was granted, not exceeding five years. (Sec. 306, Agriculture and Markets Law)

Whenever conversions of land occur, owners must notify the assessor within 90 days of the date from which the conversion commenced. If the landowner fails to make this notification within the prescribed time period, the assessing unit may impose a penalty up to two times the total payment owed. This penalty may not exceed $500 in addition to any payments owed. (Sec. 305, Agriculture and Markets Law; Sec. 306, Agriculture and Markets Law)

• *Improvements*

Structures and buildings essential to the operation of lands actively devoted to agriculture and horticulture and used and occupied for such purposes are exempt from tax if constructed or reconstructed after January 1, 1969, and before 2029. (Sec. 483(1), Real Property Tax Law) The exemption is for the increase in value of the property due to the improvements.

Exempt structures and buildings include those used:

• directly and exclusively in the raising and production for sale of agricultural and horticultural commodities or their storage;

• to provide housing for regular and essential employees and their immediate families who are primarily employed in connection with the operation of lands actively devoted to agricultural and horticultural use, but not including structures and buildings occupied as a residence by the applicant and his immediate family;

• as indoor exercise arenas exclusively for training and exercising horses in connection with the raising and production for sale of agricultural and horticultural commodities or in connection with a commercial horse boarding operation;

• in the production of maple syrup; and

• in the production of honey and beeswax, including those structures and buildings used for the storage of bees.

(Sec. 483(2), Real Property Tax Law)

The land, which must comprise at least five acres, must have been actively devoted to *bona fide* agricultural or horticultural production and operation carried on for profit. (Sec. 483(3), Real Property Tax Law) Applications for exemption must be filed with the local assessor by the taxable status date of such locality. (Sec. 483(4), Real Property Tax Law) The exemption is in force only for years within which the buildings and structures are used for agricultural or horticultural purposes, and is limited to a period of ten years. (Sec. 483(6), Real Property Tax Law) If the land or structures or buildings are converted to nonagricultural use during the period of exemption, roll-back taxes are imposed equal to the taxes that would have been imposed on the structures or buildings in each year in which the exemption was granted. (Sec. 483(7), Real Property Tax Law)

The term "agricultural and horticultural" specifically encompasses the raising, breeding, and boarding of livestock, including commercial horse boarding operations. (Sec. 483(8), Real Property Tax Law)

Farm silos, farm feed grain storage bins, commodity sheds, bulk milk tanks and coolers, and manure storage, handling and treatment facilities.—The following structures permanently affixed to agricultural land are exempt from taxation, special ad valorem levies and special assessments: (1) structures for the purpose of preserving and storing forage in edible condition; (2) farm feed grain storage bins; (3) commodity sheds; (4) bulk milk tanks and coolers used to hold milk awaiting shipment to market; and (5) manure storage, handling and treatment facilities, including composting of agricultural materials, such as livestock manure and farming wastes, food residuals or other organic wastes associated with food production or consumption with at least 50% by weight of its feedstock on an annual basis being livestock manure, farming wastes and crops grown specifically for use as composting feedstock. "Food residuals" means organic material, including, but not limited to, food scraps, food processing residue, and related soiled or unrecyclable paper used in food packaging, preparation or cleanup. (Sec. 483-a, Real Property Tax Law)

Structures permanently affixed to land for the purpose of anaerobic digestion of agricultural materials, including structures necessary for the storage and handling of the agricultural materials that are part of the digestion process, together with any equipment necessary for producing, collecting, storing, cleaning and converting biogas into forms of energy and generation, transmission, transporting, use of and/or the sale of biogas or energy on-site, off-site, and/or pursuant to an interconnection agreement with a utility; are exempt from taxation, special ad valorem levies and special assessments. (Sec. 483-e, Real Property Tax Law)

The exemption will only be granted upon the application of the owner of the property upon which the structures are located, and must be filed on or before the appropriate taxable status date with the assessor of the municipality having the power to assess real property. Once an exemption is granted, no renewal is necessary. (Sec. 483-a(2), Real Property Tax Law; Sec. 483-e(2), Real Property Tax Law)

The terms "farm feed grain storage bin" and "commodity shed" refer to limited use structures that are designed and used for the storage of grains, feed grains and other feed components, that have a flat or conical bottom, and are designed specifically for on-farm storage. (Sec. 483-a(3), Real Property Tax Law)

• *Farm worker buildings*

An exemption is enacted for farm or food processing labor camps or commissaries, as well as any other structures used to improve the health, living, and working conditions for farm laborers, provided that the structures are in compliance with applicable health, labor, and building code standards. (Sec. 483-d, Real Property Tax Law)

• *Quarantined farmland*

The Board of Supervisors of a county or the financial board of any city may grant an exemption to farmland that the state has taken possession of for the purpose of enforcing a quarantine and to fumigate or treat the lands against the spread of the golden nemotode. However, the property is subject to tax levies for school district purposes and for special assessments. The exemption continues as long as the land is in possession of the state and under quarantine. (Sec. 482, Real Property Tax Law)

• *Disclosure*

Prior to the sale, purchase or exchange of real property located wholly or partially in an agricultural district, the prospective grantor must deliver to the prospective grantee a notice which states that:

"*It is the policy of this state and this community to conserve, protect and encourage the development and improvement of agricultural land for the production of food, and other products, and also for its natural and ecological value. This notice is to inform prospective residents that the property they are about to acquire lies partially or wholly within an agricultural district and that farming activities occur within the district. Such farming activities may include, but not be limited to, activities that cause noise, dust and odors.*" (Sec. 310, Agriculture and Markets Law)

• *Orchards, vineyards, or hopyard*

A limited property tax exemption is allowed for certain land used solely for crop expansion or replanting as part of an orchard, vineyard or hopyard. The exemption is allowed for a period not exceeding six years, beginning on the first eligible taxable status date following the replanting or expansion, provided the following conditions are met:

• the land used for crop expansion or replanting is part of an existing orchard, vineyard or hopyard that:

(a) is located on land used in agricultural production within an agricultural district; or

(b) is part of an existing orchard or vineyard that is eligible for an agricultural assessment;

• the land eligible for the exemption does not in any one year exceed 20% of the total acreage of the orchard, vineyard or hopyard that is located on land used in agricultural production within an agricultural district, or 20% of the total acreage of the orchard, vineyard or hopyard eligible for an agricultural assessment; and

• the land eligible for such real property tax exemption is to be maintained as land used in agricultural production as part of the orchard, vineyard or hopyard for each year that the exemption is granted.

(Sec. 305, Agriculture and Markets Law)

Assessment of orchards, vineyards, or hopyards.—The portion of the value of such land eligible for exemption will be determined based on the average per acre assessment of all agricultural land of the specific tax parcel, as reported in a form approved by the State Board of Real Property Tax Services. (Sec. 305(7), Agriculture and Markets Law)

• *Disaster areas*

The 20% total acreage restriction discussed above does not apply to land that is located in a declared disaster area. However, the land qualifying under this provision may not exceed the total acreage damaged or destroyed by the disaster. In subsequent years, the exemption is limited to the total acreage that remains damaged. (Sec. 483(3), Real Property Tax Law)

• *Shellfish grounds*

An annual tax of $1 per acre is imposed on all state-owned underwater lands held by a franchise for shellfish cultivation. The tax is levied and assessed by the Department of Environmental Conservation before February 1 on lands held on August 1 of the prior year. The tax must be paid by April 1, and is in lieu of all other taxes on the property. (Sec. 13-0303, Environmental Conservation Law)

[¶20-135] Computer Hardware and Software

New York has no specific provisions regarding computer hardware and software. For a discussion of classification of property, see ¶20-105.

[¶20-145] Construction Work in Progress

New York has no specific provisions regarding construction work in progress. Valuation of property assessed as of a March 1 taxable status date is determined as of the preceding January 1.

[¶20-165] Energy Systems or Facilities

Energy conservation measures that are added to a one-, two-, three- or four-family home that qualifies for financing under a home conservation plan pursuant to Article VII-A of the Public Service Law, or any conservation-related state or federal tax credit are exempt from real property tax and special ad valorem levies to the extent of any increase in the property's assessed value resulting from the installation of such measures. (Sec. 487-a, Real Property Tax Law) Eligible improvements are: (Sec. 135-b, Public Service Law)

- caulking and weather stripping of all exterior doors and windows;
- furnace efficiency modifications;
- furnace and boiler retrofits;
- furnace and boiler replacements that meet minimum efficiency standards;
- heat pumps that meet minimum efficiency standards;
- clock thermostats;
- ceiling, attic, wall, foundation, air duct, heating pipe and floor insulation;
- hot water heater insulation;
- solar and wind systems; and
- load management devices and energy use meters, together with associated wiring.

Also eligible for exemption are improvements to such residences that qualify for any conservation-related state or federal tax credit or deduction.

• *Energy systems*

Real property that contains a solar or wind energy system or farm waste energy system approved by the New York State Energy Research and Development Authority is exempt from taxation for a period of 15 years to the extent of any increase in assessed value due to the system. The exemption applies to solar or wind energy systems or farm waste energy systems that are existing or constructed prior to July 1, 1988, or constructed after January 1, 1991, and before January 1, 2025. The exemption is inapplicable to any structure that satisfies the requirements for exemption under Sec. 483-e, Real Property Tax Law. (Sec. 487, Real Property Tax Law)

The exemption also applies to micro-hydroelectric energy systems, fuel cell electric generating systems, micro-combined heat and power generating equipment systems, and electric energy storage equipment and electric energy storage systems. In addition, the exemption applies to "fuel-flexible linear generation," which includes fuel-flexible linear generator electric generating equipment and fuel-flexible linear generator electric generating systems. The exemption applies to such systems that are constructed prior to January 1, 2025. The exemption is inapplicable to any structure that satisfies the requirements for exemption under Sec. 483-e, Real Property Tax Law. (Sec. 487, Real Property Tax Law)

Local option to limit tax.—Counties, cities, towns, villages and school districts may disallow exemptions for either (1) solar and wind energy systems or farm waste energy systems which began construction after January 1, 1991, or the date of the local law, whichever is later, or (2) micro-hydroelectric energy systems, fuel cell electric generating systems, micro-combined heat and power generating equipment systems, or electric energy storage equipment or electric energy storage systems constructed subsequent to January 1, 2018, or the effective date of such local law, ordinance or resolution, whichever is later, or both. The option must be exercised by counties, cities, towns and villages through adoption of a local law, and by school districts by adoption of a resolution. (Sec. 487, Real Property Tax Law)

Construction of a solar or wind energy system or a farm waste energy system is deemed to have begun upon the full execution of a contract or interconnection agreement with a utility; provided however, that if such contract or interconnection agreement requires a deposit to be made, then construction will be deemed to have begun when the contract or interconnection agreement is fully executed and the deposit is made. The owner or developer of such a system must provide written notification to the appropriate local jurisdiction or jurisdictions upon execution of the contract or the interconnection agreement. (Sec. 487, Real Property Tax Law)

*Local exemption for qualified energy systems.*A local real property tax exemption is authorized for specified energy systems and the owner of such property is not required to enter into a contract for payments in lieu of taxes (PILOT agreement). (Sec. 487(10), Real Property Tax Law) Specifically, a local exemption is authorized for the following (individually or collectively, "energy system"):

- solar or wind energy systems,
- farm waste energy systems,
- microhydroelectric energy systems,
- fuel cell electric generating systems,
- microcombined heat and power generating equipment systems,
- electric energy storage systems, or
- fuel-flexible linear generators.

(Sec. 487(10), Real Property Tax Law)

Also, any owner of property that comprises or includes an energy system is not required to enter into a contract for payments in lieu of taxes (PILOT agreement) if:

- the energy system is installed on real property that is owned or controlled by New York or a state entity; and

- New York or a state entity has agreed to purchase the energy produced by such energy system, or the environmental credits or attributes created by virtue of such energy system's operation, in accordance with a written agreement with the owner or operator of such energy system.

(Sec. 487(10), Real Property Tax Law)

The project owners would need to file applications with the local assessor. (Sec. 487(10), Real Property Tax Law)

Calculation of exemption.—Generally, the exemption is limited to the increase in the property's assessed value attributable to the energy system. If the system or its components also serve as part of the building structure, the increase in value exempt from taxation is the equal to the assessed value attributable to the system or its components, multiplied by the ratio of "incremental costs" of the system or components to the total cost of the system or components. The "incremental cost" is the increased cost of the solar or wind energy system, or farm waste energy system, that also serves as part of the building structure, above the cost for similar conventional construction, which enables its use as a solar, wind, or farm waste energy system or component. (Sec. 487, Real Property Tax Law)

Application for exemption required.—The exemption is granted only upon application by the owner of the real property on a form prescribed and made available by the state board. The applicant must furnish such information as the board requires. The application must be filed with the assessor of the appropriate county, city, town or village on or before the applicable taxable status date. A copy of the application must be filed with the Authority. (Sec. 487, Real Property Tax Law)

Definitions.—"Solar or wind energy equipment" means collectors, controls, energy storage devices, heat pumps and pumps, heat exchangers, windmills, and other materials, hardware or equipment necessary to the process by which solar radiation or wind is:

- collected,

- converted into another form of energy such as thermal, electrical, mechanical or chemical,

- stored,

- protected from unnecessary dissipation, and

- distributed.

The term does not include pipes, controls, insulation or other equipment that are part of the normal heating, cooling, or insulation system of a building. It does include insulated glazing or insulation to the extent that such materials exceed the energy efficiency standards required by law. (Sec. 487(1)(a), Real Property Tax Law)

"Solar or wind energy system" means an arrangement or combination of solar or wind energy equipment designed to provide heating, cooling, hot water, or mechanical, chemical, or electrical energy by the collection of solar or wind energy and its conversion, storage, protection and distribution. (Sec. 487(1)(b), Real Property Tax Law)

"Farm waste energy system" means an arrangement or combination of farm waste electric generating equipment or other materials, hardware, or equipment necessary to the process by which agricultural waste biogas is produced, collected, stored, cleaned, and converted into forms of energy such as thermal, electrical, mechanical, or chemical and by which the biogas and converted energy are distributed on-site. The term does not include pipes, controls, insulation, or other equipment that is part of the normal heating, cooling, or insulation system of a building. (Sec. 487(1)(f), Real Property Tax Law)

"Farm waste electric generating equipment" means equipment that generates electric energy from biogas produced by the anaerobic digestion of agricultural waste, such as livestock manure, farming waste and food processing wastes with a rated capacity of not more than 1,000 kilowatts that is:

   (i) manufactured, installed and operated in accordance with applicable government and industry standards;

   (ii) connected to the electric system and operated in conjunction with an electric corporation's transmission and distribution facilities;

   (iii) operated in compliance with the provisions of §66-j of the Public Service Law;

   (iv) fueled at a minimum of 90% on an annual basis by biogas produced from the anaerobic digestion of agricultural waste such as livestock manure materials, crop residues and food processing wastes; and

   (v) fueled by biogas generated by anaerobic digestion with at least 50% by weight of its feedstock being livestock manure materials on an annual basis.

(Sec. 487(1)(e), Real Property Tax Law)

"Fuel-flexible linear generator electric generating equipment" or "fuel-flexible linear generator" means an integrated system consisting of oscillators, cylinders, electricity conversion equipment and associated balance of plant components that directly convert the linear motion of the oscillators into electricity and which has a combined rated capacity of not more than two thousand kilowatts. "Fuel-flexible linear generator electric generating system" means an arrangement or combination of fuel-flexible linear generator electric generating equipment designed to produce electrical energy from linear motion created by the reaction of gaseous or liquid fuels, including but not limited to biogas and natural gas. (Sec. 487(1)(o) and (p), Real Property Tax Law)

¶20-165

[¶20-195] Health Care Facilities and Equipment

Municipalities cannot tax real property owned by a corporation or association organized or conducted exclusively for the purpose of acting as a hospital (this includes corporations operating hospitals for cities under Sec. 438(2), Real Property Tax Law). (Sec. 420-a(1)(a), Real Property Tax Law) See also ¶20-285 Nonprofit, Religious, Charitable, Scientific, and Educational Organizations.

[¶20-205] Homestead

There is no general, statewide homestead property tax exemption. However, homestead property may be separately taxed at a lower rate in taxing districts that have undertaken a general revaluation of real property in the district.

Homestead property consists of the following real properties: (Sec. 1901, Real Property Tax Law)

• all one-, two- or three-family dwelling residential property, including dwellings used primarily for residential purposes but also used, in part, for nonresidential purposes;

• residential real property of more than three dwelling units used as condominiums, provided they have not previously been assessed as dwellings other than condominiums;

• all vacant land parcels located in assessing units which have zoning laws or ordinances in effect, provided that the parcel does not exceed 10 acres and is located in a zone that only permits specific residential use; and

• eligible land used for agricultural production (see ¶20-115 Agriculture), including farm buildings and structures essential to the operation of agricultural or horticultural lands.

Nonhomestead property consists of all real property not included in the homestead class.

For further discussion, see ¶20-105 Classification of Property.

Local taxing bodies are authorized to enact exemptions for the residential property of senior citizens or veterans. They may also enact an exemption for living quarters provided for a parent or grandparent and a partial exemption for first-time homeowners (see discussions below). In addition, low-income homeowners and renters may be eligible for a circuit breaker property tax credit against the personal income tax. (Sec. 606(e), Tax Law)

• *Green buildings*

Enhanced benefits are allowed for improvements to real property in a city with a population between 27,500 and 28,000 (i.e., the city of Auburn), if adopted by local law, meeting certification standards for green buildings. Residential real property that has been reconstructed, altered, or improved that is certified under a certification standard approved by a city which is determined to be equivalent to the leadership in energy and environmental design (LEED) certification for the categories of certified/silver, gold, or platinum as meeting green building standards will be exempt by certain percentages. A copy of the certification for a qualified category must be filed with the assessor and the assessor must approve the application for the applicable category as meeting the requirements and the local law of the city. (Sec. 421-ff, Real Property Tax Law)

Certified/silver certification standard.—Qualified buildings will be exempt for a three-year period for 100% of the increase in the assessed value attributable to the improvements. The exemption will be decreased by 20% of the exemption base for the next four years. The "exemption base" will be the increase in assessed value due to improvements as determined by the assessor in the initial year of the seven-year period following the filing of an original application. (Sec. 421-ff, Real Property Tax Law)

Gold standard.—Qualified buildings will be exempt for a four-year period for 100% of the increase in the assessed value attributable to the improvements. The exemption will be decreased by 20% of the exemption base for the next four years. The "exemption base" will be the increase in assessed value due to improvements as determined by the assessor in the initial year of the eight-year period following the filing of an original application. (Sec. 421-ff, Real Property Tax Law)

Platinum standard.—Qualified buildings will be exempt for a six-year period for 100% of the increase in the assessed value attributable to the improvements. The exemption will be decreased by 20% of the exemption base for the next four years. The "exemption base" will be the increase in assessed value due to improvements as determined by the assessor in the initial year of the ten-year period following the filing of an original application. (Sec. 421-ff, Real Property Tax Law)

In order to qualify for the exemptions, construction of the improvements must commence as specified by local law, the project must exceed $7,500, and the owner must comply with proper documentation requirements. The exemption will be removed if the property ceases to be used primarily for eligible purposes. (Sec. 421-ff, Real Property Tax Law)

• *Capital improvements*

Municipalities other than New York City may authorize limited exemptions from tax and *ad valorem* levies for increases in the assessed value of residential buildings reconstructed, altered or improved after July 1, 1995, or the adoption of the local law authorizing the exemption. To be eligible, the building or structure must be designed and occupied exclusively for residential purposes by not more than two families. In addition, the reconstruction, alteration or improvement must be commenced after the date that the local law authorizing the exemption was enacted, the value of the modifications must exceed $3,000 and the greater portion, as determined by square footage, of the building reconstructed, altered or improved must be at least five years old. (Sec. 421-f, Real Property Tax Law)

The exemption applies for a one-year period to the extent of 100% of the increase in assessed value attributable to the modifications, and for an additional seven years. During the additional exemption period, the exemption amount is decreased by 12.5% of the initial exemption amount. (Sec. 421-f(2), Real Property Tax Law)

Exemption limit.—The exemption is limited to $80,000 of the increased market value of the property attributable to the reconstruction, alteration or improvement. Municipalities may, by local law, decrease the exemption limitation to an amount not less than $5,000. any increase in market value that exceeds $80,000 or the lower amount specified in the local law is ineligible for exemption. (Sec. 421-f(2), Real Property Tax Law)

"Market value" defined.—In special assessing units, the "market value" of a reconstruction, alteration or improvement is equal to the increased assessed value attributable to the reconstruction, alteration or improvement divided by the class I ratio. In the remainder of the state, "market value" is equal to the increased assessed value attributable to the reconstruction, alteration or improvement divided by the most recently established state equalization rate or special equalization rate. If the state equalization rate or special equalization rate equals or exceeds 95%, the increase in assessed value attributable to the reconstruction, alteration or improvement equals the market value of those modifications. (Sec. 421-f(2), Real Property Tax Law)

Modification of exemptions.—Municipalities may, by local law, reduce the exemption percentages noted above. In addition, municipalities may provide that the exemption is applicable to reconstruction, alterations, or improvements of residential dwellings or they may limit the exemption to one or more of such categories. Local laws may also limit "improvements" to include only those modifications that would otherwise result in increases in the assessed valuation of real property and that consist of additions, remodeling, or modernization to existing residential structures to prevent physical deterioration or to comply with applicable building, sanitary, health or fire codes. (Sec. 421-f(7), Real Property Tax Law)

No local laws or resolutions may reduce or repeal exemptions previously granted until the expiration of the exemption period. (Sec. 421-f(7), Real Property Tax Law)

Termination of exemption.—The exemption will terminate if an eligible building or structure ceases to be used primarily for residential purposes or if title is transferred to persons other than the owner's heirs or distributees. (Sec. 421-f(6), Real Property Tax Law)

City of Auburn.—A partial New York property tax exemption is allowed for the reconstruction, alteration, or improvements to existing housing and vacant residential buildings in a city with a population between 27,500 and 28,000 (i.e., the city of Auburn) if adopted by local law. (Sec. 421-ff, Real Property Tax Law)

Qualified buildings will be exempt for a two-year period for 100% of the increase in the assessed value attributable to the improvements. The exemption will be decreased by 20% of the exemption base for the next four years. The "exemption base" will be the increase in assessed value due to improvements as determined by the assessor in the initial year of the six-year period following the filing of an original application. (Sec. 421-ff, Real Property Tax Law)

Town of Evans.—If adopted by local law, a town with a population between 16,350 and 16,360 (the town of Evans, Erie County) is authorized to enact a partial New York property tax exemption for the improvement, modification, or renovation of residential family homes that increases the home's assessed value. The exemption is equal to 50% of the assessed value for the first year and is then decreased by 10% per year for an additional four-year period. For purposes of the exemption, "reconstruction," "alteration," or "improvement" does not include ordinary maintenance and repairs. (Sec. 421-l, Real Property Tax Law)

City of Oneonta.—If adopted by local law, city having a population of more than 13,500 inhabitants but fewer than 14,000 inhabitants (the city of Oneonta) is authorized to enact a partial New York property tax exemption applicable to multiple dwelling buildings reconstructed, altered, or converted back to an owner-occupied single family dwelling or any owner-occupied multiple dwelling that is reduced to at most two units by such reconstruction. The exemption applies for a one-year period to the extent of 100% of the increase in assessed value attributable to the modifications, and for an additional seven years. During the additional exemption period, the exemption amount is decreased each year by 12.5% of the initial exemption amount. (Sec. 421-n, Real Property Tax Law)

City of Hornell.—If adopted by local law, a city having a population of more than 8,000 inhabitants but fewer than 9,000 inhabitants located in a county with a population of more than 97,000 inhabitants but fewer than 99,000 inhabitants (the city of Hornell) is authorized to enact a partial New York property tax exemption applicable to multiple dwelling buildings reconstructed, altered, or converted back to an owner-occupied single family dwelling. The exemption applies for a one-year period to the extent of 100% of the increase in assessed value attributable to the modifications, and for an additional 11 years. During the additional exemption period, the exemption amount is decreased each year by 8 $1/3$% of the initial exemption amount. (Sec. 421-o, Real Property Tax Law)

City of Corning.—If adopted by local law, a city having a population of more than 10,000 inhabitants but fewer than 12,000 inhabitants located in a county with a population of more than 97,000 inhabitants but fewer than 99,000 inhabitants (the city of Corning) is authorized to enact a partial New York property tax exemption applicable to multiple dwelling buildings reconstructed, altered, or converted back to an owner-occupied single family dwelling. The exemption applies for a one-year period to the extent of 100% of the increase in assessed value attributable to the modifications, and for an additional 11 years. During the additional exemption period, the exemption amount is decreased each year by 8 $1/3$% of the initial exemption amount. (Sec. 421-o, Real Property Tax Law)

• *STAR program exemptions*

The school tax relief program (STAR) exempts certain residential real property from taxation for school purposes. The STAR program consists of two variations of the exemption: (1) an exemption for property used as the primary residences of homeowners, known as the "basic" STAR exemption, and (2) property of senior citizens satisfying certain requirements, known as the "enhanced" STAR exemption. (Sec. 425(2)(a), Real Property Tax Law)

Eligibility for the basic STAR exemption is limited to those with incomes of $500,000 or less. However, beginning with the 2019-2020 school year, the income limit for the basic STAR exemption is lowered to $250,000 (for purposes of the STAR credit, the existing $500,000 income limit remains intact). Income is defined as:

— income of all owners who reside primarily on the property as of taxable status date;

— income of any owners' spouses residing there;

— income from two years prior to the levy date;

— income is federal "adjusted gross income," less the taxable amount of total distributions from IRAs.

(Sec. 425.3(b-1), Real Property Tax Law)

NEW DEVELOPMENTS: Beginning with assessment rolls used to levy school district taxes for the 2016-2017 school year, the existing School Tax Relief (STAR) exemption program is closed to new applicants, and a new refundable personal income tax credit is established in its place. Current recipients of STAR exemptions are permitted to keep the exemptions as long as they continue to own their homes, but upon transfer of the property to a new owner, the new owner would only be eligible for the income tax credit program. Current STAR exemption recipients have the option of giving up their STAR exemptions in favor of the personal income tax credit, though it is not required. (Sec. 425(16), Real Property Tax Law)

If the owners of a parcel that is receiving the STAR exemption want to claim the personal income tax credit in lieu of such exemption, they made do so by switching to the credit as provided in Sec. 425(17), Real Property Tax Law. Alternatively, they may renounce the exemption and make any payments in the manner provided by Sec. 496, Real Property Tax Law. Any such switch to the credit is irrevocable. (Sec. 425(16), Real Property Tax Law)

NEW DEVELOPMENTS: The 2019-20 budget package imposes a 0% cap upon the growth in Basic and Enhanced STAR benefits for purposes of the STAR exemption, beginning with the 2019-20 school year. For purposes of the STAR credit, the existing 2% cap remains intact. (Ch. 59 (S.B. 1509, Part LL))

Exemption amount.—The exemption amount is determined by first multiplying the applicable base figure (see below) by the applicable sales price differential factor, if any, determined by the Commissioner of Taxation and Finance. The product is then multiplied by the appropriate equalization factor for the assessing unit, also determined by the commissioner to account for variances in assessing levels. Finally, the resulting amount, after the equalization factor, may not be less than 95% of the exempt amount determined for the prior levy unless the level of assessment by the school has changed by 5% or more, in which case the exemption may not be less than 95% of the exempt amount for the prior levy multiplied by the change in level of assessment factor. The commissioner must compute the exempt amount for each assessing unit in each county and certify it to the assessor of each unit and the county director of real property tax services at least 20 days prior to the last date for the filing of the tentative assessment roll. (Sec. 425(2)(g), Real Property Tax Law)

Homeowner base figures (basic exemption).—For the 2009-2010 school year and thereafter, homeowners are eligible for an exemption computed using a base figure that equals the prior year's base figure multiplied by the percentage increase in the consumer price index for urban wage earners and clerical workers (CPI-W) published by the U.S. Department of Labor, Bureau of Labor Statistics, for the third quarter of the calendar year preceding the applicable school year, as compared to the third quarter of the prior calendar year. (Sec. 425(2), Real Property Tax Law)

Senior citizen base figures (enhanced exemption).—The applicable income tax year, cost-of-living adjustment percentage, and the applicable increase percentage will be advanced by one year, and the income standard will be the previously-applicable income standard increased by the new cost-of-living adjustment percentage. (Sec. 425(2), Real Property Tax Law) For the 2009-2010 school year and thereafter, the base figure for the enhanced STAR exemption equals the prior year's base figure multiplied by the percentage increase in the consumer price index for urban wage earners and clerical workers (CPI-W) published by the U.S. Department of Labor, Bureau of Labor Statistics, for the third quarter of the calendar year preceding the applicable school year, as compared to the third quarter of the prior calendar year. (Sec. 425(2), Real Property Tax Law)

Eligibility.—To qualify for exemption the property must be a one-, two- or three-family residence, a farm dwelling, or residential property held in condominium or cooperative form of ownership. The property must also serve as the primary residence of one or more of the owners. If the property is not an eligible type of property, but a portion of the property is partially used by the owner as a primary residence, that portion that is so used is entitled to the exemption; however, the exemption may not exceed the assessed value attributable to that portion. If a farm dwelling is owned by an LLC, the exemption may be granted if the property serves as the primary residence of one or more of the owners. (Sec. 425(3) and (4), Real Property Tax Law)

Additional requirements for senior citizens.—In order for property to qualify for the senior citizens enhanced exemption:

(1) all of the owners must be at least age 65, unless the owners are husband and wife or siblings, in which case only one need be at least 65;

(2) the combined income (adjusted gross income reported on the applicant's latest available federal or state income tax return reduced by any distributions from an IRA or individual retirement annuity) of all the owners and owners' spouses residing on the property for the income tax year immediately preceding the date of application for the exemption may not exceed $60,000 increased annually by a cost-of-living adjustment (Form RP-425, Application for School Tax Relief (STAR) Exemption); and

(3) the property must serve as the primary residence of that owner. any information supplied by an applicant for a STAR exemption to verify income is deemed confidential and disclosure of such information by the assessor or any municipal official or employee, except in the course of their official duties, is a violation of the General Municipal Law.

Further, in order to qualify for the enhanced exemption, eligibility will be based upon age as of December 31 rather than the locally applicable taxable status date. (Sec. 425(4), Real Property Tax Law)

Surviving spouses.—In the case of property owned by a husband and wife, one of whom is at least 65 years of age, the enhanced exemption will not be rescinded solely because of the death of the older spouse, as long as the surviving spouse is at least 62 years of age. (Sec. 425(4), Real Property Tax Law)

Nursing home residents.—If an owner is absent from his or her residence while receiving health-related care as an inpatient of a residential health care facility, the enhanced exemption may still be granted, provided that during the owner's confinement the property is not occupied by anyone other than the owner's spouse or another co-owner. (Sec. 425(4), Real Property Tax Law)

STAR registration program.—Legislation requires the creation of a system for the registration of recipients of the STAR exemption. All owners of property initially applying for and receiving a basic STAR exemption will be required to register with the Commissioner of Taxation and Finance in the manner and on the dates prescribed by the commissioner. After the initial registration program has been implemented, the commissioner will endeavor to confirm the continuing eligibility of STAR recipients through means other than re-registration, such as by reviewing relevant data appearing on personal income tax returns. The commissioner may direct the removal or denial of a STAR exemption under specified circumstances and is required to provide the property owners with notice and an opportunity to demonstrate eligibility before taking such action. (Sec. 425(14), Real Property Tax Law)

CCH COMMENT: STAR registration program.—The New York Department of Taxation and Finance has announced the launch of an online STAR Registration platform for homeowners currently receiving the Basic STAR property tax exemption. The system will facilitate a budget initiative to eliminate inappropriate STAR property tax exemptions. The initiative follows a department investigation which showed that some homeowners were receiving the exemption on more than one property.

Homeowners will not have to re-register every year. Based on the information provided in the registration process, the department will monitor homeowners' eligibility in future years. (Press Release, New York Department of Taxation and Finance, August 20, 2013)

If late registration for the (STAR) program is accepted after the Basic STAR exemption has already been removed from the subject property, the Commissioner is authorized to remit directly to the property owner the tax savings that the exemption would have yielded had it not been removed. The Commissioner may direct the assessor to restore the exemption on a prospective basis without a new application, unless there is reason to believe the property owner is no longer eligible. (Sec. 425(14)(a)(iii), Real Property Tax Law)

Application for exemption.—An application for exemption must be jointly made by all owners of the property who primarily reside on it. When property is eligible for a local senior citizens exemption authorized under Sec. 467, Real Property Tax Law, it is deemed to be eligible for the enhanced exemption and no separate application need be filed. (Sec. 425(6), Real Property Tax Law)

In general, the application must be filed by the appropriate taxable status date, which in most cases is March 1. (Sec. 425(6), Real Property Tax Law) Applications for (STAR) and senior citizen property tax exemptions may be filed after the taxable status date in certain cases. No later than the last day for paying taxes without incurring cost or penalty, owners may submit a written request to the assessor requesting a filing extension. Requests much contain an explanation of why the deadline was missed and be accompanied by a renewal application. The assessor may extend the deadline and grant the exemption if good cause existed for failure to timely file the renewal application and if the applicant is otherwise entitled to the exemption. (Sec. 425(6)(a-2), Real Property Tax Law)

In cases where school district taxes are levied upon the prior year's assessment roll, the assessing unit may adopt a local law allowing STAR applications for each school year to be submitted by the taxable status date of the current year's assessment roll. When such a law is in effect, the eligibility of property for a STAR exemption will be based on:

- the condition of the property as of the taxable status date of the prior year's assessment roll; and

- the ownership of the property as of the taxable status date of the current year's assessment roll.

When a STAR application is approved, the prior year's assessment roll will be revised accordingly. When a STAR application is denied, the applicant may seek administrative and judicial review of the denial, subject to the same timing constraints that apply to taxpayers seeking review of assessments appearing on the current year's assessment roll. Under prior law, no special STAR provisions existed for localities having school district taxes based on prior year assessment rolls. (Sec. 425(6), Real Property Tax Law)

If an applicant is found to be ineligible for the exemption, the assessor must mail the applicant a notice indicating that the exemption has been denied for that year and specifying the reasons for the denial. However, a failure to mail any such notice will not prevent the levy, collection, and enforcement of taxes on the applicant's property. (Sec. 425(6), Real Property Law)

The State Board of Real Property Services has the power to hear and determine reviews relating to determinations of STAR eligibility made by the Department of Taxation and Finance. (Sec. 200-a, Real Property Tax Law)

Eligibility erroneously not taken into account.—Where a property owner was eligible for the STAR exemption which was not taken into account in the calculation of the taxpayer's school tax bill due to administrative error, and an excessive amount of school taxes was paid as a result, the Commissioner may remit directly to the property owner the tax savings that the exemption would have yielded if it had been properly taken into account on the taxpayer's school tax bill. (Sec. 425(15-a), Real Property Tax Law)

Income verification program for enhanced exemption.—An income verification program (IVP) is provided whereby senior citizens may elect to have their renewal application processed automatically, with annual income verification by the Department of Taxation and Finance. (Sec. 425(4)(b), Real Property Tax Law) Seniors electing to participate in the program do not need to present tax returns to their local assessors and each year they will receive a postcard indicating information on record, cost-of-living adjustment changes, and a reminder to report any changes in their status. (Sec. 425(4)(b), Real Property Tax Law) This notification process also is applicable where senior citizens designate a third party to be notified when enhanced STAR renewal applications are due. For those who do not participate in the income verification program, an enhanced exemption only applies for one year. To continue receiving the enhanced exemption, a renewal application must be filed annually. (Sec. 425(4)(b), Real Property Tax Law) However, even if a senior citizen that does not participate in the income verification program and fails to file an annual renewal application, the assessor must nevertheless grant the basic exemption that is generally available to other owners. (Sec. 425(9), Real Property Tax Law)

> **NEW DEVELOPMENTS:** Effective with applications for the exemption on 2019 assessment rolls, all enhanced STAR recipients are required to be enrolled in the IVP. This includes recipients of the senior citizen exemption, who previously received enhanced STAR automatically. Also, effective with 2020 assessment rolls, the Department of Taxation and Finance is required to annually verify that enhanced STAR exemption recipients meet the residency and age requirements, thus requiring the same eligibility verification for the enhanced STAR exemption that it has done for the basic STAR exemption. (Sec. 425(4)(b), Real Property Tax Law)

Apartment co-ops and manufactured homes.—With respect to residents of cooperative apartments and owners of trailers and mobile homes, who are allowed to apply for the STAR exemption even though the tax bill generally goes to the landowner or cooperative corporation, the assessor is required to provide the landowner or cooperative apartment corporation with a statement setting forth the exemption attributable to each eligible tenant-stockholder, trailer, or mobile home. (Sec. 425(2), Real Property Tax Law)

Cooperative apartment corporations may credit the exemption to tenant-stockholders. There are four options:

> (1) a full credit against the fees and charges of any single month within the current assessment cycle, with any balance to be credited in full for subsequent months until exhausted;

> (2) a proportional credit over six months during the current assessment cycle;

> (3) a proportional credit over 12 months during the current assessment cycle; or

> (4) a lump sum payment of the total savings to the tenant-stockholder.

The exemption must be fully credited during the assessment cycle for which each tenant-stockholder is eligible for STAR. In addition, cooperative apartment corporations are required to inform eligible tenant-stockholders about the full value of their STAR benefits and how the amounts were calculated. (Sec. 425(2)(k)(iii), Real Property Tax Law)

Escrow account reduction.—With respect to escrow accounts maintained by mortgage investing institutions to ensure the payment of real property taxes, when the granting of a STAR exemption results in an escrow overage, the homeowner is entitled to a proportionate reduction in the amount that the mortgage investing institution is authorized to collect and deposit on a monthly basis. (Sec. 953(6-a), Real Property Tax Law)

Local property tax rebate program.—When a property owner is entitled to the basic or enhanced STAR exemption, the owner or owners also may receive a local property tax rebate. (Sec. 1306-b, Real Property Tax Law)

Recoupment of improperly granted benefits.—The Department of Taxation and Finance is authorized to use data collected through the registration process to recoup improperly granted STAR property tax exemptions in the current school year or more of the three preceding school years, along with interest. Notice and grievance procedures are also enacted that govern any such recoupment proceedings. Neither assessors nor boards of assessment review have authority to consider objections to recoupment of an exemption; rather, such actions may only be challenged before the department. (Sec. 425(15), Real Property Tax Law)

Past-due property taxes.—A property owner whose primary residence is subject to past-due property taxes will not be allowed to receive a STAR credit or STAR exemption unless the past-due property taxes are paid in full on or before a specified date. (Sec. 171-w, Tax Law)

• *Voluntary STAR exemption renunciation*

A property owner may voluntarily renounce his or her claim to a school tax relief (STAR) exemption. The owner must file an application form authorized by the tax commissioner, together with a $500 application fee, with the county director of real property tax services no later than 10 years after the levy of taxes on the assessment roll. If an applicant is renouncing a STAR exemption in order to qualify for the personal income tax credit authorized by Sec. 606(eee), Tax Law, and no other exemptions are being renounced on the same application, or if the applicant is renouncing a STAR exemption before school taxes have been levied on the assessment roll upon which that exemption appears, no processing fee applies. (Sec. 496, Real Property Tax Law)

The assessed value of the property will be multiplied by the tax rate or rates that were applied to that assessment roll, and interest will be added to the product for each month or portion thereof since the levy of taxes on the assessment roll. (Sec. 496, Real Property Tax Law)

The property owner must pay the total amount due to the county treasurer within 15 days of the mailing of the form. (Sec. 496, Real Property Tax Law)

• *Exemption for living quarters for parent or grandparent*

A county, city, town, village, or school district acting through its local legislative body may adopt and amend local laws, or resolutions in the case of school districts, to provide an exemption from New York real property taxation for any increase in the assessed value of residential property resulting from the construction or reconstruction of such property for the purpose of providing living quarters for the property owner's parent or grandparent who is age 62 or older. (Sec. 469, Real Property Tax Law)

Limitations on exemption.—The exemption must not exceed the lesser of:

   • the increase in assessed value resulting from the construction or reconstruction of such property;

   • 20% of the total assessed value of such property as improved; or

- 20% of the median sale price of residential property as reported in the most recent sales statistical summary published by the New York State Board of Real Property Services for the county in which the property is located.

Also, no exemption may be granted unless:

- the property is within the geographical area in which such construction or reconstruction is permitted; and

- the property is the principal place of residence of the owner. If granted, the exemption is applicable only to construction or reconstruction that occurs after August 30, 2000, and only during taxable years in which at least one parent or grandparent maintains a primary place of residence in the living quarters.

(Sec. 469, Real Property Tax Law)

Application for exemption.—Application for the exemption must be made annually by the property owner to the local assessor by the taxable status date of the city, town, village, or county having the power to assess the property. (Sec. 469, Real Property Tax Law)

Parent or grandparent defined.—For purposes of the exemption, the term "parent or grandparent" is defined to include any natural or adopted parent or grandparent of the property owner or the property owner's spouse. (Sec. 469, Real Property Tax Law)

• *First-time homebuyers*

Localities may enact a partial exemption for a period of up to five years for newly constructed primary residential property purchased by one or more persons, each of whom is a first-time home buyer and has not been married to a homeowner in the three years prior to applying for the exemption. In the first year, 50% of the property's assessed valuation is exempt. Thereafter, the exemption amount is phased out by 10% each year. Property purchased on or after December 31, 2022, will not qualify for the exemption unless the purchase is made under a binding written contract entered into before December 31, 2022. (Sec. 457, Real Property Tax Law)

Qualifications for the exemption include a purchase price limitation and a household income limitation, both based on maximum price and income amounts set by the State of New York Mortgage Agency for the county in question under the Low Interest Rate Mortgage Program. A locality may increase the purchase price limit used for eligibility by up to 25%. (Sec. 457, Real Property Tax Law)

Reconstruction, alteration, and improvements exceeding $3,000 in value may also qualify for exemption if performed under the written contract for sale or a written contract entered into by the first-time home buyer within 90 days after the closing of the sale. (Sec. 457, Real Property Tax Law)

If a qualifying property ceases to be used primarily for residential purposes, or if title to the property is transferred to someone other than the owner's heirs or distributees, the exemption will be discontinued. In addition, an exemption granted with respect to a single family property will be discontinued if any portion of the property is found to be the subject of a lease agreement. (Sec. 457, Real Property Tax Law)

• *Family day care homes*

A residential home that is used on a limited secondary basis as a family day care home is assessed for New York property tax purposes at its value as a residence and not as commercial property. (Sec. 581-b, Real Property Tax Law)

• *Improvements in Amherst for soil subsidence damage*

A partial property tax exemption is allowed for residential construction improvements in Amherst, Erie County, for structural damage caused by soil subsidence. If approved by local law, the improvements are exempt in full for a period of one year. The exemption gradually decreases by 20% each year over the next four years and expires after the fourth year. The value of the construction improvements must be more than $10,000 and other conditions must be satisfied. (Sec. 485-l, Real Property Tax Law)

[¶20-215] Housing

Discussed below are whole or partial exemptions granted to the property of certain organizations providing housing, as well as exemptions relating to new or renovated multiple dwelling units. Publicly owned property is discussed at ¶20-190.

• *Nonprofit housing corporations*

Nonprofit housing corporations may be granted, at the option of the municipality, an exemption from local and municipal real property taxes to the extent of all or part of the value of the property included in the completed project. (Sec. 577, Private Housing Finance Law)

• *Not-for-profit housing companies*

An exemption is granted for the property of not-for-profit housing development fund companies organized under Article 11 of the Private Housing Finance Law that provide housing for low-income elderly or handicapped persons. (Sec. 422(1)(a), Real Property Tax Law)

• *Limited-profit housing companies*

An exemption is granted for limited-profit housing companies that provide housing for: (Sec. 422, Real Property Tax Law)

(1) faculty members, students, employees, medical and medical research personnel and their families in attendance or employed at colleges, child care institutions, hospitals and medical research institutes; or

(2) low-income handicapped or elderly persons.

All or part of the value of the property included in a project is exempt to the extent that it represents an increase over the assessed valuation of the real property, both land and improvements, acquired for the project at the time of its acquisition by the limited-profit housing company. (Sec. 33(c), Private Housing Finance Law) However, the amount of taxes to be paid may not be less than 10% of the annual shelter rent of carrying charges of the project. The exemption remains in force for as long as mortgage loans of the company, including additional approved mortgage loans, the proceeds of which are used primarily for the residential portion of the project, are outstanding.

Property sold by a municipality to a limited-profit housing company or a housing development fund company may be wholly exempted by local option if used for low-income, moderate-income or middle-income housing. (Sec. 414, Real Property Tax Law; Sec. 36-a(4), Private Housing Finance Law) The exemption continues as long as capital loans of the company to which the project has been sold or leased, or any approved additional loan used primarily for the residential portion of the project, remain outstanding.

In addition, a limited profit housing company development is entitled to New York property tax exemption as long as at least one building wide improvement or

alteration is part of the application for benefits even if such improvement or alteration is financed with a grant, loan, or subsidy from any federal, state or local agency.
However, it is only entitled to the exemption if it has entered into a binding and
irrevocable agreement which prohibits it from dissolving or reconstituting under
Private Housing Finance Law Sec. 35 for not less than 15 years from the commencement of the benefits. (Sec. 489(4-b), Real Property Tax Law) The abatement of taxes on
such property, including land, cannot exceed 90% of the certified reasonable cost of
such alterations or improvements, nor greater than $8^1/3\%$ of such certified reasonable
cost in any 12 month period, nor be effective for more than 20 years. The annual
abatement cannot exceed 50% of the amount of taxes payable in the 12–month period
or 50% of payments made in lieu of taxes. (Sec. 489(4-b), Real Property Tax Law)

• *Limited-dividend housing companies*

Municipalities are authorized to grant an exemption for all or part of the value of
the property that represents an increase over assessed valuation of the real property
acquired at the time of its acquisition. (Sec. 93, Private Housing Finance Law)

• *Redevelopment companies*

Municipalities may grant exemptions by contract to redevelopment company
projects, for a maximum period of 25 years. (Sec. 125(1)(a), Private Housing Finance
Law) The exemption may be granted for all or part of the increase in assessed
valuation attributable to the value of the property included in the project. The
exemption continues upon the transfer of a project to a mutual redevelopment
company, and a partial exemption may, under certain circumstances, be granted for
another 25 years.

Exemption extension.—Local legislative bodies are permitted to extend the real
property tax abatement to redevelopment companies in order to encourage the
retention of federally subsidized affordable housing within the municipality. The
abatement may be granted for up to an additional 50-year period or until such time
as the property ceases to provide affordable housing. (Sec. 125(1)(a-3), Private Housing Finance Law)

The amount of taxes paid by the redevelopment company during any additional
tax exemption period cannot be less than an amount equal to the greater of:

(1) 10% of the annual rent or carrying charges of the project, minus utilities
for the residential portion of the project; or

(2) the taxes payable by the redevelopment company for the residential
portion of the project immediately prior to the expiration of the initial tax
exemption period.

(Sec. 125(1)(a-3), Private Housing Finance Law)

Where a local legislative body has acted to extend the tax exemption of a mutual
redevelopment company for the maximum period, an additional tax exemption may
be granted for a period of up to 50 years, provided that the amount of taxes to be
paid during any such period of tax exemption may be not less than an amount equal
to the greater of (1) 10% of the annual rent or carrying charges of the project minus
utilities for the residential portion of the project, or (2) the taxes payable by such
company for the residential portion of the project during the tax year commencing
July 1, 2000, and ending on June 30, 2001. Such grant of an additional tax exemption
period will take effect upon the expiration of the maximum period provided for in
Sec. 125(1)(a-2), Private Housing Finance Law. (Sec. 125(1)(a-4), Private Housing
Finance Law)

If the exemption is not extended following the end of the contract exemption period, the property is eligible for a partial phase-out exemption for a period of nine years. Only the portion of the value of the property that was exempt from taxation under the agreement is exempt. (Sec. 423, Real Property Tax Law)

The tax payable is calculated as follows:

• 1st year after the expiration of the contract exemption, the taxes payable during the last year of the contractual exemption (the prior year), plus $1/10$ of the difference between the tax payable during that year and the taxes that would have been payable in the 1st year without the exemption;

• 2nd year after the expiration of the contract exemption, the taxes payable during the 1st year, plus $1/9$ of the difference between the tax payable during the 1st year and the taxes that would have been payable in the 2nd year without the exemption;

• 3rd year after the expiration of the contract exemption, the taxes payable during the 2nd year, plus $1/8$ of the difference between the tax payable during the 2nd year and the taxes that would have been payable in the 3rd year without the exemption;

• 4th year after the expiration of the contract exemption, the taxes payable during the 3rd year, plus $1/7$ of the difference between the tax payable during the 3rd year and the taxes that would have been payable in the 4th year without the exemption;

• 5th year after the expiration of the contract exemption, the taxes payable during the 4th year, plus $1/6$ of the difference between the tax payable during the 4th year and the taxes that would have been payable in the 5th year without the exemption;

• 6th year after the expiration of the contract exemption, the taxes payable during the 5th year, plus $1/5$ of the difference between the tax payable during the 5th year and the taxes that would have been payable in the 6th year without the exemption;

• 7th year after the expiration of the contract exemption, the taxes payable during the 6th year, plus $1/4$ of the difference between the tax payable during the 6th year and the taxes that would have been payable in the 7th year without the exemption;

• 8th year after the expiration of the contract exemption, the taxes payable during the 7th year, plus $1/3$ of the difference between the tax payable during the 7th year and the taxes that would have been payable in the 8th year without the exemption; and

• 9th year after the expiration of the contract exemption, the taxes payable during the 8th year, plus $1/2$ of the difference between the tax payable during the 8th year and the taxes that would have been payable in the 9th year without the exemption.

No exemption is applicable after the 9th year following the expiration of the contract exemption. (Sec. 423, Real Property Tax Law)

• *Urban redevelopment corporations*

Municipalities may grant exemption by local law for the real property of redevelopment corporations for a maximum period of ten years. The agreement may exempt all or part of the increase of the local tax over the maximum local tax. (Sec. 211(1), Private Housing Finance Law)

In addition, property owned by urban redevelopment corporations is entitled to the exemptions provided in Ch. 892, Laws 1941, and Ch. 845, Laws 1942. (Sec. 484, Real Property Tax Law)

• *Multiple dwellings—Improvements*

Cities to which the Multiple Dwelling Law applies are authorized to provide a 14-year exemption from tax for any increase in the assessed valuation of certain multiple dwellings resulting from improvements to eliminate substandard living conditions. The multiple dwelling law applies to all cities with a population exceeding 325,000 (New York and Buffalo), and to other cities and towns that have adopted its provisions by local law. Such cities may adopt or amend laws to exercise this authority on or before January 1, 2020, applicable to work on Class A and certain converted Class B multiple dwellings or other buildings or structures completed within 30 months of the date work was begun and before June 30, 2019. The substantial rehabilitation of a vacant class A multiple dwelling may also be exempted by such cities for a period of up to 20 years. Tax abatements may also be granted for such conversions and improvements. The local law may provide that where part of the building is used for nonresidential purposes, the value of improvements may be apportioned, so that the exemption or abatement is allowed only on the portion used for residential purposes. (Sec. 489(1), Real Property Tax Law; Sec. 3, Multiple Dwelling Law; Sec. 489(6), Real Property Tax Law; Sec. 489(2), Real Property Tax Law)

An increase in valuation resulting from improvements performed with the aid of loans made under the public housing law to owners of existing multiple dwellings may also be exempted or abated or both. (Sec. 214-a, Public Housing Law)

• *Multiple dwellings developed as a planned community*

A local law may be enacted providing that a group of multiple dwellings developed as a planned community and owned as two separate condominiums containing a total of 10,000 or more dwelling units is eligible for New York property tax exemption and abatement for alterations and improvements to eliminate fire and health hazards and for other purposes enumerated under the law. However, the exemption and abatement only apply to alterations or improvements completed prior to December 31, 2005. (Sec. 489(4)(c), Real Property Tax Law)

The exemption is available with respect to an increase in assessed valuation that results from qualifying alterations or improvements to a multiple dwelling in a planned community and continues for 30 years. After 30 years, the amount of the exempted assessed value will be reduced by 20% annually until the assessed value of the alterations or improvements is fully taxable. The exemption may commence at the beginning of any tax quarter after the start of the alterations or improvements. However, the alterations or improvements may not result in an equalization increase in the assessed valuation of any multiple dwelling forming part of the planned community where such alterations or improvements are performed. (Sec. 489(4)(c), Real Property Tax Law)

An abatement of taxes on a planned community may not exceed the greater of 150% of the certified reasonable cost of the alterations or improvements or the construction cost of the alterations or improvements. The abatement may not be effective for more than 20 years and the annual abatement in any consecutive 12-month period may not be greater than 10% of the total abatement granted and may not exceed the amount of taxes payable in such consecutive 12-month period. The abatement may begin no sooner than the first quarterly tax bill immediately following the completion of such alterations or improvements. (Sec. 489(4)(c), Real Property Tax Law)

• *New multiple dwellings in localities with rent control provisions*

Local governments other than New York City that have adopted rent control are authorized to provide a ten-year decreasing exemption for newly constructed residential buildings where the owner elects to subject the buildings to rent control. (Sec. 421-c(1), Real Property Tax Law) The exemption is permitted for ten years in the following percentages: 100% of the tax for the first two years following completion, followed by two years at 80%, followed by two years at 60%, two years at 40% and two years at 20%. (Sec. 421-c(2), Real Property Tax Law) Applications for the exemption must be filed with the assessors between February 1 and March 15. (Sec. 421-c(3), Real Property Tax Law)

• *Projects receiving Private Housing Finance Law payments*

Municipalities may adopt by local law an exemption for any cooperative, condominium, homesteading or rental project that receives payments, grants or loans pursuant to Article 18 of the Private Housing Finance Law (the Low Income Housing Trust Fund Program) or for any new construction project that receives payments, grants, or loans pursuant to Article 19 of the Private Housing Finance Law (the Low Income Turnkey/Enhanced Housing Trust Fund Program). The local law may provide a whole or partial exemption for a period of up to 20 years after the taxable status date immediately following the completion of the project, not to exceed the following:

- first 12 years after completion, 100% exemption;

- following two years, 80% exemption;

- following two years, 60% exemption;

- following two years, 40% exemption; and

- following two years, 20% exemption.

(Sec. 421-e, Real Property Tax Law)

• *Nursing home companies*

Also exempt are nonprofit nursing home companies providing nursing facilities for low-income persons, companies engaged exclusively in caring for, treating, training and educating the mentally ill or retarded, and companies whose facilities are used exclusively to provide programs, services and other facilities for the elderly. (Sec. 422(1)(a), Real Property Tax Law)

• *Residential-commercial urban exemption program*

Cities with fewer than 1 million inhabitants are authorized to adopt a local law providing a 12-year decreasing exemption with respect to the increase in assessed value attributable to the conversion of nonresidential real property to mixed-use property. The exemption amount is 100% of the exemption base in the first eight years, 80% in year 9, 60% in year 10, 40% in year 11, and 20% in year 12. Upon the adoption of such a local law by a city, the county in which the city is located and any school district located entirely or partially in the city may also exempt such property from taxation in the same manner and to the same extent as the city has done. (Sec. 485-a, Real Property Tax Law)

• *Residential investment exemption*

A partial property tax exemption is authorized for the construction of residential real property in cities having a population of at least 31,000 but no more than 32,000. (Sec. 485-h, Real Property Tax Law)

A temporary partial property tax exemption for new residential construction may be authorized by certain school districts that serve a city with a population of more than 31,000 and less than 32,000. According to legislative reports, the Jamestown School District requested the legislation. (Sec. 485-i, Real Property Tax Law)

A partial property tax exemption is authorized for the construction of residential real property that is the primary residence of the owner in cities having a population of at least 34,000 but not more than 35,000. According to legislative reports, the city of Rome, Oneida County, requested the legislation to encourage the construction of new homes within the city. (Sec. 485-i, Real Property Tax Law)

The cities of Niagara Falls, Utica (Oneida County), Amsterdam, and Dunkirk are authorized to allow a partial real property tax exemption for new home construction. The exemptions range from 50% in the first year to 5% in the tenth year. (Sec. 485-j, Real Property Tax Law)

The City of Syracuse allows a property tax exemption for those who rehabilitate certain vacant residential structures. The exemption amount ranges from 100% for the first year to 25% for the 10th year. In addition, Syracuse allows another exemption for residential structures that have been rehabilitated to be environmentally friendly and meet LEED standards. The exemption amount ranges from 100% for the first year for certified silver, gold or platinum categories, to 0% for certified silver and gold categories and to 25% for platinum for the 14th year. (Sec. 485-o, Real Property Tax Law)

The City of Jamestown is authorized to establish an owner-occupied residential property tax exemption program applicable to any construction work where (1) the creation, modernization, rehabilitation, or expansion of a single family or two family residential property that is vacant, legally condemned and has outstanding state and local building and fire code violations, the cost of remedying such violations exceeds the value of such property or (2) the construction of a new single family or two family residence of not less that 1200 square feet on a parcel where a prior structure was demolished. Eligible properties would qualify for a decreasing tax exemption over a period of 11 years. The exemption would apply to the increased value in the property generated by the construction and improvements. (Sec. 485-t, Real Property Tax Law)

• *Multiple dwellings converted to single family dwellings*

An exemption is authorized for cities having a population of more than 22,000 but less than 23,000 for former multiple dwelling residences that are converted into single family residences or two unit residences. (Sec. 421-h, Real Property Tax Law)

An exemption, at the option of a city having a population between 90,000 and 95,000 (the city of Albany), is authorized for former multiple dwelling residences that are converted into single-family residences or two-unit residences. The exemption applies to any rise in assessment values resulting from improvements to the property, and decreases each year over a seven-year period. (Sec. 421-i, Real Property Tax Law)

• *Installation of grab bars in seniors, disabled persons' residences*

Subject to the adoption of a local ordinance, off-site owners of multiple dwelling units for New York City senior citizens and disabled persons may claim a property tax abatement for the installation of grab bars on the walls of shower and bathtub stalls and adjacent to each toilet in the residential units. The amount of the abatement allowed is a maximum of:

> • $250 for the installation of grab bars that requires anchoring by screws or toggles only;

- $400 where the installation also requires removal and replacement of surrounding surface tiles; and

- $800 where the installation requires removal and replacement of surface, lines, and underlayment behind the surface tiles.

(Sec. 467-f, Real Property Tax Law)

[¶20-230] Intangible Property

All intangible property is exempt from New York property taxation because *ad valorem* taxation of intangible property is prohibited by the New York State Constitution. (Art. XVI, N.Y. Const.)

[¶20-245] Leased Property

New York statutes contain provisions making renters liable for payment of taxes on certain leased property, to take effect on the first April 1 occurring more than six months after an Internal Revenue Ruling that renters may deduct the taxes for federal tax purposes. (Sec. 304(2), Real Property Tax Law) However, the IRS has issued a Revenue Ruling to the effect that since owners are also liable for payment of the tax under the New York provisions, the economic incidence of the tax does not fall on the renter. Thus, the tax is not a tax on the renter for federal income tax purposes, and payments are not deductible. *Rev. Rul.* 79-180, 1979-1 CB 95.

[¶20-265] Manufacturing and Industrial Property

Manufacturing and industrial real property is generally taxable to the same extent as other property. Movable machinery or equipment consisting of structures to the operation of which machinery is essential, owned by a corporation subject to the Business Corporation Franchise Tax (Article 9-A), used for trade or manufacture, and not essential to the support of the building or structure in which located, is excluded from the definition of real property, and is therefore exempt. (Sec. 102(12)(f), Real Property Tax Law) (*Note:* A transition provision with respect to the movable machinery exemption applies to certain taxpayers that were transferred from Article 9 taxation to Article 9-A taxation by Ch. 63 (A.B. 11006), Laws 2000; see the footnote under Sec. 102(12)(f), Real Property Tax Law) Otherwise, all articles or other structures affixed to land or to other structures are taxed as real estate. (Sec. 102(12)(b), Real Property Tax Law) All personal property is exempt from tax (see ¶20-295 Personal Property). (Sec. 300, Real Property Tax Law)

- *Tools*

By virtue of the fact that all personal property is exempt from New York property tax, tools would be considered exempt. (Sec. 300, Real Property Tax Law)

- *Business investment exemption*

A ten-year partial exemption from taxation and special ad valorem levies is allowed for the cost of construction, alteration, installation or improvement of business property. (Sec. 485-b, Real Property Tax Law)

- *Steel manufacturing equipment*

Certain real property used in manufacturing steel is exempt if owned by a corporation subject to the franchise tax. Exempt property includes the following:

- blast furnaces and open hearth furnaces;

- soaking pits;

- coke ovens; and

- tanks, towers and stills used in processing gases and liquids produced by coke ovens.

The exempt amount may not exceed 23.85% of the total assessed valuation in cities with a population of less than 50,000. (Sec. 485-a, Real Property Tax Law; Sec. 485-c, Real Property Tax Law)

[¶20-275] Motor Vehicles

Personal property is exempt from property tax. (Sec. 300, Real Property Tax Law) Thus, motor vehicles are not taxed unless they are affixed to real property.

[¶20-285] Nonprofit, Religious, Charitable, Scientific, and Educational Organizations

There are two statutory categories of exemptions provided for real property owned by nonprofit organizations:

(1) mandatory; and

(2) permissive.

(Sec. 420-a(1)(a), Real Property Tax Law; Sec. 420-b(1)(a), Real Property Tax Law)

• *Mandatory class*

The statute mandates that municipalities cannot tax real property owned by a corporation or association organized or conducted exclusively for one or more of the following purposes: (Sec. 420-a(1)(a), Real Property Tax Law)

- religious;
- charitable;
- hospital;
- educational purposes; or
- moral or mental improvement of men, women or children. In addition, the property must be used exclusively for the exempt purposes of such an organization.

(Sec. 420-a(1)(a), Real Property Tax Law)

• *Permissive class*

Real property owned by an organization or association in this category is also generally exempt from property taxes, but the law permits a municipality to tax the property if that municipality affirmatively enacts a provision to tax them. An organization or association in this category must be organized exclusively for one or more of the following purposes and must use their property exclusively for these purposes: (Sec. 420-b(1)(a), Real Property Tax Law)

- bible, tract, benevolent, or missionary;
- infirmary;
- public playground;
- scientific;
- literary;
- bar association;
- medical society;
- library;

- patriotic;

- historical;

- the development of good sportsmanship for persons under 18 years of age through the conduct of supervised athletic games; or

- the enforcement of laws relating to children or animals.

Local enactments taxing property within the latter category of permissive exemptions may impose a tax on property used for a particular purpose, but may not tax a specific owner or property. (Sec. 420-b(1)(b), Real Property Tax Law)

If an officer, member or employee of any tax-exempt property owner receives some type of profit from the organization in excess of reasonable compensation for services, the property is taxable. (Sec. 420-a(1)(b), Real Property Tax Law; Sec. 420-b(1)(c), Real Property Tax Law)

Property held in trust by ministers or clergy of a religious denomination for the benefit of the members of their incorporated or unincorporated church, or property held by trustees named in a will or deed of trust or appointed by the Supreme Court of New York for hospital, public playground or library purposes, is granted the same exemption from taxation that it would have if held by a nonprofit corporation, provided it otherwise meets all the conditions of exemption. (Sec. 436, Real Property Tax Law; Sec. 438(1), Real Property Tax Law)

• *Actual uses*

Use of exempt property as a polling place for purposes of registration or election does not bar the exemption. (Sec. 420-a(4), Real Property Tax Law; Sec. 420-b(4), Real Property Tax Law) Property not in actual use by the tax-exempt owner due to the lack of suitable buildings or improvements is exempt if the construction is in progress or is in good faith contemplated by the organization or if the property is held with a condition that title will revert to the grantor if a suitable building is not erected on the premises. (Sec. 420-a(3), Real Property Tax Law; Sec. 420-b(3), Real Property Tax Law)

• *Lease of exempt property*

The requirement that property must be "exclusively used" for a specific, non-profit purpose does not preclude an organization from leasing its property. (Sec. 420-a(2), Real Property Tax Law; Sec. 420-b(2), Real Property Tax Law) See also ¶ 20-245 Leased Property.

Real property owned and operated as a free public hospital and property outside a city owned and used as a free public library is specifically exempt from tax and does not lose its exempt status if leased in order to obtain funds necessary for support and maintenance of the facility. (Sec. 420-a(6), Real Property Tax Law; Sec. 420-b(5), Real Property Tax Law) Real property owned and used for hospital purposes by a free public hospital that depends for maintenance and support upon voluntary charity remains exempt if a portion of the property is leased or used for purposes of income, provided the income is necessary for and is actually applied to, the maintenance and support of the hospital. (Sec. 420-a(5), Real Property Tax Law)

In addition, real property owned for more than 100 years as of January 1, 1983, by a corporation organized by a special charter of the New York Legislature and leased to an exempt educational organization for a period of more than 25 years is also exempt as if the property was owned by an education corporation and used exclusively for educational purposes. The lease must provide that the lessee is required to pay the property tax. (Sec. 420-a(7), Real Property Tax Law)

> *CCH COMMENT: START-UP NY.*—The SUNY Tax-Free Areas to Revitalize and Transform Upstate (START-UP) New York program provides a property tax exemption to promote business and job creation by transforming public higher education through tax-free communities in upstate New York and other strategically-designated locations. Private universities and colleges will maintain tax-exempt status on property that is currently tax exempt and that they subsequently lease to businesses participating in the START-UP NY program. Only the portion of the property that is used for purposes of the START-UP NY program will be exempt. (Sec. 420-a, Real Property Tax Law)

• *Parsonages*

Property owned by a religious organization and used as the residence of the officiating clergyman is exempt. Real property owned for residential use by a minister, priest or rabbi who is either working in an assignment by a church or denomination or who is unable to work due to impaired health or advanced age (over 70) is exempt from taxation to the extent of $1,500 of assessed valuation. (Sec. 462, Real Property Tax Law; Sec. 460, Real Property Tax Law)

• *Constitutionality of religious exemption*

The U.S. Supreme Court has held that the New York property tax exemption for real property owned by churches and used exclusively for religious purposes does not constitute governmental "establishment of religion" in violation of the First Amendment to the United States Constitution. (*Walz v. Tax Commission of the City of New York*, 397 U.S. 654 (1970)) The Court ruled that the First Amendment prohibition against governmental "establishment of religion, or prohibiting the free exercise thereof" requires neutrality only to the extent of barring governmental sponsorship, on the one extreme, and governmental suppression, on the other. The indirect economic benefit granted to churches by exemption from a property tax burden that must be borne by others does not amount to governmental sponsorship.

• *Academies of music*

Academies of music in cities with a population of 175,000 or more may be wholly or partially exempted by local option. The property must have been acquired with the proceeds of popular or general subscription. The exemption is not allowed in the year following any year in which the corporation earned a net annual income upon the net cost of the academy. (Sec. 434, Real Property Tax Law)

• *Agricultural societies' permanent exhibition grounds*

Property owned by an agricultural society and permanently used by it for a meeting hall or exhibition grounds is exempt from taxation. (Sec. 450, Real Property Tax Law) For a discussion of agricultural property, see ¶ 20-115.

• *Brooklyn Academy of Music*

The property of the Brooklyn Academy of Music is exempt even though a portion is leased or used for public performances or other noncommercial uses, provided the income produced is necessary for and actually applied to the maintenance and support of the Academy. (Sec. 424, Real Property Tax Law)

• *Dental societies*

Property owned by a dental society within a city with a population of 175,000 or more is partially exempt unless disallowed by local law, provided the property is used exclusively for the purposes of the dental society. In the 1st, 2nd, 10th or 11th judicial districts (New York, Richmond, Kings, Queens, Nassau and Suffolk Counties) the exemption is limited to $100,000. In all other judicial districts, the exemption is limited to $50,000. (Sec. 474, Real Property Tax Law)

• *Firefighters associations*

Property owned by an incorporated volunteer fire company is wholly exempt if used for the following purposes: (Sec. 464(2), Real Property Tax Law)

> • actual and exclusive use and occupation by the fire company or fire department for public purposes;

> • lease to the city, town, village or fire district in which the property is located and actual use and occupation by that city, town, village or fire district for fire department purposes or for the social and recreational use of the firefighters and residents of the locality, provided the rent under the lease does not exceed the amount of carrying, maintenance and depreciation charges; or

> • lease to the school district in which it is located and actual and exclusive use for school district purposes, provided the rent under the lease does not exceed the amount of carrying, maintenance and depreciation charges.

Public purposes.—Public purposes are: (Sec. 464(3), Real Property Tax Law)

> • housing, storage, repair and testing of fire department vehicles and of equipment, appliances, devices, tools, protective clothing, uniforms and supplies;

> • receipt and dispatch of alarms;

> • training, drills and instruction;

> • generators, lockers, showers, custodial quarters;

> • offices, company meetings, ready room; or

> • social and recreational use, other than for income-producing or business purposes, of both the firemen and residents of the city, town, village or fire district in which the real property is located.

In addition, property owned by an incorporated association of present or former volunteer firefighters, not organized as a business corporation, is exempt in an amount not to exceed $20,000, provided the property is used for the following purposes: (Sec. 464(1), Real Property Tax Law)

> • actual and exclusive use and occupation by the incorporated association;

> • lease to the city, town, village or fire district in which the property is located and actual use and occupation by that city, town, village or fire district for fire department purposes or for the social and recreational use of the firefighters and residents of the locality, provided the rent under the lease does not exceed the amount of carrying, maintenance and depreciation charges; or

> • lease to the school district in which it is located and actual and exclusive use for school district purposes, provided the rent under the lease does not exceed the amount of carrying, maintenance and depreciation charges.

Property owned by a corporation organized to maintain a fire patrol and salvage corporation for the public benefit and used exclusively for housing or storing property used exclusively for the purpose of the fire patrol and salvage corporation, is wholly exempt from taxation. The fire patrol and salvage service must be rendered indiscriminately and without charge for public benefit. (Sec. 468, Real Property Tax Law)

Villages may adopt an exemption for property owned by volunteer fire companies in the village, or by volunteer members of the village fire department, in an amount not to exceed $500. (Sec. 466, Real Property Tax Law)

Volunteer firefighters and ambulance workers.—A 10% exemption may be granted for the primary residences of certain volunteer firefighters and ambulance workers in the counties listed below, through the adoption of a local law, ordinance, or resolution. The exemption may not exceed $3,000 multiplied by the latest state equalization rate for the assessing unit in which the real property is located. The $3,000 multiplier cap does not apply to firefighters and ambulance personnel who reside in counties with a population of over 1.3 million but less than 1.4 million. (Sec. 466-a, Real Property Tax Law; Sec. 466-b, Real Property Tax Law)

To be eligible for the exemption, the applicant must reside in one of the listed counties, be a member of a volunteer fire or ambulance organization for a minimum of five years, the property must be the primary residence of the applicant, and the property must be used exclusively for residential purposes. (Sec. 466-a, Real Property Tax Law; Sec. 466-b, Real Property Tax Law)

The exemption applies in the following counties, based on the listed populations:

- between 26,000 and 27,500;
- between 31,000 and 32,500 (Schoharie County);
- between 43,400 and 43,600 (Wyoming County);
- between 44,100 and 44,600 (Orleans County);
- between 49,000 and 49,900;
- between 63,000 and 63,100 (Columbia County);
- between 73,000 and 74,000 (Sullivan County);
- between 79,000 and 80,000 (Clinton County);
- between 83,001 and 84,499 (Cattaraugus County);
- between 95,000 and 96,000 (Putnam County);
- between 98,700 and 99,000 (Steuben County);
- between 110,000 and 113,000;
- between 120,000 and 141,000;
- between 146,000 and 150,000;
- between 175,000 and 180,000 (Ulster County);
- between 218,000 and 223,000 (Niagara County);
- between 225,000 and 250,000 (Oneida County);
- between 261,000 and 270,000 (Rockland County);
- between 280,000 and 280,200 (Dutchess County);
- between 292,000 and 297,000 (Albany County);
- between 300,000 and 350,000 (Orange County);
- between 458,000 and 460,000 (Onondaga County);
- between 900,000 and 950,000 (Westchester County);
- between 950,000 and 960,000 (Erie County);
- between 1.3 million and 1.4 million and not located within a city with a population of 1 million or more; and
- between 1.4 million and 1.5 million.

(Sec. 466-a, Real Property Tax Law; Sec. 466-b, Real Property Tax Law; Sec. 466-c, Real Property Tax Law; Sec. 466-d, Real Property Tax Law; Sec. 466-e, Real Property Tax Law; Sec. 466-f, Real Property Tax Law; Sec. 466-g, Real Property Tax Law; Sec. 466-h, Real Property Tax Law; Sec. 466-i, Real Property Tax Law; Sec. 466-j, Real Property Tax Law)

Any municipality may provide an exemption from New York property tax for un-remarried spouses of members of volunteer fire companies or volunteer ambulance services killed in the line of duty. The un-remarried spouse must be certified by the authority having jurisdiction for the the incorporated volunteer fire company, fire department or incorporated voluntary ambulance service, the deceased volunteer must have been an active member of the volunteer organization for at least five years, and the deceased volunteer must have been previously receiving the exemption. (Sec. 466-h, Real Property Tax Law)

• *Fraternal organizations*

The grand lodge of a fraternal organization, used for its meetings or meetings of the general assembly of its members or subordinate bodies, or by other fraternal organizations for the same purpose, is exempt, provided the entire income produced by the property is used to support institutions for care of indigent members and their families. (Sec. 428, Real Property Tax Law)

• *Health maintenance organizations*

The property of not-for-profit corporations operating as health maintenance organizations and used exclusively for their corporate purposes is exempt. (Sec. 486-a, Real Property Tax Law)

• *Historical societies*

Historic sites owned by historical societies are exempt from tax, provided that no more than six acres is held in any one locality. (Sec. 444, Real Property Tax Law; Sec. 1408, Not-for-Profit Corporation Law)

• *Infant home corporations*

Property owned by an infant home corporation actually dedicated and used by the corporation exclusively as a place for the free maintenance, care and recreation of children six years old and under is exempt. (Sec. 440, Real Property Tax Law)

• *Interdenominational centers*

Property owned by a corporation organized for the purpose of establishing an interdenominational center and to promote cooperation among various religious denominations is exempt. Property leased to such a corporation for the same purpose is also exempt if the owner is a nonprofit corporation exempt under Sec. 420-a, Real Property Tax Law, or by a nonprofit corporation exempt under Sec. 420-b, Real Property Tax Law, that is not taxed by local option. (Sec. 430, Real Property Tax Law)

• *Lincoln Center for the Performing Arts*

Property of the Lincoln Center for the Performing Arts is exempt provided it is used for the production of musical and performing art and other related educational activities. The property is exempt even though a portion is leased or used for public performances or other noncommercial uses, if the income produced is necessary for and is actually applied to the maintenance and support of the corporation, provided that leasing is not the principal use made of the property. (Sec. 427, Real Property Tax Law)

- *Opera houses*

Real property owned by a corporation whose certificate of incorporation is approved by the Commissioner of Education and that is organized to sustain, encourage, and promote musical art and to educate the general public in good music, is exempt, provided:

- moneys donated to the organization as a result of popular or general appeal have been used for the acquisition of the property;

- the property is maintained for the production of opera and providing operatic and musical performance and other related educational activities.

(Sec. 426, Real Property Tax Law)

The property is exempt even though a portion is leased or used for public performances or other noncommercial uses, provided the income produced is necessary for and is actually applied to the maintenance and support of the corporation.

- *Pharmaceutical societies*

Property owned by an incorporated pharmaceutical society within a city with a population of 175,000 or more is wholly exempt unless disallowed by local law, provided:

- no rent is derived from the property;

- the society is authorized by state law to establish a college of pharmacy; and

- the property is used exclusively for the purpose of operating a college of pharmacy.

(Sec. 472, Real Property Tax Law)

- *Retirement systems*

Property owned by a private nonprofit retirement system is wholly exempt. (Sec. 488, Real Property Tax Law; Sec. 4607, Insurance Law)

- *Nonprofit property/casualty insurance companies*

An exemption is provided for nonprofit property/casualty insurance companies subject to the provisions of Insurance Law Article 67. (Sec. 6707, Insurance Law)

- *Soldiers' monument corporations*

Property owned by a soldiers' monument corporation and used for a soldiers' memorial is exempt. Property of a soldiers' monument corporation not used for memorial purposes may also be exempt as veterans' organization property if the membership of the corporation is composed of U.S. veterans of war. (Sec. 442, Real Property Tax Law; Sec. 1405, Not-for-Profit Corporation Law; Sec. 452(3), Real Property Tax Law)

- *Theatrical corporations*

Real property owned by a nonprofit theatrical corporation created by an Act of Congress used for the purpose of a theater and dramatic school and to present productions, is exempt, provided the property was acquired with moneys donated to the owning corporation as a result of a popular or general appeal. The property is fully exempt even if a portion of the property is leased or used by another corporation organized for purposes exempt under Sec. 420-a, Sec. 420-b, Sec. 422, Sec. 424, Sec. 426, Sec. 428, or Sec. 430, Real Property Tax Law, and for one or more of the purposes for which the theatrical corporation is organized, provided the property is actually used for such purposes. Likewise, the property is fully exempt even if the auditorium is leased or used for public performances and other educational noncommercial uses, provided the income produced is necessary for and actually applied to the maintenance and support of the owner corporation and is not used for acquisition of additional real property in New York State. (Sec. 432, Real Property Tax Law)

• *Veterans' associations*

Property owned by a corporation or association of veterans of the U.S. armed forces in any war is exempt if actually used by the corporation or association. The property is also exempt if some or all of the property is used by another corporation or association whose property would be entitled to exemption under Article 4 of the Real Property Tax Law, other than an organization exempt under Sec. 408 (school districts), Sec. 440 (infant homes), Sec. 466 (volunteer fire companies in village) or Sec. 478 (off-street automobile parking providing underground shelter) of the Real Property Tax Law. However, the property is taxable if the sums paid to the owning corporation or association by the corporation using the property exceeds the amount of carrying, maintenance and depreciation charges of the portion of the property used. (Sec. 452(1), Real Property Tax Law; Sec. 452(2), Real Property Tax Law)

Municipalities may exempt from local taxes any portion of property owned by veterans' organizations that is rented to community, charitable, educational, or other organizations that may not be tax-exempt entities. (Sec. 452(2), Real Property Tax Law)

Property of a soldiers' monument corporation not used for memorial purposes may also be exempt as veterans' organization property if the membership of the corporation is composed of U.S. veterans of war. See above under **Soldiers' monument corporations**.

[¶20-295] Personal Property

Property taxation in New York State is limited to real property, and exemptions are provided for both tangible and intangible personal property. Tangible personal property is exempt by statute. (Sec. 300, Real Property Tax Law) *Ad valorem* taxation of intangible property is prohibited by the New York Constitution. (Sec. 3, Art. XVI, N.Y. Const.)

For a discussion of real property, see ¶20-310.

[¶20-310] Real Property

All real property in New York is subject to taxation unless exempted by law. (Sec. 300, Real Property Tax Law) For New York property tax purposes, real property includes the following:

— land, including land above or under water, trees and undergrowth, and any minerals, fossils or quarries below the land's surface; (Sec. 102(12)(a), Real Property Tax Law)

— buildings and other structures, substructures and superstructures above or below ground, articles and structures affixed to land or other structures, bridges, wharves and piers and the value of the right to collect wharfage, dockage or cranage, but not including bulk milk tanks or coolers on a farm to hold milk before shipment, or silos located on operating farms used to store livestock feed; (Sec. 102(12)(b), Real Property Tax Law)

— railroads, whether located on the land's surface, underground or elevated, and including all railroad structures, substructures and superstructures, tracks, branches, switches and any other authorized or permitted railroad fixture; (Sec. 102(12)(c), Real Property Tax Law)

— telephone and telegraph lines, wires, poles, supports and enclosures for electrical conductors upon, above and underground, if owned by a telephone company (a regulated company providing non-cellular switched local exchange telephone service to the general public within its exchange area, at the points of origination and termination of the signal)—station connections do not constitute real property; (Sec. 102(12)(d), Real Property Tax Law)

— lines, wires, poles, supports and enclosures for electrical conductors upon, above and underground, not owned by a telephone company, and used in connection with the transmission or switching of electromagnetic voice, video and data signals between different entities separated by air, street or other public domain, other than station connections, fire and surveillance alarm system property, property used in the transmission of news wire services, or property used in transmission of news or entertainment radio, television or cable television signals; (Sec. 102(12)(i), Real Property Tax Law)

— mains, pipes and tanks used for the transmission of steam, heat, water, oil, electricity or other property capable of such transmission, which are permitted to be laid or placed in, upon, above or under any public or private street; (Sec. 102(12)(e), Real Property Tax Law)

— boilers, ventilating apparatuses, elevators, plumbing, heating, lighting, power generators, shafting other than counter-shafting, and equipment for the distribution of heat, light, power, gases and liquids (excluding movable machinery or equipment consisting of structures to the operation of which machinery is essential, owned by a corporation subject to the Business Corporation Franchise Tax (Article 9-A), used for trade or manufacture, and not essential to the support of the building or structure). (Sec. 102(12)(f), Real Property Tax Law) (*Note:* A transition provision with respect to the movable machinery exemption applies to certain taxpayers that were transferred from Article 9 taxation to Article 9-A taxation by Ch. 63 (A.B. 11006), Laws 2000; see the footnote under Sec. 102(12)(f), Real Property Tax Law);

— trailers and mobile homes that are or can be used for residential, commercial or office purposes, except those that are:

(a) within the assessment unit for less than 60 days;

(b) unoccupied and for sale; or

(c) recreational vehicles that are 400 square feet or less in size, self-propelled or towable by an automobile or light duty truck, and used as temporary living quarters for recreational, camping, travel or seasonal use; (Sec. 102(12)(g), Real Property Tax Law) and

— special franchises.

(Sec. 102(12)(h), Real Property Tax Law)

Special franchises.—Special franchises are the franchises, rights, authority or permission of utilities to construct or use above, in or under public streets and places pipes, tanks, conduits, wires or transformers for conducting water, steam, light, power, electricity, gas or other substances. (Sec. 102(17), Real Property Tax Law) Property of a municipal corporation, public benefit corporation or special district does not constitute a special franchise. Crossings of less than 250 feet in length of a public way outside a city or village are also excluded from the definition of special franchise, unless they are a continuation of an occupancy of another public way.

Relief for certain storm-damaged property.—Eligible municipalities may allow a reduction in the assessment of property that has lost value due to specified hurricane or storm damage. See the discussion at ¶20-640 Real Property Valuation.

[¶20-330] Utilities

The following constitute real property for New York property tax purposes, and therefore are not eligible for exemption as personal property:

— mains, pipes and tanks permitted or authorized to be made, laid or placed in, upon, above or under any public or private street or place to conduct steam, heat, water, oil, electricity or any property, substance or product capable of transportation or conveyance therein or that is protected thereby; (Sec. 102(12)(e), Real Property Tax Law)

— heating, lighting and power generating apparatuses and equipment for the distribution of heat, light, power, gases and liquids (however, movable machinery or equipment consisting of structures to the operation of which machinery is essential, owned by a corporation taxable under Article 9-A of the Tax Law, used for trade or manufacture, not essential for the support of the building or structure, and removable without injury to the structure, is not real property). (Sec. 102(12)(f), Real Property Tax Law) (*Note:* A transition provision with respect to the movable machinery exemption applies to certain taxpayers that were transferred from Article 9 taxation to Article 9-A taxation by Ch. 63 (A.B. 11006), Laws 2000; see the footnote under Sec. 102(12)(f), Real Property Tax Law); and

— special franchises, that is, franchises, rights, authority or permission of utilities to construct or use above, in or under public streets and places, pipes, tanks, conduits, wires or transformers for conducting water, steam, light, power, electricity, gas or other substances. (Sec. 102(17), Real Property Tax Law)

A deduction is allowed against taxes imposed on special franchises for taxes paid to an assessing unit based upon a percentage of gross earnings or other income, or a license fee or other sum paid on account of the special franchise. (Sec. 626, Real Property Tax Law)

The costs and expenses of the State Division of Taxation incurred in the assessment of special franchises are paid by an annual charge on special franchise owners, assessed to each owner in relation to the total full value of its special franchise property. (Sec. 600, Real Property Tax Law)

Property of a municipal corporation, public benefit corporation or special district does not constitute a special franchise. Crossings of less than 250 feet in length of a public way outside a city or village are also excluded from the definition of special franchise, unless they are a continuation of an occupancy of another public way.

• *Dams and reservoirs*

Dams and reservoirs, including the related right or privilege and capacity to store or provide water for power purposes, are generally taxable in the assessing unit in which they are located. The interest of a dam or reservoir owner in the use, occupation, or possession of lands occupied or submerged by a dam or a reservoir for the storage of water for power purposes, or the right to use, occupy, or possess such lands, is taxable as real property if the legal title to the occupied or submerged lands is held by the state or a person other than the owner of the dam or reservoir but the dam or reservoir owner holds an interest in the lands under an easement, right or lease for a term of 50 years or more. This provision does not apply, however, to the water supply system of a municipality. (Sec. 556(1), Real Property Tax Law)

• *Nuclear powered electric generating facilities*

Local governments and school districts in New York are authorized to adopt local laws and resolutions exempting nuclear powered electric generating facilities from property taxes, special ad valorem levies, and special assessments. Payments in lieu of taxes are required. For purposes of these provisions, "nuclear powered electric generating facility" means a facility that uses nuclear power to generate electricity for sale, directly or indirectly, to the public. The provisions apply to the land upon which such a facility is located, any equipment used in such generation, and equipment leading from the facility to the interconnection with the electric transmission system, but they do not apply to any equipment in the electric transmission system. (Sec. 485, Real Property Tax Law; Sec. 490, Real Property Tax Law; Sec. 1227, Real Property Tax Law)

• *Local public utility mass properties*

Effective January 1, 2015, applicable to assessment rolls with taxable status dates on or after that date, and expiring January 1, 2023, annual assessment ceilings are established by the Commissioner of Taxation and Finance for local public utility mass real properties located in a particular town, village, city or county assessing unit and under the same ownership. (Sec. 499-jjjj, Real Property Tax Law; Sec. 499-kkkk, Real Property Tax Law; Sec. 499-llll, Real Property Tax Law) Also, legislation extends and restructures the transitional provisions of the program so changes will be phased in gradually. Specifically, assessment ceilings are allowed to deviate from the 2014 assessments by as much as 25% in 2018, 50% in 2019 and 75% in 2020. In 2021, the ceilings will no longer be tied to the 2014 assessments. (Sec. 499-kkkk, Real Property Tax Law)

Owners of local public utility mass real property will be subject to an annual fee for any costs and expenses incurred by the commissioner in the establishment of assessment ceilings, computed according to a rule as issued by the commissioner. The valuation date will be January 1 of the year preceding the year in which the assessment roll on which such property is to be assessed, completed and filed in the office of the city or town clerk. (Sec. 499-iiii, Real Property Tax Law)

"Public utility mass real property" means real property, including conduits, cables, lines, wires, poles, supports, and enclosures for electrical conductors located on, above, and below real property, that is used in the transmission and distribution of telephone or telegraph service, and electromagnetic voice, video and data signals. (Sec. 499-hhhh, Real Property Tax Law)

[¶20-400]
RATES

[¶20-405] Rates of Tax

There is no state property tax levied. Tax rates are set by each taxing district (county, city, town, village or school district or special district) by dividing the amount of money to be raised (the tax levy) by the assessed valuation of taxable property in the taxing district, subject to constitutional tax revenue limitations.

The New York state property tax structure generally is not based on a classification system, and tax rates therefore apply to all types of property (residential, industrial, commercial, agricultural). However, property is classified in New York City and Nassau County, as well as in certain other tax districts that have undertaken a general revaluation of all property and that have adopted classification provisions.

There is no distinction between land and buildings for tax rate purposes. These general tax rates are also applied to the values of special franchises for the taxation of utilities. Since New York does not require assessment at full value, the impact of the tax rate depends on the assessment ratio, the valuation of the properties and the extent of exemptions, if any.

For New York City property tax rates, see ¶520-405.

Property tax cap.—Property tax increases by local governments are capped at 2% or the rate of inflation, whichever is less. The cap is subject to limited exceptions, such as: judgments or court orders arising out of tort actions that exceed 5% of a locality's levy; growth in pension costs where the system's average rate increases by more than 2 percentage points from the previous year (the amount of contributions above the 2 percentage points is excluded from the limit); or growth in tax levies due to economic development. (Sec. 3-c, General Municipal Law; Sec. 2023-a, Education Law)

Real property tax freeze credit.—Local governments that are subject to the provisions of Sec. 2023-a, Education Law orSec. 3-c, General Municipal Law must comply with the certain requirements in order to render its taxpayers eligible for the real property tax freeze income tax credit authorized by Sec 606(bbb), Tax Law. The credit is available to taxpayers who are STAR recipients or otherwise would be STAR-eligible, and is applicable against school district and municipal taxes levied outside of the City of New York. For more information, see discussion in the income tax division at ¶ 16-957, Other Credits--Real Property Tax Freeze Credit, and *Publication 1030*, New York Department of Taxation and Finance, July 14, 2014.

Property tax relief credit.—A property tax relief credit against the personal income tax is available for tax years 2016 through 2019. The credit is available to resident homeowners who have income not exceeding $275,000 and who live in school districts that comply with the property tax cap. The credit is not available for property located in New York City. (Sec 606(n-1), Tax Law) For more information, see discussion in the income tax division.

Deferral of tax impact for reorganized school districts.—School districts that propose to reorganize are authorized to defer the impact to school district property taxes. Where such reorganization would have an impact upon the school tax rates within the areas served by the school districts that existed prior to the reorganization, the boards of education or trustees of all participating school districts, after conducting a public hearing, may adopt a resolution at least 45 days prior to the special district meeting at which the reorganization vote will be held, to defer the tax impact for up to a one-year period and/or phase in the impact for a period not to exceed 10 years. The law provides for the calculation of school district tax rates under either scenario. (Sec. 3613, Education Law)

• *Local tax rates*

Local tax rate and levy data can be accessed on the New York State Office of Real Property Tax Services website at http://orps1.orpts.ny.gov/cfapps/MuniPro/index.cfm.

[¶ 20-500]

EXEMPTIONS

[¶ 20-505] Exemptions in General

Generally, claims for exemption must be submitted to the assessor by the taxable status date (usually, March 1), accompanied by whatever documentation may be required to substantiate the taxpayer's claim. Claims may be filed late, but by the last date for filing a complaint of assessment, if the cause is the death or illness of the claimant's spouse, child, parent, or sibling. (Sec. 467(5), Real Property Tax Law; Sec. 467(5a), Real Property Tax Law)

[¶20-600]

VALUATION, ASSESSMENT, AND EQUALIZATION

[¶20-610] Valuation Procedures

"Value" is not defined in New York statutes or regulations. However, according to Uniform Assessment Standards by the New York Department of Taxation and Finance, all property is assessed at its current full value (market value). (Uniform Assessment Standards, New York Department of Taxation and Finance)

Certain provisions do apply to the valuation process. For instance, condominium and cooperative property may not be assessed at a value higher than that at which it would have been assessed if not held on a cooperative or condominium basis. In addition, the value that a rental property might have if converted to a cooperative or condominium form of ownership may not be considered in determining value. (Sec. 581(3), Real Property Tax Law)

New York courts have generally held that the standard for tax assessment purposes is the value of property in its current use, not its value at a presumed "highest and best use." (*N.Y. Properties, L.P. v. The Commissioner of Finance & The Tax Commissioner of the City of New York*, N.Y. Supreme Court, N.Y. County, 210 N.Y.L.J. 70) One exception to this standard, however, may be the valuation of vacant land.

With respect to the value of lands and structures supporting nonresidential water-dependent activities, the law specifically provides that real property owned or leased for such activities must be assessed at a sum reflecting the current use, rather than the best possible use, of the lands. (Sec. 582-a, Real Property Tax Law)

• *Valuation methods*

For a discussion of valuation methods in general, see ¶20-615.

[¶20-615] Valuation Methods in General

The most commonly used methods for valuing property, both throughout the country and by New York, are the income method, sales method (also called the market data method), cost method, and unit method. Each method has advantages and disadvantages. A particular method often becomes associated with certain types of properties. These methods are discussed at the following paragraphs:

— income method;

— sales method;

— cost method; or

— unit method.

For a discussion of valuation procedures, see ¶20-610.

[¶20-640] Real Property Valuation

In assessing units other than New York City and Nassau County, all real property in each assessing unit must be assessed either at full value or at a uniform percentage of value (fractional assessment). (Sec. 305, Real Property Tax Law) In New York City and Nassau County, a classification system is allowed. (see ¶20-105)

All real property subject to taxation, and assessed as of a March 1 taxable status date, must be valued as of the preceding July 1. The valuation date of real property in a city or town not subject to this provision must be determined as of the date provided by law applicable to such city or town, or if not so provided, then as of the taxable status date of the city or town. (Sec. 301, Real Property Tax Law) The valuation date of the real property entered on any assessment roll shall be imprinted or otherwise indicated at the top of the first page of each volume of such roll. (Sec. 301, Real Property Tax Law) For a discussion on the taxation of real property, see ¶ 20-310.

For a discussion of valuation procedures, see ¶ 20-610.

• *Lake Ontario and Connected Waterways Assessment Relief Act*

Eligible municipalities have the option to adopt, by resolution, provisions of the Lake Ontario and Connected Waterways Assessment Relief Act, which allows a reduction in the assessment of a property that has lost value due to flood damage. (Uncodified Sec. 1, Part B, Ch. 85 (A.B. 8013), Laws 2017)

The relief program can be adopted by an eligible county and any city, town, village, school district, or special district that is wholly or partly contained within an eligible county. The provisions of the legislation are available only to taxpayers in eligible municipalities that have opted to offer the relief. (Uncodified Sec. 3, Part B, Ch. 85 (A.B. 8013), Laws 2017) "Eligible municipality" means a municipal corporation which is either: (a) an eligible county; or (b) a city, town, village, special district, or school district that is wholly or partly contained within an eligible county."Eligible counties" include counties included in the governor's Executive Order 165 of 2017, declaring a state of emergency, dated May 3, 2017. (Uncodified Sec. 2, Part B, Ch. 85 (A.B. 8013), Laws 2017) The deadline for municipalities to opt into the program is August 24, 2017. (https://www.tax.ny.gov/research/property/Lake_Ontario_Legislation.htm)

The assessment reductions range from 15% for property that has lost between 10% and less than 20% of its taxable assessed value, to 100% for property that has lost 100% of its value. The local assessor will determine the percentage reduction, subject to review by the board of assessment. (Uncodified Sec. 4, Part B, Ch. 85 (A.B. 8013), Laws 2017)

Adoption of the program by a county does not apply to other local governments within the county; each municipality, school district, or special district that wishes to offer the option to its property owners must separately adopt a resolution. (Uncodified Sec. 3, Part B, Ch. 85 (A.B. 8013), Laws 2017)

To receive relief, a property owner must submit a written request to the assessor on a form approved by the Commissioner within 120 days following the date of enactment of the Act (November 7, 2017). (https://www.tax.ny.gov/research/property/Lake_Ontario_Legislation.htm) Such request must include any and all reports prepared by, but not limited to, an insurance adjuster, real property appraiser or broker that describe in reasonable detail the damage caused to the property by the flooding and the condition of the property following the flooding and may be accompanied by any other supporting documentation. The assessor must mail written notice of findings to the property owner and the participating municipality. (Uncodified Sec. 4, Part B, Ch. 85 (A.B. 8013), Laws 2017)

• *Hurricane Irene and Tropical Storm Lee Assessment Relief Act*

Adjusted assessments are authorized for storm-damaged properties affected by floods or natural disasters. Eligible municipalities have the option to adopt, by resolution, provisions of the Hurricane Irene and Tropical Storm Lee Assessment Relief Act, which allows a reduction in the assessment of a property that has lost at least 50% of its value due to hurricane or storm damage. (Sec. 3, Part G, of Ch. 56 (S.B. 50002), Laws 2011)

The assessment reductions range from 55% for property that has lost between 50% and less than 60% of its taxable assessed value to 95% for property that has lost between 90% and less than 100% of its value. If a property has lost all of its value due to storm-related damage, the taxable assessed value is reduced to zero. The local assessor will determine the percentage reduction, subject to review by the board of assessment review, and make adjustments for any applicable exemptions. (Sec. 4, Part G, of Ch. 56 (S.B. 50002), Laws 2011)

• *Superstorm Sandy Assessment Relief Act*

Legislation allows taxing jurisdictions to provide relief to property owners for damage to the improvements on property caused by Superstorm Sandy (i.e., the storms, rains, winds, or floods during the period beginning October 29, 2012, and ending November 3, 2012). The legislation applies to all improved properties; it is not limited to residential property. The legislation effectively provides relief if an assessment roll has a taxable status date prior to October 28, 2012, for taxes levied on that roll that are payable without interest on or after October 28, 2012. (Secs. 1 through 8, Ch. 424 (A.B. 8075), Laws 2013)

The relief program can be adopted by an eligible county and any city, town, village, school district, or special district that is wholly or partly contained within an eligible county. The provisions of the legislation are available only to taxpayers in eligible municipalities that have opted to offer the relief. "Eligible county" means a county, other than a county wholly contained within a city, included in FEMA-4085-DR, the notice of the presidential declaration of a major disaster for the state of New York. Specifically, the eligible counties are Greene, Nassau, Orange, Putnam, Rockland, Suffolk, Sullivan, Ulster, and Westchester.

An eligible municipality that opts in has the further option of offering relief to those whose buildings and other property improvements lost less than 50% of their value. If the municipality opts into the legislation without opting to offer relief at levels below 50%, the relief will be available only to those whose buildings and other property improvements lost 50% or more of their value.

Adoption of the program by a county does not apply to other local governments within the county; each municipality, school district, or special district that wishes to offer the option to its property owners must separately adopt a resolution. The deadline for taxing jurisdictions to opt into the program is December 6, 2013.

To receive relief, the property owner in a participating municipality must submit a written request to the assessor (using Form RP-5849-APP), along with supporting documentation. The deadline for a property owner to apply for assessment relief is January 21, 2014.

The summary provides additional details regarding the application process, assessment reductions, relevant forms, determinations, and board of assessment review. (*Summary of Legislation, Superstorm Sandy Assessment Relief Act*, N.Y. Department of Taxation and Finance, October 2013)

The deadline is extended for the town of Smithtown to exercise the provisions of the Superstorm Sandy Assessment Relief Act. Any school district within the town of Smithtown may provide assessment relief for real property impacted by Superstorm Sandy located within the district, after passage of a resolution electing to do so, within one year of October 21, 2014. (Uncodified Sec. 1 (S.B. 6959), Laws 2014)

For a discussion of authorization of a property tax abatement for New York City taxpayers who rebuilt or repaired property after Superstorm Sandy, see ¶ 20-810.

¶20-640

• *Mohawk Valley and Niagara County Assessment Relief Act*

Eligible municipalities have the option to adopt, by resolution, provisions of the Mohawk Valley and Niagara County Assessment Relief Act, which allows a reduction in the assessment of a property that has lost value due to hurricane or storm damage. (Sec. 3, Part T, Ch. 55 (A.B. 8555), Laws 2014)

The relief program can be adopted by an eligible county and any city, town, village, school district, or special district that is wholly or partly contained within an eligible county. The provisions of the legislation are available only to taxpayers in eligible municipalities that have opted to offer the relief. "Eligible municipality" means a municipal corporation which is either: (a) an eligible county; or (b) a city, town, village, special district, or school district that is wholly or partly contained within an eligible county."Eligible counties" include Oneida, Herkimer, Madison, Montgomery, Tompkins, Cortland, Chemung, Schuyler, Steuben and Niagara. (Sec. 2, Part T, Ch. 55 (A.B. 8555), Laws 2014)

The assessment reductions range from 15% for property that has lost between 10% and less than 20% of its taxable assessed value, to 100% for property that has 100% of its value. The local assessor will determine the percentage reduction, subject to review by the board of assessment review. (Sec. 4, Part T, Ch. 55 (A.B. 8555), Laws 2014)

Adoption of the program by a county does not apply to other local governments within the county; each municipality, school district, or special district that wishes to offer the option to its property owners must separately adopt a resolution. The deadline for taxing jurisdictions to opt into the program is May 15, 2014.

To receive relief, the property owner in a participating municipality must submit a written request to the assessor (using Form RP-6361-APP), along with supporting documentation. The deadline for a property owner to apply for assessment relief is June 30, 2014. (*Summary of Legislation, Mohawk Valley and Niagara County Assessment Relief Act*, N.Y. Department of Taxation and Finance, April 2014)

Installment payments also are allowed, if adopted by local law, in certain school districts affected by floods or natural disasters. See ¶ 20-756 Payment.

[¶20-645] Personal Property Valuation

Property taxation in New York State is limited to real property, and exemptions are provided for both tangible and intangible personal property. Tangible personal property is exempt by statute. (Sec. 300, Real Property Tax Law) *Ad valorem* taxation of intangible property is prohibited by the New York Constitution. (Sec. 3, Art. XVI, N.Y. Const.)

For a discussion of valuation procedures, see ¶ 20-610.

[¶20-750]

PAYMENT, COLLECTION OF TAXES

[¶20-752] Interest

Interest is charged on late payment of property tax at the rate set by the Commissioner of Taxation and Finance pursuant to Sec. 697(j), Tax Law. The rate may not be less than 1% per month. The same rate of interest is applied to installment payments of taxes made after the interest-free period. Taxes are considered late and must be paid with interest after the later of January 31 or 31 days after receipt of the tax roll and warrant by the collecting officer. (Sec. 924-a, Real Property Tax Law; Sec. 924, Real Property Tax Law)

Village taxes remaining unpaid after July 1 bear interest at the rate of 5% for July, and at the general rate set by the Commissioner for each subsequent whole or partial month that the tax remains unpaid. (Sec. 1432, Real Property Tax Law)

[¶20-756] Payment of Tax

There are no statutory requirements for returns by real property owners in connection with New York real property taxes. Special applications and reports are required in connection with special franchises, forest lands, and certain railroads.

Special franchises.—Every person, partnership, association, or corporation acquiring a special franchise (the special franchise owner) must, within 30 days after acquisition of the special franchise, make a written report to the Commissioner of Taxation and Finance containing a full description of the special franchise, a copy of the special law, grant, ordinance, or contract under which it is held, or a reference to the general law applicable, and a statement of any conditions related to the special franchise. (Sec. 604(1), Real Property Tax Law)

Annual and supplemental reports may be required by the commissioner. (Sec. 604(2), Real Property Tax Law)

Forest lands.—Owners of eligible tracts of forest lands must file an application with the Department of Environmental Conservation for consideration of classification as forest lands. (Sec. 480-a(2), Real Property Tax Law)

Notices of forest crop cuttings must be given to the chief fiscal officers of the counties wherein the tract is located. (Sec. 480-a(5)(a), Real Property Tax Law) The notice must be filed at least 30 days before cutting.

Railroads.—Each railroad company must furnish to the Commissioner of Taxation and Finance copies of financial statements and such other reports as are required by the state board. (Sec. 489-q, Real Property Tax Law; Sec. 489-nn, Real Property Tax Law)

Payments.—Property taxes are payable to the collecting officer of the assessing unit. (Sec. 924(1), Real Property Tax Law) The collecting officer is the elected or appointed officer of the municipality or district authorized by law to receive and collect taxes. The collecting officer is required to receive taxes at the times and places indicated in the notice of receipt of the tax roll and warrant, as well as during usual business hours during the period of collection. Payment may also be sent by mail or designated delivery service to the appropriate collecting officer. (Sec. 925, Real Property Tax Law)

Partial payments.—Collecting officers are authorized to accept partial payments. Governing bodies that adopt a resolution permitting partial payments of property taxes may require a service charge of up to $10 to be paid with each partial payment. School districts within governing bodies that have adopted a resolution authorizing partial payments may also pass a resolution authorizing partial payments for school district purposes. (Sec. 928-a, Real Property Tax Law)

Optional payment extensions for STAR exemption recipients.—Senior citizens who qualify for the school tax relief (STAR) exemption are allowed a grace period of five business days to make payments of New York property taxes without penalty or interest if the governing body of a municipal corporation, other than a county, adopts this delayed payment provision. (Sec. 925-b, Real Property Tax Law)

Due date.—Taxes are due by January 31, or within 30 days of the date of receipt of the tax roll and warrant, whichever is later. (Sec. 924(2), Real Property Tax Law) Taxes are timely paid if received in an envelope bearing a U.S. postmark dated no later than the due date of the tax payment. The above reference to a U.S. postmark is treated as including any date recorded or marked by a designated delivery service, as provided in IRC Sec. 7502. Also, payment will be deemed to have been made on the date of delivery if the postmark is illegible or does not appear. (Sec. 925, Real Property Tax Law)

Mailing rules.—Generally, any tax return or document required to be filed or payment made will be deemed filed as of the U.S. postmark date stamped on the envelope. However, where delivery is made by courier, delivery messenger or similar service, the filing date will be the date the return or document is received. (Reg. Sec. 2399.2) See also Publication 55, Designated Private Delivery Services.

Extensions for payment.—Due dates for tax payments that fall on a Saturday, Sunday or public holiday are automatically extended to the first business day following the due date. (Reg. Sec. 2399.3)

During a natural disaster, the Governor may extend through the disaster period and up to 30 days afterward the final date for paying tax without penalty or interest. The governing body of a municipal corporation, other than a county, may, by resolution adopted prior to the levy of any real property taxes, extend the deadline for payment of taxes without penalty or interest up to five business days for citizens 65 years of age or older. (Sec. 925-b(1), Real Property Tax Law)

If an extension is granted due to a natural disaster or municipal corporation resolution for senior citizens and the tax is not paid, those taxes are subject to the same penalties and interest that would have applied had no extension been granted. (Sec. 925-b(1), Real Property Tax Law)

An extension of the property tax due date for the payment of taxes without interest or penalty during a state disaster emergency is allowed for up to 21 days. (Sec. 925-a, Real Property Tax Law)

Village taxes.—Village taxes may be paid without interest on or before July 1, unless the village has elected to change its fiscal year as provided in Secs. 5-510 and Sec. 17-1729 of the Village Law. (Sec. 1432(1), Real Property Tax Law)

• *Installment payments*

County legislative bodies may adopt by local law a provision for the payment of property taxes in a number of equal installments unless the taxes are paid through a real property escrow account. (Sec. 972, Real Property Tax Law)

The local law sets the number of installments and the due dates of each installment. The due date of the first installment must be no later than the last day of the month in which the taxes would otherwise be payable without interest and the last installment can be no later than the last day of the fiscal year for which it was levied. In the case of a school district, the last installment can be no later than August 31 following the conclusion of the fiscal year. Each installment, other than the first, shall be subject to interest. If an installment is not paid on or before the due date, additional interest shall be added. The installment program applies to all types of property unless the local law establishing the program limits it to one or more of the following types of property:

    • property that has been assessed as a one, two or three family residence; or

    • property that is exempt from taxation because it is owned by someone 65 years of age or older; or

    • property containing improvements that are exempt from taxation because the resident owner or member of the resident owner's family is disabled; or

    • property that is owned by, or used as, the principle residence of a person who receives supplemental security income.

(Sec. 972, Real Property Tax Law)

Cities and towns in the county may decide whether to adopt the installment payment provisions, and taxpayers may decide whether to participate in the program. (Sec. 973, Real Property Tax Law)

The governing body of a tax district may enact and amend a local law providing for the installment payment of eligible delinquent property taxes. The maximum term of installment agreements cannot exceed 36 months. The payment schedule may be monthly, bi-monthly, quarterly or semi-annually, and the required initial down payment, if any, may not exceed 25% of the eligible delinquent taxes. The properties can be either:

(1) residential property;

(2) both residential and farm property; or

(3) all properties within the tax district.

(Sec. 1184(3), Real Property Tax Law)

The waiver of interest and penalties is available for certain eligible deployed military members. (Sec. 1184(7-a), Real Property Tax Law)

Installment payments of school district taxes.—A school district may, by resolution, provide that real property tax in excess of $50 levied by the county board may be paid in three installments. The first installment must be at least 50% of the total tax due, or a lesser amount if adopted by resolution, and is due no later than the last day of the one-month collection period prescribed by law. The second payment must be at least 50% of the remaining tax due, or a lesser amount if adopted by resolution, plus interest at the rate set by law and paid by a specified date. The third and final payment must comprise the remaining tax due, plus interest, and must be paid by the date specified in the resolution for the expiration of the warrant, which is not later than the 15th day of the following November. (Sec. 1326-a.1, Real Property Tax Law)

CCH COMMENT: Installment payments—floods or natural disasters.— Property tax installment payments are allowed in certain school districts affected by floods or natural disasters. A school district that is located in a federally declared disaster county is allowed to adopt, by resolution and within the six months preceding the due date for school taxes, an installment payment schedule, with payment amounts and dates specified in the resolution. Such school district is authorized to refund any portion of taxes previously paid if the school board adopts an installment payment resolution. (Sec. 1326-b, Real Property Tax Law)

The installment program applies to all property within the school district unless it is explicitly limited to specific classes of property. (Sec. 1326-a.4, Real Property Tax Law)

The Board of Trustees of a village may adopt a resolution to provide for payment of taxes in two installments. (Sec. 1434, Real Property Tax Law)

Payments via the Internet.—any local government authorizing the payment of property taxes via the Internet must provide a confirmation page to the taxpayer following the completion of the Internet transaction. The confirmation page must include, at least, the following:

(1) the date the transaction was completed and sent by the taxpayer; and

(2) a notice to the taxpayer to print out and retain the confirmation page as his of her receipt.

(Sec. 925-c, Real Property Law)

¶20-756

[¶20-758] Assessment of Delinquent Tax

Property taxes are payable to the collecting officer of the assessing unit. (Sec. 924(1), Real Property Tax Law) The collecting officer is the elected or appointed officer of the municipality or district authorized by law to receive and collect taxes. The collecting officer is required to receive taxes at the times and places indicated in the notice of receipt of the tax roll and warrant, as well as during usual business hours during the period of collection. Payment may also be sent by mail or designated delivery service to the appropriate collecting officer. (Sec. 925, Real Property Tax Law)

Taxes are due by January 31, or within 30 days of the date of receipt of the tax roll and warrant, whichever is later. (Sec. 924(2), Real Property Tax Law) Taxes are timely paid if received in an envelope bearing a U.S. postmark dated no later than the due date of the tax payment. The above reference to a U.S. postmark is treated as including any date recorded or marked by a designated delivery service, as provided in IRC §7502. Also, payment will be deemed to have been made on the date of delivery if the postmark is illegible or does not appear. (Sec. 925 Real Property Tax Law)

[¶20-770] Penalties

Special franchise owners that fail to file required property tax reports are subject to a penalty of $100 for each failure plus $10 for each additional day that the failure continues. (Sec. 604(4), Real Property Tax Law)

Intrastate and interstate railroad companies that fail to file required property tax reports are subject to a penalty of $100 for each failure plus $50 for each additional day that the failure continues. (Sec. 489-q(4), Real Property Tax Law; Sec. 489-nn(3), Real Property Tax Law)

[¶20-800]

CREDITS, ABATEMENTS, REFUNDS, INCENTIVES

[¶20-810] Abatements

Abatements of tax are most commonly authorized for the purpose of enabling taxpayers to amortize the costs of certain tax-favored conduct, such as rehabilitation of substandard housing. They are often utilized in conjunction with a partial exemption from assessment increases resulting from construction of improvements.

A property tax abatement is allowed for eligible industrial and commercial buildings that are built, modernized, rehabilitated, expanded, or otherwise physically improved in New York City.

Property tax abatements are allowed for the construction of a "green roof" on a class one, two, or four property in New York City and for the construction of a solar electric generating system and electric energy storage on a class one, two, or four building in New York City.

For information on property tax abatements allowed for residential improvements, see ¶20-205 Homesteads.

- *Hurricane Sandy abatement for New York City*

New York City is authorized to grant a partial abatement of taxes on real property that was seriously damaged during Hurricane Sandy and has since been rebuilt. The abatement extends to New York City residents affected by the storm whose property tax bill in City Fiscal Year 2015 is greater than the corresponding tax liability from City Fiscal Year 2013. The law authorizes New York City to enact a local law granting a partial abatement of taxes on property that meets the following criteria:

— the Department of Finance reduced the assessed valuation of the building on the property for fiscal year 2014 from the assessed valuation for fiscal year 2013 as a result of damage caused by Hurricane Sandy;

— the Department of Finance increased the assessed valuation of the building for fiscal year 2015 from its assessed valuation for fiscal year 2014; and

— the assessed valuation of the building for fiscal year 2015 exceeds that for fiscal year 2013.

In the event that the repair or rebuilding resulted in an increase in the square footage of the affected building, there will be a proportional decrease in the amount of the abatement to reflect the increase in the square footage of the building. (Sec. 467-h, Real Property Tax Law)

• *Limitations to increased assessed value due to Superstorm Sandy repairs*

A limitation applies to increases in the assessed value of certain class one, class two and class four New York City properties that satisfy the following conditions:

— the Department of Finance reduced the assessed value of the building on the property on the assessment roll completed in 2013 from the assessed value on the assessment roll completed in 2012 as a result of damage caused by Superstorm Sandy; and

— the Department of Finance increased or will increase the assessed value of the building on the property as a result of the repair or reconstruction of damage caused by Superstorm Sandy on any assessment roll completed from 2014 through 2020.

For properties that satisfy these conditions and have not had repairs or reconstruction performed as of the assessment roll completed in 2015, the physical increase to their assessed value as a result of repairs or reconstruction that will be performed is limited to the amount of the physical decrease reflected on the assessment roll completed in 2013. Any increase in excess of the amount of the physical decrease reflected on the assessment roll completed in 2013 will be treated as an equalization (non-physical) increase and subject to the limitations for equalization increases prescribed in the Real Property Tax Law. The assessed values of the properties that satisfy the requisite conditions will not be higher than they would have been but for Superstorm Sandy. For class four and larger class two properties subject to transitional assessments, the limitation on physical increases applies to the lower of the actual assessed value or the transitional assessed value.

The limitations also apply to assessments of properties that have already been rebuilt. Where a property is rebuilt to a larger size than prior to the storm, the limitation on physical increases will be recalculated by multiplying the limitation by the percentage of the excess square footage of the building. (Sec. 11-240.1, N.Y.C. Adm. Code; Sec. 1805-a, Real Property Tax Law)

• *Housing*

Abatements are authorized for costs of substantial rehabilitation of specified multiple dwellings to eliminate substandard housing conditions. Such programs are discussed at ¶ 20-215 and ¶ 520-215.

¶20-810

A partial property tax abatement is allowed to certain homeowners of residential cooperative and condominium units in class-two multi-family residential properties. (see ¶520-140) The abatement, allowed for a three-year period ending in 1998, is determined on the basis of the average assessment per residential unit.

In New York City, abatements are also available for the reasonable costs of alterations or improvements to multiple dwellings to conserve the use of fuel, electricity or other energy sources. See ¶520-165.

• *Green buildings*

If adopted by local law, ordinance or resolution, a property tax abatement is authorized for construction of improvements to real property initiated on or after the January 1, 2013, that meets certification standards for green buildings, including Leadership in Energy and Environmental Design (LEED), the green building initiative's green globes rating system, the national green building standards as approved by the American National Standards Institute, or substantially equivalent standards for certification using a similar program for green buildings as determined by a municipal corporation. The law is clarified to provide that the required certification may be determined by an accredited professional under any of the named standards. (Sec. 470, Real Property Tax Law)

The exemption amount ranges from 100% in the first year for certified/silver, gold, or platinum LEED exemption, to 20% in the tenth year for platinum LEED exemption. A municipality may establish a maximum exemption amount in its local law, ordinance, or resolution. The value of the construction must exceed $10,000 and is documented by a building permit, if required, or other appropriate documentation as required by the assessor. (Sec. 470, Real Property Tax Law)

If approved by the assessor, the exemption becomes effective for the assessment roll that is prepared after the taxable status date. For purposes of the exemption, construction of improvements does not include ordinary maintenance and repairs. (Sec. 470, Real Property Tax Law)

For abatement provisions for green buildings in the city of Auburn, see ¶20-205 Homesteads.

• *Senior citizens' rental housing*

Municipalities may adopt local laws providing tax abatements for property subject to rent control containing rental units in which persons at least 62 years of age reside. Generally, the abatement amount is equal to the portion of any increase in the legal regulated rent that causes it to exceed one-third of the combined income of the household. The amount of the abatement is deducted from the legal maximum rent or legal regulated rent for the dwelling unit of the senior citizen.

• *Rehabilitation of historic property*

Abatements of New York City property taxes are authorized for the reasonable costs of alterations or improvements to the exteriors of designated historic landmark sites or structures. Details of the program are discussed at ¶520-200.

[¶20-900]

TAXPAYER RIGHTS AND REMEDIES

[¶20-906] Protest and Appeal of Assessments

There are a number of options available for protesting and appealing property tax assessments.

Discussed here in relation to property tax assessment appeals are:

— representation of taxpayers,

— limitations periods for appeals,

— informal conferences,

— local administrative hearings,

— state administrative hearings, and

— judicial appeals and remedies.

• *Representation of taxpayer*

Taxpayers may be represented in proceedings before the Division of Tax Appeals only by persons identified by statute, and a power of attorney may be required. With the exception of additional types of representation by individuals (i.e. parents, children, and other individuals), small claims representatives and representatives before the Bureau of Conciliation and Mediation Services are the same as representatives allowed in other proceedings before the Division of Tax Appeals (see below). (Sec. 2014, Tax Law; Reg. Sec. 3000.2)

CCH PLANNING NOTE: Obtain power of attorney right away.—One of the first steps a representative should take upon being retained is to obtain a power of attorney from the client and file it, together with a notice of appearance. Without it, he or she may discover that no one in the Department will discuss the case. Furthermore, it focuses the taxpayer's attention on the fact that the practitioner has been retained to handle the case. This may be useful if any question about that arises at a later point.

In a small claims hearing (see ¶ 20-906), certain persons may represent a taxpayer, in addition to the taxpayer's child or parent. Other individuals may also represent the taxpayer in a small claims hearing by special permission of the Tax Appeals Tribunal. (Reg. Sec. 2014; Reg. Sec. 3000.2(d))

• *Limitations periods for appeals*

In most communities, the deadline for submitting Form RP-524, Complaint on Real Property Assessment, is Grievance Day (the fourth Tuesday in May). However, there are exceptions:

— Cities and towns that share an assessor can adopt different Grievance Days between the fourth Tuesday in May and the second Tuesday in June;

— New York City - the Assessment Review Commission meets throughout the year, but complaints must be filed by March 15 for Class One properties and March 1 for all other properties;

— Nassau County - the Assessment Review Commission meets throughout the year, but complaints must be filed by March 1;

— Other cities - dates vary, contact your assessor or city clerk for the date;

— Suffolk County - town board of assessment review (BAR)'s meet on the third Tuesday in May;

— Westchester County - town BARs meet on the third Tuesday in June; and

— Villages that assess property - typically, the BAR meets on the third Tuesday of February; however, dates can vary - check with the village assessor or village clerk.

(*Grievance Procedures*, New York Department of Taxation and Finance, http://www.tax.ny.gov/pit/property/contest/grievproced.htm)

• *Informal conferences*

Prior to instituting the formal protest process, a good first step in most cases is to review the assessor's valuation records, which are public records, for neighboring and/or comparable properties to confirm whether any glaring inconsistencies are evident. For example, if the other properties have been assigned relatively higher values, that may caution against proceeding with a protest to avoid the risk of having an appraised value increased or otherwise alerting the assessor to what may essentially be a favorable appraisal. It also may be useful to directly contact the assessor to discuss what factors the assessor considered in valuing the property, as this may alert the parties to obvious valuation errors that the assessor may be willing to correct without requiring the property owner to pursue a formal protest.

• *Local administrative hearings*

Taxpayers may file complaints of allegedly illegal or erroneous assessments with the local assessors at any time before the time fixed for review by the local board of assessment review. (Sec. 524(1), Real Property Tax Law) The board of assessment review of each municipality or village hears complaints beginning the fourth Tuesday in May, or as many days after that date that the board deems necessary. (Sec. 512, Real Property Tax Law) If an assessor is employed by two assessing units, the governing body of an assessing unit may establish a date, no earlier than the fourth Tuesday in May and no later than the second Tuesday in June, for the meetings of the board of assessment review. (Sec. 525(1), Real Property Tax Law) The board takes testimony and hears proofs, and may require the owner of the property, or any other person, to appear before the board and be examined, and to produce papers relating to the assessment. (Sec. 525(2), Real Property Tax Law)

Following the hearing, the board of assessment review determines the final assessed valuation or taxable assessed valuation. (Sec. 525(3), Real Property Tax Law) If the original assessment is determined to be unlawful, it may be ordered stricken from the roll, or entered on to the exemption portion of the roll if appropriate.

Hearing panel.—The legislative body of a municipality or village may also establish an administrative hearing panel to hear assessment complaints. (Sec. 523-a, Real Property Tax Law) The findings of the panel do not fix the final assessment, but rather constitute recommendations to the board of assessment review. If a majority of the board disagree with the assessment determined by the panel, a hearing before the board is scheduled.

Form of complaint.—Complaints must be filed on forms provided by the Commissioner of Taxation and Finance and must consist of a statement specifying the respect in which the assessment is excessive, unequal or unlawful, or the respect in which real property is misclassified, and the reduction in assessed valuation or taxable assessed valuation or change in class designation or allocation of assessed valuation sought. (Sec. 524(3), Real Property Tax Law) The statement must also contain an estimate of the value of the real property.

The statement must be made by the person whose property is assessed, or by some person authorized in writing by the complainant or his officer or agent to make such statement who has knowledge of the facts stated therein. The written authorization must be made a part of the statement and bear a date within the same calendar year during which the complaint is filed. The statement must also contain the following:

"I certify that all statements made on this application are true and correct to the best of my knowledge and belief and I understand that the making of any willful false statement of material fact herein will subject me to the provisions of the penal law relevant to the making and filing of false instruments."

CCH COMMENT: Statement of stipulated value.—The complaint may include a statement that, if signed by both the assessor and the complainant, constitutes a stipulation to the assessed value to be applied to the subject parcel. If the stipulated assessed value is entered on the final assessment roll, no review of the assessment will be allowed.

Grounds for complaint.—A complaint may allege that the assessment is excessive, unequal or unlawful, or that the property is misclassified. (Sec. 524(2), Real Property Tax Law)

Excessive assessment.—An assessment is excessive if it:

— exceeds the full value of the property;

— failed to receive all or a portion of a partial exemption to which the property or the owner was entitled; or

— exceeds the transitional assessment limit in localities conducting a general revaluation that have adopted transitional assessment provisions.

(Sec. 522(4), Real Property Tax Law)

Unequal assessment.—An assessment is unequal if:

— it is made at a higher proportionate valuation that the assessed valuation of other property on the same tax roll assessed by the same officers; or

— it is improved by a one-, two- or three-family residence and is made at a higher proportion of full value than the assessed valuation of other residential property on the same tax roll assessed by the same officers.

(Sec. 522(9), Real Property Tax Law)

Unlawful assessment.—An assessment is unlawful if:

— the property is wholly exempt from taxation;

— the property is entirely outside the boundaries of the assessing district;

— the property cannot be identified by the assessment roll description or tax map land parcel number on the assessment roll;

— the entry of assessed valuation on the assessment roll was made by a person without the authority to do so; or

— a special franchise is assessed at a level in excess of th final assessment determined by the state board of equalization and assessment.

(Sec. 522(10), Real Property Tax Law)

Misclassified property.—Property is misclassified if:

(1) an incorrect class designation is entered on the assessment roll; or

(2) a class designation is entered on the assessment roll that results in an incorrect allocation of a parcel's assessed valuation between two or more classes.

(Sec. 522(6), Real Property Tax Law)

• *State administrative hearings*

Taxpayers may apply to the county director of real property tax services for the correction of clerical errors, unlawful entries, or errors in essential fact. A tax levying body may enact a resolution delegating its authority to correct clerical errors, unlawful entries, or certain errors in essential fact on tax rolls to officials empowered to authorize payment of bills without prior audit by the tax levying body or to officials responsible for the payment of bills upon audit of the municipal corporation. The resolution may only be in effect during the calendar year of adoption and must provide that the designated official only has correction authority if the recommended correction is $2500 or less. (Sec. 554(2), Real Property Tax Law; Sec. 554(9), Real Property Tax Law)

Clerical errors.—The following constitute clerical errors:

— an incorrect entry of assessed valuation on an assessment or tax roll that, due to a mistake in transcription, does not conform to the entry for the same parcel that appears on the property record card, field book or other final work product of the assessor, or the final verified statement of the board of assessment review;

— an entry that is a mathematical error present in the computation of a partial exemption;

— an incorrect entry of assessed valuation on an assessment or tax roll that would be eligible for a partial exemption, except for the failure on the part of the assessor to act on the partial exemption;

— an entry that is a mathematical error present in the computation or extension of the tax;

— an entry on an assessment roll or on a tax roll that is incorrect due to a mistake in the determination or transcription of a special assessment or charge based on units of service provided by a special district;

— a duplicate entry on an assessment or tax roll of the description or assessed valuation of an entire single parcel;

— an entry on an assessment or tax roll that is incorrect by reason of an arithmetical mistake by the assessor appearing on the property record card, field book or other final work product of the assessor;

— an incorrect entry on a tax roll of a relevied school tax or relevied village tax that has been previously paid;

— an entry on a tax roll which is incorrect by reason of a mistake in the transcription of a relevied school tax or relevied village tax; or

— an incorrect entry of assessed valuation on an assessment roll or a tax roll due to an assessor's failure to utilize the required assessment method pursuant to Sec. 581-a, Real Property Tax Law in the valuation of qualifying real property.

(Sec. 550(2), Real Property Tax Law)

Factual errors.—The following constitute errors in essential fact:

— an incorrect entry on the taxable portion of the assessment or tax roll of the assessed valuation of an improvement to real property that was destroyed or removed prior to the taxable status date for the assessment roll;

— an incorrect entry on the taxable portion of the assessment or tax roll of the assessed valuation of an improvement to real property that was not in existence or was present on a different parcel;

— an incorrect entry of acreage on the taxable portion of the assessment or tax roll, which was considered by the assessor in the valuation of the parcel and which resulted in an incorrect assessed valuation, where the acreage is shown to be incorrect on a survey submitted by the applicant;

— the omission of the value of an improvement present on real property prior to the taxable status date;

— an incorrect entry of a partial exemption on an assessment roll for a parcel that is not eligible for such partial exemption; or

— an entry on an assessment or tax roll pursuant to Article 19 of the Real Property Tax Law, concerning the preservation of class share in districts undertaking a general revaluation, which is incorrect by reason of a misclassification of property that is exclusively used for either residential or nonresidential purposes.

(Sec. 550(3), Real Property Tax Law)

Unlawful entries.—The following constitute unlawful entries:

— an entry on the taxable portion of the assessment roll or the tax roll, or both, of the assessed valuation of real property that is wholly exempt from taxation, other than for special assessments;

— an entry on an assessment roll or a tax roll of the assessed valuation of real property that is entirely outside the boundaries of the assessing unit, the school district or the special district in which the real property is designated as being located;

— an entry of assessed valuation on an assessment or tax roll that has been made by a person or body without the authority to make the entry;

— an entry of assessed valuation of state land subject to taxation on an assessment or tax roll that exceeds the assessment of such land approved by the state board; or

— an entry of assessed valuation of a special franchise on an assessment or tax roll that exceeds the final assessment determined by the state board.

(Sec. 550(7), Real Property Tax Law)

Investigation of errors.—The county director must investigate the circumstances of the claimed error to determine whether the error exists, within 10 days of the receipt of an application. The county director sends a written report of the investigation and recommendations for action to the tax levying body, which in turn must either approve or reject the application for correction. If the same alleged error also appears on a current assessment roll, the county director must also file a copy of the report and recommendations with the appropriate assessor and board of assessment review, who must consider the same to be the equivalent of a petition for correction under Sec. 553, Real Property Tax Law. The rejected application or notice of approval of the application is mailed to the taxpayer. (Sec. 554(4) and (5), Real Property Tax Law)

If the same clerical error or unlawful entry is made with respect to a substantial number of parcels in the preparation of a tax roll, a single application may be filed with the county director of real property tax services on behalf of all owners of property affected by the error or unlawful entry. (Sec. 556-b, Real Property Tax Law)

Small claims hearings.—A simplified review procedure of excessive or unequal assessments is available for assessments on one-, two- or three-family owner-occupied residential property, and on property that is unimproved and is not of sufficient size, as determined by the assessing unit or special assessing unit, to contain one-, two-, or three-family dwellings. (Sec. 730, Real Property Tax Law) The equalized value of this property, however, must not exceed $450,000 and the total assessment reduction requested must not exceed 25% of the assessed property value. A petition for small claim review must be filed within 30 days after the completion and filing of the final assessment roll containing the assessment, and may only be filed if the property owner has first filed an administrative complaint. (Sec. 730, Real Property Tax Law)

Grounds for review.—Grounds for small claims review are unequal or excessive assessment. Excessive assessment for small claims review purposes is an entry on the assessment roll that exceeds the full value of the property, or an entry on the assessment roll that is excessive because the property failed to receive all or a portion of a partial exemption to which the real property was entitled. (Sec. 729, Real Property Tax Law) Unequal assessment is an entry on the assessment roll of the assessed valuation of real property improved by a one-, two- or three family residential structure that is made at a higher proportion of full value than the assessed valuation of other residential property on the same roll, or at a higher proportion of full value than the assessed valuation of all real property on the same roll.

A small claims proceeding may relate only to a single parcel. (Sec. 730(5), Real Property Tax Law) A taxpayer seeking small claims review must waive the right to judicial review of the assessment. (Sec. 736, Real Property Tax Law) Further review is available only through an Article 78 proceeding.

The hearing is held within 45 days after the final day for filing petitions. (Sec. 732(1), Real Property Tax Law)

Limited partnerships; trusts.—Persons who own their homes through limited partnerships are allowed to qualify for small claims assessment review (SCAR) if certain conditions are met. In addition, the legislation clarifies that property held in trust may qualify for SCAR if certain statutory requirements have been met. (Sec. 730(1), Real Property Tax Law)

Review of special franchise assessments.—The owner of a special franchise, or the assessing unit in which it is located, may challenge a tentative special franchise assessment before the Commissioner of Taxation and Finance. The notice of tentative assessment states the date and time at which a hearing will be held. The owner or assessing unit must serve a written complaint specifying its objection at least ten days prior to the date set for the hearing if it intends to challenge the assessment. The requirement for making and serving the complaint may be waived by the Board if the special franchise owner and/or the assessing unit consent. (Sec. 610, Real Property Tax Law; Sec. 608, Real Property Tax Law)

The commissioner may establish a separate tentative and final special franchise value or assessment for physical property that was omitted when calculating special franchise values for the assessment roll of the preceding year. Values for omitted property must be calculated by the same procedures used when establishing the values for the roll from which the property was omitted. The Board may also deduct from the tentative and final values or assessments of special franchise property an amount for physical property that was incorrectly included in the values or assessments of the assessment roll for the preceding year. any amount deducted must be clearly and separately identified on the notice of tentative assessments or values and on the certificate of final assessment. (Sec. 608, Real Property Tax Law)

If either the special franchise owner or the assessing unit files a complaint concerning a special franchise assessment, the party not filing the complaint may appear at the commissioner's hearing and offer testimony. or provide written statements and supporting documents. The commissioner is required to consider any such testimoN.Y., statements, or documents along with any submission in support of the initial complaint. (Sec. 610, Real Property Tax Law)

Post-hearing procedures.—After hearing the complaints, the commissioner determines the assessment of each special franchise. (Sec. 612, Real Property Tax Law; Sec. 614, Real Property Tax Law) Certificates of final assessment or special franchises are filed with the assessing units and written notice of the final assessment is given to the special franchise owner. (Sec. 616, Real Property Tax Law; Sec. 618, Real Property Tax Law)

In addition, special franchise assessments may be reviewed in the same manner as assessments of real property. Proceedings for review must be commenced within 60 days after the notice of final assessment. The proceedings must be maintained against the commissioner. In addition, the local assessing unit may commence a proceeding on the ground of inadequate assessment. Either the special franchise owner or the assessing unit may appeal the final assessment by the Board directly to the Appellate Division of the Supreme Court. (Sec. 740, Real Property Tax Law; Sec. 744(1), Real Property Tax Law)

• *Judicial appeals and remedies*

After the assessment roll is finalized, including correction and revision of assessments and determinations by a county board of assessment review, the actions of the tax assessors and review boards are subject to judicial review by a proceeding to review an assessment.

The proceeding to review an assessment must be brought at a Special Term of the Supreme Court in the judicial district in which the assessment was made, within 30 days after the final completion and filing of the assessment roll. (Sec. 702, Real Property Tax Law) The assessment roll is not considered finally completed and filed until the last date set by law for filing the roll or notice has been given as required by law, whichever is later.

The proceeding is commenced by serving a petition together with notice in writing of an application for review returnable not less than 20 nor more than 90 days after service. In New York City, the proceeding is commenced by service of petition only. (Sec. 704, Real Property Tax Law) Failure to comply with the requirements for service of petition and notice may result in the dismissal of the petition.

Grounds for review.—The petition must set forth grounds for review. (Sec. 706, Real Property Tax Law) Grounds for review are excessive, unequal or unlawful assessment, or misclassification of property. "Excessive," "unequal," and "unlawful" assessment have the same meaning as for administrative review (discussed above), except that an assessed value of real property improved by a one-, two-, or three-family residence that is made at a higher proportion of full value than the assessed valuation of other residential property on the same roll is not included in the definition of unequal assessment for judicial review purposes. (Sec. 700, Real Property Tax Law)

Two or more proceedings involving similar issues may be consolidated for review. (Sec. 710, Real Property Tax Law)

Response.—The respondent tax authority must serve a verified answer at least five days prior to the return day, unless extended by the parties. If the answer is not made in the required time, all allegations in the petition are deemed denied. (Sec. 712, Real Property Tax Law)

Remedies.—If the court determines the assessment is illegal, the assessment is stricken from the assessment roll, and, if held erroneous or unequal, the appropriate adjustment is ordered. (Sec. 720, Real Property Tax Law) If taxes have already been paid, a refund is ordered. (Sec. 726, Real Property Tax Law) Interest is paid on refunds. (see ¶ 20-752) Where a final order is entered directing the refund of taxes collected under an excessive, unequal or unlawful assessment or as a result of a misclassification of property, interest will be paid from the date that the application for audit and payment is made. The annual rate of interest on such refunds is the lesser of 9% or the quarterly rate set by the Commissioner on January 1.

Appeals from final orders of the Supreme Court are made in the same manner as other appeals from the Supreme Court. (Sec. 724, Real Property Tax Law)

Apportionment of assessment.—A taxpayer whose property has been erroneously assessed with the property of another may apply to the county court to have the taxes on the property apportioned. (Sec. 934, Real Property Tax Law)

MISCELLANEOUS TAXES AND FEES

[¶32-220]

UNRELATED BUSINESS INCOME TAX—ORGANIZATIONS SUBJECT TO TAX

[¶32-225] In General

The New York tax on unrelated business income conforms to the comparable federal income tax on the unrelated business income of exempt organizations. (Sec. 291, Tax Law) Accordingly, exempt organizations or trusts described in IRC Secs. 511(a)(2) or 511(b)(2) that carry on unrelated trades or businesses in New York are subject to New York unrelated business income tax. (Sec. 290(a), Tax Law)

Trade or business carried on by receiver.—A receiver, referee, trustee, assignee, fiduciary or court-appointed officer or agent who carries on an unrelated trade or business of an organization or trust is subject tax in the same manner and to the same extent as if the unrelated trade or business was carried on by the agents, officers or trustees of the organization or trust. (Sec. 290(b), Tax Law)

Employee trusts.—The New York Department of Taxation and Finance has concluded that an employee trust, as described in IRC Sec. 401(a), is subject to the unrelated business income tax if it is carrying on an unrelated trade or business in New York. Accordingly, any employee trust, as described in IRC Sec. 401(a), that is carrying on an unrelated trade or business in New York must file returns (Form CT-13, Unrelated Business Income Tax Return) and pay the unrelated business income tax for tax years beginning on or after January 1, 2006. (TSB-M-06(6)C)

• *"Unrelated trade or business"*

Article 13, Tax Law, does not contain a definition of the term "unrelated trade or business." Under comparable federal provisions, however, an exempt organization is subject to tax on unrelated business income only if the trade or business regularly carried on by the organization is not substantially related (other than the need of the organization for income or funds or the use it makes of the funds derived) to the exercise or performance of the organization's exempt function. (IRC Sec. 513)

S corporation status.—For tax years beginning on or after January 1, 1998, tax-exempt organizations which are shareholders of a federal S corporation, and which are subject to the New York tax on unrelated business income, may make the New York S election with respect to such corporation. (Sec. 660(a), Tax Law; TSB-M-98(2)C)

[¶32-230]

UNRELATED BUSINESS INCOME TAX--EXEMPTIONS

[¶32-235] In General

The following entities and organizations are exempt from the New York unrelated business income tax:

(1) Corporations subject to business corporation franchise tax (Article 9-A, Tax Law). For a discussion of corporations that are exempt from Article 9-A taxes, see ¶ 10-245, Exempt Organizations.

(2) Organizations whose sole unrelated trade or business carried on in New York consist of providing commercial-type insurance, as defined by IRC Sec. 501(m)(2)(A). (Sec. 290(c), Tax Law)

See also ¶ 32-241 for a discussion of certain modifications to the tax base.

• *Income from games of chance*

Income derived from the conduct of games of chance or from the rental of premises for the conduct of games of chance pursuant to a license granted under Article 9-A, General Municipal Law, is exempt from tax.

Games of chance do not include bingo or lottery. (Instructions, Form CT-13-I)

[¶ 32-240]

UNRELATED BUSINESS INCOME TAX--BASIS OF TAX

[¶ 32-241] Adoption of Federal Base

The tax is imposed on the exempt organization's unrelated business income allocated to New York. (Sec. 292(a), Tax Law) Taxable income is based on the organization's federal unrelated business taxable income for the taxable year, with the following modifications:

(1) the amount of the state tax must be added to federal taxable income (Sec. 292(a)(1), Tax Law); and

(2) the amount of any refund or credit for overpayment of the tax is subtracted from federal income. (Sec. 292(a)(2), Tax Law)

Net operating losses.—For determination of net operating loss deductions, see ¶ 32-243.

• *TCJA fringe benefit tax increase*

New York has decoupled from a Tax Cuts and Jobs Act provision increasing nonprofit employers' unrelated business taxable income by certain fringe benefit amounts. Specifically, New York created a subtraction from nonprofits' federal unrelated business taxable income for fringe benefit amounts included under IRC Sec. 512(a)(7). (Sec. 292(a)(4), Tax Law) The subtraction is applicable to amounts paid or incurred on and after January 1, 2018. (*TSB-M-19(3)C*)

Federal provision. Under the TCJA change, an exempt organization's federal unrelated business taxable income is increased by the nondeductible amount of certain fringe benefit expenses. The fringe benefits include:

— any qualified transportation fringe;

— any parking facility used in connection with qualified parking; and

— any on-premises athletic facility.

But the increase does not apply to the extent that the amount is directly connected with an unrelated trade or business regularly carried on by the organization.

• *QPAI deduction*

An addition modification is required for the IRC § 199 deduction for qualified production activities income. (Sec. 292(a)(7), Tax Law)

Note: As a result of the Tax Cuts and Jobs Act, the federal domestic production activities deduction (DPAD) under IRC § 199 is repealed for tax years beginning after 2017.

• *Related member expenses*

Under the 2003 budget bill (as amended by the Ch. 686, Laws 2003, technical corrections legislation), New York requires an addition for certain royalty payments made to a related member. (Sec. 292(a)(6), Tax Law) These anti-PIC (passive investment company) provisions, also referred to as expense disallowance provisions, are similar to the corporate franchise tax provisions; see the detailed discussion at ¶10-620.

See also TSB-M-03(8)C.

[¶32-243] Net Operating Losses

A net operating loss deduction is allowed in computing unrelated business taxable income for New York unrelated business income tax purposes, except that federal unrelated business taxable income is modified to exclude income from activities that consist of providing commercial-type insurance. (Sec. 292(a)(3), Tax Law) The amount of the deduction is the same as that allowed under IRC Sec. 512(b)(6), except that the deduction must reflect the modifications to federal taxable income discussed at ¶32-241. (Sec. 292(a)(4)(A), Tax Law), it may not include a net operating loss sustained in a year prior to 1970 or in a year in which the taxpayer was not subject to the unrelated business tax (Sec. 292(a)(4)(B), Tax Law), and it may not exceed the allowable federal deduction. (Sec. 292(a)(4)(C), Tax Law)

A net operating loss deduction cannot be claimed for a period during which a taxpayer was not subject to unrelated business income tax. (Instructions, Form CT-13-I)

[¶32-247] Taxable Period Different from Federal Taxable Period

If the period covered by a New York unrelated business income tax return is different than the period covered by the comparable federal return, New York State unrelated business taxable income is determined by multiplying the modified federal unrelated business taxable income (see ¶32-241) by the number of calendar months, or major parts thereof, covered by the New York return, and dividing by the number of calendar months, or major parts thereof, covered by the federal return. (Sec. 292(b), Tax Law)

Determination of taxable income by Department.—If the method noted above does not properly reflect the taxpayer's income during the period covered by the return, the Department of Taxation and Finance may determine New York unrelated business taxable income solely on the basis of the taxpayer's income during the period covered by the state return.

[¶32-250]

UNRELATED BUSINESS INCOME TAX--ALLOCATION AND APPORTIONMENT

[¶32-255] Allocation of Income

The portion of a taxpayer's unrelated business taxable income that is allocated to New York is determined by multiplying its unrelated business taxable income (see ¶32-241) by a business allocation percentage. (Sec. 293, Tax Law) The business allocation factor is the average of the taxpayer's property, receipts and payroll factors.

Property factor.—The property factor is the percentage that the average value of the taxpayer's real and tangible personal property in its unrelated trade or business within New York during the period covered by the taxpayer's return bears to the average value of all the taxpayer's real and tangible personal property, wherever situated. (Sec. 293(a)(1), Tax Law) In determining the property factor, real property includes property owned by the taxpayer and property rented to it.

Receipts factor.—The receipts factor is the percentage that the taxpayer's receipts from its unrelated trade or business arising from the following sources bears to all receipts earned by the taxpayer's unrelated trade or business, whether within or without the state (Sec. 293(a)(2), Tax Law);

(1) sales of tangible personal property by the unrelated trade or business, where shipments are made to points within New York;

(2) services performed within New York by the unrelated trade or business;

(3) rentals from property of the unrelated trade or business situated within New York; and

(4) all other receipts earned by the unrelated trade or business within the state.

The receipts factor may be computed on the cash or accrual basis according to the method of accounting used in the computation of the taxpayer's unrelated business taxable income.

Payroll factor.—The payroll factor is the percentage that the total wages, salaries and other personal service compensation paid to employees of the taxpayer's unrelated trade or business within New York bears to the total wages, salaries and other personal service compensation paid to employees of the unrelated trade or business within and without New York. (Sec. 293(a)(3), Tax Law) Compensation paid to general executive officers is excluded.

"General executive officers" include the chairman, president, vice-president, secretary, assistant secretary, treasurer, comptroller and any other officer charged with the general executive affairs of the taxpayer. (Instructions, Form CT-13-I)

• *No regular place of business outside New York*

If a taxpayer does not have a regular place of business outside New York in which its unrelated trade or business is conducted, the business allocation percentage is 100%. (Sec. 293(a)(4), Tax Law)

[¶32-260]

UNRELATED BUSINESS INCOME TAX--RATE OF TAX

[¶32-265] Rate of Tax

Tax is imposed at the rate of 9% of the unrelated business taxable income or that portion of the income allocated to New York State, or $250, whichever is greater. (Sec. 290(a), Tax Law)

• *Surcharge*

An additional tax is imposed on taxable income for taxable years ending after June 30, 1990, and before July 1, 1997. (Sec. 290-A, Tax Law) The surcharge is equal to 15% of the original tax for taxable years ending after June 30, 1990, and before July 1, 1994; 12^1/$_2$%, for taxable years beginning after June 20, 1994, and before July 1, 1995; 7^1/$_2$%, for taxable years ending after June 30, 1995, and before July 1, 1996; and 2^1/$_2$% for taxable years ending after July 30, 1996 and before July 1, 1997.

[¶35-000]
HEALTH FACILITY TAX

[¶35-001] Health Facility Tax

Hospitals are subject to a health facility tax on their gross receipts for patient services. (Sec. 2807-d, Public Health Law) Hospital is broadly defined and includes general hospitals (including specialty hospitals for persons who are developmentally disabled), public health centers, dental centers, midwifery birth centers, rehabilitation centers, residential health care facility and diagnostic and treatment centers. (Sec. 2801(1), Public Health Law)

• *Basis of tax*

The health facility tax is based on the gross receipts received from all patient care services and other operating income, less personal needs allowances and refunds, on a cash basis. (Sec. 2807-d(1)(a), Public Health Law)

• *Exemptions*

Certain voluntary nonprofit and private proprietary general hospitals, voluntary nonprofit hospitals totally financed by charitable contributions or dedicated to free care of low income patients, and any facility dedicated solely to the care of police, firefighters, and emergency service personnel are exempt from the health facility tax. (Sec. 2807-d(1)(b), Public Health Law)

• *Rate of tax*

As indicated below, taxes are imposed on certain health care facilities. (Sec. 2807-d(2), Public Health Law)

General hospitals.—A general hospital is a hospital engaged in providing medical and surgical services primarily to in-patients on a 24-hour basis which also provides emergency care and has an organized medical staff and nursing service. A general hospital does not include a residential health care facility, public health center, diagnostic center, treatment center, out-patient lodge, dispensary and laboratory or central service facility serving more than one institution. (Sec. 2801(10), Public Health Law)

An assessment is imposed at the rate of 0.35% on gross receipts received by general hospitals for periods on or after April 1, 2009. (Sec. 2807-d(2)(a)(v), Public Health Law) (https://www.health.ny.gov/facilities/cash_assessment/assessment/2011-2019_assessment_rates.htm)

Residential health care facilities.—The assessment is 6.8% of each residential health care facility's gross receipts received from all patient care services and other operating income on a cash basis for periods on or after November 1, 2012, for hospital or health-related services, including adult day services. (Sec. 2807-d(2)(b), Public Health Law) (https://www.health.ny.gov/facilities/cash_assessment/assessment/2011-2019_assessment_rates.htm)

Gross receipts defined.—Gross receipts include monies received from investment income, parking lots, cafeterias, gift shops and rent, except for diagnostic and treatment centers operated by health maintenance organizations. (Sec. 2807-d(3)(d), Public Health Law)

Caps on additional tax.—Certain caps are placed on the amount of tax and additional tax that may be collected in total for certain periods from general hospitals, residential health care facilities, and diagnostic and treatment centers or other health care facilities, respectively. (Sec. 2807-d(11), Public Health Law) Amounts collected in excess of these caps are refunded based on the ratio which the taxpayer's tax for such period bears to the total tax for such period paid by such taxpayers.

- *Returns and payment of tax*

Hospitals subject to the health facility tax must make monthly estimates of the tax (Sec. 2807-d(5), Public Health Law) and file quarterly and annual reports prescribed by the Commissioner of Health. (Sec. 2807-d(7), Public Health Law) (http://www.health.ny.gov/facilities/cash_assessment/questions/general.htm)

Estimated tax payments.—Estimated payments of the health facility tax are due monthly on or before the fifteenth day following the end of a calendar month to which the assessment applies. (Sec. 2807-d(5), Public Health Law)

If the Commissioner of Health determines, based on evidence of moneys received by a hospital for that month or prior periods, that the estimated payment for a month is less than 70% of the amount due, the Commissioner may estimate the amount due, notify the hospital of the amount due at least three days before collection and have the amount withheld from any monies due the hospital from the state, a health maintenance organization operated under Article 44 of the Public Health Law, or any nonprofit medical or dental indemnity or health and hospital service corporation organized and operating under Article 43 of the New York Insurance Law. (Sec. 2807-d(6), Public Health Law) The hospital may request a hearing to present evidence on the amount due.

A 5% penalty is due on the difference between the amount owed and amount due. (Sec. 2807-d(8), Public Health Law) However, if an estimated payment for a month is determined to be less than 90% of the amount due and at least two previous estimated payments within the preceding six months were less than 90%, the Commissioner may estimate the amount due and begin the collection proceedings described above. (Sec. 2807-d(6), Public Health Law) When the estimated payment is less than 90% of the tax due, interest is charged on the difference between the amount due and the amount paid. (Sec. 2807-d(8), Public Health Law)

Residential health care facilities.—Effective April 1, 2009, an electronic report must be submitted each month by designated residential health care facility providers, even if there were no assessable cash receipts for the reporting month. (http://www.health.ny.gov/facilities/cash_assessment/rhcf_index.htm)

- *Quarterly and annual reports*

Reports related to the health facility tax on a cash basis of actual gross receipts received from all patient care services and operating income for each month must be filed on a quarterly basis. (Sec. 2807-d(7), Public Health Law) In addition, a certified annual report must be filed.

[¶35-050]

TAXICAB TRIP TAX

[¶35-051] Taxicab Trip Tax

A tax of 50 cents per taxicab trip is imposed on every trip that originates in New York City and terminates anywhere within the territorial boundaries of the Metropolitan Commuter Transportation District. (Sec. 1281, Tax Law) Although the tax is imposed on the taxicab owner, the taxicab owner must pass along the economic incidence of the tax to the passenger by adjusting the fare for the trip. (Sec. 1283, Tax Law)

Hail vehicle trips.—The Metropolitan Transportation Authority (MTA) taxicab trip surcharge is also imposed on HAIL vehicle trips. A "HAIL vehicle trip" is a HAIL vehicle trip provided to one or more passengers regardless of the number of stops, that originated by street hail, and for which the taximeter is required to be in the recording or hired position designating a street hail trip subject to the taxicab trip tax. (Sec. 1280(s), Tax Law)

A "HAIL vehicle" means a for-hire vehicle having a taximeter and a Taxi and Limousine Commission (TLC)-sanctioned trip record system, licensed by the TLC to carry passengers for hire, and authorized to accept hails from prospective passengers in certain designated areas of New York City. Prohibited are the pick-up of passengers by street hail at airports and by street hail or pre-arranged call in certain sections of Manhattan. (Sec. 1280(o), Tax Law)

The Department of Taxation and Finance has issued a memorandum that explains the 50 cents per trip tax on hail vehicle trips in the Metropolitan Commuter Transportation District (MCTD) that occur as of June 1, 2012. The tax is imposed on each hail vehicle trip that begins in New York City and ends anywhere in the MCTD. (*TSB-M-12(3)M, TSB-M-12(7)S*, Office of Tax Policy Analysis, New York Department of Taxation and Finance, May 30, 2012)

Hail bases must report and remit taxes for any taxable trips that occur during the period June 1, 2012, through June 30, 2012, when they electronically file their quarterly return for July 1 through September 30, due on October 22, 2012. However, hail bases are required to keep records of trips as soon as any vehicle affiliated with the base provides any hail trips. Records must be maintained for three years and available to the tax department. (*TSB-M-12(3)M, TSB-M-12(7)S*, Office of Tax Policy Analysis, New York Department of Taxation and Finance, May 30, 2012)

Definitions.—A "taxicab" means a motor vehicle carrying passengers for hire in the New York City, duly licensed by the taxi and limousine commission and permitted to accept hails from prospective passengers in the street. (Sec. 1280, Tax Law)

A "taxicab owner" means a person owning a taxicab and includes a purchaser under a reserve title contract, conditional sales agreement or vendor's lien agreement. In addition, an owner is deemed to include any lessee, licensee, or bailee having the exclusive use of a taxicab, under a lease or otherwise, for a period of 30 days or more. (Sec. 1280, Tax Law)

Returns and payment.—Taxicab vehicle owners must file a return for each calendar quarter on Form MT-75-MN, MTA Quarterly Tax Return for Taxicab Rides, and remit the tax. Taxicab owners must file Form MT-75-MN within 20 days after the end of the quarterly period. (Sec. 1284, Tax Law)

The department advised that it is converting from a paper return filing system to a Web-based return filing system. Medallion owners or their agents were required to file online at the department's Web site (www.nystax.gov) beginning with the quarter July 1, 2010, through September 30, 2010, and remit 50 cents tax for each applicable taxicab trip during the quarter. This return had to be filed over the Internet with electronic payment made by October 20, 2010. (*TSB-M-10(11)M*, Office of Tax Policy Analysis, New York Department of Taxation and Finance, August 13, 2010)

Because the new law took effect November 1, 2009, the first return covered the short period of November 1, 2009, through December 31, 2009. This return was due January 20, 2010. (*TSB-M-09(9)M*, Office of Tax Policy Analysis, New York Department of Taxation and Finance, October 1, 2009)

¶35-051

[¶35-100]

WATERFRONT COMMISSION GROSS PAYROLL TAX

[¶35-101] Waterfront Commission Gross Payroll Tax

Ch. 882, Laws 1953, established a joint compact between New York and New Jersey and created the Waterfront Commission of New York Harbor to regulate employment conditions within the Port of New York District. Activities of the commission are partially funded by an assessment on employer's gross payroll payments made to certain individuals performing labor or services within the Port of New York District.

Ch. 951, Laws 1970, extended the authority of the waterfront commission to airport facilities, located within 100 miles of the Port of New York District, where the total tonnage of air freight loaded and unloaded on and from aircraft exceeds 20,000 tons during a calendar year, and imposed an assessment on employers of air-freightmen and airfreightmen supervisors. This assessment, however, is contingent upon the enactment of legislation by New Jersey having an identical effect and upon the consent of Congress. Congressional consent has not been given.

• *Imposition of tax*

Employers of persons registered or licensed under the compact must pay to the commission an assessment computed on the gross payroll payments made by such employer to longshoremen, pier superintendents, hiring agents and port watchmen for work or labor performed within the Port of New York District. (Sec. 9858, Unconsolidated Laws) The assessment is in lieu of any other charge for the issuance of licenses for stevedores, pier superintendents, hiring agents and pier watchmen, for the registration of pier longshoremen, or for the use of employment information centers. (Sec. 9861, Unconsolidated Laws)

• *Basis and rate of assessment*

The assessment on employers is determined by the Waterfront Commission on the basis of its estimate of the percentage of employer gross payroll payments that will be sufficient to finance the commission's budget for the year after taking into account funds available from reserves, federal grants and other funds on hand. (Sec. 9858, Unconsolidated Laws) The tax rate may not exceed 2% of gross payroll payments. The current rate is 1.7%, effective from July 1, 2020, through June 30, 2021. For the previous period, the rate was 1.8%. (See CCH Payroll Management Guide ¶7559)

• *Returns and payment of tax*

Every employer subject to the assessment must file quarterly returns with the commission following the end of any calendar quarter-year during which payroll payments are made to longshoremen, pier superintendents, hiring agents or port watchmen for work performed within the District. (Sec. 9901, Unconsolidated Laws) Returns are due on or before the 15th day of April, July, October, and January. The assessment must be paid at the time the return is required to be filed.

Extension of time.—The commission may grant a reasonable extension of time for filing returns or for assessment payments whenever good cause exists. (Sec. 9901, Unconsolidated Laws)

• *Preservation of records*

Employers subject to assessment must maintain accurate employment records of longshoremen, pier superintendents, hiring agents and port watchmen for work performed within the district and the compensation paid. (Sec. 9901, Unconsolidated Laws) The records must be maintained for a period of three years and must be open for inspection at reasonable times. The commission may consent to the destruction of employment records upon the expiration of the three-year period, or may require that they be kept longer, but not in excess of six years.

• *Penalties and interest*

Employers who fail to file returns or pay tax in a timely manner are subject to penalties and interest fees. (Sec. 9901, Unconsolidated Laws)

Late payment of tax.—An employer who willfully fails to pay an assessment will be assessed interest at the rate of 1% per month on the amount due and unpaid, and an additional penalty of 5% of the amount due for each thirty days or part thereof that the assessment remains unpaid. (Sec. 9901, Unconsolidated Laws) The commission may abate all or any part of the penalty upon a showing of good cause.

Willful furnishing false or fraudulent information.—An employer who willfully furnishes false or fraudulent information, or willfully fails to provide pertinent information with respect to the amount of an assessment due, is guilty of a misdemeanor, punishable by a fine of not more than $1,000 or imprisonment for not more than one year, or both. (Sec. 9901, Unconsolidated Laws)

Suspension of license.—In addition to any other sanction permitted by law, the commission may revoke or suspend an employer's license, or the right of the employer to employ registered or licensed employees, for nonpayment of any assessment when due. (Sec. 9860, Unconsolidated Laws)

[¶35-150]

YONKERS INCOME TAX SURCHARGE ON RESIDENTS

[¶35-151] Yonkers Income Tax Surcharge on Residents

Article 30-A, Tax Law, authorizes the City of Yonkers to impose a city income surcharge on residents. The tax is administered by the New York State Department of Taxation and Finance. (Sec. 1321(a), Tax Law)

• *Imposition of tax*

The city income tax surcharge is imposed on every city resident, estate and trust (Sec. 1332(a), Tax Law) for tax years beginning before 2022. (Sec. 1321(a), Tax Law)

Partnerships are not subject to a city income tax surcharge. (Sec. 1322(b), Tax Law) Persons carrying on business as partners are liable for the city income tax surcharge only in their separate or individual capacities.

• *Basis and rate of tax*

Although Yonkers is authorized to impose the surcharge at a rate of up to, but not exceeding, 19.25%, the surcharge is imposed at the rate of 16.75% of the net state tax (*TSB-M-14(4)I*); prior to tax year 2014, the rate was 15%; prior to tax year 2011, the rate was 10%. (Sec. 1321(a), Tax Law; *TSB-M-06(4)I*; *TSB-M-99(3)I*) Before January 1, 2005, the rate was 5%. The rate was decreased from 10% to 5% effective January 1, 2000. (*Release*, Yonkers Department of Finance, October 25, 1999)

Prior to 1999, the surcharge was imposed at a rate of 15% of the net state tax. (*Letter to CCH*, dated March 4, 1993)

The net state tax is the sum of all taxes imposed under Article 22 less applicable credits (other than the credit for tax withheld). (Sec. 1323, Tax Law)

• *Returns and payment of tax*

The city income tax surcharge is reported on the New York State personal income tax return and is paid together with the state tax. (Sec. 1332(c), Tax Law)

• *Withholding of tax*

Withholding of the surcharge is required. (Sec. 1329(b), Tax Law)

The supplemental wage payment withholding rate for the Yonkers resident tax surcharge is 1.61135% (prior to January 1, 2015, it was 1.84704%; prior to August 1, 2014, it was 1.443%; prior to January 1, 2012, it was 1.70975%; prior to May 1, 2011, it was 0.977%; prior to January 1, 2010, it was 1.103%; prior to May 1, 2009, it was 0.735%).

The Yonkers withholding tax tables and methods are provided in NYS-50-T-Y.

[¶35-200]

YONKERS EARNINGS TAX ON NONRESIDENTS

[¶35-201] Yonkers Earnings Tax on Nonresidents

Article 30-B, Tax Law, authorizes the City of Yonkers to impose a city earnings tax on nonresidents. The tax is patterned after the former New York City nonresident earnings tax. The tax is administered by the New York State Department of Taxation and Finance. (Sec. 1340(a), Tax Law)

• *Imposition of tax*

The city earnings tax is imposed on wages earned and net earnings from self-employment within the City of Yonkers by every nonresident individual, estate and trust (Sec. 1340(c), Tax Law) for tax years beginning before 2022. (Sec. 1340(b), Tax Law)

• *Basis and rate of tax*

The tax is currently imposed at the rate of 0.5% on the wages earned and net earnings from self-employment within the City of Yonkers. (Sec. 1340(c), Tax Law; *TSB-M-06(4)I*) Before January 1, 2005, the rate was 0.25%. The rate was decreased from 0.5% to 0.25% effective January 1, 2000. (*Release,* Yonkers Department of Finance, October 25, 1999)

Exclusion.—In computing the amount of taxable wages and earnings from self-employment, the following exclusion is allowed (Sec. 1340(c), Tax Law):

Total of wages and net earnings	Exclusion Allowable
Not over $10,000	$3,000
Over $10,000 but not over $20,000	2,000
Over $20,000 but not over $30,000	1,000
Over $30,000	None

• *Returns and payment*

The city earnings tax return is attached to the New York State personal income tax return, and payment of any earnings tax due is paid at the time of filing. (Sec. 1340, Tax Law)

• *Withholding of tax*

Withholding of tax began January 1, 1985. (Sec. 1341, Tax Law)

The supplemental wage payment withholding rate for the Yonkers nonresident earnings tax is 0.50%.

The Yonkers withholding tax tables and methods are provided in NYS-50-T-Y.

- *Forms*

The following forms are in current use:

— Y-203, City of Yonkers Nonresident Earnings Tax Return

— Y-203-1, Instructions for Form Y-203

— Y-204, City of Yonkers Nonresident Partner Allocation

— Y-206, City of Yonkers Nonresident Fiduciary Earnings Tax Return

[¶35-250]
MEDICAL MARIJUANA TAX

[¶35-251] Medical Marijuana Tax

A 7% excise tax is imposed upon the gross receipts from the sale of medical marijuana by a registered organization to a certified patient or designated caregiver. The tax is to be paid by the registered organization, and may not be added as a separate charge or line item on any sales slip, invoice, receipt or other statement of price given to the retail customer.

"Registered organization" means a registered organization under Title V-A, Secs. 3364 and 3365 of the Public Health Law. A "certified patient" is a patient who is a resident of New York State or is receiving care and treatment in New York State as determined by the Commissioner in regulation, and is certified under Title V-A, Sec. 3316 of the Public Health Law. (Sec. 490, Tax Law)

Return and payment.—Registered organizations that make medical marijuana sales must file a return and pay the tax due on or before the 20th day of each month. The law expires seven years from the date of enactment. Returns must be filed even if a registered organization had no sales during the month. (Sec. 490, Tax Law)

A Department of Taxation and Finance memorandum details requirements for return filings, tax payments, and record keeping, in addition to discussing income and sales and use tax implications. (*TSB-M-16(1)M*, New York State Department of Taxation and Finance, January 7, 2016)

[¶35-275]
OPIOID EXCISE TAX

[¶35-276] Opioid Excise Tax

An excise tax imposed on the first sale of an opioid unit by a registrant in New York. There are two tax rates:

- $.0025 on each morphine milligram equivalent with a wholesale acquisition cost of less than $0.50 per unit, or

- $.015 on each morphine milligram equivalent with a wholesale acquisition cost of $0.50 or more per unit.

(Sec. 498, Tax Law) ((Opioid Excise Tax, New York Department of Taxation and Finance))

However, no such tax applies when such first sale is to any program operated as a hospice (Article 40, Public Health Law) and services for chemical dependency and compulsive gambling (Article 32, Mental Hygiene Law).

The tax must be charged against and paid by the registrant making such first sale, and accrues at the time of such sale. It is presumed that any sale of an opioid unit in New York by a registrant is the first sale of such in the state until the contrary is established, and the burden of proving that any sale is not the first sale in the state is upon the registrant. (Sec. 498, Tax Law)

Reportable sales. All first sales of an opioid unit by a registrant in New York must be reported, other than sales:

- of buprenorphine, methadone, or morphine;

- of opioids dispensed by prescription to a consumer;

- of opioids to a purchaser outside of New York, to be used or consumed outside of New York, within the same filing period; and

- that are canceled within the same filing period.

(Opioid Excise Tax, New York Department of Taxation and Finance)

Returns. Returns are required to be filed for quarterly periods ending on the last day of March, June, September, and December of each year. Registrants must use the Tax Department's Opioid Excise Tax Web File application to file their calendar quarterly excise tax returns. Returns must be filed, and the tax paid no later than the 20th day of the month following the quarter in which the opioid was sold. A return must be filed even if the registrant had no sales during the quarter. The registrant must have a Business Online Services account to file tax returns and remit the excise tax. (Sec. 498, Tax Law) The first required filing will be for an extended period beginning July 1, 2019, and ending December 31, 2019. The return for this period is due by January 21, 2020. (Opioid Excise Tax, New York Department of Taxation and Finance)

Records. All records must be retained for six years after the due date of the return they relate to, or the date the return is filed if later. Records must be sufficient to determine the total units sold or transferred, as well as determining the morphine milligram equivalent of the units. (Sec. 498, Tax Law)

Records would include, but are not limited to:

- sales slips

- invoices

- receipts

- statements or memos of sales

- documentation of a cancelled sale

- documentation of a transfer of sale out of New York

(Opioid Excise Tax, New York Department of Taxation and Finance)

The records must also show the address from which the units are shipped or delivered; and the place at which actual physical possession of the units occurred. (Sec. 498, Tax Law) (Opioid Excise Tax, New York Department of Taxation and Finance)

Definitions related to opioid tax. For purposes of the tax, an "opioid" means an "opiate" as defined in the public health law and any natural, synthetic, or semisynthetic "narcotic drug" that has agonist, partial agonist, or agonist/antagonist morphine-like activities or effects similar to natural opium alkaloids, and any derivative, congener, or combination thereof. The term "opioid" does not include bupre-norphine, methadone, or morphine. The term "unit" means a single finished dosage form of an opioid, such as a pill, tablet, capsule, suppository, transdermal patch, buccal film, milliliter of liquid, milligram of topical preparation, or any other form. (Sec. 497, Tax Law) (Opioid Excise Tax, New York Department of Taxation and Finance)

A "first sale" is any transfer of title to an opioid unit for consideration where actual or constructive possession of such opioid unit is transferred by a registrant holding title to such opioid unit to a purchaser or its designee in this state for the first time. A sale does not include either: the dispensing of an opioid unit pursuant to a prescription to an ultimate consumer, or the transfer of title to an opioid unit from a manufacturer in this state to a purchaser outside this state when such opioid unit will be used or consumed outside this state. It is presumed that every sale by a registrant in New York is the first sale unless it is established otherwise. The burden of proving that a sale does not qualify as a first sale is on the registrant. (Opioid Excise Tax, New York Department of Taxation and Finance)

"Registrant" means any person, firm, corporation, or association that holds and transfers title to an opioid unit and:

• is required to register with the New York State Department of Health as a manufacturer or distributor of a controlled substance;

• is required to register with the New York State Department of Education (NYS DOE) as a wholesaler, manufacturer, or outsourcing facility; or

• is a nonresident establishment excepted from registration with the NYS DOE under NYS Education Law § 6808-b(2).

(Opioid Excise Tax, New York Department of Taxation and Finance)

[¶35-300]
GAMING AND WAGERING TAXES

[¶35-301] Gaming and Wagering Taxes

New York imposes privilege taxes on certain gaming and wagering activities. Taxation of thoroughbred horse racing (pari-mutuel taxes), combative sports, and interactive fantasy sports are discussed below.

• *Thoroughbred racing (pari-mutuel taxes)*

Corporations and associations conducting pari-mutuel betting pay a percentage of the total pool to the Department of Taxation and Finance. For racing corporation or association pools, rates are as follows: 1.5% of regular and multiple bets, 6.75% of exotic bets, and 7.75% of super exotic bets, as well as 55% of the breaks. (Sec. 236, Racing, Pari-Mutuel Wagering and Breeding Law)

An additional $1/2$ of 1% applies to all on-track bets where a racing association or corporation failed to expend at least $1/2$ of 1% of such bets during the prior calendar year on capital improvement enhancements.

For nonprofit racing corporations or associations, the tax on the total pool of regular and multiple bets is 20% of the breaks as well as 5% of regular bets and 4% of multiple bets. Exotic bets are subject to a tax of 7.5% plus 20% of the breaks. Super exotic bets are subject to a tax of 7.5% plus 50% of the breaks. Nonprofit associations or corporations must pay 50% of the compensation received from wagers made on races simulcast outside the State to the New York State Thoroughbred Racing Capital Investment Fund. (Sec. 238, Racing, Pari-Mutuel Wagering and Breeding Law)

There is a 4% tax on admissions. (Sec. 227, Racing, Pari-Mutuel Wagering and Breeding Law)

New York City imposes a 5% surcharge on the portion of pari-mutuel wagering pools distributable to persons having placed bets at off-track betting facilities within the City. (Sec. 532, Racing, Pari-Mutuel Wagering and Breeding Law)

Every other regional off-track betting corporation and off-track betting operator imposes a similar surcharge.

• *Authorized combative sports*

Every person holding any professional or amateur boxing, sparring or wrestling match or exhibition in New York is subject to a tax at a rate of 3% of gross receipts from ticket sales and/or broadcasting rights, except that in no event may the tax exceed $50,000 for any match or exhibition. (Sec. 452, Tax Law)

On and after September 1, 2016, a gross receipts tax is imposed on authorized combative sports held in New York, other than any professional or amateur boxing, sparring or wrestling exhibition or match (i.e., kick boxing, single discipline martial arts, or mixed martial arts events in the state) at a rate of 8.5% of gross receipts from ticket sales, and 3% of the sum of (i) gross receipts from broadcasting rights, and (ii) gross receipts from digital streaming over the internet. The tax imposed may not exceed $50,000 for any match or exhibition. (Sec. 452, Tax Law; *TSB-M-16(6)M, 8(S)*, New York Department of Taxation and Finance, August 18, 2016) The tax rates on boxing, sparring or wrestling matches or exhibitions which have been in effect since October 1, 1999, and subject to the 3% rate have not been changed by the newly effective tax on combative sports. (*TSB-M-16(6)M, 8(S)*, New York Department of Taxation and Finance, August 18, 2016)

Exemptions.—Exemptions from the tax are in effect for the following:

　　— matches or exhibitions conducted under the supervision or the control of the New York State National Guard or naval militia where all of the contestants are members of the active militia;

　　— matches or exhibitions where the contestants are all amateurs, sponsored by or under the supervision of any university, college, school or other institution of learning, recognized by the regents of the state of New York;

　　— matches or exhibitions where the contestants are all amateurs sponsored by or under the supervision of the U.S. Amateur Boxing Federation or its local affiliates, or the American Olympic Association.

(Sec. 455, Tax Law)

Returns and payments.—Returns and payments of the gross receipts tax from broadcasting rights must be made on or before the last day of the month in which such gross receipts from broadcasting rights are received by the individual corporation, association or club holding such match or exhibition. Where the taxpayer receives receipts subject to tax during the last five days of a month, the required return and payment of tax is not due until the fifth day of the succeeding month. Returns and payments of the gross receipts tax from ticket sales must be made within 10 business days after the holding of the match or exhibition. (Sec. 453, Tax Law)

• *Interactive fantasy sports*

Effective August 3, 2016, a privilege tax is imposed on interactive fantasy sports contests in the state. Registrants are required to pay a tax equivalent to 15% of their interactive fantasy sports gross revenue generated within the state; in addition, registrants must pay a tax equal to 0.5%, but not to exceed $50,000 annually. (Sec. 1407, Racing, Pari-Mutuel Wagering and Breeding Law) "Interactive fantasy sports contest" or "contest" means a game of skill wherein one or more contestants compete against each other by using their knowledge and understanding of athletic events and athletes to select and manage rosters of simulated players whose performance directly corresponds with the actual performance of human competitors on sports teams and in sports events. "Interactive fantasy sports gross revenue" is defined as the amount equal to the total of all entry fees not attributable to New York state prohibited sports events that a registrant collects from all players, less the total of all sums not attributable to New York state prohibited sports events paid out as winnings to all players, multiplied by the resident percentage for New York state; provided, however, that the total of all sums paid out as winnings to players may not include the cash equivalent value of any merchandise or thing of value awarded as a prize. "Interactive fantasy sports registrant" or "registrant" means an operator that is registered by the State Gaming Commission. A registrant may utilize multiple interactive fantasy sports platforms and offer multiple contests, provided that each platform and each contest has been reviewed and approved by the commission. (Sec. 1401, Racing, Pari-Mutuel Wagering and Breeding Law)

The commission may perform audits of the books and records of an interactive fantasy sports operator with a permit or registrant, at such times and intervals as it deems appropriate, for the purpose of determining the sufficiency of tax payments. If a return required with regard to obligations imposed is not filed, or if a return when filed or is determined by the commission to be incorrect or insufficient with or without an audit, the amount of tax due will be determined by the commission. Notice of such determination must be given to the interactive fantasy sports operator liable for the payment of the tax. Such determination will finally and irrevocably fix the tax unless the person against whom it is assessed, within 30 days after receiving notice of such determination, applies to the commission for a hearing. (Sec. 1410, Racing, Pari-Mutuel Wagering and Breeding Law)

[¶35-325]
CONGESTION SURCHARGE

[¶35-326] Congestion Surcharge

A congestion surcharge is added to the charge for transportation that:

— both begins and ends in New York state, and that

— begins in, ends in, or passes through the area of New York City in the borough of Manhattan, south of and excluding 96th Street (an area known as the "congestion zone")

(Sec. 1299-A, Tax Law) (TSB-M-18(1)CS)

NOTE: Collection of the congestion surcharge was scheduled to begin on January 1, 2019. However, the onset of collections was delayed due to a temporary restraining order that was lifted by the New York State Supreme Court on January 31, 2019. As a result, the congestion surcharge must be collected beginning at 12:01 am on Saturday, February 2, 2019. (Important Notice N-19-2)

The surcharge applies to transportation in vehicles that carry people for-hire, including:

— vehicles commonly known as taxis,

— vehicles commonly known as "green cabs,"

— limousines,

— black cars,

— livery vehicles (including community cars),

— rideshare/transportation network company vehicles, and

— pool vehicles.

(TSB-M-18(1)CS)

The surcharge does not apply to the following:

— transportation provided in connection with funerals,

— transportation provided by a bus,

— transportation provided by, or pursuant to a contract with, school districts,

— transportation administered by or on behalf of the Metropolitan Transportation Authority, or

— transportation by ambulance or ambulette.

(TSB-M-18(1)CS)

The applicable surcharge is required to be passed through to passengers and be separately stated on any receipt that is provided.

• *Amount of surcharge*

The rate of the surcharge depends on the type of vehicle used to provide transportation in or through the congestion zone. (TSB-M-18(1)CS) The surcharge is generally:

— $2.75 for each for-hire transportation trip in a vehicle that is not a medallion taxicab or a pool vehicle,

— $2.50 per trip when the transportation is provided by a medallion taxicab, and

— $0.75 per pool trip.

(Sec. 1299-A, Tax Law)

• *Liability for surcharge*

Generally, the person or entity that sends a vehicle (i.e., dispatches it) to a customer is responsible for the payment of the surcharge. This includes businesses and individuals that receive transportation requests directly from customers (as opposed to bases or third-party applications) and use their own vehicles to provide such transportation. This also includes transportation network companies, as defined in Vehicle and Traffic Law Article 44-B. However, for rides provided by medallion taxicabs, the owner of the medallion that is affixed to the taxicab is responsible for the payment of the surcharge. Likewise, for rides provided by Hail vehicles that originate by street-hail, the base that the Hail vehicle is affiliated with is responsible for the payment of the surcharge. (Sec. 1299-B, Tax Law) (TSB-M-18(1)CS)

• *Registration*

Any person or entity who will be responsible for the payment of a surcharge on more than one trip in any calendar month must register by completing an online application and obtaining a certificate of registration. The certificate will be valid for the specified term on the certificate and is subject to renewal. Any person or entity who is responsible for the payment of the surcharge on no more than one trip in any calendar month is not required to register. Such person or entity, however, must file a return and pay any surcharge that is due when a surcharge liability is incurred. If the information reported on your registration has changed, you are required to update your information on a calendar quarterly basis. There is no fee to update your registration. (Sec. 1299-C, Tax Law; Reg. Sec. 700.3) (TSB-M-18(1)CS)

Fee. There is a $1.50 fee to register and $1.50 fee to renew a certificate of registration. (Sec. 1299-C, Tax Law)

- *Filing returns and paying the surcharge*

Persons liable for the surcharge must use the Tax Department's Congestion Surcharge Web File application to file monthly returns and pay the surcharge due. They must file returns and pay the surcharge due within 20 days after the end of the month for which the return covers. Persons registered for the surcharge must file a return even if they incurred no surcharges during a calendar month. In addition to any other applicable penalties and interest, any person that fails to timely pay a surcharge that is due will be subject to a penalty of 200% of the amount that is due. (Sec. 1299-D, Tax Law) (TSB-M-18(1)CS)

- *Recordkeeping*

Persons or entities liable for the surcharge must keep records that are sufficient to determine whether the surcharge was properly applied, and must electronically transmit those records to the Tax Department upon request. (Sec. 1299-E, Tax Law; Reg. Sec. 700.4) (TSB-M-18(1)CS) This includes, but is not limited to, the following for all transportation that is subject to the surcharge:

— Records of the location, date and time where each trip begins and ends, and of the route taken;

— A record of the date, time and geographic location where the for-hire vehicle used for a trip enters and/or leaves the congestion zone, if applicable;

— Records that identify pool trips, and the location, date and time where each individual or group that separately requests transportation enters and exits the vehicle;

— Records of the vehicle used for the trip, including any number assigned to the vehicle by a regulatory agency or, if none exists, the vehicle's license plate number and jurisdiction;

— Records of all amounts charged and collected for the trip, including fare, taxes, and surcharges (including the congestion surcharge); and

— True and complete copies of any records that must be kept as required by any applicable regulatory department or agency.

(Reg. Sec. 700.4)

All records must be kept for a minimum of three years after filing a return to which those records relate, or from the date such return was due, whichever is later. In the absence of a filed return, the maintenance of records from earlier periods is required. (TSB-M-18(1)CS)

Compliance with the above may be achieved by using a system or equipment that is required to be used in for-hire vehicles by a regulatory agency, so long as such system or equipment is capable of collecting, storing and electronically transmitting all required records and information. (TSB-M-18(1)CS)

- *Definitions related to congestion surcharge*

The following definitions are related to the congestion surcharge:

— "For-hire transportation trip" means transportation provided in a for-hire vehicle that is not a pool vehicle, regardless of the number of stops, for which a charge is made. But, it does not include transportation provided by, or pursuant to a contract with, school districts, or in connection with funerals.

— "For-hire vehicle" means a motor vehicle, other than an ambulance and a bus, carrying passengers for hire.

— "Pool vehicles" are vehicles that are used to provide pool trips. A pool trip is transportation between two points that is provided to a person (or to a group of people that enter and exit a vehicle together per a single request for transportation) in a vehicle that may also simultaneously transport others in trips that are requested and charged separately. To qualify as a pool trip, it is not necessary that the vehicle transport two or more persons or groups in simultaneous trips. Rather, it must be possible during the course of a trip that the vehicle will pick up and/or drop off another person or group that separately requested transportation. Whether a trip is a pool trip for purposes of the surcharge is determined on a per-ride basis.

— "Congestion zone" means the geographic area of New York City, in the borough of Manhattan, south of and excluding 96th Street.

— "Bus" is any motor vehicle with a seating capacity of at least 15 persons, excluding the driver, that does not otherwise qualify as a limousine.

— "Hail vehicle" is a motor vehicle, commonly referred to as a "green cab," that is affiliated with a base and authorized by the New York City Taxi and Limousine Commission (TLC) to accept hails from prospective passengers in the streets of New York City, but which does not have a medallion issued by the TLC affixed to it.

— "Limousine" is any vehicle with a seating capacity of up to 14 persons, excluding the driver, and any vehicle with a seating capacity of between 15 and 20 persons, excluding the driver, that has only two axles and four tires.

— "Medallion taxicab" is a motor vehicle, commonly referred to as a "yellow cab," that has a medallion issued by the New York City Taxi and Limousine Commission affixed to it.

(Sec. 1299, Tax Law; Reg. Sec. 700.1) (TSB-M-18(1)CS)

[¶35-350]

TRANSPORTATION NETWORK COMPANY SERVICES ASSESSMENT

[¶35-351] Transportation Network Company Services Assessment

A state assessment fee is imposed on transportation network company (TNC) prearranged trips that originate anywhere in the state outside the city and terminate anywhere in the state. (Sec. 1292, Tax Law)

Definitions.—"Transportation network company" or "TNC" means a person, corporation, partnership, sole proprietorship, or other entity that is license and operating within the state exclusively using a digital network to connect passengers to drivers who provide TNC prearranged trips. "TNC prearranged trip" or "trip" means the provision of transportation by a transportation network company driver to a passenger provided through the use of a TNC's digital network: (1) beginning when a transportation network company driver accepts a passenger's request for a trip through a digital network controlled by a transportation network company, (2) continuing while the transportation network company driver transports the requesting passenger in a TNC vehicle, and (3) ending when the last requesting passenger departs from the TNC vehicle. A TNC prearranged trip does not include transportation provided through shared expense carpool or vanpool arrangements, or use of a taxicab, livery, luxury limousine, or other for-hire vehicle. "Gross trip fare" means the sum of the base fare charge, distance charge and time charge for a complete TNC prearranged trip at the applicable rate charged by the TNC at the time such trip is arranged. (Sec. 1291, Tax Law; Sec. 1691, Vehicle and Traffic Law; *TSB-M-17(1)M, (1)S*, New York Department of Taxation and Finance, June 23, 2017)

Rate.—The fee is imposed at 4% of the gross trip fare of every TNC prearranged trip provided by such TNC that originates anywhere in the state outside the city and terminates anywhere in the state. (Sec. 1292, Tax Law; *TSB-M-17(1)M, (1)S*, New York Department of Taxation and Finance, June 23, 2017)

Returns and payments.—Returns must be filed on a calendar-quarterly basis showing the number of TNC prearranged trips, the total gross trip fares and the amount of fees due for the quarter. Returns and payments are due within 30 days after the end of the quarterly period covered, unless shorter periods are required by the Commissioner. (Sec. 1294, Tax Law; *TSB-M-17(1)M, (1)S*, New York Department of Taxation and Finance, June 23, 2017)

[¶37-000]

ALCOHOLIC BEVERAGES

[¶37-001] Alcoholic Beverages

New York's Alcoholic Beverage Tax is covered in Article 18 of the Tax Law. Current tax rates are:

Beer	$0.14/gallon
Still wine	$0.30/gallon
Cider containing more than 3.2% alcohol by volume	$0.0379/gallon
Artificially carbonated sparkling wines	$0.30/gallon
Artificially carbonated sparkling cider containing over 3.2% alcohol	$0.0379/gallon
Naturally sparkling wines	$0.30/gallon
Naturally carbonated sparkling cider containing over 3.2% alcohol	$0.0379/gallon
Liquors containing not more than 2% alcohol	$0.01/liter (this rate is eliminated effective 9/1/2020)
Liquors containing more than 2% alcohol but less than 24% alcohol	$0.67/liter
All other liquors	$1.70/liter

(Sec. 424(1), Tax Law; www.tax.ny.gov)

A quantity of alcoholic beverages which is a fractional part of a gallon or liter, is taxed at such fractional part of the applicable rate.

Comprehensive coverage of taxation of alcohol, as well as licensing and distribution information is provided in Wolters Kluwer, CCH Liquor Control Law Reporter. For more information go to CCHGroup.com or contact an account representative at 888-CCH-REPS (888-224-7377).

[¶37-050]
DOCUMENT RECORDING TAX

[¶37-051] Real Estate Transfer Tax

NEW DEVELOPMENTS: Enacted as part of the 2019 budget, Ch. 59 (S.B. 1509), increases the real estate transfer tax rates, including the so-called mansion tax, on conveyances of real property in New York City. Specifically, the law increases the real estate transfer tax by 0.25% for conveyances of: (i) residential real property when the consideration is $3 million or more, and (ii) any other real property (i.e., commercial property) when the consideration is $2 million or more. The increased real estate transfer tax rate is in addition to the existing 0.4% real estate transfer tax on all conveyances. The law also imposes an additional mansion tax, ranging from 0.25% on transfers of $2 million or more to 2.9% on transfers of $25 million or more. This new/additional mansion tax is in addition to the existing 1% mansion tax on transfers of residential real property of $1 million or more. As a result of these increases and additional tax, the total combined top rate is 4.55% on the sale of residential properties valued at $25 million or above in New York City. The new rates go into effect on July 1, 2019, other than conveyances that are made pursuant to binding written contracts entered into on or before April 1, 2019, provided that the date of execution of such contract is confirmed by independent evidence or other facts and circumstances.

The Department of Taxation and Finance has issued a summary of the amendments to the real estate transfer taxes enacted in the budget bill. (TSB-M-19(1)R)

Article 31, Real Estate Transfer Tax imposes a tax (the base tax) on each convey-ance of New York real property or interest in real property when the consideration exceeds $500. (Sec. 1402, Tax Law)

New York City imposes a separate real estate transfer tax.

Additional "mansion tax".—An additional real estate transfer tax (commonly referred to as the mansion tax), is imposed on each conveyance of New York real property that is or may be used in whole or in part as a personal residence when the consideration for the entire conveyance is $1 million or more. (Sec. 1402-a, Tax Law)

Additional base tax for conveyances in New York City.—Applicable to convey-ances occurring on or after July 1, 2019, the law is amended to provide for an addition to the base tax (additional base tax) on the consideration for certain conveyances of real property located in New York City. (TSB-M-19(1)R)

Supplemental tax on residences.—Applicable to conveyances occurring on or after July 1, 2019, the law is amended to add a supplemental tax on the conveyance of residential real property located in New York City where the consideration for the conveyance is $2 million or more. (TSB-M-19(1)R)

Columbia County.—Effective until December 31, 2023, Columbia County im-poses an additional tax on conveyances of interests in real property. The rate is $1 per $500 on real property conveyances. The first $150,000 on the sale of a single family residence is exempt. (Sec. 1439-b, Tax Law)

Erie County.—Erie County imposes an additional tax on conveyances of interests in real property that occur on or after June 1, 1990, unless pursuant to a written contract entered into before such date, where the consideration for the interest exceeds $500. (Sec. 1425, Tax Law; Local Law 7-2000, Erie County) Generally, the tax is administered, collected and paid in the same manner as the state transfer tax.

Peconic Bay.—Effective until December 31, 2030, any town within the Peconic Bay region may adopt a local law imposing an additional tax, subject to mandatory referendum, for the purposes of community preservation, at the rate of 2% of the consideration (where it exceeds $500) for the real property conveyance. (Sec. 1449-bb, Tax Law) However, prior to adopting such a local law, the town must establish a dedicated community preservation fund for the deposit of the tax proceeds. (Sec. 1449-bb, Tax Law)

Town of Warwick.—Until December 31, 2025, town of Warwick is authorized to impose a New York real estate transfer tax at the rate of 0.75% on all converyances of real property where the consideration exceeds $500. (Sec. 1449-bbbb, Tax Law)

- *Administration of tax*

The real estate transfer tax is administered by the Commissioner of Taxation and Finance. (Sec. 1415, Tax Law) Although returns, accompanied by the payment of tax, are normally filed with the recording officer as a prerequisite to the recording of the instrument of conveyance, provisions also permit the filing of the return and payment of tax with the Department of Taxation and Finance.

- *Property subject to tax*

A real estate transfer tax (the base tax) is imposed on each conveyance of New York real property or interest in real property when the consideration exceeds $500. (Sec. 1402, Tax Law) All conveyances of real property are presumed taxable. (Reg. Sec. 575.4)

"Conveyance" means the transfer or transfers of any interest in real property by any method, including but not limited to sale, exchange, assignment, surrender, mortgage foreclosure, transfer in lieu of foreclosure, option, trust indenture, taking by eminent domain, conveyance upon liquidation or by a receiver, or transfer or acquisition of a controlling interest in any entity with an interest in real property. (Sec. 1401(e), Tax Law) The term does not, however, include conveyances pursuant to devise, bequest or inheritance.

Interests in real property that are subject to tax include titles in fee, leasehold interests, beneficial interests, encumbrances, development rights, air space and air rights, or any other interest with the right to use or occupancy of real property or the right to receive rents, profits or other income derived from real property. (Sec. 1401(f), Tax Law) Options or contracts to purchase real property are taxable interests. A right of first refusal to purchase real property, however, is not a taxable interest.

"Real property" means every estate or right, legal or equitable, present or future, vested or contingent, in lands, tenements or hereditaments, including buildings, structures and other improvements thereon, which are located in whole or in part within the State of New York. (Sec. 1401(c), Tax Law) It does not include rights to sepulture.

Additional real estate transfer (mansion) tax.—An additional real estate transfer tax (commonly referred to as the mansion tax) is imposed on each conveyance of New York real property that is or may be used in whole or in part as a personal residence when the consideration for the entire conveyance is $1 million or more. (Sec. 1402-a(a), Tax Law) "Residential real property" includes any premises that is or may be used in whole or in part as a personal residence, including one-, two- or three-family houses, individual condominium units, or cooperative apartment units.

The New York Department of Taxation and Finance has issued a real estate transfer tax bulletin that explains how the additional tax applies to the transfer of more than three separate condominium or cooperative units to a single purchaser or to related purchasers. (*TB-RE-10*, New York Department of Taxation and Finance, November 18, 2011)

Additional base tax for conveyances in New York City.—Applicable to conveyances occurring on or after July 1, 2019, the law is amended to provide for an addition to the base tax (additional base tax) on the consideration for certain conveyances of real property located in New York City. (TSB-M-19(1)R) Specifically, the tax applies to:

- The conveyance of residential real property where the consideration for the entire conveyance is $3 million or more; and

- The conveyance of real property other thanresidential real property where the consideration for the entire conveyance is $2 million or more.

(TSB-M-19(1)R)

The seller is required to pay the additional base tax. If the seller fails to pay the tax or is exempt from the tax, the buyer is required to pay the tax. When the buyer is required to pay the tax because the seller has failed to pay, the additional base tax becomes the joint and several liability of the seller and the buyer. (TSB-M-19(1)R)

For purposes of the additional base tax, all mixed-use real property is considered residential real property. Therefore, if the consideration for the conveyance of mixed-use real property is $3 million or more, the entire consideration is subject to the additional base tax. (TSB-M-19(1)R)

Residential real property includes any premises that is or may be used in whole or in part as a personal residence, and includes a one-, two- or three-family house, an individual condominium unit or a cooperative apartment unit. (TSB-M-19(1)R)

Mixed-usereal property is real property that is used for both residential and other than residential (for example, commercial) purposes. (TSB-M-19(1)R)

Supplemental tax on residences.—Applicable to conveyances occurring on or after July 1, 2019, the law is amended to add a supplemental tax on the conveyance of residential real property located in New York City where the consideration for the conveyance is $2 million or more. (TSB-M-19(1)R)

Local transfer tax.—If adopted by resolution, certain New York municipalities would be authorized to enact a local law to impose a real estate transfer tax for the purpose of generating money for the Hudson Valley community preservation fund. The local transfer tax could not exceed 2% of the consideration for property conveyances and would be payable by the buyer to the treasurer or a recording officer acting as the treasurer's agent. (Sec. 1561, Tax Law; Sec. 1562, Tax Law; Sec. 1563, Tax Law)

The following would be exempt from the local transfer tax:

— New York or any of its agencies, instrumentalities, political subdivisions, or public corporations; and

— the United Nations, the United States or any of its agencies or instrumentalities.

(Sec. 1564, Tax Law)

Several conveyances would also be exempt from the tax, including deeds that convey real property as gifts, tax sales, corrections to previously recorded deeds, open space, parks, conservation easement property, and property conveyed to not-for-profit corporations that are operated for conservation, environmental, park or historic preservation purposes. (Sec. 1564, Tax Law)

Leaseholds and subleases.—Three possible transactions involving leases qualify as taxable conveyances of real property for transfer tax purposes:

Sublease without option to purchase.—The creation of a lease or sublease not coupled with an option to purchase is a taxable conveyance of an interest in real property only where:

(1) the sum of the term of the lease or sublease and any options for renewal exceeds 49 years;

(2) substantial capital improvements are or may be made by or for the benefit of the lessee or sublessee; and

(3) the lease or sublease is for substantially all of the premises constituting the real property.

(Sec. 1401(e), Tax Law)

"Substantially all" means 90% or more of the total rentable space of the premises, exclusive of common areas. (Reg. Sec. 575.7)

> *EXAMPLE:* Corporation Z owns a ten-story building. Corporation Z creates a 60-year lease with Corporation Y as tenant, such lease covering five floors of the building (50% of the premises). Since the lease covers less than 90% of the rentable space of the premises, the creation of the lease is not a conveyance subject to the transfer tax.

Option to purchase.—An option to purchase real property coupled with the right of use or occupancy of the property is, for transfer tax purposes, the conveyance of a taxable interest in real property. (Reg. Sec. 575.7) Accordingly, the creation of a lease coupled with the granting of an option to purchase, regardless of the term of the lease, is a conveyance subject to the transfer tax.

> *EXAMPLE:* A, as lessor, creates a lease of a building with B as lessee. The term of the lease is 20 years. The lease contains an option to purchase the building which is exercisable through the tenth year of the lease. If the option is exercised, the lease provides that the property will be transferred to B not later than six months after the option is exercised. B paid $10,000 specifically for the granting of the option. Since this is the granting of an option with use and occupancy, the transaction is subject to the transfer tax.

Assignment, surrender of lease.—The transfer of a leasehold interest by assignment or surrender, regardless of the term, is a conveyance subject to tax.

Cooperative housing corporations.—The conveyance of shares of stock in cooperative housing corporations in connection with the grant or transfer of proprietary leaseholds that occur on or after July 1, 1989, unless pursuant to the terms of a binding written contract executed on or before February 16, 1989, is subject to transfer tax. (Sec. 1405-B, Tax Law; Reg. Sec. 575.8) The tax applies to both the original conveyance of shares of stock by the cooperative housing corporation or cooperative plan sponsor and any subsequent conveyance of stock by the owner.

Controlling interests.—The acquisition or transfer of a controlling interest in an entity with an interest in real property is, for transfer tax purposes, a conveyance of a taxable interest in real property. (Sec. 1401(e), Tax Law) Where a corporation has an interest in real property, the transfer or acquisition of a controlling interest occurs when a person, or group of persons acting in concert, transfers or acquires a total of 50% or more of the voting stock in such corporation. (Reg. Sec. 575.6) In the case of a partnership, association, trust or other entity having an interest in real property, a transfer or acquisition of a controlling interest occurs when a person, or group of persons acting in concert, transfers or acquires a total of 50% or more of the capital, profits or beneficial interest in such entity.

Persons are acting in concert when they have a relationship such that one person influences or controls the actions of another. Where individuals or entities are not commonly controlled or owned, persons will be treated as acting in concert when the unity with which the sellers or purchasers have negotiated and will consummate the transfer of ownership interests indicates that they are acting as a single entity. The parties may be required to provide a sworn statement that their transfers or acquisitions are independent.

Factors that indicate whether persons are acting in concert include the following:

(1) the transfers or acquisitions are closely related in time;

(2) there are few grantors or grantees;

(3) the contracts of sale contain mutual terms;

(4) the grantors or grantees have entered into an agreement in addition to the sales contract binding themselves to a course of action with respect to the transfer or acquisition.

(Reg. Sec. 575.6)

The New York Department of Taxation and Finance has issued a real estate transfer tax bulletin that addresses four specific situations that arise when there is a transfer or acquisition of a controlling interest in a partnership, corporation, or other entity with an interest in real property. (TB-RE-885, New York Department of Taxation and Finance, November 18, 2011)

> EXAMPLE: A owns 100% of X Corporation, the only asset of which is real property. B, C, D and E, as a group, negotiate to buy all of A's interest with B, C, D and E each buying 25% of A's interest. The contracts of B, C, D and E are identical and the purchases are to occur simultaneously. B, C, D and E have also negotiated an agreement binding themselves to a course of action with respect to the acquisition of X Corporation and the terms of a shareholders agreement which would govern their relationship as owners of X Corporation. The acquisitions by B, C, D and E would be treated as a single acquisition which is subject to the real estate transfer tax.

> EXAMPLE: Partnership X, which owns real property, is composed of partners A and B, each having a 50% partnership interest. In November 1989, A and B decided to raise more capital by agreeing that they each will sell a percentage of their partnership interest. On November 20, 1989, A and B each sold a $12^1/_2$% partnership interest to C. On October 11, 1990, A and B each sold a 15% partnership interest to D. Since A and B have acted in concert and transferred a 55% interest ($12^1/_2 + 12^1/_2 + 15 + 15$) within a three year period, the transfers are subject to the real estate transfer tax. A and B would each owe transfer tax on the respective transfers of their $12^1/_2$% and 15% interests.

> EXAMPLE: Corporation X has 2 stockholders. Individual A owns 90 shares of stock (90%) and individual B owns 10 shares of stock (10%). Corporation X owns 60% of the stock of Corporation Y, which owns real property. Individual A, by virtue of owning 90% of the stock of Corporation X, has a 54% interest in Corporation Y (90% interest in Corporation X multiplied by the 60% interest Corporation X has in Corporation Y equals the 54% interest individual A has in Corporation Y). Individual A sells his 90 shares of stock in Corporation X to individual G. Individual A, by selling his 90 shares of Corporation X stock, has

transferred a controlling interest (54%) in an entity that owns real property (Corporation Y) which transfer is subject to the real estate transfer tax. The consideration used to determine the transfer tax due would be equal to 54% of fair market value of the real property owned by Corporation Y.

EXAMPLE: Corporation X is a publicly held corporation, the stock of which is owned by many unrelated shareholders. X owns an interest in real property. D, E, F and G, pursuant to a plan to gain control of X, make a tender offer of $100 per share to the public shareholders to acquire such control. As a result of the tender offer, D, E, F and G acquire, in total, 80% of the stock of X with each getting 20%. D, E, F and G would be treated as acting in concert to acquire a controlling interest, and the tax would apply to this transaction as an acquisition of a controlling interest.

Aggregation of interests.—With limited exceptions, interests acquired after June 30, 1989, are aggregated for purposes of determining whether a controlling interest has been acquired. (Reg. Sec. 575.6) Transfers or acquisitions made after June 30, 1989, will not be aggregated if made pursuant to a binding written contract that was entered into on or before February 16, 1989. The date of execution of the contract must be confirmed by independent evidence. Interests acquired beyond a three-year period will not be aggregated, unless timed as part of a plan to avoid transfer tax.

Real estate investment trusts.—Transfers of interests in real property on or after June 9, 1994, to qualified real estate investment trusts (REITs), or to a partnership or corporation in which a REIT owns a controlling interest immediately following such conveyance, where the conveyance occurs in connection with the initial formation of the REIT, are subject to a reduced real estate transfer tax. (Sec. 1402(b)(1), Tax Law)

In addition, the provision granting the reduced real estate transfer tax rates has been expanded to include transfers on or after July 13, 1996, and before September 1, 2020, to qualified existing REITS (that is, transfers that do *not* occur in connection with the formation of the REIT). For details, see note below. (Sec. 1402(b)(2)(B), Tax Law)

Transfers after June 9, 1994.—To be eligible for the reduced tax, transfers made after June 9, 1994, in connection with the initial formation of a REIT must meet the following requirements:

Retained ownership requirements.—The transferor (or transferors) must receive, as part of the consideration for the transfer, ownership interests in the REIT (or an entity controlled or to be controlled by the REIT) equal to at least 40% of the value of the equity interest in the real property or interest therein conveyed by the transferor(s) to the transferee. Ownership interests must be retained by the transferor (or owners of the transferor) for a period of not less than two years from the date of the conveyance (unless the transferor dies, in which case the two-year retention period will be deemed to be satisfied, notwithstanding any conveyance of the interest as a result of such death). (Sec. 1402(b)(2)(B)(i), Tax Law)

The equity value of the property (or interest therein) transferred to the REIT (or entity controlled or to be controlled by the REIT) is computed by subtracting from the consideration the unpaid balance of any loans secured by mortgages or other encumbrances that are liens on the real property (or interest therein) immediately prior to the transfer. In the case of a transfer of property that is a transfer or an acquisition of a controlling interest, the amount required to be subtracted from the consideration is equal to the sum of: (1) a reasonable apportionment to the ownership interests in the entity being transferred of the unpaid balance of any loans secured by encumbrances on the ownership interests in the entity being transferred, and (2) a reasonable apportionment to the ownership interests in the entity being transferred of the unpaid balance of any loans secured by mortgages or other encumbrances on the real property of the entity itself. Mortgages or other encumbrances on the real property or interest therein that are created in contemplation of the initial formation of the REIT or in contemplation of the conveyance of the real property or interest therein to the REIT or to a partnership or corporation in which the REIT owns a controlling interest immediately following the conveyance are not considered. (Sec. 1402(b)(2)(B)(i), Tax Law)

In computing the equity value of the real property or interest therein being conveyed, any mortgages or other encumbrances on the property (or interest therein) that are created primarily in contemplation of the initial formation of the REIT in order to avoid or evade tax (rather than for an adequate business purpose) may not be deducted from the consideration. In addition, unsecured liabilities may not be considered when determining the equity value of the property or interest therein being transferred.

The value of the ownership interests in the REIT or an entity controlled or to be controlled by the REIT that are received by the transferor must be computed by one of the following methods:

(1) where the real property or interest therein is transferred directly to the REIT and the consideration for the transfer includes shares in the REIT, the value of the ownership interests in the REIT received by the transferor(s) is presumed to be equal to the arithmetic mean of the opening and closing prices of the shares in the REIT (as traded on an established securities market) on the date of the transfer, multiplied by the number of shares in the REIT received by the transferor(s). If the REIT offering is not a public offering (i.e., a private placement), the value of the ownership interests in the REIT received by the transferor is presumed to be equal to the arm's-length price of the shares of the REIT, without regard to any discounts in the price of the shares, on the date of transfer, multiplied by the number of shares in the REIT received by the transferor; or

(2) where the real property or interest therein is transferred to an entity controlled or to be controlled by the REIT and the consideration for the transfer includes an ownership interest in the controlled entity, there is a presumption that the value of the ownership interests in the entity controlled (or to be controlled) by the REIT is equal to the net cash proceeds (gross proceeds less underwriting discounts) of the initial offering of the REIT used by the REIT to acquire its interest in the controlled entity, divided by the percentage interest in the controlled entity acquired by the REIT.

(Sec. 1402(b)(2)(B)(ii), Tax Law)

A taxpayer may use other reasonable methods to calculate the value of the ownership interest received if it demonstrates that the methods noted above do not result in an accurate representation of the value of the ownership interests received. (TSB-M-94(4)R)

Where a transferor receives as consideration for a REIT transfer ownership interests having a value greater than 40% of the equity value of the property (or interest therein), the transferor may subsequently transfer any portion of the ownership interests in the property that exceed such 40% equity value in the property without violating the 40% ownership condition for preferential tax treatment. The ownership condition will be satisfied so long as the transferor continues to maintain (for a period of two years following the date of the REIT transfer) ownership interests in the REIT (or an entity controlled by the REIT) having a value (as determined on the date of the transfer) of at least 40% of the property's equity value. However, if the initial REIT transfer was the transfer or acquisition of a controlling interest, if the subsequent transfer of ownership interests related to the value of the ownership interests in excess of 40% of the property's equity value (where such transfer does not otherwise qualify as a REIT transfer) results in a further transfer or acquisition of a controlling interest, the further transfer will not be eligible for preferential tax treatment.

Where an entity transfers an interest in real property to a REIT and the value of the ownership interests received by the entity as consideration for the transfer is at least 40% of the equity value of the property transferred, the ownership requirement will continue to be satisfied so long as the entity continues to retain, for a period of two years following the date of the REIT transfer, ownership interests have a value of at least 40% of the equity value of the property transferred, without regard to any changes in the beneficial ownership of the entity itself. (TSB-M-94(4)R)

75% reinvestment requirement.—75% or more of the cash proceeds received by the REIT from the sale of ownership interests in the REIT upon its initial formation must be used:

(1) to make payments on loans secured by any interest in real property (including an ownership interest in an entity owning real property) that is owned directly or indirectly by the REIT;

(2) to pay for capital improvements to real property or any interest therein owned directly or indirectly by the REIT;

(3) to pay costs, fees, and expenses (including brokerage fees and commissions, professional fees and payments to or on behalf of a tenant as an inducement to enter into a lease or sublease) incurred in connection with the creation of a leasehold or sublease pertaining to real property or an interest therein owned directly or indirectly by the REIT;

(4) to acquire any interest in real property (including an ownership interest in any entity owning real property), apart from any acquisition to which a reduced rate of tax is applicable; or

(5) for reserves established for any of the purposes noted in (1), (2) or (3), above.

The consideration for real property (or any interest therein) transferred to a REIT (or entity controlled by a REIT) must be calculated by dividing the net cash flow from operations with respect to the property for the 12-month period ending on the last day of the second month preceding the date of the conveyance, by the sum of (1) 2% and (2) the federal long-term rate compounded semi-annually by the U.S. Secretary of the Treasury pursuant to IRC Sec. 1274(d) in effect 30 days prior to the date of the conveyance.

The Commissioner of Taxation and Finance may adjust the amount upon a determination that the formula noted above does not result in an accurate representation of the fair market value, and may also prescribe other rules or regulations for determination a transfer's "fair market value."

All revenues and expense items included in the calculation of net cash flow from operations must be included under the cash basis of accounting. Items that constitute revenue must be recognized in the period in which they are actually or constructively received, and expenses must be recognized in the period in which they are paid.

Deductions for amortized portions of certain capital expense items are allowed in the calculation of net cash flow from operations. Unless other provided, for purposes of determining the term of a lease to be used in the amortization of capital expenses, the terms of the lease must include the current unexpired term of the lease and all periods pursuant to any options to renew remaining at the time the amortizable expense item was incurred, or the amortizable improvement was completed and placed into service. However, the cost of such capital expenses may be amortized over the initial lease term, without regard to any renewal periods, if the taxpayer can clearly demonstrate that the expense items were related only to the initial lease term and not to any renewal periods.

Debt service expenses (principal and interest), taxes (other than operating taxes such as real estate taxes and special assessments, payroll taxes, and sales and utility taxes) and depreciation amounts are not deductible in computing the net cash flow from operations for the property for the subject period.

CCH CAUTION: The Department of Taxation and Finance has indicated that the following REIT transfers will be regarded as transfers that occur in connection with the initial formation of the REIT and, as such, qualify for reduced tax treatment (TSB-M-94(4)R):

(1) any REIT transfer that is specifically disclosed in the prospectus for the initial offer of the REIT shares, regardless of when such transfer takes place;

(2) any REIT transfer whose consideration is paid, in part, from the proceeds of the initial offering of the REIT shares, regardless of when such transfer takes place; or

(3) any REIT transfer made within six months after the date of the initial offering of the REIT shares, without regard to (1) or (2), above.

As noted by the Department, any other transfer will be presumed not to be a transfer occurring in connection with the initial formation of the REIT. A taxpayer may, however, rebut this presumption by presenting clear and convincing evidence that the transfer in question was contemplated at the time of the initial formation of the REIT, but was unable to be consummated within six months from the initial offering of the REIT shares.

Qualified employee benefit plans.—Although it may not be considered as precedent in the Division of Tax Appeals or any New York State judicial proceeding, the New York Division of Tax Appeals, Administrative Law Judge Unit, has held that the Federal Employee Retirement Income Security Act of 1974 (ERISA) does not preempt the Division of Taxation from imposing real estate transfer tax on conveyances of real property by a trust owned by a qualified employee benefit plan.

In *In the Matter of the Petition of Net Realty Holding Trust*, the Administrative Law Judge (ALJ) rejected the taxpayer's contention that there was a direct relationship between the real estate transfer tax and employee benefit plans because the tax is paid from the plan's income and amounts available for distribution to plan beneficiaries are thereby reduced. The ALJ distinguished the real estate transfer tax from the real property gains tax, which is preempted by ERISA, noting that the transfer tax does not impose any recordkeeping or filing requirements and, therefore, does not mandate administrative procedures that are not imposed by other jurisdictions. Additionally, since the transfer tax, unlike gains tax, does not apply to earnings derived from real estate, it would not have a significant influence on the pension fund's investment strategy. Finally, the transfer tax has no counterpart in the Internal Revenue Code, while preemption of the gains tax was consistent with the favorable treatment given to benefit plans under the federal tax code, which exempts earnings on a plan's assets from federal taxation. In contrast, a direct relationship cannot be drawn between the federal policy of exempting pension plan income from federal taxes and the state's imposition of a transfer tax on the conveyance of a deed.

For the text of *Net Realty Holding Trust*, see ¶401-675.

• *Basis and rates of tax*

NEW DEVELOPMENTS: Enacted as part of the 2019 budget, Ch. 59 (S.B. 1509), increases the real estate transfer tax rates, including the so-called mansion tax, on conveyances of real property in New York City. Specifically, the law increases the real estate transfer tax by 0.25% for conveyances of: (i) residential real property when the consideration is $3 million or more, and (ii) any other real property (i.e., commercial property) when the consideration is $2 million or more. The increased real estate transfer tax rate is in addition to the existing 0.4% real estate transfer tax on all conveyances. The law also imposes an additional mansion tax, ranging from 0.25% on transfers of $2 million or more to 2.9% on transfers of $25 million or more. This new/additional mansion tax is in addition to the existing 1% mansion tax on transfers of residential real property of $1 million or more. As a result of these increases and additional tax, the total combined top rate is 4.55% on the sale of residential properties valued at $25 million or above in New York City. The new rates go into effect on July 1, 2019, other than conveyances that are made pursuant to binding written contracts entered into on or before April 1, 2019, provided that the date of execution of such contract is confirmed by independent evidence or other facts and circumstances.

The Department of Taxation and Finance has issued a summary of the amendments to the real estate transfer taxes enacted in the budget bill. (TSB-M-19(1)R)

A real estate transfer tax (the base tax) is imposed on each conveyance of an interest in real property, including the conveyance of shares in a cooperative housing corporation, when the consideration exceeds $500. (Sec. 1402, Tax Law; Sec. 1405-B, Tax Law) The rate of the base tax is $2 for each $500, or fractional part thereof, of such consideration or value. The base tax is paid by the seller (grantor). However, if the seller does not pay the tax, or is exempt from the tax, the buyer (grantee) must pay the tax. (Sec. 1402, Tax Law)

Real estate investment trust transfers.—Transfers of interest in real property on or after June 9, 1994, to qualified real estate investment trusts (REITs) or to a partnership or corporation in which the REIT owns a controlling interest immediately following such conveyance, are subject to real estate transfer tax at the rate of $1 for each $500 (or fractional part thereof) of consideration. (Sec. 1402, Tax Law)

Additional real estate transfer (mansion) tax.—An additional real estate transfer tax (commonly referred to as the mansion tax) is imposed on each conveyance of New York real property that is or may be used in whole or in part as a personal residence when the consideration for the entire conveyance is $1 million or more. The mansion tax is imposed at the rate of 1% of the consideration, or part thereof, that is attributable to the residential real property. (Sec. 1402-a(a), Tax Law) (TSB-M-19(1)R) The mansion tax is required to be paid by the buyer (grantee). Applicable to conveyances occurring on or after July 1, 2019, the law iss amended to provide that when the buyer fails to pay the tax, the seller (grantor) is required to pay. When the seller is required to pay the additional tax because the buyer failed to pay, the additional tax becomes the joint and several liability of the seller and the buyer. (TSB-M-19(1)R)

Additional base tax for conveyances in New York City.—Applicable to conveyances occurring on or after July 1, 2019, the law is amended to provide for an addition to the base tax (additional base tax) in the amount of $1.25 for each $500, or fractional part, of the consideration for certain conveyances of real property located in New York City. (TSB-M-19(1)R)

Supplemental tax on residences.—Applicable to conveyances occurring on or after July 1, 2019, the law is amended to add a supplemental tax on the conveyance of residential real property located in New York City where the consideration for the conveyance is $2 million or more. (TSB-M-19(1)R) The supplemental tax rate differs depending on the amount of the consideration for the entire conveyance as indicated below:

- if the entire conveyance is at least $2 million but less than $3 million: the rate is 0.25%;

- if the entire conveyance is at least $3 million but less than $5 million: the rate is 0.5%;

- if the entire conveyance is at least $5 million but less than $10 million: the rate is 1.25%;

- if the entire conveyance is at least $10 million but less than $15 million: the rate is 2.25%;

- if the entire conveyance is at least $15 million but less than $20 million: the rate is 2.5%;

- if the entire conveyance is at least $20 million but less than $25 million: the rate is 2.75%; and

- if the entire conveyance is $25 million or more: the rate is 2.9%.

(TSB-M-19(1)R)

The buyer is required to pay the supplemental tax. If the buyer fails to pay the tax or is exempt, the seller is required to pay the tax. When the seller is required to pay the tax because the buyer has failed to pay, the supplemental tax becomes the joint and several liability of the seller and the buyer. (TSB-M-19(1)R)

The supplemental tax is due on the conveyance of mixed use real property when the consideration for the entire property is $2 million or more. Tax is computed only on the consideration attributed to the residential portion of the property. (TSB-M-19(1)R)

Multiple transfers.—When a seller transfers more than one interest in real property to a buyer, the property interests will be treated as a single conveyance when the property interests are used in conjunction with each other or there is a clear relationship between each property interest. When multiple transfers are treated as a single conveyance, the consideration for these transfers must be added together to determine whether the additional base tax or supplemental tax are due. (TSB-M-19(1)R)

A seller making multiple transfers in New York City must complete Form 584.6-NYC, Real Estate Transfer Tax Return Schedule of Apportionment, to show how consideration is apportioned between the properties and compute the additional base tax, supplemental tax, and other applicable real estate transfer taxes. (TSB-M-19(1)R)

Taxes collected.—The base tax, additional base tax, mansion tax, and supplemental tax are all due within 15 days from the date of conveyance and are to be remitted with Form TP-584-NYC, Combined Real Estate Transfer Tax Return, Credit Line Mortgage Certificate, and Certification of Exemption from the Payment of Estimated Personal Income Tax for the Conveyance of Real Property Located in New York City. (TSB-M-19(1)R)

Erie County.—The additional tax imposed of conveyances of interests in real property located in whole or in part in Erie County is imposed at the rate of $2.50 for each $500, or fractional part thereof, of the consideration or value. (Sec. 1425, Tax Law)

Transfer recording filing fees.—A real property transfer Form RP-5217, RP-5217-NYC, or RP-5217-PDF (pilot project) is required for all real property transfers where a deed is filed. A filing fee is also required. The fees are:

— $125 for residential and farm property; and

— $250 for all other property.

(Sec. 333(3), Real Property Law)

Consideration.—Subject to the limitations noted in the following paragraphs, "consideration" is the price actually paid or required to be paid for the conveyance of an interest in real property. (Sec. 1401(d), Tax Law; Reg. Sec. 575.4) Included are:

(1) payments for an option or contract to purchase real property (whether expressed in the deed or paid or required to be paid by money, property, or any other thing of value);

(2) the cancellation or discharge of an indebtedness or obligation; and

(3) the amount of any mortgage, purchase money mortgage, lien or other encumbrance, whether or not the underlying indebtedness is assumed or taken subject to.

Property other than money.—If the consideration paid, or required to be paid, includes property other than money, the consideration is presumed to be the fair market value of the real property or interest therein. (Reg. Sec. 575.4) The presumptions may be rebutted by the person liable for payment of the tax.

"Fair market value" is the amount that a willing buyer would pay a willing seller for the interest in the property. (Reg. Sec. 575.1) It is generally determined by appraisal based upon the value of the real property at the time of conveyance.

Tax paid by transferee.—The grantor is primarily responsible for the payment of transfer tax. Where the transferee agrees, as part of the consideration, to pay the tax, the payment constitutes additional consideration and is subject to tax.

EXAMPLE: A one-family house, which is the grantor's residence, is sold for $2 million. There are no liens or other encumbrances on the property at the time of conveyance. The sales contract provides that the grantee will pay the transfer tax for the grantor. The grantee would compute the tax as follows:

$2 million ÷ $500 = 4,000 × $2 = $8,000

$2,008,000 ÷ $500 = 4,016 × $2 = $8,032 Tax Due

The payment of the transfer tax by the transferee also constitute additional consideration when computing the additional tax on residential property.

Additional tax.—When determining taxable consideration for the purpose of computing the additional tax on conveyances of interests in residential property, no deduction is allowed for continuing liens on real property or, in the case of the conveyance of cooperative shares, for any mortgage on the property owned by the cooperative corporation or any lien on the cooperative housing shares. (Reg. Sec. 575.3)

Tax paid by grantor.—The transferee is primarily responsible for the payment of the additional transfer tax. Where the transferee is personally liable, payment of the tax by the grantor is considered to be an expense connected with the conveyance of the property. The consideration received by the grantor will not be reduced by the amount of additional tax paid by the grantor. (Reg. Sec. 575.4)

> *EXAMPLE:* A one-family house, which is the grantor's residence, is sold for consideration of $1.4 million. The sales contract provides that the grantor will pay the additional tax for the grantee. The grantor would be required to pay additional tax of $14,000. (Sec. 1402(b), Tax Law× $1.4 million) The grantor would also be liable for payment of transfer tax in the amount of $5,600. ($2 for each $500, or fractional part thereof, of consideration of $1.4 million)

Foreclosure sales.—In *Petition of Indian Head Associates*, the Division of Tax Appeals, Administrative Law Judge Unit, rejected a taxpayer's claim that the consideration for property acquired at a foreclosure sale should be based on the property's fair market value. Instead, the administrative law judge agreed with the Department of Taxation and Finance's position that, when real property is conveyed pursuant to a mortgage foreclosure and the successful bidder is the mortgagee, the consideration is equal to the amount of the judgment in foreclosure or the bid price, whichever is higher, plus the amount of any other pre-existing mortgages remaining on the property after the conveyance. The administrative law judge rejected the taxpayer's contention that the definition of "consideration" applicable for real property transfer gains tax purposes applied to the real property transfer tax.

Qualifying residential property.—"Consideration" does not include the amount of any lien or encumbrance remaining at the time of sale where the conveyance involves a one-, two- or three-family house or individual residential condominium unit. (Sec. 1402, Tax Law; Reg. Sec. 575.1)

Example: A three-family house is sold for $850,000. The grantee assumed an existing $200,000 mortgage, obtained an additional $550,000 mortgage from a bank and paid $100,000 in cash. The tax is imposed upon $650,000, because the $850,000 consideration is reduced by the $200,000 mortgage which remained on the qualifying residential property at the time of the sale. However, the $850,000 cannot be reduced by the new $550,000 mortgage obtained by the grantee in connection with the sale. The result would have been the same if the grantee had purchased the property subject to an existing $200,000 mortgage which remained on the property at the time of the sale.

Consideration under $500,000.—"Consideration" does not include the amount of any lien or encumbrance remaining at the time of sale when the consideration for the conveyance is less than $500,000. (Sec. 1402, Tax Law; Reg. Sec. 575.1)

Example: A commercial building is sold for $800,000. The grantee assumed an existing $300,000 mortgage and paid $500,000 in cash. The tax is imposed on the entire $800,000, because the consideration exceeds $500,000 and the building is not qualifying residential property. No exclusion is allowed for the existing $300,000 mortgage. The result would have been the same if the grantee had purchased the property subject to an existing $300,000 mortgage and/or obtained an additional mortgage with respect to $500,000.

Leaseholds and subleases.—The creation of a taxable lease or sublease not coupled with an option to purchase is subject to tax where:

> (1) the sum of the term of the lease or sublease and any options for renewal exceeds 49 years,

> (2) substantial capital improvements are or may be made by or for the benefit of the lessee or sublessee, and

> (3) the lease or sublease is for substantially all of the premises constituting the real property.

(Reg. Sec. 575.7)

¶37-051

In such instances, the consideration used to compute transfer tax is the present value of the right to receive rental payments or other payments attributable to the use and occupancy of the real property, plus the present value of rental or other payments attributable to any renewal term. (Sec. 1401(d)(i), Tax Law)

The present value of the lease payments is determined by applying a federal discount rate to net rents. (Reg. Sec. 575.7) "Net rents" are the excess of gross rents over certain operating costs, including heat, gas, electricity, furnishings, insurance, maintenance, management, and real estate taxes. Operating expenses paid directly to third parties by the lessee are not included in gross rents, nor deductible as operating costs. If the lease requires the lessor to pay a fixed amount of operating costs, the lessor may deduct such itemized amounts from gross rents in computing net rents; if the lease does not itemize the operating costs for which the lessor is responsible, reasonable estimated operating costs may be deducted from gross rents. If the lessor pays one or more of the following operating costs, and there is no itemization in the lease for such costs, and no reasonable estimate of such costs is made and substantiated, the following percentages of gross rentals will be presumed attributable to the following costs:

Heat and Gas 15%

Electricity 5%

Furnishings 5%

The discount rate is equal to 110% of the federal long-term discount rate, compounded semiannually, determined pursuant to IRC Sec. 1274(d). An alternative discount rate, based on the fair market value of the property, will be permitted if the taxpayer establishes that the use of the 110% discount rate:

(1) is inappropriate under the particular circumstances, and

(2) will result in a calculation of consideration that exceeds the fair market value of the property.

Subleases.—With respect to the creation of taxable subleases, consideration is computed in the manner noted above, except that the value of the remaining prime lease rental payments must be subtracted. (Sec. 1401(d)(ii), Tax Law; Reg. Sec. 575.7)

EXAMPLE: A, as lessor, creates a lease with B as lessee. The lease is for a term of 60 years and covers an entire office building owned by A. The terms of the lease allow B to make substantial capital improvements to the building. The gross rents to be received by A over the term of the lease total $5 million. Operating costs are estimated to be $2 million. Net rents total $3 million (gross rents of $5 million less operating costs of $2 million paid by A). The present value of net rents is $550,000.

The taxable consideration is $550,000, the present value of net rents. The total tax due, at the rate of $2 for each $500 of consideration, is $2,200.

Lease coupled with option.—The consideration for the creation of a lease for a term of less than 49 years, coupled with the grant of an option to purchase, is the present value of the net rental payments under the lease plus the consideration paid for the granting of the option to purchase. Rental payments for periods that occur after the last date that the property may be purchased, if the option is exercised, are excluded from the calculation of the present value of rental payments.

EXAMPLE: A, as lessor, creates a lease of a building with B as lessee. The term of the lease is 20 years. The lease contains an option to purchase the building which is exercisable through the tenth year of the lease. If the option is exercised, the lease provides that the property will be transferred to B not later than six months after the option is exercised. B paid $10,000 specifically for the granting of the option. Since this is the granting of an option with use and occupancy, the transaction is subject to transfer tax. The consideration used to compute the tax would be the present value of the net rental payments to be received from the effective date of the lease through the expiration of the first ten years and six months of the lease, which is the period during which the property may be purchased pursuant to the option to purchase, plus the $10,000 paid for the granting of the option.

Assignment of lease.—The consideration for the assignment of a lease is the amount paid for the assignment by the assignee to the assignor (that is, the lessee under the lease or the person who is assigning his or her rights to purchase the property under the option or contract). Consideration does not include the value of remaining rental payments required to be made pursuant to the terms of the lease. (Sec. 1401(d)(iv), Tax Law)

No tax will be imposed on an assignment of a leasehold interest if the assignor pays consideration to the assignee to accept the assignment.

> *EXAMPLE:* A, a lessee under a 30-year lease, enters into an agreement to assign the leasehold interest to B, who will replace A as a tenant under the lease. B agrees to pay A $500,000 for the leasehold interest. The assignment of A's leasehold interest to B is subject to tax at the rate of $2 for each $500 of consideration, resulting in a tax due of $2,000.

Surrender of lease.—The consideration for the surrender of a leasehold interest is the amount paid for the surrender by the lessor to the lessee. Consideration does not include the value of remaining rental payments required to be made pursuant to the terms of the lease. (Sec. 1401(d)(iv), Tax Law)

No tax will be imposed on the surrender of a leasehold interest if the lessee pays consideration to the lessor to accept the surrender.

> *EXAMPLE:* X is the owner of a building which is leased to Z under a 20-year lease which has 10 years remaining under the terms of the lease. X wishes to cancel the lease before it expires and, therefore, enters into an agreement with Z whereby X will pay Z $400,000 to surrender the lease. The surrender of the leasehold interest by Z is subject to tax at the rate of $2 for each $500 of consideration, resulting in a tax due of $1,600.

> *EXAMPLE:* Same facts as above, except that Z is the party motivating the cancellation of the lease and, therefore, Z agrees to pay X to accept the surrender of the lease. No tax would be due since Z, the grantor, is not receiving consideration for the conveyance.

Cooperative housing corporations.—The consideration for an original conveyance of shares of stock by a cooperative housing corporation must include a proportionate share of the unpaid principal of any mortgage on the real property of the cooperative housing corporation comprising the cooperative dwelling or dwellings. (Sec. 1401(d)(v), Tax Law) The share is determined by multiplying the total unpaid principal of the mortgage by a fraction. The numerator is the number of shares of stock being conveyed in the cooperative housing corporation in connection with the grant or transfer of a proprietary leasehold, and the denominator is the total number of shares of stock in the cooperative housing corporation.

A proportionate share of the unpaid principal of a mortgage on the real property of the cooperative housing corporation must also be included as a part of the consideration received from a subsequent conveyance by the owner of stock in the corporation in connection with the grant or transfer of a proprietary leasehold for a cooperative unit other than an individual residential unit. Where an individual residential unit is to be transferred in connection with the conveyance of the cooperative corporation's stock,

Where the property to be transferred in connection with the conveyance of stock is an individual residential unit, the consideration for the conveyance must exclude the amount of any lien on the certificates of stock or other evidence of ownership interest at the time of conveyance. (Reg. Sec. 575.1) No exclusion is made, however, on account of any lien or encumbrance placed upon the property in connection with the conveyance or by reason of deferred payments of the purchase price, whether represented by notes or otherwise.

Controlling interest.—In the case of the acquisition of a controlling interest in any entity that owns real property, "consideration" is the fair market value of the interest in the real property, apportioned based on the percentage of the ownership interest transferred or acquired in the entity. (Sec. 1401(d)(iii), Tax Law)

Property located within and without New York.—Where property is situated partly within and partly without New York State, the consideration subject to transfer tax is the allocated portion of the total consideration that is attributable to the portion of the property situated within the state. (Reg Sec. 575.12)

• *Exemptions*

New York has a variety of exemptions applicable to the real estate transfer tax.

CCH COMMENT: *START-UP NY.*—The SUNY Tax-Free Areas to Revitalize and Transform Upstate (START-UP) New York program provides a real property transfer tax exemption to promote business and job creation by transforming public higher education through tax-free communities in upstate New York and other strategically-designated locations. Conveyances of real property located in tax-free NY areas to businesses located in those areas that are participating in the START-UP NY program are exempt from state and local real estate transfer tax or real property transfer tax. In addition, any lease of property to an eligible business also is exempt from any state or local real estate transfer tax or real property transfer tax. This lease provision applies to taxable years beginning on or after January 1, 2014. (Sec. 39, Tax Law)

Governmental transfers.—The following governmental organizations are exempt from payment of transfer tax:

(1) the State of New York, its agencies, instrumentalities, political subdivisions, and public corporations (including a public corporation created pursuant to agreement or compact with another state or Canada);

(2) the United Nations; and

(3) the United States, its agencies and instrumentalities.

(Sec. 1405(a), Tax Law)

Transferee liability.—The exemption of the governmental organizations noted above does not extend to the transferee. Accordingly, where an exempt governmental organization conveys property to a non-exempt individual or entity, tax is payable by the transferee. (Reg. Sec. 575.9)

Conveyances to governmental organizations.—Conveyances to any of the governmental organizations noted in the preceding paragraphs, including any agency or instrumentality of the United Nations, are exempt from tax. (Sec. 1405(b)(1), Tax Law)

Grandfathered conveyances.—A conveyance of real property occurring after June 30, 1989, that does not involve the delivery of a deed and is made pursuant to a binding written contract entered into on or before February 16, 1989, is exempt from transfer tax. (Reg. Sec. 575.5) The date of execution of the contract must be confirmed by independent evidence.

EXAMPLE: A, the owner of real property, executed a binding written contract on February 6, 1989, to lease the property with an option to purchase to B for $1,000 a month for ten years. B paid $1,000 as a deposit on the lease on that date. The final closing of the transaction occurred on July 10, 1989. The creation of the lease with the option to purchase is a grandfathered conveyance which is not subject to tax since it did not involve the delivery of a deed, was made pursuant to a binding written contract entered into on or before February 16, 1989, and the date of the execution of the contract was confirmed by independent evidence (payment of the deposit by B).

Additional tax.—A conveyance of real property that occurs after June 30, 1989, pursuant to a binding written contract entered into on or before February 16, 1989, is exempt from the additional 1% tax on residential property. (Reg. Sec. 575.5) The date of execution of the contract must be confirmed by independent evidence.

EXAMPLE: On February 1, 1989, D executed a binding written contract to sell his personal residence, a one-family home, to E for $1.2 million. E gave D a check for $10,000 as a deposit on the contract on that date. D conveyed the property to E on July 5, 1989. This conveyance is a grandfathered conveyance for purposes of the 1% additional tax since it was made pursuant to a binding written contract entered into on or before February 16, 1989, and the date of execution of the contract is confirmed by independent evidence (payment of the deposit by E). However, the conveyance remains subject to the transfer tax imposed by Sec. 1402, Tax Law.

A grandfathered contract for the conveyance of real property that is amended after February 16, 1989, will qualify for the grandfathered exemption, provided the amendment is a nonsubstantial change. (Reg. Sec. 575.5) The determination of what constitutes a nonsubstantial change is made on a case by case basis.

Change in consideration.—A change in the amount of consideration to be paid for a conveyance of real property is a substantial change and will render the grandfather exemption inapplicable. (Reg. Sec. 575.5)

EXAMPLE: A, the owner of real property, executed a binding written contract on February 6, 1989 to lease the property with an option to purchase to B for $1,000 a month for ten years. B paid $1,000 as a deposit on the lease on that date. The final closing of the transaction occurred on July 10, 1989. On June 11, 1989, the contract was amended to provide that B would pay $1,200 each month instead of $1,000. This is a change in the amount of consideration for an interest in the real property. Therefore, the conveyance is subject to tax since it no longer qualifies as a grandfathered conveyance.

Postponement of closing date.—The extension of a closing date specified within a grandfathered contract is not a substantial amendment. (Reg. Sec. 575.5) If additional payments are to be made by the grantee in return for the extension, the conveyance will remain eligible for exemption if it is shown that the additional payments do not constitute additional consideration.

Mere change of identity.—Conveyances of real property that consist of a mere change of identity or form of ownership or organization, without any change in beneficial ownership, are exempt from transfer tax. (Sec. 1405(b)(6), Tax Law) Examples include:

(1) A conveyance by tenants-in-common to a partnership or a corporation, the partnership or corporation interests being in the same *pro rata* shares that the tenants-in-common held before the conveyance.

(2) A conveyance by a corporation to its shareholders who will hold the real property as tenants-in-common in the same *pro rata* share as they own the corporation.

(3) A conveyance by a corporation to its wholly owned subsidiary, from a wholly owned subsidiary to its parent, or from one wholly owned subsidiary to another. The conveyance is exempt to the extent that there is no change in beneficial ownership.

(4) A conveyance by a person to a partnership in exchange for an interest in the partnership. The conveyance is exempt to the extent of the grantor's interest in the partnership.

(Reg. Sec. 575.10)

Cooperative housing corporations.—The mere change of identity exemption does not apply to conveyances of real property comprising a cooperative dwelling or dwellings to a cooperative housing corporation. (Sec. 1405(b)(6), Tax Law) To avoid the possibility of double taxation, however, a credit against tax is allowed.

Debt securities.—Conveyances that are or were used to secure a debt or other obligation are exempt from transfer tax,. (Sec. 1405(b)(2), Tax Law)

Supplemental and corrective conveyances.—Conveyances that, without additional consideration, confirm, correct, modify or supplement a prior conveyance, are exempt from transfer tax. (Sec. 1405(b)(3), Tax Law)

Gift, devise, bequest, or inheritance.—Conveyances of real property that are made without consideration and otherwise than in connection with a sale are exempt from transfer tax. (Sec. 1405(b)(4), Tax Law) Examples include *bona fide* gifts and conveyances by devise, bequest or inheritance. (Reg. Sec. 575.9)

Tax sales.—Conveyances given in connection with tax sales are not subject to transfer tax. (Sec. 1405(b)(5), Tax Law)

Partition deeds.—Partition deeds are not subject to transfer tax. (Sec. 1405(b)(7), Tax Law)

Bankruptcy plans.—Conveyances given pursuant to the federal bankruptcy act are exempt from transfer tax. (Sec. 1405(b)(8), Tax Law)

Conveyances without use or occupancy.—Contracts to sell real property without the use or occupancy of the property are exempt from transfer tax. (Sec. 1405(b)(9), Tax Law) The grant of an option to purchase real property without the accompanying right of use or occupancy is also exempt.

Personal residences.—An option or contract to purchase real property that includes the use or occupancy of the property, where the consideration is less than $200,000 and the property was used solely as the grantor's personal residence, is exempt from transfer tax. (Sec. 1405(b)(10), Tax Law) The property must consist of a one-, two- or three-family house, an individual residential condominium unit or the sale of stock in a cooperative housing corporation in connection with the grant or transfer of a proprietary leasehold covering an individual residential cooperative unit.

Assignment of option or contract to purchase personal residence.—The assignment of an option or contract to purchase real property that qualifies for the personal residence exemption is also exempt from transfer tax. (Reg. Sec. 575.7)

Right of first refusal.—Rights of first refusal to purchase real property are expressly excluded from the definition of "interests in real property" and, accordingly, are not subject to transfer tax. (Sec. 1401(f), Tax Law)

Industrial Development Agency.—In certain instances, conveyances of property to and from an Industrial Development Agency (IDA) are exempt from transfer tax. (Reg. Sec. 575.11)

Conveyance to IDA.—When a beneficiary of IDA financing conveys real property to the IDA in connection with the receipt of such financing, the conveyance is exempt. However, if the IDA obtains the property from a third party, at the beneficiary's direction, and subsequently leases the property to the beneficiary, the conveyance is taxable. In the latter instance, the beneficiary of the IDA financing, rather than the IDA, is deemed to be the grantee.

Conveyance from IDA.—A conveyance of real property by the IDA to the beneficiary of IDA financing is not subject to tax. However, if the IDA conveys an interest in the property to a person other than the beneficiary, where the conveyance is made at the discretion of the beneficiary, the conveyance is taxable; the beneficiary of the IDA financing is deemed to be the grantor of the conveyance.

Mortgages.—Mortgage foreclosures and transfers in lieu of foreclosure are expressly included within the statutory definition of "conveyance" and, accordingly, are subject to transfer tax. (Sec. 1401(e), Tax Law) The following mortgage transactions, however, are excluded:

(1) the creation, modification, extension, spreading, severance, consolidation, assignment, transfer, release or satisfaction of a mortgage;

(2) mortgage subordination agreements;

(3) mortgage severance agreements; and

(4) instruments given to perfect or correct a recorded mortgage.

(Reg. Sec. 575.1)

Release of tax liens.—Releases of tax liens pursuant to state or federal tax law provisions are expressly excluded from the statutory definition of "conveyance" and, accordingly, are not subject to transfer tax. (Sec. 1401(e), Tax Law)

• *Credits*

Credits against the real estate transfer tax are given for prior transfer tax paid and for qualifying conveyances of shares of stock by a cooperative housing corporation.

Credit for prior transfer tax paid.—A grantor is allowed a credit against transfer tax due on a conveyance of real property to the extent that the tax was previously paid by the grantor as the result of the creation of a prior leasehold or the grant of an option or contract to purchase all or a portion of the same property (Reg. Sec. 575.13).

Calculation of credit.—The credit is computed by multiplying the tax paid on the creation of the leasehold or on the granting of an option or contract by a fraction. The numerator is the value of the consideration used to compute the tax paid that is not yet due to the grantor on the date of the subsequent conveyance (which the grantor will not be entitled to receive after such date). The denominator is the total value of the consideration used to compute the tax paid.

Cooperative housing corporation.—New York transfer tax is imposed on both the original conveyance of shares of stock by a cooperative housing corporation in connection with the conversion of property to cooperative ownership and upon the subsequent conveyance of shares by an owner. (Sec. 1405-B, Tax Law; Reg. Sec. 575.8)

Where the property has been converted into cooperative ownership, a credit will be allowed on the subsequent conveyance of the corporation's shares of stock to the extent that the initial conveyance to the housing corporation effectuated a mere change of identity or form of ownership.

Determination of credit.—The amount of the credit is determined by multiplying the amount of tax paid upon the conveyance to the cooperative housing corporation by a percentage representing the extent to which such conveyance effectuated a mere change of identity or form of ownership and not a change in the beneficial ownership of such property. The resulting product is then multiplied by a fraction, the numerator of which is the number of shares of stock conveyed to the owner in exchange for the transfer of the realty to the coperative housing corporation and the denominator of which is the total number of shares of stock of the cooperative housing corporation (including any stock held by the corporation).

Limitations.—The credit may not reduce the tax below zero. In addition, no credit is allowed for a tax paid more than 24 months prior to the date on which occurs the first in a series of conveyances of shares of stock in an offering of cooperative housing corporation shares.

- *Payment*

Real estate transfer tax must be paid to the Commissioner of Taxation and Finance, or the Commissioner's authorized agent, within 15 days after the delivery of the instrument effecting the conveyance by the grantor to the grantee. (Sec. 1410(a), Tax Law) The date on the instrument effecting the conveyance is presumed to the date of delivery. The presumption may be rebutted by the person responsible for the payment of the tax. (Reg. Sec. 575.14)

Payment of tax is evidenced by the placement of a notation or stamps on the instrument of conveyance. (Sec. 1410(a), Tax Law) All payments received by a recording officer during each month must be forwarded to the Commissioner on the 10th day of the succeeding month.

Additional tax.—The additional 1% tax on conveyances of residential real property is payable at the same time and in the same manner as noted above. (Sec. 1402-a, Tax Law)

Returns.—A joint real estate transfer tax return must be filed by the grantor and grantee for each conveyance of an interest in real property, regardless of whether transfer tax is due except in the case of the conveyance of an easement or license to a public utility where the consideration is $2 or less and is clearly stated as actual consideration in the instrument of conveyance. The manner in which the return is filed is dependent upon the location of the property and whether the conveyance is to be recorded. If the tax is paid to the Commissioner of Taxation and Finance, the return is filed with the Commissioner at the time the tax is paid. The receipt provided by the Commissioner confirming that the tax has been paid is then filed with the county recording officer. (Sec. 1409(a), Tax Law; Reg. Sec. 575.14)

Certain conveyances involving LLCs: When a limited liability company (LLC) is the grantor or grantee in a deed transfer of a building containing one- to four-family dwelling units, the following forms cannot be accepted for filing unless accompanied by documentation that identifies all members, managers, and other authorized persons of the LLC:

- Form TP-584, Combined Real Estate Transfer Tax Return, Credit Line Mortgage Certificate, and Certification of Exemption from the Payment of Estimated Personal Income Tax; and

- Form TP-584-NYC, Combined Real Estate Transfer Tax Return, Credit Line Mortgage Certificate, and Certification of Exemption from the Payment of Estimated Personal Income Tax for the Conveyance of Real Property Located in New York City.

(Sec. 1409(a), Tax Law) (TSB-M-19(2)R)

Form TP-584 or Form TP-584-NYC must be accompanied by a list of the names and addresses of all members, managers and other authorized persons of the LLC. If any member of the LLC is itself an LLC or other business entity, a list of all shareholders, directors, officers, members, managers and/or partners of that LLC or other business entity must also be provided until ultimate ownership by natural persons is disclosed. (TSB-M-19(2)R)

The documentation requirements apply when the applicable property is partially used for commercial purposes. (TSB-M-19(2)R)

"Authorized person" means a person, whether or not a member, who is authorized by the operating agreement, or otherwise, to act on behalf of an LLC or foreign LLC. "Natural person" means a human being, as opposed to an artificial person, who is the beneficial owner of the real property. A natural person does not include: a corporation or partnership, natural person(s) operating a business under a d/b/a (doing business as), an estate (such as the estate of a bankrupt or deceased person), or a trust. (TSB-M-19(2)R)

Conveyance to be recorded.—Where a conveyance is to be recorded, the return is filed with, and accompanying tax is paid to, the recording officer of the county where the conveyance is recorded. (Reg. Sec. 575.14; TSB-M-97(1)R) Where the instrument effecting the conveyance is to be recorded in more than one county, the return is filed with the recording officer of the county where the instrument effecting the conveyance is first recorded. A recording officer will not record a conveyance until the return has been filed and any tax due has been paid. (Sec. 1410(b), Tax Law)

Conveyance not recorded.—Where a conveyance is not recorded, or will not be recorded after the expiration of the applicable time period for the payment of tax, the return, together with any tax due, must be filed with the Department of Taxation and Finance within 15 days of the conveyance. (Reg. Sec. 575.14; TSB-M-97(1)R)

Release of tax return to third party.—When a person requesting the receipted copy of a real estate transfer tax return is not the grantor or grantee, such as a legal professional or title insurance company representative, a written authorization signed by the grantor or grantee must be provided to the Department of Taxation and Finance. The Department has revised transfer tax Forms TP-584 and TP-584-REIT to incorporate this authorization as part of the signature certification. Third party filers must enclose a self-addressed, postage-paid return envelope when requesting a receipted copy. (*Important Notice N-07-13*, New York Department of Taxation and Finance, June 2007)

Filing extension.—For good cause shown, the Commissioner of Taxation and Finance may grant an extension of time, not exceeding three months, within which to file a real estate transfer tax return. The application for extension must be made in writing prior to the due date of the return. If the extension is granted, a tentative return must be filed, and estimated tax paid, on or before the original due date.

Determination of tax by commissioner.—The Commissioner of Taxation and Finance is authorized to determine the amount of the real estate transfer tax due when a return is not filed or, if filed, is incorrect or insufficient. (Sec. 1411(a), Tax Law) Notice of the determination is given to the person liable for the payment of the tax. The determination finally and irrevocably fixes the tax, unless a petition is filed with the Division of Tax Appeals within 90 days after the giving of the notice.

Assessment limitations.—Assessments of additional tax may not be made after the expiration of more than three years from the date a return was filed, but tax may be assessed at any time if no return was filed or a willfully false or fraudulent return was filed. (Sec. 1420(a), Tax Law) The period for the assessment of additional tax may be extended by the taxpayer. (Sec. 1420(b), Tax Law)

Transferee liability.—Generally, the grantor of an interest in real property is responsible for the payment of real estate transfer tax. (Sec. 1404(a), Tax Law) However, if the grantor fails to pay the tax within the applicable time limitations, or is otherwise exempt from the payment of tax, the grantee is liable. If the grantee has the duty to pay transfer tax as a result of the failure of the grantor to make the necessary payment, the tax is the joint and several liability of the grantor and the grantee.

The grantee is responsible for the payment of the 1% additional transfer tax on conveyances of residential property. (Sec. 1402-a(b), Tax Law) If the grantee is exempt, the grantor has the duty to pay the tax.

Refunds.—Anyone claiming to have erroneously paid transfer tax may file an application for refund within two years from the date of payment. (Sec. 1412, Tax Law) Where a taxpayer has consented in writing to the extension of the period for determination of tax due, the period for filing an application for a refund will not expire prior to six months after the extended period in which a determination of tax due may be made. (Reg. Sec. 575.16) (For a discussion of refunds generally, see ¶ 89-224 in the "Practice and Procedure" division).

Administrative review.—The Commissioner of Taxation and Finance may grant or deny an application for refund in whole or in part, and must notify the applicant of its determination by mail. The determination is final and irrevocable unless the applicant, within 90 days after the mailing of the determination, petitions the Division of Tax Appeals for a hearing. The Division must review the request for a hearing and mail a notice of its determination to the applicant. See, generally, ¶ 89-234 in the "Practice and Procedure" division.

Judicial review.—A proceeding pursuant to Article 78, Civil Practice Laws and Rules, may be filed to review a decision of the Tax Appeals Tribunal. As a prerequisite, the amount of the tax sought to be reviewed, with penalties and interest, must be filed with the Commissioner of Taxation and Finance. In addition, an undertaking, issued by a surety company licensed to do business in New York and approved by the Commissioner of Insurance, in an amount sufficient to pay all costs of charges that will accrue in the prosecution of the Article 78 proceeding must be filed. See, generally, in the "Practice and Procedure" division.

Interest.—Interest of $1 or more is allowed and paid on refunds. Interest is computed at the overpayment established by the Commissioner of Taxation and Finance (see ¶ 89-204 in the "Practice and Procedure" division) from the last date prescribed for payment, rather than the actual date of payment, to a date preceding the date of the refund check by not more than 30 days.

• *Penalties*

Overpayments, underpayments.—Interest is imposed on overpayments and underpayments of real property transfer gains tax at rates set by the Commissioner of Taxation and Finance. (Sec. 1416(a), Tax Law; Sec. 1416(c), Tax Law)

For current rates, see ¶ 89-204 in the "Practice and Procedure" division.

Penalties.—Any taxpayer that fails to file a return or to pay the tax within the time required is subject to a penalty equal to 10% of the amount of the tax plus an interest penalty equal to 2% for each month or fraction thereof of delay. (Sec. 1416(b), Tax Law) The interest penalty may not exceed 25% in the aggregate.

The Commissioner may remit, abate or waive the penalty if the delay was due to reasonable cause and not due to willful neglect.

[¶37-052] Mortgage Recording Tax

Mortgage recording taxes are excise taxes imposed on the recording of mortgages on real property situated in New York. (TSB-M-91(1.1)R) The following taxes are authorized to be imposed:

— the basic tax (imposed by Sec. 253(1), Tax Law);

— the additional tax (imposed by Sec. 253(2), Tax Law);

— the special additional tax (imposed by Sec. 253(1-a), Tax Law);

— the New York City tax (authorized by Sec. 253-a, Tax Law, and imposed by Sec. 11-2601, N.Y.C. Adm. Code) (for details, see ¶557-005 and following);

— the Nassau County tax (authorized by Sec. 253-c, Tax Law);

— the City of Yonkers tax (authorized by Sec. 253-d, Tax Law, and imposed by Sec. 92-123, Code of the City of Yonkers);

— the Broome County tax (authorized by Sec. 253-e, Tax Law, and imposed by Local Law INTRO. No. 9, adopted July 21, 1994);

— the Rockland County tax (authorized by Sec. 253-f, Tax Law; Form MT-15, Mortgage Recording Tax Return);

— the Westchester County tax (authorized by Sec. 253-g, Tax Law; Form MT-15, Mortgage Recording Tax Return);

— the Lewis County tax (authorized by Sec. 253-h, Tax Law);

— the Columbia County tax (authorized by Sec. 253-i, Tax Law);

— the Sullivan County tax (authorized by Sec. 253-j(1), Tax Law);

— the Hamilton County tax (authorized by Sec. 253-j(2), Tax Law);

— the Essex County tax (authorized by Sec. 253-j(3), Tax Law);

— the Schoharie County tax (authorized by Sec. 253-j(4), Tax Law);

— the Genesee County tax (authorized by Sec. 253-k, Tax Law);

— the Rensselaer County tax (authorized by Sec. 253-l, Tax Law);

— the Wayne County tax (authorized by Sec. 253-m, Tax Law);

— the Wyoming County tax (authorized by Sec. 253-n, Tax Law);

— the Chautauqua County tax (authorized by Sec. 253-o, Tax Law);

— the Albany County tax (authorized by Sec. 253-p, Tax Law);

— the Schenectady County tax (authorized by Sec. 253-r, Tax Law);

— the Steuben County tax (authorized by Sec. 253-s, Tax Law);

— the Yates County tax (authorized by Sec. 253-t, Tax Law);

— the Herkimer County tax (authorized by Sec. 253-u, Tax Law);

— the Cortland County tax (authorized by Sec. 253-v, Tax Law);

— the Warren County tax (authorized by Sec. 253-w, Tax Law);

— the Cattaraugus County tax (authorized by Sec. 253-x(1), Tax Law);

— the Greene County tax (authorized by Sec. 253-x(2), Tax Law);

— the Livingston County tax (authorized by Sec. 253-y, Tax Law)

— the Madison County tax (authorized by Sec. 253-y, Tax Law);

— the Washington County tax (authorized by Sec. 253-y, Tax Law).

The mortgage recording tax is an excise tax on the privilege of recording a document measured by the amount of principal debt or obligation secured by a mortgage on real property situated in New York State.

Every mortgage involving property situated, in whole or in part, in New York State, is subject to the basic tax and the special additional tax. Mortgages involving property situated in whole or in part in New York are also subject to the additional tax unless the imposition of the tax has been suspended by a local law, ordinance or resolution. Mortgages involving property located in whole or in part in New York City, the City of Yonkers, or Broome County are also subject to the respective local taxes.

Constitutional provisions.—No special constitutional provisions apply.

The most important constitutional question involving the mortgage recording tax concerned the effect of an amendment which prohibited the ad valorem taxation of personal property. The mortgage recording tax was held to be an excise tax on the privilege of recording and not an ad valorem tax, see *Franklin Society for Home Building and Savings v. Bennett,* (1939, NY Ct App), 282 NY 79,24 NE2d 854; app dism'd US SCt, 309 US 640, 60 SCt 894.

• *Taxable transactions*

The recording of every mortgage, unless exempt from taxation, is subject to the basic tax and the special additional tax. In addition, the recording of a mortgage is subject to the additional tax, unless the imposition of such tax was suspended by local law, ordinance or resolution; the New York City tax if the real property subject to the mortgage is located, in whole or in part, in New York City; the City of Yonkers tax if the real property subject to the mortgage is located, in whole or in part, in the City of Yonkers; and the Broome County tax if the real property subject to the mortgage is located, in whole or in part, in Broome County.

CCH COMMENT: *Federal credit unions.*—The New York Department of Taxation and Finance advises that the recording of residential mortgages given to federal credit unions is subject to all mortgage recording taxes, except the special additional tax imposed by § 253.1-a(a), Tax Law. The New York Court of Appeals held in *Hudson Valley Federal Credit Union v. New York State Department of Taxation and Finance* that the recording of mortgages securing loans made by federal credit unions is not exempt from the mortgage recording tax. Other than the exception noted below, the recording of mortgages given to federal credit unions is subject to all mortgage recording taxes imposed by and pursuant to Article 11 of the Tax Law, including the basic tax, additional tax, special additional tax, city taxes, and all county taxes.

The recording of mortgages given to federal credit unions on real property principally improved or to be improved by one or more structures containing in the aggregate not more than six residential dwelling units, each having its own separate cooking facilities, is not subject to the special additional tax imposed by § 253.1-a(a), Tax Law. (*TSB-M-12(1)R,* Taxpayer Guidance Division, New York Department of Taxation and Finance, December 6, 2012)

Real property defined.—The term "real property" means:

(1) land, whether above and under water, all buildings and other articles and structures, substructures and superstructures, erected upon, under or above, or affixed to the same;

(2) all wharves and piers (including the value of the right to collect wharfage, cranage or dockage thereon);

(3) all bridges, all telegraph lines, wires, poles and appurtenances;

(4) all supports and inclosures for electrical conductors and other appurtenances upon, above and under ground;

(5) all surface, underground or elevated railroads, including the value of all franchises, rights or permission to construct, maintain or operate the same in, under, above, on or through streets, highways or public places;

(6) all railroad structures, substructures and superstructures, tracks and the iron thereon; branches, switches and other fixtures permitted or authorized to be made, laid or placed in, upon, above or under any public or private road, street or ground;

(7) ll mains, pipes and tanks laid or placed in, upon, above or under any public or private street or place for conducting steam, heat, water, oil, electricity or any property, substance or product capable of transportation or conveyance therein or that is protected thereby, including the value of all franchises, rights, authority or permission to construct, maintain or operate, in, under, above, upon, or through, any streets, highways or public places, any mains, pipes, tanks, conduits or wires, with their appurtenances, for conducting water, steam, heat, light, power, gas, oil or other substance, or electricity or telegraphic, telephonic or other purposes;

(8) all trees and underwood growing upon land, and all mines, minerals, quarries and fossils in and under the same, except mines belonging to the state; and

(9) all the forms of housing which are adaptable to motivation by a power connected thereto or which may be propelled by a power within themselves and which are or can be used as a house or living abode or habitation of one or more persons, or for business, commercial or office purposes, either temporarily or permanently, and commonly called and hereafter referred to as "trailers"; except (a) transient trailers that have been located within the boundaries of a city, town or village for less than 60 days and (b) trailers which are for sale and which are not occupied.

(Sec. 250, Tax Law)

"Real property" also includes everything a conveyance or mortgage of which can be recorded as a conveyance or mortgage of real property under the laws of the State.

Exclusions.—The term "real property" does not include bulk milk tanks or coolers installed upon a farm to hold milk awaiting shipment to market.

Mortgage defined.—The term "mortgage" includes all instruments in writing that impose a lien on, or affect the title to, real property (or both real and personal property), where the property is used as security for the payment of money or the performance of an obligation. (Sec. 250, Tax Law; Reg. Sec. 641.6)

Applicable to mortgages recorded on or after January 17, 2005, the law is amended to specify that a contract or agreement, whereby the proceeds of any indebtedness secured by a mortgage of real property in New York City are used to reduce all or any part of a mortgagee's equity interest in a wraparound or similar mortgage of the real property, is deemed a mortgage of real property and is taxable to the extent of the amount of such proceeds so used, regardless of whether the aggregate amount of indebtedness secured by mortgages of such real property is increased or added to. (Sec. 250, Tax Law; TSB-M-04(12)R, New York Department of Taxation and Finance, December 29, 2004; TSB-M-04(9)R, New York Department of Taxation and Finance, November 22, 2004)

The New York Department of Taxation and Finance has a mortgage recording tax bulletin that discusses advances secured by a mortgage executed under a confirmed plan of reorganization in bankruptcy (*TB-MR-15*, New York Department of Taxation and Finance, November 18, 2011)

Credit line mortgages.—A "credit line mortgage" is any mortgage or deed of trust, other than a mortgage or deed of trust made pursuant to a building loan contract (as defined in Sec. 2(13), Lien Law) that states that it secures indebtedness under a note, credit agreement or other financing agreement that reflects the fact that the parties reasonably contemplate entering into a series of advances, or advances, payments and readvances, and that limits the aggregate amount at any time outstanding to a maximum amount specified in such mortgage or deed of trust. (Sec. 253-b(2), Tax Law) A "credit line mortgage" does not, however, include reverse mortgages created pursuant to Secs. 280 or 280-a, Real Property Law.

Executory contracts.—Executory contracts for the sale of real property (or both real and personal property) under which the purchaser has, or is entitled to, possession of the real property prior to the delivery of the deed are "mortgages" for purposes of mortgage recording taxes and, therefore, are subject to tax. (Reg. Sec. 643.1)

Supplemental mortgages.—Supplemental mortgages filed subsequent to the recording of a primary mortgage are taxable if they create or secure new or further indebtedness or obligations other than the principal indebtedness or obligation. (Sec. 255, Tax Law)

Applicable to mortgages recorded on or after January 17, 2005, tax applies to the recording of a spreading agreement or additional mortgage that imposes the lien thereof upon real property located in New York City and not originally covered by or described in a recorded primary mortgage, unless the real property that becomes subject to the lien of such spreading agreement or additional mortgage is owned by the mortgagor of the real property subject to the lien of such recorded primary mortgage. The Commissioner of Taxation and Finance is authorized to disregard transfers under certain circumstances, and there is a presumption that all transfers of one or both of such properties to related parties, within the 12-month period preceding the recording of the spreading agreement or additional mortgage, were undertaken for tax avoidance or evasion purposes. Such a presumption can only be rebutted with clear and convincing evidence to the contrary. (Sec. 255, Tax Law; *TSB-M-04(12)R*, Technical Services Bureau, Taxpayer Services Division, New York Department of Taxation and Finance, December 29, 2004) The New York Department of Taxation and Finance has described this provision as a loophole closer. According to the Department, tax was previously avoided by "spreading" an existing mortgage from one property with a mortgagor (owner) and mortgagee (lender) to another property with a different mortgagor and mortgagee. (*Summary of Tax Provisions in SFY 2004-05 Budget*, New York Department of Taxation and Finance, August 2004)

Mortgages for indefinite amounts.—A mortgage for an indefinite amount is one where it is not possible to determine from the terms of the mortgage itself the maximum amount of principal debt or obligation which is, or under any contingency may be, secured at the date of execution thereof or at any time thereafter. (Reg. Sec. 648.1)

A mortgage that secures the repayment of a specific sum of money, but also contains provisions that allow the mortgage to secure additional amounts in the event of the mortgagor's failure to perform a covenant or obligation under the terms of the mortgage relating to maintaining the real property, preserving its value and protecting the mortgagee's lien, the expenses in the event of a foreclosure, and interest and late payment charges (collectively referred to as "incidental amounts") is not a mortgage for an indefinite amount, provided that the failure to perform such covenant or obligation is a condition of default under the terms of the mortgage.

For examples of incidental amounts that may be secured by a mortgage without the mortgage becoming a mortgage for an indefinite amount. (Reg. Sec. 648.1)

Instruments not entitled to be recorded.—Instruments that are not entitled to be recorded but are subject to mortgage recording taxes may be presented to the recording officer of the county in which the real property (or any part of it) affected by the instrument is located. (Sec. 258-a, Tax Law) The tax is payable at this time.

• *Exemptions*

Every mortgage situated within New York State is subject to tax unless specifically exempted by statute or by operation of federal or state constitutional provisions.

Sec. 252, Tax Law, generally provides, with certain exceptions, that no mortgage of real property situated within New York is exempt from mortgage recording taxes by reason of anything contained in any other statute. (Sec. 252, Tax Law) However, as noted by the Department of Taxation and Finance in *Empire State Certified Development Corporation:*

"Notwithstanding the language of Section 252 of the Tax Law, this Department has considered claims for exemption from various public authorities in New York State based on tax exemptions in their creating statutes and has ruled in certain cases that the recording of the mortgages the authorities issued were exempt from the tax imposed by Article 11 of the Tax Law, despite the fact that Section 252 on its face makes no provision for such an exemption. This position is consistent with the general rule that where a conflict or variance exists between two enactments relating to the same general subject matter, a later special statute takes precedence against a general statute and the prior general statute must yield to the later specific or special statute." (*Williamsburg Power Plant Corp. v. City of New York*, 255 App Div 214, affd 280 NY 551; *First National Bank and Trust Co. v. Village of Saltaire*, 256 App Div 156)

Whenever an exemption is claimed, an affidavit must be filed in duplicate at the time that the mortgage is presented for recording, signed by the mortgagor, mortgagee or any other person who has knowledge of the facts, describing the mortgage and setting forth the basis for claiming the exemption. (Reg. Sec. 644.1)

Where an exemption is claimed by a voluntary non-profit hospital corporation, the affidavit must be made by a duly authorized officer of the corporation, and there must be attached to the affidavit a certified copy of the certificate of incorporation and a copy of the certificate of the Public Health Council authorizing the corporation to operate as a hospital. (TSB-M-91(1)R)

The New York Department of Taxation and Finance has issued a mortgage recording tax bulletin that discusses debtor-in-possession financing (*TB-MR-165*, New York Department of Taxation and Finance, November 18, 2011)

State-chartered credit unions.—Effective January 1, 2010, an exemption from the special additional mortgage recording tax is enacted for residential mortgages issued by state-chartered credit unions that have converted from federal credit unions on or after January 1, 2009. (Sec. 253, Tax Law) In order to claim the exemption, the credit union must submit to the recording officer an affidavit at the time the mortgage is presented for recording. The affidavit must be made in duplicate, signed by the mortgagee, and contain the following information:

(1) the mortgagee is a credit union that has been issued an authorization certificate from the Superintendent of Banks pursuant to Sec. 486 of the Banking Law indicating that the credit union has converted from a federal charter to a state charter on or after January 1, 2009, and

(2) pursuant to Sec. 486-a, Article 11 of the Banking Law, the mortgage is exempt from the special additional mortgage recording tax imposed by Sec. 253.1-a(a) of the Tax Law.

(TSB-M-08(5)R, New York Department of Taxation and Finance, October 27, 2008)

In addition, state credit unions must submit the following information:

— the mortgaged premises constitute real property that is principally improved by a structure containing a total of not more than six residential dwelling units, each with its own separate cooking facilities;

— the mortgagee is a state credit union formed under Article 11 of the Banking Law; and

— the mortgage is exempt from the SAMRT imposed by Section 253.1-a(a) of the Tax Law. Separate provisions apply to federal credit unions that have converted to state credit unions on or after January 1, 2009.

(*TSB-M-10(1)R*, Office of Tax Policy Analysis, New York Department of Taxation and Finance, March 30, 2010)

Governmental mortgages.—The recording of the following mortgages involving New York State or the federal government are exempt from mortgage recording taxes:

Mortgages involving state entities.—Mortgages where the mortgagor or mortgagee is New York State or any of its agencies, instrumentalities or political subdivisions are exempt from mortgage recording taxes, to the extent that such entities are immune from such taxation. (*Matter of City of New York v. Tully*, 88 AD2d 701, lv to app den 57 NY 2d 606)

New York Urban Development Corporation.—Property owned by the New York State Urban Development Corporation is exempt from mortgage recording tax. (Sec. 4, S.B. 7803, Laws 2004)

In an advisory opinion, the Commissioner of Taxation and Finance has held that the New York State Urban Development Corporation (UDC) is not subject to New York mortgage recording tax upon the recording of any mortgage that is a part of a project where:

(1) the UDC is named mortgagee and presents the mortgage for recording;

(2) the funds secured by the mortgage are provided by entities other than the UDC; and

(3) the proceeds of the mortgage loans are used for project development costs.

The Commissioner noted that although Article 11 of the Tax Law does not provide a specific exemption applicable to the UDC, the Urban Development Act specifies that the UDC is a state agency. As such, it is immune from taxation. Moreover, the Urban Development Act specifically provides that the UDC and its subsidiaries are not required to pay taxes of any kind. *New York State Urban Development Corporation (Advisory Opinion)*

Mortgages involving federal agencies.—Mortgages where the mortgagor or mortgagee is the United States of America or any of its agencies or instrumentalities, are exempt from mortgage recording taxes, to the extent that such entities are immune from such taxes. (*Pittman v. Home Owners Loan Corporation*, 308 US 21)

Agricultural credit association mortgages.—Mortgages of real property situated within New York that are transferred, assigned or made to agricultural credit associations within the Farm Credit System are exempt from mortgage recording taxes. (Sec. 252, Tax Law)

Federal Home Loan Bank mortgages.—Mortgages of real property situated within New York that are transferred, assigned or made to federal home loan banks are exempt from mortgage recording taxes. (Sec. 252, Tax Law)

Federal bankruptcy plan mortgages.—Mortgages made pursuant to confirmed plans under Sec. 1129, Ch. XI, Bankruptcy Code, are exempt from mortgage recording taxes. (Sec. 252, Tax Law)

Railroad redevelopment corporation mortgages.—Mortgages of real property situated within New York that are executed, given or made by a railroad redevelopment corporation during the first nine years of its existence are exempt from mortgage recording taxes. (Sec. 252, Tax Law)

Mortgages for qualifying individuals 65 years of age and older.—Mortgages given to secure obligation incurred and given pursuant to the provisions of Sec. 6-a, Banking Law, that are secured by first or second mortgages on the mortgagee's property, are exempt from mortgage recording taxes. (Sec. 252-a, Tax Law) Sec. 6-a, Banking Law, permits banking institutions to make certain types of loans to persons 65 years of age or older, with such loans being secured by first or second mortgages on the property of such person.

Reverse mortgages.—Reverse mortgages recorded on or after December 2, 1993, that conform to the provisions of Secs. 280 or 280-a, Real Property Law, are exempt from mortgage recording taxes. (Sec. 252-a, Tax Law)

Documentation required for reverse mortgages made pursuant to Sec. 280.—To claim the exemption, an affidavit must be submitted in duplicate to the recording officer at the time the mortgage is presented for recording. In the case of a reverse mortgage made pursuant to Sec. 280, Real Property Law, the affidavit must state:

(1) that the mortgage is a reverse mortgage given by a mortgagor who is, or mortgagors all of whom are, at least 60 years of age;

(2) the reverse mortgage is of real property improved by a one- to four-family residence or condominium unit that is the residence of the mortgagor or mortgagors; and

(3) the reverse mortgage conforms to all other provisions of Sec. 280, Real Property Law.

Documentation required for reverse mortgages made pursuant to Sec. 280-2.—In the case of a reverse mortgage made pursuant to Sec. 280-a, Real Property Law, the affidavit must state: (a) that the mortgage is a reverse mortgage given by a mortgagor who is, or mortgagors all of whom are, at least 70 years of age; (b) the reverse mortgage is of real property improved by a one- to four-family residence or condominium unit that is the residence of the mortgagor or mortgagors; and (c) the reverse mortgage conforms to all other provisions of Sec. 280-a, Real Property Law. (Reg. Sec. 644.1)

Failure to provide documentation.—Where documentation is not furnished, mortgage recording taxes will be calculated on the maximum principal debt or obligation that the authorized lender is obligated to lend the borrower at the time that the mortgage is executed, or at any time thereafter (determined without regard to any contingency relating to the addition of any unpaid interest to principal or relating to any percentage of the future appreciation of the property securing the loan as consideration or additional consideration for the making of the loan). If, subsequent to the recording of the mortgage, the proceeds that the authorized lender is obligated to lend the borrower are increased, the new or further indebtedness or obligations will be the measure of the tax.

Declarations or liens for common charges.—Declarations or liens for common charges are exempt from mortgage recording taxes. (Sec. 252, Tax Law; Sec. 339-ee, Real Property Law)

"Common charges", as defined in Sec. 339-e, Real Property Law, are a condominium unit's proportionate share of the common expenses in accordance with its common interest. (Sec. 339-e(2), Real Property Law) "Common expenses" include:

> (1) expenses of operating the property; and

> (2) all sums designated as common expenses by or pursuant to the provisions of Article 9-B, Real Property Law, or the condominium association's declaration or by-laws.

(Sec. 339-e(4), Real Property Law)

Voluntary nonprofit entities.—Mortgages executed by voluntary nonprofit hospital corporations are exempt from mortgage recording taxes. (Sec. 253(3), Tax Law)

Voluntary nonprofit hospital corporation defined: A "voluntary nonprofit hospital corporation" is a hospital, as defined in Sec. 2801, Public Health Law, that operates as a corporation, as defined in Sec. 102(5), Not-For-Profit Corporation Law.

Mortgages executed by voluntary fire companies and volunteer ambulance services also are exempt from mortgage recording taxes. (Sec. 253(3), Tax Law) In order to claim the exemption, the fire company or ambulance service must file two copies of an affidavit signed by the mortgagor or mortgagee that describes the mortgage. The affidavit also must state that the reason for claiming the exemption is that a volunteer fire company or ambulance service is obtaining the mortgage. (TSB-M-07(4)R, Technical Services Bureau, Taxpayer Services Division, New York Department of Taxation and Finance, August 22, 2007)

Limited dividend housing company mortgagess.—Mortgages executed by limited dividend housing companies created pursuant to Article 4, Private Housing Finance Law, are exempt from mortgage recording taxes. (Sec. 93(1), Private Housing Finance Law)

Housing development fund company mortgages.—Mortgages of housing development fund companies formed pursuant to Article 11, Private Housing Finance Law, are exempt from mortgage recording taxes. (Sec. 577(2), Private Housing Finance Law)

Limited-profit housing company mortgages.—Mortgages of a limited-profit housing company created pursuant to Article 2, Private Housing Finance Law, are exempt from mortgage recording taxes. (Sec. 33(5), Private Housing Finance Law)

Redevelopment company mortgages.—Mortgages of a redevelopment company created pursuant to Article 5, Private Housing Finance Law, issued to the federal government or any instrumentality thereof, or to any municipal housing authority or other public housing agency or instrumentality thereof whose obligations are determined to be exempt from federal taxation by the federal government, or issued to a financial institution and insured or guaranteed by the Federal Housing Administrator or any other instrumentality of the federal government, are exempt from mortgage recording taxes. (Sec. 125(2), Private Housing Finance Law.)

Community senior citizens centers and service company mortgages.—Mortgages of community senior citizens centers and service companies created pursuant to Article 7-A, Private Housing Finance Law, are exempt from mortgage recording taxes. (Sec. 357(3), Private Housing Finance Law)

Article 8-B mortgages.—Mortgages given to secure the payment of a loan made pursuant to the provisions of Article 8-B, Private Housing Finance Law, are exempt from mortgage recording taxes. (Sec. 476, Private Housing Finance Law)

Article 6-B mortgages.—Mortgages executed by a fund formed for the purpose of insuring deposits and/or depositors created pursuant to Article 6-B, Banking Law, are exempt from mortgage recording taxes. (Sec. 286, Banking Law)

Article 20 mortgages.—Mortgages of a trust created pursuant to Article 20, Arts and Cultural Affairs Law, are exempt from mortgage recording taxes. (Sec. 20.33(2), Arts and Cultural Affairs Law)

Community mental health, retardation service company mortgages.—Mortgages of a community mental health services company or community mental retardation services company created pursuant to Article 75, Mental Hygiene Law, are exempt from mortgage recording taxes. (Sec. 75.17(c), Mental Hygiene Law)

Supplemental mortgages.—Supplemental instruments or mortgages may be recorded without the payment of mortgage recording taxes, provided that such instrument or mortgage is recorded:

(1) for the purpose of correcting or perfecting the prior recorded mortgage;

(2) pursuant to some provision or covenant in the prior recorded mortgage; or

(3) for the purpose of imposing a lien upon property not originally covered by or not described in the recorded mortgage.

(Sec. 255, Tax Law; TSB-M-91(1)R)

Example: The correct tax is paid on a mortgage containing an error in the description of the property conveyed. A supplemental mortgage correcting the description may be recorded without the payment of mortgage recording taxes.

Example: The correct tax was paid upon the recording of an executory contract for the sale of real property wherein the contract vendor (seller) agreed to convey title at a later date and take back a mortgage to secure the then unpaid balance of the purchase price. The mortgage given pursuant to the terms of the contract is a supplemental mortgage.

Example: A mortgage for $10,000 is recorded covering parcel A and the correct tax was paid. A supplemental mortgage or instrument spreading the lien of the original mortgage to parcel B, so that the mortgage will cover both parcels A and B, may be recorded tax free.

A supplemental instrument or mortgage is taxable to the extent of any new or further indebtedness or obligation secured.

Affidavit in support of exemption.—Where an exemption from mortgage recording taxes is claimed upon the recording of a supplemental mortgage, an affidavit must be filed in duplicate at the time that the supplemental mortgage is recorded:

(1) the names of the mortgagor and mortgagee;

(2) the date that the prior recorded primary mortgage was executed and recorded;

¶37-052

(3) the book and the page number where the prior recorded primary mortgage was recorded;

(4) the amount of the principal debt or obligation secured or which under any contingency could have been secured by the prior recorded primary mortgage as of the date of its execution;

(5) the total amount of mortgage recording taxes paid when the prior recorded primary mortgage was recorded;

(6) the remaining principal balance of the prior recorded primary mortgage as of the date that the supplemental mortgage was executed;

(7) a description of the supplemental mortgage, including the reasons why the instrument qualifies as a supplemental mortgage, and the principal debt or obligation secured by it;

(8) a statement setting forth the amount, if any, of further indebtedness or obligation other than the unpaid balance of the principal indebtedness or obligation secured by or which under any contingency may be secured by the prior recorded primary mortgage;

(9) a statement setting forth the amount, if any, of any new funds advanced or readvanced; and

(10) a statement setting forth the maximum principal debt or obligation that is, or may be, secured under any contingency by the supplemental mortgage.

(Sec. 255, Tax Law)

The affidavit must contain the following information (Reg. Sec. 645.3):

If an exemption from mortgage recording taxes is claimed after a supplemental mortgage is recorded and taxes are paid, the affidavit must be submitted to the Department of Taxation and Finance along with an application for refund.

Not-for-profit local development corporations.—In *Empire State Certified Development Corporation* (TSB-A-93(13)R), the Department of Taxation and Finance held that mortgages given to or by Sec. 1411(f), Not-For-Profit Corporation Law, corporations are exempt from mortgage recording taxes.

CCH CAUTION: *Advisory opinions authority.*—Advisory opinions are binding upon the Department of Taxation and Finance and the Commissioner of Taxation and Finance only with respect to the person to whom the opinion is rendered and only with respect to the set of facts stated within the opinion.

Sec. 1411, Not-For-Profit Corporation Law, allows the creation of not-for-profit local development corporations to be operated for the exclusively charitable or public purposes of relieving and reducing unemployment, promoting and providing for additional and maximum employment, bettering and maintaining job opportunities, instructing or training individuals to improve or develop their capabilities for such jobs, carrying on scientific research for the purpose of aiding a community or geographical area by attracting new industry to the community or area or by encouraging the development of, or retention of, an industry in the community or area and lessening the burdens of government and acting in the public interest. (Sec. 1411, Not-For-Profit Law) Sec. 1411(f), Not-For-Profit Corporation Law, provides that the income and operations of Sec. 1411 corporations are exempt from taxation.

Unrecorded negative pledge agreements.—Reg. Sec. 641.6(b)(9) includes, within a list of examples of instruments that are considered as mortgages if given as security for a debt or the performance of an obligation, "an agreement not to transfer, sell, convey or otherwise encumber real property, otherwise known as a negative pledge agreement."

Notwithstanding said regulation, the Department of Taxation and Finance has issued a Technical Services Bureau Memorandum containing a Counsel Opinion that *unrecorded* negative pledge agreements are not mortgages for mortgage recording tax purposes. (TSB-M-95(1)R)

As noted within the Opinion:

To constitute a mortgage for purposes of the mortgage recording tax, a negative pledge agreement must either impose a lien on real property or affect title to real property. [***] A negative pledge agreement by itself does not impose a lien on real property. "The creation of a lien is an affirmative act, and the intention to do such an act cannot be implied from an express negative." (*Knott v Shepherdstown Mfg. Co.*, 5 S.E. 266 [West Virginia, 1888], quoted in Osborne, Law of Mortgages, § 44 [1971])

[***]

The intent to affect title to property may be gleaned from the instrument itself and through the parties' actions [Citation omitted. CCH]. Among the factors to be examined is whether the agreement describes particular real property and contains other indicia of such an intent. The deciding factor indicating an intent to affect title to real property in the case of a negative pledge agreement, however, is the actual recording of the instrument. The recording of the negative pledge agreement puts the public on notice of the lender's interest in the real property. By invoking the protections of the Recording Act, the parties will be demonstrating clearly an intent to affect conveyances to third parties.

IRC Sec. 501(a) nonprofit organizations.—An IRC Sec. 501(a) nonprofit organization that is the mortgagee of real property that is (or is to be) principally improved by one or more structures containing in the aggregate six or fewer residential dwelling units, with each dwelling unit having separate cooking facilities, is exempt from the payment of the special additional recording tax. (Sec. 253(1-a)(b), Tax Law) In such instances, the special additional mortgage recording tax must be paid by the mortgagor.

If both the mortgagor and mortgagee are IRC Sec. 501(a) exempt organizations, no special additional tax is imposed upon the recording of the mortgage. (Reg. Sec. 642.3)

Limitation on exemption.—Where the real property covered by the mortgage contains or will contain other improvements, the cost or fair market value of which are in excess of the cost or fair market value of the structure containing the residential dwelling units, the real property will not be deemed to be "principally improved by such structure containing in the aggregate six or less residential dwelling units," and the mortgagee will be responsible for the payment of the special additional mortgage recording tax. (Reg. Sec. 642.3)

Special additional morgtage recording tax.—A mortgagee of real property who is a natural person is exempt from the payment of special additional mortgage recording tax where the mortgaged premises consist of real property improved by a structure containing six residential dwelling units or less, each with separate cooking facilities. (Sec. 253(1-a)(b), Tax Law)

For purposes of the exemption, a "natural person" is a human being, as opposed to an artificial person, who is the owner of a mortgage (that is, a mortgagee). A "natural person" does not include:

— a corporation or partnership;

— natural persons operating a business under a "dba" (doing business as);

— an estate (including the estate of a bankrupt or deceased person);

— or a trust.

(Reg. Sec. 642.3; TSB-M-91(1)R)

The term also does not include a person who is acting in a fiduciary capacity for a mortgagee who is not a natural person, such as an executor or executrix of an estate, a trustee of a trust, a partner of a partnership or a shareholder or officer of a corporation.

Affidavit in support of exemption.—Where an exemption from special additional mortgage recording tax is claimed on the basis that the mortgagee is a natural person, as noted above, an affidavit must be submitted with the mortgage that sets forth: (a) that the mortgagee is a natural person; and (b) that the mortgaged real property as of the date of the recording of the mortgage is improved by a structure containing six residential dwelling units or less, each with separate cooking facilities. The affidavit may be made by the mortgagor, the mortgagee or any other person who has knowledge of the facts related to the mortgage.

Suspension of additional mortgage recording tax.—The imposition of the special additional tax on mortgages recorded in a county outside the City of New York, other than one of the counties comprising the Metropolitan Commuter Transportation District, the Niagara Frontier Transportation District, the Rochester-Genesee Transportation District, the Capital District Transportation District, or the Central New York Regional Transportation District may be suspended for a specified period of time or without limitation as to time by a local law, ordinance or resolution duly adopted by the local legislative body of such county. (Sec. 253(2), Tax Law)

• *Basis of tax*

The mortgage recording taxes are taxes on the privilege of recording a mortgage on real property within the state measured by the amount of principal debt or obligation which is or may be secured by the mortgage. (Sec. 253(1), Tax Law)

The first $10,000 of mortgage indebtedness on one- and two-family residences is exempt from the additional tax. (Sec. 253(2), Tax Law)

The New York Department of Taxation and Finance has issued a mortgage recording tax bulletin that discusses the $10,000 residential property exclusion on certain mortgages. (*TB-MR-5*, New York Department of Taxation and Finance, November 18, 2011)

The bases of tax in special circumstances are treated at the following paragraphs.

Pre-July 1, 1906, mortgages.—While the tax was levied on mortgages executed or made on or after July 1, 1906, the option was granted to pay tax on pre-recorded mortgages or mortgages not previously recorded, so that benefits of later transactions could apply. The tax in the following situations was based on:

— *Mortgages recorded before July 1, 1906:* The amount of the debt or obligation remaining unpaid. (Sec. 254, Tax Law)

— *Pre-July 1, 1906 unrecorded mortgages:* The amount of indebtedness remaining unpaid at the time of recordation. (Sec. 254, Tax Law)

— *Corporate trust mortgage recorded before July 1, 1906 and given to secure bonds:* The whole amount of the bond. (Sec. 264, Tax Law) Where the real property is situated partly within and partly without the state, the tax is determined by an apportionment formula. (Sec. 260, Tax Law)

— *Subsequent advances on pre-July 1, 1906 mortgages:* The amount advanced. (Sec. 264, Tax Law)

— *Mortgages to secure bonds recorded before July 1, 1906:* The value of bonds representing a portion of the principal indebtedness. (Sec. 264, Tax Law)

— *Advances on mortgages recorded before July 1, 1906 but remaining unpaid as of July 1, 1906:* The extent of indebtedness remaining unpaid. (Sec. 264, Tax Law)

Supplemental mortgages.—The recording of supplemental mortgages are subject to mortgage recording taxes to the extent that they create or secure a new or further indebtedness or obligation other than the principal indebtedness or obligation secured by or which under any contingency may be secured by the prior recorded primary mortgage. (Sec. 255, Tax Law)

The principal indebtedness or obligation secured by or which under any contingency may be secured by the prior recorded primary mortgage is equal to the remaining principal indebtedness secured or which under any contingency may be secured by such mortgage at the time that the supplemental mortgage is executed or at any time thereafter. (Reg. Sec. 645.2)

EXAMPLE: On January 1, 1990, Mr. Jones gives XYZ Bank a mortgage securing a principal debt of $100,000 and the proper mortgage recording taxes are paid. On January 1, 1991, at a time when the remaining principal indebtedness secured by such prior recorded mortgage totals $90,000. Mr. Jones gives XYZ Bank another mortgage which secures an additional $30,000. When the mortgage was presented for recording the proper taxes computed upon the $30,000 amount were paid. Simultaneously, Mr. Jones and the bank enter into an agreement which by its terms consolidates the liens of the two mortgages into one lien securing a total principal debt of $120,000. The consolidation agreement makes proper reference to the prior recorded mortgages. Therefore, the consolidation agreement constitutes a supplemental mortgage which may be recorded tax free since it does not secure any new or further indebtedness other than that secured by the prior recorded primary mortgages.

If the new $30,000 mortgage had by its terms consolidated the liens of the two mortgages into one lien securing a total principal debt of $120,000, the new mortgage itself would have constituted a supplemental mortgage. The applicable mortgage recording taxes would apply to its recording and taxes would be imposed and computed based upon the $30,000 of new or further indebtedness secured by such mortgage.

If a supplemental mortgage is recorded for the purpose of providing additional or further security for the payment of the principal debt or obligation secured by the prior recorded primary mortgage by spreading the lien of the prior recorded primary mortgage to additional real property or by imposing a new lien on the additional real property, and the additional real property covered by the supplemental mortgage is located in a county where the additional tax imposed by Sec. 253(2), Tax Law, is imposed and the prior recorded primary mortgage was on real property situated in a county that has suspended the additional tax, and such tax was not paid, the additional tax is imposed and computed based on the principal indebtedness or obligation secured by or which under any contingency may be secured by the supplemental mortgage on the date it is executed or at any time thereafter.

EXAMPLE: Mr. Smith gives Z Bank a mortgage on real property located in Schoharie County, which is a county that has suspended the imposition of the additional tax. The mortgage secures a principal debt of $50,000. The mortgage is recorded and the proper mortgage recording taxes are paid. Subsequent to the recording of such mortgage, Mr. Smith gives Z Bank a mortgage on real property located in Albany County, as additional security for the payment of the same $50,000 debt. Albany County imposes the additional tax.

The additional tax is imposed and computed upon the $50,000 debt secured by the supplemental mortgage.

Supplemental mortgage securing additional real property in City of Yonkers or Broome County.—If a supplemental mortgage is recorded for the purpose of providing additional or further security for the payment of the principal debt or obligation secured by the prior recorded primary mortgage by spreading the lien of the prior recorded primary mortgage to additional real property or by imposing a new lien on the additional real property, and the additional real property covered by the supplemental mortgage is situated within the City of Yonkers or the County of Broome, and the prior recorded primary mortgage was on real property situated outside the City of Yonkers or County of Broome, and the City of Yonkers tax imposed under Sec. 92-123, Code, City of Yonkers, or the Broome County tax imposed by Local Law INTRO. No. 9, Laws 1994, was not paid when the prior recorded primary mortgage was recorded, mortgage recording tax is imposed and computed based on the principal indebtedness or obligation secured by or which under any contingency may be secured by such supplemental mortgage at the date of execution of such supplemental mortgage or at any time thereafter.

Executory contracts.—The principal debt or obligation that is used as the basis for computing mortgage recording taxes is the portion of the purchase price under the contract that remains unpaid as of the date that the purchaser has or is entitled to possession of the real property under the contract. (Reg. Sec. 643.2)

EXAMPLE: X Corporation entered into an executory contract to sell a 10 unit apartment building located in Flushing, Queens County, New York City to Y for a purchase price of $600,000. On October 1, 1990 the contract was executed and pursuant to its terms Y was required to make a $60,000 down payment. The contract also provided that an additional payment of $100,000 was required on December 1, 1990, at which time Y was entitled to possession of the premises.

Y will be required to make 10 semi-annual payments over a 5 year period to X Corporation to pay the remaining balance due under the contract, with the final payment due on December 1, 1995. Upon receipt of the final payment X Corporation will deliver a deed to the subject premises to Y.

Since the executory contract between X Corporation and Y grants the purchaser possession of the real property prior to the delivery of the deed, such contract is a mortgage, the recording of which is subject to tax.

The taxes due upon the recording of this contract are computed as follows:

Purchase price under the contract		$600,000
Less: Downpayment—October 1, 1990	$60,000	
Additional payment—December 1, 1990	$100,000	
Total Subtractions		$160,000
Total amount remaining unpaid at the time		
Y is entitled to possession—		
December 1, 1990	$440,000	
Basic tax due (($440,000 ÷ $100) × $.50)	$2,200	
Additional tax (($440,000 ÷ $100) × $.25)	$1,100	
Special additional tax due		

(($440,000 ÷ $100) × $.25)	$1,100
New York City tax due $1.00 rate	
(($440,000 ÷ $100) × $1.00)	$4,400
Total taxes due	$8,800

Trust mortgages.—A trust mortgage is a mortgage given by a corporation to a trustee to secure the payment of bonds or obligations issued (or to be issued) by the corporation. (Sec. 259, Tax Law; Reg. Sec. 646.1) The bonds or obligations secured by the mortgage may be issued prior to or after the mortgage has been presented for recording.

Mortgage containing statement of maximum amount secured or to be to secured.—If secured bonds or obligations are issued prior to, or simultaneously with, the recording of the mortgage, the amount of the bonds or obligations are less than the maximum amount secured (or which under any contingency may be secured) by the mortgage, and the mortgage contains a statement of the amount advanced or secured by the mortgage as of the date of recording the mortgage, mortgage recording taxes are computed on the basis of the amount stated to have been advanced or accrued or that is stated to be secured thereby. (Sec. 259, Tax Law; Reg. Sec. 646.2) The statement of the amount advanced or secured is binding upon and conclusive against the mortgagee, the holders of any bonds or obligations secured by the mortgage and all persons claiming through the mortgagee any interest in the mortgage or in the mortgaged premises.

Further advances.—If a further amount is to be advanced or to become secured by a trust mortgage, applicable mortgage recording taxes are imposed based on such amount and must be paid at or before the time that the advance is made. (Reg. Sec. 646.3)

The mortgagor must, at the time of paying such tax, file a verified statement in the office of the recording officer in the county where the mortgage is first recorded and with the Commissioner of Taxation and Finance. (Sec. 259, Tax Law)

If the additional tax is not paid, the trust mortgagee may not certify any bonds or other obligations evidencing further amounts under the mortgage.

Credit line mortgages.—Mortgage recording taxes on credit line mortgages are imposed on the basis of the maximum principal amount which is, or under any contingency may be, secured by the mortgage at the date of execution or any time thereafter. (Sec. 253-b, Tax Law)

Effect of increasing maximum principal amount.—If the maximum principal amount of a credit line mortgage is increased, additional mortgage recording taxes become payable at the time an instrument evidencing the increase is recorded. (Reg. Sec. 647.2) Taxes are computed on the amount of the increase in the maximum principal amount, plus the amount of any new funds, if any.

Effect of extending/modifying draw period.—Modification and extension agreements relating to credit line mortgages that are recorded before April 1, 2000, may be recorded without the payment of any additional mortgage recording taxes, provided that the maximum principal amount secured by the lien of the credit line mortgage is not increased. (TSB-M-99(3)R)

For modifications/extension agreements recorded after March 31, 2000, a modification or extension to a credit line mortgage will be treated as a new or further debt obligation if the draw period in which a borrower may obtain loan advances is concluded or otherwise terminates before the modification and extension agreement is executed. (TSB-M-99(3)R) Consequently, tax must be paid on the recording of the extension or modification, calculated on the basis of the maximum principal amount that may be advanced to the borrower under the terms of the agreement. If the modification/extension is executed but not recorded, the taxpayer is subject to a penalty for nonpayment. Conversely, tax is not imposed if:

(1) the modification or extension of the draw period is executed before the draw period is concluded,

(2) the original mortgage or underlying loan documentation explicitly authorized an extension/modification or contained a provision that authorized the lender and borrower to change the terms of the agreement, and

(3) the maximum principal amount secured by the lien of the credit line mortgage is not increased.

If the original mortgage or loan documentation did not explicitly provide for a modification or extension of the draw period or did not contain a change of terms provision, tax will be imposed on the recording of the modification/extension, calculated on the basis of the maximum principal amount that may be advanced to the borrower under the terms of that agreement.

One- to six-family owner-occupied residences or dwellings.—The "maximum principal debt or obligation which is or under any contingency may be secured at the date of execution" of a credit line mortgage securing real property improved or to be improved by a one- to six-family owner-occupied residence or dwelling is the amount specified in the mortgage. (Sec. 253-b, Tax Law) Accordingly, where mortgage recording taxes are paid on the initial recording of the mortgage, no further taxes will become payable on the making of advances or readvances pursuant to the mortgage, or on the recording or filing of an instrument evidencing such advances or readvances, regardless of the cumulative total of advances and readvances thereunder, provided the advances and readvances are made to the original obligor (borrower) or to one or more of the original obligors named in the recorded primary credit line mortgage. (Reg. Sec. 647.4)

Sale or transfer of property.—Except as noted below, where real property improved or to be improved by a one- to six-family owner occupied residence or dwelling and encumbered by a credit-line mortgage is sold or transferred, and the lien of the credit line mortgage remains outstanding and is not to be satisfied as a result of the sale or transfer, mortgage recording taxes are imposed upon the recording of the instrument evidencing the sale or transfer. (Reg. Sec. 647.5) Tax is computed on the basis of the maximum principal amount specified in the credit line mortgage on the date when the instrument evidencing the sale or transfer is recorded, as such amount may have been increased or decreased by any instrument recorded evidencing an increase or decrease in the maximum principal amount specified in the credit line mortgage.

The following sales or transfers will not result in the imposition of mortgage recording taxes:

(1) transfers of other than a fee simple interest;

(2) transfers of a fee simple interest to a person or persons who held a fee simple interest in the real property immediately prior to the transfer;

(3) transfers of a fee simple interest to a person or persons related by blood, marriage or adoption to the original obligor or to one or more of the original obligors (hereinafter "a related person"); or to any person or entity where 50% or more of the beneficial interest in such real property after the transfer is held by the transferor or such related person or persons (as in the case of a transfer to a trustee for the benefit of a minor or the transfer to a trust for the benefit of the transferor); and

(4) transfers to a trustee in bankruptcy, a receiver, assignee or other officer of a court. However, a subsequent transfer of real property subject to a credit line mortgage by any such individuals is subject to tax unless exempt under some other provision of Article 11, Tax Law.

Statement in support of exemption.—If a claim for exemption from mortgage recording taxes is made pursuant to clauses (b), (c), or (d), above, a statement of the facts supporting the claim must be filed.

Mortgages under $3 million.—The favorable tax treatment afforded residential credit line mortgages on one- to six-family owner-occupied residences or dwellings (see discussion above) has been extended to all other credit line mortgages (nonresidential credit line mortgages), such as commercial credit line mortgages, that secure a maximum principal indebtedness of less than $3 million. (Sec. 253-b, Tax Law; Reg. Sec. 647.4; TSB-M-96(6)R)

Aggregation.—For purposes of determining if the maximum principal indebtedness secured by a non-residential credit line mortgage is less than $3 million, the maximum principal indebtedness secured by separate non-residential credit line mortgages must be aggregated under certain circumstances. (Reg. Sec. 647.5) In those cases where separate non-residential credit line mortgages form part of the same or related transactions and have the same or related mortgagors, the maximum principal indebtedness secured by all separate credit line mortgages must be added together to determine if the maximum principal indebtedness secured is less than $3 million and therefore eligible to receive the favorable tax treatment. For the purpose of determining whether this aggregation rule applies, there is a presumption that all mortgages offered for recording within a period of twelve consecutive months having the same or related mortgagors are part of a related transaction. This presumption may be rebutted only with clear and convincing evidence to the contrary, that shows that the mortgages were created solely for independent business or financial reasons and were not separately created for the purpose of receiving the favorable tax treatment.

In a Technical Services Bureau Memorandum, the Department of Taxation and Finance has indicated that the phrase "related mortgagors" within the context of the aforementioned aggregation rules will include, but not be limited to, the following relationships:

(1) members of a family, including spouses, ancestors, lineal descendants, and brothers and sisters (whether by the whole or half blood);

(2) a shareholder and a corporation in which more than 50% of the value of the outstanding stock is owned or controlled directly or indirectly by the shareholder;

(3) a partner and a partnership in which more than 50% of the interest in the capita or profits is owned or controlled directly or indirectly by the partner;

(4) a beneficiary and a trust in which more than 50% of the beneficial interest is owned or controlled directly or indirectly by the beneficiary;

(5) two or more corporations, partnerships, associations, or trusts, or any combination thereof, which are owned or controlled, either directly or indirectly, by the same person, corporation or other entity: and

(6) a grantor of a trust and such trust.

(TSB-M-96(6)R)

Non-residential credit line mortgages securing $3 million or more.—Preferential tax treatment is *not* afforded to nonresidential credit line mortgages securing a maximum principal debt of $3 million or more. Therefore, in addition to imposing mortgage recording tax on the maximum amount secured by these credit line mortgages, the recording or the filing of instruments evidencing advances and readvances continue to be subject to the mortgage recording tax.

Mortgages for indefinite amounts.—Sec. 256, Tax Law, permits a property owner, when presenting a mortgage for an indefinite amount for recording, to file a sworn statement of the maximum amount secured or which under any contingency may be secured by the mortgage at the date of execution or any time thereafter. (Sec. 256, Tax Law; Reg. Sec. 648.2) If such a statement is filed, or if a statement is contained in the mortgage that states such maximum amount, mortgage recording taxes are based and computed on the maximum amount so stated. The statement is binding upon and conclusive against the owner, the holders of any bonds or obligations secured by such mortgage and all persons claiming through the mortgagee any interest in the mortgage or the mortgaged premises.

Sworn statement not filed.—If a sworn statement as to the maximum amount secured or which under any contingency may be secured by the mortgage at the date of execution or any time thereafter, is not filed, mortgage recording taxes are computed based upon the higher of:

(1) the fair market value of the mortgaged property on the date the mortgage was executed; or

(2) the portion of such amount secured which is determinable by the terms of the mortgage.

The fair market value of the property is determined by the recording officer to whom the mortgage is presented for recording.

The determination by the recording officer of the value of the property covered by the mortgage, and copies of the requested information used as the basis for computing the fair market value of the property and computing the taxes, must be forwarded to and subject to review by the Commissioner of Taxation and Finance.

Payment tendered after mortgage is recorded.—Except as noted below, if mortgage recording taxes are first tendered after a mortgage for an indefinite amount has been recorded, the amount of taxes due must be computed based upon the higher of:

(1) the fair market value of the mortgaged property on the date that the mortgage was executed; or

(2) the portion of the amount secured by the mortgage on the date that the mortgage was executed which is determinable by the terms of the mortgage.

(Reg. Sec. 648.3)

If a mortgage for an indefinite amount is recorded without the payment of mortgage recording taxes, and it is subsequently determined by the Commissioner of Taxation and Finance that the failure to pay was due to an honest misconception on the part of the recording officer or the mortgage owner as to the nature or taxability of the mortgage, the Commissioner may make an order permitting the recording officer to file the aforesaid statement *nunc pro tunc* as of the date of the recording of the mortgage. (Sec. 256, Tax Law) The payment of the tax may be made on the basis of the statement with interest thereon at the annual rate of 6%.

Property situated in two tax districts.—Where real property secured by a mortgage is situated in more than one tax district, mortgage recording taxes are apportioned between the respective districts on the basis of the relative assessments of each parcel as it appears on the district's last assessment roll. (Sec. 260, Tax Law) If all or any part of the property covered by a mortgage is not assessed on the district's last assessment roll, or the property is assessed as a part of a larger tract so that the

308   Guidebook to New York Taxes

assessed value cannot be determined, or if improvements have been made that materially change the assessed value of the property, the Commissioner of Taxation and Finance may require the local assessors, the mortgagor, or the mortgagee to furnish sworn appraisals of the property, and use the same to determine the apportionment.

Penalty—Failure to provide requested information.—An individual or officer who fails to furnish a requested statement or other information is subject to a penalty equal to $100. (Sec. 260, Tax Law)

Property located partially in district that has suspended additional tax.—If a mortgage covers property located in more than one county, and one or more, but not all, of the counties have suspended the additional tax, the taxpayer may compute the tax according to one of the following procedures (Reg. Sec. 642.2):

— *Procedure 1:* The taxpayer may compute the tax as if the property was located entirely in any one of the counties that is authorized to collect the greatest amount of tax. The amount must be paid to the recording officer of the county where the mortgage is first recorded. The recording officer must endorse upon the mortgage the amount of tax so paid. In addition, the taxpayer should present to the recording officer a completed Form MT-15.1, "Mortgage Recording Tax Claim for Refund." The taxpayer then can proceed to record the mortgage in any other county where the property (or any part thereof) is located.

— *Procedure 2:* At the time that the mortgage is presented for recording, the taxpayer may file a completed Form MT-15, "Mortgage Recording Tax Return" and pay the amount of tax computed to be due on Form MT-15, or as adjusted by the recording officer, to the recording officer of the county where the mortgage is first recorded. The recording officer will then endorse the payment of the tax upon the mortgage so that the mortgage can be recorded without further payment of tax in the other county or counties. The return is subject to audit by the Department of Taxation and Finance and by the recording officer where the mortgage was first recorded and the tax paid. If there is an underpayment of the tax, the Commissioner will direct the recording officer where the mortgage was first recorded and the tax paid to notify the parties to the mortgage of such underpayment. If there is an overpayment of the tax, the Commissioner shall direct the appropriate recording officer to refund the amount of the overpayment to the taxpayer or his duly authorized representative.

Property situated partly within and partly without New York.—Where real property secured by a mortgage is situated partly within and partly without New York, mortgage recording taxes are determined based on an apportionment of the principal debt or obligation that is (or under any contingency may be) secured at the date of the execution of the mortgage or at any time thereafter. (Sec. 260, Tax Law) The apportionment is made by multiplying the principal debt or obligation by a fraction, the numerator of which is the net value of the mortgaged property located within New York, and the denominator of which is the net value of the mortgaged property located within and without the State. (Reg. Sec. 649.1) The "net value of the mortgaged property" is the property's fair market value less the unpaid amount of any prior existing mortgage liens that remain on the property subsequent to the mortgage's execution.

EXAMPLE: Mr. Smith borrows $100,000 from Bank X, and gives the bank a mortgage on two commercially improved parcels. One of the parcels is located in Albany, New York and the other is located in Paterson, New Jersey. The parcel located in Albany has a fair market value of $400,000, and has a prior existing mortgage lien totaling $33,000, which remains on the parcel after execution of the mortgage and which represents an amount owed to Bank Z. The parcel located in Paterson has a fair market value of $200,000, and has no prior existing mortgage liens. Therefore, the net value of the Albany parcel is $367,000 ($400,000–$33,000) and the net value of both parcels is $567,000 ($367,000 + $200,000). The portion of the $100,000 debt secured by the mortgage subject to the taxes described in Part 642 of these regulations is commuted as follows:

Net value of Albany parcel	$367,000	
	—————	× $100,000 = $64,727
Net value of both parcels	567,000	

Accordingly, $64,700 ($64,727 rounded to the nearest $100) would be the amount used to compute the mortgage recording taxes.

In determining the separate net values of mortgaged property located within and without New York, the Commissioner of Taxation and Finance may consider only tangible real and personal property. Leases of real property are deemed to be tangible property.

Request for Order of Determination and Apportionment.—A request for an order of determination and apportionment may be made prior to recording a mortgage covering real property situated partly within and partly without New York. (Reg. Sec. 649.2) The Commissioner of Taxation and Finance, after receiving such a request and the required documentation, must issue an order of determination and apportionment stating the portion of the principal debt or obligation secured by the mortgage that is subject to mortgage recording taxes.

The following documentation must be provided to the Commissioner at the time that the request for an order of determination and apportionment is made:

(1) a copy of the mortgage;

(2) book values and appraised values of the property covered by the mortgage, separated into the following categories:

(a) real property in New York;

(b) real property outside the state;

(c) tangible personal property located in New York; and

(d) tangible personal property located outside the state;

(3) assessed values of the real property located within New York by tax district as the same appears on the assessment rolls most recent to the date of recording the mortgage;

(4) a brief description of each parcel of real property, including the page of the mortgage where described; and

(5) a statement of all prior encumbrances upon the property covered by the mortgage, including a description of each encumbrance, and the amount outstanding.

Penalty—Failure to provide requested information.—An individual or officer who fails to furnish a requested statement or other information is subject to a penalty equal to $100. (Reg. Sec. 649.2)

Mortgage securing one- or two-family residence.—Where a mortgage subject to the *additional tax* secures real property that is principally improved (or is to be principally improved) by a one- or two-family residence or dwelling, the first $10,000 of principal debt or obligation is deducted from the total principal debt or obligation secured by the mortgage and the additional tax is computed on the remaining amount. (Sec. 253(2), Tax Law)

Proof of deduction required.—A statement in support of the claimed deduction must be provided to the recording officer of the county where the mortgage is first recorded. The statement, which may either be contained in the mortgage instrument or in a separate affidavit signed by the mortgagor, mortgagee or any other party with knowledge of the facts, must note the following:

(1) that the real property covered by the mortgage is improved or will be improved by a one- or two-family residence or dwelling; and

(2) that there are or will be no other improvements, the cost or fair market value of which exceed (or will exceed) the cost or fair market value of the one- or two-family residence or dwelling.

(Reg. Sec. 642.2)

The Commissioner of Taxation may require the mortgagor, the mortgagee or any other person who has knowledge of the facts to furnish additional information by affidavit in support of the claimed deduction.

Denial of deduction.—Property will not be considered to be principally improved by a one- or two-family residence or dwelling if the property covered by the mortgage contains or will contain other improvements, the cost or fair market value of which exceed the cost or fair market value of the one- or two-family residence or dwelling.

• *Rate of tax*

Mortgage recording taxes are imposed at the following rates (Form MT-15, Mortgage Recording Tax Return):

The basic tax is imposed at the rate of 50¢ for each $100 and each remaining major fraction thereof of principal debt that is, or under any contingency may be, secured at the date of execution of the mortgage or at any time thereafter. (Sec. 253(1), Tax Law) If the principal debt or obligation that is, or under any contingency may be, secured by the mortgage is less than $100, a tax of $.50 is imposed.

Additional tax.—The additional tax is generally imposed at the rate of 25¢ for each $100 and each remaining major fraction thereof of principal debt or obligation that is, or under any contingency may be, secured at the date of execution of the mortgage or at any time thereafter. (Sec. 253(2), Tax Law)

An additional mortgage recording tax is imposed in the Metropolitan Commuter Transportation District (MCTD) equal to 30¢ for each $100 of principal debt secured by a mortgage. (Sec. 253(2)(a), Tax Law)

Where a mortgage subject to the additional tax secures real property that is principally improved (or is to be principally improved) by a one- or two-family residence or dwelling, the first $10,000 of principal debt or obligation is deducted from the total principal debt or obligation secured by the mortgage and the additional tax is computed on the remaining amount.

Special additional tax.—The special additional tax is imposed at the rate of 25¢ for each $100 and each remaining major fraction thereof of principal debt or obligation that is, or under any contingency may, be secured at the date of execution of such mortgage or at any time thereafter. (Sec. 253(1-a), Tax Law)

City of Yonkers tax.—The City of Yonkers mortgage recording tax is imposed at the rate of 50¢ for each $100 and each remaining major fraction thereof of principal debt or obligation that is, or under any contingency may be, secured at the date of the execution of the mortgage or at any time thereafter, on property located in whole or in part in the City of Yonkers. (Sec. 253-d, Tax Law; Yonkers Local Law No. 11-1997) The tax is scheduled to expire August 31, 2023. A tax of 50¢ is imposed if the principal debt or obligation secured by the mortgage is less than $100. The total mortgage recording tax rate for the City of Yonkers is $1.80 for each $100 secured by a mortgage. (TSB-M-09(2)R; TSB-M-07(3)R; TSB-M-93(3.3)R)

County tax rates.—The following chart lists the total mortgage recording taxes by county. Rates are for each $100 and remaining major fraction thereof of principal debt that is secured by a mortgage.

County	Rate
Albany	$1.25 (expires 12/1/23) (TSB-M-05(8)R)
Allegany	1.00
Broome	1.00
Cattaraugus	1.25 (expires 12/1/21) (TSB-M-09(7)R)
Cayuga	1.00
Chautauqua	1.25 (TSB-M-05(7)R)
Chemung	$0.75
Chenango	0.75
Clinton	1.00
Columbia	1.25 (TSB-M-09(5)R)
Cortland	1.00 (expires 12/1/23)
Delaware	1.00
Dutchess	1.05* (TSB-M-09(9)R)
Erie	1.00
Essex	1.25 (expires 12/1/21)
Franklin	1.00
Fulton	1.00 (expires 11/30/23)
Genesee	1.25 (expires 11/1/23) (TSB-M-09(6)R)
Greene	1.25 (expires 12/1/23) (TSB-M-09(3)R)
Hamilton	1.00 (expires 12/1/23) (TSB-M-06(5)R)
Herkimer	1.00 (expires 12/1/23) (TSB-M-05(12)R)
Jefferson	0.75
Lewis	1.00 (TSB-M-07(5)R)
Livingston	1.25
Madison	1.00
Monroe	1.00
Montgomery	0.75
Nassau	1.05*
Niagara	1.00
Oneida	1.00
Onondaga	1.00
Ontario	1.00
Orange	1.05*
Orleans	1.00
Oswego	1.00

Otsego 0.75

Putnam 1.05*

Rensselaer .... 1.25 (TSB-M-07(9)R)

Rockland 1.30*

Saratoga 1.00

Schenectady .... 1.25 (TSB-M-05(9)R)

Schoharie .... 1.00 (expires 12/1/23)

Schuyler 1.00

Seneca 1.00

St. Lawrence 0.75

Steuben .... 1.25 (expires 12/1/23)

Suffolk 1.05*

Sullivan .... 1.00 (TSB-M-07(2)R)

Tioga 0.75

Tompkins .... 1.00 (TSB-M-14(1)R)

Ulster 0.75

Warren .... 1.25 (expires 12/1/23) (TSB-M-08(1)R)

Washington 1.25

Wayne .... 1.25 (TSB-M-05(6)R)

Westchester ..... 1.30 ($1.80 if the property is located in whole or in part in Yonkers)

Wyoming .... 1.25 (expires 12/1/21) (TSB-M-05(13)R)

Yates .... 1.00 (expires 12/1/23)

*Includes MCTD tax.

New York City taxes.—For mortgage recording taxes imposed in the City of New York, see ¶ 557-005 and following.

• *Credits*

A special credit is allowed against mortgage recording taxes on purchase money mortgages recorded in connection with the first conveyance of units in condominiums subject to Article 9-B, Real Property Law. (Sec. 339-ee, Real Property Law) The credit is only permitted where mortgage recording tax was previously paid on (1) a construction mortgage whose proceeds were applied to construction of the unit, or (2) a blanket mortgage whose proceeds were applied exclusively to the payment of the construction mortgage, capital expenditures or expenses for the development or operation of the condominium, or the purchase of land or buildings for the condominium (provided that such purchase was no more than two years prior to the recording of the declaration of condominium).

A credit is allowed in the case of construction or blanket mortgages recorded on or after July 1, 1989, where the first condominium unit of the condominium plan is sold more than two years after the construction or blanket mortgage was recorded. In addition, the credit does not apply to the *special additional mortgage recording tax* imposed by Sec. 253(1-a), Tax Law.

Computation of credit.—The amount of credit is determined by multiplying the basic tax (and, where applicable, the additional tax, the City of New York tax, the City of Yonkers tax and the Broome County tax) paid upon the recording of the construction or blanket mortgage by the purchaser's pro rata percentage of interest in the common elements of the condominium. (Reg. Sec. 651.2)

EXAMPLE: A $1 million construction mortgage on real property located in New York City is recorded on January 1, 1991. The proceeds of the mortgage are applied to the construction of a building, which consists of 10 residential condominium units. Each unit is allocated 10% of the common elements as provided by the condominium declaration. Upon the recording of the construction mortgage $5000 of basic tax, $2500 of additional tax, and $17,500 of City of New York tax was paid.

The first unit in the newly constructed building is sold on August 1, 1991. The purchaser, Mr. Jones, borrows $400,000 from Bank X to finance his purchase, and gives a mortgage to Bank X as security for the amount borrowed. When the $400,000 mortgage is recorded, the taxes due and credit are commuted as follows:

Basic tax on $400,000 mortgage	$2,000	
Less: Credit allowed against basic tax (10% × $5000)	500	
Basic tax due		1,500
Additional tax on $400,000 mortgage	$1,000	
*Less: Exclusion for first $10,000 of mortgage debt	25	
Balance	975	
Less: Credit allowed against additional tax (10% × 2500)	250	
Additional tax due		725
Special additional tax on		
$400,000 mortgage (no credit allowed)		1,000**
City of New York tax on		
$400,000 mortgage ($1 per $100 rate)	4,000	
Less: Credit allowed against City of New York tax (10% × 17,500)	1,750	
City of New York tax due		2,250
Total mortgage recording taxes due		$5,475

*Since the real property covered by the mortgage is a one family residence, the first $10,000 of principal debt secured by the mortgage is deducted when computing the additional tax. (See subdivision (b) of section 642.2 of these regulations.)

**Since the $400,000 mortgage is of real property which is principally improved with a residential dwelling unit, Bank X, the mortgagee, must pay the special additional tax. (See subdivision (c) of section 642.3 of these regulations.)

EXAMPLE: Same facts as noted above, except that the first unit in the building is sold on February 1, 1993. Since the first unit is sold more than two years after the construction mortgage was recorded, no credit is allowed.

EXAMPLE: Same facts as noted above, except that the construction mortgage was recorded on May 1, 1989. Since the construction mortgage was recorded prior to July 1, 1989, the credit is allowed regardless of the fact that the first unit of the condominium is sold more than two years after the date that the construction mortgage was recorded.

Also, the City of New York tax payable on the recording of the construction mortgage would be $12,500 based on the rate in effect on May 1, 1989, resulting in the credit with respect to such tax being $1,250 (10% × 12,500).

• *Returns and reports*

Since the amount of the principal indebtedness which is or may be secured by the mortgage is set forth in the instrument and tax is computed on such amount by the recording officer, no returns and reports are ordinarily required. (Sec. 253, Tax Law)

However, special situations require the filing of certain statements.

Annual statement, trust mortgages.—The mortgagor or owner of property that secures a trust mortgage debt must file an annual statement with the recording officer of the county where the mortgage was first recorded and with the Commissioner of Taxation and Finance. (Sec. 259, Tax Law) The annual statements, which must be filed on or before July 31, must be verified by the secretary, treasurer or other officer of the mortgagee and contain the following information:

(1) the names of the mortgagor and the mortgagee;

(2) the date of the mortgage and the county where it was first recorded;

(3) the maximum amount of principal debt or obligation that under any contingency may be secured by the mortgage; and

(4) the amounts advanced on such mortgage during the year ending the preceding June 30th, with the date and amount of each advance.

Annual statements must be filed until the maximum amount secured by the trust mortgage has been advanced and the taxes thereon have been paid.

A mortgagor or other person who fails to file a required annual statement is subject to a penalty of not less than $1, nor more than $100, for each $1,000 of the maximum amount of principal indebtedness that is (or under any contingency may become) secured by the mortgage. (Reg. Sec. 653.3) The penalty, which is in addition to all other interest penalties and penalties, may not exceed in the aggregate the sum of $5,000 with respect to each trust mortgage.

Metropolitan Commuter Transportation District and Erie County.—No mortgage may be recorded in any of the counties comprising the Metropolitan Commuter Transportation District or in Erie County unless a statement is included, in the mortgage or in a separate attached statement, stating whether the mortgage is a mortgage of real property principally improved or to be principally improved by a structure containing in the aggregate not more than six residential dwelling units, each unit containing separate cooking facilities. (Reg. Sec. 655.1)

A statement in the mortgage that the real property is principally improved or is to be principally improved by a one- or two-family residence or dwelling, sufficient to claim the $10,000 deduction from the additional tax is sufficient to satisfy the notice requirements.

Statements may be required in the following circumstances:

— *Optional tax on mortgages paid before July 1, 1906:* A statement describing the mortgage and unpaid indebtedness. (Sec. 254, Tax Law)

— *Unrecorded mortgages executed or delivered before July 1, 1906:* A statement showing the amount remaining unpaid and an election to incur tax on such amount. (Sec. 254, Tax Law)

— *Subsequent advances or mortgages recorded before July 1, 1906:* A statement of the principal indebtedness of mortgage. (Sec. 264, Tax Law)

— *Portion of advances remaining unpaid as of July 1, 1906:* A statement indicating the amount of the prior advances remaining unpaid. (Sec. 264, Tax Law)

Supplemental mortgages.—A statement claiming exemption from tax must be filed upon recording the supplemental mortgage. (Sec. 255(2), Tax Law)

Mortgages to secure contract performance or of indefinite amounts.—Owner of mortgage files with the recording officer a sworn statement of the maximum amount covered by the mortgage. (Sec. 256, Tax Law)

Real property within and without New York.—A statement showing net value of property within and without the state. (Sec. 260, Tax Law)

Reverse mortgages.—Reverse mortgages recorded on or after December 2, 1993, that conform to the provisions of Secs. 280 or 280-a, Real Property Law, are exempt from mortgage recording taxes, provided an affidavit is filed in duplicate with the recording officer at the time that the mortgage is presented for recording. (Sec. 252-a, Tax Law) If no affidavit is filed, mortgage recording taxes will be calculated on the maximum principal debt or obligation that the authorized lender is obligated to lend the borrower at the time that the mortgage is executed, or at any time thereafter (determined without regard to any contingency relating to the addition of any unpaid interest to principal or relating to any percentage of the future appreciation of the property securing the loan as consideration or additional consideration for the making of the loan).

Special additional mortgage recording tax exemptions.—A mortgagee of real property who is a natural person is exempt from the payment of special additional mortgage recording tax where the mortgaged premises consist of real property improved by a structure containing six residential dwelling units or less, each with separate cooking facilities, provided an affidavit setting for the grounds for the exemption is submitted with the mortgage. (Sec. 253(1-a)(b), Tax Law)

A statement in support of the claimed deduction must be provided to the recording officer of the county where the mortgage is first recorded. (Sec. 253(2), Tax Law)

• *Assessment, revision, and appeal*

Initially, the tax is assessed upon amounts fixed by the recording officer on basis of information in the documents or accompanying statements or subsequent statements when applicable.

Special formula methods are permitted for use by the recording officer in determining the tax on mortgages covering property situated partly within and partly without the state. (Sec. 260, Tax Law)

The State Tax Commission may permit the owner to file a sworn statement as of the original date of recording of the mortgage and pay tax with 6% interest if a tax on a mortgage for

    (1) an indeterminable amount or

    (2) to secure an obligation other than money, has not been paid because of error.

(Sec. 256, Tax Law)

If an unrecorded mortgage has been lost or destroyed, the State Tax Commission determines tax on proper evidence presented. (Sec. 258-a, Tax Law)

Review by commissioner.—The Commissioner of Taxation and Finance reviews the determinations of the recording officer upon application of a party to the instrument or person interested therein or property affected thereby. (Sec. 251, Tax Law) The Commissioner gives not less than three days notice to the parties at the time and place of the hearing.

The determination of the recording officer on the application for exemption of supplemental mortgages is reviewable by the Commissioner. (Sec. 255(2), Tax Law)

Determination of value of property covered by mortgages for indefinite amounts or securing performance of contracts are reviewable by the Commissioner. (Sec. 256, Tax Law)

Determinations of the Commissioner of Taxation and Finance are subject to review.

• *Payment of tax*

Mortgage recording taxes are paid to the recording officer of any county in which all or any part of the real property covered by the mortgage is situated. (Sec. 257, Tax Law) The recording officer is usually the county clerk or register. The tax is payable upon the recording of each mortgage subject to tax or, in special circumstances, at such other times as specified in the law.

Taxes on further advances under corporate trust mortgages must be paid at or before the time when the payment is advanced, accrued or secured. (Sec. 259, Tax Law)

The taxes determined to be due on mortgages covering property partly within and partly without the state must be paid within 10 days after service of certified copy of the determination by the Commissioner of Taxation and Finance. (Sec. 260, Tax Law)

Payment of tax.—Except as noted below, the amount of tax is usually paid by the borrower to the mortgagee, who then has the instrument recorded.

In cases of real property principally improved or to be improved by one or more structures containing in the aggregate not more than six residential dwelling units, each unit having its own separate cooking facilities, the special additional mortgage tax must be paid by the mortgagee, and may not be passed through, directly, or indirectly, to the mortgagor, unless the mortgagee is an exempt organization, in which case the mortgagor must pay the tax. (Sec. 253(1-a), Tax Law) For purposes of this anti-pass through provision, if the cost or fair market value of the residential units is not exceeded by the cost or fair market value of any other improvements that are or will be made to the property, the property will be regarded as "principally improved" by the residential units. (TSB-M 86(2)M)

Tax bills.—The tax is owed at the time of recording of the instrument. In the case of property partly within and partly without the state, a certified copy of the determination of tax is given to the applicable parties who have ten days to pay the tax. (Sec. 260, Tax Law)

Lost or destroyed unrecorded instrument.—Where an unrecorded instrument subject to the mortgage recording taxes has been lost or destroyed, the Commissioner of Taxation and Finance may, upon presentation of proper proofs, determine the taxable amount of the instrument. (Sec. 258-a, Tax Law)

Required proofs.—The proofs must include an affidavit made by a party to the instrument, or a person who has knowledge of the facts, affirming that the unrecorded instrument has been lost or destroyed and the maximum amount of principal debt or obligation secured at the time of execution of the lost or destroyed instrument. (Reg. Sec. 650.2)

The Commissioner may require additional proofs upon a determination that the same are necessary for the purpose of determining the taxable amount of the unrecorded instrument.

Issuance of determination.—After reviewing the affidavit and any additional information requested, the Commissioner must issue a determination fixing the taxable amount of the lost or destroyed unrecorded instrument and the amount of tax due. The determination may be presented to the recording officer of the county in which the real property or any part thereof affected by the lost or destroyed instrument is located, and the tax determined to be due must be paid to the recording officer.

Action to enforce payment of tax.—The Attorney General may enforce the payment of mortgage recording taxes by:

(1) bringing suit to sell such mortgage; or

(2) maintaining an action against:

(a) the mortgagee or his assignee or successor personally,

(b) the mortgagee or his successor in interest personally, where the mortgage stipulates that it is the duty of the mortgagor to pay the tax or where the mortgagor is liable for the special additional mortgage recording tax or

(c) the trust mortgagee, personally, in the case of a trust mortgage.

(Sec. 266, Tax Law)

Venue.—If the amount sought to be recovered is $50.00 or more, the action must be instituted in Albany County.

Interest on judgment.—Interest is added to the amount of tax included in the judgment at the rate of 1% per month. Interest is generally computed from the date on which the tax became due and payable. In the case of taxable mortgages previously recorded, upon which mortgage recording taxes have not been paid, where no penalty is prescribed by law for the nonpayment of tax, interest is added at the rate of 6% per annum.

Actions involving trust mortgages.—In actions involving trust mortgages, the Attorney General may maintain an action against the trust mortgagee personally. (Reg. Sec. 652.3)

If recovery is had personally against the trust mortgagee, and the trust mortgagee pays the amount recovered, (or voluntarily pays the mortgage recording taxes), the trust mortgagee will be deemed to have, possess and to have become subrogated to all the rights and interests in and to the tax lien. (Sec. 267, Tax Law) The trust mortgagee will be entitled to to enforce the repayment of the amount so paid with interest at the rate of 6% per annum and may maintain an action in its own name against any person, association or corporation liable to pay such taxes, or for the sale of such mortgage and the secured debt to which the lien attaches.

Refunds.—An application may be made to the Commissioner of Taxation and Finance for a refund of mortgage recording taxes paid by a mortgagor or mortgagee where:

(1) taxes were erroneously paid; or

(2) a statutory right of rescission is exercised and a discharge of the mortgage has been recorded.

(Sec. 263, Tax Law; Sec. 257-a, Tax Law; Reg. Sec. 654.1) A "statutory right of rescission" is defined in Sec. 257-a, Tax Law, as the right of a borrower (mortgagor) to rescind a consumer credit transaction in which a security interest, including a mortgage, is retained or acquired in any real property that is used or is expected to be used as a residence of the mortgagor, as such right is provided in the Sec. 125,

Consumer Protection Act ("Truth in Lending Act") and in the regulations issued by the Board of Governors of the Federal Reserve System (Sec. 257-a, Tax Law; Reg. Sec. 641.11)

Time limitations.—A claim for a refund of taxes erroneously paid must be filed within two years from the date that the erroneous payment was received by the recording officer. Where a refund is claimed as a result of a mortgagor's exercise of a statutory right of rescission, the claim for refund must be filed within the later of:

(1) two years from the date that the taxes were paid; or

(2) one year from the date that the mortgage was discharged.

Documentation required.—The application for a refund must be accompanied by a complete copy of the recorded mortgage that is the subject of the refund claim. (Reg. Sec. 654.2) If the basis for the refund claim is the mortgagor's exercise of a statutory right of rescission, the application must also be accompanied by:

(1) a copy of the recorded satisfaction or discharge of the mortgage; and

(2) an executed copy of the "Notice of Right to Cancel."

If the refund is to be paid to the mortgagor or mortgagee's legal representative, a notarized consent or assignment must be attached to the application for refund.

Interest on refund.—Interest on refunds at the rate of $1/2$ of 1% per month is allowed if the refund check is issued more that 90 days after the application is received by the Commissioner in processible form. (Sec. 263, Tax Law; Reg. Sec. 654.5) Interest will be computed for each month (or a fraction of a month) for the period from the date the application for refund is received by the Commissioner in processible form to a date preceding the date of the refund check by not more than 30 days. No interest will be issued, however, if the amount owed is less than $1.00.

• *Penalties*

Mortgage recording taxes are liens upon both the mortgage upon which tax is imposed and the underlying debt or obligation secured by the mortgage. (Sec. 265, Tax Law)

Mortgages recorded prior to July 1, 1906.—The mortgage recording tax lien on mortgages recorded prior to July 1, 1906, extends only to amounts advanced after July 1, 1906. (Sec. 265, Tax Law)

Lien from deed of trust or deed absolute.—Mortgage recording tax liens resulting from a deed of trust or a deed absolute on its face that is security for a debt or obligation will cease ten years after the the deed's recording, provided that the document is in the hands of a bona fide purchaser for value.

Nonpayment of tax, refusal to record, release, assign or discharge mortgage.— No mortgage may be recorded by a county clerk or register until applicable mortgage recording taxes are paid. (Sec. 258, Tax Law) In addition, no mortgage subject to mortgage recording taxes may be released, discharged of record or received in evidence in any action or proceeding, nor may any assignment of or agreement extending the mortgage be recorded unless applicable mortgage recording taxes are paid.

Release or discharge of mortgage where mortgagor is not subject to payment of special additional mortgage recording tax.—Where a mortgage is subject to special additional mortgage recording taxes, a mortgagor who is not liable for payment of the tax, or a subsequent owner, may obtain a release or discharge of record of the mortgage by paying the special additional tax, plus applicable penalties and interest. In such instances, the mortgagor or subsequent owner may (1) where applicable, apply for the credit allowable under Articles 9, 9-A, 32 or 33, Tax Law, or (2) maintain an action to recover the amounts so paid against the person liable for payment of the tax, or such person's subsequent assignees or owners of the mortgage or consolidated mortgage of which the mortgage is a part.

Refusal to enter judgment of foreclosure.—No judgment or final order in any action or proceeding may be made for the foreclosure or the enforcement of any mortgage subject to mortgage recording taxes or of any debt or obligation secured by any such mortgage, unless applicable mortgage recording taxes are paid. (Sec. 258, Tax Law)

Penalties.—A mortgage that is recorded without the payment of mortgage recording taxes is subject to a penalty equal to $1/2$ of 1% for each month (or fraction of a month) that the tax remains unpaid. (Sec. 258, Tax Law) In instances where it could not be determined from the face of the instrument that mortgage recording taxes were due, or where an advance has been made on a prior advance mortgage or a corporate trust mortgage without payment of mortgage recording taxes, a penalty equal to 1% will be added to the tax for each month (or fraction of a month) that the tax remains unpaid.

Partial remittance by Commissioner.—Where a taxable mortgage is recorded in good faith, and the county clerk or register determines that the mortgage is either nontaxable or taxable at a lower amount than what is subsequently determined to be due, the Commissioner of Taxation and Finance may remit the penalties in excess of $1/2$ of 1% per month.

Interest.—Interest is imposed on underpayments of mortgage recording taxes at rates set by the Commissioner of Taxation and Finance. For current rates, see ¶89-204 in the "Practice and Procedure" division.

• *Forms*

The following forms are in current use with respect to the mortgage recording tax:

— MT-12, Annual Statement

— MT-15, Mortgage Recording Tax Return

— MT-15.1, Mortgage Recording Tax Claim for Refund

— MT-17, Statement of Advance

— AU-202.1, Appraisal of Real Property Covered by Indeterminate Mortgage

Forms may be obtained from: New York State Tax Department, Taxpayer Assistance Bureau, W A Harriman Campus, Albany, New York 12227. Taxpayers requesting forms may also call toll free (from New York State only) 1-800-462-8100. From areas outside New York, call (518) 438-1073.

[¶37-053] Stock Transfer Tax

Article 12, Tax on Transfers of Stock and Other Corporate Certificates, imposes tax on transactions involving shares or certificates of stock in domestic or foreign associations, companies or corporations. (Sec. 270(1), Tax Law) The tax applies to transactions that occur within New York after June 1, 1905.

Ch. 878, Laws 1977, provided for a schedule of rebates of the stock transfer tax. Although 100% of the tax is currently rebated, the tax is maintained in order to meet certain funding requirements of the Municipal Assistance Corporation.

The Stock Transfer Tax is administered by the Stock Transfer Tax Section of the Miscellaneous Tax Bureau, Department of Taxation and Finance. The main office of the Department is located at State Campus, Albany, New York 12227.

• *Transfers subject to tax*

Tax is imposed on sales and transfers of shares of stock and certificates representing shares of stock by domestic or foreign associations, companies or corporations, businesses conducted by trustees, residents and nonresidents. (Sec. 270(1), Tax Law; Reg. Sec. 50.2) The tax applies to:

(1) shares of stock;

(2) certificates of stock;

(3) certificates of rights to stock;

(4) certificates of interest in property or accumulations;

(5) certificates of interest in a business conducted by a trustee or trustees; and

(6) certificates of deposit representing any of the foregoing.

The tax is imposed on sales, agreements to sell, memoranda of sales, deliveries and transfers of shares of stock and certificates, regardless of whether the transfer is made upon or shown by the books of the association, company, corporation, or trustee, by assignment in blank, by delivery of the stock or certificate, or by paper, agreement, memorandum or other evidence of sale or transfer. (Sec. 270(1), Tax Law)

The tax applies to both intermediate and final transfers, provided at least one taxable event occurs within New York. (Reg. Sec. 50.2) However, only one tax is payable with respect to any one transaction. For example, if a sale, delivery of the certificates and record transfer to the name of the purchaser are all made within the state, only one tax is payable. However, if any taxable event occurs within the state in connection with any transaction, the transaction is subject to tax regardless of where other transactions occur. Therefore, a transfer of record ownership on the books of a corporation within New York is subject to tax, even though the sale and delivery of the certificates may be made outside the state. The same is true of a sale or agreement to sell, or a delivery of certificates made within the state, although all other events relating to the same transaction occurred outside New York.

It is not necessary for legal title to be transferred; tax is imposed whether the transaction invests the holder of the shares or certificates with a beneficial interest, legal title, or merely with possession or use of the shares or certificates for any purpose. Further, it is not necessary that the transaction involve a sale; deliveries or transfers of shares or certificates by gift are subject to tax.

For examples of taxable stock transfers, see Reg. Sec. 50.1.

Shares and certificates.—Shares and certificates, the transfer of which are subject to tax, include the following:

(1) Shares of stock, whether or not represented by certificates, including shares subscribed for by an accommodation incorporator;

(2) Temporary or interim certificates;

(3) Certificates representing the interest of a subscriber for stock, although further payment must be made;

(4) Voting trust certificates; and

(5) Certificates of stock in a dissolved corporation.

(Reg. Sec. 50.1)

¶37-053

Calls.—Calls are agreements to sell and are subject to tax when given, regardless of whether the option is subsequently exercised. (Reg. Sec. 50.1) Where the tax has been paid, however, no tax will be payable on a sale, delivery or transfer made pursuant to the call. A certificate evidencing the payment of the stock transfer tax should be submitted to the transfer agent.

• *Exemptions*

Exemptions provided by statute generally fall into two categories: transactions that must be accompanied by an exemption certificate, and transactions exempt by operation of law that do not require an accompanying exemption certificate.

For contents of exemption certificates, see Reg. Sec. 54.1and Reg. Sec. 54.2.

Exempt transfers requiring exemption certificates.—The following transfers are specifically exempt from tax, provided the transactions are accompanied by a form setting forth the facts and such other required information to establish the reasons for exemption:

(1) Transactions on organized securities exchanges within New York that are registered with the United States Securities and Exchange Commission, involving shares or certificates of less than 100 shares and less than the unit of trading on the exchange by registered dealers. (Sec. 270(5)(a), Tax Law)

(2) Deposits of certificates as collateral security, where the certificates are not actually sold. (Sec. 270(5)(b), Tax Law)

(3) Transfers or deliveries of certificates pursuant to a statutory provision, to a trustee or public officer to secure the performance of obligations, and retransfers or redeliveries of such certificates to the transferor or depositor. (Sec. 270(5)(c), Tax Law)

(4) Transfers of certificates from the name of a fiduciary to a nominee of the fiduciary, or from one nominee of a fiduciary to another. (Sec. 270(5)(d), Tax Law) The certificates must be held by the nominee or nominees for the same purpose for which they would be held if retained by the fiduciary.

(5) Transfers of certificates from the name of the owner to a custodian, where the certificates are to be held or disposed of by the custodian for and subject to the instructions of the owner. (Sec. 270(5)(e), Tax Law) Transfers from the name of the custodian to the custodian's nominee, or from one nominee are also exempt, provided the certificates continue to be held by the nominee or nominees for the same purpose for which they would be held if retained by the original custodian.

(6) Loans of stock and certificates, or the return thereof. (Sec. 270(5)(f), Tax Law)

(7) Deliveries or transfers from the name of the owner to a broker for sale, or deliveries by or transfers from the name of a broker to a customer for whom and upon whose order the broker purchased the stock or certificates. (Sec. 270(5)(g), Tax Law)

(8) Deliveries or transfers from a corporation to its registered nominee, or from one registered nominee of the corporation to another, provided the shares or certificates continue to be held by the nominee for the same purpose for which they would be held if retained by the corporation. (Sec. 270(5)(h), Tax Law)

(9) Transfers or deliveries of shares or certificates upon the instructions of a broker, from the broker's name or from the name of a customer to the broker's

registered nominee for the purpose of holding such shares or certificates subject to the instructions of a clearing corporation affiliated with any securities exchange in New York, as agent for such broker. (Sec. 270(5)(i), Tax Law)

(10) Transfers or deliveries by a depositor in a system for the central handling of securities, from the depositor or the depositor's customer or their nominees to a nominee registered with the Department of Taxation and Finance. (Sec. 270(5)(j), Tax Law)

Certain transfers not expressly described in the law section listing the specific exemptions (see above) may be exempt, because they represent a combination of exempt transfers. (Reg. Sec. 53.1) The principle is that where all the transfers in a chain of transfers are exempt, any of the intermediate links of the chain may be omitted and the transfer will still be exempt.

Transfers through systems for the central handling of securities.—Transfers or deliveries upon the instructions of a depositor in a system for the central handling of securities (including the clearing and settling of securities transactions) from the name of the depositor, the depositor's nominee, or from the name of the depositor's or nominee's customer to the registered nominee of the central handling system are exempt from tax, provided the transfer or delivery is made for the purpose of holding the shares or certificates as the agent for the depositor. (Sec. 270(5)(j), Tax Law; Reg. Sec. 53.2) Transfers or deliveries upon the instructions of a depositor from the name of the registered nominee of central handling system to the same depositor, customer or nominee are similarly exempt.

The system for the central handling of securities must be (a) established by a national securities exchange or association registered with the Securities and Exchange Commission of the United States or (b) maintained by a clearing corporation as defined in Sec. 8-102(3), Uniform Commercial Code. (Sec. 270(5)(j), Tax Law) Each transfer must be accompanied by an exemption certificate in order for the exemption to apply.

Where a broker certifies to its affiliated clearing corporation that all of the entries in its account with the clearing corporation reflected in a daily statement of transactions represent transactions subject to the stock transfer tax upon which the tax has been paid, and/or transactions that come within one or more of the exemptions specified in Sec. 270(5), its certification will be deemed to apply to all of the transfers reflected on the daily statement that represent exempt transfers.

"Depositor" defined.—The term "depositor" includes the following individuals or organizations that have been accepted as participants in a system for the central handling of securities:

(1) securities exchanges or associations registered under federal statutes such as the Securities Exchange Act of 1934, and affiliated clearing corporations;

(2) banks, trust companies, investment companies, insurance companies and other financial organizations subject to supervision or regulation under federal or state banking laws or state insurance laws; and

(3) brokers, dealers and investment companies registered under the Securities Exchange Act of 1934 or the Investment Company Act of 1940.

(Reg. Sec. 53.2)

Exempt transfers not requiring exemption certificates.—The following transactions are exempt by operation of law:

(1) Transfers from a decedent to an executor or administrator (Sec. 270-c(1), Tax Law);

(2) Transfers from a minor to a guardian or from a guardian to a ward upon attaining majority (Sec. 270-c(2), Tax Law);

(3) Transfers from an incompetent to a committee or similar legal representative, or from a committee or similar legal representative to a former incompetent upon the removal of the disability (Sec. 270-c(3), Tax Law);

(4) Transfers from a conservatee to a conservator, or from a conservator to a former conservatee upon cessation of the conservatorship (Sec. 270-c(4), Tax Law);

(5) Transfers from a bank, trust company, financial institution, insurance company, or similar entity (including nominees, custodians, or trustees of banks and related institutions) to a public officer, commission, or person designated by the officer or commission or by a court, in connection with the complete or partial taking over of the institution's assets (Sec. 270-c(5), Tax Law);

(6) Bankruptcy and receivership transactions between the bankrupt and the trustee or receiver (Sec. 270-c(6), Tax Law);

(7) Transfers from transferees under paragraphs (1) through (6), above, to successor transferees acting in the same capacity (Sec. 270-c(7), Tax Law);

(8) Transfers from a foreign country or national thereof to the United States or any agency of the United States, or to the government of any foreign country pursuant to Sec. 5(b), Trading With the Enemy Act (40 Stat. 415) (Sec. 270-c(8), Tax Law);

(9) Transfers from trustees to surviving, substitute, succeeding or additional trustees of the same trust (Sec. 270-c(9), Tax Law);

(10) Transfers upon the death of a joint tenant or tenant by the entirety, to a survivor or survivors (Sec. 270-c(10), Tax Law);

(11) Transfers pursuant to orders of the Securities and Exchange Commission, provided the order specifies that the delivery or transfer is necessary or appropriate to effectuate the provisions of Sec. 11(b), Public Utility Holding Company Act of 1935, and specifies and itemizes the securities to be delivered or transferred (Sec. 270-c(11), Tax Law);

(12) Transfers to effectuate plans of reorganization or adjustment

(a) under a confirmed bankruptcy plan,

(b) that have been approved in an equity receivership proceeding in court involving a corporation, or

(c) pursuant to Secs. 119 through 123, Real Property Law, or Article 9, Stock Corporation Law (Sec. 270-c(12), Tax Law);

(13) Transfers to effectuate plans of reorganization or adjustment under federal or state anti-trust laws (Sec. 270-c(13), Tax Law); and

(14) Transfers of the capital stock of a corporation organized under or subject to either Article 3 or Article 7, Banking Law, in exchange for shares or other securities of a company substantially all of whose assets will be the exchanged capital stock. (Sec. 270-c(14), Tax Law)

Certificate required.—Upon request of the Commissioner of Taxation and Finance, the transactions noted above must be accompanied by a certificate setting forth the facts and such other required information to establish the reasons for exemption. (Sec. 270-c, Tax Law)

Transfers by executors or administrators.—Transfers or deliveries of stock or certificates by an executor or administrator to a legatee, heir or distributee are ordinarily subject to tax. (Reg. Sec. 50.1) The transaction will be exempt from tax, however, if it is shown to the satisfaction of the Commissioner of Taxation and Finance that the value of the shares or certificates is no greater than the amount of the tax that would otherwise be imposed. (Sec. 270(b), Tax Law)

Investment trusts.—Transfers of shares or certificates issued under a fixed-type noncorporate investment trust agreement are exempt from tax. (Sec. 270(8)(a))

Transfers involving the distribution of a management-type investment trust's shares or certificates to investors are exempt if the shareholders are entitled, upon reasonable notice, to require the trust to redeem or repurchase their shares or certificates for their proportionate interest in the property of the trust or the cash equivalent of the trust, less a 3% discount. (Sec. 270(8)(b); Reg. Sec. 50.1) Transfers involving the redemption of shares by the trust (that is, transfers between the investment trust and an underwriter, between an underwriter and a dealer in securities, or between an underwriter or dealer and an investor), are also exempt. Other transfers of shares of a management-type investment trust, however, including sales by one dealer to another, or by one investor to another, are subject to tax.

Original issue of stock.—An original issue of stock is not subject to tax. (Sec. 270(1), Tax Law)

The transfer of shares subject to a "warrant" is not taxable if the shares transferred represent an original issue of stock by the corporation making the warrant. Transfer of treasury stock by a corporation does not qualify as an original issuance of stock, and is thus a taxable transfer. (Reg. Sec. 50.1(g))

With regard to the transfer of shares in a cooperative housing corporation, only the transfer to the initial unit purchasers of shares related to specific cooperative units, and the transfer of the remaining shares to the sponsor of the cooperative conversion, are exempt from tax as an original issuance of stock by the corporation. Subsequent transfers by the initial unit purchasers of their cooperative shares, and transfers of the remaining shares in the cooperative from the sponsor to additional unit purchasers, are not exempt from tax. (Reg. Sec. 50.1(h))

Corporate reacquisition of stock.—The purchase, redemption or other reacquisition of its own shares by a corporation is exempt from tax, provided the shares are canceled upon reacquisition pursuant to Sec. 515, Business Corporation Law, or, within one year from the date of purchase, redemption or other reacquisition, the shares are canceled by an amendment to the corporation's certificate of incorporation or by action of the corporation's board of directors. (Sec. 270(1), Tax Law)

Transfers on books regularly kept outside New York.—Transfers of stock or certificates made upon books of a domestic association, company or corporation that are regularly kept at a transfer office or by a transfer agent outside New York are exempt from tax, provided the following conditions are met:

> (1) the maintenance of the books outside the state is necessary or convenient for the transaction of the ordinary business affairs of the association, company or corporation and has been approved by the Commissioner of Taxation and Finance, and

> (2) no act necessary to effect the transfer (other than the making of a record in the stock book kept in compliance with Sec. 10, Stock Corporation Law) is performed within New York.

(Sec. 270(6), Tax Law)

Transfers to or by registered clearing agencies or registered transfer agents.—By federal law, where the sole event in New York is the delivery or transfer to or by a "registered clearing agency" or a "registered transfer agent," as defined in the

Securities Exchange Act of 1934, no stock transfer tax is due and owing. However, if the sale, agreement to sell, memorandum of sale or any other delivery or transfer takes place within New York, the stock transfer tax applies.

Governmental transfers.—The stock transfer tax does not apply to any sale or transfer where the vendor or transferor is a governmental entity or international organization that is not subject to tax. (Sec. 270(3), Tax Law)

• *Basis and rate*

The stock transfer tax is measured by the number of shares sold or transferred and computed on a per share rate according to the value of the shares or certificates.

Sales.—Where shares or certificates of stock are sold, tax is imposed at the following rates (Sec. 270(2), Tax Law):

Selling price per share	Rate per share
Less than $5	1 1/4 cents
$5 or more but less than $10	2 1/2 cents
$10 or more but less than $20	3 3/4 cents
$20 or more	5 cents

Large block transactions.—The maximum tax on a single transaction involving a sale relating to shares or certificates of the same class that are issued by the same issuer may not exceed $350. (Sec. 270-e, Tax Law) Multiple transactions executed on the same day by a member of a securities exchange or by a registered dealer who is permitted or required to pay tax without the use of stamps, which are made pursuant to orders by the same person and relate to shares or certificates of the same class and issued by the same issuer, are considered a single qualifying sale.

The law formerly provided reduced rates for transactions involving nonresidents. This was held unconstitutional by the New York Court of Appeals. (*Opinion of Counsel, Department of Taxation and Finance*)

• *Assessment and collection*

The tax is generally self-assessed since it is payable by the purchase and affixing of stamps.

The person or persons making or effectuating a taxable transfer or sale, including the person or persons to whom the sale or transfer is made, is responsible for the payment of the stock transfer tax. (Sec. 270(3), Tax Law) Thus, both transferor and transferee are liable; if a transfer is made on the books of the corporation, the corporation is also liable. (Reg. Sec. 50.3)

The transferor and transferee may agree between themselves which of them will be responsible for the payment of the tax, and payment by either discharges the liability of both. (Reg. Sec. 50.3) However, if the party who has agreed to pay the tax fails to do so, the other party is not exonerated from liability as a result of such agreement, and payment may be enforced against either party.

Determination of tax by commissioner.—The Department of Taxation and Finance is authorized to make a determination of tax due if tax has not been paid on a taxable transaction within five years after its due date. (Sec. 279-a, Tax Law) Written notice must be given to the applicable party specifying the determination. The person against whom the determination is made may appeal within 30 days after mailing of the notice. Failure to appeal renders the determination final. Further review may be had under Article 78 proceedings.

Refund claims are permitted. Appeals from denials may be made within 30 days after mailing of notice of denial of claim and further appeals under Article 78 proceedings may be commenced within 90 days of denial of appeal. (Sec. 280, Tax Law)

Collection of tax.—The stock transfer tax is collected by two methods. The first involves the use of stamps provided by the Department of Taxation and Finance; the second method provides for payment of tax without use of stamps on sales executed or effected by members of a securities exchange within the state or dealers in securities who are not members of a securities exchange but have filed written notice of their election to pay tax directly to the Department of Taxation and Finance without the use of stamps.

Use of adhesive stamps.—The payment of stock transfer tax is usually indicated by the use of adhesive stamps issued by the Department of Taxation and Finance and sold through authorized transfer agents. (Sec. 271, Tax Law)

It is the duty of the person making or effectuating the sale or transfer to procure and furnish, and the duty of the association, company, corporation or trustee to affix and cancel, the stamp. (Sec. 270(4), Tax Law) Where the transaction is effected by delivery or transfer of a certificate, the stamp is placed on the surrendered certificate and canceled. If the only evidence of the transfer or sale is a change on the books of the association or corporation within the state, the stamps are affixed to the transfer books and canceled.

Memoranda of sales.—If a transaction involves an agreement to sell or a sale made by delivery of a certificate assigned in blank, the stamp is attached to the bill or memorandum of sale that the seller is required to deliver to the buyer. (Sec. 270(4), Tax Law) The bill or memorandum must include the following information:

(1) the date of the transaction;

(2) the name of the seller;

(3) the stock or other certificate to which it relates;

(4) the number of shares involved in the transaction;

(5) the selling price per share; and

(6) an identification number.

(Reg. Sec. 50.4)

The identification number also must be entered and recorded in the book of account required to be kept by Sec. 276, Tax Law. No additional tax is imposed upon the delivery of the certificate, or upon the actual issuance of a new certificate, when the original certificate is accompanied by the duly stamped memorandum of sale.

Cancellation of stamp.—The initials of the person using or affixing the stamp and the date upon which the stamp was attached or used must be marked on the stamp. (Sec. 273, Tax Law) The stamp must also be cut or perforated so that it cannot be used again.

Penalties.—Any person that makes use of an adhesive stamp to denote the payment of tax without canceling the stamp is guilty of a misdemeanor and subject to a fine of not less than $200 nor more than $500, imprisonment for not less than six months, or both. (Sec. 273, Tax Law)

Payment of tax by brokers through clearing corporations.—Members of securities exchanges (that is, brokers) within New York that are registered with the U.S. Securities and Exchange Commission are permitted to pay tax on sales, deliveries and transfers of stock or other certificates executed or effected in New York without the use of stamps. (Sec. 281-a(1), Tax Law) Instead, the tax is paid to the exchange's affiliated clearing corporation for the account of the Department of Taxation and Finance. Where a broker is a member of more than one exchange, the broker must choose the affiliated clearing corporation through which taxes on all transactions will be paid; the choice, once made, is irrevocable, unless the Commissioner of Taxation and Finance consents to a change in writing.

Each broker must file a report showing the amount of stock transfer taxes payable on all sales, deliveries or transfers executed or effected by such broker during each full business day upon which the clearing corporation is clearing or settling accounts. The report must also authorize and direct the clearing corporation to remit the taxes shown to be payable to the Division of Taxation and Finance, or its duly designated depositary, and to charge the amount to the broker's account. The report must be filed with the clearing corporation within one business day following the day for which the report is made. The amount of taxes must be shown in a separate account on the general ledger of the broker, and the postings to the account must clearly refer to the books of original entry showing separately the tax required to be reported on each exchange.

Each clearing corporation must remit the aggregate amount of all taxes received by it on the business day on which a report is received. (Reg. Sec. 52.2) The remittance must be accompanied by a report and schedule on forms prescribed by the Division of Taxation and Finance.

All reports and schedules of brokers must be preserved for a period of four years.

Payment of tax by dealers in securities who are not members of a securities exchange.—Securities dealers registered with the Attorney-General of the State of New York that are not required to pay taxes through clearing corporations may elect to pay stock transfer tax directly to the Department of Taxation and Finance without the use of stamps. Every dealer is required to make a weekly report to the commissioner on a form prescribed by the commissioner. (Sec. 281-a(1), Tax Law; Reg. Sec. 52.3) If a dealer uses a clearing agent, it may, subject to the written approval of the Department of Taxation and Finance, appoint the agent to remit tax on its behalf. The election must be made in writing and filed with the Department of Taxation and Finance.

The election, once made, is irrevocable unless the Commissioner of Taxation and Finance consents to a change in writing. (Reg. Sec. 52.3) If a dealer becomes an eligible member of a corporation formed to provide facilities for clearing transactions in over-the-counter securities and, therefore, is required to pay taxes to such corporation, the election to pay taxes directly to the Department of Taxation and Finance without the use of stamps will be terminated. In addition, the Department of Taxation and Finance may withdraw the privilege of paying tax without stamps.

Each dealer (or authorized agent) must make weekly reports to the Department of Taxation and Finance showing the daily amount of stock transfer taxes payable on all sales and transfers due for settlement within the period for which the report is filed. (Reg. Sec. 52.3) The report and remittance of tax must be mailed or delivered to the Department of Taxation and Finance not later than the second business day of the week following the week for which the report is made.

Payment of tax by dealers through authorized corporations.—Members of corporations formed to provide facilities for clearing transactions in over-the-counter securities by dealers and brokers, who do not make payments of tax through affiliated clearing corporations, must pay tax on sales, deliveries and transfers of stock and other certificates through corporations authorized by the Department of Taxation to receive the payment of the tax. (Sec. 281-a(1), Tax Law)

Each eligible member must, for each full business day upon which the authorized corporation is clearing or settling, make a report showing the amount of stock transfer taxes payable on all sales, deliveries or transfers executed or effected by the member that are due for clearance or settlement. (Reg. Sec. 52.4) The report must authorize and direct the corporation to remit the amount of taxes that the report shows to be payable, and to charge that amount to the account of the member making the report. The report must be filed with such corporation not later than one business day following the day for which the report is made.

• *Rebate*

Rebates of 100% of the stock transfer tax are allowed for transactions occurring on or after October 1, 1981. (Sec. 280-a(1), Tax Law) No rebates are allowed, however, where the Department of Taxation and Finance has determined the amount of tax due because of the failure of a taxpayer to pay required tax. (Sec. 280-a(2-a), Tax Law)

Rebates are not allowed or paid until the person, firm, company or corporation claiming the rebate complies with applicable rules, regulations and instructions of the Department of Taxation and Finance, including the furnishing of a just and true book of account of transactions within the state. (Sec. 280-a(1), Tax Law)

Claim for rebate.—Rebates are paid only upon the filing of a claim for rebate with the Department of Taxation and Finance. (Sec. 280-a(3), Tax Law) The claim for rebate must comply with rules, regulations or instructions of the Department, and must be presented within two years after the affixing and canceling of stock transfer tax stamps or other payment of the tax. Where the tax is paid by the use of stamps, the original purchase receipt for the stamps must be included with the rebate claim. (Reg. 52.1(b))

Every rebate claim must certify that the statements contained within the claim are true and accurate. (Sec. 280-a(4), Tax Law) In addition, the person or entity requesting the rebate must certify the amount of stock transfer tax that has been paid to the state and that the amount of the requested rebate is actually due and owing. The Department of Taxation and Finance, if satisfied that the tax has actually been paid, must rebate the tax on the audit and warrant of the State Comptroller on vouchers approved by the Commissioner of Taxation and Finance.

Members of securities exchanges.—Members of securities exchanges and registered dealers that are permitted or required to pay tax without the use of stamps may apply for a rebate without the filing of a formal claim. (Sec. 280-a(6), Tax Law) The amount of the rebate is determined on the basis of written reports that are required to be made to or through securities exchanges located within New York, affiliated clearing corporations or authorized agencies of the Department of Taxation and Finance. (Sec. 280-a(1), Tax Law) A broker may submit daily transaction information to its clearing corporation electronically, and these electronic submissions may be covered by a comprehensive certification with the clearing corporation that will apply to all the electronic reports of the broker. (Reg. 52.2)

• *Refunds, penalties*

Refunds for erroneously paid taxes are permitted upon proper application and review. Claims for refunds must be made in writing to the Commissioner of Taxation and Finance within two years after the erroneous affixing or payment. Review of any decision of the Commissioner with respect to the refund claim may be made under an Article 78 proceeding within 90 days after notice of determination is given by the Commissioner. A bond, approved by a justice of the Supreme Court, also must be filed to cover costs and charges of such review, if the decision is reviewed or the review is dismissed. (Sec. 280, Tax Law)

Penalties.—The following penalties apply with respect to nonpayment of taxes and failure to perform other acts under the Stock Transfer Tax:

— *Civil penalties for failure to pay tax:* $1 for each share of stock or other taxable interest involved with the non-tax-paid transaction. (Sec. 277, Tax Law)

— *Other civil penalties:* $500 for each violation under the Stock Transfer Tax. (Sec. 277, Tax Law)

— *Failure to pay tax-misdemeanor:* $500—$1000 and/or imprisonment up to six months. (Sec. 272, Tax Law)

— *Unlawful sale of stamps:* $500—$1000 and/or imprisonment up to six months. (Sec. 271-a, Tax Law)

— *Illegal use of stamps:* $500—$1000 and/or imprisonment up to one year. (Sec. 275, Tax Law)

— *Failure to cancel stamps:* $200—$500 and/or imprisonment up to six months. (Sec. 273, Tax Law)

— *Failure to register:* $100—$500 and/or imprisonment up to six months. (Sec. 275-a, Tax Law)

— *Failure to keep records:* $500—$5000 and/or imprisonment for 3 months to 1 year. (Sec. 276, Tax Law)

• *Returns and records*

The tax is ordinarily collected by the sale of tax stamps through authorized agents, affixed and canceled on the stock certificate or the memorandum of sale. In the case of transactions shown only on the books of the corporation, the stamp must be placed on such book.

Alternate methods of payment are available for members of a securities exchange in New York registered with the Securities and Exchange Commission, and certain others. Returns are required only in the case of the alternate methods.

Provisions are made for registration of brokers and dealers in securities and transfer agents and records to be maintained by brokers and dealers and transfer agents.

Registration of brokers and transfer agents.—Every person acting individually or as a trustee, firm, company, association or corporation engaged in the making or negotiating of sales, agreements to sell, deliveries or transfers of shares or certificates subject to the stock transfer tax, or conducting or transacting a stock brokerage business, must register with the Commissioner of Taxation and Finance within ten days after commencing business. Corporations, stock associations, companies and trustees that maintain principal offices or places of business within the state, or keep or cause to be kept within the state places for the sale, transfer or delivery of their stock or other taxable certificates, also must register. (Sec. 275-a, Tax Law)

Each certificate must include:

(1) the name under which the business is, or is to be, conducted or transacted,

(2) the true or real full name or names of the person or persons conducting or transacting business; and

(3) the post office address or addresses of the person or persons conducting or transacting the business.

¶37-053

A corporation or trustee must provide the address of its principal office or place of business and the date and jurisdiction of incorporation or organization. The certificate must be executed and acknowledged by the person or persons conducting or intending to conduct the business or, where applicable, by the corporation's president or secretary. (Sec. 275-a, Tax Law)

Changes in the composition of a firm or association subject to registration must be reported to the Commissioner within 10 days after the change occurs. (Sec. 275-a, Tax Law)

Brokers.—Brokers and persons dealing in securities must keep accurate records of taxable transactions at an accessible place within New York. Information required to be maintained includes the following:

(1) the date of each sale, agreement to sell, delivery or transfer of taxable shares or certificates;

(2) the name, class and number of shares;

(3) the selling price;

(4) the name, address and resident or nonresident status of the seller or transferor;

(5) the name of the purchaser or transferee;

(6) the value of the stamps affixed in payment of the tax, or payment of the tax otherwise than by the use of stamps; and

(7) the date and amount of each purchase of stock transfer stamps and from whom purchased.

(Sec. 276, Tax Law)

Brokers and persons dealing in securities must also keep all memoranda, including telegrams, teletypes and other communications relating to taxable transactions. If a taxable transaction is effected pursuant to instructions received on magnetic or punched tape, discs, cards or other media, or by wire or wireless transmission, the broker, in lieu of maintaining the original media, may retain a copy or record of such instructions. (Reg. Sec. 51.2)

Instructions in lieu of exemption certificates involving transfers through a system for the central handling of securities, effected pursuant to instructions on magnetic or punched tape, discs, cards or other media, or by wire or wireless transmission, must include either the name of or a unique alphabetic or numeric symbol identifying the broker, bank, national banking association or trust company or dealer in securities maintaining a regular place of business within the state who or which is a depositor in the system. The transfer agent or other party whose records contain the unique alphabetic or numeric symbol under this subdivision is responsible for identifying the party to whom the symbol refers. (Reg. Sec. 51.2)

Corporations, trustees, and transfer agents.—Every corporation or business conducted by a trustee or trustees, or its transfer agent, must keep a stock certificate book and a transfer ledger or register at an accessible place within New York containing the following information:

(1) the date of making every transfer;

(2) the name and number of shares thereof;

(3) the serial number of each surrendered certificate;

(4) the name of the party surrendering each certificate;

(5) the serial number of the certificate issued in exchange for the surrendered certificate;

(6) the number of shares represented by the surrendered certificate;

(7) the name of the party to whom the certificate was issued; and

(8) the value of the stock transfer stamps affixed in payment of the tax on the transfer.

(Sec. 276, Tax Law)

Out-of-state brokers and dealers in securities.—Brokers and dealers in securities who do not maintain a regular place of business within the state must maintain ledgers and books of account available for inspection by representatives of the Department of Taxation and Finance. The records must include entries on blotters or other records of original entry containing itemized records of all transactions in securities by the broker or dealer in securities, including a separate column showing the stock transfer tax paid on transactions subject to tax. In addition, the ledger or books of account must contain a New York State stock transfer tax account, a special account for securities in transfer with New York transfer agents, and the amount of tax paid on each transfer. (Reg. Sec. 54.2)

Maintenance of records.—Records must be kept for a period of at least four years from the date of the last entry. (Sec. 276, Tax Law) The Department of Taxation and Finance may permit canceled certificates to be retained outside New York within the four-year period if an examination with respect to the transactions to which such certificates relate has been completed and the parties agree that the certificates will be returned to New York for further examination within the remainder of the four-year period. (Reg. Sec. 56.1)

The Department of Taxation and Finance may consent to the destruction of surrendered or cancelled shares, certificates, memoranda and declarations, provided:

(1) an examination has been completed with respect to the transactions to which such documents relate;

(2) the Department is satisfied that there is no need to continue to preserve the original documents; and

(3) a record of the documents is recorded, copied or reproduced by a means that forms a durable medium for reproducing the originals.

(Reg. Sec. 56.1)

Penalties.—Failure to keep books of account and sales memoranda, or altering, destroying or making false entries in required records, or denying or preventing access to books and records to Department agents is a misdemeanor subject to a $500 to $5,000 fine and/or imprisonment from 3 months to 1 year. (Sec. 276(d), Tax Law)

Registration of brokers and transfer agents.—Returns associated with the payment of taxes are not normally required since the tax is paid by purchase and affixing of stamps. (Sec. 271, Tax Law)

An alternative method is permitted in the case of:

(1) sales executed or effected by a member of any securities exchange within New York State that is registered by the Securities and Exchange Commission,

(2) sales by a security dealer who is not a member of any exchange but who is registered as a dealer in securities with the Attorney General of New York, or

(3) sales by a security dealer who is an eligible member of a corporation that clears transactions in over-the-counter securities by brokers and dealers and is authorized to collect the tax from its members.

(Sec. 281-a, Tax Law)

• *Forms*

The following forms are in current use:

— MT-610.1, Certificate of Place of Sale of Stock

— MT-615, Registration Form for Brokers

— MT-651, Return of Stock Transfer Taxes—Article 12 of the Tax Law

— MT-675, Daily Report to Clearing Corporation

— MT-676, Authorization to Remit Taxes by "Authorized Corporation" and "Eligible Members"

— MT-680, Daily of Stock Transfer Taxes

— MT-680.1, Schedule of Taxes Deposited by Clearing Corporation (Accompanies MT-680)

Forms may be obtained from: New York State Tax Department, Taxpayer Assistance Bureau, W A Harriman Campus, Albany, New York 12227. Taxpayers requesting forms may also call toll free (from New York State only) 1-800-462-8100. From areas outside New York, call (518) 438-1073.

[¶37-100]

MOTOR VEHICLES

[¶37-101] Motor Vehicles

Property taxation of motor vehicles is discussed at ¶20-275 Motor Vehicles and ¶20-325 Transportation Equipment. Sales taxation of motor vehicles is discussed at ¶60-570 Motor Vehicles.

[¶37-150]

ENVIRONMENTAL TAXES AND FEES

[¶37-151] Environmental Taxes and Fees

This division discusses environmental taxes that are imposed by the state and environmental fees administered by state taxing bodies. The following are discussed: hazardous waste fees; the marine fisheries tax; oil spill prevention fees; the underground storage permit; and the waste tire management and recycling fee.

For a discussion of the paper carryout bag reduction fee, see ¶60-390 Food and Grocery Items.

• *Hazardous waste fees*

Every person engaged in the generation of hazardous waste is subject to a special assessment. Persons holding, or required to hold, permits for the storage, treatment or disposal of hazardous wastes are subject to a hazardous waste disposal special assessment. (Sec. 27-0923(1) and (2), Environmental Conservation Law)

Hazardous waste defined.—The term "hazardous waste" means any waste or combination of wastes which, because of its quantity, concentration, or physical chemical or infectious characteristics may either:

(1) cause or significantly contribute to an increase in mortality or serious irreversible or incapacitating reversible illness; or

¶37-100

(2) pose a substantial present or potential hazard to human health or the environment when improperly treated, stored, transported, disposed of or otherwise managed.

(Sec. 27-0901(3), Environmental Conservation Law)

Exemptions.—No special assessment is imposed on the resource recovery of any hazardous waste. Materials remaining from resource recovery which are hazardous wastes and are subsequently disposed of, treated or incinerated, however, are subject to the special assessments. "Resource recovery" does not include the removal of water from a hazardous waste. (Sec. 27-0923(3), Environmental Conservation Law)

"Generation of hazardous waste" does not include retrieval or creation of hazardous waste which must be disposed of due to remediation of an inactive hazardous waste disposal site in New York.

Hazardous waste residues remaining after incineration in a facility located on the site of generation, which are subsequently disposed of in an onsite landfill, are not subject to special assessment. (Sec. 27-0923(1)(e), Environmental Conservation Law)

No special assessment is imposed on the generation of universal wastes. (Sec. 27-0923(1)(f), Environmental Conservation Law)

Basis and rate of fees.—The special assessments are imposed on the tonnage of hazardous waste produced or treated. (Sec. 27-0923(1), Environmental Conservation Law) The assessments are prorated in the event of fractional tons. (Sec. 27-0923(3)(b), Environmental Conservation Law) The special assessment on generators of hazardous waste is determined as follows:

(1) $27 per ton of hazardous waste that is disposed of in a landfill on the site where the waste is generated, is designated for removal or removed from the site of generation for disposal in a landfill, or is removed from the site of generation for storage prior to disposal in a landfill;

(2) $9 per ton of hazardous waste that is designated for removal or removed from the site of generation for incineration or for storage prior to incineration;

(3) $2 per ton of hazardous waste that is incinerated on the site where the waste was generated;

(4) $16 per ton of hazardous waste that is designated for removal or removed from the site of generation for treatment or disposal, exclusive of disposal in a landfill or by incineration, or for storage prior to such treatment or disposal.

(Sec. 27-0923(1), Environmental Conservation Law)

Persons required to hold permits for the storage, treatment or disposal of hazardous waste are subject to the hazardous waste disposal special assessment as follows:

(1) $27 per ton of hazardous waste that is received for disposal in a landfill or for storage prior to disposal in a landfill;

(2) $9 per ton of hazardous waste that is received for incineration or for storage prior to incineration;

(3) $16 per ton of hazardous waste that is received for treatment or disposal, or storage prior thereto, exclusive of disposal in a landfill or by incineration.

(Sec. 27-0923(2), Environmental Conservation Law)

The hazardous waste disposal special assessment is not imposed on the disposal of hazardous waste generated by a person subject to the special assessment on hazardous waste generated.

The actual method utilized to dispose of or treat hazardous waste governs the determination of the applicable rate per ton. If an assessment is reported and paid on the basis of a rate which is greater than the rate applicable to the actual method used to dispose of or treat the waste, the difference between the amount reported and paid and the amount due using the rate applicable to the method utilized is regarded as an overpayment and must be credited or refunded. (Sec. 27-0923(3)(e), Environmental Conservation Law)

Reports, payment, and penalties.—Reports must be filed with the Department of Taxation and Finance on a quarterly basis on or before the 20th day of the month following the end of each calendar quarter. Payment of the assessment generally must accompany the report. No payment or report is required when the assessment at the end of any calendar quarter is $27 or less. (Sec. 27-0923(4), Environmental Conservation Law)

A penalty of 25% is imposed, in addition to an estimate of tax due, for failure or refusal to file a return or furnish information to the Department of Taxation and Finance. Interest is imposed at the rate of 15% per year on amounts not paid before the due date, from the date that the payment is due until the payment is made. (Sec. 27-0923(7), Environmental Conservation Law)

Administration.—The special assessments are administered by the Department of Taxation and Finance, State Campus, Albany, New York 12227. (Sec. 27-0923, Environmental Conservation Law)

• *Marine fisheries tax*

A tax of $1 per acre is imposed on state-owned underwater land held by franchise for shellfish cultivation. The Department of Taxation and Finance assesses the tax by February 1 each year on land held as of August 1 of the preceding year. (Sec. 13-0303, Environmental Conservation Law)

Payment.—The tax must be paid annually by April 1. (Sec. 13-0303, Environmental Conservation Law)

• *Oil spill prevention fees*

The Environmental Protection and Spill Compensation Fund is established to ensure the prompt cleanup and removal of petroleum spills. It is funded by license fees levied against major facilities in the state, including penalties collected against owners or operators using containment booms in violation of Sec. 174-a, Navigation Law. (Sec. 179, Navigation Law)

The owner of a major facility responsible for a petroleum spill is liable for all costs of cleanup and removal of the spill. The Department of Transportation may disburse money from the fund for the cleanup costs if the facility fails to attend to the cleanup operation. However, the fund must be reimbursed by the facility. (Sec. 181, Navigation Law)

License requirements.—Any person operating a major facility must be licensed by the Commissioner of the Department of Environmental Conservation. (Sec. 174, Navigation Law) "Major facilities" include refineries, storage or transfer terminals, pipelines, deep water ports, drilling platforms and any attachments relating to the above used to refine, produce, store, handle, transfer, process or transport petroleum. (Sec. 172, Navigation Law)

¶37-151

Vessels are major facilities if petroleum is transferred between them. Vessels that would not otherwise be considered major facilities are not considered major facilities based solely upon their rendering of care, assistance or advice consistent with the national contingency plan or as otherwise directed by the federal on-scene coordinator or by the Commissioner, or the Commissioner's designee, in response to a discharge of petroleum into or upon navigable waters. (Sec. 172, Navigation Law)

Facilities with a combined above and below-ground storage capacity of under 400,000 gallons are not major facilities. (Sec. 1742, Navigation Law) Applicants must show proof that state and federal plans and regulations for the control, containment and removal of petroleum discharges are being implemented. License applications must also show the number of barrels or other storage capacity of the facility, average daily throughput, and preliminary and contingency cleanup plan. Licenses are issued for a period not to exceed 5 years. (Sec. 174, Navigation Law)

Fees.—A license fee of 9.5¢ per barrel transferred is imposed; however, the fee on any barrel, including any products derived therefrom, subject to multiple transfer will be imposed only once at the point of first transfer. The license fee is 8¢ for major facilities that (i) transfer barrels for their own use, and (ii) do not sell or transfer the product subject to such license fee. (Sec. 174, Navigation Law) The fee is collected until the Environmental Protection and Spill Compensation Fund contains $40 million or more. No license fee is imposed subsequently unless the balance of the fund falls below $25 million or pending claims against the fund exceed 50% of the balance. (Sec. 174, Navigation Law)

The surcharge on the license fee is 4.25¢ per barrel for each barrel transferred on or after February 1, 1990. The surcharge is 13.75¢ per barrel for any barrel that is transferred but thereafter exported from the state for use outside the state. The surcharge continues to be imposed regardless of whether the license fee continues to be imposed. (Sec. 174, Navigation Law)

Reports.—Each licensee must file a certificate with the Commissioner of the Department of Environmental Conservation by the 20th day of the month following the close of the license period showing the number of barrels transferred to the facility. Payment of the license fee is required when the certificate is filed. If a certificate is not filed or is filed incorrectly, the Commissioner will determine the license fee from any available information. The taxpayer has a right to appeal the determination of the Commissioner. (Sec. 174, Navigation Law)

• *Underground storage permit*

The prospective operator of an underground storage reservoir devoted to the storage of gas or liquefied petroleum gas must obtain an underground storage permit from the Department of Environmental Conservation. The department will grant a permit within 90 days upon submission of satisfactory information. (Sec. 23-1301, Environmental Conservation Law)

Fees.—Fees for underground storage permits are:

— $10,000 for a new underground storage reservoir; and

— $5,000 for a modification of the storage capacity of an existing underground storage reservoir.

(Sec. 23-1301, Environmental Conservation Law)

Reports.—Underground storage operators are required to submit a report to the department by December 31 each year indicating any changes in:

— the estimated size in surface acreage or shape of the reservoir and the buffer zone if any;

— an estimate of total capacity of the reservoir;

— an estimate of working capacity of the reservoir; and

— other engineering, geological or operational data that may be requested by the department.

(Sec. 23-1301, Environmental Conservation Law)

• *Waste tire management and recycling fee*

Tire service providers are required to collect a fee from purchasers of new tires or new motor vehicles. The fee is scheduled for repeal on December 31, 2022. (Sec. 27-1913, Environmental Conservation Law)

Fee.—The waste tire management and recycling fee is $2.50 for each new tire sold, although sellers are entitled to retain a statutory allowance of 25¢ per tire from the fees collected. (Sec. 27-1913, Environmental Conservation Law)

Exemptions.—The waste tire management and recycling fee does not apply to:

— recapped or resold tires;

— mail-order sales; or

— the sale of new motor vehicle tires to a person solely for the purpose of resale provided the subsequent retail sale in New York is subject to the fee.

(Sec. 27-1913, Environmental Conservation Law)

Reports.—Tire service providers must file quarterly reports with the Department of Taxation and Finance until March 31, 2023, by the last day of March, June, September, and December. Copies of all reports must be retained by tire service providers for three years. (Sec. 27-1913, Environmental Conservation Law)

Tire service providers that cease to conduct business are required to file a final return and remit all fees due to the department not more than one month after discontinuing business. (Sec. 27-1913, Environmental Conservation Law)

UNCLAIMED PROPERTY

[¶37-350]

UNCLAIMED PROPERTY

[¶37-351] Unclaimed Property

Generally, property that is unclaimed by its rightful owner is presumed abandoned after a specified period of years following the date upon which the owner may demand the property or the date upon which the obligation to pay or distribute the property arises, whichever comes first.

What is unclaimed property?

Abandoned property includes all money or other personal property collected or received by the state comptroller or the Department of Taxation and Finance pursuant to state law.

COMMENT: Escheat is an area of potential federal/state conflict. A federal statute may preempt state escheat provisions, as for instance Sec. 514(a) of the Employee Retirement Income Security Act of 1974 (ERISA). Pursuant to this provision, the Department of Labor and Workforce Development has been of the opinion that funds of missing participants in a qualified employee benefit plan must stay in the plan despite a state escheat provision because ERISA preempts application of the state escheat laws with respect to such funds (Advisory Opinion 94-41A, Department of Labor, Pension and Welfare Benefit Administration, Dec. 7, 1994). Some states have challenged the federal position on this and similar narrowly delineated situations. Similar conflicts can arise with respect to SEC rules and the treatment of certain securities. Practitioners are thus advised that a specific situation where federal and state policy cross on the issue of escheat may, at this time, be an area of unsettled law. In the case of federal tax refunds, IRC Sec. 6408 disallows refunds if the refund would escheat to a state.

What are the dormancy periods for unclaimed property?

General rule. There is no general dormancy period for New York unclaimed property.

Checks and drafts. Three years of inactivity is required before uncashed checks, including certified checks held by banking corporations, are presumed abandoned.

Bank accounts. Bank and savings and loan deposits are considered abandoned after three years.

Property distributable in the course of demutualization or related reorganization of an insurance company. Any amount, security, or other distribution payable or distributable to a resident as the result of a demutualization or similar reorganization of an insurance company is deemed abandoned if, for two successive years all amounts, securities, or other distributions have remained unpaid to or unclaimed by the resident, and no written communication from the resident has been received by the holder.

Gift certificates, gift cards and credit memos. Any amount representing gift certificates remaining unclaimed by the owner for five years will be deemed abandoned property.

Stocks and other intangibles. Three years of inactivity is required before stock dividends, stocks and bonds may be presumed abandoned.

Other dormancy periods. Most states also have specified dormancy periods for:

Business association dissolutions/refunds,

Insurance policies,

IRAs/retirement funds,

Money orders,

Proceeds from class action suits,

Property held by fiduciaries,

Safe deposit boxes,

Shares in a financial institution,

Traveler's checks,

Utilities,

Wages/salaries, and

Property held by courts/public agencies.

Is there a business-to-business exemption for unclaimed property?

No, New York does not have a business-to-business exemption.

What are the notice requirements for unclaimed property?

At least 90 days prior to the applicable reporting date for the unclaimed property, the holder must send written notice by first class mail to each person appearing to be the owner of property listed in an abandoned property report. However, these requirements do not apply if the holder does not have an address for the owner or can demonstrate that the only address that the holder has pertaining to the owner is not the owner's current address.

With respect to property whose value exceeds $1,000, the holder is required to send a second written notice by certified mail, return receipt requested, at least 60 days prior to the applicable reporting date. Such notice is not required if the holder has received a claim from the owner of the property or the original mailing was returned as undeliverable. The cost of the notice by certified mail may be deducted from the property as a service charge.

Financial organizations, utilities, insurance companies, and corporations holding abandoned condemnation awards are required to publish the names of the owners of unclaimed property within 30 days of the report to the State Comptroller. An affidavit detailing proof of publication must be filed with the State Comptroller.

County treasurers or, in the case of the City of New York, the Commissioner of Finance, are similarly required to publish the names of persons believed to be the owners of abandoned court funds by February 1 of each year.

What are the reporting requirements for unclaimed property?

General requirements.

General corporations, mutual funds, state, municipal, or other public stock/bond issuers, brokers and dealers, title insurance companies. General corporations and brokers must file reports by March 10, for property unclaimed as of the prior December 31.

Banking institutions. Banking institutions holding property as of June 30 must file a preliminary report due August 1. Negative reports are due August

10, publication notices are due August 31, proof of publication is due September 10, and final reports are due November 10.

Insurance companies. For property held as of January 1 (December 31 for superannuated policies), insurance company preliminary or negative reports are due April 1, publication notices are due May 1, proof of publication is due May 10, and final reports are due September 10.

Utilities. For utilities holding property as of July 1, preliminary or negative reports are due August 1, publication notices are due August 31, proof of publication is due September 10, and final reports are due October 10.

Court funds. Court funds must be accompanied by a report and delivered to the state comptroller by April 10 for property held as of January 1.

Negative reporting. New York does not require negative reporting. (*Handbook for Reporters of Unclaimed Funds*, New York State Comptroller)

Minimum reporting. There is no minimum amount required to file in New York. (*Handbook for Reporters of Unclaimed Funds*, New York State Comptroller)

Aggregate reporting. Holders of unclaimed property may report property amounting to $20 or less in the aggregate, without specifying the name, address, or other identifying information of the owner.

Electronic reporting. Holders reporting more than 25 items are required to file electronically. (New York State Comptroller website)

Record keeping. Records must be retained for a period of five years following the end of the year in which the property was reported. Dealers and brokers must retain records for 10 years following the end of the year in which records are created.

MOTOR FUELS

[¶ 40-000]

MOTOR FUELS

[¶ 40-001] Gasoline Taxes

New York has a motor fuel excise tax and a diesel fuel excise tax. (See ¶ 40-003 Diesel Taxes) New York also participates in the International Fuel Tax Agreement (IFTA) and imposes tax on other fuels, including the petroleum business tax (¶ 40-005 Other Fuel Taxes).

The gasoline tax is an excise tax on fuel sold or used within New York State. (Sec. 284(1), Tax Law; 284-a, Tax Law)

COMPLIANCE ALERT: Hurricane Sandy relief.—The Hurricane Sandy motor fuel tax relief granted by Executive Order No. 54 (see *Important Notice N-12-13* below) expires at the end of the day on November 30, 2012. Accordingly, as of December 1, 2012, all fuel distributors and transporters are subject to the registration, licensing, certification, manifest, and record-keeping requirements provided under the Tax Law.

Fuel dealers who imported fuel into New York State during the period November 1, 2012, through November 30, 2012, while not registered as distributors of motor fuel or diesel motor fuel, must file Form FT-959, Special Fuel Tax Return for Unregistered Distributors (Hurricane Sandy Recovery Period) by December 20, 2012, and pay the applicable taxes for each gallon of motor fuel sold or used in New York State. (Important Notice N-12-19, New York Department of Taxation and Finance, November 2012)

CCH COMMENT: 2012 Hurricane Sandy.—The New York State Department of Taxation and Finance has issued an important notice stating that to aid in recovery efforts related to Hurricane Sandy, motor fuel and diesel fuel tax requirements related to registration, licensing, certification, manifest, and record keeping are suspended from November 1, 2012, until further notice. However, dealers who import fuel from outside the state but are not currently registered will have to remit applicable taxes, including excise tax, petroleum business tax, and prepaid sales tax. The department will provide additional details on how to report and pay these taxes, but returns and payments would not be due before December 20, 2012. (*Important Notice N-12-13*, New York Department of Taxation and Finance, November 5, 2012)

The statutory definition of "motor fuel" means gasoline, benzol, reformulated blend stock for oxygenate blending, conventional blend stock for oxygenate blending, E85, fuel grade ethanol that meets the ASTM International active standards specifications D4806 or D4814 or other product which is suitable for use in operation of a motor vehicle engine. (Sec. 282(2), Tax Law) By regulation, "motor fuel" means gasoline, benzol or other product, except kerosene and crude oil, which is suitable for use in the operation of a motor vehicle engine. If kerosene or crude oil is compounded or mixed with any other product or products, and the resulting compound or mixture is suitable for use in the operation of any such motor vehicle engine, such resulting compound or mixture in its entirety is motor fuel. Motor fuel includes, but is not limited to, gasoline, benzol, benzene, naphtha, ethanol, methanol, liquefied petroleum gas, compressed natural gas, propane gas, or any combination, or any other product, or combination of products, which is suitable for use in the operation of a motor vehicle engine. (Reg. Sec. 410.2)

"E85" means a fuel blend consisting of ethanol and motor fuel, which meets the ASTM International active standard D5798 for fuel ethanol. (Sec. 282(22), Tax Law)

Specific topics discussed below are:
— products subject to tax,
— point of taxation,
— license requirements,
— basis of tax,
— rate of tax
— exemptions,
— reports and payments,
— credits, refunds, and reimbursements, and
— local taxes.

• *Products subject to tax*

Although the tax is paid by the distributor, the ultimate burden of the tax falls on persons who use the public highways of the state for the operation of motor vehicles or who use New York waterways for the operation of recreational or pleasure motorboats. (Sec. 289-c(2), Tax Law)

Motor fuel brought into the state in an ordinary motor vehicle fuel tank and used directly from the tank to operate the vehicle is not considered imported. (Reg. Sec. 410.2)

A "purchaser" includes the usual meaning of the word and also includes a distributor who transfers motor fuel from its stock into a motor vehicle or into a container for later transfer to a motor vehicle. (Sec. 282(4), Tax Law)

• *Point of taxation*

The tax is imposed on motor fuels imported into the state by a distributor for use, distribution, storage, or sale, and on motor fuels that are produced, refined, manufactured or compounded by a distributor. The state collects the tax from distributors of motor fuel and diesel motor fuel who, in turn, are expected to collect the tax from the purchaser. The tax is paid to the state only once, with credits and refunds available. (Sec. 284(1), Tax Law)

• *License requirements*

Distributors.—In order to sell motor fuel in New York, a distributor must register with the Department of Taxation and Finance. (Sec. 283(1), Tax Law; Reg. Sec. 411.1) To register, a distributor must submit to the Department the following:

(1) a completed application (Form TP-128.3);

(2) current unqualified financial statements certified by a certified public accountant who has conducted an audit; and

(3) an estimate of the monthly number of gallons of motor fuel expected to be imported, produced, and distributed.

(Reg. Sec. 411.1)

¶40-001

Before a distributor may be registered, the distributor must file or deposit and maintain with the Department a bond executed by a surety company or other acceptable security. (Sec. 283(3), Tax Law; Reg. Sec. 411.2) The amount of the bond is calculated on the basis of the distributor's maximum potential tax liability, net worth, financial solvency and stability, and compliance record. (Reg. Sec. 411.2) A distributor's maximum potential tax liability is calculated on the basis of a formula.

Registration may be canceled if the distributor fails to comply with any of the statutory or regulatory provisions or to file a required bond. (Sec. 283(4), Tax Law) Such cancellation must be sent by registered mail to the distributor's address as given on his application or registration (or a later address if provided) and constitutes sufficient notice of the action. Applications for administrative review of a cancellation, suspension or denial of registration are filed with the Division of Tax Appeals. A determination of an administrative law judge (ALJ) must be issued within three months from the date that a timely application is filed. Within 15 days from the date that notice of the ALJ decision is given, an exception may be filed with the Tax Appeals Tribunal. The Tribunal must issue affirming or reversing the ALJ decision within 75 days from the date that the exception is taken.

The registration granted to a distributor is personal and may not be transferred without prior written approval of the Department. (Sec. 283(9), Tax Law; Reg. Sec. 411.8) Application for approval of a contemplated transfer is made in the same manner as an application for registration. (Reg. Sec. 411.8)

In addition to the usual meaning, a transfer of registration occurs if:

(1) a new partner is added or replaces an existing partner for a distributor that is a partnership or

(2) if more than 10% of the shares of voting stock of a distributor are acquired (25% if the entity has four or fewer shareholders).

(Reg. Sec. 411.8)

Upon the application of a person importing, manufacturing, selling, using or consuming liquefied petroleum gas identified as a fuel for use in the operation of a motor vehicle or a pleasure or recreational motor boat, the Department may issue a liquefied petroleum gas fuel permit in lieu of registration as a distributor, provided the person does not import motor fuel other than liquefied petroleum gas fuel into the state for use, distribution, storage or sale or produce, refine, manufacture or compound motor fuel other than liquefied petroleum gas fuel in the state. (Sec. 283-c, Tax Law) The Commissioner of Taxation and Finance may waive the requirement that holders of liquefied petroleum gas fuel permits file a bond or other security.

Wholesalers.—Wholesalers of motor fuel are required to register with the Department and file motor fuel tax returns. "Wholesaler of motor fuel" is defined as a person, firm, association or corporation who (1) is not a distributor of motor fuel; (2) makes a sale of motor fuel in New York other than a retail sale not in bulk; and (3) makes any purchases of motor fuel for resale within specified regions. (Sec. 282(27), Tax Law; Sec. 283-d, Tax Law; *TSB-M-16(7)M, (9)S*)

Bond or security may be required to register. (Sec. 283-d, Tax Law) Unregistered wholesalers are prohibited from making sales of motor fuel in New York other than a retail sale not in bulk. Any person not registered as a motor fuel wholesaler who makes a sale in New York other than a retail sale not in bulk may be guilty of a class E felony. (Sec. 1102(f), Tax Law; *TSB-M-16(7)M, (9)S*)

• *Basis of tax*

As a result of exemptions and refund provisions, the ultimate basis of tax is the number of gallons of motor fuel consumed in the operation of motor vehicles upon the highways of the state or in the operation of pleasure and recreational vehicles. (Sec. 289-c(2), Tax Law)

• *Rate of tax*

The total tax is 8¢ per gallon on motor fuel sold within the state, plus a petroleum testing fee, for a total rate of 8.05¢ per gallon. This rate includes the basic rate imposed of 4¢ (Sec. 284, Tax Law), an additional tax of 3¢ (Sec. 284-a, Tax Law), a supplemental tax of 1¢ (Sec. 284-c, Tax Law), and the petroleum testing fee, discussed below.

Petroleum testing fee.—A petroleum testing fee is also imposed on motor fuel imported, manufactured, or sold within New York by a distributor. The fee is equal to 1/2 of 1 mill per gallon of motor fuel. (Sec. 284-d, Tax Law)

• *Exemptions*

Sales that do not incur motor fuel tax liability generally fall into the following categories:

— fuel used to propel something other than a "motor vehicle" (Reg. Sec. 410.2(d));

— fuel not considered imported because it was brought into the state in the tank of a motor vehicle (Sec. 282(1), Tax Law);

— fuel sold to exempt government entities (Sec. 284(1), Tax Law; Reg. Sec. 412.1);

— fuel sold to qualified hospitals;

— fuel sold on U.S. military or other reservations unless the fuel sold is to be used for something other than federal purposes (Title 4, § 104, U.S.C.);

— the United Nations, as a retail purchaser of motor fuel, provided that the fuel is acquired by the United Nations for its official use. (Sec. 4, Tax Law; Reg. Sec. 414.5);

— sales of motor fuel to a registered or licensed distributor or dealer of motor fuel in another state or in a province of a foreign country provided that the fuel is exported immediately to an identified location in that state or province for purposes of selling it. (Reg. Sec. 412.1);

— fuel for immediate export (Reg. Sec. 414.1(3)); and

— fuel in foreign or interstate commerce. (Sec. 289-a, Tax Law)

Although farmers are not exempt from the motor fuel tax provisions, refunds are available for fuel used in farm vehicles that cannot be considered "motor vehicles." (TSB-M-79(6)M)

Generally, the burden of proving that a sale of motor fuel is exempt from tax is on the purchaser. (Reg. Sec. 414.1) In certain instances, the burden may also be on the person required to pass through the tax.

E85 fuel.—Sales of E85 fuel are exempt from New York motor fuel tax provided the E85 is delivered to and placed in a storage tank of a filling station to be dispensed directly into a motor vehicle for use in the operation of the motor vehicle, but is not exempt from the petroleum testing fee. This provision is repealed September 1, 2021. (Sec. 289-c.1-a.(d)(i), Tax Law; TSB-M-16(3)M, TSB-M-16(4)S)

B20.—Sales of B20 are partially exempt (20%) from motor fuel tax. This provision is repealed September 1, 2021. (Sec. 289-c.1-a.(d)(ii), Tax Law; TSB-M-16(3)M, TSB-M-16(4)S)

¶40-001

CNG, hydrogen fuel.—Sales of CNG or hydrogen for operation of a motor vehicle were exempt from motor fuel tax, but is not exempt from the petroleum testing fee. This provision is repealed September 1, 2021. (Sec. 289-c.1-a.(d)(iii), Tax Law; TSB-M-16(3)M, TSB-M-16(4)S)

Non-exempt sales.—As noted, the exemption applies only to motor fuel that is obtained for the governmental entity's own use or consumption. Accordingly, a governmental entity that does not use or otherwise consume the motor fuel on which no tax has been paid, but otherwise distributes the fuel in New York, is subject to tax on the fuel that is distributed. (Reg. Sec. 414.2)

State regulations also specifically provide that motor fuel used by contractors in connection with work done for governmental entities is not exempt from tax. (Reg. Sec. 414.2) Accordingly, where such contractors import or cause motor fuel to be imported into New York State or produce, refine, manufacture or compound motor fuel in New York, they are liable for the motor fuel tax and must be registered as distributors.

Proof of sales and delivery.—Retail sellers of motor fuel must keep a record of each tax-free sale indicating the date, quantity, name of purchaser and person to whom the fuel was delivered. (Reg. Sec. 414.2)

Refunds and reports.—Registered distributors who sell motor fuel to an exempt governmental body or agency must include such sales in their monthly returns, but can deduct that quantity to determine net gallons subject to tax. (Reg. Sec. 414.2)

Sales to volunteer fire departments, voluntary ambulance services, and volunteer rescue squads.—Motor fuel and diesel motor fuel tax paid by a volunteer fire department or company, volunteer rescue squad supported by public funds, or volunteer ambulance service is refundable.

• *Reports and payments*

Every motor fuel distributor and every wholesaler of motor fuel, must, on or before the 20th day of each month, file with the Department of Taxation and Finance a monthly return of tax on motor fuels on a form prescribed by the Department even if no tax is due. (Sec. 287, Tax Law; Reg. Sec. 413.1; Reg. Sec. 413.5) If the due date for filing the return falls on a Saturday, Sunday or a day which is a legal holiday in New York, the return is timely if filed on the next succeeding day which is not a Saturday, Sunday or legal holiday. (Reg. Sec. 2399.3)

The return must state the number of gallons of motor fuel, during the preceding calendar month, the distributor:

(1) imported or caused to be imported into New York for use, distribution, storage or sale in the state;

(2) produced, refined, manufactured or compounded in the state; or

(3) sold in the state (if the motor fuel tax had not been imposed prior to such sale).

The Department may, if it deems it necessary in order to insure the payment of any motor fuel taxes, require returns to be made at such times and covering such periods as it may determine.

The Department of Taxation and Finance has issued a publication that lists the product codes used to report fuels on New York State tax returns and reports. (*Publication 902*, New York Department of Taxation and Finance)

Certification required: Every return filed by or on behalf of a motor fuel distributor must include a certification that the statements in the return are true, correct and complete. The distributor's name and/or an individual's name signed on the certification of the return is *prima facie* evidence that the individual is authorized to sign and certify the return on behalf of the distributor and that the return was actually signed by the distributor.

Where to file: Returns are filed with the Department of Taxation and Finance, Miscellaneous Tax Bureau, P.O. Box 1833, Albany, N.Y. 12201-1883. (Reg. Sec. 413.1)

Every wholesaler, jobber or other person who is not required to file reports with the Department of Taxation and Finance, but who sells motor fuel other than exclusively at retail service stations, must file a report of sales tax prepayment on motor fuel on a prescribed form, regardless of whether any tax is due. The report must be filed monthly and is due within 20 days from the end of the month covered by the report.

Retail vendors who purchase, sell or use motor fuel must file quarterly motor fuel inventory reports by retail service stations within 25 days of the end of the sales tax quarter covered by the report.

Sales to exempt governmental bodies or agencies: Registered distributors who sell motor fuel to an exempt governmental body or agency must include such sales in their monthly returns, but can deduct that quantity to determine net gallons subject to tax. (Reg. Sec. 414.2)

Timely mailing as timely filing: For returns and other required documents, generally the date of the postmark stamped on the mailing envelope is considered the date of delivery as long as it is properly addressed, with sufficient postage and postmarked by the U.S. Post Office. (Reg. Sec. 2399.2) If the postmark is not stamped by the post office, the date of the postmark must be within the prescribed time period in order to be timely. For registered or certified mail, the date of registration or the postmark at the time of certification is treated as the date of delivery. For delivery services designated by the U.S. Secretary of the Treasury under IRC Sec. 7502, the postmark refers to any date recorded or marked in a manner described in IRC Sec. 7502. (Sec. 289-d, Tax Law) Currently there are four private delivery companies that filers can use. Here they are listed with the specific types of delivery service that qualify under IRC Sec. 7502: (1) Airborne Express (Airborne): Overnight Air Express Service; Next Afternoon Service; and Second Day Service; (2) DHL Worldwide Express (DHL): DHL "Same Day" Service and DHL USA Overnight; (3) Federal Express (FedEx): FedEx Priority Overnight; FedEx Standard Overnight; and FedEx 2 Day; and (4) United Parcel Service (UPS): UPS Next Day Air; UPS Next Day Air Saver; UPS 2nd Day Air; and UPS 2nd Day Air A.M. (*TSB-M-97(07)M*)

Payments.—Payment of the motor fuel tax and the diesel motor fuel tax is due with the return. (Sec. 287(1), Tax Law) The motor fuel tax is paid with the distributor's monthly return and the diesel fuel tax is paid with the distributor's monthly, quarterly, semi-annual or annual return.

The tax may be reported and paid in whole dollar amounts, disregarding amounts of less than 50¢ and including amounts greater than 50¢ by increasing such an amount to $1. (Reg. Sec. 413.2) Remittances are made payable to the Commissioner of Taxation and Finance.

Electronic funds transfer: New York has implemented a program requiring taxpayers to submit payments of motor fuel and diesel motor fuel taxes through electronic fund transfers (EFT) or certified checks where certain dollar threshold amounts are met. Generally, a taxpayer will be required to participate in the program if, on or after June 1 of any year, its tax liability for the June 1 through May 31 period immediately preceding the prior June 1 through May 31 period is $5 million or more. (Sec. 10, Tax Law; Reg. Sec. 2397.2)

¶40-001

Taxpayers that do not meet the dollar threshold noted above may apply for permission to participate in the program on a voluntary basis. Applications for voluntary participation will be granted unless the commissioner of taxation and finance determines that the administrative costs associated with accepting new enrollees outweigh the revenue and tax administration benefits associated with payment by EFT or certified check.

For hardship exemptions, see Reg. Sec. 2397.2(b).

Participating taxpayers must, on or before the third business day following the 22nd day of each calendar month, remit by EFT or certified check either:

(1) 75% of the motor fuel or diesel motor fuel taxes properly payable by the taxpayer for the comparable month of the preceding year; or

(2) its total liability for motor fuel or diesel motor fuel taxes during the first 22 days of the month.

(Reg. Sec. 2397.6)

No penalties or interest will be imposed if the taxpayer timely remits tax in an amount not less than 90% of the taxes finally determined to be due and payable for such period.

Any remaining tax liability owed by the taxpayer for the period must accompany the filing of the taxpayer's monthly return. Such amounts may not be submitted by electronic fund transfer.

See also Payment Methodsfor information on electronic funds transfer (EFT) payments under **Sales and use, Motor fuels, and petroleum business taxes.**

• *Credits, refunds, and reimbursements*

All refund claims must be on forms prescribed by the Department of Taxation and Finance. Such claims must include a certificate indicating that the refund claim is just, true and correct and that no part of the refund has been paid except as stated and that the balance is due and owing. The department must be satisfied that the tax was actually paid in the amount claimed and that the fuel was consumed in a manner which would entitle the taxpayer to a refund. Refunds are paid from gasoline tax revenues which are deposited with the comptroller. (Sec. 289-c(3)(c), Tax Law)

Sale to exempt governmental body or agency.—Registered distributors who sell motor fuel to an exempt governmental body or agency must include such sales in their monthly returns, but can deduct that quantity to determine net gallons subject to tax. (Reg. Sec. 414.2)

Taxicab licensees.—Taxicab licensees operating in New York are entitled to a refund of motor fuel tax paid in excess of 4¢ a gallon of the aggregate amount imposed by Secs. 284 (4¢) and 284-a (3¢), Tax Law. Therefore, the refund available to taxicab licensees for motor fuel tax paid is limited to 3¢ per gallon. (Reg. Sec. 415.3)

Nonpublic school operators.—A nonpublic school operator that purchases motor fuel is entitled to a full refund of the tax imposed provided the fuel was consumed exclusively for education-related activities. (Sec. 289-c(3)(e), Tax Law)

Voluntary ambulance services.—Any volunteer ambulance service which purchases motor fuel on which the tax has been paid is entitled to a full refund of the tax imposed provided the fuel was consumed in an ambulance vehicle operating within the state. (Sec. 289-c(3)(f), Tax Law)

A volunteer ambulance service making such a refund claim must indicate that it has paid the tax and that the tax is reimbursable within the meaning of the statute. (TSB-M-78(7)M)

See the sales tax exemption provision for volunteer fire departments, volunteer ambulance services and volunteer rescue squads, ¶ 60-020.

Commercial fishing vessels.—The determination of whether a vessel with a license to fish and sell a portion of its catch is entitled to a refund of motor fuel tax is a factual question. (*Montauk Marine Basin (Advisory Opinion)*) In making this determination, the Department of Taxation and Finance will consider collectively the provisions of Articles 12-A, 13-A, 28 and 29 as they apply to commercial fishers and commercial fishing vessels. The criteria to be met include, but are not limited to:

(1) the fact that the fisherman falls within the definition of a commercial fisherman, taking into consideration the amount of time, capital and effort that are consumed by the fisherman, as well as the percent of total gross income from all sources such fisherman has derived from the harvesting of fish for sale; and

(2) whether the commercial fishing vessel was used directly and predominantly (more than 50%) in the harvesting of fish for sale.

Fishing vessels used directly and predominantly in the harvesting of fish for sale do not include any vessel used predominantly (more than 50%) for sport fishing. If the fisherman and vessel do not fall within the provisions of Articles 12-A, 13-A, 28 and 29 as they apply to vessels engaged in commercial fishing, no reimbursement of the taxes paid on fuel used in the vessel will be allowed.

Vessels.—Motor fuel brought into the state in a fuel tank connecting with the engine of a vessel propelled by that petroleum or fuel upon which a consumption or use tax is imposed, may be eligible for a refund or credit. The tax liability is the positive difference between the gallonage consumed in the state and the gallonage purchased in the state upon which tax was imposed. A credit or refund is available for any excess of tax liability for gallonage purchased upon which tax was imposed and gallonage consumed in the state. These provisions do not apply to recreational motor boats or commercial fishing boats when the fuel is used to operate a vessel engaged in harvesting fish for sale. (Sec. 301(c), Tax Law; Sec. 301-a(b)(2), Tax Law; Sec. 301-a(c)(1)(B), Tax Law)

CCH COMMENT: *Vessel fuel consumption tax provisions invalid.*—On June 7, 2001, in *Moran Towing Corp. et al.* the Appellate Division, Third Department, declared the fuel consumption tax found in subdivisions (b)(2) and (c)(1)(B) of Sec. 301-a, Tax Law, to be unconstitutional.

Government purchases by credit card.—Credit card companies and motor fuel distributors that finance the purchase of such fuel by governmental entities using credit cards are allowed a credit or refund of New York motor fuel taxes on such purchases. (Sec. 289-c(3).(h), Tax Law) This provision is intended to conform to federal tax legislation that creates a system for credit card issuers and fuel distributors to receive refunds of the federal excise tax on fuel purchases by governmental entities using credit cards.

Credit card issuers may apply for a refund, and fuel distributors may apply for a refund or credit, of motor fuel taxes paid on purchases of fuel by government entities and paid for with a credit card or other access card if all of the following criteria are met:

— the Department must receive Form FT-505.1, Government Entity Credit Card Refund or Credit Election, signed by an authorized representative of the government entity and the credit card issuer or fuel distributor certifying that the credit card issuer or fuel distributor is the only party eligible to receive the refund or credit;

¶40-001

— if the credit card issuer is designated to apply for the refund, it must register for sales tax purposes (if not already registered), obtain a Certificate of Authority, and file sales tax returns;

— the sales and excise taxes were actually paid to the Department, and no refund or credit was previously claimed or allowed for those taxes;

— the government entity purchased the fuel for its own use or consumption and it therefore qualifies as an exempt purchase;

— the Department has not issued a notice of ineligibility to the government entity, and to either the credit card issuer or fuel distributor;

— the credit card issuer or fuel distributor designated to receive the refund or credit (1) must certify that it will not charge or otherwise receive any excise taxes from the government entity making the purchase, and (2) must file a written consent signed by an authorized representative of the government entity stating that no tax will be charged to the government entity by the credit card issuer or fuel distributor and that the government entity will not claim a refund or credit related to its purchases of fuel made by a credit card provided by the issuer. These conditions are included on Form FT-505.1 as part of the consent for filing the election;

— the credit card issuer or fuel distributor must certify that (1) the retail station or other vendor has been repaid the excise taxes it charged to the government entity on its fuel purchases, or (2) it has obtained a written consent from the retail station or other vendor to receive the refund or credit for the excise taxes; and

— the credit card issuer or fuel distributor must, upon request by the Department, provide detailed transactional and jurisdictional information related to the fuel sales in the form requested by the Department.

(*TSB-M-08(9)M*, Office of Tax Policy Analysis, New York Department of Taxation and Finance, November 5, 2008)

Applying for a refund or credit.—Fuel distributors may apply for a credit of the excise taxes paid on motor fuel by filing Form PT-101, Tax on Motor Fuels. The credit claimed on Form PT-101 is carried over to Form PT-100, Petroleum Business Tax Return and may result in a refund or credit. These forms may be filed after the end of the month in which the government entity purchased the fuel. Fuel distributors may continue to claim a credit for the prepaid sales tax on Form FT-945/1045, Report of Sales Tax Prepayment on Motor Fuel/Diesel Motor Fuel on a monthly basis. Fuel distributors may claim a refund of the additional sales tax (the difference between the retail sales tax repaid to the retail vendor and the prepaid sales tax paid by the distributor) using Form FT-500, Application for Refund of Sales Tax Paid on Automotive Fuels, after the end of the quarter in which the fuel was purchased by the government entity. (*TSB-M-08(9)M*, Office of Tax Policy Analysis, New York Department of Taxation and Finance, November 5, 2008)

Liability.—The Department may issue an assessment for tax, penalty, and interest to a credit issuer or fuel distributor for any refund or credit that was allowed or paid that was erroneous, illegal, or unconstitutional. In addition, a penalty equal to the amount of tax refunded or credited, plus applicable interest, may also be imposed on any credit card issuer or fuel distributor that files a refund application or takes a credit knowing that the fuel purchased by government entity was not for the government entity's own use or consumption. (*TSB-M-08(9)M*, Office of Tax Policy Analysis, New York Department of Taxation and Finance, November 5, 2008)

Credit in lieu of a refund.—Unless the Commissioner of Taxation and Finance withdraws the privilege, a distributor entitled to a refund may instead take a credit for it on its monthly return. (Sec. 287(2), Tax Law)

For a description of the refund process for farmers, see Technical Services Bureau Memorandum TSB-M-79(6)M.

With regard to taxpayer remedies, see ¶89-230 Taxpayer Conferences for a discussion regarding conciliation conferences.

Refunds for fuel taxed but not used for purposes subject to tax.—Any person who buys motor fuel on which the required tax has already been paid but uses the fuel in a manner other than for the operation of a motor vehicle on New York highways or the operation of a pleasure or recreational motorboat is entitled to a refund. (Reg. Sec. 415.3) A refund is not permitted, however, for the tax paid on motor fuel taken out of state in the tank of a motor vehicle for consumption outside the state. Motor fuel leaving the state in this manner is not considered an export. (Sec. 289-c(8), Tax Law; Sec. 301-b(b)(3), Tax Law)

Refund application.—The application must include all claims for the calendar month, but two or more calendar months may be combined in one application. Refund claims may be made within three years of the earliest purchase on the application. (Reg. Sec. 415.1)

Any person selling motor fuel to an exempt purchaser may exclude the amount of tax from the selling price and claim a refund or credit. (Reg. Sec. 415.2)

All motor fuel tax refund claims are subject to Reg. Sec. 415.2 provisions.

Provisions for omnibus carriers.—Two refund provisions apply to omnibus carriers. A partial refund is available to carriers operating in New York and a full refund applies to omnibus carriers using fuel for local transit service.

Omnibus carrier defined.—An omnibus carrier is any person engaged in operating an omnibus line subject to the State Department of Public Services under Article 3-A of the Public Service Law. (Sec. 282, Tax Law)This definition includes buses used for transporting school children under a contract made pursuant to provisions of the Education Law.

New York State omnibus carriers.—Omnibus carriers operating in New York are entitled to a refund of any amount paid in excess of 4¢ a gallon of the aggregate tax imposed by Secs. 284 (4¢) and 284-a (3¢), Tax Law. (Sec. 289-c(3)(b), Tax Law) As a result, the refund available to omnibus carriers for motor fuel tax paid is limited to 3¢ per gallon. (Reg. Sec. 415.3)

Omnibus carriers in local transit service.—A full refund of motor fuel tax is provided for any carrier operating an omnibus for local transit service pursuant to a certificate of convenience and necessity issued by the New York Commissioner of Transportation, the U.S. Interstate Commerce Commission or pursuant to a contract, franchise or consent of the City of New York or one of its agencies. In order to be eligible for a refund of the tax, the fuel must be used in local transit service. (Sec. 289-c(3)(d), Tax Law)

Local transit services defined.—An omnibus "in local transit service" is one that provides mass transit by carrying passengers from one point in the state to another and either:

   (1) picks up or discharges passengers at their convenience or at specific bus stops on the street or highway, or

   (2) picks up and discharges passengers at a bus terminal traveling at a distance of up to 75 miles between terminals, as measured by the bus route.

¶40-001

Excluded from this definition of local transit service are charter, contract, school bus, sightseeing or other such services. (Reg. Sec. 415.3) Note that even if the omnibus carrier is not considered "in local transit service," it may be eligible for the partial refund for omnibus carriers in New York State described in the previous paragraph.

Records.—Local omnibus carriers claiming a refund or credit must maintain a vehicular trip record for each bus including the vehicle number, date of each trip, origin and destination of each trip, points between which the refund or credit is claimed, total miles traveled, credit or refund miles claimed, gallons of fuel consumed and gallons credit or refund claimed. Without the information required, there is an insufficient basis for a credit allowance unless approved by the Department of Taxation and Finance. (Reg. Sec. 415.3)

Refund of taxes paid in error.—Fuel taxes paid may be refunded for motor fuel sold under circumstances for which the fuel would not be taxable. (Sec. 289-c(6), Tax Law)

A refund claim for taxes paid in error must be accompanied by a certificate indicating that the claim is just, true and correct, that no part of the refund had been paid except as indicated and that the balance is actually due and owing. (Reg. Sec. 415.4) Such a claim generally must be filed within two years of the erroneous payment. (Sec. 289-c(6), Tax Law) However, if the taxpayer consents to extend the limitation time for the determination of the tax, a claim for refund may be filed within six months after the expiration of the extended payment. (Sec. 289-c(7), Tax Law)

Interest on refunds.—Interest, equal to the overpayment rate set by the Commissioner of Taxation and Finance, is allowed for refunds or reimbursements paid to:

(1) distributors or purchasers registered with or licensed by another state as a motor fuel distributor or dealer with respect to fuel imported, manufactured or sold or purchased in New York State. (Sec. 289-c(8), Tax Law) For the exemption to apply, the distributor or purchaser must be registered with or licensed by the state to which the fuel is exported as a distributor or dealer in the fuel being exported; and

(2) exempt organizations under Sec. 1116(a)(4), Tax Law, which include corporations, associations, trusts, community chests, funds or foundations organized and operated exclusively for religious, charitable, scientific testing for public safety, literary or educational purposes or which are involved in fostering national or international amateur sports competition or prevention of cruelty to children or animals.

(Sec. 289-c(9), Tax Law)

No interest is allowed with respect to refunds to motor fuel distributors or dealers if the refund check is mailed within 30 days of receipt of a claim for refund in processible form or if the interest allowed is less than one dollar. (Sec. 289-c(8), Tax Law) No interest is allowed with respect to reimbursement to exempt organizations under Sec. 1116(a)(4), Tax Law, if the reimbursement check is mailed within 45 days of receipt by the Commissioner of the application for reimbursement or if the amount of interest is less than one dollar. (Sec. 289-c(9), Tax Law) For current interest rates, and rates in effect for prior periods, see ¶ 89-204.

• *Local taxes*

There are no local provisions concerning the motor fuel tax.

[¶40-003] Diesel Fuel Taxes

An excise tax is imposed on the first sale or use of diesel motor fuel within New York by a distributor. (Sec. 282-a(1), Tax Law) Except for definitions specifically considered below, the definitions applicable to motor fuels also apply to diesel motor fuels. See ¶40-001 Gasoline Taxes.

"Diesel motor fuel" means No. 1 Diesel fuel, No. 2 Diesel fuel, biodiesel, kerosene, crude oil, fuel oil or other middle distillate and also motor fuel suitable for use in the operation of an engine of the diesel type, excluding, however, any product specifically designated "No. 4 Diesel fuel" and not suitable as a fuel used in the operation of a motor vehicle engine. (Sec. 282(14), Tax Law) It does not include, however, any product specifically designated "No. 4 diesel fuel" and not suitable as a fuel used in the operation of a vehicle engine.

"Non-highway Diesel motor fuel" means any Diesel motor fuel that is designated for use other than on a public highway (except for the use of the public highway by farmers to reach adjacent lands), and is dyed Diesel motor fuel. (Sec. 282(16), Tax Law)

"Highway Diesel motor fuel" means any Diesel motor fuel which is not non-highway Diesel motor fuel. (Sec. 282(16-a), Tax Law)

The New York Department of Taxation and Finance has issued a memorandum that discusses various definitions for diesel fuel tax purposes that have been amended to conform to federal tax provisions. (TSB-M-11(6)M, TSB-M-11(11)S, Taxpayer Guidance Division, New York Department of Taxation and Finance, July 29, 2011)

Enhanced/unenhanced diesel motor fuel.—The terms "enhanced diesel motor fuel" and "unenhanced diesel motor fuel" are obsolete. It is no longer necessary to determine if the fuel is labeled as diesel fuel, No. 1 diesel fuel, No. 2 diesel fuel, or similar designation, or if it is a blended product that it will be used as diesel fuel in a motor vehicle. Also, reference the fuel's sulfur content is no longer necessary to determine its taxability. (TSB-M-11(6)M, TSB-M-11(11)S)

Specific topics discussed below are:

— persons subject to tax,

— basis of tax,

— rate of tax

— exemptions,

— reports and payments, and

— credits, refunds, and reimbursements.

• *Persons subject to tax*

The tax is imposed on distributors. (Sec. 282-a(1), Tax Law) The tax is imposed on diesel motor fuel on the removal of highway diesel motor fuel from a registered terminal other than by pipeline, barge, tanker, or other vessel. (Sec. 301-b, Tax Law)

Persons are considered distributors if they do one or more of the following within New York:

(1) import diesel motor fuel for use, distribution, storage or sale;

(2) produce, refine, manufacture or compound diesel motor fuel;

(3) who or which makes a sale or use of Diesel motor fuel in this state other than

(A) a retail sale not in bulk or

(B) the self-use of Diesel motor fuel which has been the subject of a retail sale to such person;

(4) the self-use of Diesel motor fuel which has been the subject of a retail sale to such person;

(5) who or which is registered by the department as a distributor of kero-jet fuel.

(Sec. 282(13), Tax Law)

Distributors of diesel motor fuel must be registered with the Department of Taxation and Finance. (Sec. 282-a(2), Tax Law)

Terminal operators in the State receiving, storing and dispensing diesel fuel are required to register with the Department as a terminal operator and file monthly activity returns. Additional record keeping may also be required. (Sec. 282(1)(b), Tax Law)

Wholesalers of motor fuel are required to register with the Department and file motor fuel tax returns. "Wholesaler of motor fuel" is defined as a person, firm, association or corporation who (1) is not a distributor of motor fuel; (2) makes a sale of motor fuel in New York other than a retail sale not in bulk; and (3) makes any purchases of motor fuel for resale within specified regions. (Sec. 282(27), Tax Law; Sec. 283-d, Tax Law; *TSB-M-16(7)M, (9)S*)

• *Basis of tax*

The motor fuel tax imposed by Article 12-A is based upon the number of gallons of motor fuel or diesel motor fuel sold within the state by a distributor. (Sec. 284(1), Tax Law; Sec. 282-a(1), Tax Law) The first sale or use of diesel motor fuel to occur is taxed, as well as the delivery of diesel motor fuel to a filling station or into the fuel tank of a motor vehicle for its operation, whichever occurs first, provided that the tax has not been imposed previously. (Sec. 282-a(1), Tax Law)

• *Rate of tax*

Diesel motor fuel excise tax rates effective January 1, 2020 are as follows:

— Highway diesel motor fuel . . . . 8¢
— Highway B20. . . . . 6.4¢
— Undyed kerosene . . . . 8¢
— Non-highway diesel motor fuel. . . . . none
— Non-highway B20 . . . . none
— Dyed kerosene . . . . none

(Sec. 282-a(1), Tax Law; Sec. 282-b, Tax Law; Sec. 282-c, Tax Law; *Publication 908*)

• *Exemptions*

Sales that do not incur motor fuel tax liability generally fall into the following categories:

— fuel not considered imported because it was brought into the state in the tank of a motor vehicle (Sec. 282(1), Tax Law);

— fuel sold to exempt government entities (Sec. 284(1), Tax Law; Reg. Sec. 412.1);

— fuel sold to qualified hospitals.

In addition, sales between registered distributors may be tax-free under certain circumstances. (See below under *Interdistributor sales.*)

The following sales are specifically excluded from the tax on diesel motor fuel (Sec. 282-a(3), Tax Law):

(1) sale or use of untaxed diesel motor fuel to or by New York State, its agencies, instrumentalities, public corporations (including a public corporation created under an agreement or compact with another state or Canada) or political subdivisions or the United States, and any of its agencies and instrumentalities, where the diesel motor fuel is used by the exempt organization for its own use or consumption;

(2) consumer sale or use of previously untaxed diesel motor fuel which is not enhanced and which is used exclusively for heating purposes or consumption directly and exclusively in the production of tangible personal property, gas, electricity, refrigeration or steam. (Sec. 282-a(3), Tax Law) The exemption does not apply to a sale of diesel motor fuel which involves a delivery at a filling station or into a repository equipped with a hose or other apparatus by which such fuel can be dispensed into the fuel tank of a motor vehicle;

(3) sale of previously untaxed diesel motor fuel which is not enhanced to a registered distributor of diesel motor fuel other than retail sales to registered distributors of motor fuel or sales which involve a delivery at a filling station or into a repository equipped to dispense fuel into the tank of a motor vehicle;

(4) sale or use of enhanced diesel motor fuel to or by a consumer exclusively for certain heating purposes only if the enhanced diesel motor fuel is delivered into a storage tank which is not equipped with a hose or other apparatus by which the fuel can be dispensed into the fuel tank of a motor vehicle and the storage tank is attached to a heating unit burning such fuel subject to certification requirements pertaining to gallonage;

(5) sale or use consisting of no more than 4,500 gallons of diesel motor fuel in a 30-day period to or by a consumer for use or consumption directly and exclusively in the production for sale of tangible personal property of farming if all of the fuel is delivered on the farm site and is consumed other than on the highways of New York State (except for use of the highway to adjacent farmlands). A farmer may purchase more than 4,500 gallons of diesel motor fuel in a 30-day period for use or consumption exempt from the tax with prior clearance given by the Commissioner of Taxation and Finance;

(6) sale to the consumer consisting of not more than 20 gallons of water-white kerosene to be used and consumed exclusively for heating purposes;

(7) sale to or delivery at a filling station or other retail vendor of water-white kerosene if the retail vendor or filling stations sell only water-white kerosene for heating purposes in containers of not more than 20 gallons; or

(8) sale of kero-jet fuel to an airline for use in its airplanes or a use of kero-jet fuel by an airline in its airplanes.

An exempt transaction certificate, inter-distributor sale certificate, or other relevant document provided by the Commissioner of Taxation and Finance must be shown to the seller by the purchaser at the time of, or prior to, delivery of the diesel motor fuel. (Sec. 285-b, Tax Law)

Interdistributor sales.—In addition, exemption provisions allow clear undyed diesel motor fuel to be sold in the State tax-free between registered distributors. These interdistributor sales are permitted where: (A) the highway diesel fuel is delivered by pipeline, railcar, barge, tanker or other vessel; or (B) within a registered diesel fuel terminal. (Sec. 301-b, Tax Law)

¶40-003

CCH COMMENT: Interdistributor exemption.—Sales of previously untaxed highway diesel motor fuel by a person registered as a distributor of diesel motor fuel to another person registered as a distributor of diesel motor fuel are exempt from the excise tax, petroleum business tax, and prepaid sales tax if the fuel is: delivered by pipeline, railcar, barge, tanker or other vessel to a terminal of a licensed/registered operator, or sold within a diesel fuel terminal where it was delivered.

Form FT-1001, Exemption Certificate for Diesel Motor Fuel Interdistributor Transactions, allows registered distributors of diesel motor fuel to claim the interdistributor exemption for highway diesel motor fuel. Also, any person who has the use or control, or the right to use or control, a diesel motor fuel storage facility with a storage capacity of 50,000 gallons or more (other than a facility where fuel is stored solely for retail sale at the facility or for the person's own use or consumption) must be licensed/registered as a terminal operator. (*TSB-M-13(7)M, TSB-M-13(5)S*, Taxpayer Guidance Division, New York Department of Taxation and Finance, July 11, 2013)

The New York State Department of Taxation and Finance has issued a memorandum that lists exemptions from various taxes due on diesel motor fuel or kerosene. (TSB-M-11(6)M, TSB-M-11(11)S, Taxpayer Guidance Division, New York Department of Taxation and Finance, July 29, 2011)

Kerosene.—The New York Department of Taxation and Finance has issued a memorandum concerning the motor fuels tax exemption and refund provisions for kerosene. (TSB-M-11(12)M, TSB-M-11(18)S, Taxpayer Guidance Division, New York Department of Taxation and Finance, October 6, 2011)

Partial exemptions.—Sales of B20 fuel, or diesel motor fuel mixed with 20% biodiesel, are partially exempt from motor fuel tax. The exemption is equal to 20% of the applicable taxes. Accordingly, the excise tax for B20 will be computed using 80% of the excise tax rate. The seller may exclude 20% of the amount of the tax or taxes imposed from the selling price of B20. The seller must provide the purchaser with a completed Form FT-1000, Certificate of Prepayment or Payment of Taxes on Diesel Motor Fuel, or an invoice or other billing document showing the taxes being charged on each sale of B20. The partial exemption expires September 1, 2016. (Sec. 289-c, Tax Law; *TSB-M-06(2)M*, New York Department of Taxation and Finance, August 11, 2006; *TSB-M-16(3)M, TSB-M-16(4)S*, New York Department of Taxation and Finance, July 22, 2016) If B20 sold in New York on or after September 1, 2006, and the taxes incurred by the purchaser are greater than the tax computed at 80% of the total tax, the purchaser may submit a claim for a partial credit or refund of the tax. The purchaser must provide documentary evidence of the entire amount of taxes incurred.

• *Reports and payments*

Distributors of diesel motor fuel and wholesalers of motor fuel, are required to file monthly returns and report the number of gallons of motor fuel imported, manufactured, or sold by the distributor during the preceding calendar month and the number of gallons of Diesel motor fuel imported and the number of gallons which have been sold or used. (Sec. 287, Tax Law) The Commissioner of Taxation and Finance may require returns to be filed quarterly, semi-annually or annually instead of monthly.

The Department of Taxation and Finance has issued a publication that lists the product codes used to report fuels on New York State tax returns and reports. (*Publication 902*)

Distributors of diesel motor fuel that is used exclusively for heating purposes or for use or consumption directly and exclusively in the production of tangible personal property, gas, electricity, refrigeration or steam, may elect to file quarterly. Persons who distribute kero-jet fuel exclusively may also elect to file quarterly. (Sec. 286(3), Tax Law)

Timely mailing as timely filing: For returns and other required documents, generally the date of the postmark stamped on the mailing envelope is considered the date of delivery as long as it is properly addressed, with sufficient postage and postmarked by the U.S. Post Office. (Reg. Sec. 2399.2) If the postmark is not stamped by the post office, the date of the postmark must be within the prescribed time period in order to be timely. For registered or certified mail, the date of registration or the postmark at the time of certification is treated as the date of delivery. For delivery services designated by the U.S. Secretary of the Treasury under IRC Sec. 7502, the postmark refers to any date recorded or marked in a manner described in IRC Sec. 7502. (Sec. 289-d, Tax Law) Currently there are four private delivery companies that filers can use. Here they are listed with the specific types of delivery service that qualify under IRC § 7502:

(1) Airborne Express (Airborne): Overnight Air Express Service; Next Afternoon Service; and Second Day Service;

(2) DHL Worldwide Express (DHL): DHL "Same Day" Service and DHL USA Overnight;

(3) Federal Express (FedEx): FedEx Priority Overnight; FedEx Standard Overnight; and FedEx 2 Day; and

(4) United Parcel Service (UPS): UPS Next Day Air; UPS Next Day Air Saver; UPS 2nd Day Air; and UPS 2nd Day Air A.M.

(*TSB-M-97(07)M*)

Payments.—Payment of the diesel motor fuel tax is due with the return. (Sec. 287(1), Tax Law) The tax is paid with the distributor's monthly, quarterly, semiannual or annual return.

The tax may be reported and paid in whole dollar amounts, disregarding amounts of less than 50¢ and including amounts greater than 50¢ by increasing such an amount to $1. (Reg. Sec. 413.2) Remittances are made payable to the Commissioner of Taxation and Finance.

Electronic funds transfer: New York has implemented a program requiring taxpayers to submit payments of diesel motor fuel tax through electronic fund transfers (EFT) or certified checks where certain dollar threshold amounts are met. Generally, a taxpayer will be required to participate in the program if, on or after June 1 of any year, its tax liability for the June 1 through May 31 period immediately preceding the prior June 1 through May 31 period is $5 million or more. (Sec. 10, Tax Law; Reg. Sec. 2397.2)

Taxpayers that do not meet the dollar threshold noted above may apply for permission to participate in the Program on a voluntary basis. Applications for voluntary participation will be granted unless the Commissioner of Taxation and Finance determines that the administrative costs associated with accepting new enrollees outweigh the revenue and tax administration benefits associated with payment by EFT or certified check.

¶40-003

For hardship exemptions, see Reg. Sec. 2397.2(b).

Participating taxpayers must, on or before the third business day following the 22nd day of each calendar month, remit by EFT or certified check either:

(1) 75% of the diesel motor fuel tax properly payable by the taxpayer for the comparable month of the preceding year; or

(2) its total liability for diesel motor fuel tax during the first 22 days of the month.

(Reg. Sec. 2397.6)

No penalties or interest will be imposed if the taxpayer timely remits tax in an amount not less than 90% of the taxes finally determined to be due and payable for such period. Any remaining tax liability owed by the taxpayer for the period must accompany the filing of the taxpayer's monthly return. Such amounts may not be submitted by electronic fund transfer.

For other details, see ¶ 89-106 Electronic Filing.

See also Payment Methods, ¶ 89-108 for information on electronic funds transfer (EFT) payments under **Sales and use, Motor fuels, and petroleum business taxes.**

• *Credits, refunds, and reimbursements*

All refund claims must be on forms prescribed by the Department of Taxation and Finance. Such claims must include a certificate indicating that the refund claim is just, true and correct and that no part of the refund has been paid except as stated and that the balance is due and owing. The department must be satisfied that the tax was actually paid in the amount claimed and that the fuel was consumed in a manner which would entitle the taxpayer to a refund. Refunds are paid from gasoline tax revenues which are deposited with the comptroller. (Sec. 289-c(3)(c), Tax Law)

The New York State Department of Taxation and Finance has issued a memorandum that lists the various refunds, reimbursements, or credits for taxes paid on diesel motor fuel. (TSB-M-11(6)M, TSB-M-11(11)S, Taxpayer Guidance Division, New York Department of Taxation and Finance, July 29, 2011)

Taxicab licenses.—Taxicab licensees using diesel motor fuel are entitled to a refund of the diesel motor fuel tax paid in excess of 6¢ a gallon of the aggregate amount imposed by Secs. 282-a (6¢) and 282-b (3¢), Tax Law. (Sec. 289-c(3)(b), Tax Law)

Nonpublic school operators.—A nonpublic school operator who purchases diesel motor fuel is entitled to a full refund of the tax imposed provided the fuel was consumed exclusively for education-related activities. (Sec. 289-c(3)(e), Tax Law) A "nonpublic school operator" includes any nonpublic elementary or secondary school which owns or leases and operates any vehicle exclusively for its own purposes. (Sec. 282(11), Tax Law)

Voluntary ambulance services.—Any volunteer ambulance service which purchases diesel motor fuel on which the tax has been paid is entitled to a full refund of the tax imposed provided the fuel was consumed in an ambulance vehicle operating within the state. (Sec. 289-c(3)(f), Tax Law)

A volunteer ambulance service making such a refund claim must indicate that it has paid the tax and that the tax is reimbursable within the meaning of the statute. (TSB-M-78(7)M)

See the sales tax exemption provision for volunteer fire departments, volunteer ambulance services and volunteer rescue squads, ¶ 60-020.

Vessels.—Diesel fuel brought into the state in a fuel tank connecting with the engine of a vessel propelled by that petroleum or fuel upon which a consumption or use tax is imposed, may be eligible for a refund or credit. The tax liability is the positive difference between the gallonage consumed in the state and the gallonage purchased in the state upon which tax was imposed. A credit or refund is available for any excess of tax liability for gallonage purchased upon which tax was imposed and gallonage consumed in the state. These provisions do not apply to recreational motor boats or commercial fishing boats when the fuel is used to operate a vessel engaged in harvesting fish for sale. (Sec. 301(c), Tax Law; Sec. 301-a(b)(2), Tax Law; Sec. 301-a(c)(1)(B), Tax Law)

> **CCH COMMENT:** *Vessel fuel consumption tax provisions invalid.*—On June 7, 2001, in *Moran Towing Corp. et al.,* the Appellate Division, Third Department, declared the fuel consumption tax found in subdivisions (b)(2) and (c)(1)(B) of Sec. 301-a, Tax Law, to be unconstitutional.

For a general discussion of refunds, see ¶ 89-224 Refunds.

Government purchases by credit card.—Credit card companies and motor diesel fuel distributors that finance the purchase of such fuel by governmental entities using credit cards are allowed a credit or refund of New York motor fuel taxes on such purchases. (Sec. 289-c(3)(h), Tax Law) This provision is intended to conform to federal tax legislation that creates a system for credit card issuers and fuel distributors to receive refunds of the federal excise tax on fuel purchases by governmental entities using credit cards.

Credit card issuers may apply for a refund, and fuel distributors may apply for a refund or credit, of motor fuel taxes paid on purchases of fuel by government entities and paid for with a credit card or other access card if all of the following criteria are met:

— the Department must receive Form FT-505.1, Government Entity Credit Card Refund or Credit Election, signed by an authorized representative of the government entity and the credit card issuer or fuel distributor certifying that the credit card issuer or fuel distributor is the only party eligible to receive the refund or credit;

— if the credit card issuer is designated to apply for the refund, it must register for sales tax purposes (if not already registered), obtain a Certificate of Authority, and file sales tax returns;

— the sales and excise taxes were actually paid to the Department, and no refund or credit was previously claimed or allowed for those taxes;

— the government entity purchased the fuel for its own use or consumption and it therefore qualifies as an exempt purchase;

— the Department has not issued a notice of ineligibility to the government entity, and to either the credit card issuer or fuel distributor;

— the credit card issuer or fuel distributor designated to receive the refund or credit (1) must certify that it will not charge or otherwise receive any excise taxes from the government entity making the purchase, and (2) must file a written consent signed by an authorized representative of the government entity stating that no tax will be charged to the government entity by the credit card issuer or fuel distributor and that the government entity will not claim a refund or credit related to its purchases of fuel made by a credit card provided by the issuer. These conditions are included on Form FT-505.1 as part of the consent for filing the election;

— the credit card issuer or fuel distributor must certify that (1) the retail station or other vendor has been repaid the excise taxes it charged to the government entity on its fuel purchases, or (2) it has obtained a written consent from the retail station or other vendor to receive the refund or credit for the excise taxes; and

— the credit card issuer or fuel distributor must, upon request by the Department, provide detailed transactional and jurisdictional information related to the fuel sales in the form requested by the Department.

(*TSB-M-08(9)M*, Office of Tax Policy Analysis, New York Department of Taxation and Finance, November 5, 2008)

Applying for a refund or credit.—Fuel distributors may apply for a credit of the excise taxes paid on diesel fuel by filing Form PT-102, Tax on Diesel Motor Fuels. The credit claimed on Form PT-102 is carried over to Form PT-100, Petroleum Business Tax Return and may result in a refund or credit. These forms may be filed after the end of the month in which the government entity purchased the fuel. Fuel distributors may continue to claim a credit for the prepaid sales tax on Form FT-945/1045, Report of Sales Tax Prepayment on Motor Fuel/Diesel Motor Fuel on a monthly basis. Fuel distributors may claim a refund of the additional sales tax (the difference between the retail sales tax repaid to the retail vendor and the prepaid sales tax paid by the distributor) using Form FT-500, Application for Refund of Sales Tax Paid on Automotive Fuels, after the end of the quarter in which the fuel was purchased by the government entity. (*TSB-M-08(9)M*, Office of Tax Policy Analysis, New York Department of Taxation and Finance, November 5, 2008)

Liability.—The Department may issue an assessment for tax, penalty, and interest to a credit issuer or fuel distributor for any refund or credit that was allowed or paid that was erroneous, illegal, or unconstitutional. In addition, a penalty equal to the amount of tax refunded or credited, plus applicable interest, may also be imposed on any credit card issuer or fuel distributor that files a refund application or takes a credit knowing that the fuel purchased by government entity was not for the government entity's own use or consumption. (*TSB-M-08(9)M*, Office of Tax Policy Analysis, New York Department of Taxation and Finance, November 5, 2008)

Credit in lieu of a refund.—Unless the Commissioner of Taxation and Finance withdraws the privilege, a distributor entitled to a refund may instead take a credit for it on his monthly return. (Sec. 287(2), Tax Law)

For a description of the refund process for farmers, see Technical Services Bureau Memorandum TSB-M-79(6)M.

With regard to taxpayer remedies, see ¶89-230 Taxpayer Conferences for a discussion regarding conciliation conferences.

Refunds for fuel taxed but not used for purposes subject to tax.—Any person who buys motor fuel on which the required tax has already been paid but uses the fuel in a manner other than for the operation of a motor vehicle on New York highways or the operation of a pleasure or recreational motorboat is entitled to a refund. (Reg. Sec. 415.3) A refund is not permitted, however, for the tax paid on diesel motor fuel taken out of state in the tank of a motor vehicle for consumption outside the state. Diesel fuel leaving the state in this manner is not considered an export. (Sec. 289-c(8), Tax Law; Sec. 301-b(b)(3), Tax Law)

Refund application.—The application must include all claims for the calendar month, but two or more calendar months may be combined in one application. Refund claims may be made within three years of the earliest purchase on the application. (Reg. Sec. 415.1)

Any person selling motor fuel to an exempt purchaser may exclude the amount of tax from the selling price and claim a refund or credit. (Reg. Sec. 415.2)

All motor fuel tax refund claims are subject to Reg. Sec. 415.2 provisions.

Provisions for omnibus carriers.—Two refund provisions apply to omnibus carriers. A partial refund is available to carriers operating in New York and a full refund applies to omnibus carriers using fuel for local transit service.

New York State omnibus carriers.—Omnibus carriers using diesel motor fuel are entitled to a refund of diesel motor fuel tax paid in excess of 6¢ a gallon of the aggregate amount imposed by Secs. 282-a (6¢) and 282-b (3¢) Tax Law. As a result, the refund available to omnibus carriers for diesel motor fuel tax paid is limited to 3¢ per gallon. (Reg. Sec. 415.3)

While an omnibus carrier who purchases diesel motor fuel at retail can claim a refund, a carrier who is a bulk user or retail vendor can claim a credit on his monthly return instead of a refund.

Omnibus carriers in local transit service.—A full refund of diesel motor fuel tax is provided for any carrier operating an omnibus for local transit service pursuant to a certificate of convenience and necessity issued by the New York Commissioner of Transportation, the U.S. Interstate Commerce Commission or pursuant to a contract, franchise or consent of the City of New York or one of its agencies. In order to be eligible for a refund of the tax, the fuel must be used in local transit service. (Sec. 289-c(3)(d), Tax Law) Note that even if the omnibus carrier is not considered "in local transit service," it may be eligible for the partial refund.

Records.—Local omnibus carriers claiming a refund or credit must maintain a vehicular trip record for each bus including the vehicle number, date of each trip, origin and destination of each trip, points between which the refund or credit is claimed, total miles traveled, credit or refund miles claimed, gallons of fuel consumed and gallons credit or refund claimed. (Reg. Sec. 415.3) Without the information required, there is an insufficient basis for a credit allowance unless approved by the Department of Taxation and Finance.

Refund of taxes paid in error.—Fuel taxes paid may be refunded for diesel motor fuel sold under circumstances for which the fuel would not be taxable. (Sec. 289-c(6), Tax Law)

A refund claim for taxes paid in error must be accompanied by a certificate indicating that the claim is just, true and correct, that no part of the refund had been paid except as indicated and that the balance is actually due and owing. (Reg. Sec. 415.4) Such a claim generally must be filed within three years of the erroneous payment. (Sec. 289-c(6), Tax Law) However, if the taxpayer consents to extend the limitation time for the determination of the tax, a claim for refund may be filed within six months after the expiration of the extended payment. (Sec. 289-c(7), Tax Law)

Interest on refunds.—Interest, equal to the overpayment rate set by the Commissioner of Taxation and Finance, is allowed for refunds or reimbursements paid to:

(1) distributors or purchasers registered with or licensed by another state as a diesel motor fuel distributor or dealer with respect to fuel imported, manufactured or sold or purchased in New York State. (Sec. 289-c(8), Tax Law) For the exemption to apply, the distributor or purchaser must be registered with or licensed by the state to which the fuel is exported as a distributor or dealer in the fuel being exported; and

(2) exempt organizations under Sec. 1116(a)(4), Tax Law, which include corporations, associations, trusts, community chests, funds or foundations or-

ganized and operated exclusively for religious, charitable, scientific testing for public safety, literary or educational purposes or which are involved in fostering national or international amateur sports competition or prevention of cruelty to children or animals.

(Sec. 289-c(9), Tax Law)

No interest is allowed with respect to refunds to motor fuel distributors or dealers if the refund check is mailed within 30 days of receipt of a claim for refund in processible form or if the interest allowed is less than $1. (Sec. 289-c(8), Tax Law) No interest is allowed with respect to reimbursement to exempt organizations under Sec. 1116(a)(4), Tax Law, if the reimbursement check is mailed within 45 days of receipt by the Commissioner of the application for reimbursement or if the amount of interest is less than one dollar. (Sec. 289-c(9), Tax Law)

Current rates.—For current interest rates, and rates in effect for prior periods, see ¶ 89-204 Interest Rates.

• *Hurricane Sandy recovery provisions*

The New York State Department of Taxation and Finance issued an important notice stating that to aid in recovery efforts related to Hurricane Sandy, motor fuel and diesel fuel tax requirements related to registration, licensing, certification, manifest, and record keeping were suspended from November 1, 2012, until further notice. However, dealers who imported fuel from outside the state but were not currently registered will have to remit applicable taxes, including excise tax, petroleum business tax, and prepaid sales tax. Returns and payments would not be due before December 20, 2012. (*Important Notice N-12-13*, New York Department of Taxation and Finance, November 5, 2012)

The New York Department of Taxation and Finance announced that, as part of Hurricane Sandy recovery efforts, the Internal Revenue Service extended relief to allow the use of dyed diesel motor fuel in motor vehicles on the highway. As a result, the provisions discussed in Important Notice N-12-14 (see below) was extended through December 7, 2012. (*Important Notice N-12-17*, New York Department of Taxation and Finance, November 2012)

For the period of October 30, 2012, through November 20, 2012, dyed diesel fuel could be sold and/or used in motor vehicles on New York highways and distributors could pass through the excise, petroleum business, and prepaid sales taxes when the fuel was sold to retail service stations. Retail service stations were required to pass through the excise and petroleum business taxes and charge state and local sales tax when the dyed diesel fuel was sold to consumers. In addition, dyed diesel fuel could be used in farm production without the imposition of excise, petroleum business, or sales tax. (*Important Notice N-12-14*, New York Department of Taxation and Finance, November 6, 2012)

[¶40-005] Aviation Fuel Taxes

An aviation fuel business tax is imposed on aviation fuel businesses for the privilege of engaging in business, doing business, employing capital, owning or leasing property, or maintaining an office in New York. (Sec. 301-e(a), Tax Law)

Specific topics discussed below are:

— persons subject to tax,

— basis of tax,

— rate of tax

— exemptions,

— reports and payments, and

— credits, refunds, and reimbursements.

"Kero-jet fuel and aviation gasoline consumed in this state" is presumed to mean all such fuel consumed during takeoffs from points in New York. (Sec. 301-e(e)(2), Tax Law; TSB-M-04(3)M)

• *Persons subject to tax*

The tax is imposed on aviation fuel businesses that:

(1) import or cause aviation gasoline or kero-jet fuel to be imported (including the importation in aircraft fuel tanks) into the state for use, distribution, storage or sale in the state;

(2) produce, refine, manufacture or compound aviation gasoline or kero-jet fuel in New York;

(3) sell or use kero-jet fuel in the state, other than a retail sale not in bulk or self-use of kero-jet fuel which has been subject to a retail sale to such corporation or unincorporated business; or

(4) register as a distributor of kero-jet fuel only.

(TSB-M-90(7)M)

• *Basis of tax*

The tax is equal to the sum of the aviation gasoline component and the kero jet component. The components of the tax are determined as follows:

Aviation gasoline component.—The aviation gasoline component is determined by multiplying the aviation gasoline rate by the number of gallons of aviation gasoline imported or caused to be imported for use, distribution, storage or sale in the state, or produced, refined, manufactured, or compounded in New York by the aviation fuel business.

Kero-jet fuel component.—The kero-jet fuel component is determined by multiplying the kero-jet fuel rate by:

(1) the number of gallons of kero-jet fuel imported or caused to be imported by an aviation fuel business and consumed in New York by the business in the operation of its aircraft, and

(2) kero-jet fuel, which has not been previously included in the measure of the tax, that is sold in New York by an aviation fuel business to persons other than those registered as aviation fuel businesses or consumed in the state by the aviation fuel business in the operation of its aircraft.

(Sec. 301-e(c), Tax Law)

Fuel imported in aircraft tanks.—Aviation gasoline and kero-jet fuel imported into New York in the fuel tanks of aircraft is regarded as imported for use and, therefore, is subject to tax. (Sec. 301-e(c), Tax Law)

• *Rates*

Effective January 1, 2020, aviation gasoline, supplemental aviation gasoline, and kero-jet fuel tax rates per gallon have been adjusted as follows:

— Aviation gasoline . . . . 17.4¢

— Retail sellers of aviation gasoline . . . . 7.0¢

— Kero-jet fuel . . . . 7.0¢

(*Publication 908*)

¶40-005

The rate is adjusted at the same time as the rates of the components of the petroleum business tax imposed by Sec. 301-a, Tax Law and the method of making adjustments to the kero-jet fuel rate will be the same as the method used for petroleum business tax rates.

Supplemental tax.—A supplemental tax is imposed on petroleum businesses. (Sec. 301-j, Tax Law) The supplemental aviation fuel business tax is imposed only on products included in the aviation gasoline component of the Sec. 301-e tax on aviation fuel businesses; i.e., the tax is *not* imposed on products included in the kero-jet fuel component.

• *Exemptions*

An exemption from the tax and any surcharge is provided for any aviation fuel business servicing four or more cities in New York with non-stop flights between those cities. (Sec. 301-e(f), Tax Law; TSB-M-04(3)M)

The aviation gasoline credit/refund/reimbursement is 10.6¢. (*Publication 908*)

Exemption from supplemental tax.—Commercial gallonage and railroad diesel are exempt from the supplemental tax. (Sec. 301-j(a)(2) and (3), Tax Law)

• *Reports and payments*

Generally, returns are due on or before the 20th day following the close of a taxable month. (Sec. 308(a), Tax Law; Sec. 308(b), Tax Law)

The Department of Taxation and Finance has issued a publication that lists the product codes used to report fuels on New York State tax returns and reports. (*Publication 902*)

Generally, payment of tax accompanies the return. (Sec. 308(b), Tax Law)

Quarterly returns.—The Commissioner of Taxation and Finance may permit returns to be filed on a quarterly basis by registered petroleum businesses that only make sales of diesel motor fuel solely for residential heating purposes, and by petroleum businesses registered as distributors of kero-jet fuel only. (Sec. 308(a), Tax Law)

Annual returns.—The Commissioner of Taxation and Finance may permit aviation businesses that are not airlines to pay aviation fuel business tax and file returns relating to such tax for periods covering 12 consecutive taxable months. (Sec. 301-e(a), Tax Law)

Corporations ceasing to do business or to be subject to tax.—A corporation that ceases to exercise its corporate franchise or to be subject to Article 13-A tax must file a return with the Commissioner as of the date of such cessation, or at such other time as the Commissioner may require, covering each month or period for which no return was previously filed. (Sec. 308(a), Tax Law)

• *Credit, refunds, and reimbursements*

A partial credit, refund or reimbursement of aviation fuel business tax is allowed in connection with sales of aviation gasoline. (Sec. 301-e(b)(2), Tax Law; TSB-M-95(12)M) The credit is available to:

(1) sales by motor fuel distributors to a fixed base operator registered under Art. 12-A, Tax Law, as a "retail seller of aviation gasoline" where the tax claimed as a credit or refund has been paid or assumed by the distributor and not passed on to the "retail seller of aviation gasoline;"

(2) sales of aviation gasoline by motor fuel distributors who are also registered as "retail sellers of aviation gasoline," where the gasoline is delivered

and stored at its fixed base operations premises. The credit or refund accrues at the time that the fuel is delivered and placed in the storage facility;

(3) airlines registered as motor fuel distributors that import aviation gasoline into New York for exclusive use in their airplanes; and

(4) gasoline consumed in New York by aviation fuel businesses that are subject to tax by reason of importation in the fuel tank of an airplane.

Documentary proof required.—The documentation required is copies of purchase invoices signed by the dealer or monthly statements, showing the name and address of the dealer and purchaser, date of purchase, number of gallons, and the petroleum business tax listed separately. (*Form PR-677*, Aviation Gasoline Partial Reimbursement)

Reimbursement of tax—Aviation fuel businesses.—An aviation fuel business is entitled to a reimbursement of aviation fuel business tax, less any credit allowed or refund granted, with respect to aviation gasoline or kero-jet fuel purchased in New York and consumed by the business exclusively as aviation fuel in the operation of its aircraft outside New York. The credit will be allowed only where the tax (less any applicable credit or refund) has been absorbed by the business. (Sec. 301-e(d), Tax Law) Similarly, an aviation fuel business that has imported aviation gasoline into New York is allowed a credit (less any applicable refunds or credits) on the portion of the fuel consumed in the operation of its aircraft outside New York.

Partial reimbursement.—A purchaser of aviation gasoline in New York who consumes the gasoline exclusively as aviation fuel in the operation of its aircraft is entitled to a partial reimbursement of tax with respect to aviation gasoline that was purchased by the purchaser and upon which the purchaser paid or absorbed the full amount of the tax, where:

(1) the purchaser purchases the aviation gasoline from a fixed base operator that qualifies as a retail seller of aviation gasoline but is not so registered under Art. 12-A, Tax Law; or

(2) the purchaser purchases the aviation gasoline in bulk from a registered motor fuel distributor where the distributor delivers the gasoline directly into a bulk storage facility of the purchaser that is at a fixed and permanent place at an airport within New York and is used solely to fill the fuel tanks of its aircraft for use in the operations thereof.

(Sec. 301-e(d)(3), Tax Law)

Amount of reimbursement.—The amount of the reimbursement is equal to the amount of the partial credit or refund allowed to sellers of aviation gasoline.

Documentary proof required.—Documentary proof of entitlement to the credit, refund or reimbursement is required.

Refunds for uncollectible debt.—Aviation fuel businesses may apply for refunds of petroleum and aviation fuel business taxes (including the aviation business fuel surcharge and the supplemental aviation fuel business tax) with respect to taxes paid for sales on accounts determined to be uncollectible. (Sec. 301-l(a), Tax Law)

A refund will be permitted if:

(a) the gallons have been included in reports filed by the aviation fuel business and the tax paid;

(b) the gallonage was sold in bulk by the aviation fuel business to a purchaser for the purchaser's own use and consumption; and

(c) the sale gave rise to a debt that is

(1) worthless and

(2) deducted as a worthless debt for federal income tax purposes for the taxable year covering the month in which the state refund claim is filed.

(Sec. 301-l(a), Tax Law)

A sale of motor fuel and diesel motor fuel to a filling station is deemed to be a sale in-bulk for the filling station's own use and consumption. However, a refund will not be permitted where the debt arises from a retail sale at a filling station where product is delivered directly into the fuel tank of a motor vehicle, airplane or other conveyance. (Sec. 301-l(a), Tax Law)

A refund will be apportioned if only a portion of the debt becomes worthless due to a partial payment. Interest will be allowed and paid at the overpayment rate set by the Commissioner of Taxation and Finance pursuant to Sec. 171(26), Tax Law, from the date of receipt of the refund claim to the date of the refund check. (Sec. 301-l(b), Tax Law) No interest is allowed or paid if the amount would be less than $1. (Sec. 301-l(c), Tax Law)

Federal disallowance of an uncollectible debt.—Any disallowance, for federal tax purposes, of a bad debt for which a refund of an aviation fuel business tax was paid, will be treated as a report of federal change, correction or disallowance. For purposes of the aviation fuel business tax, the change, correction or disallowance must be reported within 90 days after the final determination. An aviation fuel business corporation that has filed a combined report must report the change within 120 days. (TSB-M-94(5)M)

CIGARETTES, TOBACCO PRODUCTS

[¶55-000]
CIGARETTES, TOBACCO PRODUCTS

[¶55-001] Cigarettes

A tax is imposed on all cigarettes possessed for sale in New York (Sec. 471(1), Tax Law), with certain exceptions. Authorized agents advance and pay the tax to the Commissioner of Taxation and Finance by purchasing adhesive stamps or through the use of metering machines if prescribed by the Commissioner. (Sec. 471(2), Tax Law) The stamps are affixed to the individual packages of cigarettes, and not to cartons or large containers. (Reg. Sec. 74.3(a)(2)(i)) The tax is imposed only once on the same package of cigarettes. (Sec. 471(1), Tax Law)

The New York City cigarette tax referred to in this section is discussed beginning at NYC Tobacco.

Use tax: A complementary use tax is levied on cigarettes used in the state which are not possessed for sale. The use tax must be paid and a return filed within 24 hours after liability for the tax accrues. (Sec. 471-a, Tax Law)

Cigarettes also are subject to sales tax in the state.

Discussed here in relation to the cigarette tax are:
— Persons and products subject to tax,
— Exemptions,
— Basis of tax,
— Rate of tax,
— Reports,
— Payment,
— Credits, refunds, discounts,
— Licenses and permits, and
— Local taxes.

Cigarette and tobacco tax practice and procedure discussions begin at ¶55-010.

• *Persons and products subject to tax*

The cigarette tax is advanced and paid to the Department of Taxation and Finance by authorized agents who purchase adhesive stamps from fiscal agents appointed by the Commissioner of Taxation and Finance. Since the ultimate liability for the tax is on the consumer, however, the agent paying the tax is to collect it from the consumer by adding the amount of the tax to the sales price of the cigarettes. (Sec. 471(2), Tax Law; Reg. Sec. 74.1(b)(1))

Agent defined.—An "agent" is any person, cigarette dealer or manufacturer authorized by the Commissioner of Taxation and Finance to purchase and affix adhesive or meter stamps to packages of cigarettes. (Sec. 470(11), Tax Law) The following persons may be appointed as agents:

(1) any retail or wholesale dealer in cigarettes, who maintains a separate warehousing facility for the purposes of receiving and distributing cigarettes and conducting its business, and who receives commitments from at least two cigarette manufacturers whose aggregate market share of the New York State cigarette market is at least 40% (Reg. Sec. 71.1(a)(2)(i));

(2) any importer, exporter, or manufacturer of cigarettes, or any other person who is not a dealer (Reg. Sec. 71.1(a)(3)); and

(3) the state or city when either purchases cigarettes for distribution on a nonprofit basis. (Reg. Sec. 71.1(a)(4))

"Dealer" defined.—For purposes of the cigarette tax, a "dealer" is defined as any wholesale or retail dealer. (Sec. 470(7), Tax Law)

"Wholesale dealer" defined.—A "wholesale dealer" is any person who sells cigarettes or tobacco products to retail dealers or other persons for purposes of resale only, as well as any person who owns, operates or maintains one or more cigarette or tobacco product vending machines on premises owned or occupied by another person. (Sec. 470(8), Tax Law)

Included in this definition are manufacturers, jobbers, subjobbers, and any others who sell cigarettes in New York State to the retail trade. (Reg. Sec. 70.2) A person who customarily sells cigarettes to the retail trade is a wholesaler even though such person may be required to be registered as a retail dealer. Wholesale dealers are required to be licensed. In addition, every wholesaler that sells cigarettes in New York state at retail is also required to register as a retailer. For license requirements, see Licenses and permits.

"Retail dealer" defined.—A "retail dealer" is any person, other than a wholesale dealer, who sells cigarettes or tobacco products in New York. Effective September 1, 2020, the definition applicable to certificate of registration violations is amended to include the retailer dealer's "responsible persons" for sales tax purposes (i.e., persons required to collect tax). (Sec. 470(9), Tax Law; Reg. Sec. 70.2(h)(3))

Sales to dealers, manufacturers and others.—The Commissioner may license dealers, who maintain separate warehousing facilities for the purpose of receiving and distributing cigarettes and conducting their business and have received commitments from at least two cigarette manufacturers whose aggregate market share is at least 40% of the New York State cigarette market, and importers, exporters, and manufacturers of cigarettes, and other persons within or without New York State as agents to buy or affix stamps. (Sec. 472(1), Tax Law; Reg. Sec. 71.1(a)(2)(i); Reg. Sec. 71.1(a)(3))

Master Settlement Agreement.—New York has entered into the Master Settlement Agreement, which in part requires participating cigarette manufacturers to pay substantial sums of money to the state. Nonparticipating manufacturers must make payments into a separate escrow fund for each cigarette sold in the state and are subject to separate reporting requirements. (Sec. 1399-pp, Public Health Law)

Sales of cigarettes on Indian reservations.—Cigarettes sold to Indian nations or tribes and reservation cigarette sellers must bear tax stamps. The New York Department of Taxation and Finance has determined the annual amount of stamped tax-exempt packs of cigarettes for each of the Indian nations or tribes for the 12-month period beginning September 1, 2020, and ending August 31, 2021. (N-20-10).

• *Exemptions*

Sales in interstate commerce and foreign sales are not subject to the New York cigarette tax under provisions of the federal constitution. (Reg. Sec. 76.3) The cigarette tax law and the tobacco products tax laws specifically state that no tax will be imposed on cigarettes or tobacco products, respectively, when sold under such circumstances that New York State is without power to impose such a tax. (Sec. 471, Tax Law; Sec. 471-b(1), Tax Law)

Research tobacco products.—Medical research tobacco products are exempt from cigarette and tobacco products tax and regulatory requirements intended for commercial tobacco products. A research tobacco product is a tobacco product or cigarette that is labeled as a research tobacco product, manufactured for use in research for health, scientific, or similar experimental purposes, is exclusively used for such purposes by an accredited college, university or hospital, or a researcher affiliated with an accredited college, university or hospital, and is not offered for sale or sold to consumers for any purpose. (Sec. 470(20), Tax Law) Every accredited college, university or hospital that receives research tobacco products must, in good faith, file an annual information return on or before the last day of January reporting all research tobacco products received by such college, university or hospital or its affiliated researcher within the preceding calendar year. Any person required to file an information return who willfully fails to timely file such return or willfully fails to provide any material information required to be reported on such return may be subject to a penalty of up to $1,000. (Sec. 474(4), Tax Law)

Sales to out-of-state purchasers.—Licensed cigarette agents may sell cigarettes upon which the tax has not been prepaid and precollected, but which are within the state's taxing authority, to out-of-state purchasers without incurring any tax liability. (Reg. Sec. 76.3) In such instances, the licensed cigarette agent must receive from the out-of-state purchaser, at the time of each delivery and as proof of the exempt sale, a certificate to the effect that the cigarettes will be immediately removed from the state to an identified location for purposes of resale or use outside the state and that the cigarettes will not be returned to the state for sale or use.

For refunds provisions relating to taxes paid on cigarettes that are sold and shipped into another state for sale or use outside New York, see **Credits, refunds, discounts**.

Sales to or by the United States or its agencies.—Cigarettes sold to or by the United States of America or any of its agencies or instrumentalities, including voluntary unincorporated organizations of the U.S. Armed Forces that operate places for the sale of goods pursuant to regulations promulgated by the appropriate federal agency, are exempt from tax, provided the cigarettes are sold, used or consumed by those entities exclusively in the exercise of governmental functions or are used or consumed by authorized purchasers within the confines of a military reservation, facility or other federal area. (Sec. 471, Tax Law; Sec. 471-b(1), Tax Law; Reg. Sec. 76.2)

Sales to New York State.—No tax is imposed on cigarettes sold *to* New York State or any of its agencies or instrumentalities, provided the cigarettes are used or consumed by such entities exclusively in the exercise of governmental functions and provided the cigarettes are not sold for purposes of resale. (Reg. Sec. 76.2) Sales of cigarettes *by* New York or any of its agencies or instrumentalities are subject to tax.

Sales to the United Nations, diplomatic missions and diplomatic personnel.— No cigarette tax applies to cigarettes purchased by the United Nations for its own official use, and not for purposes of resale. (Reg. Sec. 76.5) Nor is the cigarette tax imposed upon cigarettes purchased by diplomatic missions and diplomatic personnel for their own use and consumption, and not for resale purposes. (Reg. Sec. 76.4)

Generally, diplomatic missions and diplomatic personnel, in order to receive the exemption, must establish their exempt status with the U.S. Department of State or, in the case of employees of the Coordination Council for North American Affairs, with the American Institute in Taiwan.

NEW DEVELOPMENTS: Settlement agreement between Oneida Nation, New York.—The New York Department of Taxation and Finance is notifying New York State licensed cigarette agents and federally licensed manufacturers that they may sell unstamped cigarettes directly to the Oneida Nation of New York. On March 4, 2014, the U.S. District Court, Northern District of New York in *State of New York v. Sally Jewell, Secretary, United States Department of the Interior and Oneida Nation of New York* issued a ruling ratifying the *Settlement Agreement by the*

Oneida Nation, the State of New York, the County of Madison and the County of Oneida dated May 6, 2013. Based on this decision, effective March 4, 2014, New York State licensed cigarette agents and federally licensed manufacturers may sell unstamped cigarettes directly to the Oneida Nation of New York. (*TSB-M-14(1)M, TSB-M-14(4)S,* Taxpayer Guidance Division, New York Department of Taxation and Finance, March 7, 2014)

Sales to Indian nations or tribes, nation or tribal businesses, qualified Indian consumers and registered reservation dealers.—Native American governments possess a sovereign authority that is currently protected and reserved by federal law and policies (but is subject to Congressional defeasance). Federal constitutional and statutory provisions generally preclude states from imposing cigarette excise taxes on sales of cigarettes on qualified Indian reservations to a qualified Indian for his or her own personal use or consumption. However, this exemption from tax does not apply to sales of cigarettes on qualified reservations to non-Indians or nonqualified Indians. Similarly, sales of cigarettes made outside a qualified reservations—regardless of whether the purchaser is an exempt Indian nation or tribe, an Indian nation or tribal business, a qualified Indian consumer, or a registered reservation dealer—are generally subject to tax.

As affirmed by the U.S. Supreme Court in *Department of Taxation and Finance v. Milhelm Attea & Bros., Inc.,* (1994, US SCt) 114 SCt 2028, federal statutes governing trade with Indians do not preempt New York regulations that impose recordkeeping requirements and set quotas on the number of untaxed cigarettes that wholesale distributors licensed by the Bureau of Indian Affairs can sell to tribal retailers.

CCH COMMENT: Indian tax-exempt cigarette annual amounts.—The Department of Taxation and Finance has determined the annual amount of stamped tax-exempt packs of cigarettes for each of the Indian nations or tribes for the 12-month period beginning September 1, 2019, and ending August 31, 2020. (N-19-4) For the period beginning September 1, 2020 and ending August 31, 2021, see N-20-10. The annual amount is based on the probable demand for tax-exempt cigarettes, determined by reference to, among other data, the U.S. average cigarette consumption per capita, as compiled for 2019, multiplied by the number of qualified Indians for each of the Indian nations or tribes. The annual amount is then prorated to each of the four quarters beginning with the first day of September, December, March, and June, and rounded up to the nearest case of cigarettes. Evidence relating to probable demand must be submitted to the tax department in accordance with regulations. (N-19-4)

Sales of cigarettes on Indian reservations.—All cigarettes sold to Indian nations or tribes and reservation cigarette sellers must bear tax stamps. However, a dual system is implemented to collect taxes on all cigarettes sold on an Indian reservation to non-Indians and non-members of an Indian nation or tribe. The governing body of an Indian nation or tribe may elect to participate in the Indian tax exemption coupon system or an alternate prior approval system. (Sec. 471, Tax Law)

Under both the coupon system and the prior approval system, the Department of Taxation and Finance will determine the quantity of tax-exempt cigarettes for each Indian nation or tribe annually in June, based on the probable demand of the qualified Indians on the Indian nation's or tribe's reservation plus an additional amount needed for official nation or tribal use. The department will then provide coupons or prior approvals to agents and wholesale dealers for tax-exempt sales to each nation in the amount that is determined. Both the coupon system and the prior approval system will be in place for tax-free sales taking place on or after September 1, 2010. (Sec. 471-e, Tax Law)

The department has adopted emergency regulations effective June 22, 2010, and applicable to all cigarettes sold on or after September 1, 2010, concerning the implementation of the dual tax exemption system. (Reg. Sec. 74.6; Reg. Sec. 74.7)

Nontaxable sales to agents.—Persons introducing cigarettes into the New York market for sale may sell unstamped packages of cigarettes to a licensed cigarette agent appointed by the Commissioner of Taxation and Finance. (Reg. Sec. 74.3; Reg. Sec. 76.1)

Use tax.—The cigarette use tax is not imposed on cigarettes used in the state, where:

(1) the cigarette sales tax was paid on such cigarettes;

(2) an exemption from the cigarette sales tax applies; or

(3) the number of cigarettes brought into New York State on or in the possession of any person does not exceed 400.

(Sec. 471-a, Tax Law)

If more than 400 cigarettes are brought into the state or are in the possession of any person, the first 400 cigarettes also are subject to tax. (Reg. Sec. 74.5)

Mail-order or Internet purchased cigarettes.—The above exemptions do not apply to mail-order or Internet purchased cigarettes.

• *Basis of tax*

The tax on cigarettes is imposed on the sale of cigarettes or little cigars in packs. (Sec. 471, Tax Law)

Sale defined.—The term "sale" means any transfer of title or possession, exchange or barter, conditional or otherwise, in any manner or by any means or any agreement for such transfer. (Sec. 470(4), Tax Law) For example, the giving of cigarettes as samples, prizes, or gifts, and the exchanging of cigarettes for any consideration other than money are considered sales. (Reg. Sec. 71.2)

• *Rate of tax*

The cigarette tax rate is $4.35 per pack of 20 cigarettes. If a pack of cigarettes contains more than 20 cigarettes, the tax on the cigarettes in excess of 20 is imposed at the rate of $1.0875 for each five cigarettes or fraction thereof. (Sec. 471, Tax Law; Sec. 471-a, Tax Law; *Important Notice N-10-4*, New York Department of Taxation and Finance, June 2010) Prior to July 1, 2010, the rate was $2.75 per pack and 68.75¢ for each five cigarettes in excess of 20.

The tax is imposed only once on the same package of cigarettes and it is presumed that all cigarettes in the state are subject to tax, unless it is established otherwise. The burden of proof that any cigarettes are not taxable is on the person in possession of the cigarettes. (Sec. 471, Tax Law)

Cigarette defined.—For purposes of the tax, a "cigarette" is defined as any roll for smoking, made wholly or in part of tobacco or any other substance, irrespective of size or shape and regardless of whether such tobacco or substance is flavored, adulterated or mixed with any other ingredient, the wrapper or cover of which is made of paper or any other substance or material but is not made in whole or in part of tobacco. (Sec. 470, Tax Law)

Little cigars.—Although little cigars are taxed at the same rate as cigarettes, they are still considered a "tobacco product" and a "cigar". See discussion of little cigars at Tobacco Products.

Master Settlement Agreement.—Pursuant to the terms of the Master Settlement Agreement laws in New York, after 2006 nonparticipating manufacturers are required by the model statute to make a yearly deposit into a qualified escrow account. The base escrow amount is $0.0188482 for each cigarette (unit) sold in a year, prior to the inflation adjustment. The deposit is to be made by each April 15 and no later than April 30 for units sold during the previous calendar year. (Sec. 1399-pp, Public Health Law)

• *Reports*

The Commissioner of Taxation and Finance is authorized to require the filing of returns. (Sec. 475, Tax Law) Under this power, dealers, distributors, agents and cigarette and tobacco products transporters must furnish reports to the Commissioner or keep invoices and records of all cigarettes or tobacco products received, sold or delivered, which are subject to inspection by the Commissioner. (Sec. 474, Tax Law)

Agents—Agents' monthly reports.—Licensed cigarette agents appointed by the Commissioner of Taxation and Finance are required to file monthly reports on or before the 15th day of each month covering transactions for the preceding calendar month with the Commissioner, on forms furnished by the commissioner. The reports are to show the following:

(1) the number of unstamped cigarettes

    (a) on hand at the beginning of the month,

    (b) purchased or received during the month,

    (c) on hand at the end of the month,

    (d) sold or disposed of during the month; and

(2) the number of cigarette tax stamps

    (a) on hand at the beginning of the month,

    (b) purchased during the month,

    (c) on hand at the end of the month,

    (d) affixed or otherwise disposed of during the month.

(Reg. Sec. 75.1)

Licensed cigarette agents must report the number of New York State cigarette tax stamps that they affix to cigarette packages during a monthly reporting period. (Reg. Sec. 75.1) Under the Tobacco Escrow Funds Act (Ch. 536 (S.B. 4718), Laws 1999), the New York Department of Taxation and Finance is required to determine how much New York cigarette excise tax has been paid on cigarettes sold in New York so that New York may determine its share of settlement money from tobacco companies under the Master Settlement Agreement. The agreement requires tobacco companies to compensate 46 states, including New York, for state costs of providing health care to tobacco users.

Licensed cigarette agents must attach a separate schedule to their monthly cigarette tax return itemizing the following information on tax stamps:

(1) the number of excise tax stamps affixed to cigarette packages purchased by a cigarette agent directly from the manufacturers of the cigarettes;

(2) the number of excise tax stamps affixed to cigarette packages purchased indirectly from manufacturers through suppliers, including a supplier that is a manufacturer selling another manufacturer's cigarettes;

(3) the names of all brands of cigarettes purchased from each supplier;

(4) the number of excise tax stamps affixed to each brand sold by a supplier; and

(5) the identity of the manufacturer of the cigarettes furnished by a supplier. However, if a manufacturer did not intend to sell cigarettes in the United

States, a cigarette agent must identify the person responsible for designating the cigarettes for sale in the United States.

(Reg. Sec. 75.1)

Records that support information disclosed on a schedule must be maintained. (Reg. Sec. 75.5(a)(1)(ii))

Agents' invoices.—At the time of delivering cigarettes to any person, each agent must make a duplicate invoice showing:

> (1) the date of delivery;
>
> (2) the number of packages and cigarettes in each shipment delivered; and
>
> (3) the name of the purchaser to whom delivery is made.

(Sec. 474(4), Tax Law)

All invoices and any other records must be retained for three years and are subject to examination by the Commissioner of Taxation and Finance. (Sec. 474(4), Tax Law)

Agents' records.—Every licensed cigarette agent must keep complete and accurate records showing every purchase, sale or other disposition of all cigarettes and cigarette tax stamps handled. (Sec. 474(4), Tax Law; Reg. Sec. 75.5) The records of an agent's cigarette transactions must be distinct from other transactions or else maintained entirely separately. (Reg. Sec. 75.5) If an agent is also a wholesale or retail dealer, or both, all records in each separate capacity must be maintained separately.

Agents are required to maintain and keep the records for three years. (Sec. 474(4), Tax Law) The records are subject to examination by the Commissioner of Taxation and Finance.

Dealers—Dealers' invoices.—At the time of delivering cigarettes to any person, each wholesale dealer must make a duplicate invoice containing the following information:

> (1) the date of delivery;
>
> (2) the items, quantity and wholesale price of every item in each shipment of tobacco products delivered; and
>
> (3) the name of the purchaser to whom delivery is made.

(Sec. 474(4), Tax Law)

Each dealer must obtain and retain invoices showing the following information:

> (1) the number of packages and cigarettes contained therein, in each shipment of cigarettes received;
>
> (2) the date of receipt; and
>
> (3) the name of the shipper.

(Sec. 474(4), Tax Law)

Dealers' records.—All wholesale and retail dealers must keep complete and accurate records showing every purchase, sale or other disposition of all cigarettes handled. (Sec. 474(4), Tax Law; Reg. Sec. 75.5)

All dealers must maintain and keep such records for three years. (Sec. 474(4), Tax Law) The records are subject to examination by the Commissioner of Taxation and Finance.

COMPLIANCE ALERT: *Wholesale dealers' informational returns.*—Beginning with the quarter December 1, 2013, through February 28, 2014 (due March 20, 2014), the New York Department of Taxation and Finance advises that wholesale dealers of cigarettes, including a wholesale dealer who is also an agent, will be required to either electronically upload their quarterly informational returns using their online services account or continue to file using a secure communications channel, such as MOVEit™. However, the option to file using a secure communications channel will end on June 30, 2014. Wholesale dealers of cigarettes who do not use a computer to prepare their returns may continue to file Form CG-89, Wholesale Dealer of Cigarettes Informational Return, as a paper return. In keeping with the policy announced in Important Notice N-12-2, the department will not accept returns filed on CDs, DVDs or any other form of portable media. (*Important Notice N-14-1*, New York Department of Taxation and Finance, January 2014)

Dealers' informational returns.—Wholesale dealers of cigarettes, including wholesale dealers who are also agents, are required to file an annual informational return with the Department of Taxation and Finance by the 20th day of March, June, September, and December for the quarterly periods ending on the last day of February, May, August, and November of each year. (Reg. Sec. 75.5) The return must contain the following information:

(1) the name and address of every person from whom cigarettes have been purchased or otherwise acquired and the quantity of cigarettes purchased or acquired from each such person during the year;

(2) the name, address and sales tax identification number of every person, other than consumers of the cigarettes, to whom cigarettes have been sold or otherwise disposed of and the quantity of cigarettes sold or disposed of to each such person during the year; and

(3) the location and number of cigarette vending machines in, at or upon premises owned or occupied by another person within New York State.

(Reg. Sec. 75.2(a))

CCH COMMENT: *Informational returns on magnetic tapes, CDs, DVDs, etc.*— In an effort to strengthen data security, the New York State Department of Taxation and Finance will no longer accept electronically file quarterly cigarette tax informational returns on magnetic tapes, CDs, DVDs, floppy discs, removable drives, or any other form of portable media. Beginning with the quarter December 1, 2011, through February 29, 2012, wholesale dealers of cigarettes must electronically file quarterly informational returns using a secure communications channel. (*Important Notice N-12-2*, New York Department of Taxation and Finance, February 2012)

Wholesale dealers of cigarettes, including wholesale dealers who are also agents, are also required to file quarterly updates to the prior year's annual return for the three-month periods ending with the last days of May, August and November. (Reg. Sec. 75.2(b))

Tobacco products wholesale dealers who are not also distributors must file monthly informational returns with the Department of Taxation and Finance that detail their purchases, sales, and prices of tobacco products. The returns are due by the 20th of each month and must reflect the wholesale dealer's activities for the preceding month. (Reg. Sec. 90.1; *TSB-M-08(1)M*, New York Department of Taxation and Finance, February 28, 2008)

Vending machine owners.—Wholesale dealers who own, operate or maintain one or more cigarette vending machines in, at or upon premises in New York State that are owned or occupied by another person are required to display the following information on each machine: the wholesale dealer's name, address, telephone number and wholesale license identification number. (Reg. Sec. 75.2(b))

Transporters of cigarettes.—Any person possessing or transporting unstamped cigarettes in New York State must have invoices or delivery tickets for the cigarettes in his possession. The invoices or delivery tickets must show:

(1) the name and address of the consignor or seller;

(2) the name and address of the consignee or purchaser;

(3) the quantity and brands of cigarettes transported; and

(4) the name and address of the person paying the tax.

The absence of such invoices or delivery tickets is considered prima facie evidence that the person transporting the cigarettes is a dealer and is subject to tax. (Sec. 474(1), Tax Law)

Out-of-state shippers.—The Commissioner may provide, by regulation, that whenever cigarettes are shipped into New York State, the railroad company, express company, trucking company or other public carrier transporting the shipment must file a copy of the freight bill with the Commissioner within 10 days after delivery. (Sec. 474(4), Tax Law)

Cigarette and tobacco products use tax returns.—Persons subject to the cigarette use tax or the tobacco products use tax must file a return and pay the tax due within 24 hours after liability for the tax accrues. The form of the return is prescribed by the Commissioner. (Sec. 471-a, Tax Law; Sec. 471-c, Tax Law; Reg. Sec. 75.3)

Delinquent dates; extensions of time for filing.—Cigarette and tobacco products use tax returns must be filed within 24 hours after the liability for tax accrues. (Sec. 471-a, Tax Law; Sec. 471-c, Tax Law) Agents' monthly reports must be filed on or before the 15th day of each month. (Reg. Sec. 75.1) Wholesale dealers' information returns must be filed by March 15. (Reg. Sec. 75.5) Distributors of tobacco products are required to file a return, on or before the 20th day of each month. (Sec. 473-a, Tax Law)

There are no provisions in the law or regulations allowing extensions of time for filing the required reports.

Jenkins Act.—The federal Jenkins Act (15 U.S.C. §§ 375-378), as amended in 2010 by the Prevent All Cigarette Trafficking Act of 2009 (PACT Act), Pub. L. No. 111-154, imposes certain registration and reporting requirements on those who sell, transfer, or ship (or who advertise or offer to do so) cigarettes, roll-your-own tobacco, and smokeless tobacco for profit in interstate commerce to a state, locality, or Indian country of an Indian tribe that taxes the sale or use of such products.

Registration requirement: A statement must be filed with the U.S. Attorney General and with the tobacco tax administrators of the state and place into which the products are shipped (or where advertisements or offers are directed). The statement must provide the name and trade name (if any) of the seller, transferor, or shipper, and the address of its principal place of business and of any other place of business. (15 U.S.C. § 376(a)) Additionally, the statement must include telephone numbers for each place of business, a principal e-mail address, any website addresses, and the name, address, and telephone number of an agent in the state authorized to accept service on behalf of the seller, transferor, or shipper. (15 U.S.C. § 376(a))

As an alternative to filing a statement with the U.S. Attorney General, Form 5070.1 can be filed with the Bureau of Alcohol, Tobacco, Firearms and Explosives (ATF). This federal form is available on the ATF's website at http://www.atf.gov/.

Reporting requirement: The Jenkins Act also imposes a duty to file on the 10th of each month with the relevant state tobacco tax administrator a report of the names and addresses of all of the seller's in-state cigarette and smokeless tobacco purchasers, the brand and quantity of cigarettes or smokeless tobacco, and the name, address, and phone number of the person delivering the shipment. (15 U.S.C. § 376(a)) A copy

¶55-001

of the report must be filed with the chief law enforcement officer of the local government and any Indian tribe that applies its own local or tribal taxes on the cigarettes or smokeless tobacco purchased. (15 U.S.C. § 376(a)) These reports can be used by the state tobacco tax administrators and the local chief law enforcement officers that receive them to enforce the collection of any taxes owed on the sales. (15 U.S.C. § 376(c))

The Jenkins Act was sustained in *Consumer Mail Order Ass'n of America et al. v. McGrath,* (1950), 340 US 934, 71 SCt 500, aff'g *per curiam,* 94 FSupp 705. For a similar decision under state law, see *Roberts Tobacco Co. v. Michigan Department of Revenue,* (1948), 322 Mich 519, 34 NW2d 54.

The New York Department of Taxation and Finance has issued a cigarette and tobacco products tax memorandum that describes the new and expanded reporting requirements concerning reporting to the department under the Jenkins Act, as amended by the Prevent All Cigarette Trafficking Act (PACT), effective June 29, 2010. Reports are due by the 10th day of each calendar month. The first monthly report under the new provisions, covering the month of June 2010, was due July 10, 2010. All persons required to file this report that have not yet done so should file that report immediately. (*TSB-M-10(7)M,* Office of Tax Policy Analysis, New York Department of Taxation and Finance, August 3, 2010)

Master Settlement Agreement.—Every tobacco product manufacturer selling cigarettes in the state must file a report with the New York Attorney General and the Tax Commissioner certifying that it is either a participating manufacturer under the terms of the Master Settlement Agreement, or that it is a nonparticipating manufacturer in full compliance with New York requirements for nonparticipating manufacturers. (Sec. 1399-pp, Public Health Law)

• *Payment*

Cigarette stamps are available from fiscal agents or agent banks. (Sec. 472, Tax Law; Reg. Sec. 74.2(b)(2)) Agents may purchase stamps either for cash or on 30 days credit. (Sec. 472, Tax Law; Reg. Sec. 74.2(c)) Generally, stamps are purchased over the telephone or by mail and are delivered by the U.S. Postal Service under a mail classification guaranteeing next business day delivery. However, in an emergency, agents may purchase stamps in person. (Reg. Sec. 74.2(c))

The Department of Taxation and Finance reserves the right to allow for the affixation and cancellation of cigarette tax stamps by way of metering machines. (Sec. 472, Tax Law; Reg. Sec. 74.3(2)(ii))

Affixing and canceling stamps by agent.—Each agent must affix stamps to each package of cigarettes and cancel the stamps before the cigarettes are sold or offered for sale, unless stamps have already been affixed and canceled before the agent received them. (Sec. 473, Tax Law) The stamps must be affixed to the bottoms of cigarette packages and in a manner so that they are clearly visible to purchasers. (Reg. Sec. 74.3(2)(i))

No other stamps, labels, decals, marks or signs, other than the design of the package or the required cancellation of the stamps, may appear at the bottom of cigarette packages without the prior written approval of the Department of Taxation and Finance. Approval is only granted to licensed cigarette agents who agree to purchase the additional indicia from authorized cigarette tax stamp manufacturers.

In no event may anything displayed anywhere on cigarette packages resemble the prescribed cigarette tax stamps.

A person may not:

(1) import into New York any cigarettes that have been marked for export outside the United States or that violate federal requirements for the placement of labels, warnings, or other information on the cigarette package or

(2) affix a stamp on a package of cigarettes, cigarette papers, wrappers, or tubes that has been marked for export outside the United States or that violates federal trademark and copyright laws or federal requirements for the placement of labels, warnings, or other information on the package.

(Sec. 473-b, Tax Law; TSB-M-00(1)M)

An agent may appoint a person in his or her employ to affix the stamps to any cigarettes under the agent's control. (Sec. 472(1), Tax Law)

All stamps must be canceled in ink with the identification number assigned to each licensed agent. (Reg. Sec. 74.3(2)(i))

Agents may not affix a state cigarette tax stamp to a package of cigarettes if the cigarette manufacturer has failed to give the agent required certification regarding compliance with certain New York public health law provisions. (For a discussion of the definition of a tobacco product manufacturer, see *TSB-M-01(7)M*) All product manufacturers must issue their first certification by December 28, 2001. Thereafter, certifications must be made annually, no earlier than April 16 and no later than April 30 of each year. (*TSB-M-01(7)M*)

Stamping is also prohibited if the Commissioner of Taxation and Finance has notified the agent that the manufacturer is in violation of such public health law provisions or has filed a false certification. (*TSB-M-01(7)M*) The Commissioner may impose a $5,000 penalty for each violation by an agent or by a tobacco product manufacturer, and may also suspend or cancel the violator's cigarette tax licenses. (Sec. 480-b, Tax Law; Sec. 481(1)(c), Tax Law; *TSB-M-01(7)M*) In addition, police officers and certain peace officers are authorized to seize cigarettes that have been stamped in violation of these provisions. (*TSB-M-01(7)M*)

• *Credits, refunds, discounts*

Agents, dealers and tobacco products distributors are entitled to refunds for the amount of tax paid on stamped cigarettes or tobacco products which have been sold and shipped into another state for sale or use there, have become unfit for use and consumption or unsalable, or have been destroyed. Provision is also made for the redemption of any lawfully possessed unused stamps. All refund applications must be filed with the Commissioner of Taxation and Finance within two years from the time the stamps were affixed to the cigarettes or the tax was paid on the tobacco products. (Sec. 476, Tax Law; Reg. Sec. 77.1; Reg. Sec. 77.3)

However, if an agreement has been timely made, under the provisions of Sec. 478 of the Tax Law, to extend the period for determining the tax due, the refund application period will be extended. (Sec. 476, Tax Law)

The Department of Taxation and Finance established new procedures applicable to requests for refunds with respect to cigarette tax stamps affixed to cigarettes that have become unfit for use and consumption, damage, or unsalable. The procedures apply where the cigarette retailer or cigarette wholesaler has retained possession of the product rather than returning it to the manufacturer. In this situation, the retail or wholesale dealer must submit to the Department Form CG-114, Claim for Redemption/Refund of Cigarette Tax Stamps and Prepaid Sales Tax, the corresponding stamped packages of cigarettes, and copies of the corresponding purchase invoices. A separate claim for refund of New York City cigarette tax is not required. (*Important Notice N-04-08*)

The Commissioner of Taxation and Finance may redeem unused stamps and prescribe rules and regulations concerning refunds, sales of stamps and redemptions. (Sec. 476, Tax Law; Reg. 77.1)

The Commissioner may issue stamps of sufficient value to cover the refund to a dealer of cigarettes or may, subject to audit by the Comptroller, make a refund of the tax on cigarettes or on tobacco products. (Sec. 476, Tax Law)

Refund or credit of retail dealers' application fee.—The Commissioner must refund or credit an application fee paid with respect to the registration of vending machine or retail businesses through which cigarettes or tobacco products were to be sold if the registration is returned to the Department of Taxation and Finance prior to the beginning of the calendar year to which the registration relates, or the certificate is destroyed and the dealer or machine operator accounts to the Commissioner for the missing certificate. (Sec. 480-a(1), Tax Law)

Agents' commission for affixing stamps.—As compensation for their services and expenses in affixing stamps showing payment of the state cigarette tax, agents are entitled to a commission not exceeding 5% on the par value of the stamps. (Sec. 472(1), Tax Law) Concerning stamps representing payment of New York State tax only, "par value" means the face value of the stamps. (Reg. Sec. 74.3(b)) In the case of joint stamps showing payment of both the New York State tax and the New York City tax, the par value means the face value of the stamps representing payment of state tax only at the rate imposed by law. For further details, see Reg. Sec. 74.3.

The commission must be deducted by the agent from the purchase price of the stamps at the time payment is made. (Reg. Sec. 74.3(b))

All cigarettes sold to Indian nations or tribes and reservation cigarette sellers must bear tax stamps. However, a dual system is implemented to collect taxes on all cigarettes sold on an Indian reservation to non-Indians and non-members of an Indian nation or tribe.

The governing body of an Indian nation or tribe may elect to participate in the Indian tax exemption coupon system or an alternate prior approval system. See the discussion of *Sales to Indian nations or tribes, nation or tribal businesses, qualified Indian consumers and registered reservation dealers* under Exemptions.

• *Licenses and permits*

Discussed below are license and permit provisions for wholesale dealers, retail dealers, vending machine operators, and agents. Registration requirements imposed by the federal Jenkins Act are discussed under Reports above.

Wholesale dealers.—Wholesale dealers must obtain a license from the Department of Taxation and Finance and publicly display such license in their places of business. The license may not be transferred or assigned. (Sec. 480(1), Tax Law)

The application must be made on a form prescribed by the Commissioner. Applications for licenses or re-licensing must be accompanied by proof of the applicant's financial responsibility, including, but not limited to, satisfactory proof of a minimum net worth of $25,000 if the applicant is an individual, or net worth in the capitalization of the business, if the applicant is not an individual, equal to a minimum of $25,000.

Except as noted below, an applicant for a license or re-license must also provide:

    (1) a bond in the face amount of $10,000;

    (2) satisfactory proof that the applicant will maintain a secure separate warehousing facility for the purpose of receiving and distributing cigarettes or tobacco products and conducting its wholesale business;

¶55-001

(3) satisfactory proof that the applicant will provide disability and workers' compensation insurance for its employees;

(4) proof of U.S. citizenship or eligibility to obtain employment within the United States if not a citizen.

A $1,500 fee is charged for the filing of an application for the license. For dealers who have paid the application fee during the preceding 12 months, the fee is $1,000. (Sec. 480(1), Tax Law; Reg. Sec. 72.1)

Every wholesale dealer that is engaged in the activity of selling cigarettes in New York state at retail is also required to register as a retail dealer. (Reg. Sec. 70.2; TSB-M-04(1)M)

The Commissioner of Taxation and Finance may, for cause, refuse to license an applicant and may suspend or revoke the license of any wholesale dealer. (Sec. 480(2), Tax Law; Sec. 480(3), Tax Law) The Commissioner is required to give dealers notice of proposed cancellation or suspension of a license or refusal to issue a license. (Sec. 480(5), Tax Law)

Changes of address or ownership must be reported to the Department of Taxation and Finance. (Reg. Sec. 72.1)

Any violation of the provisions of the cigarette tax law or cigarette tax regulations may be cause for cancellation or suspension of the license. (Reg. Sec. 72.3)

Retail dealers.—Retail dealers are required to register with the Commissioner of Taxation and Finance. (Sec. 480-a(1), Tax Law) The application for registration must be filed with the return due for the quarter ending on August 31 and must be accompanied by a $300 application fee for each retail place of business in the state through which the dealer sells cigarettes or tobacco products. The fee is retroactive to September 1, 2009. (Sec. 480-a(2), Tax Law)

CCH COMMENT: Registration fees for 2010 and 2011.—The New York Department of Taxation and Finance has issued a cigarette tax memorandum discussing recent legislation that reduced the annual registration fees for retail dealers and vending machine operators selling cigarettes and tobacco products. Because the new flat annual fees are retroactive to calendar years 2010 and 2011, any retail dealer or vending machine operator who paid a fee greater than the new flat fee will be issued a refund for those calendar years. Any overpayment may be used to offset any other taxes or liabilities administered by the department. Any retail dealer who paid the $100 fee allowed under the temporary restraining order will be issued a notice and demand to collect the difference in the new fee. If there is an overpayment in one year and an underpayment in the other, the two amounts will be netted. Certificates of registration for 2012 will not be issued to retail dealers or vending machine operators if their 2010 and 2011 outstanding registration fees are not paid in full. (TSB-M-11(3)M, Taxpayer Guidance Division, New York Department of Taxation and Finance, May 2, 2011)

Prior law.—Under statutory provisions, the basis for computing the New York tobacco products registration application fee imposed on cigarette and tobacco products retail dealers and vending machine owners or operators was changed, applicable to fees related to applications for registration for the 2010 calendar year and thereafter. The fee was based on the gross sales for a particular place of business or vending machine during the previous calendar year. (Former Sec. 480-a(2), Tax Law)

Under prior law, for cigarette and tobacco products retail dealers, the application fee was: $1,000 for each retail place of business with gross sales totaling less than $1 million; $2,500 for each retail place of business with gross sales totaling at least $1 million but less than $10 million; and $5,000 for each retail place of business with gross sales totaling $10 million or more. (Former Sec. 480-a(2), Tax Law) This fee schedule was never imposed due to the restraining order that was issued in September 2009.

Vending machine operators.—Persons owning or operating one or more vending machines through which cigarettes or tobacco products are sold in New York State are also required to register with the Commissioner of Taxation and Finance. (Sec. 480-a(1), Tax Law) The application for registration must be filed with the return due for the quarter ending on August 31 and must be accompanied by the payment of a fee of $100 per vending machine. The fee is retroactive to September 1, 2009. (Sec. 480-a(2), Tax Law)

Prior law.—The basis for computing the New York tobacco products registration application fee imposed on cigarette and tobacco products vending machine owners or operators was changed, applicable to fees related to applications for registration for the 2010 calendar year and thereafter. The fees were based on the gross sales for a particular place of business or vending machine during the previous calendar year. The increased fees were never imposed due to a restraining order that was issued in September 2009. (Sec. 480-a(2), Tax Law)

Under prior law, for vending machine owners and operators, the fee was: $250 for each vending machine with gross sales totaling less than $100,000; $625 for each vending machine with gross sales totaling at least $100,000 but less than $1 million; and $1,250 for each vending machine with gross sales totaling $1 million or more. (Former Sec. 480-a(2), Tax Law; TSB-M-09(7)M, New York Department of Taxation and Finance, July 31, 2009)

Any retail place of business or vending machine with zero dollars in gross sales during the previous calendar year was subject to the lowest application fee. (Former Sec. 480-a(2)(b), Tax Law)

The Commissioner may prohibit a retail dealer from selling cigarettes or tobacco products for violating any provisions of the Cigarette and Tobacco Products Tax Law. (Sec. 480, Tax Law) The Commissioner may also refuse to register a retail dealer if the dealer's place of business is at the same premises as that of a retail dealer whose registration has been revoked and such revocation is still in effect, unless the premises was acquired through an arm's-length transaction. (Sec. 480-a(1)(e), Tax Law)

Adolescent tobacco-use protection act violations.—The Commissioner must deny the registration, and may suspend or cancel an existing registration, of a retail dealer who has been convicted of selling or causing tobacco to be sold to a person younger than 18 years, or as directed by an enforcement officer pursuant to Article 13-F, Public Health Law. (Sec. 480-a(1)(d), Tax Law)

Agents.—The application fee for an agent's license is $1,500. For agents who have paid the application fee during the preceding 12 months, the fee is $1,000. (Sec. 472(1), Tax Law)

The Commissioner of Taxation and Finance may, for cause, refuse to license an applicant and may cancel or suspend the license of any agent. The Commissioner is required to give agents notice of proposed cancellation or suspension of a license or refusal to issue a license. (Sec. 472(1), Tax Law; Sec. 480(2), Tax Law; Sec. 480(3), Tax Law)

Performance bonds.—Before a person may be licensed as a cigarette agent, he or she must file or deposit and maintain, with the Commissioner of Taxation and Finance, a $1,000 performance bond executed by a surety company which is authorized to transact business in New York State, registered with and under the supervision of the New York State Insurance Department and approved by the

Superintendent of Insurance as to solvency and responsibility to guarantee the proper performance of its duties. (Sec. 472(1), Tax Law; Reg. Sec. 71.2)

For purposes of the tobacco products tax, distributors may be required to deposit with the Commissioner a bond issued by a surety company approved by the Superintendent of Insurance. (Sec. 472(3), Tax Law)

Credit bonds.—An agent may be permitted to pay for stamps within 30 days from the date of purchase. Any agent who desires to establish credit for the purchase of stamps may be required to file or deposit and maintain with the Commissioner a bond issued by a surety company approved by the Superintendent of Insurance. (Sec. 472(1), Tax Law; Reg. Sec. 71.2)

Deposit of securities.—In lieu of the performance or credit bonds, agents and distributors may deposit securities with the Commissioner. These securities may be sold by the Commissioner to recover sums due, but no sale will be held without a hearing or court determination. (Sec. 472(1), Tax Law; Sec. 472(3), Tax Law; Reg. Sec. 71.3)

Chain stores.—Chain stores, including vending machine operators, cooperative members, franchisees and large volume outlet operators, are required to register with the Commissioner of Taxation and Finance and pay a registration fee of $300. If a registration fee has been paid during the preceding 12 months, the registration fee is $200. (Sec. 489, Tax Law)

The registration fee for a chain store which is a vending machine operator and sells cigarettes at not less than 15 separate outlets is $250 (regardless of the number of vending machines operated or owned). However, if the registration fee has been paid during the preceding 12 months, the fee is $200. (Sec. 489, Tax Law)

Unlawful acts of a chain store are discussed in Reg. Sec. 82.4.

• *Local taxes*

New York City imposes a city cigarette tax. See Imposition and Rate of NYC Tax Both state and city taxes must be paid on cigarettes possessed for sale in New York City. Joint stamps covering both state and city taxes are available for purchase. (Reg. Sec. 74.2)

[¶55-005] Tobacco Products

A tax is imposed on all tobacco products possessed in New York by any person for sale, with certain exceptions. (Sec. 471-b(1), Tax Law) Distributors are responsible for payment of the tax on all tobacco products which they import or cause to be imported into New York State or which they manufacture in the state. (Sec. 471-b(2), Tax Law) Dealers are liable for the tax on all tobacco products in their possession at any time, upon which tax has not been paid or assumed by a distributor. (Sec. 471-b(3), Tax Law) A return must be filed and the tax remitted within 24 hours after liability for the tax accrues. (Sec. 471(1), Tax Law)

Use tax.—A complimentary use tax is levied on all tobacco products used in the state which are not possessed for sale. (Sec. 471-c, Tax Law) The use tax must be paid and a return filed within 24 hours after liability for the tax accrues.

Special provision—Tobacco products tax.—Persons who receive tobacco products which were excluded from tax and who, thereafter, possess such tobacco products for sale or use such tobacco products in a taxable manner or under taxable circumstances are liable for the sales or use tax on tobacco products. (Sec. 471-d, Tax Law)

Where the law treats cigarettes and other tobacco products the same, the reader will be linked to the discussion of cigarettes at ¶55-001. Topics discussed here include:

— Persons and products subject to tax,

— Exemptions,

— Basis of tax,

— Rate of tax,

— Reports,

— Payment,

— Credits, refunds, discounts,

— Licenses and permits, and

— Local taxes.

COMPLIANCE ALERT: Roll-your-own cigarette/tobacco machines.—The New York Department of Taxation and Finance has issued tobacco tax memorandums that provide guidance regarding the impact of federal legislation regarding roll-your-own cigarette/tobacco machines on the cigarette and tobacco products taxes. Any retailers, businesses, or organizations that provide roll-your-own cigarette/tobacco (RYO) machines used for making cigarettes must be licensed as a cigarette stamping agent and are required to purchase and affix cigarette tax stamps to the packages of cigarettes that are sold.

Manufacturers of cigarettes must annually certify that they are in compliance with the Master Settlement Agreement. Certain fire safety standards must be met. If a RYO machine is used for making cigars, the business or organization must apply for a license to be a distributor of tobacco products. In addition, bonding and filing requirements and penalty provisions are discussed. (TSB-M-12(5)M, New York Department of Taxation and Finance, October 2, 2012; TSB-M-14(3)M, New York Department of Taxation and Finance, July 2, 2014)

• *Persons and products subject to tax*

The distributor is liable for payment of the tax on tobacco products which he or she imports or causes to be imported into New York State, or which he or she manufactures in New York. (Sec. 471-b(2), Tax Law) A dealer is liable for the tax on all tobacco products in his or her possession at any time, upon which tax has not been paid or assumed by a distributor appointed by the Commissioner of Taxation and Finance. (Sec. 471-b(3), Tax Law)

The Commissioner may appoint dealers in tobacco products, manufacturers of tobacco products and other persons within or outside New York State as distributors and authorize them to make returns and pay the tax on tobacco products sold, shipped, or delivered by them to any person in the state. (Sec. 472(3), Tax Law)

Distributor defined.—A "distributor" is any person who imports or causes to be imported into New York State any tobacco product for sale, or who manufactures any tobacco product in New York, and any person within or without the state who is authorized by the Commissioner of Taxation and Finance to make returns and pay the tax on tobacco products sold, shipped or delivered by him to any person in the state. (Sec. 470(12), Tax Law)

Use tax.—Taxes are imposed on the use of tobacco products in the state, subject to certain exceptions. (Sec. 471-a, Tax Law; Sec. 471-c, Tax Law)

"Use" defined.—For purposes of the tax, the term "use" is defined as the exercise of any right or power, actual or constructive, and includes (but is not limited to) the

receipt, storage, keeping or retention of cigarettes for any length of time. The possession of cigarettes or tobacco products for sale is not a "use" within the meaning of the statute. (Sec. 471-a, Tax Law; Sec. 471-c, Tax Law)

• *Exemptions*

The tobacco products use tax is not imposed on tobacco products used in state when:

(1) the tobacco products sales tax was paid on such tobacco products;

(2) an exemption from the tobacco products sales tax applies; or

(3) the number of cigars brought into New York State on, or in the possession of, any person does not exceed 250 or the amount of tobacco brought into the state on, or in the possession of, any person, does not exceed five pounds.

(Sec. 471-c, Tax Law)

Research tobacco products.—Medical research tobacco products are exempt from cigarette and tobacco products tax and regulatory requirements intended for commercial tobacco products. A research tobacco product is a tobacco product or cigarette that is labeled as a research tobacco product, manufactured for use in research for health, scientific, or similar experimental purposes, is exclusively used for such purposes by an accredited college, university or hospital, or a researcher affiliated with an accredited college, university or hospital, and is not offered for sale or sold to consumers for any purpose. (Sec. 470(20), Tax Law) Every accredited college, university or hospital that receives research tobacco products must, in good faith, file an annual information return on or before the last day of January reporting all research tobacco products received by such college, university or hospital or its affiliated researcher within the preceding calendar year. Any person required to file an information return who willfully fails to timely file such return or willfully fails to provide any material information required to be reported on such return may be subject to a penalty of up to $1,000. (Sec. 474(4), Tax Law)

• *Basis of tax*

The new York tobacco products tax is based on the wholesale price on all tobacco products, other than snuff. (Sec. 471-b(1), Tax Law)

• *Rate of tax*

A tax is imposed at the rate of 75% of the wholesale price on all tobacco products, other than snuff, possessed in New York by any person for sale or used in the state by any person. Snuff is taxed at the rate of $2.00 per ounce and a proportionate rate on any fractional amount for containers with more than one ounce (for example, the tax on a 1.25 oz. container would be $2.50). (Sec. 471-b(1), Tax Law; Sec. 471-c, Tax Law)

CCH COMMENT: Wholesale price adjustment ratio for certain cigar sales.—For purposes of determining the wholesale price of cigars to calculate New York tobacco products tax when no manufacturer's invoice is available, the New York Department of Taxation and Finance has established an industry standard adjustment ratio. Generally, if a distributor of tobacco products is unable to determine the established price for which a manufacturer sold cigars, the distributor's purchase price is presumed to be the wholesale price unless:

— evidence of a lower wholesale price can be established, or

— any industry standard of markups relating to the purchase price in relation to the wholesale price is established.

Effective for cigars imported into the state on or after December 1, 2013, the adjustment ratio is 38%. To determine the wholesale price of cigars, the distributor multiplies its purchase price by the adjustment ratio. The resulting amount is multiplied by 75% to determine the tax due. This ratio applies only to cigars. It does not apply to little cigars, snuff, or other tobacco products. (TSB-M-13(12)M, Taxpayer Guidance Division, New York Department of Taxation and Finance, December 5, 2013)

Little cigars are taxed at the rate of $4.35 per pack of 20. (Sec. 471, Tax Law) Although they are taxed at the same rate as cigarettes, little cigars are still considered a "tobacco product" and a "cigar" as defined in Article 20 of the Tax Law. Packs of little cigars are not required to have tax stamps affixed to them. The New York City tax on cigarettes of $1.50 per pack does not apply to little cigars. (*TSB-M-10(4)M*, Office of Tax Policy Analysis, New York Department of Taxation and Finance, July 20, 2010; *TSB-M-10(10)M*, Office of Tax Policy Analysis, New York Department of Taxation and Finance, August 6, 2010)

Computation of tax on little cigars.—The New York Department of Taxation and Finance has issued a cigarette tax memorandum that explains the computation of tax on little cigars. The department advises that Form MT-203, Distributor of Tobacco Products Return, is being revised to simplify the computation. (*TSB-M-10(14)M*, Office of Tax Policy Analysis, New York Department of Taxation and Finance, November 5, 2010)

Floor tax.—The New York Department of Taxation and Finance advises that no floor tax will be imposed on tobacco products on August 1, 2010. Taxes on cigars and other tobacco products, little cigars, and snuff in inventory that were imported or caused to be imported into or manufactured in New York prior to August 1, 2010, do not have to be recomputed at the new rates. However, tobacco products use tax must be paid for cigars and other tobacco products, little cigars, and snuff used in the state on or after August 1, 2010, on which the tobacco products excise tax has not been paid and where the use of the product is not exempt from tax. (*TSB-M-10(4)M*, Office of Tax Policy Analysis, New York Department of Taxation and Finance, July 20, 2010)

The New York Department of Taxation and Finance issued a release that discussed the tax rate increase on cigars and tobacco products other than snuff from 46% to 75% of the wholesale price. (*Release*, New York Department of Taxation and Finance, June 22, 2010)

The tobacco products use tax is not imposed on cigars and tobacco products other than snuff and little cigars where the amount brought into New York on or in the possession of any person does not exceed 250 cigars, five pounds of tobacco, or 36 ounces of roll-your-own (RYO) cigarette tobacco. (*TSB-M-09(1)M*, Office of Tax Policy Analysis, New York Department of Taxation and Finance, April 7, 2009)

The Department of Taxation and Finance issued a memorandum that discussed the change in the method of calculating the New York tobacco products tax on snuff. (*TSB-M-08(2)M*, June 4, 2008)

The tax is imposed only once on the same tobacco product and it is presumed that all tobacco products in New York State are subject to tax, unless it is established otherwise. The burden of proof that any tobacco product is not taxable is on the person in possession of such tobacco product. (Sec. 471-b(1), Tax Law)

Tobacco products defined.—For purposes of the tobacco products tax, the term "tobacco products" includes any cigar, including a little cigar, or tobacco, other than cigarettes, intended for consumption by smoking, chewing, or as snuff. (Sec. 470(2), Tax Law)

Little cigar defined.—A "little cigar" includes any roll for smoking made wholly or in part of tobacco if the product is wrapped in any substance containing tobacco, other than natural leaf tobacco wrapper, and weighing not more than four pounds per thousand or with a cellulose acetate or other integrated filter. (Sec. 470(2), Tax Law)

¶55-005

The Department of Taxation and Finance has issued a technical bulletin discussing little cigars that includes definitions and provides guidance on distinguishing little cigars from other cigars. (*TB-TP-530*)

Snuff defined.—Snuff is defined as any finely cut, ground, or powdered tobacco that is not intended to be smoked. (Sec. 470(18), Tax Law) Snuff includes both moist and dry snuff, but does not include chewing tobaccos such as plug or twist tobacco. Snuff also does not include compressed powder tobacco lozenges. (*TSB-M-08(2)M*, June 4, 2008)

Roll-your-own tobacco defined.—The term roll-your-own (RYO) tobacco means any tobacco product that, because of its appearance, type, packaging, or labeling, is suitable for use and likely to be offered to, or purchased by, consumers as tobacco for making cigarettes. (Sec. 470(2-a), Tax Law; *TSB-M-08(8)M*, October 28, 2008)

Wholesale price defined.—For purposes of the tobacco products tax, wholesale price is the established price for which a manufacturer sells tobacco products to a distributor, before the allowance of any discount, trade allowance, rebate, or other reduction. (Sec. 470(6), Tax Law; *Important Notice N-02-14*) In the absence of the established price, the wholesale price is the manufacturer's invoice price. Generally, if the manufacturer's established price or the manufacturer's invoice price are not known, the tax would be computed on the price at which the tobacco products were purchased, without allowance of any discount, trade allowance, rebate, or other reduction. However, for purposes of the floor tax only, retail dealers may use 50% of their selling price (excluding sales tax) as the wholesale price. (*Important Notice N-02-14*) Effective October 1, 2020, the definition is changed to clarify that the wholesale price is the actual amount paid by the distributor, whether paid to a manufacturer or to some other entity. (Sec. 470(6), Tax Law)

• *Reports*

Distributors of tobacco products are required to file a return, on or before the 20th day of each month, showing the quantity and wholesale price of all tobacco products which they imported or caused to be imported into New York State or which they manufactured in the state during the preceding calendar month. (Sec. 473-a(1), Tax Law) The tax is due upon the filing of the return. (Sec. 473-a(2), Tax Law) The Commissioner may, by regulation, permit the filing of returns on a quarterly, semiannual or annual basis. (Sec. 473-a(1), Tax Law) The Commissioner may waive the filing of returns by a distributor.

CCH CAUTION: Tax Department suspends Important Notice N-13-10.—The New York Department of Taxation and Finance has suspended cigarette and tobacco products tax Important Notice N-13-10, Change in Policy Regarding the Filing of Quarterly Informational Returns by Wholesale Dealers of Cigarettes and Wholesale Dealers of Tobacco Products, which explained a change in the quarterly informational return filing requirements for wholesaler dealers of cigarettes and wholesale dealers of tobacco products. The new filing requirements discussed in that notice have been postponed until a future filing period. The department will provide more information when the new requirements take effect. (*Email*, New York Department of Taxation and Finance, December 18, 2013)

Federal Jenkins Act reporting provisions are discussed at **Cigarettes** under Reports

Reports of roll-your-own cigarette tobacco.—Reporting requirements are discussed above at **Compliance Alert** under Tobacco Products.

Non-participating manufacturers (NPMs) in the Tobacco Master Settlement Agreement (MSA) are required to include units of roll-your-own (RYO) cigarettes sold in New York in their annual escrow payments. Such distributors must complete and attach Form MT-203-ATT, Information on RYO Cigarette Tobacco Manufactured or Imported by a Distributor, to their monthly return (Form MT-203, Distributor of Tobacco Products Tax Return). A distributor that does not manufacture, import, or cause to be imported RYO cigarette tobacco for a particular month is not required to file Form MT-203-ATT for that month. (Reg. Sec. 89.4; *TSB-M-06(7)M*, Technical Services Bureau, Taxpayer Services Division, New York Department of Taxation and Finance, December 11, 2006)

The Department of Taxation and Finance will mail Form MT-203-ATT to all distributors each month along with Form MT-203. The forms and instructions may be downloaded from the Department's website (http://www.nystax.gov) and are also available by fax at 1-800-748-FORM (1-800-748-3676). Distributors also may call 1-800-462-8100 to receive a copy by mail. (*TSB-M-06(7)M*, Technical Services Bureau, Taxpayer Services Division, New York Department of Taxation and Finance, December 11, 2006)

Transporters of tobacco products.—Any person possessing or transporting tobacco products in New York State must have invoices or delivery tickets for the tobacco products in his possession. The invoices or delivery tickets must show:

(1) the name and address of the consignor or seller;

(2) the name and address of the consignee or purchaser;

(3) the quantity and brands of tobacco products transported;

(4) the name and address of the person paying the tax; and

(5) the wholesale price or the tax paid or payable.

The absence of such invoices or delivery tickets is considered prima facie evidence that the person transporting the tobacco products is a dealer and is subject to tax. (Sec. 474(2), Tax Law)

Dealers and distributors.—Dealers or distributors who possess or transport tobacco products are required to have invoices or delivery tickets for the tobacco products in their possession. (Sec. 474(3), Tax Law) The invoices or delivery tickets must show:

(1) the name and address of the consignor or seller;

(2) the name and address of the consignee or purchaser;

(3) the quantity and brands of cigarettes products transported;

(4) the name and address of the person paying the tax; and

(5) the wholesale price or the tax paid or payable.

The absence of such invoices or delivery tickets is considered prima facie evidence that the tax on tobacco products has not been paid and is due and owing. (Sec. 474(2), Tax Law)

Out-of-state shippers.—The Commissioner may provide, by regulation, that whenever tobacco products are shipped into New York State, the railroad company, express company, trucking company or other public carrier transporting the shipment must file a copy of the freight bill with the Commissioner within ten days after delivery. (Sec. 474(4), Tax Law)

• *Payment*

Distributors are liable for payment of the tax on tobacco products which they import or cause to be imported into New York, or which they manufacture in New York. Dealers are liable for the tax on all tobacco products in their possession at any time, upon which tax has not been paid or assumed by a distributor appointed by the Commissioner of Taxation and Finance. (Sec. 471-b(2), Tax Law; Sec. 471-b(3), Tax Law)

• *Credits, refunds, discounts*

For provisions concerning credits for cigarettes purchased at Indian reservations, see Credits ¶ 55-001 under Cigarettes.

• *Licenses and permits*

Every tobacco product manufacturer whose roll-your-own (RYO) cigarette tobacco is sold for consumption in New York must annually certify under penalty of perjury that as of the date of that certification, the tobacco product manufacturer is:

— a participating manufacturer as defined by Sec. 1399-pp(1) of the Public Health Law; or

— a non-participating manufacturer in full compliance with Sec. 1399-pp(2) of the Public Health Law.

(Sec. 480-c, Tax Law; *TSB-M-08(8)M*, New York Department of Taxation and Finance, October 28, 2008)

This certification must be made on Form CG-30, Certification of Tobacco Master Settlement Agreement Status, and must include a list of the brands of RYO cigarette tobacco sold for consumption in New York State. Form CG-30 must be executed by the manufacturer and delivered to the Tax Department, the attorney general of New York State, and any distributor of that manufacturer's RYO cigarette tobacco no earlier than April 16 and no later than April 30 of each year (see the instructions for Form CG-30 for additional details). (*TSB-M-08(8)M*, New York Department of Taxation and Finance, October 28, 2008)

If the manufacturer introduces a new brand of RYO cigarette tobacco after filing the annual certification, Form CG-30.1-X, Additional Information Regarding Cigarette Brands Sold in New York, must be filed with the Tax Department, the attorney general, and any distributor prior to the first sale of the new brand. (*TSB-M-08(8)M*, New York Department of Taxation and Finance, October 28, 2008)

Licensing of roll-your-own cigarette/tobacco retailers.—Licensing requirements are discussed above at **Compliance Alert** under Tobacco Products.

• *Local taxes*

No local taxes are imposed on tobacco products other than little cigars.

SALES AND USE

[¶60-000]

INTRODUCTION

[¶60-020] Application of Sales and Use Taxes

New York sales tax is imposed on retail sales of taxable tangible personal property and specified taxable services. (Sec. 1105, Tax Law) Use tax is imposed on the use of taxable items and specified taxable services in New York when the sales tax has not been paid. (Sec. 1110, Tax Law)

For a quick reference guide for taxable and exempt property and services, including examples of each, see TB-ST-740.

Which transactions are generally subject to sales tax in New York?

Sales tax is imposed on retail sales of taxable tangible personal property and specified taxable services. (Sec. 1105, Tax Law) The tax is collected from the person who purchases at retail—the consumer. Liability for the tax occurs at the time of the transaction. The point of delivery or point at which possession is transferred by the vendor to the purchaser or the purchaser's designee controls both the tax incident and the tax rate. (Reg. Sec. 525.2)

In general, sales tax applies to the following categories:

— retail sales and rentals of tangible personal property;

— utilities (i.e., gas, electricity, refrigeration, and steam) and intrastate telephone and telegraph;

— sales of food and drink by restaurants, taverns, and caterers;

— admission and amusement charges;

— dues and initiation fees paid to social and athletic clubs;

— hotel room occupancies; and

— specifically enumerated taxable services.

For examples of taxable and exempt tangible personal property and services, see TB-ST-740.

Presumption of taxability. All receipts of tangible personal property and specified services, all rents for occupancy and all amusement charges are presumed taxable, unless the contrary is established. The burden of proving exemption from tax is imposed on the person required to collect tax or the purchaser of the goods or services. However, where a properly completed resale certificate, exempt use or exempt organization statement has been furnished to the vendor, the burden of proof as to non-taxability of a receipt, amusement charge or rent is shifted to the purchaser. (Sec. 1132(c), Tax Law)

In addition, New York has a rebuttable presumption that certain sellers of taxable tangible personal property or services, using New York residents to solicit sales in the state, are sales tax vendors that are required to register for sales tax purposes and collect state and local sales taxes. (Sec. 1101(b)(8)(vi), Tax Law) TSB-M-08(3)S TSB-M-08(3.1)S For a complete discussion of the rebuttable presumption, see Nexus—Doing Business in New York.

Responsibility for collecting tax. The collection of sales tax is generally performed by "persons required to collect tax." (Sec. 1131(1), Tax Law) Those persons required to collect tax are to collect the tax from the customer when collecting the price, amusement charge or rent to which it applies. Such persons are personally liable for the tax required to be collected. (Sec. 1133(a), Tax Law) However, the liability is transferred to the purchaser in the event that the tax has not been paid to the person required to collect it. (Sec. 1133(b), Tax Law)

Advertisement of tax. Persons required to collect the tax are not permitted to advertise or to suggest to a purchaser or to the general public (whether directly or indirectly) that the tax is not considered an element of the selling price. Nor is the vendor permitted to indicate that he or she will pay the tax, or that the tax will be refunded. (Sec. 1133, Tax Law)

Sales tax definitions.

Persons required to collect tax. "Persons required to collect tax" is defined to include all vendors of tangible personal property or services, recipients of amusement charges, operators of hotels and all insurers licensed to issue physical or property damage liability insurance for motor vehicles registered in New York. Individual corporate officers, employees and partners are also included as "persons required to collect tax" under certain circumstances. (Sec. 1131(1), Tax Law)

Retail purchase and retail sale. A "retail purchase" and "retail sale" respectively, are defined as a purchase or sale of tangible personal property by or to any person for any purpose other than (1) for resale in the same form or as a physical component part of other tangible personal property, or (2) for use by such person in performing certain taxable services where the property so sold becomes a physical component part of the property upon which the services are performed or is later actually transferred to the purchaser of the service in connection with the performance of the service. (Sec. 1101(b)(4)(i), Tax Law) The definition of retail sale includes any transfer of tangible personal property to certain entities when the property would be resold to related persons or entities, including: (1) sales to a single-member LLC or its subsidiary for resale to its member or owner, when the single-member LLC or its subsidiary is disregarded as an entity separate from its owner for federal income tax purposes; (2) sales to a partnership for resale to one or more of its partners; or (3) sales to a trustee of a trust for resale to one or more beneficiaries of the trust. (Sec. 1101(b)(4)(v), Tax Law; TSB-M-17(4)S)

Certain transfers to and from corporations and partnerships are excluded from the definition of the term "retail sale," including:

— transfers of tangible personal property to a corporation, solely in consideration for the issuance of its stock, pursuant to a merger or consolidation;

— distributions of property by a corporation to its stockholders as a liquidating dividend;

— distributions of property by a partnership to its partners in whole or partial liquidation;

— transfers of property to a corporation upon its organization in consideration for the issuance of its stock; and

— contributions of property to a partnership in consideration for a partnership interest.

(Sec. 1101(b)(4)(iii), Tax Law; Reg. Sec. 526.6(d))

¶60-020

These exclusions from the definition of "retail sale" do not apply to transfers, distributions, or contributions of aircraft and vessels between affiliated entities. (Sec. 1111(q), Tax Law) For additional information, see Transportation.

Sale, selling, and purchase. The terms "sale", "selling" and "purchase" are defined as any transfer of title and/or possession, exchange or barter, rental, lease or license to use or consume (whether conditional or not) in any manner, or by any means, for a consideration, of tangible personal property or the rendering of any service subject to the sales tax. The right to reproduce computer software is specifically included in the definition of the term "sale." (Sec. 1101(b)(5), Tax Law; Reg. Sec. 526.7(d)) The term "sale" also includes the transfer of tangible personal property in a repossession or foreclosure action, which may be effected in any manner, including but not limited to, voluntary relinquishment, assignment or seizure by the mortgagee. However, the transfer of tangible personal property in a repossession or foreclosure action by the mortgagee for the purpose of resale is not a taxable transaction. The transfer of tangible personal property to a carrier, repairman, warehouseman or insurer by the owner of the property after payment for damages or other losses is not defined as a sale. (Reg. Sec. 526.7(d))

Tangible personal property. The term "tangible personal property" includes all corporeal personal property. However, for purposes other than the tax on sales of utility services, the term does not include gas, electricity, refrigeration and steam. Pre-written computer software (sold as part of a package, as a separate component, or otherwise), regardless of the medium by which such software is conveyed to the purchaser, is specifically included in the definition of the term "tangible personal property." Likewise, "tangible personal property" does not include a modular home that is permanently affixed to real property. However, if the modular home is to be removed from the realty, then the home and its component parts would be tangible personal property whether sold as a whole or as pieces. (Sec. 1101(b)(6), Tax Law)

Property sold as tangible personal property and subsequently annexed to real property, or which becomes part of real property, is nevertheless considered tangible personal property at the time of sale. (Reg. Sec. 526.8)

Examples of taxable tangible personal property (TB-ST-175) include:

— raw materials (i.e., wood, cloth, or metal);

— manufactured items such as jewelry, clothing, furniture, machinery, and appliances;

— motor vehicles, gasoline, oil, and chemicals;

— computers and prewritten computer software (canned or off-the-shelf);

— artistic items such as paintings, sculptures, photographs, and craft items;

— animals, trees, shrubs, and flowers; and

— certain grocery store items such as soda, beer, candy, and bottled water.

Which transactions are generally subject to use tax in New York?

Use tax is imposed on the use of taxable property and specified taxable services in New York when the sales tax has not been paid. (Sec. 1110, Tax Law)

Guidebook to New York Taxes

> *NOTE:* For purposes of use tax, taxable property and services are generally the same items or services that would be subject to New York sales tax if sold in New York. (TB-ST-910)

"Use" is defined as the exercise of any right or power over tangible personal property by the purchaser. This includes, but is not limited to, the receiving, storage or any keeping or retention for any length of time, withdrawal from storage, or any installation, affixation to real or personal property, or consumption of such property. The term "use" also includes the distribution of only tangible personal property, such as promotional materials. (Sec. 1101(b)(7), Tax Law; Reg. Sec. 526.9) For definitions of terminology specified in the definition of "use," see Reg. Sec. 526.9.

For a discussion of the application of use tax for businesses and individuals (including estates and trusts), see TB-ST-910 and TB-ST-913.

Situations in which businesses or individuals owe use tax.

Purchases of taxable property or services made outside of New York. Purchases of taxable property from a seller who is located outside of New York without paying New York state and local sales taxes, which are later used in New York, are subject to use tax. Property that is taken or sent out of New York to have a taxable service performed on that property, and it is then brought or shipped back into New York for use in the state, is subject to use tax. Purchases of taxable services outside New York that are used in New York are subject to use tax. Examples of these services include taxable information services and protective (security) and detective services. (TB-ST-910; TB-ST-913)

Property purchased while a nonresident of New York. No use tax is due upon tangible personal property purchased by the user while a nonresident of New York. However, use tax is imposed when a nonresident business brings tangible personal property or a taxable service into New York for use in New York unless the nonresident business has been doing business outside New York for at least six months prior to the date that the property or service is brought into New York. (Sec. 1182(2), Tax Law; TSB-M-17(4)S) This restriction on the use tax exclusion for purchases by nonresident businesses does not apply to individuals. Also, if a nonresident business paid sales or use tax in another state when it purchased the property or service subject to use tax under this provision, a reciprocal credit for sales or use tax paid in the other state may be available. (TSB-M-17(4)S)

Purchases made over the Internet, from catalogs, or by phone from out-of-state businesses. Purchases of taxable property or services over the Internet, from catalogs, or by phone without paying New York sales tax, and the seller delivers the property or service into New York, including by common carrier, are subject to use tax. (TB-ST-910; TB-ST-913)

Purchases of taxable property or services on an Indian reservation. Purchases of taxable property or services from an Indian reservation without paying New York sales tax, which are brought or delivered to New York, are subject to use tax. (TB-ST-910; TB-ST-913)

> *NOTE:* Indian arts and crafts purchased on Indian reservations are not taxable property. (TB-ST-910; TB-ST-913)

Purchases where the taxable property or services are used in a different local taxing jurisdiction than where they were purchased or where they were

delivered. Local sales tax rates vary from one jurisdiction (city, county, etc.) within New York to another. The amount of use tax a business or individual owes is generally determined by the rates in effect where the business uses the item or service or where the individual lives. Therefore, even though New York state and local sales tax may have been collected where the item or service was purchased, if the local tax was collected at a rate that is lower than the rate at the location where the business uses the item or service or the individual lives and uses the item, the business or individual will owe the difference in use tax. However, if the local tax was collected at a rate that is higher than the rate at the location where the item or service is used, the business or individual is not entitled to a refund of the difference. (TB-ST-910; TB-ST-913)

Withdrawal of taxable property from inventory. When businesses purchase taxable property (such as inventory) or services without paying taxes because they intend to resell them, but they remove an item from inventory and use it, it is subject to use tax. (TB-ST-910; TB-ST-913)

How to calculate use tax. Use tax is generally due on the consideration given or contracted to be given for the property or service, or for the use of the property or service, including any charges by the seller to the user for shipping or handling. (TB-ST-910; TB-ST-913)

"Consideration" is the dollar value of all amounts paid for any property or service. It can include:

— money;

— bartered goods or services;

— assumption of liabilities;

— fees, rentals, royalties;

— charges that a purchaser, lessee, or licensee is required to pay (i.e., delivery charge); and

— any other agreement for payment.

For a detailed discussion of the methods for calculating use tax due for businesses and individuals, see TB-ST-910 and TB-ST-913.

Does New York follow destination or origin based sourcing for general retail sales?

New York follows destination based sourcing of general interstate and intrastate retail sales. Specifically, New York sales tax is a "destination tax" for both interstate and intrastate sales. The point of delivery or point at which possession is transferred by the vendor to the purchaser, or the purchaser's designee, controls both the tax incidence and the tax rate. (Reg. Sec. 525.2(a)(3); Reg. Sec. 526.7(e)) (Publication 750)

Does New York provide any other information concerning the general applicability of sales and use taxes?

Yes. New York provides information on various aspects of sales and use tax.

Rates. New York has a standard sales and use tax rate and Metropolitan Commuter Transportation District (MCTD) rate (¶61-110), as well as various local sales and use tax rates (¶61-735).

Due dates. For a discussion of due dates, see Returns, Payments, and Due Dates (¶61-220).

Filing and payment requirements. For a discussion of filing and payment requirements, see Returns, Payments, and Due Dates (¶61-220).

Services. Services (¶60-665) are generally exempt from sales and use tax unless specifically identified as taxable.

Tax holidays. New York does not currently have any tax holidays.

Credits. New York provides various credits (¶61-270), including a credit for tax paid to out-of-state jurisdictions.

Local taxes. Counties, cities, and certain school districts may impose local sales and use taxes. For a discussion of local tax rates, see Local Tax Rates (¶61-735).

Co-vendor agreements. A co-vendor agreement applies to situations where a seller (generally a manufacturer, wholesaler, or other supplier) has independent distributors selling its products through party plans or similar arrangements (i.e., catalog, door-to-door sales, multi-level marketing, etc.). In a co-vendor situation, the supplier can request to enter into a written co-vendor agreement with the department and, once approved, takes on all the sales tax responsibilities for its independent distributors. The supplier must register for New York state sales tax purposes and collect and remit any sales taxes due. (TB-ST-142)

The independent distributor processes a customer's order paperwork and submits it directly to the supplier. The supplier then sends the items ordered to the independent distributor for delivery to the customers or sends the items directly to the customers. The supplier must collect sales tax from the independent distributor based on the retail selling price of the items purchased at the tax rate in effect where the items are delivered to the independent distributor or to the customer. (TB-ST-142)

An independent distributor whose supplier is registered and is complying with its responsibilities as a New York co-vendor is not required to register as a vendor. (TB-ST-142)

The supplier and its independent distributors remain jointly liable for any sales taxes due, even though only the supplier is actually registered and files sales and use tax returns. (TB-ST-142)

Terms of co-vendor agreements. The Department of Taxation and Finance has a standard co-vendor agreement that it will send to a supplier that requests to be treated as a co-vendor. The supplier must complete the agreement and return it to the department. In addition, the supplier must furnish:

— a detailed description of its business operation in New York;

— copies of catalogs, etc., showing the suggested retail prices of its products; and

— copies of any contracts or other agreements in place between the supplier and its independent distributors.

The agreement may be canceled or terminated by either party only upon at least 90 days written notification to the other party by certified or registered mail. However, the cancellation may only go into effect at the close of business on the last day of February, May, August, or November.

Refund or credit for sales tax refunded to distributors. The sales tax collected by a supplier from its independent distributors must be based on the catalog or suggested retail price of a taxable product. However, if the independent distributor sells a product to a customer at a price lower than the catalog or suggested retail price, the supplier may: (i) refund to the independent distributor the difference in sales tax between the amount collected based on the catalog or suggested retail price and the amount due based on the lower price at which the product was sold; and (ii) use Form AU-11, Application for Credit or Refund of Sales or Use Tax, to claim a refund or credit of the sales tax refunded to the independent distributor. (TB-ST-142)

Other reasons for claiming a refund or credit include (TB-ST-142):

— price adjustments;

— out-of-state deliveries;

— local jurisdictional adjustments;

— merchandise used for personal consumption or demonstration purposes;

— exempt sales;

— returned merchandise; and

— clerical or mathematical errors.

Sales records. Suppliers and their independent distributors must keep records of: every sale, the amount of the sale, and the sales tax collected. In addition, suppliers must maintain the names, addresses, and sales tax identification numbers (if any) of their independent distributors. (TB-ST-142)

[¶60-025] Nexus--Doing Business in State

Whether an obligation to collect New York sales or use tax attaches to a sale by an out-of-seller is determined by a combination of federal and state restrictions. At the federal level, the determination revolves around whether a nexus (or connection) between the sale and New York can be established. If there is sufficient nexus, it then must be determined whether the seller qualifies as a "retailer engaged in business" in the state.

What is sales and use tax nexus?

In the state tax area, nexus is an important concern for companies that have a multistate presence because it is a threshold issue that must be evaluated to determine whether a business has tax registration, filing, collection, and remittance obligations in a particular jurisdiction. "Sales and use tax nexus" refers to the amount and type of business activity that must be present before the business is subject to the state's taxing authority.

State tax nexus considerations differ by tax type and jurisdiction, and there has been limited guidance from tax authorities as to when nexus conclusively exists. State nexus statutes are subject to federal constitutional restrictions.

In a series of cases, the U.S. Supreme Court established a general rule of "substantial nexus" which required an out-of-state seller to have a physical presence in a state before that state could require the seller to register and collect and remit sales or use taxes. Physical presence can be created by employees or other agents, property owned or leased in the state, or other factors. There are many gray areas when it comes to determining whether nexus conclusively exists, particularly for e-commerce.

Timeline of Important U.S. Supreme Court Nexus Cases

However, in *South Dakota v. Wayfair, Inc.*, 585 U.S. __ (2018), the U.S. Supreme Court held that physical presence is no longer required to establish substantial nexus.

Rather, economic and virtual contacts in a state and minimum in-state sales thresholds can establish sales and use tax nexus.

PLANNING NOTE: Nexus determinations are based on a taxpayer's specific set of facts. Taxpayers must carefully evaluate whether specific activities or types of contact create/establish nexus in each state in which they do business, as well as how frequently such contacts must occur in order to create tax nexus. A certain combination of business activities or a specific aspect of an activity may result in a different conclusion. To have a complete picture of all tax reporting requirements, multistate businesses should conduct a nexus review. A nexus review helps businesses understand their exposure and avoid audit situations.

South Dakota v. Wayfair. In a 5 to 4 decision, the U.S. Supreme Court held that *Quill Corp. v. North Dakota*, 504 U.S. 298 (1992), and *National Bellas Hess, Inc. v. Department of Revenue of Ill.*, 386 U.S. 753 (1967), are overruled because *Quill's* physical presence rule is unsound and incorrect. As a result, physical presence is no longer required to establish sales and use tax nexus.

The Court held that the *Complete Auto* (*Complete Auto Transit v. Brady*, 430 U.S. 274 (1977)) substantial nexus requirement with the taxing state is satisfied based on both the economic and virtual contacts the respondents have with the state. As a result of this decision, states are now free to levy taxes on sales of goods and services regardless of whether the seller has a physical presence in the state. Due process requirements, unrelated to those required by the "Commerce Clause" of the Constitution still apply, as do other nexus tests of the Commerce Clause. Since the *Wayfair* decision was issued, many states have enacted economic nexus and/or marketplace nexus thresholds. (*South Dakota v. Wayfair, Inc.*, 585 U.S. ___ (2018))

How is nexus established in New York?

The collection of New York sales and use taxes is generally performed by "persons required to collect tax," which includes vendors meeting the following descriptions:

- those making sales of taxable tangible personal property or services;
- those maintaining a place of business in New York and making sales of taxable tangible personal property or services to persons within the state. A person is considered to be maintaining a place of business in New York if it has a store, salesroom, sample room, showroom, distribution center, warehouse, service center, factory, credit and collection office, administrative office or research facility in New York;
- those who solicit business by employees, independent contractors, agents or other representatives and by reason of such solicitation makes sales of taxable tangible personal property or services in New York;
- those who solicit business by the distribution of catalogs or other advertising matter (whether or not by regular or systematic solicitation) where such person has some additional connection with New York that satisfies the nexus requirement of the U.S. Constitution and by reason of such solicitation makes sales of taxable tangible personal property or services within New York. The additional connection with New York a person may have in order to qualify as a vendor include, but are not limited to having the following in New York: the operation of a retail store; the presence of traveling sales representatives; the presence of employees, independent contractors or agents; the presence of service representatives; the maintenance of a post office box for receiving re-

sponses to such person's solicitations; or the maintenance of an office, even if such office performs no activities related to the sales solicited by such person;

- those who make sales of taxable tangible personal property or services and regularly or systematically deliver the property or services in New York by means other than the U.S. mail or common carrier. A person is presumed to be regularly or systematically delivering property or services in New York if the cumulative total number of occasions such person or his agent came into New York to deliver property and/or services exceeded 12 during the immediately preceding four quarterly sales tax reporting periods;

- those who regularly or systematically solicit business in New York by distribution (regardless of the place of origination) of catalogs, advertising flyers, letters, or any other means of solicitation, and who thereby makes taxable sales to persons within New York, provided the solicitation satisfies the nexus requirement of the U.S. Constitution;

- those making sales of taxable tangible personal property where the seller retains an ownership interest in the property and where such property is brought into New York by the purchaser, who is or becomes a resident or who uses the property in any manner in carrying on any employment, trade, business or profession in New York;

- those making sales to persons within New York of taxable tangible personal property or services who are authorized by the Commissioner of Taxation and Finance to collect the tax;

- the State of New York, including its agencies and political subdivisions, when such entity sells services or property of a kind ordinarily sold by private persons; and

- the United States, its agencies and instrumentalities, and any other international organization of which the United States is a member, when engaged in selling, in New York, services or property of a kind ordinarily sold by private persons.

(Sec. 1101(b)(8)(i), Tax Law; Reg. Sec. 526.10(a))

EXAMPLE: An independent manufacturer's representative, representing many clients and acting on his own behalf, who solicits orders from New York customers is a vendor. (Reg. Sec. 526.10(a)(1))

EXAMPLE: A California based company uses independent manufacturer's representatives, who are residents of New York, to sell its product in New York. The California company is a vendor. (Reg. Sec. 526.10(a)(3))

EXAMPLE: A company with its main office in Nevada has a mail order business that solicits sales in New York via catalogs mailed directly to customers in New York. Customer orders are sent to, and all orders are filled from, the mail order headquarters in Nevada. The company also operates retail stores in New York. The company is a vendor for purposes of both the mail order business and the retail stores. (Reg. Sec. 526.10(a)(4))

EXAMPLE: A company in Ohio makes weekly deliveries of business forms in its own trucks to its customers in New York. The forms were ordered by mail or telephone. The company is presumed to be regularly or systematically delivering property in the State and is therefore presumed to be a vendor. (Reg. Sec. 526.10(a)(5))

COMPLIANCE TIP: If a business located outside New York solicits sales of taxable tangible personal property or services through employees, salespersons, independent agents, or representatives located in New York, the business must register as a vendor and obtain a Certificate of Authority for New York sales tax purposes. (Sec. 1101(b)(8), Tax Law; Reg. Sec. 526.10(a)(3))

New York also has economic nexus, click-through nexus, affiliate nexus, and marketplace provider provisions.

Exempt organizations. The term "vendor" also includes certain exempt organizations that make sales of tangible personal property through a shop or store operated by the organization, or that sell food and drink in New York. These exempt organizations include:

• posts or organizations of past or present members of the U.S. Armed Forces organized in New York (including auxiliary units, societies, trusts or foundations of such posts or organizations) which meet certain membership requirements, no part of net earnings of which inures to the benefit of any private shareholder or individual: and

• any corporation, association, trust or community chest fund or foundation organized exclusively for religious, charitable, scientific testing for public safety, literary or educational purposes or to foster national or international amateur sports competition, or for the prevention of cruelty to children or animals, subject to certain requirements. (Reg. Sec. 526.10(a))

Fulfillment companies. The definition of vendor excludes any person who purchases fulfillment services carried on in New York from a non-affiliated person and a person that owns tangible personal property located on the premises of a non-affiliated fulfillment services provider performing services for that person. The purchaser of the fulfillment services must not otherwise be a vendor. Fulfillment services are defined as: accepting orders or responding to consumer correspondence or inquiries electronically or via mail, telephone, fax, or the Internet; billing and collection activities; or shipping of orders from inventory. Persons are affiliated persons with respect to each other if one has a direct or indirect ownership interest of more than 5% in the other or if an ownership interest of more than 5%, direct or indirect, is held in each such person by another or by a group of persons that are affiliated persons with respect to each other. Thus, a foreign corporation may engage a New York fulfillment service company to fill orders for it with merchandise stored in New York and the foreign corporation will not be considered a vendor. (Sec. 1101(b)(8), Tax Law)

Internet advertising. The term "vendor" does not include a person having its advertisingstored on a server or other computer equipment located in New York or a person whose advertising is disseminated or displayed on the Internet by an individual or entity having nexus with New York. (Sec. 12, Tax Law)

Trade shows. The New York Department of Taxation and Finance has issued advisory opinions that held that out-of-state manufacturers whose only contact with New York consisted of participation in trade shows at which its products were demonstrated, but not sold, were not required to collect New York state and local taxes on goods delivered via U.S. mail or common carrier to New York customers. (TSB-A-96(62)S)

Accounting or legal services. In-state activities of an affiliate in providing accounting or legal services or advice, or in directing the activities of a seller, including but not limited to, making decisions about strategic planning, marketing, inventory, staffing, distribution, or cash management, do not make the seller a vendor. (Sec. 1101(b)(8)(i), Tax Law)

Does New York have economic nexus?

Yes. A business that has no physical presence in New York, but meets the following requirements in the immediately preceding four sales tax quarters, is required to register and collect/remit sales tax:

- makes more than $500,000 in sales of tangible personal property delivered in New York, **and**

- makes more than 100 sales of tangible personal property delivered in New York.

(Secs. 1101(b)(8)(i)(E) and 1101(b)(8)(iv), Tax Law) (Important Notice N-19-1; TSB-M-19(4)S)

NOTE: Ch. 39 (S.B. 6615) increased the economic nexus threshold from $300,000 to $500,000. The increase for businesses that have no physical presence in New York is effective retroactively to June 21, 2018. The increase for marketplace providers is effective retroactively to June 1, 2019.

Both of these conditions must be met during the lookback period. For example, a business that meets the sales threshold but has not made more than 100 transactions in that period is not required to register for sales tax.

Relief for incorrect local tax rate. A business with no physical presence in New York that registered for sales tax because of the above provisions, and in good faith, collected and remitted sales tax at an incorrect local rate, must pay the additional local sales tax due but is not liable for penalty and interest on the additional local tax. This relief applies only to sales made during the first four quarterly periods after the business was required to register. (TSB-M-19(4)S)

New York has provided answers to frequently asked questions related to economic nexus provisions that require registration for businesses with no physical presence in New York.

Marketplace providers. Marketplace providers are also required to collect and remit sales tax on taxable sales of tangible personal property that they facilitate. A "marketplace provider" is a person who, pursuant to an agreement, facilitates sales of tangible personal property by a marketplace seller(s). (Sec. 1101(e)(1), Tax Law) (TSB-M-19(2.1)S)

A person "facilitates a sale of tangible personal property" when the person meets both of the following conditions:

- such person provides the forum in which, or by means of which, the sale takes place or the offer of sale is accepted, including an Internet website, catalog, shop, store, booth, or similar forum; and

- such person or an affiliate of such person collects the receipts paid by a customer to a marketplace seller for a sale of tangible personal property, or contracts with a third party to collect such receipts. (Sec. 1101(e)(1), Tax Law)

To be a marketplace provider a person must meet both criteria in the above definition. For example, a person that provides a forum for third parties to make sales or the offer of a sale is not a marketplace provider if it (or an affiliate, as defined above) does not collect the payment paid by a customer, or if it has not contracted with a third party to collect the payments. (TSB-M-19(2.1)S)

A marketplace provider must be registered with the Department for sales tax purposes. If not already registered, the marketplace provider must register at least 20 days before beginning business in New York. (TSB-M-19(2.1)S)

A person with no physical presence in New York who facilitates sales of marketplace sellers is a marketplace provider and if required to register for sales tax purposes and collect, remit sales tax, if, in the previous four sales tax quarters:

• the cumulative total of the person's gross receipts from sales made or facilitated of tangible personal property delivered into the state exceeded $500,000; and

• such person made or facilitated more than 100 sales of tangible personal property delivered in New York.

(Sec. 1101(e)(1), Tax Law) (TSB-M-19(2.1)S)

NOTE: Ch. 39 (S.B. 6615) increased the economic nexus threshold from $300,000 to $500,000. The increase for businesses that have no physical presence in New York is effective retroactively to June 21, 2018. The increase for marketplace providers is effective retroactively to June 1, 2019.

Marketplace sellers. A marketplace seller is defined as any person who has an agreement with a marketplace provider under which the marketplace provider will facilitate sales of tangible personal property for the marketplace seller. (TSB-M-19(2.1)S)

Sales of tangible personal property. A marketplace provider is required to collect and remit sales tax on all taxable sales of tangible personal property (including sales of prewritten computer software that is downloaded or remotely accessed by the customer) that it facilitates for marketplace sellers, regardless of whether the marketplace seller is required to register for sales tax purposes. A sale is any transaction where there is as transfer of title or possession, or both, of tangible personal property for a consideration. However, a marketplace provider is not required to collect sales tax on the rental of a passenger car. (TSB-M-19(2.1)S)

A marketplace provider is not required to collect sales tax on transactions that are not considered the sale of tangible personal property, such as sales of: (i) services (for example, transportation services or electric service); (ii) restaurant food; (iii) hotel occupancy; or (iv) admissions to a place of amusement.

A marketplace seller who is registered to collect New York State sales tax and makes sales of tangible personal property in New York State by means other than through a marketplace provider remains responsible for collecting and remitting any tax due on those sales. Such a marketplace seller also remains responsible for collecting sales tax on taxable transactions facilitated by a marketplace provider that do not involve the sale of tangible personal property.

Requirements for marketplace providers. A marketplace provider has all the obligations and rights of a vendor, including, but not limited to: obtaining a Certificate of Authority; collecting tax, filing returns, and remitting the tax due; the right to accept a certificate or other documentation substantiating an exemption or exclusion from tax; and the right to receive a refund. (TSB-M-19(2.1)S)

A marketplace provider cannot refuse to collect tax on a marketplace seller's sales, even if the seller is registered for sales tax purposes. Marketplace providers must keep records and cooperate with the Tax Department to ensure the proper collection and remittance of tax imposed, collected or required to be collected. Except as provided below, a marketplace provider must issue Form

¶60-025

ST-150, Marketplace Provider Certificate of Collection, to its marketplace sellers for sales of tangible personal property that it facilitates for such sellers.

Liability relief for marketplace providers. A marketplace provider is relieved of liability for failure to collect the correct amount of tax to the extent that the marketplace provider can show that the error was due to incorrect or insufficient information given to the marketplace provider by the marketplace seller. This liability relief does not apply if the marketplace seller and marketplace provider are affiliated. (TSB-M-19(2.1)S)

Liability relief for marketplace sellers. A marketplace seller who is registered to collect New York sales tax is relieved from the duty to collect tax on a sale of tangible personal property and should not include the receipts from the sale in its taxable receipts if: (i) the marketplace seller can show that the sale was facilitated by a marketplace provider from whom the marketplace seller has received, in good faith, a properly completed Form ST-150, Marketplace Provider Certificate of Collection, certifying that the marketplace provider is registered to collect sales tax and will collect sales tax on all taxable sales of tangible personal property by the marketplace seller facilitated by the marketplace provider; and (ii) any failure of the marketplace provider to collect the proper amount of tax on a sale was not the result of the marketplace seller providing the marketplace provider with incorrect or insufficient information. (This relief of liability does not apply if the marketplace seller and marketplace provider are affiliated) (TSB-M-19(2.1)S)

Alternative to Form ST-150. A marketplace provider who has a publicly-available agreement with its marketplace sellers that includes the following statement, or one that is substantially similar, does not need to issue Form ST-150 to such sellers: [Marketplace provider name] is registered to collect New York State sales tax and will collect sales tax on all taxable sales of tangible personal property that it facilitates for marketplace sellers for delivery to a New York State address.

This provision will have the same effect as if the marketplace provider had issued Form ST-150 to its marketplace sellers. If a marketplace seller has a publicly-available agreement with a marketplace provider that includes the statement provided above, it does not need to obtain Form ST-150 from such provider.

Does New York have click-through nexus?

Yes. New York has a rebuttable presumption that certain sellers of taxable tangible personal property or services are sales tax vendors required to register for sales tax purposes and collect state and local sales taxes. Specifically, a seller that makes taxable sales of tangible personal property or services in New York is presumed to be a vendor required to be registered for sales tax purposes and required to collect sales tax on all of its taxable sales in New York, if both of the following conditions are met:

• the seller enters into an agreement(s) with a New York resident(s) under which, for a commission or other consideration, the resident representative directly or indirectly refers potential customers to the seller, whether by link on an Internet website or otherwise (i.e., a resident representative would be indirectly referring potential customers to the seller where the resident representative refers potential customers to its own website, or to another party's website which then directs the potential customer to the seller's website); and

• the cumulative gross receipts from sales by the seller to customers in New York as a result of referrals by all of the seller's resident representatives under the type of contract or agreement described above total more than $10,000 during the preceding four quarterly sales tax periods (ending on the last day of February, May, August, and November)

(Sec. 1101(b)(8)(vi), Tax Law) (TSB-M-08(3)S; TSB-M-08(3.1)S; TSB-M-08(9)S)

For purposes of this presumption, a seller meets the condition of having an agreement with a New York resident if the seller enters into an agreement with a third party under which the third party, in turn, enters into an agreement with the New York resident to act as the seller's representative. (TSB-M-08(3)S)

An agreement to place an advertisement does not give rise to the presumption. For this purpose, placing an advertisement does not include the placement of a link on a website that, directly or indirectly, links to the seller's website, where the consideration for placing the link on the website is based on the volume of completed sales generated by the link. (TSB-M-08(3)S)

Rebutting the presumption. A seller may rebut the presumption that it is soliciting sales in New York through resident representatives. The Department of Taxation and Finance deems the presumption rebutted if the seller establishes that the resident representatives' only activity in New York on behalf of the seller is a website link to the seller's website, and none of the resident representatives engage in any solicitation activity in the state targeted at potential New York customers on behalf of the seller. (Sec. 1101(b)(8)(vi), Tax Law) (TSB-M-08(3)S) Inclusion of language in a contract or agreement between a seller and a resident representative that prohibits solicitation by the resident representative is not sufficient, by itself, to rebut the presumption. The seller must be able to demonstrate both that the prohibition has been established and that the resident representative has complied with it. (TSB-M-08(3.1)S) For example, a seller may rebut the presumption by meeting both of the following conditions (TSB-M-08(3.1)S):

Contract condition. The contract or agreement between the seller and the resident representative provides that the resident representative is prohibited from engaging in any solicitation activities in New York that refer potential customers to the seller including, but not limited to, distributing flyers, coupons, newsletters and other printed promotional materials, or electronic equivalents; verbal solicitation (e.g., in-person referrals); initiating telephone calls; and sending e-mails. In addition, if the resident representative is an organization such as a club or a nonprofit group, the contract or agreement must provide that the organization's website will maintain information alerting its members to the prohibition against each of the solicitation activities described above; and

Proof of compliance condition. Annually, each resident representative must submit to the seller a signed certification stating that it has not engaged in any prohibited solicitation activities in New York, at any time during the previous year. If the resident representative is an organization, the annual certification must also include a statement from the resident organization certifying that its website includes information directed at its members alerting them to the prohibition against the solicitation activities. Also, the certification must contain a statement alerting the representative that the certification and any information submitted with it is subject to verification and audit by the Department of Taxation and Finance.

With regard to the proof of compliance condition, the following provisions also apply (TSB-M-08(3.1)S):

• Annual certification may be submitted to the seller in paper form or electronically. The certification must be signed (manually or electronically) by the resident representative. If the resident representative is an organization, the certification must be signed by a person who has the authority to execute binding contracts on behalf of the organization. The certification must also show the name and address of the resident representative (or, if it is an organization, the name and address of the person signing).

- A seller satisfies this condition if it receives the completed certifications from its resident representatives and accepts them in good faith (that is, the seller does not know or have reason to know that any certifications are false or fraudulent).

- The seller must retain copies of the certifications (hard-copy or electronic format) and make the copies available to the Department upon request.

- In weighing the significance of a seller's reliance on certifications from fewer than all its New York resident representatives, the Department will apply constitutional standards.

- There is no specific form required for this certification process. The seller may choose the form of the certification as long as it contains the required information.

COMPLIANCE TIP: If the seller meets these two conditions, it rebuts the presumption. Accordingly, the seller need not register and collect tax unless the Department subsequently determines that any of the resident representatives are actually engaging in solicitation activities in New York or that the seller is a vendor for some other reason (e.g., the seller has employees in the state). (TSB-M-08(3.1)S)

Does New York have affiliate nexus?

Yes. Under certain conditions, the definition of "vendor" includes out-of-state sellers (remote affiliates) of taxable tangible personal property or services that are affiliated with businesses in New York (New York affiliates). A New York business and an out-of-state seller are affiliated with each other if one owns, directly or indirectly, more than 5% of the other or if more than 5% of each person is owned, directly or indirectly, by the same person or by an affiliated group of persons. (Sec. 1101(b)(8)(i)(I), Tax Law) (TSB-M-09(3)S; TSB-M-09(16)S) Remote affiliates are vendors and must register for sales tax purposes and begin to collect and remit sales tax when they are affiliated with a business in New York and either of the following conditions is met (TSB-M-09(3)S):

Condition I. A New York affiliate who is a sales tax vendor uses a trademark, service mark, or trade name in New York that is the same as that used in New York by the remote affiliate; or

Condition II. A New York affiliate engages in activities in New York that benefit the remote affiliate in its development or maintenance of a market for its goods or services in New York, to the extent that those activities are sufficient for the remote affiliate to satisfy the nexus requirements of the U.S. Constitution (Condition II). Condition II will be met if the percentage of direct or indirect ownership exceeds 50% (i.e., if one owns more than 50% of the other, or if more than 50% of each is owned by the same person or by an affiliated group) and the New York affiliate engages in any activities that are more than de minimis and promote the development or maintenance of a market for the remote affiliate's products or services in New York.

The following activities will result in vendor status under Condition II (TSB-M-09(3)S):

- referring New York customers to the remote affiliate;

- accepting merchandise returns from catalog, telephone, or Internet customers of the remote affiliate;

• *Metropolitan commuter transportation district (MCTD)*

An additional New York state sales and compensating use tax rate of $3/8$ of 1% is imposed in the Metropolitan Commuter Transportation District (MCTD). (Sec. 1109(a), Tax Law) (TSB-M-05(7)S) The MCTD consists of New York City and the Counties of Dutchess, Nassau, Orange, Putnam, Rockland, Suffolk and Westchester.

If the counties of Dutchess, Orange, or Rockland withdraw from the MCTD, they can adopt, in the alternative, rates up to 3 $3/8$%, provided revenues equal to $3/8$% are set aside for mass transportation purposes. (Sec. 1210, Tax Law)

• *Energy sources and services*

There is currently no statewide sales and use tax imposed upon retail sales or uses of: fuel oil, coal, propane (except when sold in containers of less than 100 pounds), natural gas, electricity or steam when used for residential purposes and upon wood when used for residential heating purposes. (Sec. 1105-A, Tax Law) The statewide portion of this tax was phased out as of October 1, 1980. For further details, see ¶ 60-750 Utilities.

The state sales tax, however, is imposed upon: (1) diesel motor fuel delivered at a filling station or into a repository equipped to dispense fuel into the fuel tank of a motor vehicle and (2) enhanced diesel motor fuel, except when used exclusively for residential purposes and delivered into a storage tank which is not equipped with a hose or other apparatus for dispensing the fuel into the fuel tank of a motor vehicle and which tank is attached to the heating unit burning the fuel. For deliveries of fuel exceeding 4,500 gallons, a certificate signed by the purchaser and stating that the product will be used exclusively for residential purposes is required. (Sec. 1105-A, Tax Law)

Localities, including New York City, may adopt reduced rates on retail sales and uses of certain residential energy sources or may exempt such sales and uses. (Sec. 1210(i), Tax Law) See also ¶ 61-735 Local Rates.

A phased-in reduction of the rate on gas and electric services is discussed at ¶ 60-750 Utilities.

• *Passenger car rentals*

Statewide special tax.—There is an additional 6% state-only sales or use tax on the short-term rental of a passenger car rented within New York, or rented outside New York for use within New York. "Short-term rental" means any rental for less than one year. (TB-ST-825)

Special supplemental tax.—In addition to the statewide 6% passenger car rental tax, there is a 6% special supplemental tax (total of 12%) on all passenger car rentals where delivery occurs within the MCTD, or where the passenger car is rented outside the MCTD for use within the MCTD. Also, there is an additional supplemental tax of 6% is imposed on passenger car rentals outside the MCTD (total of 12%). (Sec. 1166-A, Tax Law) (TB-ST-825); Sec. 1166-a, Tax Law; Sec. 1166-b, Tax Law) (TSB-M-19(1)S)

For a complete discussion of both taxes imposed on passenger car rentals, see ¶ 60-570 Motor Vehicles.

[¶60-200]

TAXABILITY OF PERSONS AND TRANSACTIONS

[¶60-230] Admissions, Entertainment, and Dues

Generally, sales tax is imposed on admission charges in excess of 10¢ to or for the use of a place of amusement in New York (admission charges of 10¢ or less are not subject to tax). (Sec. 1105(f)(1), Tax Law; Reg. Sec. 527.10(a)(1)) (TB-ST-8)

• *Taxable admission definitions*

"Admission charge".—An admission charge is the amount paid for admission, season ticket or subscription to any place of amusement, including any service charge or any charge for entertainment or amusement or for the use of the facilities. (Sec. 1101(d)(2), Tax Law; Reg. Sec. 527.10(b)(1)(i))

Taxable charges for the use of facilities for entertainment include any charge for the use of a device, at a place of entertainment, without distinction to the manner in which payment is made. (Reg. Sec. 527.10(b)(1)(iii))

CCH COMMENT: "Free" or "complimentary" tickets.—"Free" or "complimentary" tickets furnished for athletic events are not subject to tax, since no additional consideration for the tickets is given. *(TSB-M-78(16)S)*

"Place of amusement.—"A "place of amusement" is any place where facilities for entertainment, amusement or sports are provided. The term includes:

• a theater, concert hall, opera house or other place where a performance is given;

• fairground or exhibition hall or grounds;

• golf course, athletic field, sporting arena, gymnasium, bowling alley, shooting gallery, swimming pool, bathing beach, skating rink, tennis court, handball court, billiard hall or other place for athletic exhibits; and

• a "penny arcade" or any room which includes ping pong tables and amusement devices and any amusement device, carousel, miniature fair, ferris wheel or other amusement ride (whether or not contained in an enclosure).

(Sec. 1101(d)(10), Tax Law; Reg. Sec. 527.10(b)(3))

Examples of taxable admission charges include, but are not limited to, admission charges to:

• professional or college sporting events, including: football, baseball, basketball, or hockey games; golf tournaments; tennis matches; stock car races; track and field events; and swimming or skating competitions;

• amusement parks;

• fairgrounds or exhibition halls;

• beaches;

• carnivals and rodeos;

• variety shows;

• museums;

• zoos;

• aquariums;

- play centers for children;

- trade shows open to the public, such as automobile, boat or animal shows;

- closed circuit television broadcasts of any sporting event originating outside of New York shown at a theater or other establishment in New York;

- haunted houses; and

- adult entertainment establishments.

(Reg. Sec. 527.10(b)(1)(ii)) (TB-ST-8)

• *Nontaxable admissions*

Sporting events.—Tax is not imposed upon charges for admission to: race tracks and "combative sports" taxed under another provision of New York law, dramatic or musical arts performances, or live circus performances, or sporting facilities where the patron is to be a participant (such as bowling alleys and swimming pools). (Sec. 1105(f)(1), Tax Law; Reg. Sec. 527.10(d))

Live dramatic, choreographic, or musical performances.—Admission charges to live dramatic, choreographic, or musical arts performances are exempt from tax. For sales tax purposes, variety shows, magic shows, circuses, animal acts, ice shows, aquatic shows and similar performances are not considered "dramatic or musical arts performances." (Reg. Sec. 527.10(d)(2)) (TB-ST-8)

EXAMPLE: *Dance routines.*—A theater in the round has a show which consists exclusively of dance routines. The admission is exempt since choreography is included within the term "musical arts." (Reg. Sec. 527.10(d)(2))

EXAMPLE: *Multiple show acts.*— A show is composed of several acts in which performers dressed as story book characters, appearing with musical accompaniment, and portray scenes from books, inviting audience participation. This does not qualify as a dramatic or musical arts presentation. (Reg. Sec. 527.10(d)(2))

Form ST-121.9, Exempt Purchase Certificate for Certain Property and Services Used in Dramatic and Musical Arts Performances, should be used to make tax-exempt purchases. (TB-ST-535)

Form ST-121.9 applies only to a production of a live dramatic or musical arts performance that meets all the following conditions:

- It will be presented in a theater or other similar place of assembly in New York (excluding roof gardens, cabarets, or other similar places).

- It will be performed in a facility that has seating capacity of at least 100 permanently installed seats.

- The production or performance will be presented to the public at least five times a week for a period of at least two consecutive weeks.

- The content of each production or performance is the same.

- There is a charge for admission to each production or performance.

(TB-ST-535)

The purchaser must complete Form ST-121.9, sign it, and submit it to the seller within 90 days of the delivery of the property or the performance of the service. Sales tax exemption certificates may also be issued and accepted electronically. Form ST-121.9 may be used as a single-use certificate, or as a blanket certificate covering the first and subsequent purchases for the same production or performance. (TB-ST-535)

¶60-230

Motion picture theaters.—Charges for admission to motion picture theaters for the showing of films are not subject to tax. For purposes of this exclusion, the term "motion picture theater" means any place in which people congregate for the showing of a film, and does not include booths or other devices for individual showing of films. (Reg. Sec. 527.10(d)(3)) (TB-ST-8) However, charges for admissions to closed circuit television broadcasts of any event, such as wrestling or boxing matches which originate from outside New York, are subject to tax, whether in a motion picture theater or other establishment. When the sporting event originates in New York, it may not be subject to tax. (Reg. Sec. 527.10(b)(1)(iv))

Examples of nontaxable admission charges include charges for admission to:

- grade, middle, or high school sporting events;
- admission charges taxed under any other law of this state (such as horse racing tracks and boxing, sparring, or wrestling matches or exhibitions);
- charges to go on amusement rides that are separate from the charge for admission to the place of amusement itself;
- sporting facilities or activities in which the patron is a participant, such as golf, bowling, swimming, or skiing (however, charges for the use of items such as bowling shoes, skis, towels, or lockers are taxable);
- live circus performances;
- networking events, such as singles events; and
- free tickets to any amusement, including free passes given to employees, as long as there is nothing given in return for the tickets.

(TB-ST-8)

In addition, admission charges to the following places or events are tax-exempt:

- agricultural fairs;
- historical homes and gardens; and
- historic sites, houses and shrines and museums;

provided that no part of the net earnings inures to the benefit of any stockholder. (Sec. 1116(d)(3), Tax Law)

Admissions for benefit of certain exempt entities.—Admissions, all of the proceeds of which inure exclusively to the benefit of certain exempt entities, are not subject to sales tax. Those entities include:

- a corporation, association, trust, community chest, fund or foundation, organized and operated exclusively for religious, charitable, scientific, testing for public safety, literary or educational purposes or to foster national or international amateur sports competition or for the prevention of cruelty to children or animals;
- a post or organization predominantly comprised of past or present members of the U.S. Armed Forces (including any auxiliary unit or society, trust or foundation of such post or organization) organized in New York State;
- the Cayuga, Oneida, Onondaga, Poospatuck, Saint Regis Mohawk, Seneca, Shinnecock, Tonawanda and Tuscarora Indian nations or tribes residing in New York, where such nation or tribe is the purchaser, user or consumer;
- a society or organization conducted for the sole purpose of maintaining symphony orchestras or operas and receiving substantial support from voluntary contributions;
- national guard organizations; or

- a police or fire department of a political subdivision of the state, a voluntary fire or ambulance company, or exclusively to a retirement, pension or disability fund for the sole benefit of members of the police or fire department or to a fund for the heirs of such persons.

(Sec. 1116(d)(1), Tax Law) (TB-ST-8)

The following admissions charges, although for the benefit of the exempt organizations enumerated above, are taxable:

- admissions to athletic games or exhibitions, unless the proceeds inure exclusively to the benefit of an elementary or secondary school or, in the case of an athletic game between two elementary or secondary schools, the entire gross proceeds from the game inure to the benefit of one or more religious, charitable, scientific, etc. organizations or

- admissions to carnivals, rodeos, or circuses in which any professional performer or operator participates for compensation, unless the entire net profit from the event inures exclusively to the benefit of a charitable or educational organization.

(Sec. 1116(d)(2), Tax Law)

Circuses are not subject to tax. (Sec. 1101(d)(2), Tax Law)

Volunteer fire companies.—A volunteer fire company's charge for admission to a place of amusement is not taxable if all of the proceeds from the admission charge inure exclusively to the benefit of the company. The exemption extends to the sale by a volunteer fire company of tangible personal property and food and drink at booths operated on the grounds of a firemen's field day, carnival, competition or other similar event conducted by a volunteer fire company and the proceeds of which exclusively inure to the benefit of such volunteer fire company. (*TSB-M-78(6)S*)

- *Season tickets*

Season tickets to taxable events are taxed on the total selling price of the ticket regardless of the price for admission to each event. If a season ticket covers admission to a combination of taxable and nontaxable events, the price of the season ticket should be prorated based on the number of taxable events and sales tax is computed on the prorated amount. (TB-ST-8)

EXAMPLE: A season ticket holder pays $1,000 for a season ticket to attend all home games of a professional football team. The tax is computed on the $1,000 charge for the season ticket, whether or not the ticket holder attends each game and regardless of the price at which the seat would have been sold for individual games. (TB-ST-8)

EXAMPLE: An arena has 10 events during the summer, 3 of which are subject to sales tax. An individual may purchase a season ticket for all 10 events for $240. Since 3 out the 10 events (30%) are taxable, the sales tax due on the season ticket is computed on $72 ($240 multiplied by 30%). (TB-ST-8)

- *Box seats*

A person having the permanent use or possession of a box or seat, or a lease or license (other than a season ticket) for the use of a box or seat, at a place of amusement is taxed upon the amount for which a similar box or seat is sold for each performance or exhibition at which he or she uses or reserves such box or seat. (Sec. 1105(f)(1), Tax Law; Reg. Sec. 527.10(a)(2)) (TB-ST-8) "Boxes" that are assigned and reserved for corporate purposes or to officials of or stockholders in an organization are subject to tax. (*TSB-M-78(16)S*)

Computation.—The tax imposed with respect to the permanent use or possession or a box or seat or a lease or a license other than a season ticket, of a box or seat is computed on the amount for which a similar box or seat is sold for each performance or exhibition at which the box or seat is used or reserved for an even that is subject to tax. (Reg. Sec. 527.10(c)(2))

• *Amusement parks and rides*

A charge for admission to an amusement park that only allows customers to enter the park, and does not allow them on the rides, is a charge for admission to a place of amusement and is subject to tax. However, the sale of tickets or tokens that are solely for the use of amusement rides is not subject to tax. Thus, if a customer purchases an individual ride ticket to go on a single ride, or a combination ticket or wristband that allows the customer to go on all or most of the rides, the entire charge is not subject to tax. (*TSB-M-87(15)S*; TB-ST-30)

Except at a "qualifying place of amusement", a "pay-one-price" admission that allows customers to enter the park and to ride all or most of the rides is fully subject to sales tax unless all of the following conditions are met:

• at all times, the amusement park sells both a pay-one-price ticket and an admission-only ticket, each of which shows on its face the charge for the ticket;

• the pay-one-price ticket also separately states on its face the portion of the charge for the use of the rides and the portion of the charge for admission;

• the admission-only ticket does not allow a customer to use the rides;

• the admission charge to enter the park shown on the pay-one-price ticket is the same as the charge shown on the admission-only ticket; and

• the availability of both types of tickets, and the charges for each type, are conspicuously displayed at every entrance to the park, on the amusement park's Web sites, and in all advertisements, signs, and brochures that contain information about admission policies and charges; and a customer can readily purchase either an admission-only ticket or a pay-one-price ticket.

(TB-ST-30)

If all of these conditions are met, then the portion of the pay-one-price ticket that separately states the charge for use of the rides is not subject to sales tax, while the remainder of the pay-one-price ticket is subject to sales tax. (TB-ST-30)

> *EXAMPLE:* An amusement park sells a $10 admission-only (no rides) ticket that limits the customer to admission to the park. The park also sells a $25 pay-one-price ticket, which separately shows a $15 charge for the use of the rides and a $10 charge for admission. The availability of both types of tickets is clearly communicated to all customers, and either ticket can readily be purchased. The $15 charge on the pay-one-price ticket for use of the rides is exempt from sales tax. (TB-ST-30)

Qualifying place of amusement (partial exemption).—Some amusement parks do not sell admission-only tickets and the charge for entering the amusement park and the charge for going on the rides are combined in the price that customers pay when entering the park. An admission charge to this type of amusement park is subject to sales tax on the entire amount unless the park is a qualifying place of amusement. If a park is a qualifying place of amusement, the sales tax is computed on 25% of the total admission charge (the remaining 75% of the admission charge is exempt). The exemption also applies to the tax imposed in the Metropolitan Commuter Transportation District (MCTD). (TSB-M-06(12)S; TSB-M-05(5)S; TB-ST-30)

An amusement park is a qualifying place of amusement if it meets all of these conditions:

• the amusement park is at the same location year-round, even though it may not be open year-round;

• the combined admission charge allows patrons to ride at least 75% of the rides, at no additional charge;

• the combined area of amusement rides equals at least 50% of the entire area of the amusement park. When figuring the entire area of the amusement park, don't include parking lots, hotels, picnic areas, campgrounds, lakes, administrative areas, woodlands, and undeveloped areas in the park; and

• each person who buys an admission to the park also gets a paper ticket or receipt showing the amount of the admission charge the person paid and the tax due on such charges.

(Sec. 1122, Tax Law) (TB-ST-30; TSB-M-04(7)S)

If a place of amusement is not a qualifying place of amusement, it must collect sales tax on 100% of its admission charges unless it offers an admission-only ticket. (TSB-M-06(12)S; TSB-M-04(7)S; TSB-M-05(5)S)

In its first year of operation, a place of amusement shall not be excluded from classification as a qualifying place of amusement because it has not existed or will not exist on a year-round basis, so long as it admits patrons for the portion of the year that it is open and all other conditions outlined above are met. (TSB-M-04(7)S)

An admission charge to a patron for admission to, or use of, facilities for sporting activities in which the patron will be a participant (i.e. bowling alleys and swimming pools) continues to be exempt from sales tax. (TSB-M-06(12)S; TSB-M-04(7)S; TSB-M-05(5)S)

Amusement rides include roller coasters, ferris wheels, carousels, water slides, and all other amusement rides and water rides. (TSB-M-04(7)S)

Games.—A separate charge to play a game at an amusement park is not subject to tax. (TB-ST-30)

Parking.—A separate charge for parking at an amusement park is subject to tax. (TB-ST-30)

• *Roof garden and cabaret charges*

Generally, tax is imposed upon the amount paid as charges of a roof garden, cabaret or similar place in New York. (Sec. 1105(f)(3), Tax Law) However, admission charges to a roof garden, cabaret or other similar place to attend a dramatic or musical arts performance are exempt from sales and compensating use tax, provided the following conditions are satisfied:

• the venue states the admission portion of the charge separately from the rest of its charges;

• separately stated charges for food, drink, service and merchandise are not less on a day when the place offers performances than on days when it does not offer them, or if the place is open for business only when it offers performances, separately stated charges for food, drink, service and merchandise are comparable to charges for comparable items at other similar places, restaurants and taverns; and

• the place retains and makes available the menus and any other statements of its charges, showing all of its charges for food, drink, service, merchandise and admission.

(Sec. 1123, Tax Law) (TSB-M-06(15)S)

"Roof garden, cabaret or other similar place" defined.—A "roof garden, cabaret or other similar place" is a place that furnishes a public performance for profit (Sec. 1101(d)(12), Tax Law) or a room in a hotel, restaurant, hall or other place where music and dancing privileges or entertainment are afforded the patrons in connection with the serving or selling of food, refreshment or merchandise. (Reg. Sec. 527.12(b)(2))

The phrase does not include any place where only live dramatic and musical arts performances are offered along with the "merely incidental" sale of refreshments and merchandise. (*TSB-M-86(28)S*)

> **CCH EXAMPLE:** *Theater-in-the-round dance routines.*—A theater-in-the-round has a show which consists exclusively of dance routines. During intermission, an assortment of light refreshments consisting of cider, wine and cheese are offered for sale. Since such sales are merely incidental to the performance, the admission charge is not subject to tax as an admission to a roof garden, cabaret or other similar place. (*TSB-M-86(28)S*)

"Charge of a roof garden, cabaret or other similar place" defined.—For purposes of the tax, the "charge of a roof garden, cabaret or other similar place" is defined as any charge made for admission, cover minimum, music or entertainment, refreshment, food and drink, service or merchandise at a roof garden, cabaret or other similar place. (Sec. 1101(d)(4), Tax Law; Reg. Sec. 527.12(b)(1))

See ¶ 60-390 Food and Grocery Items.

• *Live dramatic or musical performances*

Tangible personal property and services used or consumed in the production of live public dramatical or musical performances in a theater or similar place of assembly are exempt from New York sales and use tax. The theater or other similar place of assembly must have a seating capacity of 100 or more rigidly anchored chairs, with at least five performances per week for a period of at least two consecutive weeks, and with the content of each performance being the same. However, roof gardens, cabarets, or similar venues do not qualify for exemption. (Sec. 1115(x), Tax Law)

"Place of assembly" defined.—The term place of assembly is defined as a place of assembly with a stage in which scenery and scenic elements are used, and for which an approved seating plan is required to be kept. (Sec. 1115(x), Tax Law)

Services.—Services rendered with respect to exempt property and that are described in Secs. 1105(c)(2) and 1105(c)(3), Tax Laws, are also exempt. (Sec. 1115(x), Tax Law) These services include producing, fabricating, processing, printing, and imprinting performed on tangible personal property furnished by the customer, and installing, maintaining, servicing, or repairing tangible personal property not held for sale in the regular course of business. However, the exemption does not apply to tangible personal property which is permanently affixed to or becomes an integral part of a structure, building, or real property. (Sec. 1115(x), Tax Law)

• *Entertainment services provided by telephony or telegraphy*

The furnishing or providing of entertainment by means of interstate or intrastate telephony, telegraphy, telephone or telegraph service, including entertainment services provided through 800- or 900- telephone numbers, are subject to tax. However, the provision of cable television service to customers is exempt. (Sec. 1105(c)(9), Tax Law)

Additional tax.—Receipts from taxable entertainment or information services are also subject to an additional 5% tax. (Sec. 1105(c)(9), Tax Law)

See ¶ 60-665 Services.

• *Social or athletic club dues*

Dues paid to a social or athletic club in New York State are subject to tax where the dues of an active annual member (defined as a member enjoying full privileges) (Sec. 1101(d)(1), Tax Law), exclusive of the initiation fee, exceed $10 per year. (Sec. 1105(f)(2), Tax Law) The tax is imposed upon the initiation fee where such fee, regardless of the amount of dues, is more than $10.

Honorary members are exempt from tax. (Sec. 1105(f)(2), Tax Law)

If the tax applies to a particular club, the tax must be paid by all members, other than honorary members, regardless of the amount of dues payable by a particular member. (Sec. 1105(f)(2), Tax Law)

Life memberships.—The sales tax on a life membership in a social or athletic club is imposed on the amount paid as life membership dues. (Sec. 1105(f)(2), Tax Law) Life members, other than honorary members, who have been paying the tax annually, are to continue the annual payments until the total tax paid is equal to the tax which would have been due if the tax had been paid at the time the life membership was purchased. Life memberships for which no consideration is given are not subject to tax. (Reg. Sec. 527.11(a)(4))

EXAMPLE: *Annual and life memberships.*—An athletic club has two types of memberships: annual membership for $25 per year and life membership for $250. A person purchasing a life membership is required to pay tax on the $250 charge for membership at the time of purchase. (Reg. Sec. 527.11(a)(4))

"Dues" defined.—The term "dues" refers to any dues or membership fee, including assessments, and any charges for social or sports privileges or facilities (except charges for sports privileges or facilities offered to members' guests which would otherwise be exempt if paid directly by such guest). (Sec. 1101(d)(6), Tax Law; Reg. Sec. 527.11(b)(2))

EXAMPLE: *Examples of dues.*—The following are examples of calculating dues.

— A social club operates a restaurant and bar for the use of its members. The club requires of each member a minimum expenditure during the year of $200 for food and drink. If a member does not make actual expenditures totaling $200, he or she is billed for an additional amount equal to the difference between his or her actual expenditures and $200. The additional amount constitutes taxable dues or membership fees, inasmuch as such charge must be paid for the privilege of being a member of the club.

— A social club collects no regular dues or membership fees but meets its operating expenses by levying assessments on its members as funds are required. These assessments constitute taxable dues or membership fees where the fees, combined with annual dues, exceed $10.

— A social club collects $10 per year from each of its members as regular dues. Members are entitled to use the clubhouse facilities without payment of an additional charge. However, members who wish to use the golf course may do so only upon payment of an additional charge. Since the golf course is a social or athletic club facility, any charge made by the club to a member for the use of the course constitutes dues. The fact that such charges are made upon the member's election to use the course is immaterial.

— A member of an athletic club invites a guest to play a round of golf at his or her club. The member is charged a $5 greens fee for the guest. Since the greens fee would be exempt as a fee for a participating sport if paid directly by the guest, such fee paid by the member is exempt. (Reg. Sec. 527.11(b)(2))

"Initiation fee" defined.—An "initiation fee" is any payment, contribution or loan, required as a condition precedent to membership, whether or not evidenced by a certificate of interest or indebtedness or share of stock and irrespective of the person or organization to whom paid, contributed or loaned. (Sec. 1101(d)(7), Tax Law; Reg. Sec. 527.11(b)(4))

CCH EXAMPLE: Purchase of bonds.—As a condition necessary for membership in a social club, an applicant is required to purchase a $50 bond from the club. This purchase is an initiation fee subject to tax. (Reg. Sec. 527.11(b)(4))

For definitions of "honorary member," "club organization," "social club" and "athletic club," see Reg. Sec. 527.11.

Nontaxable dues.—The tax on dues does not apply to fraternal societies, orders or associations operating under the lodge system, to fraternal associations of college students, rod or gun clubs (i.e. fishing and hunting clubs). (Sec. 1105(f)(2), Tax Law; TSB-M-96(16)S)

Dues paid to organizations which have social or athletic activities that are not a material purpose of the organization are not taxable. (Reg. Sec. 527.11(c)(2))

EXAMPLE: YMCA's—A Young Men's Christian Association or a Young Men's Hebrew Association is not a social or athletic club, since the material purposes of each are philanthropic and religious even though they may have social and athletic activities. (Reg. Sec. 527.11(c)(2))

EXAMPLE: Rotary clubs.—Service organizations, such as Rotary Club or Kiwanis, even though they have social luncheons, are not social clubs. (Reg. Sec. 527.11(c)(2))

Dues paid to organizations which are organized and operated exclusively to foster national or international amateur sports competition, but which do not (either directly or indirectly) provide any athletic facilities or equipment, are exempt. (Reg. Sec. 527.11(c)(3))

Rod or gun clubs.—Dues and initiation fees paid by members to rod or gun clubs (i.e. fishing and hunting clubs) are not subject to New York state and local sales taxes. (TSB-M-96(16)S; TSB-A-04(13)S)

• *Health and fitness clubs*

Dues or membership fees paid to health and fitness clubs are not subject to New York state sales tax and are not subject to local sales taxes if the club is located outside New York City. (TB-ST-329) In addition to dues or membership fees, health and fitness clubs may charge customers separately for other items and services. Charges for the following are examples of charges that are subject to state and local sales taxes, regardless of where in New York the club is located:

- locker fees;
- water or water bottles;
- gym bags, towels, training aids, etc.;
- food sold from a snack bar or restaurant facility; and
- items sold from vending machines (other than candy, fruit drinks and soft drinks sold for 75 cents or less, and heated beverages).

(TB-ST-329)

Charges for the following are exempt from the state sales tax, but are subject to New York City sales tax if the club qualifies as a weight control salon, health salon, gymnasium, or other establishment, and is located in New York City:

- aerobic, Pilates or other exercise classes;
- child care services;
- fitness and wellness workshops;
- guest access;
- personal training services;
- use of a spa and services provided by persons who are not medical professionals (i.e., massage, facials, and body treatments); and
- tanning services.

(TB-ST-329)

Purchases by health and fitness clubs.—All purchases of taxable items for use in a health or fitness club are subject to tax unless purchased for resale to customers. If a health or fitness club is not charged tax by a seller on purchases of taxable items not intended for resale, the club must pay the unpaid sales tax or use tax. (TB-ST-329)

Coupons and discounts.—The tax due on a taxable item or service is based on the price paid by the customer after deducting a discount or coupon issued by the health or fitness club. However, if a customer uses a manufacturer's coupon to purchase a product, the tax is computed on the price for the item before subtracting the coupon. (TB-ST-329)

Yoga facilities in New York City.—Facilities in New York City that offer only instruction in various yoga disciplines are not considered to be weight control salons, health salons, or gymnasiums. As a result, charges by these facilities for yoga classes are not subject to the New York City local sales tax. (TB-ST-329) Charges to customers for the use of any tangible personal property (such as yoga mats, etc.) are subject to both state and local sales taxes. Charges for yoga instruction by a facility that otherwise qualifies as a weight control salon, health salon, or gymnasium (i.e., a facility that also offers its customers access to exercise equipment or to Pilates or aerobic classes) are subject to the New York City local sales tax. (TB-ST-329; NYT-G-12(1))

For a discussion of the imposition of New York City sales tax on health and fitness clubs, see TB-ST-329.

- *Dues paid to homeowners associations*

Dues paid by owners or residents to a homeowners association that operates social or athletic facilities (whether or not for the exclusive use by the owners or residents) are exempt from tax. (Sec. 1105(f)(2), Tax Law)

The term "homeowners association" includes cooperative housing corporations, condominium associations and cooperative housing corporations. (TSB-M-95(12)S)

To qualify for the exclusion, the homeowners association must meet the following conditions:

- the membership of the association must consist exclusively of owners or residents of residential dwelling units. For condominium associations, this means that all the members must be owners of condominiums; in instances involving cooperative housing corporations and cooperative apartment corporations, the members must be shareholders;

- the residential dwelling units must all be within a defined geographical area (such as a building, a group of buildings, a housing development or subdivision);

- the social or athletic facilities must be within the defined geographical area of the residential units; and

- the social or athletic facilities must be for use by the members of the homeowners association (use of the facilities does not have to be limited to only the members of the association).

(Sec. 1105(f)(2), Tax Law) (TSB-M-95(12)S)

Payments made by homeowners associations for purchases of maintenance and repairs (including maintenance and repairs to social or athletic facilities) remain subject to sales tax. (TSB-M-95(12)S)

[¶60-240] Advertising

Fees for the services of advertising agencies or other persons acting in a representative capacity are excluded from sales tax. (Sec. 1105(c)(1), Tax Law; Reg. Sec. 527.3(b)(5))

Sales of advertising services.—Sales of advertising services are not subject to sales tax. Advertising services consist of: (i) consultation and development of advertising campaigns; and (ii) placement of advertisements with the media, without the transfer of tangible personal property. (Reg. Sec. 527.3(b)(5)) (TB-ST-10)

Any advertising materials created by an advertising agency that are conveyed to its customer by intangible means (e.g., by digital or other electronic media) are not subject to sales tax. (TB-ST-10)

> *EXAMPLE:* An advertising agency is hired to design an advertising program and to furnish a finished advertisement to the media. The fee charged by the agency for this service is not subject to sales tax. (TB-ST-10)

Any advertising materials created by an advertising agency that are conveyed to its customer by intangible means (e.g., by digital or other electronic media) are not subject to sales tax. (TB-ST-10)

Any tangible materials used by the advertising agency that are turned over to the customer after use by the agency to furnish the advertising content to the media are considered to be incidental to the agency's sale of advertising services and are not subject to sales tax. However, if the advertising agency sells any tangible personal property, such as layouts or art work, to the customer prior to furnishing them to the media, the advertising agency is making a sale that is subject to sales tax. Additionally, any other outright sales of tangible personal property (such as layouts, printing plates, or films contained on tangible media) by an advertising agency are subject to sales tax. (Reg. Sec. 527.3(b)(5)) (TB-ST-10)

The sale of a personal report containing information derived from information services by an advertising agency is not the sale of a taxable information service. However, if an advertising agency charges only for the purpose of conducting a survey, or if a survey is separately authorized and billed to the customer, the advertising agency is making a sale of a taxable information service. (Reg. Sec. 527.3(b)(5)) (TB-ST-10)

In *Stillman Advertising, Inc.*, the Commissioner of Taxation and Finance advised that an advertising agency's total fee, whether or not itemized on the billing for its client, for producing an advertisement and placing it in a printed medium, without the transfer of tangible personal property to the client, is an exempt advertising charge. The operation of the exemption is not dependent on the selected publication's taxability or method of distribution, nor is it material whether or not the publication is for sale.

Charges for running advertisements on the Internet are not subject to tax, provided the taxpayer does not sell tangible personal property in conjunction with the services. (Sec. 1105(c)(1), Tax Law; Reg. Sec. 527.3(b)(5)) (TSB-A-95(33)S)

Purchase by advertising agencies.—Generally, purchases by an advertising agency for use in performing its services are purchases at retail subject to tax. (Reg. Sec. 527.3(c)(3)) (TB-ST-10)

> *EXAMPLE:* An advertising agency designs billboard advertisements for its customer and hires a printer to print the billboard posters. Any purchases by the advertising agency of tangible personal property that is used to create its billboards are purchases at retail subject to sales tax. Also, the advertising agency must pay sales tax on its purchases of any taxable services, such as printing services, that are used to perform its nontaxable advertising services. (TB-ST-10)

However, other sales tax exemptions may apply to the purchases of advertising agencies, such as purchases related to: (i) producing television and radio commercials and advertisements; or (ii) developing and producing printed promotional materials. (TB-ST-10)

• *Promotional material distributed out-of-state*

An exemption from sales and use taxation is provided for promotional materials that are mailed, shipped or otherwise distributed from a point within New York State, by or on behalf of vendors, to prospective customers located outside the state, for use outside the state. (Sec. 1115(n)(1), Taw Law) Moreover, services (such as mailing list services) that would otherwise be taxable as the producing, fabricating, processing, printing or imprinting of tangible personal property furnished by the purchaser, and not purchased for resale, are exempt if performed on or directly in conjunction with exempt promotional materials. (Sec. 1115(n)(2), Tax Law)

• *Shopping papers*

Materials (such as paper, ink and other tangible personal property) purchased for use in connection with the publication of a shopping paper, and which are to become a physical component part of the paper, are exempt from sales and compensating use taxes. (Sec. 1115(a)(20), Tax Law) In addition, an exemption from tax is allowed for receipts from the retail sale of a shopping paper to the publisher, as well as for receipts from the sale of printing services performed in publishing the paper. (Sec. 1115(i)(A), Tax Law)

• *Advertising supplements*

Advertising supplements, when distributed as inserts in a newspaper, periodical or shopping paper, are considered part of such newspaper, periodical or shopping paper, and are therefore exempt from tax. (Reg. Sec. 528.6(e)(1)) Also, advertising in the form of a section, purchased from a newspaper publisher pursuant to the advertising rate schedule for insertion in its newspaper, and numbered as part of the newspaper, is considered to be part of the newspaper, and not an advertising supplement. (Reg. Sec. 528.6(e)(2))

The charge by a printer to an advertiser for whom an advertising supplement is produced is taxable as a sale of tangible personal property, unless the charge is for supplements which are distributed with newspapers, periodicals or shopping papers. (Reg. Sec. 528.6(e)(3)) The charge by a newspaper to an advertiser for distribution of the advertising supplement with the newspaper is a nontaxable advertising service. (Reg. Sec. 528.6(e)(5))

A printer's purchase of materials (such as paper and ink), which become a component part of the advertising supplement, is not taxable as a sale for resale. (Reg. Sec. 528.6(e)(4))

[¶60-250] Agriculture

This paragraph concerns the taxability of tangible property used in farm production, horse boarding operations, fishing vessels, and services performed upon property used for farm production, horse boarding, or fishing purposes. The taxability of veterinary services and transactions involving racehorses are also discussed.

• *Farming and commercial horse boarding operations*

An exemption from the sales and use tax is provided for tangible personal property (whether or not incorporated in a building or structure) used or consumed directly and predominantly in either farming or in a commercial horse boarding operation, or in both. (Sec. 1115(a)(6), Tax Law) (TB-ST-244)

Definitions.—The term "farming" includes agriculture, floriculture, horticulture, aquaculture, viniculture, viticulture, and silviculture; stock, dairy, poultry, fruit or vegetable, graping, truck and tree farming (i.e., maple trees or Christmas trees); ranching; raising fur-bearing animals; operating orchards; raising, growing and harvesting crops, livestock and livestock products; and raising, growing and harvesting woodland products, including, but not limited to, timber, logs, lumber, pulpwood, posts and firewood. (TB-ST-244; TB-ST-253)

A "commercial horse boarding operation" is a business that:

- operates on at least seven acres;

- boards at least 10 horses (regardless of ownership); and

- receives $10,000 or more in gross receipts annually from fees generated from: the boarding of horses, the production for sale of crops, livestock, and livestock products, or both of these activities.

(TB-ST-244)

A commercial horse boarding operation does not include any operation where the primary on-site function is horse racing. (TB-ST-244)

"Farm production" is the production of tangible personal property for sale by farming. It begins with the preparation of the soil or other growing medium, or with the beginning of the life cycle for animals. Farm production ends when the product is ready for sale in its natural state. For farm products that will be converted into other products, farm production ceases when the normal development of the farm product has reached a stage where it will be processed or converted into a another product. (TB-ST-244; TB-ST-253)

The term "directly" means that the tangible personal property must, during the production phase of farming:

- act upon or affect a change in material to form the product to be sold, or

- have an active causal relationship in the production of the product to be sold, or

- be used in the handling, storage or conveyance of materials used in the production of the product to be sold, or

- be used to place the product to be sold in the package in which it will enter the stream of commerce.

(Reg. Sec. 528.7(d)(1))

The term "predominantly" means that the tangible personal property must be used more than 50% of the time directly in the production phase of farming. (Reg. Sec. 528.7(d)(2))

> **CCH EXAMPLE:** *Feed purchased for farm animals.*—Hay, corn, silage, grain and other feed purchased for farm animals which will produce a product for sale or which are raised for resale, is exempt. (Reg. Sec. 528.7(d)(2))

A properly completed Farmer's Exemption Certificate is used by a farmer to make exempt purchases of tangible personal property. (Reg. Sec. 528.7)

The exemption is inapplicable for New York City sales and use tax purposes (see TSB-M-81(14)S)

Cities, other than New York City, and counties and school districts which impose the entire state tax package must exclude from tax all sales of tangible property for use and consumption directly and predominantly in farm production (see TSB-M-97(9)S).

Milk crates.—Milk crates purchased by a dairy farmer or licensed milk distributor used exclusively and directly for the packaging and delivery of milk and milk products to customers are exempt. (Sec. 1115(a)(19-A), Tax Law) (TSB-M-06(16)S) The exemption does not apply to crates that are also used to package and deliver juice, juice drinks or other non-milk products. In order to claim this exemption, a diary farmer or New York licensed milk distributor who purchases qualifying milk crates must submit to the vendor a properly completed Form ST-121, Exempt Use Certificate. Part III, box M of Form ST-121 must be completed. (TSB-M-06(16)S)

Exemption certificates and refunds.—To make qualifying purchases, other than motor fuel and diesel motor fuel, without paying sales tax, a farmer or commercial horse boarding operator must fill out Form ST-125, Farmer's and Commercial Horse Boarding Operator's Exemption Certificate, and give it to the seller. Any sales tax paid on a purchase that otherwise qualifies for the exemption can be refunded. (TB-ST-244)

Machinery, equipment, and supplies.—A farmer's or commercial horse boarding operator's purchase of tangible personal property, such as machinery, equipment, and supplies, is exempt from sales tax if the property is used or consumed predominantly (more than 50% of the time) in farm production or in commercial horse boarding operations. (TB-ST-244) The bulletin provides a list of property that can be purchased exempt from sales tax.

Computers.—A computer that will be used predominantly in either farm production or in a commercial horse boarding operation, or in both, can be purchased without the payment of sales tax. This includes a computer used predominantly to: turn milking machines on and off; direct machinery and equipment used for measuring and delivering feed to livestock; turn irrigation systems on and off; maintain animal feed, weight, and health records; or perform agricultural research. (TB-ST-244)

Vehicles.—Motor vehicles, trailers, ATVs, boats, and snowmobiles that are used predominantly in farm production or in a commercial horse boarding operation, or in both, are exempt from sales and use taxes. In order to be exempt, the vehicle must be used for farm production on property actually farmed or on property actually used in a horse boarding operation, or both. Usage can be measured by hours of use or by miles traveled. (TB-ST-244)

Building materials.—Building materials that will be used to build, add to, improve, install, maintain or repair real property used predominantly in farm production or in a commercial horse boarding operation, or in both, can be purchased without paying sales tax. These tax-free purchases may be made by a farmer or commercial horse boarder, or by a contractor hired to do the work. (TB-ST-244)

Examples would be purchases of materials to build or repair:

- animal barns;
- hay and feed storage barns;
- barns or garages to park and store farm production equipment;
- fences;
- silos; and
- greenhouses.

(TB-ST-244)

The exemption for purchases of building materials by contractors, subcontractors, or repairmen is available only if the materials become an integral component part of a building, structure, or real property used predominantly in farm production or in a commercial horse boarding operation, or in both. A contractor, subcontractor or repairman should use Form ST-120.1, Contractor Exempt Purchase Certificate, to make qualifying exempt purchases. (TB-ST-244)

• *Services*

The services of installing, maintaining, servicing and repairing tangible personal property, or for maintaining, servicing, or repairing real property, used or consumed predominantly in farm production or in a commercial horse boarding operation, or in both, are tax-exempt. However, the exemption does not apply to the New York City sales and use tax. (Sec. 1105(c)(3)(vi), Tax Law; Reg. Sec. 528.7(a)(2)) (TB-ST-244)

There is no exemption from the tax imposed upon the services of maintaining, servicing and repairing real property, except when such services are rendered to a grape-trellis or silo. (Reg. Sec. 528.7(a)(3))

Services eligible for exemption may be purchased without payment of tax upon the issuance to the vendor of a timely filed and properly completed Farmer's Exemption Certificate. (Reg. Sec. 528.7(f)(1))

• *Motor fuel and highway diesel fuel*

Motor fuel (gasoline) and highway diesel motor fuel cannot be purchased without paying sales tax. However, a farmer or commercial horse boarder can use Form FT-500, Application for Refund of Sales Tax Paid on Petroleum Products, to claim a refund of sales tax paid on these products when used in farm production or in a commercial horse boarding operation, or in both. In addition, a farmer (but not a commercial horse boarder) can use Form FT-420, Refund Application for Farmers Purchasing Motor Fuel, to claim a refund of the motor fuel excise tax, the petroleum business tax, and the sales tax on motor fuel (but not diesel motor fuel) used directly and exclusively in farm production. (TB-ST-244)

• *Utilities*

Utilities used or consumed in farm production or in a commercial horse boarding operation, or in both, are also exempt from sales and use taxes. This includes: non-highway diesel motor fuel (but not motor fuel or highway diesel motor fuel); gas (natural gas, propane, etc.); electricity; refrigeration; steam; and gas, electric, refrigeration and steam services. (TB-ST-244)

Non-highway diesel motor fuel that is used in farm production or in a commercial horse boarding operation, or in both, can be purchased exempt from sales and use taxes by giving the seller Form FT-1004, Certificate of Purchases of Non-Highway Diesel Motor Fuel or Residual Petroleum Product for Farmers and Commercial Horse Boarding Operations.

• *Veterinarians*

Sales of tangible personal property designed for use in some manner relating to domestic animals or poultry, when sold to a licensed veterinarian, are deemed to be retail sales, notwithstanding a subsequent sale of the item by the veterinarian. (Reg. Sec. 526.6(b)(2))

See ¶ 60-665 Services and TB-ST-930.

• *Veterinary services*

An exemption is provided for services which constitute the practice of veterinary medicine. Other services provided by a veterinarian to pets and other animals, such as boarding, grooming and clipping, are taxable. The charges for hospitalization are also exempt, provided no separate boarding charge is made. (Sec. 1115(f), Tax Law)

Tangible personal property designed for use in some manner relating to domestic animals or poultry (such as collars, flea spray and medicine), when sold by a licensed veterinarian, is exempt. However, such property is taxable when sold to a licensed veterinarian. (Sec. 1115(f), Tax Law; Reg. Sec. 528.24(c)(2))

Drugs or medicine used on livestock or poultry used in farm production.—A refund or credit is allowed for tax paid on the sale to or use by a veterinarian of drugs or medicine which are used by him or her in rendering exempt veterinarian services to livestock or poultry used in farm production. A similar refund or credit is provided for tax paid on drugs or medicine sold to a farmer for use on livestock or poultry. Effective June 1, 2018, the existing credit or refund is converted to an up-front exemption. (Sec. 1115(f), Tax Law; Sec. 1119(a), Tax Law) (TSB-M-18(1)S) This exemption applies to:

• drugs or medicine sold to or used by a veterinarian providing exempt veterinary services to livestock or poultry used in farm production, and

• drugs or medicine sold to or used by a person on livestock or poultry used in farm production.

(TSB-M-18(1)S)

• *Racehorses*

The purchase of a racehorse is considered to be a purchase of tangible personal property and is therefore subject to sales tax, except as described below. This includes the purchase of an interest in a racehorse, trading or leasing a racehorse, and generally, the syndication of a racehorse. Also, when a horse breeder transfers ownership of a racehorse and later reacquires the same racehorse, the reacquisition is considered a purchase. Racehorses include thoroughbred, standardbred, and quarter horses. Use tax is due on the use of a racehorse purchased by a New York resident out of state and brought into New York for use here, unless an exemption applies. (Reg. Sec. 527.14) (TB-ST-755)

Any tax due on the purchase of a racehorse is computed at the tax rate in effect where delivery of the racehorse is made in New York State, whether the purchaser is a New York resident or nonresident. (Reg. Sec. 527.14(c)) (TB-ST-755)

When remitting payment of the tax due on the purchase of a racehorse, submit a copy of the original invoice showing the total price paid for the racehorse and the computations used in determining the amount of the tax due. (Reg. Sec. 527.14(c)(1)(viii))

Guidebook to New York Taxes

Exemption for qualifying thoroughbred and standardbred racehorses.—The purchase of a thoroughbred or standardbred racehorse is exempt from sales tax if the racehorse:

- is registered with the Jockey Club, the United States Trotting Association, the National Steeplechase and Hunt Association, or is no more than 24 months old and is eligible to be registered with one of these associations; and

- is purchased with the intent of entering the horse in a racing event on which pari-mutuel wagering is authorized by law.

(TB-ST-755; TB-ST-757)

To claim this exemption, The purchaser must complete Form ST-126 and give it to the seller no later than 90 days after the transfer of the horse. A separate form is required for each racehorse purchased. In addition to other sales tax recordkeeping requirements, the seller must retain documentary proof of the horse's age for three years. (TB-ST-755; TB-ST-757)

Racehorses purchased outside New York and brought into this state are not subject to use tax if the purchase otherwise qualified for this exemption. (TB-ST-755)

This exemption does not apply to:

- a quarter horse; or

- a horse that is considered to be at least four years old and has never raced in an event on which pari-mutuel wagering is authorized by law.

(TB-ST-755; TB-ST-757)

Use tax.—New York use tax is due on the purchase of a thoroughbred, standard-bred, or quarter horse (other than an exempt thoroughbred or standardbred racehorse described above) outside the state by a New York resident if the racehorse is later brought into New York. However, there is an exemption from the use tax for a racehorse that is brought into New York to enter racing events on which pari-mutuel wagering is allowed, or to prepare for such events, as long as the racehorse is entered in such events on no more than 5 days in any single calendar year. Accordingly, this exemption does not apply to any racehorse that is entered in New York racing events on more than 5 days in any single calendar year. (Reg. Sec. 527.14(d)) (TB-ST-755)

If the use tax applies, only the first $100,000 of the price of a racehorse is subject to tax. Any amount exceeding $100,000 is not taxable. (TB-ST-755)

For purposes of the imposition of New York use tax, a New York resident includes a person who:

- carries on any activity in New York in preparation for racing in New York (such as hiring grooms, trainers, jockeys, or drivers);

- maintains a stable in New York; or

- races horses on tracks within New York.

(TB-ST-755)

If sales tax is paid on the purchase of a racehorse to another state, and the racehorse later becomes subject to New York use tax, the purchaser may be entitled to a credit for the tax paid to the other state. The credit cannot exceed the New York use tax due. (TB-ST-755)

If the purchase of a racehorse qualifies for the exemption for thoroughbred and standardbred horses described above, that exemption will apply, the purchase will be fully exempt from tax, and the information on use tax outlined in the bulletin does not apply. (TB-ST-755)

Claiming races.—Sales tax is due on the purchase of a racehorse (other than an exempt thoroughbred or standardbred racehorse described above) in a claiming race in New York. (Sec. 1111(g), Tax Law) (TB-ST-755) The amount subject to sales tax is:

- the full purchase price paid for the racehorse the first time the racehorse is claimed in a calendar year; or

- the amount of the current purchase price that exceeds the highest prior purchase price paid for the same racehorse in a New York claiming race held during the same calendar year.

(TB-ST-755)

If the purchase of a racehorse qualifies for the exemption for thoroughbred and standardbred horses described above, that exemption will apply, the purchase will be fully exempt from tax, and the information on claiming races outlined in the bulletin does not apply. (TB-ST-755)

Racehorses sold for breeding purposes.—A racehorse purchased to be used predominantly (more than 50%) for breeding purposes is not subject to sales tax. The purchaser must provide the seller with a properly completed Form ST-125, Farmer's and Commercial Horse Boarding Operator's Exemption Certificate, to claim this exemption. (TB-ST-755)

Care and maintenance of racehorses.—The maintenance of a racehorse includes boarding, feeding, grooming, shoeing, walking, and riding the racehorse. If the services are rendered by a trainer licensed under the racing, pari-mutuel wagering, and breeding laws of this state or another state, the services are not taxable. If the services are not rendered by a licensed trainer, the services are subject to sales tax. Any purchases by a trainer (whether licensed or not) are taxable. (Sec. 1115(m)(1), Tax Law) (TB-ST-755) For purposes of this exemption, racehorse means a thoroughbred, standardbred or quarter horse that:

- is registered with the Jockey Club, the United States Trotting Association, the American Quarter Horse Association, or the National Steeplechase and Hunt Association, or

- is no more than 24 months old and is eligible to be registered with one of these associations.

(TB-ST-755)

- *Sales of commercial fishing vessels*

Fishing vessels used directly and predominantly in the harvesting of fish for sale are exempt from tax. Also exempt is property used by or purchased for the use of fishing vessels for fuel, provisions, supplies, maintenance and repairs. (Sec. 1115(a)(24), Tax Law)

For purposes of the exemption, the term "fishing vessel" does not include any vessels used predominantly for sport fishing purposes. (Sec. 1115(a)(24), Tax Law)

- *Services to fishing vessels*

The services of installing, maintaining, servicing or repairing fishing vessels used directly and predominantly in harvesting fish for sale and property used by or purchased for the use of such vessels for fuel, provisions, supplies, maintenance and repairs are exempt from tax. (Sec. 1105(c)(3)(vii), Tax Law)

• *Landscapers*

Landscapers are considered contractors for sales tax purposes. Whether or not a landscaper collects sales tax from a customer depends on whether the work being performed is a capital improvement to real property, or is repair, maintenance, or installation work. When landscaping work qualifies as a capital improvement, the customer should not be charged sales tax. Examples of capital improvement projects include: planting or installing a new lawn; installing retaining walls; planting shrubs and trees; installing permanent ponds and water features; planting perennials. (TB-ST-505)

The removal of shrubs and trees qualifies as a capital improvement only when done in conjunction with another capital improvement project. The removal of shrubs and trees to improve the landscape without replacement or not otherwise part of a capital improvement project is considered maintenance of real property and is a taxable service. (TB-ST-505)

Purchases.—Materials and other tangible personal property purchased for use in landscaping are taxable, whether purchased by a landscaper, subcontractor, or the customer. The sales tax paid by landscapers becomes an expense that can be passed through to the customer as part of the overall charge for the capital improvement. Landscapers do not normally sell materials to customers without installation and, therefore, cannot use Form ST-120, Resale Certificate, to make purchases exempt from tax. However, in certain circumstances, landscapers can use Form ST-120.1, Contractor Exempt Purchase Certificate, to make purchases exempt from sales tax. Materials purchased in one taxing jurisdiction in New York may be subject to a different tax rate (higher or lower) if the materials are later used in a capital improvement project in a different jurisdiction in New York. (TB-ST-505)

Billing: When performing capital improvement work, a landscaper should get a properly completed Form ST-124, Certificate of Capital Improvement, from the customer (including a customer that is an exempt organization) and should not collect sales tax from the customer for the project. Receiving Form ST-124 relieves the landscaper from liability for any tax due on the work. This exemption certificate should be kept in the landscaper's records to show why no sales tax was collected on the work. However, if no capital improvement certificate is received, the contract or other records of the project can still be used to establish that the work done constituted a capital improvement. When calculating how much to charge a customer, a landscaper may include the sales tax paid on building materials just like any other project expense. (TB-ST-505)

Repair, maintenance, or installation services.—Maintaining, servicing, and repairing real property are services that are subject to sales tax. These services cover all activities that relate to keeping real property in a condition of fitness, efficiency, readiness, or safety, or restoring it to such condition. All repair, maintenance, and installation services are taxable unless the customer gives the landscaper a properly completed exemption document. See Tax-exempt customers below. Landscapers must be registered for New York State sales tax purposes and have a valid Certificate of Authority to perform any services that are considered repair, maintenance, or installation services.

Billing: For repair, maintenance, or installation work, a landscaper must charge tax to the customer on both materials and labor for the job, including any expenses or other markups. The landscaper is eligible to take a credit for the sales tax originally paid on any materials transferred to the customer. (TB-ST-505)

Greenhouses and nurseries.—Greenhouse and nursery operators that grow the plants they sell are considered farmers for sales tax purposes. When greenhouse and nursery operators install their products, they are considered landscapers. As landscapers, any charges for installation work will be either tax-exempt capital improvements or taxable repair, maintenance, or installation services. For capital improvement projects, the landscaper must pay use tax to the Tax Department on any product removed from inventory for installation as part of the capital improvement. The amount of tax owed is based on the normal retail price charged for the product by the landscaper, at the rate in effect where the product is installed. For repair, maintenance, and installation projects, the landscaper: must charge sales tax to the customer on both materials and labor, including any expenses or other markups: and is eligible to take a credit for sales tax originally paid on materials transferred to the customer. (TB-ST-505)

[¶60-260] Alcoholic Beverages

Sales, other than sales for resale, of beer, wine, and any other alcoholic beverages are subject to tax. (Sec. 1115(a)(1), Tax Law) (TSB-M-18(1)S) Tax also applies to receipts (including cover, minimum, entertainment, and other charges) from every sale of beer, wine, or other alcoholic beverages sold in or by a restaurant, tavern or other establishment in New York or by caterers. (Sec. 1105(d)(i), Tax Law) See ¶60-390 Food and Grocery Items.

The federal gallonage taxes on distilled spirits, wines and beer, the New York State alcoholic beverages tax and the City of New York's tax on beer and liquors (where applicable) are included in the receipts on which the sales tax is computed. (Reg. Sec. 526.5(b)(1))

• *Alcoholic beverage producers*

Alcoholic beverage producers in New York may qualify for various exemptions from sales and use taxes, as discussed below. Alcoholic beverage producers include: wineries and farm wineries; cideries and farm cideries; breweries and farm breweries; and distilleries and farm distilleries. (TB-ST-15)

Exemptions for manufacturers.—Alcoholic beverage producers may qualify as manufacturers. Manufacturers can purchase tangible personal property, such as machinery, equipment, and supplies, exempt from tax if the property will be used directly and predominantly in the production of tangible personal property (alcoholic beverages) for sale. Certain services and utilities used in production may also be purchased exempt from tax. To qualify for these exemptions, 50% or more of the alcoholic beverages produced must be sold: at wholesale, or at retail for off-premises consumption. An alcoholic beverage producer will not qualify as a manufacturer if 50% or more of the beverages produced are sold at a restaurant, tavern, brew pub, wine bar, or similar establishment owned by the same legal entity as the beverage producer. This is because alcoholic beverages sold at such establishments are treated as "restaurant-type" drinks and not as tangible personal property. (TB-ST-15)

> *EXAMPLE:* A brewery produces beer, all of which is sold at an adjoining brew pub that the brewery also owns and operates. Since more than 50% of the beer produced is sold at a restaurant owned and operated by the brewery, the brewery is not considered to be producing tangible personal property for sale, and the brewery does not qualify as a manufacturer eligible for the production exemptions. (TB-ST-15)

Alcoholic beverage producers that qualify as manufacturers are eligible to purchase the following exempt from tax:

— raw materials (i.e., food items, such as grains (barley, corn, and wheat), grapes and other fruit, hops, malt, sugar, and yeast);

— machinery and equipment (i.e., barrels, bottling equipment, carboys, CO2 systems, chillers, crushers, dehydrators, destemmers, fermentation vats, heat exchangers, hydrometers, mash/lauter tuns, presses, racking equipment, refractometers, regulators, stills, tanks, and thermometers);

— parts, tools, and supplies (i.e., bowls, buckets, colanders, cleaning and sanitizing chemicals, flavoring agents, oil and grease (for exempt equipment), punch-down tools, stirring wands, strainers, and tubing);

— packaging materials (i.e., bottles, cans, boxes, caps, corks, and labels); and

— utilities and fuel (i.e., gas (natural gas, propane, etc.), coal, electricity, refrigeration, steam, wood (including wood pellets and other compressed wood products), and gas, electric, refrigeration, and steam services)

(TB-ST-15)

Alcoholic beverage producers that are also farmers.—Alcoholic beverage producers may also be farmers. The production exemption available to farmers is more expansive than the general production exemption. Property only has to be used predominantly (more than 50% of the time) - and not directly - in farm production to qualify for the exemption. Farming includes the growing and harvesting of crops used in producing alcoholic beverages for sale, such as grapes and other fruit, hops, and grains. Form ST-125, Farmer's and Commercial Horse Boarding Operator's Exemption Certificate, is used to make purchases that qualify for the farm production exemption. According to the Department of Taxation and Finance, the more expansive farm production exemption ceases when the farm product has reached a stage where it will be processed or converted into an alcoholic beverage. From that point on, only the general production exemption applies to the activities of producing the alcoholic beverages. (TB-ST-15)

> *EXAMPLE:* A brewery grows its own hops for use in making beer. Once the hops are harvested and pelletized, they are ready to be used with other ingredients in brewing beer. At that point, farm production has ceased and any other machinery or equipment used to process the hops into beer qualifies only for the general production exemption. (TB-ST-15)

Registration requirements.—Alcoholic beverage producers must be registered for sales tax purposes to make any sales of alcoholic beverages. Sales of alcoholic beverages to customers are taxable whether sold for on-premises or off-premises consumption. Sales to a distributor or retailer for the purpose of resale do not require the collection of sales tax provided the purchaser issues a properly completed Form ST-120, Resale Certificate. (TB-ST-15)

Tastings and tours.—Specific sales and use tax exemptions exist for certain items taken from inventory and furnished to customers at tastings held in conformance with the Alcoholic Beverage Control Law. These items include wine, wine product, beer, cider, liquor, or mead furnished at the tasting. Also included are bottles, corks, caps, and labels used to package these beverages. Charges for admission to tour the facilities of an alcoholic beverage producer are not taxable. (TB-ST-15)

• *Vending machine sales of drinks*

All sales of beer, wine, or other alcoholic beverages, or any other sale of drink and food by restaurants, taverns, or other establishments where the sales are made through a vending machine activated by use of coin, currency, credit card, or debit card are subject to sales tax. (Sec. 1105(d)(i)(3), Tax Law)

• *Alcoholic beverage tastings*

An exemption is provided for wine or wine product, beer or beer product, cider or cider product, liquor or liquor product, mead or mead product, and the kegs, cans, bottles, growlers, corks, caps, and labels used to package such alcoholic product, furnished by the official agent of a farm winery, winery, brewery, farm brewery, cider producer, farm cidery, distillery, farm distillery, mead producer, farm meadery, wholesaler, or importer at a tasting held in accordance with the alcoholic beverage control law to a customer or prospective customer who consumes such wine, beer, cider, liquor, or mead at such tasting. (Sec. 1115(a)(33), Tax Law) (TSB-M-15(1)S; TSB-M-16(7)S)

"Wine" means the product of the normal alcoholic fermentation of the juice of grapes, or other fruits or plants, including champagne, sparkling, and fortified wine. The alcoholic content of wine cannot exceed 24% by volume. It includes mead. "Wine product" means a beverage containing wine to which is added concentrated or unconcentrated juice, flavoring material, water, citric acid, sugar, and carbon dioxide. The alcoholic content of wine product cannot exceed 6% by volume. (TSB-M-15(1)S)

"Beer" means any fermented beverage of any name or description manufactured from malt, wholly or in part, or from any substitute for malt. "Cider" means the partially or fully fermented juice of fresh, whole apples or other pome fruits, containing more than 3.2% but not more than 8.5% alcohol by volume. "Liquor" means any and all distilled or rectified spirits, brandy, whiskey, rum, gin, cordials or similar distilled alcoholic beverages, including all dilutions and mixtures of one or more of the foregoing. (TSB-M-15(1)S)

Beer tasting exemption. For purposes of the beer tasting exemption, a beer tasting means no more than four samples of beer not exceeding four fluid ounces each, which may be provided or sold to a person in any calendar day, and each such sample must be a different beer than the others. Only a customer's first purchase during each calendar day at each licensed brewery will be exempt. (Sec. 1115(a)(45), Tax Law)

[¶60-290] Clothing

Except as noted below, sales of clothing and footwear are subject to tax as retail sales of tangible personal property. (Sec. 1105(a), Tax Law; Reg. Sec. 526.8(a)(2))

For a discussion of the treatment of clothing in New York City, see ¶560-010 NYC Exemptions.

For the local sales and use tax rates on clothing and footwear, see Publication 718-C.

• *Exemption for clothing and footwear under $110*

There is a year-round exemption from New York state sales and use taxes for clothing, footwear, and items used to make or repair exempt clothing, costing less than $110 per item or pair. (TSB-M-06(6)S; TSB-M-06(6.1)S; TSB-M-12(3)S) The exemption does not apply to locally imposed sales and use taxes unless the county or city imposing those taxes elected the exemption. (TSB-M-06(6.1)S; TSB-M-06(6.2)S; TSB-M-12(3)S)

The exemption also applies to the sales and use taxes imposed by the state in the Metropolitan Commuter Transportation District (MCTD), but only in those areas of the MCTD located in a county or city in the MCTD that elects the exemption from its own local taxes. (TSB-M-12(3)S; TSB-M-06(6)S; TSB-M-06(6.2)S) For a listing of listing of local tax rates in the counties and cities where clothing and footwear remain subject to local tax and for a listing of counties and cities where no tax applies during the exemption period, see TSB-M-06(6.1)Sand TSB-M-06(6.2)S.

The exemption applies only to clothing and footwear worn by humans. It also applies to most items that become a physical component part of exempt clothing or that are used to make or repair exempt clothing, such as most fabric, thread, yarn, buttons, snaps, hooks, zippers, and like items. (TSB-M-06(6)S) (TB-ST-122) However, such items are not exempt if they are made from pearls, precious or semi-precious stones, jewels or metals, or imitations thereof, even if the item sells for less than $110. (TB-ST-122)

Examples of exempt items include:

- aerobic clothing;
- athletic uniforms or clothing (but not equipment such as mitts, helmets, and pads);
- bathing suits;
- blouses;
- boots (climbing, fishing, riding, ski, waders);
- coats and wraps;
- dresses;
- hats;
- hosiery;
- slacks;
- shirts;
- shoes (ballet, bicycle, bowling, cleated, football, golf, jazz, soccer, etc.);
- sleepwear; and
- underwear.

(TB-ST-122)

Not all items worn on the body qualify as exempt clothing and footwear. Examples of taxable items include:

- costumes and rented formal wear (i.e., Halloween costumes);
- rented formal wear (i.e., tuxedos);
- jewelry, watches, and similar accessories;
- equipment items (i.e., tool belts, hard hats, and sport, bicycle, and motor-cycle helmets);
- protective goggles, safety glasses (other than prescription), masks, or pads for sport or occupational use;
- hockey and baseball fielders' gloves or mitts; and
- ice skates and roller skates.

(TB-ST-122)

If exempt clothing or footwear is sold with other taxable merchandise as a single unit, the full price is subject to sales or use tax, unless the price of the clothing or footwear is reasonable and separately stated. (TSB-M-06(6)S)

For a list of exempt and taxable clothing, footwear, and items used to make or repair exempt clothing, see TB-ST-530.

"Clothing and footwear" defined.—For purposes of the exemption, the term "clothing and footwear" is defined to mean:

- clothing and footwear to be worn by human beings, but not including costumes or rented formal wear; and

- fabric, thread, yarn, buttons, snaps, hooks, zippers and like items that are used or consumed to make or repair such clothing (other than costumes or rented formal wear) and become a physical component part of the clothing, but not including items made from pearls, precious or semi-precious stones, jewels or metals, or imitations thereof.

(Sec. 1101(b)(15), Tax Law)

Orders for clothing and footwear: Merchandise that is ordered by mail, telephone, the Internet, or e-mail is taxed at the rate in effect on the date the order is accepted by the vendor, regardless of when the order will be delivered. An order is accepted by the vendor when the vendor has taken an action to fill the order. Actions to fill an order include placing an in-date stamp on a mail order or assigning an order number to an order. Accordingly, the state and local exemption in effect on the date the order is accepted will apply. (TSB-M-12(3)S)

Rain checks: Sales tax on any purchase made with a rain check is based on the rate in effect at the time of the purchase, without regard to when the rain check was issued. Accordingly, any state and local exemption in effect at the time of purchase will apply. (TSB-M-12(3)S)

Layaway sales: In a layaway sale, merchandise is set aside for future delivery to a customer who makes a deposit and agrees to pay the balance of the purchase price over a period of time before the merchandise is delivered. The sales price of the merchandise includes any additional charges a vendor makes for putting the merchandise on layaway. (TSB-M-12(3)S)

Additional limitations.—The following additional limitations apply to the year-round exemption:

- The article of clothing or footwear (per pair) must be sold for less than $110 per article or pair. This "less than $110" limitation also applies to each item of fabric, thread, yarn, buttons, snaps, hooks, zippers, and like items that become a physical component part of exempt clothing or are used to make or repair exempt clothing. A charge for alterations should be included when determining whether the less than $110 limitation has been met, unless the charges are reasonable and separately stated on the receipt given to the customer.

- Costumes and rented formal wear are not eligible for exemption. The exemption also does not apply to fabric, thread, yarn, buttons, snaps, hooks, zippers, and like items which become a physical component part of costumes or rented formal wear, or are used to make or repair costumes or rented formal wear.

- Items of fabric, thread, yarn, buttons, snaps, hooks, zippers and like items used to make or repair otherwise exempt clothing are not eligible for exemption if the item used is made from real or imitation pearls, or from real or imitation precious or semiprecious stones, jewels, or metals.

- Most accessories (i.e. handbags, umbrellas, watches, and watchbands) are not considered clothing and are taxable. However, belt buckles, handkerchiefs, sweatbands, head scarves, and neck wear such as ties and scarves, are exempt.

- Fabric, thread, yarn, buttons, snaps, hooks, zippers and like items used to make or repair taxable products, are taxable.

- Monogramming of clothing prior to its sale is eligible for exemption if the monogramming is sold in conjunction with the sale of the article and the price for the monogrammed item is less than $110. However, if monogramming is done separately by a vendor for a separate charge, the charge for this service is taxable. This limitation also applies to the application of decals, logos, and like items (i.e. pictures and letters) by sewing, printing, imprinting, and silk screening, and the like.

(TSB-M-06(6)S)

Delivery charges.—Reasonable, separately stated charges by the vendor for delivery of eligible clothing and footwear are not taken into account in determining if the cost of the item is less than the $110 limitation. (TSB-M-06(6)S)

Coupons.—If a customer uses a manufacturer's coupon to pay for an article of clothing or a pair of shoes or other articles of footwear, the value of the coupon does not reduce the selling price for purposes of determining whether the article or pair is sold for less than $110. But if a customer pays for clothing or footwear using a store coupon, for which the store receives no reimbursement, the store coupon does reduce the selling price of the clothing or footwear. (TSB-M-06(6)S)

Special reporting requirements for exempt items.—Vendors who make sales of exempt clothing, footwear, and items used to make or repair exempt clothing must file Schedule H to report those sales. All sales of these items must be separately reported on Schedule H for the locality in which the sales were made. Schedule H must be completed and filed by vendors who have made sales of eligible clothing and footwear during the period covered by the return. Schedule H will be supplied to all quarterly and annual filers of Forms ST-100, ST-101, ST-102, and ST-810 with their returns. This schedule should be completed and filed along with the quarterly or annual return. (TSB-M-06(6)S)

- *Reporting clothing and footwear sales*

Sales in New York City of clothing and footwear costing $110 or more per item or pair are subject to the New York state sales and use taxes, the sales and use taxes imposed by the state in the Metropolitan Commuter Transportation District (MCTD), and the New York City sales and use tax. Sales and uses in New York City of clothing and footwear costing less than $110 per item or pair are fully exempt from state, local, and MCTD sales and use taxes. (TSB-M-07(5)S) For special transitional provisions relating to sales in New York City of clothing and footwear costing $110 or more, see Important Notice N-09-12.

For a discussion of the treatment of clothing in New York City, see ¶560-010 NYC Exemptions.

- *Farm clothing*

All clothing (including work clothes) purchased by farmers is taxable. See ¶60-250 Agriculture.

- *Services performed upon wearing apparel*

Laundering, dry-cleaning, tailoring, weaving, pressing, shoe repairing and shoe shining services are exempt. (Sec. 1105(c)(3)(ii), Tax Law) However, services by a tailor consisting of the making of new clothes are taxable. (Reg. Sec. 527.4(b); Reg. Sec. 527.4(c))

Alterations.—Reasonable and separately stated charges for alterations to all clothing are treated as tailoring and will be exempt from sales and use tax. (Reg. Sec. 527.4; Reg. Sec. 527.5) (TSB-M-02(4)S) The exemption does not depend on whether the individual articles of clothing are new or used, or on who performs the alterations.

¶60-290

CCH COMMENT: Tailoring businesses.—Businesses providing clothing alteration services should stop collecting sales tax from customers on sales of alteration services on or after September 1, 2002. However, when a customer brings material to a vendor to have a new article of clothing made, the vendor is considered to be performing the service of producing tangible personal property (making the article of clothing) for the customer. This transaction is not an alteration; instead the transaction is subject to tax as the production of clothing. (TSB-M-02(4)S)

Other services.—Monogramming of clothing or the application of decals, logos, and like items (such as pictures and letters) by sewing, printing, imprinting, silk screening, and the like, are not considered to be exempt alterations. However, such a service performed on an article of clothing prior to its sale may be eligible for the clothing exemption if the service is sold in conjunction with the sale of the article, and there is no separate charge for the service. In that case, the total charge to the customer is used to determine whether the article of clothing meets or exceeds the $110 threshold. (TSB-M-02(4)S)

• *Local rates on clothing and footwear*

For the local sales and use tax rates on clothing and footwear, see Publication 718-C.

[¶60-310] Computers, Software, and Services

In general, computer hardware and canned or prewritten computer software are subject to sales and use tax, but custom computer software and computer services are exempt.

Is computer hardware subject to sales tax in New York?

In general, computer hardware is subject to sales tax as tangible personal property. (Sec. 1105(a), Tax Law) However, certain computer system hardware is exempt. (Sec. 1115(a)(35), Tax Law)

Computer system hardware exemption. Computer system hardware used or consumed directly and predominantly in designing and developing computer software for sale is exempt. Such hardware used in providing the service, for sale, of designing and developing Internet websites is also exempt from tax. (Sec. 1115(a)(35), Tax Law) (TB-ST-243)

Computer system hardware includes the physical components from which a computer system is built, as well as associated parts and embedded software (i.e., software that comes as a part of the computer system hardware and is actually an integral part of the computer, typically in the form of a memory chip). Computer system hardware includes: microcomputers; minicomputers; mainframe computers; personal/laptop computers; tablet computers; external hard drives; portable disk drives; CD-ROM drives; external modems; monitors; keyboards; mouses; printers; scanners; servers; network interfaces; network hubs; and network routers. (TB-ST-243)

Directly and predominantly. Only the purchase of those components of the computer hardware and associated parts used directly and predominately in the design and development are exempt. "Directly" means that the hardware is actually used in, or has an active, casual relationship in, designing and developing computer software for sale or in providing the service, for sale, of designing and developing Internet websites. The use of computer system hardware in administration, production, or distribution activities is not considered direct use for purposes of the exemption. "Predominantly" means that the hardware must be used more than 50% of the time in design and development of computer software for sale or in providing the service, for sale, of designing and developing Internet websites. (TB-ST-243)

Designing and developing. "Designing and developing" includes systems analysis, program design, coding, testing, debugging, and documentation activities. (TB-ST-243)

Associated parts. The exemption for computer system hardware also extends to "associated parts," which encompass any component of, or attachment to, computer system hardware that is used in connection with and that is necessary to the performance of the hardware's operation. Examples of associated parts are: motherboards, CPUs, modems, and network wiring and cables. Although the exemption does not extend to software, embedded software that is actually an integral part of the computer (typically in the form of memory chips) is considered part of the computer system hardware for purposes of the exemption. (TSB-M-98(5)S)

Form needed for purchasing qualifying hardware. When purchasing qualifying computer system hardware, the purchaser must fill out and present Form ST-121.3, Exempt Use Certificate for Computer System Hardware, to the seller. The purchaser must complete all required entries and sign and date the form. The purchaser must give the seller a properly completed Form ST-121.3 within 90 days after the delivery of the property or performance of the service. Sales tax exemption certificates may also be issued and accepted electronically. Form ST-121.3 may be used as a single-purchase certificate, or as a blanket certificate covering the first and subsequent purchases of the same general type of property or service from the same seller. (TB-ST-243)

Taxable purchases. The following purchases are not eligible for the computer system hardware exemption: prewritten computer software, including operating system software and application software, that is not embedded software; consumable supplies or tools (i.e., toner, in, printer paper, and CD-ROMs); services of installing, maintaining, servicing, or repairing computer system hardware; and support packages and warranties. (TB-ST-243; TSB-M-98(5)S)

Computer equipment used in production. Computer equipment used directly in production qualifies for the manufacturing exemption. To qualify, the computers must be directly linked to production equipment, and have an active and necessary role in the actual production process. Computer equipment used in collateral or administrative functions (such as computer equipment linked to production equipment that merely functions to collect data for administrative use) does not qualify for the exemption. (TB-ST-552) For a general discussion of the manufacturing exemption, see Manufacturing, Processing, Assembling, or Refining.

Is computer software subject to sales tax in New York?

In general, canned or prewritten computer software is taxable, but custom computer software is exempt.

Canned or prewritten software. Prewritten computer software is taxable as tangible personal property, whether sold as part of a package or as a separate component, and regardless of how the software is conveyed to the purchaser. (Sec.

1101(b)(6), Tax Law) In other words, prewritten software is taxable whether sold on a disk or other physical medium; by electronic transmission; or by remote access. (TB-ST-128) Prewritten software that is modified or enhanced to the specifications of a particular purchaser (custom software) is subject to tax. However, if the charge for the custom modification or enhancement is reasonable and separately stated on the invoice, then the charge for the modification or enhancement is not subject to tax.

Custom software. Custom software is not subject to tax, provided it is designed and developed to the specifications of a specific purchaser (the method of delivery does not matter). However, if the custom software is sold or otherwise transferred to someone other than the person for whom it was originally designed and developed, it becomes subject to tax. (Sec. 1101(b)(14), Tax Law) (TB-ST-128; TSB-A-99(31)S)

Incidental use of programming languages. The incidental use of programming languages (for example, COBOL, FORTRAN, BASIC, C, etc.) or of libraries of "prewritten" functions or routines in designing and developing a "custom" software program to the specifications of a specific purchaser will not, in and of itself, make a sale of an otherwise custom program taxable. If prewritten components of a custom program are sold separately, however, they are subject to tax. (TSB-M-93(3)S)

Transfer of public domain software. The transfer of public domain software without charge is exempt because there is no consideration. (TSB-M-93(3)S)

Shareware. Payments for the right to use shareware (computer software initially provided without charge for a trial period for which a customer, to be entitled to the continued use of the product, pays a registration fee or donation) or to receive technical support or upgrades of shareware, are subject to tax. (TSB-M-93(3)S)

Affiliated group transfers. Custom software is exempt from tax when resold or transferred directly or indirectly by the purchaser of the software to either: (i) a corporation that is a member of an affiliated group of corporations that includes the original purchaser of the custom software; or (ii) a partnership in which the original purchaser of the custom software and other members of the affiliated group have at least a 50% interest in capital or profits. However, the exemption does not apply if the sale or transfer is part of a plan having as its principal purpose the avoidance or evasion of tax, or if the sale is prewritten software that is available to be sold to customers in the ordinary course of business. (TB-ST-128)

Software upgrades. In general, the sale of a revision or upgrade of prewritten software is subject to tax. If, however, the software upgrade is designed and developed to the specifications of a particular purchaser, then its sale to that specific purchaser is exempt as a sale of custom software. (TB-ST-128)

Remotely accessed software. The sale to a purchaser in New York of a license to remotely access software is subject to tax. The location of the sale for determining the proper local tax rate is the location from which the purchaser uses or directs the use of the software, not the location of the code embodying the software. Therefore, if a purchaser has employees who use the software located both in and outside of New York, the seller of the software should collect tax based on the portion of the receipt attributable to the users location in New York. (TB-ST-128)

Are computer services taxable?

Many services related to computer software are exempt from tax. However, when these otherwise exempt services are provided in conjunction with the sale of prewritten software, the charge for the service is exempt only when it is reasonable and separately stated on the invoice or billing statement given to the customer. Examples of exempt services include: training; consulting; instruction; troubleshooting; installing; programming; systems analysis; repairing; maintaining; and servicing. (Sec. 1115(o), Tax Law) (TB-ST-128)

EXAMPLE: Charge for services. A computer vendor sells an "off-the-shelf" software program to a customer. The vendor charges additional fees for installing the software, on-site training and diagnostic and trouble-shooting customer support. The sale of the software is taxable since it is prewritten. However, the charges for installation, on-site training and customer support services are not taxable if reasonable and separately stated on an invoice or billing statement given to the customer. (TSB-M-93(3)S)

Software maintenance agreements. Separately stated and reasonable charges for maintaining, servicing, or repairing software are exempt from sales tax. However, if a software maintenance agreement provides for the sale of both taxable elements (such as upgrades to prewritten software) and nontaxable elements, then the charge for the entire maintenance agreement is subject to tax unless the charges for the nontaxable elements are: reasonable and separately stated in the maintenance agreement, and billed separately on the invoice or other document of sale given to the purchaser. (TB-ST-128)

EXAMPLE: A vendor of computer systems sells a maintenance agreement to provide on-site training, repairs, software upgrades, and customer support by telephone for a customer's computer system (hardware and prewritten software). The portion of the cost of the agreement allocated to prewritten software upgrades and for maintenance of the computer system hardware is taxable. However, the portion of the cost allocated for on-site training, repairs and maintenance of the prewritten software and telephone support is exempt if the cost is reasonable and separately stated in the written agreement and the customer invoice. (TSB-M-93(3)S)

Data entry services. Data entry services performed by independent or temporary service contractors or similar service providers are exempt from tax, regardless of who provides the medium on which the data is recorded. The Department of Taxation and Finance has indicated that these services will be treated in the same manner as nontaxable typing and word processing services for sales and use tax purposes."Data entry service" is the transcribing and entering of data (words or numbers) by a person directly to a magnetic tape, punch card, disc, or computer via an alphanumeric keyboard or other data entry device. The term does *not* include the design and development of custom software or prewritten software. (TSB-M-96(8)S)

Computer bulletin board systems. Charges by a system operator ("sysop") to persons in New York for membership or "on-line" time, for the purpose of exchanging information or software programs, are subject to tax. The system operator must register as a vendor and collect the appropriate sales and use taxes on its sales. The rate is determined by the location of where the software is delivered or where the service occurs. Exchanges of public domain software or other copyrighted software that are not offered for sale and for which no fee or charge is made or demanded are not subject to tax. If the system operator merely serves as a conduit, there is no requirement for the sysop to collect tax on transfers of free software. Charges or other consideration requested by the sysop in exchange for the transfer, however, are subject to tax. (TSB-M-93(3)S)

EXAMPLE: The system operator of a commercial on-line computer information service charges a fee to its customers for downloading prewritten software programs and for access to a computer bulletin board which has features on software support and technical advice by computer experts regarding the prewritten software. Charges for the software program are taxable as the sale of tangible personal property. Charges for access to the software support and technical advice are subject to tax as information services. The manner of delivery to the customer of the software or information services does not affect the taxable status of the transactions. (TSB-M-93(3)S)

Is cloud computing taxable?

The taxability of cloud computing depends on the category under which the activity is classified. Cloud computing is a term used to describe the delivery of computing resources, including software applications, development tools, storage, and servers over the Internet. Rather than purchasing hardware or software, a consumer may purchase access to a cloud computing provider's hardware or software. Cloud computing offerings are generally divided into three categories: software as a service (SaaS), infrastructure as a service (IaaS), and platform as a service (PaaS).

Software as a service. Under the SaaS model, a consumer purchases access to a software application that is owned, operated, and maintained by a SaaS provider. The consumer accesses the application over the Internet. The software is located on a server that is owned or leased by the SaaS provider. The software is not transferred to the customer, and the customer does not have the right to download, copy, or modify the software.

Sales tax authority on SaaS transactions is still evolving. Some states have taken the position that SaaS transactions are a sale of software, reasoning that using software by electronically accessing it is no different than downloading it. Other states have deemed it a service based on the fact that no software is transferred. In some states, the taxability may depend on the specific facts and whether the object of the transaction is the use of software or some other purpose.

New York has no specific authority on the taxability of SaaS. However, the Department of Taxation and Finance has issued various Advisory Opinions on software accessed remotely. See, e.g., TSB-A-13(22)S (sales of access to forms via software stored on the taxpayer's website are subject to sales tax when accessed by a customer located in New York because the taxpayer's product is prewritten computer software); TSB-A-09(44)S (discusses the sales and use tax treatment of various Internet advertising, set-up, support, and service fees relating to real estate listings, including application service provider (ASP) fees for website functionality that are considered receipts from the sale of prewritten computer software and are subject to tax); TSB-A-09(25)S (web based software applications developed by the taxpayer for use by homecare agencies to track patient care and employee time and attendance, and for billing purposes, are subject to sales tax); TSB-A-09(15)S (charges for online access to "loan origination and processing services," which, among other things, allowed customers to complete and print certain loan processing documents, constituted receipts from the sale of prewritten computer software); and TSB-A-08(62)S (license to use software product that allowed a customer to upload and image to a website and manipulate the image to show various colors and views, constituted the sale of prewritten computer software).

It should be noted that the Department issued an Advisory Opinion (TSB-A-15(2)S) that access to computing power is a nontaxable service.

Infrastructure as a service. IaaS providers sell access to storage, networks, equipment, and other computing resources that the provider operates and maintains.

A consumer purchases the ability to store data or deploy and run software using the provider's equipment. The consumer does not manage or control the cloud infrastructure but has control over its applications and data.

New York has no specific authority on the taxability of IaaS. However, the Department of Taxation issued an Advisory Opinion (TSB-A-15(2)S) that access to computing power is a nontaxable service. Also, the Department has issued various Advisory Opinions on software accessed remotely.

Platform as a service. Under the PaaS model, the provider sells access to a platform and software development tools that a consumer uses to create its own applications. A consumer deploys the applications it creates onto the provider's infrastructure. The consumer has control over its deployed applications but does not control the underlying infrastructure.

New York has no specific authority on the taxability of PaaS. However, the Department of Taxation issued an Advisory Opinion (TSB-A-15(2)S) that access to computing power is a nontaxable service. Also, the Department has issued various Advisory Opinions on software accessed remotely.

Does a sales tax holiday apply to computer items in New York?

No, New York does not currently have any sales tax holidays.

[¶60-330] Construction

In general, construction materials and supplies, as well as construction related services, are taxable. (Sec. 1101(b), Tax Law; Sec. 1105(c)(3)(iii), Tax Law; Sec. 1105(c)(5), Tax Law) However, charges for capital improvements are exempt.

Are construction materials and supplies taxable in New York?

In general, sales of tangible personal property to a contractor, subcontractor or repairman for use or consumption in erecting a structure or building and adding to, altering, improving, maintaining, servicing or repairing real property are taxable. Accordingly, contractors must pay sales tax upon purchases of materials or supplies used by them in fulfilling contracts. (Sec. 1101(b)(4), Tax Law)

The sale of a new mobile home to a contractor, subcontractor or repairman who, in that capacity, installs the new mobile home is not a taxable retail sale. (Sec. 1101(b)(4), Tax Law)

Capital improvements. Tangible personal property sold by a contractor to someone other than an exempt organization for whom the contractor is adding to or improving real property by a capital improvement is not subject to tax, provided that the property becomes an integral component part of the structure or real property. (Sec. 1115(a)(17), Tax Law; Reg. Sec. 528.18) (TB-ST-104)

> *EXAMPLE:* A contractor builds a home for a customer that includes the sale of a free standing refrigerator. The contractor is required to collect the tax on the sale of the refrigerator. (Reg. Sec. 528.18)

The customer must issue a Certificate of Capital Improvement to the contractor in order to exempt the purchase of an addition or improvement to real property. (Reg. Sec. 541.5)

"Capital improvement" defined. The term "capital improvement" is defined as an addition or alteration to real property that:

— substantially adds to the value of the real property or appreciably prolongs its useful life;

— becomes part of the real property or is permanently affixed to it so that removal would cause material damage to the property or article itself; and

— is intended to become a permanent installation.

(Sec. 1101(b)(9), Tax Law) (TB-ST-104)

The work performed must meet all three of these requirements to be considered a capital improvement. (TB-ST-113)

For example, building a deck, installing a hot water heater, or installing kitchen cabinets are all capital improvement projects. Repairing a broken step, replacing a thermostat on a hot water heater, or painting existing cabinets are all examples of taxable repair and maintenance work. (TB-ST-104)

Floor covering (such as carpet, carpet padding, linoleum and vinyl roll flooring, carpet tile, linoleum tile and vinyl tile), when installed as the initial finished floor covering in new construction or as a new addition to or total reconstruction of existing construction, constitutes a capital improvement. (Sec. 1101(b)(9), Tax Law)

Purchases of materials. Purchases of building materials and other tangible personal property for capital improvement work are taxable, whether purchased by a contractor, subcontractor, repairman, or homeowner. The sales tax paid by contractors becomes an expense that can be passed through to the customer as part of the overall charge for the capital improvement. Contractors do not normally sell building materials to customers without installation and, therefore, cannot use Form ST-120, Resale Certificate, to make purchases of building materials exempt from tax. However, in certain situations, contractors can use Form ST-120.1, Contractor Exempt Purchase Certificate, to make purchases exempt from sales tax. For example, a contractor is hired to build a house, and the contract requires the contractor to provide certain freestanding appliances such as a refrigerator, washer, and dryer. The installation of these appliances does not qualify as a capital improvement, since freestanding appliances do not become part of the real property, as do building materials. The contractor can use Form ST-120.1 to purchase the appliances exempt from sales tax. However, the contractor must collect sales tax on the charge to the customer for the appliances. Purchases of materials in one taxing jurisdiction in New York may be subject to a different tax rate (higher or lower) if the materials are later used in a different jurisdiction in New York. (TB-ST-104)

Capital improvement billing. When calculating how much to charge a customer, a contractor may include the sales tax paid on building materials just like any other project expense. The sales tax that the contractor paid on the materials is an expense that the contractor builds into the price charged to the customer. However, because the work is a capital improvement, there is no sales tax due on the charge to the customer. (TB-ST-104)

Leasehold improvements. Additions or alterations to real property made by or for a tenant, rather than the owner of the property, may be considered to be temporary in nature, rather than permanent. As a result, certain work that may otherwise qualify as a capital improvement may not qualify if the tenant's lease does not transfer ownership of the improvement to the property owner. For example, some leases require the tenant to return the property to its original state when the lease expires. In those cases, nothing that was installed over the term of the lease can be considered permanent, since it will have to be removed if the tenant moves. This fact means that the work performed cannot qualify as a capital improvement. (TB-ST-104)

¶60-330

EXAMPLE: A contractor installs sinks and related plumbing fixtures for a hair salon that is a tenant in a building. Installing a sink normally qualifies as a capital improvement. However, the hair salon's lease stipulates that the premises must be returned to their original condition when the lease ends. Because the sinks must be removed at the end of the lease, they do not qualify as a permanent installation, and their installation is not a capital improvement.

Exemption certificates. When performing capital improvement work, a contractor should get a properly completed exemption certificates, Form ST-124, Certificate of Capital Improvement, from the customer and should not collect sales tax from the customer for the project. (TB-ST-104)

Construction equipment and motor vehicles. The purchase, rental, lease or license to use construction equipment and motor vehicles by a contractor is subject to tax. However, a nonresident's purchase of a motor vehicle is not taxable, even if delivery is made within New York, provided that the contractor furnishes the dealer with a properly completed exemption certificate for purchase of the motor vehicle. Equipment and motor vehicles purchased out-of-state by a nonresident contractor are not subject to compensating use tax upon subsequent use within New York. (Reg. Sec. 541.9)

A taxable rental or leasing of equipment occurs where dominion and control of equipment supplied with an operator or driver transfers to the contractor. The operator's or driver's wages may be excluded from the taxable receipts if such wages are both reasonable and separately stated. Where dominion and control of equipment supplied with an operator or driver remains with the lessor, there is no taxable rental or leasing of equipment to the contractor. However, the service performed may constitute a taxable installation and repair or real estate maintenance and repair service. (Reg. Sec. 541.9)

Contractors who lease equipment are liable for the combined New York state and local sales or use tax on the total charges at the highest rate in effect in any jurisdiction in which the equipment is used during the lease payment period. The total amount of the lease charge is subject to tax. Interest and other expenses paid by a lessor on the purchase of tangible personal property leased to a contractor, even though separately stated on the bill, must be included in the receipts subject to tax. In addition, all expenses incurred by the lessor in determining the amount charged for rental of tangible personal property to a contractor, such as "setting up, assembling, installing and/or dismantling," are elements of the total receipt subject to tax (regardless of their taxable status and whether they are separately billed to the lessee). (Reg. Sec. 541.9)

Property used for exempt organizations. An exemption is provided for tangible personal property sold to a contractor, subcontractor or repairman for use in erecting a structure of an exempt organization or for adding, altering, improving, maintaining, servicing or repairing real property of such organization, if the property becomes an integral component part of the structure or real property. (Sec. 1115(a)(15), Tax Law; Sec. 1115(a)(16), Tax Law; Reg. Sec. 528.16; Reg. Sec. 528.17) The exemption applies, whether the contract is on a lump sum, time and materials, cost-plus or other basis. (Reg. Sec. 541.3)

EXAMPLE: An exempt organization contracts to have a building erected on its land. Purchases by its contractor of tangible personal property, such as nails, sheetrock and plywood that become part of the structure, are exempt. (Reg. Sec. 528.16(a))

EXAMPLE: The owner of real property enters into a contract to erect a building to be leased, under a long-term lease, to an exempt organization. The contractor's purchases are not exempt as the owner of the building is not an exempt organization. (Reg. Sec. 528.16(a))

EXAMPLE: Lumber and other materials that are used to build forms are not exempt since they do not become a component part of the structure. (Reg. Sec. 528.16(a))

EXAMPLE: Equipment rentals such as cranes, bulldozers, backhoes, etc. for use in building a structure for an exempt organization are subject to tax. (Reg. Sec. 528.16(a))

EXAMPLE: A painting contractor uses masking tape on a contract for an exempt. The tape is subject to tax since it will not become an integral component part of the real property. (Reg. Sec. 528.17)

Form of contract. The form of contract entered into between an exempt organization and its contractor is not relevant. Purchases of tangible personal property by subcontractors and repairmen are accorded the same treatment as purchases by contractors. (Reg. Sec. 528.16(b))

EXAMPLE: A building is being erected for an exempt organization. Glass in the windows has been broken, and a glazier has been engaged by the general contractor to repair the windows. The charges for such repairs are exempt, and the purchase of new glass is exempt. (Reg. Sec. 528.16(b))

Materialmen and pay-when-paid option. Materialmen who make qualified sales to contractors may be able to postpone payment of the sales tax until they receive payment from the contractor. (Sec. 1132(a), Tax Law) (TB-ST-555) A "materialman" is any person or business that sells any of the following to a property owner, contractor, subcontractor, or repairman to be used for the improvement of real property:

— building materials;

— machinery, tools, or equipment;

— compressed gases for welding or cutting; or

— fuel or lubricants for the operation of machinery or motor vehicles.

(TB-ST-555)

Tools and supplies. Charges for tools or supplies (including safety apparel) purchased by a contractor are subject to state and local sales or use taxes. Resident contractors are also liable for state and local use taxes on tools or supplies purchased outside New York and later used in the state. (Reg. Sec. 541.10)

EXAMPLE: A masonry contractor sets forms for pouring a foundation footing in the performance of a non-agency contract for the erection of a building for an exempt organization. The walls are set upon the footing and the foundation is backfilled. The supplies used in making forms are left in the ground since the cost of removal is more than the salvage value. Although the supplies stay with the job they are considered abandoned and not transferred to the customer as a component part of the project. The cost of the supplies is taxable to the contractor. (Reg. Sec. 541.10)

Production machinery and equipment. A contractor may make an exempt purchase of production machinery or equipment qualifying for the manufacturer's exemption by issuing a properly completed contractor exempt purchase certificate to the supplier. (Reg. Sec. 541.6) Services performed on production machinery and equipment are exempt.

How does New York tax construction related services?

Charges for the services of repairing, maintaining or installing tangible personal property and for repairing or maintaining real property are generally taxable. (Sec. 1105(c)(3)(iii), Tax Law; Sec. 1105(c)(5), Tax Law) However, charges for the installation of property that, when installed, will constitute an addition or capital improvement are exempt. The tax also does not apply for real estate maintenance or repair services when rendered by a person who does not offer such services to the public in a regular trade or business. Fabricators and manufacturers who install their fabricated or manufactured product into real property are treated as contractors. (Reg. Sec. 541.11)

> *EXAMPLE:* A contractor-fabricator purchases steel beams from a manufacturer and pays the sales tax on the cost. The fabricator's employees fabricate the beams to job specifications and install the beams in a capital improvement job. The fabricator is not subject to a use tax on the value added by the fabrication. (Reg. Sec. 541.11)

> *EXAMPLE:* A contractor purchases steel beams which must be fabricated before they can be installed. The work is subcontracted out for fabrication. The fabricator's charge to the contractor for the fabrication of the steel beams which the contractor will install is subject to the tax. (Reg. Sec. 541.11)

Likewise, retailers (such as department stores), when installing tangible personal property that constitutes a capital improvement to a customer's real property, are acting as contractors. (Reg. Sec. 541.13)

> *EXAMPLE:* A retailer with a hardware and plumbing department, sells hot water tanks with or without installation. When the tank is sold, installed by the retailer and the customer presents a properly completed certificate of capital improvement to the retailer, the retailer is acting as a contractor and is liable for the compensating use tax based upon its cost for the tank. The retailer must report the cost of the hot water tank as a purchase subject to use tax on its sales tax return. (Reg. Sec. 541.13)

Repair services to construction equipment or motor vehicles. The total charge for repairs (including parts, materials and labor) to a contractor's equipment or motor vehicles is subject to tax when delivered in New York or delivered to a resident contractor in another state and subsequently returned to New York. For equipment or motor vehicles owned by a contractor and repaired by the contractor's employees, the wages, salaries and other compensation paid by the contractor to the employees are not subject to tax. However, the cost of the parts and materials is taxable. (Reg. Sec. 541.9)

Charges for repairs on rented or leased equipment and motor vehicles are taxable to the contractor-lessee when the contractor is responsible for any repairs incurred. The contractor owes the tax due on repairs performed on the equipment and motor vehicles made within the state. If such equipment or motor vehicle is repaired outside the state for a resident contractor, the contractor owes the tax when the equipment or motor vehicle is subsequently returned to New York. (Reg. Sec. 541.9)

When the lessor is responsible for any repairs to the equipment or motor vehicle, the repair charges are exempt if the equipment or motor vehicles are purchased exclusively for rental. If the contractor has repairs made to rented or leased equipment or motor vehicles and is fully reimbursed by the lessor, the lessor may claim a refund or credit for the amount of tax the lessor reimbursed to the contractor. (Reg. Sec. 541.9)

Mixed use equipment or motor vehicles. Charges for repairs to equipment or motor vehicles that have a mixed use (for self use and for rental or lease purposes) are taxable. (Reg. Sec. 541.9)

Credit for tax paid to other state. If another state's sales tax was paid by the contractor to an out-of-state vendor on repairs, which are not reimbursed by the lessor, and the other state has a reciprocal agreement with New York, a claim for credit may be submitted by the contractor for the other state's tax rate paid against any New York tax owed (but not to exceed the New York and local compensating use tax rate due). (Reg. Sec. 541.9)

Services performed on production machinery and equipment. Charges for installing, maintaining, servicing or repairing qualifying production machinery and equipment are exempt. (Reg. Sec. 541.6)

Temporary facilities at construction sites. The New York Department of Taxation and Finance provides guidance (TSB-M-14(15)S) on its policy regarding the application of state and local sales and use taxes to temporary scaffolding, temporary protective pedestrian walkways (sidewalk bridges), and temporary hoisting systems (referred to collectively as scaffolding systems) that are used at construction sites.

Scaffolding services provided in capital improvement projects. When provided in connection with a capital improvement project, a scaffolding service is one of the services covered by the exclusion from sales tax described in Reg. Sec. 541.8(a). As a result, amounts charged by a subcontractor for scaffolding services qualify as charges for a "temporary facility" that are not subject to sales tax provided that the underlying construction project qualifies as a capital improvement project. Accordingly, all charges made by a subcontractor for materials and labor necessary to provide a scaffolding service at a construction site are not subject to sales tax if the end result of the underlying construction project, when viewed as a whole, qualifies as a capital improvement project and is supported by the issuance of a valid Form ST-124, Certificate of Capital Improvement. Both lump sum and separately stated contracts are treated the same for sales tax purposes. (TSB-M-14(15)S)

However, when a subcontractor provides scaffolding services in connection with a construction project that qualifies as a capital improvement project, the subcontractor is liable for the payment of sales tax on its own purchases or rentals of materials acquired to provide the scaffolding service because these purchases and rentals do not qualify as purchases for resale. This sales tax liability also applies to purchases and rentals of materials from a related entity. That is, if the subcontractor purchases or rents a scaffolding system from a related entity, the charge for the purchase or rental is subject to tax. Moreover, the charge must be reasonable in view of prevailing market sale or rental prices for the scaffolding system. (TSB-M-14(15)S)

Scaffolding services provided in installation, maintenance, servicing, or repair projects. A scaffolding service provided as part of a taxable installation, maintenance, servicing, or repair project is subject to sales tax whether billed on either a lump sum or separately stated basis. The rental, installation, and dismantling of the scaffolding system are all elements of the total receipts for the scaffolding service that are subject to sales tax. The subcontractor or repairman must charge sales tax to the prime contractor on the complete lump sum charged for the scaffolding service or, alternatively, on all of the separately stated charges including dismantling of the scaffolding system. (TSB-M-14(15)S)

When a subcontractor or repairman provides scaffolding services in connection with a taxable installation, maintenance, servicing, or repair project, the subcontractor or repairman is liable for payment of sales tax on its purchases of the materials obtained to provide the scaffolding service because the subcontractor or repairman is using the materials for its own purposes to perform construction activities subject to tax. The materials do not become a "physical component part" of the property serviced and are not actually transferred to the customer as required for application of the exclusion from tax under Tax Law §1101(b)(4)(i). Moreover, the purchase of the scaffolding service by the prime contractor does not qualify as a purchase for resale because the prime contractor is using the service for its own purposes and will not be reselling it. (TSB-M-14(15)S)

Scaffolding materials purchased by persons other than contractors, subcontractors, or repairmen. When scaffolding materials are purchased by a person exclusively for the purpose of reselling or renting the scaffolding materials to others (i.e., without the lessor providing any accompanying services), the scaffolding materials may be purchased for resale without payment of sales tax. The purchaser should furnish its supplier with a properly completed Form ST-120, Resale Certificate. Charges by the purchaser for the sale or rental of the scaffolding materials to a related entity must be reasonable in view of prevailing market sale or rental prices. (TSB-M-14(15)S)

Scaffolding materials purchased outside of New York. A subcontractor's out-of-state purchases or rentals of materials that are used to provide scaffolding services within New York are subject to use tax on the date the materials are first brought into New York. The tax is based on the purchase price of the materials, unless: (i) the materials are used outside New York by the subcontractor for more than six months prior to their use in New York, in which case the tax is based on the lesser of the purchase price or the fair market value of the materials (but not to exceed their cost) at the time of first use in New York; or (ii) the materials brought into New York (other than for complete consumption) will be used for a period of less than six months, in which case the subcontractor may elect to pay the use tax based on the fair rental value of the materials for the period of use within New York. The subcontractor may be eligible for a reciprocal tax credit against the use tax due for sales or use tax paid in another state, provided the other state provides a reciprocal credit for sales or use taxes paid to New York. (TSB-M-14(15)S)

On-site assembly. On-site assembly performed by a manufacturer-installer or a contractor hired by the manufacturer is recognized as a continuation of the manufacturing process in those instances where it is demonstrated that machinery and equipment by virtue of its size, weight, and the like could not be completely assembled prior to delivery to the customer. (Reg. Sec. 541.6) The cost of assembly becomes part of the selling price of the machinery and equipment. In order for the charge by the contractor to the manufacturer to be exempt as a service to property being resold, the contractor must obtain a resale certificate from the manufacturer. The vendor's charge for assembly is taxable if the machinery and equipment is subject to sales or use tax and exempt if the machinery and equipment is exempt from sales and use taxes. Regarding lump-sum contracts to furnish and install machinery and equipment involving on-site assembly and installation charges, reasonable engineering estimates may be used to determine the amount of the price relating to the taxable installation after on-site assembly has been completed.

On-site assembly is completed at the point where the machinery and equipment is assembled into a completed unit. Any further charges are charges for the installation, maintenance and servicing of machinery and equipment, and may be subject to local sales and use taxes (including New York City sales and use taxes). Installation charges include the wiring from the electrical panel to the machinery and equipment to make it operational as well as attaching the machinery and equipment by bolts or other means to a foundation. (Reg. Sec. 541.6)

Charges by a contractor for installing and/or assembling machinery or equipment owned by the customer prior to hiring the contractor are not part of the selling price of the machinery or equipment. Such charges may be subject to local sales and use taxes, including New York City sales and use taxes. (Reg. Sec. 541.6)

Trash removal. A contractor's purchase of trash or debris removal service is exempt from tax as a purchase for resale if:

— the contractor generated the trash or debris as a result of maintaining, servicing, or repairing real property, property, or land;

— the contractor's agreement with the owner provides that the contractor is responsible for having the trash or debris removed; and

— the contractor furnishes a contractor's exempt purchase certificate to the person performing the trash or debris removal service.

(Reg. Sec. 541.7) (TSB-M-00(5)S)

A contractor's purchase of trash or debris removal service is also exempt if:

— the contractor performs work that constitutes a capital improvement;

— the contractor generated the trash or debris as a result of such work;

— the contractor obtains a certificate of capital improvement from the contractor's customer; and

— the contractor furnishes a copy of the certificate to the person performing the trash or debris removal service.

(Reg. Sec. 541.7)

Guaranty or warranty work. Payments by a contractor to another contractor to perform maintenance, service and repair of real and tangible personal property, when purchased to fulfill a guarantee or warranty, are not subject to tax. However, where a contractor services real or tangible personal property and a charge is made to the customer, the charge is subject to the tax even though some of the work is performed partially under a guarantee or warranty. (Reg. Sec. 541.1) A refund or credit may apply for guarantee work.

Drilling test wells and related services. The New York Department of Taxation and Finance provides guidance on the application of sales and use taxes to the service of drilling test wells and other associated services. The guidance does not address drilling services provided with respect to the production of gas or oil and related activities. Drilling services rendered directly with respect to real property, property, or land used or consumed directly and predominantly in the production for sale of gas or oil are exempt from sales tax. (TSB-M-10(4)S)

Tax treatment of drilling services. Drilling services are generally taxable as repair or maintenance services to real property. However, drilling services performed as a constituent part of a capital improvement to real property are not subject to tax. When drilling services are performed in conjunction with a remediation project or a construction project, the sales tax treatment of the drilling services will be determined by the overall nature of the project performed. If a project results in a capital improvement, the charge for the drilling services is not subject to tax. If a project is determined to be the service of maintaining, servicing, or repairing real property, the charge for the drilling service is subject to tax. A determination as to whether a remediation project or a construction project constitutes a capital improvement is a question of fact based on the circumstances in each particular instance. (Note: The drilling of a new water well or the deepening of an existing water well are considered capital improvements to real property and are not subject to sales tax. Therefore, where the service of a drilling company results in the installation of a new water well, or the deepening of an existing well, the service is not subject to sales tax.) (TSB-M-10(4)S)

Drilling services for engineering firms. Engineering services are not taxable. Drilling services are often provided to engineering firms in conjunction with their projects. Generally, an engineering firm will subcontract for drilling services as support services to the overall service that the firm is providing to its customer. (TSB-M-10(4)S) Charges for drilling services that are performed on real property, such as the drilling of test wells on the property of an engineering firms client, are generally subject to sales tax, unless performed as a constituent part of a capital improvement project. While an engineering firm is not required to charge sales tax when billing its clients for engineering services, it must pay sales tax on its purchases of taxable property and services. Therefore, the fact that a drilling contractor's customer is an engineering firm is not relevant to determining the taxability of the drilling services provided. (TSB-M-10(4)S)

Drilling services in conjunction with geological research and development services. Certain companies primarily provide geologic site characterization reports. In these cases, a company will do its own drilling and sampling, rather than subcontract those tasks to a third party, and furnish a written report to its customer. Geologic site characterization includes obtaining information pertaining to the depth of the water table from the land surface, the depth to the bedrock from the land surface, the direction of the flow of subsurface water, soil conditions, and underground water quality and quantity. The information obtained is used to define hydrogeologic conditions for geologic site characterization reports. These reports are similar to reports containing results of scientific laboratory analysis of environmental samples and are not subject to sales tax. If a company providing a geologic site report to its customer subcontracts for the necessary drilling services, these services are taxable unless performed as a constituent part of a capital improvement to real property. (TSB-M-10(4)S)

Are labor charges taxable in New York?

In general, the services of installing, maintaining, servicing, or repairing tangible personal property are taxable. (Sec. 1105(c)(3), Tax Law; Reg. Sec. 527.5(a)) Likewise, tax is generally imposed on the maintenance, servicing or repair of real property. However, the services of adding to or improving real property by a capital improvement are not subject to tax. (Sec. 1105(c)(5), Tax Law; Reg. Sec. 527.7(b)(1))

What incentives or credits are available for contractors in New York?

In general, a contractor can take a sales tax credit on their return if they:

— paid sales tax on building materials to a supplier;

— transferred those materials to a customer in a taxable repair, maintenance, or installation service; and

— charged sales tax to a customer.

(TB-ST-130)

In most cases, this means that a contractor can take a credit when the work they perform is classified as a taxable repair, maintenance, or installation service, but not when it is classified as a capital improvement. (Sec. 1119(c), Tax Law) (TB-ST-130)

A contractor may apply for a refund of the sales tax instead of a credit. If a contractor is not required to be registered for sales tax purposes, the contractor must apply to the Department for refund of sales tax. (TB-ST-130)

Economic transformation and facility redevelopment program. Participants in the Economic Transformation and Facility Redevelopment Program, or their contractors, may claim a refund of state sales or use tax paid on tangible personal property that is used in constructing, expanding or rehabilitating industrial or commercial real property located in an ETA. The tangible personal property must become an "integral component part" of the real property in order to qualify for the refund. The refund is available for property purchased after the participant receives its certificate of eligibility and used before a certificate of occupancy is issued for the real property. The participant or contractor may only apply for a refund once per sales tax quarter and the amount may not be claimed as a credit on a sales tax return. The provisions are scheduled to expire on December 31, 2021. (Sec. 1119(f), Tax Law) For additional information, see TSB-M-11(9)Sand Enterprise Zones and Similar Tax Incentives.

For a discussion of sales tax credits that may be available to contractors, see Credits and TB-ST-130.

For a discussion of sales tax incentives that may be available to contractors, see Enterprise Zones and Similar Tax Incentives.

What certificate or form must a contractor use to claim an exemption in New York?

New York has the following exemption certificates that may be of interest for contractors:

— ST-120.1, Contractor Exempt Purchase Certificate; and

— ST-124, Certificate of Capital Improvement.

For a discussion of these forms and other exemption certificates or forms that might be related to contractors, see Exemption Certificates.

Does New York have special rules concerning subcontractors?

No. Subcontractors are treated the same as contractors because they are included within the definition of a "contractor." (Reg. Sec. 541.2)

Does New York have any other provisions related to construction?

Yes. New York has various other provisions related to construction.

Certification requirements for businesses that contract with New York state. In certain instances, businesses that are awarded contracts with New York state are required to certify that they are registered to collect New York state and local sales and use taxes on sales delivered to locations within New York. The purpose of this requirement is to ensure that contractors do not get state work unless they, their affiliates, and their subcontractors making sales of tangible personal property or taxable services are registered to collect New York sales tax. This means that certain businesses, including in some cases out-of-state businesses not currently registered to collect New York sales taxes, will need to register for New York sales tax purposes. (Sec. 5-a, Tax Law) (TB-ST-118)

Certification requirements. Certain contractors that are awarded state contracts valued at more than $100,000 must certify to the Tax Department that they are registered to collect sales tax. This certification is made by filing a properly completed Form ST-220-TD, Contractor Certification, with the Tax Department. This certification only has to be filed once, as long as the information it contains remains correct and complete. (TB-ST-118)

Contractors who have made sales of tangible personal property or services with a cumulative value in excess of $300,000, delivered by any means to locations within New York, must certify that they are registered to collect sales tax. The $300,000 threshold in cumulative sales is measured over the four sales tax quarters that immediately precede the sales tax quarter in which Form ST-220-TD is filed. Sales tax quarters are March-May, June-August, September-November, and December-February. (TB-ST-118)

Contractors must also certify that each affiliate and subcontractor who exceeds the $300,000 sales threshold during the specified period is registered to collect sales tax. If the contractor, affiliate, or subcontractor did not make sales of property or taxable services in excess of $300,000 during the specified period, it must indicate this on Form ST-220-TD. (Sec. 5-a, Tax Law) (TB-ST-118)

When determining whether the $300,000 sales threshold has been met, contractors must take into account all sales of tangible personal property and taxable services within New York during the specified period (not merely sales to covered agencies). This also includes the amount of any sales made that are exempt from sales tax (for example, sales made to an exempt organization). (TB-ST-118)

In addition to filing Form ST-220-TD, certifying that the contractor (and any affiliates or subcontractors) is registered to collect sales tax, the contractor must also certify to the procuring covered agency that it filed Form ST-220-TD with the Tax Department, and that the filing is correct and complete. Contractors must make this certification by filing Form ST-220-CA, Contractor Certification to Covered Agency, with the procuring covered agency. (TB-ST-118)

Exempt contracts. Certain contracts are exempt from the contractor certification requirements. A contract is exempt if the procuring covered agency and the Office of the State Comptroller (or other contract reviewer) find in writing that the contract is necessary to:

— address an emergency (defined in the State Finance Law as an urgent and unexpected requirement where health and public safety or the conservation of public resources is at risk); or

— ensure the public health, safety, or welfare when an urgent event with a compelling public purpose arises.

(Sec. 5-a(4), Tax Law) (TB-ST-118)

In addition, the agency's and contract reviewer's written finding must explain the reasons supporting the determination. (TB-ST-118)

Temporary construction of world's fair. The New York compensating use tax is not imposed upon property used exclusively for the temporary construction, improvement, alteration or repair of any building, structure or exhibit located entirely on land owned by New York City and leased by it to a corporation organized for the sole purposes of holding a world's fair and confining its operations solely to preparing for and conducting such fair. (Sec. 1118(6), Tax Law)

[¶60-340] Drop Shipments

A drop shipment is a shipment of tangible personal property from a seller directly to the purchaser's customer, at the direction of the purchaser. These sales are also known as third-party sales because they require that there be, at arm's length, three parties and two separate sales transactions. Generally, a primary seller (generally a retailer) accepts an order from a customer, places this order with a third party seller, usually a manufacturer or wholesale distributor, and directs the third party seller to ship the goods directly to the primary seller's customer or to the primary seller's unaffiliated fulfillment services provider. Drop shipments are examined as two transactions: (1) the sale from the third-party seller to the primary seller, and (2) the sale from the primary seller to the primary seller's customer. (TB-ST-190)

- *New York treatment of drop-shipment sales*

When all the parties are located in the state, the retailer furnishes a resale certificate to the primary seller, rendering the first sale a nontaxable transaction. The retailer then collects sales tax on behalf of the state on the secondary sale to its customer. However, different considerations arise when one or more of the parties are not within the state.

New York will exempt the sale of the primary (or initial) seller to an out-of-state retailer not doing business in New York provided that the retailer presents a resale certificate or other appropriate evidence that the sale is made for resale. If the out-of-state secondary seller does not have New York nexus and consequently cannot be held liable for tax on the sale to its New York customer, then the customer becomes liable for use tax. (Sec. 1110, Tax Law)

The New York State Tax Department permits qualified out-of-state vendors not registered in New York to use Form ST-120, *Resale Certificate*, in connection with purchases for resale that are exempt from New York sales and use taxes. (*TSB-M-98(3)S*)

- *Use of Form ST-120, Resale Certificate*

When the primary seller is registered for New York sales tax purposes, and the third-party seller and the primary seller's customer are located in New York State, the primary seller should furnish Form ST-120, Resale Certificate, to the third-party seller. The third-party seller then delivers the order to the primary seller's customer or to the seller's unaffiliated fulfillment services provider. The primary seller collects the sales tax from the customer, reports the sale and remits the sales tax to the department on the appropriate sales tax return. (TB-ST-190)

If the primary seller is a qualified out-of-state purchaser he or she can also use the form to make tax-exempt purchases of tangible personal property for resale. A qualified out-of state purchaser is one that: is not registered or required to be registered for sales tax purposes with the New York State Tax Department; is registered with another state, the District of Columbia, a province of Canada, or other country, or has its only location in a state, province, or country that does not require registration; and is purchasing items for resale that will be either: delivered to the purchaser's customer or unaffiliated fulfillment services provider located in New York State; or delivered to the purchaser in New York State, but resold from a business located outside the state. (TB-ST-190)

Misuse of this exemption certificate may result in serious civil and criminal sanctions in addition to the payment of any tax and interest due. (TB-ST-190)

- *Unaffiliated fulfillment services providers*

A seller who has a place of business or salespeople in New York, or that owns or leases tangible personal property in New York, is required to register for New York sales tax purposes. However, a seller who is not otherwise required to register in New York may purchase fulfillment services from a New York fulfillment services provider who is not an affiliated person without being required to register in New

York. A New York fulfillment services provider may provide one or more of the following services for a seller that is not an affiliated person and that is not otherwise required to be registered without causing that seller to have to register for New York sales tax purposes: store the seller's inventory on its premises; accept orders electronically or by mail, telephone, fax, or Internet; respond to consumer correspondence and inquiries electronically or by mail, telephone, fax, or Internet; perform billing or collection activities; and ship orders from an inventory of products offered for sale by the seller. Fulfillment services providers located in New York State must be registered for New York sales tax. (TB-ST-190)

[¶60-360] Enterprise Zones and Similar Tax Incentives

New York offers sales and use tax credits or refunds for qualified empire zone enterprises (QEZEs) under the Empire Zone (EZ) Program. The credits or refunds do not apply for local sales and use tax purposes unless the city, county, or school district imposing the tax elects to provide the QEZE credit or refund. (Sec. 14, Tax Law; Sec. 1119(d), Tax Law) (TSB-M-02(5)S; TSB-M-09(12)S; TSB-M-09(16)S; Important Notice N-09-14) Businesses currently certified as QEZEs may continue to claim an exemption from tax using Form ST-121.6 only through August 31, 2009. As of September 1, 2009, vendors that have been issued Form ST-121.6 must begin charging full state and local sales taxes on all sales to QEZEs. (Important Notice N-09-14)

CCH Note: All Empire Zone designations expired on June 30, 2010.

With the expiration of the Empire Zones designations, the sales tax refund or credit on certain building materials used in an Empire Zone under Tax Law § 1119(a)(6) is discontinued. Tax Law § 1119(a)(6) allows a refund or credit for the state portion of sales and use taxes paid on building materials used in the construction, expansion, or rehabilitation of qualifying real property located in an Empire Zone. In addition, the local taxing authority within which the Empire Zone is located may also provide a similar refund or credit for the local sales and use tax paid under those circumstances. However, the refund or credit may only be claimed after the building materials are physically incorporated into the qualifying real property. As a result of the expiration of the Empire Zone designations, it is the position of the Department that the refund or credit of state sales tax, and if applicable, local sales tax, will be allowed only for those building materials that were purchased on or before June 30, 2010, and physically incorporated on or before August 31, 2010, into qualifying real property located in an Empire Zone. No refund or credit will be allowed for building materials physically incorporated into the real property after August 31, 2010, even if the materials were purchased or a building project was started before July 1, 2010. (TSB-M-10(6)S)

For a discussion of the continuing eligibility for Empire Zone tax benefits after the June 30, 2010 expiration date, see TSB-M-11(4)S. Specifically, the memorandum provides guidance on whether certain actions or events may lead a business enterprise or taxpayer that was certified as an EZ business on or before June 30, 2010, to subsequently lose eligibility to receive EZ benefits.

• *Issuance of Empire Zone Retention Certificates*

Article 18-B of the General Municipal Law requires Empire Zone Development (ESD) to review all certified Empire Zone business enterprises and apply certain criteria for continued certification of businesses wishing to retain Empire Zone benefits. ESD will issue an Empire Zone Retention Certificate (EZRC) to businesses meeting the criteria for continued certification. However, a business that receives an EZRC is not automatically eligible for the QEZE sales tax benefits provided under the Tax Law. A business that receives an EZRC must still meet all eligibility requirements under the Tax Law (including passing the QEZE employment test each year) to qualify for QEZE sales tax benefits. (TSB-M-09(12)S)

• *Eligibility requirements*

A QEZE must apply for a refund or credit of tax paid on qualifying purchases pursuant to Sec. 1119(d), Tax Law. A business enterprise must receive an EZRC from ESD before applying for the refund or taking the credit. In addition, the business enterprise must still meet all eligibility requirements under the Tax Law (including passing the QEZE employment test each year) in order to claim a refund or a credit. (TSB-M-09(12)S)

A business enterprise's eligibility for the refund or credit provided by Sec. 1119(d), Tax Law depends on when the business enterprise is certified by ESD and whether or not it has been issued Form DTF-81, Qualified Empire Zone Enterprise (QEZE) Sales Tax Certification, by the Department of Taxation and Finance:

— A business enterprise certified by ESD before April 1, 2009, that has already been issued Form DTF-81 is eligible for a refund or credit of tax paid on or after September 1, 2009, on qualifying purchases after it receives its EZRC from ESD. The sales tax benefit period for the business is unaffected and continues to run for 120 months from the effective date on Form DTF-81. The business must pass the employment test for the tax year in which a refund or credit is claimed.

— A business enterprise certified by ESD before April 1, 2009, that has received an EZRC but has not yet applied for Form DTF-81 is eligible for a refund or credit after it has filed the appropriate QEZE application (see Forms DTF-82, DTF-83, and DTF-84) and received Form DTF-81 from the Department. QEZE sales tax benefits are not retroactive; the benefit period is 120 months from the effective date on Form DTF-81. The business must pass the employment test for the tax year in which a refund or credit is claimed.

— A business enterprise certified by ESD on or after April 1, 2009, is eligible for a refund or credit of tax paid on qualifying purchases during the first month after certification by ESD, based on the date on the Certificate of Eligibility and on the EZRC issued to it by ESD. The business must pass the employment test for the tax year in which a refund or credit is claimed. However, a business certified by ESD on or after April 1, 2009, is eligible for a refund or credit of any taxes paid only if the locality in which the purchase is made has elected to provide the Sec. 1119(d), Tax Law, refund or credit. If the locality has not made this election, no refund or credit of any taxes paid is available.

(TSB-M-09(12)S)

• *How to claim the refund or credit*

The Department is creating a new form specifically for refund claims made under Sec. 1119(d). This new form must be used for all refund claims. A claim for a refund under Sec. 1119(d) may be filed only once each sales tax quarter. No interest is payable on any claim for refund. Form AU-11, Application for Credit or Refund of Sales or Use Tax, cannot be used to claim a refund under Sec. 1119(d). (TSB-M-09(12)S)

QEZEs that are registered for sales tax purposes will also be able to claim the credit allowed under Sec. 1119(d) on their periodic sales and use tax returns. Claims for the credit cannot be made on returns filed more often than quarterly. The Department is developing a schedule to be used to claim the credit. Pursuant to Sec. 1119(a), a credit may be claimed with a return due coincident or immediately subsequent to the time the new QEZE refund form is filed. (TSB-M-09(12)S)

However, no refund applications will be approved or paid prior to January 2, 2010. QEZEs that are also registered for sales and use tax purposes may begin claiming credits for qualifying purchases beginning with the December 1, 2009, through February 28, 2010, reporting period. (TSB-M-09(12)S)

• *Purchases eligible for a QEZE refund or credit*

For purchases and uses of property and services to be eligible for a refund or credit, the property or services (other than the Sec. 1105(b) consumer utility services) must be directly and predominantly used or consumed by the QEZE in an Empire Zone in which the QEZE has qualified for benefits. For purposes of the refund or credit, predominantly means 50% or more (or at least 50%). (TSB-M-09(12)S)

A QEZE's use of a motor vehicle or property related to a motor vehicle will be found to occur predominantly in an Empire Zone where the QEZE has qualified for benefits if:

— the QEZE uses the vehicle at least 50% exclusively in such a zone;

— at least 50% of the vehicle's use is in activities originating or terminating in such a zone; or

— at least 50% of its use is a combination of use exclusively in such a zone and in activities originating or terminating in such a zone.

(TSB-M-09(12)S)

The QEZE may choose to compute the usage of the vehicle based on either hours of use or miles traveled. Property related to a motor vehicle includes a battery, diesel motor fuel, an engine, engine components, motor fuel, a muffler, tires, and similar tangible personal property used in or on a motor vehicle. (Note: To apply for a refund of sales taxes paid on qualifying purchases of diesel motor fuel or motor fuel, complete Form FT-500, Application for Refunds of Sales Taxes Paid on Automotive Fuels.) The QEZE refunds or credits pertaining to motor vehicles are also applicable to the special taxes imposed under Article 28-A of the Tax Law on passenger car rentals. (TSB-M-09(12)S)

Consumer utility services (other than telephony and telegraphy, telephone and telegraph services, and telephone answering services) must be used or consumed directly and exclusively (i.e., 100%) by a QEZE in an Empire Zone in which the QEZE has qualified for benefits. These services include sales of gas, electricity, refrigeration, and steam, as well as gas, electric, refrigeration, and steam services of whatever nature. Telephony and telegraphy, telephone and telegraph services, and telephone answering services must be delivered and billed to the QEZE at an address in the zone in which the QEZE has qualified for benefits in order for the refund or credit to apply. Mobile telecommunications services purchased by a QEZE will qualify for the refund or credit if provided to end users whose business locations are in the zone where the QEZE is certified. (TSB-M-09(12)S)

The QEZE refund or credit does not apply to the taxes imposed under Sec. 1105(b) on sales of food or drink at restaurants, taverns, or other establishments, or to sales by caterers; nor does the refund or credit apply to rent for hotel occupancy or amusement charges subject to tax under sections Sec. 1105(e) and (f), respectively. (TSB-M-09(12)S)

• *QEZE employment tests*

A business enterprise must pass the applicable employment test in order to be eligible to claim a refund or credit under Sec. 1119(d).

For a business enterprise certified by ESD **prior to April 1, 2005**, the employment test is met if:

— the business enterprise's employment number in all empire zones for the tax year equals or exceeds its employment number in all empire zones for the base period; and

— the business enterprise's employment number in New York outside of empire zones for the tax year equals or exceeds its employment number in New York outside of empire zones for the base period.

(TSB-M-09(12)S; TSB-M-05(16)S)

For a business enterprise certified by ESD prior to April 1, 2005, the base period is the five tax years immediately preceding the test year (i.e., the tax year ending before the test date, which is the date the business enterprise was first certified, or July 1, 2000, whichever is later).

A business enterprise certified by ESD **between August 1, 2002, and March 31, 2005**, that has a base period of zero years and an employment number in empire zones of greater than zero with respect to a tax year will meet the employment test only if the business enterprise qualifies as a new business. The new business test will also apply to a business enterprise certified prior to August 1, 2002, that has a base period of zero years or zero employment in the base period. If such a business enterprise is substantially similar in ownership and operation to an existing or previously existing taxpayer, it may qualify as a new business only if it was formed for a valid business purpose and not solely to gain empire zone benefits. (TSB-M-09(12)S)

For business enterprises certified **on or after April 1, 2005**, the business enterprise will include its employees within empire zones in its statewide employment numbers, and the number of employees in the tax year being measured must exceed (not merely be equal to) the number in the base period for both empire zones and the state in order to pass the employment test. The new business test will apply to business enterprises with a base period employment of zero in addition to those with a base period of zero years. The base period for these business enterprises is shortened from five years to three years. (TSB-M-09(12)S)

For employment tests using a tax year beginning **on or after January 1, 2005**, a business enterprise that was certified on or after April 1, 2005, will meet the employment test if:

— its employment number in all EZs for the tax year exceeds its employment number in all EZs for the base period; and

— its employment number in New York State for the tax year exceeds its employment number in New York State for the base period (see below).

(TSB-M-09(12)S)

If the business enterprise has a base period of zero years or its base period employment is zero and it has an employment number in the Empire Zone greater than zero in the tax year, the employment test will be met only if the business enterprise qualifies as a new business. (TSB-M-09(12)S)

For purposes of the sales and use tax benefit period, if the business enterprise is certified by ESD during its first tax year and otherwise qualifies as a new business, the employment test will be met for that tax year in any month in which its employment number exceeds zero. (TSB-M-09(12)S)

• *Certificates*

All sales to QEZEs are fully taxable as of September 1, 2009. Starting with the September—November 2009 sales tax quarter, vendors should no longer file any of the following schedules, which will be discontinued:

— Schedule Q, Report of Sales to a Qualified Empire Zone Enterprise (QEZE) Eligible for Exemption;

— Schedule B-ATT, Consumer's Utility and Fuel Taxes for Nonresidential Gas, Electricity, Refrigeration, and Steam Sold to a Qualified Empire Zone Enterprise (QEZE); and

— Schedule T-ATT, Consumer's Utility Tax for Telephone Services, Telephone Answering Services, and Telegraph Services Sold to a Qualified Empire Zone Enterprise (QEZE).

(Important Notice N-09-14)

• *Economic Transformation and Facility Redevelopment Program*

Under the Economic Transformation and Facility Redevelopment Program (Article 18, Secs. 400- 404), incentives are provided to attract new businesses and jobs in communities affected by the closing of certain correctional and youth facilities. Generally, an economic transformation area means an area limited to the site of a closed facility or an area within a certain radius of a closed facility. The designation of the size of an economic transformation area will vary depending on factors including, but not limited to, the closed facility's location and the population density, poverty rate, unemployment rate, and the loss of jobs at that facility and in the region. Special rules apply for areas within the Metropolitan Commuter Transportation District and the Port Authority District. (TSB-M-11(9)S)

A closed facility means a correctional facility as defined in section 2(4)(a) of the Correction Law that has been selected by the governor of New York State for closure after April 1, 2011, but no later than March 31, 2021; or a facility operated by the Office of Children and Family Services under Article 19-G of the Executive Law that is closed under the authority of that office, provided the Commissioner of Economic Development has been properly notified of the closure.

The economic transformation area(s) must be established by the Empire State Development Corporation (ESDC) before applications for the program can be accepted. To be eligible for the tax benefits available under this program, a participant must:

— qualify as a new business;

— apply for and receive a Certificate of Eligibility from ESDC based on a projected creation of at least five net new full-time jobs and the making of certain qualified investments in an economic transformation area. The value of investments combined with wages and benefits paid to the net new jobs must be at least 10 times the amount of projected tax benefits (i.e., a benefit-cost ratio of 10:1);

— demonstrate that it has created at least five net new full-time jobs and met its benefit-cost ratio;

— be in compliance with all worker protection and environmental laws and regulations;

— not owe past-due federal or state taxes or local property taxes (unless those taxes are being paid through an executed payment plan); and

— have the location of its business for which it seeks tax benefits wholly located within the economic transformation area.

(TSB-M-11(9)S)

The following business entities are not eligible to participate in this new program:

— a retail business if the application is for any facility or business location that will be primarily used in making retail sales to customers who personally visit the facility;

— a business engaged in offering professional services licensed by the state or by the courts of this state; and

— a business that is or will be principally operated as a real estate holding company or as a landlord for retail businesses or entities offering professional services licensed by the state or by the courts of this state.

(TSB-M-11(9)S)

Refund of sales and use tax.—In addition to the economic transformation and facility redevelopment tax credit available, a participant may also be eligible for a refund of New York state sales or use tax paid for certain purchases of tangible personal property. The tangible personal property must be used in construction, expansion, or rehabilitation of industrial or commercial real property and must become an integral part of the property that is located within an economic transformation area. To qualify, the tangible personal property must be purchased or contracted to be purchased after the participant receives its Certificate of Eligibility and be incorporated into real property before a certificate of occupancy is issued for the real property. (Sec. 1119(f), Tax Law) (TSB-M-11(9)S)

A refund is also available for sales tax paid on certain purchases of tangible personal property used by contractors. The tangible personal property must be used in erecting a structure or building after the participant has received its Certificate of Eligibility, or in adding, altering, or improving a participant's real property, property, or land. To qualify, the tangible personal property must become an integral part of the property improvements and the structure, building, real property, property, or land and must be located within an economic transformation area. The tangible personal property must be in the contractor's inventory on or after the day the participant receives its Certificate of Eligibility, or the contractor must purchase or be contracted to purchase the property after the participant receives its Certificate of Eligibility. The tangible personal property must be incorporated into the real property before a certificate of occupancy is issued. There is no refund available for tax paid on services that the contractor may provide in relation to the tangible personal property, including the services of installing the tangible personal property. The refunds described above are applicable only to the 4% state portion of the sales tax paid. They do not apply to any local sales tax imposed by a county or city and do not apply to the sales tax imposed in the Metropolitan Commuter Transportation District (MCTD). The participant or contractor may only apply for a refund once per sales tax quarter, and the amount cannot be claimed as a credit on a sales tax return. Refunds must be claimed within three years after the tax was payable to the department. The provisions are scheduled to expire on December 31, 2021. (Sec. 1119(f), Tax Law) (TSB-M-11(9)S)

• *START-UP NY program*

Legislation created a START-UP NY program that provides tax benefits to approved businesses that locate in vacant space or land of approved New York state public and private colleges and universities, approved strategic state assets, and New York state incubators affiliated with private universities or colleges that are designated as tax-free NY areas. The program is administered by Empire State Development (ESD). Approved businesses will be issued a certificate of eligibility by the sponsoring campus, university, or college. The benefits are available for taxable years beginning on or after January 1, 2014, sales tax quarters beginning on or after March 1, 2014, or transactions occurring on or after January 1, 2014, depending upon the benefit. Sales tax benefits are available for a period of 120 consecutive months beginning with the month during which the business locates in the tax-free NY area. (Sec. 430, Tax Law; Sec. 432, Tax Law; Sec. 433, Tax Law; Sec. 434, Tax Law; Sec. 39, Tax Law) (TSB-M-13(7)S) Certain correctional facilities are also eligible for participation in the START-UP NY program. (Sec. 431, Economic Development Law; Sec. 435, Economic Development Law.

An approved business that is located in a tax-free NY area is eligible for a credit or refund of New York State and local sales and use taxes, including the 3/8% tax imposed by the state in the MCTD (MCTD state sales tax), imposed on the sale of tangible personal property, utility services, and services taxable under Tax Law Sec. 1105(c). In addition, a credit or refund is available for certain purchases of tangible personal property by contractors, subcontractors, and repairmen that is used in constructing, improving, maintaining, servicing, or repairing real property of an approved business that is located in a tax-free NY area. The credit or refund is allowed for 120 consecutive months beginning with the month during which the business locates in the tax-free NY area. (TSB-M-13(7)S)

Note: An approved business located in a tax-free NY area that makes sales subject to sales and use tax is still required to be registered as a sales tax vendor and to collect and remit the appropriate state and local sales tax on its sales. (TSB-M-13(7)S)

Purchases by an approved business eligible for a refund or credit.—For purchases and uses of property and services to be eligible for a credit or refund, the property or services (other than the Tax Law Sec. 1105(b) consumer utility services discussed below) must be directly and predominantly used or consumed by an approved business at its location in a tax-free NY area. For purposes of the credit or refund, predominantly means more than 50%. (TSB-M-13(7)S)

Consumer utility services (other than telephony and telegraphy, telephone and telegraph services, and telephone answering services) and prepaid telephone calling services must be used or consumed directly and exclusively (100%) by an approved business at its location in a tax-free NY area. Consumer utility services include sales of gas, electricity, refrigeration, and steam, as well as gas, electric, refrigeration, and steam services of whatever nature. Telephony and telegraphy, telephone and telegraph services, and telephone answering services must be delivered and billed to the approved business at an address at its location in the tax-free NY area. Mobile telecommunications services purchased by an approved business will qualify for the credit or refund where the approved business's place of primary use is at its location in a tax-free NY area. (TSB-M-13(7)S)

The credit or refund for an approved business located in a tax-free NY area does not apply to:

   — the sales tax imposed under Tax Law Sec. 1105(d) on sales of food or drink at restaurants, taverns, or other establishments, or by caterers;

   — the sales tax on rent for hotel occupancy imposed under Tax Law Sec. 1105(e);

   — the sales tax on admission charges and dues imposed under Tax Law Sec. 1105(f); and

   — the sales tax on transportation services imposed under Tax Law Sec. 1105(c)(10).

(TSB-M-13(7)S)

Contractors, subcontractors, and repairmen.—Contractors, subcontractors, and repairmen are eligible to claim a credit or refund for New York State and local sales and use tax, including the MCTD state sales tax, paid on purchases of tangible personal property used in erecting a structure or building for an approved business at its location in a tax-free NY area; or for use in adding to, altering, improving, maintaining, servicing, or repairing real property, property, or land of an approved business at its location in a tax-free NY area. This credit or refund is available for purchases of tangible personal property that becomes an integral component part of the approved business's structure, building, real property, property, or land. (TSB-M-13(7)S)

Tangible personal property that becomes an integral component part of the approved business's structure, building, real property, property, or land includes items such as building and landscaping materials, but does not include items such as tools, equipment, and supplies that are used or consumed by the contractor, subcontractor, or repairman. (TSB-M-13(7)S)

How to claim the credit or refund.—A claim for credit or refund for the sales and use tax paid on eligible purchases must be made by filing Form AU-11, Application for Credit or Refund of Sales or Use Tax. Taxpayers may submit Form AU-11 electronically using Sales Tax Web File. An approved business may file a claim for credit or refund only once each sales tax quarter. No interest is payable on any credit allowed or refund made. (TSB-M-13(7)S)

Penalties for fraud.—If the Commissioner of Economic Development makes a final determination that an approved business participating in the START-UP NY program has acted fraudulently in connection with its participation in the program, the business will be: (1) immediately terminated from the program; (2) subject to criminal penalties, including but not limited to the felony crime of offering a false instrument for filing in the first degree in accordance with Penal Law Sec. 175.35; and (3) required in that year to add back to tax the total value of all of the tax benefits provided under the START-UP program that the business and the employees of the business have received up to the date of the final determination. The amount required to be added back is reported on the business's corporation franchise tax return if the business is taxed as a corporation or is a corporate partner of a partnership, or on a personal income tax return if the owner of the business is a sole proprietor, an individual partner in a partnership, or a shareholder of a New York S corporation. (TSB-M-13(7)S)

[¶60-390] Food and Grocery Items

Generally, food, food products, beverages, dietary foods and health supplements sold for human consumption are not subject to tax. (Sec. 1115(a)(1), Tax Law) The terms "food" and "food products," for sales tax purposes, refer to edible commodities (whether prepared, processed, cooked, raw, canned or in any other form) which are generally regarded as food. (Reg. Sec. 528.2(a)(2)) This includes the following:

— meat and meat products;

— milk products;

— cereals and grain products;

— baked goods;

— vegetables and vegetable products;

— fruits and fruit products;

— poultry;

— fish and seafood;

— frozen entrees and desserts;

— jellying agents;

— fats, oils and shortenings;

— condiments;

— spices;

— sweetening agents;

— food preservatives;

— food coloring;

— frozen dinners; and

— snacks (except candy and confections).

(Reg. Sec. 528.2(a)(2)) (TB-ST-283)

For a listing of examples of exempt and taxable foods and beverages, see TB-ST-525.

However, the exemption does not apply to the following:

— candy and confectionery (discussed below);

— fruit drinks which contain less than 70% of natural fruit juice;

— soft drinks, sodas and beverages (other than coffee, tea and cocoa) ordinarily dispensed at soda fountains; and

— beer, wine and other alcoholic beverages (see ¶60-260 Alcoholic Beverages).

(Sec. 1115(a)(1), Tax Law; Reg. Sec. 528.2(b)(1))

For a listing of examples of exempt and taxable foods and beverages, see TB-ST-525.

• *Candy and confectionery*

Most sales of candy and confectionery are subject to sales tax. Candy and confectionery includes candy of all types, and similar products that are regarded as candy or confectionery based on their normal use or marketing. (TB-ST-103) Candy and confectionery also generally includes preparations of fruits, nuts, popcorn, or other products in combination with chocolate, sugar, honey, candy, etc. Some examples of candy and confectionery include: candy bars; chocolates; fruit, nuts, and popcorn covered with caramel, chocolate, honey, sprinkles, or other similar coatings; honey-roasted nuts; chewing gum; fudge; maple sugar candy; candy or chocolate covered marshmallows in decorative shapes; mints; peanut brittle; cotton candy; licorice; dietetic candy; and candied apples. (TB-ST-103)

Products that are not considered candy and confectionery.—Candy and confectionery does not include:

— baked goods, including cupcakes, cookies, pretzels, donuts, and pastries, or any similar products such as granola or cereal bars;

— baking or cooking ingredients, such as candied fruitcake ingredients, chocolate chips or bars, and marshmallows of any size (other than the candy or chocolate covered marshmallows described above);

— maple sugar products, unless labeled candy or confection or advertised as candy; and

— dried fruit, including Craisins, Fruit Roll-Ups, or other similar snacks (unless coated or covered in candy, etc., as described above).

(TB-ST-103)

Packaging and marketing.—In determining whether a product is taxable as candy or confectionery, or exempt as food, a number of factors are considered, including how the product is labeled, packaged, advertised, displayed, and sold. For example, pure maple sugar products are exempt as food unless displayed, labeled, or advertised as candy or confectionery. They are not candy merely because they are molded in the shape of a maple leaf or sold in individual quantities. (TB-ST-103)

Exempt sales.—Sales of candy and confectionery are not taxable if: (i) the purchaser is exempt from sales tax and gives the seller a properly completed exemption certificate, or (ii) the candy or confectionery is sold from a vending machine for $1.50 or less. (TB-ST-103)

• *Food and drink sold by food stores, beverages centers, restaurants, and similar establishments*

Food and food products sold by food stores.—In general, food and food products sold by food stores are exempt from sales tax. However, there are exceptions. The Department of Taxation and Finance has issued a bulletin that explains what kinds of foods are subject to sales tax and which are exempt when sold by food stores and similar establishments, including supermarkets, grocery stores, convenience stores, etc. (see TB-ST-283) (Sec. 1105(d), Tax Law; Reg. Sec. 527.8(k)) The following are examples of foods and food products that are exempt, unless sold under the conditions described in TB-ST-283 that would render them taxable:

— canned goods;

— dairy products;

— fruits;

— vegetables;

— meat, poultry, fish;

— bakery products, including bread, rolls, donuts, cakes, and pies;

— snack items such as potato chips, pretzels, popcorn, and corn chips (however, if any of these items are sugar-coated, chocolate-coated, or candy-coated, they are taxable);

— frozen foods, including frozen dinners or entrees;

— baking ingredients, including baking chocolate;

— cookies and snack cakes;

— packaged salads sold by the pound;

— granola and cereal bars;

— dried fruits, including raisins and Craisins (however, if any of these items are sugar-coated, chocolate-coated, or candy-coated, they are taxable);

— nuts, unless honey-roasted, chocolate, or candy-coated;

— food coloring, food preservatives, and sweeteners;

— Fruit Gushers, Fruit Roll-Ups, and fruit snacks; and

— baby food.

(TB-ST-283)

Generally, food sold at food stores is taxable when sold under any of the following conditions:

— it is sold heated;

— it is sold for consumption on the premises; or

— it has been prepared by the seller and is ready to be eaten, whether for on premises or off premises consumption.

(TB-ST-283)

Also, these categories of food are taxable:

— sandwiches (whether heated or unheated) (see TB-ST-835);

— carbonated beverages;

— candy and confectionery (see TB-ST-103); and

— pet foods.

(TB-ST-283)

Beverages sold by food stores, beverage centers, and similar establishments.— Most beverages sold by food stores, beverage centers, and similar establishments are subject to sales tax. A bulletin explains which beverages are taxable and which are exempt when sold for human consumption off the premises (see TB-ST-65). Bottle deposits are not subject to sales tax. (TB-ST-65)

Restaurants and similar establishments.—Sales tax is imposed on receipts from the sale, other than sale for resale, of food and beverages (whether alcoholic or nonalcoholic) by a restaurant, tavern or similar establishment in New York, or by a caterer, where:

— the sale is for consumption on the premises where sold (regardless of whether it is hot or cold);

— the vendor, or another person whose services are arranged for by the vendor, after delivery of the food or drink for consumption off the premises of the vendor, serves or assists in serving, cooks, heats or provides other services with respect to such food or drink; or

— the sale is for consumption off the premises of the vendor.

(Sec. 1105(d)(i), Tax Law) (TB-ST-695)

Cover, minimum, entertainment or other charges are included in the taxable amount. (Sec. 1105(d)(i), Tax Law)

The tax is not applicable to sales of food (other than sandwiches) or drink for off-premises consumption, which are (a) sold in an unheated state and (b) of a type commonly sold for off-premises consumption in the same form and condition in food stores not principally engaged in selling foods prepared and ready to be eaten. (Sec. 1105(d)(i), Tax Law)

"Restaurant-type" food can generally be described as food or drink that is sold in a form ready to be eaten. It includes the following:

— food or drink sold for on-premises consumption;

— sandwiches;

— self-service salad bars;

— food or drink sold in a heated state; and

— unheated food or beverages sold for off-premises consumption that are not sold in the same form, condition, quantities and packaging as they are ordinarily sold in grocery stores.

(TB-ST-695)

When food or drink is sold for on-premises consumption, it is taxable, whether it is sold hot or cold. On-premises consumption includes consumption at: restaurants and diners; tables in a food court at a mall; and picnic tables located outside a drive-in restaurant. (TB-ST-806)

When the food and drink is sold by a restaurant to-go, it is taxable unless the food (other than sandwiches) or drink is being sold unheated, and is being sold in the same way (in the same form, condition, quantities, and packaging) you would normally find it in a supermarket or grocery store. (TB-ST-806)

All sales of heated food are taxable whether sold by a restaurant or a supermarket. Heated food is food sold at a temperature warmer than the surrounding air temperature. If you are keeping food warm by using a heat lamp or warming trays, sales of the food are all subject to sales tax. Heated food sold as a sit-down dinner at a fine dining restaurant, sold as take-out from the window of a drive-through, or sold at a deli is taxable. (TB-ST-806)

Resale exclusion: Sales of otherwise taxable food and beverages by restaurants, caterers, and similar establishments can be made for resale and not subject to sales tax. (TSB-M-18(1)S) Examples of food and beverages that can be sold for resale include:

— cooked meat or vegetable dishes,

— cooked pasta dishes,

— cooked rotisserie chicken,

— deli or sandwich platters (such as cold cuts, subs, or burgers),

— hot coffee,

— meals purchased from restaurants to be resold,

— premade sandwiches,

— soups,

— subcontracted catering services, and

— vegetable platters.

(TSB-M-18(1)S)

Corkage fee: Corkage fees charged to customers who bring their own wine to a restaurant are another form of a service charge and are taxable as part of the total charge for the taxable food and beverage. (TB-ST-806)

Cover charges: All cover, drink minimum, entertainment, or other charges to customers are taxable. (TB-ST-806)

Coupons: When a customer uses a coupon as a discount on the purchase price of food or beverage, there are times when you may subtract the value of the coupon before calculating the sales tax on the bill. This depends on the type of coupon being used. Coupons and discounts offered by individual restaurants that are printed in coupon books, mailers, and newspapers that reduce the cost of the food or beverage are generally subtracted from the total bill before the sales tax is calculated. However, if the restaurant accepts the coupon as partial payment for the meal, and is then reimbursed that amount by a third party, the sales tax is calculated on the full amount of the bill before subtracting the value of the coupon or discount. (TB-ST-806)

Gift certificates and gift cards: Gift certificates for a set dollar amount, whether given away for no charge or sold to a customer, are not subject to sales tax. When the gift certificate is used, the sales tax is charged if a taxable purchase is made. The customer uses the gift certificate as if it were cash to pay for his or her purchases. If the purchase is subject to tax, the customer must also pay the tax, either by using the gift certificate or with additional cash. (TB-ST-806)

Restaurant meals purchased with certain third-party discount certificates and coupons: When computing the sales tax on restaurant meals where the customer purchasing one or more meals presents a discount certificate or coupon for which the restaurant will not be reimbursed, the restaurant must deduct the value of the certificate or coupon from the bill and then calculate the sales tax on the remaining amount. Sales tax is due only on the discounted amount billed to the customer. (TSB-M-10(13)S)

Convenience stores and bodegas.—For a bulletin explaining which sales made by convenience stores and bodegas (i.e., sales of food items, beverages, general merchandise, kerosene, and gasoline and diesel sales) are subject to tax, including examples, see TB-ST-135.

Dietary foods and health supplements.—In general, sales of dietary foods and health supplements are not taxable. Dietary foods include any food labeled for special dietary use by people. Dietary foods are intended to substitute for or supplement an ordinary diet, or substitute for natural foods. The label of a dietary food must have a statement describing the product's nutritional and dietary properties. Health supplements, such as vitamins and minerals, are products that are intended to substitute for or supplement natural food in an ordinary diet. If a product qualifies as a dietary food or health supplement, it is exempt from sales tax regardless of the form in which it is sold (i.e., sold as a solid, liquid, pill, or powder). (TB-ST-160)

Carbonated beverages, sports drinks, and energy drinks do not qualify as dietary foods or health supplements. However, products that supplement and replenish the body after intense exercise may qualify as nontaxable dietary foods if they aree labeled and sold as a nutritional shake, protein drink, or similar product. Examples of products that are exempt include: antioxidant supplements; Carnation Instant Breakfast; Ensure; fiber bars or wafers; health, energy or protein bars; herbal supplements; meal replacement mixes; mineral supplements; nutritional or protein powders; protein bars; Slim-Fast; and vitamins and multivitamins. Examples of products that are taxable include: 5-Hour Energy; Gatorade; Monster Energy Drink; Powerade; Red Bull; Rockstar Energy Drink; smartwater, and vitaminwater. (TB-ST-160)

Student meals.—No tax is imposed upon sales of food or drink by a restaurant or cafeteria located on school premises to:

— nursery school, kindergarten, elementary or secondary school students or

— college students, pursuant to a contractual arrangement whereby cash is not paid at the time the student is served.

(Sec. 1105(d)(ii), Tax Law)

Employee meals.—Food and drink furnished by an employer to employees are not taxable if the employer receives no cash or other consideration for the food and drink from the employees and the value of the food and drink is not income for the employees under the federal and state income tax laws. The employer is liable for tax, however, on the cost of any taxable components of such food and any taxable drink furnished to employees. (Reg. Sec. 527.8(j)) (TB-ST-695)

Any charge by an employer to an employee for food or drink is subject to tax, whether paid in cash by the employee or withheld from the employee's wages. (Reg. Sec. 527.8(j))

Subsidized employee cafeteria and food service operations: An employer who engages a caterer or food service contractor to provide food and drink or service to employees at the employer's expense is the purchaser of food and drink and subject to the sales tax. Sales of food, drink or service to employees through a cafeteria on the employer's premises are subject to the sales tax. (Reg. Sec. 527.8(k)) Any subsidy given by an employer to a caterer or food service contractor (whether termed a management fee, guarantee of profit or other designation) is taxable as a receipt from the sale of food and drink. Where the subsidy is paid by an employer in addition to a specific amount paid by the employee, both amounts are taxed as the receipt from the sale of food and drink. (Reg. Sec. 527.8(k))

EXAMPLE: Subsidized operations.—Employer E provides food and drink to employees without charge. E contracts with a food service contractor, F, to prepare and serve the food and drink for a fee to be paid by E. The fee paid by E is subject to tax as a receipt from the sale of food and drink. (Reg. Sec. 527.8(k))

EXAMPLE: Subsidized operations.—Employer E maintains a cafeteria or restaurant on his premises for the purposes of selling food and drink to the employees. The sale of the food and drink to the employees is taxable. (Reg. Sec. 527.8(k))

EXAMPLE: Subsidized operations.—Caterer C agrees to charge employer E's employees a scheduled amount for each item of food and drink it sells to them. E agrees to pay caterer C an amount, in addition to the employees' payments, which would guarantee a 12.50% profit from the sales to the employees. The amount paid by E to the caterer is a taxable receipt from the sale of food and drink. (Reg. Sec. 527.8(k))

EXAMPLE: Subsidized operations.—Employer E will pay 50¢ to a caterer for each sale of food and drink to E's employees. E's employees will pay any amount due which exceeds the 50¢ paid by E. Both the amount paid by the employee and the 50¢ paid by E are taxable receipts from the sale of food and drink. (Reg. Sec. 527.8(k))

Self-service salad bar.—Sales of salad ingredients at a self-service salad bar located in a grocery store or supermarket, which items are chopped or otherwise prepared by store personnel so that they are ready to be eaten, and which items may be selected by the customer and placed in containers available at the salad bar, are prepared foods constituting a meal or part of a meal, and are subject to sales tax (whether sold by weight or by volume). (TSB-M-86(18)S)

- *Gratuities and service charges*

For sales tax purposes, the term "gratuity" means money a customer gives a wait person, server, housekeeper, or other person as an expression of appreciation for service rendered, such as a tip at a restaurant or bar. When a customer chooses to leave a gratuity, it is considered a voluntary gratuity. Voluntary gratuities that a customer leaves are not taxable. (TSB-M-09(13)S; TB-ST-320) Mandatory gratuities are different because they are not automatically added onto the bill given to the customer. However, a mandatory gratuity is not taxable if all of these conditions are met:

— the charge is shown separately on the bill;

— the charge identified as a gratuity; and

— the business gives the entire separately stated gratuity amount to its employees.

(TB-ST-320)

If any of these conditions is not met, the mandatory gratuity is taxable, along with the rest of the bill. (TB-ST-320)

In some cases, an establishment may use part of an employee's gratuities to pay part of the employee's tax liability (for example, withholding tax or the employee's portion of social security) and give the remainder of the gratuities to the employee. Since the end result of this situation is that 100% of the gratuities are, in effect, turned over to the employee, the gratuities charge is not subject to sales tax. However, if the establishment keeps any part of the gratuities or uses any part of the gratuities to pay its own liabilities, such as the employee's wages or the employer's portion of social security, the entire gratuities charge is subject to sales tax. (TSB-M-09(13)S)

Service charges.—Service charges or other charges not specifically listed as gratuities on a bill or invoice are subject to sales tax. (TB-ST-320; TSB-M-09(13)S)

Union contract or other agreement.—The existence of a union contract or other agreement regarding gratuities does not determine the taxability of mandatory gratuities. However, in situations involving union contracts, businesses must be careful to establish that the conditions stated above have been met. (TB-ST-320)

• *Caterers and catering services*

In general, all charges by caterers related to a customer's event are taxable. This includes a caterer's charges for food, beverages, and any services provided for a customer's event. Any expenses incurred by the caterer for an event that are included in the overall charge to the customer are also taxable. This is true even if the charges are separately listed on the customer's bill or invoice. (Reg. Sec. 527.8(f)(1)) (TB-ST-110) Sales of otherwise taxable food and beverages by caterers can be made for resale and not subject to sales tax. (TSB-M-18(1)S)

Food and beverages.—The sale of food and beverages (both alcoholic and nonalcoholic) that have been prepared or are served by caterers is taxable. This includes everything from butler-served hors d'oeuvres and sit-down dinners to breakfast buffets. Prepared food also includes food items typically found at the deli or supermarket, such as cold cut platters, vegetable platters, cheese platters, fruit platters, dessert trays, subs, and sandwiches. (TB-ST-110)

Room rental charges.—Hotel and banquet facilities may charge a separate fee for the use of a room to hold a banquet or other catered event. When the catering service is sold by a hotel or a caterer hired by the hotel, the charge for rental of the room is part of the charge for the event and is taxable. It doesn't matter if the room charge is separately stated on the bill to the customer or included in the charge for catering. When a customer rents a room from a banquet facility but hires a separate caterer to conduct the event, the room rental charge is not taxable. (TB-ST-110)

Gratuities and service charges.—Gratuities and tips that a customer leaves voluntarily for the wait staff are not taxable. A mandatory gratuity is not taxable if all of these conditions are met: the charge is show separately on the bill, the charge is identified as a gratuity, and all of the money collected is given to the employees. (TB-ST-110)

Many caterers bill a service charge on banquets or on parties of more than eight or ten people. Since these charges are not specifically listed as gratuities on the bill or invoice, the service charge is always subject to sales tax. (TB-ST-110)

Purchases and rentals by caterers.—A caterer may need to purchase or rent items or an event. Although many purchases or rentals may be used on a specific customer request, the caterer is using the items to provide its catering services and is not reselling the items to its customers. Therefore, a caterer must pay sales tax to its supplier on the purchase or rental of items such as:

— tables,

— chairs,

— tents,

— portable bars or dance floors,

— children's games (i.e., inflatable slides, obstacle courses, ball ponds, bounces, etc.),

— linens, napkins, chair covers,

— silverware, glassware, serving utensils,

— audio/visual equipment,

— fountains,

— ice used to chill food or drinks before serving,

— ice carvings, and

— uniforms for wait staff.

(TB-ST-110)

A caterer's entire charge to its customer is taxable, even if charges for these types of items are separately listed on the bill or invoice. Also, a caterer cannot claim a credit on its sales tax returns for the tax paid on these purchases. (TB-ST-110)

Nontaxable food and beverages.—Certain food and beverage items, such as produce, seafood, meat, canned goods, and similar food items, are not taxable. No exemption certificate is needed to make these purchases without paying sales tax. Other nontaxable food and beverages include:

— fruit juices that contain 70% or more natural fruit juice,

— bar accompaniments like olives, cherries, lemons, limes, etc.,

— pastries,

— wedding cakes, and

— desserts.

(TB-ST-110)

Purchases for resale.—A caterer does not have to pay sales tax on its purchases of beverages (except for hot beverages such as hot coffee) that will be resold to customers as part of a catering event. A caterer can issue Form ST-120, Resale Certificate, to its suppliers for purchases of:

— liquor,

— soft drinks,

— bottled water,

— beer,

— wine,

— champagne,

— juices containing less than 70% natural fruit juice,

— cocktail mixers, and

— ice served in drinks.

(TB-ST-110)

Other food items, such as candy and confectionery, can also be purchased without paying sales tax by using Form ST-120, Resale Certificate. (TB-ST-110)

Flowers.—When a caterer purchases flowers for an event, if can use Form ST-120, Resale Certificate, to purchase the flowers without paying sales tax and later collect the sales tax from its customers, as long as all of the following are met:

— the customer must have the choice to deal directly with the florist or to not purchase any flowers at all;

— the customer must have complete control over the selection and arrangement of the flowers;

— the customer or the customer' guests must have the right to take the flowers with them;

— the customer must keep records showing the customers, florists, and flowers purchased for resale;

— the caterer cannot use one customer's flowers for another customer's event; and

— the caterer must collect sales tax from the customer on its entire charge.

(TB-ST-110)

Kitchen and serving equipment and supplies.—Kitchen equipment and supplies that are used to prepare, cook, and serve food and beverages are taxable when purchased, leased, or rented by a caterer. (TB-ST-110)

Services.—Often caterers are responsible for extra services in addition to the provision of food and beverages. A caterer's employees may provide these services or it may hire a third-party vendor. When a caterer purchases a taxable service (i.e., decorating and design services, parking services, security services, or portable toilets (i.e., waste removal services)), it must pay sales tax to the service provider. The caterer must charge and collect sales tax from its customer when including expenses for taxable services in its bill, even if charges for these expenses are separately stated. (TB-ST-110)

A caterer may also purchase nontaxable services for an event (i.e., band or disc jockey, bartenders, photographers, wait staff, and staff to perform valet parking service). Again, the caterer must charge and collect ales tax from its customer when including expenses for nontaxable services in its bill. (TB-ST-110)

• *Vending machine sales of food and beverages*

Sales of food and beverages from vending machines are generally taxed in the same manner as sales of the same items in food stores. (TB-ST-280) Examples of taxable food and beverage items sold from vending machines include:

— sandwiches;

— food arranged on a plate or prepared and ready to eat;

— bottled water; and

— any food that is heated by or kept warm in the vending machine (including soup, but not including broth or any other hot beverage).

(TB-ST-280)

However, there are two exceptions to this general rule: hot beverages sold from a vending machine are always exempt; and certain items that are taxable when sold by food stores are exempt when they are sold from a vending machine for $1.50 or less. (TB-ST-280) For instance, the following items are exempt from sales and use tax when sold for $1.50 or less through any vending machine activated by the use of a coin, currency, credit card, or debit card:

— candy and confectionery, including chocolate bars, chewing gum, honey-roasted nuts, and candy- or chocolate-coated nuts, popcorn, pretzels, etc.;

— soda, pop, lemonade, sports drinks, fruit drinks which contain less than 70% of natural fruit juice;

— soft drinks, sodas and beverages (other than coffee, tea and cocoa) ordinarily dispensed at soda fountains;

— beer, wine and other alcoholic beverages; and.

— bottled water.

(Sec. 1115(a)(1), Tax Law) (TB-ST-280) (TSB-M-19(1)S)

The exemption amount is $2 or less for candy, fruit drinks, soft drinks, and bottled water sold from a vending machine that accepts forms of payment other than coin or currency (whether or not it also accepts coin and currency). For vending machines that only accept coin and currency, the exemption applies to candy, fruit drinks, soft drinks, and bottled water sold for $1.50 or less. (TSB-M-19(1)S)

The following items are exempt from sales tax when sold from a vending machine, regardless of their price:

— Unheated foods (other than sandwiches and other prepared foods), such as whole fruit; cookies, donuts, pastries, cereal bars, granola bars, and diet bars; pretzels, popcorn, potato chips, plain or salted nuts, and crackers; ice cream, fruit bars, and fruit snacks; single-serving cereal packets; and canned foods.

— Unheated beverages, other than soft drinks, such as milk, chocolate milk, and diet shakes; vegetable juices; fruit drinks that contain 70% or more natural juice; and iced tea and iced coffee.

— Hot beverages, including coffee, tea, cocoa, and broth.

(TB-ST-280)

The sales tax on beer, wine, or other alcoholic beverages, or any other sale of drink and food by restaurants, taverns, or other establishments includes those instances where the sale is made through a vending machine that is activated by use of coin, currency, credit card, or debit card. (Sec. 1105(d)(i), Tax Law) However, food and drink sold through vending machines is exempt from the tax if it would be exempt when sold at retail. (Sec. 1105(d)(i), Tax Law)

Food and drink sold through a coin-operated bulk vending machine at 25¢ or less is exempt only when the bulk vending machine is located on premises which have no facilities provided for customers for on-premises consumption. (Reg. Sec. 528.14(b)(1)(ii))

Vending machine operations carried on in premises where facilities such as tables, chairs, benches, counters, etc. are provided for customers are considered to be eating establishments selling food or drink for on-premises consumption, and sales made through such machines are taxable. (Reg. Sec. 527.8(g)(1)) But, when food or drink is sold through vending machines and no facilities are provided for customers, such sales are deemed to be for off-premises consumption, and are taxed accordingly. (Reg. Sec. 527.8(g)(3))

Computing sales tax on vending machine sales.—If a taxpayer is selling taxable food or beverages, they should include the amount of the sales tax in the selling price of the item, and use the sales tax rate in the local taxing jurisdiction where the machines are located. To file sales tax returns, the taxpayer will need to separate the amount of sales made from the sale tax collected. To do this, divide the total amount of your sales subject to sales tax (which will include the sales tax collected) by one plus the sales tax rate in the particular jurisdiction, expressed as a decimal. (TB-ST-280)

Audit policy.—The Tax Commission has adopted an audit policy which creates a rebuttable presumption that 66 $2/3$% of the vending machine sales of nontaxable food (such as pastries, cartons of milk, ice cream, fruit) are considered for off-premises consumption. (*TSB-M-79(2)S*) This presumption may be rebutted by a vendor who can submit evidence to prove that the sales for off-premises consumption are in excess of 66 ^{2}/$_3$%. The ratio is not to be applied to those food items that are subject to tax (such as soda, candy, hot coffee or other prepared foods).

• *Production equipment and utilities used to prepare food*

Supermarkets, grocery stores, and delis can purchase machinery and equipment used directly and predominantly (more than 50% of the time) in the production of tangible personal property for sale without paying sales tax. To be exempt from tax, equipment must be used directly and predominantly in production of food commonly sold by grocery stores, and not used to prepare "restaurant-type" food (i.e., food or drink sold for on-premises consumption, sandwiches, self-service salad bars, food or drink sold in a heated state, and unheated beverages that are not sold in the same form, condition, quantities and packaging as they are ordinarily sold in grocery stores). (TB-ST-690)

Butcher shop.—Machinery and equipment used more than 50% of the time to process and package meat for ale can be purchased tax free. (Sec. 1115(a)(12), Tax Law) This includes:

— power meat saws, cubers, and grinders;

— sausage stuffers and hamburger patty machines;

— power tenderizers;

— scales used to weigh processed meat for labeling; and

— coolers and freezers used to store unprocessed product.

(TB-ST-690)

Deli area.—Only equipment that is used more than 50% of the time to process food for sale at food stores may be purchased tax free. Equipment used to cook, prepare, or package restaurant-type food for sale is taxable. Coolers and display cases used predominantly to store items not yet ready for sale (e.g., meats and cheeses not yet sliced or packaged for sale) can be purchased without paying sales tax. Coolers and display cases used predominantly to store packaged salads or other foods finished and ready for sale cannot be purchased without paying sales tax. Equipment used in the preparation of deli platters for sale, and coolers and display cases that are used to store products that are packaged and ready for sale, do not qualify for exemption. (TB-ST-690)

Bakery area.—Equipment used more than 50% of the time to prepare, bake, and package bakery items for sale may be purchased tax free as long as the baked goods are being sold for off premises consumption. Some examples of machinery and equipment that would qualify include:

— mixers;

— scales;

— proof boxes;

— ovens;

— cooling racks; and

— bread slicers.

(TB-ST-690)

Produce area.—Generally, machinery, equipment, and supplies used in the produce section of the supermarket are not considered to be used in production. Any washing, trimming, and repackaging of produce is considered part of the distribution or sale of the product. (TB-ST-690)

Utilities.—Fuel, gas, electricity, refrigeration, and steam (collectively, "utilities") used in the production of tangible personal property for sale may qualify to be exempt from tax. Utilities are exempt when used directly and exclusively in the production process. Therefore, if machinery and equipment have both taxable and exempt uses, the portion of the utilities used in the production process will qualify for exemption, even if the machinery itself does not. (TB-ST-690) Utilities used for general lighting and front-end operations, or for freezers, coolers, and display cases used throughout the supermarket or deli predominantly for the storage of goods packaged and ready for sale, do not qualify for the sales tax exemption. This includes the frozen food, dairy, and meat sections of the store. (TB-ST-690) For further information on utilities, see ¶ 60-750 Utilities.

• *Paper carryout bag reduction fee*

New York authorizes counties and cities to impose a five-cent paper carryout bag reduction fee on paper carryout bags, other than an exempt bag, that certain sales tax vendors provide to customers. The paper bag fee applies to each paper carryout bag provided to a customer, even if the sales tax vendor does not sell any tangible personal property or service to a customer, and regardless of whether the tangible personal property or service sold is exempt from sales tax. New York also bans businesses from providing plastic carryout bags to customers, unless such bags are exempt bags. (Paper carryout bag reduction fee, New York Department of Taxation and Finance website) (Publication 718-B)

Localities imposing fee. The following localities impose the five-cent fee, effective December 1, 2020:

- Albany County;
- Troy (city) (Rensselaer County);
- Suffolk County;
- Tompkins County;
- White Plains (city) (Westchester County); and
- New York City.

(Publication 718-B)

• *Eligible food purchased with food stamps*

Receipts from the sale of food eligible to be purchased with coupons issued pursuant to the Federal Food Stamp Act of 1977 from retail stores and other approved participants are exempt, when food is purchased with such coupons. (Sec. 1115(k), Tax Law)

For a listing of participating establishments which are included under the exemption, see Reg. Sec. 528.27(a)(2).

For a listing of eligible foods which qualify for the exemption, see Reg. Sec. 528.27(a)(3) and Reg. Sec. 528.27(a)(4).

For a discussion of the rules for applying food stamps to the purchase of eligible food and for applying food stamps when certain discount coupons are tendered, see Reg. Sec. 528.27(d) and Reg. Sec. 528.27(e).

• *Sales by a senior citizen independent housing community*

Receipts from sales of food or drink (other than beer, wine, or other alcoholic beverages) by a senior citizen independent housing community to residents or guests of residents for consumption on the premises of the community are exempt from state and local sales and use taxes. The food or drink must be served in the residents' rooms or in the community's dining facility that is not open to the public. The exemption does not apply to food or drink sold through vending machines. (Sec. 1115(w), Tax Law)

For purposes of the exemption, the term "senior citizen" means a person at least 55 years of age and the term "senior citizen independent housing community" means a residential facility with or without additional facilities such as recreational facilities, which is designed for senior citizens, the residents of which are senior citizens, spouses of the senior citizens or any other person, not necessarily related, who has resided with a senior citizen for at least six months, and persons hired to provide live-in long term care to a resident and who are actually providing such care to the resident for compensation. (TSB-M-01(4)S)

Purchases from caterers.—Where the community purchases prepared food or drink from a caterer or other person and resells the food or drink to its residents or their guests, the community must pay sales tax to the caterer or other person at the time of purchase. (TSB-M-01(4)S) However, no tax is required to be collected by the community when the food or drink is resold to the resident or their guests and the community would be eligible for a credit or refund of the sales tax paid on the food or drink that it resold. (TSB-M-01(4)S)

• *Cosmetic and toilet articles*

Cosmetics and toilet articles (notwithstanding the presence of medical ingredients) are taxable. (Sec. 1115(a)(3), Tax Law)

"Cosmetics" defined.—The term "cosmetics" refers to articles intended to be rubbed, poured, sprinkled or sprayed on, introduced into or otherwise applied to the human body for cleansing, beautifying, promoting attractiveness or altering the appearance, as well as articles intended for use as a component of any such article. Cold creams, suntan lotions and makeup are examples of taxable cosmetics. (Reg. Sec. 528.4(c))

"Toilet articles" defined.—The term "toilet articles" includes any article advertised or held out for grooming purposes or which is customarily used for such purposes (regardless of the name by which it is known). Examples of taxable "toilet articles" are soap, tooth paste and hair spray. (Reg. Sec. 528.4(d))

• *Food and drink sold to airlines*

Food or drink sold to an airline for consumption in flight is not subject to tax. (Sec. 1105(d)(ii), Tax Law)

• *Food for animals*

Pet foods are not deemed to be "sold for human consumption," and are, therefore, taxable. (Reg. Sec. 528.2(a)(3)) However, food used for farm animals is covered by the agricultural exemption. See ¶ 60-250 Agriculture.

• *Cooking and baking items*

Items advertised and sold for use in cooking and baking, such as chocolate morsels and glazed fruit, are exempt from tax. (Reg. Sec. 528.2(a)(5))

• *AV equipment used by hotels or other establishments*

A memorandum clarifies the application of sales and use taxes to the purchase, rental and use of audio/visual (AV) equipment by hotels, restaurants, taverns, banquet houses, caterers, and similar establishments for customer events. When a hotel or other establishment provides or arranges for the provision of AV equipment for a charge to a customer in connection with the sale of food and drink to that customer, the AV equipment is considered part of the sale of the food and drink and is subject to tax. However, if a hotel or other establishment rents or purchases AV equipment for a customer who is not purchasing food and drink, the rental or purchase is exempt from tax as a purchase for resale. In this case, the hotel is not required to pay sales tax on the purchase or rental of AV equipment, but must collect sales tax on the sale or rental of the AV equipment to the customer. The purchase or rental of AV equipment by the customer directly from a vendor that is unrelated to the hotel where the event is held is not taxable; whereas, the purchase or rental of AV equipment from a related vendor may be taxable. (TSB-M-10(3)S)

[¶60-420] Government Transactions

Sales and amusement charges by or to: (1) the United States, its agencies and instrumentalities, (2) New York State, its agencies, instrumentalities, public corporations (including public corporations created pursuant to agreement or compact with another state or Canada) and political subdivisions, or (3) the United Nations or any international organization of which the United States is a member, are exempt from tax, where such entity is the purchaser, user or consumer or sells services or property of a kind not ordinarily sold by private persons. (Sec. 1116(a), Tax Law; Reg. Sec. 529.2(a)(2))

Agent of a New York governmental agency.—In order for a taxpayer to make tax exempt sales to a private entity as an agent for a New York governmental entity, the taxpayer must obtain from the private entity a properly completed Form ST-122, Exempt Purchase Certificate for an Agent of a New York Governmental Entity, or Form FT-122, Fuel Tax Exempt Purchase Certificate for an Agent of a New York Governmental Entity. A copy of Form DTF-122, Certification of Agency Appointment by a New York Governmental Entity, must be attached to Form ST-122 or Form FT-122. (Important Notice N-05-9)

New York Urban Development Corporation.—The New York State Urban Development Corporation is exempt from sales tax. (Reg. Sec. 541.3)

Any use or occupancy by such entities is also entitled to exemption. The tax is imposed, however, upon sales of food or drink in a restaurant or tavern operated by New York State, its agencies and instrumentalities, where the purchaser is not an exempt organization. (Sec. 1116(b)(2), Tax Law)

States other than New York State, their agencies and political subdivisions do not qualify for exemption. (Reg. Sec. 529.1(c))

The terms "agencies and instrumentalities," "public corporation" and "public subdivision" are defined by regulation. See Reg. Sec. 529.1—Reg. Sec. 529.3.

For additional information explaining how sales and use tax applies to purchases and sales by New York and U.S. governmental agencies, see *TB-ST-700.*

• *Motor fuel*

Purchases of motor fuel and diesel motor fuel by the United States or New York State, their agencies and instrumentalities for their own use or consumption are not subject to the prepaid tax or to sales and use taxes. (Sec. 1116(b)(5), Tax Law)

Purchases of motor fuel by exempt fire companies, fire departments or voluntary ambulance services for their own use and consumption for use in firefighting vehicles, apparatus or equipment, or emergency rescue or first aid response vehicles, apparatus or equipment, owned and operated by the department, company or service are also exempt. (Sec. 1116(b)(5), Tax Law)

See ¶60-560 Motor Fuels.

• *Governmental contractors*

Tangible personal property incorporated into real property owned by a governmental entity is exempt from tax, regardless of whether the contract is on a lump sum, time and material, cost-plus or other basis. (Reg. Sec. 541.3(d)(1)) Charges for maintaining, installing, repairing and servicing tangible personal property and real property are not subject to tax, provided that the exempt entity is the payer of record. (Reg. Sec. 541.3(d)(2)) However, where such charges are billed to and paid by a tenant which does not qualify as an exempt entity, the charges are taxable on the full invoice price.

Sales of tangible personal property to a contractor, subcontractor or repairman for use in erecting, repairing, adding to or altering a structure or building owned by an exempt organization are not subject to tax, where they are to become an integral component part of the structure or building. Moreover, tangible personal property purchased by a contractor and which remains tangible personal property after installation is not taxable, if purchased for and sold to an exempt entity. (Reg. Sec. 541.3(d)(2))

The tax is imposed, however, upon a contractor's purchases of construction supplies which do not become part of an exempt entity's real property and are used or consumed by the contractor and upon taxable services (such as electricity) used by the contractor. (Reg. Sec. 529.1(c))

• *Government employee occupancy of hotel rooms*

Employees of New York or the federal government on official business may rent hotel or motel rooms in New York exempt from sales tax using Form ST-129, Exemption Certificate - Tax on Occupancy of Hotel or Motel Rooms. The exemption includes the $1.50 hotel unit fee in New York City but does not include locally imposed and administered hotel occupancy taxes, also known as bed taxes. (*TB-ST-315*)

Government employees must complete and sign Form ST-129 and give it to the operator of the hotel or motel no later than 90 days after the last day they rented the room when paying with: cash; a personal check; or a personal credit card or debit card. Employees staying at more than one location while on official business must complete a certificate for each establishment. If a group of employees is travelling on official business, each employee must complete a separate certificate. Government employees paying with a government voucher or a government credit card do not need to use Form ST-129. However, government employees must show the operator appropriate and satisfactory identification whether or not they are using Form ST-129. (*TB-ST-315*)

Misuse of this exemption certificate may subject a taxpayer to serious civil and criminal sanctions in addition to the payment of any tax and interest due. (*TB-ST-315*)

• *Industrial Development Agencies*

New York provides guidance on how Industrial Development Agencies (IDAs) work with their agents, operators, and contractors on economic development projects to provide sales and use tax benefits. The guidance also explains the requirements and responsibilities that apply to IDAs and their agents, operators, and contractors with respect to the Department of Taxation and Finance. (TSB-M-14(1.1)S; TB-ST-385)

General information.—IDAs are public benefit corporations established under the GML and the PAL. IDAs are established to promote, develop, encourage, and assist in the acquisition, construction, reconstruction, improvement, maintenance, equipping, and furnishing of industrial, manufacturing, warehousing, commercial, research, and recreational facilities in New York. The purpose of IDAs is to advance job opportunities, and the health, general prosperity, and economic welfare of the people of New York. (*TSB-M-14(1.1)S*)

Appointing an agent.—As a government entity, an IDA is exempt from paying sales and use taxes on its purchases. However, it is not normal practice for an IDA itself to make purchases related to an industrial development project. Typically, an IDA appoints as its agent for this purposes a: business and/or developer, contractor, or subcontractor. (TB-ST-385)

Purchases made by a properly appointed agent within the authority granted to it by the IDA are deemed to be purchases made by the IDA and are exempt from sales tax. The IDA must file Form ST-60, IDA Appointment of Project Operator or Agent For Sales Tax Purposes, each time it appoints an agent to receive sales tax benefits. The IDA must file Form ST-60 within 30 days of appointing an agent. If the IDA authorizes an agent to appoint other persons as agents of the IDA, the agent making the appointment must inform the IDA that it has appointed someone as agent and the IDA must file Form ST-60 within 30 days of the date of the new agent's appointment. (*TSB-M-14(1.1)S*; TB-ST-385)

In addition, an IDA must include the terms and conditions described in General Municipal Law § 875(3) (including provisions regarding recapture of benefits) in each resolution or project document that: establishes a project, or appoints an agent. Each agent appointed by an IDA must agree to those terms and conditions prior to receiving any sales tax exemption benefits. (TB-ST-385)

Purchases by agents.—Once appointed, agents can make purchases to acquire, build, or equip a project exempt from sales tax, including the additional $f\%$ sales tax in the Metropolitan Commuter Transportation District (if applicable). However, exempt purchases are only allowable to the extent provided by the terms of the agent's IDA project contract. To make qualifying purchases exempt from sales tax, agents use: Form ST-123, IDA Agent or Project Operator Exempt Purchase Certificate, or Form FT-123, IDA Agent or Project Operator Exempt Purchase Certificate for Fuel. (TB-ST-385)

Amending or revoking an agent's appointment.—If an IDA amends, revokes, or cancels its appointment of an agent, or if an agent's appointment becomes invalid for any reason, the IDA must, within 30 days, file a statement with the Department at the address listed on Form ST-60 that identifies the agent and explains that the agent's appointment has been: amended, revoked, canceled, or is otherwise no longer valid; and the effective date of the change. The IDA should attach a copy of the original Form ST-60 filed for the agent's appointment to the letter. (*TSB-M-14(1.1)S*; TB-ST-385)

Recordkeeping and reporting requirements.—An IDA must keep records of the sales tax exemption benefits it provides. It is also required to report the sales tax exemption benefits it provides to an agent by filing Form ST-60 with the Tax Department within 30 days of conferring the exemption benefit. If the IDA fails to report the sales tax exemption benefits or make records available to the Department upon request, the IDA shall be prohibited from providing sales tax benefits until the IDA comes into compliance with all such requirements. (*TSB-M-14(1.1)S*; TB-ST-385)

After the end of each calendar year, each agent appointed directly by an IDA must filewith the Tax Department Form ST-340, Annual Report of Sales and Use Tax Exemptions Claimed by Agent/Project Operator of Industrial Development Agency/ Authority (IDA). Form ST-340 is used to report the total value of all state and local sales and use taxes exemptions claimed during a calendar year under the terms of the project contract, including the value of the exemptions claimed by: the agent itself;

and the agent's sub-agents, contractors, subcontractors, consultants, and others, whether or not appointed as agents of the IDA. (TB-ST-385)

Form ST-340 is due on the last day of February in the following calendar year. (TB-ST-385)

Note: Agents that were not appointed directly by an IDA, such as sub-agents appointed by an IDA agent, are not required to file Form ST-340. (TB-ST-385)

Recapture requirements.—An IDA must recapture any state sales tax exemption benefits that were claimed by an agent whenever the benefits were:

— not entitled or authorized to be taken,

— in excess of the amounts authorized,

— for unauthorized property or services, or

— for property or services not used according to the terms of the project contract with the IDA.

(*TSB-M-14(1.1)S*; TB-ST-385)

An IDA must remit recaptured sales tax exemption benefits to the Tax Department using Form ST-65, IDA Report of Recaptured Sales and Use Tax Benefits. The IDA must file Form ST-65 within 30 days from when the IDA comes into possession of the recaptured funds. (TB-ST-385)

An agent must cooperate with the IDA in its effort to recapture state sales tax exemption benefits. Where an agent fails to cooperate, IDAs have an obligation to commence an action or proceeding against an agent to recover unauthorized sales tax if necessary. (TB-ST-385)

Any failure by an agent to pay over improper sales tax exemption benefits to an IDA could also result in an assessment to the agent for the state sales tax due, plus applicable penalties and interest. The IDA must cooperate with the Department, for example, by sharing the relevant documents and information in the event that the Department elects to issue an assessment. (TB-ST-385)

Annual compliance report.—An IDA must file Form ST-62, IDA Annual Compliance Report - State Sales Tax Recapture, within 90 days of the end of the IDA's fiscal year. The report must include details of: the terms and conditions of each of its projects; the IDA's activities and efforts to recapture any state sales tax exemption benefits due; and any other information required by either the Commissioner of Taxation and Finance or Commissioner of Economic Development. The IDA must file the report with the: Commissioner of Taxation and Finance, Director of the Budget, Commissioner of Economic Development, State Comptroller, and municipality's governing body. (TB-ST-385)

• *Federal financial institutions*

National banks and federal savings and loan associations are subject to sales and use taxes. (Tit. 12, Sec. 548 U.S.C.; Tit. 12, Sec. 1464 U.S.C.) However, federal law prohibits the imposition of state sales and use taxes upon other federal financial institutions, including federal credit unions. (Tit. 12, Sec. 1768 U.S.C.)

• *Public educational institutions*

Sales of food or drink by a restaurant or cafeteria located on school premises to: (1) nursery school, kindergarten, elementary or secondary school students or (2) college students, pursuant to a contractual arrangement whereby cash is not paid at the time the student is served are tax-exempt. (Sec. 1105(d)(ii), Tax Law) See ¶ 60-390 Food and Grocery Items.

¶60-420

Private schools and post-secondary schools are discussed at ¶60-580 Nonprofit Organizations, Private Schools, and Churches.

• *Police and fire departments*

Admissions, all of the proceeds of which inure exclusively to the benefit of a police or fire department or volunteer fire or ambulance company or exclusively to a retirement, pension or disability fund for the sole benefit of police or fire department members or their heirs, are not subject to tax. (Sec. 1116(d)(1)(D), Tax Law) See 60-230 Admissions, Entertainment, and Dues and 60-580 Nonprofit Organizations, Private Schools, and Churches.

• *Trash removal services rendered by or on behalf of a municipal corporation*

An exemption from tax is provided for trash removal services rendered by a municipal corporation of New York State (except New York City) or on its behalf, under an agreement with such municipal corporation. (Sec. 1116(e), Tax Law)

• *Military decorations*

Purchases of certain military decorations (i.e. ribbons, medals, mini-medals, and lapel pins) by a veteran or active member of the United States military are exempt from New York sales and use tax. In order to make the purchase exempt from sales tax, the purchaser must provide the seller with a copy of Form ST-121, Exempt Use Certificate. In addition, the purchaser must show proof of his or her status in the form of discharge papers or other official documentation of actual military service. However, the vendor is not required to retain a copy of this proof. (Sec. 1115(a)(11-A), Tax Law; *TSB-M-06(15)S*)

[¶60-445] Internet/Electronic Commerce

Sales or use tax may apply to a variety of transactions in an electronic commerce environment. Such transactions include (1) purchases over the Internet of taxable services and property that are delivered in a nonelectronic form and (2) purchases of services or property that are delivered electronically and that may or may not be the equivalent of services or property that also can be delivered by nonelectronic means. General principles concerning the taxability of such transactions are discussed below.

Taxes on sales of computer software and services are discussed at ¶60-310 Computer Software and Services.

In an electronic commerce environment, the seller may have nexus with the taxing jurisdiction and be required to collect and remit sales tax.

The federal Internet Tax Freedom Act (ITFA) and its amendments (P.L. 105-277, 112 Stat. 2681, 47 U.S.C. 151 note, amended by P.L. 107-75, P.L. 108-435, P.L. 110-108, P.L. 113-164, P.L. 113-235, P.L. 114-113, and P.L. 114-125) permanently bar state and local governments from imposing multiple or discriminatory taxes on electronic commerce and taxes on Internet access. The Internet Tax Freedom Act and its amendments are discussed below.

• *Taxability of transactions in electronic commerce*

The federal Internet Tax Freedom Act (ITFA) defines "electronic commerce" as any transaction conducted over the Internet or through Internet access, comprising the sale, lease, license, offer, or delivery of property, goods, services, or information, whether or not for consideration, and includes the provision of Internet access.

Transactions involving nonelectronic delivery.—Sales over the Internet may include the purchase of services that are delivered in a nonelectronic form, tangible personal property that is commonly delivered by mail or common carrier, or property in an electronic form capable of being processed by a computer ("digital property") that is stored on tangible storage media that is commonly delivered by mail or common carrier.

The taxability of such sales over the Internet generally is governed by the same rules as the purchase of such services or property in a traditional Main Street environment. However, the obligation of the seller to collect tax on such remote sales depends on whether the seller has nexus with the taxing jurisdiction, which is discussed below. If a sale is taxable and the seller does not collect tax, then the buyer generally is responsible for remitting use tax on the transaction.

A state may consider digital property stored on tangible storage media to be included in the definition of "tangible personal property" and, therefore, subject to the same taxability standard. While New York does not have any laws or regulations regarding the status of digital property as tangible or intangible property, advisory opinions have been issued indicating that the taxability of digital property is determined by other aspects of the transaction. For example, the sale of artwork transmitted through the internet is not taxable but artwork transmitted by diskette is taxable. (TSB-A-99(48)S, November 12, 1999) In addition, the sale of digital ID's are not taxable unless the ID's are sold as apart of a lump-sum transaction including computers. (TSB-A-00(7)S, February 2, 2000) Many states have special rules concerning the taxability of software and these are discussed at ¶60-310 Computers, Software, and Services.

Transactions involving electronic delivery.—Sales over the Internet may also include the purchase of digital property, services, or information delivered electronically. While most states impose sales and use tax generally on all sales of tangible personal property, the taxability of sales of digital property delivered electronically varies among the states. In some states, a sale of certain types of digital property delivered electronically is considered a taxable sale of tangible personal property. In other states, such a sale is treated as not involving the transfer of tangible personal property and, therefore, is nontaxable. In yet other states, sales of some software delivered electronically are taxable while sales of other items delivered electronically are nontaxable.

Prewritten computer software: Under New York law, prewritten computer software is specifically deemed to be tangible personal property for sales and use tax purposes, regardless of the medium by which the software is conveyed to the purchaser. Therefore, software that is otherwise taxable remains subject to sales tax even if conveyed to the purchaser electronically. (Sec. 1101(b)(6), Tax Law)

> **EXAMPLE:** *Shareware programs.*—A New York resident downloads a shareware program from a computer bulletin board system, and the creator of the shareware requests a $75 registration fee or required "donation" for its use. The cost of the shareware program is subject to state and local sales taxes because the amount paid to the creator constitutes consideration paid upon the transfer or possession of prewritten computer software at retail. (TSB-M-93(3)S)

Custom software: However, custom software (i.e., software designed and developed to the specifications of a specified purchaser) is exempt from tax regardless of the form of delivery. (Sec. 1101(b)(14), Tax Law)

> **EXAMPLE:** *Website development.*—With respect to a company engaged in web site development, which involved the designing and computer programming of websites, the Commissioner of Taxation and Finance noted that each of the websites at issue was created from start to finish for a particular client. Consequently, the sites were distinguishable from prewritten computer software and tangible personal property, as defined in the Tax Law, and the company's

receipts were therefore exempt from sales and use tax. (TSB-A-97(43)S) For additional discussion of website development and maintenance, see TSB-A-02(7)S.

Further, otherwise taxable software may be exempt if it is provided as part of an Internet access service. As discussed in more detail at ¶ 60-720 Telecommunications, the exemption for Internet access services specifically includes navigation, communication, and e-mail software, as well as web site space, news headlines, and other website services, as long as these items and services are offered in conjunction with, and merely incidental to, the provision of an Internet connection. (Sec. 1115(v), Tax Law)

Digital products.—The sales of digital products transferred electronically (i.e., downloaded music, ringtones, movies, books, etc.) are not subject to New York sales and use taxes. (TSB-A-08(63)S and 08(8)C; TSB-A-07(16)S; TSB-A-07(14)S)

e-books: The Department's current policy is that the sale of a book delivered electronically (e-book) does not constitute the sale of an information service subject to state and local sales and use tax. (TSB-M-11(5)S) However, the e-book must meet all of the following conditions:

— the purchase of the product does not entitle the customer to additional goods and services and any revisions done to the e-book are for the limited purpose of correcting errors;

— the product is provided as a single download;

— the product is advertised or marketed as an e-book or a similar term;

— if the intended or customary use of the product requires that the product be updated or that a new or revised edition of the product be issued from time to time (i.e., an almanac), the updates or the new or revised editions are not issued more frequently than annually; and

— the product is not designed to work with software other than the software necessary to make the e-book legible on a reading device (i.e., Kindle, Nook, iPad, iPhone or personal computer).

(TSB-M-11(5)S)

This policy on e-books is limited to products that are not, or do not include, prewritten computer software or any other product that constitutes tangible personal property under Tax Law Sec. 1101(b)(6). (TSB-M-11(5)S)

Some states may also draw a distinction based on whether the digital property delivered electronically would be considered tangible personal property if the same content were transferred on tangible storage media. That is, some states may only tax sales involving the electronic delivery of property if the property is the digital equivalent of tangible personal property.

Most states apply a true object of the transaction test in making taxability determinations. For example, if a state does not tax legal services, the delivery of a will electronically would not be taxable even if the state taxes the digital equivalent of tangible personal property, just as delivery of a will prepared on paper would not be taxable as the sale of tangible personal property.

Electronic periodicals: Electronic periodicals are exempt from sales and use tax. (Sec. 1115(gg))

Services.—The taxability of services varies among the states. In New York, sales tax is imposed on receipts from retail sales of tangible personal property and on a broad range of specified services, which are discussed at ¶ 60-665 Services.

EXAMPLE: Website service charges.—Amounts charged for website development, domain registration, InterNIC registration, host site maintenance, and creation of interactive games for web pages were not subject to sales or use tax because such services were not included among the list of enumerated services subject to tax in New York. (TSB-A-97(87)S)

The taxability of information services and information databases also varies among the states. In New York, certain information and entertainment services that may be provided electronically are specifically subject to sales and use tax. (Sec. 1105(c)(1), Tax Law; Sec. 1105(c)(9), Tax Law)

In addition, a specific exemption from the tax on information services has been provided for electronic newspapers that meet certain requirements. (Sec. 1101(b)(6), Tax Law) The exemption is explained at ¶60-640 Publishing and Broadcasting.

See also ¶60-665 Services and ¶60-310 Computers, Software, and Services.

EXAMPLE: Checking account verification.—A checking account verification service, whereby financial institutions are advised over the telephone or by online computer whether applicants have had prior accounts closed for lack of sufficient funds, is subject to sales tax as an information service. (TSB-A-95(14)S)

Although an otherwise taxable service in New York may still be subject to tax if performed electronically, services other than those enumerated as taxable in the Tax Law will be exempt.

EXAMPLE: Computer bulletin board system.—A New York resident is charged an annual membership fee of $30 by a computer bulletin board system. State and local sales taxes are due and payable on the fee, which is taxable as the purchase of an information service. (TSB-M-93(3)S)

EXAMPLE: Transmissions through telephone lines.—A corporation that transmits financial information to its New York subscribers through leased telephone lines that are linked to its central computer facility is considered to be selling taxable information services. (TSB-A-93(61)S)

Electronic news services: Electronic news services are exempt from sales and use tax. (Sec. 1115(gg)) (TSB-M-12(1)S)

Internet data centers.—Machinery, equipment, and other tangible personal property purchased by the operator of an Internet data center located in New York where such property is to be placed or installed in an Internet data center and is directly related to the provision of Internet website services for sale by the operator of the center are exempt from sales and use tax. (Sec. 1115(a)(37), Tax Law; Sec. 1115(y), Tax Law) (TSB-M-00(7)S; TB-ST-405)

• *Federal Internet Tax Freedom Act*

The federal Internet Tax Freedom Act (ITFA) and its amendments (P.L. 105-277, 112 Stat. 2681, 47 U.S.C. 151 note, amended by P.L. 107-75, P.L. 108-435, P.L. 110-108, P.L. 113-164, P.L. 113-235, P.L. 114-113, and P.L. 114-125) permanently bar state and local governments from imposing multiple or discriminatory taxes on electronic commerce and taxes on Internet access. For a discussion of the ITFA and its effect on New York sales tax, see TSB-M-08(4)C, (2)S and TSB-M-08(4.1)C, TSB-M-08(2.1)S.

Tax on Internet access.—The term "tax on Internet access" applies regardless of whether such a tax is imposed on a provider of Internet access or a buyer of Internet access and regardless of the terminology used to describe the tax. However, the term "tax on Internet access" does not include taxes on or measured by net income, capital stock, net worth, or property value, or other state general business taxes, such as gross receipts taxes, that are structured in such a way as to be a substitute for or supplement the state corporate income tax.

Grandfather provision.—A state or local government may continue to tax Internet access if the tax was generally imposed and actually enforced prior to October 1, 1998. However, this grandfather clause does not apply to any state that, prior to November 1, 2005, repealed its tax on Internet access or issued a rule that it no longer applies such a tax.

Internet access definition.—For purposes of the federal moratorium, "Internet access" means a service that enables users to connect to the Internet to access content, information, or other services. The definition includes the purchase, use, or sale of telecommunications by an Internet service provider to provide the service or otherwise enable users to access content, information, or other services offered over the Internet. It also includes incidental services such as home pages, electronic mail, instant messaging, video clips (i.e. movie previews and portions or short clips of a complete video), and personal electronic storage capacity. These services are included in the federal moratorium regardless of whether they are furnished as part of the Internet connection service, or if they are purchased and furnished separately. However, any form for telephony (i.e. private telecommunications networks), including Voice over Internet Protocol (VOIP), network services and data transmission services, other than telecommunications services used by an Internet Service Provider (ISP) to connect customers to the Internet, are not included under the federal moratorium. Accordingly, these forms of telephony continue to be subject to New York state and local sales taxes. (TSB-M-08(4)C, (2)S)

Telecommunications services.—Under amendments to the Act in 2007, state and local governments that continue to impose tax on telecommunications service purchased, used, or sold by a provider of Internet access have until June 30, 2008, to end these disputed taxes. However, this provision only operates if a public ruling applying such a tax was issued prior to July 1, 2007, or such a tax is the subject of litigation that was begun prior to July 1, 2007. It is the position of the Department of Taxation and Finance that the excise tax imposed by Tax Law Sec. 186-e on the telecommunications purchased, used, or sold by ISPs to provide Internet access was preempted by federal law on and after November 1, 2005. The Department believes this interpretation is more consistent with the intent of Congress. Accordingly, those telecommunications services were no longer subject to the excise tax effective November 1, 2005. (see TSB-M-08(4.1)C, TSB-M-08(2.1)S)

CCH COMMENT: Disputed taxes on telecommunications.—Some states dispute the assertion that taxes they impose on telecommunications service purchased by Internet service providers to connect their customers to the Internet (so-called "backbone" services) were prohibited by Congress in the 2004 renewal of the moratorium. The 2007 amendment and the revised definition of "Internet access" (discussed above) are intended to resolve this issue and end state and local taxation of Internet "backbone" service. According to the Congressional Budget Office, as many as eight states (Alabama, Florida, Illinois, Minnesota, Missouri, New Hampshire, Pennsylvania, and Washington) and several local governments in those states were collecting such taxes in 2007.

Bundled services.—The Act allows the taxation of otherwise exempt Internet access service charges that are aggregated (i.e. bundled) with and not separately stated from charges for telecommunications or other taxable services, unless the Internet access provider can reasonably identify the charges for Internet access from its books and records kept in the regular course of business.

Discriminatory taxes.—Under the Act, prohibited discriminatory taxes are defined as:

— taxes imposed on electronic commerce transactions that are not generally imposed and legally collectible on other transactions that involve similar property, goods, services or information;

— taxes imposed on electronic commerce transactions at a different rate from that imposed on other transactions involving similar property, goods, services or information, unless the rate is lower as part of a phase-out of the tax over a five-year or lesser period;

— collection or payment obligations imposed upon a different person or entity than would apply if the transaction were not transacted via electronic commerce;

— classification of Internet access service providers or online service providers for purposes of imposing on such providers a higher rate of tax than is imposed on providers of similar information delivered through other means;

— collection obligations imposed on a remote seller on the basis of the in-state accessibility of the seller's out-of-state computer server; and

— collection obligations imposed on a remote seller solely because the Internet access service or online service provider is deemed to be the remote seller's agent on the basis of the remote seller's display of information or content on the out-of-state server or because orders are processed through the out-of-state server.

Multiple taxes.—Prohibited multiple taxes are taxes imposed by a state or local government on the same, or essentially the same, transactions in electronic commerce that are also subject to a tax imposed by another state or local government without a corresponding credit or resale exemption certificate for taxes paid in other jurisdictions.

The moratorium against multiple taxes does not include taxes imposed within a state by the state or by one or more local governments within the state on the same electronic commerce.

The moratorium against multiple taxes does not prohibit other taxes from being imposed on persons who are engaged in electronic commerce even though that commerce has been subject to a sales or use tax.

State Internet access taxes.—New York does not tax Internet access and is prohibited from doing so under the current federal Internet Tax Freedom Act moratorium. (Sec. 1115(v), Tax Law)

[¶60-460] Leases and Rentals

Leases and rentals of tangible personal property are subject to New York sales and use tax. (Sec. 1101(b)(5), Tax Law; Sec. 1110, Tax Law; Reg. Sec. 526.7)

Are leases and rentals taxable in New York?

Yes. Leases and rentals of tangible personal property are subject to sales and use tax because the definition of "sale, selling or purchase" includes rentals, leases or licenses to use or consume tangible personal property for a consideration. (Sec. 1101(b)(5), Tax Law; Sec. 1110, Tax Law; Reg. Sec. 526.7)

Leases and rentals of hotel rooms and other accommodations and construction equipment are discussed separately.

¶60-460

Lease or rental with option to purchase. Where a lease (other than certain leases of motor vehicles, vessels and noncommercial aircraft) with an option to purchase has been entered into and the option is exercised, tax is payable on the consideration given when the option is exercised. This tax is in addition to any taxes paid or payable on each lease payment. (Reg. Sec. 526.7(c)(2))

Purchases for subsequent lease or rental. The purchase of tangible personal property for lease or rental may be exempt as a sale for resale. (Sec. 1101(b), Tax Law; Sec. 1105(a), Tax Law)

> *EXAMPLE:* An advisory opinion held that a lease constitutes a "sale, selling or purchase" in accordance with the Tax Law, therefore, when an item is purchased with the intent to lease it, the transaction is considered a purchase for resale and does not constitute a retail sale of tangible personal property subject to sales tax. (TSB-A-98(89)S)

Lease or rental as security agreement. A lease that has been entered into merely as a security agreement, but that does not in fact represent a transaction in which there has been a transfer of possession from the lessor to the lessee, is not a taxable "sale". (Reg. Sec. 526.7(c)(3))

Lease or rental containing property and service components. When a lease of equipment includes the services of an operator, possession is deemed to be transferred and sales tax is imposed if the lessee has the right to direct and control the use of the equipment. The operator's wages, if separately stated, are excluded from the taxable receipts, provided that such wages reflect prevailing wage rates. (Reg. Sec. 526.7(e)(6))

> *EXAMPLE:* A company enters into an agreement to lease a crane, together with the services of the operator of the crane. The operator will take instructions from the company's foreman, and the company determines the working hours and locations. The operator's wages are separately stated. This transaction is within the definition of a taxable sale, and the transfer of possession has occurred by reason of the company's right to direct and control the use of the equipment by the operator. The taxable receipt excludes the operator's wages. (Reg. Sec. 526.7(e)(6))

Leased departments. Every person making sales from a concession or department leased from a vendor and operated under the name of another vendor, is considered to be a "vendor" required to register for sales tax purposes and file sales tax returns. Leased departments and concessions that collect and account for their sales independently from the lessor-vendor are required to undertake all of the responsibilities of a vendor. (Reg. Sec. 526.10(f)) Where a leased department or concession must account for and pay over its receipts to the lessor-vendor, the lessor is responsible for reporting sales and remitting the tax. (Reg. Sec. 526.10(f)(3)) In such instances, however, the leased department or concession must:

— file a return reporting only its sales;

— state that the lessor is responsible for reporting sales and remitting tax due;

— attach a statement to the effect that it is a leased department or concession; and

— identify the lessor by name, address and vendor identification number.

Both the leased department or concession and the lessor-vendor are jointly responsible for the collection and remittance of the taxes on the sales made by the leased department or concession. (Reg. Sec. 526.10(f)(3))

For further information concerning reporting requirements, see Return, Payments, and Due Dates (¶ 61-220).

Lease of storage space. While tax is imposed on the service of providing storage space, it is not imposed on the lease of real property for storage. A lease can be distinguished from the provision of storage space, in that under a lease, the tenant contracts for a certain amount of footage in a specific location, the tenant has unlimited control of access to the space, and may supply his own racks, cabinets and other physical facilities. (Reg. Sec. 527.6(b)(2)) For a discussion of the taxability of storage space, see Services (¶ 60-665).

Deposits. A charge made by a vendor to a customer as a deposit on tangible personal property rented, leased or loaned is not a taxable receipt, but is collateral security for return of the property. Upon the return of the rented, leased or borrowed tangible personal property, any amount not refunded by the vendor constitutes a taxable receipt. (Reg. Sec. 526.5(j))

Interest paid by lessor. Interest paid by a lessor on the purchase of tangible personal property intended to be leased to a customer is an expenditure of the lessor and is subject to tax. (Reg. Sec. 526.5(h)(3))

EXAMPLE: A lessor purchases equipment for a lessee on credit. The agreement provides that the lessee is to pay $100 per month for equipment rented and $7 per month to reimburse the lessor for interest paid. The tax is to be collected on $107. (Reg. Sec. 526.5(h)(3))

Penalty, late fee or demurrage. A charge by a vendor to a customer for the retention of tangible personal property beyond a stipulated time is taxable. The designation of the charge as a penalty, late fee or demurrage in no way affects its taxable status. (Reg. Sec. 526.5(i)(1))

Leases and rentals of motor vehicles, aircraft and vessels. For a discussion of leases and rentals or motor vehicles, aircraft, and vessels, see Motor Vehicles and Transportation. (¶ 60-570 and ¶ 60-740)

Car rental facilities in airports. Vehicle rental companies that operate car rental facilities in airports can separately state and recover a consolidated facilities charge and a concession recovery fee from its vehicle renters. The consolidated facility charge and concession recovery fee constitute expenses of the rental vehicle company. Thus, regardless of whether the vehicle rental company separately states the fees on its bill to the renter, the fees are taxable. (TSB-M-04(8)S; TSB-M-06(15)S)

Supplemental tax on passenger car rentals in MCTD. A special supplemental sales and use tax is imposed on passenger car rentals within the Metropolitan Commuter Transportation District (MCTD). For a complete discussion, see Motor Vehicles (¶ 60-570).

Definitions for leases and rentals.

Consideration. The term "consideration" includes monetary consideration, exchange, barter, the rendering of any service, or any agreement. "Monetary consideration" includes assumption of liabilities, fees, rentals, royalties or any other charge that a purchaser, lessee or licensee is required to pay. (Reg. Sec. 526.7)

Rental, lease or license to use. The terms "rental," "lease" and "license to use" refer to all transactions in which there is a transfer for a consideration of possession of tangible personal property without a transfer of title to the property. Whether a transaction is a "sale" or a "rental, lease or license to use" is determined in accordance with the provisions of the agreement. (Reg. Sec. 526.7(c)(1))

Transfer of possession. "Transfer of possession" with respect to a rental, lease or license to use, means that one of the following attributes of property ownership has been transferred:

— custody or possession of the tangible personal property, actual or constructive;

— the right to custody or possession of the tangible personal property; or

— the right to use, or control or direct the use of tangible personal property. (Reg. Sec. 526.7(e)(4))

It is not essential for a transfer of possession to include the right to move the tangible personal property which is the subject of a rental, lease or license to use.

Are there any special exemptions for leases or rentals in New York?

Yes. New York has two sales and use tax exemptions for certain purchases of tangible personal property and services related to new commercial office space leases (as opposed to ground leases) of 10 years or more commencing on or after September 1, 2005 for a defined period of time. The exemptions differ based on the location of the leased premises in two specific eligible areas. The first area (Eligible Area A) consists of a broad area of lower Manhattan below City Hall. The second area (Eligible Area B) consists of the World Trade Center site, the World Financial Center, and the Battery Park City area. (Sec. 1115(ee), Tax Law) (TSB-M-05(12)S) The exemptions provided for in Eligible Area B are broader in scope and longer in duration than those provided for in Eligible Area A. Accordingly, for leased commercial office space located within both eligible areas, the broader exemptions granted in Eligible Area A apply. (Sec. 1115(ee), Tax Law) (TSB-M-05(12)S) The date by which a qualifying commercial lease must commence in Eligible Area A is September 1, 2020 and the exemption for Eligible Area A will expire on December 1, 2021. The date by which a qualifying commercial lease must commence in Eligible Area B is September 1, 2022 and the exemption for Eligible Area B will expire on December 1, 2023. (Sec. 1115(ee), Tax Law) (TSB-M-09(14)S; TSB-M-14(10)S; TSB-M-17(5)S)

The exemptions apply to the state and local sales and use taxes imposed in New York City, including the additional tax imposed by the state within the Metropolitan Commuter Transportation District (MCTD). The exemptions do not apply to sales and use taxes imposed by other counties or cities within New York. To make a purchase of tangible personal property or installation service exempt from sales and use taxes, the tenant or landlord must issue a completed Form ST-121, Exempt Use Certificate, using Part III, Box T, to the vendor at the time of purchase. To be granted this exemption, contractors making qualifying purchases of tangible personal property or installation service must submit to the vendor a properly completed Form ST-120.1, Contractor's Exempt Purchase Certificate. (TSB-M-05(12)S)

Anyone (i.e., tenants, landlords, and contractors) who paid sales tax on otherwise qualifying purchases are eligible to apply for a credit or refund of the tax paid at the time of the sale. A credit or refund of sales tax paid on such qualifying purchases may be claimed by filing Form AU-11, Application for Credit or Refund of Sales or

Use Tax. Form AU-11 may be submitted electronically. A claim must generally be filed within three years after the date when the tax was required to be paid. Where Form AU-11 has been filed and a credit has been claimed by a person required to file sales tax returns, the applicant may take such credit on the return that is due coincident with or immediately subsequent to the time that the applicant filed the application for credit. (TSB-M-05(12)S; TSB-M-14(10)S)

[¶60-480] Lodging

Rents paid for occupancies of rooms in hotels or similar establishments in New York State are subject to tax. However, the tax is not imposed upon a permanent resident or where the rent is $2 or less per day. (Sec. 1105(e), Tax Law) "Hotels" are defined as buildings, or portions of buildings, which are regularly used and kept open for the lodging of guests. The term "hotel" also includes apartment hotels, motels, inns, boarding houses, certain clubs, beds and breakfasts, resorts, ski lodges, apartment hotels, dude ranches, and certain bungalows, condos, cottages, and cabins. (Sec. 1101(c)(1), Tax Law) (TB-ST-331) (*TSB-M-92(7)S*)

For a sales and use tax guide geared specifically for hotel and motel operators, see Publication 848.

• *Room remarketers*

State and local sales taxes must be paid on the full amount charged to customers by businesses such as Web-based travel companies (room remarketers) for hotel occupancy in New York (including markups). (TSB-M-10(10)S; TSB-M-10(18)S) However, a state and local sales tax exemption is provided for rent paid by a room remarketer to a hotel operator for an occupancy that the room remarketer intends to sell to its customers. The exemption also applies to the $1.50 per unit, per day fee imposed on hotel occupancy in New York City. To claim this exemption, a room remarketer must give the hotel operator a properly completed Form ST-120.2, Room Remarketer's Exempt Purchase Certificate, within 90 days of the date it purchases the occupancy from the hotel operator. However, the exemption does not apply to rent paid by a room remarketer to another room remarketer. A room remarketer may still claim this refund or credit for any tax it paid. (Sec. 1105(e)(2), Tax Law; Sec. 1115(kk), Tax Law) (TSB-M-16(2)S)

A room remarketer is a person who reserves, arranges for, conveys, or furnishes occupancy, whether directly or indirectly, to an occupant for rent in an amount determined by the room remarketer, directly or indirectly, whether pursuant to a written or other agreement. If a business meets the definition of a room remarketer, its ability or authority to reserve, arrange for, convey, or furnish occupancy, directly or indirectly, and to determine rent therefore, is referred to as the "rights of a room remarketer". (Sec. 1101(c), Tax Law; Sec. 1119, Tax Law) (TSB-M-10(10)S; TSB-M-10(18)S)

Businesses, such as travel agencies, that reserve rooms on behalf of their customers and do not have the right to determine the amount of rent that their customer pays for the room (i.e., the rent is fixed and determined by the hotel, and is not allowed to be marked-up by the business that reserves the room on behalf of its customer), are not room remarketers. (TSB-M-10(10)S)

Computation of taxable portion of bill when occupancy is sold with other items for single price (bundled sales).—When occupancy is provided for a single consideration with property, services, amusement charges, or any other items, whether or not such other items are taxable, the rent portion of the consideration for such transaction must be computed as follows: either the total consideration received by the room remarketer multiplied by a fraction, the numerator of which is the consideration payable for the occupancy by the room remarketer and the denominator of which is such consideration payable for the occupancy plus the consideration payable by the remarketer for the other items being sold, or by any other method as may be authorized by the Commissioner of Taxation and Finance. If the room remarketer fails to separately state the tax on the rent so computed on a sales slip, invoice, receipt, or other statement given to the occupant or fails to maintain records of the prices of all components of a transaction, the entire consideration shall be treated as rent subject to tax. (Sec. 1111(r)(1), Tax Law) (TSB-M-12(8)S)

In addition, room remarketers are permitted to provide the information about the amount of the sales tax due on any invoice given to the customer prior to the completion of the occupancy. (Sec. 1111(r)(2), Tax Law) (TSB-M-12(8)S)

Rent for occupancy paid and received by room remarketers.—A room remarketer constitutes an operator of a hotel to the extent that the room remarketer has acquired the rights of a room remarketer with respect to a room or rooms in a hotel. In addition, rent subject to the sales tax on occupancy of a room or rooms in a hotel now includes any service or other charge or amount paid as a condition of occupancy to a room remarketer. Accordingly, the full amount charged by a room remarketer to its customer for the right to occupy a room in a hotel in New York constitutes rent for occupancy of a room in a hotel, and is subject to state and local sales tax. Furthermore, since the law provides that in these circumstances a room remarketer is an operator of a hotel, the room remarketer must collect the sales tax, and where applicable, the $1.50 hotel unit fee imposed on every occupancy of a unit in a hotel located in New York City (NYC $1.50 fee) from its customer, and remit the amount collected to the Tax Department. (TSB-M-10(10)S) However, an exemption is provided for the purchase of hotel room occupancies by room remarketers when those purchases are made from hotels for later resale. (Sec. 1105(e)(2), Tax Law; Sec. 1115(kk), Tax Law)

The full amount paid by a room remarketer to a hotel operator, for the ability or authority to reserve rooms in a hotel, to convey the rights of occupancy of the rooms to their customers, and to determine the amount of rent the room remarketer charges its customers for occupancy of the rooms, constitutes rent for hotel occupancy subject to sales tax, and, where applicable the NYC $1.50 fee. (TSB-M-10(10)S)

Reporting and payment.—Room remarketers are required to report such sales tax due on the return due for the filing period in which the occupancy ends. (Sec. 1111(r)(3), Tax Law) (TSB-M-12(8)S)

Refund or credit for sales tax and NYC unit fee paid by room remarketer.—A room remarketer is allowed a refund or credit against the sales tax and, where applicable, the NYC $1.50 fee. The amount of the refund or credit is the New York state and local sales tax on rent for hotel occupancy, and, where applicable, the NYC $1.50 fee, paid to the operator of a hotel by a room remarketer. (Sec. 1119, Tax Law) (TSB-M-10(10)S)

However, in order to qualify for the refund or credit for any sales tax quarterly period, the room remarketer must, for that quarter: (1) be registered as a person required to collect sales tax under Tax Law § 1134 and must collect sales tax on rent for hotel occupancy, and, where applicable, the NYC $1.50 fee, from its customers; and (2) furnish the Certificate of Authority number of the operator of the hotel to whom the room remarketer paid the tax, if required on the room remarketer's application for refund or credit, or if otherwise requested by the Tax Department. (TSB-M-10(10)S) A room remarketer can provide the name, business address, telephone number, and the address of the hotel where the occupancy took place if the room remarketer requests the hotel operator's certificate of authority number and is not provided that number. (Sec. 1119, Tax Law)

An application for refund or credit must be filed by a room remarketer using Form AU-11, Application for Credit or Refund of Sales or Use Tax, within three years after the date the tax was payable to the Tax Department by the operator of the hotel to whom the tax was paid by the room remarketer. If an application for credit has been filed, the room remarketer may immediately take the credit on the return that is due coincident with the application for credit, or immediately after the room remarketer files the application for credit. However, the taking of the credit on the return is deemed to be part of the application for credit. (TSB-M-10(10)S)

Treatment of hotel occupancy when sold with nontaxable products or services.— The amendments also clarify that where occupancy of a room or rooms in a hotel is sold together with property, services, amusement charges, or any other items that are not subject to sales tax (other nontaxable sales) for one charge, the one charge is subject to sales tax as rent for hotel occupancy. However, the amendments further clarify that if the hotel operator, including a room remarketer, gives a sales slip, invoice, receipt, or other statement to the occupant, which states the amount of rent for occupancy, separately from the nontaxable charges, only the separately stated rent for occupancy is subject to sales tax. This is so only if the separately stated rent for occupancy is reasonable in relation to the amount charged for the nontaxable sales. (TSB-M-10(10)S)

• *Nontaxable hotel occupancies*

*Permanent residents.—*No sales tax is due from hotel guests who are considered permanent residents, which is a guest who stays in a hotel room for at least 90 consecutive days without interruption. (Sec. 1101(c)(5), Tax Law) (TB-ST-331) In New York City only, the local sales tax applies until a guest has stayed for at least 180 consecutive days. State and local sales tax must be charged to a guest until 90 consecutive days of occupancy is reached. At that time, the total can stop charging the guest tax. The hotel may credit the guests account or refund the tax already paid. If the hotel does not credit or refund the sales tax, the guest can apply directly to the state for a refund. In New York City only, the local sales tax applies until a guest has stayed for at least 180 consecutive days. (TB-ST-331)

A business can also qualify as a permanent resident if it meets these conditions: (1) the business rents the hotel rooms for use by its employees or clients; (2) the business must pay the hotel room rental charge and not be reimbursed by the employee, customer, client, or other person who physically occupies the room; and (3) the rooms are rented by the business for at least 90 consecutive days (at least 180 consecutive days in New York City for the local sales tax). (TB-ST-331)

The customer does not have to be in the same room within the hotel to meet the 90/180-day requirement. (TB-ST-331)

*Other miscellaneous occupancies.—*In addition, the following occupancies are not subject to the tax on hotel occupancies:

— a room or suite of rooms containing no sleeping facilities and used solely as a place of assembly;

— nursing homes, rest homes, convalescent homes, maternity homes for expectant mothers, residences or homes for adults or retarded persons;

— summer camps;

— college dormitories; and

— bungalows, where no housekeeping, food or other common hotel services (including entertainment or planned activities) are furnished by the lessor (Effective On March 16, 2012), the Department of Taxation and Finance announced its new policy eliminating the one-week stay test to determine whether the rental of a bungalow or similar living unit is subject to the sales tax imposed on hotel occupancy (see TSB-M-12(4)S),

(Reg. Sec. 527.9(e)) (TB-ST-331)

In addition, the rental of a place of assembly is not subject to sales tax. However, the rental of a place of assembly in conjunction with the sale of food or drink is generally subject to tax. (TB-ST-331)

> *EXAMPLE:* A senior citizen's lodging facility which only furnishes hotel facilities and services and does not furnish services or special care provided by attendants is a hotel. (Reg. Sec. 527.9(e))

Rents received from room occupancies in a hotel operated by a religious, charitable, scientific, etc. organization, in furtherance of the activities of the non-profit organization, are also tax-exempt. (Sec. 1116(c), Tax Law) See ¶60-580 Nonprofit Organizations, Private Schools, and Churches.

For a sales and use tax guide geared specifically for hotel and motel operators, see Publication 848 and TB-ST-331.

• *Hotel services*

The Department of Taxation and Finance issued a bulletin that discusses the taxability of many different services offered by hotels and motels that are in addition to their providing occupancy, as discussed below.

Taxable sales and services.—The following sales and services are taxable:

— Safe deposit rental: A hotel's charges to its guest to store items in a safe deposit box, whether it's located in the guest's room or elsewhere in the hotel (e.g., a vault in the manager's office) are taxable;

— Check room for coats, hats, luggage, etc.: Any charges to check a guest's coat, luggage, or packages, etc. are taxable. Optional tips or gratuities given to the employees working in the storage areas are not taxable;

— Television and in-room movies: Any charges by a hotel to its guest for television, pay-per-view movies, video games, or optional programming are taxable. It's treated as part of the charge for hotel occupancy even if listed separately on the bill or receipt;

— Fax service: A hotel's charge to send or receive a fax is taxable. If the fax transmission is intrastate, meaning the call that sends the fax both begins and ends in New York State, the charge is taxable. However, if the fax transmission is interstate or international, meaning the call either begins or ends outside of New York State, the charge is not taxable;

— Copy services: A hotel's charges to make copies for a guest are taxable. However, if a guest uses a coin-operated copy machine that charges 50 cents or less per copy, the charges are not taxable.;

— Telephone service: A hotel's charges for providing telephone equipment and in-house calls, such as calling room to room are taxable. Per-call charges by a hotel for local or intrastate telephone service are also taxable. However, per-call charges for interstate or international telephone service are not taxable;

— Room service: A hotel's service or delivery charges added to a bill for room service are taxable. Optional tips and gratuities are not taxable;

— Rental of recreation equipment or other items: A hotel's charges for the rental of beach chairs, umbrellas, canoes, paddle boats, golf carts, etc. are taxable;

¶60-480

— Separately stated service charges: A hotel's separately stated service charges or other charges related to a taxable sale that are not specifically listed as gratuities on a bill or invoice are taxable;

— Sporting and other event tickets: Sales of tickets to sporting events where the guest will be a spectator, such as baseball or football games, stock car races, and college athletic events, or tickets to exhibitions, such as a boat or car show are taxable. However, sales of tickets to horse racing tracks and "combative sports", are not taxable. Sales of certain other types of tickets are also not taxable; and

— Transportation services: A hotel's charges for certain types of transportation to and from airports, attractions, and local businesses are taxable.

(TB-ST-333)

Nontaxable sales and services.—The following sales and services are not taxable:

— Internet access: A hotel's separately stated charges for Internet access are not taxable;

— Valet and laundry services: A hotel's charges for laundering clothing, dry cleaning, tailoring, or shoe shining are not taxable;

— Admission charges: A hotel's charges to a guest for admission to a sporting event where the guest will participate are not taxable. This includes activities like swimming, golf, tennis, and skiing;

— Theater and similar tickets: Sales of theater tickets, movie tickets, or tickets to other dramatic or musical arts performances are not taxable; and

— Gratuities and tips: Gratuities and tips that a customer leaves voluntarily (e.g., for housekeeping staff or the wait staff in a restaurant) are not taxable. Mandatory gratuities related to a taxable sale are different because they are automatically added onto the bill given to the customer. A mandatory gratuity is not taxable if all of these conditions are met: (i) the charge is shown separately on the bill, (ii) the charge is identified as a gratuity, and (iii) all the money collected is given to the employees. If any of these conditions is not met, the mandatory gratuity is taxable.

(TB-ST-333)

• *Cancellation fees and guaranteed no-show fees*

A cancellation fee is not taxable because the customer never has the right to occupy the room and the fee is not considered to be rent for occupancy. However, guaranteed no-show fees are taxable as charges for hotel occupancy. (TB-ST-331)

• *College and university-operated hotels*

Colleges and universities that operate hotels containing 100 or more rooms must collect sales tax from customers who do not qualify for a sales tax exemption pursuant to Sec. 1116(a), Tax Law. (Sec. 1116(b)(7), Tax Law)

Room rentals to organizations exempt from sales and use tax under Sec. 1116(a), Tax Law, remain exempt from tax, regardless of the number of rooms within the hotel. In addition, where an individual rents an otherwise taxable rooms at a college or university hotel, the room rental is not subject to tax if the individual is doing business on behalf of an organization exempt from tax under Sec. 1116(a), Tax Law. To claim the exemption, the occupant must provide the appropriate exemption documentation to the hotel operator.

Taxable room rentals to students as guests of the hotel are not to be confused with nontaxable sales of college or university provided room and board to students in dorms, fraternity houses, etc. (*TSB-M-96(6)S*) In addition, rent paid for hotel occupancy by attendees of seminars and other educational events is not considered student room and board. It is, in the absence of any other applicable exemption, taxable.

• *Complimentary accommodations*

The tax is not collected where a hotel furnishes complimentary accommodations to persons for which there is no consideration paid and no rental charged. Where there is consideration (such as the bringing of future business to the hotel by a tour guide, travel representative or another person who at the time of negotiations receives his or her accommodations free of charge), the accommodation is subject to tax on the normal rent of the room except when the normal rent is less than $2 a day. (Reg. Sec. 527.9(f)) (TB-ST-331)

> **EXAMPLE:** A hotel advertises that for every 12 days of occupancy of one of its rooms by one individual it will offer that individual one day's accommodation of the same type without charge. This additional occupancy is not subject to tax. (Reg. Sec. 527.9(f))

• *Employee lodging*

Lodging furnished by an employer to employees is not subject to tax if the employer receives no cash or other consideration for the lodging from the employees and the value of the lodging is not income for the employees under the federal and state income tax laws. (Reg. Sec. 527.9(g)) (TB-ST-331) An employer is liable for the tax for any expenses incurred which would ordinarily be taxable for the operator of a hotel. Any charge by an employer to an employee for lodging is subject to tax, whether paid in cash by the employee or withheld from the employee's wages. (Reg. Sec. 527.9(g))

• *Exempt organizations*

Certain exempt organizations, such as religious groups, youth sports groups, and charitable organizations, can purchase hotel occupancy without paying sales tax. In order to qualify for the exemption the group must:

— be identified on the hotel bill or invoice along with the individual who occupied the room;

— be the direct payor of record when payment is made directly from the funds of the organization, such as with a check from the organization, with the organization's credit card, cash or other funds. If the employee or representative pays the hotel bill with a personal check, personal credit card or other personal funds, the exemption does not apply; and

— give the hotel operator a properly completed Form ST-119.1, Exempt Organization Exempt Purchase Certificate.

(TB-ST-331)

• *Governmental employees*

Employees of New York or the federal government on official business that may rent hotel or motel rooms in New York using Form ST-129, Exemption Certificate–Tax on Occupancy of Hotel or Motel Rooms. The exemption includes the $1.50 hotel unit fee in New York City but does not include locally imposed and administered hotel occupancy taxes, also known as bed taxes. Government employees must complete and sign Form ST-129 and give it to the operator of the hotel or motel no later than 90 days after the last day they rented the room when paying with: cash; a personal check; or a personal credit card or debit card. Employees staying at more than one location while on official business must complete a certificate for each establishment. If a group of employees is travelling on official business, each employee must complete a separate certificate. Government employees paying with a government voucher or a government credit card do not need to use Form ST-129. However, government employees must show the operator appropriate and satisfactory identification whether or not they are using Form ST-129. (TB-ST-331; TB-ST-315)

• *Authorized representative of veterans' organizations*

Authorized representatives of veterans' posts or organizations, while on official business of the post or organization, may occupy hotel or motel rooms in New York exempt from all state-administered state and local hotel occupancy taxes. (Sec. 1116(g), Tax Law) (*Important Notice N-93-29; Important Notice N-93-30*) The exemption applies to state-administered state and local sales taxes in effect in the area where the transaction occurs, including the 5% special hotel occupancy tax, the .2% Hudson River Valley Greenway Fee and the tax imposed in the Metropolitan Commuter Transportation District (MCTD) (see ¶60-110 Rate of Tax). The exemption does not apply to locally administered bed taxes or charges for food or drink, entertainment services, safety deposit services or for any other taxable sales or services.

To claim the exemption, the representative must present the hotel or motel room operator with a properly completed Form ST-119.5, "Exempt Organization Certification for Hotel and Motel Occupancy by Representatives of Veterans' Organizations." The certification must contain the original signature of both the representative and an officer (other than the representative) of the post or organization. Photocopied signatures will not be accepted. A copy of Form ST-119, "Exempt Organization Certificate," must be attached to Form ST-119.5.

Food services offered by hotels.—A hotel operating on the American plan, modified American plan or other similar plan must, for the first 90 days, collect tax on the total charge for both rooms (if the charge is more than $2 per night) and meals. (Reg. Sec. 527.9(h)) When the occupant becomes a permanent resident, the operator will discontinue collecting tax on the room charge. In lieu of establishing a separate charge for meals, the operator may use the following schedule to determine the percentage of the total charge to be apportioned to meals furnished and collect tax based on that amount.

Total charge includes	Room	Meals
room, breakfast, lunch, dinner	50%	50%
room, lunch, dinner	60%	40%
room, breakfast, dinner	60%	40%
room, breakfast, lunch	70%	30%
room, dinner	75%	25%
room, lunch	85%	15%
room, breakfast	85%	15%

If the hotel operator neither separately states the charge for room and meals nor uses the above schedule, the entire charge is taxable, whether or not the occupant is a permanent resident. (Reg. Sec. 527.9(h))

A hotel offering a free continental breakfast (juice, pastry and coffee) may not separately state a reasonable value for the breakfast or use the American plan schedule. (Reg. Sec. 527.9(h)) Rather, the entire charge is subject to tax as rent for the room.

The separately stated charges for food and drink at a restaurant facility operated by a hotel are taxable. (Reg. Sec. 527.9(h)) See ¶60-390 Food and Grocery Items.

Charges for room service constitute part of the receipt from the sale of food or drink and are taxable. (Reg. Sec. 527.9(h))

- *Miscellaneous transactions*

Charges for certain telephone service are considered incidental to hotel occupancy and are taxable as part of the occupancy. A hotel may not claim a credit or refund for taxes paid to the phone company on that portion of the service which has been furnished to the guests. (Reg. Sec. 527.9(i))

Additional charges made by hotels which are taxable include:

— charges for in-room use of movies;

— charges for rentals of tangible personal property, such as recreational equipment;

— charges for safekeeping of a guest's valuables, including the use of safe deposit boxes; and

— charges for a cabaret facility operated by a hotel.

(Reg. Sec. 527.9(i))

The following are examples of purchases made by hotel that are subject to tax:

— fuel, gas, electricity, steam, telephony and telegraphy and other utilities;

— furniture used in guest rooms and elsewhere;

— soap, paper products and other supplies used in the operation of the hotel; and

— items which will be used for recreational purposes, such as golf carts, pool chairs or other recreational equipment.

(Reg. Sec. 527.9(i))

[¶60-510] Manufacturing, Processing, Assembling, or Refining

In general, a manufacturer's purchases of certain materials and equipment are exempt from tax, but its sales of the resulting tangible personal property are taxable. (Sec. 1115(a)(12), Tax Law; Reg. Sec. 528.13(a)(1)(i))

Are purchases by manufacturers, processors, assemblers, or refiners taxable in New York?

No. An exemption is provided for machinery and equipment used or consumed directly and predominantly in the production of tangible personal property for sale by manufacturing, processing, generating, assembling, refining, mining or extracting (the exemption also applies to New York City sales and use taxes). (Sec. 1115(a)(12), Tax Law; Sec. 1107(a), Tax Law; Reg. Sec. 528.13(a)(1)(i)) However, the exemption does not include parts with a useful life of one year or less or tools or supplies used in connection with the machinery or equipment. (Sec. 1115(a)(12), Tax Law) Likewise, machinery and equipment used in the administration and distribution phases of the manufacturing process do not qualify for the exemption. (Reg. Sec. 528.13(b)(2)) (TB-ST-552)

The determination of when production begins depends on the procedure used in a plant. If on receiving raw materials, the purchaser weighs, inspects, measures, or tests the material prior to placement into storage, then production begins with placement into storage and the prior activities are administrative. However, if the materials are unloaded and placed in storage for production without the other activities, then the unloading is the beginning of production. (Reg. Sec. 528.13(b)(3))

Definitions related to manufacturing, processing, assembling, or refining. The following definitions apply to manufacturing, processing, assembling, or refining.

Administration. The administration phase of the manufacturing process includes sales, promotion, accounting, purchasing, general facility maintenance, clerical work, and the receiving and testing of raw materials. (TB-ST-552)

Assembling. "Assembling" is a manufacturing operation, or a process associated with a manufacturing operation, that produces goods by fitting together various parts to make a complete product. (Reg. Sec. 531.2(c)) (TB-ST-552)

EXAMPLE: A company combines pre-cut glass, plastic, aluminum extrusions, and rubber gaskets to make storm windows. Such combining of materials is assembling. (Reg. Sec. 531.2(c))

EXAMPLE: A manufacturer of cars has a production line where various components (engines, frames, doors, windows, etc.) are put together in the process of making a finished car. This is an assembly operation. (TB-ST-552)

Directly. "Directly" means that during the production phase the machinery or equipment must:

— act upon or effect a change in material to form the product to be sold;

— have an active and necessary role in the production of the product for sale;

— be used in handling, storage, or conveyance of materials or the product to be sold; or

— be used to package the product for sale.

(TB-ST-552)

Usage in activities collateral to the actual production process is not deemed to be use directly in production. (Reg. Sec. 528.13(c)(2))

EXAMPLE: A manufacturer has two forklifts. One forklift is used to unload the raw materials to be weighed and inspected before being placed in storage. The forklift does not qualify for the exemption because weighing and inspecting of raw materials is an administrative function. The second forklift is used to move materials throughout the production line. This forklift qualifies for the exemption. (TB-ST-552)

EXAMPLE: Plating racks, used during the process of electroplating products for sale are deemed to be equipment used directly in the production of tangible personal property. (Reg. Sec. 528.13(c))

EXAMPLE: A private water company purchases pumps, chlorinators, valves, aerators, motors, and motor controls to be used in the processing of water for sale. Such machinery and equipment is used directly in the production of water. (Reg. Sec. 528.13(c))

Distribution. The distribution phase of the manufacturing process includes everything that takes place after the products are packaged and ready for sale, including storing, loading, shipping, displaying, and selling finished products. (TB-ST-552)

Manufacturing. "Manufacturing" generally results in the creation of a product that is substantially different from its component parts in form, character, composition, and usefulness. It includes the production of standardized items as well as the production of items to a customer's specifications. (Reg. Sec. 531.2(b)) (TB-ST-552)

EXAMPLE: A steel manufacturer combines iron with carbon to make commercial steel. This is a manufacturing operation. (TB-ST-552)

EXAMPLE: A company furnishes concrete that is poured into foundations. Cement, water, and aggregates are mixed in a truck en route to the job to form concrete. The concrete is a manufactured product. (Reg. Sec. 531.2(b))

EXAMPLE: A company combines metal, wood, glass, and other component parts into structural panel sections that are joined to form the bearing walls of a building. These panels are manufactured products. (Reg. Sec. 531.2(b))

Predominantly. "Predominantly" means that the machinery or equipment is used more than 50% of the time in a production activity. This is generally determined by hours of operation. (Reg. Sec. 528.13(c)(4)) (TB-ST-552)

Machinery or equipment used in production by someone other than its owner is exempt under the same conditions as other machinery and equipment. (Reg. Sec. 528.13(c)(5))

Computer equipment used directly in production also qualifies for the sales tax exemption. To qualify, the computers must be directly linked to production equipment and have an active and necessary role in the actual production process. Computer equipment used in collateral or administrative functions (such as computer equipment linked to production equipment that merely functions to collect data for administrative use) does not qualify for the exemption. (TB-ST-552)

EXAMPLE: A company purchases a machine to produce new paper machine rolls and to recondition old paper machine rolls for its customers. The machine is to be used for production 70% of the time and for reconditioning 30% of the time. Reconditioning is a repair service to tangible personal property, and machinery used for that purposes is not in production. However, because the machine will be used directly in production over 50% of the time, it qualifies for exemption. (Reg. Sec. 528.13(c)(4))

EXAMPLE: A fork lift is used 60% of the time on an assembly line and 40% of the time for loading finished products onto railroad cars for delivery. The fork lift is used predominantly in production. (Reg. Sec. 528.13(c)(4))

EXAMPLE: An overhead crane is located near the end of an assembly line. It is used to carry materials along the assembly line and also to load finished products onto railroad cars for shipment to customers. It is used for assembly line operations 40% of the time and 60% of the time for the loading of the finished products. The crane is taxable as it is not predominantly used in the production phase of the operation. (Reg. Sec. 528.13(c)(4))

Processing. "Processing" is the performance of any service on tangible personal property that effects a change in the nature, shape, or form of the property. (Reg. Sec. 531.2(e)) (TB-ST-552)

EXAMPLE: To make decorative landscaping stone, chunks of rock are passed through a series of crushers which reduce the chunks into smaller sizes. This is a processing operation. (TB-ST-552)

Production. "Production" covers a variety of activities, including manufacturing, processing, generating, assembling, refining, mining and extracting. (TB-ST-552) It also includes the actual production process, starting with the handling and storage of raw materials at the plant site, continuing through the production and quality control testing of products, and ending with the last step of production where the resulting products are packaged and ready for sale. (Reg. Sec. 528.13(b)(1)(ii))

EXAMPLE: A food processor sells canned food in cases of 48 cans. The canned food is stacked for later labeling and casing. The line of production is deemed to extend through the labeling and casing operation. (Reg. Sec. 528.13(b))

Refining. "Refining" is the operation by which impurities or unwanted elements are removed from a product. (TB-ST-552)

EXAMPLE: Production of gasoline, motor fuels, and fuel oils from crude oil is a refining operation. (TB-ST-552)

Parts, tools, and supplies. Parts, tools and supplies can be purchased exempt from tax if they are used directly and predominantly in production. This includes receipts from retail sales of (1) tools and supplies used or consumed directly and predominantly in the production of tangible personal property, gas, electricity, refrigeration, or steam for sale by manufacturing, processing, generating, assembling, refining, mining, or extracting; (2) telephone central office equipment, station apparatus, or comparable telegraph equipment used directly and predominately in receiving at destination or initiating and switching telephone or telegraph communication, or in receiving, amplifying, processing, transmitting and retransmitting telephone or telegraph signals; and (3) parts, tools, and supplies for use or consumption directly and predominantly in the production for sale of gas or oil by manufacturing, processing, generating, assembling, refining, mining, or extracting. (Sec. 1105-B(a), Tax Law; Sec. 1115(a)(36), Tax Law; Reg. Sec. 528.13(e)(1)) (TSB-M-96(5)S) (TB-ST-552) However, the exemption does not include parts with a useful life of one year or less or tools or supplies used in connection with such machinery or equipment. (Sec. 1115(a)(12), Tax Law)

EXAMPLE: A compressor motor used for production painting is replaced after the machine has been in operation for six months. The normal useful life of this type of motor is two years. A replacement motor may be purchased tax-exempt. Likewise, a replacement blade for a bench saw used in production has a useful life of six months and, therefore, is a part which is exempt. (Reg. Sec. 528.13(e)(1))

Parts. "Parts" are components of machinery or equipment that are actually attached to the machinery or equipment. A part cannot accomplish the work for which it was designed independent of the machine for which it is intended to be a component. (Reg. Sec. 528.13(e)(1)) (TB-ST-552) Examples of parts (TB-ST-552) are:

— saw blades,

— motors,

— gears, and

— bits.

Tools. "Tools" are manually operated implements for performing a task. (Reg. Sec. 528.13(e)(2)) Common examples of tools are:

— wrenches,

— sheet metal shears,

— utility knives,

— hammers,

— vises, and

— drills. (TB-ST-552)

Supplies. "Supplies" are items used in the maintenance of exempt machinery or equipment, and items used or consumed in production. (Reg. Sec. 528.13(e)(3)) (TB-ST-552) Examples include:

¶60-510

— oil, grease, and coolant to keep engines running properly,

— sandpaper,

— paper patterns, and

— welding rods, acetylene, and propane gas used with welding equipment. (TB-ST-552)

Fuel and utilities. Fuel, utilities (gas, electricity, refrigeration and steam), and utility services used or consumed directly and exclusively in the production for sale of tangible personal property, gas, electricity, refrigeration, or steam by manufacturing, processing, assembling, generating, or refining are not subject to tax. (Sec. 1115(c), Tax Law) The exemption includes all pipe, pipeline, drilling rigs, service rigs, vehicles and associated equipment used in the drilling, production and operation of oil, gas, and solution mining activities to the point of sale to the first commercial purchaser. (Sec. 1115(a)(12), Tax Law; Reg. Sec. 528.13(a)(1)(i)) However, fuel, gas, electricity, refrigeration, steam, and like services are subject to tax when used or consumed in the heating, cooling, or lighting of buildings; in the preparation of food and drink; or in the storage of tangible personal property. (Reg. Sec. 528.22(a)(2))

Raw materials. A manufacturer may purchase raw materials that will become part of the finished product without paying tax by issuing to its supplier Form ST-120, Resale Certificate. (TB-ST-552)

EXAMPLE: A manufacturer of fragrances purchases oils, dyes, and chemical compounds used in the production of perfume for sale. The manufacturer may purchase these items without paying sales tax by issuing Form ST-120, Resale Certificate, to the supplier. (TB-ST-552)

EXAMPLE: A furniture manufacturer purchases pine boards to make dining room tables. The furniture manufacturer may purchase the pine boards for resale without paying sales tax. (TB-ST-552)

Subcontractors. Work performed by a subcontractor that becomes part of the finished product is considered exempt production work. (TB-ST-552)

EXAMPLE: A custom motorcycle manufacturer sends parts to a paint shop to be painted prior to being installed on the motorcycle. The work performed at the paint shop is part of the production process. (TB-ST-552)

EXAMPLE: A door manufacturer has custom stained glass produced by a subcontractor that will be inlaid in the doors for sale. The process of creating the stained glass that will become a component part of the door is part of the production process. (TB-ST-552)

Are sales by manufacturers, processors, assemblers, or refiners taxable in New York?

Yes, retail sales of tangible personal property by manufacturers, processors, assemblers, or refiners are subject to tax. Since New York does not have any specific provisions for sales by manufacturers, processors, assemblers, or refiners, manufacturers would be taxable on sales of tangible personal property under the general taxability statutes. (Sec. 1105, Tax Law; Sec. 1110, Tax Law)

Donations to an exempt organization. Tangible personal property manufactured, processed, or assembled and donated to an exempt organization by a manufacturer, processor, or assembler is exempt from tax, provided that the manufacturer, processor, or assembler offers the same kind or property for sale in the regular course of business and has not made any other use of the donated property. No refund or credit is allowed for sales and use taxes properly paid. (Sec. 1115(l), Tax Law)

Are self-produced goods used in manufacturing, processing, assembling or refining taxable in New York?

No. Machinery used to produce other machinery or equipment or parts for self-use in production is considered to be used directly in production and not taxable. (Reg. Sec. 528.13(c)(3)) The mere storage, keeping, retention or withdrawal from storage of tangible personal property by the manufacturer, processor, or assembler is also not taxable. (Sec. 1110, Tax Law)

Are labor and services related to manufacturing, processing, assembling or refining taxable in New York?

The services of producing, fabricating, processing, printing or imprinting tangible personal property are taxable. This includes those services performed for a person who directly or indirectly furnishes the tangible personal property that is not purchased by that person for resale. (Sec. 1105(c)(2), Tax Law; Reg. Sec. 527.4(a))

Indirectly furnishing. Furnishing "indirectly" means that items of tangible personal property are supplied to the person performing the enumerated services by an agent or other person on behalf of the customer or, when the items of tangible personal property are not supplied by the person performing the enumerated services, at the direction of the customer. (Reg. Sec. 527.4(a)(3))

Producing. "Producing" means the manufacture of a product from one or more raw materials and any process in which a raw material loses its identity when the production process is completed. (Reg. Sec. 527.4(b))

Processing. "Processing" is the performance of any service on tangible personal property for the owner which effects a change in the nature, shape, or form of the property. (Reg. Sec. 527.4(d))

When such services are combined with the sale of property by the person performing the services, the entire transaction is subject to tax as a retail sale. (Reg. Sec. 527.4(a)(4))

For a general discussion of the taxability of sales of services, see Services (¶60-665).

Installing, repairing, maintaining, or servicing exempt machinery and equipment. Charges to a manufacturer for installing, maintaining, servicing, or repairing exempt production machinery and equipment are exempt from tax. Installing means setting up or putting something in place for use. For example, the installation of plumbing or electrical fixtures needed for the operation of production equipment is exempt from sales tax. Maintaining, servicing, and repairing are terms used to cover all activities that relate to keeping things in a condition of fitness, efficiency, readiness, or safety, or restoring them to such condition. (TB-ST-552)

On-site assembly. If machinery and equipment cannot be completely assembled prior to delivery to the customer due to the size and weight of the item, then on-site assembly performed by a manufacturer-installer or a contractor hired by the manufacturer to perform such assembly is recognized as a continuation of the manufacturing process. The cost of assembly is part of the selling price of the machinery and equipment and, presumably, exempt from tax. Also, in order for the charge by the contractor to be exempt as a service to property being resold, the contractor must obtain a resale certificate from the manufacturer. (Reg. Sec. 541.6(d)) For further details, see Construction (¶60-330).

¶60-510

Are there refund and/or credit provisions for manufacturing, processing, assembling or refining in New York?

Yes, a credit or refund is allowed for tax paid on the sale or use within New York of tangible personal property, not purchased for resale, if the use of the property is restricted to fabricating (including incorporating it into or assembling it with other tangible personal property), processing, printing or imprinting the property and then shipping it out of the state for use outside the state.

In addition, a credit or refund is allowed, in an amount equal to the sales or use tax imposed and paid on the sale or use of tangible personal property, where the property is subsequently used by the purchaser in performing certain taxable services and becomes a physical component part of the property upon which the service is performed, or where the property is subsequently transferred to the purchaser of the service in conjunction with the performance of the service. Taxable services for which the refund or credit against the tax may be claimed include processing and printing services. (Sec. 1119(c), Tax Law)

For a general discussion of refunds and credits, see Credits (¶61-270) and Application for Refund (¶61-610).

[¶60-520] Medical, Dental, and Optical Supplies and Drugs

This paragraph discusses the taxability of medical, dental and optical supplies, equipment and drugs, as well as other health supplies.

For a discussion of how sales tax applies to items commonly sold by drugstores and pharmacies, including charts that list taxable cosmetic and toiletries, as well as taxable general merchandise, see TB-ST-193.

• *Drugs and medicines*

An exemption from sales and use taxes is provided for drugs and medicines intended for use (either internally or externally) in the cure, mitigation, treatment or prevention of illnesses or diseases in human beings. (Sec. 1115(a)(3), Tax Law) This includes both prescription and nonprescription drugs and medicines that are recognized by the United States Pharmacopeia, the Homeopathic Pharmacopeia of the United States, or the National Formulary. (TB-ST-193) The exemption also applies to products consumed by humans for the preservation of health (other than cosmetics or toilet articles). (Reg. Sec. 528.4(a)(1))

"Drugs" and "medicines" defined.—The terms "drugs" and "medicines" refer to: (1) articles (regardless of whether a prescription is required) recognized as such in the U.S. Pharmacopoeia, Homeopathic Pharmacopia of the U.S. or National Formulary and intended for use in the diagnosis, cure, mitigation, treatment or prevention of disease in humans and (2) articles (other than food) intended to affect the structure or any function of the human body. (Reg. Sec. 528.4(b)(1))

"Products consumed by humans for the preservation of health" defined.—"Products consumed by humans for the preservation of health" include other substances used internally or externally which are not ordinarily considered drugs or medicines. (Reg. Sec. 528.4(b)(3)) Analgesics, antiseptics, antacids, cough and cold remedies, laxatives and medical oxygen are examples of "products consumed by humans for the preservation of health" and, therefore, qualify for exemption.

The base or medium used to contain the drug or medicine (i.e. oil, ointment, cream, talc, or alcohol), and the medium used for delivery of the drug or medicine (i.e. disposable wipe, atomizer, syringe, or saturated pad) will not affect its tax exempt status. (Publication 840)

EXAMPLE: Exempt drugs or medicines.—The following are examples of drugs and medicines that are exempt from sales and use tax: analgesics, antiseptics, antacids, cough and cold remedies, laxatives, aspirin, boric acid ointment, cod liver oil and castor oil; antibiotics, sulfa drugs, and birth control pills; and any diagnostic drug, chemical or other substance which is used internally or externally on a human.

(Reg. Sec. 528.4(b)(3))

Prescription drugs and medicines.—Prescription drugs and medicines are used under the supervision of a licensed physician and must be obtained from a licensed pharmacist. They include: antibiotics, narcotics, and controlled substances. (TB-ST-193)

Nonprescription drugs and medicines.—Nonprescription or over-the-counter drugs and medicines can also be purchased exempt from sales tax. They include: pain relievers (aspirin, ibuprofen, etc.), antacids, cough and cold remedies, and dandruff shampoo and treatments. (TB-ST-193)

Other medicinal products.—Other medicinal products used internally or externally by humans for the preservation of health, and products (other than food) that are intended to affect the structure or a function of the human body, are also exempt from sales tax. These products, which are not ordinarily considered drugs or medicines, include: acne preparations, contact lens preparations, eye drops, laxatives, lip balm intended to treat or prevent chapped lips, petroleum jelly that is uncolored and unscented, products that treat nicotine withdrawal symptoms, products that prevent or treat athlete's foot or other fungus infections, products intended to treat sunburns, sunscreens, and vaginal creams, foams, ointments, and jellies that treat specific medical conditions. (TB-ST-193)

• *Oxygen, insulin, and blood*

Oxygen.—Medical oxygen and nitrous oxide are exempt from sales and use tax. (Reg. Sec. 528.4) Oxygen provided in connection with furnishing oxygen therapy services is exempt from tax. The operation of oxygen therapy equipment by a technician was also not taxable. (*Opinion of Counsel*, New York Department of Taxation and Finance) In addition, medical equipment used to dispense oxygen (i.e. regulators, humidifies, ring stands, etc.) is exempt from tax. (*Nichols Oxygen Service, Inc.*)

Insulin.—Insulin packaged with disposable syringes is exempt from sales and use tax. (Reg. Sec. 528.4)

Blood and plasma.—Blood and its derivatives are exempt from sales and use tax. (Reg. Sec. 528.4)

• *Optical*

Eyeglasses and artificial devices (including component parts) purchased to correct or alleviate physical incapacity in human beings are exempt from sales and use taxes. (Sec. 1115(a)(4), Tax Law)

Replacement parts.—Replacement parts for eyeglasses and artificial devices may be purchased exempt from tax, provided that they are identifiable at the time the retail sale is made. (Reg. Sec. 528.5(c)(1))

Supplies used in connection with eyeglasses.—Supplies used in conjunction with eyeglasses and artificial devices are subject to tax. Accordingly, lens tissue for cleaning glasses and cushioned nose pads for glasses are taxable supplies. (Reg. Sec. 528.5(c)(2))

Requirements to qualify for exemption.—In order to qualify for the exemption, the item is required to satisfy the following criteria:

— it must either completely or partially replace a missing body part or function of a permanently inoperative or permanently malfunctioning body part;

— it must be primarily and customarily used for such purposes; and

— it must not be generally useful in the absence of illness, injury or physical incapacity.

(Reg. Sec. 528.5(b)(1))

The exemption applies to such items as artificial limbs, false teeth, cardiac pacemakers, guide dogs for the blind and Braille typewriters. (Reg. Sec. 528.5(b)(1))

• *Dental*

Dental supplies, other than drugs and medicines, used by a dentist in providing dental care for compensation are subject to sales tax. (TSB-M-06(5)S) (See *John O. Butler Co. v. State Tax Commission; Mohawk Dental Supply Co., Inc.,*)

Products used in the restorations of teeth.—Dental supplies include all products used or consumed by the dentist in the practice of dentistry, such as direct-filling materials used in the restoration of patients' teech, but do not include prosthetic dental devices. A dentist is not considered to be purchasing dental supplies for resale to patients as part of his or her dental practive, nor are such supplies considered to be used by the dentist in the production of any tangible personal property for sale. (TSB-M-06(5)S) Prosthetic dental devices (including their component parts, but not related supplies) that completely or partially replace missing teeth or the functions of permanently inoperative or permanently malfunctioning teeth are prosthetic devices exempt from sales tax. These prosthetic dental devices include implants, dentures, bridges, full and partial crowns (both temporary and permanent), onlays, and inlays. Prosthetic dental devices do not include any products that are not primarily and customarily used for such purposes and that are generally useful in the absence of illness, injury, or physical incapacity. This includes products that are cosmetic in nature, such as laminate veneers, decorative caps, and specialty or jewelry teeth. (TSB-M-06(5)S)

• *Hearing aids*

Hearing aids and other artificial devices (including component parts) purchased to correct or alleviate physical incapacity are exempt from sales and use taxes. (Sec. 1115(a)(4), Tax Law) See *Publication 822*, Taxable Status of Medical Equipment and Supplies, Prosthetic Devices, and Related Items.

Replacement parts.—Replacement parts for hearing aids and other artificial devices may be purchased exempt from tax, provided that they are identifiable at the time the retail sale is made. For example, batteries for hearing aids which are clearly labeled as such by the manufacturer are exempt replacement parts. When the replacement parts are not identifiable parts, the purchaser must pay the tax at the time of purchase. In such instances, the purchaser may apply to the Sales Tax Bureau for a refund if he or she can show that the replacement parts were used on exempt prosthetic aids. (Reg. Sec. 528.5(c)(1))

Supplies used in connection with hearing aids.—Supplies used in conjunction with hearing aids are subject to tax. (Reg. Sec. 528.5(c)(2))

Requirements to qualify for exemption.—The requirements to qualify for the exemption for hearing aids are the same as for optical items discussed above.

(TB-ST-193)

• *Prosthetic devices*

Prosthetic aids and artificial devices (including component parts) purchased to correct or alleviate physical incapacity in human beings are exempt from sales and use taxes. (Sec. 1115(a)(4), Tax Law) (TSB-M-14(8)S) See Publication 822, Taxable Status of Medical Equipment and Supplies, Prosthetic Devices, and Related Items.

Power lift chairs.—The Department of Taxation and Finance has determined that power lift chairs qualify as prosthetic aids. Power lift chairs are chairs that feature a powered lifting mechanism that raises the entire chair up from or down to its base, assisting the user to move more easily into either a standing or a sitting position. (TSB-M-14(8)S)

Requirements to qualify for exemption.—The requirements to qualify for the exemption for prosthetic devices are the same as for optical items discussed above.

Component or replacement parts for prosthetic aids.—Component or replacement parts for exempt prosthetic aids are exempt. If a component part is clearly identified as a part of such aid, the part may be purchased exempt from tax. If a component part is not clearly identified as a part for such aid, the purchaser must pay sales tax at the time of purchase and file a claim for refund using Form AU-11, Application for Credit or Refund of Sales or Use Tax. (Reg. Sec. 528.5(c)(1)) (TSB-M-14(8)S)

Supplies used in connection with prosthetic aids.—Supplies used in conjunction with prosthetic aids and artificial devices are subject to tax. (Reg. Sec. 528.5(c)(2))

Special devices and attachments for handicapped persons.—The exemption for prosthetic devices does apply for parts, special attachments and special lettering that are added to or attached to tangible personal property (such as appliances) so that a handicapped person can use them. If tangible personal property is sold with special controls, lettering or devices and the charge for the added feature is separately stated on the bill, the portion of the sales receipt attributable to the added feature is exempt. (Reg. Sec. 528.5(b)(2))

CCH EXAMPLE: *Braille books and games.*—That portion of the price of braille books and braille games which is attributable to those features of the books and games that enable the affected person to use them, if separately stated on the bill, is excluded from the amount upon which the sales tax is computed. In determining the reasonableness of the amount of the exclusion, like items must be compared. One such example is the comparison of the price of a hard cover braille edition of a book with the same hard cover edition of a non-braille book. (Reg. Sec. 528.5(b)(2))

Services performed on exempt prosthetic devices.—Receipts from the installation, maintenance, servicing or repair of exempt prosthetic aids, hearing aids, eyeglasses or artificial devices are also exempt from tax. (Sec. 1115(g), Tax Law) Where tangible personal property with special controls or attachments for use by handicapped persons is repaired, maintained, or serviced, the exemption applies only to the portion of the charge attributable to the added feature and only if the charge is separately stated on the service bill. (Reg. Sec. 528.5(d))

• *Medical equipment and vehicles*

Medical equipment (including component parts) and supplies required for medical use or to correct or alleviate physical incapacity are also exempt. (Sec. 1115(a)(3), Tax Law) (TSB-M-14(8)S) See Publication 822, Taxable Status of Medical Equipment and Supplies, Prosthetic Devices, and Related Items. However, medical equipment and supplies (other than drugs and medicines) purchased at retail by a person performing medical or similar services for compensation are taxable. Accordingly, such items as stethoscopes when purchased by a physician, stretchers when purchased by an ambulance service or dental supplies (including porcelain, amalgam and dental floss) when purchased by a dentist are subject to sales and use taxes. (Reg. Sec. 528.4(h)(1)) (TSB-M-14(8)S)

The following items qualify as exempt medical equipment if purchased and used for medical purposes (except if purchased by paid providers of medical services):

— bath chairs and seats;

— bath safety grab bars, handles, and rails;

— over-bed tables;

— prefabricated wheelchair ramps; and

— wheelchair trays.

(TSB-M-14(8)S)

"Medical equipment" defined.—The term "medical equipment" means machinery, apparatus and other devices (except prosthetic aids, hearing aids, eyeglasses and artificial devices) which are intended for use in the cure, mitigation, treatment or prevention of illnesses or diseases or the correction or alleviation of physical incapacity in human beings. (Reg. Sec. 528.4(e)(1))

To qualify for exemption as "medical equipment," the equipment must be primarily and customarily used for medical purposes and not be generally useful in the absence of illness, injury or physical incapacity. (Reg. Sec. 528.4(e)(2)) Examples of "medical equipment" include hospital beds, respirators, wheel chairs and orthodontic appliances.

"Medical supplies" defined.—"Medical supplies" are defined as supplies used in the cure, mitigation, treatment or prevention of illnesses or diseases or for the correction and alleviation of physical incapacity. Examples include colostomy bags, bandages, gauze, dressings and disposable hypodermic syringes and litmus paper used by diabetics. (Reg. Sec. 528.4(g)(1))

Component or replacement parts for medical equipment.—Component or replacement parts for exempt medical equipment are also exempt from tax. If a component part is clearly identified as a part of such equipment, the part may be purchased exempt from tax. If a component part is not clearly identified as a part for such equipment, the purchaser must pay sales tax at the time of purchase and file a claim for refund using Form AU-11, Application for Credit or Refund of Sales or Use Tax. (Reg. Sec. 528.4(e)(3)) (TSB-M-14(8)S)

Services performed upon exempt medical equipment.—Services of installing, maintaining, servicing, and repairing exempt medical equipment and component parts of medical equipment are exempt from tax unless performed for doctors and other paid providers of medical services. (Sec. 1115(g), Tax Law) (TSB-M-14(8)S)

Orthopedic or corrective shoes.—Shoes made to specifications prescribed by a podiatrist, orthopedist or other physician for the purpose of treating or preventing illness or disease or to correct physical incapacity are deemed to be "medical equipment" and are, therefore, tax-exempt. (Reg. Sec. 528.4(f)(1)) Accordingly, shoes made from a mold of a foot or shoes with special devices to straighten malformed bones are exempt.

Similarly, stock orthopedic shoes modified to the specifications of a podiatrist, orthopedist or other physician qualify for exemption. (Reg. Sec. 528.4(f)(5)) However, the charge for an ordinary shoe which is modified (by the insertion of a lift, wedge or arch support) to specifications prescribed by a podiatrist, orthopedist or other physician for medical purposes is taxable, although any reasonable separately stated charge for the modification is tax-exempt. (Reg. Sec. 528.4(f)(3))

The entire charge for ordinary shoes modified for more comfortable fit (e.g. heel pad inserted or insole added), improved styling or other similar purpose is taxable. The tax is also imposed upon any separately stated amount for modification. (Reg. Sec. 528.4(f)(4)) The tax likewise applies to shoes made to order for special fitting problems (such as narrow heels or extra large feet). (Reg. Sec. 528.4(f)(2))

• *Guide, hearing, and service dogs*

Sales or uses of any goods or services necessary for the acquisition, sustenance or maintenance of a guide dog, a hearing dog, or a service dog are exempt from sales and use taxes. The guide, hearing or service dog must be used by a person with a disability to compensate for an impairment to the person's sight, hearing or movement. Those eligible to claim this exemption are a person with a disability and an individual whose dependent is a person with a disability. People who have been given express authority by an eligible person to make purchases on the eligible person's behalf may also claim the exemption. (Sec. 1115(s), Tax Law) (TB-ST-245)

"Person with a disability" defined.—The term "person with a disability" means any person with a physical or medical impairment resulting from an anatomical, physiological, or neurological condition which prevents the exercise of a normal bodily function, or which is demonstrable by medically accepted clinical or laboratory diagnostic techniques. (TB-ST-245)

"Guide dog", "hearing dog" and "service dog" defined.—The terms "guide dog" and "hearing dog," respectively, refer to any dog that is trained and actually used to aid a person who is blind or has a hearing impairment. The terms also refer to any dog owned by a recognized training center located within New York during the period that it is being trained or bred for such purposes. (Sec. 108(9), Agriculture and Markets Law; Sec. 108(21), Agriculture and Markets Law) (TB-ST-245)

The term "service dog" is defined to mean any dog that is trained to and used to aid: a person with a physical impairment that is permanent and that severely limits a person's mobility, or a person who is unable to move about without the use of a wheelchair or without the aid of a prosthetic device. (TB-ST-245)

The purchase of a guide, hearing or service dog by or on behalf of a person with a disability, or by a person whose dependent is a person with a disability, is exempt from sales or compensating use tax if the dog is utilized to completely or partially replace the function of a missing body part, or the function of a permanently inoperative or permanently malfunctioning body part. In addition, purchases of goods or services for the guide, hearing or service dog are exempt from sales and compensating use taxes. (TSB-M-95(10)S) (TB-ST-245)

Exempt products: Items of tangible personal property that may be purchased exempt include:

— backpacks specifically designed for domestic dogs;

— beds, linen, blankets, pillows, cushions etc., specifically designed and manufactured for use by a domestic dog;

— dental care products specifically designed and manufactured for use on domestic dogs;

— deodorant sprays specifically designed and manufactured for use on a domestic dog;

— de-worming products designed for the treatment or prevention of worms (roundworms, tapeworms, hookworms, etc.);

— dog collars and leads;

— dog food, including dog biscuits and dog treats;

— dog harnesses (e.g., pulling harness used by a service dog to pull a wheelchair);

— dog leashes, including work leashes and exercise leashes;

— dog shampoos;

— dog waste disposal supplies and equipment (e.g., "pooper scoopers");

— ear care products specifically designed and manufactured for use on domestic dogs;

— ear treatments, anti-bacterial shampoos, sprays, and lotions, dry eye ointments, etc. specifically designed for use on domestic dogs;

— first aid kits designed for the care and treatment of domestic dogs;

— flea or tick collars, powders, sprays, or shampoos;

— grooming articles specifically designed and manufactured for use on domestic dogs, such as grooming brushes, rakes, combs, hair clippers, scissors, shears, and nail clippers;

— pharmaceutical supplies (e.g., non-prescription antibiotics, aspirin, non-prescription)

— prescription and nonprescription drugs and pharmaceuticals used to care for the dog;

— travel kennels, cages, crates and other carriers specifically designed and manufactured for use in transporting a domestic dog;

— vitamin supplements specifically designed and manufactured for use by domestic dogs; and

— water and food dishes designed for use by a domestic dog.

(TSB-M-95(10)S; TB-ST-245)

Exempt services: Services that may be purchased exempt include:

— boarding services;

— dental services;

— grooming and clipping services; and

— veterinarian services (note: veterinarian services are exempt for all animals)

(TSB-M-95(10)S) (TB-ST-245)

CCH PLANNING NOTE: *Claiming the exemption.*—To claim the exemption, use Form ST-860, *Exemption Certificate for Purchases Relating to Guide, Hearing and Service Dogs.* (*TSB-M-95(10)S*) The exemption must be claimed by a person with a disability, or by a person whose dependent is a person with a disability. Purchases made by third parties on behalf of a person with a disability qualify for the exemption; in such cases, Form ST-860 must be completed in the name of the person with a disability on whose behalf the purchases are made. The exemption certificate must be signed by the person making the purchase. When the purchaser is not the person with a disability, the purchaser must indicate his or her relationship (e.g., family member, shopping volunteer, etc.) to the person with the disability on whose behalf purchases are being made.

For discussions relating to the following, see the appropriate referenced paragraph:

Veterinary medicine, see ¶ 60-250 Agriculture.

Hospitals, see ¶ 60-580 Nonprofit Organizations, Private Schools, and Churches.

Beauty aids, see ¶ 60-390 Food and Grocery Items.

• *Medical marijuana*

The sale of medical marijuana is exempt from sales tax. Sales of related products purchased to administer medical marijuana are also exempt. While registered organizations will not be making any taxable sales, they must register as a vendor in order to issue and accept certain sales tax exemption certificates, including Form ST-120, Resale Certificate, and Form ST-121, Exempt Use Certificate. As a registered vendor, the organization will be required to Web File periodic sales and use tax returns. (TSB-M-16(1)M)

A registered organization may also be able to use certain exemption forms related to farming. These include: Form ST-125, Farmer's and Commercial Horse Boarding Operator's Exemption Certificate, and Form FT-1004, Certificate for Purchases of Non-Highway Diesel Motor Fuel or Residual Petroleum Product for Farmers and Commercial Horse Boarding Operations. (TSB-M-16(1)M)

Instead, a 7% excise tax is imposed on the gross receipts from the sale of medical marijuana by a registered organization to certified patients and designated caregivers. For a complete discussion, see ¶ 35-251 Medical Marijuana Tax and TSB-M-16(1)M.

• *Family planning*

Products sold to reduce the chance of pregnancy are not taxable. These products may be sold by prescription or over the counter. Examples of these items include: birth control pills, condoms, contraceptive creams, foams, jellies, or sponges, diaphragms, and vaginal suppositories. (TB-ST-193)

• *Feminine hygiene products*

Feminine hygiene products are exempt from state and local sales and use taxes. (Sec. 1115(a)(3-a), Tax Law) Feminine hygiene products include the following:

— sanitary napkins;

— tampons;

— panty liners;

— douches;

— feminine hygiene syringes; and

— vaginal creams, foams, ointments, jellies, powders, and sprays used for hygiene purposes.

(Sec. 1115(a)(3-a), Tax Law) (TSB-M-16(6)S)

• *Cosmetics and toiletries*

Cosmetic and toiletry products are used for cleansing, personal grooming, beautifying, or altering your appearance. These products are taxable even if they contain some medicinal ingredients. (TB-ST-193)

¶ 60-520

• *Insurance coverage*

The taxability of an item does not change when payment is made under medical insurance coverage, including: personal insurance, an employer-sponsored medical plan, Medicaid, or Medicare. Nontaxable items remain nontaxable regardless of the method of payment. Taxable items remain taxable even when paid for under insurance coverage. (TB-ST-193)

[¶60-560] Motor Fuels

The following paragraph discusses the taxability of motor fuel and diesel motor fuel, including alternative fuels. Aircraft and vessel fuels are also discussed.

For a discussion of the exemptions and refunds available for the purchase of different types of fuel (motor fuel, highway diesel motor fuel, and non-highway diesel motor fuel) used in production, see TB-ST-587.

For a discussion of home heating fuel, see ¶60-750 Utilities.

For a discussion of alternative fuel vehicles, see ¶60-570 Motor Vehicles.

• *Motor fuel*

Retail sales of motor fuel are generally subject to tax as "retail sales of tangible personal property". (Sec. 1101(b)(4)(ii), Tax Law; Sec. 1105(a), Tax Law; Reg. Sec. 561.1(f)) Similarly, the use of motor fuel is subject to the compensating use tax. (Sec. 1110, Tax Law) The retail vendor must collect the sales tax based on the actual selling price of the motor fuel, which price does not include the amount of prepaid state and local sales and use taxes required to be paid by distributors of motor fuel. (Sec. 1111(d), Tax Law; Reg. Sec. 561.1(c))

The sales tax on motor fuel is 8 cents per gallon outside the Metropolitan Commuter Transportation District (MCTD) and 8-3/4 cents per gallon within the MCTD. (Sec. 1111(m), Tax Law; Important Notice N-16-7) Counties and cities, including New York City, are allowed to change their percentage rate sales tax to a cents per gallon method. (TSB-M-06(8)S)

The state and local cents per gallon method applies only to qualified fuel. (Sec. 1111(m)(7), Tax Law) (TSB-M-06(8)S) Credit for prepaid sales tax paid on fuel that is not qualified fuel may be claimed on Schedule FR, Sales and Use Tax on Motor Fuel and Diesel Motor Fuel. (Important Notice N-07-17)

Although the sales are not reported on Schedule FR, the credit for the prepaid sales tax may be claimed in Step 6 of the schedule. If a taxpayer does not report sales of qualified fuel on Schedule FR, claiming the credit for the prepaid sales tax will result in a credit balance in box 18 of Schedule FR, Adjusted tax. Taxpayers should precede the credit entry in box 18 with a minus sign. (Important Notice N-07-17)

Sales of fuel that is not qualified fuel must continue to be reported on the appropriate jurisdiction line on Form ST-100, New York State and Local Quarterly Sales and Use Tax Return; Form ST-810, New York State and Local Quarterly Sales and Use Tax Return for Part-Quarterly Filers; and Form ST-101, New York State and Local Annual Sales and Use Tax Return. Examples of the types of sales reported in this manner include fuel sold for commercial heating purposes or sales by fixed base operators of aviation gasoline or kero-jet fuel for use in an aircraft. (Important Notice N-07-17)

Qualified fuel means motor fuel or diesel motor fuel that is (1) sold for use directly and exclusively in the engine of a motor vehicle; or (2) sold by a retail gas station (other than water-white kerosene sold exclusively for heating purposes in containers of no more than twenty gallons). (Sec. 1111(m)(7), Tax Law) (TSB-M-06(8)S)

Any vendor of fuels that is not a retail gas station must compute the sales tax due using the percentage rate method unless the purchaser gives the vendor, within 90 days of sale, a properly completed Form ST-121, Exempt Use Certificate, using Part III, Box T. If the vendor receives and accepts a properly completed ST-121, the vendor should treat the fuel as qualified fuel and should compute and collect tax using the cents per gallon method. (TSB-M-06(8)S)

If the purchaser actually uses the fuel for purposes other than in the engine of a motor vehicle, the purchaser is subject to any additional sales or use taxes due, based on the difference between the tax paid and the tax that would have been due if the fuel had not been treated as qualified fuel. (TSB-M-06(8)S) If the purchaser does not give the vendor a properly completed Form ST-121, the vendor should not treat the fuel as qualified fuel and should compute and collect tax using the percentage rate sales tax method. However, if the purchaser actually uses the fuel in the engine of a motor vehicle, the purchaser may claim a credit on its sales tax return or file a claim for a refund for any overpayment of sales tax for the portion of the fuel that is actually used directly and exclusively in the engine of a motor vehicle. (TSB-M-06(8)S)

For sales made on or after July 1, 2006, vendors must resume computing and collecting the state and, if applicable, the MCTD sales tax on motor fuel that is not qualified fuel using the percentage rate sales tax method. In addition, vendors must continue to compute and collect the local tax on this fuel using the percentage rate sales tax method. That is, the tax is computed on these sales by multiplying the taxable receipt by the combined state and local tax percentage rate in the jurisdiction where the sale occurred. (TSB-M-06(8)S)

Retail vendors of motor fuel are entitled to a refund or credit in the amount by which the prepaid tax exceeds the retail sales tax. (Reg. Sec. 561.1(d))

Exempt purchasers of motor fuel.—Retail sales of motor fuel to the following purchasers for their own use or consumption, however, are tax-exempt:

— the United States, its agencies and instrumentalities;

— New York State, its agencies, instrumentalities, public corporations (including those created pursuant to an agreement or compact with another state or Canada) and political subdivisions (including school districts);

— hospitals which qualify as exempt organizations;

— airlines purchasing kero-jet fuel for use in their own aircraft or for use in aircraft under their control;

— exempt Indian nations or tribes making purchases from a retail service station on a qualified reservation and individual members of exempt Indian nations or tribes making purchases from a retail service station on a qualified reservation where they reside;

— diplomatic missions and diplomatic personnel purchasing motor fuel with credit cards issued by oil companies; and

— purchases of motor fuel and diesel motor fuel by a fire company, fire department, or a voluntary ambulance service, for its own use and consumption for use in firefighting vehicles, apparatus or equipment, or emergency rescue or first aid response vehicles, apparatus or equipment, owned and operated by the company, department or service.

(Reg. Sec. 561.7(c))

"Motor fuel" defined.—The term "motor fuel" means gasoline, benzol, reformulated blend stock for oxygenate blending, conventional blend stock for oxygenate blending, E-85, fuel-grade ethanol that meets ASTM International active standards specifications D4806 or D4814, or other product suitable for use in operation of a motor vehicle engine. "Motor fuel" includes: gasoline, naptha, liquefied petroleum gas, compressed natural gas, propane gas or any other product or combination of products (except diesel motor fuel) which is suitable for use in the operation of a motor vehicle engine. Propane is not deemed to be motor fuel, for purposes of the sales tax, until pumped into the fuel tank of a motor vehicle for use in its operation. (Reg. Sec. 561.2(a)(1)) (TSB-M-11(8)S, TSB-M-11(5)M)

"Kero-jet fuel" defined.—"Kero-jet fuel" refers to a quality, highly refined kerosene product or derivative which meets kerosene-type jet fuel specifications and is primarily used for commercial turbojet and turboprop aircraft engines. (Reg. Sec. 561.2(a)(4))

Prepayment of tax by distributors of motor fuel.—Distributors are required to prepay New York State and local sales and use taxes on every gallon of motor fuel which they either:

— import or cause to be imported into New York state for use, distribution, storage or sale in the state;

— produce, refine, manufacture or compound in New York State; or

— sell in New York State (if not previously taxed prior to such sale).

(Sec. 1102(a)(1), Tax Law)

The prepaid tax does not apply where imposition of the tax is precluded by the U.S. Constitution or federal law or where the motor fuel is purchased by the U.S. or New York State, their agencies and instrumentalities or by a hospital classified as an exempt organization. Nor is the prepaid tax imposed upon kero-jet fuel when imported by an airline for use in its airplanes. (Sec. 1102(a)(1), Tax Law)

In addition, a distributor may import motor fuel into New York State without payment and pass-through of the prepaid sales tax, where the distributor (with prior approval of the Department of Taxation and Finance or of an Indian Nation or tribe, if applicable) sells and delivers the fuel to an exempt Indian nation or tribe, a qualified Indian consumer or a registered dealer. (Reg. Sec. 561.2(b)(2))

• *Diesel motor fuel*

Retail sales of diesel motor fuel are generally subject to tax as "retail sales of tangible personal property." (Sec. 1101(b)(4)(ii), Tax Law; Sec. 1105(a), Tax Law; Reg. Sec. 561.15) Similarly, the use of diesel motor fuel is subject to the compensating use tax. (Sec. 1111(d), Tax Law)

CCH COMMENT: Treatment of motor fuel revised.—The 2011-2012 budget package (Ch. 61 (S.B. 2811), Laws 2011) updated the manner in which diesel motor fuel is classified for purposes of the sales and use taxes, among other taxes, imposed on diesel motor fuel. Specifically, the bill changes the statutory definitions related to the taxation of diesel motor fuel to be consistent with federal laws, effective September 1, 2011. Currently, the taxation of diesel motor fuel is based upon whether the diesel motor fuel is "enhanced." The bill removes the concept of "enhancement" from the Tax Law, and amends the Tax Law to incorporate federal dyeing rules.

The bill also creates two categories of diesel motor fuel: non-highway diesel motor fuel and highway diesel motor fuel. Non-highway diesel motor fuel is defined as any diesel motor fuel that is designated for use other than on a public highway (except for the use of the public highway by farmers to reach adjacent lands) and dyed in accordance with the federal regulation for dyeing diesel motor fuel. Highway diesel motor fuel is defined as any diesel motor fuel that is not non-highway diesel motor fuel. Highway diesel motor fuel is subject to the prepaid sales tax when it is first sold in New York. Non-highway diesel motor fuel is exempt from the prepaid sales tax. (TSB-M-11(11)S)

The bill also amends the definition of motor fuel to include E85 and fuel grade ethanol. The definition of E85 is amended to describe it as a fuel blend consisting of ethanol and motor fuel that meets the American Society for Testing and Materials (ASTM) International active standard D5798 for fuel ethanol. Currently, the law defines E85 as consisting of 85% ethanol and the remainder of which is motor fuel. As a result of these changes, the sales and use tax law, in addition to other Tax Law articles, is amended to change the references to "automotive fuel" to "petroleum product" to avoid confusion with the use of that term as defined in Article 12-A and 13-A and in order to avoid the unintended consequence of changing the sales tax base. Article 37, related to crimes and other offenses as well as seizures and forfeitures, is amended to conform to the definitional changes made to the diesel fuel tax structure and to add a seizure provision for diesel motor fuel that would parallel the existing seizure provisions that already exist for motor fuel. Conforming changes are made to sections of the Criminal Procedures Law that were necessitated by the definitional changes made in Article 28. Also, various provisions of the Tax Law and the New York City Administrative Code are repealed because they are either outdated or have expired. (TSB-M-11(11)S; TSB-M-11(8)S; TSB-M-11(9)S)

The 2012-2013 budget package (Ch. 59 (A.B. 9059)), Laws 2012 makes technical amendments to the classification of diesel motor fuel. For instance, the prepaid sales tax on diesel motor fuel will not apply to the sale of previously untaxed qualified biodiesel to a person registered under Article 12-A as a distributor of diesel motor fuel other than (1) a retail sale to such person or (2) a sale to such person that involves a delivery at a filling station or into a repository that is equipped with a hose or other apparatus by which such qualified biodiesel can be dispensed into the fuel tank of a motor vehicle. Also, the bill deletes crude oil from the definition of "diesel motor fuel."

The Department of Taxation and Finance has also issued a memorandum discussing changes in the taxation and classification of diesel motor fuel beginning September 1, 2011, as a result of the budget bill (see TSB-M-11(11)S.) The Department has also issued a memorandum that explains how exemptions and refund (credit) provisions apply to sales of kerosene. (see TSB-M-11(12)M, TSB-M-11(18)S)

The sales tax on diesel motor fuel is 8 cents per gallon outside the Metropolitan Commuter Transportation District (MCTD) and 8-3/4 cents per gallon within the MCTD. (Sec. 1111(m), Tax Law; Important Notice N-16-7) Counties and cities, including New York City, are allowed to change their percentage rate sales tax to a cents per gallon method. (TSB-M-06(8)S)

Credit for prepaid sales tax paid on fuel that is not qualified fuel may be claimed on Schedule FR, Sales and Use Tax on Motor Fuel and Diesel Motor Fuel. (Important Notice N-07-17)

Although the sales are not reported on Schedule FR, the credit for the prepaid sales tax may be claimed in Step 6 of the schedule. If a taxpayer does not report sales of qualified fuel on Schedule FR, claiming the credit for the prepaid sales tax will result in a credit balance in box 18 of Schedule FR, Adjusted tax. Taxpayers should precede the credit entry in box 18 with a minus sign. (Important Notice N-07-17)

Sales of fuel that is not qualified fuel must continue to be reported on the appropriate jurisdiction line on Form ST-100, New York State and Local Quarterly Sales and Use Tax Return; Form ST-810, New York State and Local Quarterly Sales and Use Tax Return for Part-Quarterly Filers; and Form ST-101, New York State and Local Annual Sales and Use Tax Return. Examples of the types of sales reported in this manner include fuel sold for commercial heating purposes or sales by fixed base operators of aviation gasoline or kero-jet fuel for use in an aircraft. (Important Notice N-07-17)

Qualified fuel means motor fuel or diesel motor fuel that is (1) sold for use directly and exclusively in the engine of a motor vehicle; or (2) sold by a retail gas station (other than water-white kerosene sold exclusively for heating purposes in containers of no more than twenty gallons). (Sec. 1111(m), Tax Law) (TSB-M-06(8)S)

Any vendor of fuels that is not a retail gas station must compute the sales tax due using the percentage rate method unless the purchaser gives the vendor, within 90 days of sale, a properly completed Form ST-121, Exempt Use Certificate, using Part III, Box T. If the vendor receives and accepts a properly completed ST-121, the vendor should treat the fuel as qualified fuel and should compute and collect tax using the cents per gallon method. (TSB-M-06(8)S)

If the purchaser actually uses the fuel for purposes other than in the engine of a motor vehicle, the purchaser is subject to any additional sales or use taxes due, based on the difference between the tax paid and the tax that would have been due if the fuel had not been treated as qualified fuel. (TSB-M-06(8)S) If the purchaser does not give the vendor a properly completed Form ST-121, the vendor should not treat the fuel as qualified fuel and should compute and collect tax using the percentage rate sales tax method. However, if the purchaser actually uses the fuel in the engine of a motor vehicle, the purchaser may claim a credit on its sales tax return or file a claim for a refund for any overpayment of sales tax for the portion of the fuel that is actually used directly and exclusively in the engine of a motor vehicle. (TSB-M-06(8)S)

For sales made on or after July 1, 2006, vendors must resume computing and collecting the state and, if applicable, the MCTD sales tax on diesel motor fuel that is not qualified fuel using the percentage rate sales tax method. In addition, vendors must continue to compute and collect the local tax on this fuel using the percentage rate sales tax method. That is, the tax is computed on these sales by multiplying the taxable receipt by the combined state and local tax percentage rate in the jurisdiction where the sale occurred. (TSB-M-06(8)S)

Exempt purchasers of diesel motor fuel.—An exemption from tax is provided, however, for the following purchases:

— purchases of diesel motor fuel, for its own use or consumption, by the U.S., New York State, their agencies and instrumentalities;

— purchases of diesel motor fuel, for its own use or consumption, by a hospital which qualifies as an exempt organization; and

— purchases of diesel motor fuel, for its own heating use and consumption, by an organization organized and operated exclusively for religious, charitable, scientific, testing for public safety, literary or educational purposes or to foster certain national or international amateur sports competitions or for the prevention of cruelty to children or animals.

(Sec. 1116(b)(5), Tax Law)

Fuel used in farm production.—The exemption also applies to sales and uses of non-highway diesel motor fuel for use or consumption either in the production for sale of tangible personal property by farming or in a commercial horse boarding operation, or in both, but only if all of such fuel is consumed other than on the public highways of New York (except for the use of the public highways to reach adjacent farmlands or adjacent lands used in a commercial horse boarding operation, or both). (Sec. 1115(j), Tax Law) (TSB-M-00(8)S). See ¶ 60-250 Agriculture and ¶ 60-750 Utilities.

"Diesel motor fuel" defined.—The term "diesel motor fuel" means No. 1 diesel fuel, No. 2 diesel fuel, biodiesel, kerosene, fuel oil, or other middle distillate. It also includes motor fuel suitable for operating a diesel engine (excluding any product specifically designated "No. 4 diesel fuel" and not suitable for operating a motor vehicle engine). (Reg. Sec. 561.2(a)(2)) (TSB-M-11(11)S)

Prepayment of tax by distributors or diesel motor fuel.—Distributors are required to prepay New York state and local sales and use taxes based upon the number of gallons of diesel fuel sold or used in the State of New York. If not already imposed, the tax is levied when the fuel is delivered to a retail service station.

The prepaid tax does not apply where imposition of the tax is precluded by the U.S. Constitution or federal law. Nor is the prepaid tax applicable to the sale of previously untaxed diesel fuel, which is not enhanced, to registered distributors, except for:

(1) sales involving delivery at a filling station or into a repository equipped with a hose or other apparatus to dispense the fuel into the fuel tank of a motor vehicle; and

(2) sales to or deliveries at a filling station or other retail vendor of water-white kerosene sold exclusively for heating purposes in containers of 20 gallons or less.

Nonroad, locomotive, and marine diesel fuel.—The federal Environmental Protection Agency (EPA) has been phasing in regulations regarding the standards, uses and labeling for nonroad, locomotive, and marine diesel fuel (NRLM), which are discussed in a memorandum issued by the Department of Taxation and Finance (TSB-M-07(2)M, TSB-M-07(4)S). Since June 1, 2007, EPA regulations have limited the sulfur content of NRLM diesel fuel to no greater than 500 parts per million (ppm). EPA regulations also provide that distributors must accurately and clearly designate this fuel as 500 ppm sulfur NRLM diesel fuel. (TSB-M-07(2)M, TSB-M-07(4)S)

The Department of Taxation and Finance has determined that diesel fuel designated as 500 ppm sulfur NRLM diesel fuel or similar designations (e.g., 500 ppm dyed low-sulfur nonroad diesel fuel) is unenhanced diesel motor fuel for sales tax purposes. (TSB-M-07(2)M, TSB-M-07(4)S; TSB-M-08(4)M, TSB-M-08(7)S) Accordingly, provided such fuel is not delivered to a filling station or into a storage tank or other respository equipped with a nozzle or similar apparatus capable of dispensing the fuel into a motor vehicle tank, the following rules apply:

— a registered distributor may sell 500 ppm sulfur NRLM diesel fuel or other unenhanced diesel motor fuel to other registered distributors and retailers of heating oil only (ROHOs) without passing through the prepaid sales tax. A Form FT-1001, the exemption certificate for diesel motor fuel interdistributor transactions, must be received from the purchaser;

— a registered distributor or ROHO may sell 500 ppm sulfur NRLM diesel fuel or other unenhanced diesel motor fuel for use directly and exclusively in the production, for sale, of tangible personal property by manufacturing, processing, or assembly exempt from sales tax. A Form FT-1012, the manufacturing certification for diesel motor fuel and residual petroleum product, must be received from the purchaser;

¶60-560

— a registered distributor or ROHO may sell 500 ppm sulfur NRLM diesel fuel or other unenhanced diesel motor fuel for use directly and exclusively in the production, for sale, of tangible personal property by refining, mining, or extracting exempt from sales tax. A Form FT-1020, the exemption certificate for certain taxes imposed on diesel motor fuel and propane, must be received from the purchaser;

— a registered distributor or ROHO may sell 500 ppm sulfur NRLM diesel fuel or other unenhanced diesel motor fuel for use directly and exclusively in the production, for sale, of gas, electricity, refrigeration, or steam exempt from sales tax. A Form FT- 1020, the exemption certificate for certain taxes imposed on diesel motor fuel and propane, must be received from the purchaser; and

— a registered distributor or ROHO may sell 500 ppm sulfur NRLM diesel fuel or other unenhanced diesel motor fuel to exempt organizations qualified under Tax Law § 1116(a)(4) for nonresidential heating purposes exempt from sales tax. A Form FT-1021-A, the certification for purchases of unenhanced diesel motor fuel, residual petroleum product, or dyed diesel motor fuel, by certain exempt organizations, must be received from the purchaser.

(TSB-M-07(2)M, TSB-M-07(4)S)

The Department issued an additional memorandum to clarify that NRLM diesel fuel will be treated as unenhanced diesel motor fuel when both of the following criteria are met: (1) the diesel fuel has a sulfuer content greater than 15 ppm but not greater than 500 ppm; and (2) the diesel fuel is designated as 500 ppm sulfur NRLM or has a similar designation. Diesel fuel with a sulfur content of 15 ppm or less is enhanced diesel motor fuel for petroleum business, motor fuel, and sales tax purposes. (TSB-M-08(4)M, TSB-M-08(7)S)

Effective August 1, 2010, the EPA regulations further reduced the maximum sulfur content of nonroad (NR) diesel fuel to 15 ppm. The maximum sulfur content for locomotive and marine (LM) diesel fuel (currently 500 ppm) is not required to meet the 15 ppm standard until June 1, 2012. The department has issued a memorandum explaining how NRLM diesel motor fuel that meets the 15 ppm (maximum) sulfur standard is treated for sales tax purposes. (see TSM-10(13)M, TSB-M-10(17)S) Since NRLM diesel fuel meeting the 15 ppm (maximum) sulfur standard is enhanced diesel fuel, it is not included in the definitions of manufacturing gallonage, commercial gallonge, or nonautomotive-type diesel motor fuel. Therefore, the following limitations apply:

— the fuel does not qualify for the manufacturing exemption or the commercial gallonage rate. Rather, the full automotive diesel motor fuel rate now applies.

— the fuel does not qualify for the Article 13-A utility credit or reimbursement.

— a registered distributor may not sell the fuel to other registered distributors and ROHOs without passing through the excise tax, petroleum business tax, and prepaid sales tax.

— ROHOs are not permitted to sell the fuel. A ROHO that wants to sell this fuel must first become registered as a distributor of diesel motor fuel.

— registered distributors and ROHOs may no longer accept certain certification forms (Forms FT-1001, FT-1012, and FT-1020) for the fuel. Form FT-1021-A may only be accepted for sales of dyed NRLM diesel fuel meeting the 15 ppm (maximum) sulfur standard and for sales of other dyed diesel motor fuel when box 2, Dyed diesel motor fuel, is checked.

— registered distributors may not report as exempt, or partially exempt, on Form PT-102 or applicable schedules, NRLM diesel fuel meeting the 15 ppm (maximum) sulfur standard or other enhanced diesel motor fuel: (1) sold or used in manufacturing, (2) sold to registered diesel motor fuel distributors (except sales of dyed diesel motor fuel to holders of a direct pay permit), (3) sold for use and consumption directly and exclusively in the production of tangible personal property for sale by refining, extracting, and mining, or (4) sold for use and consumption in the production of gas, electricity, (except sales to rate-regulated electric corporations) refrigeration, or steam, for sale.

(TSM-10(13)M, TSB-M-10(17)S)

Refund/reimbusement: Purchasers of NRLM diesel fuel meeting the 15 ppm (maximum) sulfur standard or other enhanced diesel motor fuel who use or consume the fuel directly and exclusively in the production of tangible personal property, gas, electricity, refrigeration or steam, for sale, by manufacturing, processing, assembling, generating, refining, mining or extracting may apply for a refund of the State and local sales taxes under Article 28 and 29 of the Tax Law on Form FT- 500, Application for Refund of Sales Tax Paid on Automotive Fuels. (TSM-10(13)M, TSB-M-10(17)S)

Exemptions and refunds related to kerosene.—The Department of Taxation and Finance has issued a memorandum discussing how sales and use tax exemption and refund (credit) provisions apply to sales of kerosene. The memorandum also discusses the exemptions and refunds for kerosene applicable to the excise tax and petroleum business tax. (TSB-M-11(12)M, TSB-M-11(18)S)

Ultra-low sulfur kerosene.—The Department of Taxation and Finance has also determined that all of the exemptions and provisions pertaining to unenhanced diesel motor fuel are allowed for dyed ultra-low sulfur kerosene for sales tax purposes, as well as excise and petroleum business taxes. "Ultra-low kerosene" means kerosene meeting the federal Environmental Protection Agency standard of 15 parts per million (maximum) sulfur content. (TSB-M-11(2)M, TSB-M-11(2)S)

No exemption is allowed if the dyed ultra-low sulfur kerosene is delivered to a filling station or into a storage tank or other repository equipped with a nozzle or similar apparatus capable of dispensing the fuel into the tank of a motor vehicle. However, the delivery of water-white kerosene at a filling station or other retail vendor for resale exclusively as heating fuel in containers of no more than 20 gallons is exempt. (TSB-M-11(2)M, TSB-M-11(2)S)

Ultra-low sulfur kerosene (whether it is dyed or not) is subject to tax as enhanced diesel motor fuel if:

— it is combined or blended with any other substance and the resulting product constitutes diesel motor fuel;

— it is designated as No. 1 diesel fuel, No. 2 diesel fuel or any similar designation indicating that it is to be used or sold for use in a motor vehicle; or

— it is dispensed into the fuel tank of a motor vehicle.

(TSB-M-11(2)M, TSB-M-11(2)S)

• *Motor fuel and diesel motor fuel used in production*

The New York Department of Taxation and Finance has issued a bulletin that describes the sales tax exemptions and refunds available for the purchase of different types of fuel (motor fuel, highway diesel motor fuel, and non-highway diesel motor fuel) used in production. (TB-ST-587) To qualify for the exemption or refund, the fuel must be used directly and exclusively (100%) in the production phase. To qualify as being used directly in production, fuel must be used or consumed during the production phase to:

— operate exempt production machinery or equipment;

— create conditions necessary for production; or

— perform an actual part of the production process.

(TB-ST-587)

Exempt production machinery or equipment is machinery or equipment that:

— acts upon or changes material to form the product to be sold;

— has an active and necessary role in the production of the product;

— is used in handling, storage, or conveying materials or product produced through the production line; or

— is used to package the product for sale.

(TB-ST-587)

Fuel used in the administration or distribution phases does not qualify for the exemption. Therefore, fuel does not qualify for the exemption if it is used or consumed in:

— the lighting of buildings;

— the heating and cooling of buildings;

— the preparation of food and drink subject to tax imposed by Tax Law § 1105(d); or

— the storage of tangible personal property.

(TB-ST-587)

Motor fuel and highway diesel motor fuel.—Motor fuel and highway diesel motor fuel cannot be purchased without the payment of sales tax. However, the sales tax paid on fuel used directly and exclusively in production is eligible for a refund using Form FT-500, Application for Refund of Sales Tax Paid on Petroleum Products. Motor fuel includes: gasoline; compressed natural gas (CNG); liquefied natural gas (LNG); and liquefied petroleum gas (LPG). Highway diesel motor fuel includes any diesel motor fuel that is not non-highway diesel motor fuel. (TB-ST-587)

Non-highway diesel motor fuel.—Non-highway diesel motor fuel (includes dyed diesel motor fuel that is designated for use other than on a public highway) that will be used directly and exclusively in production can be purchased without paying sales tax by using either: Form FT-1012, Manufacturing Certification for Non-Highway Diesel Motor Fuel and Residual Petroleum Product, or Form FT-1020, Exemption Certificate for Certain Taxes Imposed on Diesel Motor Fuel and Propane. In order to qualify for the exemption, non-highway diesel motor fuel cannot be delivered into a storage tank equipped to dispense fuel into the fuel tank of a motor vehicle, or otherwise used on the highways of this state. (TB-ST-587)

Fuel used to produce gas, electricity, refrigeration, and steam for sale.—Fuel used to produce gas, electricity, refrigeration, and steam for sale is exempt from the New York state sales and use taxes and from local taxes outside New York City. However, the fuel is subject to New York City's local sales tax rate when used or consumed in New York City. (TB-ST-587)

Farm production.—The production exemption available for farm production is more expansive than the general production exemption. Fuel only has to be used predominantly (more than 50% of the time) - and not directly - in farm production to qualify for the exemption. (TB-ST-587)

• *Alternative fuels*

The following types of alternative fuels are fully exempt from the state cents-per-gallon sales tax and the local cents-per-gallon or percentage rate sales taxes, provided they are used or consumed directly and exclusively in motor vehicle engines:

— E85 (a fuel blend consisting of ethanol and motor fuel that meets the American Society for Testing and Materials (ASTM) International active standard D5798 for fuel ethanol);

— Compressed natural gas (CNG) (fuel composed primarily of methanol suitable for motor fuel use);

— Purchase and use of natural gas that will be converted into CNG, for use or for sale for use or consumption directly and exclusively in the engine of a motor vehicle; and

— Hydrogen (fuel composed primarily of molecular hydrogen suitable for motor vehicle use).

(Sec. 1115(a)(42), Tax Law) (TSB-M-13(3)S; TSB-M-06(10)S)

These exemptions are deemed repealed on September 1, 2021. (TSB-M-16(4)S)

To claim the exemption for the purchase and use of natural gas that will be converted into CNG, for use or for sale for use or consumption directly and exclusively in the engine of a motor vehicle, the purchaser must provide the vendor with a properly completed Form ST-121, Exempt Use Certificate, using Part 3, Box U. If a portion of the natural gas purchased is used for a non-exempt purpose (e.g., a portion of the natural gas is used for nonresidential heating purposes), the amount paid that is attributable to the portion of the natural gas used for the non-exempt purpose must be reported as a purchase subject to use tax on the purchaser's sales and use tax return (or, if applicable, on Schedule B, Taxes on Utilities and Heating Fuels). If the purchaser does not give the vendor a properly completed Form ST-121 or other exemption certificate, the vendor should compute and collect the state and local sales from the purchaser on the selling price of the natural gas. However, if the purchaser ultimately converts all or a portion of the natural gas purchased into CNG for use or consumption directly and exclusively in the engine of a motor vehicle, the purchaser may file a claim for a refund or credit using Form AU-11, Application for Credit or Refund of Sales or Use Tax, for the sales tax that was paid that is attributable to the portion of the natural gas used for this exempt purpose. (TSB-M-13(3)S)

For various definitions related to the exemptions and reductions for alternative fuels, see TSB-M-06(10)S.

In addition, a partial (20%) exemption exists for qualified B20 fuel so that the sales and use tax is imposed at 80% of the cents per gallon rate. (Sec. 1111(n), Tax Law) (TSB-M-06(10)S) Accordingly, the state cents-per-gallon rate for qualified B20 sold or used outside the Metropolitan Commuter Transportation District (MCTD) is 6¢ per gallon. In the MCTD, the state tax is 6.6¢ per gallon. (TSB-M-06(10)S; TSB-M-11(8)S; TSB-M-11(9)S)

If a county or city imposes is local tax on qualified fuel using the cents-per-gallon method, the law provides that its cents-per-gallon rate on the sale or use of qualified B20 in the locality is 80% of the rate that applies to qualified fuel (the regular rate). If a county or city currently imposes its local sales tax on qualified fuel using the percentage method and does not make the cents per gallon election, the local sales taxes are determined by multiplying 80% of the taxable receipts (or in the case of use tax, 80% of the consideration) by the percentage rate for the locality. (Sec. 1111(n), Tax Law) (TSB-M-06(10)S)

"B20" means a mixture consisting by volume of 20% biodiesel and 80% diesel motor fuel. (Sec. 282(22), Tax Law) For additional definitions related to the exemptions and reductions for alternative fuels, see TSB-M-06(10)S.

This exemption is deemed repealed on September 1, 2021. (TSB-M-16(4)S; TSB-M-06(10)S; TSB-M-11(13)S; TSB-M-12(10)S)

Special rules for vendors who are not retail gas stations.—Sales of qualified CNG, hydrogen and E85 fuel by vendors other than retail gas stations where such fuel is used directly and exclusively in the engine of a motor vehicle (e.g., such fuel sold by a distributor to a bulk purchaser who will use the fuel exclusively in its fleet of rental cars) are eligible for the new exemptions for CNG, hydrogen, and E85 fuels or the reduced cents-per-gallon rate or taxable receipt on qualified B20 as described above. (TSB-M-06(10)S) However, any vendor that is not a retail gas station must compute and collect the sales taxes on such fuel on the total taxable receipt and at the regular applicable percentage rate of state and local sales taxes, unless the purchaser gives the vendor, within 90 days of sale, a properly completed Form ST-121, Exempt Use Certificate, using Part III, Box U. For this purpose, purchasers of motor fuel or diesel motor fuel who are not required to have a Certificate of Authority are not required to list a Certificate of Authority number on Form ST-121. (TSB-M-06(10)S)

• *Local tax rates*

Local sales taxes imposed on motor fuel and diesel motor fuel are calculated using form New York Form ST-100.10, Quarterly Schedule FR. For a list of applicable combined state and local tax rates, see ¶61-735 Local Rates.

Localities are allowed to change their method of computing the local tax to a cents per gallon rate method. (TSB-M-06(8)S) Localities that change to a cents per gallon method may revert to a percentage rate method for that fuel on the first day of a subsequent sales tax quarter. In addition, localities that do not elect the cents per gallon method are allowed to change to a cents per gallon method beginning on the first day of a subsequent sales tax quarter. (TSB-M-06(8)S)

For the local sales tax collection charts for qualified motor fuel or highway diesel motor fuel sold at retail, see Publication 873The charts show the amount of the local sales tax component in any given pump price of a gallon of qualified motor fuel or highway diesel motor fuel. They are to be used to verify the sales tax due, not to establish pump prices. Also, this publication should be used only to compute the local sales tax due in jurisdictions that continue to impose and compute their sales tax on qualified motor fuel or highway diesel motor fuel using a percentage sales tax rate. This method does not apply in those localities that have changed to a cents-per-gallon method of computing the local sales tax due. The publication contains charts for the local sales tax components for jurisdictions inside and outside the Metropolitan Commuter Transportation District (MCTD). The publication also contains instructions for computing gross sales, taxable sales and self-use, and sales tax due. For the local sales and use tax rates on qualified motor fuel, diesel motor fuel, and B20 biodiesel, see Publication 718-F.

Fuel used in commercial and general aviation aircraft.—All retail sales of fuel for use in commercial aircraft or general aviation aircraft are exempt from all local sales taxes. However, such fuel remains subject to the state sales tax and the sales tax imposed in the Metropolitan Commuter Transportation District. Retailers must collect the state sales tax and the sales tax imposed in the MCTD and report those sales on either the New York State only or the New York State/MCTD line when filing their periodic sales and use tax returns. (Sec. 1210(a)(1)(i), Tax Law) (TSB-M-17(2)M, (7)S; N-17-17)

• *Price reductions*

Distributors of automotive fuel are required to reduce the price they charge their customers for automotive fuel by any reductions in the prepaid sales taxes paid by the distributor. (TSB-M-06(8)S) Likewise, retail vendors are required to reduce the price they charge their customers for automotive fuel to reflect the lower sales tax as a result of the new cents-per-gallon computation method. A penalty of up to $5,000 per day for each violation may be imposed if a seller or distributor is found to be in violation of the price reduction requirements. (TSB-M-06(8)S)

• *Fuel sold to airline for use in airplanes*

Fuel sold to an airline for use in its airplanes is tax-exempt. (Sec. 1115(a)(9), Tax Law)

For definition of "airline," see Reg. Sec. 528.10(b).

The taxability of fueling services furnished to an airline for use in its airplanes is dependent upon when title to the fuel vests in the airline. (Reg. Sec. 528.10(c)(1)) The charge for defueling an airplane is a taxable service to the airline as a service to tangible personal property. (Reg. Sec. 528.10(c)(2))

Sales and uses of kero-jet fuel are exempt, including prepayment of the sales tax on motor and diesel motor fuels. (Sec. 1115(j), Tax Law)

• *Fuel used by commercial vessels engaged in interstate commerce*

An exemption is provided for fuel used by commercial vessels primarily engaged in interstate or foreign commerce. (Sec. 1115(a)(8), Tax Law) See ¶60-740 Transportation.

• *Fuel used by commercial fishing vessels*

Fuel used by commercial fishing vessels which are engaged directly and predominantly in the harvesting of fish for sale is exempt from tax. For purposes of the exemption, the term "fishing vessel" does not include any vessel used predominantly for sport fishing purposes. (Sec. 1115(a)(24), Tax Law) See also Agriculture at ¶60-250 and Utilities at ¶60-750.

[¶60-570] Motor Vehicles

Sales of motor vehicles are generally taxable as sales of tangible personal property. (Sec. 1105(a), Tax Law) However, there are certain transactions involving motor vehicles that are tax-exempt, which are discussed below.

Any allowance or credit for a motor vehicle which a vendor accepts in part payment on the purchase of a new motor vehicle and which vehicle is intended for resale by such vendor is to be excluded when arriving at the receipt subject to tax. (Sec. 1101(b)(3), Tax Law)

The taking of a motor vehicle by an insurance company following an accident as a result of which such vehicle is declared a total loss is not considered a taxable "sale". However, the purchase of another vehicle by the owner of the damaged vehicle with the proceeds of the insurance is deemed to be a taxable "retail sale." (Reg. Sec. 526.7(a)(5))

Banks and car rental agencies which sell repossessed motor vehicles qualify as "vendors" of such vehicles for sales tax purposes. As "vendors," these banks and car rental agencies are required to collect the appropriate tax at the time a sale takes place, unless they accept a properly completed exemption document. (TSB-M-80(11)S)

The Department of Taxation and Finance has issued a guide to sales tax for automobile dealers. The publication provides a general explanation of sales tax, and includes information about sales tax registration and record keeping requirements. It also explains which sales and services are subject to tax; how to apply sales tax to lease or rental transactions; general use tax rules for such topics as demonstrators, mixed-use, and loaner vehicles; how sales tax applies to sales and purchases of parking, garaging, and storage; how to determine the correct tax rate; dealer purchases and exempt sales; sales to exempt organizations; and the lemon law. In addition, the appendix includes definitions; record keeping and return information; and general information about the sale, transfer, or assignment of business assets. For details, see Publication 838.

See ¶ 60-740 Transportation.

• *Prepayment of tax*

Motor vehicle registration.—New registration certificates for motor vehicles, trailers, snowmobiles and all terrain vehicles will only be issued by the Commissioner of Motor Vehicles upon the furnishing of acceptable proof that the sales or use tax has been paid or that no tax is due. (Sec. 1132(f), Tax Law)

The Department of Taxation and Finance requires purchasers of a motor vehicle obtained through a private (non-dealer) transaction to present a Sales Tax Clearance Certificate to the Department of Motor Vehicles at the time of registration and to pay the tax due. (TSB-M-80(13)S) A list of generally encountered transactions, the clearance certificates necessary for registration and their form numbers is provided in TSB-M-80(13)S.

• *Exemptions*

Sales of fuel to government entities.—Credit card issuers and fuel distributors are allowed to apply for refunds or credits of state and local sales taxes on motor fuel and diesel motor fuel sold to exempt government entities when certain criteria are met. (Sec. 301-m, Tax Law; Sec. 1139, Tax Law) (TSB-M-08(12)S and TSB-M-08(9)M) For additional information, including the required criteria, see ¶ 60-580 Nonprofit Organizations, Private Schools, and Churches.

Motor vehicles sold between close family members.—An exemption is provided for motor vehicles sold between spouses or from parent to child or from child to parent, unless the vendor is a dealer. (Sec. 1115(a)(14), Tax Law; Reg. Sec. 528.15(b)(1))

The term "motor vehicles," for purposes of the exemption, is defined in accordance with Sec. 125, Vehicle and Traffic Law. Trailers are not considered to be "motor vehicles". The term does include every vehicle operated or driven upon a public highway which is propelled by power other than muscular power, except for snowmobiles, electrically driven wheelchairs and vehicles which run only upon rails or tracks. (Reg. Sec. 528.15(b)(1))

The term "dealer," as defined in Sec. 415 of the Vehicle and Traffic Law, refers to a person engaged in the business of dealing in motor vehicles, motorcycles or trailers (other than mobile home trailers) at retail or wholesale. Any person who obtains motor vehicles for the purposes of resale and offers for sale more that five such vehicles in a calendar year or displays at least three such vehicles in a calendar month on premises that the person owns or controls is regarded as a "dealer". (Reg. Sec. 528.15(b)(2))

> **CCH EXAMPLE:** *Parent and child.*—A parent purchases an automobile for his child's use. Title is in the parent's name. A year later, the child assumes payment of the note, and title is transferred to him. A sales tax would ordinarily

be due on the transfer of a car in exchange for the assumption of liabilities; but as this is a transaction between a parent and a child, the exemption applies. (Reg. Sec. 528.15(b)(2))

Motor vehicles sold to certain nonresidents.—Sales of motor vehicles to certain nonresidents are not taxable, despite the purchaser's taking of physical possession within New York State. (Sec. 1117(a), Tax Law) For the exemption to apply, the purchaser must, at the time of taking delivery:

- be a nonresident of New York;

- have no permanent place of abode in New York; and

- not be engaged in carrying on any employment, trade, business or profession in New York in which the motor vehicle will be used in the state.

(Sec. 1117(a), Tax Law)

Prior to taking delivery, the purchaser is required to furnish the vendor with an affidavit, statement or such additional evidence (documentary or otherwise) as the Commissioner of Taxation and Finance may require. (Sec. 1117(a), Tax Law)

A vendor is relieved of liability for failure to collect the tax due where the vendor, prior to making delivery, obtains the required affidavit, statement or other additional evidence and keeps it available for inspection by the Commissioner of Taxation and Finance. The vendor must not have known the evidence to be false prior to making physical delivery of the motor vehicle. (Sec. 1117(b), Tax Law)

The exemption applies only where (1) the vendor does not issue a temporary certificate of registration pursuant to Sec. 420(7), Vehicle and Traffic Law, or temporary registration pursuant to Sec. 420-a, Vehicle and Traffic Law, or similar certificate or registration, to the purchaser and (2) the purchaser does not register the vehicle in New York prior to registering it in another state or jurisdiction. (Sec. 1117(a)(2), Tax Law)

- *Long-term motor vehicle leases*

Accelerated sales tax payment provisions apply to long-term leases of motor vehicles having a gross vehicle weight of 10,000 pound or less. (Sec. 1111(i), Tax Law) In general, all receipts due or consideration given, or contracted to be given, for the leased motor vehicle for the entire period of the lease (including any option to renew or similar provision) are subject to sales tax at the inception of the lease, even if the payments are not required to be made at that time. The total sales tax due must be paid by and collected from the lessee on the date the first lease payment is due or the date the vehicle is registered with the New York Department of Motor Vehicle (DMV), whichever is earlier. (Sec. 1111(i), Tax Law; Publication 839)

For a guide that explains the rules for computing state and local sales and use taxes on long-term motor vehicle leases, see Publication 839.

Computing the tax.—The sum of the following payments, fees, and charges due from the lessee is subject to sales tax:

- any down payment, up-front payment, or due-on-signing payment;

- the total of the monthly (or other periodic) payments due for the entire term of the lease, including any option to renew (special rules apply to leases vehicles that are primarily used in a business or trade). Renewal options are included in the computation of tax, whether or not they are exercised or are for a period of one year or more, individually or cumulatively. (Reg. Sec. 527.15)

- acquisition fees, bank fees, certain documentation fees, disposition fees, warranty fees, such as extended service programs and maintenance programs, transportation and destination charges, advertising charges, dealer preparation fees, and any other fees or charges that are charged at the start of the lease period, if the fee or charge is not already included as part of the monthly payment under the lease; and

• the amount of any rebate or incentive provided or reimbursed by the manufacturer or any other third party that is assigned or paid to the dealer and applied against the amount due under the lease, such as a factory rebate, first-time buyer incentive, college student incentive, or other similar rebate or payment.

(Publication 839)

The following charges and fees associated with a long-term motor vehicle lease are also subject to sales tax. However, the tax is due at the time the charge or fee is actually paid by the lessee:

• excess mileage or use charges;

• excess wear charges;

• damage, repair and similar charges;

• lease transfer or lease assumption fees;

• the charge to purchase the vehicle at the end of the lease term, if the lessee decides to purchase the vehicle; and

• any disposition fee or any other fee if the amount of the fee is charged at the end of the lease term.

(Publication 839)

The following charges, fees, and incentives are generally not subject to tax:

• vehicle registration and title fees if the amount charged by the dealer is the exact amount charged by DMV and the charge is not included in the monthly payment;

• certain documentation fees;

• any security deposit that is refunded to the lessee at the end of the lease term;

• the charge for "gap insurance" if the charge is reasonable, separately stated, and not included in the monthly payment; and

• any rebates, discounts, or similar incentives provided by the vendor and not reimbursed by the manufacturer or any other third party.

(Publication 839)

Where a lessor accepts tangible personal property for resale as a trade-in on a lease agreement, the total receipts do not include the value of the trade-in. Receipts from excess mileage or use charges, excess wear charges, damage assessments, repair or similar charges are subject to tax at the time they are paid by or are due from the lessee. (Reg. Sec. 527.15)

Where the initial term of a lease covers a period of less than one year but, because of the availability of renewal options the lease qualifies as a lease for a period of one year or more, all renewal options are included in determining the receipts due for the computation of the tax. This is so whether or not the renewal options are exercised and whether or not such options, individually or cumulatively, are for a period of one year or more. (Reg. Sec. 527.15)

Vehicle registration and title fees.—If a dealer obtains the vehicle's DMV registration or title documents for the lessee, and the dealer separately states the actual

DMV vehicle registration and title fees on the lease document or other memorandum of the price given to the lessee, the fees would not be subject to sales tax. These fees would also not be subject to tax if the dealer charges the lessee a separately stated, estimated amount (DMV fee deposit) for registration and title fees, does not include the deposit in the monthly payment, and later refunds to the customer the amount of the deposit that exceeded the exact DMV charge. However, if the dealer charges the lessee more than the amount charged by DMV, the excess amount is taxable. In addition, if the dealer builds the registration and title fees into the monthly payments due under the lease, the fees would be subject to tax. (Publication 839)

Documentation fees.—Documentation fees are fees charged by the dealer to prepare, on behalf of the purchaser/lessee, the paperwork necessary to obtain a title and/or registration for the vehicle. These fees are subject to sales tax unless both of the following conditions are met:

- the fee is separately stated in the lease or contract, the fee is reasonable, and it is not included in the monthly payment;

- the customer has the option to avoid paying the fee by preparing his or her own paperwork and taking the paperwork to DMV.

(Publication 839)

If a dealer is contractually obligated to the leasing company to ensure that the vehicle is properly registered to the lessee and titled to the leasing company, the lessee/customer may not have the option of preparing his or her own paperwork and taking it to DMV. In that case, the dealer's charges to the customer for documentation fees would be subject to tax. (Publication 839)

Security deposits.—A charge by the dealer for a refundable security deposit on a leased vehicle is considered collateral security and is not subject to sales tax. However, when the lessee returns the vehicle at the end of the lease, any portion of the deposit not returned to the lessee is subject to sales tax at that time. (Publication 839)

Refunds and credits.—A regulation provides that no refund or credit is allowed based upon the fact that receipts are not actually paid as in the case of early termination of a lease, failure to exercise an option to renew a lease or bad debt because, as noted, all payments are deemed to have been paid. (Reg. Sec. 527.15)

Fleet leases.—If the lessee of the motor vehicle certifies in writing that more than 50% of the use of the vehicle will be in the lessee's trade or business, and the lease includes an indeterminate number of options to renew (or other similar contractual provision) or at least 36 monthly options to renew beyond the initial term, all receipts due or consideration given or contracted to be given under the lease for (1) the first 32 months or (2) the period of the initial term of the lease, whichever is greater, will be deemed to have been paid or given, and are subject to tax. Accelerated tax payment provisions do not apply to any payments due or contracted to be given upon the exercise of an option to renew (or similar provision) after the first 32 months or the initial term, if longer. (Sec. 1117(a), Tax Law)

Exemptions.—Accelerated payment provisions do not apply to leases to federal and state agencies and instrumentalities and other qualified organizations exempt from tax pursuant to Sec. 1116, Tax Law. (TSB-M-80(11)S)

Collection of tax.—Where an agreement to lease a motor vehicle for a term of one year or more is entered into, the lessor must collect the tax at the inception of the lease, based on the rate of tax in effect for the local jurisdiction in which the vehicle is regularly garaged or stored. (Reg. Sec. 527.15; Publication 839)

Determining the tax rate.—The rate of tax to be paid and collected on leases of motor vehicles is the rate in effect in the locality (county or city) where the lessee resides at the time the tax is due, not the locality where the dealership or finance company is located. Therefore, when filing its sales tax return, the dealer or finance company should report tax collected from the lessee under the lease, or any other taxable transaction related to the lease, as a sale in the locality where the lessee resides. (Publication 839)

Compensating use tax.—Where a lease for a term of one year or more is entered into outside New York State, but the vehicle is subsequently brought by the lessee into New York State, any remaining receipts due or consideration to be given attributable to the use of the property in New York will be subject to tax as if the lease had been entered into for the first time within New York if:

• at the time of entering into the lease, the lessee was a resident of New York and leased the property for use outside the State but subsequently brings the property into the State for use here, or

• at the time of entering into the lease, the lessee was not a resident of New York but subsequently becomes a resident and brings the property into the State for use in the State.

(Sec. 1117(a), Tax Law; Reg. Sec. 527.15)

The lessee is liable for the combined State and local sales and use tax on the total of any remaining receipts due or consideration to be given beginning with the day the property is first used in New York by the lessee as a resident of New York. The tax is based upon the rate in effect in the jurisdiction where the vehicle is regularly garaged or stored. (Reg. Sec. 527.15)

CCH EXAMPLE: Determining local compensating use tax.—Mr. W, a New York State resident, enters into a 48-month lease of a motor vehicle with an out-of-state lessor for use of the vehicle outside New York State. If the vehicle is subsequently used in New York, such use will be subject to the New York State and local compensating use tax. The amount of tax due is to be determined as if the original lease had been entered into in New York State, except that the receipts subject to tax will be the total of any remaining receipts due or consideration to be given under the lease after the lessee first used the motor vehicle in New York State. (Reg. Sec. 527.15)

However, where a lessee pays sales or use taxes to another state or jurisdiction within such state on the lease of a motor vehicle, the use of which becomes subject to the New York state and local compensating use taxes, the lessee may be eligible to claim a credit for the tax paid to such other state or local jurisdiction may be allowed where:

— the tax was legally due and paid to the other state or jurisdiction without any right to a refund or credit thereof; and

— a similar credit is allowed by the other state or jurisdiction for the New York State and local sales and compensating use taxes paid under similar circumstances.

(Reg. Sec. 527.15(f))

The reciprocity credit is computed based upon the rate of tax paid to the other state and locality and the rate of tax to be paid to New York State and local jurisdictions within New York State, not on the dollar amounts of tax paid. The claim for credit will be allowed only to the extent that the rate used to determine the tax paid to the other state and locality does not exceed the New York State and local compensating use tax rate used to determine such tax due to New York State and its local jurisdictions. Where the New York State and local rate exceeds the other state's rate, the lessee will only be required to remit tax based on the difference in tax rates and on any remaining receipts due or consideration to be given under the lease, renewal option or combination of them beginning with the day the property is first used in New York State. The credit described in this subdivision may only apply to the extent that taxes have been paid to another state or jurisdiction based upon such remaining receipts or consideration. (Reg. Sec. 527.15(f)(3))

Lease with option to purchase.—Where a lease with an option to purchase has been entered into and the option exercised, the tax is payable on the consideration given when the option is exercised plus the taxes paid or payable on each lease payment. (Reg. Sec. 526.7(c)(2)) See ¶60-460 Leases and Rentals.

• *Determining proper tax rate for sales, leases of motor vehicles, vessels, and trailers*

Generally, the sale of tangible personal property in New York is subject to sales tax at the rate in effect where the property is delivered to the purchaser. However, a special rule applies to sales (including leases) of motor vehicles, vessels, and trailers, which provides that the sales tax is imposed based on the tax rate in effect where the purchaser resides. (TB-ST-590) The special rule for sales of motor vehicles, vessels, and trailers applies if the purchaser is:

— a nonresident of New York; or

— a resident of a taxing jurisdiction in New York other than the jurisdiction where the motor vehicle, vessel, or trailer is delivered.

(TB-ST-590)

In either case, the purchaser must submit a properly completed Form DTF-820, Certificate of Nonresidency of New York State and/or Local Taxing Jurisdiction, to the seller at the time of sale in order to establish that the special rule applies. (TB-ST-590)

If a purchaser does not submit Form DTF-820, the seller must collect the sales tax at the rate in effect where the motor vehicle, vessel, or trailer is delivered to the purchaser (usually the rate in effect where the dealer's premises are located). (TB-ST-590)

Nonresidents.—A nonresident purchaser is a purchaser that:

— does not have a permanent place of abode in this state;

— is not carrying on any employment, trade, business, or profession in this state in which the motor vehicle, vessel, or trailer will be used; and

— will not register the motor vehicle, vessel, or trailer in New York (including any temporary registration).

(TB-ST-590)

Sales to nonresident purchasers are exempt from both state and local sales tax. (TB-ST-590)

Residents of another New York taxing jurisdiction.—Sales to a purchaser who is a resident of a taxing jurisdiction in New York other than the jurisdiction where the motor vehicle, vessel, or trailer is delivered are subject to sales tax at the rate in effect for the New York jurisdiction where the purchaser resides. If the purchaser is an individual, the applicable rate is the combined state and local rate in effect in the taxing jurisdiction where the purchaser has a permanent place of abode. If the purchaser is a business, the applicable rate is the combined state and local rate in effect in the taxing jurisdiction where the motor vehicle, vessel, or trailer will be principally garaged or moored. (TB-ST-590)

• *Motor vehicles purchased by military personnel*

Purchases of motor vehicles in New York State made by members of the U.S. Armed Forces who live in the state are subject to the New York State sales tax. This includes motor vehicles purchased by military personnel who occupy housing located on a federal military base or reservation in New York State. (Important Notice No. N-90-27) However, military service members are allowed, upon their return to New York, an exemption from New York state sales and use taxes when he or she can show proof that tax was paid to another state in order to obtain title to the motor vehicle. In order to qualify for the exemption, the military service member (or former member) must have purchased the vehicle while in the military service of the United States and have proof when registering the motor vehicle in New York state of tax paid to another state (whether the payment was made by the seller or the purchaser). A receipt from the other state showing payment of sales, use, excise, usage, or a highway use tax on the purchase of the vehicle is considered proof of tax paid to another state. Military service members who purchase a motor vehicle that qualifies for this exemption must submit a properly completed Form DTF-803, Claim for Sales and Use Tax Exemption - Title/Registration, to the New York Department of Motor Vehicles upon registration of the vehicle. Military service members must mark an X in box 12a of Form DTF-803, complete the information required by that form, and be able to show military ID or other documentation as proof of military service. (Sec. 1115(a)(14-a), Tax Law) (TSB-M-14(11)S)

• *Use of motor vehicles held in car dealer's inventory*

Motor vehicles held in inventory exclusively for resale but used for purposes of demonstration to prospective customers are not taxable to the dealer if used solely for demonstration purposes. (TSB-M-02(3)S; TSB-M-87(2)S; TSB-M-83(13)S) Also, no tax is due from dealers for vehicles held in inventory and loaned without charge to a high school driver education program. (TSB-M-02(3)S)

Mixed use vehicles.—Vehicles held in inventory solely for resale (including a vehicle used for demonstration purposes) but used occasionally for business or pleasure by the dealer or an officer or employee of the company is subject to state and local use tax as a mixed use vehicle. (TSB-M-02(3)S; TSB-M-87(2)S) A mixed use vehicle also includes any vehicle held in a dealer's inventory for resale, but loaned to a customer while the customer's vehicle is under repair by the dealer, provided there is no separate charge attributable to use of the vehicle by the customer, or the charge does not reflect a fair market rental rate for such use (a "loaner vehicle"). (TSB-M-02(3)S)

The use tax due on these mixed use vehicles must be reported and paid with the dealer's sales and use tax return that covers the period of use. Since no purchase, sale or trade occurs when the taxable use begins or ends, and since a particular vehicle in inventory will usually be used in this manner for only a short period of time before being sold, dealers are allowed to pay tax based on 1% depreciation instead of tax normally due on a sale. (TSB-M-02(3)S; TSB-M-87(2)S)

A motor vehicle dealer may apply the 1% depreciation method to a mixed use vehicle provided that the vehicle is held in inventory, is available for sale, and the vehicle is used by the dealer: (1) for six months or less with no mileage restrictions, or (2) for more than six months but no more than one year, and the mileage does not exceed 15,000 miles for the entire year. (TSB-M-02(3)S) If the vehicle's mileage exceeds 15,000 miles and it is used for more than six months, or, regardless of mileage, if the vehicle is used for more than one year, use tax must be computed based on the dealer's total cost of the vehicle plus interest and penalties, computed from the date that a return for the occasion of first use would have been due. Credit for use tax paid under either the 1% method or the previous 2% method (prior to June 1, 2002) is allowed. (TSB-M-02(3)S)

In addition, a dealer does not qualify for the 1% method of computing use tax if: (1) the dealer seeks or intends to seek a trade-in allowance on the vehicle, regardless of whether the dealer operates as a single entity or as more than one entity; or (2) the dealer depreciates or takes an investment tax credit with respect to the vehicle. If a dealer is disqualified under either of these conditions, but had already been computing use tax using the 1% or 2% depreciation method, use tax is due on the dealer's total cost of the vehicle plus interest and penalties, computed from the date that a return for the occasion of first use would have been due, minus a credit for use tax paid under the particular depreciation method used. (TSB-M-02(3)S)

Rate of depreciation: The rate of depreciation is 1% per month (or any part of a month), computed on an amount equal to the total invoiced cost to the dealer (including delivery) for any vehicle purchased new. Where a motor vehicle is purchased used or taken in trade, the tax is computed on the purchase price or trade allowance plus the value of any repairs made to the vehicle. TSB-M-02(3)S; TSB-M-87(2)S

Record keeping requirements: A dealer must maintain adequate records to verify the use of a vehicle as a mixed use vehicle. For a list of what information must be maintained by the dealer for each mixed use vehicle, see TSB-M-02(3)S.

• *Motor vehicle maintenance and repairs*

Installation, maintenance, servicing and repair work performed upon a motor vehicle is a taxable service. The tax is, therefore, imposed upon the charge for the service of lubricating a motor vehicle and the charge for washing an automobile (whether the washing is performed manually or by a coin-operated machine). (Sec. 1105(c)(3), Tax Law; Reg. Sec. 527.5(a)(3))

Products and supplies purchased for use in performing installation, maintenance, servicing or repair work upon a motor vehicle are purchased for resale and hence not subject to tax, where such items become a physical component part of the vehicle repaired. (Reg. Sec. 526.6(c)(6)) Accordingly, a service station may purchase grease to be used for lubricating automobiles without payment of tax, since the grease will be transferred to the customers in connection with the performance of a taxable service.

• *Auto repair and body shops*

In general, most charges by a repair or body shop are taxable, including the total charge for parts and labor for repair services and parts and supplies sold directly to customers. (TB-ST-40)

Towing and transportation.—Towing or transporting a disabled vehicle is taxable. However, the transportation of vehicles that are not broken down or otherwise disabled is not taxable (i.e., transportation of antique cars to a car show, transporting reposed vehicles, or hauling a vehicle from one location to another). (TB-ST-40)

Storage.—Charges for storing a vehicle are taxable. For example, charges to store a repaired vehicle that is not picked up by its owner by a certain date are taxable. (TB-ST-40)

New York state inspections.—The charge for a New York state motor vehicle inspection is not taxable. However, any charges for additional repair work required for the vehicle to pass inspection are taxable. (TB-ST-40)

Warranty work and service contracts.—Charges to a warranty company for repair work that is covered under a service contract or warranty is not taxable provided the warranty company provides a Form ST-120, Resale Certificate. Only warranty companies that are registered vendors with New York can issue a properly completed resale certificate. Any additional charges billed to the customer (such as charges for repairs not covered by the warranty) are taxable. (TB-ST-40)

Insurance claims and repairs.—When repair work is covered by insurance and the insurance company is billed, both materials and labor are taxable. (TB-ST-40)

> **EXAMPLE:** A customer brings his vehicle to your shop after it was damaged in an accident. You inspect the vehicle and determine you need to replace the fender, front quarter panel, and passenger-side door, and paint the repaired parts of the vehicle. You complete the work and send the bill to the insurance company. The entire bill is taxable. (TB-ST-40)

Parts purchases.—Tax is not imposed on purchases of parts that are transferred to customers as part of a repair job. The repair or body shop should give Form ST-120, Resale Certificate, to its supplier. Examples of parts that can be purchased for resale include: brake pads, rotors; shocks, struts; tires; filters; fan belts; electronic sensors; headlights and brake lights; starters, alternators; windshields; rear-view mirrors; doors; and fenders. (TB-ST-40)

Tools and equipment purchases.—Purchases, leases, or rentals of tools or equipment for a repair shop are taxable. Tools and equipment are used to perform repair services, but are not transferred to the customer as part of the job. Taxable tools and equipment include: wrenches and sockets; screwdrivers and nut drivers; pliers; impact tools; clamps; hammers; torches; jumper cables; lifts; wheel balancers; engine analyzers; pipe benders; alignment equipment; air compressors; welding equipment; and paint booths. (TB-ST-40) However, purchases of enhanced emissions inspections equipment can be made without paying sales tax as long as the following conditions are met: (i) the New York Department of Environmental Conservation has certified the equipment for use in an enhanced emissions inspection and maintenance program as required by the federal Clean Air Act and the New York Clean Air Compliance Act; and (ii) the shop is an official inspection station licensed by the Commissioner of Motor Vehicles and authorized to conduct the enhanced emission inspections required by the federal Clean Air Act. (TB-ST-40)

Supplies purchases.—Supplies that are actually transferred to the customer as part of a repair or maintenance job can be purchased exempt from tax. This includes items such as: brake fluid; transmission fluid; antifreeze; bearing grease; motor oil; paint; automotive body fillers; flux; sheet metal; and thinners and solvents. (TB-ST-40)

Supplies that are used in and around a repair shop to perform repair and maintenance work that are not actually transferred to the customer cannot be purchased exempt from tax. This includes items such as: shop towels; cleaners; paper floor mats; office supplies; sandpaper; drop cloths; face masks; masking tape; and polishing and buffing pads. (TB-ST-40)

• *Motor vehicle parking, garaging and storing services*

Except as noted below, receipts from vehicle parking, garaging or storing services, when performed by a person operating a garage, parking lot or similar place of business engaged in providing such services, are taxable. (Sec. 1105(c)(6), Tax Law) No sales tax is imposed, however, when:

> — the garage is part of premises occupied solely as a private one- or two-family dwelling;

> — the facilities are owned and operated by a public corporation, other than a public benefit corporation, created by interstate compact or at least half of

¶60-570

whose members are appointed by the governor, or any agency or instrumentality of a municipal corporation or district corporation; or

— parking charges are paid to a homeowner's association by its members. This includes parking charges paid by members of a homeowner's association to a person leasing a parking facility from the homeowner's association.

(Sec. 1105(c)(6), Tax Law)

A vendor who sells or rents motor vehicles cannot use an exempt use certificate when purchasing parking services. (TSB-M-08(4.1)S) Therefore, vendors of parking services are required to collect sales tax from vendors who sell or rent motor vehicles on charges made for parking, garaging, or storing motor vehicles. (TSB-M-08(4.1)S)

See ¶ 60-665 Services.

New York City parking tax.—New York City also imposes a 6% tax on parking, which tax is administered as part of the combined city and state sales and use tax. (Sec. 1107(c), Tax Law).

• *Special tax on passenger car rentals*

A special tax at the rate of 6% is imposed on receipts from the rental of motor vehicles, other than motorcycles, designed for passenger transportation, having a gross vehicle weight of 9,000 pounds or less with a seating capacity of nine persons or fewer. This tax is in addition to the applicable state and local sales and use taxes. (Sec. 1160(a), Tax Law) (TSB-M-09(1)S)

To the extent not otherwise subject to the special tax on passenger car rentals, passenger cars rented by persons for use within New York are subject to use tax. The use tax is computed on the basis of the consideration given or contracted to be given for the use of the vehicle, excluding any credit for tangible personal accepted in part payment and intended for resale. The tax, which is in addition to all other taxes imposed by New York, applies whether the customer is a resident or nonresident and regardless of whether or not the passenger car is required to be registered in New York. (Important Notice No. N-90-26)

Exemptions.—Federal and state agencies and instrumentalities and other qualified organizations that are exempt from tax pursuant to Sec. 1116, Tax Law, are also exempt from the special tax. Long-term leases of motor vehicles subject to accelerated sales tax payment provisions are also exempt. The exemption for property or services upon which tax is paid to other jurisdictions is applicable only to the extent that the rate of the retail sales or use tax paid to any other state or jurisdiction within another state, exceeds the aggregate rate of the use tax and any city, county or school district use tax imposed. (Sec. 1160(a), Tax Law)

Administration.—The special tax on passenger car rentals is administered and collected pursuant to the provisions of Article 28, Sales and Use Tax. (Sec. 1165, Tax Law) Vendors required to collect the tax must report and remit the tax quarterly, regardless of the their sales tax filing status. (*Important Notice No. N-90-26*)

Additional tax on rentals in and outside MCTD.—A special additional supplemental 6% sales and use tax is imposed on passenger car rentals within the Metropolitan Commuter Transportation District (MCTD) and those outside of the MCTD. (Sec. 1166-A, Tax Law) (TSB-M-19(1)S) The special supplemental tax is in addition to the applicable state and local sales and use taxes and the statewide special tax on the rental of passenger cares (statewide special tax). The special supplemental tax uses the same rules as the statewide special tax and therefore is calculated, administered, and collected in the same manner as that tax, except that it is only imposed on rentals or uses within the MCTD. Accordingly, if a rental of a passenger car within the MCTD is subject to the statewide special tax, it will also be subject to the special supplemental tax. (TSB-M-09(6)S)

¶60-570

Vendors who provide the rental of passenger cars within the MCTD are required to collect the special supplemental tax from their customers and pay the special supplemental tax in the same manner and at the same time in which they remit the statewide special tax. In addition, the vendor must separately account for and report sales within the MCTD subject to the special supplemental tax. The department has added a new line and reporting code to the sales tax returns to allow vendors to report and remit the special supplemental tax. (TSB-M-09(6)S)

- *Waste tire management and recycling charges*

A waste tire management and recycling fee of $2.50 is imposed by tire sellers on every new tire sold, of which an allowance of 25¢ is retained by the seller to cover its costs associated with collecting the fee. This state-imposed fee is not subject to state and local sales taxes. A seller's waste tire management and recycling costs in excess of the 25¢ allowance may be included in the advertised price of the tire, or the seller may choose to impose a separate charge for those costs. If the seller chooses to impose the separate charge, the charge is limited to $2.50, or the actual waste tire management and recycling costs of the seller reduced by the 25¢ allowance, whichever is less. In addition, the amount of the charge must be separately stated on the invoice, and the invoice must state that the charge is imposed at the sole discretion of the seller. Unlike the state-imposed waste tire management and recycling fee, any additional waste tire management and recycling charges made by the tire seller, whether included in the price of the tire or separately stated, is considered part of the total selling price of the tire and is subject to sales tax. (TSB-M-08(6)S)

- *Payments under federal CARS Act*

The Department of Taxation and Finance has issued a memorandum discussing the sales or use tax treatment of payments made under the federal Consumer Assistance to Recycle and Save Act of 2009 (CARS Act) (Pub. L. 111-32, §§1301-02). The CARS Act directs the National Highway Traffic Safety Administration to establish a program to provide incentives to replace vehicles that are not fuel efficient. Under the program, a payment is provided by the federal government when an owner of a vehicle meeting statutorily specified criteria turns in that vehicle and purchases or leases a new vehicle meeting certain requirements. When a dealer sells or leases a vehicle under this program to a New York resident, the dealer must collect state and local sales or use tax based on the full amount of the sale or lease price. Because payments under the program represent partial payment for the purchase of an eligible new vehicle, those payments constitute receipts from the sale of tangible personal property that are subject to tax. The dealer's acceptance of the vehicle turned in by the consumer is required by the program and is not in part payment of the new vehicle's purchase price because the dealer receives full payment for the new vehicle in the form of cash from the consumer and the payment amount under the program from the federal government. However, any separate credit given by the dealer to the consumer for the scrap value of the vehicle being turned in that actually reduces the overall purchase or lease price of the new vehicle would be allowed as a reduction in the total receipt subject to tax. (TSB-M-09(11)S)

- *Refunds—Motor vehicles returned by customers as lemons*

Purchasers or lessees of a new motor vehicle who return the vehicle to the manufacturer pursuant to the provisions of the "New Car Lemon Law" and receive a full or partial refund of the purchase price or capitalized cost are entitled, within three years of the date that they receive the refund from the manufacturer, to apply to the Commissioner of Taxation and Finance for a refund of any tax paid on the purchase price or capitalized costs plus fees and charges refunded by the manufacturer which is not in excess of the receipts and proportionate to the taxable receipts. (Sec. 1139(f), Tax Law) Interest is payable commencing three months after the date the application for refund in processible form is received. The term "capitalized cost," for purposes of the refund, refers to the aggregate deposit and rental payments previously paid to the lessor for the leased vehicle minus any service fees (defined as the portion of a lease payment attributable to earned interest calculated at an annual rate equal to two points above the prime rate in effect on the date that the lease is executed plus any insurance or other costs expended by the lessor for the benefit of the lessee). (*TSB-M-86(9.1)S*)

[¶60-580] Nonprofit Organizations, Private Schools, and Churches

Sales or amusement charges by or to certain entities, as well as any use or occupancy by such entities, are exempt from tax. (Sec. 1116(a), Tax Law)

For a guide to sales tax in New York for exempt organizations, see Publication 843Publication 843,.

• *Non-taxable entities*

The following are non-taxable entities:

— New York state governmental entities (other states and their agencies and political subdivisions do not qualify for sales tax exemption) (Sec. 1116(a)(1), Tax Law);

— United States governmental entities (Sec. 1116(a)(2), Tax Law);

— the United Nations or any international organization of which the U.S. is a member, as well as diplomatic missions and diplomatic personnel, where such entity or person is the purchaser, user or consumer or sells services or property of a kind not ordinarily sold by private persons; (Sec. 1116(a)(3), Tax Law; Reg. Sec. 529.5(c))

— any corporation, association, trust, community chest, fund, foundation, or limited liability company organized and operated exclusively for religious, charitable, scientific, testing for public safety, literary or educational purposes or to foster national or international amateur sports competition (but only if part of its activities involve the provision of athletic facilities or equipment) or for the prevention of cruelty to children or animals; provided that (a) no part of the net earnings of such entity inures to the benefit of any private shareholder or individual, (b) no substantial part of the activities of such entity is carrying on propaganda or otherwise attempting to influence legislation (except as otherwise provided in IRC Sec. 501(h)) and (c) the entity does not participate in or intervene (including the publishing or distributing of statements) in any political campaign on behalf of or in opposition to a candidate for public office (Sec. 1116(a)(4), Tax Law);

— a post or organization of past or present members of the U.S. Armed Forces or an auxiliary unit or society of or trust or foundation for any such post or organization, provided that: (a) it is organized in New York State, (b) has at least 75% of its membership comprised of past or present members of the U.S. Armed Forces, as defined in Sec. 13-a of the General Construction Law, and substantially all of its remaining membership comprised of cadets or spouses, widows, widowers, ancestors, or lineal descendants of past or present members of the U.S. Armed Forces or of cadets, and (c) no part of its net earnings inures to the benefit of any private shareholder or individual (Sec. 1116(a)(5), Tax Law) (TSB-M-04(8)S);

— a nonprofit health maintenance organization (HMO) subject to the provisions of Article 44 of the Public Health Law (Sec. 1116(a)(7), Tax Law); and

— any cooperative and foreign corporation doing business in New York pursuant to the Rural Electric Cooperative Law. (Sec. 1116(a)(8), Tax Law)

(Publication 843)

Qualified settlement funds or grantor trusts set up to deal with claims arising from the Holocaust, World War II, or Nazi persecution, are exempt from state and local use taxes. (Sec. 13, Tax Law)

For further details (including definitions and qualifications for exemption), see Reg. Sec. 529.4*et seq. et seq.* and Reg. Sec. 529.10.

The requirement that no part of the activities of an organization organized to foster national or international amateur sports competition involve the provision of athletic facilities or equipment does not apply to "qualified amateur sports organizations." A "qualified amateur sports organization" is as an organization organized and operated exclusively to foster national or international amateur sports competition, which organization is also organized and operated primarily to conduct national or international competition in sports or to support and develop amateur athletes for national or international competition in sports. (Sec. 1116(f), Tax Law)

As an exempt organization, a volunteer fire company is not subject to the New York state and local sales and use taxes upon its purchases of tangible personal property and services or upon hotel rents and amusement charges properly paid by it. A volunteer fire company must, however, claim exemption by filing an Exempt Organization Certificate (Form ST 119-2) with the State Tax Bureau in accordance with the instructions on the form. Once the volunteer fire company has been determined to be an exempt organization, it must then furnish Form ST 119-1 to its vendors in order to make purchases tax free. (*TSB-M-78(6)S*)

The exemption also covers sales by a volunteer fire company of tangible personal property, as well as food and drink at booths operated on the grounds of a firemen's field day, carnival, competition or other similar event conducted by a volunteer fire department and the proceeds of which exclusively inure to the volunteer fire company's benefit. (*TSB-M-78(6)S*)

Tangible personal property sold to a contractor, subcontractor or repairman for use in erecting a structure or building of a nonprofit organization or adding to, altering, improving, maintaining, servicing or repairing real property of such an organization is specifically exempted from the tax, where such property is to become an integral component part of the structure, building or real property. (Sec. 1115(a)(15), Tax Law; Sec. 1115(a)(16), Tax Law) See ¶60-330 Construction.

Tangible personal property manufactured, processed or assembled and donated by the manufacturer, processor or assembler to a nonprofit organization is exempt from tax, provided that such manufacturer, processor or assembler offers the same kind of property for sale in the regular course of business and has not made any other use of the donated property. No refund or credit is allowed for sales and use taxes properly paid. (Sec. 1115(l), Tax Law) See ¶60-510 Manufacturing, Processing, Assembling, or Refining.

Rents received from room occupancies in a hotel operated by a religious, charitable, scientific, etc. organization in furtherance of the activities of the nonprofit organization are also tax-exempt. (Sec. 1116(c), Tax Law) In addition, duly authorized representatives of posts or organizations comprised of past or present members of the

U.S. Armed Forces, when acting on behalf of these organizations, are not subject to hotel room occupancy taxes and are not required to pay sales tax on hotel room occupancies. (Sec. 1116(g), Tax Law) See ¶ 60-480 Lodging.

The tax is not imposed upon any admissions where the entire proceeds inure exclusively to the benefit of: (1) an exempt religious, charitable, scientific, etc., organization, (2) an organization predominantly comprised of past or present members of the U.S. Armed Forces, (3) an organization conducted solely for the purposes of maintaining symphony orchestras or operas and receiving substantial support from voluntary contributions or (4) a voluntary fire or ambulance company. (Sec. 1116(d)(1), Tax Law)

Admission charges to the following places or events are also tax-exempt:

— agricultural fairs,

— historic homes and gardens, and

— historic sites, houses and shrines and museums,

provided that no part of the net earnings inures to the benefit of any private stockholder or individual. (Sec. 1116(d)(3), Tax Law)

See ¶ 60-230 Admissions, Entertainment, and Dues.

• *U.S. Department of State diplomatic tax exemption cards*

The U.S. Department of State, Office of Foreign Missions (OFM) issues diplomatic tax exemption cards to eligible foreign diplomats and consular missions and their personnel and eligible families. Diplomatic missions and personnel use the tax exemption cards to make purchases exempt from New York sales tax. OFM recently issued newly designed tax exemption cards. Previously issued cards contained colored stripes that indicated the type and level of exemption granted to the cardholder. Those cards have been replaced with cards that contain animal images. (Important Notice N-11-11) The following types of tax exemption cards have been issued:

— Buffalo image card: exempts the cardholder from sales tax on official mission purchases, subject to the restrictions listed on the card;

— Owl image card: exempts the cardholder from sales tax on all official mission purchases;

— Deer image card: exempts the cardholder from sales tax on personal purchases, subject to the restrictions listed on the card; and

— Eagle image card: exempts the cardholder from sales tax on all personal purchases.

(Important Notice N-11-11)

Diplomatic missions and personnel may continue to make purchases exempt from sales tax by presenting vendors with a properly completed Form DTF-950, Certificate of Sales Tax Exemption for Diplomatic Missions and Personnel, Single Purchase Certificate, accompanied by their tax exemption card. (Important Notice N-11-11)

Because of this change, notices N-86-25, Notices Regarding Tax Exemption for Diplomats, Diplomatic Missions and Related Personnel, and N-85-29, National Diplomatic Tax Exemption Cards, are obsolete and should no longer be relied upon. (Important Notice N-11-11)

¶60-580

• *Purchases by New York governmental entities*

Generally, a New York governmental entity is exempt from payment of sales tax on its purchases when the entity is the purchaser, user or consumer of tangible personal property or services, or when an employee of the entity, on official business, is the occupant of a hotel room, or a patron at a place of amusement, club, or similar place. To claim exemption from sales tax, a New York governmental entity must provide vendors with a governmental purchase order, government credit card, or the appropriate exemption document. (Publication 843)

• *Taxable sales involving exempt entities*

Tangible personal property sold at retail in a shop or store operated by a religious, charitable, scientific, etc. organization or by an organization of past or present members of the U.S. Armed Forces are subject to sales and use taxes. (Sec. 1116(b)(1), Tax Law) Similarly, sales of food or drink in a restaurant or tavern operated by a religious, charitable, scientific, etc. organization or an organization of past or present members of the U.S. Armed Forces are generally taxable. The tax also applies to motor vehicle parking, garaging or storage services provided by a religious, charitable, scientific, etc. organization or by an organization of past or present members of the U.S. Armed Forces, where such entity operates a garage (other than a garage which is part of premises occupied solely as a private one or two family dwelling), parking lot or similar place of business. (Sec. 1116(b)(2), Tax Law; Sec. 1116(b)(3), Tax Law) (Publication 843)

All nonprofit tax-exempt organizations are required to collect sales and compensating use tax on additional retail sales, including online and mail-order catalogue sales, and rentals or leases of tangible personal property. (Sec. 1116(b)(1), Tax Law) (TSB-M-08(5)S; TSB-M-08(9)S) Specifically, the following exempt organization sales are subject to state and local sales and compensating use taxes:

— retail sales of tangible personal property by any shop or store operated by an exempt organization;

— any utility services provided under Tax Law § 1105(b) and any service to real property described under § 1105(c)(5), whether or not sold from the exempt organization's shop or store. Utility services include gas, electricity, refrigeration, and steam; and gas, electricity, refrigeration, and steam service of any nature. These services also include telephony, telegraphy, and telephone and telegraph service of any nature, except interstate and international telephony, telegraphy, and telephone and telegraph services; telephone answering services; prepaid telephone calling services; and mobile telecommunications services. Taxable services to real property include, but are not limited to, painting and cleaning services, landscaping and lawn services, snow plowing, and property repair services; or

— any retail sales of tangible personal property where the sale is made by remote means, such as by telephone, mail order (including e-mail), over the Internet, or by other similar methods, provided the exempt organization makes such sales with a degree of regularity, frequency, and continuity.

(Sec. 1116(b)(1), Tax Law) (TSB-M-08(5)S; TSB-M-08(9)S)

Such sales are subject to tax whether or not they are made from a shop or store. (TSB-M-08(5)S; TSB-M-08(9)S)

Sales and use taxes are also imposed upon sales of tangible personal property or services by cooperative and foreign corporations doing business in New York State pursuant to the Rural Electric Cooperative Law, unless the purchaser is an exempt entity. (Sec. 1116(b)(4), Tax Law)

Motor fuel and diesel motor fuel.—In general, motor fuel and diesel motor fuel purchased by a nonprofit organization are subject to the prepaid tax and the retail sales tax. However, purchases of motor fuel and diesel motor fuel by a hospital classified as an exempt organization, for its own use and consumption, as well as purchases of diesel motor fuel by exempt religious, charitable, etc. organizations, for its own heating use and consumption, are exempt from both the prepaid tax and retail sales and use taxes on such fuels. (Sec. 1116(b)(5), Tax Law) See ¶60-560 Motor Fuels.

Sales of fuel to government entities.—Credit card issuers and fuel distributors are allowed to apply for refunds or credits of state and local sales taxes on motor fuel and diesel motor fuel sold to exempt government entities when certain criteria are met. (Sec. 301-m, Tax Law; Sec. 1139, Tax Law) (TSB-M-08(12)S and TSB-M-08(9)M) Credit card issuers may apply for a refund, and fuel distributors may apply for a refund or credit, of sales and excise taxes paid on purchases of fuel by government entities and paid for with a credit card or other access card if all of the following criteria are met:

— The Department must receive Form FT-505.1, Government Entity Credit Card Refund or Credit Election, signed by an authorized representative of the government entity and the credit card issuer or fuel distributor certifying that the credit card issuer or fuel distributor is the only party eligible to receive the refund or credit.

— If the credit card issuer is designated to apply for the refund, it must register for sales tax purposes (if not already registered), obtain a Certificate of Authority, and file sales tax returns.

— The sales and excise taxes were actually paid to the Department, and no refund or credit was previously claimed or allowed for those taxes.

— The government entity purchased the fuel for its own use or consumption and it therefore qualifies as an exempt purchase.

— The Department has not issued a notice of ineligibility to the government entity, and to either the credit card issuer or fuel distributor.

— The credit card issuer or fuel distributor designated to receive the refund or credit (1) must certify that it will not charge or otherwise receive any sales and excise taxes from the government entity making the purchase, and (2) must file a written consent signed by an authorized representative of the government entity stating that no tax will be charged to the government entity by the credit card issuer or fuel distributor and that the government entity will not claim a refund or credit related to its purchases of fuel made by a credit card provided by the issuer. These conditions are included on Form FT-505.1 as part of the consent for filing the election.

— The credit card issuer or fuel distributor must certify that (1) the retail station or other vendor has been repaid the sales and excise taxes it charged to the government entity on its fuel purchases, or (2) it has obtained a written consent from the retail station or other vendor to receive the refund or credit for the sales and excise taxes.

— The credit card issuer or fuel distributor must, upon request by the Department, provide detailed transactional and jurisdictional information related to the fuel sales in the form requested by the Department.

(TSB-M-08(12)S and TSB-M-08(9)M)

Applying for a refund or credit: Credit card issuers may claim a refund of the sales and excise taxes paid on fuel by filing Form FT-505, Claim for Refund of Taxes

Paid on Government Entity Credit Card Purchases of Fuel, after the end of the sales tax quarter in which the government entity purchased the fuel. The refund form must be accompanied by any additional documentation required by the form's instructions. (TSB-M-08(12)S and TSB-M-08(9)M)

Fuel distributors may apply for a credit of the excise taxes paid on motor fuel by filing Form PT-101, Tax on Motor Fuels, and/or excise taxes paid on diesel motor fuel by filing Form PT-102, Tax on Diesel Motor Fuels. The credit claimed on Form PT-101 and/or Form PT-102 is carried over to Form PT-100, Petroleum Business Tax Return and may result in a refund or credit. These forms may be filed after the end of the month in which the government entity purchased the fuel. Fuel distributors may continue to claim a credit for the prepaid sales tax on Form FT-945/1045, Report of Sales Tax Prepayment on Motor Fuel/Diesel Motor Fuel on a monthly basis. Fuel distributors may claim a refund of the additional sales tax (the difference between the retail sales tax repaid to the retail vendor and the prepaid sales tax paid by the distributor) using Form FT-500, Application for Refund of Sales Tax Paid on Automotive Fuels, after the end of the quarter in which the fuel was purchased by the government entity. (TSB-M-08(12)S and TSB-M-08(9)M)

Liability: The Department may issue an assessment for tax, penalty, and interest to a credit issuer or fuel distributor for any refund or credit that was allowed or paid that was erroneous, illegal, or unconstitutional. In addition, a penalty equal to the amount of tax refunded or credited, plus applicable interest, may also be imposed on any credit card issuer or fuel distributor that files a refund application or takes a credit knowing that the fuel purchased by government entity was not for the government entity's own use or consumption. (TSB-M-08(12)S and TSB-M-08(9)M)

• *Taxable admissions involving exempt entities*

The tax is imposed upon certain admissions, including admissions to the following:

— any athletic game or exhibition; unless the proceeds inure exclusively to the benefit of elementary or secondary schools or, in the case of an athletic game between two elementary or secondary schools, the entire gross proceeds from the game inure to the benefit of one or more religious, charitable, scientific, etc. organizations; and

— carnivals, rodeos, or circuses in which any professional performer or operator participates for compensation, unless the entire net profit from such event inures exclusively to the benefit of a charitable or educational organization (circuses are no longer be taxable under this provision).

(Sec. 1116(d)(2), Tax Law)

See ¶60-230 Admissions, Entertainment, and Dues.

• *College textbooks*

Textbooks purchased by full- and part-time college students for use in courses taken at an institution of higher education are exempt from state sales and compensating use tax. To qualify for the exemption, a textbook must be required or recommended by the instructor or the institution for the student's course. (Sec. 1115(a)(34), Tax Law) (TB-ST-125; TSB-M-98(4)S) The student may have to complete Form ST-121.4, Textbook Exemption Certificate, and give it to the seller. (TB-ST-126)

The term "textbooks" includes new and used textbooks, related workbooks, or course-packs, written, designed, or produced for educational, instructional, or pedagogical purposes, but specifically required or recommended for a course at an institution of higher education. An "institution of higher education" is one that is either recognized or approved by the regents of the University of the State of New York, or accredited by another accrediting agency or association that is also recognized by the regents of the University of the State of New York. Institutions of higher education include colleges, universities, professional and technical schools, and libraries or museums that conduct educational programs leading to a post-secondary degree, certificate, or diploma. (TB-ST-125; TSB-M-98(4)S)

Qualifications for exempt purchase.—For a purchase to be exempt from sales tax:

— the textbook must be purchased by a full-time or part-time student who is enrolled at an institution of higher education and be for use in his or her course;

— the textbook must be required or recommended for the student's course, either by the instructor or by the institution;

— the student must provide a valid student identification card or other evidence of enrollment at the time of purchase; and

— the vendor must either have a list of eligible textbooks or receive a properly completed Form ST-121.4, Textbook Exemption Certificate, from the student.

(TB-ST-125; TSB-M-98(4)S)

Exempt purchases.—Purchases may be made from any bookstore, including college or university bookstores, retail bookstores, by mail order (including e-mail), over the Internet, or by other means. The textbook must be for a course the student is taking that is offered by an educational institution. However, the course does not have to be part of the curriculum for a particular degree, certificate, or diploma. (TB-ST-125)

The exemption applies to purchases of new or used textbooks. This includes course-packs and workbooks required or recommended by the institution or instructor. The exemption applies whether the textbook is in printed form or on CD-ROM, DVD, or other optical disc. The exemption does not apply to supplies, notebooks, etc., or to books not required or recommended for a course. (TB-ST-125)

Student identification.—If a student is purchasing a textbook in person, the student must show the vendor a valid identification card issued by an institution of higher education. If the student does not have an identification card, the student must provide other evidence of enrollment. The student must give the vendor the name and address of the institution where he or she is enrolled and his or her student identification number, if the institution has assigned one. (TB-ST-125)

If a student is purchasing a textbook over the Internet or by mail order, the student must furnish his or her name, address, valid student identification number and the name and address of the institution, except where the identification number is the student's social security number. In such a situation, the student should tell the vendor the identification number and social security number is the same, and the vendor is required to record that information with the sale and include the name and address of the educational institution. Where the institution does not issue student identification cards, the student must provide other evidence of enrollment to the vendor. (TB-ST-125; TSB-M-98(4)S)

Vendor requirements.—If the educational institution or the course instructor has given the vendor a list of eligible textbooks, the vendor may sell any book on the list exempt from tax to an eligible student. If the institution or instructor has not given a list of eligible books to the vendor, the student may obtain a copy of the list and give it to the vendor. The vendor may then sell any book on the list exempt from tax to the student. If the textbook is not available at the time of purchase, the vendor may sell a textbook exempt from tax if the student gives the vendor a properly completed Form ST-121.4, Textbook Exemption Certificate (TB-ST-125)

If the student purchases a book in person and claims the textbook exemption, the vendor must check the student's identification to verify that he or she is a current student at an educational institution. To substantiate exempt sales to students, the vendor must keep the following:

— a copy of the required or recommended list of books from the course instructor or school;

— a copy of the list furnished by the student; or

— Form ST-121.4, Textbook Exemption Certificate, required to be furnished by a student.

(TB-ST-125; TSB-M-98(4)S)

If the student purchases a book over the Internet or by mail order and claims the textbook exemption, in addition to a copy of the list of books or Form ST-121.4, the vendor must retain and associate the student identification card number and other student identification information with the sales record for the transaction. (TB-ST-125; TSB-M-98(4)S)

Where the educational institution does not issue student identification cards, the student must provide other evidence of enrollment, such as (1) a receipt showing payment of paid tuition, with the name of the institution and the student's name, (2) a dated registrar's statement confirming enrollment as a student at the institution, (3) a list or schedule, issued by the institution, indicating the student's name, the institution's name, the scheduled courses, with the period of enrollment, or (4) other documentation currently issued by the institution that indicates the name of the student, the name of the institution, and the period of enrollment. (TSB-M-98(4)S)

How to use Form ST-121.4.—A student purchaser must use this certificate if the seller does not have, and you cannot give the seller, a list of required or recommended textbooks for the course you are taking at the institution where you are enrolled. The exemption applies only to textbooks described above. It does not apply to other required supplies, notebooks, or books not required or recommended for a course. You must show the seller at the time of purchase your valid student ID card issued by the institution of higher education where you are enrolled as a full- or part-time student. If the institution where you are enrolled does not issue student ID cards, enter school does not issue student IDs in the Student's ID number box and provide the seller with other valid evidence of enrollment at an institution of higher education, as described in the instructions for Form ST-121.4. If you are purchasing eligible textbooks over the Internet or by mail, you must provide the seller your name, address, valid student ID number, and the name and address of the institution where you are enrolled. (TB-ST-126)

Recordkeeping.—The seller must check the student ID (if available) to verify that the purchaser is a student currently enrolled at an institution of higher education. To substantiate an exempt sale, the seller must keep: a copy of the required or recommended list of textbooks furnished by the course instructor or institution of higher education; a copy of the instructor's or institution's list furnished by the student; or a properly completed certificate. If the purchase was made over the Internet or by mail, in addition to a copy of the list of books or this certificate, the seller must retain and associate the student ID card number and other student ID information with the sales record of the transaction. See Tax Bulletin College Textbooks (TB-ST-125), for more information. If the seller does not have a copy of the list of textbooks as described above, the seller will be protected from liability for the tax if the seller accepts in good faith a properly completed Form ST-121.4 (and related documentation) within 90 days of the date of sale. (TB-ST-126)

Penalties.—Misuse of this exemption certificate may result in serious civil and criminal sanctions in addition to the payment of any tax and interest due. (TB-ST-126) These include:

— a penalty equal to 100% of the tax due;

— a $50 penalty for each fraudulent exemption certificate issued; and

— criminal felony prosecution, punishable by a substantial fine and a possible jail sentence.

(TB-ST-126)

• *Nonprofit property/casualty insurance companies*

An exemption is provided for nonprofit property/casualty insurance companies subject to the provisions of Insurance Law Article 67. (Sec. 6707, Insurance Law)

• *Terrorist organizations*

New York law includes a provision that revokes the New York tax-exempt status of terrorist organizations whose federal tax-exempt status has been revoked by the IRS. When an organization's sales tax-exempt status is revoked, it must collect sales and use taxes on all of its taxable sales. If an organization whose tax-exempt status has been revoked does not collect the proper sales and use taxes on its taxable sales, the purchaser owes and is required to pay the taxes due. The purchaser will not be held liable for any penalty or interest for failing to file a return or to pay the sales and use taxes if the purchaser files a return and pays the tax due within 30 days of the date the purchaser learns that the tax is owed. (TSB-M-04(8)S)

In addition, when an organization is notified by the Tax Department that its tax-exempt status is revoked for sales and use tax purposes, the organization must immediately surrender its *Exempt Organization Certificate* and cease usings its corresponding tax exemption number and exempt purchase certificate(s) to make purchases exempt from sales and use taxes. (TSB-M-04(8)S)

An organization whose tax-exempt status is restored by the IRS is required to submit a new application and be approved before tax-exempt status is restored with respect to any tax or fee administered by the New York Commissioner of Taxation and Finance. (Sec. 27, Tax Law) (TSB-M-04(8)S)

• *Veterans*

Sales by veterans for benefit of veteran's service organization.—An exemption is provided for tangible personal property manufactured and sold by a veteran for the benefit of a veteran's service organization, provided that such person or any member of his or her household does not conduct a trade or business in which similar items are sold. The exemption applies to the first $2,500 of receipts from such sales in a calendar year. (Sec. 1115(a)(18-a), Tax Law)

Veteran's home gift shops.—Retail sales of tangible personal property by any gift shop located in a veteran's home are exempt. (Sec. 1115(ff), Tax Law) (TSB-M-06(15)S) For purposes of this exemption, the term "veterans' home" means any of the five veterans' nursing homes operated by New York state for veterans disabled by age, disease, or otherwise who by reason of such disability are incapable of earning a living. (TSB-M-06(15)S)

The exemption applies regardless of the amount of the retail sale or who the purchaser is. In other words, the exemption is not limited to sales made solely to residents of the facility. (TSB-M-06(15)S)

¶60-580

• *START-UP NY program*

Legislation created a START-UP NY program that provides tax benefits to approved businesses that locate in vacant space or land of approved New York state public and private colleges and universities, approved strategic state assets, and New York state incubators affiliated with private universities or colleges that are designated as tax-free NY areas. The program is administered by Empire State Development (ESD). Approved businesses will be issued a certificate of eligibility by the sponsoring campus, university, or college. The benefits are available for taxable years beginning on or after January 1, 2014, sales tax quarters beginning on or after March 1, 2014, or transactions occurring on or after January 1, 2014, depending upon the benefit. Sales tax benefits are available for a period of 120 consecutive months beginning with the month during which the business locates in the tax-free NY area. (Sec. 430, Tax Law; Sec. 432, Tax Law; Sec. 433, Tax Law; Sec. 434, Tax Law; Sec. 39, Tax Law) (TSB-M-13(7)S) Certain correctional facilities are also eligible for participation in the START-UP NY program. (Sec. 431, Economic Development Law; Sec. 435, Economic Development Law)

An approved business that is located in a tax-free NY area is eligible for a credit or refund of New York State and local sales and use taxes, including the 3/8% tax imposed by the state in the MCTD (MCTD state sales tax), imposed on the sale of tangible personal property, utility services, and services taxable under Tax Law Sec. 1105(c). In addition, a credit or refund is available for certain purchases of tangible personal property by contractors, subcontractors, and repairmen that is used in constructing, improving, maintaining, servicing, or repairing real property of an approved business that is located in a tax-free NY area. The credit or refund is allowed for 120 consecutive months beginning with the month during which the business locates in the tax-free NY area. (TSB-M-13(7)S)

Note: An approved business located in a tax-free NY area that makes sales subject to sales and use tax is still required to be registered as a sales tax vendor and to collect and remit the appropriate state and local sales tax on its sales. (TSB-M-13(7)S)

Purchases by an approved business eligible for a refund or credit.—For purchases and uses of property and services to be eligible for a credit or refund, the property or services (other than the Tax Law Sec. 1105(b) consumer utility services discussed below) must be directly and predominantly used or consumed by an approved business at its location in a tax-free NY area. For purposes of the credit or refund, predominantly means more than 50%. (TSB-M-13(7)S)

Consumer utility services (other than telephony and telegraphy, telephone and telegraph services, and telephone answering services) and prepaid telephone calling services must be used or consumed directly and exclusively (100%) by an approved business at its location in a tax-free NY area. Consumer utility services include sales of gas, electricity, refrigeration, and steam, as well as gas, electric, refrigeration, and steam services of whatever nature. Telephony and telegraphy, telephone and telegraph services, and telephone answering services must be delivered and billed to the approved business at an address at its location in the tax-free NY area. Mobile telecommunications services purchased by an approved business will qualify for the credit or refund where the approved business's place of primary use is at its location in a tax-free NY area. (TSB-M-13(7)S)

The credit or refund for an approved business located in a tax-free NY area does not apply to:

— the sales tax imposed under Tax Law Sec. 1105(d) on sales of food or drink at restaurants, taverns, or other establishments, or by caterers;

— the sales tax on rent for hotel occupancy imposed under Tax Law Sec. 1105(e);

— the sales tax on admission charges and dues imposed under Tax Law Sec. 1105(f); and

— the sales tax on transportation services imposed under Tax Law Sec. 1105(c)(10).

(TSB-M-13(7)S)

Contractors, subcontractors, and repairmen.—Contractors, subcontractors, and repairmen are eligible to claim a credit or refund for New York State and local sales and use tax, including the MCTD state sales tax, paid on purchases of tangible personal property used in erecting a structure or building for an approved business at its location in a tax-free NY area; or for use in adding to, altering, improving, maintaining, servicing, or repairing real property, property, or land of an approved business at its location in a tax-free NY area. This credit or refund is available for purchases of tangible personal property that becomes an integral component part of the approved business's structure, building, real property, property, or land. (TSB-M-13(7)S)

Tangible personal property that becomes an integral component part of the approved business's structure, building, real property, property, or land includes items such as building and landscaping materials, but does not include items such as tools, equipment, and supplies that are used or consumed by the contractor, subcontractor, or repairman. (TSB-M-13(7)S)

How to claim the credit or refund.—A claim for credit or refund for the sales and use tax paid on eligible purchases must be made by filing Form AU-11, Application for Credit or Refund of Sales or Use Tax. Taxpayers may submit Form AU-11 electronically using Sales Tax Web File. An approved business may file a claim for credit or refund only once each sales tax quarter. No interest is payable on any credit allowed or refund made. (TSB-M-13(7)S)

Penalties for fraud.—If the Commissioner of Economic Development makes a final determination that an approved business participating in the START-UP NY program has acted fraudulently in connection with its participation in the program, the business will be: (1) immediately terminated from the program; (2) subject to criminal penalties, including but not limited to the felony crime of offering a false instrument for filing in the first degree in accordance with Penal Law Sec. 175.35; and (3) required in that year to add back to tax the total value of all of the tax benefits provided under the START-UP program that the business and the employees of the business have received up to the date of the final determination. The amount required to be added back is reported on the business's corporation franchise tax return if the business is taxed as a corporation or is a corporate partner of a partnership, or on a personal income tax return if the owner of the business is a sole proprietor, an individual partner in a partnership, or a shareholder of a New York S corporation. (TSB-M-13(7)S)

[¶60-650] Resales

Sales for resale in New York are not subject to sales and use tax because the sales and compensating use taxes are imposed only upon "retail sales" of tangible personal property and selected services. (Sec. 1105, Tax Law; Reg. Sec. 526.6(c)(2))

Sales for resale include the following sales of tangible personal property:

— sales for resale in the same form as purchased;

— sales for resale as a physical component part of tangible personal property; and

— sales for use by the purchaser in performing certain taxable services where the property sold becomes a physical component part of the property upon which the services are performed or is later actually transferred to the purchaser of the taxable service in connection with that service. Those services include:

(a) information services;

(b) processing and printing services;

(c) installation, maintenance and repair services upon tangible personal property;

(d) real estate maintenance, service or repair;

(e) interior decorating and designing services; and

(f) protective and detective services.

(Sec. 1101(b)(4), Tax Law)

> **EXAMPLE:** *Book publisher's leather purchase.*—A book publisher purchases leather for making book bindings and then sells the books directly to the public. The leather has become a physical component part of the books sold to the public and, therefore, has been purchased for resale by the book publisher and is not subject to the tax. (Reg. Sec. 526.6(c)(5))

> **CCH EXAMPLE:** *Grease purchased by a service station.*—A service station purchases grease to be used for lubricating automobiles, without payment of tax, as the grease will be transferred to the customers in connection with the performance of a taxable service. (Reg. Sec. 526.6(c)(6))

See ¶ 61-020 Exemption Certificates

• *Resale certificates*

Unless a vendor receives a properly completed resale certificate, a sale is presumed not to be excluded from tax as a purchase for resale. A vendor who accepts a properly completed resale certificate is not liable for a failure to collect tax, even if the purchaser erroneously gave such certificate, unless the vendor has actual knowledge that the certificate is false. (Sec. 1132(c), Tax Law; Reg. Sec. 526.6(c)(2))

Form of resale certificate.—A sale for resale will be recognized only if the vendor receives a properly completed official resale certificate, Form ST-120, *Resale Certificate.* Such certificate is considered to be properly completed when it contains the following:

— the date prepared;

— name and address of the purchaser;

— name and address of the vendor;

— identification number of the purchaser as shown on its certificate of authority;

— signature of the purchaser or the purchaser's authorized representative; and

— any other information required to be completed on the particular certificate or document.

(Reg. Sec. 532.4(b)(2)(ii))

The resale certificate must be received within 90 days after the delivery of the property or the rendition of the service. (Reg. Sec. 532.4(b)(2)(iii))

Receipts from the sale of property purchased under a resale certificate are not subject to tax at the time of purchase by the person who will resell the property. Instead, the receipts are taxable at the time of the retail sale. (Reg. Sec. 526.6(c)(3))

See ¶ 61-020 Exemption Certificates.

Blanket resale certificates.—A purchaser may provide the vendor with a blanket resale certificate to cover additional purchases of the same general type of property or service. Each vendor accepting a resale certificate must, for verification purposes, maintain a method of associating a sale made for resale with the resale certificate on file. A blanket certificate has no definitive expiration date. Instead, it is valid as long as it is properly completed and the purchaser information on the form remains accurate. (Reg. Sec. 532.4(d))

Out-of-state purchasers.—The New York State Tax Department allows qualified out-of-state vendors not registered in New York State to use Form ST-120, *Resale Certificate*, in connection with purchases for resale that are exempt from New York sales and use taxes. (*TSB-M-98(3)S*)

Nonregistered out-of-state purchasers who qualify may use Form ST-120 when the New York vendor will drop-ship the item purchased for resale to the purchaser's customer in New York or to its unaffiliated fulfillment service provider in the state, or when the purchaser takes delivery of the item in New York for resale from a business located outside the state.

Form ST-120 may be used by qualified out-of-state purchasers either as a single-use certificate or as a blanket certificate, the latter choice covering the first and any subsequent purchases of the same general type of property or service purchased for resale.

New York registered vendors that accept Form ST-120 in lieu of collecting tax from an out-of-state purchaser must check to see that this certificate was timely issued and properly completed or corrected. The New York registered vendor should also have a method of associating the exemption certificate with corresponding invoices for exempt sales made to that purchaser.

MTC Uniform Sales and Use Tax Certificate.—New York does not currently allow vendors to accept the MTC Uniform Sales and Use Tax Certificate for resales.

Validity period.—Resale certificates do not have a stated expiration period. However, the resale certificate must be received within 90 days after the delivery of the property or the rendition of the service. (Reg. Sec. 532.4(b)(2)(iii)) (ST-120)

Retention of resale certificate.—The resale certificate must be retained for at least three years after the due date of the return to which it relates, or the date the return was filed, if later. (Form ST-120)

Revocation/cancellation of resale certificate.—Any purchaser that intentionally issues a fraudulent resale certificate may lose their certificate of authority. (Form ST-120)

• *Electronic resale certificates*

The New York Department of Taxation and Finance authorizes the use and acceptance of electronic versions of certain sales and use tax resale and exemption documents (e-certificates). The new policy does not require the use or acceptance of e-certificates. The paper resale and exemption forms prescribed by the Department may still be used. The change in policy only pertains to the manner in which resale and exemption documents may be executed. (TSB-M-07(1)S) For a complete discussion of e-certificates, see ¶61-020 Exemption Certificates.

E-certificates are not available from the Department. At their discretion, purchasers and sellers may establish the means to electronically issue and receive e-certificates. The Department does not prescribe specific technologies or technical specifications for executing e-certificates nor does the Department require the use of particular types of hardware or software. However, an e-certificate must reproduce in its entirety the current paper resale or exemption form issued by the Department. Although the electronic version does not need to be a facsimile or an exact copy of the paper form, it must contain all of the language that is on the current paper form. When electronically reproducing the Department's documents, it is incumbent on the purchasers and sellers that they use the current forms as the bases for their e-certificates, even if it has been updated by the Department. If a purchaser or a seller wishes to use an e-certificate that has modified language, including any additions or deletions, prior approval must be obtained from the Department. (TSB-M-07(1)S)

An e-certificate in its entirety, which includes all applicable instructions, must be available to both the purchaser and the seller. However, it is not necessary that the instructions be included when issuing an e-certificate to the seller in order for the e-certificate to be considered accepted in good faith or properly completed. If the paper resale or exemption form may be issued as a blanket certificate or as a single-purchase certificate, the corresponding e-certificate may also be issued as a blanket certificate or as a single-purchase certificate. In addition to reproducing all of the language (including all certifications) that is on the paper resale form, an e-certificate must contain specific e-certification and electronic signature language (see TSB-M-07(1)S for the specific language)

Electronic signatures.—To be relieved of liability for failure to collect tax, a seller must accept in good faith an e-certificate that is properly completed within 90 days after delivery of the property or the rendition of the service. A properly completed e-certificate includes the purchaser's (or authorized representative's) signature. In the case of an e-certificate, this requires an electronic signature that is in lieu of any written signature required on the paper counterpart. There is no requirement to affix a physical signature on the e-certificate. An electronic signature has the same validity and effect as a handwritten signature. (TSB-M-07(1)S)

Recordkeeping.—Sellers must keep e-certificates as part of the records required to be kept under the Tax Law and sales and use tax regulations. An e-certificate must comply with all of the requirements for retaining records, including the requirements that it be capable of being accurately reproduced so as to be perceptible by human sensory capabilities and be capable of being accessed by the Department if requested. (TSB-M-07(1)S)

• *Services*

Tangible personal property purchased for use in performing a non-taxable service is not purchased for resale. (Reg. Sec. 526.6(c)(7))

EXAMPLE: *Leather purchased by a shoe repairman.*—A shoe repairman purchases leather to be used for resoling shoes. The shoe repairman's purchase of the leather is not a purchase for resale even though the leather will be transferred to the customer in connection with the performance of the service, because the service that the shoe repairman is performing is not taxable. (Reg. Sec. 526.6(c)(7))

The resale exclusion also applies to a sale of service. (Reg. Sec. 526.6(c)(8))

¶60-650

Guidebook to New York Taxes

EXAMPLE: Jewelery services.—A jeweler sends a customer's watch to a repairman for servicing. The charge by the jeweler to the customer is taxable. The charge to the jeweler by the repairman is not taxable because the service was purchased for resale by the jeweler. (Reg. Sec. 526.6(c)(8))

• *Promotional material*

Tangible personal property which is purchased and given away without charge, for promotional or advertising purposes, is subject to tax as a retail sale to the purchaser. (Reg. Sec. 526.6(c)(4)(i)) Likewise, tangible personal property which is purchased for promotional or advertising purposes and sold for a minimal charge which does not reflect its true cost, or which is not ordinarily sold by that person in the operation of his or her business, is a retail sale to the purchaser. (Reg. Sec. 526.6(c)(4)(ii))

• *Withdrawals from inventory*

The compensating use tax is due upon the use of tangible personal property that was purchased for resale or an exempt use and is subsequently withdrawn from or diverted to a taxable use by the purchaser. (Reg. Sec. 531.3(a)(2))

EXAMPLE: Desk removed from inventory.—A retail store purchased a dozen desks at $75 each for sale to its customers at $125 each. It subsequently withdrew one of the desks from inventory to be used in its office. A compensating use tax is due for the desk withdrawn from inventory. The tax is computed on the $75 that the store paid. (Reg. Sec. 531.3(a)(2))

EXAMPLE: Drill press withdrawn from production lines.—A machine shop which produces machine tools for sale withdraws a drill press from its production line for use in its building maintenance shop. The drill press was originally purchased exempt from tax for use in production. The use of the drill press in the building maintenance shop is a use subject to the compensating use tax at cost or fair market value, whichever is lower. (Reg. Sec. 531.3(a)(2))

[¶60-665] Services

Services are generally exempt from sales and use tax in New York unless specifically identified as taxable. (Sec. 1105(c), Tax Law)

The New York Department of Taxation and Finance provides a quick reference guide for taxable and exempt property and services, including examples of each, and required exemption documents. (TB-ST-740)

What services are taxable in New York?

The taxable services include:

Auto repair and body shops

Credit reporting

Hotel services

Information services

Interior decorating and design

Motor vehicle parking, garaging, and storage

Pest control

Producing, fabricating, processing, printing, and imprinting

Protective and detective services

Repair, installation, and maintenance

Safe deposit rental

Storage

Telecommunications

Transportation

Utilities

Veterinarians

Beauty salons, barber shops, and hair restoration services (New York City only)

Hair removal services (New York City only)

Manicures and pedicures (New York City only)

Massage services (New York City only)

Tanning salons (New York City only)

Tattooing and permanent make-up services (New York City only)

What about transactions that also involve tangible personal property?

When tangible personal property is provided as an incidental addition to an exempt service, the entire transaction generally remains exempt. (*Sharon I. Burkert d/b/a Sharon't Nail Fashions*; TSB-A-88(22)S)

How is tangible personal property purchased by the service provider treated?

An item sold to a service provider is not subject to tax if the item becomes a physical component of the property upon which taxable services are performed or if the item is later transferred to the purchaser of the service. A sale for resale also is not subject to tax. Tangible personal property purchased for use in performing a nontaxable service is not considered to be purchased for resale and is subject to tax. (Sec. 1101(b)(4), Tax Law; Reg. Sec. 526.6(c)(7)) See Resales. (¶ 60-650)

Does New York provide any detailed guidance on specific services?

Yes, the Department of Taxation and Finance has issued detailed guidance on many of the services found below.

Auto repair and body shops. Most charges by a repair or body shop are taxable. Auto repair and body shops must collect sales tax on the total charge for parts and labor for the repair services they provide, as well as on parts or supplies (i.e., windshield wipers or motor oil) sold directly to their customers. (TB-ST-40) For further discussion of auto repair and body shops, see Motor Vehicles. (¶ 60-570)

Beauty salons, barber shops, and hair restoration services. Beautician, barbering, and hair restoration services are exempt from state and local sales tax everywhere in New York outside New York City, but subject to New York City's local sales tax when sold in New York City. Hair restoration services performed in New York City by a licensed physician are not taxable. Beautician, barbering, and hair restoration services include: haircuts, hair coloring, shampooing, blow drying, permanents, hair extensions, hair straightening, and hair restorations. (TB-ST-60)

Sales of products. Sales of products to customers, such as shampoos, conditioners, and hair styling products, are subject to sales tax throughout New York. Sales of all dandruff preparations, including dandruff shampoos, are not taxable. In addition, sales of products that are intended as a hair regrowth treatment (such as Rogaine) for use by people who have hair loss or gradual thinning of the hair are not taxable. (TB-ST-60)

Purchases of products. A business may purchase products that it intends to resell to customers without paying sales tax by giving their supplier a properly completed Form ST-120, Resale Certificate. However, any products a business buys to be used in providing beautician, barbering, or hair restoration services cannot be purchased for resale, and the business must pay sales tax to the supplier at the time of purchase. Also, any items bought for resale that are later used in providing services are subject to use tax. (TB-ST-60)

EXAMPLE: The owner of a beauty salon keeps an inventory of various shampoos, conditioners, and other hair styling products available for retail sale to her customers. Occasionally she takes some of those products for her own use in providing beautician services at the salon. The owner of the salon must pay use tax on her cost for the products used in providing services at the salon.

Purchases of equipment. All purchases of equipment for use in such business are subject to sales tax at the time of purchase, including scissors, brushes, combs, mirrors, hair dryers, capes, razors, and barber chairs. (TB-ST-60)

Booth rentals. Charges for booth rentals that give the renter the right to use certain space are considered to be charges for the rental of real property and are not subject to sales tax. (TB-ST-60)

Utilities. All charges for utilities used in providing beautician, barbering, and hair restoration services are subject to sales tax. (TB-ST-60)

Hair removal services. Sales of hair removal services are exempt from state and local sales tax everywhere in New York outside New York City, but subject to New York City's local sales tax when sold in New York City. Hair removal services include electrolysis, waxing, and laser treatments. (TB-ST-326)

Sales of products. Sales of products to customers, such as shave gels and depilatory creams, razors, pulsed light hair removal systems, and hair trimmers, are subject to tax throughout New York. (TB-ST-326)

Purchases of products. A business may purchase products that it intends to resell to its customers without paying sales tax by giving its supplier a properly completed Form ST-120, Resale Certificate. However, any products a business buys to be used in providing hair removal services cannot be purchased for resale, and it must pay sales tax to its supplier at the time of purchase. Also, any items that a business buys for resale that it later uses in providing its services are subject to use tax. (TB-ST-326)

Purchases of equipment. All purchases of equipment for use in the business are subject to sales tax at the time of purchase, including epilators, wax warmers, electrolysis hair removal systems, hair trimmers, and laser hair removal workstations. (TB-ST-326)

Booth rentals. Charges for booth rentals that give the renter the right to use certain space are considered to be charges for the rental of real property and are not subject to sales tax. (TB-ST-326)

Utilities. All charges for utilities used in providing hair removal services are subject to sales tax. (TB-ST-326)

Interior decorating and design services. Anyone who sells interior decorating or design services must register for New York sales tax purposes if they deliver services in New York or if they have a place of business in the state. Except for the New York City local sales tax, these services are taxable at the full state and local sales tax rate, including the Metropolitan Commuter Transportation District (MCTD) sales tax.

Interior decorating and design services generally relate to the planning and design of interior spaces. Such services are not limited to services performed on residential or commercial properties for property owners or tenants. (TB-ST-400)

Architecture and engineering. Interior decorating and design services do not include services that consist of the practice of architecture or engineering. However, when a licensed architect or engineer performs interior decorating or design services that do not constitute architecture or engineering, those services are taxable. (TB-ST-400)

Sales to, or uses by, licensed architects and engineers. Drawings, plans, renderings, and other interior decorating and design services sold to a licensed architect or engineer are taxable, unless the services will be resold or used by the architect or engineer in performing a taxable decorating or design service. The fact that a sale is made to a licensed architect or engineer does not make the sale exempt from sales tax as a service that consists of the practice of architecture or engineering. Also, the use of an interior decorating or design service by an architect or engineer is subject to use tax. (TB-ST-400)

An architect or engineer who purchases a decorating or design service and incorporates it into architectural or engineering plans for a customer cannot purchase the decorating or design service for resale because the interior decorating and design service is not resold by the architect or engineer as an interior decorating and design service.

Applicable tax rate. The point of delivery determines the sales tax rate applicable to a sale of interior decorating or design services. (TB-ST-400)

Sales of furniture, fixtures, and other services. Interior decorating or design services that are performed in conjunction with the sale of tangible personal property or other taxable services will be subject to state and local sales tax if the tangible personal property or services associated with the decorating service are delivered to the customer in New York. (TB-ST-400)

Manicures and pedicures. Sales of manicure and pedicure services are exempt from state and local sales tax everywhere in New York outside New York City, but subject to New York City's local sales tax when sold in New York City. Manicure and pedicure services include: nail shaping, cuticle trimming, nail strengthening applications, applying acrylic or gel nails, nail fills, exfoliation treatments, foot and calf massage, and paraffin treatments. (TB-ST-551)

Sales of products. Sales of products to customers, such as nail polish, nail files, soaking liquids, scrubs, and creams, are subject to tax throughout New York. Sales of products designed to treat a medical nail problem, such as nail fungus, are exempt from sales tax if the product contains a recognized drug or medicine. (TB-ST-551)

Purchases of products. A business may purchase products that it intends to resell to its customers without paying sales tax by giving its supplier a properly completed Form ST-120, Resale Certificate. Any products a business buys that are to be used in providing manicure and pedicure services cannot be purchased for resale, and the business must pay sales tax to the supplier at the time of purchase. Also, any items bought for resale that are later used in providing services are subject to use tax. (TB-ST-551)

Purchases of equipment. All purchases of equipment for use in such business are subject to sales tax at the time of purchase, including chairs, soaking tubs and bowls, disposable slippers and toe separators, scrubs, exfoliants, and creams. (TB-ST-551)

Booth rentals. Charges for booth rentals that give the renter the right to use certain space are considered to be charges for the rental of real property and are not subject to sales tax. (TB-ST-551)

Utilities. All charges for utilities used in providing manicure and pedicure services are subject to sales tax. (TB-ST-551)

Massage services. Sales of any massage services are exempt from state and local sales tax everywhere in New York outside New York City. However, sales of typical massage services are subject to New York City's local sales tax when sold in New York City. Sales of typical massage services are taxable in New York City even if a person is a licensed massage therapist under Title VIII of the Education Law. However, massage services performed by a licensed physician, physiotherapist, or chiropractor for medical reasons are not subject to New York City's local sales tax. (TB-ST-554)

Sales of products. Sales of products to customers, such as, electronic massagers, massage oils, lotions or creams, hot and cold packs, herbal wraps, and pillows, are subject to tax throughout New York. (TB-ST-554)

Purchases of products. A business may purchase products that it intends to resell to its customers without paying sales tax by giving its supplier a properly completed Form ST-120, Resale Certificate. Any products a business buys to be used in providing massage services cannot be purchased for resale, and the business must pay sales tax to its supplier at the time of purchase. Also, any items that are bought for resale that are later used in providing services are subject to use tax. (TB-ST-554)

Purchases of equipment. All purchases of equipment for use in such business are subject to sales tax at the time of purchase, including electronic massagers, massage tables, massage chairs and stools, hot towel cabinets, and facial systems. (TB-ST-554)

Booth rentals. Charges for booth rentals that give the renter the right to use certain space are considered to be charges for the rental of real property and are not subject to sales tax. (TB-ST-554)

Utilities. All charges for utilities used in providing massage services are subject to sales tax. (TB-ST-554)

Medical emergency response services. Sales of alarm call services designed specifically to respond to medical emergencies are exempt from sales and use taxes. (Sec. 1115(r), Tax Law)

Motor vehicle parking, garaging, and storing services. Sales tax is imposed on the services of parking, garaging, or storing motor vehicles in a garage, parking lot, or other place of business that provides these services (but not if the garage is part of a private one-or two-family residence). (Sec. 1105(c)(6), Tax Law) (TB-ST-677; Important Notice No. N-90-21)

Any person making a charge for parking, garaging or storing of motor vehicles is a vendor for the purpose of collecting sales tax. (Important Notice No. N-90-21) It is the Department of Taxation and Finance's position that a vendor engaged in the business of selling or renting motor vehicles cannot use an exempt use certificate when purchasing parking, garaging, or storage services from a person operating a garage, parking lot, or similar place of business, for vehicles that are held for rental or sale. Therefore, vendors of parking services are required to collect sales tax from vendors who sell or rent motor vehicles on charges made for parking, garaging, or storing motor vehicles. (TSB-M-08(4.1)S)

Examples of vendors engaged in providing taxable parking services include (TB-ST-677):

— public parking garages and lots;

— airports, train stations, etc., that charge for parking;

— a hotel that charges guests for parking in its garage;

— owners or operators of sports stadiums, ski centers, civic centers, beaches, racetracks, amusement parks, concert grounds, and similar places;

— hospitals that charge visitors, employees, or patients for parking;

— a business that charges its employees for parking;

— landlords who charge tenants for parking;

— a state agency selling permits that allow state residents unlimited parking at any of the state parks;

— a school that charges for parking during athletic events;

— a person at a private residence who charges for parking on a lawn during the week of a county fair; and

— marinas that charge for parking motor vehicles (other than docking charges for boats).

Calculating the sales tax due. Vendors should calculate the amount of sales tax due by multiplying the parking charge by the combined state and local rate in the jurisdiction where the vehicle is parked, garaged or stored. Sales tax must be separately stated on any receipt given to the customer, or the seller may be held liable for failing to collect tax. If a seller does not give its customers a receipt or similar evidence of payment, the seller must conspicuously post a sign explaining that the charges include sales tax. (TB-ST-677)

Nontaxable leases of real property. Payments made under a lease or rental agreement that includes parking, garaging, or storing of motor vehicles, where the agreement constitutes a lease of real property, are not subject to sales tax. (TB-ST-677; TSB-M-08(14)S) If a person who enters into an agreement to obtain parking, garaging, or storage of motor vehicles that qualifies as a lease of real property not subject to tax subsequently uses any part of the parking, garaging, or storage facility to provide parking, garaging, or storage services to other persons, the receipts from the sales of those services are subject to tax. (TSB-M-08(14)S) A transaction, including a concession agreement or similar agreement, will be treated as a nontaxable lease of real property if there is a written agreement between the parties and all of the following conditions are satisfied:

— the lessee has the exclusive right to occupy either the entire premises of the lessor, or a fixed and specific area;

— the lessor gives up the right to enter the leased premises except to perform activities normally required of a landlord, such as collecting rent and making repairs;

— the lessee, its employees, or agents have an unlimited right to enter the property during normal business hours; and

— the lessee has an insurable interest in the property.

(B-ST-677; TSB-M-08(14)S)

Homeowner's association. Charges paid by members of a homeowner's association to the association for parking, or charges paid by members of a homeowner's association to a person leasing the parking facility from the homeowner's association, are not subject to tax. The association's membership must be comprised exclusively of owners or residents of residential dwelling units and the association must own or operate the facility in which the services are provided or performed. (Sec. 1105(c)(6), Tax Law) (TB-ST-677; TSB-M-01(3)S)

Exempt organizations. Tax exempt organizations are not required to pay sales tax on their purchases of parking, garaging, or storage services. An exempt organization that sells parking services must collect sales tax on its charges for parking, garaging, and storing motor vehicles. (TB-ST-677)

New York City. Parking, garaging and storing of motor vehicles within New York City are subject to the state tax, the New York City local tax, and the Metropolitan Commuter Transportation District (MCTD) tax. Also, parking in Manhattan is subject to an additional 8% parking tax unless the purchaser is a certified exempt resident. (TB-ST-677) For additional information on New York City parking tax, see New York City Parking Tax. (¶ 560-030)

Moving services and related transactions. The service of transporting household goods (moving service) is not subject to sales tax unless the charge is included as part of the bill for the sale of taxable property or services (i.e., a charge for shipping as part of the sale of taxable tangible personal property). Moving services include moving household goods to and from any destination, whether local, intrastate, interstate or international. Moving services also include moving items from a building to a truck, from a truck to a building, or moving items within a building, whether or not truck transportation is provided. Office moves are treated the same as household moves. (TB-ST-341) Charges for general storage unrelated to moving services are subject to tax, as discussed below.

Storage in transit in relation to moving service. The Department of Taxation and Finance will recognize storage in transit (TB-ST-341) as incidental to the provision of an exempt transportation service, and as a result not taxable, if all of the following conditions are met:

— The mover is providing its customer a transportation service. That is, the mover provides its customer with a bill of lading specifying a destination address that is: different from the address where the mover picks up the property to be moved, and different from the location where the mover would provide storage.

— The mover is responsible to the customer for any loss or damage to the property during the storage-in-transit period.

— The mover remains responsible, during the storage-in-transit period, to complete the moving process.

— Any charge for storage in transit made or identified prior to the commencement of the transportation service does not exceed the amount of the charge for the transportation.

Storage in transit occurs in the context of a moving service when events delay the delivery of goods by the mover to the customer's destination, and the stored property is the responsibility of the mover. (TB-ST-341)

Movers should keep complete and accurate records to substantiate a period of exempt storage in transit and when that period ends. When providing exempt storage in transit a mover cannot purchase the storage for resale and must pay sales tax to any third party from which the mover purchases storage services. (TB-ST-341)

Sales to exempt entities. If the customer is an exempt governmental entity, the mover does not need to collect sales tax on its sales of any taxable storage services provided the mover receives a governmental purchase order or a government contract to document the exempt sale. If the customer is an exempt organization claiming a sales tax exemption, the customer must give the mover or warehouser a properly completed Form ST-119.1, Exempt Organization Exempt Purchase Certificate, to verify the customer's exempt status. If the mover pays a third party to provide the storage, the mover can issue Form ST-120, Resale Certificate, to the storage provider to purchase the storage for resale. However, if the mover pays a third party to provide storage during a period of storage in transit, that payment is subject to sales tax. (TB-ST-341)

Packing materials sold to customers. Any sales of cartons, boxes, barrels, covers, crates, paper for padding, bubble wrap, Styrofoam peanuts, and like materials directly to a customer for use by that customer in packing are taxable if the customer takes possession of the materials in New York. A mover that makes these sales must be registered for sales tax purposes. Packing materials that are resold to the customer and become the property of the customer will not be subject to tax when purchased by the mover if the mover furnishes the supplier with a properly completed Form ST-120, Resale Certificate. A mover who pays tax on the purchase of packing materials may be entitled to a credit or refund of tax if those materials are later resold to and become the property of the mover's customer. (TB-ST-341)

Materials used by movers. All items used and consumed by a mover in providing moving services (i.e., tape, markers, paper for padding, bubble wrap, Styrofoam peanuts, cartons, boxes, etc.) are subject to tax at the time of purchase by the mover. If the mover purchases materials without paying sales tax (i.e., the mover purchases these items from an out-of-state vendor who does not collect New York state and local sales taxes) and uses the materials as part of its moving services, the purchase price of the materials is subject to use tax at the rate in effect where the mover first uses the items. (TB-ST-341)

Services provided by movers. The services of packing, unpacking, loading, and unloading goods, etc., by a mover are considered incidental to the moving services and are not taxable. Charges for packing services provided in connection with a move into or out of permanent storage, when the mover is a third party and not the provider of the storage service, are considered part of the overall moving services. When a mover hires a third party to crate an item for transport, the entire charge by the third party to the mover is subject to sales tax. When the mover charges the customer for the crating services, the charge is part of the moving services and is not taxable. (TB-ST-341)

Disassembly and dismantling services. Separately stated and reasonable charges by the mover to its customer, or charges by a third party to the mover, for disassembly and dismantling services are not subject to sales tax. (TB-ST-341)

Assembly and installation services. Whether separately stated charges by the mover to its customer for assembly or installation services performed inside New York are subject to sales tax depends on the nature of the service performed. Similarly, the nature of the services performed determines whether charges by a third party to the mover for assembly or installation services are subject to tax. If the property installed does not become an integral part of the real property at the customer's destination (i.e., beds, pianos, exercise machines, pool tables, etc.), charges by the mover to its customer, or charges by a third party to the mover, for the assembly or installation services are subject to tax. However, if the property does become an integral part of the real property at the customer's destination (i.e., certain appliances, chandeliers, certain hot tub installations, etc.) the installation services may qualify as a capital improvement. (TB-ST-341)

Unpacking and removal of packing materials. Most household movers will unpack a customer's belongings at the customer's destination for an additional fee. This service usually includes the removal of boxes, packaging, and other packing materials once the unpacking is complete. The mover's service of unpacking a customer's belongings and removing any packing materials is considered part of the overall moving services and is not subject to tax. If the mover hires a third party to remove packing materials, the charge by the third party to the mover is subject to sales tax at the rate in effect where the service is performed in New York. When the mover passes these charges through to the customer, the charges are part of the overall moving services and are not taxable. (TB-ST-341)

Municipal services. Services provided by a municipality, which are of a type ordinarily provided by a private person, are not taxable when the charge for the services is a tax based on the assessed valuation of the property in a municipality rather than specific charges for such services. (Reg. Sec. 527.7(d)) Charges for services rendered by municipalities are subject to tax when such charges are for services of a type ordinarily provided by private persons and the charges are arrived at based solely on the services rendered to a specific person, family or location. The fact that a charge is added to a real property tax bill for the purposes of collection and levy does not change the taxability of the charge.

Pest control services. Pest control and rodent services are taxable. (Sec. 1105(c)(5), Tax Law)

Processing and printing services. Tax is imposed upon the services of producing, fabricating, processing, printing or imprinting tangible personal property, when performed for a person who directly or indirectly furnishes the tangible personal property (not purchased for resale) upon which such services are performed. (Sec. 1105(c)(2), Tax Law) When such services are combined with the sale of property by the person performing the services, the entire transaction is taxable. (Reg. Sec. 527.4(a)(4))

Production services relating to mailing lists are exempt from tax if mailed, shipped or otherwise distributed from a point within New York to customers or prospective customers located outside New York, for use outside New York. (Sec. 1115(n)(2), Tax Law)

Use of tangible property not acquired for resale upon which processing or printing services have been performed. The use tax is imposed at the rate of 4% of the consideration given or contracted to be given for the processing or printing service, including the consideration for any tangible personal property transferred in connection with the performance of the service, plus any charges for shipping and delivery of the property so transferred and of the tangible personal property upon which the service was performed. (Sec. 1110, Tax Law)

The terms "producing," "fabricating," and "processing," are defined in Reg. Sec. 527.4.

Where sales or use tax has been paid on purchases of tangible personal property used in connection with a taxable processing or printing service there is a right to a refund or credit, subject to specified conditions. (Sec. 1119(c), Tax Law) Provisions governing eligibility for such a refund or credit are discussed at Credits. (¶ 61-270)

Protective and detective services. Tax is imposed on the sale of protective and detective services, whether or not any tangible personal property is transferred in connection with the service. (Sec. 1105(c)(8), Tax Law)

Protective and detective services include, but are not limited to:

— all types of protective services, including the operation of alarm and protection systems or services of whatever nature (i.e., fire, burglar, medical, contamination, mechanical breakdown or malfunction, or any similar alarm or protection system or service);

— detective agency services;

— private investigator services;

— armored car services;

— bonded courier services;

— watchman and patrol services;

— fingerprinting services;

— lie detection services;

— guard services;

— bodyguard services; and

— guard dog services.

(Sec. 1105(c)(8), Tax Law) (Important Notice No. N-90-20)

However, the term protective and detective services does not include those services performed by a licensed port watchman. (Sec. 1105(c)(8), Tax Law)

Vendors of protective and detective services who are not already registered to collect sales tax must file a Certificate of Registration with the Tax Department and have a valid Certificate of Authority at the time the taxable service is rendered. (Important Notice No. N-90-20)

Physical location of service. The physical location of the real or personal property being protected determines whether or not certain protective services (alarm and protection systems, patrol, guard dog, watchmen services, etc.) are taxable in New York. (Important Notice No. N-90-20) Where the service is taxable in New York, physical location is also a determining factor for the purposes of computing the correct local tax. The application of the tax to armored car services and the services of bonded couriers is determined by the place in which the items protected are delivered, regardless of where the items are picked up. When detective and investigative services are performed and an investigative report is rendered as a result, the tax consequence of that service is determined by the point of delivery of the report rather than the location of the subject of the report.

New York City. In New York City, the state sales tax must be collected in addition to the city sales tax already being collected on charges for protective and detective services. (Important Notice No. N-90-20) Sales of the following services in New York City are not reported on Part 3 of Schedule N, Taxes on Selected Sales and Services in New York City Only (quarterly ST-100.5, ST-810.5, annual ST-101.5): interior cleaning and maintenance services (regardless of the length of the contract); protective and detective services; and interior decorating and design services. The listed services must be reported on the main sales tax return (quarterly ST-100 or ST-810, annual ST-101). Vendors making sales of such services outside New York City are required to report the tax on their regular sales and use tax return. (Important Notice No. N-90-20)

Safe deposit rental. The rental of safe deposit boxes or similar spaces are subject to tax. (Sec. 1105(c)(4), Tax Law; Reg. Sec. 527.6(b)(2))

Storage. General storage services and the services of storing tangible personal property not held for sales in the regular course of business are generally subject to sales tax. (Sec. 1105(c)(4), Tax Law; Reg. Sec. 527.6(b)(2)) However, the rental of real property for storage and storage services delivered to a purchaser outside of New York are not subject to tax. (Reg. Sec. 527.6(b)(2)) (TB-ST-340) The service of transporting household goods (moving service) is discussed separately.

"General storage" refers to storage services that are provided outside the context of a moving service. The purpose of a general storage transaction is to have property stored at a facility by the storage service provider for period of time. Its purpose is not to have property stored temporarily in the process of being moved from point A to point B. (TB-ST-340) "Storage" is defined as the provision of a place for the safekeeping of goods, without regard to the manner of payment or length of time of the service. (Reg. Sec. 527.6(a))

Separate charges associated with storage services. Separate charges listed as pull charges, warehouse labor, and pickup and delivery shown on the invoice for storage service are part of the taxable receipts for the storage service, regardless of the duration of the storage. (TB-ST-340)

Location of storage services. Storage services are considered to be delivered at the location where the storage service provider takes possession of the property to be stored, without regard to the location of the storage facility itself. Therefore, where a storage service provider takes possession of property in New York, the sale is subject to New York state and local sales taxes. Where a storage provider takes possession of property at a point outside New York, no New York state sales tax is due. (TB-ST-340)

Storage services vs. rental of real property. Although charges for storage services are subject to tax, charges for the rental or lease of real property, even though used by the tenant for storing property, are not subject to sales tax. Indicators of a rental or lease of real property include:

— the tenant contracts for a certain amount of footage in a specific location;

— the tenant has unlimited control of access to the space and exclusive possession of the space (where a self-storage facility is not open to customers at all hours, a customer is considered to have unlimited control as long as the customer has access to the space during hours when other similar commercial storage facilities are generally accessible);

— the tenant's possession and control of the space must be to the exclusion of the proprietor (the tenant's exclusive possession of the space may be established by means of a lock, either the proprietor's or the tenant's, on the door of the enclosed space, under the control of the tenant). Exclusive possession will still be recognized if the proprietor has a duplicate or master key and, as a result, has access to the space, but the written lease agreement specifically provides that the proprietor has no right of access to the space during the term of the rental except to collect rent, make necessary repairs, or in an emergency;

— the tenant is allowed to supply racks, cabinets, and other facilities for the tenant's own use in the leased space; and

— the proprietor does not provide any additional services that require the tenant to give up possession and control of his or her property to the proprietor (such as receiving, handling, storing, or forwarding of the tenant's personal property). If the proprietor provides such additional services that require the tenant to give up possession and control of the stored goods to the proprietor, a lease may be deemed to constitute a taxable storage service. (Reg. Sec. 527.6(b)(2)) (TB-ST-340)

Portable storage and moving containers. The use of portable storage and moving containers by a customer on the customer's premises is a rental of tangible personal property subject to sales tax if the customer's premises are located in New York. Charges for initial delivery of an empty container to the customer and for pick-up of the container for return are part of the rental charge subject to sales tax. The charge for picking up a loaded container at a customer's location and delivering it to a storage facility, and the charge for delivering a loaded container from a storage facility to a customer's location, are subject to sales tax. However, the charge for moving a container from the customer's location to a different location, without delivery to a storage facility, is a charge for a moving service and is not subject to tax if the charge is reasonable and is separately stated on the bill or invoice given to the customer. (TB-ST-340)

Rental of self-service mini-storage units. The rental of self-service mini-storage units is not subject to tax. Such transaction constitutes a lease of real property for storage, rather than the taxable service of providing storage space. (TSB-M-86(3)S)

Demurrage. A vendor's charge to a customer for a delay by the customer in removing tangible personal property from the vendor's premises is a charge for the storage of such tangible personal property. (Reg. Sec. 526.5(i)(2))

Motor vehicles. While tax is imposed on storage of motor vehicles, it is not imposed on parking or garaging of vehicles. (Reg. Sec. 527.6(b)(3))

Tanning salons. Sales of tanning services, whether paid on a per-visit basis or paid for in advance (i.e., 10 visits for $50.00), are exempt from state and local sales tax everywhere in New York outside New York City, but subject to New York City's local sales tax when sold in New York City. (TB-ST-853)

Sales of products. Sales of products to customers, such as, lotions, creams, protective goggles, and jewelry, are subject to tax throughout New York. Sales of sunscreens are not taxable. (TB-ST-853)

Purchases of products. A tanning salon may purchase products that it intends to resell to its customers without paying sales tax by giving its supplier a properly completed Form ST-120, Resale Certificate. Any products a tanning salon buys to be used in providing tanning services cannot be purchased for resale, and the salon must pay sales tax to its supplier at the time of purchase. Also, any items that are bought for resale that are later used in providing services are subject to use tax. (TB-ST-853)

Purchases of equipment. All purchases of equipment for use in such a business are subject to sales tax at the time of purchase, including tanning beds, lamps, towels, clothes racks, and sanitation kits. (TB-ST-853)

Utilities. All charges for utilities used in providing tanning services are subject to sales tax. (TB-ST-853)

Tattooing and permanent make-up services. Sales of tattooing and permanent make-up services are exempt from state and local sales tax everywhere in New York outside New York City, but subject to New York City's local sales tax when sold in New York City. Tattooing is a cosmetic process that uses needles and colored ink to permanently put a mark or design on a person's skin. Applying permanent make-up, such as eyelining and other permanent colors to enhance the skin of the face, lips, eyelids, and eyebrows, is also a cosmetic service. Tattooing services performed in New York City for medical reasons (i.e., cancer radiation therapy) by a person who is licensed under Title VIII of the Education Law are not taxable. (TB-ST-855)

Sales of products. Sales of products to customers, such as, jewelry, or aftercare ointments, lotions, or creams, are subject to tax throughout New York. (TB-ST-855)

Purchases of products. A business may purchase products that it intends to resell to customers without paying sales tax by giving its supplier a properly completed Form ST-120, Resale Certificate. Any products the business buys that are to be used in providing tattoo or permanent make-up services cannot be purchased for resale, and the business must pay sales tax to its supplier at the time of purchase. Also, any items that are bought without paying tax that are later used in providing services are subject to use tax. (TB-ST-855)

Purchases of equipment. All purchases of equipment for use in such a business are subject to sales tax at the time of purchase. (TB-ST-855) This includes purchases of:

— needles;

— chairs or beds;

— lights;

— mirrors;

— coil and/or rotary machines; and

— sterilization and sanitation kits.

Booth rentals. Charges for booth rentals that give the renter the right to use certain space are considered to be charges for the rental of real property and are not subject to sales tax. (TB-ST-855)

Utilities. All charges for utilities used in providing tattooing and permanent make-up services are subject to sales tax. (TB-ST-855)

Training seminars. There are no specific provisions in New York regarding training seminar services. Since New York taxes only specified services, and training seminars are not specifically enumerated, such services are not subject to tax. (Sec. 1105(c), Tax Law)

Travel agencies. There are no specific provisions in New York regarding travel agency services. Since New York taxes only specified services, and travel agency services are not specifically enumerated, such services are not subject to tax. (Sec. 1105(c), Tax Law)

Veterinarians. No sales tax is due on charges for services provided by a licensed veterinarian (TB-ST-930) relating to the health care of pet or farm animal, including:

— diagnosing and treating the illness or disease of an animal;

— providing wellness visits;

— administering vaccines;

— hospitalization required for medical reasons (as opposed to boarding);

— grooming and clipping (if performed as a necessary part of the practice of veterinary medicine, such as clipping before surgery); and

— services that would otherwise be taxable, but are provided to a guide, hearing, or service do (such as grooming, nail clipping, or boarding).

However, sales tax is due on charges for taxable services not relating to health care of animals, including:

— boarding;

— grooming and clipping (except when provided as a necessary part of the practice of veterinary medicine);

— pet cremation; and

— pet burial services.

Purchases made by veterinarians. All tangible personal property or taxable services purchased by a veterinarian for use in the practice of veterinary medicine or for performing taxable services are taxable at the time of purchase. (TB-ST-930) Taxable purchases include:

— medical equipment and supplies;

— drugs and medicines;

— office equipment and supplies;

— boarding equipment and supplies;

— cleaning supplies;

— equipment repair; and

— landscaping and lawn maintenance.

However, a refund or credit is available for sales tax paid on a veterinarian's purchases of drugs or medicines used to provide veterinary services to livestock or poultry if the livestock or poultry is used in the production of tangible personal property for sale by farming. The refund or credit is also available if the drugs or medicines are sold to a person engaged in farming for use on such livestock or poultry. Effective June 1, 2018, the existing credit or refund is converted to an upfront exemption. (Sec. 1115(f)(2), Tax Law) (TB-ST-930)

This exemption applies to: (i) drugs or medicine sold to or used by a veterinarian providing exempt veterinary services to livestock or poultry used in farm production; and (ii) drugs or medicine sold to or used by a person on livestock or poultry used in farm production. (TSB-M-18(1)S)

Nontaxable sales of items by veterinarians. No sales tax is due on sales by a veterinarian of items designed for use in the care of domestic animals, poultry, or guide, hearing, and service dogs. (TB-ST-930) These items include, but are not limited to:

— drugs, medicines, and bandages;

— leashes, collars, and pet beds;

— flea and tick collars, sprays and medications;

— pet food;

— grooming tools; and

— pet cages and carriers.

However, a veterinarian must pay sales tax when purchasing these items.

Taxable sales of items by veterinarians. Sales tax is due on the sale by a veterinarian of an animal (except for guide, hearing, and service dogs), and on the sale of other property that is not for use in the care of domestic animals or poultry (i.e., calendars, mugs, T-shirts, pictures, key rings, etc.). However, items intended for resale that are not for use in the care of domestic animals or poultry may be purchased without paying sales tax. A veterinarian must have a Certificate of Authority and must give the seller a properly completed Form ST-120, Resale Certificate, to make purchases for resale. (TB-ST-930)

Sales to tax-exempt purchasers. Sales by veterinarians to certain purchasers are exempt from tax. When eligible, these exempt purchasers must give the veterinarian a properly completed exemption certificate or other documentation to claim an exemption from tax. Exempt purchasers include (TB-ST-930):

— farmers (when making purchases relating to animals used in farm production);

— commercial horse boarders;

— owners of guide, hearing, or service dogs;

— the United Nations, diplomatic missions, and diplomatic personnel;

— certain religious, charitable, scientific, and educational institutions;

— certain organizations organized and operated for the prevention of cruelty to children or animals;

— certain Indian nations; and

— certain organizations consisting of past and present members of the armed forces of the United States.

[¶60-740] Transportation

In general, transportation equipment and supplies are exempt, but transportation services are taxable. (Sec. 1115, Tax Law; Sec. 1101(b)(17), Tax Law; Sec. 1105, Tax Law)

How does New York tax transportation equipment and supplies?

In general, transportation equipment and supplies are exempt from sales and use tax. (Sec. 1115, Tax Law; Sec. 1101(b)(17), Tax Law; Sec. 1105, Tax Law)

Non-commercial vessels. An exemption from state and local sales and use tax is provided for receipts in excess of $230,000 from the sale of a vessel, including any outboard motor or trailer sold in conjunction with the vessel (vessels costing $230,000 or less are taxable). (Sec. 1115(jj), Tax Law) (TSB-M-15(2)S) The following amounts are included in computing the price of a vessel for purposes of the exemption:

— the price of the vessel itself, including: (i) property affixed to the vessel for its equipping, such as furniture, fixtures, built-in appliances, window coverings, climate control systems, navigation equipment, or entertainment systems; and (ii) property that the vessel is outfitted with at the time of sale that is necessary for its normal operation, such as an anchor, a flare gun, flotation devices, pumps, ropes, cables, chains, lifeboat or life raft;

— the price of any outboard motor sold with the vessel;

— the price of any trailer sold with the vessel; and

— any charges by the seller for shipping or delivery. (TSB-M-15(2)S)

The combined price of these items is reduced by the amount of any trade-in allowance. (TSB-M-15(2)S)

The cap of $230,000 also applies in determining the maximum amount subject to sales or use tax for:

— leases of vessels subject to the accelerated tax payment provisions of Tax Law § 1111(i);

— transfers of vessels that qualify as retail sales under Tax Law §1111(q)); and

— a vessel that is qualified property subject to use tax under Tax Law § 1118(2) purchased out of state by a nonresident that is used primarily to carry certain individuals who were residents of New York at the time the vessel was purchased.

(TSB-M-15(2)S)

Accessories. Any accessories added to or included in the purchase of a vessel (i.e., décor, including paintings, sculptures, vases, etc.; tableware, glass-ware, or cookware; small appliances; deck furniture; linens, pillows, or towels; personal watercraft; or other ancillary property) are not included in computing the price of the vessel for purposes of the exemption. Such items remain fully taxable and should be invoiced separately from the price of the vessel itself. (TSB-M-15(2)S)

Vessels sold to nonresidents. The sale of a vessel to an out-of-state purchaser who takes possession of the vessel in New York is excluded from New York sales tax if:

— the purchaser, at the time of delivery, is a nonresident of New York; has no permanent place of abode in New York; and is not using the vessel in New York in carrying on any employment, trade, business, or profession in New York;

— the vendor does not assign a New York registration number to the vessel or issue a temporary registration to the purchaser for the vessel;

— the purchaser does not register the vessel in New York before registering it in another state or jurisdiction; and

— prior to taking delivery the purchaser furnishes the vendor a properly completed Certificate of Nonresidency of New York State and/or Local Taxing Jurisdiction (Form DTF-820).

(Sec. 1117, Tax Law) (TSB-M-01(4)S)

Payment of use tax. For a vessel that is purchased by a New York resident outside the state and subsequently used in New York, the use tax is not due until the first of these events occurs:

— the date that the vessel is required to be registered with the Department of Motor Vehicles;

— the date that the vessel is actually registered with the Department of Motor Vehicles; or

— the date when the purchaser of the vessel uses the vessel in New York for more than 90 consecutive days.

(Sec. 1118(13), Tax Law) (TSB-M-15(2)S)

The amount subject to New York use tax is the lesser of $230,000, the purchase price of the vessel, or the current fair market value of the vessel if the vessel was used by the purchaser outside of New York for more than six months prior to its first use in New York. (TSB-M-15(2)S)

Limitation on reciprocal credit. The reciprocal credit under Tax Law § 1118(7) for sales or use tax paid to another state or jurisdiction is limited to the amount of tax paid on the purchase price of the vessel up to $230,000, regardless of the actual purchase price or actual amount of tax paid to the other state or jurisdiction. (TSB-M-15(2)S)

Commercial vessels. Commercial vessels primarily engaged in interstate or foreign commerce, as well as property used by or purchased for the use of such vessels for fuel, provisions, supplies, maintenance and repairs (other than articles purchased for the original equipping of a new ship), are not subject to tax. (Sec. 1115(a)(8), Tax Law; Sec. 1105(c)(3)(iv), Tax Law; Reg. Sec. 527.5(b)(5)(i))

Receipts from services rendered to marine cargo containers used by or for commercial vessels engaged in foreign or interstate commerce are also excluded from tax. (Reg. Sec. 527.5(b)(5)(iv)) Examples of exempt services include: painting, hull cleaning, carpentry, hold cleaning and ship sealing, as well as repair and maintenance of radar, navigational aids, onboard cargo handling equipment, marine cargo containers, canvas and office equipment. (Reg. Sec. 528.9(d)(1)) Services that are not exempt include: stevedoring, cargo weighing, piloting and clerking and checking during cargo handling. (Reg. Sec. 528.9(d)(2))

"Commercial vessel" defined. A "commercial vessel" is any type of water craft used or engaged in the transportation for hire of persons or property on water. Any vessel used or engaged for other purposes on more than an occasional basis is not a commercial vessel. A commercial vessel is "primarily engaged in interstate or foreign commerce" where more than 50% of the receipts from the vessel's activities are derived from interstate or foreign commerce. (Reg. Sec. 527.5(b)(5)(ii))

Property used by or purchased for the use of commercial vessels. Examples of property used by or purchased for the use of commercial vessels that are exempt include:

— sea stores—all articles, supplies and provisions taken on board a vessel, necessary for the sustenance and maintenance of its passengers and crew during a voyage (such as foods, medicines, soap, toilet articles, etc.);

— ships stores—all articles, materials or supplies taken aboard a vessel, necessary and used for the maintenance of the ship during a voyage (such as spare parts, hand tools, grease, oil, etc.); and

— ships equipment—all articles which are necessary for navigation or operation of the vessel or for the safety or accommodation of persons or cargo aboard (such as anchors, cables, rigging, lifeboats, search lights, etc.). (Reg. Sec. 528.9(c))

Commercial fishing vessels. Fishing vessels used directly and predominantly in the harvesting of fish for sale are exempt from tax. (Sec. 1115(a)(24), Tax Law) For a complete discussion, see Agriculture (¶ 60-250).

General aviation aircraft. A sales and use tax exemption is provided for general aviation aircraft, and machinery or equipment to be installed on such aircraft. For purposes of the exemption, "general aviation aircraft" means an aircraft that is used in civil aviation and that is not a commercial aircraft, military aircraft, unmanned aerial vehicle or drone. (Sec. 1115(a)(21-a), Tax Law) (TSB-M-15(3)S)

For the sale (including a lease or rental) of a general aviation aircraft, the exemption applies to the receipts for (TSB-M-15(3)S):

— the aircraft itself;

— other property that is affixed to the aircraft for its equipping, such as furniture, fixtures, built-in appliances, window coverings, climate control systems, or entertainment systems; and

— property that the aircraft is outfitted with at the time of sale that is necessary for its normal operation, such as avionics, radios, weather radar systems, and navigation and emergency lighting.

However, any accessories added to the purchase price of the aircraft (i.e., items of décor, including paintings or other artwork; tableware, glassware, or cookware; small appliances; linens, pillows, or towels; or other ancillary property) are not exempt. Such items remain fully taxable and should be invoiced separately from the price of the aircraft itself. (TSB-M-15(3)S)

Machinery or equipment that is installed on a general aviation aircraft subsequent to its purchase and that is necessary for the aircraft's equipping or the aircraft's normal operation is also exempt from sales tax. Form ST-121, Exempt Use Certificate, should be used to claim the exemption by marking an X in the Other box and entering Machinery or equipment to be installed on exempt general aviation aircraft in the space provided. (TSB-M-15(3)S)

Commercial aircraft. An exemption is available for commercial aircraft. (Sec. 1115(a)(21), Tax Law) Commercial aircraft qualify for the exemption if the aircraft produces at least 50% of total income from the activity of transporting persons or property for compensation within New York or between states or countries. (TSB-M-80(4)S) An aircraft may also qualify if used to transport tangible personal property in the conduct of the purchaser's business. (TSB-M-96(14)S)

An aircraft used primarily to transport a purchaser's personnel or those of an affiliated entity does not qualify for the exemption. For purposes of the exemption, persons are affiliated persons with respect to each other where one of the persons has an ownership interest of more than 5% (whether direct or indirect) in the other, or where an ownership interest of more than 5% (whether direct or indirect) is held in each of the persons by another person or by a group of other persons that are affiliated persons with respect to each other. (Sec. 1101(b)(17), Tax Law; Sec. 1115(a)(21), Tax Law) (TSB-M-09(4)S)

Also, use tax is imposed on an aircraft that does not meet the definition of commercial aircraft, and is: purchased outright by and delivered to a New York resident, outside of New York, and subsequently used in New York by the New York resident; or, leased outside New York and subsequently used in New York by a lessee of the aircraft, who is a New York resident. (TSB-M-09(4)S)

Air cargo containers. A commercial airline's purchase of air cargo containers (which containers are of a permanent character suitable for repeated use and are specifically designed to facilitate the carriage of goods on aircraft) are an integral part of the aircraft and are not subject to tax. Nor does the tax apply to receipts from repairs to such containers. (TSB-M-80(4.1)S)

Fueling services. The taxability of fueling services furnished to an airline for use in its airplanes is dependent upon when title to the fuel vests in the airline. The charge for defueling an airplane is a taxable service. (Reg. Sec. 528.10(c)) However, fuel sold to an airline for use in its airplanes is exempt from tax. (Sec. 1115(a)(9), Tax Law) See ¶ 60-560 Motor Fuels.

Installation, maintenance or repair services to commercial aircraft. Installation, maintenance or repair services rendered to commercial aircraft primarily engaged in intrastate, interstate or foreign commerce are exempt from tax. (Sec. 1105(c)(3)(v), Tax Law) Also exempt are the services of installing, maintaining or repairing machinery or equipment on such commercial aircraft. Moreover, the tax is not imposed upon property used by or purchased for the use of such aircraft for maintenance and repairs, including flight simulators purchased by commercial airlines. (Sec. 1115(a)(21), Tax Law)

Foreign airlines. Use tax is not imposed upon the spare parts (including engines), consumable technical supplies and maintenance and ground equipment for use exclusively in the operation or handling of aircraft and aircraft stores brought into New York from a foreign country by a foreign airline holding a foreign air carrier permit to engage in foreign air transportation. In order for the exemption to apply, the following conditions must be met: (1) the property must be used on aircraft (or directly in the operation, handling or maintenance of the aircraft) of the airline providing foreign air transportation services (or the aircraft of another eligible foreign airline); and (2) the property must not be subject to taxes imposed in the foreign country in which the particular foreign airline is based if brought into that country by a U.S. airline operating in that country. (Sec. 1118(8), Tax Law)

Aircraft maintenance. Sales and use tax exemptions are allowed for maintenance and certain other services performed on aircraft, as well as tangible personal property purchased and used in performing the services, where such property becomes a physical component part of the property upon which the services are performed or where such property is a lubricant applied to aircraft. An exemption is also allowed for the storing of an aircraft by such service providers, when the storing is rendered in conjunction with the provision of such services to the aircraft. (Sec. 1115(dd), Tax Law) (TSB-M-09(18)S; TSB-M-04(8)S) In addition, the sale of any service that keeps an aircraft in a condition of fitness, efficiency, readiness or safety or restoring it to such condition, is also exempt. (TSB-M-09(18)S; TSB-M-04(8)S)

Exempt **services** to aircraft include, but are not limited to:

— cleaning, repairing or replacing upholstery of seating, walls, etc.;

— painting and repairing the interior or exterior of aircraft;

— interior and exterior cleaning of aircraft, including ordinary janitorial services (i.e. dusting, cleaning and washing of walls, floors and windows);

— mechanical services;

— ramp services to aircraft, such as emptying lavatories and de-icing; and

— operating tugs to tow an aircraft or operating other equipment to provide maintenance, service or repair to the aircraft.

(TSB-M-09(18)S; TSB-M-04(8)S)

Exempt **items** (provided they are purchased by the person who performs an exempt service to aircraft and the item becomes a physical component part of the aircraft) include, but are not limited to:

— machinery and equipment installed on the aircraft;

— engine parts;

— waxing and polishing agents;

— headsets that are hardwired into the aircraft and plug-in headsets used by the flight crew;

— paint;

— light bulbs; and

— cloth and other material purchased to repair or replace upholstery of seating, walls, etc.

(TSB-M-09(18)S; TSB-M-04(8)S)

Lubricants. Lubricants applied to aircraft (i.e. engine oil, grease, etc.) are also exempt, if purchased by the person performing an exempt service. Glycol or other antifreeze sprayed on aircraft for de-icing is not exempt, since it is not a lubricant and does not become a physical component part of the aircraft. (TSB-M-09(18)S; TSB-M-04(8)S)

¶60-740

Aircraft and vessels transferred between affiliated entities. The transfer of an aircraft or vessel to or by affiliated corporations or partnerships, or between corporations or partnerships and their shareholders or partners/members is a retail sale subject to state and local sales tax, unless the exception with regard to mergers between "unaffiliated persons" or another exemption applies. However, in certain situations a refund or credit is provided for the sales and use tax previously paid by the seller. (TSB-M-10(14)S) Entities are affiliated with respect to each other where (i) more than 5% of their combined shares are owned by members of the same family; (ii) one of the entities has an ownership interest of more than 5% (whether direct or indirect) in the other; or (iii) another person or group of other persons that are affiliated persons with respect to each other hold an ownership interest of more than 5% (whether direct or indirect) in each of the entities. (Sec. 1111(q), Tax Law)

Computation of tax. Sales tax on the transfer of an aircraft or vessel that qualifies as a retail sale is computed based on the price paid for the aircraft or vessel upon its acquisition by the transferor/seller. However, if the transferor/seller or transferee/purchaser affirmatively shows that the seller owned the aircraft or vessel for six months prior to making the transfer that qualifies as a retail sale, the sales tax is computed on the lesser of the current market value of the aircraft or vessel, or the price paid for the aircraft or vessel when it was acquired. (Sec. 1111(q), Tax Law; TSB-M-10(14)S) "Current market value" must not exceed the cost of the aircraft or vessel. (Sec. 1111(q), Tax Law)

Refund or credit. The transferee/purchaser of an aircraft or vessel, the transfer of which is taxable, may apply for a refund or credit against the sales or use tax due as a result of the transfer. The refund or credit is the amount of the sales or use tax paid to New York or any other state on the transferor's/seller's purchase or previous use of the aircraft or vessel, but not more than the sales tax due on the transfer or the use tax due on the purchaser's use in New York of the aircraft or vessel. In addition, the refund or credit based on the tax paid on the transferor's/seller's purchase or previous use of the aircraft or vessel is allowable regardless of the date on which the transferor/seller purchased or used the aircraft or vessel. (Sec. 1111(q), Tax Law) (TSB-M-10(14)S)

An application for refund or credit must be filed using Form AU-11, Application for Credit or Refund of Sales or Use Tax, within three years after the date the tax due from the transferee/purchaser was payable to the department. If the transferee/purchaser is registered for sales tax purposes, and where an application for refund or credit has been filed, the applicant may take the credit on the return which is due coincident with or immediately subsequent to the time the application for credit is filed. However, the taking of the credit on the return is deemed to be part of the application for credit. (TSB-M-10(14)S)

The Department of Taxation and Finance has the discretion to waive the requirement that an application for refund or credit be filed in order to claim the refund or credit where the refund or credit is equal to the amount of the tax due from the transferee/purchaser. In these cases the department will waive the requirement for an application for a refund or credit to be filed. In addition, no interest is allowed or paid on any refund or credit that is granted relating to these transfers. (TSB-M-10(14)S)

Trucks, tractors, trailers or semi-trailers. The purchase of a truck, trailer or tractor-trailer combination for rental or lease to an authorized carrier, pursuant to a written contractual agreement, for use in the transportation for hire of tangible personal property as augmenting equipment by the carrier, is deemed to be a retail sale and is, therefore, taxable. (Sec. 1101(b)(4), Tax Law) However, the actual rental or lease of such trucks, tractors or tractor-trailer combinations to an authorized carrier are exempt, provided that under such rental, lease or license to use, the owner of any such vehicle or any employee of such owner operates the vehicle. (Sec. 1115(a)(22), Tax Law)

Tractors, trailers and semi-trailers with gross vehicle weight in excess of 26,000 pounds. Tractors, trailers or semi-trailers, when used in combinations which have a gross vehicle weight in excess of 26,000 pounds, are exempt from tax. Property installed in tractors, trailers or semi-trailers for their equipping, maintenance or repair is also exempt. (Sec. 1115(a)(26), Tax Law)

The exemption does not apply with respect to the following (Reg. Sec. 528.26(a)(3)):

— trucks;

— motor fuel and/or diesel fuel;

— shop equipment;

— tools (other than tools sold as part of original equipment);

— tractors, trailers and semi-trailers when used in combinations which have gross vehicle weights of 26,000 pounds or less; and

— mobile homes and/or factory manufactured homes.

Installation, maintenance or repair services. Installation, maintenance or repair services performed on qualifying tractors, trailers, or semi-trailers used in combination with a gross vehicle weight in excess of 26,000 pounds are tax-exempt. Installation, maintenance or repair services performed on property installed on qualifying tractors, trailers or semitrailers for purposes of equipping, maintenance or repair are also exempt from tax. The exemption applies only when the receipts from the retail sale of the tractors, trailers, or semitrailers or property are exempt. (Sec. 1115(a)(26), Tax Law)

Definitions of tractor, trailer, and semi-trailer. A "tractor" is a motor vehicle designed and used as the power unit in combination with a semi-trailer or trailer, or two such trailers in tandem. It may not carry cargo, except that a tractor and semi-trailer engaged in the transportation of automobiles may transport motor vehicles on part of the power unit. (Reg. Sec. 528.26(b)(1)) A "trailer" is any vehicle not propelled by its own power, drawn on the public highways by a motor vehicle, except for: (1) motorcycle sidecars; (2) vehicles being towed by a non-rigid support; and (3) vehicles designed and primarily used for other purposes and only occasionally drawn by a motor vehicle. (Reg. Sec. 528.26(b)(3)) A "semi-trailer" is any trailer which is designed such that, when operated, the forward end of its body or chassis rests upon the body or chassis of the towing vehicle. (Reg. Sec. 528.26(b)(2))

Exemption Form ST-121.1. Exempt purchases or leases of qualifying vehicles, property, and services may be made using Form ST-121.1, Exemption Certificate for Tractors, Trailers, Semitrailers, or Omnibuses. (TB-ST-890) Specifically, the following can be purchased or leased exempt from sales tax using Form ST-121.1: a qualifying tractor, trailer, or semitrailer; tangible personal property for installation on qualifying tractors, trailers, or semitrailers, for their equipping, maintenance or repair; and installation, maintenance, or repair services performed on qualifying tractors, trailers, or semitrailers, or performed on tangible personal property installed on these vehicles. A qualifying tractor, trailer, or semitrailer is a vehicle being used in combination where the gross vehicle weight of the combination exceeds 26,000 pounds. (TB-ST-890)

A qualifying purchaser should fill out Form ST-121.1 and give it to the seller. The instructions for the form provide detailed definitions of the vehicles and other property that are eligible for the exemptions. The purchaser must give the seller a properly completed form within 90 days after the delivery of the property or performance of the service. Sales tax exemption certificates may also be issued and accepted electronically. Form ST-121.1 may be used as a single-purchase certificate, or as a blanket certificate covering the first and subsequent purchases of the same general type of property or service from the same seller. (TB-ST-890)

Form ST-121.1 cannot be used to purchase the following: nonqualifying vehicles or omnibuses; motor fuel or diesel motor fuel; services for, or property to be installed on, nonqualifying vehicles; equipment not installed as part of a qualifying tractor, trailer, or semitrailer (e.g., hand tools, road flares, and road reflectors), unless sold as part of the original equipment; or shop equipment (e.g., service jacks, tire changers, part washers, battery chargers, and truck and tractor washers). (TB-ST-890)

Ferry boats. Ferry boats used directly and predominantly to provide ferry service for vehicles and passengers within a county or counties by a ferry company whose rates are regulated by the county or counties in which that service is provided are exempt from sales and use taxes. Likewise, fuel, provisions, and supplies used in operating an exempt ferry boat and property purchased or used to maintain or repair an exempt ferry boat are also exempt from sales tax. However, these exemptions do not apply to charges for the service of maintaining, servicing, or repairing an exempt ferry boat or related property. (Sec. 1115(a)(43), Tax Law) (TSB-M-08(11)S)

A ferry boat company that purchases a boat or related property that qualifies for these exemptions, other than for fuel, must submit a properly completed Form ST-121, Exempt Use Certificate, to the vendor. To complete Form ST-121, the purchaser must check the "Other" box in Part III of the form and write "Property purchased to operate, maintain, or repair an exempt ferry boat (Tax Law Section 1115(a)(43))" in the box. Form ST-121 must be submitted to the vendor within 90 days after the delivery of the exempt boat or property. (TSB-M-08(11)S)

Refund of tax paid on fuel. Sales tax must be paid at the time of purchase on fuel used to operate an exempt ferry boat. However, the ferry boat company may apply for a refund of sales tax paid on purchases of fuel if the fuel is used to operate an exempt ferry boat, by filing Form FT-500, Application for Refund of Sales Tax Paid on Automotive Fuels. This form must be filed within three years of the date the tax was paid. (TSB-M-08(11)S)

Railroads.

Railroad rolling stock. Tax does not apply to the services of installing, maintaining and repairing railroad rolling stock primarily engaged in carrying freight in intrastate, interstate or foreign commerce. However, the tax is imposed upon any charge for parts or other tangible personal property, whether such property has become a physical component part of the property upon which the services are performed or has been transferred to the purchaser of the services in connection with the performance of the service. (Sec. 1105(c)(3)(viii), Tax Law)

Sales by railroad in reorganization to profitable railroad. Sales of tangible personal property by a railroad in reorganization to a profitable railroad, as part of a plan of reorganization and restructuring under the Regional Rail Reorganization Act of 1973, are exempt from the retail sales and compensating use taxes. (Sec. 1115(h), Tax Law; Reg. Sec. 528.25(a)) For purposes of the exemption, the term "profitable railroad" means any railroad which is not a railroad in reorganization. The term does not include the Consolidated Rail Corporation, the National Railroad Passenger Corporation, or a railroad leased, operated or controlled by a railroad in reorganization in the region. (Reg. Sec. 528.25(b))

Marine container terminals. Purchases or uses of machinery and equipment used directly and predominantly in loading, unloading, and handling cargo at a marine terminal facility located in New York City that handles more than 350,000 twenty-foot equivalent units (TEUs) are exempt from state sales and use tax. The exemption also applies to the sales and use taxes for the Metropolitan Commuter Transportation District (MCTD). The exemption does not apply to the local sales and use taxes imposed in New York City. (Sec. 1115(a)(41), Tax Law) (TSB-M-05(14)S)

For purposes of the exemption, the term "twenty-foot equivalent unit" is used to express the relative number of containers based on the equivalent length of a twenty-foot container. (Sec. 1115(a)(41), Tax Law) (TSB-M-05(14)S)

New York City sales tax collected by the vendor must be reported on the New York City-local tax only line of the sales tax return. Machinery and equipment that qualifies for the exemption and that is delivered to the purchaser outside of New York City is exempt from state and local sales and use taxes in that other jurisdiction. However, when the purchaser brings the machinery or equipment into New York City for use at the qualified marine terminal, the purchaser would owe the New York City compensating use tax. (TSB-M-05(14)S)

> **Forms.** A contractor making a purchase qualifying for the exemption should use Form ST-120.1, Contractor Exempt Purchase Certificate, to claim the exemption. A person other than a contractor making a purchase qualifying for the exemption should use Form ST-121, Exempt Use Certificate. (TSB-M-05(14)S) For a discussion of exemption certificates, see Exemption Certificates (¶ 61-020).

What is the tax treatment of transportation services in New York?

Sales tax is imposed on specified transportation services (i.e., limousines, black cars, etc.), whether or not any tangible personal property is transferred in conjunction with the service, and regardless of whether the charge is paid in New York or out-of-state, as long as the service is provided in New York. (Sec. 1105(c)(10), Tax Law) (TSB-M-09(2)S; TSB-M-09(7)S; TSB-M-09(16)S)

For purposes of the tax, "transportation service" is defined to include the service of transporting, carrying or conveying a person or persons by livery service, whether to a single destination or to multiple destinations, and whether the compensation paid by or on behalf of the passenger is based on mileage, trip, time consumed or any other basis. (Sec. 1101(b)(34), Tax Law) A "livery service" means service provided by limousine, black car or other motor vehicle (i.e. community cars or vans), with a driver, but excludes a taxicab, bus, affiliated livery vehicle in New York City, and any scheduled public service. (TSB-M-09(7)S) A "limousine" means any vehicle with a seating capacity of up to 14 people, excluding the driver. It also means any vehicle with a seating capacity of between 15 and 20 people (excluding the driver), that has only two axles and four tires. (Sec. 1101(b)(34), Tax Law) (TSB-M-18(1)S) "Bus" means any motor vehicle with a seating capacity of at least 15 people (excluding the driver), that does not otherwise qualify as a limousine. Transportation services provided by buses are not subject to sales tax. (Sec. 1101(b)(34), Tax Law) (TSB-M-18(1)S) "Black car" means a for-hire vehicle dispatched from a central facility. (Sec. 1101(b)(34), Tax Law)

Receipts from the sale of a transportation service subject to tax include any handling, carrying, baggage, booking service, administrative, mark-up, additional, or other charge, of any nature, made in conjunction with the transportation service.

Transportation service also includes transporting, carrying, or conveying property of the person being transported, whether owned by or in the care of such person. However, transportation service does not include interstate services or services provided in connection with funerals. Also, taxable transportation service does not include ambulance, ambulette, or emergency service transportation. (Sec. 1101(b)(34), Tax Law) (TSB-M-09(7)S)

Receipts from the sale of transportation service are subject to sales tax only if the service begins and ends in New York (intrastate service). If the service begins and ends in New York, it is taxable even if it passes outside the state during a portion of the trip. A charge for transportation service made outside the state is taxable as long as the service begins and ends in New York. Transportation services that begin or end outside the state (interstate service) are not subject to tax. If a round-trip service starts in New York and proceeds to a destination in another state, and then later the return leg of the round-trip service ends up back in New York, a single charge for that round-trip service would not be taxable, since the trip was interstate in nature. (Sec. 1101(b)(34), Tax Law) (TSB-M-09(7)S)

Transportation network company (TNC) prearranged trips. Transportation network company (TNC) prearranged trips that are subject to the state assessment fee imposed under Article 29-B are not subject to sales and use tax because they are not considered a transportation service for sales and use tax purposes. "Transportation network company" or "TNC" is any person or entity that is licensed by the New York State Department of Motor Vehicles (DMV) that operates in New York exclusively through the use of a digital network to connect passengers with drivers to provide TNC prearranged trips. "TNC prearranged trip" or "trip" is the transportation provided by a TNC driver to a passenger that is arranged through the use of a TNC's digital network; begins when a TNC driver accepts a passenger's trip request, continues through the transport of the passenger, and ends when the last requesting passenger exits the vehicle. A TNC prearranged trip does not include transportation provided through any of the following: shared expense carpool or vanpool arrangements; and use of a taxicab, livery, luxury limousine, or other for-hire vehicle. (Sec. 1101(b)(34), Tax Law; Sec. 1291, Tax Law; Sec. 1292, Tax Law) (TSB-M-17(1)S) For additional information, see Transportation Network Company Services Assessment (¶35-351).

Hail vehicle trips. Hail vehicle trips that are subject to the 50 cents-per-trip tax under Article 29-A are exempt from sales tax imposed on transportation services. A "hail vehicle trip" is a trip provided to one or more passengers regardless of the number of stops, that originated by street hail, and for which the taximeter is required to be in the recording or hired position designating a street hail trip subject to the 50 cents-per-trip tax. (TSB-M-12(7)S)

Purchases by transportation service providers. When a transportation service provider purchases a vehicle for use in its business, it must pay state and local sales or compensating use taxes on that purchase. Likewise, if the service provider purchases maintenance or repair services or parts for the vehicle, those purchases are also subject to sales tax. A vendor of transportation can purchase transportation services for resale from another vendor of transportation services, in appropriate circumstances. A qualified empire zone enterprise (QEZE) must pay tax on its purchase of taxable transportation services, and it cannot apply for a refund or credit of the tax it paid on those services. (TSB-M-09(7)S)

Omnibus carriers. Omnibus carriers are entitled to a refund or credit for sales and use taxes paid on maintenance, servicing or repairs purchased and used by them

¶60-740

in the operation of an omnibus. (Sec. 1119(b), Tax Law) To qualify for the refund or credit, the carrier must provide local transit service in New York and operate pursuant to a certificate of public convenience and necessity issued by the New York State Commissioner of Transportation or by an appropriate federal agency, or under contract, franchise or consent with New York City. A refund or credit is also permitted for sales and use taxes paid on any omnibus and/or on parts, equipment, lubricants, motor fuel or diesel motor fuel purchased and used by an omnibus carrier in the operation of an omnibus. (TSB-M-97(12)S)

Omnibuses which are used to transport persons for hire by a carrier operating pursuant to a New York or United States certificate of authority and the parts, equipment and lubricants needed for their operation are exempt. (Sec. 1115(u), Tax Law) When these receipts have been exempted, they may not also qualify for the refund or credit. (Sec. 1115(a)(32), Tax Law) The exemptions do not apply to the purchase of motor fuel or diesel fuel. (TSB-M-97(12)S)

Exemption Form ST-121.1. Exempt purchases or leases of qualifying vehicles, property, and services may be made using Form ST-121.1, Exemption Certificate for Tractors, Trailers, Semitrailers, or Omnibuses. The following can be purchased or leased exempt from sales tax using Form ST-121.1: a qualifying omnibus; parts, equipment, and lubricants used in operating a qualifying omnibus; and installation, maintenance, or repair services performed on a qualifying omnibus, or performed on parts, equipment, or lubricants used in the operation of the qualifying omnibus. A qualifying omnibus is a motor vehicle weighing at least 26,000 pounds and measuring at least 40 feet in length that is used to transport persons for hire by an omnibus carrier operating with a certificate or permit issued by the New York State Department of Transportation, or by an appropriate agency of the United States. (TB-ST-890)

A qualifying purchaser should fill out Form ST-121.1 and give it to the seller. The instructions for the form provide detailed definitions of the vehicles and other property that are eligible for the exemptions. The purchaser must give the seller a properly completed form within 90 days after the delivery of the property or performance of the service. Sales tax exemption certificates may also be issued and accepted electronically. The form may be used as a single-purchase certificate, or as a blanket certificate covering the first and subsequent purchases of the same general type of property or service from the same seller. Form ST-121.1 cannot be used to purchase the following exempt from tax: nonqualifying vehicles or omnibuses; motor fuel or diesel motor fuel; services for, or property to be installed on, nonqualifying vehicles; equipment not installed as part of a qualifying tractor, trailer, or semitrailer (e.g., hand tools, road flares, and road reflectors), unless sold as part of the original equipment; or shop equipment (e.g., service jacks, tire changers, part washers, battery chargers, and truck and tractor washers). However, omnibus carriers not eligible for the exemption may qualify for a refund or credit of taxes paid on certain vehicles, property, services, and fuel if they are providing a local transit service. If eligible, the omnibus carrier can use Form AU-11, Application for Credit or Refund of Sales or Use Tax, to apply for a refund for taxes paid on property or services. Additionally, the omnibus carrier can use Form FT-500, Application for Refund of Sales Tax Paid on Petroleum Products, to apply for a refund of taxes paid on qualifying fuel purchases. (TB-ST-890)

Gratuities. A mandatory charge for gratuities is taxable unless all of the following conditions are met: (1) the gratuity charge is separately stated on the bill, invoice, or other statement given to the customer, (2) the charge is specifically designated as a gratuity, and (3) the service provider pays the entire amount of the charge to the driver. If a passenger gives a gratuity directly to the driver voluntarily, that is not a charge for transportation service and is not subject to sales tax. (TSB-M-09(7)S)

Transportation services provided by affiliated livery vehicles. Charges for transportation services provided by affiliated livery vehicles wholly within New York City are excluded from the state and local sales taxes on transportation services (i.e., only charges for trips that begin and end in New York City are not taxable). (Sec. 1101(b)(34), Tax Law) (TSB-M-10(15)S) In addition, the exclusion applies to charges for transportation services provided by affiliated livery vehicles for trips that either begin or end in New York City. For example, charges for transportation services provided by affiliated livery vehicles for trips that begin in New York City and end in Nassau County are excluded from sales tax. Similarly, charges for transportation services that begin in Nassau County and end in New York City are also excluded from sales tax. (TSB-M-13(2)S)

For purposes of this exclusion, "affiliated livery vehicle" means a for-hire motor vehicle with a seating capacity of up to six persons, including the driver, other than a black car or luxury limousine, that is authorized and licensed by the taxi and limousine commission of a city of one million or more to be dispatched by a livery base station located in such a city and regulated by such taxi and limousine commission. In addition, the charges for service provided by an affiliated livery vehicle must be on the basis of flat rate, time, mileage, or zones and not on a garage-to-garage basis. The term "luxury limousine" has the same meaning as limousine (i.e., a vehicle with a seating capacity of up to 14 people, excluding the driver). (Sec. 1101(b)(34), Tax Law) (TSB-M-10(15)S)

Exempt organizations.

Sales of transportation services by exempt organizations. Transportation services sold by exempt organizations are either subject to tax or exempt, depending on the type of organization making the sale. Sales of transportation services are exempt from sales tax when sold by an organization described in Tax Law § 1116(a)(4), (5), or (7), such as a private not-for-profit school, or a church or charity, armed services post, health maintenance organization, or other exempt organization. However, transportation services sold by other exempt organizations are taxable. (TSB-M-09(2)S; TSB-M-09(7)S)

Purchases of transportation services by exempt organizations. Transportation services are exempt from sales tax when purchased by any organization exempt from tax under Tax Law § 1116(a), including New York and its municipalities and their agencies and instrumentalities. In each case, the exempt organization purchasing the service must establish its right to the exemption by submitting the proper exemption certificate to the vendor of the service or other required documentation. However, New York State, a New York municipality, or an agency or instrumentality of either of them must use its letterhead or purchase order to make an exempt purchase. A New York government employee on official business can use Form AC-946, Tax Exemption Certificate, to purchase service exempt from tax in appropriate circumstances. (TSB-M-09(7)S)

Refund of charge for transportation service. If a vendor of transportation service charges its customer the wrong amount for its service, or if the vendor charges for service that it ends up not providing, and the vendor returns the charge, or a portion of the charge, to the customer, the vendor must also refund to the customer the amount of the sales tax collected on the amount of the returned charge. If the vendor has already remitted the tax, it may apply for a credit or refund for the amount of the tax refunded to the customer that it already paid. When the application for credit has been filed, the vendor may immediately take a credit on its next return and attach a copy of the application indicating on the application it has already applied for the credit. (TSB-M-09(7)S)

Bad debt refund or credit. If a vendor of transportation services determines that an amount due from its customer is uncollectible and the vendor has actually charged off the amount for federal income tax purposes, the vendor may apply for a refund or credit in the amount of the tax that the vendor paid with its tax return on such amount. Only the amount attributable to the sales tax imposed and remitted by the vendor to the department remaining unpaid by the customer is allowable as a refund or credit. When an application for credit has been filed, the vendor may immediately take a credit on its next return and attach a copy of the application indicating on the application if it has already applied for the credit. (TSB-M-09(7)S)

Registration. Providers of transportation services that will be subject to sales tax must register for sales tax purposes and obtain a Certificate of Authority to provide these services and to collect tax on them. Except for the special rule relating to the rental or lease of a vehicle to an unrelated person, the provider of the transportation service is the person or entity that collects the transportation charge from the customer. Accordingly, the provider of a transportation service may be the person (corporation, partnership, LLC, individual, governmental entity, etc.) that owns the vehicle used to provide the service, the base that dispatches the vehicle used to provide the service, or the owner-driver that provides the service. (TSB-M-09(2)S; TSB-M-09(7)S)

Special rule for rental or lease of a vehicle to an unrelated person. The Tax Law provides a special rule regarding who must register for sales tax purposes and collect the tax when a driver rents or leases a limousine, black car, or other vehicle from an unrelated person and uses the vehicle to provide a transportation service. In these cases, the owner or lessor of the vehicle is considered to provide the transportation service. Accordingly, the owner or the lessor is considered to be the vendor (provider); is required to register; and is required to collect the tax from the driver based on 200% of the daily or shift rental charge. An unrelated person is a person other than a related person as defined in § 14 the Tax Law. Thus, if a person rents or leases a vehicle to an unrelated driver, they must register for sales tax purposes. (TSB-M-09(2)S; TSB-M-09(7)S)

Vessels providing local transit service. A refund or credit is allowed for tax paid on the sale to or use by a vessel operator of a vessel with a seating capacity of more than 20 passengers used for the transportation on water of passengers for hire. The provision also applies with respect to parts, equipment, lubricants, diesel motor fuel, maintenance, servicing, or repair purchased and used in the operation of any such vessel by the operator. In order to qualify, the vessel operator must provide local transit service in New York and operate under a certificate of public convenience and necessity issued by the New York Commissioner of Transportation or a like officer or agency of the United States or pursuant to a contract, franchise, or consent between the operator and New York City. (Sec. 1119(b), Tax Law; Reg. Sec. 534.10) (TSB-M-04(8)S)

The credit or refund amount will be calculated based on the operator's vessel hours in local transit service compared to the total hours operated in New York. If the "local transit service percentage" is:

— less that 10%, there is no credit or refund;

— 10%, there is a credit or refund of 10%;

— greater than 10% but less that 70%, the credit or refund is 10% plus the product of 1.5 times each whole percentage in excess of 10%; and

— 70% or more, there is a 100% credit or refund.

(Sec. 1119(b), Tax Law; Reg. Sec. 534.10) (TSB-M-04(8)S)

Local transit service. "Local transit service" means a mass transit service provided by a vessel operator in which passengers are carried by a vessel from one point in New York to another point in New York and in performance of which the vessel:

— regularly picks up and discharges such passengers as scheduled, or at their convenience, at designated piers, slips, docks, or other landings along waterways (as distinguished from buildings or similar facilities used as terminals or stations);

— picks up and discharges passengers at terminals or stations, the distance between which is not more than 75 miles (5,280 feet per mile), measured along the route traveled by the vessel; or

— picks up and discharges passengers as described in both clauses above. (Reg. Sec. 534.10(a)(3))

Local transit does not include charter, contract, excursion, sight-seeing, or other passenger service. (Reg. Sec. 534.10(a)(3))

Vessel hours. "Vessel hours" means the number of hours that all vessels are operated by a vessel operator in the performance of local transit service, plus the number of idle hours used to reach the point at which such service begins and from the point at which service terminates. Such hours only include those hours operated in New York. (Reg. Sec. 534.10(a)(4))

Total hours operated. "Total hours operated" means the vessel hours, plus the number of hours used in charter, contract, excursion, sight-seeing, and all other passenger service, which hours are not included in the meaning of vessel hours. Such hours only include hours operated in New York. (Reg. Sec. 534.10(a)(5))

Tugboats. Tugboat services are considered to be exempt transporting services. (Reg. Sec. 528.9(d)(3))

Passenger tickets. State and local governments are prohibited by federal legislation from taxing passenger tickets purchased by individuals traveling by motor carrier from one state to another, such as bus tickets purchased for travel from a city or town in Arizona to a location in Wyoming. *Interstate Commerce Commission Termination Act of 1995*, P.L. 104-88 (H.R. 2539) Passenger tickets for travel within a state are taxable. The ban on taxation specifically bars the collection or levy of a tax, fee, head charge, or other charge on: (1) a passenger traveling in interstate commerce by motor carrier; (2) the transportation of a passenger traveling in interstate commerce by motor carrier; (3) the sale of passenger transportation in interstate commerce by motor carrier; or (4) the gross receipts from the transportation of passengers in interstate commerce by motor carrier.

Local taxes. When a transportation service begins in one jurisdiction (county or city) in New York but ends in another jurisdiction in New York, the local tax that applies is the tax imposed by the jurisdiction where the service begins (in some counties, cities also impose tax and if the service begins in that city, then the local tax is the combined county and city tax). The service begins at the point where the passenger is picked up. (TSB-M-09(7)S)

[¶60-750] Utilities

Generally, receipts from every sale (other than for resale) of gas, electricity, refrigeration and steam are subject to tax. Similarly, receipts from the provision of gas, electric, refrigeration and steam services are also subject to tax. For tax to apply, however, the utility or services must be furnished in an identifiable sale transaction as a commodity or article of commerce. (Sec. 1105(b), Tax Law)

In *Debevoise & Plimpton v. New York State Department of Taxation and Finance*, the New York Court of Appeals rejected the Department's argument that additional rent paid by a commercial tenant for overtime heating, ventilation and air conditioning (HVAC) services provided by a landlord incidental to the rental of office space were subject to tax. The Court held that tax was authorized only on receipts from transactions that can be identified as independent sales of utility or utility services.

However, the situation in *Debevoise & Plimpton*, was distinguished in *Mutual Redevelopment Houses, Inc.*, New York Division of Tax Appeals, Tax Appeals Tribunal. In *Mutual Redevelopment Houses, Inc.*, the New York Tax Appeals Tribunal held that charges for electricity furnished to residential and commercial tenants of a cooperative housing development, measured through the use of a meter for each tenant, pursuant to their occupancy agreements or leases were subject to New York sales tax because the charges were separately identifiable sales transactions, not incidents of the occupancy agreements or leases or as part of the rental of their premises. When the landlord began to separately meter its tenants' actual electric usage, separately bill for such service based on actual consumption, and identified them separately from rental income on its annual financial statements, the service became taxable. This was distinguished from the situation where the tenant was paying rent and all electricity was included as part of the rental. In addition, the terms of the lease were instructive since it mandated that tenants must purchase electric service from the landlord as a separate sales transaction and was not payment of additional rent.

Exemptions concerning sales of fuel or utilities are discussed in the subheads that follow.

• *Electricity or gas purchased from out-of-state supplier*

New York use tax is specifically imposed on the use of gas or electricity. (Sec. 1110(a)(H), Tax Law) Thus, any disparity in taxation favoring out-of-state sellers is eliminated. See TSB-M-00(4)S.

• *Residential energy sources and services*

Certain residential energy sources and services are not subject to New York sales and use tax. The following tangible personal property and services used for residential purposes constitute residential energy sources and services not subject to sales and use tax:

— natural gas;

— propane sold in containers of 100 pounds or more;

— electricity;

— steam;

— fuel oil;

— non-highway diesel motor fuel (purchases of highway diesel motor fuel used for residential heating purposes are subject to sales tax at the time of purchase but are eligible for a refund of any sales tax paid);

— coal;

— wood (including wood pellets and other compressed wood products) for heating purposes only (the exemption does not apply to other pellets or other compressed products that are made from non-wood material, or other non-wood products, such as corn or corn kernels); and

— gas, electric, and steam services.

(Sec. 1105-A(a), Tax Law) (TSB-M-07(3)S; TB-ST-775)

Wood pellets and other pellets.—Wood pellets and other compressed wood products designed to be used in a stove or fireplace used for residential heating purposes constitute wood. Accordingly, purchases of these products for residential heating purposes are also exempt from state sales tax. (TSB-M-07(3)S) The tax treatment of wood pellets and compressed wood products does not apply to other pellets or other compressed products that are made from non-wood material, or other non-wood products, such as corn or corn kernels. Vendors must collect sales tax on receipts from the sales of these non-wood products at the combined New York sales tax rate and regular local sales tax rate in the locality where the products are delivered to the customer. (TSB-M-07(3)S) For these rates, see Publication 718.

Mixed use properties.—Where energy sources or services billed on a single meter are used for both residential and nonresidential purposes, and residential purposes constitute 75% or more of the usage, the entire amount billed is considered as being used for residential purposes and is exempt from state sales and compensating use tax. If the percentage of residential use is less than 75%, the amount billed is allocated. The percentage attributable to residential use is determined by dividing the total area of the space used for residential purposes, excluding common areas, by the total area of the premises (residential and nonresidential), excluding common areas, rounded to the nearest 10%. (Sec. 1105-A(d), Tax Law; Reg. Sec. 527.13) (TB-ST-775)

Motor fuel.—The New York State sales tax is imposed upon diesel motor fuel delivered at a filling station or into a repository equipped to dispense fuel into the fuel tank of a motor vehicle. For deliveries of fuel exceeding 4,500 gallons, a certificate signed by the purchaser and stating that the product will be used exclusively for residential purposes is required. (Sec. 1105-A(a), Tax Law)

Counties and localities.—Counties and localities that impose a local sales tax may choose to either tax or exempt residential energy sources and services. The localities that choose to impose a local tax on residential energy sources and services may further choose to tax these sources and services at their regular rate or at a reduced local rate. (Sec. 1210(a)(3)(i), Tax Law) (TSB-M-07(3)S) Part 2 of Publication 718-R, Local Sales and Use Tax Rates on Residential Energy Sources and Services, lists the jurisdictions that impose a local tax on residential energy sources and services with the applicable rate. Localities not listed in Publication 718-R do not impose a local tax on residential energy sources and services. (TSB-M-07(3)S) See Publication 718-R.

• *Utilities used in production*

Fuel, utilities (gas, electricity, coal, refrigeration, steam, and wood) and utilities services used or consumed directly and exclusively in the production for sale of tangible personal property, gas, electricity, refrigeration or steam by manufacturing, processing, assembling, generating, refining, mining, extracting, farming, agriculture, horticulture, floriculture, or commercial horse boarding operations, are not subject to the New York State sales and use taxes. (Sec. 1115(c), Tax Law) (TSB-M-00(8)S) (TB-ST-917)

To qualify for the exemption, the utilities must be used directly and exclusively (100%) in the production phase. (TB-ST-917) To qualify as being used directly in production, utilities must be used or consumed during the production phase to:

— operate exempt production machinery or equipment;

— create conditions necessary for production; or

— perform an actual part of the production process.

(TB-ST-917)

Exempt production machinery or equipment is machinery or equipment that:

— acts upon or changes material to form the product to be sold;

— has an active and necessary role in the production of the product;

— is used in the handling, storage, or conveyance of materials or product produced through the production line;

— or is used to package the product for sale.

(TB-ST-917)

Utilities used in the administration or distribution phases do not qualify for the exemption. Therefore, utilities do not qualify for the exemption if they are used or consumed in:

— the lighting of buildings;

— the heating and cooling of buildings;

— the preparation of food and drink subject to tax imposed by Tax Law § 1105(d); or

— the storage of tangible personal property.

(TB-ST-917)

Making tax-exempt purchases.—Registered vendors should use Form ST-121 to purchase utilities used or consumed directly and exclusively in the production of tangible personal property for sale. These purchases are exempt from both the New York state and local sales taxes. Form ST-121 may also be used to purchase utilities used or consumed directly and exclusively in the production of gas, electricity, refrigeration, and steam for sale. These purchases are exempt from the New York state sales and use taxes and from local taxes outside New York City. However, these purchases are subject to New York City's local sales tax rate when used or consumed in New York City. The department notes that Form ST-121 cannot be used to purchase motor fuel and diesel motor fuel exempt from tax even if the fuel will be used in production activities. (TB-ST-917)

Allocating utilities to compute the percentage of exempt use.—Utilities must be used directly and exclusively (100%) in production to be exempt from tax. If a separate meter tracks utilities used directly and exclusively in production, the utilities can be purchased exempt from tax by issuing Form ST-121 to the utility supplier. However, some types of utilities are normally received by a purchaser in bulk or in a continuous flow and may be used for both exempt (production) and taxable (lighting, heating, etc.) purposes. (TB-ST-917) In these circumstances, the purchaser can either:

— pay sales tax on the purchase of the utilities and use Form AU-11, Application for Credit or Refund of Sales or Use Tax, to apply for a credit or refund of sales tax paid on the portion of the utilities used for exempt purposes; or

— use Form ST-121 to purchase the utilities exempt from sales tax, provided the purchaser pays any state and local taxes due on the taxable portion of the utilities when filing its sales and use tax return.

(TB-ST-917)

The purchaser must substantiate the amounts used for exempt and taxable purposes using alternative methods where direct, separate metering is not available. To substantiate its allocation, the purchaser may use an engineering survey or other formula to arrive at the amounts used in an exempt manner. (TB-ST-917)

New York City.—The exemption also generally applies against New York City sales and use tax, except for fuel, gas, electricity, refrigeration and steam, gas, electric, refrigeration and steam service used or consumed directly and exclusively in the production of gas, electricity, refrigeration or steam. (Sec. 1107(b)(1), Tax Law)

"Fuel" defined.—"Fuel" eligible for the exemption includes any commodity which produces heat or energy. It includes wood, coal, radio-active materials and petroleum (except lubricants). (Reg. Sec. 528.22(b)(1))

"Directly" defined.—For purposes of the exemption, the term "directly" means that the fuel, gas, electricity, refrigeration and steam and like services must, during the production phase of a process, either:

— operate exempt production machinery or equipment;

— create conditions necessary for production; or

— perform an actual part of the production process.

(Reg. Sec. 528.22(c)(1))

Usage in activities collateral to the actual production process is not deemed to be used directly in production. (Reg. Sec. 528.22(c)(2))

EXAMPLE: *Direct Use.*—A welding shop produces stainless steel railings. In order to carry out the production, the railings must be welded in an inert atmosphere. The welding shop purchases an inert gas which is used to create the inert atmosphere. The gas is used directly in production. (Reg. Sec. 528.22(c)(2))

"Exclusively" defined.—The term "exclusively" means that the fuel, gas, electricity, refrigeration and steam and like services are used in total (100%) in the production process. (Reg. Sec. 528.22(c)(3)(i))

• *Commercial fuel cell electricity generating systems equipment*

An exemption is provided for commercial fuel cell electricity generating systems equipment and the service of installing and maintaining such systems. For purposes of the exemption, "fuel cell electricity generating systems equipment" means an electric generating arrangement or combination of components installed upon non-residential premises and that utilizes one of the following types of fuel cells: solid oxide, molten carbonate, proton exchange membrane, phosphoric acid, or a linear generator. (Sec. 1115(kk)(1), Tax Law) (TSB-M-16(3)S) A contractor who purchases fuel cell electricity generating systems equipment must submit to the vendor a properly completed Form ST-120.1, Contractor Exempt Purchase Certificate, to claim the exemption. (TSB-M-16(3)S)

Sales of electricity and hydrogen gas.—An exemption is also provided for the sales of nonresidential electricity and hydrogen gas. To qualify, the sales must be made pursuant to a written agreement by a person primarily engaged in the sale of: fuel cell electricity generating systems equipment, electricity that is generated by such or equipment, or both. The electricity or hydrogen gas must be sold to the person with whom the seller has a written agreement, and it must be generated by commercial fuel cell electricity generating systems equipment that is: (a) owned by a person other than the purchaser of such electricity; (b) installed on the nonresidential premises of the purchaser of such electricity; (c) placed in service; and (d) used to provide heating, cooling, hot water or electricity to such premises. (Sec. 1115(kk)(2), Tax Law) (TSB-M-16(3)S)

Sales are exempt from local sales and use taxes only if the jurisdiction imposing the tax elects to provide this exemption. For a listing of local tax rates on commercial fuel cell systems equipment, electricity, and hydrogen, see Publication 718-FC a.

• *Utilities used in farm production or commercial horse boarding*

Utilities used or consumed in farm production or in a commercial horse boarding operation, or in both, are also exempt from sales and use taxes. (TB-ST-244) For additional information, see ¶ 60-250 Agriculture.

• *Gas or electricity used for gas or electric service*

An exemption from state and local sales and use taxes is provided for certain purchases of gas or electricity used to provide gas or electric service. Specifically, the exemption applies to gas or electricity, or gas or electric service, used or consumed directly and exclusively to provide gas or electric service consisting of operating a gas pipeline or distribution line or an electric transmission or distribution line and ensuring the necessary working pressure in an underground gas storage facility. The exemption includes, but is not limited to, gas or electricity or gas or electric service used or consumed directly and exclusively for the following:

— to ensure necessary working pressure in a gas pipeline used to transport, transmit, or distribute gas;

— to operate compressors used to transport, transmit, or distribute gas through a gas pipeline or distribution line or used to ensure necessary working pressure in a storage facility;

— to operate heaters to prevent gas in a pipeline or distribution line from freezing;

— to operate equipment that removes impurities and moisture from gas in a pipeline or distribution line;

— to operate substations and equipment related to electric transmission and distribution lines, such as transformers, capacitors, meters, switches, communication devices, and heating and cooling equipment; and

— to ensure the reliability of electricity or electric service transmitted or distributed through such lines, for example, by operating reserve capacity machinery and equipment.

(Sec. 1115(w), Tax Law)

See also TSB-M-00(4)S.

• *Gas or electric services*

Every sale of gas service or electric service of whatever nature (including the transportation, transmission or distribution of gas or electricity, but not including gas or electricity) is not subject to sales and use tax. However, tax is imposed on the transportation, transmission, or distribution charges for gas or electricity when the transportation, transmission or distribution is by the vendor of the commodity. Such tax is imposed regardless of whether such charges are separately stated in the written contract, if any, or on the bill rendered to such purchaser, and regardless of whether such transportation, transmission, or distribution is provided by such vendor or a third party. However, where the transportation, transmission or distribution of gas or electricity is sold wholly within a service area of New York wherein the public service commission has approved a single retailer model for the regulated utility which has the responsibility to serve that area, the charge for such transportation, transmission or distribution when made by the provider who also sells, other than as a sale for resale, the gas or electricity, will not be subject to tax. (Sec. 1105-C, Tax Law)

Beginning on June 1, 2019, the state and local sales and use tax exemption for the transportation, transmission, or distribution of gas or electricity when purchased from someone other than the vendor of the gas or electricity is repealed. This change applies to sales made and services rendered on or after that date regardless of when a service contract began. As a result of this change, the services of transporting, transmitting, or distributing gas or electricity (T&D) are subject to both state and local sales tax when the sale of the commodity is also subject to state and local sales tax. (TSB-M-19(1)S)

Sales of gas and electricity for commercial purposes are subject to both state and local sales tax and, therefore, the charges for T&D are also subject to state and local sales tax. Sales of residential energy continue to be exempt from state sales tax and, therefore, charges for T&D residential energy are also exempt from state tax. Where sales of residential energy are subject to local sales tax, the charges for T&D related to those sales are also subject to local sales tax. (TSB-M-19(1)S)

• *Natural gas used for personal residence consumption*

Natural gas used for personal residence consumption by a landowner from (or provided in exchange for gas from) a natural gas well located on the property is tax-exempt, where the gas has been set aside for the property owner's use by lease. (Sec. 1115(a)(25), Tax Law)

• *Water*

Water, when delivered to the consumer through mains or pipes, is exempt from tax. (Sec. 1115(a)(2), Tax Law) The tax, however, is imposed upon water sold in bottles or by means other than through mains or pipes. (Reg. Sec. 528.3(b)) In addition, water sold as ice or in any other form is taxable. (Reg. Sec. 528.3(c))

> **EXAMPLE:** *Bottled Water.*—A person purchases three gallons of bottled spring water at a supermarket. The bottled spring water is taxable. (Reg. Sec. 528.3(c))

> **EXAMPLE:** *Swimming Pool.*—A person contracts with a firm to furnish 20,000 gallons of water to fill a swimming pool. The water is delivered by a tank truck and is taxable. (Reg. Sec. 528.3(c))

• *Water and sewer service line protection programs*

Receipts from sales of and fees associated with water and sewer service line protection programs sold to residential property owners are exempt from sales and use tax. The exemption applies to state and local sales taxes, including the tax imposed by the state in the Metropolitan Commuter Transportation District. Water and sewer service line protection programs cover a homeowner's costs associated with repairing damaged water and sewer lines that run from the homeowner's home to the connection to the municipal service line. The maintenance of the lines that run from the home to the connection to the municipal service line is the homeowner's responsibility. (Sec. 1115(ii), Tax Law) (TSB-M-14(14)S)

• *Energy distributed to cooperative corporation tenants*

Sales of electricity, steam, and refrigeration (utilities) and electric, steam, and refrigeration services that are metered and generated or produced by a cogeneration facility owned or operated by certain cooperative corporations are exempt from New York sales and compensating use taxes. (Sec. 1115(b)(iii), Tax Law) (TSB-M-06(3)S) In order to qualify for the exemption, the cooperative corporation must have at least 1,500 apartments and the energy or energy services must be distributed to the tenants or occupants of such cooperative corporations. (Sec. 1115(b)(iii), Tax Law) (TSB-M-06(3)S) For definitions of a "cogeneration facility" and "cooperative corporation" for purposes of the exemption, see (Sec. 1115(b)(iii)(B) and (C), Tax Law, and TSB-M-06(3)S)

The exemption only applies to sales of utilities and utility services produced by a cogeneration facility that was in operation before January 1, 2004. However, the exemption will continue to apply if the cooperative corporation replaces the cogeneration facility that was in operation before January 1, 2004, with another cogeneration facility. (TSB-M-06(3)S)

Fuel, gas, electricity, refrigeration and steam, gas, electric, refrigeration and steam service used or consumed in the production of the utilities and utility services that are exempt are not entitled to the exemption for utilities and utility services used or consumed directly and exclusively in the production of tangible property, gas, electricity, refrigeration or steam, for sale, as provided in Tax Law Sec. 1115(c)(1). (TSB-M-06(3)S) Further, machinery or equipment purchased by a cooperative corporation for use or consumption directly and predominantly in the production for sale of the exempt utilities and utility services described in this memorandum may be purchased exempt from New York state and local sales and compensating use taxes based on Tax Law Sec. 1115(a)(12). (TSB-M-06(3)S)

• *Garbage collection*

The service of trash removal from buildings is taxable. (Sec. 1105(c)(5), Tax Law)

Municipal services.—Services provided by a municipality, which are of a type ordinarily provided by a private person, are not taxable when the charge for the services is a tax based on the assessed valuation of the property in a municipality rather than specific charges for such services. (Reg. Sec. 527.7(d)(1)) Charges for services rendered by municipalities are subject to tax when such charges are for services of a type ordinarily provided by private persons and the charges are arrived at based solely on the services rendered to a specific person, family or location. (Reg. Sec. 527.7(d)(2)) The fact that a charge is added to a real property tax bill for the purposes of collection and levy does not change the taxability of the charge. (Reg. Sec. 527.7(d)(4))

> *EXAMPLE: Municipal Services.*—A town levies a tax based on assessed valuation of all taxpayers for garbage removal services. This tax is not subject to the sales tax. (Reg. Sec. 527.7(d)(4))

> *EXAMPLE: Municipal Services.*—A town charges a fee to residents who desire garbage removal, at a rate of $15 quarterly, and rents dumpsters for a fee of $5 quarterly. The fees are subject to tax. (Reg. Sec. 527.7(d)(4))

Refund or credit provision.—Where sales or use tax has been paid on purchases of tangible personal property used in connection with a taxable real estate maintenance, service or repair of real property; there is a right to a refund or credit, subject to specified conditions. (Sec. 1119(c), Tax Law) Provisions governing eligibility for such a refund or credit are discussed at ¶61-270 Credits.

• *North Country Power Authority*

Legislation enacted in 2010 created the North Country Power Authority NCPA for the purpose of providing electric power services in its service area, consisting of portion of Franklin and St. Lawrence Counties. Under the legislation, the NCPA is a public benefit corporation, constituting an exempt organization for sales tax purposes under Tax Law § 1116(a)(1). Therefore, the NCPA is exempt from state and local sales and use taxes on all its purchases. However, NCPA is required to collect sales and use tax on its sales of property or services of a kind ordinarily sold by private persons. Therefore, since private persons do regularly sell electric power, and the NCPA will sell electric power, the NCPA will be required to register with the Tax Department for sales tax purposes, collect sales tax on its taxable sales, comply with the sales tax record keeping requirements, file sales tax returns, and remit sales tax required to be collected with its returns. (TSB-M-11(1)S)

[¶61-000]

EXEMPTIONS

[¶61-020] Exemption Certificates

All receipts of tangible personal property and specified services, all rents for occupancy, and all amusement charges are presumed taxable unless the contrary is established. (Sec. 1132(c), Tax Law; Reg. Sec. 532.4(a)) The burden of proving exemption from tax is imposed on the person required to collect tax or the purchaser of the goods or services. (Sec. 1132(c), Tax Law; Reg. Sec. 532.4(b)(1)) However, where a properly completed exemption certificate or statement has been furnished to the vendor, the burden of proof as to nontaxability of a receipt, amusement charge or rent is shifted to the purchaser. The vendor will not be required to collect tax from a purchaser who furnishes a certificate of resale, an exempt organization statement, or other exemption certificate in proper form, unless the purchaser's certificate of authority had been suspended, revoked or has expired. (Sec. 1132(c), Tax Law; Reg. Sec. 532.4(b)(2)(i))

The Department of Taxation and Finance has issued a Tax Bulletin on exemption certificates that explains the following: who may use exemption certificates, how to use them properly, and the various exemption certificates that are available. (TB-ST-240)

Resale certificates are discussed at ¶ 60-650 Resales.

Direct payment permits are discussed at ¶ 61-250 Direct Payment Permits.

• *Exemption certificates*

A vendor who in good faith accepts a properly completed exemption certificate not later than 90 days after delivery of the property or the rendition of the service is relieved of liability for failure to collect sales tax with respect to that transaction. The timely receipt of the certificate itself will satisfy the vendor's burden of proving the nontaxability of the transaction and relieve the vendor of responsibility for collecting tax from the customer. (Sec. 1132(c), Tax Law; Reg. Sec. 532.4(b)(2)(i)) (TB-ST-240)

Exemption certificates of other states or countries are not valid to claim exemption from New York state and local sales and use tax. (TB-ST-240)

The term "90 days after the delivery of the property" means that day which is 90 days after the date actual possession of the property or a portion of it is transferred to the purchaser. If actual possession is not transferred to the purchaser (such as in a "sale and leaseback" transaction or where the property is delivered by the vendor at the direction of the purchaser to a third party), it shall mean that day which is 90 days after the earlier of transfer of title or constructive transfer of possession to the purchaser. (Reg. Sec. 532.4(b)(2)(iii))

An exemption certificate is considered to be properly completed when it contains the following information:

— date prepared;

— name and address of the purchaser;

— name and address of the seller;

— identification number of the purchaser as shown on its certificate of authority, or exempt organization number as shown on the exempt organization certificate;

— signature of the purchaser or the purchaser's authorized representative; and

— any other information required to be completed on the particular certificate or document.

(Sec. 1132(c), Tax Law; Reg. Sec. 532.4(b)(2)(ii)) (TB-ST-240)

Sellers have the right to refuse an exemption certificate, even if it is correct and properly completed. A seller that refuses a certificate must charge the purchaser sales tax. The purchaser may apply for a refund of the sales tax using Form AU-11, Application for Credit or Refund of Sales or Use Tax. (TB-ST-240)

Certain sales to all purchasers are exempt from sales tax. Therefore, the purchaser is not required to provide an exemption document to claim the exemption. These exemptions include, but are not limited to, sales of:

— food, food products, beverages, dietary foods, and health supplements that are sold by food markets for human consumption (note: sales of candy, confections, soft drinks, alcoholic beverages, fruit drinks that contain less than 70% natural fruit juice, sandwiches, and heated foods are subject to sales tax);

— drugs and medicines intended for use, internally or externally, in the diagnosis, cure, mitigation, treatment, or prevention of illnesses or diseases in human beings;

— medical equipment and supplies (note: medical equipment and supplies purchased for use in providing medical or similar services for compensation, such as services of physicians, hospitals, clinical laboratories, and ambulance companies, are subject to sales tax);

— newspapers, magazines, and other periodicals;

— prosthetic aids and devices, hearing aids and eyeglasses;

— services of laundering and dry cleaning;

— shoe repair; and

— services of a licensed veterinarian constituting the practice of veterinary medicine.

(Publication 750)

Blanket certificates.—Instead of providing a single transaction exemption certificate for each transaction, a purchaser may provide a blanket exemption certificate. This certificate may be used for the current sale as well as for subsequent sales made to that purchaser. A blanket exemption certificate may only be used by a purchaser to cover additional sales of the same general type of property or service. (Publication 750; TB-ST-240) (Form ST-121, Exempt Use Certificate)

If a purchasers address, identification number, or any other information on the blanket certificate changes, the purchaser must give the seller an updated blanket certificate. The seller has the right to ask a purchaser for an updated blanket certificate at any time. Otherwise, the blanket certificate remains in effect as long as the purchaser is making exempt purchases from the seller. (TB-ST-240)

Good faith acceptance.—For an exemption to be recognized, the vendor must, in good faith, accept a properly completed exemption certificate. (Sec. 1132(c), Tax Law; Reg. Sec. 532.4(b)(2)(i)) An exemption certificate is "accepted in good faith" when a vendor has no knowledge that the exemption certificate or other document issued by the purchaser is false or is fraudulently presented. If reasonable ordinary due care is exercised, knowledge will not be imputed to the seller required to collect the tax. (Reg. Sec. 532.4(b)(2)(i))

Retroactive acceptance.—A certificate or document in substantiation of an exempt sale is considered timely received by the vendor when it is received within 90 days after the delivery of the property or the rendition of the service. (Reg. Sec. 532.4(b)(2)(iii)) If an exemption certificate is received after the 90-day period, both the vendor and purchaser assume the burden of proving the sale was exempt, and additional substantiation may be required. Also, both the vendor and purchaser may be liable for any tax, penalties, and interest due in the event the sale is taxable. (Publication 750) (Form ST-121, Exempt Use Certificate)

Recordkeeping requirements.—Generally, records must be kept for a minimum of three years from the due date of the return to which they relate, or the date the return is filed, if later. Records must be made available to the Tax Department upon request. (Reg. Sec. 533.2) (Publication 750) Exemption certificates must be dated and retained in order to prove exempt sales. (Reg. Sec. 533.2)

A single transaction exemption certificate, where required, associated with each exempt sale made must be kept for a minimum of three years after the due date of the sales tax return to which it relates, or the date the return was filed, if later. Records may be kept in electronic format. A vendor must keep a blanket exemption certificate as long as he or she continues to do business with the purchaser and for three years after the due date of the most recent sales tax return to which it relates, or the date the most recent return was filed, if later. (Reg. Sec. 533.2) (Publication 750)

Penalties for misuse.—Any purchaser issuing a false or fraudulent resale or other exemption certificate may be subject to the following penalties:

— 100% of the tax that would have been due had the misuse of the certificate not occurred;

— $50 penalty for each fraudulent exemption certificate issued;

— other monetary penalties as imposed under the Tax Law;

— a misdemeanor penalty (consisting of imprisonment for up to one year and fines not to exceed $10,000 for an individual or $20,000 for a corporation); and

— revocation of the purchaser's Certificate of Authority, if required to be registered as a vendor.

(Reg. Sec. 532.4(c)(3))

Expiration date.—Single purchase exemption certificates have no definitive expiration date. Instead, it is valid as long as it is properly completed and the purchaser information on the form remains accurate. (Telephone Conversation, New York Department of Taxation and Finance, February 4, 2011) Likewise, a blanket exemption certificate has no definitive expiration date. Instead, a blanket exemption certificate remains in effect until the purchaser give written notice of revocation, the vendor has knowledge that the certificate is false or was fraudulently presented, or until the Tax Department notifies the vendor that the purchaser may not make exempt purchases. (Form ST-121, Exempt Use Certificate) (TB-ST-240) (Telephone Conversation, New York Department of Taxation and Finance, February 4, 2011)

• *Specialized certificates*

New York has other commonly used exemption certificates that include, but are not limited to, the following (certificates marked with an asterisk (*) may be used as blanket certificate):

— DTF-801, Certificate of Individual Indian Exemption from State Taxes on Property or Services Delivered on a Reservation (in order to be exempt, the purchase must meet all of the conditions listed on the form);

— DTF-803, Claim for Sales and Use Tax Exemption – Title/Registration Motor Vehicle, All-Terrain Vehicle (ATV), Vessel (Boat), or Snowmobile;

— DTF-950, Certificate of Sales Tax Exemption for Diplomatic Missions and Personnel;

— ST-119.1, Exempt Organization Certificate (available only by calling the Department of Taxation and Finance);

— ST-119.2, Application for an Exempt Organization Certificate;

— ST-119.5, Exemption Certificate for Hotel or Motel Occupancy by Veterans Organizations (must be issued with photocopy of the organization's Exempt Organization Certificate);

— ST-120*, Resale Certificate (not for use by construction contractors);

— ST-120.1, Contractor Exempt Purchase Certificate (for contractors to use instead of ST-120);

— ST-121*, Exempt Use Certificate (covers many exemptions) (see discussion below and TB-ST-235);

— ST-121.1*, Exemption Certificate for Tractors, Trailers, Semitrailers, or Omnibuses;

— ST-121.2*, Certificate of Exemption for Purchases of Promotional Materials;

— ST-121.3*, Exempt Use Certificate for Computer System Hardware;

— ST-121.4, Textbook Exemption Certificate;

— ST-121.5*, Exempt Use Certificate for Operators of Internet Data Centers (Web Hosting);

— ST-121.9*, Exempt Use Certificate for Certain Theatrical Productions (certain restrictions on blanket certificates);

— ST-124, Certificate of Capital Improvement (contractor need not have a Certificate of Authority to accept ST-124);

— ST-125*, Farmer's and Commercial Horse Boarding Operator's Exemption Certificate;

— ST-126, Exemption Certificate for Purchase of Racehorses;

— ST-129, Exemption Certificate: Tax on Occupancy of Hotel Rooms (may be accepted only by hotel operators. Does not provide exemption from locally administered occupancy taxes);

— ST-860*, Exemption Certificate for Purchases Relating to Guide, Hearing and Service Dogs; and

— TP-385*, Certification of Residential Use of Energy Purchases (only if residential use is less than 75%).

¶61-020

For more information on the various certificates, see TB-ST-240.

Form ST-121, Exempt Use Certificate.—Manufacturers, certain service providers, and other types of businesses may use Form ST-121, Exempt Use Certificate, to purchase, rent, or lease certain tangible personal property or services exempt from sales tax. (TB-ST-235) A bulletin issued by the Department of Taxation and Finance discusses this certificate (see TB-ST-235).

If you are the purchaser, fill out Form ST-121 and give it to the seller. You must complete all required entries and sign and date the form. The seller keeps the certificate and may then sell you certain property or services without charging sales tax. You must give the seller a properly completed Form ST-121 within 90 days after the delivery of the property or performance of the service. Sales tax exemption certificates may also be issued and accepted electronically. You may use Form ST-121 as a single-purchase certificate, or as a blanket certificate covering the first and subsequent purchases of the same general type of property or service from the same seller. Except as noted in the bulletin and in the instructions for Form ST-121, you must have a valid Certificate of Authority when you use Form ST-121 to make tax-free purchases. (TB-ST-235)

The bulletin issued by the Department also explains what kinds of property and services can be purchased exempt from sales tax using the certificate, and provides examples (with general descriptions) of tangible personal property and services related to production, transfer stations, and demolition facilities that a taxpayer may purchase exempt from sales tax with Form ST-121, as well as other general exemptions. (TB-ST-235)

Misuse of this exemption certificate may subject a taxpayer to serious civil and criminal sanctions in addition to the payment of any tax and interest due. These include the following:

— a penalty equal to 100% of the tax due;

— a $50 penalty for each fraudulent exemption certificate issued; and

— criminal felony prosecution, punishable by a substantial fine and a possible jail sentence, and revocation of your Certificate of Authority, if you are required to be registered for sales tax purposes.

(TB-ST-235)

Form ST-124, Certificate of Capital Improvement.—When performing capital improvement work, a contractor should get a properly completed Form ST-124, Certificate of Capital Improvement, from the customer (including a customer that is an exempt organization) and should not collect sales tax from the customer for the project. Receiving Form ST-124 relieves the contractor from liability for any tax due on the work. The contractor should keep this exemption certificate in his or her records to show why no sales tax was collected on the work. However, if no capital improvement certificate is received, the contract or other records of the project can still be used to establish that the work done constituted a capital improvement. If a contractor hires a subcontractor to work on a capital improvement project, the contractor should give the subcontractor a copy of the capital improvement certificate issued by the customer, so that the subcontractor's charges will be exempt from sales tax. All records must be kept for a minimum of three years. (TB-ST-104) For a discussion of capital improvements, see ¶ 60-330 Construction.

New York has other exemption certificates, as discussed below.

Certificates for prepayment of motor fuel and diesel motor fuel.—Upon each sale of motor fuel, other than a sale at retail, the seller must give to the purchaser a certification containing such information as the Commissioner of Taxation and Finance requires, including a statement to the effect that if the seller is a registered distributor, the seller has assumed the payment of or paid the tax required to be prepaid or that the seller is passing through the tax which was so previously assumed or paid by an identified registered distributor and passed through to the seller. (Sec. 1132(h)(1)(iii), Tax Law)

Where the required certification has been furnished to the purchaser by the seller at delivery and accepted in good faith, the burden of proving that the tax required to be paid was assumed or paid by a registered distributor and passed through is solely on the seller. (Sec. 1132(h)(1)(iii), Tax Law) If the certification required is not furnished by the seller at delivery of the motor fuel, it will be presumed that the tax required to be prepaid has not been assumed or paid by a registered distributor and that the purchaser in such case is jointly and severally liable for the tax.

A certification of tax payment is considered to be properly completed when it contains the following information:

— the seller's name and address;

— the seller's sales tax identification number;

— the seller's motor fuel tax registration number, if any;

— the purchaser's name and address;

— the number of gallons of each type of fuel (leaded, unleaded or premium);

— a separately stated amount for the prepaid sales tax and the motor fuel taxes charged to the customer;

— the date of delivery and the respective invoice or other billing or shipping document numbers;

— the name of the person who paid the motor fuel tax and prepaid sales tax or assumed lability for the payment of such taxes and that person's sales tax registration and motor fuel tax registration number; and

— if the seller is the registered distributor responsible for payment of the motor fuel tax and the prepaid sales tax, a signed statement to the effect that it has assumed the payment of or paid such taxes and, in each case, is passing through such taxes; or

if the seller is other than the registered distributor responsible for payment of the motor fuel tax and the prepaid sales tax, a signed statement to the effect that it is passing through such taxes which were previously paid or assumed by a registered distributor and which were passed through to it.

(Reg. Sec. 561.5)

Where the certification is contained on an invoice or other billing or shipping document, no signature is required if the seller is a registered motor fuel distributor. In all other cases, the certification must be signed.

Similar certification requirements apply for diesel motor fuel.

Preliminary certification.—The Commissioner of Taxation and Finance may authorize the delivery of motor fuel, without proper certification, if due to the circumstances of delivery, it is not possible to issue the required certification. (Sec. 1132(h)(1)(iii), Tax Law) In such instances, the Commissioner of Taxation and Finance will authorize the use of a preliminary certification. (Reg. Sec. 561.6) An example of where such authorization may be granted is the circumstance where motor fuel is sold through a terminal operated by a third person at which the seller has no agents or employees and the information necessary for a complete certification is not available. For additional information, see Reg. Sec. 561.6.

Interdistributor sale certificate.—The exemption from the required prepayment of tax on diesel motor fuel is established by means of an interdistributor sale certificate. Where the exemption is applicable, the purchaser is to furnish the certificate to the seller at the time of or prior to delivery of the diesel motor fuel. (Sec. 1132(h)(2)(iii), Tax Law) The certificate must contain: (1) the name and address of the purchaser; (2) the purchaser's registration number; and (3) an affirmation by the purchaser that the purchaser is registered as a distributor of diesel motor fuel and that such registration has not been suspended or canceled. Both the purchaser and the seller are required to sign the certificate. The certificate must also be in such form and contain such other information as the Commissioner of Taxation and Finance requires.

Where a proper and complete interdistributor sale certificate has been furnished and accepted by the seller in good faith, the seller is relieved of the burden of proving that the diesel motor fuel covered by the certificate is exempt from the required prepayment of tax. (Sec. 1132(h)(2)(iii), Tax Law) A seller will not be deemed to have accepted such a certificate in good faith if the purchaser's registration is invalid because it has been suspended or canceled or if the purchaser is not registered and the Commissioner of Taxation and Finance has furnished registered distributors with information identifying all those persons then validly registered as distributors of diesel motor fuel and those persons whose registrations have been suspended or canceled. Any purchaser who furnishes a false or fraudulent interdistributor sale certificate to the seller for the purpose of establishing an exemption is jointly and severally liable for the tax.

For more information on the various certificates, see TB-ST-240.

Empire zone credit or refund.—There is no longer an up-front exemption from tax for purchases made by a Qualified Empire Zone Enterprise (QEZE); a QEZE must apply for a refund or credit of tax paid on qualifying purchases. As of September 1, 2009, Form ST-121.6 Qualified Empire Zone Enterprise (QEZE) Exempt Purchase Certificate, is invalid. See ¶60-360 Empire Zones and Similar Incentives for further details on this credit or refund.

• *Electronic exemption certificates*

The New York Department of Taxation and Finance authorizes the use and acceptance of electronic versions of certain sales and use tax resale and exemption documents (e-certificates). The new policy does not require the use or acceptance of e-certificates. The paper resale and exemption forms prescribed by the Department may still be used. The change in policy only pertains to the manner in which resale and exemption documents may be executed. (TSB-M-07(1)S)

E-certificates are not available from the Department. At their discretion, purchasers and sellers may establish the means to electronically issue and receive e-certificates. The Department does not prescribe specific technologies or technical specifications for executing e-certificates nor does the Department require the use of particular types of hardware or software. However, an e-certificate must reproduce in its entirety the current paper resale or exemption form issued by the Department. Although the electronic version does not need to be a facsimile or an exact copy of the paper form, it must contain all of the language that is on the current paper form. When electronically reproducing the Department's documents, it is incumbent on the purchasers and sellers that they use the current forms as the bases for their e-certificates, even if it has been updated by the Department. If a purchaser or a seller wishes to use an e-certificate that has modified language, including any additions or deletions, prior approval must be obtained from the Department. (TSB-M-07(1)S)

An e-certificate in its entirety, which includes all applicable instructions, must be available to both the purchaser and the seller. However, it is not necessary that the instructions be included when issuing an e-certificate to the seller in order for the e-certificate to be considered accepted in good faith or properly completed. If the paper resale or exemption form may be issued as a blanket certificate or as a single-purchase certificate, the corresponding e-certificate may also be issued as a blanket certificate or as a single-purchase certificate. In addition to reproducing all of the language (including all certifications) that is on the paper resale form, an e-certificate must contain specific e-certification and electronic signature language (see TSB-M-07(1)S for the specific language)

Electronic signatures.—To be relieved of liability for failure to collect tax, a seller must accept in good faith an e-certificate that is properly completed within 90 days after delivery of the property or the rendition of the service. A properly completed e-certificate includes the purchaser's (or authorized representative's) signature. In the case of an e-certificate, this requires an electronic signature that is in lieu of any written signature required on the paper counterpart. There is no requirement to affix a physical signature on the e-certificate. An electronic signature has the same validity and effect as a handwritten signature. (TSB-M-07(1)S)

Recordkeeping.—Sellers must keep e-certificates as part of the records required to be kept under the Tax Law and sales and use tax regulations. An e-certificate must comply with all of the requirements for retaining records, including the requirements that it be capable of being accurately reproduced so as to be perceptible by human sensory capabilities and be capable of being accessed by the Department if requested. (TSB-M-07(1)S)

For a discussion of resales, see ¶ 60-650 Resales.

• *Multiple point of use certificates (MPUs)*

New York does not have any provisions for MPUs.

• *MTC and SST certificates*

New York does not accept any of the following exemption certificates:

— the MTC Uniform Sales and Use Tax Certificate as an exemption certificate;

— the Streamlined Sales and Use Tax (SST) Agreement exemption certificate; or

— other state's exemption certificates.

(Telephone Conversation, New York Department of Taxation and Finance, November 3, 2008; E-mail, New York Department of Taxation and Finance, January 13, 2017)

The Streamlined Sales and Use Tax (SST) Agreement is discussed further at ¶ 60-098 Streamlined Sales and Use Tax Agreement—New York Conformity.

The Multistate Tax Compact is discussed further at ¶ 60-096 Multistate Agreements and Initiatives.

• *Direct payment permit holders*

Direct payment permit holders are required to notify vendors from whom they make purchases of their status by submitting a copy of the direct payment permit with the first purchase order. (Reg. Sec. 532.5(e)(3))

Direct payment permits are discussed at ¶ 61-250 Direct Payment Permits

¶61-020

[¶61-100]

BASIS OF TAX

[¶61-110] Tax Base

In general, the New York State sales and use taxes are imposed on receipts from every retail sale of taxable tangible personal property and specified services. (Sec. 1105, Tax Law; Sec. 1110, Tax Law)

• *"Receipt" defined*

The term "receipt" is defined as the amount of the sales price of any item of property or the charge for any service subject to the sales or use tax, including gas and gas service and electricity and electric service of whatever nature, valued in money (whether received in money or otherwise). (Sec. 1101(b)(3), Tax Law; Reg. Sec. 526.5(a)) Included in the taxable receipts are any amounts for which credit is allowed by the vendor to the purchaser, without any deduction for expenses or early payment discounts and any charges by the vendor to the purchaser for shipping or delivery or—with respect to gas, gas service, electricity, and electric service—for transportation, transmission, or distribution (regardless of whether such charges are separately stated in the written contract or on the bill rendered to the purchaser and regardless of whether such shipping or delivery—or such transportation, transmission, or distribution—is provided by the vendor or by a third party). The sales and use taxes on delivery charges are imposed upon tangible personal property actually delivered and services actually rendered after August 31, 1991, although delivered or rendered under a prior contract. The taxable receipts do not include any credit for tangible personal property accepted in part payment and intended for resale.

A vendor's separately stated charges to ship or deliver promotional materials to a purchaser's customers or prospective customers by means of the United States postal service are exempt from tax. (Sec. 1115(n)(3), Tax Law)

• *Withdrawals from inventory*

The compensating use tax is due upon the use of tangible personal property which was purchased for resale or an exempt use and is subsequently withdrawn from or diverted to a taxable use by the purchaser. (Reg. Sec. 531.3(a)(2))

> **CCH EXAMPLE:** *Desk removed from inventory.*—A retail store purchased a dozen desks at $75 each for sale to its customers at $125 each. It subsequently withdrew one of the desks from inventory to be used in its office. A compensating use tax is due for the desk withdrawn from inventory. The tax is computed on the $75 that the store paid. (Reg. Sec. 531.3(a)(2))

> **CCH EXAMPLE:** *Drill press withdrawn from production lines.*—A machine shop which produces machine tools for sale withdraws a drill press from its production line for use in its building maintenance shop. The drill press was originally purchased exempt from tax for use in production. The use of the drill press in the building maintenance shop is a use subject to the compensating use tax at cost or fair market value, whichever is lower. (Reg. Sec. 531.3(a)(2))

• *Expenses*

Expenses (including telephone, telegraph and other service charges) incurred by a vendor in making a sale, regardless of their taxable status and regardless of whether they are billed to a customer, are not deductible from the receipts. (Reg. Sec. 526.5(e)) (TB-ST-860)

• *Demurrage*

A charge by a vendor to a customer for the retention of tangible personal property beyond a stipulated time is deemed to be a taxable receipt from the rental or lease of tangible personal property retained. The designation of such charge as a penalty, late fee or demurrage in no way affects its taxable status. (Reg. Sec. 526.5(i)(1))

The vendor's charge to a customer for a delay by the customer in removing tangible personal property from the vendor's premises is a charge for the storage of such tangible personal property. (Reg. Sec. 526.5(i)(2))

A charge to a shipper or consignee for the retention of a railroad car, trailer, semi-trailer, vessel or marine-cargo container is considered part of the transportation charge and not subject to the sales or compensating use tax, although such charge may be designated as "demurrage." (Reg. Sec. 526.5(i)(3))

• *Deposits*

If a vendor charges a deposit on items that it rents, leases, or loans, the charge is not considered to be part of the taxable receipt. If the vendor keeps any portion of the deposit when the property is returned, that portion of the deposit is subject to sales tax at that time as part of the charge for the rental or lease of the item. (Reg. Sec. 526.5(j)) (TB-ST-860)

• *Interest, account service fees, and late fees*

In general, if a vendor charges interest, service fees, or late fees for extending credit to its customers in order for them to pay over a period of time, these charges are not part of the purchase price of the item or service and therefore, are not subject to sales tax. However, if vendor charges a late fee when taxable goods are not returned on time, the additional charge is not for the extension of credit. The late fee is part of the charge for the rental of the goods and is part of the taxable receipt subject to sales tax. For example, a late fee for returning a video a day late is really a charge for an additional day's rental, and would be subject to sales tax. (TB-ST-860)

• *Special basis provisions*

Special basis provisions are provided for specific transactions, such as leases. Listed below, in alphabetical order, are the special basis provisions with a cross-reference for each to the paragraph numbers at which they are discussed in detail:

Information services, interior decorating and designing services and protective and detective services . . . . ¶ 60-665

Long term leases of certain motor vehicles, vessels and noncommercial aircraft . . . . ¶ 60-460, ¶ 60-570, ¶ 60-740

Motor fuel and diesel motor fuel sold at retail and such fuels subject to prepayment of tax . . . . ¶ 60-560

New mobile homes . . . . ¶ 60-540

Retail sales of cigarettes and tobacco products . . . . ¶ 60-730

Sales of racehorses made through claiming races within New York State . . . . ¶ 60-250

Tangible property not acquired for resale upon which processing and printing services; installation, repair and maintenance services; or interior decorating and designing services have been performed . . . . ¶ 60-630, ¶ 60-645, ¶ 60-665

¶61-110

Tangible property purchased outside the state by a New York State resident for out-of-state use which subsequently becomes subject to the compensating use tax . . . . ¶ 60-450

Tangible property when manufactured, processed or assembled and used by the manufacturer, processor or assembler in the regular course of business . . . . ¶ 60-510

Use of tangible property purchased at retail . . . . ¶ 60-020

[¶61-200]

RETURNS, PAYMENT, AND RECORDS

[¶61-220] Returns, Payment, and Due Dates

Every person who is required to register with the Commissioner of Taxation and Finance, or who voluntarily registers, is required to file sales tax returns and pay sales tax due. (Sec. 1136(a), Tax Law) Taxpayers are required to file annually, quarterly, or part-quarterly, depending on the amount of taxable sales or sales tax collected. Taxpayers must file a sales tax return on time, even if no tax is due for the filing period. (Publication 900, Important Information for Business Owners)

Any person required to file quarterly returns whose total tax due for the four most recent quarterly periods for which data is available for such person within the most recent six quarters for which data is available did not exceed $3,000 may file a return annually in lieu of filing quarterly. (Reg. Sec. 533.3(d)) Payment of tax accompanies the return. (Sec. 1137(e)(1), Tax Law) Monthly returns are due by the 20th day of the following month. (Sec. 1136 (b), Tax Law) Quarterly returns are due on or before March 20, June 20, September 20 and December 20 for the three-month periods ending with the last day of February, May, August and November, respectively. (Reg. Sec. 533.3(d)) The annual return covers the period from March 1st through the end of the following February. (Reg. Sec. 533.3(d)) Returns on other dates for other periods may be authorized or permitted. (Sec. 1137-A(b), Tax Law)

For additional information on filing and payment requirements, see Publication 900, Important Information for Business Owners; TB-ST-265; and TB-ST-275.

For a discussion of amendments to the Tax Law and the Administrative Code of New York City in relation to penalties imposed upon tax return preparers who fail to electronically file (e-file), to authorize reasonable correction periods for electronic tax filings and payments, and to prohibit tax return preparers and software companies from charging separately for electronic filing of New York tax documents, see TSB-M-10(18)S.

For a discussion of legislation that excluded enrolled agents from the definition of "tax return preparer" under the Tax Preparer Registration Program, see TSB-M-11(1)S.

• *Persons required to file monthly returns*

Every person whose taxable receipts, amusement charges, rents, and purchases subject to use tax, total $300,000 or more in any quarter of the preceding four quarters, or a distributor of petroleum products with sales of 100,000 gallons or more in any quarter of the preceding four quarters, must file a return each month. Persons required to file monthly may elect to file either a long-form or short-form, part-quarterly return. (Sec. 1136(a), Tax Law) The Commissioner has the discretion, when he or she deems it necessary to protect state and local sales and use tax revenues, to require a vendor that files only quarterly returns to file either short-form or long-form quarterly returns. (Sec. 1136(a)(1), Tax Law)

A "long-form, part-quarterly return" reports the actual sales and use taxes for the preceding month. A person filing a "long-form, part-quarterly return" for each of the months contained in a quarter is also required to file a quarterly return for the quarter. (Sec. 1136(a), Tax Law)

A "short-form, part-quarterly return" may be used for the first two months of any quarter to report sales and use taxes for each month on the basis on one-third of the combined state and local sales and use taxes paid in the comparable quarter of the preceding year. (Sec. 1136(a), Tax Law)

The quarterly return serves as a monthly return for the last month of a quarter and a reconciliation for the quarter. (Reg. Sec. 533.3 (b))

• *Persons required to file quarterly returns*

Persons with taxable receipts of $300,000 or less or distributors whose sales of petroleum products total less than 100,000 gallons in every quarter of the preceding four quarters must file quarterly returns. (Sec. 1136(a), Tax Law)

• *Election to file annual returns*

Vendors and other persons required to file sales and use tax returns may elect to file an annual return, in lieu of the monthly or quarterly returns normally required if the total tax for the succeeding 12-month period reasonably can be expected not to exceed $3,000 and such election is made on a specified form by the 20th day of their annual period. The period covered by the annual return will be from March 1st through the end of the following February. (Reg. Sec. 533.3(d))

Annual filers can use the Department's new fill-in version of Form ST-101, New York State and Local Annual Sales and Use Tax Return. The new fill-in form can be used by filers of Form ST-101 and by filers of Form ST-102-A, New York State and Local Annual Sales and Use Tax Return for a Single Jurisdiction. (Important Notice N-07-7)

• *Amended returns*

Amended returns may be required to be filed within 20 days after notice and to contain the information specified in the notice. (Sec. 1136(d), Tax Law)

• *Final returns*

Vendors who cease business operations, sell (transfer or assign) their business, or change the organizational form of the business must file a final return clearly marked at the top, "Final Return," indicating the actual period covered by the return, calculated from the first day of the period in which the event occurred to the final day of business. (Reg. Sec. 533.3(e)) A final return must be filed within 20 days after ceasing business operations or the sale, transfer, or change occurs. The back of the sales tax Certificate of Authority must be completed, and the certificate must be surrendered with the final return. (TB-ST-265)

A final return must include the same information that would be included on a regular return. (TB-ST-265)

Web Filing the final return.—A taxpayer must register to Web File their final return. If the Web File return for the correct filing period is available at the time the final return is due, use the Web File return. When you Web File your final return, check the box indicating that it is a final return. Once you've completed the final return on the Web, you'll be given an address to send your Certificate of Authority. You must surrender the certificate to the Tax Department; complete the questions on the back of the certificate, and mail it to the address provided. (TB-ST-265)

There are certain instances when you will need to file a paper final return instead of Web Filing. If you are required to file Schedule N-ATT, Taxes on Parking Services in New York City, or Schedule FR, Sales and Use Tax on Qualified Motor Fuel and Diesel Motor Fuel, with your part-quarterly, quarterly, or annual sales tax return, you cannot Web File. You must file a paper final return. If you normally Web File and the return for the final sales tax period of your business is not yet available, you must file a paper final return 20 days after you stop doing business or are otherwise required to surrender your Certificate of Authority. (TB-ST-265)

Filing a paper final return.—The Department does not produce a separate paper form for use as a final return. If a taxpayer files a final paper return, they will need to modify the return appropriate for the filing status. (TB-ST-265)

Filing period indicators.—For a discussion of filing period indicators on final sales tax returns, see TB-ST-270. The bulletin explains the following: where to find the filing period indicator on a return, how to determine whether it is correct, and how to change it if it is not correct. However, the bulletin is only applicable to a business that files a paper final return. The filing period indicator on a Web File return cannot be changed. (TB-ST-270)

• *Annual information returns*

In addition to all other returns, the following persons must file annual information returns:

— every insurer licensed to issue motor vehicle physical damage or motor vehicle property damage liability insurance for motor vehicles registered in New York if, during the period covered by the return, it has paid consideration or an amount under an insurance contract for the servicing or repair of a motor vehicle on behalf of an insured. For each person to whom the insurer paid the consideration, the return must report the total amount paid for that period, along with other required information;

— every franchisor that has at least one franchisee that is required to be registered for sales and use tax purposes. For each franchisee, the return must include the gross sales of the franchisee in New York reported by the franchisee to the franchisor, the total amount of sales by the franchisor to the franchisee, and any income reported to the franchisor by each franchisee, along with additional information; and

— every wholesaler, if it has made a sale of an alcoholic beverage, without collecting sales or use tax during the period covered by the return, except (i) a sale to a person that has furnished an exempt organization certificate to the wholesaler for that sale; or (ii) a sale to another wholesaler whose license under the alcoholic beverage control law does not allow it to make retail sales of the alcoholic beverage. For each vendor, operator, or recipient to whom the wholesaler has made a sale without collecting sales or compensating use tax, the return must include the total value of those sales made during the period covered by the return and the vendor's, operator's or recipient's state liquor authority license number, along with other information.

(Sec. 1136(i)(2), Tax Law) (TSB-M-09(8)S; TSB-M-09(8.1)S; TSB-M-09(9)S; TSB-M-09(9.1)S; TSB-M-09(10)S; TSB-M-09(10.1)S)

The first information returns required under the new law are due on or before September 20, 2009, and will cover the period March 1, 2009 through August 31, 2009. If the required information cannot be obtained or compiled by the required due date of the first information return (September 21, 2009), the party may apply electronically for an automatic 90-day extension of time to file the return. The application for the extension must be made on or before September 21, 2009, to extend the due date

Guidebook to New York Taxes

of the first information return to December 21, 2009. (TSB-M-09(8)S; TSB-M-09(8.1)S; TSB-M-09(9)S; TSB-M-09(9.1)S; TSB-M-09(10)S; TSB-M-09(10.1)S)

The next information returns will be due on or before March 20, 2010, and will cover the period September 1, 2009 through February 28, 2010. Subsequently, annual information returns will be due on or before March 20th of each year, and will cover the period from March 1 of the previous year through February 28 or 29 of the current year. (TSB-M-09(8)S; TSB-M-09(8.1)S; TSB-M-09(9)S; TSB-M-09(9.1)S; TSB-M-09(10)S; TSB-M-09(10.1)S)

Exclusions from filing.—Licensed farm wineries, farm distilleries, farm cideries, farm breweries, and brewers who produce less than 60,000 barrels of beer a year are excluded from the sales tax annual information return filing requirements imposed by Tax Law § 1136(i). (TSB-M-12(11)S) (TSB-M-15(6)S) Also excluded are businesses operating under a winery license (as provided in Sec. 76 of the Alcoholic Beverage Control Law) that produce less than 150,000 finished gallons of wine a year. Businesses that meet this statutory provision are not required to file annual sales tax information returns due on or after March 20, 2016. Businesses operating under a farm winery license continue to be excluded from this filing requirement (Sec. 76-A of the Alcoholic Beverage Control Law). (Sec. 1136(i)(1)(C), Tax Law) (TSB-M-16(1)S)

Filing.—The information returns must be electronically filed annually on or before March 20 and must cover the four sales tax quarterly periods immediately preceding such date. (Sec. 1136(i)(1), Tax Law)

Penalties.—Failure to comply with the information return filing requirements can result in various penalties. A waiver of penalties is allowed in certain cases. For a discussion of these, and other penalties, see TSB-M-09(8)S; TSB-M-09(8.1)S; TSB-M-09(9)S; TSB-M-09(9.1)S; TSB-M-09(10)S; and TSB-M-09(10.1)S.

For a discussion of the requirements for the filing of information returns for insurers of motor vehicles, see TSB-M-09(8)S and TSB-M-09(8.1)S.

For a discussion of the requirements for the filing of information returns for franchisors, see TSB-M-09(9)S and TSB-M-09(9.1)S.

For a discussion of the requirements for the filing of information returns for alcoholic beverage wholesalers, see TSB-M-09(10)S and TSB-M-09(10.1)S.

• *Electronic filing*

The Department of Taxation and Finance is authorized to require electronic filing (e-file) and electronic payment (e-pay) of all tax documents. (Sec. 29, Tax Law) (TSB-M-08(9)S) In addition, if a tax return preparer prepared authorixed tax documents for more than 10 different taxpayers during any calendar year beginning on or after January 1, 2012, and if in any succeeding year that preparer prepares one or more authorized tax documents using tax software, then all authorized tax documents prepared by that preparer must be filed electronically. An "authorized tax document" means a tax document which the commissioners has authorized to be filed electronically, provided however that any return or report that includes one or more tax documents that cannot be filed electronically are not deemed to be an authorized tax document. This requirement sunsets on December 31, 2019. (Sec. 29, Tax Law)

Many sales tax returns can be filed online using the Department's Web File system. Most registered sales tax vendors may use the Web File program to file returns and make payments. Taxpayers can even file a simplified return online when they have no tax due. (TB-ST-275)

The Department requires certain part-quarterly (monthly) sales tax filers to Web File their sales tax returns and make the payments associated with those returns by electronic withdrawal from their bank accounts. Quarterly filers are also required to use Sales Tax Web File beginning with the quarterly sales tax return due on June 20, 2011. As a quarterly or monthly sales filer, a taxpayer must Web File if its business meets all three of the following conditions:

— it does not use a tax preparer to prepare the required filings;

— it uses a computer to prepare, document, or calculate the required filings or related schedules, or is subject to the corporation tax e-file mandate; and

— it has broadband Internet access.

(TB-ST-275) (*E-file—Business tax e-file mandate for businesses that self-file tax returns,* New York Department of Taxation and Finance, May 2011)

Subscribers can view information on e-filing mandate for businesses.

However, if a taxpayer files either Form ST-100.5-ATT or Form ST-810.5-ATT, they cannot e-file their return and the mandate does not apply. (TB-ST-275)

Web filing the final return.—A taxpayer must register to Web File their final return. (TB-ST-265) There are certain instances when you will need to file a paper final return instead of Web Filing, which are discussed in TB-ST-265.

Penalty provisions.—The following penalty and interest provisions apply to taxpayers for taxes other than personal income tax. (TSB-M-11(9)S) A taxpayer who is required to electronically pay any liability is assessed a penalty of $50 for each failure to electronically pay the liability. The penalty will be imposed unless the taxpayer can show that the failure was due to reasonable cause and not willful neglect. The following additional penalties also apply to a taxpayer who is required to e-file any authorized document that fails to e-file the authorized tax document:

— a penalty of $50 for each failure to e-file unless the taxpayer can show that the failure was due to reasonable cause and not willful neglect, and

— a penalty under the applicable article for the failure to file a return or report, whether a paper return or report has been filed or not.

(TSB-M-11(9)S)

If a taxpayer who is required to e-file any authorized document fails to e-file the authorized tax document, the taxpayer will not be eligible to receive interest on any overpayment until the document is filed electronically. (TSB-M-11(9)S)

Requirements for tax return preparers.—Sales tax documents for PrompTax, monthly, and quarterly filers must be filed electronically. Beginning with the return due on March 20, 2012, tax preparers will also be required to electronically file returns for annual sales tax filers. (*E-file mandate for tax preparers,* New York Department of Taxation and Finance)

• *Casual sales*

Except for sales of motor vehicles, snowmobiles, vessels and all-terrain vehicles required to be registered or titled by the Department of Motor Vehicles, any person making a taxable sale of tangible personal property or services, or who makes a purchase subject to the compensating use tax, and who is not otherwise required to register as a vendor, must file a report of casual sale. (Reg. Sec. 533.3(g))

Reports.—Reports of casual sales must show the amount of sales of tangible personal property and services, food and drink, amusement charges, and rents and the amount of purchases subject to use tax, for each jurisdiction, as well as totals of all jurisdictions. (Reg. Sec. 533.3(g))

• *Persons purchasing or selling property for resale*

Persons required to register only because they are purchasing or selling tangible property for resale, and who are not required to collect any tax or pay any tax directly to the Commissioner, must file an annual information return. (Sec. 1136(a)(3), Tax Law)

• *Sales to itinerant vendors*

The Commissioner of Taxation and Finance may requiring persons registered or required to be registered to file reports regarding sales for resale within New York of tangible personal property or services to itinerant vendors. (Sec. 1136(h), Tax Law)

• *Vendors of petroleum products*

A person who is required to register and who is selling petroleum products, but is not a distributor of motor fuel, must file an information return quarterly, or if deemed necessary by the Commissioner, must file a return monthly in a form prescribed by the Commissioner. (Sec. 1136(a), Tax Law)

Returns of sellers of petroleum products.—The return of any seller of petroleum products must show the number of gallons of petroleum products sold and the taxable receipts from the sale of petroleum products and motor fuel, together with any additional information as the Commissioner may require in order to certify the amount of taxes, penalties and interest payable to local taxing jurisdictions imposed on the sale or use of petroleum products. (Sec. 1136(a), Tax Law)

• *Retail service stations*

Every retail vendor purchasing, selling or using motor fuel must file, in addition to any other sales tax return or report, a report of motor fuel inventory. (Reg. Sec. 561.13(b)(4)) The report must be filed quarterly within 25 days of the end of the sales tax quarter covered by the report.

• *Lessors of amusement places*

Owners, licensees or lessees of places of amusement, roof gardens, cabarets or other similar places may be required by regulation to file information returns with the Commissioner showing all leases, subleases and licenses to use granted to persons who take amusement charges. The Commissioner is authorized to prescribe the form of the returns, the time when they are to be filed and the information to be contained in them. (Sec. 1136(e), Tax Law)

• *Show promoters (flea markets, antique shows, craft shows, etc.)*

Show promoters must file monthly reports, within 20 days after the end of the preceding month, for all shows that they promoted during the preceding month. (Sec. 1136(f), Tax Law)

Show promoters must list on the monthly reports the date and place of each show and the name, address and certificate of authority number, by show, of every person whom the promoter permits to display for sale or to sell tangible personal property or services subject to tax at each show. Persons who display for sale or sell tangible personal property or services subject to tax are required to supply the promoter with their names, addresses and certificate of authority numbers for the promoter's use in filing the report. (Sec. 1136(f), Tax Law)

• *Entertainment promoters*

Entertainment promoters must file monthly reports for all entertainment events that they promoted during the preceding month. Each report must be filed within 20 days after the end of the preceding month. (Sec. 1136(g), Tax Law)

Reports.—The monthly reports filed by entertainment promoters must list the date and place of each event, and the name, address and certificate of authority number, by event, of every vendor who made taxable sales of tangible personal property at the event. Entertainment vendors are required to supply the promoter with their names, addresses and certificate of authority numbers for the promoter's use in filing the report. (Sec. 1136(g), Tax Law)

• *Prepaid sales tax reports*

Every distributor of motor fuel and every person selling motor fuel not exclusively at retail must file, in addition to other required sales tax returns or reports, a report of sales tax prepayment on motor fuel. The report must be filed monthly within 20 days after the end of the preceding month to which the report applies. The reports of distributors must be accompanied by payment of the full amount of prepaid sales tax due. (Reg. Sec. 561.13(b)(2))

• *Customers*

In the event that a customer fails to pay tax to the person required to collect the tax, it is the duty of the customer to file a return with the Commissioner and to pay the tax within 20 days after the date on which the tax was required to be paid. (Sec. 1133(b), Tax Law)

The Commissioner is authorized to prescribe regulations requiring customers to file returns and pay tax directly to the Commissioner. (Sec. 1133(c), Tax Law)

• *Motor vehicle parking, garaging and storing services*

Taxpayers required to pay state sales and use taxes, New York City temporary municipal assistance sales and use tax and New York City sales and use tax on parking services in Manhattan must file reports or schedules or make separate entries on the return for each separate place of business providing motor vehicle parking, garaging or storing services. The return must identify the specific location, address and licensed capacity of each place of business, include applicable license numbers and schedules of information prescribed by the Commissioner of Taxation and Finance and accompany the state and state-administered local sales and use tax returns. Taxpayers may be exempt from these requirements provided the annual limited sales and use tax liability incurred creates undue hardship. (Sec. 1142-A, Tax Law; Reg. Part 538.1)

• *Returns covering other periods*

The Commissioner may permit or require returns to be made covering other periods according to dates as the Commissioner may specify. If the Commissioner deems it necessary in order to insure payment of the taxes imposed by Article 28, the Commissioner may require returns to be made for shorter periods than those prescribed and upon such dates as the Commissioner may specify. (Sec. 1136(d), Tax Law)

• *Returns of estimated tax no longer required*

The requirement of an estimated return has been eliminated. Receipts for the month of March and the tax due thereon are to be reported on the regular monthly return due on April 20. (Sec. 1137-A(c), Tax Law)

• *Fees*

There is no provision for payment of fees in connection with the filing of returns.

See ¶ 61-220 Returns, Payment, and Due Dates.

• *Contents*

Returns must be made on forms prescribed by the Commissioner of Taxation and Finance and must contain all information deemed necessary to administer the law. (Sec. 1136(d), Tax Law; Reg. Sec. 533.3(a)(1))

Vendor returns.—The return of a vendor of tangible personal property or services must indicate receipts from sales, the aggregate value of tangible personal property and services sold, the use of which is subject to tax, and the amount of tax required to be collected. (Sec. 1136(a), Tax Law)

Returns of recipients of amusement charges.—The return of the recipient of amusement charges must indicate all amusement charges and the amount of tax imposed. (Sec. 1136(a), Tax Law)

Returns of hotel operators.—A hotel operator's return must show all rents received or charged and the amount of tax imposed. (Sec. 1136(a), Tax Law)

• *Payment and computation of tax*

All sales and use tax required to be collected is due and payable to the Commissioner of Taxation and Finance on or before the date set for the filing of the return for the reporting period, without regard to whether a return is filed and whether the return filed is correct or complete. The tax is due and payable whether or not it has been collected by the vendor from the purchaser. (Reg. Sec. 533.4(a))

All moneys collected as tax, purportedly in accordance with a tax schedule, whether or not the receipts are subject to tax, must be remitted at the time a return is filed.

All vendors (except utilities).—Every person subject to tax must pay 4% of the total of all taxable receipts, amusement charges and rents, plus the amount imposed on receipts, amusement charges and rents by the locality. In addition, payment must be made of 5% on receipts from every rental of a passenger car which is a retail sale of the car. (Sec. 1137(a), Tax Law; Sec. 1160, Tax Law) Within the Metropolitan Commuter Transportation District, an additional charge must be remitted (see ¶60-110 Rate of Tax). (Reg. Sec. 530.1(c))

A person filing a short-form, part-quarterly return, however, must pay, at the time of filing, one-third of the total state and local sales and compensating use taxes payable in the comparable quarter of the immediately preceding year. (Sec. 1137(c)(1), Tax Law)

Vendors of utility services.—Vendors selling utilities can select one of two methods provided for computing the amount of tax which is to be remitted:

— General method: Persons remitting tax must pay all state and local taxes imposed, as well as any amounts collected by them acting or purporting to act under the state and local tax laws.

— Elective method using effective rates of tax: The Commissioner of Taxation and Finance is authorized to fix effective rates of tax for any person, group, or classification of persons. The effective rate is intended to require payment of all state and local taxes imposed. Use of the method of computing the amount of tax to be remitted which involves use of effective rates is optional with the taxpayer, and subject to the approval of the Commissioner.

(Sec. 1137(d), Tax Law)

This method may not be used with short-form, part-quarterly returns. (Sec. 1137(c)(1), Tax Law)

• *Electronic Fund Transfer Program*

New York has implemented a program requiring certain vendors to submit payments of tax through electronic fund transfers (EFT) or certified checks. Generally, a taxpayer will be required to participate in the program if, on or after June 1 of any year, its tax liability for the immediately preceding June 1 through May 31 period exceeds certain dollar thresholds. (Sec. 10, Tax Law; Reg. Sec. 2397.2) See ¶89-108 Payment Methods.

• *Due dates*

Returns must be filed within 20 days after the end of the period being reported. The Commissioner of Taxation and Finance may permit or require returns to be made covering other periods and specify other due dates. (Sec. 1136(c), Tax Law) Returns may be required for shorter periods than those prescribed and due on different dates if the Commissioner deems it necessary in order to insure the payment of taxes.

If a due date falls on a Saturday, Sunday or a day which is a legal holiday in the State of New York, filing will be timely if it is performed on the next succeeding day which is not a Saturday, Sunday or legal holiday. (Reg. Sec. 2399.3)

Monthly returns.—Returns required to be filed monthly must be filed for monthly periods ending on the last day of each month. Each return is due within 20 days after the end of each prior month. (Sec. 1136(b), Tax Law)

Quarterly returns.—Returns required to be filed quarterly must be filed for quarterly periods ending on the last day of February, May, August and November of each year. Each return must be filed within 20 days after the end of the quarterly period being reported. (Sec. 1136(b), Tax Law)

Annual returns.—Annual filers must file their returns for annual periods beginning on March 1st and ending with the last day of February in the subsequent year. The returns must be filed with the department on or before March 20th of each such subsequent year. (Reg. Sec. 533.3(d)(4)(i))

Information returns.—Information returns that are required to be filed annually must be filed for 12-month periods ending on the last day of May each year. Each information return must be filed within 20 days following the 12-month period covered by the return. (Sec. 1136(b), Tax Law)

Monthly reports of promoters of entertainment and shows (flea markets, antique shows, craft shows, etc.).—Entertainment and show promoters must file monthly reports for all entertainment events and shows that they promoted during the preceding month. Each report is to be filed within 20 days after the end of the preceding month. (Sec. 1136(f), Tax Law; Sec. 1136(g), Tax Law)

Customers' returns.—Customers failing to pay the tax to the person required to collect the tax must file a return with the Commissioner of Taxation and Finance, and pay the tax, within 20 days from the date when payment was due. (Sec. 1133(b), Tax Law) The Commissioner is authorized to issue regulations requiring customers to file returns and pay the tax directly to the Commissioner at the same time that the returns and payment are due from the persons required to collect the tax. (Sec. 1133(c), Tax Law)

Amended returns.—The Commissioner may require amended returns to be filed within 20 days after notice. (Sec. 1136(d), Tax Law)

Final returns.—Vendors who cease operations, sell a business, or change the organizational form of the business must file a final return within 20 days after the occurrence of such event. (Reg. Sec. 533.3(f))

Casual sale reports.—Where the casual sale occurs in New York, the report must be filed within 20 days from the date of the sale. When a resident of New York purchases tangible personal property outside the state and brings the property into the state, the report must be filed within 20 days from the date on which the purchases are brought into New York. (Reg. Sec. 533.3(g))

Extension of time for filing.—The Commissioner of Taxation and Finance is authorized to extend, for cause shown, the time of filing any return or report for a period not exceeding three months. (Sec. 1142(2), Tax Law)

Delinquent returns.—There are no specific statutory delinquent dates other than the due dates.

[¶61-240] Vendor Registration

If a taxpayer will be making sales in New York that are subject to sales tax, they must register with the Department of Taxation and Finance. Specifically, the following persons must register:

— every person required to collect sales and use taxes commencing business or opening a new place of business;

— every person purchasing or selling tangible personal property for resale commencing business or opening a new place of business;

— every person selling petroleum products, including persons who are not distributors;

— every person heretofore described who takes possession of or pays for business assets under a bulk sale; and

— every person required to register whose certificate of authority has been revoked.

(Sec. 1134(a)(1), Tax Law) (TB-ST-175) (Publication 900)

Upon registration, the Department of Taxation and Finance will issue a certificate of authority to collect the tax together with duplicate certificates for any additional places of business. (Sec. 1134(a)(2), Tax Law) (See Publication 750, A Guide to Sales Tax in New York State) There is no registration fee.

All current sales tax vendors are required to re-register and pay a one-time $50 application fee. A person may be subject to the re-registration requirement even if such person holds a certificate of authority that has not been in effect for a period of at least three years. Small vendors who file on an annual basis will not have to pay the fee when they re-register. (Ch. 57 (S.B. 6807), Part LL-1, Laws 2008, ¶104-970m) (TSB-M-08(9)S) The re-registration program also applies to show and entertainment vendors. (TSB-M-08(13)S)

Once a taxpayer has registered as a sales tax vendor, its obligations include, but are not limited to:

— collecting the proper amount of state and local sales tax from customers;

— keeping adequate records related to business activities as a sales tax vendor;

— filing timely sales tax returns, even if no tax is due;

— paying any sales taxes due with returns; and

— keeping registration data up-to-date with the Department of Taxation and Finance.

(Publication 900)

For additional information on who is required to register and what kinds of goods and services are generally subject to tax, see TB-ST-175.

• *Certain installation, repair and maintenance services*

If you are in the business of installing, repairing, maintaining, or servicing tangible personal property, you are required to register for sales tax. This includes services such as:

> — motor vehicle repair;
>
> — dog grooming;
>
> — appliance repair;
>
> — computer repair; and
>
> — installation of car stereos.

(TB-ST-175)

If you are in the business of performing repair and maintenance services to real property, you are required to register for sales tax. This includes services such as:

> — lawn mowing;
>
> — interior or exterior painting of an existing house or structure;
>
> — snow removal services;
>
> — plumbing repairs;
>
> — electrical repairs; and
>
> — swimming pool maintenance.

(TB-ST-175)

• *Out-of-state businesses*

Even though a business is located in another state, if it has customers in New York, it may be required to register as a vendor for New York sales tax purposes if the business has sufficient connection with New York State. (See ¶ 60-025 Nexus—Doing Business in New York) (TB-ST-175) (See also Publication 750, A Guide to Sales Tax in New York State)

• *Wholesalers*

If a business will be selling tangible personal property to other wholesalers or retailers, it must register for sales tax purposes in order to issue and accept most exemption certificates. (TB-ST-175)

• *Manufacturers*

Manufacturing includes a variety of operations, including manufacturing and processing, along with mining and extracting. In most cases, manufacturers do not have to collect sales tax on the sales that they make, because the products will later be resold. However, a manufacturer must register for sales tax for other reasons. Manufacturers must be registered for sales tax to accept resale certificates from their customers, and to buy certain items (such as raw materials, machinery, equipment and electricity used in production) without paying sales tax. (TB-ST-175)

• *Show vendors, entertainment vendors, and temporary vendors*

Show vendors, temporary vendors, and entertainment vendors must also register with the Commissioner of Taxation and Finance. (Sec. 1134(a)(2), Tax Law) (TB-ST-175)

Show vendor—A "show vendor" is any person who displays for sale or sells, at a show, taxable tangible personal property or services. (Sec. 1131(7), Tax Law) (See Publication 750, A Guide to Sales Tax in New York State and Publication 900)

Temporary vendor.—A "temporary vendor" is any person who makes sales of taxable tangible personal property or services (other than at a show or entertainment event) in not more than two consecutive quarterly periods in any 12-month period. (Sec. 1131(11), Tax Law)

Issuance of certificates of authority.—The Department will no longer issue Form DTF-726. In December 2008, currently registered show and entertainment vendors that have timely filed sales tax returns and paid the applicable taxes due will instead automatically receive Form DTF-17-A, Certificate of Authority, effective January 1, 2009. Also starting in December 2008, any person who applies as a show or entertainment vendor for the first time will be issued Form DTF-17-A. In either case, Form DTF-17-A issued to a show or entertainment vendor will not have an expiration date and will remain in effect until it is suspended or revoked or until it becomes subject to the re-registration program. Any show or entertainment vendor that has not timely filed its sales tax returns or paid the proper amount of taxes due will not automatically receive Form DTF-17-A in December 2008. Instead, the Department will notify the vendor of its filing and payment status and explain how the vendor can resolve its account in order to receive a new Certificate of Authority. (TSB-M-08(13)S)

Previously, show and entertainment vendors were issued Form DTF-726, Certificate of Authority for Show and Entertainment Vendors. This certificate was valid for one calendar year and expired on the last day of the calendar year for which it was issued. If a show or entertainment vendor timely filed its sales tax returns and paid the applicable taxes due, the Department automatically reissued the vendor's certificate of authority by sending the vendor a new Form DTF-726 that was valid for the next calendar year. (TSB-M-08(13)S)

For purposes of the re-registration program that the Department is required to conduct for every person that holds a sales tax Certificate of Authority, the Department will contact all such persons, including show and entertainment vendors, when it is time to re-register and obtain a new Certificate of Authority under this re-registration program. (TSB-M-08(13)S)

• *Exceptions to registration requirement and thresholds for registration*

Exceptions to registration requirement.—Unless certain thresholds are met, registration is not required by:

(1) a person who sells tangible personal property or services, the use of which is taxed, and who regularly or systematically delivers the property or services by means other than the U.S. mail or common carrier;

(2) a person who regularly or systematically solicits business in New York by the distribution, without regard to the place of origin, of catalogs, advertising flyers or letters, or by any other means, and thereby makes sales to persons within the state of tangible personal property, the use of which is taxed, provided that the solicitation satisfies the nexus requirement of the U.S. Constitution; or

(3) a person making sales of tangible personal property, the use of which is subject to tax, where the seller retains an ownership interest in the property and where such property is brought into the state by the purchaser, who is or becomes a resident or who uses the property in carrying on any employment, trade, business, or profession in New York.

(Sec. 1134(a)(1), Tax Law; Sec. 1101(b)(8)(i)(D), (E), and (F))

¶61-240

Thresholds for registration.—The exceptions for the three categories of vendors noted in the paragraph above do not apply if the vendor's activities meet certain thresholds. Vendors who sell tangible personal property or services by means other than the U.S. mail or common carrier, as noted in (1) above, must file with the Commissioner of Taxation and Finance a certificate of registration within 30 days after the day on which the cumulative total number of occasions that the vendor came into New York to deliver property or services exceeds 12, for the immediately preceding four quarterly periods ending on the last day of February, May, August and November. (Sec. 1134(a)(1), Tax Law; Sec. 1101(b)(8)(i)(D))

Vendors that solicit business in New York by the distribution of catalogs, advertising flyers, or letters, as noted in (2) above, are required to file with the Commissioner a certificate of registration within 30 days after the day on which the cumulative total of the vendor's gross receipts from sales in the state exceed $500,000 and the number of sales exceeds 100, for the immediately preceding four quarterly periods ending on the last day of February, May, August and November. (Sec. 1134(a)(1), Tax Law; Sec. 1101(b)(8)(i)(E))

Vendors that make sales of tangible personal property but retain an ownership interest in the property, as noted in (3) above, must file a certificate of registration with the Commissioner within 30 days after the date on which the property is brought into the state by the purchaser, where the purchaser becomes or is a resident or uses the property in carrying on any trade, business, or profession in the state. (Sec. 1134(a)(1), Tax Law; Sec. 1101(b)(8)(i)(F))

• *Show promoters (flea markets, antique shows, craft shows, etc.)*

At least 10 days before the opening of a show, a show promoter must file with the Commissioner of Taxation and Finance a notice stating the location and dates of the show, in a form prescribed by the Commissioner. (Sec. 1134(b)(1), Tax Law) Within five days after the receipt of the notice, the Commissioner will issue to the show promoter, without charge, a permit to operate the show. (Sec. 1134(b)(2), Tax Law) If a permit is denied, the show promoter has a right to a hearing in the Division of Tax Appeals.

Show promoter described.—Every person who has no permanent place of business in the state who intends to display for sale or sell tangible personal property or services subject to tax at a flea market, craft show, antique show, coin show, stamp show, comic book show, fair, or any similar show must file an application for a certificate of authority for show vendors. (Reg. Sec. 533.1(b)(1)) (See Publication 750, A Guide to Sales Tax in New York State)

Displaying the permit.—The permit must be prominently displayed at the main entrance to the show. If a permit has not been received by the show promoter in time, and if a notice has been properly filed, the requirement to display the permit is considered to have been complied with, unless and until the show promoter receives the permit or receives a notice from the Commissioner denying the permit. (Sec. 1134(b)(2), Tax Law)

Restrictions.—A show promoter cannot rent, lease or grant a license to use space for a show or operate a show without a permit. (Sec. 1134(b)(2), Tax Law) A show promoter may not permit any person to sell taxable tangible personal property or perform taxable services at a show unless that person is registered with the Commissioner and displays a certificate of registration. (Sec. 1134(b)(4), Tax Law)

Penalties.—A show promoter who fails to file a notice of a show, operates a show without a permit, fails to file a report of a show, files a report which is willfully false, or otherwise fails to comply with provisions concerning show permits, is subject to the revocation of all existing permits issued to operate a show, and may be issued an order denying future permits to operate a show for a period of not more than six months from the date of the order. These penalties will be in addition to all other penalties. (Sec. 1134(b)(5), Tax Law)

• Entertainment promoters

At least 20 days before an entertainment event, an entertainment promoter must file with the Commissioner of Taxation and Finance a notice and application for an entertainment promoter certificate stating the location and date of the event, in a form prescribed by the Commissioner. Within ten days after the receipt of the notice, the Commissioner will issue to the entertainment promoter, without charge, an entertainment promoter certificate. If a certificate is denied, the entertainment promoter has a right to a hearing in the Division of Tax Appeals. (Sec. 1134(c)(1), Tax Law)

"Promoter" defined.—A promoter is any person who directly or indirectly rents, leases or grants a license to use space to any person for the conduct of more than three shows in a calendar year, or operates more than three shows in a calendar year. For purposes of determining whether three shows have been held, the conduct of a show on one day alone or up to seven consecutive days constitutes a single show. (Reg. Sec. 533.1(c)(3))

Displaying the certificate.—The certificate must be prominently displayed at the main entrance to the event. If a certificate has not been received by the entertainment promoter in time for the beginning of the event, and if a notice has been properly filed, the requirement of displaying the certificate is considered to have been complied with, unless and until the entertainment promoter receives the certificate or receives a notice from the Commissioner denying the certificate. (Sec. 1134(c)(1), Tax Law)

Restrictions.—Without a certificate, an entertainment promoter cannot permit an entertainment vendor to make taxable sales at the event. Furthermore, an entertainment promoter cannot authorize any person to make taxable sales of tangible personal property at the entertainment event unless that person is registered with the Commissioner and displays a certificate of registration. (Sec. 1134(c)(2), Tax Law)

Penalties.—An entertainment promoter who fails to comply with provisions concerning entertainment event certificates is subject to the revocation of all existing certificates issued to operate an event and may be issued an order denying future certificates to operate an event for a period of not more than six months from the date of the order. (Sec. 1134(c)(4), Tax Law)

• At-home businesses

If you operate a trade or business from your home, you have the same responsibilities as any other vendor making the same types of taxable sales in New York State. Whether you run your business from a store or your home, or whether you work full time or part time is not what determines your requirement to be registered for sales tax. Instead, whether or not you are required to register is based on what types of items you sell, or what kind of services you provide. If the items or services that you sell are subject to sales tax, you are required to register. This also includes items that you sell on a regular basis through online auction or other Web sites. (TB-ST-175; TB-ST-807) Examples of businesses that you may operate out of a home that will require you to register and collect sales tax are:

— landscaping;

— event parking;

— contracting;

— small engine repair; and

— craft businesses.

(TB-ST-807)

Also, you are required to register to collect sales tax if you make items at your home and bring them to other locations to sell or sell them over the Internet, if the items that you are selling are subject to sales tax. Items commonly sold at craft fairs and through online auction sites, such as knitted and crocheted items, homemade soaps and candles, holiday decorations, woodworking projects, and homemade candy, are examples. (TB-ST-175; TB-ST-807)

• *Time of registration*

Persons required to register must file a certificate of registration at least 20 days prior to commencing business or opening a new place of business or purchasing or taking of possession or payment, whichever comes first. (Sec. 1134(a)(1), Tax Law)

The time of registration for vendors meeting certain thresholds is discussed above under the heading "Exceptions to registration requirement and thresholds for registration."

• *Certificates of authority*

A Certificate of Authority authorizes a business to collect sales tax on taxable sales and to issue and accept New York sales tax exemption certificates. A certificate or duplicate must state the place of business to which it applies and be prominently displayed. (Sec. 1134(a)(2), Tax Law) (Publication 750, A Guide to Sales Tax in New York State) When applying for a Certificate of Authority, a business must select a NAICS code that best describes its business. (TB-ST-640) A business does not have to renew its Certificates of Authority unless it is notified to do so by the Department of Taxation and Finance. (Publication 900)

The Department of Taxation and Finance issues two types of Certificate of Authority for sales tax purposes: (1) regular and (2) temporary. (TB-ST-360) The type of Certificate of Authority needed is based on the expected duration of the business activities. The same form and application process are used for both types of certificates. However, the temporary certificate will be issued with a beginning and ending date. (TB-ST-360)

Regular Certificate of Authority.—A taxpayer must apply for a regular Certificate of Authority if they will be making taxable sales from their home, a shop, a store, cart, stand, or any other facility from which it regularly conducts business. It does not matter whether they own or rent the facility. If you make sales at a show or entertainment event, such as a craft show, antique show, flea market, or sporting event, you must apply for a regular Certificate of Authority, even if your sales are only on an isolated or occasional basis. The department no longer issues the Certificate of Authority for Show and Entertainment Vendors that was previously issued for these vendors. (TB-ST-360)

Temporary Certificate of Authority.—If you expect to make taxable sales in New York for no more than two consecutive sales tax quarters in any 12-month period, you may apply for a temporary Certificate of Authority. Show and entertainment vendors may not apply for a temporary Certificate of Authority; they must apply for a regular Certificate of Authority. To request a temporary Certificate of Authority, you must indicate when you expect your business operation to begin and end. The temporary certificate will only authorize you to collect tax and conduct your business between those dates. (TB-ST-360)

Multiple locations.—Taxpayers must have a Certificate of Authority for each business location. Taxpayers can choose to file one sales tax return for combined sales at all locations or a separate return for each location. (TB-ST-360)

Transfer of ownership and organizational changes.—A Certificate of Authority cannot be transferred or assigned. If you are buying an existing business, or taking over the ownership of a family business, you must apply for your own Certificate of Authority. You cannot use the Certificate of Authority that we issued to the previous owner. You must also apply for a new Certificate of Authority if you are changing the organizational structure (legal form) of your business, such as switching from a sole proprietorship to a corporation. The new business must have its own Certificate of Authority before it begins business. (TB-ST-360); (Publication 900)

Amending a Certificate of Authority.—A taxpayer must amend its Certificate of Authority within 20 days whenever its business changes any of the following:

— business name;

— business address, including a new additional business location;

— federal identification number;

— business telephone number;

— owner, officer, or responsible person information; or

— business activity.

(TB-ST-25)

Suspension of revocation of a Certificate of Authority.—A certificate may be suspended or revoked for any of the following:

— willfully fail to file a report or return required under the sales tax law;

— willfully file, cause to be filed, give, cause to be given a report, certificate, or affidavit required under the sales tax law that is false;

— willfully fail to collect, truthfully account for, or pay over any state and local sales tax;

— willfully fail to keep adequate records and were convicted of a crime for that willful failure;

— have been convicted of a crime under the Tax Law and the conviction occurred within one year of the date of such revocation or suspension; and

— willfully fail to file a bond or establish a trust account and make payments as provided in Tax Law § 1137(e)(2) or (3), if notified by the Department of Taxation and Finance to do so.

(Publication 900)

Surrendering a Certificate of Authority.—A taxpayer must turn in a Certificate of Authority if it:

— stops doing business;

— sells, transfers or assigns the business; or

— changes the form of the business (i.e., changes from a sole proprietorship to a corporation).

(TB-ST-25)

For additional information on amending or surrendering a Certificate of Authority, see TB-ST-25

¶61-240

• *North American Industry Classification System (NAICS) Codes*

Businesses that plan to sell taxable goods or services in New York must register with the Tax Department for sales tax purposes and receive a sales tax Certificate of Authority. (TB-ST-640) When applying for a Certificate of Authority, a business must select a NAICS code that best describes its business. Department for sales tax purposes and receive a sales tax Certificate of Authority. The NAICS is an industry classification system developed and used to classify businesses according to their principal business activity, using a six-digit code. A business's principal business activity is that which generates its greatest New York state gross sales. It is possible that the principal business activity may not be the business activity that required the business to register for sales tax purposes. Also, if a business has another business activity that is unrelated to its principal business activity, the business can choose to provide a secondary NAICS code when registering for a Certificate of Authority. The department uses NAICS codes to do the following: identify vendors that should be targeted to receive important information related to specific industries, and help collect, compile, and analyze statistical data related to taxation issues. (TB-ST-640)

Changing NAICS codes.—Businesses can change their NAICS code by contacting the department. Reasons for changing NAICS codes include a change in the nature of a business's principal activity or finding that a different NAICS code better reflects the business's current principal business activity. (TB-ST-640)

Multiple locations.—If a business registers multiple locations and plans to file a single sales tax return covering all locations, it should choose a NAICS code that reflects the principal business activity when all the locations are combined together. If a business registers multiple locations and plans to file a separate sales tax return for each location, it should choose a NAICS code that reflects the principal business activity at each specific business location. (TB-ST-640)

Out-of-state business.—If a taxpayer registers a business located outside New York, the taxpayer should select the NAICS code based on the business activity that generates the greatest New York state gross sales. (TB-ST-640)

• *Voluntary registration*

A person not otherwise required to register who makes sales of tangible personal property or services to persons within New York State, the use of which is subject to tax, may elect to register. The Department may, in its discretion, issue a certificate of authority to collect the compensating use tax. (Sec. 1134(a)(3), Tax Law)

• *Contractors and subcontractors*

Contractors and subcontractors (including affiliates) are required to register for New York sales and use tax purposes if they enter into contracts for sales deliveries to locations within New York of tangible personal property or taxable services having a value in excess of $300,000 during the immediately preceding consecutive four sales tax quarters. If they are not registered, such contracts would not be valid. Once registered, such contractor, subcontractor, or affiliate will be a vendor subject to Articles 28 and 29 of the Tax Law. (Sec. 5-a, Tax Law) (TSB-M-06(12)S) For further discussion, see ¶ 60-330 Construction.

• *Suspension or revocation of registration*

The Commissioner may suspend or revoke a certificate of authority where a person:

— willfully fails to file a required report or return;

— willfully files, causes to be filed, gives or causes to be given a required report, return, certificate or affidavit which is false;

— willfully fails to post a surety bond or establish a trust account after notice from the Commissioner;

— willfully fails to collect, truthfully account for or pay over any tax imposed; or

— has been convicted of a crime.

(Sec. 1134(a)(4), Tax Law) (Publication 900, Important Information for Business Owners)

• *Penalties*

A person required to obtain a certificate of authority who, without possessing a valid certificate of authority: (1) sells tangible personal property or services subject to tax, receives amusement charges or operates a hotel; (2) purchases or sells tangible personal property for resale; or (3) sells automotive fuel; will, in addition to any other penalty, be subject to a penalty in an amount not exceeding $500 for the first day on which the sales or purchases are made, plus an amount not exceeding $200 for each subsequent day on which the sale or purchases are made, not to exceed $10,000 in the aggregate. (Sec. 1145(a)(3), Tax Law)

A person who fails to surrender a certificate of authority when a notice of revocation or suspension has become final, in addition to any other penalty, is subject to a penalty in an amount not exceeding $500 for the first day of the failure, together with a penalty in an amount not exceeding $200 for each subsequent day of the failure, not to exceed $10,000 in the aggregate. (Sec. 1145(a)(3), Tax Law)

Failure to file a certificate of registration, in addition to any other penalty required by law, results in a maximum $200 penalty. (Sec. 1145(a)(3), Tax Law)

Failure to display a certificate of authority, in addition to any other penalty required by law, results in a penalty of $50. If the Commissioner determines that the failure was due to reasonable cause and not due to willful neglect, he may remit all or part of the penalty. (Sec. 1145(a)(3), Tax Law)

For factors resulting in a refusal by the Commissioner to issue a certificate of authority, see Sec. 1134(a)(3), Tax Law.

• *Requirement of surety bond or trust account*

Where the Commissioner has suspended, revoked or refused to issue a certificate of authority, the retention or issuance of the certificate of authority may be conditioned upon the filing of a surety bond or the deposit of tax in a bank trust account. (Sec. 1134(a)(4), Tax Law)

Internet advertisers.—A person will not be deemed to be a vendor solely by reason of having its advertising stored on a server or other computer equipment located in New York or by having its advertising disseminated by a person with nexus to New York. (Sec. 12, Tax Law) However, this exemption does not apply when the server or other computer equipment located in New York State is owned or leased by such person. (*TSB-M-97(1.1)C, TSB-M-97(1.1)S*) In addition, a person who provides telecommunication services or Internet access service is not considered a vendor solely by virtue of the fact that the provider's customers advertise and sell products and services through the provider's server or other computer equipment.

[¶61-270] Credits

If a vendor is registered for sales tax purposes, it can claim a credit for sales taxes overpaid, paid by mistake, or collected but then repaid to customers. The vendor can then apply the credit to reduce the tax they owe on their sales tax return. (TB-ST-810)

Credits and refunds for state and local sales and use taxes are authorized, subject to the following conditions and limitations:

— on the purchase of tangible personal property used in a specified manner;

— on the purchase of tangible personal property or services used by specified omnibus carriers to provide local transit service;

— on the purchase of tangible personal property used in the performance of specified taxable services on a retail sale by a contractor; and

— on the purchase of tangible personal property by a contractor, subcontractor or repairman who was required to pay tax on the purchase if the property was sold at retail by the contractor, subcontractor or repairman. In addition, credits and refunds are allowed for canceled sales and returned merchandise, for bad debts, and for any taxes, penalty or interest which was erroneously, illegally or unconstitutionally paid or collected.

(Reg. Sec. 534.1(a))

Vendors are also entitled to a credit equal to 1.5% of the state portion of the sales and use tax.

In general, in order to apply for a credit, the taxpayer must send in a properly completed Form AU-11, Application for Credit or Refund of Sales or Use Tax. When the Form AU-11 is filed, the taxpayer must explain the reason for the credit claim. (TB-ST-810) A credit must be claimed within three years from the date the sales tax return was due, or two years from the date the tax was paid to the Department, whichever is later. (TB-ST-810)

Taxpayers should send copies of all of the documents needed to prove a claim for credit (i.e., invoices, receipts, exemption certificates, proof of payment of tax, etc.). Taxpayers should send in photocopies and keep the originals. (TB-ST-810)

• *Vendor collection credit*

Businesses that make taxable sales are required to collect sales tax and remit tax on their sales tax returns. When a business files its sales tax return and pays the full amount due on time, it may be eligible to claim a vendor collection credit. This credit will reduce the amount of money that must be sent to the state with their sales tax return. (TB-ST-925)

A business is eligible for the vendor collection credit if it files sales tax returns on a quarterly basis (Form ST-100, New York State and Local Quarterly Sales and Use Tax Return) or on an annual basis (Form ST-101, New York State and Local Annual Sales and Use Tax Return). To qualify, a business must file its return on time and pay what they owe in full. A business can't claim the credit on an amended return or on a past-due return. Also, the credit can't be carried over to a future return. (TB-ST-925) The following businesses are no longer eligible for the vendor collection credit: businesses that file, or are required to file, their sales tax returns on a monthly basis (Form ST-809, New York State and Local Sales and Use Tax Return for Part Quarterly [Monthly] Filers; and Form ST-810, New York State and Local Quarterly Sales and Use Tax Return for Part-Quarterly [Monthly] Filers); and businesses enrolled in the PrompTax program for sales tax. (TB-ST-925)

Calculating the credit.—The vendor credit is equal to 5% of the taxes and fees reported on a return, up to a maximum of $200 for each quarterly or annual reporting period. (Sec. 1137(f), Tax Law) (TSB-M-06(12)S; TB-ST-925) The following taxes and fees are included when calculating the credit:

— state sales and use taxes;

— county, city, and school district sales and use taxes;

- special state sales taxes on passenger car rentals;

- additional state sales tax on certain information services;

- additional state sales tax on certain entertainment services;

- net credit for prepaid sales tax on sales of fuel (from Schedule FR, box 17); and

- New York City hotel unit fee.

(TB-ST-925)

Businesses should not include the taxes reported on Schedule NJ when calculating the credit. (TB-ST-925)

The credit must be taken only on the return for the quarterly or longer period to which the credit applies. (Sec. 1137(f), Tax Law) No refund, carryforward or carryback of credit, nor application for credit or refund of tax, penalty or interest, will be allowed. The claim for credit must be filed with the original return on which the credit is claimed. The credit may be disallowed if the vendor claims a credit in an amount greater than that allowed or under circumstances where the credit is not authorized, or where the vendor later becomes subject to certain penalties or is found guilty of a crime or offense under Sec. 1817, Tax Law, relating to the period during which the credit was claimed. (Sec. 1137(f), Tax Law) (TB-ST-925)

• *Reciprocal credit*

A state and local reciprocal use tax credit may be allowed for sales or use tax paid in another state or in another locality in New York. Resident purchasers that owe New York state and local use tax may have paid a sales or use tax in the state and/or locality where they purchased and took possession of the item or service. (TB-ST-765) A reciprocal credit for sales or use tax paid to another state and/or locality in that state may be available if all the following conditions are met:

- the state and/or locality where the purchase was made allows a corresponding credit for sales or use tax paid to New York state and/or localities in New York;

- the purchaser was legally liable for the tax and paid the tax to the other state and/or locality;

- the tax paid to the other state and/or locality on the purchase is a sales or use tax;

- the purchaser has no right to a refund or credit of the tax paid to the other state and/or locality; and

- the purchaser has proof of payment, such as a receipt showing the amount or rate of tax paid to the other state and/or locality.

(TB-ST-765)

Federal excise taxes and customs duties, and taxes and fees paid in foreign countries are not allowed as a credit against New York state or local use tax. (TB-ST-765)

New York may provide a reciprocal credit on a rate-to-rate basis for sales or use taxes paid to another state only where, and to the extent that, the other state provides a reciprocal credit for sales or use taxes paid to New York state and/or its localities. (TB-ST-765) Therefore, a New York reciprocal credit may be available for:

- both the state and local sales and use taxes paid in another state;

- only state sales and use taxes paid in another state; or

- only local sales and use taxes paid in another state.

(TB-ST-765)

Full reciprocal credit.—Where another state allows a reciprocal credit for both New York's state tax and its local taxes, New York's reciprocal credit is the sum of the other state's state and local taxes. If the total tax paid in the other state exceeds the total use tax due in New York, no New York use tax is due, but the excess amount will not be refunded. (TB-ST-765)

Partial reciprocal credit.—Where another state allows a reciprocal credit only for New York's state tax, New York's reciprocal credit is allowed only against New York's state tax and only for the other state's state tax. If the state tax paid in the other state exceeds the state use tax due in New York, no New York state use tax is due, but the excess amount will not be refunded and cannot be used to reduce the amount of local use tax due in New York. Similarly, if another state allows a reciprocal credit only for New York's local taxes, New York's reciprocal credit is allowed only against New York's local taxes and only for the other state's local tax. If the local tax paid in the other state exceeds the local use tax due in New York, no New York local use tax is due, but the excess amount will not be refunded and cannot be used to reduce the amount of state use tax due in New York. (TB-ST-765)

Claiming a reciprocal credit.—When claiming a reciprocal credit, a taxpayer should be able to substantiate:

— proof of payment to the other state, such as with a receipt showing the amount or rate of sales or use tax paid to the other state and/or locality;

— that the state and/or locality where you made the purchase allows a credit for sales or use tax paid to New York state and/or its localities;

— that you were legally liable for the tax and paid the tax to the other state and/or locality; and

— that you have no right to a refund or credit of the tax paid to the other state and/or locality.

(TB-ST-765)

Alternative basis for computing New York state and local use tax on certain property: There are two instances where the New York state and local use taxes due on items purchased by a New York resident are not based on the item's purchase price:

— If an item is used outside of New York (or outside the county/city of residence) for more than six months prior to the New York resident bringing the item or service into New York (or into the county/city of residence), the amount subject to tax is the lesser of the purchase price or the fair market value at the time the item is brought into New York (or into the county/city of residence); and

— In the case of tangible personal property brought into New York to be used in the performance of a contract for a period of less than six months, the amount subject to tax may, at the election of the user, be based on the fair rental value of the property for the period of use within New York, but only if the property is not completely consumed in New York or is not incorporated into real property in New York.

(TB-ST-765)

In either of these cases, where the amount subject to New York state use tax is an amount other than the purchase price of the item or service, the amount of use tax due must be computed by comparing the rate of tax paid to the other state and/or locality and the applicable rate of state and/or local tax due in New York that is allowed as a reciprocal credit. (TB-ST-765)

• *Property or services upon which tax is paid to other jurisdictions*

Credit is also allowed for use tax paid to out-of-state jurisdictions which allow a corresponding exemption. Where the tax imposed is at a higher rate than that imposed by the first taxing jurisdiction, tax must be collected to the extent of the difference in rates. (Sec. 1118(7)(a), Tax Law)

• *Refund applications*

The Commissioner of Taxation and Finance will credit or refund any tax, penalty or interest erroneously, illegally or unconstitutionally collected or paid if an application for the credit or refund is filed with the Commissioner within three years after the tax payment due date. (Sec. 1139(a), Tax Law) However, no refund or credit will be made until it is established to the satisfaction of the Commissioner that the tax has been repaid to the customer. (Reg. Sec. 534.8(a))

Where a taxpayer is requesting a refund of an overpayment of sales tax, the refund claim must be filed within three years from the time the return was filed or two years from the time the tax was paid, whichever is later. If no return was filed, the taxpayer must file the refund claim within two years from the time the tax was paid. (Sec. 1139(c), Tax Law)

See ¶ 61-610 Application for Refund.

• *Property incorporated into realty outside the state*

A credit or refund is allowed for tax paid on the sale or use of tangible personal property if the purchaser, or user, in the performance of a contract, later incorporates that tangible personal property into real property located outside the state. (Sec. 1119(a), Tax Law)

• *Bulk purchase of property temporarily stored in state*

A credit or refund is allowed for tax paid on the sale or use of tangible personal property purchased in bulk, or any portion thereof, which is stored and not used by the purchaser within the state, and is subsequently reshipped out of the state by the purchaser for use outside the state. (Sec. 1119(a), Tax Law)

• *Construction contracts*

The contractor in a lump sum or unit price construction contract irrevocably entered into prior to the date of a statewide sales and use tax rate increase (or a contract resulting from the acceptance by a governmental agency of a bid accompanied by a bond or other performance guaranty which was irrevocably submitted prior to such date) will be allowed a credit or refund of the increase in sales or use tax in respect of the purchases of tangible personal property used solely in the performance of the contract. (Sec. 1119(a), Tax Law; Reg. Sec. 534.3(d))

• *Fabrication of property shipped and used outside state*

A credit or refund is allowed for tax paid on the sale or use within the state of tangible personal property, not purchased for resale, if the use of the property is restricted to fabricating (including incorporating it into or assembling it with other tangible personal property), processing, printing or imprinting the property and then shipping it out of the state for use outside the state. (Sec. 1119(a), Tax Law)

¶61-270

• *Veterinarians and farmers*

A credit or refund is allowed for tax paid on the sale to or use by a veterinarian of drugs or medicine in rendering exempt veterinary services to livestock or poultry used in the production for sale of tangible personal property by farming (see ¶60-250 Agriculture). Effective June 1, 2018, the existing tax credit or refund is converted to an upfront exemption. (Sec. 1115(f)(2), Tax Law; Sec. 1119(a), Tax Law) A similar credit or refund is allowed for tax paid on the sale of drugs or medicine to a person entitled to the farmer's exemption (see ¶60-250 Agriculture).

• *Empire zone credits (sales and use tax incentive)*

A refund or credit is provided for tax paid on qualifying purchases made by a qualified empire zone enterprise (QEZE). Previously, an upfront exemption was provided for on certain purchases and uses of tangible personal property and services by a QEZE. (Important Notice N-09-14; TSB-M-09(12)S) However, all Empire Zone designations expired on June 30, 2010.

With the expiration of the Empire Zones designations, the sales tax refund or credit on certain building materials used in an Empire Zone under Tax Law §1119(a)(6) is discontinued. Tax Law §1119(a)(6) allows a refund or credit for the state portion of sales and use taxes paid on building materials used in the construction, expansion, or rehabilitation of qualifying real property located in an Empire Zone. In addition, the local taxing authority within which the Empire Zone is located may also provide a similar refund or credit for the local sales and use tax paid under those circumstances. However, the refund or credit may only be claimed after the building materials are physically incorporated into the qualifying real property. As a result of the expiration of the Empire Zone designations, it is the position of the Department that the refund or credit of state sales tax, and if applicable, local sales tax, will be allowed only for those building materials that were purchased on or before June 30, 2010, and physically incorporated on or before August 31, 2010, into qualifying real property located in an Empire Zone. No refund or credit will be allowed for building materials physically incorporated into the real property after August 31, 2010, even if the materials were purchased or a building project was started before July 1, 2010. (TSB-M-10(6)S)

• *Limitation on credits or refunds—Certain uses of tangible personal property*

To qualify for a credit or refund, the tangible personal property, the sale or use of which was taxed by the vendor, must have been incorporated into real property, reshipped, or used within three years after the date on which the tax was payable to the Commissioner by the vendor. The same limitation applies where the tax on the sale or use of tangible personal property was paid by the applicant for the credit or refund directly to the Commissioner. (Sec. 1119(a), Tax Law)

• *Omnibus carriers providing local transit service*

A credit or refund is allowed for tax paid on the sale to or use by a certified omnibus carrier providing local transit service in a city with a population of more than one million, of any omnibus, and the parts, equipment, lubricants, motor fuel, diesel motor fuel, maintenance, servicing or repair purchased and used in the omnibus' operation. (Sec. 1119(b), Tax Law) The amount of the credit or refund is to be determined by computing the local transit service percentage—the proportion of the carrier's local vehicle mileage in the preceding calendar year compared to the carrier's total statewide mileage. For an omnibus carrier not engaged in local transit service in the preceding calendar year, the percentage is to be determined by using the proportion that such a carrier's vehicle mileage in local transit service in the first three months of operation bears to the carrier's total statewide mileage for the same period. (Sec. 1119(b), Tax Law)

The credit or refund allowed on the combined state and local tax paid is then calculated as follows: (Sec. 1119(b), Tax Law)

If the local transit service percentage is: (1) less that 10%, there is no credit or refund; (2) 10%, there is a credit or refund of 10%; (3) greater than 10% but less that 70%, the credit or refund is 10% plus the product of 1.5 times each whole percentage in excess of 10%; and (4) 70% or more, there is a 100% credit or refund. (Sec. 1119(b), Tax Law)

Omnibus.—An omnibus is a motor vehicle with a seating capacity of more than seven passengers used for the transportation of passengers for hire. (Reg. Sec. 534.4(a)(2))

Local transit service.—Local transit service is a mass transit service provided by an omnibus carrier in which passengers are carried from one point in the state to another point in the state and in performance of which the omnibuses pick up and discharge passengers either (1) regularly at their convenience or at bus stops on the street or highway; or (2) at bus terminals or stations no more than 75 miles apart. (Reg. Sec. 534.4(a)(3))

• *Vessels providing local transit service*

Provisions similar to those discussed above for omnibus carriers are applicable with respect to certain vessel operators providing local transit service. (Sec. 1119(b), Tax Law) For details, see ¶60-740 Transportation.

• *Property used for certain taxable services*

A credit or refund against the sales and compensating use tax is allowed, in an amount equal to the sales or use tax imposed and paid on the sale or use of tangible personal property, where the property is subsequently used by the purchaser in performing certain taxable services and becomes a physical component part of the property upon which the service is performed, or where the property is subsequently transferred to the purchaser of the service in conjunction with the performance of the service. (Sec. 1119(c), Tax Law) Taxable services for which the refund or credit against the tax may be claimed are:

— Information services;

— Processing and printing services;

— Installation and maintenance services;

— Real estate maintenance and service;

— Interior decorating and designing services; and

— Protective and detective services.

• *Contractors*

In general, a contractor can take a sales tax credit on their return if they:

— paid sales tax on building materials to a supplier;

— transferred those materials to your customer in a taxable repair, maintenance, or installation service; and

— charged sales tax to a customer.

(TB-ST-130)

In most cases, this means that a contractor can take a credit when the perform they perform is classified as a taxable repair, maintenance, or installation service, but not when it is classified as a capital improvement. (Sec. 1119(c), Tax Law) (TB-ST-130)

¶61-270

Materials used in a taxable repair, maintenance or installation service.—When a contractor buys materials from its supplier and those materials are transferred to your customer as part of a taxable repair, maintenance, or installation service, you must pay sales tax at the time of purchase. However, the tax you paid on these materials qualifies for a sales tax credit. This includes materials such as: plywood, drywall, shingles, and 2 x 4s; nails, screws, bolts, and staples; electrical materials; plumbing materials; and landscaping materials. A contractor cannot claim a credit for sales tax paid on materials, supplies, or other items that are not transferred to your customer as part of the job you perform. This is true even if the cost of those materials, supplies, or other items was included in your charge to your customer for the job performed. Some typical items used by contractors that you may not take a credit for include: tools, such as hammers, paint brushes, etc.; consumable supplies, such as sandpaper and garbage bags; cell phones, pagers, and office supplies; drop cloths; uniforms, clothing, and work boots; equipment or tools you rent; gases used in plumbing, welding, etc.; and vehicles and fuels used in vehicles. (TB-ST-130)

When and how to take a credit.—A contractor is allowed to take a credit and subtract the credit amount from the amount of sales tax due when you file your sales tax return. Any credits claimed must be reported in Step 5 of the sales tax return. In addition, the contractor must file a completed Form AU-11, Application for Credit or Refund of Sales or Use Tax, and attach proof of eligibility for the credit. The taxable sale and the tax due on the sale are reported on the sales tax return that covers the period when the work is performed, even if the contractor has not yet received payment from a customer. In certain jobs, it may take longer than one reporting period to complete the job. The contractor cannot take a credit for tax paid on materials at the time of purchase until they are used in the performance of a job, and are reported on the return. If a contractor purchases certain items in bulk and use them over a period of time, they have to wait and take the sales tax credit as you use the items in jobs where you charge sales tax to your customer. (TB-ST-130)

Work performed for exempt organizations and governmental entities.—If a contractor performs a job for an exempt organization or governmental entity, they will not charge sales tax on the work, whether it's a capital improvement or repair and maintenance job. Building materials transferred to the customer in performance of the job can be purchased without the payment of sales tax using Form ST-120.1, Contractor Exempt Purchase Certificate. If the contractor did not use the exemption certificate when it purchased the materials, the contractor may take a credit for sales tax paid on the purchase of materials that were used in the project. The contractor cannot take a credit for sales tax paid on other supplies even though they may be used in an exempt job. (TB-ST-130)

Other situations where contractor may take a credit.—If a contractor purchases materials and pays sales tax in New York and later uses these materials in a job outside New York, the contractor is allowed to take a credit for the sales tax paid to New York. (TB-ST-130) A contractor can also take a credit in the following situations:

— you charged your customer sales tax in error and later give the customer a refund of the tax;

— you overpaid the sales tax; and

— you paid sales tax by mistake.

(TB-ST-130)

Lump-sum contracts.—If a contractor enters into a unit-price construction contract or has a preexisting lump-sum contract with a customer, and during the contract period the state or local sales tax rate is increased, the contractor may be eligible for a credit for the additional sales tax they pay on property purchased after the rate change has gone into effect that is incorporated into the project. (TB-ST-130)

Guaranty work refund or credit.—A contractor is not entitled to a refund or credit of the tax paid on the purchase of tangible personal property used in guarantee or warranty work in the performance of a capital improvement. If the guarantee or warranty work is on a repair to real property or tangible personal property that remains tangible personal property after installation, a refund or credit may be claimed by the contractor for the tax paid on the materials and parts transferred to the customer (whether or not a charge is made to the customer for the guarantee or warranty work). But, if any charge is made to the customer, the charge is subject to tax. (Reg. Sec. 541.1)

Documentation.—A contractor will need to document any credit with copies of the following:

— purchase invoices showing sales tax paid to a supplier on the purchase of the materials;

— contracts or sales invoices to a customer for services documenting the materials that were used to complete the project, or bills or invoices showing that materials or supplies were resold as a retail sale;

— customer contracts, bills or invoices showing that the service rendered was a repair, maintenance, or installation service; or

— any other documentation, including copies of exemption certificates received from customers, showing that the contractor is entitled to a credit for tax paid.

(TB-ST-130)

All purchase invoices must separately state the sales tax due and paid, and all customer invoices must separately state the sales tax collected. All contracts that are executed as cost-plus contracts must clearly state that the estimate is based on cost-plus in order for the purchase and sales invoices to accurately document the sales tax credit due. (TB-ST-130)

• *Canceled sales and returned merchandise*

When a sale is canceled, or the property is returned within the reporting period in which the sale was made, the vendor may exclude the tax from the return. If a sale has been canceled or property returned and the tax collected has been refunded to the customer, but has already been paid and reported on the vendor's return, an application for a refund or credit must be filed with the Commissioner within three years of the date on which the tax was paid. The vendor may take the credit on the return due coincidentally or immediately subsequent to the date of the refund application. (Reg. Sec. 534.6(a))

• *Bad debts*

Where a receipt, amusement charge, or hotel rent has been ascertained to be uncollectible, either in whole or in part, the vendor may apply for a refund or credit of the tax paid within three years from the date on which the tax was payable. A refund or credit is not available for transactions financed by a third party or for a debt assigned to a third party. Only the amount of the uncollectible debt that is attributable to sales tax is allowable as a refund or credit. (Reg. Sec. 534.7(b))

• *Erroneous, illegal, or unconstitutional payment or collection of tax*

Any person who has repaid to a customer tax that was erroneously, illegally or unconstitutionally collected, may claim a credit or refund. However, no refund or credit will be made until it is established to the satisfaction of the Commissioner that the tax has been repaid to the customer. (Sec. 1119(b), Tax Law)

• *Motor fuel and diesel motor fuel*

A credit or refund of prepaid tax on motor fuel or diesel motor fuel is allowed only to the extent that the tax paid by or passed through to the retail vendor, purchaser, consumer or user exceeds the amount of tax required to be collected or remitted. (Sec. 1120(f), Tax Law) A claim for a credit of prepaid tax may not exceed the amount of tax actually paid by or passed through to the taxpayer. (Sec. 1120(g), Tax Law)

A vendor of motor fuel or diesel motor fuel required to collect sales tax is allowed a refund or credit against the amount of tax collected and required to be remitted to the Commissioner upon the retail sale of motor fuel or diesel motor fuel. (Sec. 1120(a)(1), Tax Law) The refund or credit is in the amount of the tax on the fuel prepaid by or passed through to and included in the price paid by the vendor. The vendor is also allowed a refund or credit for the tax prepaid by or passed through to and included in the price paid by the vendor upon the fuel, if the fuel is sold at retail by the vendor under circumstances where taxes are not required to be collected and remitted. (Sec. 1120(a)(2), Tax Law)

A retail purchaser, user or consumer of motor fuel or diesel motor fuel is allowed a credit against the use tax required to be paid to the Commissioner in the amount of the tax prepaid by or passed through to and included in the price paid by the purchaser, user or consumer. (Sec. 1120(b), Tax Law)

A registered motor fuel distributor or a purchaser registered by the taxing authorities of another state as a distributor or dealer of motor fuel is allowed a refund or credit of the prepaid tax on motor fuel imported, manufactured, sold, or purchased in New York for sale outside the state, provided the fuel is immediately exported to an identified facility in the state in which the distributor or purchaser is registered or licensed. The refund or credit is also available to registered diesel motor fuel distributors for the prepaid tax on enhanced diesel motor fuel. (Sec. 1120(e), Tax Law)

• *Tractors, trailers, semitrailers*

A credit or refund is allowed for sales taxes paid for tractors, trailers or semitrailers, and property installed on such vehicles for their equipping, maintenance or repair, provided the vehicle is used in combination where the gross vehicle weight of such combination exceeds 26,000 pounds. A credit or refund is further allowed for sales taxes paid on services performed on such tractors, trailers, and semitrailers, or property installed on these vehicles. (Sec. 1139(g), Tax Law)

• *Restrictions on credits and refunds*

Amounts representing estimated assessments will not be credited or refunded if the taxpayer has had a hearing or an opportunity for a hearing, as provided by statute, or has failed to avail himself of the remedies. (Sec. 1139(c), Tax Law) However, persons who have filed consents to have the tax fixed earlier than under ordinary procedure, before a determination assessing the tax has been issued, are not disqualified from applying for a credit or refund so long as the application is made within the ordinary assessment limitation period or within two years of the date of payment of the amount assessed in accordance with the consent, whichever is later, but the application is limited to the amount of such payment.

Estimated assessments, after final determination, may not be credited or refunded unless found to be erroneous, illegal, improper or unconstitutional.

• *Interest for overpayment of tax*

The interest rate applicable to overpayments of tax is set by the Commissioner of Taxation and Finance. (Sec. 1139(d), Tax Law)

[¶61-600]

TAXPAYER REMEDIES

[¶61-610] Application for Refund

To claim a refund or credit for any tax, penalty or interest collected or paid, a person must file an application with the Department of Taxation and Finance within three years from the date the tax was due, or two years from the date tax was paid, whichever was later. The application must be in a form prescribed by the department. However, no refund or credit of tax, penalty or interest erroneously, illegally or unconstitutionally collected or paid will be made until it is established, to the satisfaction of the department, that the tax has been repaid to the customer. (Sec. 1139(a), Tax Law) (TB-ST-350)

The Commissioner must grant or deny such an application, in whole or in part, within six months after receiving it and must notify the applicant by mail accordingly. The Commissioner's determination will be final and irrevocable unless the applicant petitions the Division of Tax Appeals for a hearing within 90 days after the notice of determination is mailed. (Sec. 1139(b), Tax Law) The Commissioner's determination will be final and irrevocable unless the applicant petitions the Division of Tax Appeals for a hearing within 90 days after the notice of determination is mailed. Review by the Division of Tax Appeals is discussed at ¶61-620 Administrative Remedies.

For information on how to apply for a refund, see TB-ST-350. This bulletin explains the following: who is eligible to claim a refund, which form to use to apply for a refund, what other documents are needed to support a refund claim, and when and where to send a refund claim.

• *Form of application*

An application for a refund or credit must contain:

— the applicant's vendor identification number (if the applicant is registered);

— a full explanation of the facts on which the claim is based, including substantiation of the basis for and the amount of the claim; and

— a certification that no part of the tax paid for which the claim is made has been refunded or credited to the applicant by the person to whom it was paid, or, in the case of an application by a vendor, a certification and evidence satisfactory to the Commissioner that the tax has been refunded to the customer.

(Reg. Sec. 534.2)

• *Application procedures*

Where an application for credit has been filed, the applicant may immediately take the credit on the return which is due coincident with or immediately subsequent to the time the credit application is filed. The taking of the credit on the sales and use tax return is deemed to be part of the credit application. The application for credit, or a copy of the application if filed earlier, must be attached to the return on which the credit is taken. (Sec. 1119(a), Tax Law)

• *Documentation to substantiate refund claim*

Taxpayers seeking a refund should include all invoices, receipts, contracts, or any other documents that provide you paid the sales tax. Photocopies are acceptable. If documents are voluminous, you may submit a summary in table form or a schedule. The department may ask for additional information or documentation as needed. Also, you must include an explanation of the basis for the refund claim. (TB-ST-350)

• *Timeliness of applications*

An application for a refund or credit must be filed within the following time limitations:

— where the tax was paid by the applicant to a person required to collect tax, within three years after the date the tax was payable by the person who collected the tax. (Sec. 1139(a), Tax Law);

— where the tax, penalty or interest was paid by the applicant directly to the Commissioner, within three years after the date the tax, interest or penalty was payable. (Sec. 1139(a), Tax Law); or

— where a taxpayer is requesting a refund of an overpayment of sales tax, the refund claim must be filed within three years from the time the return was filed or two years from the time the tax was paid, whichever is later. If no return was filed, the taxpayer must file the refund claim within two years from the time the tax was paid. (Sec. 1139(c), Tax Law)

If a taxpayer has consented in writing to the extension of the period for assessment, the period for filing an application for credit or refund does not expire prior to six months after the expiration of the period within which the assessment may be made. (Sec. 1147(c), Tax Law)

• *Forms to use to apply for a refund*

When a special application form is not required (see specialized application forms below), taxpayers should use Form AU-11, Application for Credit or Refund of Sales or Use Tax. (TB-ST-350)

Specialized application forms including the following:

— Qualified Empire Zone Enterprises (QEZE): Form AU-12, Application for Credit or Refund of Sales or Use Tax—Qualified Empire Zone Enterprise (QEZE).

— Motor vehicles: Form DTF-806, Application for Refund and/or Credit of Sales or Use Tax Paid on Casual Sale of Motor Vehicle.

— Motor fuels: Form FT-500, Application for Refund of Sales Tax Paid on Automotive Fuels.

— Motor fuels sold to government entities: Form AU-629, Application for Refund/Reimbursement of Taxes Paid on Fuel Sold to Governmental Entities by Registered Distributors.

— Motor fuels purchased by government entities: Form FT-504, Claim for Refund of Taxes Paid on Fuel by a Government Entity, and Form FT-505, Claim for Refund of Taxes Paid on Government Entity Credit Card Purchases of Fuel.

— Prepaid sales tax on motor fuel sold at retail service stations: Form FT-950, Application for Refund of Prepaid Sales Tax on Motor Fuel Sold at Retail Service Stations.

— Prepaid sales tax on motor fuel sold other than at retail service stations: Form FT-949, Application for Refund of Prepaid Sales Tax on Motor Fuel Sold Other Than at Retail Service Stations.

— Prepaid sales tax on diesel motor fuel sold at retail service stations: Form FT-1007, Application for Refund of Prepaid Sales Tax on Diesel Motor Fuel Sold at Retail Service Stations.

— Prepaid sales tax on diesel motor fuel sold other than at retail service stations: Form FT-1010, Application for Refund of Prepaid Sales Tax on Diesel Motor Fuel Sold Other Than at Retail Service Stations.

— Motor fuels purchased by farmers: Form FT-420, Refund Application for Farmers Purchasing Motor Fuel.

— Fuels used by commercial fishermen: Form AU-631, Claim for Refund/Reimbursement of Taxes Paid on Fuel Used in a Vessel Engaged in Commercial Fishing.

(TB-ST-350)

• *Repayment of tax to a customer*

Any person who has erroneously, illegally, or unconstitutionally collected any tax from a customer and remitted the tax to the Commissioner must repay the tax to the customer before the Commissioner may issue a refund. An accurate record of the amount of tax repaid to each customer, the reason for repayment and proof of repayment must be kept and made available to the Commissioner upon request. (Reg. Sec. 534.8)

• *Motor vehicles*

If a consumer receives a manufacturer's refund of the purchase price of a returned motor vehicle, a sales tax refund will be issued in the amount of tax paid on the purchase price refunded, not in excess of the receipts subject to tax, provided the refund request is made within three years of receipt of the manufacturer's refund. (Sec. 1139(f), Tax Law)

• *Allowance of interest*

Interest is only allowed on refunds or credits granted for any tax, penalty, or interest which was erroneously, illegally, or unconstitutionally collected or paid. (Sec. 1139(d), Tax Law) Interest accrues from the date that the claim for credit or refund is made. However, no interest is paid if the Department of Revenue processes the claim within 90 days. (Sec. 1139(d), Tax Law) (TSB-M-09(16)S)

There is no interest paid on refunds or credits due to an overpayment made with a short form part quarterly return. (Reg. Sec. 534.2) Interest does not attach to refunds and credits on tax payments attributable to canceled sales, returned or defective merchandise (Reg. Sec. 534.6) or bad debts. (Reg. Sec. 534.7) In addition, there is no interest on refunds and credits for tax paid on the purchase of tangible personal property for certain specified uses (Reg. Sec. 534.2), on the purchase of certain services (Reg. Sec. 534.5), or on purchases of property or services by omnibus carriers engaged in local transit service. (Reg. Sec. 534.4)

• *Empire Zones*

Certain taxpayers may claim a refund or credit for the sales and use tax paid on tangible personal property purchased for use in constructing, expanding, or rehabilitating qualifying industrial or commercial real property located in an empire zone (see ¶ 60-360 Enterprise Zones and Similar Tax Incentives).

• *Economic Transformation and Facility Redevelopment Program*

Participants in the Economic Transformation and Facility Redevelopment Program, or their contractors, may claim a refund of state sales or use tax paid on tangible personal property that is used in constructing, expanding or rehabilitating industrial or commercial real property located in an ETA. The tangible personal property must become an "integral component part" of the real property in order to qualify for the refund. The refund is available for property purchased after the participant receives its certificate of eligibility and used before a certificate of occupancy is issued for the real property. The participant or contractor may only apply for a refund once per sales tax quarter and the amount may not be claimed as a credit on a sales tax return. The provisions are scheduled to expire on December 31, 2021. (Sec. 1119(f), Tax Law) For additional information, see TSB-M-11(9)S and ¶60-360 Enterprise Zones and Similar Tax Incentives.

[¶61-620] Administrative Remedies

A taxpayer who is notified that the Commissioner of Taxation and Finance has made a determination of tax due may apply to the Division of Tax Appeals for a hearing. Such an application must be made within 90 days of the date of the mailing of the notice of such determination. If no application is made, the determination becomes irrevocably fixed, unless the Commissioner on its own motion makes a redetermination. A taxpayer may also apply for a hearing following denial of an application for refund or credit. (Sec. 1138(a)(1), Tax Law)

An administrative law judge (ALJ) will conduct the hearing and render a determination within six months after the completion of the hearing or the submission of briefs, whichever is later. The ALJ may, for good cause shown, extend the six-month period for three additional months. If no determination is rendered within the six-month period (or the extended period), the petitioner may institute an Article 78 proceeding to compel the issuance of such determination. (Sec. 2010(3), Tax Law)

The determination of the Administrative Law Judge is reviewable by the Tax Appeals Tribunal (TAT). The taxpayer may institute an Article 78 proceeding for review of the decision of the Tax Appeals Tribunal.

• *Jeopardy assessments*

The 90-day period in which an application may be made for a hearing applies also to jeopardy assessments. Property seized for the collection of tax under the jeopardy assessment may not be sold by the Commissioner until the time to apply for a hearing has expired. If a hearing application has been timely filed, then the sale of seized property is further stayed until four months after the Commissioner has given notice of its hearing determination to the person against whom the jeopardy assessment is made. (Sec. 1138(b), Tax Law)

• *Bond requirement*

There is no specific provision for review of a notice by the Commissioner of Taxation and Finance requiring a vendor to file a proper bond to protect the tax revenues. The determination of the Commissioner on the necessity, propriety and amount of the bond is final unless, within five days from the notice to him requiring the bond, the vendor makes a request in writing for a hearing. (Sec. 1137(e)(2), Tax Law)

The taxpayer may resolve a dispute quickly and inexpensively without a formal hearing by requesting a conciliation conference; see discussion at ¶89-230 Taxpayer Conferences.

[¶61-700]

LOCAL TAXES

[¶61-735] Local Tax Rates

Below are charts of local sales and use tax rates imposed in cities and counties. The local taxes are in addition to the 4% state rate and the additional Metropolitan Commuter Transit District (MCTD) tax (see ¶60-110 for the MCTD rate), where applicable.

A Tax Bulletin issued by the Department of Taxation and Finance lists and describes the various publications issued by the Department that are related to tax rates. (TB-ST-820) The Department has also issued a Tax Bulletin that explains how to identify the correct rates and compute tax due, jurisdiction reporting codes and rate changes, and other sales taxes and fees. (TB-ST-825)

• *Combined state and local rates*

A current table of combined state and local sales tax rates imposed is provided below:

Albany County	8%
Allegany County	8 $1/2$%
Auburn (city) (Cayuga Co.)	8%
*Bronx—see New York City	
*Brooklyn—see New York City	
Broome County	8%
Cattaraugus County	8%
Cayuga County	8%
Chautauqua County	8%
Chemung County	8%
Chenango County	8%
Clinton County	8%
Columbia County	8%
Cortland County	8%
Delaware County	8%
*Dutchess County	8 $1/8$%
Erie County	8 $3/4$%
Essex County	8%
Franklin County	8%
Fulton County	8%
Genesee County	8%
Glens Falls (city) (Warren County)	7%
Gloversville (city) (Fulton County)	8%
Greene County	8%

Hamilton County 8%

Herkimer County . . . . $8^1/4$%

Ithaca (city) (Tompkins County) 8%

Jefferson County 8%

Johnstown (city) (Fulton County) 8%

*Kings (Brooklyn)—see New York City

Lewis County 8%

Livingston County 8%

Madison County 8%

*Manhattan—see New York City

Monroe County 8%

Montgomery County 8%

*Mount Vernon (city) (Westchester Co.) . . . . $8\,^3/8$%

*Nassau County . . . . $8\,^5/8$%

*New Rochelle (city) (Westchester Co.) . . . . $8\,^3/8$%

*New York City . . . . $8\,^7/8$%

Niagara County 8%

Norwich (city) (Chenango County) 8%

Olean (city) (Cattaraugus Co.) 8%

Oneida County . . . . $8^3/4$%

Oneida (city) (Madison Co.) 8%

Onondaga County 8%

Ontario County . . . . $7\,^1/2$%

*Orange County . . . . $8\,^1/8$%

Orleans County 8%

Oswego County 8%

Oswego (city) (Oswego County) 8%

Otsego County 8%

*Putnam County . . . . $8\,^3/8$%

*Queens—see New York City

Rensselaer County 8%

*Richmond (Staten Island)—see New York City

*Rockland County . . . . $8\,^3/8$%

Rome (city) (Oneida Co.) . . . . $8^3/4$%

St. Lawrence County 8%

Salamanca (city) (Cattaraugus Co.) 8%

Saratoga County 7%

Saratoga Springs (city) (Saratoga Co.) 7%

Schenectady County 8%

Schoharie County 8%

Schuyler County 8%

Seneca County 8%

*Staten Island—see New York City

Steuben County 8%

*Suffolk County . . . . 8 $5/8$%

Sullivan County 8%

Tioga County 8%

Tompkins County 8%

Ulster County 8%

Utica (city) (Oneida Co.) . . . . 8 $3/4$%

Warren County 7%

Washington County 7%

Wayne County 8%

*Westchester County . . . . 8 $3/8$%

*White Plains (city) (Westchester Co.) . . . . 8 $3/8$%

Wyoming County 8%

Yates County 8%

*Yonkers (city) (Westchester County) . . . . 8 $7/8$%

Hotel Room Occupancy and/or Food and Drink

Long Beach (city only) . . . . 8$5/8$%

Nassau County (outside city of Long Beach) . . . . 8$5/8$%

Hotel Room Occupancy Only

Niagara Falls City 8%

Niagara County (outside cities of Niagara Falls and Lockport) 8%

Lockport City 8%

Food and Drink Only

Lockport City 8%

Niagara County (outside cities of Niagara Falls and Lockport) 8%

Niagara Falls City 8%

Admissions, Club Dues, and Cabaret Charges

Lockport City 8%

Niagara County (outside cities of Lockport and Niagara Falls) 8%

Niagara Falls City 8%

The rates are taken from Publication 718, New York State Sales and Use Tax Rates by Jurisdiction, and include the additional state tax within the Metropolitan

Commuter Transportation District (MCTD), where applicable (rates in jurisdictions marked with an (*) include the $3/8$% imposed for the benefit of the MCTD). The effective dates of the rates are listed in Publication 718A, Enactment and Effective Dates of Sales & Use Tax Rates.

The tables of local sales taxes imposed on hotel room occupancy, food and drink, and admission, club, and cabaret charges, is condensed from schedule A of form ST-100 (New York State and Local Quarterly Sales and Use Tax Return).

• *Additional tax rates*

In general, localities may levy the additional local tax at a rate no greater than 3%. However, certain localities are authorized to impose the additional local tax at the rate of 0.50%, 1%, 1.50%, 2%, 2.50% or 3%, and are subject to rate ceilings and specific applicability periods. (Sec. 1210, Tax Law) The following localities may impose an additional 1% tax for a total local rate of 4% for the specified periods (see *Publication 718-A*, Enactment and Effective Dates of Sales and Use Tax Rates):

Albany County (September 1, 1992—November 30, 2023)

Broome County (March 1, 1994—November 30, 2023)

Cattaragus County (March 1, 1986—November 30, 2023)

Cayuga County (September 1, 1992—November 30, 2023)

Chautauqua (December 1, 2015—November 30, 2023) (see discussion below for authorization of additional taxes)

Chemung County (December 1, 2002—November 30, 2023)

Chenango County (September 1, 2002—November 30, 2023)

Clinton County (December 1, 2007—November 30, 2023)

Columbia County (March 1, 1995—November 30, 2023)

Cortland County (September 1, 1992—November 30, 2023)

Delaware County (September 1, 2002—November 30, 2023)

Erie County (January 10, 1988—November 30, 2023) (see discussion below for authorization of additional taxes)

Essex (December 1, 2013—November 30, 2023) (see discussion below for authorization of additional taxes)

Franklin County (June 1, 2006—November 30, 2023)

Fulton County (September 1, 2005—November 30, 2023)

Genesee County (September 1, 1994—November 30, 2023)

Greene County (March 1, 1993—November 30, 2023)

Hamilton County (December 1, 2013—November 30, 2023)

Herkimer County (September 1, 1994—November 30, 2023) (see discussion below for authorization of additional tax)

Jefferson (December 1, 2015—November 30, 2023)

Lewis County (December 1, 2013—November 30, 2023)

Livingston County (June 1, 2003—November 30, 2023)

Madison County (June 1, 2004—November 30, 2023)

Monroe County (December 1, 1993—November 30, 2023)

Guidebook to New York Taxes — **620**

Montgomery County (June 1, 2003—November 30, 2023)

New Rochelle, City of (September 1, 1993—December 31, 2023)

Niagra (March 1, 2003—November 30, 2023)

Oneida County (September 1, 1992—November 30, 2023) (see discussion below for authorization of additional tax)

Onondaga County (September 1, 2004—November 30, 2023)

Orleans County (June 1, 1993—November 30, 2023)

Oswego (city of) (September 1, 2004—November 30, 2023)

Oswego County (September 1, 2004—November 30, 2023)

Otsego County (December 1, 2003—November 30, 2023)

Putnam County (September 1, 2007—November 30, 2023)

Rensselaer County (September 1, 1994—November 30, 2023)

Schoharie County (June 1, 2004—November 30, 2023)

Schuyler County (September 1, 1999—November 30, 2023)

Seneca County (December 1, 2002—November 30, 2023)

St. Lawrence (December 1, 2013—November 30, 2023)

Steuben County (December 1, 1992—November 30, 2023)

Suffolk (June 1, 2001—November 30, 2023) (see discussion below for authorization of additional tax)

Tioga County (December 1, 2005—November 30, 2023)

Tompkins County (December 1, 1992—November 30, 2023) (see discussion below for authorization of additional tax)

Ulster County (September 1, 2002—November 30, 2023)

Wayne County (December 1, 2005—November 30, 2023)

Westchester (August 1, 2019—November 30, 2023)

Wyoming County (September 1, 1992—November 30, 2023)

Yates County (September 1, 2003—November 30, 2023)

For a discussion of actual rates enacted, including their effective dates, see Publication 718-A, Enactment and Effective Dates of Sales and Use Tax Rates.

Allegany.—In addition to the general 3% local tax permitted, an additional tax at the rate of 1.5% is authorized for the period beginning December 1, 2004, and ending November 30, 2023. (Sec. 1210(i)(8), Tax Law)

Chautauqua.—In addition to the general 3% local tax permitted, an additional tax at the rate of 0.5% is authorized for the period beginning December 1, 2015, and ending November 30, 2023. (Sec. 1210(i)(38), Tax Law)

Dutchess.—In addition to the general 3% local tax permitted, an additional tax at the rate of 0.75% is authorized for the period beginning March 1, 2003, and ending November 30, 2023. (Sec. 1210(i)(29), Tax Law)

Erie.—In addition to the general 3% local tax authorized, the following additional taxes are authorized: 1.0% (between January 10, 1988, and November 30, 2023) and 0.75% (between December 1, 2011, and November 30, 2023). (Sec. 1210(i)(4), Tax Law)

Essex.—Essex County is authorized to impose a 5% hotel and motel tax.

¶61-735

Herkimer.—In addition to the general 3% local tax permitted and the additional 1% authorized, an additional tax at the rate of 0.25% is authorized for the period beginning December 1, 2005, and ending November 30, 2023. (Sec. 1210, Tax Law; Sec. 1210-E, Tax Law)

Nassau.—In addition to the general 3% local rate permitted, an additional 0.75% tax (between January 1, 1986, and November 30, 2023) and an additional 0.5% tax (between September 1, 1991, and November 30, 2023) are authorized. (Sec. 1210, Tax Law)

Niagara.—Niagara County is authorized to impose a 5% hotel or motel tax (between March 1, 2003—November 30, 2023). (Sec. 1202-t, Tax Law)

Oneida.—In addition to the general local tax authorized and the additional 1.0% tax authorized (between September 1, 1992, and November 30, 2023), an additional 0.75% or 0.5% tax is authorized for the period beginning December 1, 2008 and ending November 30, 2023. (Sec. 1210(i)(13), Tax Law)

Ontario.—In addition to the general 3% local tax authorized, an additional tax at the rate of .125% is authorized for the period beginning June 1, 2006, and ending November 30, 2023, and an additional tax at the rate of 0.375% for the period beginning September 1, 2009 and ending November 30, 2023. (Sec. 1210(i)(40), Tax Law)

Orange.—In addition to the general 3% local tax permitted, an additional tax at the rate of 0.75% is authorized for the period beginning June 1, 2004, and ending November 30, 2023. (Sec. 1210(i)(35), Tax Law)

Rockland.—In addition to the general 3% local tax permitted and the additional 0.625% tax authorized (between beginning March 1, 2002 and November 30, 2023), an additional 0.375% tax is authorized for the period beginning March 1, 2007, and ending November 30, 2023. (Sec. 1210(i)(23), Tax Law)

Schenectady.—In addition to the general 3% local tax permitted, an additional tax at the rate of 0.5% is authorized for the period beginning September 1, 1998 and ending August 31, 2038, in order to fund the Schenectady Metroplex Development Authority (SMDA). (Sec. 1210-C, Tax Law) The county is also authorized to impose another additional tax at the rate of 0.5% for the period beginning June 1, 2003, and ending November 30, 2023. (Sec. 1210(i)(31), Tax Law)

Suffolk.—An additional tax at the rate of 1% is authorized for the period beginning June 1, 2001, and ending November 30, 2023. Further, the county may impose a 0.25% additional tax between December 1, 1984 and November 30, 2030 as part of the Suffolk County Drinking Water protection program. (Sec. 1210-A, Tax Law)

Sullivan.—In addition to the general 3% local tax permitted, an additional tax at the rate of 0.5% is authorized for the period beginning June 1, 2003, and ending November 30, 2023. (Sec. 1210(i)(33), Tax Law) In addition, Sullivan County is authorized to impose another additional local sales and use tax at the rate of 0.5% for the period beginning June 1, 2007, and ending November 30, 2023. (Sec. 1210(i)(33), Tax Law)

Tompkins.—In addition to the general 3% local tax permitted, an additional tax at the rate of 0.5% or 1% is authorized between December 1, 1992, and November 30, 2023. (Sec. 1210(i)(11), Tax Law)

White Plains.—The city of White Plains may levy additional taxes at the rate of 0.5%, 0.25%, and 0.25% through August 31, 2021. (Sec. 1210(ii)(3), Tax Law)

Local jurisdictions may adopt the entire state tax package, with exemptions provided for items used in the production of tangible personal property and sales of utilities or telephone central office equipment, station apparatus or comparable telegraph equipment used in receiving at destination or in initiating and switching telephone or telegraph communication or in receiving, amplifying, processing, transmitting and retransmitting telephone or telegraph signals. The credit or refund for tangible personal property used to rehabilitate property in an economic development zone is allowed only when specifically provided by a local jurisdiction. (Sec. 1210(a)(1), Tax Law)

In the alternative, the local jurisdictions may adopt one or more of the taxes included in the entire state tax package, except that the sales and use taxes on tangible personal property and on services may only be adopted as part of the entire state tax package. (Sec. 1210(b)(1), Tax Law) Local jurisdiction not adopting the entire state tax package may tax telephone answering services but only if they also impose the compensating use tax upon such services. The jurisdiction is determined by the location of the person or business for whom the telephone answering service is being provided, regardless of the location of the telephone answering service. (TSB-M-91(13)S)

Upon either election, the provisions of the local tax must be uniform. (Sec. 1210(a)(1), Tax Law; Sec. 1210(b)(1), Tax Law)

Yonkers.—The city of Yonkers is authorized to impose an additional tax at the rate of 1% and 0.5% (the 0.5% authorization is for the period beginning September 1, 2015 and ending November 30, 2023). (Sec. 1210(a)(ii)(1), Tax Law)

New York City—A 4.5% New York City local tax is imposed in addition to the 4% state tax, and the revenues therefrom are paid to the Municipal Assistance Corporation for the City of New York. (Sec. 1210, Tax Law) New York City also imposes a tax on selected services (see ¶560-005 Persons and Sales Subject to NYC Tax).

No transaction may be taxed by any county or by any city within such county, or by both, at an aggregate rate in excess of the highest rate set for that jurisdiction. Where a transaction is taxed by both a county and a city, the rate of tax on the transaction imposed by the county or city is deemed to be reduced (or the entire tax eliminated) to the extent necessary to avoid exceeding the maximum tax rate. (Sec. 1223, Tax Law)

Counties having one or more cities of less than one million have prior right to impose local sales taxes on the entire state tax package to the extent of one-half the maximum rate authorized. (Sec. 1224(a), Tax Law) Each city in such a county has prior right to impose local sales taxes on the entire state tax package to the extent of one-half the maximum rate authorized. (Sec. 1224(b)(2), Tax Law) Where the entire state tax package is not adopted, each city in a county having one or more cities of less than one million has prior right to impose local sales taxes on sales of: utilities; food and drink sold by restaurants; hotel room occupancies; and admissions charges, social or athletic club dues and roof garden or cabaret charges. (Sec. 1224(b)(1), Tax Law)

• *Residential energy sources*

Local governments, including New York City, may exempt or impose reduced rates on retail sales and uses of certain residential energy sources. (Sec. 1210(a)(3)(i),

Tax Law) For a list of local sales and use tax rates on sales and installations of residential solar energy systems equipment, see Publication 718-S.

• *Fuel and utilities used in manufacturing*

New York City must, for purposes of its tax, omit the statewide exemption for fuel and utilities used or consumed in producing tangible personal property and utilities. (Sec. 1107(b), Tax Law)

• *Additional tax on sales of utility services for school district purposes*

School districts that are coterminous with or partly or wholly within cities having a population of less than 125,000 may impose a tax on sales and uses of utility services at a rate of up to 3%. Such tax is in addition to the state, city and county taxes. (Sec. 1212(a), Tax Law)

The Newburgh Enlarged City School District, Peekskill City School District, Poughkeepsie City School District, and the Rye City School District, each impose a 3% local sales tax on consumer utilities. (ST-09-3, ST-09-4, ST-14-4, and ST-19-2, New York Department of Taxation and Finance)

• *Determining the rate of local tax to be collected*

The place of delivery is controlling for purposes of determining the applicable local tax rate. (Sec. 1213, Tax Law)

• *Local rates on clothing and footwear*

For the local sales and use tax rates on clothing and footwear, see Publication 718-C. For a discussion of the taxability of clothing, see ¶ 60-290 Clothing.

• *Empire zones refund rates*

Certain taxpayers may claim a refund or credit for the sales and use tax paid on tangible personal property purchased for use in constructing, expanding, or rehabilitating qualifying industrial or commercial real property located in an empire zone (see ¶ 60-360 Enterprise Zones and Similar Tax Incentives).

• *Sales to a qualified empire zone enterprise*

Qualified empire zone enterprises (QEZEs) are granted credits or refunds from New York state sales and use taxes on purchases of certain goods and services used in an empire zone in which the QEZE has qualified for benefits (see ¶ 60-360 Enterprise Zones and Similar Tax Incentives).

TRANSPORTATION AND TRANSMISSION COMPANIES

[¶80-000]

TRANSPORTATION AND TRANSMISSION COMPANIES

[¶80-010] Imposition of Tax

Generally, every domestic corporation, joint-stock company or association formed for or principally engaged in the conduct of a transportation or transmission business is subject to a tax on issued capital stock (Sec. 183, Tax Law), and a tax on gross earnings from sources within New York (Sec. 184, Tax Law). (Sec. 183(1)(b), Tax Law; Sec. 184(1), Tax Law)

"Principally engaged" means that over 50% of the taxpayer's gross receipts are derived from the particular activity or activities. (New York Department of Taxation and Finance Corporation Tax Audit Guidelines.)

Sec. 183, Tax Law, contains the words "formed for." However, whether a corporation is properly classified and held subject to taxation under Art. 9 or under Art. 9-A is determined from an examination of the nature of its business activities; neither the laws under which the business was incorporated, nor the provisions of its certificate of incorporation, are controlling (*Matter of McAllister Bros., Inc. v. Bates*, 272 App Div 511 [3d Dept 1947], lv denied 279 NY 1037; *Matter of Holmes Electric Protective Services v. McGoldrick*, 262 App Div 514, affd 228 NY 635).

In *McAllister Bros., Inc.*, the Appellate Division set forth the following *de facto* test:

[I]t has firmly been established that classification for franchise tax purposes is to be determined by the nature of [the corporation's]business and that the purposes for which the corporation was organized are immaterial. This rule with respect to classification for franchise tax purposes applies especially to corporations organized under the general business corporation laws which have within their certificates of incorporation a wide variety of charter powers.

Neither Art. 9 nor Art. 9-A contains a definition of the term "transportation;" therefore, a corporation's principal business activities is determined by deciding whether such activities constitute transportation within the plain and ordinary sense of that word (*Matter of Newton Creek Towing Co. v. Law*, 205 App Div 209, 211 [3rd Dept 1923], affd 237 NY 578). In turn, "transportation" has been described as follows:

[i]n its ordinary sense, 'transportation' comprehends any real carrying about or movement from one place to another. It implies the taking up of persons or property at some point and putting them down at another, and signifies at least a movement of some sort between termini or places. *Matter of RVA Trucking, Inc. v. New York State Tax Commission*, 135 AD2d 938.

Statutory examples of businesses subject to Sec. 183 and Sec. 184 taxes include: domestic companies formed for or principally engaged in the conduct of railroad, canal, steamboat, ferry (other than ferry businesses operating between New York City boroughs under a City contract), express, navigation, pipe line, transfer, baggage express, omnibus, trucking, taxicab, telegraph, palace car or sleeping car businesses. (Sec. 183(1)(b), Tax Law; Sec. 184(1), Tax Law)

For additional examples of businesses that have been determined to be transportation and transmission companies, see the annotations below.

Businesses engaged in the transportation, transmission, or distribution of gas, electricity, or steam are not subject to these taxes. Instead, they are subject to the corporate franchise tax under Article 9-A. (Sec. 183(1)(b), Tax Law; Sec. 184(1), Tax Law)

Relinquishment of supervision and control: The leasing of vehicles with drivers has been held to be the conduct of a transportation business subject to tax under Secs. 183 and 184. (*People ex rel Peter J. Curran Funeral Serv. Co. v. Graves*, 257 App Div 888,12 NYS2d 153 [1939], lv denied 281 NY 888). However, in several cases, taxpayers have attempted to avoid taxation by claiming that, by relinquishing control and supervision over their vehicles and personnel, they are not involved in a "transportation" company. *McAllister Bros., Inc., supra; Peter J. Curran Funeral Service v. Graves, supra.*

However, as noted more recently by the Tax Appeals Tribunal, the totality of a company's business, of which the dispatching of drivers and the details of delivery are just small parts, is dispositive. In *Dave's Motor Transportation*, the taxpayer, although it did not dispatch the transportation crew, was still held to be conducting a transportation business. The taxpayer argued that it did not maintain control over ground transportation because (1) its employees did not dispatch the drivers or unload the cargo; (2) the cargo vehicles bore the American Airlines insignia and were numbered to correspond to American Airlines, Inc. flights; and (3) Air Cargo, Inc., an agent for American Airlines, Inc., coordinated the vehicle manifests. The Tribunal, after defining transportation and trucking and noting that "[t]he leasing of vehicles with drivers has been held to be the conduct of a transportation business subject to tax under sections 183 and 184 of the Tax Law," indicated that the "[p]etitioner's activities, i.e., the pickup and delivery of air cargo . . . are within these definitions".

See also, *Petition of Walton Hauling & Warehouse Corp.*.

For exemptions, see ¶ 80-020.

• *Telephone businesses*

For taxable years beginning prior to 1995, both Sec. 183 and Sec. 184, Tax Law, included telephone businesses within the list of transportation and transmission companies subject to tax on issued capital stock and gross earnings. For taxable years beginning after 1994, however, Sec. 184 limits the gross earnings tax with respect to telecommunication providers only to entities formed for or principally engaged in the conduct of a "local" telephone business.

For purposes of Sec. 184, the term "local telephone business" means the provision or furnishing of telecommunication services for hire wherein the service furnished by the provider consists of carrier access service or the service originates and terminates within the same local access and transport area ("LATA"). (Sec. 184(1), Tax Law) Local access and transport areas are geographic areas established, approved and in existence as of July 1, 1994, pursuant to the modification of final judgment in *United States v. Western Electric Company* (Civil Action No. 82-0192) in the United States District Court for the District of Columbia, or within the LATA-like Rochester non-associated independent area.

The term "telecommunication services" has the same meaning set forth in Sec. 186-e, Tax Law (see ¶ 80-410).

Mobile telecommunication service providers.—Mobile telecommunication service providers are not taxable under Sec. 184. (TSB-M-15(6)C)

• *Foreign transportation and transmission companies*

Transportation and transmission corporations, joint-stock companies and associations organized, incorporated or formed under the laws of a foreign state, county or sovereignty are subject to tax under Secs. 183 and 184, Tax Law, if their activities include one of more of the following:

(1) doing business in New York in a corporate or organized capacity or in a corporate form;

(2) employing capital in New York in a corporate or organized capacity or in a corporate form;

(3) owning or leasing property in New York in a corporate or organized capacity or in a corporate form; or

(4) maintaining an office in New York. (Sec. 183(6), Tax Law; TSB-M-82(13)C).

"Doing business:" Foreign transportation and transmission companies that own or hold property in New York are generally considered to be doing business within the state. (Sec. 183(7), Tax Law) Exceptions to the general rule include:

(1) foreign ferry companies operating vessels between New York City boroughs under a lease granted by New York City; and

(2) property owned or held in New York for use exclusively in interstate or foreign commerce.

In addition, foreign transportation and transmission companies will not be deemed to be doing business, employing capital, owning or leasing property, or maintaining an office in New York by reason of any, or a combination of any, of the following:

(1) the maintenance of cash balances with banks or trust companies in New York;

(2) the ownership of shares of stock or securities kept in a safe deposit box, vault or similar rented receptacle in New York or, if pledged as collateral security, or deposited with one or more banks or trust companies, or brokers who are members of a recognized security exchange, in safekeeping or custody accounts;

(3) the taking of any action by a bank or trust company or broker that is incidental to the rendering of safekeeping or custodian service to the corporation;

(4) the maintenance of an office in New York by one or more officers or directors of the foreign corporation who are not corporate employees (provided the corporation does not otherwise do business, employ capital or own or lease property in New York); or

(5) the keeping of corporate books or records in New York, provided the books or records are not kept by corporate employees and the corporation does not otherwise do business, employ capital, own or lease property or maintain an office in New York.

• *"Corporation" defined*

The term "corporation" includes publicly traded partnerships treated as corporations for federal income tax purposes, associations within the meaning of IRC Sec. 7701(a)(3) (including limited liability companies), and businesses conducted by a trustee or trustees where interest or ownership is evidenced by certificates or other written instruments. (Sec. 184(1), Tax Law; Sec. 183(1)(a), Tax Law)

[¶80-020] Exemptions

The following transportation and transmission companies are exempt from both Sec. 183 and Sec. 184 taxes:

(1) ferry companies operating between New York City boroughs under a lease granted by New York City;

(2) corporations, joint-stock companies or associations principally engaged in the conduct of aviation (including air freight forwarders acting as principal and like indirect air carriers);

(3) corporations principally engaged in providing telecommunication services between aircraft and dispatcher, aircraft and air traffic control or ground station and ground station (or any combination of the foregoing), where: (a) at least 90% of the corporation's voting stock is owned, directly or indirectly, by air carriers; and (b) the corporation's principal function is to fulfill the requirements of the Federal Aviation Administration or the International Civil Aviation Organization (or successors thereto) relating to communication systems between aircraft and dispatchers, aircraft and air traffic control or ground station and ground station (or any combination thereof) for the purposes of air safety and navigation;

(4) corporations, joint-stock companies or associations formed for or principally engaged in the transportation, transmission, or distribution of gas, electricity, or steam; and

(5) corporations, joint-stock companies or associations subject to bank franchise taxes under Art. 32, Tax Law. (Sec. 183(1)(b), Tax Law; Sec. 184(1), Tax Law)

• *Railroad and trucking companies*

For taxable years beginning before 1998, businesses formed for or principally engaged in the conduct of a railroad, palace car, sleeping car or trucking business, or formed for or principally engaged in the conduct of two or more of such businesses, were subject to Art. 9 taxes. Effective for taxable years beginning after 1997, however, such businesses are subject to Art. 9-A business corporation franchise tax (see ¶ 10-210 C Corporations) or Art. 32 bank franchise tax (see ¶ 12-001 and following in the "Banks—Income Tax" division), *unless* they elect to continue to be taxed under Art. 9. Businesses subject to Art. 9 taxes for the taxable year ending December 31, 1997, had to make their election on or before March 15, 1998. Businesses *not* subject to Sec. 183 and Sec. 184 tax for the taxable year ending December 31, 1997, but that would thereafter be subject to Art. 9-A or 32 tax if the election were not made, must make their election by the first day on which they would be required to file a return or report (without regard to extensions) under Art. 9, 9-A, or 32. (Sec. 183(1)(b), Tax Law; Sec. 183(10), Tax Law)

An election, once made, continues in effect until revoked.

• *Corporation owned by municipality*

Effective June 2, 1940, a corporation whose capital stock is owned by a New York municipal corporation is exempt from all Art. 9 taxes. (Sec. 207-a, Tax Law)

• *Corporations operating vessels in interstate or foreign commerce*

A corporation formed for or principally engaged in the operation of vessels, whose only activity in New York is (1) the maintenance of an office for the employing of capital in New York and (2) the use of property exclusively in interstate or foreign commerce, is exempt from tax under Sec. 184. (Sec. 183(7-a), Tax Law)

• *Taxicab and omnibus corporations*

Taxicab and omnibus corporations, other than those noted below, are exempt from tax during such period that the state tax on motor fuel, computed without regard to any reimbursement allowable under Sec. 289-c(3)(d), Tax Law, exceeds 2¢ per gallon. During such period, taxicab and omnibus corporations are subject to Art. 9-A business corporation franchise taxes. (Sec. 183(1)(c), Tax Law; Sec. 184(2)(a), Tax Law)

Foreign taxicab or omnibus corporations.—A taxicab or omnibus corporation that is organized, incorporated or formed under the laws of a foreign state, country or sovereignty, and neither owns nor leases property in New York in a corporate or organized capacity, nor maintains an office in New York in a corporate or organized capacity, but is doing business or employing capital in New York by conducting at least one but fewer than 12 trips into New York during a calendar year, is exempt from tax under Sec. 183, Tax Law, and is subject to a tax of $15 per trip under Sec. 184, Tax Law. The taxicab or omnibus corporation will not be deemed to be owning or leasing property in New York if the only property it owns or leases within the state is a vehicle or vehicles used to conduct trips. (Sec. 183(9)(a), Tax Law; Sec. 184(2)(b)(1), Tax Law)

A foreign taxicab or omnibus corporation will be considered to be conducting a trip into New York when one of its vehicles enters New York and transports passengers to, from, or to and from a location within the state. It will not be considered to be conducting a trip into New York if its vehicle only makes incidental stops at locations in the state while in transit between locations outside New York. (Sec. 183(9)(b), Tax Law; Sec. 184(2)(b)(3), Tax Law)

The number of trips that a corporation conducts into New York is calculated by adding together the total number of trips that each vehicle owned, leased or operated by the corporation conducts into New York.

• *Telephone companies*

For taxable years prior to January 1, 1995, the Sec. 184 tax on gross earnings applied to all telephone companies. For taxable years beginning after 1994, however, Sec. 184 limits the gross earnings tax with respect to telecommunication providers only to entities formed for or principally engaged in the conduct of a "local" telephone business. Accordingly, corporations not exclusively engaged in providing a local telephone business are exempt from Sec. 184 tax.

[¶80-030] Basis and Rate of Tax--Issued Capital Stock Tax (Sec. 183, Tax Law)

The tax on the capital stock of transportation and transmission companies is computed annually on the amount of capital stock within New York during the preceding year (that is, the base year). (Sec. 183(1)(b), Tax Law)

Measure of capital stock: The amount of a corporation's capital stock allocated to New York is the portion of the issued capital stock that the gross assets employed in any business within New York bear to the gross assets wherever employed in business. (Sec. 183(2), Tax Law)

The amount of capital stock of corporations that is taxable under Sec. 183 solely for the privilege of holding property is deemed to be the same portion of the issued capital stock as the gross assets located within New York bear to the corporation's total gross assets, wherever located.

The capital of a corporation invested in the stock of another corporation is deemed to be assets located where the issuing corporation's assets (other than patents, copyrights, trademarks, contracts and good will) are located.

In measuring a corporation's capital stock, obligations issued by the United States and cash on hand and on deposit, are not included in a corporation's gross assets.

• *Tax rate*

The minimum tax imposed on transportation and transmission companies is the greater of;

(1) $75.00;

(2) 1.5 mills on each dollar of the net value of issued capital stock allocated to New York; or

(3) 0.375 mills for each 1% of dividends paid, provided dividends paid on any kind of the corporation's capital stock during the preceding calendar year amounted to 6% or more. (Sec. 183(3), Tax Law)

However, for taxable years beginning on or after January 1, 2002, the provision discussed in (3), above, does not apply to any corporation, joint stock company, or association formed for or principally engaged in the conduct of a telephone business that is subject to the gross earnings tax under Sec. 184, Tax Law, and that has no more than one million access lines in New York. (Sec. 183(3), Tax Law)

Tax calculated on net value: The "net value" of a corporation's issued capital stock is deemed to be the greater of the following:

(1) the total number of shares of stock outstanding at the end of the base year, multiplied by the net value per share of stock outstanding at the end of the year, but not less than $5 per share;

(2) the difference between a corporation's assets and liabilities, computed as of the end of the base year; or

(3) the total number of shares of stock outstanding at the end of the base year, multiplied by the average price at which they sold during the year.

Tax calculated on dividends: The dividend rate on par-value capital stock is computed on the par value of the stock. (Sec. 183(3), Tax Law) If dividends on other classes of stock amount to less than 6%, the 1.5 mills method of taxation applies.

If a corporation, joint-stock company or association has more than one kind of capital stock, and pays a dividend amounting to 6% or more upon the par value of one kind of stock, and on the other class of stock pays dividends amounting to less than 6%, the 1.5 mills method of taxation applies. (Sec. 183(4), Tax Law)

Corporations having stock without nominal or par value will pay a dividend rate that is determined by dividing the amount paid as dividends during the year by the amount paid in on such stock. (Sec. 183(5), Tax Law) If the rate is 6% or more, the 0.375 mills method of taxation applies.

For purposes of the tax, all distributions or payments in value to stockholders out of earnings, profits or appreciation are considered dividends, as well as any consideration given by a corporation for the purchase of its own stock in excess of the consideration received by it for issuance of such stock. The amount of earned surplus at the time of a change in classification of a corporation that was formerly taxed under Art. 9-A, Tax Law, is excluded in determining the amount of dividends paid.

It should be noted that the dividend tax is used only when it results in a tax that is higher than that computed under other methods. For purposes of this tax, dividends are not taxed *per se,* but are used as a basis of rate determination.

• *Corporations engaged in operation of vessels in foreign commerce*

The measure of the capital stock of a corporation engaged in the operation of vessels in foreign commerce is the portion of the issued capital stock as the aggregate number of working days in New York territorial waters of all vessels bears to the aggregate number of working days of all vessels. (Sec. 183(8), Tax Law) The dividend rate for such a corporation is determined by dividing the amount paid as a dividend or dividends on all classes of stock during the year by the amount of paid-in capital and, if the rate is 6% or more, the .375 mill rate for each 1% of dividends will be applied to the amount of such paid-in capital.

"Working days:" The Department of Taxation and Finance has indicated that "working days" are days during which a vessel is sufficiently staffed for the transportation of persons or cargo or when it has cargo aboard. (Instructions, Form CT-183/184-I.) The working time in New York territorial waters and the working time elsewhere are computed for each vessel in hours and minutes. At the end of the year, the time is totaled for all vessels, and the sum is converted into days.

Instead of records indicating actual time in New York territorial waters, a taxpayer may compute time from records showing when Ambrose Light Station was passed on the way in and out of port.

[¶80-035] Basis and Rate of Tax--Gross Earnings Tax (Sec. 184, Tax Law)

Except as noted below (see comments under "Railroad and trucking companies"), the additional gross earnings tax is computed at the rate of $3/4$ of 1% on gross earnings from all sources within New York. (Sec. 184(1)(a), Tax Law) For taxable years ending in the year 2000, the rate is reduced to $3/8$ of one percent effective July 1, 2000 with the result that the applicable rate for the year shall be $9/16$ of one percent. For years commencing after 2000, the rate shall be $3/8$ of one percent. Unlike the Sec 183 tax, there is no minimum tax.

In *Matter of Howgen Transport Co., Inc.*, the Tax Appeals Tribunal held that a trucking company was not entitled to deduct the cost of hired trucks in computing its gross earnings under Sec. 184, Tax Law. In that opinion, the Tribunal held that "gross earnings" as used in Sec. 184 includes receipts from all sources without deduction, except those receipts which represent the "replacement of capital," essentially raw materials that are either incorporated into goods sold or materials resold exactly as purchased. Expenditures for trucks used to provide transportation services, whether purchased or leased, were held not deductible from gross earnings.

In *Matter of Group W Cable* the Division of Tax Appeals, Administrative Law Judge Unit, held that uncollectible debts that are written off for federal tax purposes are excluded from a taxpayer's gross earnings. However, it is the petitioner's burden to establish the amount of the uncollectibles in each tax year in issue.

The New York Department of Taxation and Finance Corporation Tax Audit Guidelines state that "gross earnings" means all receipts arising from or growing out of the employment of capital, whether the capital is employed in transportation or transmission or otherwise (New York Department of Taxation and Finance Corporation Tax Audit Guidelines). Besides receipts directly and incidentally related to transportation and transmission, receipts from the following sources in New York are also subject to tax under Sec. 184:

(1) advertising;

(2) charges for photostats;

(3) interest on bank accounts;

(4) on leased property: rental income, real property taxes paid by lessees, improvements made by lessees;

(5) interest and dividends on investments, allocated on the basis of the payor's issuer's allocation percentage. *Note:* interest earned on obligations of the United States and its instrumentalities, and of New York State and its political subdivisions and instrumentalities, is not taxable;

(6) interest on federal income tax refunds;

(7) capital gains from the sale or exchange of property. Profit on the sale or exchange of real or tangible personal property is computed on the basis of original cost (*not* depreciated cost), less any expenses incurred in making the sale. Capital gains may not be reduced by capital losses. Gain is allocated where the property is located or used;

(8) capital gains from the sale or exchange of securities, except stock, where the situs is in New York. This includes gains from the sale or exchange of U.S. government and New York State government securities. "Gain" is computed on the basis of original cost; brokerage expenses may be deducted in computing the gain. Capital

gains may not be reduced by capital losses. Capital losses may not be used to reduce other receipts. These gains are allocated to the domiciliary office unless the security is held, managed and controlled by an office outside the domiciliary state. Gains from the sale or exchange of stock should be allocated by the issuer's allocation percentage of the corporation whose stock is being sold.

(9) receipts from royalties, which are taxable and are allocated where earned; and

(10) gross receipts from all other sources within New York State, including those received by non-air freight forwarders acting as principals.

Railroad and trucking companies: For taxable years beginning after 1996 and ending before 2001, the gross earnings tax on railroad and trucking businesses is imposed at a rate equal to $6/10$ of one percent on gross earnings from all sources within New York. (Sec. 184(1)(a), Tax Law) For taxable years ending in the year 2000, the rate is reduced to $3/8$ of one percent effective July 1, 2000 with the result that the applicable rate for the year shall be $39/80$ of one percent. For years commencing after 2000, the rate shall be $3/8$ of one percent. In computing gross earnings, surface railroads will not include earnings derived from business of an interstate or foreign character.

• *Allocation of gross earnings*

Except as noted in the following paragraphs, a transportation or transmission corporation must determine gross earnings from transportation and transmission services within New York by multiplying its gross earnings from transportation and transmission within and without the state by a fraction, the numerator of which is the taxpayer's mileage within New York, and the denominator of which is the taxpayer's mileage within and without the state during the period covered by the report. (Sec. 184(4), Tax Law) Nonrevenue mileage, such as deadheading, should be excluded. (TSB-M-82(9)C)

In an advisory opinion, the Commissioner of Taxation and Finance has held that, in allocating gross earnings from transportation services, an overnight delivery company could not include the revenue mileage of independent contractors that it hired as drivers for its overnight delivery service. Only the taxpayer's own mileage was to be included in the calculation (*Hurry Wagon, Inc.*).

Corporations engaged in the operation of vessels: A corporation principally engaged in the operation of vessels must allocate its gross earnings to New York by multiplying its gross earnings from transportation services within and without the state by the percentage that represents the ratio of the aggregate number of working days on New York territorial waters of the vessels it owns or leases to the aggregate number of working days of all the vessels it owns or leases during such period.

Railroad companies: A corporation, joint-stock company or association formed for or principally engaged in the conduct of a non-steam railroad business, whose property is leased to another railroad corporation, is not taxed on gross earnings. (Sec. 184(3), Tax Law) Instead, an annual tax is imposed at the rate of 4.5% on dividends paid during the preceding calendar year in excess of 4% of the company's capital stock. However, if the leased property is operated by a receiver and the gross earnings are not included with the lessee's gross earnings, the receiver is subject to the gross earnings tax.

Publicly traded partnerships and associations: The gross earnings of a taxpayer who is a partner, member or associate of a publicly traded partnership or an association that is subject tax under Sec. 184, Tax Law, must include the amount received with respect to the partnership or association that is required to be reported as dividends to the U.S. Treasury Department. (Sec. 184(1-a), Tax Law)

¶80-035

• *Telephone and telegraph companies*

Prior to 1995, the gross earnings of a telegraph or telephone company were determined by totaling the corporation's gross operating revenue from transmission services performed wholly within New York, plus the portion of revenue from interstate and foreign transmission service attributable to New York during the applicable reporting period. However, for taxable years beginning after 1994, the legislature has limited the gross earnings tax on telecommunication providers only to entities formed for or principally engaged in the conduct of a "local" telephone business, and requires such businesses to exclude from earnings 100% of separately charged inter-LATA, interstate or international telecommunications service derived from sales for ultimate consumption of telecommunications service to its customers. In addition, effective January 1, 1996, 30% of separately charged receipts from intra-LATA toll charges (including any interregion regional calling plan service) must be excluded from the local telephone company's earnings.

The effect of the 1995 amendments is to eliminate long-distance telephone service receipts and a portion of local toll call receipts from the Sec. 184 gross earnings tax base. (TSB-M-95(3)C)

For a definition of "local telephone business," see ¶ 80-010.

[¶80-040] Metropolitan Commuter Transportation District Surcharge

Note: The surcharges were made permanent by the 2014 budget legislation.

Tax surcharges are imposed on transportation and transmission companies exercising their corporate franchise, doing business, employing capital, owning or leasing property, or maintaining an office in the Metropolitan Commuter Transportation District. The surcharge is computed at the rate of 17% of the taxpayer's Sec. 183 or Sec. 184 tax liability attributable to its business activities carried on within the District. For purposes of the surcharge, for taxable years beginning in 2000 and thereafter, the tax imposed under Sec. 184 is deemed to be imposed at a rate of 0.75% except that for eligible corporations, joint stock companies or associations that elect to be subject to the provisions of Sec. 183, the Sec. 184 tax is deemed to have been imposed at a rate of 0.6%. (Sec. 183-a(1), Tax Law; Sec. 184-a(1), Tax Law)

The Metropolitan Commuter Transportation District consists of the Counties of New York, Bronx, Kings, Queens, Richmond, Dutchess, Nassau, Orange, Putnam, Rockland, Suffolk and Westchester. (TSB-M-83(2)C)

• *Surcharge on taxicab rides*

A 50-cent surcharge is imposed on taxicab rides that originate in New York City and terminate anywhere within the territorial boundaries of the New York City metropolitan commuter transportation district (MCTD). Taxicab owners are required to pass along the surcharge to passengers by adjusting the fares, and taximeters must be adjusted to include the tax. This provision is effective November 1, 2009, applicable to taxi rides commencing on or after that date. (Sec. 1281, Tax Law)

Returns and payment.—Persons liable for the surcharge must file returns with the Department of Taxation and Finance within 20 days after the end of each quarterly period ending on the last day of March, June, September, and December. Such persons also must file a return by January 20, 2010, for the period of November and December 2009. Payment of the tax is due with returns filed with the Department or to designated financial institutions. Returns and reports must be retained for three years. (Sec. 1284, Tax Law; Sec. 1285, Tax Law)

• *Allocation of Sec. 183 tax*

The amount of a taxpayer's Sec. 183 tax that is subject to the surcharge is determined by multiplying its Sec. 183 tax by a fraction, the numerator of which is the taxpayer's average gross assets employed in any business within the District, and the denominator of which is the taxpayer's average gross assets employed in any business within New York State. Obligations issued by the United States, cash on hand and cash on deposit are excluded from both the numerator and denominator of the fraction. (Reg. Sec. 40.2)

The average gross assets used in determining the fraction are the assets employed during the year preceding the privilege period for the Sec. 183 tax upon which the surcharge is based.

Rolling equipment.—Gross assets consisting of trucks and other rolling equipment of corporations principally engaged in trucking are located within the District in accordance with the ratio that the mileage of the trucks and other rolling equipment traveled within the District bears to the mileage of the trucks and other rolling equipment traveled within the state.

• *Allocation of Sec. 184 tax*

A taxpayer's Sec. 184 tax that is attributable to business activity carried on within the Metropolitan Commuter Transportation District is determined by multiplying its Sec. 184 tax liability by a fraction, the numerator of which is the taxpayer's mileage within the District, and the denominator of which is the taxpayer's mileage within the entire state during the period covered by the report. (Sec. 184-a(2), Tax Law)

Telephone and telegraph companies.—A telephone or telegraph corporation must allocate its business activity to the Metropolitan Commuter Transportation District by multiplying its Sec. 184 tax liability by the ratio that its total gross operating revenue from transmission services performed wholly within the District bears to its total gross operating revenue from transmission services performed within the entire state during the period covered by the report. (Sec. 184-a(2), Tax Law)

• *Corporations principally engaged in operation of vessels*

The amount of the Sec. 183 or Sec. 184 tax of a corporation principally engaged in the operation of vessels that is subject to the surcharge is determined by multiplying the Sec. 183 tax by the percentage that the aggregate number of working days of the vessels owned or leased by the taxpayer in all navigable lakes, rivers, streams and waters within the District bears to the aggregate number of working days of all vessels owned or leased by the taxpayer in all navigable lakes, rivers, streams and waters within New York State territorial waters. (Sec. 184-a(2), Tax Law; Reg. Sec. 40.4)

The "number of working days" is the number of working days during the year preceding the privilege period for the Sec. 183 tax upon which the surcharge is based.

TAX ON FURNISHING OF UTILITY SERVICES

[¶80-200]
TAX ON FURNISHING OF UTILITY SERVICES

[¶80-210] Imposition of Tax

Utilities that are subject to the supervision of the New York Department of Public Service and, for the prior calendar year, have gross income in excess of $500, are subject to a tax on gross income. (Sec. 186-a(1), Tax Law) A similar tax is imposed on the gross operating income of utilities not subject to the Department of Public Service that, for the same period, have gross operating income in excess of $500.

As part of the 2000 budget legislation, under Ch. 63 (A.B. 11006), significant reductions in the taxes imposed under Sec. 186-a, Tax Law, are being implemented; for details, see ¶80-230.

• *"Utility" defined*

For purposes of the tax on gross income, the term "utility" is given a broader meaning than the term usually implies. (Sec. 186-a(2), Tax Law, Reg. Sec. 44.1) Utilities subject to tax are divided into two classes:

Utilities of the first class: Utilities of the first class include every person (including telecommunication services providers) subject to the supervision of the Department of Public Service, except:

(1) persons engaged in operating, on state public highways, omnibuses having a seating capacity of more than seven persons; and

(2) persons engaged in the business of operating or leasing sleeping and parlor railroad cars or of operating railroads other than street surface, rapid transit, subway and elevated railroads.

Utilities of the first class are taxed on gross income.

Utilities of the second class: Utilities of the second class include those that would not usually be classified as utilities, but are made utilities by statute for purposes of the Sec. 186-a tax on gross income. (Reg. Sec. 44.2) The term includes every person (whether or not subject to the supervision of the Department of Public Service) who sells gas, electricity, steam, water, or refrigeration, delivered through mains, pipes, or wires, or furnishes gas, electric, steam, water, or refrigerator service, by means of mains, pipes, or wires. Ordinarily, although with exceptions, utilities in the second class resell services purchased from utilities in the first class.

Second class utilities are taxed on gross operating income.

• *"Person" defined*

The word "person" means persons, corporations, companies, associations, joint-stock companies or associations, partnerships and limited liability companies, estates, assignee of rents, any person acting in a fiduciary capacity, or any other entity, and persons, their assignees, lessees, trustees or receivers.

For exemptions from tax, see ¶80-220.

• *Natural gas brokers*

In an advisory opinion, the Commissioner of Taxation and Finance has stated that a natural gas broker that (1) never takes title to the gas; (2) never has possession or control of the gas; (3) never bears any risk of loss with respect to the gas; (4) indicates in its brokerage agreements that it is acting as a broker and it does not engage in the business of selling or buying gas; (5) only includes its commission in its gross income on its federal income tax returns; and (6) has a separate account into which it deposits payments it receives from end-users, and only retains its commissions is not engaged in the business of supplying gas through mains or pipes and is not subject to tax under Sec. 186-a, Tax Law (*Nixon, Hargrave, Devans & Doyle*, TSB-A-95(12)C). A New York limited liability company that engages in similar activities is also exempt from Sec. 186-a tax (*Iroquois Energy Brokers, LLC*).

[¶80-220] Exemptions

The following utilities are exempt from tax:

(1) first class utilities with gross income for the prior calendar year of $500 or less;

(2) second class utilities with gross operating income for the prior calendar year of $500 or less;

(3) sleeping and parlor railroad car companies and railroads (other than street surface, rapid transit, subway and elevated railroads);

(4) omnibus carriers, operating on New York public highways and omnibuses having a seating capacity of more than seven persons;

(5) the State of New York, its municipalities, political and civil subdivisions of the state or municipality, and public districts (provided that, with respect to gas, electricity, and gas or electric service—including the sale of the transportation, transmission, or distribution of gas or electricity—such municipalities, subdivisions, and public districts will fall under this exclusion if they own and operate facilities that are used to generate or distribute electricity or to distribute gas, and they distribute and sell such gas or electricity solely at retail and solely within their respective jurisdiction; in addition, with respect to the sale of electricity or the transportation, transmission, or distribution of electricity, a municipality will fall under the exclusion if it sells electricity at retail and all such electricity (excluding temporary substitution power during outages or periods of reduced output) has been generated solely by, and purchased solely from, the state or a public authority of the state);

(6) corporations and associations that are organized and operated exclusively for religious, charitable or educational purposes, no part of the net earnings of which inures to the benefit of any private shareholder or individual, and that are described under Sec. 1116(a)(4), Tax Law, where such organization resells such gas or electricity, or gas or electric service, as landlord to its tenants in buildings owned by the organization; and

(7) corporations organized and operated exclusively for the purpose of leasing from a city a water-works system designed to supply water at cost to users for discharge, either before or after industrial use, into a river within the city in order to improve the flow and condition of the river and thereby to provide a means to relieve the river from pollution. (Sec. 186-a(2), Tax Law)

Limited dividend housing corporations organized under the State Housing Law are exempt from Sec. 186-a taxes. (Reg. Sec. 44.3)

See also ¶80-230 for a discussion of tax reductions and phase-outs enacted under Ch. 63 (A.B. 11006) as part of the 2000 budget legislation.

• *Cooperative corporations*

Certain cooperative utility corporations that are organized without capital stock and qualify for federal tax exemption pursuant to IRC Sec. 501(c)(12) are also exempt from the gross income tax imposed by Sec. 186-a. (Sec. 77(2), Cooperative Corporations Law)

Until January 1, 2020, in lieu of tax, qualifying cooperative utilities had to pay an annual fee of $10 to the Commissioner of Taxation and Finance. The fee was eliminated by the 2019 budget legislation (TSB-M-19(3)C).

However, the exemption under Sec. 77 continues to apply. (Sec. 77(3), Cooperative Corporations Law)

[¶80-230] Basis and Rate of Tax

Tax is imposed at the rate of 2.5% (prior to January 1, 2000, 3.25%) on the gross income of telecommunication service providers subject to the supervision of the Department of Public Service. (Sec. 186-a(1), Tax Law)

For other utilities subject to the supervision of the Department of Public Service, the tax was also imposed on gross income at the rate of 3.25% through December 31, 1999, with a reduction to 2.5% becoming effective January 1, 2000. Following enactment of the 2000 budget legislation, however, the gross income tax base for such utilities is broken into two parts, and the 2.5% rate is reduced, as follows: (1) on the portion of gross income derived from the transportation, transmission, or distribution of gas or electricity by conduits, mains, pipes, wires, lines, or similar means, the rate is reduced to 2.45% on January 1, 2001, 2.4% on January 1, 2002, 2.25% on January 1, 2003, 2.125% on January 1, 2004, and 2% on January 1, 2005; (2) on other gross income (i.e., charges for the commodity of gas or electricity), the rate is 2.1% effective January 1, 2000, with further reductions to 2% on January 1, 2001, 1.9% on January 1, 2002, 0.85% on January 1, 2003, 0.4% on January 1, 2004, and 0% beginning January 1, 2005. (Sec. 186-a(1), Tax Law)

Finally, for other utilities *not* subject to the supervision of the Department of Public Service, the tax, which is imposed on gross operating income, is being phased out. The rate is reduced to 2.1% effective January 1, 2000, with further reductions to 2% on January 1, 2001, 1.9% on January 1, 2002, 0.85% on January 1, 2003, 0.4% on January 1, 2004, and 0% beginning January 1, 2005. (Sec. 186-a(1), Tax Law)

For all of the above, no tax is imposed if gross income or gross operating income for the year is $500 or less. (Sec. 186-a(1), Tax Law)

For surcharges, see ¶ 80-240.

• *IMB Credit*

Industrial and manufacturing businesses (IMB) are allowed a refundable credit against the corporate franchise (income) tax or personal income tax equal to the sum of the utility (gross receipts) tax under Sec. 186-a, Tax Law, the natural gas importer tax under Sec. 189, Tax Law, and the related Metropolitan Commuter Transportation District surcharges under Sec. 186-c and Sec. 189-a, Tax Law, paid by or passed through to the IMB on or after January 1, 2000, but only with regard to gas, electricity, steam, water, and refrigeration—or gas, electric, steam, water, or refrigeration services—consumed by the IMB in New York. (Sec. 14-a, Tax Law)

Any person collecting such taxes from, or passing such taxes through to, an IMB must provide the IMB with sufficient information concerning the tax to enable the IMB to correctly compute this credit. (Sec. 14-a, Tax Law)

These provisions are applicable to taxable years ending after January 1, 2000, and will expire for taxable years ending on and after January 1, 2007.

• *Pass-through of tax*

Prior to 2000, the tax imposed by Sec. 186-a was specifically designated by statute as part of the utility's operating costs. (Sec. 186-a(6), Tax Law) Accordingly, the tax was charged against and paid by the utility, and it could not be added as a separate item to bills rendered by the utility to customers or others. Now, however, that prohibition has been eliminated. Upon request, a utility must furnish its customers with a statement showing the amount of the tax imposed. As noted above (see "IMB Credit"), certain businesses may obtain a credit for the amount of such tax that has been passed through by the utility.

[¶80-240] Metropolitan Commuter Transportation District Surcharge

Note: The surcharge was made permanent by the 2014 budget legislation.

A surcharge is imposed on utilities doing business in the Metropolitan Commuter Transportation District. The surcharge is imposed at the rate of 17% of the taxpayer's Sec. 186-a tax liability, after the deduction of credits otherwise allowable, except any utility credit provided by Article 13-A, Tax Law. Commencing January 1, 2000, with respect to the tax imposed under Sec. 186-a(1)(a) (i.e., relating to providers of telecommunications services), the surcharge is calculated as if the tax imposed under Sec. 186-a was imposed at a rate of 3.5%. The tax is applied only to the portion of the taxpayer's Sec. 186-a tax liability that is attributable to the taxpayer's gross income or gross operating income attributable to the taxpayer's business activity carried on within the District. (Sec. 186-c, Tax Law)

The surcharge is not allowed as a deduction in the computation of any state or local tax surcharge. Credits otherwise allowable under Article 9, Tax Law, are not be allowed against the surcharge. In addition to the extent that the surcharge is deducted in determining federal adjusted gross income, it must be added back for state tax purposes.

On and after May 1, 2015, an additional surcharge is imposed on the gross receipts from mobile telecommunication services relating to the metropolitan commuter transportation district, at the rate of 0.721%. (Sec. 186-c(1)(b)(2), Tax Law)

• *Allocation of income*

The amount of a taxpayer's tax attributable to business activity carried on within the District is determined by multiplying the tax imposed by Sec. 186-a by the ratio that the taxpayer's gross income (or gross operating income) from all sources within the District bears to its gross income (or gross operating income) from all sources within New York.

• *Metropolitan Commuter Transportation District*

The Metropolitan Commuter Transportation District consists of the Counties of New York, Bronx, Kings, Queens, Richmond, Dutchess, Nassau, Orange, Putnam, Rockland, Suffolk and Westchester. (TSB-M-83(2)C)

[¶80-400]

TELECOMMUNICATION SERVICES PROVIDERS

[¶80-410] Imposition of Tax

Sec. 186-e, Tax Law, imposes an annual excise tax on gross receipts from sales of telecommunication services by telecommunication services providers. (Sec. 186-e(2)(a)(1), Tax Law)

Special provisions concerning mobile telecommunications services are discussed below.

Surcharge.—Telecommunication services providers were subject to a surcharge on gross receipts from sales of telecommunication services for years ending on December 31, 1995 (7.5%), and December 31, 1996 (2.5%). (Sec. 188(1), Tax Law)

The state wireless communications service surcharge is discussed at ¶80-445.

Metropolitan Commuter Transportation District surcharge.—A surcharge is imposed on gross receipts from sales of telecommunication services relating to the Metropolitan Commuter Transportation District. (Sec. 186-c(1)(b)(1), Tax Law) For details, see ¶80-440.

On and after May 1, 2015, an additional surcharge is imposed on the gross receipts from mobile telecommunication services relating to the metropolitan commuter transportation district, at the rate of 0.721%. (Sec. 186-c(1)(b)(2), Tax Law)

• *"Telecommunication services" defined*

The term "telecommunication services" means telephony or telegraphy, or telephone or telegraph service. (Sec. 186-e(1)(g), Tax Law) The term includes any transmission of voice, image, data, information and paging, through the use of wire, cable, fiber-optic, laser, microwave, radio wave, satellite or similar media or any combination thereof. The term also includes services that are ancillary to the provision of telephone service (such as, but not limited to, dial tone, basic service, directory information, call forwarding, caller-identification, call-waiting and the like), plus any equipment and services provided therewith.

The term does not include:

(1) separately stated charges for any service that alters the substantive content of the message received by the recipient from that sent; or

(2) cable television services. (Sec. 186-e(2)(b)(2), Tax Law) "Cable television services" involve the transmitting to subscribers of programs broadcast by one or more television or radio stations or any other program originated by any person by means of wire, cable, microwave or any other means.

Internet access.—The purchase of telephone service from telecommunications providers to access the Internet does not fall within the scope of the exemptions from telecommunications excise tax for Internet access service. (TSB-M-97(1.1)C, TSB-M-97(1.1)S) Start-up charges by the provider of Internet access service for the installation of equipment necessary to provide Internet access are not subject to telecommunications excise tax. Internet access charges for communications software, navigation software, an e-mail address, e-mail software, news headlines, space for a website, and other website services are considered a part of the Internet access service and are not subject to telecommunications excise tax if these services are incidental to providing Internet access.

- *"Telecommunication services provider" defined*

A "telecommunication services provider" is any person who furnishes or sells telecommunications services, regardless of whether such activities are the main business of the person or are only incidental thereto. (Sec. 186-e(1)(e), Tax Law)

- *Constitutionality*

The constitutionality of Sec. 186-e, Tax Law has not been addressed by any New York court. However, in *American Telephone and Telegraph Co. v. New York State Department of Taxation and Finance*, the New York Supreme Court, Appellate Division, noted that New York may tax long distance carriers on gross receipts attributable to their doing business in New York, subject to the limitation that carriers doing most of their business within the state cannot be taxed at a lower effective rate than carriers doing most of their business without the state. In addition, the constitutionality of a comparable state telecommunications excise tax was upheld by the U.S. Supreme Court in *Goldberg v. Sweet* (1989 US SCt) 488 US 252.

- *Mobile telecommunications services*

New York provisions have been amended to conform to the federal Mobile Telecommunications Sourcing Act (P.L. 106-252). (Sec. 186-e(1)(a), Tax Law; Sec. 186-e(1)(h), Tax Law; Sec. 186-e(2)(a), Tax Law; Sec. 186-e(2)(b)(4), Tax Law; Sec. 186-e(7)(b), Tax Law) (*TSB-M-02(4)C; TSB-M-02(5)C*)

Under the amended provisions, the excise tax is imposed on gross receipts from charges for mobile telecommunications service where the customer's place of primary use is within New York State, regardless of where the mobile telecommunications service originates, terminates, or passes through. The Department of Taxation and Finance has issued a memorandum that includes a number of examples illustrating the application of the new sourcing provisions and rules for computing taxable gross receipts. (*TSB-M-02(4)C; TSB-M-02(5)C*)

Additionally, on and after May 1, 2015, an excise tax is imposed on the sale of mobile telecommunications services at the rate of 2.9% of gross receipts from any mobile telecommunications service provided by a home service provider where the mobile telecommunications customer's place of primary use is within New York State. (Sec. 186-e(2)(a)(2), Tax Law)

[¶80-420] Exclusions

The following sales of telecommunication services are excluded from tax (Sec. 186-e(2)(b), Tax Law):

- *Sales for resale*

For taxable years beginning on or after January 1, 2009, an exclusion applies to all telecommunication services sold to a provider of such services for resale (for taxable years beginning before that date, the exclusion applies only if the provider purchasing the telecommunication services for resale is an interexchange carrier or a local carrier; see the discussion below). If the telecommunication services provider obtains a properly completed certificate of resale from the purchaser within 90 days after providing the services, then the certificate constitutes conclusive proof that the services were sold for resale as telecommunication services, the provider is relieved of liability for the tax due on the sale of those services, and the burden of proving that the gross receipt is not taxable is on the purchaser. (Sec. 186-e(2)(b)(1), Tax Law)

If the exclusion is not allowed (e.g., because a properly completed certificate of resale was not provided), then a purchaser that resells telecommunication services may still apply for a credit equal to the amount of tax imposed; see ¶ 80-450. (Sec. 186-e(4)(a)(1), Tax Law)

Taxable years beginning before 2009.—Sales of telecommunication services to a telecommunication services provider that is an interexchange carrier or a local carrier are excluded from tax where the services are purchased by the provider for resale as telecommunication services to its purchasers.

"Interexchange carrier" defined: An "interexchange carrier" is any provider of telecommunication services between two or more exchanges that qualifies as a common carrier. (Sec. 186-e(1)(b), Tax Law) A "common carrier" is any person engaged as a common carrier for hire in intrastate, interstate or foreign telecommunication services.

"Local carrier" defined: A "local carrier" is any provider of telecommunication services for hire to the public, which is subject to the supervision of the public service commission and is engaged in providing carrier access service to a switched network. (Sec. 186-e(1)(b), Tax Law)

Note: For purposes of the sale for resale exclusion, a reference to an "interexchange carrier" or "local carrier" includes a cellular common carrier that is a facilities-based cellular common carrier, without regard to whether the carrier is providing local or interexchange service.

• *Cable television services*

Since sales of cable television services are specifically exempted from the definition of telecommunications services (see ¶ 80-410), receipts from sales of cable television services are beyond the scope of the tax imposed on telecommunication services providers. (Sec. 186-e(2)(b), Tax Law)

However, in an advisory opinion, the Commissioner of Taxation and Finance has indicated that sales by a transmission company of voice, data and video transmission services to cable television operators and public television stations were subject to tax (*EMI Communication Corp.*). In *EMI Communication Corp.,* the provider did not come within the exclusion for cable television services because it did not transmit programs or television entertainment to its subscribers.

• *Air safety and navigation services*

Sales of telecommunication services to air carriers solely for the purpose of air safety and navigation are excluded from the tax, provided: (1) the service is provided by an organization, at least 90% of which (or, if a corporation, 90% of the voting stock of which) is owned, directly or indirectly, by air carriers; and (2) the organization's principal function is to fulfill the requirements of (a) the Federal Aviation Administration (or the successor thereto) or (b) the International Civil Aviation Organization (or the successor thereto), relating to the existence of a communication system between aircraft and dispatcher, aircraft and air traffic control or ground station and ground station (or any combination of the foregoing) for the purposes of air safety and navigation.

• *Internet access charges*

Internet access is not considered a telecommunications service subject to the annual excise tax on gross receipts from sales of telecommunication services. (Sec. 179, Tax Law)

In addition, beginning July 1, 2008, telecommunications services purchased, used, or sold by ISPs to provide Internet access are no longer be subject to the excise tax; see the discussion below.

ITFAAA.—The New York Department of Taxation and Finance has issued a memorandum (TSB-M-08(4)C, as revised by TSB-M-08(4.1)C) discussing the sales and telecommunications excise tax effects of the federal Internet Tax Freedom Act Amendments Act of 2007 (ITFAAA) (P.L. 110-108). Under the ITFAAA, the federal moratorium on the imposition of state and local taxes on Internet access was extended for seven years, until November 1, 2014.

In addition, the ITFAAA amended the federal definition of "Internet access" for purposes of the moratorium to include certain closely related Internet communications services, such as electronic mail and instant messaging services. Therefore, Internet access now includes the following services: home page; electronic mail; instant messaging; video clips (e.g., movie previews and portions or short clips of a complete video); and personal electronic storage capacity. These services are included in the federal moratorium regardless of whether they are furnished as part of the Internet connection service or are purchased and furnished separately.

However, any forms of telephony (e.g., private telecommunications networks), including Voice over Internet Protocol (VOIP), network services, and data transmission services, other than telecommunications services used by an Internet Service Provider (ISP) to connect customers to the Internet, are not included under the federal moratorium. Accordingly, these forms of telephony continue to be subject to New York state and local sales taxes and the telecommunications excise tax.

The ITFAAA also amended various grandfather provisions. The new seven-year grandfather provision has no effect for New York sales and telecommunications excise tax purposes because Internet access was previously exempted under statutory and administrative provisions.

The Department initially indicated that telecommunications services purchased, used, or sold by ISPs to provide Internet access continued to be subject to New York's excise tax until June 30, 2008. (TSB-M-08(4)C) Upon reconsideration, however, it is the Department's view that the appropriate interpretation is that the excise tax imposed by Tax Law Sec. 186-e on the telecommunications purchased, used, or sold by ISPs to provide Internet access is preempted by federal law on and after November 1, 2005. The Department believes this interpretation is more consistent with the intent of Congress. Accordingly, those telecommunications services were no longer subject to the excise tax effective November 1, 2005. (TSB-M-08(4.1)C)

• *Federal limitations*

The telecommunication services provider tax does not apply to sales of telecommunication services under circumstances that would preclude the application of such tax by reason of the U.S. Constitution or any federal laws enacted pursuant thereto.

Direct-to-home satellite services: The federal Telecommunications Act of 1996 prohibits *local* taxation of direct-to-home satellite services. (Sec. 602, P.L. 104-104.) However, this law does not prohibit taxation at the *state* level. For additional details, see discussion at ¶ 80-501.

[¶ 80-430] Basis and Rate of Tax

The telecommunications service tax is imposed at the rate of 2.5% of gross receipts from:

(1) any intrastate telecommunication services;

(2) any interstate and international telecommunication services (other than interstate and international private telecommunication services, and mobile telecommunications taxable under Sec. 186-e(2)(a)(2), Tax Law, as discussed below) that originate or terminate in New York and are charged to a New York State service address (regardless of where the amounts charged for the services are billed or ultimately paid); and

(3) interstate and international private telecommunication services subject to apportionment rules discussed at ¶ 80-435. (Sec. 186-e(2)(a)(1), Tax Law)

Additionally, on and after May 1, 2015, an excise tax is imposed on the sale of mobile telecommunications services at the rate of 2.9% of gross receipts from any mobile telecommunications service provided by a home service provider where the mobile telecommunications customer's place of primary use is within New York State. (Sec. 186-e(2)(a)(2), Tax Law)

Effective May 1, 2015, the surcharge rate imposed on the sale of mobile telecommunication services relating to the Metropolitan Commuter Transportation District (MCTD) is 0.721%. This rate applies to a home service provider's gross receipts received on or after May 1, 2015, for mobile telecommunication services provided on or after that date where the customer's place of primary use is within the MCTD. Sales of telecommunication services other than sales of mobile telecommunication services continue to be subject to the MTA surcharge at the rate of 0.595%. (*TSB-M-15(5)C*, Taxpayer Guidance Division, New York Department of Taxation and Finance, July 24, 2015)

• *Mobile telecommunications services*

For special provisions concerning mobile telecommunications services, see ¶ 80-410.

• *"Gross receipt" defined*

"Gross receipt" means the amount received in or by reason of any sale, conditional or otherwise, of telecommunication services or in or by reason of the furnishing of telecommunication services. (Sec. 186-e(1)(a), Tax Law) The "amount received," for purposes of the definition of gross receipt, is the amount charged for the provision of a telecommunication service.

"Gross receipt" is expressed in money, whether paid in cash, credit or property of any kind or nature, and is determined without any deduction on account of the cost of the service sold or the cost of materials, labor or services used or other costs, interest or discount paid, or any other expenses. A deduction is allowed, however, for bad debts with respect to charges previously subjected to tax when the debt has become worthless in accordance with generally accepted accounting principles consistently applied by the taxpayer.

Enhanced emergency telephone system surcharge fees: Surcharges collected or administrative fees retained by a telecommunication services provider acting as a collection agent for a municipality pursuant to the provisions of Art. 6, County Law, are not considered as, nor included in the determination of, the provider's gross receipt. (Sec. 186-e(8), Tax Law)

• *"Service address" defined*

Generally, a "service address" is the location of the telecommunication equipment from which the telecommunication is originated or at which the telecommunication is received from the telecommunication services provider. (Sec. 186-e(1)(f), Tax Law)

The foregoing general rule is subject to the following special provisions, which are listed in order of priority of application:

(1) if the telecommunication originates or terminates in New York, and the service is charged to telecommunication equipment that is not associated with the origination or termination of the telecommunication (for example, by the use of a calling card or third party billing) and the location of such equipment is in New York, the service address of the telecommunication will be deemed to be in New York;

(2) if the service is obtained through the use of a credit or payment mechanism such as a bank, travel, credit or debit card, or if the service is obtained by charging telecommunication equipment that is not associated with the origination or termination of the telecommunication (for example, by the use of a calling card or third party

billing) and the equipment is not located in the state of origination or termination, then the service address will be deemed to be the location of the origination of the telecommunication; and

(3) if the service address is not a defined location, as in the case of mobile telephones, paging systems, maritime systems, air-to-ground systems and the like, the term "service address" means the location of the subscriber's primary use of the telecommunication equipment as defined by telephone number, authorization code, or location in New York where bills are sent, provided. The location of the mobile telephone switching office or similar facility in New York that receives and transmits the signals of the telecommunication will be deemed the service address where the mobile telephone switching office or similar facility is outside the subscriber's assigned service area.

• *"Private telecommunication service" defined*

A "private telecommunication service" is a dedicated telecommunication service that entitles the user or users to the exclusive or priority use of a communications channel or group of channels from one or more locations to one or more locations. (Sec. 186-e(1)(d), Tax Law) "Exclusive" means that the user-subscribers have use of a communications channel to the exclusion of all others who are not authorized to use the channel. "Priority" means that only authorized user-subscribers, as opposed to unauthorized persons, receive preferential use of a communications channel, but not necessarily a preference to the use of such channel with respect to each other.

[¶80-435] Apportionment--Private Telecommunication Services Providers

The gross receipt of an interstate or international private telecommunication services provider, if not separately ascertainable for each use of the service, is apportioned to New York as follows (Sec. 186-e(3), Tax Law):

(1) 100% of the charge imposed at each channel termination point within New York;

(2) 100% of the charge imposed for the use of a channel between channel termination points within New York; and

(3) (a) if each segment between each termination point is separately billed and the amounts so billed are fairly reflective of New York origination and/or termination traffic, then 100% of the charge imposed at each termination point in New York and for service in New York between those points and 50% of the charge imposed for service between a channel termination point outside the state and a point inside the state measured by the nearest termination point inside the state to the first termination point outside the state relative to the point inside the state, or (b) if each segment of the interstate or international circuit between each channel termination point is not separately billed or if such billing does not fairly reflect the New York origination and/or termination traffic handled by the private telecommunication service, an allocated portion of the interstate and international channel charge with respect to points in New York and points outside the state based on the ratio that the number of channel termination points in New York bears to the total number of channel termination points within and without the state.

The Commissioner of Taxation and Finance may prescribe other allocation methods if the procedure noted above does not fairly and equitably reflect private telecommunication services attributable to New York.

[¶80-440] Metropolitan Commuter Transportation District Surcharge

Note: The surcharge was made permanent by the 2014 budget legislation.

A surcharge is imposed on gross receipts from telecommunication services relating to the Metropolitan Commuter Transportation District at the rate of 17% of the state tax rate under Sec. 186-e, Tax Law. Since October 1, 1998, the surcharge has been calculated as if the tax was imposed at a state tax rate of 3.5%. (Sec. 186-c(1)(b), Tax Law)

The surcharge applies to: (1) any intra-district telecommunication services; (2) any inter-district telecommunication services that originate or terminate in the district and are charged to a service address in the district regardless of where the amounts charged for the services are billed or ultimately paid; and (3) as apportioned to the district, private telecommunication services.

For special provisions concerning mobile telecommunications services, see ¶80-410.

The Metropolitan Commuter Transportation District consists of the Counties of New York, Bronx, Kings, Queens, Richmond, Dutchess, Nassau, Orange, Putnam, Rockland, Suffolk and Westchester. (TSB-M-83(2)C)

[¶80-445] Wireless Communications Service Surcharge

A New York public utilities surcharge is imposed on wireless communications service provided to wireless communications customers with a place of primary use in New York at the rate of $1.20 per month. "Wireless communications service" means all commercial mobile services, including, but not limited to, all broadband personal communications services, wireless radio telephone services, geographic area specialized and enhanced specialized mobile radio services, and incumbent-wide area specialized mobile radio licensees, which offer real time, two-way voice or data service that is interconnected with the public switched telephone network or otherwise provides access to emergency communications services. (Sec. 186-f, Tax Law; *TSB-M-17(1)WCS*, New York Department of Taxation and Finance, November 8, 2017)

A surcharge of 90¢ is imposed on the retail sale of each prepaid wireless communications service, whether or not any tangible personal property is sold therewith. "Prepaid wireless communications service" means a prepaid mobile calling service as defined in Sec. 1101(b)(22), Tax Law. (Sec. 186-f, Tax Law; TSB-M-17(2)WCS) Also, a "prepaid wireless communications service" includes a prepaid phone card, recharge or refill authorization code that can be used on a mobile phone to make or receive calls, or to send or receive text messages. (TSB-M-18(1)WCS) For example, the following purchases are subject to the surcharge:

— long distance and international calling cards that can be used on both landlines and mobile phones; and

— cards, PINs, or codes that give access to only text services.

(TSB-M-18(1)WCS)

Purchases of cards, PINs, or codes that only give access to data services are considered purchases of Internet access and are not subject to the surcharge. However, cards, PINs, or codes that give access to data services in addition to voice or texting services and are sold together for one price are subject to the surcharge. (TSB-M-18(1)WCS)

Lifeline consumers, the State of New York, the United States of America, the United Nations, and nonprofit property/casualty insurance companies are exempt from surcharges. (Sec. 186-f, Tax Law; *TSB-M-17(1)WCS*, New York Department of

Taxation and Finance, November 8, 2017; *TSB-M-17(2)WCS*, New York Department of Taxation and Finance, November 8, 2017)

Reports and payments are due by the 20th day of the month following each quarterly period ending on the last day of February, May, August, and November. (Sec. 186-f, Tax Law)

Wireless communications service suppliers that timely file returns and remit taxes may retain as administrative fees: (1) 1.749% of the total New York State surcharge collected, and (2) 3% of the total local surcharge collected. *TSB-M-17(1)WCS*, New York Department of Taxation and Finance, November 8, 2017; *TSB-M-17(2)WCS*, New York Department of Taxation and Finance, November 8, 2017

The New York Department of Taxation and Finance has issued two publications providing information on wireless communications surcharge rates on both prepaid and postpaid wireless communications services, including local rates. (Publication 451; Publication 452)

Enhanced 911 system surcharge.—Municipalities are authorized to impose a surcharge, not to exceed 35¢ per access line per month, to pay for the costs associated with obtaining, operating and maintaining the telecommunication equipment and telephone services needed to provide an enhanced 911 emergency telephone system. (Sec. 303, County Law)

• *Local surcharges*

New York City or counties outside of New York City are authorized under the Tax Law to impose a surcharge on wireless communications services at a rate of 30¢ per month, and on prepaid wireless communications services at a rate of 30¢ per retail sale. Lifeline consumers, the State of New York, the United States of America, the United Nations, and nonprofit property/casualty insurance companies are exempt. (Sec. 186-g, Tax Law; *TSB-M-17(1)WCS*, New York Department of Taxation and Finance, November 8, 2017; *TSB-M-17(2)WCS*, New York Department of Taxation and Finance, November 8, 2017)

Reports and payments are due by the 20th day of the month following each quarterly period ending on the last day of February, May, August, and November. (Sec. 186-g, Tax Law)

Wireless communications service suppliers that timely file returns and remit taxes may retain as administrative fees: (1) 1.749% of the total New York State surcharge collected, and (2) 3% of the total local surcharge collected. *TSB-M-17(1)WCS*, New York Department of Taxation and Finance, November 8, 2017; *TSB-M-17(2)WCS*, New York Department of Taxation and Finance, November 8, 2017

The New York Department of Taxation and Finance has issued two publications providing information on wireless communications surcharge rates on both prepaid and postpaid wireless communications services, including local rates. (Publication 451; Publication 452)

Local enhanced wireless 911 emergency telephone surcharge.—The counties of Madison, Onondoga and Tompkins are authorized to impose a surcharge, not to exceed 65 cents per access line per month, to pay for the costs associated with obtaining, operating and maintaining the telecommunication equipment and telephone services needed to provide an enhanced 911 (e911) emergency telephone system. (County Law Sec. 334; County Law Sec. 335)

[¶80-450] Refunds and Credits

The following credits or refunds are allowed against the tax on telecommunication services providers. Although amounts credited or refunded are considered as overpayments of tax, no interest will be paid on the amount credited or refunded. (Sec. 186-e(4), Tax Law)

• *Priority of credits*

Credits allowable under Article 9 of the Tax Law must be applied in the following order:(Sec. 187-f, Tax Law) (*TSB-M-02(5)C*)

(1) non-carryover credits that are not refundable;

(2) carryover credits with limited carryover periods;

(3) carryover credits with unlimited carryover periods; and

(4) refundable credits.

• *Resold telecommunication services*

A credit, equal to the amount of tax imposed on telecommunication services, is allowed to purchasers that are providers of telecommunication services where (1) the telecommunication services purchased are later resold by the purchaser as telecommunication services and (2) the sale for resale exclusion (discussed at ¶ 80-420) is not allowed. (Sec. 186-e(4)(a), Tax Law) To accomplish this result, the credit is determined by computing the tax on the resold service so that the tax is imposed on the difference between the amount of the charge made by the provider to the purchaser and the amount of the charge made by the purchaser for the resold service.

• *Like taxes paid to other jurisdictions*

A credit is allowed to interstate or international telecommunication services for like taxes imposed by other states, countries or jurisdictions on sales of telecommunication services. (Sec. 186-e(4)(a), Tax Law) To be entitled to the credit, the provider or purchaser must prove that it paid a like tax on the sale of telecommunications services subject to tax under Sec. 186-e, Tax Law.

The amount of the credit is be the amount of tax lawfully due and paid to the other state. The total credit may not exceed the tax due to New York.

• *Special additional mortgage recording taxes*

A telecommunication services provider is *not* allowed a credit against Sec. 186-e tax for special additional mortgage recording taxes paid by the provider. (Sec. 253(1-a), Tax Law)

• *Foreign corporations—Annual maintenance fees*

Foreign telecommunication services providers are allowed a credit against Sec. 186-e tax for the amount of annual maintenance fees (imposed prior to 2015) paid for the calendar year. (Sec. 181(2), Tax Law)

• *Security training tax credit*

For qualified building owners, the law authorizes a security training tax credit against the New York corporate franchise, bank franchise, insurance franchise, personal income, and Article 9 corporation taxes, applicable to taxable years beginning on and after January 1, 2005. The credit amount equals the sum of the number of qualified security officers providing protection to buildings owned by the taxpayer, multiplied by $3,000. Any credit amount not deductible in a taxable year will be treated as an overpayment of tax to be credited or refunded without interest. Qualified security officers must have completed a qualified security training program. "Qualified building owner" means a building owner whose building entrances, exits, and common areas are protected by security personnel licensed under Article 7-A of the General Business Law, whether or not such personnel are employed directly by the building owner or indirectly through a contractor. The New York Office of Homeland Security may issue credit certifications for taxpayers meeting the applicable standards and demonstrating that they have provided (or will provide within the year) the appropriate training to all employees for whom the credit will be claimed. The maximum aggregate amount of tax credits allowed in any calendar year will be $5 million. (Sec. 26, Tax Law; Sec. 187-n, Tax Law)

Application process

In the event that subtraction of the credit allocations of all the eligible applications received on a given day would result in a zero or negative balance of the legislative cap, the tax credits would be allocated among such qualified building owners for that day on a pro rata basis. Each qualified building owner's request would be allowed at a reduced rate equivalent to the percentage created by dividing the unallocated tax credits by the aggregate tax credits requested on such date. Applications that were not filed on time would not be considered for the tax credit. (Reg. Sec. 1000.3)

Qualified building owners must file a complete application according to the specified method of transmittal to the Office of Homeland Security within the filing period. This information includes, but is not limited to, affirmation by the qualified building owner that the certified training has been provided to each security officer; dates and places of training; hours worked by each qualified security officer for which the taxpayer is applying; and verification that all information has been provided to the best of the qualified building owner's knowledge. All applications postmarked on the first day of the filing period by the required method of transmittal shall be treated as having been filed on the first day of the application period and shall be given priority with all other applications filed on the same day in the awarding of tax credits over all applications postmarked on subsequent days. The Office of Homeland Security will, within 45 days of the end of the filing period, issue certificates of tax credit and/or letters of disapproval, as appropriate. (Reg. Sec. 1000.3)

Eligibility in subsequent years.--Any qualified building owner who is allocated a credit in the first calendar year and who applies for credit in the second calendar year would, upon successful application, have priority of their percentage amount awarded in the previous year over all other taxpayers who file a complete application in the succeeding calendar year. (Reg. Sec. 1000.3)

LOCAL UTILITY TAXES

[¶80-500]
LOCAL UTILITY TAXES

[¶80-501] General Taxing Authority

Sec. 20-b, General City Law (Ch. 21, C.L.) authorizes cities to impose a 1% tax on gross income or gross operating income of utilities, similar to the state $3^1/_2$% tax. All cities except Sherril impose the tax. Buffalo, Rochester and Yonkers are authorized to impose the tax at a rate not exceeding 3%.

In addition, villages may impose a 1% tax on the gross income or gross operating income of utilities within the territorial limits of the village. (*Handbook of New York State and Local Taxes*, New York Department of Taxation and Finance, July 2011)

• *Direct-to-home satellite services*

The federal Telecommunications Act of 1996 prohibits local taxing jurisdictions from imposing fees or taxes on direct-to-home satellite services. The term "direct-to-home satellite service" means only programming transmitted or broadcast by satellite directly to the subscriber's premises without the use of ground receiving or distribution equipment, except at the subscriber's premises or in the uplink process to the satellite. (Sec. 602, P.L. 104-104)

The term "local taxing jurisdiction" means any municipality, city, county, township, parish, transportation district, or assessment jurisdiction, or any local jurisdiction in the territorial jurisdiction of the United States with the authority to impose a tax or fee, but does not include a state. (Sec. 602, P.L. 104-104)

[¶80-510] Cable Television Systems

Municipalities may impose a fee, tax or charge on a cable television company, if, when added to the state fee, the total does not exceed 1% of the company's annual gross receipts. (Sec. 818, Executive Law)

All cable television systems must be franchised by each municipality in which they intend to provide or extend service. (Sec. 819, Executive Law)

[¶80-530] Enhanced Emergency Telephone System Surcharge

Municipalities may impose a telephone system surcharge to pay for the cost of providing enhanced emergency telephone systems. The surcharge may not exceed 35¢ per access line per month, nor may it be imposed on more than 75 access lines per customer per location. Lifeline customers, public safety agencies, and municipalities that have enacted a surcharge are exempt from the surcharge. Telephone service suppliers must pay the surcharge on a monthly basis, and are entitled to retain an administrative fee equal to 2% of its collections. The surcharge will not be considered in the determination of gross income or gross operating income of the corporation for purposes of the additional tax on utility services. (Sec. 303, County Law; Sec. 304, County Law; Sec. 305, County Law; Sec. 306, County Law)

New York City surcharges are discussed at ¶580-310. The New York state wireless communications service surcharge is discussed at ¶80-445.

[¶80-540] Erie County Transportation Business Tax

Erie County is authorized to imposing an additional tax on utility companies. The tax is similar to the state tax imposed under Sec. 186-a, Tax Law, except that the tax may not be less than $1/_2$%, nor more than $3/_4$% of the utility's gross income or gross operating income, as the case may be, that is attributable to Erie County. (Sec. 186-d, Tax Law)

INSURANCE

[¶88-000]

INSURANCE

[¶88-010] Companies Subject to Tax

Non-life insurance corporations are subject to a premiums tax under Tax Law Sec. 1502-a, as well as the MTA surcharge.

Life insurance corporations are subject to several taxes: (1) a tax measured by allocated entire net income (or by one of three alternative bases if a higher tax results) under Tax Law Sec. 1502(a); (2) a tax on subsidiary capital under Tax Law Sec. 1502(b); (3) a tax on premiums under Tax Law Sec. 1510(b)(1); and (4) the MTA surcharge. For life insurance corporations, Tax Law Sec. 1505(a)(2) sets a limitation on the tax amount, and Tax Law Sec. 1505(b) sets a floor limitation on the tax.

For details, see ¶88-020, Basis of Tax, and ¶88-030, Rates.

For purposes of the tax imposed by Article 33, an "insurance corporation" includes a corporation, association, joint stock company or association, person, society, aggregation or partnership, by whatever name known, doing an insurance business. (Sec. 1500(a), Tax Law) It further includes a risk retention group, the state insurance fund, and a corporation, association, joint stock company or association, person, society, aggregation or partnership doing an insurance business as a member of the New York Insurance Exchange. Certain captive insurance companies, unauthorized insurers, and health maintenance organizations (HMOs) are also included in the definition.

• *Unauthorized insurance corporations*

The Department of Taxation and Finance has issued a memorandum providing guidance on the filing requirements and tax calculation for unauthorized insurance corporations (i.e., those that do not have a certificate of authority to conduct an insurance business in New York). (TSB-M-12(4)C)

Life insurance corporations.—Because unauthorized life insurance corporations are not subject to the additional premiums tax imposed under Sec. 1510(b)(1), the tax on such corporations is not limited by Sec. 1505(a)(2). Accordingly, unauthorized life insurance corporations are required to pay the tax on the highest of the four bases plus any applicable tax on allocated subsidiary capital computed pursuant to Sec. 1502. For taxable years beginning on or after January 1, 2012, these taxes are not limited pursuant to Sec. 1505(a)(2).

Non-life insurance corporations.—Tax Law Sec. 1502-a imposes a tax on premiums in lieu of the taxes imposed under Sec. 1501 (and computed under the provisions of Sec. 1502) on every non-life insurance corporation authorized by the Superintendent of Insurance to transact business in New York, on risk retention groups, and on for-profit HMOs. The provisions of Sec. 1502-a do not apply to unauthorized non-life insurance corporations that are not risk retention groups or HMOs. Therefore, unauthorized non-life insurance corporations that are not risk retention groups or HMOs are subject to tax under Sec. 1501 and must compute their tax due under Sec. 1502. Therefore, unauthorized non-life insurance corporations that are not risk retention groups or HMOs are required to pay the tax on the highest of the four bases plus any applicable tax on allocated subsidiary capital pursuant to Sec. 1502.

• *Captive REITs and RICs*

The 2008 budget legislation added provisions relating to the combination of a captive REIT or a captive RIC with a corporation subject to tax under Sec. 1501 of Article 33 (life insurance corporation), as well as the determination of entire net income of a captive REIT or captive RIC included in a combined return. (Sec. 1515(f)(4) and (5), Tax Law)

The insurance franchise tax provisions parallel amendments made under the Article 9-A general corporation franchise tax. (TSB-M-08(12)C)

These amendments were originally to have been repealed January 1, 2011, for taxable years beginning on or after that date, but were made permanent by the 2010 budget legislation.

• *HMOs*

The 2009-10 budget changed how for-profit HMOs are taxed effective for taxable years beginning on or after January 1, 2009. For-profit HMOs are now subject to the franchise tax on insurance corporations under Article 33 of the Tax Law rather than the corporate franchise tax under Article 9-A of the Tax Law. For-profit HMOs are subject to tax on the higher of two bases: a tax on premiums or a fixed dollar minimum tax. Previously, for-profit HMOs were not taxed on premiums. The law also provides that non-profit HMOs remain exempt from tax and that taxable premiums do not include premiums that New York is prohibited from taxing under federal law. (Tax Law Sec. 1502-a; Sec. 1510(c), Tax Law; TSB-M-09(7)C)

• *Surplus lines brokers and nonadmitted insurance*

A tax is imposed on excess line brokers where New York is the insured's home state. (Sec. 2118(d), Insurance Law)

In addition, a special tax is imposed under Article 33-A on independently procured insurance. For taxable insurance contracts having an effective date on or after July 21, 2011, the tax is imposed on any person whose home state is New York and who purchases or renews a taxable insurance contract from an insurer not authorized to transact business in New York under a certificate of authority from the Superintendent. (Sec. 1551, Tax Law; TSB-M-11(7)C)

The term "home state" is defined in Tax Law Sec. 1550(d) and discussed in TSB-M-11(7)C.

If the taxable insurance contract covers risks located or resident both within and outside New York and the taxpayer's home state is New York, then 100% of the premiums are allocable to New York. (Sec. 1552, Tax Law)

Prior to enactment of the provisions discussed above, the tax under Article 33-A was based on premiums for risks located or resident in New York, irrespective of the location of the insured. In cases where premiums were paid for risks that were both within and outside New York, taxpayers were required to allocate the premiums and pay tax on the amount of premiums allocated to New York. (TSB-M-11(7)C)

• *Captive insurance companies*

Captive insurance companies are subject to a special tax on all gross direct premiums and assumed reinsurance premiums, less return premiums, written on risks located or resident in New York. (Sec. 1502-b, Tax Law) For details, see ¶ 88-030.

Captive insurance companies may not be required to file combined returns with their parent corporations. (Sec. 1515(f), Tax Law; Instructions, Form CT-33-C)

Combinable captive insurance companies.—A combinable captive insurance company is excluded from the definition of an insurance corporation that is subject to tax under Article 33. (Sec. 1500(a), Tax Law) Such corporations are now required to be included in a combined return under Article 9-A with the closest controlling stockholder. (TSB-M-09(9)C; Instructions, Form CT-33-C)

• *Retaliatory taxes*

New York has retaliatory provisions that subject out-of-state insurance companies to not less than the rates of tax that their home states impose on New York insurance companies. (Sec. 1112, Insurance Law)

Credit against retaliatory taxes.—Where retaliatory taxes are assessed, the out-of-state insurance company is to be given a credit for any taxes paid under Article 33, Tax Law. (Sec. 1511(b), Tax Law)

The New York Court of Appeals held that a statutory provision (former Sec. 1505-a(d)(8), Tax Law) that prohibited foreign insurers from including Metropolitan Commuter Transportation District surcharges in the computation of retaliatory taxes is unconstitutional. In *United Services Automobile Association v. Curiale,* the Court held that, absent a legitimate purpose, a state may enforce a retaliatory tax only to the extent that it aims to equalize the tax burden of domestic and foreign insurers. The generation of revenue is not a legitimate public purpose. Noting the domestic insurance companies could include the Metropolitan Commuter Transportation Tax when calculating their retaliatory taxes imposed by other states, the Court concluded that denying a credit to foreign insurers against retaliatory taxes for the amount of the surcharge produced retaliation beyond the point of equalization and, therefore, violated the federal equal protection clause.

For the text of *United Services Automobile Association.*

Credit for Retaliatory Taxes Paid to Other Jurisdictions.—If an insurance company organized or domiciled in New York is required to pay retaliatory taxes to a foreign state for the privilege of doing business there, a credit is allowed against New York insurance franchise taxes in an amount equal to 90% of such retaliatory tax. (Sec. 1511(c), Tax Law) The credit may not be greater than the insurance franchise tax payable for the taxable year with respect to which the retaliatory tax has been imposed. To the extent that the credit exceeds the amount of the insurance franchise tax payable for the taxable year, the difference between the amount allowed as a credit and the tax payable will be credited or refunded, without interest.

The credit is claimed on Form CT-33-R.

"Retaliatory tax" defined: A retaliatory tax is a tax that a New York insurance company is required to pay to a foreign state because the corporate and insurance franchise taxes that are imposed by New York upon foreign insurers are greater than those required of domestic New York insurers by the foreign state for the privilege of doing business there. (Sec. 1511(c), Tax Law)

Credit for retaliatory Sec. 2807-t taxes paid to other jurisdictions.—A credit is allowed to New York domiciled corporations that are required to pay retaliatory taxes to other jurisdictions as a result of amounts required to be paid to New York by foreign corporations pursuant to Sec. 2807-t, Public Health Law. (Sec. 1511(i), Tax Law) The amount of the credit may not exceed 90% of the amount of the retaliatory taxes required to be paid. In addition, the credit may not be greater than the insurance franchise tax payable for the taxable year with respect to which the retaliatory tax has been imposed. To the extent that the credit exceeds the amount of the insurance franchise tax payable for the taxable year, the difference between the amount allowed as a credit and the tax payable will be credited or refunded, without interest.

Documentation in support of credit required: Insurers claiming the credit must attach to their returns a computation identifying the credit attributable to taxes paid to other states because of the amounts imposed and required to be paid pursuant to

Sec. 2807-t, Public Health Law. The computation must reflect amounts and taxable years to which the retaliatory taxes giving rise to the credit relate.

[¶88-015] Exemptions

The taxes imposed on insurance corporations by Article 33 of the Tax Law do not apply to the following:

(1) Federal, state and local governments and instrumentalities thereof;

(2) Any charitable, religious, missionary, educational or philanthropic nonstock corporation exempted by the Insurance Law in effect immediately prior to January 1, 1940;

(3) Any retirement system or pension fund which does exclusively an annuity business;

(4) Any nonprofit medical expense indemnity or hospital service corporation;

(5) Any incorporated or unincorporated fraternal benefit society or, in the event of the conversion of any such society into a mutual life insurance company or the reinsurance of the business of such society by the Superintendent of Insurance pursuant to an order of liquidation, premiums payable under insurance benefit certificates issued by such society prior to the conversion or reinsurance;

(6) Any domestic corporation for the insurance of domestic animals on the cooperative or assessment plan;

(7) A town or county cooperative insurance corporation;

(8) Any not-for-profit voluntary employees' beneficiary association which is exempt for federal income tax purposes;

(9) Any nonprofit property/casualty insurance company organized under Insurance Law Sec. 6703; and

(10) A nonprofit HMO required to obtain a certificate of authority under Public Health Law Art. 44. (Sec. 1512(a), Tax Law)

A person is not subject to tax merely because the person stores advertising on a server or other computer equipment located in New York State, or has advertising disseminated or displayed on the Internet. However, this exemption does not apply when the server or other computer equipment located in New York State is owned or leased by such person. (TSB-M-97(1.1)C, TSB-M-97(1.1)S)

• *Premiums tax*

Premiums from the following types of insurance are excluded or deducted in determining premiums subject to tax (Sec. 1510(c), Tax Law; Instructions, Form CT-33; Instructions, Form CT-33-NL):

(1) Annuity contracts;

(2) Joint underwriting of group health insurance for persons 65 years of age or older under Sec. 4236, Insurance Law;

(3) Ocean marine insurance.

Other exemptions.—In addition to the above, the tax on premiums does not apply to the following (Sec. 1512(b), Tax Law):

(1) Any insurance on property or risks located or resident outside New York written by a nonprofit fire or life insurance company organized and operated exclusively for the benefit of charitable, religious, missionary, educational or philanthropic institutions on insurance and annuity contracts issued to and for the benefit of such institutions for their employees and members of the immediate families of such employees.

(2) Any insurance on risks resident outside New York written by a nonprofit life insurance company exempt from federal income tax, organized to establish a non-profit voluntary employees beneficiary association and operated to provide life, sick, accident or other benefits to eligible employees or their beneficiaries.

(3) Except in the case of foreign and alien title insurance corporations, premiums (other than those for accident and health insurance) written, procured or received in New York for insurance on property or risks located or resident outside the United States.

• *Member of the New York Insurance Exchange*

The franchise tax, the premiums tax, and the additional franchise tax do not apply to any corporation, association, joint stock company or association, person, society, aggregation or partnership doing an insurance business as a member of the New York Insurance Exchange. (Sec. 1512(c), Tax Law) Corporations, associations, persons, societies, aggregations or partnerships must compute an allocated entire net income (See ¶ 88-020 for allocation of entire net income) and transmit a return to the Commissioner of Taxation and Finance.

The New York Insurance Exchange itself is exempt from taxes, except that direct premiums written by exchange members on risks within New York are reportable by the Exchange, which must pay the tax. (Sec. 6302, Insurance Law)

[¶88-020] Basis of Tax

For non-life insurance corporations, the tax is based on all gross direct premiums, less return premiums thereon, written on risks located or resident in New York. (Sec. 1502-a, Tax Law)

For life insurance corporations, the applicable tax bases and allocation provisions are discussed under the bullet headings below.

Captive insurance companies.—The tax on captive insurance companies is based on gross direct premiums and assumed reinsurance premiums, less return premiums, written on risks located or resident in New York. (Sec. 1502-b, Tax Law; Instructions, Form CT-33-C)

Independently procured insurance.—The tax on independently procured insurance is based on the premiums paid (or to be paid), less returns. (Sec. 1551, Tax Law; TSB-M-11(7)C)

If the taxable insurance contract covers risks located or resident both within and outside New York and the taxpayer's home state is New York, then 100% of the premiums are allocable to New York. (Sec. 1552, Tax Law)

For a discussion of the term "taxable insurance contract", see TSB-M-11(7)C.

• *Entire net income base*

The entire net income of a taxpayer is its total net income from all sources, which is presumably the same as the life insurance company taxable income (see information below concerning stock life insurance companies), taxable income of a partnership or taxable income, but not alternative minimum taxable income, which the taxpayer is required to report to the U.S. Treasury Department, for the taxable year or, in the case of a corporation exempt from federal income tax (other than the tax on unrelated business taxable income imposed under IRC Sec. 511) but not exempt from New York insurance tax under Sec. 1501, the taxable income which the taxpayer would have been required to report but for such exemption, except for certain modifications. (Sec. 1503(a), Tax Law)

Under the 2019 budget legislation, the definition of entire net income (ENI) was amended for certain stock life insurance companies to conform to a change made to the Internal Revenue Code in the Tax Cuts and Jobs Act. ENI for stock life insurance companies that have an existing policyholder's surplus account no longer includes the amount of direct and indirect distributions during the tax year to shareholders from that account. Instead, one-eighth of the balance in an existing policyholder's surplus account, as determined as of the close of the company's last taxable year beginning before January 1, 2018, is included in ENI. The change is effective for taxable years beginning on or after January 1, 2018, through taxable years beginning on or before January 1, 2025. (*TSB-M-19(3)C*)

Bonus depreciation.—For taxable years beginning after 2002, and applicable to property placed in service on or after June 1, 2003, the New York insurance franchise tax is decoupled from federal accelerated depreciation provisions, except with respect to qualified Resurgence Zone property and qualified New York Liberty Zone property. (Sec. 1503(b)(1)(R), (b)(2)(T), (b)(14), (15), and (16), Tax Law)

GILTI.—For taxable years beginning after 2018, a subtraction is allowed for 95% of the income required to be included in the taxpayer's federal gross income under IRC Sec. 951A(a), without regard to the IRC Sec. 250 deduction, generated by a corporation that is not part of the taxpayer's combined report. (Sec. 1503(b)(1)(U), Tax Law)

A subtraction is also allowed for any amount treated as a dividend received by the taxpayer under IRC Sec. 78 that is attributable to the GILTI. (Sec. 1503(b)(1)(V), Tax Law)

An addition modification is required for the amount of the federal deduction allowed under IRC Sec. 250(a)(1)(B). (Sec. 1503(b)(2)(Y), Tax Law)

QPAI deduction.—Under the 2008 budget legislation, applicable to taxable years beginning after 2007, an addition modification is required for the IRC § 199 deduction for qualified production activities income. (Sec. 1503(b)(2)(U), Tax Law)

Note: As a result of the Tax Cuts and Jobs Act, the federal domestic production activities deduction (DPAD) under IRC § 199 is repealed for tax years beginning after 2017.

Related member expenses.—New York requires an addition for certain royalty payments made to a related member. (Sec. 1503(b)(14), Tax Law) These anti-PIC (passive investment company) provisions, also referred to as expense disallowance provisions, are similar to the corporate franchise tax provisions; see the detailed discussion at ¶ 10-620.

See also TSB-M-03(8)C.

Exception for combined returns: Under the 2007 budget legislation, there is an exception from the addback requirement for any taxpayer included in a combined return with a related member under Sec. 1515(f). (Sec. 1503(b)(14), Tax Law)

Exclusions from entire net income.—The following are not included in the computation of entire net income (Sec. 1503(b)(1), Tax Law; Sec. 1503(b)(10), Tax Law):

(1) Income, gains and losses from subsidiary capital which do not include the amount of a recovery in respect of any war loss;

(2) 50% of dividends other than from subsidiaries, except that in the case of a life insurance company, such modification applies only with respect to the company's share of the dividends (percentage obtained by dividing the company's share of the net investment income for the taxable year by the net investment income for the taxable year);

(3) Any refund or credit of tax imposed under Article 33 (tax on insurance companies) or the special mortgage recording tax credit in effect, to the extent properly included as income for federal income tax purposes, for which no exclusion

or deduction was allowed in determining the taxpayer's entire net income under Article 33 for any prior year;

(4) The portion of wages or salaries paid or incurred for the taxable year for which a deduction is not allowed under IRC Sec. 280-C (relating to certain expenses for which credits are allowable);

(5) In the case of a taxpayer who is separately, or as partner of a partnership, doing an insurance business as a member of the New York Insurance Exchange, any item of income, gain, loss or deduction of such business which is the taxpayer's distributive or pro rata share for federal income tax purposes or which the taxpayer is required to take into account separately for federal income tax purposes;

(6) Except with respect to property which is a qualified mass commuting vehicle described in IRC Sec. 168(f)(8)(D), any amount which is included in the taxpayer's taxable income for federal income tax purposes solely as a result of an election made pursuant to IRC Sec. 168(f)(8), as it was in effect for agreements entered into prior to January 1, 1984;

(7) Except with respect to property which is a qualified mass commuting vehicle described in IRC Sec. 168(f)(8)(D), any amount which the taxpayer could have excluded from its taxable income for federal income tax purposes had it not made the safe harbor lease election under IRC Sec. 168(f)(8), as it was in effect for agreements entered into prior to January 1, 1984;

(8) Except with respect to property subject to the provisions of IRC Sec. 280-F (concerning luxury automobiles) and property subject to the provisions of IRC Sec. 168 (concerning the federal accelerated cost recovery system) which is placed in service in New York in taxable years beginning after December 31, 1984, and provided a deduction has not been excluded from the determination of entire net income for amounts claimed as a deduction for federal income tax purposes solely as a result of safe harbor lease election, as it was in effect for agreements prior to January 1, 1984, a taxpayer is allowed with respect to property which is subject to the provisions of IRC Sec. 168 (concerning the federal accelerated cost recovery system), the depreciation deduction allowable under IRC Sec. 167 as such section would have applied to property placed in service on December 31, 1980. With regard to property placed in service outside New York State in tax years 1985—1993, taxpayers may elect to utilize either the IRC Sec. 167 or 168 depreciation deduction (TSB-M-99(1)I and (1)C.);

(9) Upon the disposition of property subject to the provisions of IRC Sec. 168, except for property subject to the provisions of IRC Sec. 280-F (concerning luxury automobiles) and property subject to the provisions of IRC Sec. 168 (concerning the federal accelerated cost recovery system) which is placed in service in New York in taxable years beginning after December 31, 1984, and provided a deduction has not been excluded from the determination of entire net income for the amounts made solely as a result of a safe harbor lease election, the amount, if any, by which the aggregate of the amount allowed as a deduction determined under IRC Sec. 168 exceeds the amount allowable as a depreciation deduction under IRC Sec. 167;

(10) The amount of unearned premiums on outstanding business at the end of the taxable year included in premiums earned under IRC Sec. 832(b)(4)(B);

(11) The amount of unearned premiums on outstanding business at the end of the taxable year included in premiums earned under IRC Sec. 832(b)(7)(B)(i);

(12) The amount included in premiums earned under IRC Sec. 832(b)(8)(A)(i), which is the difference between the amount of discounted unearned premiums on outstanding business at the end of the taxable year and the amount of unearned premiums on outstanding business at the end of the taxable year;

(13) For taxable years beginning after December 31, 1986 and before January 1, 1992, the amount of unearned premiums on outstanding business included in premiums earned under IRC Secs. 832(b)(4)(C) and 832(b)(7)(b)(ii);

(14) The amount which is the difference between the amount of discounted unpaid losses at the end of the taxable year used in the computation of losses incurred under IRC Sec. 832(b)(5)(A), and the amount of unpaid losses that would be used in such computation for the taxable year if the losses were not discounted under IRC Sec. 846(a);

(15) The amount by which losses incurred as defined in IRC Sec. 832(b)(5)(A) are reduced in accordance with IRC Sec. 832(b)(5)(B);

(16) The amount included in federal gross income pursuant to IRC Secs. 847(5) and (6);

(17) Repatriated income under IRC § 965 received from a corporation not included in a combined report with the taxpayer (but an addback is required for the amount of the federal deduction allowed under IRC § 965(c));

(18) Any amount excepted, for purposes of IRC Sec. 118(a), from the term "contribution to the capital of the taxpayer" by IRC Sec. 118(b)(2);

(19) An attorney-in-fact for a reciprocal insurer or a mutual insurance company that is an interinsurer subject to tax under Sec. 1510(a) is provided with a subtraction from federal taxable income in computing entire net income, if the reciprocal insurer or interinsurer has made the election provided for under IRC Sec. 835. (TSB-M-03(2)C and TSB-M-03(1)I) The subtraction is the difference between the amount paid or incurred in the tax year by the reciprocal insurer or interinsurer to the AIF, and the deduction allowed to the insurer pursuant to the IRC Sec. 835 election. (TSB-M-03(2)C and TSB-M-03(1)I) In addition, there are limited exceptions to the secrecy provisions to facilitate the administration of the AIF subtraction from federal taxable income. (TSB-M-03(2)C and TSB-M-03(1)I)

Inclusions in entire net income.—Entire net income is determined without the exclusion, deduction or credit of, (Sec. 1503(b)(2), Tax Law):

(1) The amount of any specific exemption or credit allowed in any law of the United States imposing any tax on, or measured by, the income of corporations;

(2) Any part of any income from dividends or interest on any kind of stock, securities or indebtedness;

(3) Taxes paid or accrued to the United States on, or measured by, income or premiums;

(4) Taxes imposed under Article 33 (tax on insurance companies) and taxes imposed before June 1, 1990, under Article 13-A (petroleum business tax);

(5) In those instances where a credit for the special mortgage recording tax is allowed, the amount allowed as an exclusion or deduction for the special mortgage recording tax in determining the entire net income which the taxpayer is required to report to the U.S. Treasury department for such taxable year;

(6) Unless the special mortgage recording tax credit is reflected in the computation of the gain or loss so as to result in an increase in the gain or a decrease in the loss, for federal income tax purposes, from the sale or other disposition of the property with respect to which the special additional mortgage recording tax was paid, the amount of the special mortgage recording tax which was paid and which is reflected in the computation of the basis of the property;

(7) 90% of interest on indebtedness directly or indirectly owed to any stockholder or shareholder (including subsidiaries of a corporate stockholder or shareholder), or members of the immediate family of an individual stockholder or shareholder,

owning in the aggregate in excess of 5% of the issued capital stock of the taxpayer, except that such interest may be deducted:

(a) Up to an amount not exceeding $1,000;

(b) In full to the extent that it is paid to a federally licensed small business investment company or to the extent that it relates to bonds or other evidences of indebtedness issued, with stock, under a bona fide plan of reorganization, to persons who, prior to such reorganization, were bona fide creditors of the corporation or its predecessors, but were not stockholders or shareholders;

(8) In the discretion of the Commissioner of Taxation and Finance, any amount of interest directly or indirectly and any other amount directly attributable as a carrying charge or otherwise to subsidiary capital or to income, gains, or losses from subsidiary capital (or to repatriated income or GILTI);

(9) In the case of a life insurance company, the inclusion of any part of income from dividends or interest on any kind of stock, securities or indebtedness does not apply to the policyholder's share (100% of the excess above the percentage obtained by dividing the company's share of the net investment income for the taxable year by the net investment income for the taxable year);

(10) In the case of a taxpayer who is separately, or as a partner of a partnership, doing an insurance business as a member of the New York Insurance Exchange, the taxpayer's distributive or pro rata share of the allocated entire net income of the business as determined under Secs. 1503 and 1504, Tax Law, provided, however, that in the event that such allocated entire net income is a loss, the taxpayer's distributive or pro rata share of the loss is not subtracted from federal taxable income in computing entire net income;

(11) Except with respect to property which is a qualified mass commuting vehicle described in IRC Sec. 168(f)(8)(D), any amount which the taxpayer claimed as a deduction for federal income tax purposes solely as a result of the safe harbor lease election made under IRC Sec. 168(f)(8), in effect for agreements entered into prior to January 1, 1984;

(12) Except with respect to property which is a qualified mass commuting vehicle under IRC Sec. 168(f)(8)(D), any amount which the taxpayer would have been required to include in the computation of its taxable income for federal income tax purposes had it not made the election permitted under IRC Sec. 168(f)(8), in effect for agreements entered into prior to January 1, 1984;

(13) In the case of property placed in service in taxable years beginning before 1994, except with respect to property subject to the provisions of IRC Sec. 280-F (relating to luxury automobiles) and property subject to the provisions of IRC Sec. 168 (concerning the federal accelerated cost recovery system) which is placed in service in New York in taxable years beginning after December 31, 1984, the amount allowable as a deduction determined under IRC Sec. 168;

(14) Upon the disposition of property subject to the provisions of IRC Sec. 168 (concerning the federal accelerated cost recovery system) which is placed in service in New York in taxable years beginning after December 31, 1984, and provided a deduction has not been excluded for the safe harbor lease election made for federal income tax purposes, as it was in effect for agreements entered into prior to January 1, 1984, a taxpayer is allowed, with respect to property which is subject to the provisions of IRC Sec. 168, the depreciation deduction allowable under IRC Sec. 167, as such section would have applied to property placed in service on December 31, 1980;

(15) The amount of unearned premiums on outstanding business at the end of the preceding year excluded from premiums earned under IRC Sec. 832(b)(4)(B);

(16) The amount of unearned premiums on outstanding business at the end of the preceding year excluded from premiums earned under IRC Sec. 832(b)(7)(B)(i);

(17) The amount excluded from premiums earned under IRC Sec. 832(b)(8)(A)(i) which is the difference between the amount of discounted unearned premiums on outstanding business at the end of the taxable year and the amount of unearned premiums on outstanding business at the end of the preceding taxable year;

(18) The amount which is the difference between the amount of discounted unpaid losses at the end of the preceding federal taxable year used in the computation of losses incurred for the taxable year under IRC Sec. 832(b)(5)(A), and the amount of unpaid losses at the end of the preceding taxable year that would have been used in the computation for the taxable year if such losses were not discounted under IRC Sec. 846(a) (Sec. 1503(b)(2), Tax Law);

(19) The amount of the special deduction allowed for certain special estimated tax payments pursuant to IRC Sec. 847(1);

(20) For taxpayers claiming special estimated tax payment deductions, pursuant to IRC Sec. 847(1), in taxable years beginning after December 31, 1987, and ending before January 1, 1993, the amount included in federal gross income, pursuant to IRS Secs. 847(5) and (6), for taxable years beginning after December 31, 1992, as a result of the deduction claimed in taxable years beginning after December 31, 1987, and before January 1, 1993, divided by 3 (Sec. 1503(b)(11), Tax Law). This quotient is included in the taxpayers' entire net income for the first three taxable years beginning on or after January 1, 1993.

(21) The amount of the federal deduction allowed under IRC §965(c) (i.e. the repatriated income deduction);

(22) The amount of the federal deduction allowed under IRC §250(a)(1)(A) (i.e., foreign-derived intangible income (FDII)).

Subtraction from federal base—Interest on indebtedness.—In determining entire net income, a subtraction is allowed, to the extent not deductible in determining federal taxable income, for (Sec. 1503(b)(3), Tax Law): (1) interest on indebtedness incurred or continued to purchase or carry obligations or securities, the income from which is subject to tax under Article 33 (tax on insurance companies), but exempt from federal income tax; (2) ordinary and necessary expenses paid or incurred during the taxable year attributable to income which is subject to the tax on insurance companies, but exempt from federal income tax; and (3) the amortizable bond premium for the taxable year on any bond, the interest on which is subject to tax under Article 33, but exempt from federal income tax.

Net operating loss deduction.—Any "net operating loss deduction" or "operations loss deduction" allowable under IRC Secs. 172 or 810, respectively, which is allowable to the taxpayer for federal income tax purposes must be adjusted to reflect other modifications required in computing entire net income and may not exceed any deduction allowable to the taxpayer for the taxable year for federal income tax purposes. (Sec. 1503(b)(4), Tax Law) Additionally, it may not include any loss incurred in a taxable year beginning prior to January 1, 1974, or during any taxable year in which the taxpayer was not subject to the franchise tax.

Property acquired prior to January 1, 1974.—In the case of property of a taxpayer acquired prior to January 1, 1974, and disposed of thereafter, the computation of entire net income is modified as follows (Sec. 1503(b)(5), Tax Law):

(1) no gain is deemed to have been derived if either the cost or the fair market price or value on January 1, 1974, exceeds the value realized;

(2) No loss is deemed to have been sustained if either the cost or the fair market price or value on January 1, 1974, is less than the value realized; and

(3) Where both the cost and the fair market price or value on January 1, 1974, are less than the value realized, the basis for computing gain is the cost, the fair market price or value on that date, whichever is higher; and

(4) Where both the cost and the fair market price or value on January 1, 1974, are in excess of the value realized, the basis for computing the loss is the cost, the fair market price or value on that date, whichever is lower.

Capital loss carryforward.—An exclusion from the computation of entire net income is allowed, for any amount allowed as a deduction for federal income tax purposes for the taxable year under IRC Sec. 1212 as a capital loss carryforward to the taxable year which resulted from a capital loss occurring, in any taxable year in which the taxpayer was not subject to the franchise tax on insurance companies. (Sec. 1503(b)(6), Tax Law)

Income or gain from the sale of real or personal property.—There is excluded from the computation of entire net income the amount of any income or gain from the sale of real or personal property which is includable in determining federal taxable income for the taxable year under the installment method under IRC Sec. 453, to the extent the income or gain is from a sale of the property which occurred in a taxable year when the taxpayer was not subject to the franchise tax on insurance companies. (Sec. 1503(b)(7), Tax Law)

Gain from emerging technology investments.—The gain from the sale of any emerging technology investment acquired on or after March 12, 1998, and held for more than 36 months will be recognized for New York State insurance company franchise (income) (and corporate franchise (income), bank franchise (income), and personal income) tax purposes only to the extent that the gain realized exceeds the cost of any qualified emerging technology investment purchased by the taxpayer within 365 days from the date of the sale (Sec. 1503(b)(12), Tax Law, Ch. 56 (S.B. 6094-B), Laws 1998). The amount deferred will be added to federal taxable income when the reinvestment is sold (Sec. 1503(b)(13), Tax Law, Ch. 56 (S.B. 6094-B), Laws 1998).

Alternative tax for certain small companies.—Entire net income is computed without regard to IRC Sec. 831(b) (alternative tax for certain small companies). (Sec. 1503(b)(8), Tax Law)

Additional modifications.—In computing the entire net income of a fire or life insurance company organized and operated, without profit to any private shareholder or individual, exclusively for purposes of aiding and strengthening charitable, religious, missionary, educational or philanthropic institutions, by issuing insurance annuity contracts only to or for the benefit of the institutions, to individuals engaged in the services of the institutions and to members of the immediate families of such individuals, or a life insurance company which has been organized for purposes of establishing a nonprofit voluntary employees' beneficiary association to provide life, sick, accident or other benefits to eligible employees or their beneficiaries, and is operated exclusively for those purposes and without profit to any private shareholder or individual, and is duly exempt from federal income taxation, the life insurance taxable income (which includes, in the case of a stock life insurance company which has an existing policyholders' surplus account, the amount of direct and indirect distributions during the taxable year to shareholders from such account) or taxable income, as the case may be, of such taxpayer is computed without regard to any income, gains, losses, deductions, reserves, surplus or any other items, derived from, or attributable or allocable to, contracts described in IRC Sec. 1818(a). (Sec. 1503(b)(9), Tax Law)

Attribution of income to different taxable years.—The Commissioner of Taxation and Finance may, whenever necessary in order to reflect the entire net income of any taxpayer, determine the year or period in which any item of income or deduction must be included, without regard to the method of accounting employed by the taxpayer. (Sec. 1503(c), Tax Law)

• *Business and investment capital base*

The business and investment capital base is one of the alternative bases (entire net income, income-plus-salaries, minimum tax being the others) to utilize for computation if a greater tax will result. (Sec. 1502(a), Tax Law)

Investment capital defined.—The term "investment capital" means investment in stocks, bonds, and other securities, corporate and governmental, not held for sale to customers in the regular course of business, exclusive of subsidiary capital and stock issued by the taxpayer. (Sec. 1500(i), Tax Law) However, the Commissioner of Taxation and Finance has the discretion to deduct from investment capital any liabilities payable by their terms on demand or within one year from the date incurred, other than loans or advances, outstanding for more than a year as of any date during the year covered by the return, which are attributable to investment capital.

Business capital defined.—The term "business capital" means all assets, other than subsidiary capital, investment capital and stock issued by the taxpayer, less liabilities not deducted from subsidiary capital or investment capital which are payable on demand or within one year from the date incurred, other than loans or advances outstanding for more than a year beyond a date during the year covered by the return, except that cash on hand and on deposit is treated as investment or as business capital, as the taxpayer may elect. (Sec. 1500(j), Tax Law)

Reserves.—The fair market value of assets and investments held to maintain reserves required under Secs. 1303, 1304 and 1305, Insurance Law, is excluded in determining business and investment capital subject to tax. (Sec. 1500(i), Tax Law; Sec. 1500(j), Tax Law) If a company does not set aside, and therefore cannot identify, specific assets and investments held to maintain reserves, the fair market value of assets and investments held to maintain reserves must be calculated by multiplying the average value of reserves required under Secs. 1303, 1304 and 1305, Insurance Law, as reported on the annual statement filed with the Superintendent of Insurance, by the ratio of the fair market value of admitted and non-admitted assets to the average value of admitted and non-admitted reported on the annual statement. (TSB-M-93(3)C)

• *Income plus salaries base*

The income-plus-salaries base provides an alternative to the entire net income, business and investment capital, or minimum tax bases if a higher tax will result. It is computed on the basis of 9% on 30% of the taxpayer's entire net income, plus salaries and other compensation paid to the taxpayer's elected or appointed officers and every stockholder owning more than 5% of its issued capital stock, minus $15,000 and any net loss for the reported year, or the portions of the sum allocated within New York. (Sec. 1502(a), Tax Law)

• *Fixed dollar minimum tax*

The flat fee minimum tax for any period (exclusive of the tax measured by subsidiary capital) is $250, and is applicable if it will result in a higher tax than that computed utilizing one of the other bases. (Sec. 1502(a)(4), Tax Law)

For purposes of the Sec. 1502-a tax on premiums, a $250 minimum tax amount also applies. (Sec. 1502-a)

• *Subsidiary capital base*

The tax on subsidiary capital is computed on 0.8 of a mill for each dollar on the portion of the taxpayer's subsidiary capital allocated within New York. (Sec. 1502(b), Tax Law)

¶88-020

The term "subsidiary capital" means investment in the stock of subsidiaries and any indebtedness from subsidiaries, exclusive of accounts receivable acquired in the ordinary course of trade or business for services rendered or for sales of property held primarily for sale to customers, whether or not evidenced by a written instrument, on which interest is not claimed and deducted by the subsidiary for purposes of taxation under Article 60, Tax Law. (Sec. 1500(h), Tax Law) However, the Commissioner of Taxation and Finance has the discretion to deduct from subsidiary capital any liabilities payable by their terms on demand within one year from the date incurred, other than loans or advances outstanding for more than one year beyond any date during the taxable year covered by the return, which are attributable to subsidiary capital.

The tax on subsidiary capital is imposed in addition to the tax on the alternative bases discussed above.

• *Life insurance premiums*

The life insurance premiums tax is based on gross direct premiums, less return premiums, written on risks resident in New York. (Sec. 1510(b), Tax Law)

Premium defined.—The term "premium" includes all amounts received as consideration for insurance or reinsurance contracts, other than for annuity contracts, and includes premium deposits, assessments, policy fees, membership fees and every other compensation for the contract. (Sec. 1510(c)(1), Tax Law)

Determination of direct premiums.—In ascertaining the amount of direct premiums upon which tax is payable, a determination must first be made of the amount of total gross premiums or deposit premiums or assessments, less returns, on all policies, certificates, renewals, policies subsequently canceled, insurance and reinsurance executed, issued or delivered on property or risks located or resident in New York, including premiums written, procured or received in the state on business which cannot specifically be allocated or apportioned and reported as taxable premiums, or which have been used as a measure of a tax on business of any other state. In the case of special risk premiums, direct premiums include only those premiums written, procured or received in New York on property or risks located or resident in the state. The reporting of premiums for the purpose of the tax is on a written basis or on a paid-for basis consistent with the basis required by the annual statement filed with the Superintendent of Insurance.

Premiums not included in "gross direct premiums".—The term "gross direct premiums" does not include premiums for joint policies underwriting group health insurance for persons aged 65 and over, and premiums for insurance upon hulls, freights, or disbursements, or upon goods, wares, merchandise and all other personal property and interests, in the course of exportation from or importation into any country, or transportation coastwise, while being prepared for and awaiting shipment, and during any delays, storage, transshipment or reshipment incident thereto, including war risks and marine builder's risks. (Sec. 1510(c)(2), Tax Law)

Deductions.—After determining the amount of total gross premiums, less return premiums thereon, the following items are deducted:

(1) premiums, less return premiums thereon, which have been received by way of reinsurance from corporations or other insurers authorized to transact business in New York;

(2) certain reinsurance premiums received from insurers not authorized by the Superintendent of Insurance to transact business in New York (to qualify for the deduction, the reinsurance premiums must relate to transactions authorized under Insurance Law Sec. 2105 and be subject to the premiums tax on excess line brokers under Insurance Law Sec. 2118)—see also *TSB-M-03(3)C*, and *TSB-M-03(3.1)C*;

(3) dividends on such direct business, including unused or unabsorbed portions of premium deposits paid or credited to policyholders, but not including deferred dividends paid in cash to policyholders on maturing policies, nor cash surrender values. (Sec. 1510(c)(3), Tax Law)

Allocation of premiums.—In determining the amount of direct premiums taxable in New York, all such premiums written, procured or received in the state are deemed written on property or risks located or resident in New York, except premiums properly allocated or apportioned and reported as taxable or which have been used as a measure of a tax of any other state. However, in the case of special risk premiums, direct premiums include only those premiums written, procured or received in New York on property or risks located or resident within the state. (Sec. 1510(c)(4), Tax Law)

• *Allocation*

The portion of a taxpayer's entire net income to be allocated within New York State is the amount determined by multiplying such income by the income allocation percentage as follows (Sec. 1504(a), Tax Law):

(1) ascertaining the percentage which the taxpayer's New York premiums for the taxable year bear to the taxpayer's total premiums for the taxable year, and multiplying that percentage by nine;

(2) ascertaining the percentage which total wages, salaries, personal service compensation and commissions for the taxable year of employees, agents and representatives of the taxpayer within New York, bear to the total wages, salaries, personal service compensation and commissions for the taxable year of all the taxpayer's employees, agents and representatives;

(3) adding the amounts determined under (1) and (2) and dividing the sum by ten.

If it should appear to the Commissioner of Taxation and Finance that the income allocation percentage does not properly reflect the activity, business or income of a taxpayer within the sate, the Commissioner has the discretion to adjust it by (Sec. 1504(d), Tax Law):

(1) excluding one or more factors;

(2) including one or more other factors, such as expenses, purchases, receipts other than premiums, real property or tangible personal property;

(3) or any other similar or different method calculated to effect a fair and proper allocation of the income and capital reasonably attributable to New York.

Business and Investment Capital Base Allocation.—The portion of the taxpayer's business and investment capital to be allocated within New York State is determined by multiplying the amount by the allocation percentage (see discussion above). (Sec. 1504(c), Tax Law)

Income and Salaries Base Allocation.—The income-plus-salaries base is allocable as provided for entire net income (see discussion above). (Sec. 1502(a)(3))

Subsidiary Capital Base Allocation.—The portion of the taxpayer's subsidiary capital to be allocated within New York State is determined as follows (Sec. 1504(c)(2), Tax Law):

(1) Multiplying the capital invested in each subsidiary during the period covered by the return by the percentage of the entire capital, issued capital stock, or net income of such subsidiary allocated within New York on the returns filed by the subsidiary during the preceding year; and

(2) Adding together the products obtained.

[¶88-025] Deductions

Return premiums are excluded from taxation. (Sec. 1502-a, Tax Law; Sec. 1510(b), Tax Law)

After determining the amount of total gross premiums, less return premiums thereon, the following items are deducted:

(1) premiums, less return premiums thereon, which have been received by way of reinsurance from corporations or other insurers authorized to transact business in New York;

(2) certain reinsurance premiums received from insurers not authorized by the Superintendent of Insurance to transact business in New York (to qualify for the deduction, the reinsurance premiums must relate to transactions authorized under Insurance Law Sec. 2105 and be subject to the premiums tax on excess line brokers under Insurance Law Sec. 2118)—see also *TSB-M-03(3)C*, and *TSB-M-03(3.1)C*;

(3) dividends on such direct business, including unused or unabsorbed portions of premium deposits paid or credited to policyholders, but not including deferred dividends paid in cash to policyholders on maturing policies, nor cash surrender values. (Sec. 1510(c)(3), Tax Law)

See ¶88-020, Basis of Tax, for further discussion, including modifications applicable to the entire net income tax base for life insurance corporations.

[¶88-030] Rates

For non-life insurance corporations, the premium tax is imposed at the rate of 1.75% for accident and health insurance contracts and 2% for other non-life insurance premiums. The tax may not be less than $250. (Sec. 1502-a, Tax Law)

For life insurance corporations, the various applicable rates are noted below.

First, the franchise tax on life insurance corporations is the greatest of the following (Sec. 1502, Tax Law):

(1) 7.1% of the taxpayer's allocated entire net income, or portion thereof allocated within New York State, for the taxable year; or

(2) 1.6 mills for each dollar of the taxpayer's total business and investment capital allocated within New York State for the taxable year; or

(3) 9% on 30% of the taxpayer's entire net income plus salaries and other compensation paid to the taxpayer's elected or appointed officers and to every stockholder owning in excess of 5% of its issued capital stock minus $15,000 and any net loss for the reported year, or the portion of the sum allocated within New York State; or

(4) $250;

plus 0.8 of a mill for each dollar of the taxpayer's subsidiary capital allocated within New York for the taxable year.

In addition, life insurance corporations are required to pay a 0.7% tax on gross direct premiums, less return premiums. (Sec. 1510(b), Tax Law)

Floor limitation.—For life insurance corporations, there is a minimum floor limitation on the tax pursuant to Tax Law Sec. 1505(b)—i.e., the total franchise tax prior to the application of credits cannot be less than 1.5% of the premiums subject to tax under Sec. 1510. (TSB-M-03(9)C)

Maximum tax.—For life insurance corporations, there is also a maximum tax limitation pursuant to Sec. 1505(a)(2)—i.e., the tax cannot exceed an amount equal to the premium tax computed under Sec. 1510, calculated at the rate of 2%.

If more than 95% of an insurance corporation's premiums are received as consideration for annuity contracts or are for policies and insurance described in Sec. 1510(c)(2), Tax Law, then in determining the amount of tax computed solely under Sec. 1510 gross direct premiums subject to tax under that section include such amounts received as consideration for annuity contracts and premiums for policies and insurance, including any separate costs assessed by the corporation upon its policyholders, described in (c)(2) of that section that exceed 95% of all premiums received, including consideration for annuity contracts and premiums for policies and insurance (and any separate costs assessed on policyholders) described in (c)(2) of that section. (Sec. 1505(c), Tax Law)

Sec. 1505(c), Tax Law, does not define the term "premiums" for purposes of the 95% determination. However, in two advisory opinions, the Department of Taxation and Finance has held that, since the limitation contained in Sec. 1505 is based on the amount of tax that would be computed under the premiums tax imposed under Sec. 1510, it is appropriate to use the definition contained in the first sentence of Sec. 1510(c)(1), modified as required by Sec. 1505(b), [now 1505(c)] for purposes of computing the limitation. Accordingly, in *Royal Life Insurance Company of New York*, the Department held that the term "premiums" includes all amounts received as consideration for insurance contracts or reinsurance contracts, including annuity contracts, and includes premium deposits, assessments, policy fees, membership fees, any separate costs by carriers assessed upon their policyholders and every other compensation for such contract. Similarly, in *John Alden Life Insurance Company of New York* and *First Alexander Hamilton Life Insurance Company*, the Department noted that the term includes all amounts received as consideration for reinsurance contracts, regardless of whether the insurer paying the reinsurance premiums is licensed to transact business in New York or is an affiliated insurer. The term also includes all direct premiums received by an insurance company, both on risks resident in New York and outside of New York.

• *Captive insurance companies*

The tax on captive insurance companies is imposed on all gross direct premiums at a rate of 0.4% on all or any part of the first $20 million of premiums, 0.3% on all or part of the second $20 million of premiums, 0.2% on all or part of the third $20 million of premiums, and 0.075% on each dollar of premiums thereafter. (Sec. 1502-b, Tax Law)

Further, the tax imposed on assumed reinsurance premiums is 0.225% on all or any part of the first $20 million of premiums, 0.150% on all or any part of the second $20 million of premiums, 0.050% on all or any part of the third $20 million of premiums, and 0.025% on each dollar of premiums thereafter. (Sec. 1502-b, Tax Law)

The tax cannot be less than the minimum tax of $5,000. (Sec. 1502-b, Tax Law; Instructions, Form CT-33-C)

Captive insurance companies are not subject to the MTA surcharge. (Instructions, Form CT-33-C)

No credits can be claimed against the tax. (Instructions, Form CT-33-C)

• *Excess line brokers and independently procured insurance*

The tax on independently procured insurance is imposed at the rate of 3.6%. (Sec. 1551, Tax Law; TSB-M-11(7)C)

The rate of 3.6% also applies to excess line brokers. (Sec. 2118(d), Insurance Law)

• *HMOs*

For-profit HMOs are subject to tax on the higher of two bases: a tax on premiums or a fixed dollar minimum tax of $250. The premiums tax is imposed at a rate of

1.75% on accident or health premiums, and 2% on any other premiums. For-profit HMOs are also subject to the MTA surcharge. (Tax Law Sec. 1502-a; Sec. 1510(c), Tax Law; TSB-M-09(7)C)

• *MTA Surcharge*

Note: The surcharge was made permanent by the 2014 budget legislation.

Domestic, foreign or alien insurance corporations and life insurance corporations exercising their corporate franchise, doing business, employing capital, or owning or leasing property in the Metropolitan Commuter Transportation District for all or any part of their taxable years commencing after 1981 must pay annually a tax surcharge equal to 17% of the tax imposed. The surtax is taken after the deduction of any credits otherwise allowable, as allocated to the District. Even though the franchise tax rate and tax cap for insurance companies were reduced effective July 1, 2000, the surcharge continues to be calculated as though the franchise tax rate is 9% and the tax cap is 2.6%. (Sec. 1505-a, Tax Law)

The Metropolitan Commuter Transportation District includes the City of New York and Counties of Dutchess, Nassau, Orange, Putnam, Rockland, Suffolk and Westchester. (Sec. 1263, Public Authorities Law)

Allocation of taxes to District.—For the method of allocating taxes to such District for purposes of computing the tax surcharge for life insurance companies, see ¶ 85-351. For non-life insurance companies subject to the premiums tax under Sec. 1502-a, a special allocation provision applies. (Sec. 1505-a(2), Tax Law) See also TSB-M-03(8)C.

If it should appear to the Commissioner of Taxation and Finance that the application of the methodology, procedures and computation do not properly reflect the activity, business or income of a taxpayer within the Metropolitan Commuter Transportation District, the Commissioner is authorized to adjust the methodology, procedures and computation for the purposes of allocating such taxes by:

(1) excluding one or more of the factors;

(2) including one or more of the factors, such as expenses, purchases, receipts other than premiums, real property or tangible personal property; or

(3) any other similar or different method which allocates taxes by attributing a fair and proper portion of the taxes to the Metropolitan Commuter Transportation District. (Sec. 1505-a, Tax Law)

Credit for retaliatory taxes paid to other states.—Any insurer which is organized or domiciled in New York State and subject to the business tax surcharge and which is required to pay retaliatory insurance business privilege taxes in other states because of the surcharge, is allowed a credit for the taxes paid to the other states. (Sec. 1505-a, Tax Law)

An insurer claiming a credit is required to attach to the returns a computation identifying the credit attributable to taxes paid to other states because of the tax surcharge, broken down to reflect amounts and taxable years to which the retaliatory taxes giving rise to the credit relate.

The credit attributable to taxes paid to other states because of the tax surcharge is the difference between:

(1) the credit which would be claimed by the insurer if the tax surcharge were permitted in the computation of the credit; and

(2) the credit which is claimed by the insurer.

No credit against taxes paid to other jurisdictions is allowed for any surcharge paid by domestic insurance corporations, including life insurance corporations subject to tax.

Note: In *United Services Automobile Association v. Curiale,* the New York Court of Appeals ruled that the statutory provision prohibiting foreign issuers from including Metropolitan Commuter Transportation District surcharges in the computation of retaliatory taxes was unconstitutional.

PRACTICE AND PROCEDURE

[¶89-100]

RETURN FILING AND PAYMENT OF TAX

[¶89-102] Returns and Payments in General

The return filing and payment requirements for New York corporate franchise, personal income, and sales and use taxes are summarized here.

Tax return preparers are authorized to use alternative methods (i.e., rubber stamp, mechanical device, or computer software program) in signing original tax returns, amended tax returns, refund claims, and requests for extension of time to file. This policy applies to tax returns, amended tax returns, refund claims, and requests for extension of time to file for all other taxes and fees administered by the New York Department of Taxation and Finance. (*TSB-M-05(1)C, TSB-M-05(1)I, TSB-M-05(1)S*, and *TSB-M-05(1)M*, February 1, 2005)

What returns must be filed in New York?

Corporate franchise tax. Every domestic and foreign corporation or other entity doing business, employing capital, owning or leasing property, maintaining an office, or deriving receipts from activity in New York is required to file an annual franchise tax return. All general business corporations must file corporate franchise tax returns using Form CT-3, General Business Corporation Franchise Tax Return, or Form CT-3-A for combined groups. (Instructions, Form CT-3, New York General Business Corporation Franchise Tax Return) In addition, every corporation that continues in business after it is dissolved is required to file an annual return.

Consolidated returns/combined reports. New York does not allow the filing of a consolidated return except for corporate shareholders of a tax-exempt DISC, who file consolidated reports with the DISC on Form CT-3C. Certain affiliated unitary corporations are permitted or required to file combined reports.

Short period returns. A taxpayer that is not part of a federal consolidated group but becomes part of such a group on a day other than the first day of the taxpayer's federal taxable year must file a short period return. Short period returns are also required when a taxpayer ceases to be part of a federal consolidated group or leaves one group to join another. A short period return may also be required of a target corporation whose entire stock was purchased by another corporation.

Information returns. A foreign corporation, which is not a taxpayer, but which has an employee, including any officer, within New York, must file an information report. An exempt DISC is also required to file an information report.

Final report. Every taxpayer that ceases to exercise its franchise or to be subject to the corporation franchise tax must file a report with the Commissioner on the date of cessation or at such other time as the Commissioner may require covering any period for which a report was previously not filed.

Attachments. A complete copy of the taxpayer's federal return must be attached to the New York return. (Instructions, Form CT-3, New York General Business Corporation Franchise Tax Return)

Pass-through entities.

S corporations. Every federal S corporation for which an election to be treated as a New York S corporation is in effect must file a New York return if the corporation does business, employs capital, owns or leases property, or maintains an office in the state. New York S corporations must file Form CT-3-S, New York S Corporation Franchise Tax Return.

> **Attachments.** Taxpayers must attach a copy of the following: (1) federal Form 1120S as filed; (2) Form CT-34-SH; (3) Form CT-60, if applicable; (4) any applicable credit claim forms, and (5) Form CT-225, if applicable. (Form CT-3-S, New York S Corporation Franchise Tax Return)

Partnerships. Every partnership having a resident partner or having any income derived from New York sources must file a New York return on Form IT-204, Partnership Return.

> **Attachments.** A copy of federal Form 1065 is no longer required to be attached to the New York return. (*Important Notice N-08-1*)

LLCs. New York conforms with the federal classification of LLCs and, thus, an LLC that is treated as a partnership for federal income tax purposes will be treated as a partnership for New York corporate income tax purposes. LLCs treated as partnerships must file Form IT-204, Partnership Return. Domestic or foreign LLCs that are required to file a New York partnership return are also required to file Form IT-204-LL, Limited Liability Company/Limited Liability Partnership Filing Fee Payment Form. (*TSB -M-*) Form IT-204-LL may not be attached to Form IT-204.

LLPs. New York conforms with the federal classification of LLPs and, thus, an LLP that is treated as a partnership for federal income tax purposes will be treated as a partnership for New York corporate income tax purposes. Partnerships must file Form IT-204, Partnership Return. Domestic or foreign LLPs that are required to file a New York partnership return are also required to file Form IT-204-LL, Limited Liability Company/Limited Liability Partnership Filing Fee Payment Form. (*TSB-M-11(4)C*, New York Department of Taxation and Finance, April 8, 2011)

SMLLCs. A single member limited liability company (SMLLC) must file Form IT-204-LL, Limited Liability Company/Limited Liability Partnership Filing Fee Payment Form.

Information returns. When an entity has elected to be excluded from the partnership provisions of IRC Sec. 761 and state and federal partnership returns are not required, but where federal information returns (IRS Form 1099) are required to be filed, similar information returns may be required to be furnished to New York.

Composite returns. A New York pass-through entity is permitted to file a New York group nonresident personal income tax return on behalf of its qualified nonresident shareholders, partners, or members who elect to have the entity file on their behalf. For S corporations, a group return may be filed if 11 qualified shareholders elect to be included and prior approval is obtained. Participants must have the same accounting period. (Instructions, Form IT-203-S, Group Return for Nonresident Shareholders of New York S Corporations) For partnerships, Form IT-203-GR is used. Form TR-99, Application for Permission to File a Group Return, should be used by a New York pass-through entity to request permission to file a group nonresident return.

Exempt organizations. Exempt organizations that have unrelated business income are required to file a New York business income tax return on Form CT-13.

Attachments. A complete copy of the federal return must be attached to the New York return. (Form CT-13) For additional attachment requirements, see "Amended returns" and "Reporting federal audit changes" below.

Amended returns. A taxpayer filing an amended return must mark an "X" in the *Amended return* box on the top of Form CT-13. If an amended federal return is filed, the taxpayer must file an amended New York return within 90 days. (Sec. 211(3), Tax Law; Instructions, Form CT-13)

To claim a credit or refund resulting from the carryback of an NOL to a prior year, a taxpayer must file an amended return within 90 days from the date of the document indicating approval of the federal refund or credit. The following must be attached to the amended return: (Instructions, Form CT-13)

— federal claim Form 1139, *Corporation Application for Tentative Refund*, or federal amended Form 990-T, *Exempt Organization Business Income Tax Return*;

— a copy of the New York return for the loss year; and

— proof of federal refund approval, *Statement of Adjustment to Your Account*.

To claim any refund type that requires an amended return, other than an NOL carryback, a taxpayer must file an amended New York return for the year being amended and, if applicable, attach a copy of the claim form filed with the IRS (usually amended Form 990-T) and proof of federal refund approval, *Statement of Adjustment to Your Account*. (Instructions, Form CT-13)

Reporting federal audit changes. If a taxpayer's federal unrelated business taxable income has been changed or corrected by a final determination of the Commissioner of Internal Revenue, the taxpayer must file an amended New York return reflecting the federal changes within 90 days of the final federal determination. (Sec. 211(3), Tax Law; Reg. Sec. 6-1.3)

A copy of federal Form 4549, *Income Tax Examination Changes*, must be attached to the amended return. (Instructions, Form CT-13)

Personal income tax. Form IT-201 is the New York resident income tax return. Nonresidents and part-year residents use Form IT-203.

An income tax return must be filed for every resident individual:

(1) required to file a federal income tax return for the taxable year;

(2) having federal adjusted gross income for the taxable year in excess of $4,000, or in excess of the individual's New York standard deduction, if lower;

(3) subject to the minimum income tax; or

(4) having received during the taxable year a lump sum distribution any portion of which is subject to the separate tax on the ordinary income portion of a lump sum distribution.

A return must be filed by every nonresident or part-year resident individual:

(1) having New York source income for the taxable year, and having federal adjusted gross income for the taxable year, increased by the amounts required to be added to federal adjusted gross income, in excess of the individual's standard deduction;

(2) subject to the minimum income tax; or

(3) having received during the taxable year a lump sum distribution any portion of which is subject to the separate tax on the ordinary income portion of a lump sum distribution.

Attachments. The following federal forms and schedules must be attached to the state return if relevant: Form 4797; Schedules C, C-EZ, D, E, and F. (Instructions, Form IT-201)

Information returns. The Commissioner of Taxation and Finance is authorized to prescribe regulations and instructions requiring information returns to be made and filed as to the payment or crediting in any calendar year of amounts of $600 or more to any taxpayer. The returns may be required of any person having the control over the payment of interest, rents, salaries, wages, premiums, annuities, compensations, remunerations, emoluments or other fixed or determinable gains, profits or income.

Estates or trusts. Returns must be filed by every resident estate or trust:

(1) required to file a federal income tax return for the taxable year;

(2) having any New York taxable income for the taxable year;

(3) subject to the minimum income tax; or

(4) having received during the taxable year a lump sum distribution any portion of which is subject to the separate tax on the ordinary income portion of a lump sum distribution.

A nonresident estate or trust or part-year resident trust must file a return if it:

(1) has New York source income for the taxable year;

(2) is subject to the minimum income tax; or

(3) has received during the taxable year a lump sum distribution any portion of which is subject to the tax on the ordinary income portion of a lump sum distribution.

Nonresident groups cannot include any estates or trusts in their nonresident group returns. The filing of a nonresident group return is considered a group of separate returns that meets the individual filing requirements under New York's personal income tax. (*Important Notice N-09-5*, Department of Taxation and Finance, March 2009)

Husband and wife. Generally, the New York filing status of a husband and wife is determined by the filing status selected for federal income tax purposes. Accordingly, separate New York returns are normally required if separate federal income tax returns are filed, and joint New York returns are required if federal tax liability is determined on the basis of a joint return. If no federal returns are filed, a husband and wife may elect to file either joint or separate New York returns.

Missing/alienated spouses. Separate New York returns may be required, notwithstanding the filing of a joint federal tax return, where one spouse demonstrates that the address or whereabouts of the other spouse is unknown, reasonable efforts have been made to locate the missing spouse, and good cause exists for the failure to file a joint New York return. Separate returns may also be required if a spouse demonstrates that the other spouse has refused to sign a joint New York return, reasonable efforts have been made to have the spouse sign the return, objective evidence of alienation of the spouse exists, and good cause exists for the failure to file a joint New York return.

Election to be treated as New York resident. Where one spouse is a resident and the other a nonresident or part-year resident, separate New York returns are required unless (1) a joint federal return is filed and (2) both spouses elect to determine their joint New York taxable income as if both were residents.

Nonresident spouse without New York source income. New York cannot require a nonresident without New York source income to file a joint New York return solely because his or her nonresident spouse earned New York source income and the couple filed a joint federal tax return. In *Brady v. State of New York,* the New York Court of Appeals held that out-of-state cohabitation with a spouse having New York income and the filing of a joint federal income tax return by the couple was not sufficient to establish the necessary minimum connection for the extraterritorial exercise of New York's taxing power.

COMMENT: *Department of Taxation and Finance interpretation of Brady.*— The New York Department of Taxation and Finance has interpreted *Brady* as holding that a nonresident spouse without New York source income cannot be required to sign a joint return and cannot be held liable for tax, penalty or interest that may be due. Accordingly, a joint New York return is still required where a joint federal return has been filed and (1) both spouses are nonresidents but only one has New York source income or (2) one spouse is a part-year resident and the other is a nonresident with no New York source income. Where these conditions are met, only the spouse with New York source income (or the part-year resident spouse) should sign the return. (*Important Notice N-92-31*, Department of Taxation and Finance, December 1992)

Group nonresident income tax return for nonresident partners. A partnership required to file a New York State partnership return may be granted approval to file a group New York State nonresident personal income tax return on behalf of 10 or more qualified partners who elect to have the partnership file on their behalf. The same rules apply for a LLP, or LLC treated as a partnership for federal tax purposes.

Qualified electing nonresident partners. Qualified electing nonresident partners are allowed to make the election to file on a group basis.

Group nonresident income tax return for nonresident professional athletes. A professional athletic team may request permission to file a group income tax return on behalf of its qualified nonresident athletes who elect to participate in the group return instead of each athlete filing a New York personal income tax return. All members participating in the group return must have the same accounting period.

Group nonresident returns for nonresident shareholders of New York S corporations. A New York S corporation is permitted to file a New York group nonresident personal income tax return on behalf of its qualified nonresident shareholders who elect to have the S corporation file on their behalf. The rules pertaining to group filing for partnerships and nonresident partners are applicable to such S corporations.

Group returns for nonresidents with New York source income from more than one source. A nonresident person who would otherwise qualify to participate in a group return, except that the nonresident (or a spouse) has New York source income from sources other than the group, is permitted to participate in the group return if:

(1) the income from other sources is only from a partnership, professional athletic team, New York S corporation, or other group that files a proper group return;

(2) the nonresident properly participates in the group return for each partnership, professional athletic team, New York S corporation, or group for the tax year; and

(3) the nonresident person, if deriving New York City or City of Yonkers source income from more than one source, elects to waive the right to claim the exclusion against the total wages and total net earnings from self-employment for purposes of the City of New York or City of Yonkers nonresident earnings taxes, and so informs any entity that is authorized to make, file, or execute the group returns that report such New York City or City of Yonkers source income on behalf of the nonresident.

A nonresident may not participate in more than 10 group returns for any taxable year.

Decedents. The personal income tax return for any deceased individual must be filed by his executor, administrator, or other person charged with his property.

Minors, incompetents, and other persons under a disability. The personal income return for a person who is unable to make a return by reason of minority or other disability must be made and filed by the individual's guardian, conservator, committee, fiduciary or other person charged with the care of the individual's person or property (other than a receiver in possession of only a part of the individual's property), or by the individual's duly authorized agent. A minor may file his or her own return.

Fiduciary income tax. Fiduciary income tax returns are filed on Form IT-205, Fiduciary Income Tax Return.

Withholding tax. Every employer required to deduct and withhold tax is required to file a withholding return. Withholding return forms may be accessed at https://www.tax.ny.gov/forms/withholding_cur_forms.htm.

Filing requirement. All employers required to withhold tax from wages are required to file Form NYS-45, Quarterly Combined Withholding, Wage Reporting, and Unemployment Insurance Return, each calendar quarter (Sec. 674(a)(4), Tax Law). If less than $700 is withheld during a calendar quarter, the employer should remit taxes withheld with its quarterly return, Form NYS-45. If $700 or more is withheld during a calendar quarter the employer must remit the tax with Form NYS-1, Return of Tax Withheld, within 3 or 5 business days after the payroll that caused the accumulated tax withheld to equal or exceed $700.

Effective for calendar quarters beginning on or after January 1, 2019, employers are required to complete all of Part C, *Employee wage and withholding information*, including columns d and e, each calendar quarter for all employees. (TSB-M-18(4)I) Previously, employers were required to report annual wage and withholding totals for every employee they employed during the year on the last Form NYS-45 filed for the calendar year.

Additional information is provided on the Department's withholding tax site.

Seasonal employers. An employer who, due to the seasonal nature of its business, does not make payment of wages that are subject to both federal and New York income tax withholding to any employee during a calendar quarter, is not required to file either Part A or Part B of the quarterly combined withholding and wage reporting return for the calendar quarter. However, such employers must, on or before the due date for filing the quarterly combined withholding and wage reporting return covering the last calendar quarter of the year, file the annual employee specific withholding reconciliation portion of Part B of the return.

If a seasonal employer discontinues business or permanently ceases to pay wages during the calendar year, the annual employee specific withholding reconciliation information must be furnished on the employer's final quarterly combined withholding and wage reporting return.

Sales and use tax. Every person required to register with the Department of Taxation and Finance, or who voluntarily registers, is required to file sales tax returns. This includes vendors, persons purchasing or selling tangible personal property for resale, persons selling petroleum products, and persons who purchase business assets from persons required to collect sales and use tax. Registered vendors must timely file a return even if they have no tax due during the filing period. (*Publication 750, A Guide to Sales Tax in New York State*, New York Department of Taxation and Finance)

Quarterly filing. Persons whose taxable receipts, amusement charges, or rents are less than $300,000, and distributors of petroleum products who sell less than 100,000 gallons in every quarter of the proceeding four quarters, must file a quarterly return on Form ST-100. Such persons can choose to file monthly returns in addition to the quarterly returns. In addition, the Department has the discretion to require a vendor that files only quarterly returns to file either short-form or long-form part quarterly returns. The quarters covered by the returns end on the last day of February, May, August, and November of each year.

Monthly filing. Persons whose taxable receipts, amusement charges, rents, and purchases subject to tax for one of the preceding four quarters total $300,000 or more, and distributors of petroleum products who sell 100,000 gallons or more, must file monthly returns in addition to quarterly returns. Vendors of petroleum products fuel that are not classified as distributors under Tax Law Article 12-A are required to file monthly returns only if taxable receipts for one of the preceding four quarters total $300,000 or more. All of the taxpayer's locations must be combined for purposes of determining taxable sales under the monthly filing requirements regardless of whether consolidated filing or separate filing for each location is used.

Monthly returns are filed on Form ST-809, which contains both the long-form and short-form returns. Tax calculated on the long form is based on actual sales figures for each month. Tax on the short form is calculated by taking $1/3$ of the tax paid for the corresponding quarter of the previous year. Taxpayers who have filed quarterly returns for the previous four quarters can file either the long form or the short form. All other taxpayers must file the long form.

Quarterly returns on Form ST-810 must be filed by all persons filing monthly returns and are used to reconcile the returns filed for the previous two months.

Annual filing. Persons who are required to register with the Department of Taxation and Finance only because they purchase or sell tangible personal property for resale and who are not required to collect or pay sales tax only have to file an information return annually on Form ST-101. Persons otherwise required to file quarterly returns whose total tax is $250 or less for the four quarterly periods ending May 31 can elect to file an annual return instead of the quarterly returns if the returns and payments for the four quarters ending May

31 of the previous year were filed and paid on time; and the total tax for the four quarters for which the election is being filed is reasonably expected not to exceed $250. The election to file an annual return must be filed no later than June 20 for the year starting June 1 and ending the following May 31. If the total tax due at any time during such year exceeds $250, the taxpayer must start filing quarterly returns.

Final returns. Vendors who ceases operation, sells the business, or changes the organizational form of the business must file a final return, clearly marked "Final Return" at the top. Final returns are generally filed on quarterly return forms (Form ST-100) and must cover the first day of the period in which the event occurred through the final day of business. Monthly filers are also required to file a final quarterly return.

Casual sales. Except for sales of motor vehicles, snowmobiles, vessels and all-terrain vehicles required to be registered or titled by the Department of Motor Vehicles, any person making a taxable sale of tangible personal property or services in New York, who is not required to file periodic returns, must collect the tax on the sale and file a report of casual sale.

When the property sold consists of a motor vehicle, snowmobile, vessel or all-terrain vehicle, and the seller is not a person required to file periodic returns, the seller should not collect the sales tax on the sale. Instead, the purchaser must pay any tax due to the county clerk, to the Commissioner of Motor Vehicles, or directly to the Department of Taxation and Finance.

Show vendors. Holders of a certificate of authority for show vendors are required to file a New York sales and use tax return whether or not the vender participated in a show or made any sales in the period covered by the return.

Show promoters. Each promoter of a show must submit a report of show, including the promoter's information, location of show and permit number, dates of show, all participating vendors and their information, and signature and date.

A separate listing is required of all vendors making tax exempt sales, including name, address, identification number, if any, and type of goods or services sold. However, vendors selling only nontaxable foods need not be listed.

The permit to operate a show must be surrendered with the report of show covering the last show for which the permit was issued.

Places of amusement. The Department of Taxation and Finance can require lessors of any place of amusement to file information returns showing all leases, subleases, and licenses granted to persons who make amusement charges.

Amended returns. An amended return is required if an amended federal return is filed or if a federal audit of the return changes any item of income or deduction or tax preference item. An amended partnership return must also be filed to correct any error on the original New York partnership return, whether or not an amended federal partnership return was filed for the year. Generally, amended returns are filed by denoting "Amended return" on the front page of the original return forms.

When are returns due?

If a due date falls on a Saturday, Sunday, or a day which is a legal holiday in New York, the filing will be timely if filed on the next business day.

Corporate franchise tax. Through tax year 2015, returns are required to be filed annually with the Department of Taxation and Finance on or before the 15th day of the third month following the close of the taxable year (March 15 for calendar-year taxpayers). For tax years beginning on or after January 1, 2016, the due date is the 15th day of the fourth month following the close of the taxable year (April 15 for calendar-year taxpayers). DISC reports are due by September 15, or by the 15th day of the 9th month following the end of the fiscal year.

Short period returns. Except for the filing of amended returns, the due dates for New York short period returns are the same as the due dates for the filing of federal short period returns.

Federal return changes. If the amount of any taxpayer's reported federal taxable income is changed or corrected by a final determination, the taxpayer is required to report to the Commissioner of Taxation and Finance such changed or corrected taxable income within 90 days after the final determination (120 days, in case of taxpayer making a combined report). Such taxpayers must also report the renegotiation of a federal government contract or subcontract that results in a change of federal taxable income or alternative minimum taxable income. The taxpayer must either concede the accuracy of a final determination or state why it is erroneous. Any deficiency notice issued in connection with the federal tax is a final determination unless a petition to redetermine has been filed in the U.S. Tax Court. If a petition is filed, the judgment of the court of last resort is the final determination. (Sec. 211(3), Tax Law; Reg. Sec. 6-1.3)

Any taxpayer which files an amended return with the Internal Revenue Service must file an amended return with the New York Commissioner of Taxation and Finance within 90 days. (Sec. 211(3), Tax Law; Reg. Sec. 6-1.4)

Pass-through entities.

S corporations. Returns must be filed within two-and-a-half months after the end of the reporting period (i.e., if reporting for the calendar year, the return is due by March 15). (Instructions, Forms CT-3-S, and CT-3-S-ATT, New York S Corporation Franchise Tax Returns and Attachment) Composite returns are due April 15. (Instructions, Form IT-203-S, Group Return for Nonresident Shareholders of New York S Corporations)

In the termination year of an S corporation (the year the corporation allows its S corporation election to lapse and become a C corporation), a return is filed for both the S short year and the C short year, which are treated as separate taxable years. The due date for the S short year is the same as that for the C short year. (Instructionss, Forms CT-3-S, and CT-3-S-ATT, New York S Corporation Franchise Tax Returns and Attachment)

Partnerships, LLCs, LLPs, and SMLLCs. Through tax year 2015, calendar year taxpayers' returns (Form IT-204) are due on April 15 following the end of the calendar year. Fiscal year returns are due the 15th day of the fourth month after the end of the tax year. For tax years beginning after 2015, the due date is the 15th day of the 3rd month following the close of the tax year (March 15 for calendar-year taxpayers). Form IT-204-LL, the Partnership, LLC, LLP Filing Fee Payment Form, is due on or before the 15th day of the 3rd month following the close of the tax year. (*TSB-M-11(4)C*, New York Department of Taxation and Finance, April 8, 2011) Group or composite returns are due on April 15. (Instructions, Form IT-203-GR)

Exempt organizations. Generally, the return is due on the 15th day of the fifth month following the close of the taxable year.

Personal income tax. Returns are due on or before April 15 for calendar-year taxpayers, and on or before the 15th day of the fourth month following the close of the calendar year for fiscal-year taxpayers. A due date, including a due date pursuant to an extension of time, which falls on a Saturday, Sunday or legal holiday in New York State is automatically extended to the next succeeding day which is not a Saturday, Sunday or legal holiday.

Information returns are due on or before February 28 of each year. If a final return of a decedent is for a fractional part of a year, the due date of the return is the 15th day of the fourth month following the close of the 12-month period which began with the first day of the fractional part of the year. The due date for the filing of a New York personal income tax return for a nonresident alien individual is the same as the due date for the nonresident alien's federal return.

Fiduciary income tax. Returns must be filed by April 15, or the 15th day of the 4th month after the close of the taxpayer's fiscal year. (Instructions, Form IT-205)

Withholding tax.

Returns after the making of any payroll where cumulative aggregate amount of withholdings not paid during calendar quarter is $700 or more. Employers who were required to remit a cumulative aggregate amount of at least $15,000 in withholding tax during the calendar year preceding the previous calendar year must make a withholding tax return and remittance after any payroll within three business days of such payroll. If the cumulative aggregate withholding tax amount was less than $15,000 during the calendar year preceding the previous calendar year the withholding tax return and remittance must be made within five business days following such payroll.

Returns and remittances on a quarterly basis (due one month after last day of calendar quarter). An employer who has deducted and withheld, but not paid over, a cumulative aggregate amount of less than $700 of withholding tax at the close of a calendar quarter must remit the tax with the quarterly combined withholding and wage reporting tax return as described above.

Education organizations and health care providers. Educational organizations and health care providers are required to make the return and remittance within five business days following such payroll, without regard to the amount of cumulative aggregate withholding tax during the calendar year preceding the previous calendar year.

The quarterly combined return is due no later than the last day of the month following the last day of each calendar quarter.

Employers making more than one payroll per week. In determining the applicability of filing and payment provisions, employers making more than one payroll per week generally must consider the last payroll made within the week. However, if the end of the calendar quarter occurs between the making of payrolls, any tax required to be deducted and withheld in those payrolls prior to the end of the quarter must be paid over with the quarterly combined return (if the criteria for returns and remittances on a quarterly basis are met) or on or before the third or fifth business day following the date of the last payroll in the quarter (depending upon the amount of the employer's required cumulative aggregate withholding during the calendar year preceding the previous calendar year).

Sales and use tax. Quarterly returns must be filed within 20 days after the end of the quarter. In other words, a quarterly return must be filed on March 20 (for the period December 1 of the prior year to the last day of February), June 20 (for the period March 1 through May 31), September 20 (for the period June 1 through August 31), and December 20 (for the period September 1 through November 30).

Monthly returns must be filed within 20 days after the end of month for which they are being filed. No monthly returns are required for months that end a quarter, i.e., February, May, August and November.

Annual returns must be filed no later than June 20.

Final returns. Final returns are due within 20 days after a vendor ceases operation, sells the business, or changes the organization form of the business.

Casual sales. Reports must be filed within 20 days from the date of the sale.

Amended returns.

Income tax. Any taxpayer that files an amended return with the Internal Revenue Service must file an amended return with the New York Department of Taxation and Finance within 90 days.

If the amount of any taxpayer's reported federal taxable income is changed or corrected by a final determination, the taxpayer is required to report to the Department such changed or corrected taxable income within 90 days after the final determination (120 days, in case of taxpayer making a combined report). Such taxpayers must also report the renegotiation of a federal government contract or subcontract that results in a change of federal taxable income or alternative minimum taxable income.

Sales and use tax. The Department can require a taxpayer to file an amended return within 20 days after notice. The amended return must contain the information specified in the notice.

Extensions.

Corporate franchise tax. The Department may grant a reasonable filing extension if good cause exists.

An automatic six-month filing extension is allowed if the taxpayer files an application for extension on the prescribed Form CT-5 and a properly estimated tax is paid by the regular due date. A filing extension does not extend the due date for payment of tax.

On or before the expiration of the automatic six-month extension of time for filing a report, the Department may grant additional three-month extensions of time for filing reports when good cause exists. No more than two additional three-month extensions of time for filing a report for any taxable year may be granted. An application for each additional three-month extension must be made in writing before the expiration of the previous extension.

S corporations. If the deadline cannot be met, taxpayers should file Form CT-5.4, Request for Six-Month Extension to File New York S Corporation Franchise Tax Return, and pay estimated franchise tax on or before the original due date of the return. Additional extensions will not be granted beyond six months. (Instructions, Forms CT-3-S, and CT-3-S-ATT, New York S Corporation Franchise Tax Returns and Attachment; Instructions, Form CT-5.4, Request for Six-Month Extension to File New York S Corporation Franchise Tax Return)

Partnerships, LLCs and LLPs. New York Form IT-370-PF must be filed by the due date of the return in order to receive an automatic extension. (Instructions, Form IT-370-PF) The automatic extension period for partnership returns is 6 months. (TSB-M-16(9)C, (7)I)

¶89-102

Exempt organizations. A taxpayer may request an extension of the filing date by completing and filing Form CT-5, Request for Six-Month Extension to File, and paying the tax due on or before the original due date of the return. (Instructions, Form CT-13)

Fiduciary income tax. An automatic 5 1/2-month extension (i.e., until September 30) may be obtained by filing Form IT-370-PF. (Instructions, Form IT-205; TSB-M-16(9)C, (7)I)

Personal income tax. An individual who is required to file a New York personal income tax return for any taxable year will be allowed an automatic six-month extension of time to file such return if an application is prepared on Form IT-370, Application for Automatic Extension of Time to File for Individuals. An extension may not exceed six months unless the taxpayer is abroad or in military service.

An automatic 90-day extension is available for paying personal income taxes or filing a personal income tax return when a taxpayer's spouse dies within 30 days prior to the April 15 deadline. No penalties or interest will be assessed or imposed upon a taxpayer during the extension.

Sales and use tax. An extension of time for filing a return of up to three months may be granted for good cause shown. The application for the extension must be in writing and must explain why the extension is needed. If the extension is granted, the taxpayer must file a "tentative" return on the ordinary due date, showing an estimated amount of tax due, remit the total estimated tax, file a "completed" return on or before the extended due date, and remit the total tax less the total tax previously paid, if any.

How and when are tax payments made?

Payments are generally due at the time of the return. See Payment Methods for additional information, including information on Electronic Funds Transfer (EFT) payments.

Corporate franchise tax. Any amount due that is in excess of the estimated tax payments that have been made is paid with the annual return or with the taxpayer's final report in the case of a taxpayer ceasing to exercise its franchise.

Withholding tax. When filing a combined quarterly return, the employer must pay, in a single remittance, the unemployment insurance contributions and aggregate withholding taxes required to be paid with the return. Any overpayment of unemployment insurance contributions or aggregate withholding taxes made by an employer with the quarterly combined return may be credited only against the employer's liability for such contributions or taxes, respectively.

All taxpayers, except health care providers, required to deduct and withhold $35,000 or more of tax for either of the semi-annual periods ending June 30 or December 31 must pay tax through electronic fund transfers (EFT) or certified checks.

Where else can I find information on returns and payments?

New York tax calendars are found at ¶89-012 (annual schedule), ¶89-014 (quarterly schedule), and ¶89-016 (monthly schedule).

Additional information on returns and payments can be found at the following locations:

Estimated payments and returns

E-filing

Penalties and interest

Insurance companies, gross premiums

Property tax

Motor fuels tax

Cigarette and tobacco products tax

Severance tax

[¶89-104] Estimated Payments and Returns

New York requires estimated tax payments for corporate franchise, pass-through entity, and personal income taxes. Estimated sales and use tax payments are not required by the state, though prepayment of taxes may be required in certain circumstances. For a discussion of Metropolitan Commuter Transportation Mobility Tax (MCTMT) estimated payment requirements (including information on group returns for partners), see *TSB-M-09(1)MCTMT*, and *TSB-M-09(2)MCTMT*. For MCTMT estimated payment changes affecting self-employed individuals for tax years beginning on or after January 1, 2015, see *TSB-M-14(1)MCTMT*.

Are payments of estimated tax required?

Corporate franchise tax. Corporations subject to the corporation franchise tax under Article 9-A are required to file declarations of estimated tax if their tax liability for the taxable year can reasonably be expected to exceed $1000. (Instructions, Form CT-3, General Business Corporation Franchise Tax Return) The declaration must cover a calendar-year accounting period if the taxpayer files its report on the basis of a calendar year, or a full fiscal year if the taxpayer files a report on the basis of a fiscal year, unless a declaration for a short period is required. No declaration may be made for a period of more than 12 months.

If a taxpayer subject to the foregoing requirement is also subject to the Metropolitan Commuter Transportation District Surcharge, the taxpayer must also make a declaration of its estimated tax surcharge.

"Estimated tax" and "estimated tax surcharge" are defined as the amount of the tax and tax surcharge estimated to be imposed, respectively, under Sec. 209, Tax Law and Sec. 209-B, Tax Law, less estimated credits against the tax and tax surcharge.

Short periods. If a taxpayer is required to make a declaration of estimated tax and a short taxable year is involved, a declaration for the fractional part of the year is required. No declaration is required if the short taxable year is a period of five months or less.

Amended declaration. Amended or revised declarations may be made in any case in which the taxpayer finds that its estimated tax differs from the estimated tax reflected in its most recent declaration of estimated tax. However, an amended declaration may only be made on an installment date. No refunds will be issued as a result of the filing of an amended declaration.

Pass-through entities. Pass-through entities that have income from New York sources are required to pay estimated taxes on behalf of nonresident individual partners, members, shareholders, or C corporation partners on their distributive or pro rata shares of such income. (*TSB-M-04(1)I*; Instructions, Form IT-2658, Report of Estimated Tax for Nonresident Individual Partners and Shareholders; Instructions, Form CT-2658, Report of Estimated Tax for Corporate Partners)

These provisions do not apply with respect to a partner, member, or shareholder if the estimated tax required to be paid by the entity for that partner, member, or shareholder does not exceed $300 for the taxable year or if the partner, member, or shareholder has elected to be included in an authorized group return. In addition, the Commissioner may issue a waiver with respect to partners, members, or shareholders who are not subject to New York income tax (or who establish that they are filing New York income tax returns and paying estimated taxes when due) and in other circumstances when it is determined that withholding is not necessary to ensure collection of income tax on New York source income allocable to the nonresident or C corporation. (*TSB-M-04(1)I*) Further, estimated tax payments are not required for partners and shareholders who are resident S corporations, partnerships, limited liability partnerships (LLPs), or limited liability corporations (LLCs). (Instructions, Form IT-2658, Report of Estimated Tax for Nonresident Individual Partners and Shareholders; Instructions, Form CT-2658, Report of Estimated Tax for Corporate Partners)

The term "estimated tax" refers to a partner's, member's, or shareholder's distributive or pro rata share of the entity income derived from New York sources, multiplied by the highest rate of tax prescribed by Sec. 601, Tax Law for the taxable year for any partner, member, or shareholder who is an individual taxpayer, or by Sec. 210(1)(a), Tax Law for the taxable year for any partner, member, or shareholder that is a C corporation, and reduced by the distributive or pro rata share of certain credits derived from the entity.

There are no provisions specifically requiring withholding of estimated tax by pass-through entities.

Personal income tax. New York residents and part-year residents with New York source income are required to make annual payments of estimated tax when they expect to owe, after withholding and credits, New York, New York City or Yonkers tax for the current tax year, and their withholding and credits are expected to be less than the smaller of (a) 90% of the tax shown for the current tax year, or (b) 100% of the tax shown on the prior year's return (provided a return was filed and the taxable year consisted of 12 months).

Married taxpayers. A husband and wife may make joint or separate estimated tax payments, unless they are separated under a decree of divorce or separate maintenance or have different taxable years. If a joint payment is made, both spouses are jointly and severally liable for the payment of tax. If a joint payment is made but the parties file separate returns, the estimated tax for the year may be divided between them as they elect.

Trusts and estates. With two exceptions, trusts and estates must make estimated tax payments in the same manner as individuals. Estimated tax payments are not required if (1) an estate is within the first two years following the decedent's death; or (2) a grantor trust that is to receive the residue of a decedent's estate (or, if no will is admitted to probate, that is the trust primarily responsible for paying debts, taxes and expenses of administration) is within the first two years following the decedent's death.

Where estimated tax payments are required, a trustee may elect to treat any portion of an estimated tax payment by the trust as a payment made by a beneficiary of the trust. If the election is made, the amount paid must be treated as paid or credited to the beneficiary on the last day of the taxable year, and must be treated as a payment of estimated tax made by the beneficiary on the January 15th following the end of the trust's tax year. The election must be made on or before the 65th day following the close of the trust's tax year.

For estates and trusts that began after 1991 and use the annualized method of computing estimated tax installments, the annualization period must end one month prior to the due date of the installment. (*Important Notice N-92-15*)

Limitations on use of preceding year's tax. If the New York adjusted gross income shown on the return of an individual exceeds $150,000, the required annual payment will be the lesser of 90% of the tax shown on the return for the taxable year, or 110% of the tax shown on the return of the individual for the preceding taxable year. In the case of a husband and wife who file separate returns, the required annual payment will be the lesser of 90% of the tax shown on the return for the taxable year, or 110% of the tax shown on the prior year's return if New York adjusted gross income shown on the return exceeds $75,000.

Nonresident partners, S corporation shareholders, and LLC members. A partnership, LLP, S corporation, or LLC that has elected to file a group return on behalf of its nonresident partners, shareholders, or members may make estimated tax installments on behalf of the electing partners, shareholders, or members. However, should the entity determine that a member will not be participating or does not qualify, the entity is required to notify the Department of Taxation and Finance by the 15th day of the third month following the close of the taxable year to enable the Department to credit the installments to the individual member.

Professional athletes. A professional athletic team filing a group return for its nonresident members that otherwise would be required to file nonresident individual income tax returns may make estimated tax installments on behalf of the electing members in the same manner as partnerships.

Nonresidents selling real property. Nonresidents who sell certain New York real property, including cooperative units, are required to compute the gain and pay any estimated personal income tax due. (Sec. 663(a), Tax Law) The computation is done using the highest personal income tax rate. (Sec. 663(b), Tax Law) There are various exceptions (e.g., for sales of a principal residence). (Sec. 663(c), Tax Law)

How are payments of estimated tax made?

Corporate franchise tax. The amount of estimated corporate franchise tax due as shown on a declaration of estimated tax may be paid in installments or, at the election of the taxpayer, may be paid in full at the time of filing the declaration.

Corporations are generally required to make estimated tax payments during the year equal to 91% of the current year's tax, although higher payments are required of large corporations.

Pass-through entities. Pass-through entities may pay the entire amount due with the first payment, or pay in four equal installments. (*TSB-M-04(1)I*; Instructions, Form IT-2658, Report of Estimated Tax for Nonresident Individual Partners and Shareholders)

Any payment by an entity with respect to a partner, member, or shareholder who is an individual is deemed to be a payment of estimated tax by the partner, member, or shareholder. In addition, with respect to estimated tax payments made by an entity on behalf of taxpayers subject to tax under Article 9, Article 9-A, and Article 33, such taxpayers are permitted to apply the payments against their estimated tax under those articles.

Personal income tax. Estimated personal income taxes are generally due in four equal installments, though a taxpayer may elect to pay the entire amount of estimated tax with the filing of the return. However, fewer installments may be required depending upon when the individual meets the threshold for filing estimated tax.

For a nonresident selling real property, the estimated tax payment is made to the recording officer when the deed is presented for recording. (Sec. 663, Tax Law; Instructions, Form IT-2663) However, for a cooperative unit, the payment is mailed to the state tax department. (Sec. 663(i), Tax Law; Instructions, Form IT-2664)

What are due dates for estimated tax?

Corporate franchise tax. Declarations are due on or before June 15 for calendar-year taxpayers. However, if the requirements (that is, expected tax liability exceeding $1,000) are first met after May 31 and before September 1, the declaration is due on or before September 15; if requirements are first met after August 31 and before December 1, the declaration is due on or before December 15. Instead of the declaration due on December 15, these taxpayers may elect to file a completed report, with payment of any unpaid balance of tax by February 15. Corresponding dates apply to fiscal year taxpayers.

The amount of estimated tax due may be paid in full at the time of filing the declaration. If the taxpayer elects to pay estimated tax in installments, the first payment must accompany the declaration.

First installment. If the tax liability for the second preceding tax year is more than $1,000, the first installment of estimated tax for the current year is due using Form CT-300 on or before the 15th day of the 3rd month following the close of the taxable year (TSB-M-16(10)C). This first installment, generally 25% of the second preceding year's tax, is required regardless of the taxpayer's income forecasts for the current year. The first installment amount is 40% in cases where the second preceding year's tax exceeded $100,000. (*TSB-M-02(5)C*) For life insurance companies, the first installment is equal to 40% of the estimated tax due. (Instructions, Forms CT-400, Estimated Tax for Corporations)

This advance payment may be used to offset estimated tax payments if they are required. If not, the payment is credited against the tax due with the next annual report. Any overpayment of tax resulting from payment of the first installment is refunded with interest.

"Preceding year's tax," is defined as the tax imposed for the preceding calendar or fiscal year, or the amount estimated as the tax for the preceding year when an extension of time has been filed.

Other installments. For calendar-year taxpayers filing declarations on or before June 15, the amount of estimated tax is paid in three equal installments (after deducting the amount of any first installment based on the preceding year's tax liability) on June 15, September 15, and December 15. If the declaration is required to be filed on or before September 15, any estimated tax due (after deducting the amount of the first installment) is paid in two equal installments on September 15 and December 15. If the declaration is not required to be filed before September 15, any estimated tax due (after deducting the first installment) is paid at the time of filing the declaration. Corresponding dates apply to fiscal year taxpayers. Any installment may be paid prior to the due date.

Although the Commissioner may grant an extension of up to three months for payment of any installment, the delayed payment is subject to interest at the underpayment rate.

Pass-through entities. Estimated payments for pass-through entities are due on April 15, June 15, September 15, and January 15 of the next year. Entities may elect to pay the entire amount due with the first payment (April 15). The payments must be made by these dates whether the entity keeps its books on a calendar-year basis or a fiscal-year basis. (*TSB-M-04(1)I*; Instructions, Form IT-2658, Report of Estimated Tax for Nonresident Individual Partners and Shareholders; Instructions, Form CT-2658, Report of Estimated Tax for Corporate Partners)

Within 30 days after the estimated tax is paid, an entity is required to furnish a written statement to its partners, members, and shareholders showing the estimated taxes paid on their behalf. The statement must show that the payment is to be treated as a payment of estimated tax when the partners or shareholders file their New York returns; the statement cannot be a federal form W-2 or any other form or document that would indicate that the payment is income tax withheld. (*Important Notice N-04-11*) The entity is also required to provide certain information to the Commissioner, including information necessary to identify the estimated tax paid by the entity for each partner, member, or shareholder.

Personal income tax. The dates upon which installments of estimated personal income tax become due are dependent upon when the requirements to make estimated tax payments are first met. For calendar-year taxpayers whose requirements are met before April 1, estimated tax payments are due in four equal installments on April 15, June 15, September 15, and January 15 of the following tax year. When the requirements to make estimated tax payments are first met after March 31 and before June 1, 50% of the required annual payment is due on June 15, 25% is due on September 15, and 25% is due on the following January 15. When the requirements are met after May 31 and before September 1, 75% of the required annual payment is due on September 15, and 25% is due on the following January 15. Finally, when the requirements are met after August 31, 100% of the required annual payment is due on the following January 15.

Corresponding dates apply to fiscal-year taxpayers; that is, payments are generally due on the 15th day of the fourth, sixth, and ninth month of the current taxable year, and the 15th day of the first month of the following taxable year. Any installment may be paid before its due date.

Farmers and fishermen. Qualified farmers and fishermen may elect to make one payment of estimated tax, equal to 66 $2/3$% of their total tax liability, on January 15 of the following tax year. Alternatively, estimated tax payments will not be required if the New York return is filed, and total amount due is paid, on or before March 1.

An individual will be regarded as a farmer or fisherman for a taxable year if federal gross income from farming or fishing (including oyster farming) for the year is at least $2/3$ of total federal gross income from all sources for the year or if federal gross income from farming or fishing (including oyster farming) shown on the individual's return for the preceding taxable year is at least $2/3$ of the total federal gross income from all sources shown on such return.

Nonresidents selling real property. For a nonresident selling real property, the estimated tax payment is made to the recording officer when the deed is presented for recording. (Sec. 663, Tax Law; Instructions, Form IT-2663) However, for a cooperative unit, the payment is due within 15 days after delivery of the instrument effecting the sale or transfer. (Sec. 663(i), Tax Law; Instructions, Form IT-2664)

What forms are required for filing estimated tax?

Corporate franchise tax. Form CT-400, Estimated Tax for Corporations, is used to file estimated taxes. Form CT-300 is used for the mandatory first installment.

¶89-104

Pass-through entities. New York pass-through entities must file Form IT-2658, Report of Estimated Tax for Nonresident Individual Partners and Shareholders, and Form IT-2658-ATT, Attachment to Report of Estimated Tax for Nonresident Individual Partners and Shareholders, to make estimated tax payments on behalf of partners or shareholders who are nonresident individuals. Partnerships, LLPs, and LLCs must file Form CT-2658, Report of Estimated Tax for Corporate Partners, and Form CT-2658-ATT, Attachment to Report of Estimated Tax for Corporate Partners, to make estimated tax payments on behalf of partners that are C corporations.

Personal income tax. Personal income tax estimated payments are filed with Form IT-2105, Estimated Tax Payment Voucher for Individuals. For nonresidents selling real property, Form IT-2663 is generally used, but Form IT-2664 is used for sales of cooperative units.

Where can I find other information on estimated tax payments and returns?

New York has a comprehensive listing of its tax forms and publications on its website. (https://www.tax.ny.gov/)

Annual returns and payments are discussed at ¶89-102, and electronic filing is discussed at ¶89-106. See ¶89-206 for information on civil penalties.

[¶89-106] Electronic Filing

Electronic filing is generally required, as discussed below. Electronic payment options are discussed at ¶89-108.

The electronic filing mandate has been extended through 2024. (TSB-M-19(3)C, TSB-M-19(4)I)

• *Corporation tax returns*

New York participates in the Modernized e-File (MeF) program for corporation tax returns. (Publication 116)

Mandates and options.—As a result of the 2012 budget legislation, for returns filed beginning in 2013, the electronic filing mandate threshold is based on the number of taxpayers for whom documents are prepared (previously, a five-document threshold applied). Specifically, if a tax return preparer prepares authorized tax documents for more than 10 different taxpayers during any calendar year beginning on or after January 1, 2012, and if in any succeeding calendar year he or she prepares one or more authorized tax documents using tax software, then for that succeeding calendar year and each subsequent calendar year, all authorized tax documents prepared by that preparer must be filed electronically. (Sec. 29, Tax Law)

Electronic filing is also mandated for corporations that do not use a tax preparer to prepare Article 9-A general business corporation and S corporation tax returns, use tax preparation software approved by the state, and have broadband Internet access. (Sec. 29, Tax Law; E-file Mandate for Business Tax Filers)

Waiver and taxpayer opt-out.—There is no taxpayer opt-out. (Sec. 29, Tax Law; E-file Mandate for Tax Return Preparers)

Penalties.—Preparers are subject to a $50 per-document penalty for failure to e-file. Taxpayers are also subject to a $50 per-document penalty, as well as a $50 penalty for failure to pay electronically. Penalties may be waived if reasonable cause is shown. (Sec. 29, Tax Law; E-file Mandate for Tax Return Preparers; E-file Mandate for Business Tax Filers)

Forms and schedules.—Form CT-3, Form CT-3-A, and Form CT-3-S as well as related schedules are accepted for e-filing.

Extension requests.—Extension requests must be filed electronically. (E-file Mandate for Business Tax Filers; E-file Mandate and Filing/Payment Methods)

• *Partnership, LLP, and LLC returns*

New York participates in the Modernized e-File (MeF) program for partnership, limited liability partnership (LLP), and limited liability company (LLC) tax returns. (Publication 96)

Mandates and options.—As a result of the 2012 budget legislation, for returns filed beginning in 2013, the electronic filing mandate threshold is based on the number of taxpayers for whom documents are prepared (previously, a five-document threshold applied). Specifically, if a tax return preparer prepares authorized tax documents for more than 10 different taxpayers during any calendar year beginning on or after January 1, 2012, and if in any succeeding calendar year he or she prepares one or more authorized tax documents using tax software, then for that succeeding calendar year and each subsequent calendar year, all authorized tax documents prepared by that preparer must be filed electronically. (Sec. 29, Tax Law)

Electronic filing is also mandated for taxpayers that do not use a tax preparer to prepare their tax returns, use tax preparation software approved by the state, and have broadband Internet access. (Sec. 29, Tax Law; E-file Mandate for Business Tax Filers)

Waiver and taxpayer opt-out.—There is no taxpayer opt-out. (Sec. 29, Tax Law; E-file Mandate for Tax Return Preparers)

Penalties.—Preparers are subject to a $50 per-document penalty for failure to e-file. Taxpayers are also subject to a $50 per-document penalty, as well as a $50 penalty for failure to pay electronically. Penalties may be waived if reasonable cause is shown. (Sec. 29, Tax Law; E-file Mandate for Tax Return Preparers; E-file Mandate for Business Tax Filers)

Forms and schedules.—Form IT-204 and Form IT-204-LL as well as related schedules are accepted for e-filing.

Extension requests.—Extension requests must be filed electronically. (E-file Mandate for Business Tax Filers; E-file Mandate and Filing/Payment Methods)

• *Individual income tax returns*

New York participates in the fed/state e-filing program and the Modernized e-File (MeF) program for individual income tax returns. (Publication 93)

Driver license requirement.—Beginning with tax year 2016, the taxpayer's driver license or state identification information is required. For details, see https://www.tax.ny.gov/tp/driverlicense.htm.

Mandates and options.—As a result of the 2012 budget legislation, for returns filed beginning in 2013, the electronic filing mandate threshold is based on the number of taxpayers for whom documents are prepared (previously, a five-document threshold applied). Specifically, if a tax return preparer prepares authorized tax documents for more than 10 different taxpayers during any calendar year beginning on or after January 1, 2012, and if in any succeeding calendar year he or she prepares one or more authorized tax documents using tax software, then for that succeeding calendar year and each subsequent calendar year, all authorized tax documents prepared by that preparer must be filed electronically. (Sec. 29, Tax Law; E-file Mandate for Tax Return Preparers)

During 2012 through 2024, electronic filing is also mandated for individuals who do not use a tax preparer, but instead prepare their own income tax returns using software. This mandate is due to sunset on December 31, 2024. (Sec. 29, Tax Law; *TSB-M-11(12)I*)

¶89-106

Waiver and taxpayer opt-out.—There is no taxpayer opt-out. (Sec. 29, Tax Law; E-file Mandate for Tax Return Preparers; E-file Mandate for Individuals)

Penalties.—Preparers are subject to a $50 per-document penalty for failure to e-file. Penalties may be waived if reasonable cause is shown. (Sec. 29, Tax Law; E-file Mandate for Tax Return Preparers)

A $25 penalty was originally imposed on taxpayers failing to e-file, but it was eliminated by the 2012 budget legislation. (*Important Notice N-12-4*)

Forms and schedules.—Form IT-201 and related schedules are accepted for e-filing.

Extension requests.—Extension requests must be filed electronically. (E-file Mandate for Individuals)

• *Fiduciary returns*

New York participates in the fed/state e-filing program for fiduciary returns. (Publication 90)

Mandates and options.—As a result of the 2012 budget legislation, for returns filed beginning in 2013, the electronic filing mandate threshold is based on the number of taxpayers for whom documents are prepared (previously, a five-document threshold applied). Specifically, if a tax return preparer prepares authorized tax documents for more than 10 different taxpayers during any calendar year beginning on or after January 1, 2012, and if in any succeeding calendar year he or she prepares one or more authorized tax documents using tax software, then for that succeeding calendar year and each subsequent calendar year, all authorized tax documents prepared by that preparer must be filed electronically. (Sec. 29, Tax Law; E-file Mandate for Tax Return Preparers)

Electronic filing is also mandated for taxpayers using software to prepare their returns. (Sec. 29, Tax Law; Instructions, Form IT-205)

Waiver and taxpayer opt-out.—There is no taxpayer opt-out. (Sec. 29, Tax Law; E-file Mandate for Tax Return Preparers)

Penalties.—Preparers are subject to a $50 per-document penalty for failure to e-file. Penalties may be waived if reasonable cause is shown. (Sec. 29, Tax Law; E-file Mandate for Tax Return Preparers)

Forms and schedules.—Form IT-205 is accepted for e-filing.

Extension requests.—Extension requests may be filed online at http://www.tax.ny.gov/pit/file/ext.htm. Requests are not accepted for e-filing through the fed/state program. (Publication 90; E-file Mandate and Filing/Payment Methods)

• *Sales and use*

Sales tax taxpayers can Web File most forms and schedules, including: monthly, quarterly, and annual sales tax returns (most monthly and quarterly filers are required to Web File); PrompTax filers submitting Form ST-810; no-tax-due returns and final returns; the Sales Tax Record of Advance Payment (ST-330); and most sales tax schedules. (*Sales Tax Web File*, New York Department of Taxation and Finance, October 2011) In addition, tax preparers must electronically file sales tax documents for PrompTax, monthly, and quarterly filers. Beginning with the return due on March 20, 2012, tax preparers will also be required to electronically file returns for annual sales tax filers. (*E-file mandate for Tax Preparers*, New York Department of Taxation and Finance, October 2011)

For a discussion of amendments to the Tax Law and the Administrative Code of New York City in relation to penalties imposed upon tax return preparers who fail to electronically file (e-file), to authorize reasonable correction periods for electronic tax filings and payments, and to prohibit tax return preparers and software companies from charging separately for electronic filing of New York tax documents, see TSB-M-10(18)S.

• *Quarterly sales and use tax electronic filing*

New York state local quarterly sales and use tax returns (ST-100) and New York state local sales and use tax returns for a single jurisdiction (ST-102) may now also be filed online, through an approved E-service provider. (*Press Release*, New York Department of Taxation and Finance, November 20, 2001) Businesses wishing to enroll in this program may obtain enrollment information from the Department of Taxation and Finance or through the Department's website at www.tax.state.ny.us. (*Press Release*, New York Department of Taxation and Finance, November 20, 2001)

• *Electronic signatures*

Taxpayers using a tax return preparer or other electronic return originator to electronically file their return must sign and date the applicable e-file authorization (Form TR-579) to authorize electronic filing. Taxpayers may use electronic signatures on all TR-579s. (*TSB-M-20(1)C, (2)I*)

The Commissioner is authorized to provide for electronic signatures with respect to certain documents filed electronically with the Department of Taxation and Finance, and such signatures will have the same validity and effect as the use of a signature affixed by hand. (Sec. 171-k, Tax Law; *TSB-M-02(5)C*)

Applicable for personal income tax returns e-filed for taxable years beginning on or after January 1, 2014, any return, statement or other document required to be made that is signed by the taxpayer in accordance with the regulations or instructions prescribed by the Commissioner and received electronically by the tax preparer will satisfy the signature requirements. (Sec. 653(a)(2), Tax Law)

Alternative signing methods for tax return preparers, effective February 1, 2005, are discussed in *TSB-M-05(1)C, TSB-M-05(1)I, TSB-M-05(1)S,* and *TSB-M-05(1)M,* February 1, 2005.

[¶89-108] Payment Methods

Certain taxpayers are required to make tax payments by electronic funds transfer (EFT) or certified check. In addition, the Department of Taxation and Finance will accept credit card payments for certain tax liabilities. (see further discussion below)

• *Corporate franchise tax*

For taxpayers required to file electronically (see ¶89-106), the Commissioner may require tax liability or other amounts due on the return to be paid electronically. (Sec. 29(d), Tax Law)

See also http://www.tax.ny.gov/bus/efile/elf_busn_mandate.htm.

• *Personal income taxes*

All taxpayers (other than health care providers) who are required to deduct and withhold an aggregate of $35,000 or more of New York state personal income tax, New York City personal income tax, New York City income tax surcharge, City of Yonkers income tax, or nonresident city earnings tax (repealed effective July 1, 1999) must pay the tax by electronic funds transfer on or before the due date to a bank, banking house, or trust company designated by the Commissioner of Taxation and Finance. (Sec. 9(b), Tax Law) Alternatively, taxpayers may elect to pay by certified check. (Reg. Sec. 2396.7)

Every taxpayer which is identified by either its own separate Federal employer identification number, or its own separate New York state employer identification number, shall be treated as a separate withholding taxpayer for purposes of determining whether the $35,000 or more threshold is met.

Exemption.—Taxpayers are exempt from participation in the EFT Program if the aggregate tax withheld, pursuant to their most recent annual reconciliation of withholding required to be filed, is less than $100,000. (Sec. 9(d), Tax Law; Reg. Sec. 2396.3(b)(1))

Voluntary participation.—Any withholding tax taxpayer which is not required to participate in the EFT Program may, at any time, submit a request to the Commissioner of Taxation and Finance for permission to participate in such Program on a voluntary basis. (Reg. Sec. 2396.3(d)(1))

Standard: Any taxpayer that seeks permission to participate in the EFT Program must be granted permission unless the Commissioner determines that the administrative costs associated with accepting new enrollees into the Program (including, but not limited to, increasing systems capacities, adding depository bank resources, and adding Program specialists within the Department) outweigh the revenue and tax administration benefits associated with electronic filing and payment. (Reg. Sec. 2396.3(d)(2))

Notice: Within 30 calendar days after receipt of the request, the Commissioner must notify the taxpayer of his decision. If the Commissioner grants the taxpayer permission to voluntarily participate, the notice must include certain information and instructions, and must also specify the date by which the taxpayer is required to file its first return and make its first payment of tax by an EFT payment option. (Reg. Sec. 2396.3(d)(3))

Duration of participation: A taxpayer accepted to voluntarily participate in the Program after June 30, 1990 is required to continue in such Program through at least the succeeding June 30. (Reg. Sec. 2396.3(d)(5))

Ceasing voluntary participation: The following circumstances provide for stopping voluntary participation in the EFT Program.

Automatic taxpayer election: No later than March 31, 1990 or by March 31 in succeeding years, as applicable, a taxpayer voluntarily participating in the Program may notify the Commissioner in writing that it no longer elects to participate in the Program beyond the applicable date. The Commissioner must advise the taxpayer of the date of its final filing and payment by an EFT method, within 30 calendar days of receipt of such notice. (Reg. Sec. 2396.3(d)(5)(ii)(a))

Taxpayer hardship: A taxpayer may, at any time, apply to the Commissioner to cease its voluntary participation in the Program based on hardship. Within 30 calendar days of receipt of the request, the Commissioner must advise the taxpayer of his decision. The Commissioner will not grant such request unless the taxpayer demonstrates that continuation of its voluntary participation will result in hardship to such taxpayer. If the Commissioner grants such request, he will advise the taxpayer of the date for final filing and payment by an EFT method. (Reg. Sec. 2396.3(d)(5)(ii)(b))

Commissioner's determination: The Commissioner may at any time after enrollment and on 30 business days notice, advise the taxpayer that it will no longer be permitted to participate in the Program on a voluntary basis. (Reg. Sec. 2396.3(d)(5)(ii)(c))

• *Sales and use, motor fuel, and petroleum business taxes*

The Department of Taxation and Finance has implemented a program requiring tax payments by electronic fund transfers (EFT) or certified check by taxpayers whose sales and use taxes, prepaid sales and use taxes on motor fuel and diesel motor fuel, or petroleum business taxes exceed certain statutory thresholds. (Sec. 10, Tax Law) (See below)

Initial eligibility determination.—Under the terms of this program, the Department will make an initial eligibility determination within 45 days after June 1 of each year by examining the taxpayer's tax liability for the June 1 through May 31 period preceding the June 1-May 31 period that precedes the initial determination

> **CCH EXAMPLE:** *Initial determination of eligibility.*—A taxpayer's tax liability for the period June 1, 1999 through May 31, 2000, will be used as the basis for the initial determination of whether the taxpayer is required to participate in the 2000-2001 program and the taxpayer will be notified by July 15, 2000.

Threshold amounts.—The threshold amounts for the applicable June 1 through May 31 period are:

— $500,000 of state and local sales and use taxes (excluding the tax on paging devices);

— more than $5 million of prepaid state and local sales and use taxes on motor fuel and diesel motor fuel; or

— more than $5 million of the total of the tax on motor fuel and diesel motor fuel and the tax on petroleum businesses (excluding the tax on carriers).

A taxpayer will be required to participate in the program only with respect to taxes for which the applicable dollar thresholds noted above have been met. In determining whether the threshold has been met, every taxpayer who is identified by either its own federal employer identification number or its own separate New York state employer identification number is treated as a separate taxpayer. (Reg. Sec. 2397.2)

Voluntary participation.—Taxpayers who do not meet the dollar thresholds noted above may apply for permission to participate in the Program on a voluntary basis. Applications for voluntary participation will be granted unless the Commissioner determines that the administrative costs associated with accepting new enrollees outweigh the revenue and tax administration benefits associated with payment by EFT or certified check.

Hardship exemption.—A taxpayer may, within 20 calendar days of the postmark date of the notice informing the taxpayer of its required participation in the Program or after having already enrolled in the Program, apply to the Department of Taxation and Finance for a hardship exemption. However, if one of the following is demonstrated, the taxpayer will not be required to participate in the program for the remaining quarters of the sales tax year ending on the next May 31st and for the immediately succeeding four sales tax quarters:

(1) for the two most recent consecutive quarters, the state and local sales and use taxes properly payable by the taxpayer are less than 50% of the taxes properly payable by such taxpayer for the comparable two quarters of the preceding year; and

(2) the sum of the taxpayer's state and local sales and use tax liability for the most recent consecutive quarters together with the state and local sales and

use taxes properly payable by the taxpayer for the two consecutive quarters immediately preceding the two most recent consecutive quarters referred to (1), above, multiplied by the percentage arrived at under (1), are less that $250,000.

Prepaid state and local sales and use taxes.—A taxpayer who meets the statutory threshold for mandatory participation in the EFT program because it is liable for more than $5 million of prepaid state and local sales and use taxes on motor fuel and diesel motor fuel, or more than $5 million of the total of petroleum business, motor fuel and diesel motor fuel taxes, may obtain a hardship exemption if it is able to demonstrate that:

(1) for the most recent six-month period, (a) the prepaid state and local sales and compensating use taxes on motor fuel and diesel motor fuel, or (b) the total motor fuel, diesel motor fuel and petroleum business taxes, are less than 50% of the applicable taxes payable by such taxpayer for the comparable six-month period of the preceding year; and

(2) the sum of the taxpayer's liability for those taxes for the most recent six months together with the applicable taxes properly payable by the taxpayer for the six-month period immediately preceding the most recent six-month period referred to in subparagraph (1) multiplied by the percentage arrived at under (1) is less than $2.5 million.

(Sec. 10, Tax Law)

A taxpayer who demonstrates the above to the Department will not be required to participate in the Program for the remaining months of the period ending on the next May 31 and for the immediately succeeding 12 months.

Taxpayers newly required to participate in the EFT program must make their first payment by the applicable due date for the month of September.

Penalties.—Penalties are provided for taxpayers failing to comply with the above requirements.

Taxpayers liable for alcoholic beverage taxes under Art. 18 are no longer considered for electronic payment requirements.

Payment of tax.—A taxpayer required to participate in the EFT program because its sales and use tax liability exceeds the statutory threshold must remit by electronic funds transfer or certified check:

— 75% of $1/3$ of the state and local sales and use taxes properly payable by the taxpayer for the comparable quarter of the preceding year; or

— its total liability for state and local sales and compensating use taxes during the period from the first 22 days of the month.

(Reg. Sec. 2397.6)

Any remaining tax liability must accompany the taxpayer's part-quarterly and quarterly return, and may not be submitted by EFT.

Prepaid motor fuel and diesel motor fuel use tax.—A taxpayer required to participate in the EFT Program because its prepaid motor fuel and diesel motor fuel use tax liability exceeds $5 million must, on or before the third business day following the 22nd day of each calendar month, remit by EFT or certified check:

— 75% of the prepaid state and local sales and use taxes on motor fuel and diesel motor fuel properly payable by the taxpayer for the comparable month of the preceding year; or

— its total liability for prepaid state and local sales and use taxes on motor fuel and diesel motor fuel during the first 22 days of the month. (Reg. Sec.

2397.6) No penalties or interest will be imposed if the taxpayer timely remits not less than 90% of the taxes as finally determined to be due and payable for such period.

Motor fuel and diesel motor fuel and petroleum business tax.—A taxpayer required to participate in the EFT Program because it is liable for more than $5 million of the total of the tax on motor fuel and diesel motor fuel and the tax on petroleum businesses (excluding the tax on carriers) must, on or before the third business day following the 22nd day of each calendar month, remit by EFT or certified check either:

— 75% of the total of the Article 12-A or 13-A taxes properly payable by the taxpayer for the comparable month of the preceding year; or

— the total liability for such taxes during the first 22 days of the month.

Any remaining tax liability owed by the taxpayer for the period must accompany the filing of the taxpayer's monthly return. Such amounts may not be submitted by EFT.

Materialmen.—A taxpayer is permitted to remit state and local sales and compensating use taxes by EFT or certified check at the same time that payment is required to be made for Art. 28 and 29 part-quarterly and quarterly returns if it can demonstrate to the satisfaction of the Commissioner that:

— its liability for state and local sales and compensating use taxes was less than $4 million during the applicable period; and

— in any two sales tax quarters within the most recent four consecutive sales tax quarters, it was a materialman within the meaning of Sec. 2, Lien Law, primarily engaged in furnishing building materials to contractors, subcontractors or repairmen for the improvement of real property improved or to be improved with a residential dwelling unit, and authorized by such law to file a mechanic's lien upon such real property and improvement.

(Sec. 10, Tax Law)

• *Credit card payments*

The New York Department of Taxation and Finance accepts credit cards for many types of income tax payments or to pay a bill; see http://www.tax.ny.gov/pay/all/pay_by_credit_card.htm.

CAUTION NOTE: Beginning June 16, 2015, individuals will not be able to use a credit card to pay a balance due when filing a 2014 personal income tax return or to make an estimated tax payment. The department anticipates that individuals will be able to resume using credit cards starting in January 2016. (*Important Notice N-15-8*, New York Department of Taxation and Finance, June 2015.)

• *Payments via the Internet*

The governing body of any local government may, by local law, ordinance or resolution, provide for the acceptance of penalties, rents, rates, taxes, fees, charges, revenue, financial obligations or other amounts, including penalties, special assessments or interest via a municipal Internet website. However, submission via the Internet may not be the only method allowed. (Sec. 5-b, General Municipal Law)

Payments received via the Internet are considered received by the appropriate officer and paid by the taxpayer at the time the Internet transaction is completed and sent by the taxpayer. Any local government authorizing the payment of taxes via the

Internet shall provide a confirmation page to the taxpayer following the completion of the Internet transaction. (Sec. 5-b, General Municipal Law)

[¶89-130]
AUDITS

[¶89-144] Limitations Period for Audits

Generally, New York law places a three-year statute of limitations on tax audits, beyond which the Department of Taxation and Finance may not perform an audit without a taxpayers' written consent. A written consent to extend the statute of limitations must be obtained prior to expiration of the statutory period. The statute of limitations does not apply, however, for any period during which a taxpayer failed to file a return, failed to report federal changes, or filed a false or fraudulent return to evade tax.

Specific rules for determining the time within which an assessment may be made are determined by the specific tax type, as discussed in the paragraphs below.

• *Corporate franchise tax*

Corporate franchise tax assessments can generally be made up to three years after the return was filed. (Sec. 1083(a), Tax Law) When a return is filed before the due date, it is deemed to have been filed on the due date. (Sec. 1083(b), Tax Law) However, the taxpayer and the Commissioner may, within the limitation period for assessment of tax, consent in writing to an extension of the assessment limitation period. Subsequent extensions may be made if they are made within the limitation period as extended. (Sec. 1083(c)(2), Tax Law)

In addition, a tax may be assessed at any time if: (i) no report is filed; (ii) a false or fraudulent report is filed with the intent to evade tax; or (iii) the taxpayer fails to file a report or an amended report. (Reg. Sec. 8-1.2)

For a discussion of assessments of delinquent tax, see ¶89-164.

Waiver or extension agreements.—The taxpayer may agree in writing to an extension of the limitation period. (Sec. 1083(c)(2), Tax Law; Reg. Sec. 8-1.2(b)(2))

Substantial understatement of tax.—When a taxpayer omits income amounting to more than 25% of the gross income stated in the return, the limitation period is six years after the return was filed. (Sec. 1083(d), Tax Law; Reg. Sec. 8-1.2(c)) Similarly, a tax may be assessed at any time within six years after the return was filed if a taxpayer omits from the sum of its items of tax preference and adjustments required in the computation of minimum taxable income an amount in excess of 25% of the sum stated in the return.

The term "gross income" means gross income for federal income tax purposes as reportable on a business corporation return under Article 9-A of the Tax Law. An amount is not deemed to be omitted if sufficiently disclosed on the return or on an attached statement.

Fraud or failure to file.—When no return or a fraudulent return is filed, there is no period of limitation on assessment. (Sec. 1083(c)(1), Tax Law; Reg. Sec. 8-1.2(b))

Amended returns.—Under the 2018 budget legislation, the statute of limitations was extended for assessments based on changes or corrections reported on an amended return. Accordingly, the department can generally now issue an assessment on an amended return until the later of:

— one year from the date the amended return was filed, or

— three years from the date the original return was filed.

This applies to amended returns filed on or after April 12, 2018. (Sec. 1083(c)(12), Tax Law; *TSB-M-18(3)C*)

Report of federal changes or correction.—When the taxpayer fails to report any change of federal taxable income or federal tax or fails to file a required amended return (see ¶89-102 for reporting requirements), there is no period of limitation on assessment. When the taxpayer has reported federal changes, assessment may be made within two years of the report or amended return. (Sec. 1083(c)(3), Tax Law; Reg. Sec. 8-1.2(b))

Carrybacks.—Deficiencies attributable either to a net operating loss carryback or a capital loss carryback may be assessed at any time that a deficiency for the taxable year of the loss may be assessed. (Sec. 1083(c)(4), Tax Law; Reg. Sec. 8-1.2)

Accelerated assessment.—Dissolving corporations may request prompt assessment to facilitate the winding up of their affairs. (Sec. 1083(c)(6), Tax Law) When such a written request is made, assessment must be made within 18 months of the request.

Eligible business facility.—When a report is filed reflecting the revocation or modification of a certificate of eligibility upon which a credit was taken against tax, an assessment relating to the credit may be made within three years after the filing of the report. (Sec. 1083(c)(8), Tax Law)

Erroneous refund.—When an erroneous refund has been made, assessment of a deficiency arising from the refund may be made within two years of the making of the refund or within five years if it appears that any part of the refund was induced by fraud or misrepresentation. (Sec. 1083(c)(5), Tax Law)

Suspension of period.—The running of the period of limitation for assessment is suspended during the period after the mailing of a notice of deficiency until the assessment is deemed made following expiration of the appeal period. (Sec. 1083(e), Tax Law)

• *Personal income tax*

Personal income taxes must generally be assessed within three years after the return was filed. (Sec. 683(a), Tax Law)

For a discussion of assessments of delinquent tax, see ¶89-164.

No return filed.—If no return was filed, taxes may be assessed at any time. (Sec. 683(c)(1), Tax Law) (For a discussion of tax returns, see ¶89-102)

False or fraudulent return with intent to evade tax.—If a false or fraudulent return has been filed with intent to evade the tax, taxes may be assessed at any time. (Sec. 683(c)(1), Tax Law)

Amended returns.—Under the 2018 budget legislation, the statute of limitations was extended for assessments based on changes or corrections reported on an amended return. Accordingly, the department can generally now issue an assessment on an amended return until the later of:

— one year from the date the amended return was filed, or

— three years from the date the original return was filed.

This applies to amended returns filed on or after April 12, 2018. (Sec. 683(c)(12), Tax Law; *TSB-M-18(4)I*)

Report of federal change.—If the taxpayer, employer, or payor fails to report a federal change or correction in federal taxable income, federal items of tax preference, total taxable amount, ordinary income portion of a lump sum distribution or credit for employment-related expenses, or if no amended New York return is filed when a federal return is amended, taxes may be assessed at any time. (Sec. 683(c)(1), Tax Law)

If the report is made or an amended return is filed, taxes may be assessed within two years after the filing of the report or amended return (if the assessment is not deemed to have been made upon the filing of the report or amended return). (Sec. 683(c)(3), Tax Law) This provision relates only to tax attributable to the change or correction.

Extension by agreement.—The taxpayer and the Commissioner of Taxation and Finance may agree to extend the period of time for assessment of tax. (Sec. 683(c)(2), Tax Law)

Deficiency attributable to net operating loss carryback.—If a deficiency is attributable to the application to the taxpayer of a net operating loss carryback, it may be assessed at any time that a deficiency for the taxable year of the loss may be assessed. (Sec. 683(c)(4), Tax Law)

Erroneous refund.—An assessment of a deficiency arising out of an erroneous refund may be made at any time within two years from the making of the refund, or five years in the case of a refund induced by fraud or misrepresentation of a material fact. (Sec. 683(c)(5), Tax Law)

"Erroneous refund" defined: An "erroneous refund" is a refund which is issued as a result of an error made by an employee of the Department of Taxation and Finance. (Reg. Sec. 107.7)

Estate of decedent requesting prompt assessment.—If a return is required for a decedent or for his estate during the period of administration, the tax will be assessed within 18 months after a written request (made after the return is filed) by the executor, administrator or other person representing the estate of the decedent, but not more than three years after the return was filed. (Sec. 683(c)(6), Tax Law)

Omission of income in excess of 25%.—The tax may be assessed at any time within six years after the return was filed if:

— an individual omits from his New York adjusted gross income, the sum of his or her items of tax preference, or the total taxable amount or ordinary income portion of a lump sum distribution an amount properly included therein which is in excess of 25% of the amount of New York adjusted gross income, the sum of the items of tax preference, or the total taxable amount or ordinary income portion of a lump sum distribution stated in the return;

— an estate or trust omits income from its return in an amount in excess of 25% of its income determined as if it were an individual computing his or her New York adjusted gross income;

— an estate or trust omits from the sum of its items of tax preference an item properly includable therein which is in excess of 25% of the sum of the items of tax preference stated in the return;

— an estate or trust omits from the amount of the total taxable amount or ordinary income portion of a lump sum distribution an amount properly includable therein which is in excess of 25% of the amount of the total taxable amount or ordinary income portion of a lump sum distribution, respectively, stated in the return; or

— a trust omits from the amount of includable gain of a trust an amount properly includable therein which is in excess of 25% of the amount of includable gain stated in the return.

(Sec. 683(d), Tax Law)

¶89-144

Report concerning waste treatment facility, air pollution control facility or eligible business facility.—Tax may be assessed within three years after the filing of a return concerning change of use. (Sec. 683(c)(8), Tax Law)

Suspension of running of period of limitation.—The running of the period of limitations on assessment or collection of tax will, after the mailing of a notice of deficiency, be suspended for the period of time during which the Commissioner is prohibited from making the assessment or collecting by levy. (Sec. 683(e), Tax Law)

• *Sales and use tax*

The limitation periods for any proceeding or action taken by the state or the Commissioner of Taxation and Finance to levy, appraise, assess, determine or enforce the collection of any tax or penalty supersede any limitation periods set forth in the Civil Practice Law and Rules for the assessment of taxes. (Sec. 1147(b), Tax Law)

For a discussion of assessments of delinquent tax, see ¶ 89-164.

Burden of proof.—In order to establish a statute of limitations defense, a taxpayer must go forward with a prima facie case showing the date on which the limitations period commences, the expiration of the statutory period, and receipt or mailing of the statutory notice after the running of the period. (*Matter of Jencon, Inc.,* Division of Tax Appeals, Tax Appeals Tribunal, DTA No. 800868 (1990))

Return filed—not willfully false or fraudulent.—No assessment of additional tax will be made after the expiration of more than three years from the date of the filing of a return. A return filed before the last day prescribed by law or regulation for the filing of the return, or before the last day of any extension for filing the return, is deemed to be filed on such last day. (Sec. 1147(b), Tax Law)

Return filed—willfully false or fraudulent with intent to evade tax.—When a taxpayer files a willfully false or fraudulent return with the intent to evade the tax, no limitation period runs against assessment. A purchaser who furnishes a vendor with a false or fraudulent certificate of resale or other exemption certificate or other document with the intent to evade the tax may be taxed at any time. (Sec. 1147(b), Tax Law)

No return has been filed as provided by law.—Where no return has been filed, there are no time limitations on assessment. (Sec. 1147(b), Tax Law)

Date of filing.—A return filed before the last day prescribed for the filing, or before the last day of any extension of time for filing, will be deemed to be filed on the last day. (Sec. 1147(b), Tax Law) (For a discussion of returns, see ¶ 89-102)

Extension of limitation period.—The period in which the Commissioner may make an assessment may be extended if the taxpayer, prior to the expiration of the limitation period, consents in writing to such an extension. (Sec. 1147(c), Tax Law) Additional consents to extend the limitation period are permissible.

CCH CAUTION: Consent signed by corporate taxpayer.—Consents signed by a corporate taxpayer to extend the statute of limitations may not necessarily be binding upon corporate officers and directors. The plain language of Sec. 1138(c) and Sec. 1147(c), Tax Law, is that the only tax that can be addressed during an extended period is the tax of the taxpayer who signed the consent extending the period of limitation. (*Petition of On-Site Petroleum Unlimited, Inc., et al.,* DTA Nos. 811604, 811605, 811606)

Suspension of limitation period when notice appealed.—The period in which the Commissioner may make an assessment is suspended until the time for filing a petition contesting the notice of assessment has expired or where a petition is timely filed, until the decision of the Administrative Law Judge or Tax Appeals Tribunal becomes final. (Sec. 1147(d), Tax Law) A decision by an Administrative Law Judge is final when entered, unless a party requests review by the Tax Appeals Tribunal within 90 days of the assessment. A decision of the Tax Appeals Tribunal is final upon the expiration of the period specified in Sec. 1138(a)(4), Tax Law for filing an application for review, generally within four months after the notice of the decision is served on all parties; upon expiration of the time for all further judicial review; or upon the rendering of a decision by the Tax Appeals Tribunal under mandate by the court on review.

• *Motor fuels tax*

A determination of motor fuels tax may be made by the Commissioner of Taxation and Finance within three years after an incorrect or insufficient return has been filed by a distributor. (Sec. 288, Tax Law) An assessment may be made at any time, however, for a distributor who has not registered, has failed to file a return, or has filed a willfully false or fraudulent return with an intent to evade the tax. The taxpayer may agree in writing to waive the limitation period for the determination of tax.

For a discussion of assessments of delinquent tax, see ¶ 89-164.

An overpayment of a refund may be determined by the Commissioner and recovered from the claimant within two years after the date of the erroneous or excessive payment. (Sec. 289-c(3)(c), Tax Law)

Such determinations of tax by the Commissioner are final unless a hearing is requested. (Sec. 288, Tax Law)

• *Cigarette and tobacco products tax*

If any person files an incorrect or insufficient cigarette and tobacco products tax return, the Commissioner of Taxation and Finance may determine the amount of tax due at any time within three years after the return was filed, whether or not it was filed on or after the due date. (Sec. 478, Tax Law) However, if no return is filed or the return is willfully fraudulent, the determination may be made at any time.

For a discussion of assessments of delinquent tax, see ¶ 89-164.

The Commissioner may, however, enter into an agreement to extend the period for determination of the tax. (Sec. 478, Tax Law)

Any determination made under Sec. 478, Tax Law will be final unless the person against whom the tax is assessed applies, within 90 days after notice of the determination was given, to the Division of Tax Appeal for a hearing. (Sec. 478, Tax Law)

[¶ 89-160]

COLLECTION OF TAX

[¶ 89-164] Assessment of Delinquent Tax

Where the taxpayer either fails to file a return or files a return showing a tax due that is less than the correct tax, the Department of Taxation and Finance may assess a tax deficiency. (Sec. 681, Tax Law; Sec. 1081, Tax Law) As a general rule, deficiency assessments may not be summarily made. Certain procedural requirements must be satisfied in connection with assessing a deficiency in tax to afford the taxpayer an opportunity for review prior to assessment and collection.

Before assessment and collection of a deficiency, the taxpayer is entitled to a notice of the proposed assessment. (Sec. 681(a), Tax Law; Sec. 1081(a), Tax Law) The taxpayer is also entitled to a statutory waiting period after notice during which assessment and collection may not be made. (Sec. 681(c), Tax Law; 1081(c), Tax Law) This period is intended to give the taxpayer an opportunity to petition the Department for a redetermination of the deficiency.

• *Notice of deficiency*

Once the Department of Taxation and Finance determines that a deficiency exists, it must send a notice of deficiency to the taxpayer's last known address by certified or registered mail. This notice is sent to the fiduciary if the Department has received notice that a fiduciary relationship exists with respect to the taxpayer. (Sec. 681(a), Tax Law; Sec. 1081(a), Tax Law)

> **CCH EXAMPLE:** *Valid notices.*—The following are examples of valid deficiency notices.
>
> — A notice of deficiency mailed to the taxpayer's last known address is valid despite the taxpayer's failure to receive it. (*Matter of Yegnukian*, DTA Nos. 802957, 802958 (1990)) The Audit Division, however, must prove mailing to a petitioner's last known address, or actual receipt of the notice, to establish a valid notice of deficiency.
>
> — A notice sent to the petitioner's attorney, whose address was listed on bulk sale documents filed, was valid because the attorney actually received it, although the taxpayer claimed it never had notice due to a deteriorating relationship with the attorney. (*Matter of Charbru Restaurant, Inc.*, DTA No. 807524 (1993))
>
> — An incorrectly addressed notice of deficiency is valid if the taxpayer actually receives it. (*Matter of Demattia*, DTA Nos. 803620, 804749 (1990))
>
> — However, a notice sent to the wrong zip code was valid even though the taxpayer did not receive it, because the zip code was not an integral part of the taxpayer's address. (*Matter of Karolight, Ltd.*, DTA No. 802708 (1992))
>
> — A notice of deficiency to a corporation was held to be invalid where the notice was mailed only to the home of the corporation's president and not to the corporate address. (*Matter of C Riegel, Inc.*, TSB-H-86(21)C (1986))
>
> — A deficiency notice issued to a taxpayer's nickname is valid if the notice is properly addressed, delivered and accepted and the taxpayer is not misled by the use of the nickname. (*Matter of Kleinberger*, DTA No. 806241 (1991))

The presumption of delivery of a notice of deficiency does not arise where the Division's only proof of mailing is a mailing log. Corroborative evidence of mailing, such as a return receipt, affidavits as to the accuracy of the log or testimony relating to office mailing practices, is required. (*Matter of Colosimo*, DTA No. 805078 (1998)) No proof of mailing practices is required, however, where the taxpayer concedes that the notice was received and is merely arguing that it was untimely.

Factual basis.—A notice of deficiency is not valid unless it has a factual basis.

> **EXAMPLE:** *Notice of deficiency invalid because of no factual basis.*—A notice of deficiency in which employee business expenses were disallowed was held to be invalid because the disallowance had no factual basis and the Division had not requested substantiation of the expenses. (*Matter of Houser*, DTA No. 804801 (1998))

• *Corporate franchise tax*

New York assessment procedure for corporate franchise (income) tax parallels that of federal law, whereby after 90 days from the mailing of a notice of deficiency, the notice becomes an assessment of the amount of tax specified in the notice, together with interest, additions, and penalties. (Sec. 1081, Tax Law) Deficiencies may not be assessed unless a notice has been mailed to the taxpayer. (Sec. 1081(c), Tax Law)

Notice of deficiency.—The Commissioner, after examining the return and determining that additional tax is due, mails a notice of deficiency to the taxpayer by certified or registered mail at its last known address. (Sec. 1081, Tax Law)

90-day time period.—After 90 days (150 days if the taxpayer's last known address is outside the United States), the notice is an assessment of the amount of tax, additions to tax, and interest and penalties specified in the notice, except for amounts for which the taxpayer has filed a petition for redetermination of the deficiency. The Commissioner, as soon as practicable, then issues a notice and demand for assessed but unpaid tax. (Sec. 1092(b), Tax Law)

Payment of taxes.—Payment of taxes due must be made within 21 calendar days after notice and demand for assessed but unpaid taxes (10 business days if the amount for which the notice and demand is made is equal to or greater than $100,000). (Sec. 1084(h), Tax Law) The Commissioner then has six years from the date of assessment to issue a warrant to the sheriff for levy and sale.

Mathematical or clerical errors.—If an underpayment is due to mathematical or clerical error, which is not defined by statute, the Commissioner will send a notice to the taxpayer of the amount due. (Sec. 1081(d), Tax Law) This notice is not deemed to be a notice of deficiency. No interest is charged if the return was timely filed and the additional tax is paid within three months of the due date (or extended due date) of the return. (Sec. 1084(c), Tax Law) (For a discussion of interest, see ¶ 89-202)

No return filed.—If no return has been filed, the Commissioner is authorized to estimate the taxpayer's New York tax liability from any information in its possession and to mail a notice of deficiency to the taxpayer. (Sec. 1081, Tax Law)

Federal changes.—If no report of federal change is made or no amended New York return is filed when a federal return is amended, the Commissioner may assess a deficiency based upon increased federal taxable income. (Sec. 1081(e), Tax Law) The additional tax is deemed assessed 30 days after the notice is mailed (rather than the standard 90-day period described above) unless the taxpayer files the required report of change or amended return before the 30-day period has lapsed, together with a statement showing that the federal determination was erroneous.

Combined reports.—The Commissioner may determine a deficiency against any taxpayer that was included in a combined report or that might have been included in a combined report. (Sec. 1081(g), Tax Law; Reg. Sec. 8-1.3)

Allocation of income or capital not to be changed in certain assessments.—No change of the allocation or income or capital may be made during an additional limitation period in which a deficiency is assessed:

    — where the taxpayer has failed to file a report or amended return to report an increase of decrease in federal taxable income or federal tax;

    — which is based on a report of changed or corrected federal income which is treated as if it were a deficiency for federal income tax purposes; or

— which is attributable to a net operating loss carry-back of an Article 9-A corporation.

(Sec. 1083(c)(7), Tax Law)

No change of the allocation of income or capital may be made in a proceeding on the taxpayer's claim for refund or on a petition for redetermination of a deficiency involving the above.

• *Personal income tax*

The amount of personal income tax which a return shows to be due, or the amount of personal income tax which a return would have shown to be due but for a mathematical or clerical error, will be deemed to be assessed on the date of filing of the return. (Sec. 682(a), Tax Law)

If, upon examination of the taxpayer's return, the Commissioner of Taxation and Finance determines that there is a deficiency of income tax, he or she may mail a notice of deficiency to the taxpayer. (Sec. 681(a), Tax Law) If a taxpayer fails to file a required income tax return, the Commissioner is authorized to estimate the taxpayer's New York taxable income and tax thereon from any information in its possession, and to mail a notice of deficiency to the taxpayer. The notice of deficiency must be mailed by certified or registered mail to the taxpayer at his last known address. After 90 days from the mailing of a notice of deficiency, the notice will be considered an assessment of the amount of tax specified in the notice, together with the interest, additions to tax and penalties stated in the notice. (For a discussion of interest and penalties, see ¶ 89-202)

If the notice of deficiency is addressed to a person outside of the United States, the period will be 150, rather than 90 days. (Sec. 681(b), Tax Law)

Restriction on assessment and levy.—No assessment of a deficiency in tax and no levy or proceeding in court for its collection may be made, begun or prosecuted until a notice of deficiency has been mailed to the taxpayer, until the expiration of the time for filing a petition contesting such notice, and, if a petition with respect to the taxable year has been filed, until the decision of the Commissioner has become final. (Sec. 681(c), Tax Law)

Mathematical or clerical errors.—If an underpayment of tax is due to a mathematical or clerical error, the Commissioner will send a notice to the taxpayer of the amount due. (Sec. 681(d), Tax Law) This notice will not be deemed to be a notice of deficiency.

No report of federal change.—If no report of federal change or correction in federal taxable income, federal items of tax preference, total taxable amount, ordinary income portion of a lump sum distribution or credit for employment-related expenses is made or no amended New York return is filed when a federal return is amended, the Commissioner may assess a deficiency based upon the increased or decreased federal taxable income. (Sec. 681(e), Tax Law) The deficiency, interest, additions to tax and penalties due will be deemed to be assessed on the date of the mailing of the notice of additional tax due unless a report of the federal changes or an amended return is filed within 30 days after the mailing of the notice, accompanied by a statement showing in what way the federal determination and the notice of additional tax due are erroneous.

• *Sales and use tax*

The sales and use tax is self-assessed since the person required to collect the tax (such as a vendor) or the person required to pay the tax (such as a customer who has not paid the tax at the time of purchase) computes the tax and pays the tax at the time of filing returns. The Commissioner of Taxation and Finance, however, determines the tax if the return when filed is incorrect or insufficient, or if the return is not filed. (Sec. 1138(a)(1), Tax Law) The Commissioner, or duly authorized agents or employees of the Commissioner, may inspect the records of the taxpayer and may, if necessary, estimate the tax on the basis of external indices.

A notice of the determination of the tax due will be mailed by registered or certified mail, to the person liable for the collection or payment of the tax. (Sec. 1147(a)(1), Tax Law) The determination will finally and irrevocably fix the tax unless the person against whom it is assessed, within 90 days, applies to the Division of Tax Appeals for a hearing, or unless the Commissioner redetermines the tax. (Sec. 1138(a)(1), Tax Law) If an application for a hearing has been filed on behalf of an entity and a determination of personal liability has been made on behalf of the person under a duty to act, only one application for hearing is required to be filed on behalf of the corporation, dissolved corporation, partnership, or individual proprietorship and on behalf of the personally liable individual.

The Commissioner is also authorized to make jeopardy assessments.

Fixing of tax by consent.—A person liable for the collection or payment of tax (whether or not a determination assessing tax has been issued) is entitled to have the tax due finally and irrevocably fixed prior to the statutory 90-day period by filing a signed statement in writing with the Commissioner. (Sec. 1138(c), Tax Law) Where a determination assessing tax has not been issued by the Commissioner, such a consent does not disqualify the taxpayer from later claiming a refund or credit. (For a discussion of refunds, see ¶ 89-224)

Bulk sale.—However, such procedure for the acceleration of the final fixing of the tax is not applicable to the liability of a purchaser, transferee, or assignee arising from a bulk sale. (Sec. 1138(d), Tax Law)

Mailing of notice—presumptive evidence of receipt—computation of time.—Any notice of determination may be sent, by registered or certified mail, to the person for whom it was intended at the address given in the last return filed or in any application made by that person, or if no return has been filed or application made, then to any address obtainable. (Sec. 1147(a)(1), Tax Law) Any period of time which is determined by the giving of notice will commence to run on the date of the mailing of the notice.

If any return, claim, statement, notice, application, or other document required to be filed, or any payment required to be made on or before a prescribed date, is delivered by mail to the destination required for filing or payment, the date of the U.S. postmark stamped on the envelope will be deemed to be the date of delivery. (Sec. 1147(a)(2), Tax Law) For delivery services designated by the U.S. Secretary of the Treasury under IRC Sec. 7502, the postmark refers to any date recorded or marked in a manner described in IRC Sec. 7502. (Sec. 1147(a)(4), Tax Law)

Assessment to recover erroneous refunds.—The law provides no specific power for assessment to recover erroneous refunds. The Commissioner, however, has authority to make, adopt and amend rules and regulations appropriate to the carrying out of Article 28 and the purposes thereof, and the power to assess, determine, revise and readjust the taxes imposed by Article 28.

• *Transportation and transmission companies*

New York assessment procedures for transportation and transmission companies parallel that of federal law, whereby after 90 days from the mailing of a notice of deficiency, the notice becomes an assessment of the amount of tax specified in the notice, together with interest, additions, and penalties. (Sec. 1081, Tax Law) (For a discussion of interest and penalties, see ¶ 89-202)

Deficiencies may not be assessed unless a notice has been mailed to the taxpayer. (Sec. 1081(c), Tax Law)

• *Motor fuels tax*

A determination of tax may be made by the Commissioner of Taxation and Finance within three years after an incorrect or insufficient return has been filed by a distributor. (Sec. 288, Tax Law) An assessment may be made at any time, however, for a distributor who has not registered, has failed to file a return, or has filed a willfully false or fraudulent return with an intent to evade the tax. The taxpayer may agree in writing to waive the limitation period for the determination of tax.

An overpayment of a refund may be determined by the Commissioner and recovered from the claimant within two years after the date of the erroneous or excessive payment. (Sec. 289-c(3)(c), Tax Law)

Such determinations of tax by the Commissioner are final unless a hearing is requested. (Sec. 288, Tax Law)

• *Cigarette and tobacco products tax*

If any person files an incorrect or insufficient return, the Commissioner of Taxation and Finance may determine the amount of tax due at any time within three years after the return was filed, whether or not it was filed on or after the due date. (Sec. 478, Tax Law) However, if no return is filed or the return is willfully fraudulent, the determination may be made at any time.

The Commissioner may, however, enter into an agreement to extend the period for determination of the tax. (Sec. 478, Tax Law)

Any determination made under Sec. 478, Tax Law, will be final unless the person against whom the tax is assessed applies, within 90 days after notice of the determination was given, to the Division of Tax Appeal for a hearing. (Sec. 478, Tax Law)

• *Deficiency assessments due to federal changes*

Deficiencies resulting from federal changes are summarily assessed if conceded. If such changes are not conceded, usual proceedings apply, except that (1) the Department of Taxation and Finance may assess within two years of the taxpayer's filing report of change (if longer than usual period of limitations), and (2) where the taxpayer does not report federal changes, the Department must give 30 days' notice to challenge it.

Report conceding federal changes.—Taxpayers are required to report any change in their federal return that has the effect of changing New York tax liability. (Sec. 659, Tax Law; Sec. 211(3), Tax Law) The term "taxpayer" includes partnerships having a resident partner having any income from New York sources and corporations reporting any changes during a tax year in which the New York S election is in effect. A federal income tax return includes all returns required to be filed by partnerships and S corporations. (Sec. 659, Tax Law)

Where an amended return or report that concedes the accuracy of a change to the taxpayer's federal return and creates a deficiency in state tax is filed with the state, the deficiency is deemed assessed on the date the taxpayer files the return or report. This is a summary assessment and is not subject to the procedural requirements otherwise imposed on deficiency assessments. Furthermore, this type of assessment is timely without regard to the limitations period otherwise applicable to deficiency assessments. (Sec. 682(a); Sec. 1082(a)(2), Tax Law)

Report or return filed—no concession.—Where the taxpayer files a required report or amended return with the state to reflect a change in the taxpayer's federal return but does not concede the correctness of the adjustment, the usual deficiency procedures apply and the Department of Taxation and Finance must mail a notice of deficiency to the taxpayer. In this case, however, the limitations period for assessments is extended and the Department may assess a deficiency resulting from the federal change within two years from the date the report or amended return was filed by the taxpayer, or within the normal limitations period for assessments, whichever is longer. (Sec. 683(c)(3); Sec. 1083(c)(3), Tax Law)

Failure to file or report.—Where a taxpayer fails to report a change or file an amended return as required to reflect a change in the taxpayer's federal return, the Department of Taxation and Finance may assess any deficiency based on the federal change by mailing a notice of additional tax due to the taxpayer specifying the amount of the deficiency. (Sec. 681(e)(1); Sec. 682(a); Sec. 1081(e)(1); Sec. 1082(a)(2), Tax Law)

Assessment is perfected on the date the notice is mailed unless, within 30 days of the mailing, the taxpayer files with the state the required report of change or amended return and a statement showing that the federal change and notice of additional tax due are erroneous. If the taxpayer challenges the notice of additional tax due within the 30-day period, the normal deficiency assessment procedures must be followed. In commencing the normal assessment procedures, the notice of additional tax due is not deemed the equivalent of a notice of deficiency. (Sec. 681(e)(2); Sec. 1081(e)(2), Tax Law)

• *Statute of limitations*

The statute of limitations period for assessment of delinquent taxes is covered in the discussion of limitations periods for audits.

[¶89-186] Agreements in Compromise of Tax Due

General provisions concerning offers in compromise are discussed below.

In addition, a voluntary disclosure and compliance program was enacted by the 2008 budget bill. (Sec. 1700, Tax Law)

• *Offer in compromise program*

The New York State Offer in Compromise Program authorizes the Commissioner of Taxation and Finance to compromise tax liability. The commissioner is empowered to compromise taxes for qualifying taxpayers for liabilities considered fixed and final (Sec. 171.15th, Tax Law); for liabilities still subject to administrative review (Sec. 171.18th-a, Tax Law); and for certain joint personal income tax liabilities. (Sec. 171.18th-d, Tax Law) The department will not necessarily, however, accept every offer in compromise.

CCH COMMENT: New hardship eligibility guidelines.—The New York Department of Taxation and Finance has announced new reform measures that will improve tax administration on behalf of all taxpayers in the state. New eligibility consideration for severe economic hardship will allow the department to offer more favorable payment terms to taxpayers with overwhelming tax liabilities. The new eligibility factors will be added to the department's existing liability settlement program known as the Offer in Compromise Program.

The department may now consider factors other than insolvency or bankruptcy that can make it unduly burdensome for a taxpayer to pay a liability in full. These factors may include extraordinary individual or family health care costs or unemployment. In addition, the department will implement a fixed 20-year statute of limitations. (*Release*, New York Department of Taxation and Finance, September 15, 2011)

The Commissioner of Taxation and Finance is allowed to accept offers in compromise that are a lesser amount of taxes, penalties, and interest in order to increase the pool of applicants for a potential offer, including those offers based on undue economic hardship that collection in full would impose. An offer in compromise will not be accepted for any reason where acceptance of such an offer would not be in the best interests of the state or would undermine voluntary compliance with the Tax Law. Offers in compromise cannot be used as a tax planning device by businesses or individuals. (Sec. 171.15th, Tax Law; Sec. 171.18th-a, Tax Law)

The New York Department of Taxation and Finance has issued a memorandum explaining recently enacted legislation that revised the department's offer in compromise program. Eligibility to participate in the program includes individual taxpayers who can prove that collection in full of any liability administered by the department will cause the taxpayer undue economic hardship. This expanded eligibility is in addition to the existing criteria that allow participation if a taxpayer has been discharged in a bankruptcy proceeding or is proven to be insolvent. Approval by a justice of the New York State Supreme Court is required for fixed and final liabilities if the amount to be compromised is over $100,000, exclusive of penalties and interest. With respect to liabilities that are not fixed and final, the threshold is raised for requiring an opinion of counsel before an offer can be finalized to $50,000 or more, including penalty and interest. (*TSB-M-11(9)C, (9)I, (10)M, (2)MCTMT, (2)R, (14)S*, New York Department of Taxation and Finance, August 29, 2011)

For a discussion of the Offer in Compromise Program, see *Publication 220*. Note, however, that recent changes to the program in 2011 are not yet reflected in the publication.

Insolvency.—A taxpayer is considered insolvent when the taxpayer's liabilities (including tax liabilities) exceed the fair market value of his or her assets. The taxpayer must conclusively demonstrate his insolvency. (Publication 220)

The New York Department of Taxation and Finance has issued a memorandum that discusses the voluntary disclosure and compliance (VDC) program that was enacted by the 2008 budget bill and that applies to all taxes. (*TSB-M-08(6)I, TSB-M-08(11)C, TSB-M-08(6)M, TSB-M-08(4)R, and TSB-M-08(10)S*, New York Department of Taxation and Finance, September 3, 2008)

• *Filing*

Form.—Offers in compromise are filed on a form prescribed by the Commissioner of Taxation and Finance, which is available from his office or from persons designated by him. (Reg. Sec. 5000.3(c); Reg. Sec. 5005.1(c)) Forms are available on written request. A brief explanation of the reason why a taxpayer is seeking a compromise is required.

Form DTF-4, Offer in Compromise; or DTF-4.1, Offer in Compromise—Fully Determined Liability, must be filed to request an offer in compromise. In addition, a completed Form DTF-5, Statement of Financial Condition and Other Information, must be submitted with the last three years of federal income tax returns, a credit report less than 30 days old, the last 12 months of bank statements, and Form DTF-4 or DTF-4.1. (*Publication 220*)

Supporting documents.—Offers in compromise must be accompanied by appropriate documents. The information that must be contained in those documents depends on the theory underlying the offer.

Offers in compromise based on a doubt as to liability must be supported by documents and briefs that focus on legal and factual arguments casting doubt on the Department of Taxation and Finance's likelihood of prevailing in future proceedings. The Department's amenability toward the offer depends on the hazards of litigation, that is, the degree of doubt found in a particular case. (Reg. Sec. 5000.5(b)(1))

Offers based on doubt as to collectibility require a showing that the taxpayer has been discharged in bankruptcy or is insolvent. This requires a statement of the taxpayer's financial condition, such as an analysis of assets, liabilities, gross receipts and disbursements, and any other related information required on Form DTF-5. (Reg. Sec. 5000.5(b)(2); Reg. Sec. 5005.1(c))

CCH PLANNING NOTE: *Offer made on behalf of a corporation.*—If an offer based on doubt as to collectibility is made on behalf of a corporation, the Department generally requires a showing that the corporation's officers, directors and shareholders (i.e., responsible persons) are also insolvent. In all cases, the taxpayer should show the Department that the amount offered is more than the Department could obtain from any other source.

Offers in compromise should generally be accompanied by a remittance representing the amount of the offered compromise, or a deposit if the offer by its terms provides for future installment payments. If final payment of an accepted offer is contingent upon the immediate or contemporaneous release of a tax lien (whether in whole or in part), such payment must be in cash or in the form of a certified check, cashier's check or treasurer's check drawn on a bank or trust company incorporated in the United States, or by a U.S. Postal Service, bank, express or telegraph company money order. (Reg. Sec. 5000.3(a); Reg. Sec. 5005.1(c)) The taxpayer also may be required to provide the Department certain other assurances, such as collateral or security for installment payments or an agreement to pay a fixed percentage of future earnings. (Reg. Sec. 5005.1(c)(2))

Stay of proceedings.—Offers in compromise parallel the administrative review process but have no direct or immediate effect on these proceedings or on collection efforts.

The filing of an offer in compromise constitutes neither the filing of a request for a conciliation conference (see ¶ 89-230) nor the filing of a petition for a hearing before the Division of Tax Appeals. (see ¶ 89-234) (Reg. Sec. 5000.3(b)) The filing does not automatically operate to stay collection efforts with respect to the tax liability at issue (Reg. Sec. 5000.3(b)(1); Reg. Sec. 5005.1(c)(5)), or constitute cause for postponement of a conciliation conference or a hearing before the Division. (Reg. Sec. 5000.3(b)(2)) It also does not suspend the running of the statute of limitations for filing a request for a conciliation conference or a hearing before the Division. (Reg. Sec. 5000.3(b)(3)) Enforcement of collection may be deferred by the Department in cases where the offer is based on doubtful collectibility, however, if the interests of the Department are not jeopardized. (Reg. Sec. 5005.1(c)(5))

• *Review of offer*

The Counsel of the Department of Taxation and Finance is generally required to review offers in compromise and to submit a recommendation to the Commissioner of Taxation and Finance to accept or reject the offer. The Commissioner has exclusive

¶89-186

authority and jurisdiction over offers in compromise. The Division of Tax Appeals lacks authority to accept or even consider such offers. (Reg. Sec. 5000.6(a))

CCH PLANNING NOTE: Oral communications have minimal value.—The Department has expressed its desire to base its recommendations solely on the terms of offers, along with any documents submitted by taxpayers in support of them. The regulations specifically state that oral communications with the Commissioner, the Counsel or any other officer or employee of the Department regarding an offer will be considered to have minimal probative value and are strongly discouraged. (Reg. Sec. 5000.6(a)(3))

Doubt as to liability.—When an offer in compromise is based on doubt as to the taxpayer's liability, a conciliation conferee, an attorney from the Office of Counsel or the Commissioner of Taxation and Finance, must obtain an expert legal opinion from the Department of Taxation and Finance to confirm or dispute the alleged doubt. Accordingly, all such offers are forwarded to the Department's Counsel, who may request advice from either the Director of the Department's Audit Division or the Director of the Taxpayer Services Division. These officials have 60 days in which to recommend acceptance or rejection of the taxpayer's offer. The Counsel is not bound by their advice in making recommendations. (Reg. Sec. 5000.6(a)(1))

Where the Counsel's recommendation to accept an offer involves a total liability (including tax, interest and penalties) of $2,500 or more, the Counsel must also prepare a formal opinion for transmittal to the Commissioner. (Reg. Sec. 5000.6(a)(1))

Upon receipt of the Counsel's opinion and/or recommendation, the Commissioner is free to accept or reject the taxpayer's offer in compromise. Either action requires prompt notification of the taxpayer in writing. (Reg. Sec. 5000.6(b))

Doubt as to collectibility.—Where an offer in compromise is based on doubt as to collectibility, it is reviewed by the Tax Compliance Division. (Reg. Sec. 5005.1(d)) An expert opinion on the taxpayer's financial status from the Director of the Tax Compliance Division is required before action can be taken regarding the offer. The Director of Tax Compliance has 60 days in which to recommend acceptance or rejection of the offer. (Reg. Sec. 5000.6(b))

Where the total liability is less than $2,500 (including tax, interest and penalties), the Director's recommendation is submitted directly to the Commissioner of Taxation and Finance. (Reg. Sec. 5000.6(b))

Where the total liability (including tax, interest and penalties) is $2,500 or more, the Director's recommendation is forwarded to the Counsel for the Department of Taxation and Finance, who recommends acceptance, rejection or modification of the proposed offer. If the Counsel recommends acceptance, he must prepare a formal opinion for transmittal to the Commissioner along with the recommendation of the Director of Tax Compliance. (Reg. Sec. 5000.6(b))

Upon receipt of a recommendation, the Commissioner is free to accept or reject the taxpayer's offer in compromise. Either action requires prompt notification of the taxpayer in writing. (Reg. Sec. 5000.6(b))

• *Acceptance, rejection or withdrawal*

The Commissioner of Taxation and Finance has the ultimate authority to accept or reject a taxpayer's offer in compromise, and this duty cannot be delegated to any other person. (Reg. Sec. 5000.6(b); Reg. Sec. 5005.1(d)(2)(i))

Acceptance.—No offer in compromise can be accepted unless the taxpayer making the offer waives the running of the statute of limitations on collection of the liability involved for the period during which the offer is pending, or during which any installment payment remains unpaid, and for one additional year thereafter. (Reg. Sec. 5000.3(e); Reg. Sec. 5005.1(c)(3)) In addition, an acceptable offer based on doubt as to collectibility must reflect all that can be collected from a taxpayer's income (both present and prospective) after giving due effect to all priorities granted to the state's taxing authority. (Reg. Sec. 5000.5(b)(2))

As a condition to accepting any offer in compromise, the Commissioner may require a taxpayer to enter into collateral agreements (for example, pledging future income) or to post security deemed necessary for the protection of the state's revenue interests. A further condition is that a taxpayer must agree that the Department of Taxation and Finance may proceed with appropriate collection procedures provided for by the Tax Law as if the Commissioner had acquired an assessment no longer subject to administrative or judicial review. (Reg. Sec. 5000.3(c); Reg. Sec. 5005.1(c)(2)) This condition essentially requires taxpayers to waive the protection of the Tax Law insofar as the collection of an accepted offer is concerned.

Frivolous offers or offers filed for the purpose of delaying the collection of a tax liability are immediately rejected. (Reg. Sec. 5000.3(d); Reg. Sec. 5005.1(e)(2))

An offer in compromise is considered accepted or rejected only when the taxpayer who made the offer is so notified in writing. (Reg. Sec. 5000.3)

Record of acceptance: If the unpaid amount of the total liability compromised (including tax, interest and penalties) is $2,500 or more, a record of the opinion of Counsel of the Department of Taxation and Finance with respect to such compromise must be filed by the Commissioner of Taxation and Finance. (Reg. Sec. 5000.4) The Counsel's opinion must include a statement of:

— the amount of the tax and other issues that were the subject of the compromise;

— the amount of any interest, additions to the tax or penalties imposed on the taxpayer; and

— the amount actually paid, or required to be paid, in accordance with the terms of the compromise.

(Reg. Sec. 5000.4)

Rejections.—The following exemplify reasons for rejecting an offer in compromise:

— failure to meet the statutory requirements (i.e., the taxpayer has not been discharged in bankruptcy or is not insolvent and/or the Department can collect more through legal proceedings than the amount being offered in compromise);

— making a frivolous offer or filing an offer for the purpose of delaying the collection of tax liabilities;

— failure to verify financial information, where required;

— failure to make full financial disclosure;

— where there is evidence of conveyance of assets for less than fair market value;

— for public policy considerations;

— where the taxpayer has not demonstrated a good faith effort to repay/resolve the tax debt (i.e., where the taxpayer has displayed a wanton disregard for the tax debt over an extended period of time and disposed of significant assets and other holdings); or

— where the tax liability sought to be compromised directly relates to any crime for which the taxpayer has been convicted.

(Reg. Sec. 5005.1)

An offer in compromise is considered accepted or rejected only when the taxpayer who made the offer is so notified in writing. (Reg. Sec. 5000.3)

If an offer is rejected, any amount tendered with the offer must be refunded to the taxpayer (without interest) unless the taxpayer has agreed that the amount should be applied to reduce whatever liability is ultimately determined to be payable. (Reg. Sec. 5000.3; Reg. Sec. 5005.1(e)(3))

Withdrawal.—A taxpayer can withdraw an offer in compromise at any time before the Commissioner of Taxation and Finance's acceptance or rejection of the offer. (Reg. Sec. 5000.3(d); Reg. Sec. 5005.1(e)(1)) Withdrawn offers are a nullity. Thus, in the event of a timely withdrawal, a taxpayer can submit another offer regarding the same tax controversy. Once the Commissioner has acted on the offer, however, no more offers are permitted. (Reg. Sec. 5000.3(f)) When based upon the taxpayer's bankruptcy or insolvency, the Department may hold an offer made by the taxpayer in abeyance if the application or other required information is incomplete, in which case the taxpayer will usually have 30 days from notification in which to submit the information required to complete the application. (Reg. Sec. 5005.1(e)(1)) More time may be granted if the taxpayer can demonstrate to the Department's satisfaction that it is needed. If the required information is not timely submitted to the Department, the offer will be deemed to be formally withdrawn.

The taxpayer is entitled to a refund (without interest) of any amounts tendered in connection with a withdrawn offer unless he has agreed that such amounts should be applied to reduce whatever tax liability is ultimately determined to be payable. (Reg. Sec. 5000.3(d); Reg. Sec. 5005.1(e)(3)) For a discussion of refunds, see ¶ 89-224.

Default.—A taxpayer, whose offer in compromise is accepted based upon bankruptcy or insolvency, who fails to comply with the conditions of the offer, including any requirements with respect to collateral agreements, or who has made a substantial misrepresentation of a material fact discovered subsequent to acceptance by the Department of Taxation and Finance, has defaulted on the offer in compromise. (Reg. Sec. 5005.1(f)) In case of a default, the Department may reimpose the full tax liability, including all applicable interest and penalties. The Department may apply all amounts previously deposited under the offer against the amount of the liability sought to be compromised and may proceed to collect the balance of the original liability.

• *Bankruptcy and insolvency*

A taxpayer that has been discharged in bankruptcy or shown to be insolvent may make an offer in compromise of any New York tax liability that has been finally fixed and when the taxpayer has exhausted all administrative remedies. (Reg. Sec. 5005.1) The compromise amount may not be less than the amount the Department of Taxation and Finance could collect through legal proceedings and an offer in compromise may not be accepted because of hardship or any other issue that does not have a direct bearing on the Department's legal ability to collect. However, an amount less than the tax may be accepted if it is in the best interest of the parties and the amount reasonably reflects collection potential. A compromise offer must be accompanied by a remittance representing the amount of the offer or a down payment if the offer provides for future installments. As a condition to accepting an offer in compromise, a taxpayer must submit a statement of financial condition.

Where the amount owing for taxes or the warrant or judgment, exclusive of any penalties and interest, is more than $100,000, the compromise will be effective only when approved by a justice of the New York Supreme Court. (Sec. 171, Tax Law)

No offer in compromise is accepted unless the taxpayer:

— agrees that the Commissioner may keep all amounts collected, including all amounts to which the taxpayer may be entitled through overpayment of other taxes;

— agrees to return to the Commissioner any refunds of overpayments of other taxes;

— agrees not to contest in court the amount compromised;

— agrees to waive the statutory period of limitations;

— agrees to comply with filing of returns and paying of taxes for a period of five years; and

— is in compliance with all filing and payment requirements for periods not covered in the offer.

• *Disclosure of information*

The New York Department of Taxation and Finance has issued a memorandum that discusses recent amendments to the voluntary disclosure and compliance (VDC) program that applies to all taxes. The Tax Department is permitted to disclose any return or report filed by a taxpayer under the VDC program to the Secretary of the U.S. Treasury, his or her delegates, including the Internal Revenue Service (IRS), or the proper tax officer of any state or city, as otherwise permitted in the Tax Law. The amended law is effective April 7, 2009, and applies only to returns or reports filed under the VDC program on or after that date. The amendment does not apply to any other information obtained from a taxpayer during the voluntary disclosure process, including the taxpayer's actual disclosure under the VDC program. (*TSB-M-09(6)I, TSB-M-09(6)C, TSB-M-9(5)M, TSB-M-09(1)R, TSB-M-09(5)S*, Office of Tax Policy Analysis, New York Department of Taxation and Finance, May 13, 2009)

[¶89-200]

INTEREST AND PENALTIES

[¶89-202] Interest and Penalties in General

New York has separate provisions on interest and penalties for various tax types, in addition to general administrative provisions for all taxes. For a discussion of applicable interest rates, see ¶89-204. For civil penalties, see ¶89-206. For provisions relating to abatement of taxes, interest, and penalties, see ¶89-210.

Interest and penalties are reported on Form IT-201 for an individual taxpayer and on Form CT-3 for a corporate taxpayer.

[¶89-204] Interest Rates

The interest rates on underpayments and overpayments of New York taxes are set quarterly based on the federal short-term rate established by the U.S. Secretary of the Treasury for Internal Revenue Code purposes, rounded to the nearest full percentage or increased to the next full percentage (in the case of 0.5% multiple).

The underpayment rate may not be less than 7.5% per year. (Sec. 171, Tax Law; Sec. 684, Tax Law; Sec. 697, Tax Law; Sec. 1084(a), Tax Law; Sec. 1096(e)(1), Tax Law; Sec. 1145, Tax Law)

For personal income tax, the interest rate is calculated as the federal short-term rate plus 5.5% for underpayments or plus 2% for overpayments. (Sec. 697(j), Tax Law)

Finally, interest on any sales and use tax not paid is 14.5% per annum or the federal short-term rate plus seven percentage points, whichever is greater, imposed from the due date to the date paid, regardless of whether any extension of time for payment was granted. (Sec. 1145(a)(1), Tax Law) (*TSB-M-02(7)S; TSB-M-09(17)S*)

• *Corporate franchise (income) tax*

For corporate franchise (income) tax, the underpayment rate is the sum of the federal short-term interest rate plus 7% and the overpayment rate is the sum of the federal short-term interest rate plus 2%. If no rates are established, the rate will be deemed to be set at 7.5%. See below for current rates.

Underpayments.—Interest on underpayments of corporate franchise (income) tax accrues from the payment's due date (determined without regard to whether any extension of time for payment has been granted). (Sec. 1084(a), Tax Law) No interest due paid if the amount is less than $1.

Interest is payable upon notice and demand and may be assessed and collected at any time during the period within which the tax or other amount to which the interest applies may be assessed and collected. (Sec. 1092(b), Tax Law) Interest will not accrue between the date of the notice and the date of payment, provided payment is made within 21 calendar days (10 business days if the amount for which the notice and demand is made is equal to or more than $100,000). (Sec. 1084(h), Tax Law)

Tax reduced by carryback.—Where tax for a prior year is reduced by reason of a carryback of net operating loss or capital loss, the reduction of tax will not affect the computation of interest for the period ending with the filing date for the taxable year during which the net operating loss or capital loss arose. (Sec. 1084(e), Tax Law)

Estimated tax.—Interest at the underpayment rate is assessed for underpayments of estimated tax from the due date of the installment until the 15th day of the fourth month following the taxable year. (Sec. 1085(c)(1), Tax Law)

Mathematical or clerical error.—No interest is imposed on an underpayment of tax due solely to mathematical or clerical error if the return has been filed on time and the amount of underpayment is paid within three months after the due date of the return, as it may be extended. (Sec. 1084(c), Tax Law)

Suspension of interest—deficiencies.—If a waiver of restriction on assessment of a deficiency is filed by a taxpayer, and a notice and demand for payment of deficiency is not made within 30 days after the filing of the waiver, interest is suspended for the period beginning immediately after such 30th day and ending with the date of the notice and demand. (Sec. 1084(d), Tax Law)

Penalties and additions to tax.—Interest accrues on assessable penalties and additions to tax if they are not paid within 21 calendar days of notice and demand (10 business days if the amount for which the notice and demand is made is equal to or more than $100,000). (Sec. 1084(g), Tax Law) Accrual is from the date of notice and demand.

Fraud or misrepresentation.—Erroneous refunds induced by fraud or misrepresentation are subject to interest at the underpayment rate. (Sec. 1084(j), Tax Law)

Overpayments.—In the absence of a request for refund, overpayments of corporate franchise tax are applied to a taxpayers's estimated tax for the following year. (Sec. 1086(a), Tax Law) If the Commissioner notifies the taxpayer that the overpayment has been credited to the following year's estimated tax within three months after the last date prescribed (or permitted by extension of time) for filing the return, or within three months after such return was filed, whichever is later, and the taxpayer subsequently makes a claim for refund, no interest is allowed prior to the date of the claim for refund. (Sec. 1088(c), Tax Law)

Where a refund is requested, interest is allowed and paid to a date no more than 30 days preceding the date of the refund check. (Sec. 1088(a), Tax Law) No interest is paid if the amount is less than $1. No interest is paid where the overpayment is refunded or credited within three months of the last date prescribed (or permitted by extension of time) for filing the return on which the overpayment is claimed or three months from the date of filing, whichever is later. (Sec. 1088(c), Tax Law) Where an amended return or claim for credit or refund is filed on which an overpayment is claimed, no interest is paid if the overpayment is refunded or credited within three months from the date of filing. In computing the applicable three-month period, amended returns or claims for credit or refund are regarded as being filed on the last day prescribed (or permitted by extension of time) for the filing of the return of tax, rather than the actual date of filing.

Refund caused by carryback.—Where an overpayment of tax is caused by reason of a carryback of a net operating loss (NOL) or capital loss, the overpayment will be deemed not to have been made prior to the filing date of the taxable year in which the operating loss occurred. (Sec. 1088(d), Tax Law)

Overpayment applied against legally enforceable debt.—As of the date that the Commissioner receives notification of a past-due legally enforceable debt owed to a state agency, no interest will accrue on the portion of any overpayment that is to be credited against the debt. (Sec. 1088(f), Tax Law)

• *Current period*

The interest rates per annum, compounded daily, are specified below for refunds of tax and late payments and assessments of tax for the period October 1 through December 31, 2020. For all previous interest rates, see https://www.tax.ny.gov/pay/all/interest_indexes/int-all-years.htm

---

> **CCH CAUTION:** *Certain taxes repealed.*—The tax on gains derived from certain real property transfers was repealed, applicable to transfers of real property occurring on or after June 15, 1996. The gift tax was repealed, applicable to gifts made on or after January 1, 2000. The generation-skipping transfer tax was repealed, applicable to any distributions or terminations made after March 31, 2014.

Tax	Refunds	Late Payments and Assessments
Alcoholic Beverage	2%	7.5%
Authorized Combative Sports	2%	7.5%
Beverage Container Deposits	2%	7%
Cigarette	NA	7.5%
Congestion Surcharge	2%	7.5%
Corporation **	2%	7.5%
Diesel Motor Fuel	2%	7.5%
Estate	2%	7.5%
Fuel Use Tax	***	***
Generation-Skipping Transfer	2%	7.5%
Hazardous Waste	2%	15%
Highway Use	2%	7.5%
Income **	2%	7.5%
Medical Marijuana	2%	7.5%
New York City Taxicab and Hail Vehicle Trip Tax	2%	7.5%
Metropolitan Commuter Transportation Mobility Tax	2%	7.5%
Mortgage Recording	2%	7.5%

Tax	Refunds	Late Payments and Assessments
Motor Fuel	2%	7.5%
Opioid excise tax	2%	7.5%
Paper carryout bag reduction fee	2%	14.5%*
Petroleum Business	2%	7.5%
Real Estate Transfer	2%	7.5%
Sales and Use	2%	14.5% *
Tobacco Products	NA	7.5%
Transportation Network Company Assessment	2%	7.5%
Waste Tire Fee	2%	7.5%
Wireless communications surcharge	2%	14.5%*
Withholding	2%	7.5%

* The interest rate on sales tax assessments or late payments is required to be set at 14.5% for this quarter. However, if the commissioner determines that the failure to pay or delay in payment is due to reasonable cause and not willful neglect, the commissioner may impose interest at the corporate franchise (income) tax late payment and assessment rate. That rate is 7.5% for this quarter.

* * There are a number of state and local governmental bodies that have interest rates tied to the overpayment and underpayment rates contained in either Sec. 697(j), Tax Law (Income Tax) or Sec. 1096(e), Tax Law (Corporation Tax). For purposes of Sec. 697(j), Tax Law and Sec. 1096(e), Tax Law, the overpayment rate for this period is 2%. For purposes of Sec. 697(j), Tax Law, the underpayment rate for this period is 7.5%. For purposes of Sec. 1096(e), Tax Law, the underpayment rate for this period is 7.5%.

*** Under § 527(f) of the Tax Law, the interest rates relating to the fuel use tax are set pursuant to the International Fuel Tax Agreement (IFTA). For more information, see https://www.iftach.org/.

Interest is allowed on refunds of the alcoholic beverage and highway use taxes, but only where payments were made in error. Interest on alcoholic beverage tax refunds is paid to a date preceding the date of the refund check by not more than 30 days, and no interest is allowed for reimbursements. (Sec. 434, Tax Law; Sec. 513, Tax Law)

The tax on lubricating oil (Article 24, Tax Law) was repealed effective September 1, 1994. Notwithstanding such repeal, provisions relating to criminal and civil penalties applicable to violations of Article 24 continue in effect with respect to all taxes, including penalties and interest, accrued up to the effective date of repeal.

When reasonable cause is shown, the Commissioner of Taxation and Finance may waive the interest in excess of the statutory rate.

The payment of interest on overpayments of cigarette and tobacco products taxes is prohibited. (Sec. 171(26), Tax Law)

• *Article 21-A fuel use tax (IFTA)*

The underpayment and overpayment interest rates for the Article 21-A fuel use tax is set by law rather than by action of the Commissioner of Taxation and Finance. The rate is 1% per month for both underpayments and overpayments.

[¶89-206] Civil Penalties

Civil penalties are administered under specific provisions which cover procedures to be followed in cases of failure to file a return, failure to pay tax shown on return, deficiencies due to negligence or fraud, underpayment of estimated tax, and other situations warranting the imposition of penalties.

• *Failure to timely file and/or pay*

When a taxpayer fails to file a return on the due date, including extensions to file, a penalty of 5% per month is imposed, up to a maximum aggregate amount of 25%. The penalty is imposed on the difference between the amount shown as due on the return, less withholding, estimated payments, partial payments and other credits to which the taxpayer is entitled. (Sec. 685(a)(1), Tax Law; Sec. 1085(a)(1), Tax Law) If no tax is owed, therefore, a taxpayer who files late does not incur this penalty.

For a failure to pay, the penalty is 0.5% per month, up to a maximum of 25%. (Sec. 685(a)(2), (3), Tax Law; Sec. 1085(a)(2), (3), Tax Law)

Waiver.—The penalty for failure to file can be waived if the taxpayer can demonstrate that the failure to file was due to reasonable cause and not to willful neglect.

Time limitation.—The late filing penalty runs from the due date of the return (including extensions to file) to the date the return is actually received. It is not uncommon for a taxpayer to incur both failure to file and failure to pay delinquency penalties. If both penalties apply for a given month or part of a month, the penalty for failure to file is reduced by the penalty for failure to pay tax when due. (Sec. 685(a)(4)(A), Tax Law; Sec. 1085(a)(4)(A), Tax Law)

Additional penalties.—A minimum nonfiling penalty applies where the return is more than 60 days late. The penalty is equal to the lesser of $100 or 100% of the tax due, i.e., liability reduced by payments and credits. (Sec. 685(a)(1)(B), Tax Law; Sec. 1085(a)(1)(B), Tax Law) Thus, there is no minimum penalty if there is no tax liability, even where a return nonetheless must be filed. As in the case of the basic penalty (5% of tax per month, up to a maximum of 25%), this minimum penalty may not be imposed where the failure to file is shown to have been due to reasonable cause and not due to willful neglect. Unlike the basic penalty, it is not reduced by the failure to pay penalty.

A similar penalty is imposed for failure to pay a deficiency within 21 calendar days of notice and demand for payment (10 calendar days if the amount for which the notice and demand is made equals or exceeds $100,000). The amount to which the penalty rate is applied is the tax stated in the notice reduced by any partial payments. This penalty also may be waived if shown to be due to reasonable cause and not willful neglect. (Sec. 685(a)(3), Tax Law; Sec. 1085(a)(3), Tax Law)

Disasters.—In the case of disasters declared by the President or Governor, the Commissioner of Taxation and Finance may extend deadlines for payment of taxes for up to 90 days. (Sec. 171(28), Tax Law) In addition, regarding state disaster emergencies declared by the Governor, the deadlines for payment may be extended until the conclusion of the disaster (or up to 30 days thereafter).

• *Negligence*

Where any part of a deficiency is due to negligence or intentional disregard of the law, rules and regulations, but not to fraud, a two-part penalty applies. The first part of the penalty is equal to 5% of the deficiency. (Sec. 685(b)(1), Tax Law; Sec. 1085(b)(1), Tax Law) Once negligence or intentional disregard is found for any part of the deficiency, the 5% penalty is imposed on the entire underpayment. The second part of the penalty is equal to 50% of the interest otherwise due on the portion of the underpayment that is due to negligence or intentional disregard. The period for measuring the interest starts on the due date for payment of the tax (excluding extensions) and ends on the earlier of the date of assessment or payment. (Sec. 685(b)(2); Sec. 1085(b)(2), Tax Law)

In computing the amount of the deficiency on which the negligence penalty is imposed, the taxpayer's correct tax liability is reduced by any tax shown on a timely filed return (including extensions to file). (Sec. 685(m), Tax Law; Sec. 1085(i), Tax Law)

Where an underpayment is due in any part to a failure to include dividends, patronage dividends or interest required to be reported under the Internal Revenue Code, it is treated as being due to negligence in the absence of clear and convincing evidence to the contrary. (Sec. 685(b)(3), Tax Law; Sec. 1085(b)(3), Tax Law)

Negligence defined.—Negligence generally is lack of due care, or failure to do what a reasonable and ordinarily prudent person would do under the circumstances.

• *Fraud*

If any part of a deficiency is due to fraud, a penalty is imposed equal to two times the deficiency. (Sec. 685(e)(1), Tax Law; Sec. 1085(f)(1), Tax Law)

If a fraud penalty is assessed, no negligence penalties or penalties for failure to timely file or pay tax may be imposed. (Sec. 685(e)(2), Tax Law; Sec. 1085(f)(2), Tax Law)

In computing the amount of the deficiency on which the fraud penalty is imposed, the taxpayer's correct tax liability is reduced by any tax shown on a timely filed return (including extensions to file). (Sec. 685(m), Tax Law; Sec. 1085(i), Tax Law)

Joint returns.—In the case of a joint return, the fraud penalty does not apply with respect to the tax of a spouse unless some part of the underpayment is due to his or her fraud. (Sec. 685(e)(3), Tax Law)

Aiding or assisting.—A penalty of up to $5,000 for personal income tax or $10,000 for corporate taxes may be imposed for aiding or assisting in the making of a fraudulent return. (Sec. 685(r), Tax Law; Sec. 1085(l), Tax Law)

Document penalty.—In addition, any taxpayer that submits a false or fraudulent document to the department is subject to a penalty of $100 per document or $500 per tax return. (Sec. 685(cc), Tax Law; Sec. 1085(u), Tax Law; *TSB-M-09(10)C*)

Related provisions.—If a notice imposes a fraud penalty, there is a shortened period of time for requesting a conciliation conference; see ¶ 89-230.

The limitations period for assessments related to fraudulent returns is discussed at ¶ 89-144.

Criminal penalties are discussed at ¶ 89-208.

• *Substantial understatement of liability*

A 10% penalty is imposed against taxpayers for substantial understatements of tax liability. A substantial understatement is an omission of tax on an annual return equal to at least 10% of the correct tax or $2,000 ($5,000 for corporations), whichever is greater. Since substantial understatements of tax can result from incorrect positions taken in good faith, taxpayers are excused for any portion of an understatement attributable to tax treatment of an item for which there was substantial authority, or where the facts affecting the taxpayer's treatment of the item are adequately disclosed in the return or in a statement attached to the return. The Commissioner of Taxation and Finance may waive all or part of the penalty on the taxpayer's showing of good faith and reasonable cause for all or part of the understatement. (Sec. 685(p), Tax Law; Sec. 1085(k), Tax Law)

The corporate tax procedure and personal income tax regulations provide an explanation of how a taxpayer may establish reasonable cause for a substantial understatement of tax liability. First, the rules relating to reasonable cause for the failure to file returns or pay taxes also apply to substantial understatements where pertinent. Second, reasonable cause exists only where the taxpayer has acted in good faith. Relevant grounds indicating reasonable cause and good faith that apply only to the substantial understatement penalty include:

(1) an honest misunderstanding of fact or law that is reasonable in light of the education, experience and knowledge of the taxpayer;

(2) a computational or transcriptional error;

(3) reasonable reliance on written information or professional advice that the taxpayer has no reason to question; and

(4) the filing of an amended return before the taxpayer is contacted by the Department of Taxation and Finance concerning an audit or examination of a return.

(Reg. Sec. 2392.1(g), Tax Law)

• *Fraudulent failure to perform required act*

In addition to other penalties, the Commissioner of Taxation and Finance may impose a penalty of up to $1,000 against any person who, with fraudulent intent, fails to pay tax due or fails to make, sign, or certify any return, or supply information within the time required. This penalty may, in the discretion of the Commissioner, be waived, reduced, or compromised. (Sec. 685(i), Tax Law; Sec. 1085(g), Tax Law) (See ¶ 89-210)

• *Underpayment of estimated taxes*

A taxpayer who underpays estimated tax is subject to a penalty based on the amount and duration of the underpayment. (Sec. 685(c), Tax Law; Sec. 1085(c), Tax Law)

Individuals.—For individuals, the amount of the penalty for underpayment of estimated taxes is computed by applying to the underpayment the interest rate in effect for the period as established by the Commissioner of Taxation and Finance. (Sec. 685(c)(1), Tax Law) (For a list of interest rates, see ¶ 89-204) The underpayment for penalty purposes is the difference between the actual payment and the required installment. (Sec. 685(c)(2), Tax Law) The required installment is the lower of:

(1) 25% of the required annual payment, which in turn is the lesser of:

(a) 90% of the tax shown on the return (or if no return is filed, of the tax for such year), or

(b) 100% of the tax shown on the return filed for the preceding tax year, provided that the individual filed a return for that year and that it was a full tax year (12 months); (Sec. 685(c)(3), Tax Law) or

(2) an annualized income installment, which means in essence:

(a) annualizing the taxable income and minimum taxable income for the months ending before the due date for the installment, and computing the tax that would be due on such amounts,

(b) multiplying that tax by 22.5% for the first installment, 45% for the second installment, 67.5% for the third installment or 90% for the fourth installment, and

(c) subtracting from the product the aggregate of prior estimated tax payments.

(Sec. 685(c)(4), Tax Law)

Withheld tax generally is treated as a payment of estimated tax and is applied equally to the four installments. The taxpayer, however, may establish the actual dates and amounts of withholding, in which case these amounts are treated as payments of estimated tax on the actual withholding dates. (Sec. 685(c)(5)(A), Tax Law)

If a return for the year is filed and the full amount of tax computed on the return as payable is paid by the following January 31, no penalty applies to underpayment of the fourth installment. (Sec. 685(c)(5)(B), Tax Law)

Penalty exceptions.—Various exceptions apply to the imposition of the addition to tax, whereby no penalty is imposed:

— A de minimis rule prohibits imposition of a penalty where the tax (reduced by credits, including that for tax withheld) is less than $100 ($300 with regard to tax years beginning on or after January 1, 1999);

— Taxpayers who had no tax liability for the preceding year;

— Installments due on or after the taxpayer's death;

— Where the Department of Taxation and Finance determines that "by reason of casualty, disaster or other unusual circumstances the imposition of such addition to tax would be against equity and good conscience"; or

— Where the taxpayer retired after age 62 or became disabled, either in the tax year for which estimated tax payments were required or in the preceding tax year, and the Department determines that the underpayment was due to reasonable cause and not willful neglect.

(Sec. 685(d), Tax Law) (See ¶89-210)

Corporations.—Corporations are generally required to make estimated tax payments during the year equal to 91% of the current year's tax, although higher payments are required of large corporations, discussed below. If a corporation fails to pay all or any part of a required installment of estimated tax, it is subject to a penalty for underpayment of estimated tax. The amount of the penalty is computed, on Form CT-222, by applying to the underpayment the interest rate in effect for the period as established by the Commissioner of Taxation and Finance. (See ¶89-204) If the corporation makes installment payments equaling 80% (rather than the required applicable percentage) of the current year's tax liability, the penalty is reduced to 75% of the amount otherwise determined. (Sec. 1085(c)(1), Tax Law)

Large corporations.—For large corporations, defined as corporations that had (or whose predecessors had) allocated entire net income of at least $1 million for any of the three tax years immediately preceding the tax year involved, estimated tax payments during the year must equal 100% of the current year's tax. (Sec. 1085(e)(2), Tax Law)

Metropolitan Commuter Transportation District.—The penalty for underpayment of estimated tax also applies to underpayment of estimated Metropolitan Commuter Transportation District tax surcharge. (Sec. 1085(c)(3), Tax Law) This provision is effective for tax years beginning on or after January 1, 1991.

Penalty exception.—No penalty is due on an installment if the total of estimated tax payments made on or before the installment due date equals or exceeds the amount that would have been required to be paid on or before such date if the estimated tax were the smallest of:

(1) The tax shown on the return for the preceding tax year (if it was a period of 12 months). (Sec. 1085(d)(1), Tax Law) This exception does not apply to large corporations. A large corporation is one that had (or whose predecessor

had) allocated taxable income of at least $1 million for any of the three tax years immediately preceding the tax year involved (for insurance companies subject to tax under Sec. 1502-a, a special provision applies). (Sec. 1085(e)(1), Tax Law)

(2) An amount equal to the tax computed using current tax rates and last year's facts and law. (Sec. 1085(d)(2), Tax Law) This exception does not apply to large corporations (as defined in (1), above). (Sec. 1085(e)(1), Tax Law)

(3) The applicable percentage (91 or 100%) of the tax for the current year computed on an annualized basis. (Sec. 1085(d)(3); Sec. 1085(e)(2), Tax Law)

(4) The applicable percentage (91 or 100%) of the tax for the current year computed on a recurring seasonal income basis. (Sec. 1085(d)(4), Tax Law; Sec. 1085(e)(2), Tax Law)

A reduction in an estimated tax payment resulting from using annualized income or seasonal income exceptions (exceptions (3) and (4), above) must be made up in the next payment. (Sec. 1085(d)(5), Tax Law)

• *Withholding penalties*

There are several penalties for noncompliance with withholding requirements. These penalties apply even if the tax required to be withheld is ultimately paid by an employee. (Sec. 676, Tax Law)

Failure to furnish withholding statements.—An employer who fails to furnish withholding statements to employees, or furnishes fraudulent statements to them, is subject to a $50 penalty per violation. No maximum aggregate of penalties applies. (Sec. 685(j), Tax Law)

Failure to pay withholding tax.—An employer's nonwillful failure to collect and pay over withholding taxes is subject to a penalty equal to 5% of the tax due per month of deficiency, (Sec. 685(f), Tax Law) up to a maximum of 25% of the tax due. (Sec. 685(a)(1), Tax Law) If, however, the failure is willful, the penalty is equal to the sum of (1) the total amount of the tax evaded, or not collected, or not accounted for and paid over, and (2) the interest that has accrued on the total amount of tax evaded on the date this penalty is first imposed, until the penalty is paid with interest. (Sec. 685(g), Tax Law) Moreover, where the failure is due to the fraudulent intent of an employer, an additional penalty, not to exceed $1,000, is imposed. (Sec. 685(i), Tax Law)

Willful failure to collect and pay over.—Persons required to collect and pay over withholding taxes are personally liable for their willful or fraudulent failure to perform this duty. (Sec. 685(g), Tax Law) Such persons are financially responsible officers, employees or members of the employer. (Sec. 685(n), Tax Law) The penalty is separate from the employer's liability for unpaid withholding taxes.

A responsible corporate officer is liable for the full amount of unpaid withholding even though another responsible corporate officer exists. There is no authority, however, to make responsible officers indirectly liable for interest and penalties asserted against the corporation that are not included in the responsible officer's penalty. (*Matter of Phillips*, DTA Nos. 812455, 812456 (1994)) Officer assessments cannot be used to collect penalties and interest due from a corporation where the total tax due has been paid. (*Matter of Muffoletto*, DTA Nos. 801567, 802284 (1997))

The Commissioner of Taxation and Finance has discretionary authority to abate the penalty. (Sec. 685(g), Tax Law) (See ¶ 89-210)

Responsible persons.—The following are examples of persons found liable for the penalty for failure to collect and pay over withholding taxes:

— executive director of hospital with authority over hospital's staff and payroll; (*Allen v State Tax Commission*, 126 AD2d 51, 512 NYS2d 916 (1987))

— 10% owner of restaurant who had no responsibility for hiring or firing, vendor payments or handling of books and records, but who was aware of restaurant's financial difficulties, loaned restaurant substantial sums of money and had fiduciary responsibility to see that taxes were collected and paid; (*Matter of Krone*, DTA No. 806485 (1991))

— 2% general partner in limited partnership; (*Matter of Hopper*, DTA No. 807025 (1994)) and

— president and majority shareholder, even though she did not have any daily responsibilities or any involvement with financial affairs; (*Matter of Ross*, DTA Nos. 812383, 812383 (1995))

Not responsible persons.—The following persons have been found *not* to be responsible for collecting and paying over withholding taxes:

— chief operating officer with no authority to draft checks and no payroll responsibilities; (*Matter of McGarigal*, DTA No. 803697 (1988))

— corporate officer who signed checks and returns but was essentially a front for higher authority; (*Matter of Vose*, TSB-H-85-(84)-I (1985))

— corporate president, after assignment for benefit of creditors; (*Matter of Cody*, TSB-H-85-I (1985))

— corporate officer and majority shareholder who resigned his position and pledged stock as security but remained as manufacturing manager for corporation; (*Matter of Cox*, TSB-H-85-(173)-I (1985))

— assistant secretary and 25% shareholder who had rarely exercised check signing authority and was not involved in day-to-day affairs of corporation's main office; (*Matter of Gallo*, DTA No. 800007 (1988))

— vice president whose duties did not include financial management of company; (*Matter of Gallo*, DTA No. 800007 (1988))

— jobsite foreman who had authority to, but never signed, corporate checks; (*Matter of Palmese*, DTA No. 63054 (1987))

— employee with control over one corporate division's day-to-day operations but who lacked corporate-wide responsibility; (*Matter of Orville*, TSB-H-87-(184)-I (1987))

— former president who had no authority to manage corporate affairs or to sign checks; (*Matter of King*, DTA No. 810776 (1993)) and

— president of company involved in takeover related to organized crime. (*Matter of Defeo*, DTA No. 809712 (1995)).

The burden of disproving responsibility for withholding taxes is on the assessed party. (*Malkin v Tully*, DTA Nos. 815716-815722 (1998))

Disproving willfulness.—the following factors disproved a finding of willfulness:

— Director-shareholder believed that bank would honor checks for withholding taxes. (*Matter of Hahn*, TSB-H-85-(152)-L (1985))

— Vice president and 50% shareholder received no compensation from the corporation, was primarily concerned with another business and had delegated authority over financial matters to accountants. (*Matter of Lyon*, DTA No. 52750 (1987))

— Chief executive officer was not aware checks for withholding taxes had been dishonored. (*Matter of Rounick*, DTA No. 803076 (1991))

— Officer was deliberately deceived by employees as to whether the corporation was meeting its withholding obligations. (*Matter of Russack*, DTA No. 813087 (1996))

False information by employee regarding withholding.—A $500 penalty applies for each false statement made by an employee with respect to withholding (i.e., regarding withholding exemptions). This penalty may be waived if the taxpayer's credits or estimated tax payments exceed his tax liability. (Sec. 685(s), Tax Law)

• *Failure to file information returns*

New York imposes penalties on the failure to file returns of information at source (viz., Forms IT-2102 and IT-2102.1, similar to federal Forms W-2 and 1099), or annual information returns of partnerships, S corporations or trusts. The penalty applicable to returns of information at source is $50 per statement (up to an annual maximum of $10,000). The penalty applicable to partnership or S corporation information returns for each month of failure (up to five months) is equal to $50 multiplied by the number of partners or shareholders who were in the partnership or S corporation for any part of the tax year and were subject to tax for any part of that year. The penalty applicable to a trust is equal to $150 a month up to a maximum of $1,500 per taxable year. (Sec. 685(h), Tax Law) (For a discussion of penalties, see ¶ 89-202)

These penalties do not apply where the failure is due to reasonable cause and not due to willful neglect.

• *Failure to supply identifying numbers*

For failure to include one's identifying number in any return, statement or other document, a $5 penalty applies. For failure to furnish one's identifying number to another person or to include the identifying number of another person in a return, statement or other document, a $50 penalty applies. The maximum total amount of all such penalties during a calendar year is $10,000. The penalty for failure to supply one's own identifying number is not imposed unless the person fails to supply the number within 30 days after the Department of Taxation and Finance requests it. It is also not imposed if the failure is shown to be due to reasonable cause and not willful neglect. (Sec. 685(k), Tax Law) Grounds that may establish reasonable cause include good faith reliance on an incorrect identifying number, waiting for the issuance of an identifying number, and failure to obtain an identifying number after repeated documentable attempts. (Reg. Sec. 2392.1(f))

• *Frivolous tax returns and submissions*

A penalty of up to $5000 is imposed for filing a frivolous return. A return is frivolous where:

(1) it does not contain enough information on which to judge the substantial correctness of the self-assessment, or indicates on its face that the self-assessment is substantially incorrect; and

(2) it takes a position that is frivolous or evinces an intent to delay or impede the administration of the tax. (Sec. 685(q), Tax Law)

For a discussion of tax returns, see ¶ 89-102.

Specified frivolous submissions.—A $5,000 penalty applies to any person who submits a specified frivolous submission. Specified submissions include a request for conciliation conference, a petition to the division of tax appeals, an application for an installment payment agreement, or an offer in compromise. However, if the commissioner provides an individual with notice that a submission is a specified frivolous submission and that person withdraws the submission within 30 days after the notice, then the penalty will not apply. (Sec. 685(q), Tax Law)

• *Aiding or assisting in fraudulent returns and other information*

A penalty of up to $1,000 ($10,000 for corporations) applies to persons who, for a fee or other compensation and with intent to evade tax, aid, assist in, procure, counsel or advise the preparation or presentation (in connection with an income tax or franchise tax matter) of any return, report, declaration, statement or other document that is fraudulent or false as to any material matter. Also proscribed is supplying false or fraudulent information. The penalty is imposed whether or not the falsity or fraud is with the knowledge or consent of the taxpayer. (Sec. 685(r); Sec. 1085(l), Tax Law)

• *Return preparer penalties*

For failure to sign a personal income tax return, there is a penalty of $250 for each failure, up to a maximum of $10,000 per calendar year. But if the tax return preparer was already penalized for this in a preceding year, then the penalty is $500 per failure with no annual cap. (Sec. 685(u)(1), Tax Law)

For failure to furnish an identifying number on a personal income tax return, there is a penalty of $100 for each failure, up to a maximum of $2,500 per calendar year. But if the tax return preparer was already penalized for this in a preceding year, then the penalty is $250 per failure with no annual cap. (Sec. 685(u)(2), Tax Law)

The penalty for failure to furnish a copy of the return or refund claim to the taxpayer is $50 per return or claim, up to $25,000 per year. (Sec. 685(u)(3), Tax Law)

The penalty for failure to retain a copy of the return or refund claim or a list of taxpayers is $50 for each such failure, with a $25,000 maximum for any calendar year. (Sec. 685(u)(4), Tax Law)

These penalties are not imposed where the failure is due to reasonable cause and not willful neglect.

For a discussion of amendments to the Tax Law and the Administrative Code of New York City in relation to penalties imposed upon tax return preparers who fail to electronically file (e-file), to authorize reasonable correction periods for electronic tax filings and payments, and to prohibit tax return preparers and software companies from charging separately for electronic filing of New York tax documents, see TSB-M-10(18)S.

Penalties for disclosure of client information are listed at Sec. 6511 and rule 29.10.

Unsupported positions. If a tax preparer takes a position that he or she knew (or should have known) was improper, and it was not adequately disclosed on the personal income tax return, then a penalty of between $100 and $1,000 applies. If the tax preparer acts with reckless or intentional disregard of the law, then the penalty will be between $500 and $5,000. (Sec. 685(aa), Tax Law)

• *Failure to file report of information relating to certain interest payments*

For failure by corporations to report payments of interest to shareholders owning more than 50% of the capital stock of the corporation, (Sec. 211(2-a), Tax Law) a penalty of $500 is imposed unless it is shown that the failure was due to reasonable cause and not due to willful neglect. (Sec. 1085(n), Tax Law)

• *Failure relating to issuer's allocation percentage*

A $500 penalty applies against corporate taxpayers where a return does not contain the taxpayer's issuer's allocation percentage or the information necessary to compute the taxpayer's issuer's allocation percentage, unless it is shown that the failure is due to reasonable cause and not due to willful neglect. (Sec. 1085(o), Tax Law)

• *Failure regarding quarterly combined withholding and wage reporting return*

Penalties are imposed for failures by employers required to file quarterly combined withholding and wage reporting returns. (Sec. 685(v), Tax Law) (For a discussion of returns, see ¶ 89-102)

An employer who fails to include required wage reporting information relating to individual employees on the return, or to include true and correct wage reporting information, and who fails to correct the failure for more than 30 days after notification of the failure is subject to the following penalty:

(1) up to $1 for each employee for the first failure for one reporting period in any eight consecutive reporting periods;

(2) up to $5 for each employee for the second failure for one reporting period in any eight consecutive reporting periods; and

(3) up to $25 for each employee for the third failure for any reporting period in any eight consecutive reporting periods, and for each such failure in any eight consecutive reporting periods that is subsequent to the third such failure.

(Sec. 685(v), Tax Law)

An employer who fails to file a required quarterly combined withholding and wage reporting return in timely fashion is subject to a penalty of the greater of $1,000 or the product of $50 times the number of employees of the employer, up to $10,000 for any failure. The penalty is abated, however, if the employer files the return within 30 days after notification of the failure is sent by the Department of Taxation and Finance. (Sec. 685(v), Tax Law)

Failure by an employer to include all of the quarterly (before 2019, annual) withholding information relating to individual employees required to be shown on a return covering each quarter (before 2019, the last quarter) of the year results in a penalty equal to $50 times the number of employees for whom information is inaccurate or incomplete, up to $10,000. (Sec. 685(v)(3), Tax Law)

Failure to include required quarterly information not relating to individual employees on a quarterly combined return, or to include information that is true and correct, subjects the employer to a penalty of 5 percent of the quarterly withholding tax liability required to be shown by the employer for the quarter, up to $10,000, although the penalty is abated if the employer corrects the failure within 30 days after notification by the Department. The penalty is also not imposed if the Department is able to verify and reconcile the withholding and wage reporting information using the information provided by the employer. (Sec. 685(v), Tax Law)

If an employer fails to use the correct format in filing a quarterly combined return, he is deemed to have failed to file a return and is subject to a penalty of $50 per statement. (Sec. 685(v), Tax Law)

These penalties do not apply where the failure is due to reasonable cause and not due to willful neglect.

• *Bad check fee*

A $50 fee is imposed for bad checks, bad money orders, or failed electronic funds withdrawals intended for payments of any taxes, fees, or assessments imposed by the Department of Taxation and Finance. This provision applies to authorized tax documents required to be filed for tax years beginning on or after January 1, 2009. (Sec. 30, Tax Law)

[¶89-210] Abatement of Interest, Penalties, or Additions to Tax

The New York Commissioner of Taxation and Finance is authorized to abate interest, penalties and additions to tax.

For a discussion of interest rates, see ¶89-204.

For a discussion of civil penalties, see ¶89-206.

• *Departmental delays, errors in performing ministerial, managerial acts*

The Commissioner may abate all or any part of interest for any period that is attributable, in whole or in part, to any error or delay by a Department of Taxation and Finance officer or employee, acting in his or her official capacity, in performing a ministerial act. (Sec. 3008, Tax Law) Effective for interest accruing due to deficiencies or payments for taxable periods beginning and taxable events occurring after September 10, 1997, an abatement may be granted for unreasonable error or delay and extends to managerial acts. An unreasonable error or delay will be taken into account only if no significant aspect can be attributed to the taxpayer.

• *Abatement of interest attributable to misappropriated payments*

The Commissioner is authorized to abate interest with respect to misappropriated payments of all New York taxes. "Misappropriation" means circumstances in which a person wrongfully intercepts a taxpayer's payment tendered to the Department prior to the Department crediting the taxpayer's account, and obtains use of the taxpayer's funds. (Sec. 3008(d), Tax Law; *TSB-M-03(6)C, TSB-M-03(7)I, TSB-M-03(7)S, TSB-M-03(6)M, TSB-M-03(6)R*)

The Commissioner may abate any assessment or final determination of interest attributable to the misappropriation of a taxpayer's payment, for a specific period of time, where (1) the taxpayer timely makes payment to the Department for a liability incurred for any tax, and the taxpayer's account with the Department is not properly credited for the payment as a result of a misappropriation of the payment; (2) the taxpayer does not cause or contribute to the misappropriation of the payment; and (3) the taxpayer makes a replacement payment to the Department for the original amount of tax due no later than one year from the mailing date of the Department's notice for failure to pay.

• *Reliance upon erroneous written advice*

The Commissioner must abate any portion of penalty, addition or excess interest attributable to erroneous written advice furnished to a taxpayer by a Department of Taxation and Finance officer or employee acting in his or her official capacity, provided:

> (1) the written advice was reasonably relied upon by the taxpayer and was in response to the taxpayer's specific written request;

> (2) the portion of the penalty or addition to tax or excess interest did not result from a failure by the taxpayer to provide adequate or accurate information; and

> (3) the advice was requested on or after December 1, 1992.

• *Assessments attributable to mathematical errors*

Where an income tax return is prepared by a Department officer or employee acting in his or her official capacity to provide assistance to taxpayers, and a

¶89-210

deficiency attributable in whole or in part to a mathematical error described in IRC Sec. 6213(g)(2)(A) occurs, the Commissioner may abate all or any part of the interest for any period ending on or before the tenth day following the date of notice and demand by the Commissioner for payment of the deficiency. The right of abatement applies to assessments of tax imposed or pursuant to the authority of Article 22, 30, 30-A or 30-B, Tax Law, or Article 2-E, General City Law, where the mathematical error occurs on or after December 1, 1992.

• *Consolidated penalty abatement regulation*

A consolidated regulation regarding the abatement of penalties and other additions to tax for reasonable cause outlines when a taxpayer's reliance on professional advice may constitute reasonable cause and allows an honest misunderstanding of fact or law or reasonable reliance on written advice, professional advice, or other facts to establish reasonable cause for purposes of the abatement of delinquency penalties. (Reg. Sec. 2392.1)

• *Victims of disasters*

The Commissioner is authorized to postpone personal income and other tax deadlines, including any liability for outstanding interest, penalties, additional amounts or additions to the tax, for a period of up to 90 days in the event of disasters declared by the President of the United States or the governor of New York. (Sec. 171(28), Tax Law) A presidentially declared disaster is defined as a disaster that occurs in an area that the President determines requires assistance by the federal government under the Disaster Relief and Emergency Act. The postponement provisions are applicable to any period for performing an act that has not expired before January 1, 1998.

Postponed deadlines.—For those affected by a disaster, the tax deadlines that can be postponed for 90 days include the deadlines for:

— filing an income tax return; (except withholding tax)

— payment of income tax (except withholding) or any liability to the state in respect thereof;

— filing a petition or application;

— allowance of credit or refund of income tax;

— filing claim for credit or refund;

— assessment of income tax;

— giving or making notice or demand for payment of tax or liability to the state with respect thereto;

— collection of any liability in respect of income tax;

— bringing of suit by or on behalf of the state in respect of any income tax liability; or

— any other act required or permitted by Article 22 or specified in regulations prescribed under Sec. 696.

Additionally, a determination of the amount of any tax credit or refund may also be postponed for the 90-day period. However, a determination of the amount of interest on any overpayment of tax cannot be postponed.

Reasonable cause for abatement of late filing and late payment penalties presumed for those affected by terrorist attacks of September 11, 2001.—The New York Department of Taxation and Finance allowed the late filing of New York personal income and corporate franchise tax returns for general business corporations (Art. 9-A), banking corporations (Art. 32), and insurance corporations (Art. 33), and late payment of the tax on those returns, to have been due to reasonable cause and not willful neglect if the due date for filing the corresponding federal tax return under the IRS disaster provisions was later than the due date for the New York state tax return. For a complete discussion of the deadline extensions for those affected by the terrorist attacks, see *Important Notice N-01-14*, *Important Notice N-01-16*, and *Important Notice N-01-19*.

[¶89-220]

TAXPAYER RIGHTS AND REMEDIES

[¶89-224] Refunds

New York provisions concerning refunds are discussed below.

• *Income tax*

If a taxpayer has paid an amount in excess of his or her tax liability for a given year (i.e., an overpayment), he or she may seek a refund or credit of the overpayment by filing a claim for refund or credit within the statutory period of limitations. (Sec. 687(a), Tax Law; Sec. 1087(a), Tax Law) An overpayment is a payment in excess of the amount that should have been assessed and collected as tax. (Sec. 686, Tax Law; Sec. 1086, Tax Law) Any tax assessed or collected after the applicable period of limitations has expired (Sec. 686(g), Tax Law; Sec. 1086(d), Tax Law), and any withholding taxes or estimated taxes paid in excess of actual tax imposed for the year (Sec. 686(b), Tax Law), are treated as overpayments.

For refund and credit purposes, advance remittances, such as withholding or estimated taxes, are considered paid on the due date. (Sec. 687(i), Tax Law; Sec. 1087(i), Tax Law) In determining the overpayment, the tax is the correct tax as redetermined after audit.

In addition, if the period of limitations on assessment and collection has run, the Commissioner of Taxation and Finance may still take into account any time-barred deficiency found to exist for the year in determining the extent to which a taxpayer has actually overpaid his tax. (Sec. 689(d)(2), Tax Law; Sec. 1089(d)(2), Tax Law) Moreover, rather than refund an overpayment, the Commissioner may credit it against any other tax liability of the taxpayer, or against any liability the taxpayer might have for past-due support or a past-due debt owed to a state agency. (Sec. 686(a), Tax Law; Sec. 1086(a), Tax Law)

If an overpayment of corporate tax is claimed on a return or report, a refund is made only if application for the refund is made on the return or report. In the absence of such application, the overpayment is credited against the tax liability for the following year and against the estimated tax for the year, regardless of whether the taxpayer claims the overpayment as a credit in the declaration of estimated tax for the year. The Commissioner notifies the taxpayer that the overpayment has been so credited, and the taxpayer may, prior to the due date of the taxpayer's return for the year to which the overpayment has been credited, claim a refund of the overpayment. (Sec. 1086(a), Tax Law)

The person authorized by the statutes to file refund claims is the taxpayer. (Sec. 687(a), Tax Law; Sec. 1087(a), Tax Law)

Crediting against estimated tax.—Overpayment may be credited against estimated tax for the following tax year. To the extent so credited, a claim for refund is generally not allowed. (Sec. 686(e), Tax Law; Sec. 1086(b), Tax Law)

However, effective September 23, 2011, the law was amended to permit the reversing of an election to credit a personal income or corporate franchise tax overpayment against estimated tax for the succeeding taxable year, if good cause is shown by the taxpayer. The taxpayer's request must be made on or before the last day prescribed for filing the return for the succeeding taxable year, including any extension granted. The decision of the Commissioner of Taxation and Finance to grant or deny the request is final and not subject to further administrative or judicial review. (Sec. 686(e), Tax Law; Sec. 1086(b), Tax Law)

Period of limitations.—To be timely, a claim for refund or credit of an overpayment must generally be filed within three years of the date the return is filed or two years from the date the tax is paid, whichever is later. Where a claim is filed during the three-year period, it is limited to the tax paid during the three years plus any extension for filing the return. (Sec. 687(a), Tax Law; Sec. 1087(a), Tax Law)

> *EXAMPLE: Claim limited to tax period during period.*—If a taxpayer makes timely estimated tax payments but files his return more than three years late, a refund claim filed within three years of the filing of the return is timely, but the refund is limited to zero because that is the amount of tax paid within the three-year period preceding the filing of the refund claim. (*Matter of Wallace*, DTA No. 803801 (1989))

Since estimated taxes and withholding taxes are deemed paid on the due date for filing the return (Sec. 687(i), Tax Law; Sec. 1087(i), Tax Law), these amounts may be claimed even if actually remitted more than three years from the date of filing the claim. For this purpose, a return filed early is deemed filed on the due date. (Sec. 687(h), Tax Law; Sec. 1087(h), Tax Law) Where a claim is made within the two-year period, the refund or credit is limited to the portion of the tax paid during the two years. If a taxpayer fails to file a return, recovery is limited to amounts paid within the two-year period before the claim is filed.

A refund claim sent by mail is considered filed on the date of the postmark. The rule establishing the date of mailing as the date of filing applies, however, only if the document mailed is actually received. The risk of mishandling, either by the post office or the Department of Taxation and Finance, is on the taxpayer. (*Matter of Filler*, DTA No. 803976 (1989))

Special refund authority.—Under a special refund authority, the Department of Taxation and Finance can refund personal income taxes and corporation taxes at any time, without regard to any period of limitations, where no questions of fact or law are involved and the tax was erroneously or illegally collected, or paid under a mistake of fact. (Sec. 697(d), Tax Law; Sec. 1096(d), Tax Law)

> *EXAMPLE: Mistake discovered after statute of limitations.*—The special refund authority was used where a taxpayer mistakenly included his N.Y.S. pension in N.Y. adjusted gross income and did not discover his mistake until after the statute of limitations for refund claims had expired. (*Matter of Nathel*, DTA No. 812280 (1995))

> *EXAMPLE: Overwithholding claim filed after statute of limitations.*—The special refund authority has also been used where a refund claim resulted from overwithholding and the claim was filed one day after the end of the two-year limitations period. (*Matter of Filler*, DTA No. 803976 (1989))

Extension by agreement.—A written agreement between the taxpayer and the Commissioner of Taxation and Finance to extend the period of limitations for assessment of tax also extends the period of limitations for a claim for refund or credit for the same period, plus an additional six months. If a claim is made within the additional six months, the amount of refund or credit may include not only the portion of the tax paid after the agreement but all of the tax that could have been refunded had a claim been filed on the date the extension agreement was executed. (Sec. 687(b); Sec. 1087(b), Tax Law)

Claims relating to federal changes.—If an overpayment results from a change in the federal return required to be reported to the state, the claim for refund must be filed within two years from expiration of the 90-day period (120-day period for corporations filing a combined return) in which the report of change or amended return was due. If the claim is made outside the normal limitations period, the amount of the refund may not exceed the reduction in state tax attributable to the federal change. (Sec. 687(c); Sec. 1087(c), Tax Law) For corporate taxpayers, the refund must be computed without change of allocation of income or capital. (Sec. 1087(c)(1), Tax Law)

Loss carrybacks.—For corporate taxpayers claiming a credit or refund resulting from the carryback of a net operating loss to a prior year, an amended return should be filed within 90 days (120 days if filing an amended combined return) from the date of the document indicating approval of the federal refund or credit. (Reg. Sec. 3-8.9; Form CT-3 Instructions; Important Notice N-09-2)

The following must be attached to the amended return:

— federal claim Form 1139, Corporation Application for Tentative Refund, or federal Form 1120X, Amended U.S. Corporation Income Tax Return;

— a copy of the New York state return for the loss year; and

— proof of federal refund approval, Statement of Adjustment to Your Account.

A federal S corporation that files as a New York C corporation subject to Article 9-A must file the applicable New York State return for the prior year by checking the Amended return box on the front of the return and attaching a copy of federal Form 1120S, U.S. Income Tax Return for an S Corporation, for the loss year. The amended return must be filed within 15 months from the end of the loss year. (Form CT-3 Instructions; Important Notice N-09-2)

A claim for refund when the overpayment results from the carryback of a net operating loss (and/or capital loss for corporate taxpayers) must be made within (1) three years from the due date of the return (including extensions) for the tax year when the loss occurred, (2) six months after expiration of an agreement to extend the time for assessment of a deficiency for the year of the loss, or (3) the period for filing a claim based on a federal change for the carryback year, whichever expires latest. (Sec. 687(d), Tax Law; Sec. 1087(d), Tax Law)

If an overpayment results from the carryback of a net operating loss (and/or capital loss for corporate taxpayers), the overpayment is considered to have occurred on the filing date of the loss year, without regard to extensions. (Sec. 688(d), Tax Law; Sec. 1088(d), Tax Law)

Redetermination of deficiency.—If a taxpayer has filed a petition for redetermination of a deficiency, the Commissioner of Taxation and Finance has jurisdiction to determine that the taxpayer has overpaid tax for the year in question and to allow a credit or refund without requiring a separate claim by the taxpayer. (Sec. 687(f); Sec. 1087(f), Tax Law) Similarly, if on judicial review of a decision of the Commissioner a court disallows the deficiency in whole or in part, the amount of disallowed deficiency, if previously paid, may be refunded or credited without a separate claim. (Sec. 690(d), Tax Law; Sec. 1090(d), Tax Law)

Interest on overpayments.—A taxpayer is entitled to interest on an overpayment of tax from the date of the overpayment until no more than 30 days before the date of the refund check, or if the overpayment is credited, to the due date of the amount against which the credit is taken.

No interest is payable if the amount is less than $1.49. If an overpayment is refunded within three months (45 days for overpayments of personal income tax) after the due date of the return (or date of actual filing if the return is filed after the due date), no interest is payable on the overpayment. (Sec. 688(c), Tax Law; Sec. 1088(c)(1), Tax Law) Interest on a refund claimed by filing an amended return may be paid for the period preceding the filing of the amended return or claim, but no interest will be paid on the period between the filing of the amended return or claim and the refund, if the refund is provided within 45 days after the filing of the return or claim. (Sec. 688(c), Tax Law) Regarding an overpayment of corporate tax that is credited due to the absence of an application by the taxpayer for refund, if the Commissioner of Taxation and Finance notifies the taxpayer of the crediting within three months after the later of the due date of the return on which the overpayment was claimed or the date the return was filed, and the taxpayer subsequently makes a claim for refund of the overpayment, no interest is payable on the overpayment. (Sec. 1088(c)(2), Tax Law)

Overpayments credited against past-due support, against a past-due legally enforceable debt, against a defaulted guaranteed student, state university or city university loan, or (effective August 20, 2004) against a New York City tax warrant judgment debt cease to bear interest on the date that the Commissioner certifies the amount of the credit to the Comptroller. (Sec. 688(f), Tax Law; Sec. 1088(f), Tax Law)

For a discussion of interest rates, see ¶ 89-202.

For a list of current rates, see ¶ 89-204.

If a refund or credit claim results from a change in the federal return and the report of change or amended return is not filed within the required 90-day period (120-day period for corporations filing combined returns), interest does not accrue after the 90th (or 120th) day. (Sec. 687(c), Tax Law; Sec. 1087(c), Tax Law)

Late-filed returns.—If a return is filed after the due date (including extensions), no interest is allowed for any day before the date the return is filed. (Sec. 688(a)(3), Tax Law; Sec. 1088(a)(3), Tax Law) This limitation does not apply, however, if the change of an item from one year to another causes an overpayment in one year and an underpayment in another year and the taxpayer is required to pay interest on the underpayment for the same period. (Sec. 688(a)(4), Tax Law; Sec. 1088(a)(4), Tax Law)

Petitions for refund.—A taxpayer may file a petition with the Commissioner of Taxation and Finance for refund of an overpayment if six months have expired since a timely claim was filed, or the Commissioner has mailed to the taxpayer a notice of disallowance, in whole or in part, of the refund. If a notice of disallowance has been mailed, the petition for refund must be filed within two years of the mailing date unless the period has been extended by written agreement between the taxpayer and the Commissioner. The taxpayer may file a written waiver of the requirement that he be mailed a notice of disallowance of refund, in which case the two-year period for filing the petition runs from the date the waiver is filed. (Sec. 689(c), Tax Law; Sec. 1089(c), Tax Law)

In determining whether the taxpayer is entitled to a refund on petition, the Commissioner may determine all issues relating to whether an overpayment for the tax year has been made, and may offset overpayments against deficiencies for the same year that are time-barred. (Sec. 689(d)(2) Tax Law; Sec. 1089(d)(2), Tax Law)

A taxpayer may not file a petition for refund if a petition for redetermination of a deficiency for the same tax year has been timely filed, unless the petition for refund relates to a separate claim involving a federal change, amounts collected in excess of those required by a final determination of the Commissioner, amounts collected after the period of limitations on collections has expired or overpayments determined by a final decision of the Commissioner. (Sec. 689(c), Tax Law; Sec. 1089(c), Tax Law)

Judicial review.—The taxpayer is entitled to judicial review of a determination on a petition for refund by way of a CPLR Article 78 proceeding. The application must be made within four months from the date that notice of the decision of the Tax Appeals Tribunal is mailed to the taxpayer. (Sec. 690, Tax Law; Sec. 1090, Tax Law)

• *Disclosure of taxpayer's overpayment*

The Department of Taxation and Finance has authority to disclose to a taxpayer all instances of tax overpayments made by the taxpayer and discovered by the Department during the course of an audit, assessment, collection, or enforcement proceeding. For tax overpayments disclosed under this provision, a taxpayer may apply for a refund or claim a credit within 120 days from the date on which the notice of disclosure is given to the taxpayer. A failure to apply within 120 days will result in the loss of the right to apply for a refund or credit. However, this limitation will not reduce the time within which a taxpayer may claim a credit or refund of a tax overpayment under any other applicable provision. (Sec. 3004-a, Tax Law)

This provision may not be construed as requiring or permitting the payment of a refund or the granting of a credit with respect to any period that, because of a period of limitations, is not open for assessment or refund when the overpayment is discovered by the Department. (Sec. 3004-a, Tax Law)

[¶89-230] Taxpayer Conferences

Conciliation conferences, conducted informally by a conciliation conferee, seek to resolve taxpayer disputes in a quick and inexpensive manner without resorting to a formal hearing. (Sec. 170(3-a), Tax Law) The taxpayer's representative presents his or her side of the case, and an auditor presents the views of the Department of Taxation and Finance. The conciliation conferee then attempts to resolve any disagreements by narrowing the facts or legal issues in dispute. Relevant facts and legal arguments are tendered by each party in an informal manner through testimony, affidavits, briefs, letters, and other means. (Reg. Sec. 4000.5(c))

As an incentive to taxpayers to employ this settlement process, the Commissioner of Taxation and Finance may delegate to the conferee his authority to waive or modify penalties, interest, or other additions to tax. (Reg. Sec. 4000.5(c)) (See ¶89-210)

CCH PLANNING NOTE: Taxpayers should request a conciliation conference.—Conciliation conferences are strongly advised. Only in rare circumstances should they be bypassed, for example, where it is clear that nothing will be accomplished by a conference except the disclosure of information that the taxpayer's representative at this point chooses not to disclose. Conferences will usually result in a clearer definition of the issues, the elimination of agreed-upon matters, and a smoother formal hearing. Moreover, the Division of Tax Appeals has the authority to refer matters to the Bureau of Conciliation and Mediation Services for a conciliation conference where one has not been conducted, upon the request of a taxpayer and with the consent of the Office of General Counsel if the taxpayer intended to file a request rather than a petition for a formal hearing or if the conference would serve a useful purpose. (Sec. 3000.3(e), Tax Law)

• *Request for conference*

Conciliation conferences usually begin with the filing of a written request and conformed copy with the Bureau of Conciliation and Mediation Services, Department of Taxation and Finance. (Reg. Sec. 4000.3)

Form of request.—A request for a conciliation conference should be typewritten if possible and contain the following information (Reg. Sec. 4000.3(a)):

(1) the name and address of the taxpayer and, if applicable, the taxpayer's representative; (Reg. Sec. 4000.3(b)(1))

(2) the taxable years or periods involved and the amount of tax in controversy; (Reg. Sec. 4000.3(b)(1)(iii))

(3) the action(s) of the operating division or bureau that are protested; (Reg. Sec. 4000.3(b)(1)(iv))

(4) the relevant facts and law as they appear to the taxpayer; (Reg. Sec. 4000.3(b)(1)(v))

(5) the signature of the taxpayer or the taxpayer's representative beneath a statement that the request is made with knowledge that a willfully false representation is a misdemeanor; (Reg. Sec. 4000.3(b)(1)(vi))

(6) a legible copy of the statutory notice being protested; (Reg. Sec. 4000.3(b)(1)(vii)) and

(7) if applicable, the original or a legible copy of the power of attorney. (Reg. Sec. 4000.3(b)(1)(viii))

The Bureau of Conciliation and Mediation Services may request additional information in order to process the request for a conference and to resolve outstanding issues.

CCH PLANNING NOTE: Use of official forms.—The Bureau of Conciliation and Mediation Services has prepared two forms that may be used to request conciliation conferences.

Form DTF-966.5, Request for Conciliation Conference, is usually included in the materials taxpayers receive with their statutory notice. It is a bare-bones request that uses a fill-in-the-blank format. More important, when timely filed, it protects a taxpayer's statutory rights. Once Form DTF-966.5 is filed, the Bureau may request additional information. A more detailed request form, Form CMS-1, Request for Conciliation Conference, resembles the petition forms used by the old Tax Appeals Bureau. This form should be used to detail a taxpayer's position and to state the facts and law that support it.

Use of official forms is always preferred, but an informal letter containing the necessary information is sufficient.

• *Time limitations*

Requests for conciliation conferences must be filed within the statutory time limitations for filing petitions for hearing in the Division of Tax Appeals. (Reg. Sec. 4000.3)

CCH COMMENT: Time limit for filing.—Most petitions must be filed within 90 days of the issuance of a statutory notice, but there are some exceptions that require petitions within 30 days; e.g., if a notice imposes a fraud penalty, the request for review must be made within 30 days. (Sec. 170(3-a)(h), Tax Law)

No extensions of time are permitted. (Sec. 170(3-a)(a), Tax Law) A timely request for a conference suspends the running of the period of limitations for the filing of a petition for hearing with the Division of Tax Appeals. (Sec. 170(3-a)(b), Tax Law) It does not, however, suspend the accrual of any amount due as additions to tax, interest or penalties.

CCH CAUTION: Requests by ordinary mail.—In *Dattilo v. Urbach*, the New York Supreme Court, Appellate Division, rejected as untimely a request for a conciliation conference filed by a taxpayer by ordinary mail. In so doing, the Court held that mailing rules contained within Sec. 691(a), Tax Law, provide the exclusive means for proving the timely filing of a document, and rejected the taxpayer's argument that the traditional "mailbox rule" created a rebuttable presumption of delivery upon proof of mailing. Accordingly, a taxpayer that uses ordinary mail to file a document does so at his or her own risk; if ordinary mail does not result in actual delivery, the taxpayer cannot resort to extrinsic means to prove delivery and timely filing.

Referral of petition by Department of Tax Appeals.—Where a conciliation conference has not been conducted and it appears that the taxpayer intended to file a request for a conciliation conference or that one would serve a useful purpose, the Division of Tax Appeals may, at the request of the taxpayer, refer a tax appeal to the Bureau of Conciliation and Mediation Services. (Reg. Sec. 3000.3) In such instances, the taxpayer will be deemed to have requested the conference as of the date that the petition was filed. (Reg. Sec. 4000.3)

• *Representation of parties*

A taxpayer who requests a conciliation conference may appear personally or be represented by persons identified by statute. (i.e. a spouse, parent or child). (Reg. Sec. 4000.2) In certain circumstances, a power of attorney may be required.

A minor under 18 years of age may be represented by his or her adult spouse, parent, guardian or by the person who prepared the minor's return. Anyone having a proper interest in doing so may appear on behalf of a taxpayer who is mentally or physically incapable of filing a petition or appearing on his or her own behalf.

Representation by permission of Director.—Attorneys, certified public accountants (CPAs) or licensed public accountants authorized to practice or licensed in jurisdictions outside New York may appear and represent a taxpayer for a particular matter by special permission of the Director of the Bureau of Conciliation and Mediation Services.

• *Hearing procedures*

The Bureau of Conciliation and Mediation Services will acknowledge and review requests for conferences. (Reg. Sec. 4000.5) Where a request is not filed in a timely manner, a conciliation order will be issued denying the request. Otherwise, parties will be given 30 days written notice of the time and place of the first conciliation conference.

By regulation, the conciliation conference is to take place at an office of the Department of Taxation and Finance that is most convenient to the taxpayer who requested it. In addition, either party to the proceeding (the taxpayer or the Department) may ask for a preference in scheduling, which will be honored to the extent possible.

CCH PLANNING NOTE: Asking for preferred location.—Taxpayers should ask for their preferred conference location in their request for a conference or in a cover letter to the Bureau of Conciliation and Mediation Services. Conciliation conferences are generally available in locations where the Department maintains a district office, including Albany, Binghamton, Buffalo, Hauppauge (Suffolk County), Hempstead (Nassau County), New York City, Rochester, and Rye Brook (Westchester County). If a prompt conference is desired, this should be stated in the request. Asking for a conference in Albany should also be considered.

Written notice.—Written notice of the time and place of an initial conciliation conference is mailed to the parties at least 30 days before its date. Notices of adjourned or continued conferences must be mailed to the parties at least 10 days before the scheduled date of the continued or adjourned conference. (Reg. Sec. 4000.5(b)(1)(i)) A taxpayer may waive the 30-day notice requirement and request an expedited conference.

Adjournments.—A conciliation conference (other than an expedited conference) may be adjourned by either party if a request based on good cause is made in writing at least 15 days before the scheduled conference date. An adjournment may be granted on less notice in the event of an emergency. (Reg. Sec. 4000.5(b)(2))

Expedited matters.—In cases involving the denial of an application for a license, permit or registration, or the cancellation, suspension or revocation of a license, permit or registration, a conciliation conference is to be held within 20 business days of the day the Bureau of Conciliation and Mediation Services receives a request for a conference. (Reg. Sec. 4000.5(b)(1)(ii))

In addition, taxpayers can expedite any matter by waiving the 30-day notice of a conciliation conference. (Reg. Sec. 4000.5(b)(1)(i))

CCH COMMENT: Notice by telephone.—Due to the time constraints involved, the Bureau attempts to contact taxpayers by telephone to set up a conference. When possible, these telephone arrangements are confirmed by letter. (Reg. Sec. 4000.5(b)(1)(ii))

• *Defaults*

The rules governing defaults differ depending on whether the party who fails to make an appearance is the taxpayer or the representative of the Department of Taxation and Finance.

Taxpayer defaults.—Where a taxpayer fails to appear personally or by representative and no adjournment has been granted, the conferee may issue an order dismissing the request for nonappearance. (Reg. Sec. 4000.5(b)(3)) Once a dismissal order has been issued, a taxpayer has 90 days to file a petition for a hearing in the Division of Tax Appeals regarding the original statutory notice. Where, however, a taxpayer can demonstrate a reasonable excuse for his or her nonappearance (i.e. the taxpayer never received the notice scheduling the conference), a dismissal order can be vacated if the taxpayer so requests, in writing, within 30 days of the order.

Department of Taxation and Finance defaults.—When a conference has been scheduled but the representative of the Department of Taxation and Finance fails to appear, the conference is still held. (Reg. Sec. 4000.5(b)(4)) The taxpayer may make his or her presentation, and the conferee will issue an order based on the record, which consists of:

(1) the taxpayer's entire presentation (including documentary evidence);

(2) the statutory notice at issue;

(3) correspondence or other written information given to the taxpayer by the Division of Taxation before the conference; and

(4) any post-conference evidence or submission made by the taxpayer. (Reg. Sec. 4000.5(b)(4)) In addition, the conferee may contact either party to clarify any issues or facts in dispute.

CCH PLANNING NOTE: Present complete case.—Since a statutory notice is considered valid on its face, a taxpayer faced with a default should present a complete case to the conciliation conferee. The taxpayer still has the burden of proof on most issues and must overcome the presumption that the assessment is valid.

• *Discontinuances*

At any time prior to the issuance of the conciliation order the taxpayer may discontinue the conciliation conference by filing a request for a discontinuance with the Bureau of Conciliation and Mediation Services. The taxpayer will then have 90 days from the time the request for discontinuance is filed to petition for a hearing in the Division of Tax Appeals. (See ¶ 89-234) (Reg. Sec. 4000.6) If the taxpayer fails to file a timely petition, the assessment as stated in the statutory notice becomes final, and the Department of Taxation and Finance cannot be enjoined from initiating collection proceedings against the taxpayer absent allegations of fraud.

• *Consents*

After the conclusion of a conference, the conciliation conferee will review the evidence, testimony and other materials submitted by the parties and attempt to work out a resolution of the matter in the form of a consent. If there is confusion as to particular issues or facts, a conferee can contact either party for clarification. (Reg. Sec. 4000.5(c)(3)(i))

If a taxpayer agrees with the terms of a proposed consent, he must execute it within 15 days. Execution concludes the matter, and the taxpayer waives all rights to a hearing before the Division of Tax Appeals. (Reg. Sec. 4000.5(c)(3))

If a taxpayer does not agree to a proposed consent or fails to execute it within 15 days, the conciliation conference is deemed to have been concluded without a resolution. An order to that effect will be rendered by the conferee within 30 days of the deemed conclusion date. (Reg. Sec. 4000.5(c)(3)(iii))

• *Conciliation conference orders*

Within 30 days of the conclusion of a conciliation conference (including any time consumed by the submission of additional evidence, affidavits, briefs, etc.), the conciliation conferee must issue an order resolving the matter. (Sec. 170(3-a)(e), Tax Law; Reg. Sec. 4000.5(c)(3)(iii)) The issuance date of a conciliation order is the date the order is mailed, not the date indicated on the face of the order or the date the order was signed by the conferee.

CCH COMMENT: Postmarked envelope.—Because the 90-day period allowed to the taxpayer to protest a conciliation order starts from the issuance date, the taxpayer would be well-advised to save the postmarked envelope in which the order was delivered and compare this date to the date on the face of the order itself.

An order provides one of the following:

—the case against the taxpayer (or the Department of Taxation and Finance in a refund or licensing action) should be dismissed;

—the case against the taxpayer should continue to the next stage without resolution; or

—the case should be settled based on some agreement reached during the conference.

Force and effect.—Absent a showing of fraud, malfeasance or misrepresentation of a material fact, conciliation orders are binding on the Division of Taxation. Conciliation orders are not, however, considered precedent, nor are they given any force or effect in any subsequent conciliation conference with regard to the taxpayer or any other taxpayer. In fact, a taxpayer cannot use a prior conciliation order in a subsequent conference even if it involves identical legal issues.

> *CCH PLANNING NOTE: Persuasive effect.*—Nevertheless, since virtually all evidence is relevant at a conciliation conference, a taxpayer should still be able to use a prior favorable conciliation conference as evidence of the reasonableness of his or current position. The old order should have persuasive, if not precedential, effect.

[¶89-234] Administrative Appeals

Taxpayers seeking administrative review of controversies with the New York Department of Taxation and Finance may request a formal hearing with the Division of Tax Appeals. The Division of Tax Appeals is intended to promote fairness, efficiency, and quality in the administrative review of tax matters. It is an autonomous unit of the Department of Taxation and Finance that is completely independent of the Commissioner of Taxation and Finance. (Sec. 2000, Tax Law; Sec. 2002, Tax Law)

Where the amount in controversy does not exceed $20,000 ($40,000 with respect to cases involving sales and compensating use taxes), excluding penalties or interest, the parties may consent to have the proceedings conducted in the Small Claims Unit. (Reg. Sec. 3000.13) Otherwise, matters are conducted within the Administrative Law Judge Unit.

However, effective December 1, 2004, the former State practice with respect to the availability of hearings on notice and demands and notices of additional tax due issued for amounts assessed because of mathematical or clerical errors, federal changes, or failure to pay tax shown on the return which are deemed to be self-assessed is restored. Specifically, a notice and demand is used when the tax shown due exceeds the amount remitted by the taxpayer or in other self-assessed situations, such as cases involving math errors on the tax return or where failure to perform a certain act (i.e. failure to timely file a return) gives rise to a penalty. The Tax Law requires that these assessment cases be issued a notice of demand without being afforded formal hearing rights. As such, taxpayers will have 21 calendar days to remit the payments. (Sec. 173-a, Tax Law; *Summary of Tax Provisions in SFY 2004-05 Budget*, New York Department of Taxation and Finance, August 2004)

An organizational chart of the Division of Tax Appeals is located on the following page:

DIVISION OF TAX APPEALS

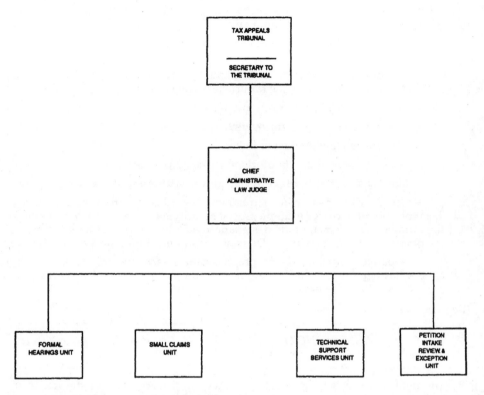

• *Authority of ALJs*

Once pleadings have been submitted (see below), the tax controversy is scheduled for a hearing before an administrative law judge (ALJ) designated by the Tax Appeals Tribunal (if a small claims hearing has not been elected). (Reg. Sec. 3000.15(a)) Administrative law judges, who must be attorneys, are appointed by the Tax Appeals Tribunal and function as impartial arbiters of tax controversies. (Sec. 2010(1), Tax Law) They are not supposed to be familiar with any of the facts underlying a controversy before hearing the case. The judges are directed to conduct their hearings in as fair a manner as possible and should permit parties to offer all relevant evidence. (Sec. 2000, Tax Law; Sec. 2010(2), Tax Law)

In addition, ALJs are authorized to:

— administer oaths and affirmances;

— sign and issue subpoenas;

— regulate the course of hearings;

— set the time and place for continued hearings;

— fix the time for filing legal memoranda and other documents;

— rule upon questions of evidence; and

— render a determination after the hearing.

(Reg. Sec. 3000.15)

• *Petition for hearing*

All proceedings in the Division of Tax Appeals are commenced by the timely filing of a typewritten petition containing the following information:

— the name, address and telephone number of the petitioner and, if applicable, the petitioner's representative;

— the division, bureau or unit of the department that sent the statutory notice, the date of the notice, the tax article involved, and the nature of the tax;

— the taxable years or periods involved;

— the amount of tax in controversy;

— the relief sought by the petitioner;

— a legible copy of the statutory notice being protested;

— the original or a legible copy of a power of attorney, if applicable;

— an identifying number or numbers prescribed by the Commissioner of Taxation and Finance (for example, social security numbers, employer identification numbers or other numeric designations suitable for proper identification of the petitioner), to be used by the Division for administration purposes only; and

— separately numbered paragraphs stating each error that the taxpayer alleges has been made, and a statement of the facts upon which the taxpayer relies to establish each error.

(Reg. Sec. 3000.3(b))

CCH PLANNING NOTE: *Standard form for petitions.*—A standard form is available for petitions. (Form TA-10)

The petition for a hearing must be signed by the taxpayer, or the taxpayer's representative, and contain an acknowledgement that the petition is made with knowledge that a willfully false representation is a misdemeanor.

Determining timeliness of petition.—For purposes of determining the timeliness of the petition, a legible copy of the order of the conciliation conferee must be provided or, if no such order was previously issued, a legible copy of the statutory notice being protested.

Filing of petition.—The original and two conformed copies of the petition are filed with the Supervising Administrative Law Judge, State of New York Division of Tax Appeals, Agency Building 1, Empire State Plaza, Albany, New York 12223.

• *Time limitations*

Petitions for administrative review within the Division of Tax Appeals must be filed within the following statutory time limitations:

— appeal from a notice of deficiency involving personal income (Sec. 681(b), Tax Law), franchise (Sec. 315, Tax Law), petroleum business (Sec. 1081(b), Tax Law) and gift taxes (Sec. 1007(b), Tax Law), 90 days (150 days if addressed to a taxpayer whose last known address is outside the U.S.);

— appeal from a notice of determination of sales and use (Sec. 1138(a)(1), Tax Law), alcoholic beverage (Sec. 430, Tax Law), tobacco (Sec. 478, Tax Law), highway use (Sec. 510, Tax Law), real property transfer (Sec. 1411(a), Tax Law), lubricating oil (Sec. 809(a), Tax Law), real property transfer gains (Sec. 1444(1), Tax Law), mortgage recording (Sec. 251, Tax Law) and motor fuels taxes (Sec. 288(5), Tax Law), 90 days;

— appeal from a notice of determination of stock transfer (Sec. 279-a, Tax Law) and motor fuel taxes (Sec. 288, Tax Law), 30 days; or

— petition for refund (Sec. 689(c), Tax Law), two years.

As a general rule, the above statute of limitations run from the mailing of the statutory notice by the Commissioner of Taxation and Finance, and not from its receipt by the taxpayer.

Mailing.—A petition is considered timely filed if it is mailed bearing a U.S. postmark dated within the limitations period. (Reg. Sec. 3000.22(a)(1)) A petition sent by metered mail, however, is timely only if the metered postmark bears a date that falls within the limitations period and the petition is received by the Division of Tax Appeals within the normal time period for receiving such an envelope mailed through the U.S. Postal Service. (Reg. Sec. 3000.22(b)(1)) The taxpayer has the burden of proving timely filing, and proof of ordinary mailing is insufficient to prove delivery. By using the U.S. mail, the petitioner bears the burden that the postmark will not be timely affixed or that the document may not be delivered at all. (For a discussion of mailing rules and legal holidays, see ¶ 89-110)

EXAMPLE: *Petition mailed by express mail.*—A petition deposited in a U.S. Express Mail mailbox before 5:00 p.m. on the 90th day of the statutory period but not collected and postmarked until the following day was held to be untimely. (*Matter of Seymour Epstein Enterprises, Inc.*, New York Division of Tax Appeals, Tax Appeals Tribunal, DTA No. 808661, September 12, 1991)

CCH PLANNING NOTE: *Suggested mailing of petition.*—While the receipt of a petition is acknowledged by the Supervising Administrative Law Judge, and such acknowledgment probably constitutes adequate proof of delivery, (Reg. Sec. 3000.3(c)(1)) to be on the safe side it is strongly advised that a taxpayer send the petition by registered or certified mail, return receipt requested, in case a question of receipt or timeliness is raised. Since only a U.S. Postal Service postmark is recognized, private overnight mail services provide no real benefit.

Extensions.—The limitation periods noted above cannot be extended. (Reg. Sec. 3000.3) The periods are, however, suspended during the period a timely request for a conciliation conference is pending before the Bureau of Conciliation and Mediation Service. (See ¶ 89-230)

• *Review of petition*

All petitions for hearings are acknowledged and reviewed by the Supervising Administrative Law Judge.

Corrections.—The Supervising Administrative Law Judge has 20 days to return defective petitions to the taxpayer, along with a statement outlining the reasons that the petition in not in proper form. (Reg. Sec. 3000.3) If the petition is not in the correct form, the taxpayer will be extended an additional 30 days in which to file a corrected petition. Failure to file a corrected petition within the 30-day period will result in the entry of a determination dismissing the petition.

CCH CAUTION: *Preparing original petition.*—Taxpayers should take extreme care in preparing the original petition, as well as any corrections. The petition is part of the record during the review of the case, including judicial review. It would not be wise to rely on correction procedures to set forth the facts in more detail, or to develop a persuasive narrative exposition of the taxpayer's case.

Referral to Bureau of Conciliation and Mediation Services.—The Division of Tax Appeals may, at the request of the taxpayer and with the consent of the Office of Counsel of the Division of Taxation, suspend action on a petition, and refer the matter to the Bureau of Conciliation and Mediation Services if the taxpayer has not made a request for a conciliation conference where:

— it appears that the taxpayer intended to request such a conference; or

— a conference would serve a useful purpose.

(Reg. Sec. 3000.3(e))

• *Answer to petition*

Once the petition is properly filed, it is forwarded to the Law Bureau for preparation of the answer. The Law Bureau must file an answer within 75 days from the date that the Supervising Administrative Law Judge acknowledges receipt of a petition in the proper form. (Reg. Sec. 3000.4) Upon written request, the Supervising Administrative Law Judge may extend the time for filing an answer to no more than 90 days. (Reg. Sec. 3000.4(b)(1))

If the Division of Taxation fails to file an answer within the prescribed time, all material allegations of fact set forth within the petition will be deemed to be admitted.

The Division of Taxation's answer must fully and completely advise the taxpayer of the Division's defenses, and contain numbered paragraphs that correspond to those in the taxpayer's petition. (Reg. Sec. 3000.4(a)(2)) In addition, the answer must contain:

— specific admissions or denials of each material allegation of fact contained in the taxpayer's petition;

— a statement of any additional facts to be proven by the Division of Taxation; and

— the relief sought by the Division of Taxation.

(Reg. Sec. 3000.4(a)(2))

Material allegations of fact set forth in the taxpayer's petition that are neither expressly admitted or denied in the answer are deemed admitted by the Division of Taxation. (Reg. Sec. 3000.4(a))

• *Reply to answer*

The taxpayer may serve a reply on the Division of Taxation within 20 days after service of the Division's answer. A copy of the reply, together with proof of service on the Division of Taxation, must be filed with the Division of Tax Appeals as well. (Reg. Sec. 3000.4(c))

• *Amended pleadings*

Amended pleadings, although not frequently used, offer practitioners the opportunity to correct defects in original pleadings. They can be used to add claims for relief derived from information received after the filing of the original pleading, or based on legal theories derived from case law. Amended pleadings can be as of right or by consent of the Supervising Administrative Law Judge.

As of right.—Both the taxpayer and the Division of Taxation have the right to amend a pleading once, as long as the amended pleading is served on the opposing party before the period for responding to the original pleading expires (i.e., the time period for serving an answer (75 days) or a reply (20 days)). (Reg. Sec. 3000.4(d))

Since this first amendment is of right, it does not involve prior notice to, or permission of, the Division of Tax Appeals.

> *CCH PLANNING NOTE: Review pleading.*—Within a short time after service of a pleading, it is a good idea to review it to get a fresh look at its assertions. Practitioners in a law firm may choose to ask another attorney to review the original filing. If an issue has not been adequately presented, there is frequently still time to submit amended pleadings as of right.

A taxpayer's amended pleading should be served on both the Division of Tax Appeals (with the Supervising Administrative Law Judge) and the Division of Taxation's Office of Counsel. (Reg. Sec. 3000.3(c); Reg. Sec. 3000.4(b)) If service is by mail, the amended pleading is deemed served on the date of the U.S. postmark on the envelope. If a machine-metered stamp is used and the pleading is received by the opposing party within the normal time period for receiving such an item mailed through the U.S. Postal Service, the pleading is deemed served on the date of the postmark. Where delivery is made by courier, delivery, messenger or similar service, the date of service is the date the opposing party receives the document. (Reg. Sec. 3000.22)

> *CCH PLANNING NOTE: Proper mailing.*—To pinpoint or ensure the date of mail service, it is advisable to obtain a U.S. Postal Service (rather than machine-metered) postmark and to mail the amended pleading by certified or registered mail, return receipt requested. Since only a U.S. Postal Service postmark is recognized, private overnight mail services provide no real benefit.

*By consent.*After expiration of the time periods described above, or after a pleading has already been amended once, amendments are allowed only with the consent of the Supervising Administrative Law Judge, or the administrative law judge or small claims presiding officer assigned to the matter. (Reg. Sec. 3000.4(d)(1))

Consent is usually requested in the form of a motion. This motion is quite similar to the amended pleading motion described by CPLR Rule 3025. A request for permission to amend should state the reasons for the amended pleading (e.g., new evidence, a new precedent, etc.). It should also include the language of the proposed amendment or the text of the amended pleading. Generally, the Division of Tax Appeals allows an amendment unless it will result in substantial prejudice to a party.

At the hearing.—Requests to amend pleadings are usually made before commencement of a formal hearing; however, there is a regulatory exception to this practice. If an issue not raised by the hearing is tried by express or implied consent of the parties, the pleadings are treated as if they were amended to raise the new issue. (Reg. Sec. 3000.4(d)(2)) Previously, a formal motion to conform the pleadings to the proof at hearing was required, but no such motion is necessary under the new rules.

> *CCH PLANNING NOTE: Motion to conform pleadings should be filed.*—Although a motion to conform the pleadings to the proof is no longer required where issues have been tried by consent, these motions are still permitted. (Reg. Sec. 3000.4(d)(2)) Practitioners are strongly urged to make a motion if they wish an issue to be preserved, even when they believe that the issue was tried by consent. The motion prevents any arguments (by either side) that the express or implied consent was never given, and ensures that the issue is, indeed, before the court. In addition, as a practical matter, by making the motion and asking the other party to identify whether it has any new issues that it believes have been tried by consent, a level of comfort that no surprise issues will appear in the briefs after the record has closed is achieved.

Although leave to amend shall be freely given, the administrative law judge or small claims presiding officer must decide whether an offered amendment would prejudice a party in the action, affect a person not present at the hearing or unduly delay the proceeding. These would be grounds to deny leave. He may also allow a pleading to be amended while directing a general continuance of the case to give the opposing party an opportunity to prepare a response to the new allegations. (Reg. Sec. 3000.4(d))

On the other hand, the judge or presiding officer should permit the amendment if he concludes that the performance of, or reason for, a test period audit was obscured by the auditor and had not been revealed in subsequent proceedings with the auditor or the Office of Counsel of the Division of Taxation. The judge or presiding officer might also find that an attack on the audit method is a standard taxpayer offense, routinely anticipated by the Office of Counsel, and one that does not require such specific and detailed delineation in the pleadings that the Division of Taxation would be prejudiced by amendment.

Additionally, the judge or presiding officer could allow the pleading to be amended while granting the Office of Counsel a continuance to respond and prepare its case.

Response.—Absent an order from an administrative law judge or a small claims presiding officer to the contrary, an adverse party must respond to an amended pleading if a response would have been required by the original pleading. The time for response is the same as that which applies to the amended pleadings, i.e., 75 days for an answer and 20 days for a reply. (Reg. Sec. 3000.4(d)(1))

Time-barred issues.—No amended pleading can revive an issue barred by the statute of limitations, unless the original pleading gave adequate notice of it. (Reg. Sec. 3000.4(d)(2)) If such notice was not given by the original pleading, the timeliness of the amended pleading's assertions are measured from the date the amended pleading was served.

• *Hearing procedures (ALJ)*

Once the pleadings have been filed, the petition is assigned to an administrative law judge (ALJ) and scheduled for a hearing. (Reg. Sec. 3000.15) Parties must be given at least 30 days' notice of the first hearing date, and at least 10 days' notice of any adjourned or continued hearing date. The regulations do not prescribe the content of a notice. Requests by either party for a preference in scheduling will be honored to the extent possible.

Hearing memoranda.—Each party must prepare and submit a hearing memorandum to the Supervising Administrative Law Judge and to the opposing party not less than 10 days before the hearing date specified in the hearing notice. (Reg. Sec. 3000.14) Each memorandum must contain the following information:

— a list of all witnesses to be called to testify and a very brief summary of the anticipated testimony of such witnesses;

— a list of all exhibits to be introduced;

— a brief statement of the legal issues being contested;

— a statement of the legal authorities relied on; and

— if the parties have reached stipulation on any facts, a copy of the stipulation.

The administrative law judge may preclude the testimony of witnesses or introduction of evidence not included in the hearing memorandum if a party fails to make a good faith effort to prepare and submit a hearing memorandum as noted above; the failure to comply with these procedures, however, will not preclude documents and testimony introduced only for purposes of rebuttal or to impeach a witness. (Reg. Sec. 3000.14(d)(2))

CCH PLANNING NOTE: Division issued hearing memorandum form.—The Division of Tax Appeals includes a form hearing memorandum when it issues its calendar call for scheduling of the hearing. Filling in all sections of that form should be sufficient to satisfy the requirements for a hearing memorandum.

Failure to appear.—If a party (or a party's representative) fails to appear at a scheduled hearing and an adjournment has not been granted, the ALJ may render a default determination against the party failing to appear. A default determination may be vacated, upon written application to the supervising administrative law judge, upon a showing of an excuse for the default and a meritorious case.

Adjournments.—At least 15 days before the scheduled date of a hearing, a party can request (in writing) an adjournment upon a showing of good cause (i.e. sickness or unavailability of witnesses). Less notice is required in the case of an emergency. (Reg. Sec. 3000.15(b)(2))

CCH PLANNING NOTE: Only request adjournment when truly necessary.—An adjournment, however, should be requested only if it is truly necessary, and never as a dilatory tactic. If an administrative law judge feels that the proceedings have been delayed continually without good cause by a party, he or she may enter a default determination against such party. (Reg. Sec. 3000.15(b)(1))

Defaults.—A default determination may be entered against a party that uses adjournments as a dilatory tactic (Reg. Sec. 3000.15(b)(1)), or against a party that fails to appear at a scheduled hearing without giving prior notice. A default determination against either the Division of Taxation or the taxpayer results in a final determination of the case. (Reg. Sec. 3000.15(b)(2)) Denial of a motion for default is not a final determination, however, and thus is not subject to review by the Tax Appeals Tribunal. (*Macbet Realty Corp.*, DTA No. 804684 (1990))

A default determination may be vacated if a party has a reasonable excuse for the default. This excuse (e.g., lack of notice of a hearing) must be presented to the Supervising Administrative Law Judge in a written application. A party must also show that it has a meritorious case. (Reg. Sec. 3000.15(b)(3)) If a party is unable to vacate a default determination, its only recourse is a CPLR Article 78 proceeding in the state courts.

CCH EXAMPLE: Reasonable excuse for default.—A default determination was entered by an administrative law judge against a taxpayer that was represented at a hearing by an unqualified person (i.e., a law student). The Tax Appeals Tribunal affirmed the determination of default, but held that since the taxpayer's attorney appeared on the afternoon of the hearing date and the taxpayer had a reasonable excuse for the default, the default should have been vacated upon the taxpayer's request. (*Morano's Jewelers of Fifth Ave, Inc.*, DTA No. 800971 (1989))

CCH EXAMPLE: No reasonable excuse for default.—A taxpayer's representative's denial of being aware of the hearing notice or of having a copy of the hearing notice in his file was not sufficient to establish reasonable cause, especially since the representative was not appointed until two years after the hearing notice was mailed. The taxpayer also failed to demonstrate a meritorious case. In another matter, a taxpayer's request to vacate a personal income tax default determination was denied because the taxpayer did not present an acceptable excuse for the default and did not provide any evidence of a meritorious case. The default determination was appropriately issued when neither the taxpayer nor the taxpayer's representative appeared at a scheduled hearing. The taxpayer's explanation that a hearing adjournment had been requested but denied was insufficient to overcome the taxpayer's burden of demonstrating an excuse for the default. Also, the taxpayer's statement that no taxes were due failed to demonstrate a meritorious case absent a detailed statement of reasons and/or corroborating evidence supporting the claim. (*Zavalla*, DTA No. 811105 (1995))

Burden of proof.—The petitioner generally bears the burden of proof at the hearing. (Reg. Sec. 3000.15(d)(5)) The issues on which the Division of Taxation bears the burden of proof include:

— whether the taxpayer has been guilty of fraud with the intent to evade tax;

— whether the petitioner is liable as the transferee of property of a taxpayer (but not to show that the original taxpayer was liable for the tax);

— whether the taxpayer is liable for an increase in a deficiency where the increase is first asserted after a notice of deficiency was mailed and a petition filed, unless the increase results from a change or correction of any federal tax item that was required to be reported to the Division of Taxation;

— whether the taxpayer is liable for the civil penalty for filing frivolous returns; and

— whether the taxpayer is liable for the civil penalty for aiding in the making of fraudulent tax returns.

(Sec. 689(e); Sec. 1089(e), Tax Law)

CCH PLANNING NOTE: Presumptions and rules of construction.—Petitioners can benefit from certain presumptions and rules of construction to satisfy his burden of proof. For example, although exemptions are construed narrowly and create a presumption in favor of taxation, exclusions are construed broadly in favor of the taxpayer. Ambiguities in the Tax Law are also construed against the Department of Taxation and Finance. (*Fairland Amusements, Inc. v State Tax Commission*, (NYCtAp) 498 NYS2d 796 (1985)) Such distinctions should be stressed in pleadings, briefs and oral argument.

• *Conduct of hearing (ALJ)*

Tax appeals hearings before administrative law judges are conducted formally. (Reg. Sec. 3000.15) The parties may call and examine witnesses, introduce exhibits, cross-examine opposing witnesses on any relevant matters, impeach the credibility of witnesses, and rebut the evidence against them. Technical rules of evidence will, however, be disregarded to the extent permitted by the decisions of New York courts, provided the evidence offered appears to be relevant and material to the issues. Except as otherwise provided by law, the burden of proof is on the taxpayer.

Opening statement.—The hearing is the petitioner's only opportunity to present his entire case in a tax controversy. Before the hearing, the petitioner only has an opportunity to confer with the Division of Taxation's Office of Counsel before the Bureau of Conciliation and Mediation Services, or an auditor, in an attempt to work out a settlement of the alleged tax deficiency or to discuss items that are the subject of discovery. After a hearing, the petitioner who continues to pursue his case is relegated to a review by the Tax Appeals Tribunal (see below) or an appellate argument in a CPLR Article 78 proceeding. Accordingly, it is incumbent upon the petitioner to make the most of this singular opportunity to present his complete case.

CCH PLANNING NOTE: Limit opening statement.—In light of the importance of the formal hearing, the practitioner can easily recognize that every opportunity should be taken to present a client's argument. It is generally not a good idea to begin a formal hearing with an extremely lengthy opening statement. The opening statement should present the crucial facts that will be uncovered during the hearing and should explain the proper legal analysis of those facts. It should not be used to explain the specific facts to be entered into evidence or how a witness will testify. Surprises and changes of strategy occur quite frequently during a formal hearing, and the practitioner should not needlessly bind himself to a particular line of questioning or the use of a particular witness. Moreover, as many practitioners can attest, no one can ever be quite sure of exactly how a witness is going to testify.

A concise statement of the ultimate facts and the legal ramifications of those facts serves to focus the hearing officer's attention on these issues. It also gives everyone a better idea of what the petitioner is attempting to accomplish. After explaining the big picture in the opening statement, the practitioner can use the hearing itself to focus on each of the details to be established.

Presentation of the case.—A case is generally presented in the following manner. The Division of Taxation (through its Office of Counsel attorney) begins the hearing by putting all of the jurisdictional papers into evidence. These papers usually consist of the notice of assessment (the 90-day letter), the petition, the Office of Counsel's answer to the perfected petition, the petitioner's power of attorney (if he is not representing himself) and copies of any other pleadings that may have been served by any party to the controversy. Copies of the taxpayer's returns dealing with the tax and time period at issue may also be submitted into evidence at this time.

After the Office of Counsel's presentation of the jurisdictional papers, the administrative law judge usually asks the Office of Counsel attorneys to make their opening statement. The petitioner is then given an opportunity to restate or otherwise respond to this explanation, and to make his opening statement. The presentation of witnesses begins after the petitioner's opening statement.

Direct examination.—The Office of Counsel attorney usually begins with direct examination of the auditor who performed the audit, and perhaps the auditor's supervisor. This direct examination usually begins with a discussion of their credentials and experience as auditors, and then moves into a discussion of what took place during the audit, e.g., whether the petitioner was cooperative, consented to any particular audit technique, and so forth. After testifying to the facts in the case, the auditor is generally asked how he determined that the petitioner owed additional taxes. In response to this line of questioning, the auditor explains the facts of the case, the audit results and the application of relevant statutory provisions of the Tax Law as well as regulations and internal audit guidelines. The Office of Counsel may also submit exhibits during this testimony. After the auditor has testified, the Office of Counsel's case is generally complete, though additional witnesses may be called.

CCH PLANNING NOTE: Calling the auditor as a witness.—Since the burden of proof generally rests with the taxpayer, (Reg. Sec. 3000.15(d)(5)) the Office of

Counsel could merely submit the jurisdictional papers and conclude its case without presenting an auditor as a witness. If this occurs, the taxpayer will no doubt want to place the auditor on the stand to explore the audit methodology.

Cross-examination.—After direct examination of each of the Office of Counsel's witnesses, the petitioner may begin cross-examination. He has the right to cross-examine the Office of Counsel's witness on any matter relevant to the issues, even if it was not covered in direct examination. (Reg. Sec. 3000.15(d)(1)) The petitioner can also use all of the standard impeachment techniques (i.e, reliability, credibility, veracity) against the Office of Counsel's witnesses. When cross-examination has concluded, the Office of Counsel can conduct a redirect examination of its witnesses. The petitioner's use of a limited form of re-cross-examination is generally allowed by the hearing officer as well.

After the Office of Counsel has presented its case and after the petitioner has had the opportunity for cross-examination, the petitioner can present his witnesses. These witnesses are subject to the same cross-examination techniques as the Office of Counsel's witnesses. (Reg. Sec. 3000.15(d)(1)) Similarly, the petitioner can introduce into evidence any exhibits that support his case. After the petitioner's witnesses have testified and been subjected to cross-examination, the hearing officer asks for closing arguments. The Office of Counsel generally presents its closing arguments first. The hearing concludes with the petitioner's closing statement.

Evidentiary considerations.—Oral testimony and the submission of exhibits form the basis for the hearing. Hearing officers are generally liberal about what can be submitted into evidence. This comports with the rule providing that "technical rules of evidence will be disregarded to the extent permitted by the decisions of the courts of this State, provided the evidence offered appears relevant and material to the issues." Full effect is given to all rules of privilege recognized by the state of New York. (Reg. Sec. 3000.15(d)(1))

Evidence submitted to the Department of Taxation and Finance's attorney but not submitted to the administrative law judge is not considered, since the Division of Taxation and the Division of Tax Appeals are autonomous units of the Department of Taxation and Finance.

Objections.—All objections to offers in evidence are considered by the hearing officer and noted in the record. The hearing officer, who usually rules on an objection at the time it is made, can ask for the basis of the objection and the opposing party's response to it. He can also question witnesses directly when it appears to him that the record may be unclear. (Reg. Sec. 3000.15(d)(1))

Documentary evidence.—When dealing with documentary evidence, it should be noted that a party can request substitution of a copy for the original of any book, record, paper or other document when the original has been entered into evidence. (Reg. Sec. 3000.15(d)(2)) Affidavits may also be submitted into evidence in lieu of the oral testimony of the person making the affidavit. (Reg. Sec. 3000.15(d)(1)) The hearing officer can assign as much or as little weight to such affidavits as he chooses.

CCH PLANNING NOTE: Photocopies as evidence.—Photocopies may be introduced into evidence instead of originals, since the best-evidence rule is not strictly applied. Taxpayers should always bring the original to the hearing when possible, however, because an objection that a copy has been altered can make introduction of that copy, in lieu of the original, difficult.

Federal determinations.—A copy of any federal determination relating to a matter at issue can be received into evidence to show the existence of the determination. (Reg. Sec. 3000.15(d)(1)) This may be very important in a case arising out of an adjustment made by or a ruling from the Internal Revenue Service.

Closing statements.—After each side has presented its case, the parties are given the opportunity to summarize orally the application of the law to the facts as presented during the hearing. (Reg. Sec. 3000.15(d)(6)) This oral presentation can have a great deal of impact. Accordingly, a good deal of time should be spent preparing for the closing statement.

Post-hearing submissions.—At the conclusion of a hearing, the parties are given an opportunity to submit written legal memoranda in support of their positions. The time for submission of these documents is determined by the administrative law judge. Each party must serve a copy of its written memorandum on the opposing party and on the administrative law judge. (Reg. Sec. 3000.15(d)(6))

CCH PLANNING NOTE: Extensions.—Typically, the taxpayer files its brief first and the schedule should allow a reasonable amount of time from the anticipated arrival date of the transcript within which to prepare that brief. The Division of Taxation is then given the opportunity to reply to the taxpayer's initial brief-typically within 30 days. Taxpayers then are given the opportunity to reply to the Division of Taxation's brief-typically within 15 days. Timing of briefs is flexible and is established at the conclusion of the hearing with the participation of both parities and the administrative law judge. The judge confirms the briefing schedule in writing following the hearing. Practitioners should note that it is the policy of the Division of Tax Appeals to allow extensions of time to file briefs only when a request is made in writing prior to the scheduled filing date.

• *Planning considerations*

The importance of the formal hearing cannot be overstated. Experience indicates that proper presentation of a case is best accomplished with thorough preparation. Accordingly, the following is an attempt to assist petitioner's counsel in preparing for the formal hearing:

(1) Review the facts underlying the case. This may generally include discussions with individuals having some knowledge of the facts, and in particular such additional efforts as making an on-site inspection of operations or property at issue. In fact, an on-site inspection is one of the best ways to prepare for a case. The practitioner may be better able to explain an activity or the function of a particular piece of property after he has seen it in use.

(2) Review and analyze all of the pleadings, records and other documentary evidence in the case. The practitioner should be intimately familiar with the contents of all documents he seeks to use to persuade the hearing officer, including the auditor's audit guidelines, work papers and reports. Nothing is more embarrassing than being surprised by an inconsistency or significant omission in a document. If inconsistencies exist, be prepared to explain them.

(3) Review each witness's testimony with the witness before the hearing. The practitioner should prepare a list of questions to ensure that all relevant and material facts are covered. He should then discuss these questions with the witness to be prepared for the witness's response to them.

(4) Formulate legal arguments based on the facts. There is no substitute for legal research. It should include the Tax Law, the regulations and memoranda, advisory opinions and formal hearing decisions promulgated by the Department of Taxation and Finance.

(5) Attempt to anticipate the arguments that will be asserted by the Division of Taxation's Office of Counsel and your response to them. This better prepares the practitioner for the time when those arguments are in fact asserted. It also points out areas of the practitioner's own argument that could be strengthened. Consider requesting a copy of the Department of Taxation and Finance's file under the Freedom of Information Act.

(6) Prepare for the presentation at the formal hearing.

Outline the opening statement-simply explain the facts that should ultimately be found and the legal ramification of these facts. Remember that the opening statement should not last longer than five minutes.

Prepare for the logical and orderly presentation of the case, including the order of the witnesses' testimony and the submission of documentary evidence.

Prepare a list of the areas where the auditors can be cross-examined. Some of these can be determined beforehand and others will arise during the hearing itself.

Outline the closing statement. This statement should summarize the evidence presented at the hearing and the legal ramifications of those facts. Also use this opportunity to point out inconsistencies and inaccuracies in the Office of Counsel's case. The closing statement is also the proper time to refute the arguments made by the Office of Counsel against the petitioner. Be sure to explain the basis for the legal conclusions asserted.

(7) After the hearing, review the transcript for inaccuracies and begin preparation of a thorough legal memorandum in support of petitioner's position. Briefly recount the facts (using record citations for each factual finding) and argue the applicability of the law. Here again, there is no substitute for solid legal research.

• *Representation of parties (ALJ)*

A taxpayer may appear in proceedings before the Division of Tax Appeals personally or be represented by his or her spouse. (Sec. 2014(1), Tax Law; Reg. Sec. 3000.2) In certain situations, a power of attorney may be required. A minor under 18 years of age may be represented by his or her adult spouse, parent, guardian or by the person who prepared the minor's return. A taxpayer who is mentally or physically incapable of filing a petition or appearing on his or her own behalf, may be represented by anyone having a proper interest in doing so.

A partnership may act through one of its general partners. A corporation may be represented by an officer.

Power of attorney.—A power of attorney is required whenever a petitioner acts through a representative. The representative will not be recognized until a power of attorney in proper form is filed with the division of tax appeals. The power of attorney must contain a declaration, signed by the petitioner's representative, stating that:

(1) the representative agrees to represent the petitioner in the matter for which the power of attorney is being executed, and

(2) the representative is authorized to act as a taxpayer representative.

Representation by permission of Tribunal.—An attorney, certified public accountant or licensed public accountant authorized to practice or licensed in jurisdictions outside New York may appear and represent a petitioner for a particular matter by special permission from the Tribunal. (Reg. Sec. 3000.2)

Representation of Division of Taxation.—The Division of Taxation is represented in all proceedings before the Division of Tax Appeals by the Chief Counsel of the Division of Taxation, or the Chief Counsel's representative.

- *Determinations (ALJ)*

The ALJ must render a determination within six months after completion of the hearing or the submission of briefs, whichever is later. (Sec. 2010(3), Tax Law; Reg. Sec. 3000.15) The six-month period may be extended, for good cause shown, for an additional three months.

The determination of the ALJ is a final determination of any matters in controversy unless a party takes exception by timely requesting review by the Tax Appeals Tribunal. (Sec. 2010(4), Tax Law) Determinations of administrative law judges are not considered precedent, nor are they given any force or effect in other proceedings in the Division of Tax Appeals. (Sec. 2010(5), Tax Law)

Expedited hearings.—Special rules govern expedited hearings for certain types of protests. Expedited hearings are available when a taxpayer receives a statutory notice regarding:

— the denial of an application for a license, permit, registration or certificate of authority; or

— an increase in the amount of a bond or other security required to be filed.

(Reg. Sec. 3000.18(a))

With the exception of time limits, the same rules relating to pleadings and amended pleadings apply in connection with expedited hearings. Petitions, however, are acknowledged by the Supervising Administrative Law Judge and reviewed for timeliness and acceptability. Within ten business days of the receipt of a petition in proper form, the Supervising Administrative Law Judge schedules the hearing in the offices of the Division of Tax Appeals in Albany. (Reg. Sec. 3000.18(a); Reg. Sec. 3000.1(q))

A determination in the controversy must be made within 30 days from the date of the petition for the expedited hearing. If exception is taken to the determination, the Tax Appeals Tribunal must issue its decision within three months from the date of a petition for an expedited hearing. Any request by the taxpayer that delays the expedited hearing process also serves to extend the preceding limitations periods. (Reg. Sec. 3000.18(b); Reg. Sec. 3000.1(b))

- *Tax Appeals Tribunal*

The Tax Appeals Tribunal is in charge of the Division of Tax Appeals. (Sec. 2002, Tax Law) It consists of three commissioners appointed by the Governor with the advice and consent of the State Senate.

The functions, powers, and duties of the Tax Appeals Tribunal include:

— authority to adopt regulations governing practice and procedure in the Division of Tax Appeals; (Sec. 2006(14), Tax Law)

— the power to reorganize units in the Division of Tax Appeals; (Sec. 2006(1), Tax Law)

— authority over employees of the Division of Tax Appeals; (Sec. 2006(2), Tax Law)

— responsibility over the financial needs of the Division of Tax Appeals; (Sec. 2006(3), Tax Law)

— authority over the formal administrative review process; (Sec. 2006, Tax Law)

— the obligation to make administrative law judge determinations and Tax Appeals Tribunal decisions available to the public; (Sec. 2006(9), Tax Law)

— the power to impose, modify, or waive interest, additions to tax and civil penalties to the same extent as the Commissioner of Taxation and Finance; (Sec. 2006(12), Tax Law) (For a discussion of civil penalties, see ¶ 89-206) and

— authority to collect, compile, and prepare for publication statistics and other data with respect to the operations of the Division of Tax Appeals. (Sec. 2006(13), Tax Law)

• *Tax Appeals Tribunal review process*

ALJ determinations are reviewable if either party, within 30 days after the giving of notice of the determination, files an exception with the Secretary of the Tax Appeals Tribunal. (Sec. 2006(7), Tax Law; Reg. Sec. 3000.17) The 30-day period will be extended, provided an application for extension is filed and served on the other party within such period and good cause for the extension is shown. Copies of the exception must be served on the other party. Where the Division of Taxation is the other party, the exception is served on the Director of the Law Bureau. Either party may request oral argument.

Form of exception.—The exception must contain the following information:

— the particular findings of fact and conclusions of law with which the party disagrees;

— the grounds of the exception with references, where possible, to the relevant pages of the transcript of hearing and exhibits; and

— alternative findings of fact and conclusions of law.

(Reg. Sec. 3000.17(b)(1))

Form TA-14 is available for filing an exception. This form does not contain spaces for, or instructions regarding, the grounds for exception, and the grounds are not defined by the Tax Law or regulations.

CCH PLANNING NOTE: *List grounds for exception separately.*—The grounds of exception are likely to be implicit in the disagreements that the party has with actual findings of fact or conclusions of law. Nevertheless, to track the requirements of the regulations, parties are advised to list separately the grounds for taking the exception.

The Tax Appeals Tribunal is not required to review issues raised in an untimely exception or untimely response. While the Tax Appeals Tribunal has the power to review any aspect of an administrative law judge's determination, it may decline to exercise this discretion. (*Sabel*, DTA No. 802535 (1991))

CCH PLANNING NOTE: *Request an extension of time within which to file an exception.*—It should be noted that the regulations make no provision for extending the 30-day time limit for exceptions to cross-exceptions in response to the opponent's exceptions in main. This differs from the Civil Practice Law and Rules (CPLR), where the time period for taking an appeal is automatically extended for cross-appeals if the other party takes an appeal. The absence of an extended time period for taking a cross-exception can have importance when a party is successful on one of its alternative arguments but not others. For example, in a sales tax case, a taxpayer may obtain a decision that an item of property it purchased was exempt from tax on the grounds that it constituted a capital improvement to real property but simultaneously lose on its alternative theory that the property was exempt as production equipment. Obviously, the taxpayer would not choose to take exception to the determination canceling the assessment, regardless of the fact that it lost on the alternative theory. The taxpayer might, however, wish to preserve the alternative production equipment theory in the event that the Division of Taxation takes exception to the administrative law judge's determination on the capital improvement issue. If the taxpayer waits for the Division of Taxation to appeal on the 30th day, it will likely be too late to take exception on the alternative theory and that theory will, as a result, be waived. The Tax Appeals Tribunal does, however, allow for extensions of time for filing an exception for good cause shown. (Reg. Sec. 3000.17(a)(2)) It has indicated that a request for such an extension premised on preserving an alternative theory if the other party excepts constitutes good cause and routinely grants such requests. Accordingly, a party that is victorious on one issue but not others should request an extension of time within which to file an exception to prevent the possibility of waiving an otherwise valid alternative theory if the opposing party takes exception.

Brief.—A brief in support of the exception may be submitted at the time the exception is filed or within 30 days thereafter. Briefs opposing the exception must be submitted within 30 days after service of the brief in support.

Review.—The Tribunal reviews the record and may, to the extent necessary or desirable, exercise all of the powers that it could have exercised if it had made the earlier determination. (Reg. Sec. 3000.17) A decision affirming, reversing, modifying, or remanding the ALJ's determination must be issued within six months from the date that the exception was filed, the briefs were submitted, or oral argument was concluded, whichever is later.

The Department may not seek judicial review of a Tax Appeals Tribunal decision. A taxpayer may seek judicial review in the Appellate Division of the State Supreme Court by instituting an Article 78 proceeding. (Sec. 2016, Tax Law; Reg. Sec. 3000.20)

[¶89-240] Limitations Period for Appeals

A decision of the Tax Appeals Tribunal which is not subject to any further administrative review will finally and irrevocably decide all the issues which were raised in proceedings before the Division of Tax Appeals upon which such decision is based, unless, within four months after notice of such decision is served by the Tax Appeals Tribunal upon every party to the proceedings before such Tribunal, the petitioner who commenced the proceeding petitions, by certified mail or personal service, for judicial review in the manner, as provided by Art. 78 of the Civil Practice Law and rules. (Sec. 2016, Tax Law; Reg. Sec. 3000.20) The proper venue for an Article 78 proceeding to review a decision of the Tax Appeals Tribunal is in the Supreme Court, Appellate Division, Third Department. (Sec. 2016, Tax Law)

> **CCH COMMENT:** *Filing tolls the statute of limitations.*—The filing of the notice of petition and petition with the clerk of the Appellate Division is sufficient to toll the statute of limitations. In *Matter of Leonard Spodek v. New York State Commissioner of Administration*, 85 NY2d 760, 651 NE2d 1275, 628 NYS2d 256 (1995), the issue was whether the CPLR "commencement-by-filing" provisions apply to Sec. 2016 proceedings originating in the Appellate Division. In concluding that they do, the Court noted:

"Respondents correctly observe that the new filing provisions specifically refer only to proceedings commenced in Supreme Court and County Court and establish certain procedures and requirements which would tend not to be applicable or practicable in a proceeding originating in the Appellate Division. However, this irregularity alone does not compel the conclusion that the Legislature intended to exclude these proceedings from the scope of CPLR 304. Nowhere in the commencement-by-filing amendments and the corresponding legislative history is there a distinction between special proceedings originating in supreme or county court and those originating in the Appellate Division. Moreover, while the Legislature specifically excluded certain lower courts (New York City Civil Court, City Courts, District Courts, and Justice Courts) from the operation of CPLR 304 by contemporaneously amending the statutes regulating the procedure in those courts, it took no such action with regard to proceedings originating in the Appellate Division."

The limitations period is measured from the Tribunal's service of notice of its decision, not from the taxpayer's receipt of the notice. (Sec. 2016, Tax Law) Service by certified mail is the normal method, and this is complete "upon deposit of [the] notice, enclosed in a post-paid properly addressed wrapper, in a post office or official depository under the exclusive care and custody of the United States Postal Service." (Sec. 2016, Tax Law) In other words, the date of mailing (i.e. the date on the face of the notice in nearly all instances) is counted as day one for purposes of measuring the four-month statutory period.

    CCH EXAMPLE: Calculation of four-month period.—If the Tribunal's decision is mailed on June 15, the period of limitations expires on October 15. If the decision is mailed on July 31, a four-month statute expires on November 30, not December 1.

NEW YORK CITY CORPORATE INCOME

[¶505-200]

NYC CORPORATE INCOME TAXPAYERS AND RATES

[¶505-205] NYC Corporate Income Taxpayers

Under corporate tax reform legislation enacted in 2015, the New York City corporate income tax system was significantly revised, generally applicable to taxable years beginning on or after January 1, 2015. (Subchapter 3-A, Corporate Tax of 2015; Sec. 11-651, N.Y.C. Adm. Code, *et. seq.*)

However, S corporations and qualified subchapter S subsidiaries remain subject to the existing, pre-reform general corporation tax provisions. (Sec. 11-602.1, N.Y.C. Adm. Code)

A memorandum explains transitional filing provisions for taxpayers affected by the corporate tax reform legislation. (*Finance Memorandum 15-2*, April 17, 2015)

Among the changes made by the reform legislation are the following:

— merging the banking and general corporation taxes;

— in place of the general 8.85% tax rate, allowing a reduced rate for certain small businesses and qualified manufacturing corporations;

— applying a 9% tax rate to certain financial corporations having more than $100 billion in assets;

— adopting combined reporting for unitary corporations that meet a more-than-50% stock ownership test;

— replacing the entire net income tax base with a business income tax base;

— adopting the phase-in of a single receipts factor, as previously contained in the general corporation tax;

— applying customer-based sourcing rules;

— eliminating the separate treatment of subsidiary capital and income;

— modifying the definitions of "investment capital" and "investment income" and exempting both from tax;

— for pre-2015 net operating losses (NOLs), providing for a prior NOL conversion subtraction;

— allowing a three-year carryback for NOLs incurred in tax years beginning after 2014;

— repealing the alternative minimum tax base for income plus compensation;

— eliminating the tax on assets for banks; and

— increasing the maximum capital base tax to $10 million, but allowing a $10,000 reduction for all capital base tax calculations.

• *Pre-reform general corporation tax*

Note: The provisions discussed below generally apply to taxable years beginning before 2015. As noted above, however, they continue to apply to S corporations. (Sec. 11-602.1, N.Y.C. Adm. Code)

Domestic or foreign corporations are subject to city general corporation tax when they perform any of the following activities: doing business, employing capital, owning or leasing property in the city in a corporate or organized capacity, or maintaining an office in the city, for all or any part of the tax year (Sec. 11-603(1), N.Y.C. Adm. Code).

Receivers, referees, trustees, assignees or other fiduciaries who conduct the business of a corporation are subject to tax in the same manner as if the business were conducted by the officers of the corporation (Sec. 11-603(3), N.Y.C. Adm. Code). A dissolved corporation which continues to conduct business is also subject to tax.

Real estate investment trusts (REITs) or regulated investment companies (RICs) are subject to tax only in taxable years in which they are subject to federal income taxation (Sec. 11-603(7), N.Y.C. Adm. Code, Sec. 11-603(8), N.Y.C. Adm. Code).

The New York City provisions closely parallel those of the state corporation franchise tax law. Differences principally reflect geographical and jurisdictional limitations; for example, the city's tax is not imposed on the privilege of exercising a corporate franchise, since the franchise is a creation of the state.

As in the case of the state, the city imposes the tax on organizations that are not literally corporations. For purposes of the tax, "corporation" is defined to include a joint-stock company or association, and a business conducted by trustees wherein interest or ownership is evidenced by certificate or other instrument (Sec. 11-602(1), N.Y.C. Adm. Code).

Effective January 1, 1996, the term "corporation" also includes associations that are classified as corporations pursuant to IRC Sec. 7701(a)(3) (including limited liability companies that are so classified) and publicly-traded partnerships that are treated as corporations for federal tax purposes pursuant to IRC Sec. 7704. (*Note:* an unincorporated organization that would be treated as a corporation under the new definition, but was subject to city unincorporated business tax for its 1995 taxable year, may make a one time election to remain subject to the unincorporated business tax. For details, see discussion at ¶519-110).

However, for taxable years beginning after 2001, the law specifically provides that a corporation does not include an entity classified as a partnership for federal income tax purposes. (Sec. 11-602(1)(c), N.Y.C. Adm. Code) Thus, an entity classified as a partnership for federal income tax purposes will be subject to the unincorporated business tax, rather than the general corporation tax, even if it is incorporated. (*Finance Memorandum 02-4*)

The city does not adopt federal provisions as to corporations electing S corporation treatment. Such corporations are subject to New York City's general corporation tax (Instructions to Form NYC-4S).

A domestic international sales corporation is subject to tax.

For exemptions, see ¶505-220.

[¶505-215] Nexus Standard of Taxability in New York City

Under corporate tax reform legislation enacted in 2015, the New York City corporate income tax system was significantly revised, generally applicable to taxable years beginning on or after January 1, 2015. (Subchapter 3-A, Corporate Tax of 2015; Sec. 11-651, N.Y.C. Adm. Code, *et. seq.*)

However, S corporations and qualified subchapter S subsidiaries remain subject to the existing, pre-reform general corporation tax provisions. (Sec. 11-602.1, N.Y.C. Adm. Code)

Under the new provisions, the business corporation tax retains the existing, pre-reform nexus standards for the privilege of doing business, employing capital, owning or leasing property, or maintaining an office in New York City. In addition, the new tax incorporates the banking corporation tax credit card nexus standard of 1,000 customers, according to mailing address and merchant locations. (Sec. 11-653, N.Y.C. Adm. Code)

• *Pre-reform provisions*

The New York City General Corporation Tax is imposed for the privilege of doing business, of employing capital, of owning or leasing property, or of maintaining an office in New York City (Sec. 11-603(1), N.Y.C. Adm. Code). Although these activities are not defined in the statute, the following activities are specifically declared not to be sufficient to establish nexus (Sec. 11-603(2), N.Y.C. Adm. Code):

(1) the maintenance of cash balances with banks or trust companies in the city;

(2) the ownership of stocks or securities which are kept in a safe deposit box or other receptacle rented for the purpose, or if pledged as collateral, or if deposited in safekeeping or custodial accounts with banks, trust companies or brokers who are members of a recognized security exchange;

(3) the taking of any action by any such bank or trust company or broker, which is incidental to the rendering of safekeeping or custodian service to such corporation;

(4) the maintenance of an office by officers or directors who are not employees of the corporation if the corporation otherwise is not doing business in the city, and does not employ capital or own or lease property in the city;

(5) the keeping of books or records of a corporation in the city if such books or records are not kept by employees and the corporation does not otherwise do business, employ capital, own or lease property or maintain an office in the city;

(6) effective for taxable years beginning on or after January 1, 1998, the trading of stocks, securities, or commodities by a foreign corporation for the corporation's own account, whether the trading is conducted by the corporation or its employees, or by a broker, commission agent, custodian, or other agent (Sec. 11-603(2-a), N.Y.C. Adm. Code; Rule Sec. 11-04(c)(3)). This exemption is not available to dealers of stocks, securities, or commodities; or

(7) any combination of the foregoing activities.

Trade shows.—Applicable to taxable years beginning after 2001, a New York City general corporation tax rule has been amended to provide that participation in trade shows for not more than 14 days, or parts thereof, in the aggregate during the taxable year will not cause a foreign corporation to be subject to tax, regardless of whether the corporation has employees or other staff present at such trade shows, as long as the corporation's activities at the trade shows are limited to displaying goods or promoting services, no sales are made, and any orders received are sent outside New York state for acceptance or rejection and are filled from outside the state. (Rule Sec. 11-04(c)(1)(vi))

• *New York City interpretation of P.L. 86-272 limitations*

A domestic or foreign corporation that falls within the categories creating a taxable status is subject to the tax notwithstanding that its activities are wholly or partly in interstate or foreign commerce. A foreign corporation will not be subject to the General Corporation Tax, however, if it conducts only minimum activities within the city. Such activities are protected if they are limited to those described in Public Law 86-272 (15 U.S.C. § 381), i.e., the solicitation of orders by its representatives or independent contractors for sales of tangible personal property when the orders are sent outside New York State for approval or rejection, and, if approved, are filled by shipment or delivery from a point outside the state.

Trade shows.—Applicable to taxable years beginning after 2001, in the case of a foreign corporation that is otherwise exempt from tax under P.L. 86-272, participation in one or more trade shows for not more than 14 days, or parts thereof, in the aggregate during the taxable year will be considered ancillary to soliciting orders. (Rule Sec. 11-04(b)(11)(iv)(I))

[¶505-220] NYC Exempt Corporations

The following corporations are exempt from the New York City general corporation tax:

Corporations subject to other New York City taxes: (1) Banks and other financial corporations subject to the city financial corporation tax (Sec. 11-603(4), N.Y.C. Adm. Code);

(2) Insurance companies formerly subject to premium tax under Subchapter 3 and 4 of Chapter 6 of Title 11 of the New York City Administrative Code (Instructions to Form NYC-3L);

(3) Utility companies subject to Chapter 11, Article 11, the city utilities excise tax. Companies subject to the tax as vendors of utilities services, but which are not utility companies under the supervision of the State Department of Public Service or (for taxable years beginning on or after August 1, 2002) a utility as defined in Sec. 11-1101(6), N.Y.C. Adm. Code, are also subject to the general corporation tax, but are allowed a reduction in allocated business income based on the portion of gross operating income subject to Chapter 11 tax (Sec. 11-603(4), N.Y.C. Adm. Code).

Other exempt corporations include:

(1) Bank holding companies which file consolidated returns with affiliated corporations subject to the New York City financial corporation tax;

(2) A trust company organized under New York State law, all the stock of which is owned by at least 20 New York savings banks;

(3) Limited-profit housing companies organized under Article 2 of the Private Housing Finance Law;

(4) Housing development fund companies organized pursuant to Article 11 of the Private Housing Finance Law;

(5) Nonstock corporations organized and operated exclusively for nonprofit purposes (Rule Sec. 11-04);

(6) New York corporations exclusively engaged in operating vessels in foreign commerce (Sec. 11-603(4), N.Y.C. Adm. Code; Rule Sec. 11-04); and

(7) New York corporations which are principally engaged in the conduct of a ferry business and operate between any of the boroughs of New York City under a lease granted by the city and a corporation principally engaged in the conduct of an aviation, steamboat, ferry or navigation business, or two or more of such businesses, all of the capital stock of which is owned by a municipal corporation of New York State (Sec. 11-603(4), N.Y.C. Adm. Code).

In addition, an exemption is provided for organizations organized exclusively for the purpose of holding title to property (under Sec. 501(2) and (25) of the Internal Revenue Code), and which turn over the net income so derived to an exempt organization. (Sec. 11-603(9), N.Y.C. Adm. Code)

An entity that is treated for federal income tax purposes as a real estate mortgage investment conduit (REMIC) is not subject to the general business corporation tax. A REMIC is not treated as a corporation, partnership or trust for purposes of the general corporation tax, and the assets of a REMIC are not included in the calculation of any tax liability under the general corporation tax. The exemption does not apply to holders of regular or residual interests, as defined in IRC Sec. 860G, or on income from such interests. (Sec. 11-122, N.Y.C. Adm. Code)

For taxable years ending before December 31, 1988, transportation companies were subject to the Transportation Corporation tax and were exempt from the general corporation tax.

[¶505-251] NYC Corporate Tax Rates

Under corporate tax reform legislation enacted in 2015, the New York City corporate income tax system was significantly revised, generally applicable to taxable years beginning on or after January 1, 2015. (Subchapter 3-A, Corporate Tax of 2015; Sec. 11-651, N.Y.C. Adm. Code, *et. seq.*)

However, S corporations and qualified subchapter S subsidiaries remain subject to the existing, pre-reform general corporation tax provisions. (Sec. 11-602.1, N.Y.C. Adm. Code)

A memorandum explains transitional filing provisions for taxpayers affected by the corporate tax reform legislation. (*Finance Memorandum 15-2*, April 17, 2015)

Under the corporate tax reform legislation, for taxable years beginning after 2014, the business income base is the primary tax base, and the business capital and fixed dollar minimum tax bases are alternative minimum tax bases. The rates are as noted below. (Sec. 11-654, N.Y.C. Adm. Code)

Business income base: The rate for qualified manufacturing corporations ranges from 4.425% to 8.85%, depending on the amount of business income.

The rate for small businesses ranges from 6.5% to 8.85%, depending on the amount of business income.

For financial corporations, the rate is 9%.

For other taxpayers, the rate is 8.85%.

Capital base: The rate is 0.04% for cooperative housing corporations and generally 0.15% for other taxpayers. However, a 0.075% tax rate applies to the portion of total business capital directly attributable to stock in a subsidiary that either would be taxable as a utility, within the meaning of the New York City utility tax, or would have been taxable as an insurance corporation under the former New York City insurance corporation tax. (Sec. 11-654(1)(e)(1)(ii), N.Y.C. Adm. Code; Finance Memorandum 17-2)

The maximum tax is $10 million, and a $10,000 reduction applies to all capital tax calculations. (Sec. 11-654(1)(e)(1)(ii), N.Y.C. Adm. Code)

Fixed dollar minimum: The fixed dollar minimum amounts range from $25 to $200,000, depending on the amount of New York City receipts.

• *Pre-reform general corporation tax*

Note: The provisions discussed below generally apply to taxable years beginning before 2015. As noted above, however, they continue to apply to S corporations. (Sec. 11-602.1, N.Y.C. Adm. Code)

For taxable years beginning before 2024, tax is imposed at whichever of the following rates will produce the highest tax:

(1) 8.85% of allocated entire net income;

(2) $1^1/_2$ mills on each dollar of allocated business and investment capital (for cooperative housing corporations, $4/_{10}$ mill), not to exceed $1 million (for taxable years beginning before 2009, $350,000) (Sec. 11-604(1)(F), N.Y.C. Adm. Code);

(3) 8.85% of an allocated income-plus-compensation base (see ¶505-470 for details); or

(4) a graduated minimum tax based on New York City receipts, as set forth below (for taxable years beginning before 2009, the tax was $300):

— $25 (if New York City receipts are not more than $100,000)

— $75 (if $100,001 -- $250,000)

— $175 (if $250,001 -- $500,000)

— $500 (if $500,001 -- $1,000,000)

— $1,500 (if $1,000,001 -- $5,000,000)

— $3,500 (if $5,000,001 -- $25,000,000)

— $5,000 (if more than $25,000,000)

(Sec. 11-604(1)(E), N.Y.C. Adm. Code)

Plus: $3/_4$ mill for each dollar of allocated subsidiary capital.

Under special provisions, real estate investment trusts and regulated investment companies are subject to tax only at the rates noted at (1) and (4) above, whichever is greater. (Sec. 11-603(7) and (8), N.Y.C. Adm. Code)

For determination of the bases to which the tax rates are applied, see "Computation of Tax Base" at ¶505-401. For allocation, see "Allocation and Apportionment" at ¶506-501.

[¶505-400]

NYC CORPORATE INCOME COMPUTATION OF TAX

[¶505-401] Federal Taxable Income as NYC Starting Point--NYC Computation of Tax Base--In General

The New York City business corporation tax, like the state corporate income tax, has several possible bases, as discussed in the following paragraphs.

Any tax base (except the minimum tax) may be subject to allocation in order to determine the actual amount subject to tax (see "Allocation and Apportionment" at ¶506-501). For the rates of tax applicable to the various bases, see ¶505-251.

The primary tax is computed on the business income base, which is federal taxable income (¶505-405), with certain additions (¶505-410 and following) and subtractions (¶505-425 and following). Additional elective deductions from allocated income are provided (¶505-450).

If a higher payment will result, the tax will be based on business capital (¶505-460) or paid as a flat-rate minimum.

¶505-400

[¶505-405] Federal Taxable Income as NYC Starting Point-- Business Income--Adoption of Federal Base

Under corporate tax reform legislation enacted in 2015 (see ¶505-205), the New York City corporate income tax system was significantly revised, generally applicable to taxable years beginning on or after January 1, 2015. (Subchapter 3-A, Corporate Tax of 2015; Sec. 11-651, N.Y.C. Adm. Code, *et. seq.*)

However, S corporations and qualified subchapter S subsidiaries remain subject to the existing, pre-reform general corporation tax provisions. (Sec. 11-602.1, N.Y.C. Adm. Code)

Under the new provisions, the business income base is the primary tax base and the business capital and fixed dollar minimum tax bases are alternative minimum bases (Sec. 11-654, N.Y.C. Adm. Code); see ¶505-251 for the rates.

The legislation modified the definitions of "investment capital" and "investment income" and exempted both from tax. (Sec. 11-652, N.Y.C. Adm. Code)

The starting point for the business income base is federal taxable income (FTI) for U.S corporations and effectively connected income (ECI) for foreign corporations not deemed domestic under the IRC. Taxpayers are required to add back treaty benefits to ECI, consistent with the previous treatment of foreign banks under the banking corporation tax. The requirement that taxpayers add back the amount of foreign taxes paid is eliminated. Most of the other existing general corporation tax modifications are continued. (Sec. 11-652, N.Y.C. Adm. Code; *Corporate Tax Reform Outline*, New York City Department of Finance)

The exemptions for income from subsidiary capital and 50% of dividends from non-subsidiaries are eliminated. (Sec. 11-652, N.Y.C. Adm. Code; *Corporate Tax Reform Outline*, New York City Department of Finance)

Income is reclassified as investment income, other exempt income, or business income. (Sec. 11-652, N.Y.C. Adm. Code; *Corporate Tax Reform Outline*, New York City Department of Finance)

Business income equals entire net income (ENI), minus investment income and other exempt income. (Sec. 11-652, N.Y.C. Adm. Code; *Corporate Tax Reform Outline*, New York City Department of Finance)

Business income includes the following (Sec. 11-652, N.Y.C. Adm. Code; *Corporate Tax Reform Outline*, New York City Department of Finance):

— interest income and gains and losses from debt instruments or other obligations, unless the income cannot be included in allocable business income under the U.S. Constitution;

— gains and losses from stock of a corporation conducting a unitary business with the taxpayer;

— dividends and gains and losses from stock held in a non-unitary corporation for one year or less or otherwise not qualifying as investment capital,

— dividends and gains from stocks that do not qualify as investment income because gross investment income exceeds 8% of ENI; and

— income from cash.

GILTI.—Net GILTI, which is the GILTI recognized under IRC Sec. 951A less the allowable IRC Sec. 250(a)(1)(B)(i) deduction, is included in entire net income under the business corporation tax; for a complete discussion, see *Finance Memorandum 18-9*, New York City Department of Finance.

Business interest deduction limitation.—For information on New York City's treatment of the IRC Sec. 163(j) limitation on deducting business interest expense, see ¶505-422 and *Business Tax Practitioner Newsletter,* Vol. 1, May 2019. See also *Finance Memorandum 18-11* regarding the attribution of interest deductions for taxpayers with IRC Sec. 163(j) limitations.

Pre-reform general corporation tax.—The provisions discussed below generally apply to taxable years beginning before 2015. As noted above, however, they continue to apply to S corporations. (Sec. 11-602.1, N.Y.C. Adm. Code)

"Allocated net income" is one of the alternative bases for the New York City general corporation tax. (Sec. 11-604(1)(E), N.Y.C. Adm. Code) The first step in the computation of "allocated net income" is the determination of "entire net income". (Sec. 11-604(3), N.Y.C. Adm. Code) "Investment income" is then computed (see ¶506-505) and subtracted from "entire net income." The result is "business income." "Business income" and "investment income" are then multiplied by their respective allocation percentages and the products are added to arrive at "allocated net income."

GCT treatment of IRC Sec. 965 Repatriation income.—IRC Sec. 965 income is a component of federal taxable income, and there are no specific statutory modifications under the GCT that exclude this income from City tax computations. Accordingly, for purposes of the GCT, the net IRC Sec. 965 income reported to the IRS must be incorporated into the starting point of City tax calculations. (*Finance Memorandum 18-10,* New York City Department of Finance)

GCT treatment of GILTI.—There are no specific statutory modifications under the GCT that exclude GILTI income. Therefore, taxpayers subject to the GCT must incorporate GILTI into the starting point of their City tax computations. Likewise, there are no specific statutory modifications under the GCT that exclude the GILTI deduction from City tax computations. Therefore, taxpayers subject to the GCT are permitted to calculate entire net income by taking the GILTI deduction into account. (*Finance Memorandum 18-10,* New York City Department of Finance)

• *Starting point of federal taxable income (GCT)*

Federal taxable income is the starting point for the computation of "entire net income". (Sec. 11-602(8), N.Y.C. Adm. Code) "Entire net income" is specifically defined to conform to the computation of entire net income under New York State law. Thus, the term is defined to mean total net income from all sources, as modified, that (1) the taxpayer must report federally; (2) the taxpayer would have been required to report federally had it not made a federal Subchapter S election; (3) in the case of a taxpayer that is exempt from federal income tax but subject to tax under New York City law, the amount that the taxpayer would have been required to report federally but for the exemption; or (4) the taxpayer would have been required to report federally if no election had been made to treat the taxpayer as a qualified subchapter S subsidiary.

Hence, corporations subject to the New York City general corporation tax begin computation of the "entire net income" base with "taxable income before net operating loss and special (dividend) deductions," line 28 of federal Form 1120. Once "entire net income" has been determined, the computations described above are made to arrive at "allocated net income," one of the alternative bases for the New York City general corporation tax. As in the case of the state franchise tax, the federal figure is taxable income before federal net operating loss and special deductions. Therefore, New York City provisions allowing deductions for dividends (¶505-428) and net operating loss (¶505-431) are treated as subtractions.

¶505-405

Generally, the definition of any term used in federal income tax law is adopted when the same term is used in the city law, in a comparable context. (Sec. 11-601(8), N.Y.C. Adm. Code)

• *City/state modifications that are the same (GCT)*

Modifications for the following items are made in the same manner for New York City purposes as for New York State purposes:

(1) Capital losses (see ¶10-635) (Sec. 11-602(8), N.Y.C. Adm. Code);

(2) Depreciation, including ACRS allowance on property placed in service in New York State in post-1984 years (see ¶10-670) (Sec. 11-602(8)(j), N.Y.C. Adm. Code);

(3) Dividends received (see ¶10-630) (Sec. 11-602(8)(a)(2), N.Y.C. Adm. Code);

(4) Federal and foreign income taxes (see ¶10-615) (Sec. 11-602(8)(b)(3), N.Y.C. Adm. Code);

(5) Foreign dividend gross-up (see ¶10-810) (Sec. 11-602(8)(a)(2-a), N.Y.C. Adm. Code);

(6) Income and deductions attributable to subsidiary capital (see ¶10-645) (Sec. 11-602(8)(a)(1), N.Y.C. Adm. Code; Sec. 11-602(8)(b)(6), N.Y. C. Adm. Code);

(7) Income received to operate school buses (see ¶10-845) (Sec. 11-602(8)(a)(4), N.Y.C. Adm. Code);

(8) Pre-1989 interest on indebtedness to stockholders (Former Sec. 11-602(8)(b)(5), N.Y.C. Adm. Code);

(9) Interest on federal obligations (see ¶10-610) (Sec. 11-602(8), N.Y.C. Adm. Code);

(10) Interest on mergers and consolidations (pre-2000) (Former Sec. 11-602(8)(b)(6-a), N.Y.C. Adm. Code);

(11) Interest on state and local obligations (see ¶10-610) (Rule Sec. 11-27);

(12) Investment income (Sec. 11-602(5), N.Y.C. Adm. Code);

(13) Related member expenses and income (see ¶505-417);

(14) Stock transfer taxes paid by security dealers (Sec. 11-602(8)(b)(4-a)(A), N.Y.C. Adm. Code);

(15) Sales and use taxes paid for production machinery and equipment. (Sec. 11-602(8)(b)(4-a)(B), N.Y.C. Adm. Code; Sec. 11-602(8)(b)(4-g), N.Y.C. Adm. Code)

Detailed descriptions of the modifications (additions or subtractions) permitted or required to convert the federal starting point into entire net income are provided in the following paragraphs.

• *Special "entire net income" definitions (GCT)*

For a real estate investment trust, "entire net income" means "real estate investment trust income" as defined in the Federal Internal Revenue, subject to modifications. (Sec. 11-603(7), N.Y.C. Adm. Code) For a regulated investment company, "entire net income" means "investment company taxable income" as defined in the federal I.R.C., subject to modifications. (Sec. 11-603(8), N.Y.C. Adm. Code)

S corporations use the federal taxable income figure that would have applied if the Subchapter S election had not been made. (Sec. 11-602(8), N.Y.C. Adm. Code; Rule Sec. 11-27) Federal S corporation taxpayers are required to complete Form NYC-

ATT-S-CORP, Calculation of Federal Taxable Income for S Corporations, and include it with their general corporation tax filing. (Instructions, Form NYC-3L)

The entire net income of an international bridge commission, also the same as for state tax purposes, is its gross income less the expense of maintaining and operating the properties, the annual interest on its bonds and other obligations, and the annual charge for the retirement of the bonds and obligations at maturity. (Sec. 11-602(8)(e), N.Y.C. Adm. Code; Rule Sec. 11-29)

A corporation included in a federal consolidated group must compute its federal taxable income, for purposes of calculating entire net income, as if it had computed its federal taxable income on a separate basis for federal income tax purposes. For a target corporation that is a member of a selling consolidated group, when an election under I.R.C. Sec. 338(h)(10) (recognition of gain or loss by the target corporation, together with nonrecognition of gain or loss on stock sold by the selling consolidated group) has been made, the federal taxable income of the target corporation includes any gain or loss on the deemed asset sale by the target corporation recognized by virtue of such election. The federal taxable income of a member of the selling consolidated group that is subject to the general corporation tax does not include gains or losses on the sale or exchange of stock of the target corporation not recognized because of the election. (Rule Sec. 11-27)

Effective February 4, 2002, and applicable to all open years, the Department of Finance will recognize and give effect to a federal election made under IRC Sec. 338(h)(10) in all cases except where the target corporation is an S corporation for federal income tax purposes. (Rule Sec. 11-27)

Utility partnerships.—For taxable years beginning on or after August 1, 2002, in the case of a taxpayer that is a partner in a partnership subject to the City utility tax as a utility, as defined in Sec. 11-1101(6), N.Y.C. Adm. Code, entire net income does not include the taxpayer's distributive or pro rata share for federal income tax purposes of any item of income, gain, loss, or deduction of such partnership, or any item of income, gain, loss, or deduction of such partnership that the taxpayer is required to take into account separately for federal income tax purposes. (Sec. 11-602(8)(a-1), N.Y.C. Adm. Code)

• *Accounting periods*

Taxpayers compute taxable income using the same period as is used for federal purposes. (Rule Sec. 11-12)

• *Accounting methods*

Taxpayers also generally use the same accounting methods to compute taxable income for the general corporation tax as are used to compute income for federal purposes. (Rule Sec. 11-30) However, the Finance Administrator reserves the right to require other methods when necessary to properly reflect entire net income.

[¶505-410] NYC Additions To Federal Base--Taxes

Under corporate tax reform legislation enacted in 2015, the New York City corporate income tax system was significantly revised, generally applicable to taxable years beginning on or after January 1, 2015. (Subchapter 3-A, Corporate Tax of 2015; Sec. 11-651, N.Y.C. Adm. Code, *et. seq.*)

However, S corporations and qualified subchapter S subsidiaries remain subject to the existing, pre-reform general corporation tax provisions. (Sec. 11-602.1, N.Y.C. Adm. Code)

For an overview of the corporate tax reform changes, see ¶505-205.

The Department of Finance's outline notes that the requirement for taxpayers to add back the amount of **foreign taxes** paid has been eliminated. Most of the other existing GCT modifications are continued under the business corporation tax. (Sec. 11-652, N.Y.C. Adm. Code)

Pre-reform provisions.—To the extent that the following taxes were deducted or excluded from income for federal purposes, they are added back to federal taxable income in computing entire net income:

(1) Income taxes payable to the United States, its possessions, or a foreign country, or taxes in lieu of income imposed by a foreign country or U.S. possession. (Sec. 11-602(8)(b)(3), N.Y.C. Adm. Code) Generally, income taxes paid to the U.S. were not deductible on the federal return and consequently do not have to be added back.

(2) Other state (including the District of Columbia) income taxes, including franchise taxes measured by income. (Sec. 11-602(8)(b)(3-a), N.Y.C. Adm. Code)

(3) The New York corporation tax, the corporation franchise tax, the petroleum business tax (see caution note below) and the banking corporation tax. (Sec. 11-602(8)(b)(3), N.Y.C. Adm. Code)

(4) The New York City general corporation tax and financial corporation tax. (Sec. 11-602(8)(b)(4), N.Y.C. Adm. Code)

These addback modifications are the same as those for state purposes except that (1) the New York City general corporation tax is added back for city but not for state purposes and (2) in post-1987 tax years, the New York City banking corporation tax must also be added back.

CCH CAUTION: Sec. 11-602(8)(b)(3), N.Y.C. Adm. Code, as noted above, requires a corporation's net income to be determined without the exclusion, deduction or credit of Article 13-a petroleum business tax. In (*Castle Oil Corp. et al. v. City of New York*), the New York Supreme Court, Appellate Division, held that this prohibition was unconstitutional to the extent that it exceeded the authorization granted by the Enabling Act.

• *Taxes or deductions for which credits are provided*

Certain New York taxes or business deductions for which special credits against the general corporation tax are allowed are added back to federal taxable income up to the amount of the credit. This requirement applies to the following taxes or deductions:

(1) New York's stock transfer tax as imposed on market-making transactions (Sec. 11-602(8)(b)(4-a)(A), N.Y.C. Adm. Code);

(2) The New York City sales and use tax in the amount of the credit on manufacturing equipment (see ¶507-020) (Sec. 11-602(8)(b)(4-a)(B), N.Y.C. Adm. Code);

(3) Relocation expense attributable to increased real estate taxes (see ¶507-010) (Sec. 11-602(8)(b)(4-b), N.Y.C. Adm. Code);

(4) Relocation expense in the amount of credits given for commercial and industrial opportunity relocation (see ¶507-015) (Sec. 11-602(8)(b)(4-c), N.Y.C. Adm. Code);

(5) The New York City sales and use tax in the amount of the credit (Sec. 11-602(8)(b)(4-d), N.Y.C. Adm. Code) for (1) electricity used in manufacturing,

processing or assembling or (2) electricity purchased at retail from the Power Authority of the State of New York or the Port Authority of New York and New Jersey, including purchases or uses by a nonresidential fuel user of fuel or fuel service;

(6) Deductions for energy charges (Sec. 11-602(8)(b)(4-e), N.Y.C. Adm. Code) and for discounts by suppliers (Sec. 11-602(8)(b)(4-f), N.Y.C. Adm. Code) in the amount of the energy cost saving credit. However, these provisions are repealed, effective November 1, 2000.

• *Refunds*

Refunds of those taxes paid in prior years that were required to be added back to federal taxable income (enumerated above) are subtracted from federal taxable income to prevent double counting of income; see ¶505-440.

[¶505-413] NYC Additions To Federal Base--NYC Dividends and Interest Received

Under corporate tax reform legislation enacted in 2015, the New York City corporate income tax system was significantly revised, generally applicable to taxable years beginning on or after January 1, 2015. (Subchapter 3-A, Corporate Tax of 2015; Sec. 11-651, N.Y.C. Adm. Code, *et. seq.*)

However, S corporations and qualified subchapter S subsidiaries remain subject to the existing, pre-reform general corporation tax provisions. (Sec. 11-602.1, N.Y.C. Adm. Code)

For an overview of the corporate tax reform changes, see ¶505-205.

The Department of Finance's outline notes that most of the existing GCT modifications are continued under the business corporation tax. (Sec. 11-652, N.Y.C. Adm. Code)

Pre-reform provisions.—The federal deduction for dividends received is not allowed for New York City purposes. (Sec. 11-602(8)(b)(2), N.Y.C. Adm. Code) However, since computation of entire net income begins with federal taxable income before the special (dividends) deduction (see ¶505-405), no addback is required. New York City allows a 100% deduction of dividends from subsidiaries and a 50% deduction of all dividends received from corporations other than subsidiaries, to the extent included in federal taxable income. These deductions are discussed at ¶505-425 and ¶505-428.

Interest expense.—Interest paid to a corporate stockholder owning more than 50% of issued and outstanding stock is added back into the federal base on lines 3 (directly attributable) and 4 (indirectly attributable) of Schedule B to Form NYC-3L, the New York City General Corporation Return. (Rule Sec. 11-27) A more detailed discussion is provided at ¶505-419.

Interest income.—Interest from New York State and local government bonds and from bonds of other state and local governments, less interest expense incurred to carry such investments, is included in New York City entire net income even though exempt for federal purposes. (Rule Sec. 11-27) Also added back to federal taxable income is any interest on federal obligations that is exempt from federal tax. Investment income to be added may be reduced by the amount of interest expense incurred to carry the investments, to the extent that the expense has not been deducted for federal purposes. (Rule Sec. 11-27(b)(1)(i))

[¶505-416] NYC Additions To Federal Base--NYC Depreciation Adjustments

Under corporate tax reform legislation enacted in 2015, the New York City corporate income tax system was significantly revised, generally applicable to taxable years beginning on or after January 1, 2015. (Subchapter 3-A, Corporate Tax of 2015; Sec. 11-651, N.Y.C. Adm. Code, *et. seq.*)

However, S corporations and qualified subchapter S subsidiaries remain subject to the existing, pre-reform general corporation tax provisions. (Sec. 11-602.1, N.Y.C. Adm. Code)

For an overview of the corporate tax reform changes, see ¶505-205.

The Department of Finance's outline notes that most of the existing GCT modifications are continued under the business corporation tax. (Sec. 11-652, N.Y.C. Adm. Code)

Pre-reform provisions.—New York City depreciation rules are generally the same as federal and state (ACRS/MACRS) for property placed into service in New York after 1984. (Sec. 11-602(8)(b)(11), N.Y.C. Adm. Code, Sec. 11-652(8)(b)(11), N.Y.C. Adm. Code) Adjustments are required, however, for taxpayers who have used federal ACRS for properties placed into service either outside of New York or before 1985. These taxpayers are required to use pre-ACRS federal rules for New York purposes. (26 U.S.C. § 167, as in effect 12/31/80; Sec. 11-602(8)(j), N.Y.C. Adm Code, Sec. 11-652(8)(j), N.Y.C. Adm. Code) Differences between federal and New York treatment are reported on Form NYC 399 and the resulting adjustments, which may be additions or subtractions, are carried forward to NYC 3L (or the appropriate city tax return). In the same manner, differences in basis are reported on Form NYC 399 when the property is sold and are then carried forward to Form CT-3. (Sec. 11-602(8)(b)(12), N.Y.C. Adm. Code, Sec. 11-652(8)(b)(12), N.Y.C. Adm. Code)

CCH CAUTION: The practical effect of the above is as follows: A taxpayer subject to New York City general corporation tax that takes accelerated depreciation deductions under IRC Sec. 168 in calculating its federal taxable income must add that amount back to its entire net income base if the deduction is for property placed in service outside New York. Under Sec. 11-602(j), N.Y.C. Adm. Code, the taxpayer may take a deduction for that property under IRC Sec. 167. For property placed in service *within* New York, however, a taxpayer may take *either* the IRC Sec. 167 deduction or the IRC Sec. 168 ACRS deduction.

In *R.J. Reynolds v. City of New York Department of Finance*, the New York Supreme Court, Appellate Division, held that, by overtly differentiating between property placed in service within and without New York, based solely on the situs of the corporate taxpayer's activities, the City violated federal Commerce Clause principles. In addition, by only allowing taxpayers to take advantage of the accelerated depreciation scheme for property placed in service within New York, the City code provisions created a distinct commercial advantage to local businesses, thereby discriminating against taxpayers whose property was located outside New York.

New York City permits an elective double depreciation of business property that is similar to the New York State former investment deduction. This subtraction adjustment is discussed at ¶505-450.

• *Federal bonus depreciation--partial decoupling*

With respect to certain provisions enacted by the federal Job Creation and Worker Assistance Act of 2002 (P.L. 107-147) (JCWAA) and the Jobs and Growth Tax Relief Reconciliation Act of 2003 (P.L. 108-27) (JGTRRA), including additional 30% and 50% depreciation deductions allowed in the first year "qualified property" is placed in service, New York City law has been amended to generally limit the depreciation deduction for qualified property to the deduction that would have been allowed for such property under IRC Sec. 167 had the property been acquired by the taxpayer on September 10, 2001. However, the depreciation deductions for qualified Resurgence Zone property, qualified New York Liberty Zone property, and qualified New York Liberty Zone leasehold improvements, as well as the additional first-year expense deduction under IRC Sec. 179 for qualified New York Liberty Zone property, are the same for New York City general corporation and business corporation tax purposes as for federal tax purposes. (Sec. 11-602(8)(a)(12), (8)(b)(16), (8)(k), and (8)(m), N.Y.C. Adm. Code, Sec. 11-652(8), N.Y.C. Adm. Code; *Finance Memorandum 02-3*, October 29, 2003)

As amended, the New York City law also requires appropriate adjustments to the amount of any gain or loss included in entire net income upon the disposition of any property for which the federal and New York City depreciation deductions differ. (Sec. 11-602(8)(l), N.Y.C. Adm. Code; Sec. 11-652(8)(l), N.Y.C. Adm. Code; *Finance Memorandum 02-3*, October 29, 2003)

For purposes of Sec. 11-602(8)(b)(16) and Sec. 11-602(8)(k), as well as Sec. 11-652(8), N.Y.C. Adm. Code, "qualified resurgence zone property" and "qualified New York liberty zone property" described in IRC Sec. 1400L(b)(2) do not include any sport utility vehicle that is not a passenger automobile as defined in IRC Sec. 280F(d)(5). (Sec. 11-602(8)(o), N.Y.C. Adm. Code; Sec. 11-652, N.Y.C. Adm. Code)

For taxable years beginning on or after January 1, 2004, in the case of a passenger motor vehicle or a sport utility vehicle subject to the provisions of Sec. 11-602(8)(o) (see "Sport utility vehicles" below), the limitation under IRC Sec. 280F(a)(1)(A)(i) applicable to the amount allowed as a deduction under Sec. 11-602(8)(k) must be determined as of the date such vehicle was placed in service and not as of September 10, 2001. (Sec. 11-602(8)(k), N.Y.C. Adm. Code; Sec. 11-652, N.Y.C. Adm. Code)

• *Sport utility vehicles*

For taxable years beginning on or after January 1, 2004, in the case of a taxpayer that is not an eligible farmer, no deduction may be taken for the amount allowable as a deduction under IRC Sec. 167, IRC Sec. 168, and IRC Sec. 179 with respect to a sport utility vehicle that is not a passenger automobile as defined in IRC Sec. 280F(d)(5). (Sec. 11-602(8)(b)(17), N.Y.C. Adm. Code; Sec. 11-652, N.Y.C. Adm. Code)

Instead, the deduction must be computed *as if* the sport utility vehicle *were* a passenger automobile as defined in IRC Sec. 280F(d)(5). (Sec. 11-602(8)(a)(13), (8)(o), N.Y.C. Adm. Code; Sec. 11-652, N.Y.C. Adm. Code)

The Department of Finance has provided schedules setting forth the applicable New York City SUV limits; see *Finance Memorandum 19-1*, March 2, 2020.

Upon the disposition of property to which Sec. 11-602(8)(o) applies, the amount of any gain or loss includible in entire net income must be adjusted to reflect the above inclusions and exclusions from entire net income attributable to such property. (Sec. 11-602(8)(p), N.Y.C. Adm. Code; Sec. 11-652, N.Y.C. Adm. Code)

[¶505-417] NYC Additions To Federal Base--NYC Related Member Expenses

Under corporate tax reform legislation enacted in 2015, the New York City corporate income tax system was significantly revised, generally applicable to taxable years beginning on or after January 1, 2015. (Subchapter 3-A, Corporate Tax of 2015; Sec. 11-651, N.Y.C. Adm. Code, *et. seq.*)

However, S corporations and qualified subchapter S subsidiaries remain subject to the existing, pre-reform general corporation tax provisions. (Sec. 11-602.1, N.Y.C. Adm. Code)

For an overview of the corporate tax reform changes, see ¶505-205.

The Department of Finance's outline notes that most of the existing GCT modifications are continued under the business corporation tax. (Sec. 11-652, N.Y.C. Adm. Code)

Pre-reform provisions.—The following provisions concerning royalty expense addbacks are parallel to similar state provisions discussed at ¶10-620. The City provisions were enacted by A.B. 8388, Laws 2003, and modified by a technical corrections bill, Ch. 686, Laws 2003. (Sec. 1201(m), Tax Law; Sec. 11-602(8)(n), N.Y.C. Adm. Code) The 2013 budget legislation further revised them; among other changes, the income exclusion provision was eliminated.

For the purpose of computing a taxpayer's entire net income or other applicable taxable basis, royalty payments made by the taxpayer to a related member during the taxable year must be added back, to the extent deductible in calculating the taxpayer's federal taxable income. (Sec. 11-602(8)(n)(2), N.Y.C. Adm. Code)

For taxable years beginning on or after January 1, 2013, the addback is not required if (Sec. 11-602(8)(n), N.Y.C. Adm. Code; Summary, New York Department of Taxation and Finance):

— the amount was included in the related member's tax base, the related member paid all or part of the amount to an unrelated party, and the transaction between the taxpayer and the related member had a valid business purpose;

— the related member paid significant taxes on the amount;

— the related member was organized in a foreign country, the income from the transaction was subject to a comprehensive income tax treaty, the related member was taxed by the foreign country at a rate at least equal to New York's rate, and the amount was paid in a transaction with a valid business purpose and arm's-length terms; or

— the taxpayer and the Department agree to alternative adjustments.

For taxable years beginning before 2013, the addback of royalty payments was not required to the extent that such payments met either of the following conditions:

—the related member during the same taxable year directly or indirectly paid or incurred the amount to a person or entity that was not a related member, and such transaction was done for a valid business purpose and the payments were made at arm's length; or

—the royalty payments were paid or incurred to a related member organized under the laws of a country other than the United States, were subject to a comprehensive income tax treaty between such country and the United States, and were taxed in such country at a tax rate at least equal to that imposed by New York. (Sec. 11-602(8)(n)(2)(B), N.Y.C. Adm. Code)

A "valid business purpose" is one or more business purposes, other than the avoidance or reduction of taxation, which alone or in combination constitute the primary motivation for some business activity or transaction, which activity or transaction changes in a meaningful way, apart from tax effects, the economic position of the taxpayer. The economic position of the taxpayer includes an increase in the market share of the taxpayer, or the entry by the taxpayer into new business markets. (Sec. 11-602(8)(n)(1)(D), N.Y.C. Adm. Code)

For purposes of these provisions, "royalty payments" are defined as payments directly connected to the acquisition, use, maintenance or management, ownership, sale, exchange, or any other disposition of licenses, trademarks, copyrights, trade names, trade dress, service marks, mask works, trade secrets, patents and any other similar types of intangible assets as determined by the Commissioner. The definition includes amounts allowable as interest deductions under IRC Sec. 163 to the extent such amounts are directly or indirectly for, related to or in connection with the acquisition, use, maintenance or management, ownership, sale, exchange or disposition of such intangible assets. (Sec. 11-602(8)(n)(1)(C), N.Y.C. Adm. Code)

"Related member" means a related person as defined in IRC § 465(b)(3)(c), except that "50%" is substituted for "10%." (Sec. 11-602(8)(n)(1), N.Y.C. Adm. Code)

[¶505-419] NYC Additions To Federal Base--NYC Interest, Carrying Charges, and Losses Attributable to Subsidiary Capital

Under corporate tax reform legislation enacted in 2015, the New York City corporate income tax system was significantly revised, generally applicable to taxable years beginning on or after January 1, 2015. (Subchapter 3-A, Corporate Tax of 2015; Sec. 11-651, N.Y.C. Adm. Code, *et. seq.*)

However, S corporations and qualified subchapter S subsidiaries remain subject to the existing, pre-reform general corporation tax provisions. (Sec. 11-602.1, N.Y.C. Adm. Code)

For an overview of the corporate tax reform changes, see ¶ 505-205.

Pre-reform provisions.—Because corporations are exempt from tax on income received from subsidiaries (Sec. 11-602(8)(a)(1), N.Y.C. Adm. Code), expenses, including interest expense, directly or indirectly attributable to subsidiary capital and income that were deducted in computing federal taxable income must generally be added back. (Sec. 11-602(8)(b)(6), N.Y.C. Adm. Code; Rule Sec. 11-27(b)(1)(ix)) However, such an addback may not be required, at the discretion of the Commissioner of Finance. (Rule Sec. 11-27(b)(1)(ix)) All losses from a subsidiary that were deducted in computing federal taxable income must also be added back.

The amount of interest expense indirectly attributable to subsidiary capital is determined by multiplying the total interest expense by the ratio of subsidiary capital to total assets (*Petition of Pfizer*). For methodology and examples of direct attribution and indirect attribution to subsidiary capital, see Bulletin 2-84 at505-419.40 below.

[¶505-422] NYC Additions To Federal Base--Other NYC Additions to Federal Base

Under corporate tax reform legislation enacted in 2015, the New York City corporate income tax system was significantly revised, generally applicable to taxable years beginning on or after January 1, 2015. (Subchapter 3-A, Corporate Tax of 2015; Sec. 11-651, N.Y.C. Adm. Code, *et. seq.*)

However, S corporations and qualified subchapter S subsidiaries remain subject to the existing, pre-reform general corporation tax provisions. (Sec. 11-602.1, N.Y.C. Adm. Code)

For an overview of the corporate tax reform changes, see ¶ 505-205.

• *Items included in entire net income—New business corporation tax*

Repatriated income deduction.—Under the 2018 budget legislation, an addback is required for the amount of the federal deduction allowed under IRC § 965(c). (Sec. 11-652(8)(b)(20), N.Y.C. Adm. Code; *Finance Memorandum 18-9*, New York City Department of Finance)

Foreign-derived intangible income (FDII).—An addback is also required for the amount of the federal deduction allowed under IRC § 250(a)(1)(A). (Sec. 11-652(8)(b)(21), N.Y.C. Adm. Code; *Finance Memorandum 18-9*, New York City Department of Finance)

Business interest expense deduction.—An addition modification is required for the amount of the increase in the federal interest deduction allowed under IRC Sec. 163(j)(10). This relates to the federal CARES Act amendment increasing the cap of the business interest expense limitation and allowing an election to use 2019 adjusted taxable income for 2020. The modification is required for taxable years beginning in 2019 and 2020. (Sec. 11-652(8)(b)(22), N.Y.C. Adm. Code; *Finance Memorandum 20-6*)

QPAI deduction.—An addition modification is required for the IRC § 199 deduction for qualified production activities income. (Sec. 11-652(8)(b)(18), N.Y.C. Adm. Code)

Safe-harbor adjustments (pre-1984).—Except for qualified mass commuting vehicles and property of a taxpayer principally engaged in the conduct of an aviation, steamboat, ferry, or navigation business that is placed in service before taxable years beginning in 1989, the amount claimed as a deduction in computing federal taxable income solely as a result of the safe harbor lease election made under IRC Sec. 168(f)(8) as it was in effect for agreements entered into prior to January 1, 1984 (Sec. 11-652(8)(b)(9), N.Y.C. Adm. Code), or the amount a taxpayer would have been required to include in the computation of its federal taxable income had it not made the safe harbor lease election is included in entire net income. (Sec. 11-652(8)(b)(10), N.Y.C. Adm. Code)

• *Items included in entire net income—Pre-reform provisions (GCT)*

Foreign-derived intangible income (FDII).—An addback is required under the GCT for the amount of the federal deduction allowed under IRC § 250(a)(1)(A). (Sec. 11-602(8)(b)(20), N.Y.C. Adm. Code; *Finance Memorandum 18-10*, New York City Department of Finance)

Business interest expense deduction.—An addition modification is required for the amount of the increase in the federal interest deduction allowed under IRC Sec. 163(j)(10). This relates to the federal CARES Act amendment increasing the cap of the business interest expense limitation and allowing an election to use 2019 adjusted taxable income for 2020. The modification is required for taxable years beginning in 2019 and 2020. (Sec. 11-602(8)(b)(21), N.Y.C. Adm. Code; *Finance Memorandum 20-6*)

Foreign-source income.—In the case of a taxpayer organized outside the United States, all income from sources outside the United States, less all allowable deductions attributable thereto, that was not taken into account in computing federal taxable income is included. (Sec. 11-602(8)(c), N.Y.C. Adm. Code; Rule Sec. 11-27(b)(1)(viii))

QPAI deduction.—Under the 2008 budget legislation, applicable to taxable years beginning after 2007, an addition modification is required for the IRC § 199 deduction for qualified production activities income. (Sec. 11-602(8)(b)(18), N.Y.C. Adm. Code)

Business on New York Insurance Exchange.—Corporations whose only insurance business is that conducted on the New York Insurance Exchange (out-of-state risks) are not required to file Form CT-33, the franchise tax return for insurance corporations. Such corporations add back the taxpayer's distributive or pro rata share of items of loss or distributive or pro rata share of net loss. (Sec. 11-602(8)(b)(8), N.Y.C. Adm. Code)

Safe-harbor adjustments (pre-1984).—Except for qualified mass commuting vehicles and property of a taxpayer principally engaged in the conduct of an aviation, steamboat, ferry, or navigation business that is placed in service before taxable years beginning in 1989, the amount claimed as a deduction in computing federal taxable income solely as a result of the safe harbor lease election made under IRC Sec. 168(f)(8) as it was in effect for agreements entered into prior to January 1, 1984 (Sec. 11-602(8)(b)(9), N.Y.C. Adm. Code), or the amount a taxpayer would have been required to include in the computation of its federal taxable income had it not made the safe harbor lease election is included in entire net income. (Sec. 11-602(8)(b)(10), N.Y.C. Adm. Code)

Addback for acquisition interest (pre-2000).—For taxable years beginning before 2000, up to 5% of the amount of interest paid by an acquiring taxpayer in the year of acquisition and for the next three years was added to federal taxable income. The amount was limited to the ratio of the taxpayer's total interest represented by acquisition cost divided by total debt. The provisions did not apply, however, if total interest (for the taxpayer singly or the taxpayer together with an affiliated group) was less than $1 million or if the acquisition ratio described above had not increased more than 60% from the preceding year. (Former Sec. 11-602(8)(b)(6-a), N.Y.C. Adm. Code)

Dividends related to sale of assets by target corporations (pre-2000).—For taxable years beginning before 2000, the exclusion for subsidiary dividends (see ¶ 505-425) was not permitted when there was a 50% reduction in the assets of the targeted acquisition within an 18-month period. When such a disposition of assets by the subsidiary occurred, those dividends had to be added to the income of the acquiring corporation. (Former Sec. 11-602(8)(b)(13)—(15), N.Y.C. Adm. Code)

Federal credits.—Although a statute denies to New York City taxpayers the amount of any specific federal exemption or credit against income, federal credits are in fact deducted on the federal return after the point at which New York City taxable income is determined (for starting point, see ¶ 505-405). Consequently, no adjustment is necessary. (Sec. 11-602(8)(b)(1), N.Y.C. Adm. Code)

Industrial business zone credit.—An addition to entire net income is required for the amount of the industrial business zone credit allowed (see ¶ 507-006), to the extent that relocation costs were deducted in the current or preceding tax year. (Sec. 11-604(17-b)(f), N.Y.C. Adm. Code)

[¶ 505-425] NYC Subtractions From Federal Base--NYC Income from Subsidiary Capital

Under corporate tax reform legislation enacted in 2015, the New York City corporate income tax system was significantly revised, generally applicable to taxable years beginning on or after January 1, 2015. (Subchapter 3-A, Corporate Tax of 2015; Sec. 11-651, N.Y.C. Adm. Code, *et. seq.*)

However, S corporations and qualified subchapter S subsidiaries remain subject to the existing, pre-reform general corporation tax provisions. (Sec. 11-602.1, N.Y.C. Adm. Code)

For an overview of the corporate tax reform changes, see ¶ 505-205.

Pre-reform provisions.—Income, gains, and losses from subsidiary capital are excluded from federal taxable income in computing New York City entire net income. (Sec. 11-602(8)(a), N.Y.C. Adm. Code) The income to be excluded includes all dividends, interest, and gains from subsidiary capital, but not any other income from subsidiaries. (Rule Sec. 11-27) No exclusion is allowed for amounts representing recovery of a war loss.

Losses from subsidiary capital must be added back to the federal base (see ¶ 505-419).

[¶505-428] NYC Subtractions From Federal Base--NYC Dividends

Under corporate tax reform legislation enacted in 2015, the New York City corporate income tax system was significantly revised, generally applicable to taxable years beginning on or after January 1, 2015. (Subchapter 3-A, Corporate Tax of 2015; Sec. 11-651, N.Y.C. Adm. Code, *et. seq.*)

However, S corporations and qualified subchapter S subsidiaries remain subject to the existing, pre-reform general corporation tax provisions. (Sec. 11-602.1, N.Y.C. Adm. Code)

For an overview of the corporate tax reform changes, see ¶ 505-205.

Under the new business corporation tax, a subtraction from federal taxable income is allowed for amounts of foreign dividend gross-up under IRC § 78, to the extent the dividends are not deducted under IRC § 250. (Sec. 11-652(8)(a)(2-a), N.Y.C. Adm. Code)

The specific exclusions for income from subsidiary capital and 50% of dividends from non-subsidiaries were repealed (see "Pre-reform provisions" discussed below).

However, subtractions are allowed for investment income and "other exempt income," which is defined as the sum of exempt CFC income and exempt unitary corporation dividends. (Sec. 11-652, N.Y.C. Adm. Code)

IRC Sec. 965 Repatriation income.—Under the 2018 budget legislation, the definition of "exempt CFC income" is expanded to encompass repatriated income received from a corporation not included in a combined report with the taxpayer (*Finance Memorandum 18-9*, New York City Department of Finance). However, an addback is required for the amount of the federal deduction allowed under IRC § 965(c) (see also ¶ 505-422).

Pre-reform provisions (GCT).—Subtractions from federal taxable income are provided for the following dividends:

(1) All dividends from subsidiaries (see ¶ 505-425);

(2) All amounts of foreign dividend gross-up determined under federal law (Sec. 11-602(8)(a)(2-a), N.Y.C. Adm. Code; 26 U.S.C. § 78); and

(3) 50% of other dividends on shares of stock conforming to IRC provisions concerning deductions for dividends received. (Sec. 11-602(8)(a)(2), N.Y.C. Adm. Code)

The 50% dividend exclusion does not apply to real estate investment trusts (Sec. 11-603(7), N.Y.C. Adm. Code; Rule Sec. 11-27(g)) or to regulated investment companies. (Sec. 11-603(8), N.Y.C. Adm. Code)

[¶505-431] NYC Subtractions From Federal Base--NYC Depreciation Adjustments

Under corporate tax reform legislation enacted in 2015, the New York City corporate income tax system was significantly revised, generally applicable to taxable years beginning on or after January 1, 2015. (Subchapter 3-A, Corporate Tax of 2015; Sec. 11-651, N.Y.C. Adm. Code, *et. seq.*)

However, S corporations and qualified subchapter S subsidiaries remain subject to the existing, pre-reform general corporation tax provisions. (Sec. 11-602.1, N.Y.C. Adm. Code)

For an overview of the corporate tax reform changes, see ¶505-205.

The Department of Finance's outline notes that most of the existing GCT modifications are continued under the business corporation tax. (Sec. 11-652, N.Y.C. Adm. Code)

Pre-reform provisions.—Adjustments made to the federal base as the result of differing federal/city treatment of depreciable property placed into service outside New York state or prior to 1985 may be additions or subtractions depending upon the depreciation method chosen. (Sec. 11-602(8)(a)(10), N.Y.C. Adm. Code; Sec. 11-602(8)(j), N.Y.C. Adm. Code) The manner of applying adjustments is discussed at ¶505-416. Adjustments may also be required upon disposition of property to reconcile federal and city depreciation methods. (Sec. 11-602(8)(a)(11), N.Y.C. Adm. Code)

Note: In *R.J. Reynolds v. City of New York Department of Finance*, the New York Supreme Court, Appellate Division, held that, by overtly differentiating between property placed in service within and without New York, based solely on the situs of the corporate taxpayer's activities, the City violated federal Commerce Clause principles. For details, see discussion at ¶505-416.

[¶505-432] NYC Subtractions From Federal Base--NYC Related Member Income

Applicable to taxable years beginning after 2002 and before 2013, a taxpayer was allowed to deduct royalty payments received from a related member during the taxable year, to the extent included in the taxpayer's federal taxable income, unless the royalty payments were not required to be added back under the expense disallowance provisions discussed at ¶505-417 or other similar provisions. (Sec. 11-602(8)(n)(3), N.Y.C. Adm. Code)

The royalty income exclusion described above was eliminated by the 2013 budget legislation. (Summary, New York Department of Taxation and Finance)

[¶505-434] NYC Subtractions From Federal Base--NYC Wages Related to Federal Credits

Under corporate tax reform legislation enacted in 2015, the New York City corporate income tax system was significantly revised, generally applicable to taxable years beginning on or after January 1, 2015. (Subchapter 3-A, Corporate Tax of 2015; Sec. 11-651, N.Y.C. Adm. Code, *et. seq.*)

However, S corporations and qualified subchapter S subsidiaries remain subject to the existing, pre-reform general corporation tax provisions. (Sec. 11-602.1, N.Y.C. Adm. Code)

For an overview of the corporate tax reform changes, see ¶505-205.

The Department of Finance's outline notes that most of the existing GCT modifications are continued under the business corporation tax. (Sec. 11-652, N.Y.C. Adm. Code)

Pre-reform provisions.—An exclusion from federal taxable income is allowed for the portion of wages and salaries not allowed as a business expense deduction for federal purposes because the federal employment tax credits were taken. (Sec. 11-602(8)(a)(7), N.Y.C. Adm. Code; 26 U.S.C. §51, 52, 280C)

[¶505-437] NYC Subtractions From Federal Base--NYC Net Operating Loss Deduction

Under corporate tax reform legislation enacted in 2015, the New York City corporate income tax system was significantly revised, generally applicable to taxable years beginning on or after January 1, 2015. (Subchapter 3-A, Corporate Tax of 2015; Sec. 11-651, N.Y.C. Adm. Code, *et. seq.*)

However, S corporations and qualified subchapter S subsidiaries remain subject to the existing, pre-reform general corporation tax provisions. (Sec. 11-602.1, N.Y.C. Adm. Code)

For pre-2015 net operating losses (NOLs), the new provisions allow a prior NOL conversion subtraction (Sec. 11-654.1, N.Y.C. Adm. Code), which is computed on Form NYC 2.3.

The new business corporation tax provisions allow a three-year carryback for NOLs incurred in tax years beginning after 2014, but no NOL earned after 2014 can be carried back to a tax year before 2015. A 20-year carryforward is allowed. (Sec. 11-654.1, N.Y.C. Adm. Code).

Pre-reform provisions. Pre-reform provisions are discussed below.

Note: The law has been amended to provide that, for taxable years beginning before 2021, any amendment to IRC Sec. 172 made after March 1, 2020, does not apply. Accordingly, the New York City general corporation tax does not conform to federal CARES Act amendments, including (1) a five-year carryback period for NOLs arising in tax years beginning in 2018, 2019, and 2020, and (2) suspension of the 80% of taxable income limitation for those years. (Sec. 11-602(8)(f)(6), N.Y.C. Adm. Code; *Finance Memorandum 20-6*)

A net operating loss deduction is allowed in computing entire net income for New York City general corporation tax purposes. (Sec. 11-602(8)(f), N.Y.C. Adm. Code) The federal carryover and carryback periods are generally followed, although carrybacks are limited to the first $10,000 of loss in any taxable year ending after June 30, 1989.

With respect to the extended five-year NOL carryback period provided by the federal Job Creation and Worker Assistance Act of 2002 (P.L. 107-147) (JCWAA) for certain NOLs arising in tax years ending in 2001 and 2002, the New York City Department of Finance has advised that the same NOL carryback periods allowed for federal tax purposes apply for New York City general corporation tax purposes. However, the $10,000 limitation noted above, and all other City modifications to the federal NOL deduction, will apply to NOLs eligible for the five-year carryback period. (*Finance Memorandum 02-3*, October 29, 2003)

The New York City deduction, whose computation begins with the federal deduction under IRC Sec. 172, is subject to the following limitations:

(1) The net loss is computed using the modifications to entire net income that are made for city purposes. These include the allowable deduction of the cost of industrial waste treatment facilities and air pollution control facilities and the disallowance of gain attributable to years before 1966;

(2) The loss deduction does not include losses sustained in years in which the corporation was not subject to the general corporation tax; and

(3) The New York NOL deduction may not exceed the deduction allowable for federal purposes.

The New York City General Tax Regulations include detailed administrative provisions dealing with net operating loss, together with helpful examples. (Rule Sec. 11-28)

• *S corporations*

Inasmuch as S corporations are subject to the general corporation tax, the net operating loss of an S corporation is computed as though the federal Subchapter S election had not been made. (Instructions to Form NYC-3L)

• *RICs and REITs*

Net operating losses may not be deducted by real estate investment trusts (Sec. 11-603(7), N.Y.C. Adm. Code; Rule Sec. 11-27(g)) or regulated investment companies. (Sec. 11-603(8), N.Y.C. Adm. Code)

• *Acquisitions and consolidations (pre-2000)*

For taxable years beginning in or after 1989 and before 2000, net operating losses attributable to acquisitions (whether by purchase, merger, or consolidation) were not includable. (Former Sec. 11-602(8)(f)(2-a), (2-b), (2-c), N.Y.C. Adm. Code) The transactions that incorporated this limitation of the NOL are detailed below. The treatment was identical to that of the state (¶ 10-805).

Acquisitions.—For taxable years beginning on or after January 1, 1989, and before 2000, the net operating loss deduction for a taxable year in which the taxpayer was a target corporation in a subdivision (15) corporate acquisition, or any subsequent taxable year, could not include a net operating loss sustained by the target corporation in its taxable year during which the acquisition occurred or in any prior taxable year. (Former Sec. 11-602(8)(f)(2-a), (2-b), (2-c), N.Y.C. Adm. Code) A "subdivision fifteen corporate acquisition" was a corporate acquisition in which the taxpayer was the target corporation and (1) the ratio of average aggregate debt to average aggregate equity, for the taxable year in which the acquisition occurred, increased by more than 100% over the ratio for the immediately preceding taxable year, and (2) the ratio of average aggregate debt to average aggregate assets, for the taxable year in which the acquisition occurred, increased by more than 60% over the ratio for the immediately preceding taxable year, and (3) the total of the acquiring person's interest paid or accrued during its taxable year in which the acquisition occurred was more than $1 million. (Former Sec. 11-602(15), N.Y.C. Adm. Code)

Mergers.—Also, for taxable years beginning on or after January 1, 1989, and before 2000, the deduction for a taxable year in which the taxpayer was a surviving corporation in a subdivision (16) corporate merger or any subsequent taxable year could not include any net operating loss sustained by any target corporation in its taxable year during which the merger occurred or in any prior taxable year. (Former Sec. 11-602(8)(f)(2-a), (2-b), (2-c), N.Y.C. Adm. Code)

Consolidations.—The net operating loss deduction, for a taxable year in which the taxpayer was a consolidated corporation in a subdivision (18) corporate consolidation, or for any subsequent taxable year, could not include any net operating loss sustained by any target corporation in its taxable year ending immediately prior to the consolidation or in any prior taxable year.

A "subdivision sixteen corporate merger" or "corporate consolidation" was a corporate merger or corporate consolidation in which the taxpayer was the surviving or consolidated corporation and that met the same criteria applicable for subdivision 15 acquisitions (above) (Former Sec. 11-602(16), N.Y.C. Adm. Code): the ratio of average aggregate debt to average aggregate equity, for the taxable year in which the merger or consolidation occurred, increased by more than 100% over the ratio for the immediately preceding taxable year, (2) the ratio of average aggregate debt to average aggregate assets, for the taxable year in which the merger or consolidation occurred, increased by more than 60% over the ratio for the immediately preceding taxable year; and (3) the total interest paid or accrued by the surviving or consolidated corporation during its taxable year in which the merger or consolidation occurred was more than $1 million.

[¶505-440] NYC Subtractions From Federal Base--NYC Air Pollution Control Facilities

Under corporate tax reform legislation enacted in 2015, the New York City corporate income tax system was significantly revised, generally applicable to taxable years beginning on or after January 1, 2015. (Subchapter 3-A, Corporate Tax of 2015; Sec. 11-651, N.Y.C. Adm. Code, *et. seq.*)

However, S corporations and qualified subchapter S subsidiaries remain subject to the existing, pre-reform general corporation tax provisions. (Sec. 11-602.1, N.Y.C. Adm. Code)

For an overview of the corporate tax reform changes, see ¶505-205.

The Department of Finance's outline notes that most of the existing GCT modifications are continued under the business corporation tax. (Sec. 11-652, N.Y.C. Adm. Code)

Pre-reform provisions.—A taxpayer may elect to subtract from the federal base any expenditures made during the taxable year for air pollution control facilities, as defined, for depreciable property situated in New York City and used in the taxpayer's trade or business that is certified as meeting applicable standards. (Sec. 11-602(8)(g), N.Y.C. Adm. Code)

The deduction may not be taken with respect to property for which the taxpayer has elected the double depreciation deduction from allocated net income (see ¶505-450).

When the deduction is elected, no further deduction may be taken in the same year or future years for the expenditures, or for depreciation or amortization of the same property to the extent that its basis is attributed to the expenditures. Therefore, any federal deductions must be reduced accordingly or added back to the base. The city deduction is disregarded in computing gain or loss on disposition of the property, which is reported instead on the basis of gain or loss reported on the federal return.

[¶505-444] NYC Subtractions From Federal Base--NYC Pre-1966 Capital Gain Deduction

Gain derived from the sale or disposition of capital asset property acquired prior to January 1, 1966, is modified to eliminate the gain attributable to the period before 1966. (Rule Sec. 11-27) The modification is made if the pre-January 1, 1966, property had a federal adjusted basis on January 1, 1966, which is lower than its fair market value on January 1, 1966.

• *Computation*

A deduction from entire net income is allowed for the difference between (1) the amount of the taxpayer's federal taxable income and (2) the amount of the taxpayer's federal taxable income computed by using the special New York City basis for the property, plus or minus adjustments to basis if smaller than (1). (Rule Sec. 11-27)

For the purpose of computing the modification, the basis of the property may be taken to be the lower of:

(1) The fair market value on January 1, 1966, or the date of its sale or other disposition prior to January 1, 1966, plus or minus all adjustments to basis for federal income tax purposes for periods on and after January 1, 1966, or

(2) the amount realized from its sale or other disposition.

• *Limitation on total modification*

The total modification for gain on such property may not exceed the taxpayer's net gain from the sale or other disposition of all such property. (Sec. 11-602(8)(h), N.Y.C. Adm. Code)

[¶505-447] NYC Subtractions From Federal Base--Other NYC Subtractions from Federal Base

Under corporate tax reform legislation enacted in 2015, the New York City corporate income tax system was significantly revised, generally applicable to taxable years beginning on or after January 1, 2015. (Subchapter 3-A, Corporate Tax of 2015; Sec. 11-651, N.Y.C. Adm. Code, *et. seq.*)

However, S corporations and qualified subchapter S subsidiaries remain subject to the existing, pre-reform general corporation tax provisions. (Sec. 11-602.1, N.Y.C. Adm. Code)

For an overview of the corporate tax reform changes, see ¶ 505-205.

The Department of Finance's outline notes that most of the existing GCT modifications are continued under the business corporation tax. (Sec. 11-652, N.Y.C. Adm. Code)

Pre-reform provisions.—To the extent that any of the following items were included in determining federal taxable income, they are subtracted from the federal base in computing New York City entire net income. In addition, certain elective deductions are discussed at ¶ 505-450.

(1) *Gifts:* Bona fide gifts. (Sec. 11-602(8)(a)(3), N.Y.C. Adm. Code) Gifts are generally not taxable on the federal return (26 U.S.C. 102) so that no adjustment is necessary on the New York City return;

(2) *School bus income:* Receipts from school districts and from nonprofit religious, charitable, or educational organizations for the operation of school buses. (Sec. 11-602(8)(a)(4), N.Y.C. Adm. Code) The subtraction applies to receipts only from

transportation for school activities, and must reflect the elimination of any related deductions allowed for federal purposes (Rule Sec. 11-27(b)(2)(iv));

(3) *Tax refunds:* A refund or credit of any previously paid New York City general corporation tax, New York City banking corporation tax, or New York state taxes imposed by Tax Law Articles 9 (corporation tax), 9-A (business corporation tax) or 32 (banking corporation tax) (Sec. 11-602(8)(a)(5), N.Y.C. Adm. Code);

(4) *Business on New York Insurance Exchange:* Corporations whose only insurance business is that conducted on the New York Insurance Exchange (out-of-state risks) subtract any items of income and any distributive or pro rata share of the income of the business reported on the federal return. (Sec. 11-602(8)(a)(6), N.Y.C. Adm. Code)

(5) *Safe harbor leases (pre-1984):* Amounts are subtracted that are included in federal taxable income as a result of former federal law (26 U.S.C. §168(f)(8)) that allowed the purchaser/lessor to take depreciation and investment tax credit deductions. (Sec. 11-602(8)(a)(8), N.Y.C. Adm. Code; Sec. 11-602(8)(a)(9), N.Y.C. Adm. Code)

(6) *Contributions to capital:* A subtraction is allowed for any amount excepted, for purposes of IRC Sec. 118(a), from the term "contribution to the capital of the taxpayer" by IRC Sec. 118(b)(2). (Sec. 11-602(8)(a)(14), N.Y.C. Adm. Code)

[¶505-450] NYC Subtractions From Federal Base--NYC Elective Adjustments: Double Depreciation of Business Property--One-Year Write-Off of Research and Development Property

A corporation may elect to take, for any taxable year, double the allowable federal depreciation for certain newly constructed, reconstructed, erected, or acquired tangible business property having a New York City situs. (Sec. 11-604(3)(e), N.Y.C. Adm. Code) To qualify, property must be principally used by the taxpayer in the production of goods by manufacturing, processing, assembling, refining, mining, extracting, farming, or fishing. Air pollution control facilities are specifically made eligible; however, taxpayers are required to choose between the double-depreciation election and the option for cost deduction described at ¶505-440.

The total of all depreciation deductions on the property may not exceed the basis of the property multiplied by the applicable business allocation percentage for the first year the double depreciation is claimed. The federal depreciation deduction is added back prior to allocation. The New York City deduction is taken from allocated income.

Currently there is not a comparable state deduction. However, the election is similar to the former state investment deduction applicable to property acquired between 1963 and 1969.

• *Research and development property*

Expenditures for the construction, reconstruction, erection, or acquisition of depreciable tangible business property having a New York City situs and used for research and development purposes may be deducted, at the election of the taxpayer, in the taxable year in which paid or incurred. (Sec. 11-604(3)(e), N.Y.C. Adm. Code) Research and development purposes include only experimental or laboratory purposes.

The deduction is limited to the amount of the expenditures paid or incurred in the taxable year multiplied by the taxpayer's business allocation percentage. Unused deductions may be carried over until exhausted. Taxpayers deducting the expenditures are not permitted to also depreciate the property.

When the property is sold or otherwise disposed of, the New York City basis is substituted for the federal basis in determining gain or loss on the property.

[¶505-460] NYC Alternative Bases--NYC Business Capital--Computation of Base

Under corporate tax reform legislation enacted in 2015 (see ¶505-205), the New York City corporate income tax system was significantly revised, generally applicable to taxable years beginning on or after January 1, 2015. (Subchapter 3-A, Corporate Tax of 2015; Sec. 11-651, N.Y.C. Adm. Code, *et. seq.*)

However, S corporations and qualified subchapter S subsidiaries remain subject to the existing, pre-reform general corporation tax provisions. (Sec. 11-602.1, N.Y.C. Adm. Code)

Under the new provisions, the business income base is the primary tax base and the business capital and fixed dollar minimum tax bases are alternative minimum bases (Sec. 11-654, N.Y.C. Adm. Code); see ¶505-251 for the rates.

The legislation modified the definitions of "investment capital" and "investment income" and exempted both from tax. (Sec. 11-652, N.Y.C. Adm. Code)

Because there is a separate tax rate applicable to the portion of total business capital directly attributable to stock in a subsidiary that either would be taxable as a utility or would have been taxable as an insurance corporation under the former New York City insurance corporation tax (see tax rate discussion at ¶505-251), the department must attribute liabilities between general business capital and insurance/utility capital to determine the amount of net business capital taxable in each tax rate category. Accordingly, for purposes of attributing liabilities within net business capital, the department will extend the methodology that applies to attributing liabilities between particular items of investment capital both directly and indirectly. The department has issued a memorandum that includes a worksheet providing a framework for extending the methodology. If the value of all liabilities attributable to business capital exceeds the value of such capital for the year, then net business capital is zero for purposes of the capital base and no attribution between tax rate categories is necessary. (Sec. 11-654(1)(e)(1)(ii), N.Y.C. Adm. Code; Finance Memorandum 17-2)

• *Pre-reform general corporation tax*

Note: The provisions discussed below generally apply to taxable years beginning before 2015. As noted above, however, they continue to apply to S corporations. (Sec. 11-602.1, N.Y.C. Adm. Code)

The New York City general corporation tax is based on the corporation's business and investment capital, or the portion thereof allocated to New York City, if a higher tax will result than from the other alternative bases of tax. The capital base does not apply to regulated investment companies (RICs) or to real estate investment trusts (REITs). (Sec. 11-603(7), N.Y.C. Adm. Code; Sec. 11-603(8), N.Y.C. Adm. Code)

Business capital.—"Business capital" means all assets (exclusive of stock issued by the taxpayer or assets constituting subsidiary or investment capital) less liabilities, to the extent such liabilities are not deducted in computed subsidiary capital or investment. (Sec. 11-602(6), N.Y.C. Adm. Code) The term includes loans to a subsidiary, if not evidenced by securities and if the subsidiary is allowed to take the interest as a deduction for purpose of New York City corporation taxes. (Rule Sec. 11-36)

¶505-460

Investment capital.—"Investment capital" means investments in stocks, bonds, and other securities issued by a corporation (other than the taxpayer or a subsidiary) or by any government or governmental entity. (Sec. 11-602(4), N.Y.C. Adm. Code; Rule Sec. 11-37; Instructions, Form NYC-3L)

Liabilities: Liabilities directly or indirectly attributable to investment capital may be deducted. (Sec. 11-602(4), N.Y.C. Adm. Code; Rule Sec. 11-38(b); Instructions, Form NYC-3L)

Cash.—Cash on hand and on deposit may, at the election of the taxpayer, be treated as either business capital or as investment capital. (Sec. 11-602(5), N.Y.C. Adm. Code) The difference in allocation percentages accorded to each will affect which characterization is more favorable to a taxpayer. No election to treat cash as investment capital may be made when the taxpayer has no other investment capital. (Rule Sec. 11-37)

Determination of business and investment capital.—A taxpayer's "business capital" is determined by taking the total average fair market value, during the period covered by the report, of all the assets of the taxpayer that constitute business capital, less certain current liabilities ("investment capital"). (Sec. 11-604(2), N.Y.C. Adm. Code; Rule Sec. 11-38)

A taxpayer's "investment capital" is determined by adding the average value and net value of each item of investment capital. The "net value" is determined by subtracting from the item's average value average liabilities that are directly or indirectly attributable to the item.

The average value of a marketable security included in investment capital is its average fair market value. The average value of an item of investment capital that is not a marketable security is the average value shown (or which should have been shown, if not so shown) on the books and records of the taxpayer in accordance with generally accepted accounting principles.

"Fair market value" defined: The fair market value of an asset owned by a taxpayer is the price at which a willing seller, not compelled to sell, will sell and a willing buyer, not compelled to buy, will buy. (Rule Sec. 11-39) The fair market value, on any date, of stocks, bonds and other securities regularly dealt in on an exchange, or in the over-the-counter market, is the mean between the highest and lowest selling prices on that date. If there were no sales on the valuation date, the fair market value is the mean between the highest and the lowest selling prices on the nearest date, within a reasonable time, on which there were sales. If actual sales within a reasonable time are not available, the fair market value is the mean between the bona fide bid and asked prices on the valuation date or the nearest date within a reasonable time.

If a taxpayer consistently values its stocks, bonds and other securities on some other basis, such as the last selling price on the valuation date, such method of valuation may be accepted by the Commissioner of Finance, provided a complete explanation of the method of valuation is provided to the Commissioner.

"Average fair market value" defined: In determining average fair market value, allowances must be made for variations in the amount of assets held by a taxpayer during the period covered by the report, as well as variations in market prices. (Rule Sec. 11-40) Average fair market value generally is computed on a quarterly basis where the taxpayer's usual accounting practice permits of such computation. However, at the option of the taxpayer, a more frequent basis (such as a monthly, weekly or daily average) may be used. A semi-annual or annual computation may be used if (1) the taxpayer's usual accounting practice does not permit a quarterly or more frequent computation of average fair market value, and (2) no distortion of average fair market value will result. The Commissioner may require averaging on a more

frequent basis upon a determination that annual, semi-annual or more frequent averaging does not adequately reflect average fair market value.

The average fair market value of real and tangible personal property owned by a taxpayer is determined by the same method used to determine the amount of taxpayer's capital. (Rule Sec. 11-64) The fair market value of real property that is rented to a taxpayer is determined by multiplying the gross rents payable during the period covered by the report by eight. "Gross rents" is the actual sum of money or other consideration payable, directly or indirectly, by the taxpayer or for its benefit for the use or possession of the property and includes:

(1) any amount payable for the use or possession of real property, or any part thereof, whether designated as a fixed sum of money or as a percentage of sales, profits, or otherwise;

Example: A taxpayer, pursuant to the terms of a lease, pays the lessor $1,000 per month and at the end of the year pays the lessor one percent of its gross sales of $400,000. Its gross rent is $16,000.

(2) any amount payable as additional rent or in lieu of rent, such as interest, taxes, insurance, repairs or any other amount required to be paid by the terms of a lease or other arrangement;

Example: A taxpayer, pursuant to the terms of a lease, pays the lessor $24,000 per annum and also pays real estate taxes in the amount of $4,000 and interest on a mortgage in the amount of $2,000. Its gross rent is $30,000.

(3) a proportionate part of the cost of any improvement to real property made by or on behalf of the taxpayer which reverts to the owner or lessor upon termination of a lease or other arrangement, based on the unexpired term of the lease commencing with the date the improvement is completed (or the life of the improvement if its life expectancy is less than the unexpired term of the lease), provided, however, that where a building is erected on leased land by or on behalf of the taxpayer, the value of the land is determined by multiplying the gross rent by eight, and the value of the building is determined in the same manner as if owned by the taxpayer. The proportionate part of the cost of an improvement (other than a building on leased land) is generally equal to the amount of amortization allowed in computing entire net income, whether the lease does or does not contain an option of renewal.

Example: A taxpayer enters into a 21-year lease of certain premises at a rental of $20,000 per annum and after the expiration of one year installs a new store front at a cost of $10,000 which reverts to the owner upon the expiration of the lease. Its gross rent for the first year is $20,000. However, for subsequent years its gross rent is $20,500 ($20,000 annual rent plus 1/20th of $10,000, the cost of the improvement apportioned on the basis of the unexpired term of the lease).

Example: A taxpayer leases a parcel of vacant land for 40 years at an annual rental of $5,000 and erects thereon a building which costs $600,000. The value of the land is determined by multiplying the annual rent of $5,000 by eight, and the value of the building is determined in the same manner as if owned by the taxpayer.

Gross rents do not include:

(1) intercompany rents if both the lessor and lessee are taxed on a combined basis;

(2) amounts payable as separate charges for water and electric service furnished by the lessor;

(3) amounts payable for storage provided no designated space under the control of the taxpayer as a tenant is rented for storage purposes;

(4) the portion of any rental payment, which, in the discretion of the Commissioner of Finance is applicable to property subleased by the taxpayer and not used by it.

Example: A taxpayer leases certain premises, all of which are of equal value, at a rental of $20,000 per annum and subleases 50 percent of such premises to one or more subtenants receiving a total of $10,000 per annum as rent from such subtenants. Since 50 percent of the rent paid by the taxpayer is applicable to the portion of the premises subleased, 50 percent thereof or $10,000 is excluded in computing the taxpayer's gross rent for such premises.

Once a particular method of determining average fair market value has been adopted by a taxpayer and accepted by the Commissioner, a new method of determining average fair market value cannot be utilized without the consent of the Commissioner.

[¶505-470] NYC Alternative Bases--NYC Income-Plus-Compensation--Computation of Base

Under corporate tax reform legislation enacted in 2015 (see ¶505-205), the New York City corporate income tax system was significantly revised, generally applicable to taxable years beginning on or after January 1, 2015. (Subchapter 3-A, Corporate Tax of 2015; Sec. 11-651, N.Y.C. Adm. Code, *et. seq.*)

However, S corporations and qualified subchapter S subsidiaries remain subject to the existing, pre-reform general corporation tax provisions. (Sec. 11-602.1, N.Y.C. Adm. Code)

Under the new provisions, the income-plus-compensation tax base has been eliminated.

Pre-reform general corporation tax.—The provisions discussed below generally apply to taxable years beginning before 2015. As noted above, however, they continue to apply to S corporations. (Sec. 11-602.1, N.Y.C. Adm. Code)

An alternative basis for measuring the New York City general corporation tax is entire net income plus certain compensation with various adjustments (or the portion of such sum allocable to New York City), if this calculation results in a higher amount than that computed on any of the other three alternative bases. (Sec. 11-604, N.Y.C. Adm. Code; Rule Sec. 11-34)

This base does not apply to real estate investment trusts or regulated investment companies (see ¶505-251).

Beginning on or after January 1, 2007, the alternative income plus compensation tax base and the capital tax base under the General Corporation Tax are eliminated for corporations that (1) have less than $250,000 in gross income, (2) allocate 100% to the City, and (3) have no investment or subsidiary capital or income. Additionally, any such corporation that is not a New York State S corporation may now elect to pay its tax based on its New York State entire net income (modified by adding back New York City corporate tax) rather than separately calculating New York City entire net income. (Sec. 11-604, N.Y.C. Adm. Code)

• *Computation of tax base*

For taxable years beginning prior to January 1, 2007, the base of the income-plus-compensation tax is 30% of the amount computed by adding, to the taxpayer's entire net income or net loss, the salaries and other compensation paid to every stockholder owning more than 5% of its issued capital stock (but only to the extent that a deduction was allowed for such salaries and compensation in computing entire net income or net loss), subtracting a fixed statutory exemption, and applying appropriate allocation rules. For taxable years beginning on or after January 1, 2007, the percentage is reduced from 30% to 15% in four equal yearly increments. For the taxable year beginning on or after January 1, 2007, and before January 1, 2008, the percentage used in the computation will be 26.25%. For the taxable year beginning on or after January 1, 2008, and before January 1, 2009, the percentage used in the computation will be 22.50%. For the taxable year beginning on or after January 1, 2009, and before January 1, 2010, the percentage used in the computation will be 18.75%. For the taxable year beginning on or after January 1, 2010, the percentage used in the computation will be 15%. Prior to July 1, 1999, a portion of the salaries and compensation paid to elected or appointed officers was also included in the computation. (Sec. 11-604, N.Y.C. Adm. Code; Rule Sec. 11-34)

For taxable years beginning on or after July 1, 1999, the tax base is determined as follows:

(1) add, to the taxpayer's entire net income (or net loss), 100% of all salaries and other compensation paid to every stockholder (including a stockholder who is also a corporate officer) owning in excess of 5% of the taxpayer's issued capital stock, but only to the extent that a deduction was allowed for such salaries and compensation in computing entire net income or net loss;

(2) deduct from such total: $40,000 (or a proportionate part thereof in the case of a return for less than a year); and

(3) multiply the balance by the percentage being used for that taxable year (for example, 30% for taxable years beginning prior to January 1, 2007.) (Sec. 11-604, N.Y.C. Adm. Code; Rule Sec. 11-34)

A rule provides detailed examples illustrating the computation of the tax base. (Rule Sec. 11-34(f))

Prior years.—For taxable years beginning before July 1, 1996, the tax base was determined as follows:

(1) add, to the taxpayer's entire net income, all salaries and other compensation paid to the taxpayer's elected or appointed officers and to every stockholder owning in excess of 5% of the taxpayer's issued capital stock;

(2) deduct from such total: (i) $15,000 (or a proportionate part thereof in the case of a return for less than a year); and (ii) any net loss for the fiscal or calendar year upon which the report is based to the extent not considered above in subparagraph (i); and

(3) multiply the balance by 30%. (Sec. 11-604, N.Y.C. Adm. Code; Rule Sec. 11-34)

For taxable years beginning on or after July 1, 1996, but before July 1, 1997, the tax base was determined as follows:

(1) add, to the taxpayer's entire net income, 75% of all salaries and other compensation paid to the taxpayer's elected or appointed officers and 100% of all salaries and other compensation paid to every stockholder (including a stockholder who is also a corporate officer) owning in excess of 5% of the taxpayer's issued capital stock;

(2) deduct from such total: (i) $15,000 (or a proportionate part thereof in the case of a return for less than a year); and (ii) any net loss for the fiscal or calendar year upon which the report is based to the extent not considered above in subparagraph (i); and

(3) multiply the balance by 30%. (Sec. 11-604, N.Y.C. Adm. Code; Rule Sec. 11-34)

For taxable years beginning on or after July 1, 1997, but before July 1, 1998, the tax base was determined as follows:

(1) add, to the taxpayer's entire net income, 75% of all salaries and other compensation paid to the taxpayer's elected or appointed officers and 100% of all salaries and other compensation paid to every stockholder (including a stockholder who is also a corporate officer) owning in excess of 5% of the taxpayer's issued capital stock;

(2) deduct from such total: (i) $30,000 (or a proportionate part thereof in the case of a return for less than a year); and (ii) any net loss for the fiscal or calendar year upon which the report is based to the extent not considered above in subparagraph (i); and

(3) multiply the balance by 30%. (Sec. 11-604, N.Y.C. Adm. Code; Rule Sec. 11-34)

For taxable years beginning on or after July 1, 1998, but before July 1, 1999, the tax base was determined as follows:

(1) add, to the taxpayer's entire net income, 50% of all salaries and other compensation paid to the taxpayer's elected or appointed officers and 100% of all salaries and other compensation paid to every stockholder (including a stockholder who is also a corporate officer) owning in excess of 5% of the taxpayer's issued capital stock;

(2) deduct from such total: (i) $40,000 (or a proportionate part thereof in the case of a return for less than a year); and (ii) any net loss for the fiscal or calendar year upon which the report is based to the extent not considered above in subparagraph (i); and

(3) multiply the balance by 30%. (Sec. 11-604, N.Y.C. Adm. Code; Rule Sec. 11-34)

• *Entire net income component*

The entire net income component of the base is determined in the same way as it is for the city's primary income base (see ¶505-405—¶505-450).

• *Compensation component*

"Elected or appointed officer" defined.—An elected or appointed officer includes the chairman, president, vice-president, secretary, assistant secretary, treasurer, assistant treasurer, comptroller, and also any other officer, irrespective of his title, who is charged with and performs any of the regular functions of any officer. A director is not an elected or appointed officer unless he performs duties ordinarily performed by an officer. However, there must be included all compensation received by an officer from the corporation in any capacity, including director's fees. (Rule Sec. 11-34)

"Stockholder owning in excess of 5% of the taxpayer's issued capital stock" defined.—A stockholder owning in excess of 5% of the corporation's issued capital stock is a person or corporation who is the beneficial owner of more than 5% of the capital stock of the taxpayer, issued and outstanding. (Rule Sec. 11-34) Rules for determining the beneficial ownership of stock are set forth in Rule Sec. 11-46(a).

Adjustment of salaries by Commissioner.—The Commissioner of Finance may disallow deductions claimed for unreasonable salaries in computing entire net income.

[¶505-490] NYC Alternative Bases--NYC Subsidiary Capital--Computation of Base

Under corporate tax reform legislation enacted in 2015 (see ¶505-205), the New York City corporate income tax system was significantly revised, generally applicable to taxable years beginning on or after January 1, 2015. (Subchapter 3-A, Corporate Tax of 2015; Sec. 11-651, N.Y.C. Adm. Code, *et. seq.*)

However, S corporations and qualified subchapter S subsidiaries remain subject to the existing, pre-reform general corporation tax provisions. (Sec. 11-602.1, N.Y.C. Adm. Code)

Under the new provisions, the separate treatment of subsidiary capital and income has been eliminated.

Pre-reform general corporation tax.—The provisions discussed below generally apply to taxable years beginning before 2015. As noted above, however, they continue to apply to S corporations. (Sec. 11-602.1, N.Y.C. Adm. Code)

A tax is imposed on the portion of a corporation's subsidiary capital, if any, that is allocated within the city. (Sec. 11-604(1), N.Y.C. Adm. Code) The tax imposed is in addition to the tax based on the greater of the alternative bases detailed in preceding paragraphs.

A "subsidiary" is defined to mean a corporation in which the taxpayer owns more than 50% of the voting stock. (Sec. 11-602(2), N.Y.C. Adm. Code) Control of a corporation, so that it is a "subsidiary" for purposes of these provisions, depends on actual beneficial ownership of stock, rather than mere record title, and on the actual legal situation with regard to voting rights. Only a first tier subsidiary is considered a subsidiary for purposes of the general corporation tax. (Rule Sec. 11-46)

"Subsidiary capital" means investments in the stock of subsidiaries and any indebtedness from subsidiaries on which an interest expense is not deducted by the subsidiary for tax purposes. (Sec. 11-602(3), N.Y.C. Adm. Code) Subsidiary capital does not include accounts receivable acquired in the ordinary course of trade or business for services rendered or for sales of property that is primarily held for sales to customers.

The statute provides that liabilities are deducted from assets but does not define or list qualifying liabilities. Chapter 525, Laws 1988, amended the law to permit the deduction of all liabilities, both long- and short-term, when computing business, investment, and subsidiary capital. (Instructions to Form NYC-3L, General Corporation Tax Return) The applicable regulation, last amended in 1978, is out of date in that it limits qualifying liabilities to those payable on demand or within one year from the date incurred. (Rule Sec. 11-46)

• *Acquired subsidiaries (pre-2000)*

For taxable years beginning in or after 1989 and before 2000, the city limited the investments that could be characterized as subsidiary stock in certain situations in which the controlling subsidiary stock or the majority of the assets of the subsidiary were sold off within 18 months of the acquisition date. (Sec. 11-602(3), N.Y.C. Adm. Code) The stock of a target corporation did not constitute subsidiary capital to the acquiring corporation if the target corporation sold or disposed of 50% or more of its assets within 18 months of the acquisition. The period for which the stock did not constitute subsidiary capital of the acquiring corporation ran from the first day of the taxable year in which the triggering disposition occurred until 18 months after the date of the disposition.

¶505-490

Similarly, if within 18 months of a corporate acquisition the acquisitor sold or otherwise disposed (including by redemption) of stock of the target corporation reducing the acquisitor's holdings to 50% or less of the stock immediately after the disposition, the stock of the target corporation did not constitute subsidiary capital of the taxpayer for the entire taxable year in which the disposition occurred.

Similar restrictions existed for state corporate franchise tax purposes. The state provisions were repealed effective for taxable years beginning after 1999 (see TSB-M-99(4)C). However, the state repeal was subsequently extended retroactively to taxable years beginning after 1996 (see TSB-M-00(2)C).

Effects of disqualification.—A Technical Services Bureau memorandum issued by the state explained the effects of the state statutes, which were identical to the city provisions. (TSB-M-89(17)C, Corporation Tax) The memorandum noted that several consequences would result from the denial of subsidiary capital treatment as a result of premature sales of stock or assets. The parent was required to include in the computation of its entire net income interest and dividends received from the target corporation and gains from such stock sales. (Sec. 11-602(8)(a)(1), N.Y.C. Adm. Code; Former Sec. 11-602(8)(b)(15), N.Y.C. Adm. Code) In addition, entire net income had to be increased by the amount of dividends excluded in the year prior to the disposition. (Former Sec. 11-602(8)(b)(13), (14), N.Y.C. Adm. Code) In both situations, a 50% dividend deduction was not allowed. (Sec. 11-602(8)(a)(2), N.Y.C. Adm. Code) The subsidiary capital base was reduced by the amount of the disqualified stock. Subsidiary stock that ceased to qualify as "subsidiary stock" was then treated as "investment stock". (Sec. 11-602(5), N.Y.C. Adm. Code)

- *Determination of amount of subsidiary capital*

The amount of subsidiary capital is determined by taking the average value of the gross assets, less deductible liabilities. (Sec. 11-604(2), N.Y.C. Adm. Code) If it is other than a period of 12 calendar months, the period covered by the report is prorated by multiplying the value by the number of calendar months or major parts thereof included in the period, and dividing the product thus obtained by 12. Real property and marketable securities will be valued at fair market value, and the value of personal property other than marketable securities will be the value shown on the books and records of the taxpayer in accordance with generally accepted accounting principles.

- *Combined report—Tax measured by combined subsidiary capital*

Combined subsidiary capital includes the subsidiary capital of all corporations included in the combined report and not just subsidiaries of corporations included in the report that have independent nexus to New York City. (Rule Sec. 11-48)

[¶506-500]

NYC ALLOCATION AND APPORTIONMENT

[¶506-501] NYC Allocation and Apportionment--In General

Under corporate tax reform legislation enacted in 2015, the New York City corporate income tax system was significantly revised, generally applicable to taxable years beginning on or after January 1, 2015. (Subchapter 3-A, Corporate Tax of 2015; Sec. 11-651, N.Y.C. Adm. Code, *et. seq.*)

However, S corporations and qualified subchapter S subsidiaries remain subject to the existing, pre-reform general corporation tax provisions. (Sec. 11-602.1, N.Y.C. Adm. Code)

The new business corporation tax provisions adopt the phase-in of a single receipts factor, as previously contained in the general corporation tax (see ¶ 506-515). The single receipts factor will be fully effective for tax years beginning on or after January 1, 2018. (Sec. 11-654.2, N.Y.C. Adm. Code)

However, taxpayers having $50 million or less of receipts allocated to the City are allowed a one-time election (in their first tax year commencing on or after January 1, 2018) to continue using the 2017 three-factor business allocation percentage formula (93% sales, 3.5% property, 3.5% payroll) to allocate income in tax years beginning on or after January 1, 2018. (Sec. 11-654(3)(a)(10)(xii), N.Y.C. Adm. Code)

In addition, the business corporation tax provisions apply customer-based sourcing rules. (Sec. 11-654.2, N.Y.C. Adm. Code)

• *Allocation for alternative bases*

Entire net income is allocated to the city by multiplying business income by a business allocation percentage, and investment income by an investment allocation percentage, and adding the two products (see ¶ 506-505). The capital base is similarly allocated by multiplying business capital by a business allocation percentage determined in the same way that it is for the entire net income base and multiplying investment capital by an investment allocation percentage determined as it is for entire net income. The two products are then added together. The income-and-salaries base is allocated to the city by means of the allocation percentages applicable to the entire net income procedure. Investments in subsidiary capital are multiplied by the issuer's allocation percentage to allocate the subsidiary capital base.

• *State tax discussion*

The provisions of the city law generally parallel those of the state franchise (income) law with respect to allocation, but there are various differences as noted in the paragraphs following.

An overview of the allocation and apportionment process, including an explanation of the Uniform Division of Income for Tax Purposes Act (UDITPA) and the Multistate Tax Compact (MTC), is presented at ¶ 11-505 in the "Corporate Income" division. New York State has not adopted UDITPA, MTC, or the traditional distinction between business and nonbusiness income. The criteria used to determine whether corporations are subject to allocation are discussed at ¶ 11-505. Combined reporting for related corporations is discussed at ¶ 11-550.

[¶ 506-503] NYC Combined Reports

Under corporate tax reform legislation enacted in 2015, the New York City corporate income tax system was significantly revised, generally applicable to taxable years beginning on or after January 1, 2015. (Subchapter 3-A, Corporate Tax of 2015; Sec. 11-651, N.Y.C. Adm. Code, *et. seq.*)

However, S corporations and qualified subchapter S subsidiaries remain subject to the existing, pre-reform general corporation tax provisions. (Sec. 11-602.1, N.Y.C. Adm. Code)

The new provisions adopt combined reporting for unitary corporations that meet a more-than-50% stock ownership test. (Sec. 11-654.3, N.Y.C. Adm. Code)

Domestic corporations and foreign corporations, to the extent of their U.S. effectively connected income, may be permitted or required to file a combined report if they conduct a unitary business and have common ownership or control (more than 50% of voting stock). (Sec. 11-654.3, N.Y.C. Adm. Code)

Commonly owned groups may also elect to a file a combined return, regardless of whether they conduct a unitary business, and the election is effective for 7 years. (Sec. 11-654.3, N.Y.C. Adm. Code)

Note: For a limited time (until June 1, 2018), certain taxpayers can withdraw the commonly owned group election made on a 2015 or 2016 combined business corporation tax return. For the withdrawal to be allowed, all corporations in the original combined group must follow all of the required procedures by June 1, 2018. See Finance Memorandum 18-3.

Combined filers use Form NYC-2A. (Instructions, Form NYC-2A)

Pre-reform provisions.—The provisions discussed below generally apply to taxable years beginning before 2015.

Starting in 2009, filing a combined return became mandatory where there were substantial intercorporate transactions among related corporations, regardless of the transfer prices charged in those transactions. Additionally, a captive RIC or a captive REIT had to be included in a combined return with a related New York City taxpayer where a greater-than-50% ownership test was met. (Sec. 11-605(4), N.Y.C. Adm. Code; Finance Memorandum 09-2)

Combined filers used Form NYC-3A. Additional details are provided in the form instructions.

The Department of Finance has issued an e-mail that discusses combined reporting for corporations having different tax years.

Generally, before 2009, every corporation subject to the New York City general corporation tax was considered a separate entity and had to file its own report on an individual basis. (Rule Sec. 11-91) However, two or more corporations meeting certain capital stock ownership and unitary business tests could be permitted or required to file combined reports if filing on a separate basis would distort the activities, business, income, or capital of the taxpayers.

[¶506-505] NYC Entire Net Income Method of Allocation

Under corporate tax reform legislation enacted in 2015, the New York City corporate income tax system was significantly revised, generally applicable to taxable years beginning on or after January 1, 2015. (Subchapter 3-A, Corporate Tax of 2015; Sec. 11-651, N.Y.C. Adm. Code, *et. seq.*)

However, S corporations and qualified subchapter S subsidiaries remain subject to the existing, pre-reform general corporation tax provisions. (Sec. 11-602.1, N.Y.C. Adm. Code)

The new business corporation tax provisions adopt the phase-in of a single receipts factor, as previously contained in the general corporation tax (see ¶506-515). The single receipts factor will be fully effective for tax years beginning on or after January 1, 2018. (Sec. 11-654.2, N.Y.C. Adm. Code)

However, taxpayers having $50 million or less of receipts allocated to the City are allowed a one-time election (in their first tax year commencing on or after January 1, 2018) to continue using the 2017 three-factor business allocation percentage formula (93% sales, 3.5% property, 3.5% payroll) to allocate income in tax years beginning on or after January 1, 2018. (Sec. 11-654(3)(a)(10)(xii), N.Y.C. Adm. Code)

In addition, the business corporation tax provisions apply customer-based sourcing rules. (Sec. 11-654.2, N.Y.C. Adm. Code)

Pre-reform provisions.—After the taxpayer's entire net income has been ascertained (see ¶505-405 and following), the portion allocated to New York City and subject to City general corporation tax is determined by multiplying business income by a business allocation percentage, and investment income by an investment allocation percentage, and adding the two products. (Sec. 11-604(3)(a)—(c), N.Y.C. Adm. Code)

• *"Investment income" defined*

"Investment income" broadly defined, is all income that is derived from investment capital less, in the discretion of the Commissioner of Finance, deductions allowable in computing entire net income that are directly or indirectly related to the investment income and less a portion of the net operating loss deduction equal to the ratio of investment income to entire net income. (Sec. 11-602(5), N.Y.C. Adm. Code) The city definition is the same as the definition for state purposes.

Income from investment capital includes:

(1) dividends from investment capital, interest from investment capital and capital gains in excess of capital losses from the sale or exchange of investment capital;

(2) gain (or loss) from closing out a position in a futures or forward contract if such contract substantially diminishes the taxpayer's risk of loss from holding one or more positions in assets that constitute investment capital. However, if a taxpayer holds more positions in futures or forward contracts than are reasonably necessary to substantially diminish its risk of loss from holding such positions in assets constituting investment capital, the gain (or loss) attributable to any such excess positions in futures or forward contracts is not investment income;

(3) gain (or loss) from short sales of assets that constitute investment capital;

(4) gain (or loss) from closing out a position in a futures or forward contract if the contract substantially diminishes the taxpayer's risk of loss from making short sales of assets that constitute investment capital. Again, if a taxpayer holds more positions in futures or forward contracts than are reasonably necessary to substantially diminish its risk of loss from such sales, the gain (or loss) attributable to any such excess positions in futures or forward contracts is not investment income; and

(5) premium income from an unexercised covered call option if the item that covers the call is an asset constituting investment capital. (Rule Sec. 11-69)

Caution: Premium income from unexercised naked call options and premium income from unexercised put options is not investment income.

Investment income may not be greater than entire net income. If a taxpayer has no business income, its investment income is deemed to be equal to its entire net income.

Dividends and interest: In computing investment income, dividends and interest from investment capital are includible in the same manner and to the same extent as in computing entire net income. Thus, where only one half of dividends from nonsubsidiary corporations is included in computing entire net income under Sec. 11-602.8(a)(2), N.Y.C. Adm. Code, only one half of such dividends is included in computing investment income. Capital gains and losses are included in computing entire net income in the same manner and to the same extent as for federal income tax purposes, subject to the modification provided in Sec. 11-602.8(h). Accordingly, in computing investment income, capital gains and losses from sales and exchanges of assets constituting investment capital are included in the same manner and to the same extent as for Federal income tax purposes, subject to the modification provided in Section 11-602.8(h).

Deduction of expenses: Investment income must be reduced by any deductions, allowable in computing entire net income, that are directly or indirectly attributable to investment capital or investment income. (Rule Sec. 11-69) Deductions allowable in computing investment income are not taken into account in computing business income.

Deductions allowable in computing entire income that are directly attributable to investment capital or investment income include: interest incurred to carry investment capital; safe deposit box rentals; financial news subscriptions; salaries of officers and employees engaged in the management and conservation of stocks; bonds and other securities included in investment capital; investment counsel fees; custodian fees; the cost of insurance and fidelity bonds covering investment capital; and legal expenses relating to investment capital.

Net operating loss deduction: Investment income is reduced by such portion of any net operating loss deduction allowable in computing entire net income as the investment income before such deduction bears to entire net income before such deduction. The effect of the reduction is to apportion the net operating loss deduction between business and investment income for the current year in the proportion that such income bears to entire net income for the current year, so that a portion of the net operating loss deduction will be allocated on the basis of the allocation percentage applicable to the current year's investment income and a portion on the basis of the allocation percentage applicable to the current year's business income.

- *"Business income" defined*

The term "business income" means entire net income minus investment income. (Sec. 11-602(7), N.Y.C. Adm. Code) The city definition is the same as that of the state.

- *Allocation percentages*

The business allocation percentage is derived by means of a three-factor formula using the ratios of property, receipts and payroll within and outside New York City; however, beginning in 2009, a single sales factor is being phased in over a 10-year period (see ¶506-515).

The investment allocation percentage is determined by a fraction reflecting the city tax allocation of corporations whose securities are included in the taxpayer's investment capital (¶506-525).

The Commissioner is authorized to adjust elements of the allocation percentages, or to use other methods of allocation (¶506-540).

[¶506-515] NYC Business Allocation Percentage

Under corporate tax reform legislation enacted in 2015, the New York City corporate income tax system was significantly revised, generally applicable to taxable years beginning on or after January 1, 2015. (Subchapter 3-A, Corporate Tax of 2015; Sec. 11-651, N.Y.C. Adm. Code, *et. seq.*)

However, S corporations and qualified subchapter S subsidiaries remain subject to the existing, pre-reform general corporation tax provisions. (Sec. 11-602.1, N.Y.C. Adm. Code)

The new business corporation tax provisions adopt the phase-in of a single receipts factor, as previously contained in the general corporation tax (see discussion below). The single receipts factor will be fully effective for tax years beginning on or after January 1, 2018. (Sec. 11-654.2, N.Y.C. Adm. Code)

However, taxpayers having $50 million or less of receipts allocated to the City are allowed a one-time election (in their first tax year commencing on or after January

1, 2018) to continue using the 2017 three-factor business allocation percentage formula (93% sales, 3.5% property, 3.5% payroll) to allocate income in tax years beginning on or after January 1, 2018. (Sec. 11-654(3)(a)(10)(xii), N.Y.C. Adm. Code)

In addition, the business corporation tax provisions apply customer-based sourcing rules. (Sec. 11-654.2, N.Y.C. Adm. Code)

Pre-reform provisions.—Beginning in 2009, a single sales factor is being phased in over 10 years. (Sec. 11-604(3)(a)(10), N.Y.C. Adm. Code; Finance Memorandum 09-2)

Specifically, the receipts factor is increased, and the payroll and property factors decreased, as indicated for the taxable years below:

— for 2009, 40% receipts—30% payroll—30% property;

— for 2010, 46%—27%—27%;

— for 2011, 53%—23.5%—23.5%;

— for 2012, 60%—20%—20%;

— for 2013, 67%—16.5%—16.5%;

— for 2014, 73%—13.5%—13.5%;

— for 2015, 80%—10%—10%;

— for 2016, 87%—6.5%—6.5%;

— for 2017, 93%—3.5%—3.5%; and

— after 2017, 100% receipts.

Prior to 2009, the business allocation percentage was determined using the three factors of property, receipts and payroll, equally weighted. (Sec. 11-604(3), N.Y.C. Adm. Code)

"Regular place of business" requirement: For taxable years beginning before July 1, 1996, a taxpayer that did not have a regular place of business outside New York City (other than a statutory office) was required to use a business allocation percentage of 100%. However, for taxable years beginning after June 30, 1996, this "regular place of business" requirement has been eliminated.

Restrictions of use of business allocation percentage: A taxpayer may not use the business allocation percentage if it has only investment income, or if it has investment income and a business loss. In such cases, only the investment allocation percentage (see ¶506-525) is used. (Rule Sec. 11-69) Some taxpayers were eligible to elect to use only one percentage in taxable years prior to 1989 (see ¶506-530).

When one or two of the factors are missing (lacking both a numerator and a denominator), the total is divided by the reduced number of factors. (Rule Sec. 11-63(c))

Manufacturing corporations: For taxable years beginning on or after July 1, 1996, and before January 1, 2011, manufacturing corporations may elect to "double weight" the receipts factor of their business allocation percentage (that is, add together their property, payroll and receipts percentages, plus an additional percentage equal to their receipts percentage, and divide the total by four). For details, see discussion at ¶506-517.

¶506-515

[¶506-516] NYC Business Allocation Percentage--Property Factor

Under corporate tax reform legislation enacted in 2015, the New York City corporate income tax system was significantly revised, generally applicable to taxable years beginning on or after January 1, 2015. (Subchapter 3-A, Corporate Tax of 2015; Sec. 11-651, N.Y.C. Adm. Code, *et. seq.*)

However, S corporations and qualified subchapter S subsidiaries remain subject to the existing, pre-reform general corporation tax provisions. (Sec. 11-602.1, N.Y.C. Adm. Code)

The new business corporation tax provisions adopt the phase-in of a single receipts factor, as previously contained in the general corporation tax (see ¶506-515). The single receipts factor will be fully effective for tax years beginning on or after January 1, 2018. (Sec. 11-654.2, N.Y.C. Adm. Code)

However, taxpayers having $50 million or less of receipts allocated to the City are allowed a one-time election (in their first tax year commencing on or after January 1, 2018) to continue using the 2017 three-factor business allocation percentage formula (93% sales, 3.5% property, 3.5% payroll) to allocate income in tax years beginning on or after January 1, 2018. (Sec. 11-654(3)(a)(10)(xii), N.Y.C. Adm. Code)

In addition, the business corporation tax provisions apply customer-based sourcing rules. (Sec. 11-654.2, N.Y.C. Adm. Code)

The property factor of the business allocation percentage is the following fraction:

$$\frac{\text{Average Value of Real and Tangible Personal Property in New York City}}{\text{Average Value of Real and Tangible Personal Property Everywhere}}$$

The property factor of the business allocation percentage is determined by comparing the average value of the taxpayer's real and tangible personal property, whether owned or rented, within New York City during the period covered by its report to the average value of all the taxpayer's real and tangible personal property wherever situated (Sec. 11-604(3)(a)(1), N.Y.C. Adm. Code).

The value of the taxpayer's real and tangible personal property is the adjusted bases of the properties for federal income tax purposes. However, the taxpayer may make a one-time, revocable election to use fair market value as the value of all of its real and tangible personal property. The election must be made on or before the due date for filing a report for the taxpayer's first taxable year beginning on or after January 1, 1988. The election does not apply to any taxable year to which the taxpayer is included on a combined report unless each of the taxpayers included on the report has made an election which remains in effect for the year. Prior to the 1988 taxable year, value was measured by fair market value.

Rental property: Rental property is valued by multiplying the gross rents payable for the period by eight (Sec. 11-604(3)(a)(1), N.Y.C. Adm. Code; Rule Sec. 11-64(b)).

• *Equipment in transit, rolling equipment*

Property in transit is not counted in the factor (Rule Sec. 11-64(a)). This treatment differs from that of the state, which locates property in transit at its destination.

Working trucks and other rolling equipment may be allocated to New York City either on the percentage that the mileage within the city bears to the total mileage everywhere or on a similar comparison with amount of time spent (Rule Sec. 11-64(a), Rule Sec. 11-65(d)). Appropriate methods may also be specified by the Finance Administrator.

[¶506-517] NYC Business Allocation Percentage--Receipts Factor

Under corporate tax reform legislation enacted in 2015, the New York City corporate income tax system was significantly revised, generally applicable to taxable years beginning on or after January 1, 2015. (Subchapter 3-A, Corporate Tax of 2015; Sec. 11-651, N.Y.C. Adm. Code, *et. seq.*)

However, S corporations and qualified subchapter S subsidiaries remain subject to the existing, pre-reform general corporation tax provisions. (Sec. 11-602.1, N.Y.C. Adm. Code)

The new business corporation tax provisions adopt the phase-in of a single receipts factor, as previously contained in the general corporation tax (see ¶506-515). The single receipts factor is fully effective for tax years beginning on or after January 1, 2018. (Sec. 11-654.2, N.Y.C. Adm. Code)

However, taxpayers having $50 million or less of receipts allocated to the City are allowed a one-time election (in their first tax year commencing on or after January 1, 2018) to continue using the 2017 three-factor business allocation percentage formula (93% sales, 3.5% property, 3.5% payroll) to allocate income in tax years beginning on or after January 1, 2018. (Sec. 11-654(3)(a)(10)(xii), N.Y.C. Adm. Code)

In addition, the business corporation tax provisions apply **customer-based sourcing rules**. (Sec. 11-654.2, N.Y.C. Adm. Code)

GILTI. Under both the business corporation tax (Sec. 11-654.2(5-a), N.Y.C. Adm. Code) and the general corporation tax (Sec. 11-604(3)(a)(2)(E), N.Y.C. Adm. Code), net global intangible low-taxed income is included in the denominator of the apportionment fraction, but not in the numerator.

Pre-reform provisions.—The receipts factor of the business allocation percentage is the following fraction:

$$\frac{\text{Receipts from Sales of Tangible Personal Property, Services, Rentals, Royalties and Other Business Receipts Attributable to New York City}}{\text{Receipts from Sales, Etc., Within and Without New York City}}$$

The receipts factor is determined by comparing the taxpayer's receipts from the following sources to the total amount of the taxpayer's receipts from all sources, whether within or outside New York City:

(1) Sales of its tangible personal property where shipments are made to points within New York City (however, see "Dock sales" discussion below);

(2) Services performed within New York City.

(3) Rentals from property situated and royalties from the use of patents or copyrights, within New York City and all other business receipts earned within New York City. (Sec. 11-604(3)(a)(2) and (5), N.Y.C. Adm. Code; Rule Sec. 11-65(a))

Single sales factor.—As discussed at ¶506-515, a single sales factor is being phased in over a 10-year period, beginning in 2009.

• *Dock sales*

Taxpayers having receipts from dock sales for tax periods beginning after 1999 may request permission to allocate those receipts in a manner consistent with New York State Reg. Sec. 4-4.2, which was amended to set forth a destination rule with respect to dock sales. Existing New York City tax law requires taxpayers to include in the numerator of the receipts factor any receipts from sales of tangible personal property where shipment is made to a point within the city. Under the amended state regulation, however, receipts from sales of tangible personal property are allocated to New York State under the following circumstances:

(1) where shipment is made to a point within the state;

(2) where possession of the property is transferred to the purchaser or the purchaser's designee within the state, unless the destination of the property is a point outside New York; or

(3) where possession of the property is transferred to the purchaser or designee outside the state but the destination of the property is within the state.

The regulation establishes a presumption that the destination of property is where the possession is transferred, unless the taxpayer provides sufficient evidence to establish the destination.

Prior to filing a return for tax periods beginning after 1999, a New York City taxpayer having dock sales will be allowed to request advance permission to allocate the receipts according to the amended state regulation. The request should contain a statement setting forth the reasons why the taxpayer believes the use of the dock sales rule is necessary to properly reflect the taxpayer's income within and outside the city, a detailed explanation of how the business allocation percentage would be calculated using the dock sales method, and a comparison of the receipts factor calculated using the dock sales rule and using the point of shipment rule. Taxpayers who receive permission to use the dock sales rule must attach a copy of the Department's response when filing the return. (*Statement of Audit Procedure: Audits of Taxpayers Having Receipts from Dock Sales*, New York City Department of Finance, Audit Division, December 28, 2000)

• *Manufacturing corporations*

For taxable years beginning on or after July 1, 1996, and before January 1, 2011, a manufacturing corporation, in determining its business allocation percentage, may elect to double weight its receipts factor. (Sec. 11-604(3)(a)(8), N.Y.C. Adm. Code; Rule Sec. 11-63(c))

The election must be made on a timely filed (determined with regard to extensions granted) original report for the taxable year and, once made, is irrevocable for that year. Separate elections must be made for each taxable year. (Sec. 11-604(3)(a)(8), N.Y.C. Adm. Code; Rule Sec. 11-63(c))

Failure to make the election will preclude the corporation from double weighting its receipts factor, unless the Commissioner of Finance determines that permission should be granted in the interests of fairness and equity due to a change in circumstances resulting from an audit adjustment. (Sec. 11-604(3)(a)(8), N.Y.C. Adm. Code; Rule Sec. 11-63(c))

"Manufacturing corporation" defined.—The term "manufacturing corporation" means a corporation primarily engaged in the manufacturing and sale of tangible personal property. The term "manufacturing" includes the process (including the assembly process)

(i) of working raw materials into wares suitable for use or

(ii) that gives new shapes, new qualities or new combinations to matter which already has gone through some artificial process, by the use of machinery, tools, appliances and other similar equipment. (Sec. 11-604(3)(a)(8), N.Y.C. Adm. Code; Rule Sec. 11-63(c))

To qualify as manufacturing, a process must result in a significant change in the raw materials or component parts so that the end product is substantially different in nature or form from the raw materials or component parts. Manufacturing does not include the mere packaging or labeling of goods and includes finishing partially finished goods only if the goods are not usable for their intended purpose in their unfinished state. (Rule Sec. 11-63(c))

Manufacturing may include printing, under certain circumstances, and may also include the design and development of pre-written computer software. However, manufacturing does not include the furnishing of information services subject to sales tax under Sec. 1105(c)(1), Tax Law, regardless of whether the information is provided in tangible form. In addition, a corporation that performs services for a customer, including manufacturing services, on property or raw materials belonging to the customer will not be considered a manufacturing corporation. (Rule Sec. 11-63(c))

A corporation will be deemed to be primarily engaged in the manufacturing and sale of tangible personal property if more than 50% of its gross receipts for the taxable year are derived from the sale of tangible personal property manufactured by the taxpayer. (Sec. 11-604(3)(a)(8), N.Y.C. Adm. Code; Rule Sec. 11-63(c))

Manufacturing corporations filing combined reports.—A otherwise eligible manufacturing corporation that is required or permitted to make a report on a combined basis with one or more other corporations will only be permitted to make the election if all of the corporations included in the report would qualify as a manufacturing corporation if they were treated as a single corporation. In making this determination, intercorporate transactions are eliminated. (Sec. 11-604(3)(a)(8), N.Y.C. Adm. Code; Rule Sec. 11-63(c))

> *EXAMPLE:* —A rule issued by the Department of Finance sets forth a number of examples illustrating the application of the provisions discussed above. (Rule Sec. 11-63(c))

[¶506-518] NYC Business Allocation Percentage--Payroll Factor

Under corporate tax reform legislation enacted in 2015, the New York City corporate income tax system was significantly revised, generally applicable to taxable years beginning on or after January 1, 2015. (Subchapter 3-A, Corporate Tax of 2015; Sec. 11-651, N.Y.C. Adm. Code, *et. seq.*)

However, S corporations and qualified subchapter S subsidiaries remain subject to the existing, pre-reform general corporation tax provisions. (Sec. 11-602.1, N.Y.C. Adm. Code)

The new business corporation tax provisions adopt the phase-in of a single receipts factor, as previously contained in the general corporation tax (see ¶506-515). The single receipts factor will be fully effective for tax years beginning on or after January 1, 2018. (Sec. 11-654.2, N.Y.C. Adm. Code)

However, taxpayers having $50 million or less of receipts allocated to the City are allowed a one-time election (in their first tax year commencing on or after January 1, 2018) to continue using the 2017 three-factor business allocation percentage formula (93% sales, 3.5% property, 3.5% payroll) to allocate income in tax years beginning on or after January 1, 2018. (Sec. 11-654(3)(a)(10)(xii), N.Y.C. Adm. Code)

In addition, the business corporation tax provisions apply customer-based sourcing rules. (Sec. 11-654.2, N.Y.C. Adm. Code)

The payroll factor of the business allocation percentage is the following fraction. (Sec. 11-604(3)(a)(3), N.Y.C. Adm. Code; Rule Sec. 11-66)

Wages, Salaries and Other Personal Service Compensation of Employees Within New York City
Wages, Salaries and Other Personal Service Compensation Within and Without New York City

The payroll factor is determined by comparing the total wages, salaries and other personal service compensation of employees within New York City, except general executive officers, to the total compensation of all the taxpayer's employees within and outside New York City, except general executive officers. (Sec. 11-604(3)(a)(3), N.Y.C. Adm. Code)

[¶506-525] NYC Investment Allocation Percentage

Under corporate tax reform legislation enacted in 2015, the New York City corporate income tax system was significantly revised, generally applicable to taxable years beginning on or after January 1, 2015. (Subchapter 3-A, Corporate Tax of 2015; Sec. 11-651, N.Y.C. Adm. Code, *et. seq.*)

However, S corporations and qualified subchapter S subsidiaries remain subject to the existing, pre-reform general corporation tax provisions. (Sec. 11-602.1, N.Y.C. Adm. Code)

Among other changes, the new business corporation tax provisions modified the definitions of "investment capital" and "investment income" and exempted both from tax. For more details, see ¶505-205.

Pre-reform provisions.—The investment allocation percentage, computed in the same manner for city as for state purposes, is determined by (1) multiplying the amount of a company's investment capital (see definition at ¶505-460) invested in each stock, bond, or other security (other than government securities) during the period covered by its report by the allocation percentage of the issuer or obligor, as explained below; (2) adding together the sums obtained; and (3) dividing the result by the total of the company's investment capital that was invested during the period in stocks, bonds, and other securities, including government securities (Sec. 11-604(3)(b), N.Y.C. Adm. Code; Rule Sec. 11-68(b))

• *Determination of issuer's allocation percentage*

For purposes of the calculation discussed above, the allocation percentage of each issuer or obligor is determined in the following manner. The issuer's allocation percentage is the percentage of the appropriate measure that is required to be allocated to New York City on the report required for the preceding year.

Appropriate measure: (1) For those subject to the general corporation tax or the Subchapter 3-A business corporation tax, the appropriate measure is entire capital.

(2) For those subject to the transportation corporation tax, the measure is issued capital stock.

(3) For those subject to the utility corporation tax, the measure is gross income.

(4) For those subject to the banking corporation tax, the issuer's allocation percentage is its alternative entire net income allocation percentage for the preceding year. When the banking corporation's alternative entire net income for the preceding year is derived exclusively from business carried on within the city, the issuer's allocation percentage is 100%.

A non-U.S. banking corporation determines its issuer's allocation percentage by dividing the (1) loans and financing leases within New York City and all other business receipts earned within the city with respect to the issuer or obligor from all sources by (2) the gross income of the issuer or obligor from all sources within and outside the United States for the preceding year.

In the case of a corporation in which 65% or more of the voting stock is owned or controlled by a bank or trust company or is registered under the Federal Bank Holding Company Act, is registered as a savings and loan holding company (except for a diversified savings and loan holding company), or is closely related to banking, managing or controlling banks, the allocation percentage is determined by dividing the portion of the corporation's entire capital allocable to the city for the preceding year by the corporation's entire capital, wherever located, for the preceding year.

Lack of report: If a report for the preceding year is not filed, or if it does not contain information needed for determination of the allocation percentage, then the allocation percentage to be used is, at the discretion of the Commissioner of Finance, either (1) the allocation percentage derived from the most recently filed report or reports of the issuer or obligor or (2) a percentage calculated by the Commissioner of Finance to indicate the degree of economic presence in the city of the issuer or obligor during the preceding year. The New York City Bureau of Tax Collection furnishes an annual list of investment allocation percentages for corporate securities. Information on percentages for companies not on the list may be obtained from the Department of Finance.

No stock, bond investments: If a taxpayer's investment allocation percentage is zero, interest received on bank accounts, is multiplied by the business allocation percentage. (Sec. 11-604(3)(b), N.Y.C. Adm. Code)

Limitations on use of percentage: A taxpayer may not use the investment allocation percentage if it has only business income, or if it has business income and an investment loss. In such cases, only the business allocation percentage is used. (Rule Sec. 11-69)

Adjustment of percentage: The Commissioner of Finance may adjust any investment allocation percentage that does not properly reflect the investment activity, business, income, or capital of the taxpayer in New York City. (Sec. 11-604(8), N.Y.C. Adm. Code; Rule Sec. 11-68(c))

[¶506-540] Discretionary Allocation by NYC Commissioner

Under corporate tax reform legislation enacted in 2015, the New York City corporate income tax system was significantly revised, generally applicable to taxable years beginning on or after January 1, 2015. (Subchapter 3-A, Corporate Tax of 2015; Sec. 11-651, N.Y.C. Adm. Code, *et. seq.*)

However, S corporations and qualified subchapter S subsidiaries remain subject to the existing, pre-reform general corporation tax provisions. (Sec. 11-602.1, N.Y.C. Adm. Code)

The new business corporation tax provides for discretionary allocation. (Sec. 11-654.2(11), N.Y.C. Adm. Code)

Pre-reform provisions.—The Commissioner of Finance is authorized to adjust elements entering into the calculation of the business or investment allocation percentage, or to substitute other methods, if the statutory methods do not properly reflect the activity, business, income or capital of a taxpayer (Sec. 11-604(8), N.Y.C. Adm. Code).

A taxpayer may request an adjustment of the formula for allocation of business income or capital. (Rule Sec. 11-67)

The Department of Finance has announced that, if a taxpayer believes that using the statutory method of allocation does not lead to a result that fairly and equitably reflects New York City income, the taxpayer may obtain the department's consent to use a different allocation method by submitting a written request, separate and apart from the tax return, describing the alternative method. The request, which is applicable only to a single tax year, may be made before or after the filing of the return. Unless consent to use an alternative method is granted prior to the filing of the return, the statutory method for allocation must be used on the return. (*Notice,* New York City Department of Finance, February 2, 2012)

The written request must fully explain the proposed alternative allocation method. The explanation must provide full information regarding the nature and scope of the business activities carried on within and outside New York City and provide complete details of how the proposed method would allocate income on a more equitable basis than the statutory method. The taxpayer must submit calculations of the tax due under both the statutory method and the proposed alternative method. (*Notice,* New York City Department of Finance, February 2, 2012)

Subscribers can view the announcement.

[¶507-000]

NYC CREDITS

[¶507-001] Overview of NYC credits

Under corporate tax reform legislation enacted in 2015, the New York City corporate income tax system was significantly revised, generally applicable to taxable years beginning on or after January 1, 2015. (Subchapter 3-A, Corporate Tax of 2015; Sec. 11-651, N.Y.C. Adm. Code, *et. seq.*)

However, S corporations and qualified subchapter S subsidiaries remain subject to the existing, pre-reform general corporation tax provisions. (Sec. 11-602.1, N.Y.C. Adm. Code)

The Department's outline notes that the GCT credits are transitioned into Subchapter 3-A, except for obsolete credits. Subchapter 3-A provides for the carry forward of credits that were allowed under Subchapter 2 in tax years prior to January 1, 2015. The credit in Subchapter 3-A for Unincorporated Business Taxes paid is modified to take into account the elimination of the alternative income plus compensation base and also the varying tax rates provided for small corporations and manufacturing corporations.

New York City allows credits against general corporation (income) tax for the following purchases, activities, and practices:

• *Enterprise zone credits*

   NYC relocation and employment assistance (REAP) credit (¶507-005)

   Industrial business zone credit (¶507-006)

• *Job creation/hiring credits*

   Employers relocated in NYC—Credit for payments to landlord for real estate taxes (¶507-010)

   Employers relocated in NYC—Credit for relocation costs (¶507-015)

• *Economic development credits*

   Beer production credit (¶507-018)

• *Other credits*

NYC credit for sales tax paid on production machinery and equipment (¶507-020)

NYC credit for distributions from partnerships subject to unincorporated business tax (¶507-025)

NYC credit for sales and use taxes for services related to production machinery, equipment, parts, tools, and supplies (¶507-030)

NYC Biotechnology credit (¶507-032)

• *Estimated tax*

All payments made as estimated tax are applied as a credit toward the tax due. (Sec. 11-608, N.Y.C. Adm. Code)

• *Overpayment of taxes*

The Commissioner of Finance, within the applicable period of limitations, may credit an overpayment of tax and interest on such overpayment against any liability in respect of any tax imposed on the taxpayer who made the overpayment. (Sec. 11-677(1), N.Y.C. Adm. Code)

• *Credit carryforward*

With limited exceptions, credits not used in one year may be carried forward to subsequent years. Specific carryforward provisions are provided for in each particular credit.

• *Recapture*

Recapture rules may apply if property ceases to remain in qualified use. Any applicable recapture provisions are provided for in each credit.

[¶507-005] NYC Enterprise Zone Credits--NYC Relocation and Employment Assistance (REAP)

Note: Under the business corporation tax, this credit is provided by Sec. 11-654(17).

Taxpayers that have conducted substantial business operations outside New York City or at locations south of 96th Street in Manhattan for 24 months prior to relocation, and that relocate all or part of these operations to eligible premises in other parts of the city (i.e., the "eligible area") may be entitled to a nonrefundable credit against the general corporation tax, provided there is an increase in employment after relocation. (Sec. 11-604(17); Sec. 22-621, N.Y.C. Adm. Code; Rule Sec. 30-01—30-09)

This REAP credit is discussed immediately below.

Benefits available to certain businesses relocating *to* Lower Manhattan are discussed further below.

• *REAP credit*

The credit is taken prior to any other credit against the general corporation tax, except the credit for unincorporated business tax paid (see ¶507-025). (Sec. 11-604(17)(c), N.Y.C. Adm. Code)

No credit is allowed under this provision to a taxpayer that has elected to take the credit against the New York City utility tax. (Sec. 11-604(17)(a), N.Y.C. Adm. Code)

Qualification.—In order to qualify, taxpayers must either (1) on or after May 27, 1987, enter into a contract to purchase or lease eligible premises, or a parcel on which eligible premises will be constructed, or (2) as of May 27, 1987, own a parcel or eligible premises if they have not applied for an exemption from real property taxation for certain industrial and commercial properties prior to that date. No credit is allowed for relocation of any retail activity or hotel services. (Sec. 11-604(17), N.Y.C. Adm. Code; Sec. 22-621(a), N.Y.C. Adm. Code)

A minimum expenditure for improvements to eligible premises is required. (Sec. 22-621(e), N.Y.C. Adm. Code)

Credit is allowed for the first taxable year during which the eligible aggregate employment shares are maintained with respect to the premises and for any of the 12 succeeding taxable years during which the shares are maintained. (Sec. 11-604(17)(b), N.Y.C. Adm. Code)

Revitalization areas.—An expanded credit is available to businesses that relocate to certain districts zoned as revitalization areas. Specifically, for businesses that have obtained a certification of eligibility dated after June 30, 2000, for a relocation to eligible premises located within a revitalization area, the normal credit amount is increased (see below). (Sec. 11-604(17)(a), N.Y.C. Adm. Code)

Definitions: Applicable definitions are set forth below.

Aggregate employment share.—"Aggregate employment share" means the sum of all employment shares maintained by an eligible business in a taxable year. (Sec. 22-621(h), N.Y.C. Adm. Code; Rule Sec. 30-01)

Eligible aggregate employment shares.—"Eligible aggregate employment shares" means the amount, if any, by which the number of aggregate employment shares maintained by an eligible business in the eligible area in the taxable year in which such eligible business claims the credit exceeds the number of aggregate employment shares maintained by an eligible business in the eligible area in the taxable year immediately preceding the taxable year during which such eligible business first relocates. Certain limitations apply. (Sec. 11-604(17)(a); Sec. 22-621(i), N.Y.C. Adm. Code)

Employment share.—A single "employment share" is roughly equivalent to a full work year of a full-time employee. (Sec. 22-621(g), N.Y.C. Adm. Code)

Eligible area.—The area of the city excluding that area lying south of the center line of 96th Street, in the borough of Manhattan constitutes an "eligible area." (Sec. 22-621(f), N.Y.C. Adm. Code; Rule Sec. 30-01)

Base year.—The "base year" is the taxable year preceding the taxable year during which an eligible business first relocates. (Rule Sec. 30-01)

For other definitions, see Sec. 22-621, N.Y.C. Adm. Code and Rule Sec. 30-01.

Credit amount: For the initial year and the 11 succeeding taxable years during which shares are maintained, the amount of the credit is determined by multiplying $1,000 ($500, in the case of taxpayers that have received certificates of eligibility dated prior to June 30, 1995) by the number of the eligible aggregate employment shares maintained by the taxpayer with respect to particular eligible premises during the taxable year. (Sec. 11-604(17)(a), N.Y.C. Adm. Code)

During the 12th year, the credit is determined by multiplying the number of eligible aggregate employment shares maintained with respect to the premises in the 12th year by the lesser of one and a fraction, the numerator of which is the number of days in the taxable year of relocation less the number of days the eligible business maintained employment shares in the eligible premises in the taxable year of relocation, and the denominator of which is the number of days in the 12th year during which the shares are maintained with respect to the premises. (Sec. 11-604(17)(a), N.Y.C. Adm. Code)

Revitalization areas.—An expanded credit is available to businesses that relocate to certain districts zoned as revitalization areas. Specifically, for businesses that have obtained a certification of eligibility dated after June 30, 2000, for a relocation to eligible premises located within a revitalization area, the normal $1,000 figure used to compute the credit is increased to $3,000. Thus, under these provisions, the credit amount is computed by multiplying $3,000 by the number of eligible aggregate employment shares maintained by the taxpayer during the taxable year with respect to particular premises to which the taxpayer has relocated. (Sec. 11-604(17), N.Y.C. Adm. Code)

Planning considerations: Various planning considerations are noted below.

Carryforward provisions.—Unused credit may be carried over for five years.

Revitalization areas: For taxpayers that have obtained a certification of eligibility within a revitalization area for the expanded credit, the credit amounts allowed for the taxable year of relocation and the four succeeding taxable years may not be carried over. Instead, for such taxable years, the credit amounts are deemed to be tax overpayments, to be credited or refunded to the taxpayer without interest. (Sec. 11-604(17)(d), N.Y.C. Adm. Code)

Expiration date.—No certification of eligibility for the credit will be issued to an eligible business on or after July 1, 2025, unless the business meets certain statutory requirements. (Sec. 22-622(b), N.Y.C. Adm. Code)

Multiple relocations.—If an eligible business has obtained certifications for more than one relocation, the portion of the total amount of eligible aggregate employment shares to be multiplied by the applicable dollar amount for each certification of a relocation is the number of total attributed eligible aggregate employment shares determined with respect to such relocation under Sec. 22-621(o). (Sec. 11-604(17)(a), N.Y.C. Adm. Code)

Additional or replacement premises.—Under A.B. 11459, Laws 2004, effective July 1, 2003, provisions are added to allow certain businesses to continue receiving REAP benefits after moving to designated additional or replacement premises. (Sec. 22-621(q), N.Y.C. Adm. Code; Sec. 22-622(e), N.Y.C. Adm. Code)

Moving more than 100 jobs out of Lower Manhattan.—Under A.B. 11459, Laws 2004, the New York City Mayor is authorized to reduce REAP benefits in certain cases when an eligible business moves more than 100 jobs out of Lower Manhattan. (Sec. 22-622(f), N.Y.C. Adm. Code)

• *Lower Manhattan Relocation and Employment Assistance Program*

Note: Under the business corporation tax, this credit is provided by Sec. 11-654(19).

Effective July 1, 2003, under the provisions of A.B. 11459, Laws 2004, REAP benefits are extended to certain eligible businesses relocating from outside New York City to Lower Manhattan. This is referred to as the Lower Manhattan REAP, or LMREAP, credit. The credit amount is $3,000 multiplied by the number of eligible aggregate employment shares maintained by the taxpayer during the taxable year with respect to eligible premises to which the taxpayer has relocated. (Sec. 11-604(19), N.Y.C. Adm. Code; Sec. 22-623, N.Y.C. Adm. Code; Sec. 22-624, N.Y.C. Adm. Code)

Additional information regarding the LMREAP credit for eligible businesses (LMREAP-EB) is available on the Department of Finance website:

http://www.nyc.gov/html/dof/html/property/
property_tax_reduc_reap_lm.shtml

¶507-005

Special eligible businesses.—Under Part E of Ch. 2 (S.B. 5930), Laws 2005, the LMREAP credit is extended to taxpayers referred to as Special Eligible Businesses (SEBs). An SEB is a firm whose purchase contract or lease for eligible space is entered into after June 30, 2005, and that had employees in Manhattan before its relocation, a disqualifying condition under the preexisting LMREAP. In order to be eligible for the credit, an SEB must actually relocate to eligible premises at least 250 employees or a sufficient number of employees to increase its payroll in the City by 25%, whichever is less. Various limits apply in determining the number of jobs that are eligible for the credit, including, in years following the year of relocation, limits on the number of qualifying jobs added through expansion rather than relocation. (Sec. 22-623, N.Y.C. Adm. Code; Sec. 22-624, N.Y.C. Adm. Code; *2005 Legislative Summary*, Dept. of Finance)

Additional information regarding the LMREAP credit for special eligible businesses (LMREAP-SEB) is available on the Department of Finance website:

http://www.nyc.gov/html/dof/html/property/ property_tax_reduc_reap_lm_seb.shtml

[¶507-006] NYC Enterprise Zone Credits--Industrial Business Zones

Note: Under the business corporation tax, this credit is provided by Sec. 11-654(17-b).

Under 2005 legislation, credits against the New York City general corporation tax and unincorporated business tax are available to eligible taxpayers that are engaged in industrial and manufacturing activities and that relocate to an industrial business zone, applicable to taxable years beginning after 2005. The credit amount equals $1,000 per full-time employee, not to exceed the lesser of actual relocation costs or $100,000. The legislation provides for the creation of an Industrial Business Zone Boundary Commission that is authorized to designate industrial business zones. (Sec. 11-604(17-b))

[¶507-010] NYC Job Creation/Hiring Credits--Employers relocated in NYC--Payments to Landlord for Real Estate Taxes

Note: Under the business corporation tax, this credit is provided by Sec. 11-654(13).

A taxpayer relocating to New York City may be entitled to a credit against the general corporation (income) tax for additional rent paid solely as a result of increased real estate taxes on the leased relocation premises. (Sec. 11-604(13), N.Y.C. Adm. Code)

Qualifications.—To qualify for the credit:

(1) The taxpayer must have relocated to the city from outside New York state; (Sec. 11-604(13)(a)(2), N.Y.C. Adm. Code)

(2) The relocation must have created and filled at least 100 full-time (30 hours per week) industrial or commercial jobs; (Sec. 11-604(13)(a)(2), N.Y.C. Adm. Code)

(3) There must be a written lease for the relocation premises providing for rent escalation tied to real estate tax increases; (Sec. 11-604(13)(a)(1), N.Y.C. Adm. Code) and

(4) The New York City Industrial and Commercial Incentive Board must approve and certify that the taxpayer is entitled to the credit. (Sec. 11-604(13)(a)(1), N.Y.C. Adm. Code)

Limitations.—The credit is available only if the taxpayer does not claim a deduction for the same amounts (i.e., the rent increase due to the real estate tax escalation as specified in the lease). In addition, the credit must be used annually by the taxpayer for the length of the lease term, or for a period not to exceed 10 years from the date of relocation, whichever is shorter. (Sec. 11-604(13)(a)(1), N.Y.C. Adm. Code)

• *Definitions*

Employment opportunity.—"Employment opportunity" is defined as the creation of full time position of gainful employment for an industrial or commercial employee and the actual hiring of such employee for said position. (Sec. 11-604(13)(a)(2), N.Y.C. Adm. Code)

Industrial employee.—An "industrial employee" is one engaged in the manufacturing or assembling of tangible goods or the processing of raw materials. (Sec. 11-604(13)(a)(2), N.Y.C. Adm. Code)

Commercial employee.—A "commercial employee" is one engaged in the buying, selling or otherwise providing of goods or the processing of raw materials. (Sec. 11-604(13)(a)(2), N.Y.C. Adm. Code)

• *Credit amount*

The credit is in the amount of any increased real estate taxes for which the employer becomes liable to the landlord under a written lease. (Sec. 11-604(13), N.Y.C. Adm. Code) The credit may be used annually for the term of the lease or for 10 years, whichever period is shorter. (Sec. 11-604(13), N.Y.C. Adm. Code)

• *Planning considerations*

Refund of excess credit.—The credit for any taxable year is deemed to be an overpayment of tax to be credited or refunded, without interest. (Sec. 11-604(13)(b), N.Y.C. Adm. Code)

Recapture.—To the extent of the credit, any deduction of the payments as a business expense for federal income tax purposes must be added back to the federal base (see ¶ 505-410).

[¶507-015] NYC Job Creation/Hiring Credits--Employers relocated in NYC--Relocation costs

Note: Under the business corporation tax, this credit is provided by Sec. 11-654(14).

An employer who relocates in the city from outside New York State, and thereby creates at least 10 full-time industrial or commercial employment opportunities, is entitled to a credit against the general corporation (income) tax for relocation expenses. (Sec. 11-604(14), N.Y.C. Adm. Code)

The credit is available only if the taxpayer does not claim a deduction for the same amount and may be taken, in whole or in part, in the year of relocation or in either or both of the two succeeding years. (Sec. 11-604(14)(a)(1), N.Y.C. Adm. Code)

No credit is allowed under this provision for industrial employment opportunities relocated to premises that are within an industrial business zone and for which a binding contract to purchase or lease was first entered into by the taxpayer on or after July 1, 2005. (Sec. 11-604(14)(a)(1), N.Y.C. Adm. Code)

- *Definitions*

Qualified employment opportunity relocation costs.—The credit is available only for "qualified employment opportunity relocation costs", defined as costs of: (Sec. 11-604(14)(a)(2), N.Y.C. Adm. Code)

(1) moving furniture, files, papers and office equipment;

(2) moving and installing machinery and equipment;

(3) installing telephones and other communications equipment needed as a result of the relocation;

(4) purchasing office furniture and fixtures needed as a result of the relocation; and

(5) renovating the premises to be occupied, but only to the extent of 75 cents per square foot of the total area utilized by the taxpayer.

Industrial employment opportunity.—"Industrial employment opportunity" means a full-time (30 hours per week) position for an employee engaged in manufacturing or assembling tangible goods or processing raw materials. (Sec. 11-604(14)(a)(2), N.Y.C. Adm. Code)

Commercial employment opportunity.—"Commercial employment opportunity" means a full-time (30 hours per week) position for an employee engaged in buying, selling or otherwise providing goods or services other than on a retail basis. (Sec. 11-604(14)(a)(2), N.Y.C. Adm. Code)

- *Credit amount*

The maximum credit is $500 for each industrial employment opportunity, and $300 for each commercial employment opportunity. (Sec. 11-604(14)(a)(1), N.Y.C. Adm. Code) The credit may be taken in whole or in part in the year of relocation or in either of the two succeeding years. (Sec. 11-604(14), N.Y.C. Adm. Code)

- *Planning considerations*

Carryforward provisions.—The credit may be taken, in whole or in part, in the year of relocation or in either or both of the two succeeding years. (Sec. 11-604(14)(a)(1), N.Y.C. Adm. Code)

Refund of excess credit.—The credit is treated as an overpayment of tax to be credited or refunded, without interest.

Recapture.—To the extent of the credit, any deduction of the relocation expenses for federal income tax purposes must be added back to the federal base (see ¶505-422). (Sec. 11-604(14)(b), N.Y.C. Adm. Code)

[¶507-018] NYC Economic Development Credits--Beer Production Credit

Legislation enacted in 2016 created a beer production credit available against the New York City unincorporated business, general corporation, and business corporation taxes, applicable to taxable years beginning on or after January 1, 2017. The law provides taxpayers with a credit of 12 cents per gallon for the first 500,000 gallons produced in New York City and 3.86 cents per gallon for the next 15 million gallons produced in New York City in the taxable year. To be eligible for the credit, a taxpayer must be registered as a distributor under Tax Law Article 18 and must produce 60 million or fewer gallons of beer in the state during the taxable year. (Sec. 11-503(p), N.Y.C. Adm. Code; Sec. 11-604(22), N.Y.C. Adm. Code; Sec. 11-654(22), N.Y.C. Adm. Code)

[¶507-020] Other NYC Credits--NYC Sales Tax Paid on Production Machinery and Equipment

A credit is allowed against New York City general corporation (income) tax for sales or use taxes paid on the purchase or use by the taxpayer of machinery or equipment used directly and predominantly in the production of tangible personal property, gas, electricity, refrigeration, or steam for sale. (Sec. 11-604(12), N.Y.C. Adm. Code)

Production for purposes of this provision includes manufacturing, processing, generating, assembling, refining, mining, and extracting. Telephone central office equipment, station apparatus, or comparable telegraph equipment used directly and predominantly in receiving at the destination or initiation or for switching telephone or telegraph communication are also eligible for the credit. (Sec. 11-604(12), N.Y.C. Adm. Code)

Parts having a useful life of one year or less and supplies used in connection with the production equipment are not eligible for the credit.

A credit is allowed for sales and use tax paid after July 1, 1977, on the purchase or use of machinery or equipment used in production. However, those purchases were exempted from sales and use tax effective December 1, 1989. (Form NYC-9.5)

• *Planning considerations*

Refunds of excess credits.—Refunds of excess credit are allowed. However, interest is not paid on refunds arising from application of the credit. (Sec. 11-604(12), N.Y.C. Adm. Code) (*Letter of Deputy Commissioner for Legal Affairs*)

Filing requirements.—If the credit claimed is on the purchase of machinery or equipment, form NYC-9.5 for 1990 or other prior year must be used. (Form NYC-9.5)

[¶507-025] Other NYC Credits--Distributions from Partnerships Subject to NYC Unincorporated Business Tax

Note: Under the business corporation tax, this credit is provided by Sec. 11-654(18).

A credit against New York City general corporation (income) tax is provided to corporations that are partners in unincorporated businesses subject to the New York City unincorporated business tax based on either entire net income or entire net income plus salaries and other compensation. (Sec. 11-604(18), N.Y.C. Adm. Code)

To be eligible for the credit, the corporation must be required to include in entire net income its distributive share of income, gain, loss and deductions of, or guaranteed payments from, the unincorporated business.

The credit must be deducted before any other general corporation tax credits, and may not be used to change the basis on which the corporation's tax is computed. (Sec. 11-604(18), N.Y.C. Adm. Code; Rule Sec. 11-50)

• *Credit amount*

The credit is equal to the lesser of the following:

(1) the sum of (a) the unincorporated business tax reported and paid by the unincorporated business for its tax year ending within or with the tax year of the

corporation and (b) the amount of any unincorporated business tax credit or credits taken by the unincorporated business, other than the fixed dollar credit, to the extent that such credit or credits do not reduce the unincorporated business's tax below zero, multiplied by a fraction, the numerator of which is the net total of the corporation's distributive share of income, gain, loss and deductions of, and guaranteed payments from, the unincorporated business for its taxable year, and the denominator of which is the sum of the net total distributive shares of income, gain, loss and deductions of, and guaranteed payments to, all partners in the unincorporated business for whom or which such net total (as separately determined for each partner) is greater than zero for the taxable year; or

(2) the excess of (a) the tax computed under Sec. 11-604(1)(e)(a)(1), N.Y.C. Adm. Code, without allowance of any credits, over (b) the tax so computed, determined as if the corporation had no such distributive share or guaranteed payments with respect to the unincorporated business, multiplied by $^{400}/_{885}$. The amounts computation is subject to the following modifications:

(i) the amounts are computed without taking into account any carryforward or carryback by the partner of a net operating loss;

(ii) if, prior to taking into account any distributive share or guaranteed payments from any unincorporated business or any net operating loss carryforward or carryback, the entire net income of the partner is less than zero, the entire net income is treated as zero; and

(iii) if the partner's net total distributive share of income, gain, loss and deductions of, and guaranteed payments from, any unincorporated business is less than zero, the net total is treated as zero.

The amount determined under (2) may not be less than zero. (Sec. 11-604(18)(a), N.Y.C. Adm. Code)

Corporations subject to tax calculated on entire net income base.—In the case of a corporation that, before the application of any credits, is liable for the tax on entire net income under Sec. 11-604(1)(e)(a)(1), N.Y.C. Adm. Code, the credit or the sum of the credits that may be taken by the corporation for a taxable year with respect to an unincorporated business or unincorporated businesses in which it is a partner may not exceed the tax so computed, without allowance of any credits, multiplied by $^{400}/_{885}$.

Corporations subject to tax calculated on entire net income plus salaries.— Although the tax is always calculated as if the taxpayer were subject to tax computed on the entire net income base, the credit may, with certain limitations, be taken against the alternative tax measured by entire net income plus compensation paid to officers and certain shareholders (see ¶505-470). In such instances, each dollar of credit will be applied to reduce the tax by $0.6638, and the maximum credit that may be taken in any taxable year is the amount that reduces the tax, without allowance of any credits, to zero.

No credit may be taken in a taxable year by a taxpayer that, in the absence of such credit, would be liable for the tax computed on the basis of business and investment capital under Sec. 11-604(1)(e)(a)(4), N.Y. City Adm. Code (see ¶505-460) or the fixed-dollar minimum tax. In addition, no credit may be taken against the tax computed on the basis of subsidiary capital under Sec. 11-604(1)(e)(b), N.Y.C. Adm. Code (see ¶505-490).

Corporations filing combined reports.—Corporations that file combined reports must compute the credit as if the combined group were the partner in each unincorporated business from which any of the members of the group had a distributive share or guaranteed payments. However, if more than one member of the combined group is a partner in the same unincorporated business, for purposes of the calculation required above, the numerator of the fraction must be the sum of the net total distributive shares of income, gain, loss and deductions of, and guaranteed payments from, the unincorporated business of all of the partners of the unincorporated business within the combined group for which the net total (as separately determined for each partner) is greater than zero, and the denominator must be the sum of the net total distributive shares of income, gain, loss and deductions of, and guaranteed payments from, the unincorporated business of all partners in the unincorporated business for whom or which such net total (as separately determined for each partner) is greater than zero.

• *Planning considerations*

Carryforward provisions.—For corporations subject to tax calculated on entire net income base, excess credit may be carried forward and used in any of the seven immediately succeeding taxable years. Credits first arising in a particular year must be taken before any credit carryforward, and credit carryforwards to an earlier year must be taken before any carryforwards attributable to a subsequent year. For corporations subject to tax calculated on entire net income plus salaries, excess credit may be carried forward and used, in order, in any of the seven immediately succeeding taxable years.

[¶507-030] Other NYC Credits--NYC Sales and Use Taxes Paid for Services Related to Production Machinery, Equipment, Parts, Tools, and Supplies

A credit against general corporation (income) tax is allowed for sales and use taxes imposed during a taxable year, less any credits or refunds of such taxes, related to installing, repairing, maintaining or servicing machinery, equipment, parts, tools and supplies used in production. (Sec. 11-604(17-a), N.Y.C. Adm. Code) Interest paid by a taxpayer in connection with the payment of such sales and use taxes will likewise be allowed as a credit. (Sec. 11-604(17-a)(a), N.Y.C. Adm. Code)

CCH COMMENT: Services exempted from sales and use tax effective September 1, 1996.—The services described above were exempted from sales and use tax effective September 1, 1996, however, a credit is available for sales and use tax due and paid on those services during the current tax year with respect to periods prior to September 1, 1996. (Form NYC-9.5)

• *Planning considerations*

Refund of excess credit.—The credit will be deemed to be an overpayment of tax by the taxpayer to be credited or refunded, without interest. (Sec. 11-604(17-a)(b), N.Y.C. Adm. Code)

Credit recapture.—Where a refund or credit of any sales and use tax (or interest) for which a credit against general corporation tax was claimed in a prior tax year is subsequently refunded or credited, the amount of the refund or credit must be added back to the general corporation tax. Such amount must also be subtracted in computing entire net income for the taxable year. (Sec. 11-604(17-a)(c), N.Y.C. Adm. Code)

[¶507-032] Other NYC Credits--NYC Biotechnology Credit

Note: Under the business corporation tax, this credit is provided by Sec. 11-654(21).

A refundable credit is allowed for biotechnology businesses. (Sec. 11-604(21), N.Y.C. Adm. Code; as authorized by Sec. 1201-a, Tax Law)

In order to claim the credit, a biotechnology firm must be a qualified emerging technology company and must meet the following requirements:

— have 100 or fewer full-time employees, with at least 75% of those employees employed in New York City;

— have a ratio of research and development funds to net sales of at least 6%; and

— have gross revenues not exceeding $20 million for the immediately preceding year.

For biotechnology firms that have increased their employment in the city by at least 5%, are newly formed, or are newly located to the city, the credit is provided as follows, up to $250,000:

— 18% for the acquisition of research and development property and related costs and fees;

— 9% for qualified research expenses; and

— 100% of certain training expenses, up to $4,000 per employee.

The law allows existing biotechnology firms that have not increased their employment by at least 5% to be eligible for the credit, but at half the rate, up to $125,000.

The total credits for a given year are capped at $3 million. If credits in a given year exceed the cap, the credit will be allocated on a prorated basis by the New York City Department of Finance. The credit is allowed for three consecutive years and is currently applicable for taxable years beginning on or after January 1, 2010, and before January 1, 2019.

Subscribers can view a set of Frequently Asked Questions regarding the credit.

In addition, the Department of Finance has adopted the following rules:

§ 48-02, regarding the application process

§ 48-03, regarding allocation of the credit

§ 48-04, regarding evaluation criteria

§ 48-05, regarding examination of records

[¶510-200]

NYC BANKS INCOME TAXPAYERS AND RATES

[¶510-201] NYC Banks Income Taxpayers and Rates--In General

Under corporate tax reform legislation enacted in 2015, the New York City corporate income tax system was significantly revised, generally applicable to taxable years beginning on or after January 1, 2015. (Subchapter 3-A, Corporate Tax of 2015; Sec. 11-651, N.Y.C. Adm. Code, *et. seq.*)

Among other changes, affected banking corporation taxpayers are transitioned to taxation under Subchapter 3-A, Corporate Tax of 2015; see ¶505-205.

However, S corporations and qualified subchapter S subsidiaries remain subject to the existing, pre-reform banking corporation tax provisions. (Sec. 11-639(a)(2), N.Y.C. Adm. Code)

A memorandum explains transitional filing provisions for taxpayers affected by the corporate tax reform legislation. (*Finance Memorandum 15-2*, April 17, 2015)

Pre-reform banking corporation tax: The provisions discussed below generally apply to taxable years beginning before 2015. As noted above, however, they continue to apply to S corporations. (Sec. 11-639(a)(2), N.Y.C. Adm. Code)

The banking corporation tax (BCT) is imposed for the privilege of doing business in New York City in a corporate or organized capacity, for each of the taxpayer's taxable years, as reported for federal tax purposes. (Sec. 11-639(a), N.Y.C. Adm. Code; Sec. 11-638(b), N.Y.C. Adm. Code)

For purposes of the tax, a banking corporation means:

(1) every corporation or association organized under New York law which is authorized to do a banking business or which is doing a banking business;

(2) every corporation or association organized under the laws of any other state or country which is doing a banking business;

(3) every national banking association organized under the authority of the United States which is doing a banking business;

(4) every federal savings bank which is doing a banking business;

(5) every federal savings and loan association which is doing a banking business;

(6) a production credit association organized under the Federal Farm Credit Act, which is doing a banking business and all of whose stock held by the Federal Production Credit Corporation has been retired;

(7) every other corporation or association organized under the authority of the United States which is doing a banking business;

(8) the Mortgage Facilities Corporation; and

(9) any corporation 65% or more of whose voting stock is owned or controlled, directly or indirectly, by a corporation or corporations subject to Article 3-A of the banking law, or registered under the Federal Bank Holding Company Act of 1956, as amended, or registered as a savings and loan holding company (but excluding a diversified savings and loan holding company) under the Federal National Housing Act, as amended, or by a corporation or corporations described in (1) through (8) above, provided that the corporation whose voting stock is so owned or controlled is

principally engaged in a business, regardless of where conducted, which either (a) might be lawfully conducted by a corporation subject to Article 3 of the banking law or by a national banking association, or (b) is so closely related to banking or managing or controlling banks, as to be deemed a proper incident thereto. (Sec. 11-640(a), N.Y.C. Adm. Code; Rule Sec. 3-01)

Under Ch. 298, Laws 1985 (which was extended numerous times), a sunset provision applied to many bank tax provisions; i.e., after the sunset, the tax would not be applicable to corporations other than savings banks and savings and loan associations, although the provisions relating to the alternative minimum tax measured by taxable assets would continue to apply to all taxpayers. (Sec. 11-640(a), N.Y.C. Adm. Code)

However, the sunset was eliminated and the provisions were made permanent by the 2011 budget legislation. (Ch. 61 (S.B. 2811), Part J)

Economic Nexus for Credit Card Companies--Effective in 2011, credit card companies with customers having a mailing address in New York City will be subject to the banking corporation tax regardless of whether the credit card company has any physical location within New York City. (Sec. 11-640(c), N.Y.C. Adm. Code)

• *Transitional provisions—Gramm-Leach-Bliley Act of 1999*

Under Part HH of Ch. 63 (A.B. 11006), Laws 2000, transitional provisions relating to the enactment and implementation of the federal Gramm-Leach-Bliley Act of 1999 allowed certain corporations that were taxed under the general corporation tax or the banking corporation tax in 1999 to maintain that taxable status in 2000. The legislation also permitted certain corporations that were owned by financial holding companies or were financial subsidiaries of banks to elect to be taxed under either the general corporation tax or the banking corporation tax for the 2000 taxable year. (Sec. 11-640(g), N.Y.C. Adm. Code; Sec. 11-646(f)(2)(iv), N.Y.C. Adm. Code) (*Summary of Tax Provisions in SFY 2000-01 Budget*, New York Department of Taxation and Finance, Office of Tax Policy Analysis)

Ch. 383 (S.B. 5828), Laws 2001, enacted similar provisions, (1) allowing certain corporations that were taxed under the general corporation tax or the banking corporation tax in 2000 to maintain that taxable status in 2001 and 2002, and (2) permitting certain corporations that were owned by financial holding companies or that were financial subsidiaries of banks to elect to be taxed under either the general corporation tax or the banking corporation tax for the 2001 and 2002 taxable years. Also, banking corporations that elected under the earlier transition provisions to be taxed as general corporations were allowed to revoke the election. (Sec. 11-640(g), N.Y.C. Adm. Code; Sec. 11-646(f)(2)(iv), N.Y.C. Adm. Code; Sec. 11-640(h), N.Y.C. Adm. Code)

2003 budget.—Under A.B. 2106, Laws 2003, similar amendments extended the transitional provisions through taxable years beginning before 2004. (Sec. 11-640(i), N.Y.C. Adm. Code; Sec. 11-646(f)(2)(iv), N.Y.C. Adm. Code)

2004 budget.—Under Ch. 60 (S.B. 6060), Laws 2004, similar amendments extended the transitional provisions through taxable years beginning before 2006. (Sec. 11-640(j), N.Y.C. Adm. Code; Sec. 11-646(f)(2)(iv), N.Y.C. Adm. Code)

2006 budget.—Under Ch. 62 (S.B. 6460), Laws 2006, similar amendments have extended the transitional provisions through taxable years beginning before 2008. (Sec. 11-640(k), N.Y.C. Adm. Code; Sec. 11-646(f)(2)(iv), N.Y.C. Adm. Code)

2007 budget.—Under Ch. 60 (S.B. 2110), Laws 2007, similar amendments have extended the transitional provisions through taxable years beginning before 2010. (Sec. 11-640(l), N.Y.C. Adm. Code; Sec. 11-646(f)(2)(iv), N.Y.C. Adm. Code)

2009 and 2010 legislation.—Under Ch. 24 (A.B. 10096), Laws 2010, similar amendments have extended the transitional provisions through taxable years beginning before 2011. (Sec. 11-640(l), N.Y.C. Adm. Code; Sec. 11-646(f)(2)(iv), N.Y.C. Adm. Code)

In addition, under A.B. 8867, Laws 2009, if a corporation meets the certain conditions set forth, it will be subject to the bank tax even if it had previously elected to be subject to the GCT, or had been grandfathered as subject to GCT, under the Gramm Leach Bliley transitional provisions. (Sec. 11-640(m), N.Y.C. Adm. Code)

2011 budget.—Under Ch. 61 (S.B. 2811), Laws 2011, similar amendments have extended the transitional provisions through taxable years beginning before 2013. (Sec. 11-640(l), N.Y.C. Adm. Code; Sec. 11-646(f)(2)(iv), N.Y.C. Adm. Code)

2012 budget.—Under Ch. 59 (A.B. 9059), Laws 2012, similar amendments have extended the transitional provisions through taxable years beginning before 2015. (Sec. 11-640(l), N.Y.C. Adm. Code; Sec. 11-646(f)(2)(iv), N.Y.C. Adm. Code) However, only a corporation that meets the definition of a "banking corporation" is allowed to remain a BCT taxpayer under the transitional provisions. (Sec. 11-640(l), N.Y.C. Adm. Code)

2014 budget.—Under Ch. 59 (S.B. 6359), Laws 2014, similar amendments extended the transitional provisions through taxable years beginning before 2017. (Sec. 11-640(l), N.Y.C. Adm. Code; Sec. 11-646(f)(2)(iv), N.Y.C. Adm. Code)

2017 legislation.—Under Ch. 302 (A.B. 7863), Laws 2017, similar amendments extended the transitional provisions through taxable years beginning before 2020. (Sec. 11-640(n), N.Y.C. Adm. Code; Sec. 11-646(f)(2)(iv), N.Y.C. Adm. Code)

[¶510-225] NYC Exempt Corporations

Under corporate tax reform legislation enacted in 2015, the New York City corporate income tax system was significantly revised, generally applicable to taxable years beginning on or after January 1, 2015. (Subchapter 3-A, Corporate Tax of 2015; Sec. 11-651, N.Y.C. Adm. Code, *et. seq.*)

Among other changes, affected banking corporation taxpayers are transitioned to taxation under Subchapter 3-A, Corporate Tax of 2015; see ¶ 505-205.

However, S corporations and qualified subchapter S subsidiaries remain subject to the existing, pre-reform banking corporation tax provisions. (Sec. 11-639(a)(2), N.Y.C. Adm. Code)

A memorandum explains transitional filing provisions for taxpayers affected by the corporate tax reform legislation. (*Finance Memorandum 15-2*, April 17, 2015)

Pre-reform banking corporation tax: The provisions discussed below generally apply to taxable years beginning before 2015. As noted above, however, they continue to apply to S corporations. (Sec. 11-639(a)(2), N.Y.C. Adm. Code)

Corporations subject to the New York City general corporation tax (Sec. 11-640(d), N.Y.C. Adm. Code), and any trust company all of whose capital stock is owned by 20 or more savings banks (Sec. 11-640(c), N.Y.C. Adm. Code) are exempt from tax. Corporations subject to tax under Article 33, Tax Law (New York State tax on insurance corporations) are exempt from tax. The exemption does not apply to savings and insurance banks conducting life insurance business. (Sec. 11-640(e), N.Y.C. Adm. Code)

Effective for taxable years beginning on or after January 1, 1998, foreign corporations (i.e., corporations incorporated outside the U.S.) whose only activity in New York City is trading stocks, securities, or commodities for their own accounts are exempt from the New York City banking corporation tax. Their trading activity is not considered to be doing business in the city, and a tax may be imposed only against corporations that are doing business in the city. The exemption from tax applies whether trading is conducted by the corporation or its employees or by a broker, commission agent, custodian, or other agent. The tax exemption does not apply to dealers of stocks, securities, or commodities. (Sec. 11-640(f), N.Y.C. Adm. Code)

[¶510-250] NYC Rates

Under corporate tax reform legislation enacted in 2015, the New York City corporate income tax system was significantly revised, generally applicable to taxable years beginning on or after January 1, 2015. (Subchapter 3-A, Corporate Tax of 2015; Sec. 11-651, N.Y.C. Adm. Code, *et. seq.*)

Among other changes, affected banking corporation taxpayers are transitioned to taxation under Subchapter 3-A, Corporate Tax of 2015; see ¶505-205.

However, S corporations and qualified subchapter S subsidiaries remain subject to the existing, pre-reform banking corporation tax provisions. (Sec. 11-639(a)(2), N.Y.C. Adm. Code)

A memorandum explains transitional filing provisions for taxpayers affected by the corporate tax reform legislation. (*Finance Memorandum 15-2*, April 17, 2015)

Pre-reform banking corporation tax: The provisions discussed below generally apply to taxable years beginning before 2015. As noted above, however, they continue to apply to S corporations. (Sec. 11-639(a)(2), N.Y.C. Adm. Code)

The basic tax is imposed at the rate of 9% of entire net income allocated to New York City. (Sec. 11-643.5(a), N.Y.C. Adm. Code)

• *Alternative minimum tax (used if a higher tax results)*

The alternative minimum tax is the largest of the following:

(1) $1/10$ of a mill on each dollar of taxable assets allocated to New York City;

(2) 3% of alternative entire net income allocated to New York City; or

(3) Flat fee minimum: $125. (Sec. 11-643.5(b), N.Y.C. Adm. Code; Rule Sec. 3-03)

A special alternative minimum tax applies to banks organized under the laws of foreign countries. (Sec. 11-643.5(b), N.Y.C. Adm. Code)

For tax years beginning after 2010, one of the alternative taxes under the Bank Tax's alternative minimum tax will be based on taxable assets allocated to the city even if the bank is organized under the laws of a country other than the United States. Under this amendment, most banks will be subject to a tax of $1/10$ of a mill, or one $1/100$ of a cent, for every dollar of taxable assets allocated to New York City, as banks organized in the United States are currently. However, certain banks with a net worth ratio of under 5% will be taxed on their allocated assets at a lower rate, and a bank will not be subject to the allocated asset tax for any part of a period in which that bank has outstanding net worth certificates issued under a certain provision of the Federal National Housing Act. (Sec. 11-643.5(b), N.Y.C. Adm. Code)

[¶510-400]

NYC BANKS COMPUTATION OF INCOME

[¶510-401] NYC Banks Computation of Income--In General

Federal taxable income is the starting point for computing entire net income taxable by New York City. (see ¶510-410) (Sec. 11-641(a), N.Y.C. Adm. Code)

City law provides for specific additions to (see ¶510-420) and subtractions from (see ¶510-430) the federal base, as well as for other modifications (see ¶510-433—¶510-440), which may result in increases or decreases, depending on the circumstances in each case.

¶510-250

The resulting "entire net income" figure is New York City taxable income if all of the income is derived from business carried on in the city. If the taxpayer does business within and outside the city, the entire net income is subject to allocation.

[¶510-410] NYC Adoption of Federal Base

Under corporate tax reform legislation enacted in 2015, the New York City corporate income tax system was significantly revised, generally applicable to taxable years beginning on or after January 1, 2015. (Subchapter 3-A, Corporate Tax of 2015; Sec. 11-651, N.Y.C. Adm. Code, *et. seq.*)

Among other changes, affected banking corporation taxpayers are transitioned to taxation under Subchapter 3-A, Corporate Tax of 2015; see ¶505-205.

However, S corporations and qualified subchapter S subsidiaries remain subject to the existing, pre-reform banking corporation tax provisions. (Sec. 11-639(a)(2), N.Y.C. Adm. Code)

A memorandum explains transitional filing provisions for taxpayers affected by the corporate tax reform legislation. (*Finance Memorandum 15-2*, April 17, 2015)

Business interest deduction limitation.—For information on New York City's treatment of the IRC Sec. 163(j) limitation on deducting business interest expense, see ¶510-420 and *Business Tax Practitioner Newsletter*, Vol. 1, May 2019. See also *Finance Memorandum 18-11* regarding the attribution of interest deductions for taxpayers with IRC Sec. 163(j) limitations.

Treatment of IRC Sec. 965 Repatriation income.—IRC Sec. 965 income is a component of federal taxable income, and there are no specific statutory modifications under the banking corporation tax that exclude this income from City tax computations. Accordingly, for purposes of the banking corporation tax, the net IRC Sec. 965 income reported to the IRS must be incorporated into the starting point of City tax calculations. (*Finance Memorandum 18-10*, New York City Department of Finance)

Treatment of GILTI.—There are no specific statutory modifications under the banking corporation tax that exclude GILTI income. Therefore, taxpayers subject to the banking corporation tax must incorporate GILTI into the starting point of their City tax computations. Likewise, there are no specific statutory modifications under the banking corporation tax that exclude the GILTI deduction from City tax computations. Therefore, taxpayers subject to the banking corporation tax are permitted to calculate entire net income by taking the GILTI deduction into account. (*Finance Memorandum 18-10*, New York City Department of Finance)

Treatment of FDII.—There is no specific statutory modification under the banking corporation tax that excludes the FDII deduction from the City tax computation. Therefore, taxpayers subject to the banking corporation tax are permitted to calculate entire net income by taking the FDII deduction into account. (*Finance Memorandum 18-10*, New York City Department of Finance)

Pre-reform banking corporation tax: The provisions discussed below generally apply to taxable years beginning before 2015. As noted above, however, they continue to apply to S corporations. (Sec. 11-639(a)(2), N.Y.C. Adm. Code)

"Entire net income" is total net income from all sources, which is the same as the entire taxable income (but not alternative minimum taxable income) (Sec. 11-641(a), N.Y.C. Adm. Code; Rule Sec. 3-03):

(1) which the taxpayer is required to report to the U.S. Treasury Department; or

(2) which the taxpayer, in the case of a corporation which is exempt from federal income tax (other than the tax on unrelated business taxable income), but which is subject to the New York City banking corporation tax, would have been required to report to the U.S. Treasury Department, but for the exemption; or

(3) which, in the case of a corporation organized under the laws of a country other than the United States, is effectively connected with the conduct of a trade or business within the United States determined under IRC Sec. 822; or

(4) which the taxpayer would have been required to report federally if an election under subchapter S had not been made; or

(5) which the taxpayer would have been required to report federally if no election had been made to treat the taxpayer as a qualified subchapter S subsidiary, subject to certain modifications and adjustments. (see ¶510-420—¶510-440) (Sec. 11-641(a), N.Y.C. Adm. Code, Rule Sec. 3-03)

A corporation included in a federal consolidated group must compute its federal taxable income, for purposes of calculating entire net income, as if it had computed its federal taxable income on a separate basis for federal income tax purposes. For a target corporation that is a member of a selling consolidated group, when an election under I.R.C. Sec. 338(h)(10) (recognition of gain or loss by the target corporation, together with nonrecognition of gain or loss on stock sold by the selling consolidated group) has been made, the federal taxable income of the target corporation includes any gain or loss on the deemed asset sale by the target corporation recognized by virtue of such election. The federal taxable income of a member of the selling consolidated group that is subject to the banking corporation tax does not include gains or losses on the sale or exchange of stock of the target corporation not recognized because of the election. (Rule Sec. 3-03)

Effective February 4, 2002, and applicable to all open years, the Department of Finance will recognize and give effect to a federal election made under IRC Sec. 338(h)(10) in all cases except where the target corporation is an S corporation for federal income tax purposes. (Rule Sec. 3-03)

• *Alternative entire net income*

Alternative entire net income is the same as entire net income, except that deductions equal to 17% of interest income from subsidiary capital, 60% of dividend income, gains and losses from subsidiary capital, and $22^{1}/2\%$ of interest income on obligations of New York State (or its political subdivisions or the United States) are not allowed. (see ¶510-422) (Sec. 11-641.1, N.Y.C. Adm. Code)

• *Utility partnerships*

For taxable years beginning on or after August 1, 2002, in the case of a taxpayer that is a partner in a partnership subject to the City utility tax as a utility, as defined in Sec. 11-1101(6), N.Y.C. Adm. Code, entire net income does not include the taxpayer's distributive or pro rata share for federal income tax purposes of any item of income, gain, loss, or deduction of such partnership, or any item of income, gain, loss, or deduction of such partnership that the taxpayer is required to take into account separately for federal income tax purposes. (Sec. 11-641(n), N.Y.C. Adm. Code)

[¶510-420] NYC Additions to Federal Base

Any of the following items, to the extent included or deducted in arriving at federal taxable income, must be added to the base in the New York City computation (Sec. 11-641(b), N.Y.C. Adm. Code; Sec. 3-03):

(1) Dividend or interest income (see ¶510-422);

(2) Any taxes on, or measured by, income or profits paid or accrued to the U.S., its possessions or a foreign country, New York State franchise taxes imposed under Tax Law Articles 9 (corporation tax), 9-A (business corporation tax), 13-A (tax on petroleum business) and 32 (banking corporation tax) and the New York City general corporation and banking corporation taxes;

(3) Any net operating loss for the taxable year allowable for federal income tax purposes;

(4) For taxable years beginning after 1981 (except for qualified mass commuting vehicles), the amount claimed as a deduction in computing federal taxable income solely as a result of a safe harbor lease election under IRC Sec. 168(f)(8) as it was in effect for agreements entered into prior to January 1, 1984.

(5) For taxable years beginning after 1981 (except for qualified mass commuting vehicles), the amount which would have to be included in federal taxable income had the safe harbor lease election under IRC Sec. 168(f)(8) not been made as it was in effect for agreements entered into prior to January 1, 1984.

(6) The amount allowed as a deduction under IRC Sec. 168. The provisions do not apply to property subject to the provisions of IRC Sec. 280-F, relating to luxury automobiles, and property subject to the provisions of IRC Sec. 168 which is placed in service in New York State for taxable years beginning after December 31, 1984.

(7) Upon the disposition of property (except for property subject to IRC Sec. 280-F, relating to luxury automobiles, and property subject to the provisions of IRC Sec. 168 which is placed in service for taxable years beginning after 1984), the amount, if any, by which the depreciation deduction under IRC Sec. 167 exceeds the aggregate of the accelerated cost recovery deduction under IRC Sec. 168;

(8) In the case of an eligible energy user, the amount allowed as an exclusion or deduction for energy charges in determining the entire taxable income required to be reported to the U.S. Treasury Department, but only the portion of the exclusion or deduction which is not in excess of the sum of certain special rebates (This provision is repealed, effective November 1, 2000);

(9) In the case of a taxpayer that is a supplier of fuel services, the entire amount allowed as an exclusion or deduction for certain discounts for energy services in determining the entire taxable income required to be reported to the U.S. Treasury Department (This provision is repealed, effective November 1, 2000);

(10) Applicable for taxable years beginning before January 1, 2010, in the case of taxpayers subject to the provisions of IRC Sec. 585(c) (pertaining to large banks), the amount allowed as a deduction under IRC Sec. 166 (relating to bad debts); and

(11) Applicable for taxable years beginning before January 1, 2010, 20% of the excess of the amount computed under Sec. 11-641(i) (see ¶510-435) over the amount which would have been allowable had the institution maintained its bad debt reserve for all taxable years on the basis of actual experience.

• *Federal bonus depreciation—partial decoupling*

With respect to certain provisions enacted by the federal Job Creation and Worker Assistance Act of 2002 (P.L. 107-147) (JCWAA) and the Jobs and Growth Tax Relief Reconciliation Act of 2003 (P.L. 108-27) (JGTRRA), including additional 30% and 50% depreciation deductions allowed in the first year "qualified property" is placed in service, New York City law has been amended to generally limit the depreciation deduction for qualified property to the deduction that would have been allowed for such property under IRC Sec. 167 had the property been acquired by the taxpayer on September 10, 2001. However, the depreciation deductions for qualified Resurgence Zone property, qualified New York Liberty Zone property, and qualified New York Liberty Zone leasehold improvements, as well as the additional first-year expense deduction under IRC Sec. 179 for qualified New York Liberty Zone property, are the same for New York City banking corporation tax purposes as for federal tax purposes. (Sec. 11-641(b)(13), (n), and (p), N.Y.C. Adm. Code; *Finance Memorandum 02-3*, October 29, 2003)

As amended, the New York City law also requires appropriate adjustments to the amount of any gain or loss included in entire net income upon the disposition of any property for which the federal and New York City depreciation deductions differ. (Sec. 11-641(o), N.Y.C. Adm. Code; *Finance Memorandum 02-3*, October 29, 2003)

For taxable years beginning on or after January 1, 2004, in the case of a passenger motor vehicle or a sport utility vehicle subject to the provisions of Sec. 11-641(r) (see "Sport utility vehicles" below), the limitation under IRC Sec. 280F(a)(1)(A)(i) applicable to the amount allowed as a deduction under Sec. 11-641(n) must be determined as of the date such vehicle was placed in service and not as of September 10, 2001. (Sec. 11-641(n), N.Y.C. Adm. Code)

• *Sport utility vehicles*

For taxable years beginning on or after January 1, 2004, in the case of a taxpayer that is not an eligible farmer, no deduction may be taken for the amount allowable as a deduction under IRC Sec. 167, IRC Sec. 168, and IRC Sec. 179 with respect to a sport utility vehicle that is not a passenger automobile as defined in IRC Sec. 280F(d)(5). (Sec. 11-641(b)(14), N.Y.C. Adm. Code)

Instead, the deduction must be computed *as if* the sport utility vehicle *were* a passenger automobile as defined in IRC Sec. 280F(d)(5). (Sec. 11-641(r), N.Y.C. Adm. Code)

The Department of Finance has provided schedules setting forth the applicable New York City SUV limits; see *Finance Memorandum 19-1*, March 2, 2020.

Upon the disposition of property to which Sec. 11-641(r) applies, the amount of any gain or loss includible in entire net income must be adjusted to reflect the above modification attributable to such property. (Sec. 11-641(s), N.Y.C. Adm. Code)

• *Business interest expense deduction*

An addition modification is required for the amount of the increase in the federal interest deduction allowed under IRC Sec. 163(j)(10). This relates to the federal CARES Act amendment increasing the cap of the business interest expense limitation and allowing an election to use 2019 adjusted taxable income for 2020. The modification is required for taxable years beginning in 2019 and 2020. (Sec. 11-641(b)(17), N.Y.C. Adm. Code; *Finance Memorandum 20-6*)

• *2008 Budget—QPAI deduction*

Under the 2008 budget legislation, applicable to taxable years beginning after 2007, an addition modification is required for the IRC § 199 deduction for qualified production activities income. (Sec. 11-641(b)(15), N.Y.C. Adm. Code)

• *2003 Budget—Related member expenses*

Under the 2003 budget bill (as amended by the Ch. 686, Laws 2003, technical corrections legislation), New York City requires an addition for certain royalty payments made to a related member. (Sec. 11-641(q), N.Y.C. Adm. Code) These anti-PIC (passive investment company) provisions, also referred to as expense disallowance provisions, are similar to the general corporation tax provisions; see the detailed discussion at ¶ 505-417.

¶510-420

[¶510-422] NYC Additions to Federal Base--Certain Dividend or Interest Income

For corporations organized under the laws of a country other than the United States, entire net income is computed without the deduction or exclusion of:

(1) any part of income from dividends or interest on any kind of stock, securities or indebtedness, but only if the income is treated as effectively conducted with a trade or business in the United States under IRC Sec. 864;

(2) any income exempt from federal taxable income under any treaty obligation of the United States, but only if the income would be treated as effectively connected in the absence of the exemption, provided that the treaty obligation does not preclude the taxation of income by a state;

(3) any income which would be treated effectively connected if the income were not excluded from gross income under IRC Sec. 103(a).

In the case of any other corporation, entire net income is computed with the deduction or exclusion of any part of any income from dividends or interest on any kind of stock, securities or indebtedness. (Sec. 11-641(b)(1), N.Y.C. Adm. Code)

Amounts treated as dividends under IRC Sec. 78 (pertaining to dividends received from certain foreign corporations by domestic corporations choosing foreign tax credit) and amounts which are treated as subtractions for New York City purposes equal to 17% of interest income from subsidiary capital, 60% of dividend income, gains and losses from subsidiary capital, and $22^1/2$% percent of interest income on obligations of New York State, its political subdivisions or the United States (see ¶510-430) are not included in the addition. (Sec. 11-641(b)(1), N.Y.C. Adm. Code)

[¶510-430] NYC Subtractions from Federal Base

Entire net income does not include any refund or credit of tax for which no exclusion or deduction was allowed in determining entire net income for New York City general corporation and banking corporation tax purposes for any prior year. (Sec. 11-641(d), N.Y.C. Adm. Code; Rule Sec. 3-03)

In addition, the following will be allowed as a deduction in determining entire net income, to the extent not deductible in determining federal taxable income:

(1) interest on indebtedness incurred or continued to purchase or carry obligations or securities, the income from which is subject to New York City banking corporation tax but exempt from federal income tax;

(2) ordinary and necessary expenses paid or incurred during the taxable year attributable to income which is subject to New York City banking corporation tax but exempt from federal income tax; and

(3) the amortizable bond premium for the taxable year on any bond, the interest on which is subject to New York City banking corporation tax but exempt from federal income tax. (Sec. 11-641(e), N.Y.C. Adm. Code)

A deduction is allowed for the portion of wages and salaries paid or incurred for the taxable year and not allowed as a business expense deduction under IRC Sec. 280C because federal employment credits and federal incentive program (WIN) credit were claimed. (Sec. 11-641(e), N.Y.C. Adm. Code)

Deductions are also allowed for money and property received from the Federal Deposit Insurance Corporation pursuant to Sec. 13 of the Federal Deposit Insurance Act, and money and property received from the Federal Savings and Loan Insurance Corporation pursuant to Sec. 406 of the Federal National Housing Act. (Sec. 11-641(e), N.Y.C. Adm. Code)

A deduction is also allowed for 17% of interest income from subsidiary capital and 60% of dividend income, gains and losses from subsidiary capital. (Sec. 11-641(e), N.Y.C. Adm. Code)

Also deductible is 22$^{1}/_{2}$% of interest income on obligations of New York State, or of any political subdivision of New York State, or on obligations of the United States, other than obligations held for resale in connection with regular trading activities. (Sec. 11-641(e), N.Y.C. Adm. Code)

Applicable for taxable years beginning before January 1, 2010, in the case of a taxpayer that recaptured its balance of the reserve for losses on loans for federal income tax purposes under IRC Sec. 585(c) (pertaining to large banks), a deduction was allowed for any amount included in federal taxable income under IRC Sec. 585(c). Also applicable for taxable years beginning before January 1, 2010, a deduction was allowed for taxpayers subject to the provisions of IRC Sec. 585(c) (regarding large banks) for any amount included in federal taxable income as a result of a recovery of a loan. (Sec. 11-641(e), N.Y.C. Adm. Code)

Banks are permitted to have a net operating loss (NOL) deduction for losses incurred in tax years after 2008. However, the deduction will only be allowed for NOLs carried forward to future tax years. No NOLs may be carried back to past years. (Sec. 11-641(k-1), N.Y.C. Adm. Code)

Note: The law has been amended to provide that, for taxable years beginning before 2021, any amendment to IRC Sec. 172 made after March 1, 2020, does not apply. Accordingly, the New York City banking corporation tax does not conform to federal CARES Act amendments, including (1) a five-year carryback period for NOLs arising in tax years beginning in 2018, 2019, and 2020, and (2) suspension of the 80% of taxable income limitation for those years. (Sec. 11-641(k-2), N.Y.C. Adm. Code; *Finance Memorandum 20-6*)

For subtractions concerning safe harbor leases and ACRS deductions, see ¶510-432. For deductions relating to international banking facilities, see ¶510-433. For other modifications, see ¶510-438—¶510-440.

[¶510-432] NYC Subtractions from Federal Base--Safe Harbor Leases and ACRS Deductions

A deduction is allowed for the following in determining entire net income, to the extent not deductible in determining federal taxable income:

(1) For taxable years beginning after 1981, except for qualified mass commuting vehicles, the amount includable in federal taxable income solely as a result of a safe harbor lease election made under IRC Sec. 168(f)(8) as it was in effect for agreements entered into prior to January 1, 1984 (Sec. 11-641(e)(5), N.Y.C. Adm. Code; Rule Sec. 3-03);

(2) For taxable years beginning after 1981, except for qualified mass commuting vehicles, the amount which could have been excluded from federal taxable income had the safe harbor lease election under IRC Sec. 168(f)(8) not been made as it was in effect for agreements entered into prior to January 1, 1984. (Sec. 11-641(e)(6), N.Y.C. Adm. Code; Rule Sec. 3-03)

(3) A deduction is allowed equal to the amount with respect to property which is subject to the provisions of IRC Sec. 168 allowable as the depreciation deduction under IRC Sec. 167 as that section would have been applied to property placed in service on December 31, 1980, provided a deduction has not been excluded from entire net income as a result of a safe harbor lease election. However, this deduction does not apply with respect to property subject to the provisions of IRC Sec. 280-F (relating to luxury automobiles) or to property subject to the provisions of IRC Sec. 168 which is placed in service in New York State after 1984. (Sec. 11-641(e)(7), N.Y.C. Adm. Code; Rule Sec. 3-03)

Upon the disposition of property (except for property subject to the provisions of IRC Sec. 280-F, relating to luxury automobiles, and property subject to the provisions of IRC Sec. 168 which is placed in service for taxable years beginning after 1984) the amount, if any, by which the aggregate of the accelerated cost recovery system deduction allowed under IRC Sec. 168 exceeds the aggregate of the depreciation deduction under IRC Sec. 167. (Sec. 11-641(e)(8), N.Y.C. Adm. Code; Rule Sec. 3-03)

[¶510-433] NYC Modifications to Federal Base--International Banking Facilities

In determining entire net income, a deduction is allowed to the extent not deductible in determining federal taxable income, for the adjusted eligible net income of an international banking facility. (Sec. 11-641(f)(1-4), N.Y.C. Adm. Code; Rule Sec. 3-03)

The eligible net income of an international banking facility is the amount remaining after subtracting applicable expenses from eligible gross income. (Sec. 11-641(f)(1-4), N.Y.C. Adm. Code; Rule Sec. 3-03) Applicable expenses are any expenses or other deductions attributable, directly or indirectly, to eligible gross income.

Eligible gross income is the gross income derived by an international banking facility from (Sec. 11-641(f)(1-4), N.Y.C. Adm. Code; Rule Sec. 3-03):

(1) making, arranging for, placing or servicing loans to foreign persons. Provided, however, that substantially all the proceeds of the loan are intended for use outside of the United States in the case of a foreign person which is an individual, or which is a foreign branch of a domestic corporation (other than a bank), or which is a foreign corporation or foreign partnership 80% or more owned or controlled either directly or indirectly by one or more domestic corporations (other than banks), domestic partnerships or resident individuals;

(2) making or placing deposits with foreign persons which are banks (including foreign subsidiaries or foreign branches of the taxpayer) or with other international banking facilities; or

(3) entering into foreign exchange trading or hedging transactions.

Adjusted eligible net income is determined by subtracting from eligible net income the ineligible funding amount, and by subtracting from the amount then remaining the floor amount. (Sec. 11-641(f)(1-4), N.Y.C. Adm. Code; Rule Sec. 3-03)

• *Ineligible funding*

The ineligible funding amount is the amount, if any, determined by multiplying eligible net income by a fraction. (Sec. 11-641(f)(5), N.Y.C. Adm. Code) The numerator is the average aggregate amount for the taxable year of all liabilities, including deposits and other sources of funds of the international banking facility which were not owed to or received from foreign persons, and the denominator is the average aggregate amount for the taxable year of all liabilities, including deposits and other sources of funds of the international banking facility.

• *Floor amount*

The floor amount is the amount, if any, determined by multiplying the amount remaining after subtracting the ineligible funding amount from the eligible net income by a fraction which is not greater than one. (Sec. 11-641(f)(6), N.Y.C. Adm. Code)

The numerator is (1) a percentage (see below for amounts of percentage) of the average aggregate amount of the taxpayer's loans to foreign persons and deposits with foreign branches of banks (including foreign subsidiaries or foreign branches or the taxpayer), which were recorded in the financial accounts of the taxpayer for its branches, agencies and offices within New York State for taxable years 1976 and 1977, *minus* (2) the average aggregate amount of the loans and the deposits for the taxable year of the taxpayer (other than the loans and deposits of an international banking facility). The amounts determined under (2) may not exceed the amounts determined under (1). (Sec. 11-641(f)(6), N.Y.C. Adm. Code)

The denominator is the average aggregate amount of the loans to foreign persons and deposits with foreign persons which are banks or foreign branches of banks (including foreign subsidiaries or foreign branches of the taxpayer), which were recorded in the financial accounts of the taxpayer's international banking facility for the taxable year. (Sec. 11-641(f)(6), N.Y.C. Adm. Code)

The percentages for the numerator are 100% for the first taxable year in which the taxpayer establishes an international banking facility and 100% for the next succeeding four taxable years. (Sec. 11-641(f)(6), N.Y.C. Adm. Code) The percentage declines to 80% for the fifth, 60% for the sixth, 40% for the seventh and 20% for the eighth taxable year next succeeding the year the taxpayer established the international banking facility, and 0% in the ninth succeeding year and thereafter.

In the event eligible net income is a loss, the loss is added to entire net income. (Sec. 11-641(f)(7), N.Y.C. Adm. Code)

In lieu of the above deduction, a taxpayer may elect to modify on an annual basis its income allocation percentage. (see ¶ 510-605)

[¶510-438] NYC Modification--Elective Double Depreciation

At the election of the taxpayer, a deduction is allowed from the portion of entire net income allocated within New York City, up to double the amount of federal depreciation on qualified tangible property (except personal property leased to others) in lieu of the amount of normal depreciation. The deduction is allowed only upon the condition that entire net income is computed without any deduction for depreciation or amortization of the same property, and the total depreciation deductions allowed under former New York City banking corporation provisions (Part 1 and Parts 2 of Subchapter 3, Ch. 6) in any taxable year may not exceed its cost or other basis. The original use of the property must commence with the taxpayer and the property must be (Sec. 11-641(k), N.Y.C. Adm. Code):

(1) depreciable tangible property under IRC 167;

(2) constructed, reconstructed, erected or acquired after December 31, 1965, and on or before December 31, 1967, subject to certain conditions; and

(3) have a situs in New York City and used in the taxpayer's business.

Any unused optional depreciation may be carried over forward to succeeding taxable years and may be deducted from the portion of the taxpayer's allocated entire net income. (Sec. 11-641(k), N.Y.C. Adm. Code)

When property is sold or otherwise disposed of for which the above elective double depreciation had been allowed or under Secs. 11-621(12) or 11-629(j), the gain or loss entering into the computation of federal taxable income is disregarded in computing entire net income. (Sec. 11-641(k), N.Y.C. Adm. Code) Instead, gain or loss upon the sale or other disposition is added to or subtracted from the portion of entire net income allocated within New York City. An adjustment is required for the elective double depreciation deduction allowed under Sec. 11-641(k)(1) (see above).

[¶510-440] NYC Adjustment of Gain or Loss

In the case of the sale or exchange of property where the property has a higher adjusted basis for city tax purposes than for federal tax purposes, there will be allowed as a deduction from entire net income the portion of any gain or loss on the sale which equals the difference in the basis. (Sec. 11-641(c)(1), N.Y.C. Adm. Code)

[¶510-600]

NYC BANKS ALLOCATION AND APPORTIONMENT

[¶510-601] NYC Allocation of Entire Net Income

If a taxpayer's entire net income is derived from business carried on both within and without New York City, the portion which is derived from business carried on within New York City is determined by multiplying its entire net income by the income allocation percentage. The income allocation percentage is determined by adding together the payroll, receipts, and deposits percentages (see ¶510-602—¶510-604), plus an additional percentage equal to the receipts percentage and an additional percentage equal to the deposits percentage, and dividing the result by five. (Sec. 11-642(b), N.Y.C. Adm. Code)

However, banking corporations that substantially provide management administrative or distributive services to investment companies are phasing in a single sales factor to replace the current three-factor allocation formula. The new allocation formula will be phased in over a 10-year period, beginning in 2009. (Sec. 11-642(b)(1-a), N.Y.C. Adm. Code)

For the determination of the income allocation percentage of an international banking facility, see ¶510-605.

[¶510-602] NYC Income Allocation Percentage--Payroll Factor

The payroll factor is the percentage which 80% of the total wages, salaries and other personal service compensation during the taxable year of employees within New York City (except wages, salaries and other personal service compensation of general executive officers) bears to the total wages, salaries and other personal service compensation during the taxable year of all the taxpayer's employees within and without New York City (except wages, salaries and other personal service compensation of general executive officers). (Sec. 11-642(a)(1), N.Y.C. Adm. Code; Rule Sec. 3-04)

However, banking corporations that substantially provide management administrative or distributive services to investment companies are phasing in a single sales factor to replace the current three-factor allocation formula. The new allocation formula will be phased in over a 10-year period, beginning in 2009. (Sec. 11-642(b)(1-a), N.Y.C. Adm. Code)

[¶510-603] NYC Income Allocation Percentage--Receipts Factor

The receipts factor is computed by ascertaining the percentage which the receipts of the taxpayer arising during the taxable year from loans (including a taxpayer's portion of a participation in a loan) and financing leases within New York City and all other business receipts earned within New York City, bears to the total amount of the taxpayer's receipts from loans (including a taxpayer's portion of a participation in a loan) and financing leases and all other business receipts within and without New York City. (Sec. 11-642(a)(2), N.Y.C. Adm. Code; Rule Sec. 3-04)

The receipts factor is weighted twice, except in computing alternative entire net income. (Sec. 11-642(b)(1) and (c)(1), N.Y.C. Adm. Code)

However, banking corporations that substantially provide management administrative or distributive services to investment companies are phasing in a single sales factor to replace the current three-factor allocation formula. The new allocation formula will be phased in over a 10-year period, beginning in 2009. (Sec. 11-642(b)(1-a), N.Y.C. Adm. Code)

• *Interest*

All interest from loans and financing leases is located where the greater portion of income-producing activity related to the loan or financing lease occurred. However, special rules apply for exempt corporations. (Sec. 11-642(a)(2), N.Y.C. Adm. Code)

• *Lease transactions*

Receipts from lease transactions other than financing leases are located where the property subject to the lease is located. (Sec. 11-642(a)(2), N.Y.C. Adm. Code)

• *Bank, travel, and entertainment cards*

Interest, fees, and penalties in the nature of interest from bank, credit, travel and entertainment card receivables are earned within New York City if the mailing address of the card holder in the records of the taxpayer is in New York City. Service charges and fees from such cards are earned within New York City if the card is serviced in New York City. Receipts from merchant discounts are earned within New York City if the merchant is located within New York City. (Sec. 11-642(a)(2)(D), N.Y.C. Adm. Code)

• *Trading activities*

The portion of total net gains and other income from trading activities (including but not limited to foreign exchange, options and financial futures) and from investment activities which are attributed to New York City is ascertained by multiplying the total net gains and other income by a fraction. The numerator is the average value of the trading assets and investment assets attributable to New York City, and the denominator is the average value of all trading assets. A trading asset or investment asset is attributable to New York City if the greater portion of income-producing activity related to the trading asset or investment occurred within New York City. (Sec. 11-642(a)(2), N.Y.C. Adm. Code)

• *Letters of credit, travelers checks, money orders*

Fees or charges from the issuance of letters of credit, travelers' checks and money orders are earned within New York City if the letters of credit, travelers checks or money orders are issued within New York City. (Sec. 11-642(a)(2), N.Y.C. Adm. Code)

• *Services to investment company*

For tax years beginning after 2000, in calculating the receipts factor of the business allocation percentage, receipts from management, administrative, or distribution services performed for regulated investment companies are deemed to arise from services performed in New York City in the same proportion as the regulated investment company's shares are held by New York state domiciliaries. (Sec. 11-642(a)(2), N.Y.C. Adm. Code)

• *Resident employees*

Receipts for services performed by the taxpayer's employees who are regularly connected with, or working out of, a New York City office of the taxpayer are allocated to New York City if the services are performed within New York City.

¶510-603

When allocating receipts for services performed, it is immaterial where the receipts are payable or where they are actually received. Where services are performed both within and without New York City, the portion of the receipt attributable to services performed within New York City is determined on the basis of the relative value, or amount of time spent in performance of such services within New York City, or by some other reasonable method. (Rule Sec. 3-04)

• *Royalties*

Receipts of royalties from the use of patents, copyrights and trademarks are allocated within New York City if the taxpayer's actual seat of management or control is located within New York City. Royalties include all amounts received by the taxpayer for the use of patents, copyrights or trademarks, whether or not the patents, copyrights or trademarks were issued to the taxpayer. (Rule Sec. 3-04)

• *Securities*

Income from securities used to maintain reserves against deposits to meet federal and state reserve requirements are allocated to New York City based upon the ratio that total deposits in New York City bears to total deposits everywhere. A receipt from the sale of a capital asset is not a business receipt and is not included in the receipts factor. (Rule Sec. 3-04)

• *Combined returns*

The receipts factor on a combined return is computed as though the corporations included in the return were one corporation. All intercorporate receipts between the corporations included in the combined return are eliminated in computing the receipts factor. (Rule Sec. 3-04)

[¶510-604] NYC Income Allocation Percentage--Deposits Factor

The deposits factor is computed by ascertaining the percentage which the average value of deposits maintained at branches within New York City during the taxable year bears to the average value of all the taxpayer's deposits maintained at branches within and without New York City during the taxable year. (Sec. 11-642(a)(3), N.Y.C. Adm. Code; Rule Sec. 3-04)

The deposits factor is weighted twice, except in computing alternative entire net income. (Sec. 11-642(b)(1) and (c)(1), N.Y.C. Adm. Code)

However, banking corporations that substantially provide management administrative or distributive services to investment companies are phasing in a single sales factor to replace the current three-factor allocation formula. The new allocation formula will be phased in over a 10-year period, beginning in 2009. (Sec. 11-642(b)(1-a), N.Y.C. Adm. Code)

[¶510-605] NYC Income Allocation Percentage--International Banking Facilities

In lieu of the modification for the adjusted eligible net income (see ¶510-433) of an international banking facility (IBF), a taxpayer may elect to modify, on an annual basis, its income allocation percentage in the following manner:

(1) Wages, salaries and other personal service compensation properly attributable to the production of eligible gross income of the taxpayer's international banking facility is not included in the computation of wages, salaries and other personal compensation of employees within New York City;

(2) Receipts properly attributable to the production of eligible gross income of the taxpayer's international banking facility is not included in the computation of receipts within New York City;

(3) Deposits from foreign persons which are properly attributable to the production of eligible gross income of the taxpayer's international banking facility is not included in the computation of deposits maintained at branches within New York City. (Sec. 11-642(b)(2), N.Y.C. Adm. Code; Rule Sec. 3-04)

For taxable years beginning on or after January 1, 1999, the election to the use the IBF formula allocation method for a taxable year is made with the filing of the return for that taxable year (previously, within 45 days after the beginning of the taxable year). In addition, the election may be made or changed with the filing of an amended return for the taxable year in question. (Rule Sec. 3-04)

[¶510-606] NYC Allocation of Alternative Entire Net Income

If a taxpayer's alternative entire net income is derived from business carried on both within and without New York City, the portion which is derived from business carried on within New York City is determined by multiplying its alternative entire net income by the alternative entire net income allocation percentage. (Sec. 11-642(c), N.Y.C. Adm. Code; Rule Sec. 3-04)

The alternative entire net income allocation percentage is determined in the same manner as the entire net income allocation percentage (see ¶510-602—¶510-604) with the following exceptions:

(1) The payroll factor is recomputed to include total (instead of 80% of) wages, salaries or other personal service compensation (other than general executive officers) within New York City; and

(2) The payroll, receipts and deposit factors are weighted as one. (Sec. 11-642(c), N.Y.C. Adm. Code)

For the computation of the income allocation percentage for international banking facilities, see ¶510-605.

[¶510-607] NYC Allocation of Taxable Assets

If the taxpayer's taxable assets are derived from business carried on both within and without New York City, the portion which is derived from business carried on within the city is determined by multiplying the taxpayer's taxable assets by an asset allocation percentage determined in the same manner as the income allocation percentage (see ¶510-602—¶510-604) when the international banking facility elects to modify its income allocation percentage, (see ¶510-605) except that the modifications made by the international banking facility do not apply. (Sec. 11-642(d), N.Y.C. Adm. Code; Rule Sec. 3-04)

[¶510-608] Allocation Percentage--Determination by NYC Commissioner

If it appears to the Commissioner of Finance that allocation percentages for entire net income, alternative entire net income, and taxable assets (see ¶510-601—¶510-607) do not properly reflect the activity, business, income or assets of a taxpayer within New York City, the Commissioner of Finance is authorized in his or her discretion to adjust it by:

(1) excluding one or more of the factors;

(2) including one or more other factors; or

(3) employing any other similar or different method calculated to effect a fair and proper allocation of the income or assets reasonably attributable to New York City. (Sec. 11-642(a)(6), N.Y.C. Adm. Code)

[¶510-800]
NYC BANKS CREDITS

[¶510-820] NYC Relocation and Employment Assistance Credit

Note: Under corporate tax reform legislation enacted in 2015, the New York City corporate income tax system was significantly revised, generally applicable to taxable years beginning on or after January 1, 2015. (Subchapter 3-A, Corporate Tax of 2015; Sec. 11-651, N.Y.C. Adm. Code, *et. seq.*)

Among other changes, affected banking corporation taxpayers are transitioned to taxation under Subchapter 3-A, Corporate Tax of 2015; see ¶505-205.

However, S corporations and qualified subchapter S subsidiaries remain subject to the existing, pre-reform banking corporation tax provisions. (Sec. 11-639(a)(2), N.Y.C. Adm. Code)

A memorandum explains transitional filing provisions for taxpayers affected by the corporate tax reform legislation. (*Finance Memorandum 15-2*, April 17, 2015)

Pre-reform banking corporation tax: The provisions discussed below generally apply to taxable years beginning before 2015. As noted above, however, they continue to apply to S corporations. (Sec. 11-639(a)(2), N.Y.C. Adm. Code)

A credit is allowed to businesses that have conducted substantial business operations at one or more business locations outside New York City or south of 96th Street in Manhattan for 24 months prior to relocation, and that relocate all or part of the business operations to eligible premises in other parts of the city. (Sec. 11-643.7(a), N.Y.C. Adm. Code; Sec. 22-621(a), N.Y.C. Adm. Code; Rule Sec. 30-01)

Relocations to Lower Manhattan: Effective July 1, 2003, REAP benefits are extended to certain eligible businesses relocating from outside New York City to Lower Manhattan. (Sec. 11-643.9, N.Y.C. Adm. Code; Sec. 22-623, N.Y.C. Adm. Code; Sec. 22-624, N.Y.C. Adm. Code) For further discussion, see ¶507-005.

• *Eligible premises*

"Eligible premises" are nonresidential premises which are wholly contained in real property which is receiving benefits pursuant to the exemption for industrial and commercial properties, subject to certain requirements. (Sec. 22-621(e), N.Y.C. Adm. Code) To qualify as "eligible premises," the following conditions must have been met:

(1) the premises have been improved by construction or renovation;

(2) expenditures have been made for improvements to real property in excess of 50% (25%, in the case of industrial property) of the value at which the real property was assessed for tax purposes for the tax year in which the improvements commenced;

(3) the expenditures have been made within 36 months (72 months if the improvement expenditures exceed $50 million) from the commencement of improvements;

(4) the real property is located in an area of the City other than in Manhattan south of 96th Street. (Sec. 22-621(e) and (f), N.Y.C. Adm. Code; Rule Sec. 30-01)

Certain other nonresidential premises may also qualify (e.g., those wholly contained in, or situated on, real property that either (1) has been leased from the New

York City Industrial Development Agency (IDA), and which is constructed or renovated subsequent to the approval by the IDA, or (2) is owned by New York City, or which has been leased from the New York State Urban Development Corporation (or subsidiary of the New York State Urban Development Corporation), and where the premises were constructed or renovated subsequent to the lease approval or execution). (Sec. 22-621(e)(2), N.Y.C. Adm. Code; Rule Sec. 30-01)

For relocations after June 30, 2003, A.B. 11459, Laws 2004, expands the definition of "eligible premises" to include nonresidential premises for which a minimum expenditure exceeding $25 per square foot has been made for improvements. If the premises are leased, the lease must have a term that does not expire until three years after the date of relocation or the lease commencement date, whichever is later. (Sec. 22-621(e)(3), N.Y.C. Adm. Code)

• *Particular premises*

For purposes of determining the credit, the term "particular premises" includes all premises occupied by an eligible business within a single building. If there are eligible and non-eligible premises in the same building, the eligible and non-eligible premises constitute separate particular premises. (Sec. 22-621(p), N.Y.C. Adm. Code; Rule Sec. 30-01)

• *Relocation*

For purposes of determining eligibility for the credit, "relocation" is defined as the transfer of pre-existing business operations or the establishment of new business operations which are not retail activities or hotel services. A relocation is not deemed to have taken place unless at least one employee of the eligible business is transferred to the eligible premises from pre-existing business operations. The date of relocation is generally the day that the first employee who is transferred begins to work at the eligible premises. (Sec. 22-621(j), N.Y.C. Adm. Code; Rule Sec. 30-01)

No claim for credit or refund of an overpayment of tax is allowed which is otherwise barred by any statute of limitations. The election of the relocation date is irrevocable. (Rule Sec. 30-01)

An eligible business may relocate only once to any particular premises. (Sec. 22-621(j), N.Y.C. Adm. Code)

• *Amount of credit*

Credit is allowed for the first taxable year during which the eligible aggregate employment shares are maintained with respect to the premises and for any of the 12 succeeding taxable years during which the shares are maintained. For the initial year and the 11 succeeding taxable years during which shares are maintained, the amount of the credit is determined by multiplying $1,000 ($500, in the case of taxpayers that received certificates of eligibility dated before July 1, 1995) by the number of the eligible aggregate employment shares maintained by the taxpayer with respect to particular eligible premises during the taxable year. During the 12th year, the credit is determined by multiplying the number of eligible aggregate employment shares maintained with respect to the premises in the 12th year by the lesser of one and a fraction, the numerator of which is the number of days in the taxable year of relocation less the number of days the eligible business maintained employment shares in the eligible premises in the taxable year of relocation, and the denominator of which is the number of days in the 12th year during which the shares are maintained with respect to the premises. (Sec. 11-643.7(a), N.Y.C. Adm. Code)

No credit is available for the relocation of any retail activity (including retail banking activities) or hotel services. (Sec. 11-643.7(a), N.Y.C. Adm. Code)

An "employment share" is the sum of (1) the number of full-time work weeks worked by each employee, partner or sole proprietor, divided by the number of weeks in the taxable year, and (2) the number of part-time work weeks worked by each employee, partner, or sole proprietor, divided by an amount equal to twice the number of weeks in the taxable year. (Sec. 22-621(g), N.Y.C. Adm. Code; Rule Sec. 30-01)

An "eligible aggregate employment share" is the amount, if any, by which the number of aggregate employment shares maintained by an eligible business in the taxable year which the business claims the credit, exceeds the number of aggregate employment shares maintained in the taxable year immediately preceding the taxable year during which the business first relocated. The amount of eligible aggregate employment shares is subject to certain limitations. (Sec. 22-621(i), N.Y.C. Adm. Code; Rule Sec. 30-01)

For further criteria and examples involving the determination of "employment share," and "eligible aggregate employment shares," see Rule Sec. 30-01 at ¶509-719.

If the amount of the credit allowable for a taxable year exceeds the tax imposed for such year, the excess may be carried over, in order, to the five immediately succeeding taxable years and, to the extent not previously deductible, may be deducted from tax. (Sec. 11-643.7(b), N.Y.C. Adm. Code)

The credit must be deducted prior to the deduction of other credits, except the credit for unincorporated business tax paid. (Sec. 11-643.7(c), N.Y.C. Adm. Code)

No credit is allowed under this provision to a taxpayer that has elected to take the credit against the New York City utility tax. (Sec. 22-622, N.Y.C. Adm. Code)

• *Revitalization areas*

An expanded credit is available to businesses that relocate to certain districts zoned as revitalization areas. Specifically, for businesses that have obtained a certification of eligibility dated after June 30, 2000, for a relocation to eligible premises located within a revitalization area, the normal $1,000 figure used to compute the credit is increased to $3,000. Thus, under these provisions, the credit amount is computed by multiplying $3,000 by the number of eligible aggregate employment shares maintained by the taxpayer during the taxable year with respect to particular premises to which the taxpayer has relocated. (Sec. 11-643.7(a) and (d), N.Y.C. Adm. Code; Sec. 22-621(n), N.Y.C. Adm. Code)

For taxpayers that have obtained such a certification of eligibility, the credit amounts allowed for the taxable year of relocation and the four succeeding taxable years may not be carried over. Instead, for such taxable years, the credit amounts are deemed to be tax overpayments, to be credited or refunded to the taxpayer without interest. (Sec. 11-643.7(a) and (d), N.Y.C. Adm. Code)

• *Multiple relocations*

If an eligible business has obtained certifications for more than one relocation, the portion of the total amount of eligible aggregate employment shares to be multiplied by the applicable dollar amount for each certification of a relocation is the number of total attributed eligible aggregate employment shares determined with respect to such relocation under Sec. 22-621(o). (Sec. 11-643.7(a), N.Y.C. Adm. Code)

• *Additional or replacement premises*

Under A.B. 11459, Laws 2004, effective July 1, 2003, provisions are added to allow certain businesses to continue receiving REAP benefits after moving to designated additional or replacement premises. (Sec. 22-621(q), N.Y.C. Adm. Code; Sec. 22-622(e), N.Y.C. Adm. Code)

• *Moving jobs out of Lower Manhattan*

Under A.B. 11459, Laws 2004, the New York City Mayor is authorized to reduce REAP benefits in certain cases when an eligible business moves more than 100 jobs out of Lower Manhattan. (Sec. 22-622(f), N.Y.C. Adm. Code)

• *Certification process*

Prior to receiving the credit, the business must receive initial certification of eligibility from the Deputy Commissioner of Tax Operations. Initial certification is required for the number of aggregate employment shares maintained by the eligible business (1) within the eligible area, (2) outside the eligible area and (3) at the particular eligible premises to which it relocates in the taxable year preceding the taxable year of relocation.

Additional initial certification is required if an eligible business subsequently relocates to a separate particular eligible premise (Rule Sec. 30-02).

A denial for initial eligibility or a contest of the number of aggregate employment shares certified must be made within 90 days of the denial of eligibility or certification of shares. The appeal must be made in writing to the Commissioner of Finance. (Rule Sec. 30-02)

An eligible business must obtain annual certification from the Department of Finance of the number of eligible aggregate employment shares maintained by the eligible business in the eligible area and in each particular eligible premise for the eligible business's taxable year. (Rule Sec. 30-02)

No certification of eligibility for the credit will be issued to an eligible business on or after July 1, 2025, unless the business meets certain statutory requirements. (Sec. 22-622, N.Y.C. Adm. Code)

[¶510-825] Credit for Distributions From Partnerships Subject to NYC Unincorporated Business Tax

A credit is allowed to banking corporations that are partners in unincorporated businesses that are subject to unincorporated business tax (see ¶519-005 and following in the "N.Y. City—Unincorporated Business" division). To be eligible for the credit for taxable years beginning after 1995, the banking corporation must be required to include in entire net income its distributive share of income, gain, loss and deductions of, or guaranteed payments from, the unincorporated business (for taxable years beginning before 1996, the credit was calculated with reference to the base on which the taxpayer would pay bank franchise tax in the absence of the credit). (Sec. 11-643.8, N.Y.C. Adm. Code)

• *Calculation of credit*

The credit is equal to the lesser of the following:

(1) the sum of (a) the unincorporated business tax reported and paid by the unincorporated business for its taxable year ending within or with the taxable year of the banking corporation and (b) the amount of any unincorporated business tax credit or credits taken by the unincorporated business, other than the fixed dollar credit (see ¶519-405 in the "N.Y. City—Unincorporated Business" division), to the extent that such credit or credits do not reduce the unincorporated business's tax below zero, multiplied by a fraction, the numerator of which is the net total of the corporation's distributive share of income, gain, loss and deductions of, and guaranteed payments from, the unincorporated business for its taxable year, and the denominator of which is the sum of the net total distributive shares of income, gain, loss and deductions of, and guaranteed payments to, all partners in the unincorporated business for whom or which such net total (as separately determined for each partner) is greater than zero for the taxable year; or

¶510-825

(2) the excess of (a) the basic tax computed pursuant to Sec. 11-643.5(a), N.Y.C. Adm. Code (see ¶510-250), without allowance of any credits allowed by this part, over (b) the basic tax so computed, determined as if the banking corporation had no such distributive share or guaranteed payments with respect to the unincorporated business, multiplied by $4/9$. The amounts so computed are subject to the following modifications:

(i) the amounts are computed without taking into account any carryforward or carryback by the partner of a net operating loss;

(ii) if, prior to taking into account any distributive share or guaranteed payments from any unincorporated business or any net operating loss carryforward or carryback, the entire net income of the partner is less than zero, the entire net income is treated as zero; and

(iii) if the partner's net total distributive share of income, gain, loss and deductions of, and guaranteed payments from, any unincorporated business is less than zero, the net total is treated as zero.

•*Credit limitations*

Banking corporations subject to basic tax.—The maximum credit or credits that may be taken in any particular year by a banking corporation that, before the application of any credits, is subject to the basic tax, is limited to its basic tax liability multiplied by $4/9$. Excess credit may be carried forward and used in any of the seven immediately succeeding taxable years. Credits first arising in a particular year must be taken before any credit carryforward, and credit carryforwards to an earlier year must be taken before any carryforwards attributable to a subsequent year.

Banking corporations subject to alternative minimum tax on alternative entire net income.—Although the tax is always calculated as if the taxpayer were subject to tax computed on the entire net income base, the credit may, with certain limitations, be taken against the alternative minimum tax on alternative entire net income. In such instances, each dollar of credit will be applied to reduce the alternative minimum tax by $.75, and the maximum tax that may be taken in any taxable year may not reduce the taxpayer's tax liability to an amount below zero. Excess credit may be carried forward and used, in order, in any of the seven immediately succeeding taxable years.

No credit may be taken in a taxable year by a taxpayer that, in the absence of the credit, would be liable for the tax computed on the basis of taxable assets, the tax computed on the basis of issued capital stock, or the fixed-dollar minimum tax.

Combined reports.—A banking corporation that files a combined report must compute its credit as if the combined group were the partner in each unincorporated business from which any of the members of the group had a distributive share or guaranteed payments. If more than one member of the combined group is a partner in the same unincorporated business, the numerator of the fraction described above must be the sum of the net total distributive shares of income, gain, loss and deductions of, and guaranteed payments from, the unincorporated business of all of the partners of the unincorporated business within the combined group for which the net total (as separately determined for each partner) is greater than zero, and the denominator of such fraction is the sum of the net total distributive shares of income, gain, loss and deductions of, and guaranteed payments from, the unincorporated business of all partners in the unincorporated business for whom or which the net total (as separately determined for each partner) is greater than zero.

[¶515-000]

NYC PERSONAL INCOME TAX ON RESIDENTS

[¶515-020] NYC Administration

The New York State Department of Taxation and Finance administers the New York City personal income tax. In practice, the state and city taxes are collected on a combined return.

The regulations issued in connection with the New York State personal income tax are made applicable to the city tax. (Reg. Sec. 290.1; Reg. Sec. 290.2)

[¶515-200]

NYC TAXPAYERS AND RATES

[¶515-210] Persons Subject to NYC Tax—"NYC Resident Individual" Defined

The term "city resident individual" is defined as an individual who is domiciled in New York City, unless certain conditions exist, or an individual who maintains a permanent place of abode in the city and spends in the aggregate more than 183 days of the taxable year in the city, whether or not domiciled in New York City for any portion of the taxable year, unless the individual is in active service in the armed forces. (Sec. 11-1705(b)(1), N.Y.C. Adm. Code)

[¶515-215] Persons Subject to NYC Tax—"NYC Resident Estate or Trust" Defined

The term "city resident estate or trust" is defined as the estate of a decedent who at his or her death was domiciled in New York City, a trust or portion of a trust consisting of property transferred by will of a decedent who at his or her death was domiciled in the city or a trust or portion of a trust consisting of property transferred by will of a decedent who at his or her death was domiciled in the city, or a trust or portion of a trust consisting of the property of a person domiciled in the city at the time the property was transferred to the trust, if such trust or portion of a trust was then irrevocable, or of a person domiciled in New York City at the time such trust or portion of a trust became irrevocable, if it was revocable when such property was transferred to the trust but has subsequently become irrevocable. (Sec. 11-1705(b)(3), N.Y.C. Adm. Code)

A trust or portion of a trust is revocable if it is subject to a power, exercisable immediately or at any future time, to revest title in the person whose property constituted such trust or portion of a trust. A trust or portion of a trust becomes irrevocable when the possibility that such power may be exercised has been terminated. (Sec. 11-1705(b)(3), N.Y.C. Adm. Code)

A resident trust is not subject to tax if all of the following conditions are satisfied: (1) all the trustees are domiciled outside New York City; (2) the entire corpus of the trusts, including real and tangible property, is located outside New York City; and (3) all income and gains of the trust are derived from or connected with sources outside New York City and are determined as if the trust were a nonresident trust. Intangible property is considered to be located in New York City if at least one of the trustees is domiciled in the city. A banking corporation located outside New York City continues to be a nonresident corporate trustee even if it later becomes an office or branch of a corporate trustee domiciled in New York City. (Sec. 11-1705(b)(3), N.Y.C. Adm. Code)

Changes made by 2014-15 Budget Bills-- The budget legislation closed the so-called "resident trust loophole" by treating resident trusts as grantor trusts for the purposes of calculating New York income tax. This change is effective for income earned **after June 1, 2014**. The change in tax treatment of these trusts causes the trust income to be included in the grantor's taxable income, for purposes of New York personal income computation. (Sec. 11-1712(b)(36), N.Y.C. Adm. Code)

The **2014-2015 budget legislation** also addresses Incomplete Gift Non-grantor Trusts ("ING trusts") which were reputed to be "tax avoidance vehicles." The budget legislation states that the "ING trusts" must be treated as grantor trusts, for New York personal income tax computation purposes. Therefore, the "ING trust" settlor must pay New York personal income tax on the income of the "ING trust." This particular change applies to taxable years beginning on or after January 1, 2014, but does not apply to income from a "ING trust" liquidated before June 1, 2014. (Sec. 11-1712(b)(37), N.Y.C. Adm. Code)

[¶515-220] Persons Subject to NYC Tax--Separate NYC Tax on Ordinary Income Portion of Lump Sum Distributions

The New York City provisions imposing a separate tax on the ordinary income portion of lump sum distributions of qualified pension, profit-sharing, and stock bonus plans are the same as state law. (Sec. 11-1703, N.Y.C. Adm. Code; Sec. 11-1724(a), N.Y.C. Adm. Code).

[¶515-300] NYC Tax Rates--In General

There are two New York City personal income taxes imposed on New York City residents, estates and trusts:

(1) the base tax imposed by Sec. 11-1701, N.Y.C. Adm. Code (see ¶515-301); and

(2) the additional tax surcharge imposed by Sec. 11-1704.1, N.Y.C. Adm. Code, for taxable years beginning after 1990 and before 2024 (see ¶515-315).

• *Minimum income tax (repealed)*

For tax years before 2014, in addition to other taxes, a tax was imposed for each taxable year on the city minimum taxable income of every city resident individual, estate or trust. For details, see ¶515-305.

• *Supplemental tax (expired)*

The tax benefit recapture provisions described below have expired for tax years beginning after 2005. (*TSB-M-06(4)I*)

For taxable years beginning after 2002 and before 2006, as part of the 2003 budget bill, a supplemental tax was imposed for the purpose of recapturing the benefit of the tax tables and eliminating the graduated income tax rates for higher income individuals. The supplemental tax was determined by multiplying the sum of the tax table benefits by their respective fractions, the numerator of which was the lesser of $50,000 or the excess of the taxpayer's New York adjusted gross income for the taxable year over $150,000, and the denominator was $50,000. (Sec. 1304-D, Tax Law; Sec. 11-1701(h), N.Y.C. Adm. Code)

The tax table benefit was the difference between:

(1) the amount of taxable income specified in a taxpayer's tax table that was not subject to the highest or second highest rate of tax for the taxable year, multiplied by such rate; and

(2) the highest or second highest dollar denominated tax set forth in the tax table applicable to the taxable year. (Sec. 1304-D, Tax Law; Sec. 11-1701(h), N.Y.C. Adm. Code)

For taxpayers with adjusted gross income over $500,000, the fraction was one. Provided, however, that the total tax prior to the application of any tax credit could not exceed the highest rate of tax set forth in the tax table multiplied by the taxpayer's taxable income. (Sec. 1304-D, Tax Law; Sec. 11-1701(h), N.Y.C. Adm. Code)

• *Temporary surcharge*

A temporary tax surcharge was imposed on the City taxable income of city residents, estates, and trusts by Sec. 11-1704, N.Y.C. Adm. Code, for taxable years beginning after 1989 and before 1999 (see ¶515-310).

• *Blended tax rates*

For blended tax schedule, which combines the basic tax and surcharges, see ¶515-320.

[¶515-301] NYC Tax Rates--NYC Base Tax

The base tax, imposed by the New York City Administrative Code (Sec. 11-1701(a) and (b), N.Y.C. Adm. Code), is authorized under the Tax Law. (Secs. 1301, and 1304, Tax Law) Rate schedules, broken down by filing status and taxable year, are set forth in the charts below. For the additional tax surcharge imposed on city residents, estates and trusts, see ¶515-315. For blended rate schedules, which combine the basic tax and surcharge, see ¶515-320.

For 2003 through 2005, instead of the regular base tax and additional tax surcharge, special rates applied under Tax Law Sec. 1304-D and N.Y.C. Adm. Code Sec. 11-1701(g); these rates are discussed at ¶515-320.

Resident married individuals filing joint returns and resident surviving spouses

Taxable years beginning after 2016

If the New York City taxable income is:	The tax is:
Not over $21,600	2.7% of the city taxable income
Over $21,600 but not over $45,000	$583 plus 3.3% of excess over $21,600
Over $45,000 but not over $90,000	$1,355 plus 3.35% of excess over $45,000
Over $90,000	$2,863 plus 3.4% of excess over $90,000

Taxable years beginning after 2014 and before 2017

If the New York City taxable income is:	The tax is:
Not over $21,600	2.55% of the city taxable income
Over $21,600 but not over $45,000	$551 plus 3.1% of excess over $21,600
Over $45,000 but not over $90,000	$1,276 plus 3.15% of excess over $45,000
Over $90,000 but not over $500,000	$2,694 plus 3.2% of excess over $90,000
Over $500,000	$16,803 plus 3.4% of excess over $500,000

Taxable years beginning after 2009 and before 2015

If the New York City taxable income is:	The tax is:
Not over $21,600	2.55% of the city taxable income
Over $21,600 but not over $45,000	$551 plus 3.1% of excess over $21,600
Over $45,000 but not over $90,000	$1,276 plus 3.15% of excess over $45,000
Over $90,000 but not over $500,000	$2,694 plus 3.2% of excess over $90,000
Over $500,000	$15,814 plus 3.4% of excess over $500,000

Taxable years beginning in 2001 and 2002 or after 2005 and before 2010

If the New York City taxable income is:	The tax is:
Not over $21,600	2.55% of the city taxable income
Over $21,600 but not over $45,000	$551 plus 3.1% of excess over $21,600
Over $45,000 but not over $90,000	$1,276 plus 3.15% of excess over $45,000
Over $90,000	$2,694 plus 3.2% of excess over $90,000

Taxable years beginning after 2023

If the New York City taxable income is:	The tax is:
Not over $21,600	1.18% of the city taxable income
Over $21,600 but not over $45,000	$255 plus 1.435% of excess over $21,600
Over $45,000 but not over $90,000	$591 plus 1.455% of excess over $45,000
Over $90,000	$1,245 plus 1.48% of excess over $90,000

Resident heads of households

Taxable years beginning after 2016

If the New York City taxable income is:	The tax is:
Not over $14,400	2.7% of the city taxable income
Over $14,400 but not over $30,000	$389 plus 3.3% of excess over $14,400
Over $30,000 but not over $60,000	$904 plus 3.35% of excess over $30,000
Over $60,000	$1,909 plus 3.4% of excess over $60,000

Taxable years beginning after 2014 and before 2017

If the New York City taxable income is:	The tax is:
Not over $14,400	2.55% of the city taxable income
Over $14,400 but not over $30,000	$367 plus 3.1% of excess over $14,400
Over $30,000 but not over $60,000	$851 plus 3.15% of excess over $30,000
Over $60,000 but not over $500,000	$1,796 plus 3.2% of excess over $60,000
Over $500,000	$16,869 plus 3.4% of excess over $500,000

Taxable years beginning after 2009 and before 2015

If the New York City taxable income is:	The tax is:
Not over $14,400	2.55% of the city taxable income
Over $14,400 but not over $30,000	$367 plus 3.1% of excess over $14,400
Over $30,000 but not over $60,000	$851 plus 3.15% of excess over $30,000
Over $60,000 but not over $500,000	$1,796 plus 3.2% of excess over $60,000
Over $500,000	$15,876 plus 3.4% of excess over $500,000

Taxable years beginning in 2001 and 2002 or after 2005 and before 2010

If the New York City taxable income is:	The tax is:
Not over $14,400	2.55% of the city taxable income
Over $14,400 but not over $30,000	$367 plus 3.1% of excess over $14,400
Over $30,000 but not over $60,000	$851 plus 3.15% of excess over $30,000
Over $60,000	$1,796 plus 3.2% of excess over $60,000

Taxable years beginning after 2023

If the New York City taxable income is:	The tax is:
Not over $14,400	1.18% of the city taxable income
Over $14,400 but not over $30,000	$170 plus 1.435% of excess over $14,400
Over $30,000 but not over $60,000	$394 plus 1.455% of excess over $30,000
Over $60,000	$830 plus 1.48% of excess over $60,000

Resident unmarried individuals, resident married individuals filing separate returns and resident estates and trusts

Taxable years beginning after 2016

If the New York City taxable income is:	The tax is:
Not over $12,000	2.7% of the city taxable income
Over $12,000 but not over $25,000	$324 plus 3.3% of excess over $12,000
Over $25,000 but not over $50,000	$753 plus 3.35% of excess over $25,000
Over $50,000	$1,591 plus 3.4% of excess over $50,000

Taxable years beginning after 2014 and before 2017

If the New York City taxable income is:	The tax is:
Not over $12,000	2.55% of the city taxable income
Over $12,000 but not over $25,000	$306 plus 3.1% of excess over $12,000
Over $25,000 but not over $50,000	$709 plus 3.15% of excess over $25,000
Over $50,000 but not over $500,000	$1,497 plus 3.2% of excess over $50,000
Over $500,000	$16,891 plus 3.4% of excess over $500,000

Taxable years beginning after 2009 and before 2015

If the New York City taxable income is:	The tax is:
Not over $12,000	2.55% of the city taxable income
Over $12,000 but not over $25,000	$306 plus 3.1% of excess over $12,000
Over $25,000 but not over $50,000	$709 plus 3.15% of excess over $25,000
Over $50,000 but not over $500,000	$1,497 plus 3.2% of excess over $50,000
Over $500,000	$15,897 plus 3.4% of excess over $500,000

Taxable years beginning in 2001 and 2002 or after 2005 and before 2010

If the New York City taxable income is:	The tax is:
Not over $12,000	2.55% of the city taxable income
Over $12,000 but not over $25,000	$306 plus 3.1% of excess over $12,000
Over $25,000 but not over $50,000	$709 plus 3.15% of excess over $25,000
Over $50,000	$1,497 plus 3.2% of excess over $50,000

Taxable years beginning after 2023

If the New York City taxable income is:	The tax is:
Not over $12,000	1.18% of the city taxable income
Over $12,000 but not over $25,000	$142 plus 1.435% of excess over $12,000
Over $25,000 but not over $50,000	$328 plus 1.455% of excess over $25,000
Over $50,000	$692 plus 1.48% of excess over $50,000

[¶515-315] NYC Tax Rates--Additional NYC Tax Surcharge

In addition to other taxes, city residents, estates and trusts are subject to an additional tax surcharge for taxable years beginning after 1990 and before 2024. (Sec. 1304-B, Tax Law; *TSB-M-06(4)I*; TSB-M-09(3)I)

The surcharge is imposed at the rate of 14% of the city personal income tax. (Sec. 11-1704.1, N.Y.C. Adm. Code)

However, the additional tax surcharge was suspended for tax years 2003 through 2005, during which a temporary rate increase was in effect for certain high-income taxpayers. (Sec. 11-1701, N.Y.C. Adm. Code) For the rates applicable during this period, see ¶515-320.

• *Reduction for 2001*

For the 2001 taxable year, the surcharge was reduced, as described below. (TSB-M-02(1)I)

(1) For resident married individuals filing joint returns and resident surviving spouses, the surcharge is imposed at the rate of 5.25% if the New York City personal income tax is based on city taxable income of $90,000 or less. However, if the tax is based on city taxable income of more than $90,000, then the surcharge equals the sum of 5.25% of the tax on income up to $90,000 and 12.25% of the tax on the excess income. (Sec. 11-1704.1, N.Y.C. Adm. Code) (TSB-M-01(3)I)

(2) For resident heads of households, the surcharge rate is 5.25% if the New York City personal income tax is based on city taxable income of $60,000 or less. However, if the tax is based on city taxable income of more than $60,000, then the surcharge equals the sum of 5.25% of the tax on income up to $60,000 and 12.25% of the tax on the excess income. (Sec. 11-1704.1, N.Y.C. Adm. Code) (TSB-M-01(3)I)

(3) For resident unmarried individuals, resident married individuals filing separate returns, and resident estates and trusts, the surcharge rate is 5.25% if the New York City personal income tax is based on city taxable income of $50,000 or less. However, if the tax is based on city taxable income of more than $50,000, then the surcharge equals the sum of 5.25% of the tax on income up to $50,000 and 12.25% of the tax on the excess income. (Sec. 11-1704.1, N.Y.C. Adm. Code) (TSB-M-01(3)I)

CCH CAUTION: TSB-M-01(2)I and forms no longer applicable.—As a result of New York City Local Law #37, Laws 2001, which amended Sec. 11-1704.1 of the Administrative Code of the City of New York to reduce the additional tax on residents that is imposed under that section applicable to tax years beginning in 2001, the New York City tax rates for 2001 set forth in TSB-M-01(2)I and in the 2001 versions of Forms IT-2105-I (individuals) or IT-2105-I-F (fiduciaries), Instructions for Form IT-2105, are no longer applicable.

• *Blended tax rates*

For blended tax schedule, which combines the basic tax and surcharges, see ¶515-320.

[¶515-320] NYC Tax Rates--Blended NYC Tax Rates

Reflecting both the base tax and the additional tax surcharge, the combined New York City personal income tax rates for tax years 2017, 2018, 2019, and 2020 are as follows (Form IT-2105 Instructions):

Married filing joint returns and qualifying widow(er)s

If the New York City taxable income is:	The tax is:
Not over $21,600	3.078% of NYC taxable income
Over $21,600 but not over $45,000	$665 plus 3.762% of excess over $21,600
Over $45,000 but not over $90,000	$1,545 plus 3.819% of excess over $45,000
Over $90,000	$3,264 plus 3.876% of excess over $90,000

Heads of households

If the New York City taxable income is:	The tax is:
Not over $14,400	3.078% of NYC taxable income
Over $14,400 but not over $30,000	$443 plus 3.762% of excess over $14,400
Over $30,000 but not over $60,000	$1,030 plus 3.819% of excess over $30,000
Over $60,000	$2,176 plus 3.876% of excess over $60,000

Single and married filing separately

If the New York City taxable income is:	The tax is:
Not over $12,000	3.078% of NYC taxable income
Over $12,000 but not over $25,000	$369 plus 3.762% of excess over $12,000
Over $25,000 but not over $50,000	$858 plus 3.819% of excess over $25,000
Over $50,000	$1,813 plus 3.876% of excess over $50,000

Prior to 2015.—Reflecting both the base tax and the additional tax surcharge, the combined New York City personal income tax rates for tax years beginning after 2009 and before 2015 were as follows (TSB-M-10(7)I):

Married filing joint returns and qualifying widow(er)s

If the New York City taxable income is:	The tax is:
Not over $21,600	2.907% of NYC taxable income
Over $21,600 but not over $45,000	$628 plus 3.534% of excess over $21,600
Over $45,000 but not over $90,000	$1,455 plus 3.591% of excess over $45,000
Over $90,000 but not over $500,000	$3,071 plus 3.648% of excess over $90,000
Over $500,000	$18,028 plus 3.876% of excess over $500,000

Heads of households

If the New York City taxable income is:	The tax is:
Not over $14,400	2.907% of NYC taxable income
Over $14,400 but not over $30,000	$419 plus 3.534% of excess over $14,400
Over $30,000 but not over $60,000	$970 plus 3.591% of excess over $30,000
Over $60,000 but not over $500,000	$2,047 plus 3.648% of excess over $60,000
Over $500,000	$18,098 plus 3.876% of excess over $500,000

Single and married filing separately

If the New York City taxable income is:	The tax is:
Not over $12,000	2.907% of NYC taxable income
Over $12,000 but not over $25,000	$349 plus 3.534% of excess over $12,000
Over $25,000 but not over $50,000	$808 plus 3.591% of excess over $25,000
Over $50,000 but not over $500,000	$1,706 plus 3.648% of excess over $50,000
Over $500,000	$18,122 plus 3.876% of excess over $500,000

Prior to 2010.—Reflecting both the base tax and the additional tax surcharge, the combined New York City personal income tax rates for tax years beginning after 2005 were as follows (*TSB-M-06(4)I*; TSB-M-09(3)I):

Married filing joint returns and qualifying widow(er)s

If the New York City taxable income is:	The tax is:
Not over $21,600	2.907% of NYC taxable income
Over $21,600 but not over $45,000	$628 plus 3.534% of excess over $21,600
Over $45,000 but not over $90,000	$1,455 plus 3.591% of excess over $45,000
Over $90,000	$3,071 plus 3.648% of excess over $90,000

Heads of households

If the New York City taxable income is:	The tax is:
Not over $14,400	2.907% of NYC taxable income
Over $14,400 but not over $30,000	$419 plus 3.534% of excess over $14,400
Over $30,000 but not over $60,000	$970 plus 3.591% of excess over $30,000
Over $60,000	$2,047 plus 3.648% of excess over $60,000

Single and married filing separately

If the New York City taxable income is:	The tax is:
Not over $12,000	2.907% of NYC taxable income
Over $12,000 but not over $25,000	$349 plus 3.534% of excess over $12,000
Over $25,000 but not over $50,000	$808 plus 3.591% of excess over $25,000
Over $50,000	$1,706 plus 3.648% of excess over $50,000

2003-2005 (temporary increases).—Under temporary rate increases enacted by the 2003 budget legislation, the following tax rate schedules were used by New York City residents for computing New York City tax: (Sec. 1304-D, Tax Law; Sec. 11-1701(g), N.Y.C. Adm. Code; TSB-M-04(1)I)

Married filing joint returns and qualifying widow(er)s

For taxable years beginning in 2005

If the New York City taxable income is:	The tax is:
Not over $21,600	2.907% of NYC taxable income
Over $21,600 but not over $45,000	$628 plus 3.534% of excess over $21,600
Over $45,000 but not over $90,000	$1,455 plus 3.591% of excess over $45,000
Over $90,000 but not over $150,000	$3,071 plus 3.648% of excess over $90,000
Over $150,000 but not over $500,000	$5,260 plus 4.05% of excess over $150,000
Over $500,000	$19,435 plus 4.45% of excess over $500,000

For taxable years beginning in 2004

If the New York City taxable income is:	The tax is:
Not over $21,600	2.907% of NYC taxable income
Over $21,600 but not over $45,000	$628 plus 3.534% of excess over $21,600
Over $45,000 but not over $90,000	$1,455 plus 3.591% of excess over $45,000
Over $90,000 but not over $150,000	$3,071 plus 3.648% of excess over $90,000
Over $150,000 but not over $500,000	$5,260 plus 4.175% of excess over $150,000
Over $500,000	$19,872 plus 4.45% of excess over $500,000

For taxable years beginning in 2003

If the New York City taxable income is:	The tax is:
Not over $21,600	2.907% of NYC taxable income
Over $21,600 but not over $45,000	$628 plus 3.534% of excess over $21,600
Over $45,000 but not over $90,000	$1,455 plus 3.591% of excess over $45,000
Over $90,000 but not over $150,000	$3,071 plus 3.648% of excess over $90,000
Over $150,000 but not over $500,000	$5,260 plus 4.25% of excess over $150,000
Over $500,000	$20,135 plus 4.45% of excess over $500,000

Heads of households

For taxable years beginning in 2005

If the New York City taxable income is:	The tax is:
Not over $14,400	2.907% of NYC taxable income
Over $14,400 but not over $30,000	$419 plus 3.534% of excess over $14,400
Over $30,000 but not over $60,000	$970 plus 3.591% of excess over $30,000
Over $60,000 but not over $125,000	$2,047 plus 3.648% of excess over $60,000
Over $125,000 but not over $500,000	$4,418 plus 4.05% of excess over $125,000
Over $500,000	$19,605 plus 4.45% of excess over $500,000

For taxable years beginning in 2004

If the New York City taxable income is:	The tax is:
Not over $14,400	2.907% of NYC taxable income
Over $14,400 but not over $30,000	$419 plus 3.534% of excess over $14,400
Over $30,000 but not over $60,000	$970 plus 3.591% of excess over $30,000
Over $60,000 but not over $125,000	$2,047 plus 3.648% of excess over $60,000
Over $125,000 but not over $500,000	$4,418 plus 4.175% of excess over $125,000
Over $500,000	$20,075 plus 4.45% of excess over $500,000

For taxable years beginning in 2003

If the New York City taxable income is:	The tax is:
Not over $14,400	2.907% of NYC taxable income
Over $14,400 but not over $30,000	$419 plus 3.534% of excess over $14,400
Over $30,000 but not over $60,000	$970 plus 3.591% of excess over $30,000
Over $60,000 but not over $125,000	$2,047 plus 3.648% of excess over $60,000

If the New York City taxable income is:	The tax is:
Over $125,000 but not over $500,000	$4,418 plus 4.25% of excess over $125,000
Over $500,000	$20,356 plus 4.45% of excess over $500,000

Single and married filing separately

For taxable years beginning in 2005

If the New York City taxable income is:	The tax is:
Not over $12,000	2.907% of NYC taxable income
Over $12,000 but not over $25,000	$349 plus 3.534% of excess over $12,000
Over $25,000 but not over $50,000	$808 plus 3.591% of excess over $25,000
Over $50,000 but not over $100,000	$1,706 plus 3.648% of excess over $50,000
Over $100,000 but not over $500,000	$3,530 plus 4.05% of excess over $100,000
Over $500,000	$19,730 plus 4.45% of excess over $500,000

For taxable years beginning in 2004

If the New York City taxable income is:	The tax is:
Not over $12,000	2.907% of NYC taxable income
Over $12,000 but not over $25,000	$349 plus 3.534% of excess over $12,000
Over $25,000 but not over $50,000	$808 plus 3.591% of excess over $25,000
Over $50,000 but not over $100,000	$1,706 plus 3.648% of excess over $50,000
Over $100,000 but not over $500,000	$3,530 plus 4.175% of excess over $100,000
Over $500,000	$20,230 plus 4.45% of excess over $500,000

For taxable years beginning in 2003

If the New York City taxable income is:	The tax is:
Not over $12,000	2.907% of NYC taxable income
Over $12,000 but not over $25,000	$349 plus 3.534% of excess over $12,000
Over $25,000 but not over $50,000	$808 plus 3.591% of excess over $25,000
Over $50,000 but not over $100,000	$1,706 plus 3.648% of excess over $50,000
Over $100,000 but not over $500,000	$3,530 plus 4.25% of excess over $100,000
Over $500,000	$20,530 plus 4.45% of excess over $500,000

Tax table benefit recapture (expired)—For taxable years beginning after 2002 and before 2006, as part of the 2003 budget bill, a supplemental tax was also imposed for the purpose of recapturing the benefit of the tax tables and eliminating the graduated income tax rates for higher income individuals. These provisions, which have expired for tax years beginning after 2005, are discussed in more detail at ¶515-300.

Prior years—For the **2002 tax year**, the New York City 2002 combined tax rate schedules are as follows (TSB-M-02(1)I):

Married filing joint returns and qualifying widow(er)s

If the New York City taxable income is:	The tax is:
Not over $21,600	2.907% of NYC taxable income
Over $21,600 but not over $45,000	$628 plus 3.534% of excess over $21,600
Over $45,000 but not over $90,000	$1,455 plus 3.591% of excess over $45,000
Over $90,000	$3,071 plus 3.648% of excess over $90,000

Heads of households

If the New York City taxable income is:	The tax is:
Not over $14,400	2.907% of NYC taxable income
Over $14,400 but not over $30,000	$419 plus 3.534% of excess over $14,400
Over $30,000 but not over $60,000	$970 plus 3.591% of excess over $30,000
Over $60,000	$2,047 plus 3.648% of excess over $60,000

Single and married filing separately

If the New York City taxable income is:	The tax is:
Not over $12,000	2.907% of NYC taxable income
Over $12,000 but not over $25,000	$349 plus 3.534% of excess over $12,000
Over $25,000 but not over $50,000	$808 plus 3.591% of excess over $25,000
Over $50,000	$1,706 plus 3.648% of excess over $50,000

For the **2001 tax year**, based on a reduction in the New York City additional tax surcharge (see ¶515-315), the New York City 2001 combined tax rate schedules are as follows (TSB-M-01(3)I):

CCH CAUTION: TSB-M-01(2)I and forms no longer applicable.—As a result of New York City Local Law #37, Laws 2001, which amended Sec. 11-1704.1 of the Administrative Code of the City of New York to reduce the additional tax on residents that is imposed under that section applicable to tax years beginning in

¶515-320

2001, the New York City tax rates for 2001 set forth in TSB-M-01(2)I and in the 2001 versions of Forms IT-2105-I (individuals) or IT-2105-I-F (fiduciaries), Instructions for Form IT-2105, are no longer applicable.

Married filing joint returns and qualifying widow(er)s

If the New York City taxable income is:	The tax is:
Not over $21,600	2.683875% of NYC taxable income
Over $21,600 but not over $45,000	$580 plus 3.26275% of excess over $21,600
Over $45,000 but not over $90,000	$1,343 plus 3.315375% of excess over $45,000
Over $90,000	$2,835 plus 3.592% of excess over $90,000

Heads of households

If the New York City taxable income is:	The tax is:
Not over $14,400	2.683875% of NYC taxable income
Over $14,400 but not over $30,000	$386 plus 3.26275% of excess over $14,400
Over $30,000 but not over $60,000	$895 plus 3.315375% of excess over $30,000
Over $60,000	$1,890 plus 3.592% of excess over $60,000

Single and married filing separately

If the New York City taxable income is:	The tax is:
Not over $12,000	2.683875% of NYC taxable income
Over $12,000 but not over $25,000	$322 plus 3.26275% of excess over $12,000
Over $25,000 but not over $50,000	$746 plus 3.315375% of excess over $25,000
Over $50,000	$1,575 plus 3.592% of excess over $50,000

For the **2000 tax year**, the following table is used by City residents in computing City personal income tax liability:

Married filing joint returns and qualifying widow(er)s

If the New York City taxable income is:	The tax is:
Not over $21,600	3.021% of NYC taxable income
Over $21,600 but not over $45,000	$653 plus 3.6651% of excess over $21,600
Over $45,000 but not over $90,000	$1,511 plus 3.7221% of excess over $45,000
Over $90,000	$3,186 plus 3.7791% of excess over $90,000

Heads of households

If the New York City taxable income is:	The tax is:
Not over $14,400	3.021% of NYC taxable income
Over $14,400 but not over $30,000	$435 plus 3.6651% of excess over $14,400
Over $30,000 but not over $60,000	$1,007 plus 3.7221% of excess over $30,000
Over $60,000	$2,124 plus 3.7791% of excess over $60,000

Single and married filing separately

If the New York City taxable income is:	The tax is:
Not over $12,000	3.021% of NYC taxable income
Over $12,000 but not over $25,000	$363 plus 3.6651% of excess over $12,000
Over $25,000 but not over $50,000	$839 plus 3.7221% of excess over $25,000
Over $50,000	$1,770 plus 3.7791% of excess over $50,000

For the **1999 tax year**, the following table is used by City residents in computing City personal income tax liability:

Married filing joint returns and qualifying widow(er)s

If the New York City taxable income is:	The tax is:
Not over $21,600	3.0495% of NYC taxable income
Over $21,600 but not over $45,000	$659 plus 3.7136% of excess over $21,600
Over $45,000 but not over $90,000	$1,528 plus 3.7706% of excess over $45,000
Over $90,000	$3,225 plus 3.8276% of excess over $90,000

Heads of households

If the New York City taxable income is:	The tax is:
Not over $14,400	3.0495% of NYC taxable income
Over $14,400 but not over $30,000	$439 plus 3.7136% of excess over $14,400
Over $30,000 but not over $60,000	$1,018 plus 3.7706% of excess over $30,000
Over $60,000	$2,149 plus 3.8276% of excess over $60,000

Single and married filing separately

If the New York City taxable income is:	The tax is:
Not over $12,000	3.0495% of NYC taxable income
Over $12,000 but not over $25,000	$366 plus 3.7136% of excess over $12,000

If the New York City taxable income is:	The tax is:
Over $25,000 but not over $50,000	$849 plus 3.7706% of excess over $25,000
Over $50,000	$1,792 plus 3.8276% of excess over $50,000

For the **1997 and 1998 tax years**, the following table is used by City residents in computing City personal income tax liability:

Married filing joint returns and qualifying widow(er)s

If the New York City taxable income is:	The tax is:
Not over $14,400	3.08% of NYC taxable income
Over $14,400 but not over $21,600	$444 plus 3.66% of excess over $14,400
Over $21,600 but not over $27,000	$708 plus 4.34% of excess over $21,600
Over $27,000 but not over $45,000	$942 plus 4.39% of excess over $27,000
Over $45,000 but not over $90,000	$1,732 plus 4.40% of excess over $45,000
Over $90,000	$3,712 plus 4.46% of excess over $90,000

Heads of households

If the New York City taxable income is:	The tax is:
Not over $7,350	3.08% of NYC taxable income
Over $7,350 but not over $9,200	$226 plus 3.56% of excess over $7,350
Over $9,200 but not over $14,400	$292 plus 3.66% of excess over $9,200
Over $14,400 but not over $17,250	$482 plus 4.34% of excess over $14,400
Over $17,250 but not over $28,750	$606 plus 4.39% of excess over $17,250
Over $28,750 but not over $30,000	$1,111 plus 4.34% of excess over $28,750
Over $30,000 but not over $60,000	$1,165 plus 4.40% of excess over $30,000
Over $60,000	$2,485 plus 4.46% of excess over $60,000

Single and married filing separately

If the New York City taxable income is:	The tax is:
Not over $8,400	3.08% of NYC taxable income
Over $8,400 but not over $12,000	$259 plus 3.66% of excess over $8,400
Over $12,000 but not over $15,000	$391 plus 4.34% of excess over $12,000
Over $15,000 but not over $25,000	$521 plus 4.39% of excess over $15,000
Over $25,000 but not over $50,000	$960 plus 4.40% of excess over $25,000
Over $50,000	$2,060 plus 4.46% of excess over $50,000

For the 1996 tax year, the following table is used by City residents in computing City personal income tax liability:

Married filing joint returns and qualifying widow(er)s

If the New York City taxable income is:	The tax is:
Not over $14,400	2.96% of taxable income
Over $14,400 but not over $27,000	$426 plus 4.00% of excess over $14,400
Over $27,000 but not over $45,000	$930 plus 4.39% of excess over $27,000
Over $45,000 but not over $108,000	$1,720 plus 4.40% of excess over $45,000
Over $108,000	$4,492 plus 4.46% of excess over $108,000

Heads of households

If the New York City taxable income is:	The tax is:
Not over $7,350	2.96% of taxable income
Over $7,350 but not over $9,200	$218 plus 3.44% of excess over $7,350
Over $9,200 but not over $9,600	$282 plus 3.55% of excess over $9,200
Over $9,600 but not over $17,250	$296 plus 4.00% of excess over $9,600
Over $17,250 but not over $18,000	$602 plus 4.05% of excess over $17,250
Over $18,000 but not over $28,750	$632 plus 4.39% of excess over $18,000
Over $28,750 but not over $30,000	$1,104 plus 4.34% of excess over $28,750
Over $30,000 but not over $72,000	$1,158 plus 4.40% of excess over $30,000
Over $72,000	$3,006 plus 4.46% of excess over $72,000

Single and married filing separately

If the New York City taxable income is:	The tax is:
Not over $8,000	2.96% of taxable income
Over $8,000 but not over $8,400	$237 plus 3.42% of excess over $8,000
Over $8,400 but not over $15,000	$251 plus 4.00% of excess over $8,400
Over $15,000 but not over $25,000	$515 plus 4.39% of excess over $15,000
Over $25,000 but not over $60,000	$954 plus 4.40% of excess over $25,000
Over $60,000	$2,494 plus 4.46% of excess over $60,000

¶515-320

For the 1995 tax year, the following table is used by City residents in computing City personal income tax liability:

Married filing joint returns and qualifying widow(er)s

If the New York City taxable income is:	The tax is:
Not over $14,400	2.57% of the New York taxable income
Over $14,400 but not over $27,000	$370 plus 3.83% of excess over $14,400
Over $27,000 but not over $45,000	$853 plus 4.39% of excess over $27,000
Over $45,000 but not over $108,000	$1,643 plus 4.40% of excess over $45,000
Over $108,000	$4,415 plus 4.46% of excess over $108,000

Heads of households

If the New York City taxable income is:	The tax is:
Not over $7,350	2.57% of the New York taxable income
Over $7,350 but not over $9,200	$189 plus 3.04% of excess over $7,350
Over $9,200 but not over $17,250	$245 plus 3.83% of excess over $9,200
Over $17,250 but not over $28,750	$553 plus 4.39% of excess over $17,250
Over $28,750 but not over $69,000	$1,058 plus 4.40% of excess over $28,750
Over $69,000	$2,869 plus 4.46% of excess over $69,000

Single and married filing separately

If the New York City taxable income is:	The tax is:
Not over $8,000	2.57% of the New York taxable income
Over $8,000 but not over $8,400	$206 plus 3.25% of excess over $8,000
Over $8,400 but not over $15,000	$219 plus 3.83% of excess over $8,400
Over $15,000 but not over $25,000	$472 plus 4.39% of excess over $15,000
Over $25,000 but not over $60,000	$911 plus 4.40% of excess over $25,000
Over $60,000	$2,451 plus 4.46% of excess over $60,000

[¶515-400]
NYC PERSONAL INCOME TAX COMPUTATION

[¶515-405] NYC Personal Income Tax Computation--In General

The New York City provisions relating to the computation of income are, for the most part, the same as state law.

The New York City Administrative Code provisions are:

Section Paragraph

11-1711 City taxable income of a city resident individual . . . .

11-1712 City adjusted gross income of a city resident individual . . . .

11-1713 City deduction of a resident individual . . . .

11-1714 City standard deduction of a city resident individual . . . .

11-1715 City itemized deduction of a city resident individual . . . .

11-1716 City exemptions of a city resident individual . . . .

11-1718 City taxable income of a resident estate or trust . . . .

11-1719 Share of a resident estate, trust, or beneficiary in city fiduciary adjustment . . . .

11-1722 City minimum taxable income of a city resident individual . . . .

For computation of income for state purposes, see ¶ 15-505 and following.

• *Itemized deduction limit for high-income taxpayers*

Under the 2010 budget legislation (as extended by the 2013, 2015, 2017, and 2019 budget bills), for tax years 2010 through 2024, provisions limit the amount of the New York itemized deduction allowed for an individual whose New York adjusted gross income exceeds $10 million to 25% of the individual's federal itemized deduction for charitable contributions. No other federal itemized deductions of the individual will be allowed for New York purposes. (Sec. 11-1715(g), NYC Adm. Code; TSB-M-19(4)I)

The 2010 law contained provisions allowing New York City to elect not to have the state itemized deduction limitation apply when computing the New York City resident tax. A memorandum noted that, if the City did make the election, additional guidance would be issued by the New York Department of Taxation and Finance. (TSB-M-10(8)I)

See also TSB-M-09(11)I regarding the limit for individuals having New York adjusted gross income exceeding $1 million.

For additional discussion, see ¶ 15-545 in the New York State Tax Reporter.

[¶516-400]

NYC CREDITS AGAINST TAX

[¶516-405] NYC Credits Against Personal Income Tax

Various New York City personal income tax credits are available, as discussed below.

• *Earned income tax credit*

New York City provides for a New York City personal income tax credit equal to 5% of the earned income credit allowed under IRC Sec. 32. The credit is available for taxable years beginning after 2003. (Sec. 11-1706(d)(1), N.Y.C. Adm. Code; Sec. 1310(f)(1), Tax Law; TSB-M-04(6)I)

Change of status.—If a taxpayer changes his or her status during the taxable year from City resident to City nonresident, or from City nonresident to City resident, the credit is limited to the amount determined by multiplying the amount of such credit by a fraction. The numerator is the taxpayer's City adjusted gross income for the period of residence, and the denominator is such taxpayer's City adjusted gross income determined as if he or she were a City resident for the entire taxable year. (Sec. 11-1706(d)(3), N.Y.C. Adm. Code; Sec. 1310(f)(3), Tax Law)

Husband and wife.—In the case of a husband and wife who file a joint return, but who are required to determine their City personal income taxes separately, the credit may be applied against the tax of either or divided between them as they may elect. In the case of a husband and wife who are not required to file a federal return, the credit is allowed only if such taxpayers file a joint City personal income tax return. (Sec. 11-1706(d)(4), N.Y.C. Adm. Code; Sec. 1310(f)(4), Tax Law)

• *Unincorporated business income tax credit*

New York City provides for a credit against City personal income tax for a portion of the New York City unincorporated business income tax (see ¶519-005) paid by a City resident. (Sec. 11-1706(c), N.Y.C. Adm. Code) A New York City resident may be eligible for a credit of up to 100% of New York City unincorporated business income tax paid by an unincorporated business conducted by the resident and/or the proportionate share of the tax paid (after adding back the partnership credits under Sec. 11-503(j) and (m), Tax Law) by a partnership in which the city resident is a partner, as calculated under a formula. If the resident's City taxable income is $42,000 or less, the amount of the credit is 100% of the tax paid. If City taxable income is more than $42,000 but less than $142,000, the credit percentage is calculated as follows: subtract from 100% a percentage determined by subtracting $42,000 from City taxable income, dividing the result by $100,000, and multiplying by 77%. For income of $142,000 or more, the credit is 23%. (Sec. 11-1706(c), N.Y.C. Adm. Code)

For taxable years beginning before 2007, if the resident's City taxable income was $42,000 or less, the amount of the credit was 65% of the tax paid. For each increment of $200 between $42,001 and $142,000, the percentage was reduced by $1/10$ of a percentage point. For income above $142,000 the credit was 15%. (Sec. 11-1706(c), N.Y.C. Adm. Code)

The City is authorized to increase the credit in future years, but may not reduce it.

• *Credit for GCT paid by S corporation*

For taxable years beginning on or after January 1, 2014, and before July 1, 2019, a credit is allowed to a city resident individual, estate, or trust for certain general corporation tax payments made by a New York S corporation or an exempt QSSS. (Sec. 11-1706(f), N.Y.C. Adm. Code)

If city taxable income is $35,000 or less, the credit is 100% of the applicable pro rata amount of tax paid. If city taxable income is more than $35,000 but less than $100,000, the credit percentage is calculated as follows: subtract from 100% a percentage determined by subtracting $35,000 from city taxable income, dividing the result by $65,000, and multiplying by 100%. If city taxable income is $100,000 or more, no credit is allowed. (Sec. 11-1706(f), N.Y.C. Adm. Code)

In addition, a formula is provided for calculating the credit for any taxable year that encompasses days occurring after June 30, 2019. (Sec. 11-1706(f), N.Y.C. Adm. Code)

No credit will be allowed for any amount of general corporation tax imposed on a combined group of corporations including a New York S corporation or an exempt QSSS, except where the combined group consists exclusively of one or more New York S corporations and one or more exempt QSSSs of such corporations, provided that each of the New York S corporations included in the group is wholly owned by the same interests and in the same proportions as each other New York S corporation included in the group. (Sec. 11-1706(f), N.Y.C. Adm. Code)

• *Credit for trust distribution*

New York City provides a credit against tax to a trust beneficiary receiving an accumulation distribution. (Sec. 11-1721, N.Y.C. Adm. Code) The City credit parallels state law (Sec. 11-1706(f), N.Y.C. Adm. Code).

New York City also allows as a credit the amount of taxes withheld from wages.

The **2014-15 budget legislation** allows a personal income tax credit for trust beneficiaries for income tax imposed on the trust for the taxable year or any prior taxable year by another state, political subdivision, or the District of Columbia, upon income both derived from and subject to New York personal income tax. The credit applies to taxable years beginning on or after January 1, 2014. (Sec. 621(b), Tax Law)

• *Credit relating to net capital gain*

A credit is allowed equal to $1/2$ of 1% of net capital gain includable in city adjusted gross income for the taxable year. (Sec. 11-1706(a), N.Y.C. Adm. Code) The credit may not exceed the amount of the tax, reduced by the credit for a trust beneficiary receiving an accumulation distribution and the household credit.

• *State school tax reduction credit*

Under the 2016 budget legislation, the New York City school tax relief credit (Sec. 1310(e), Tax Law; Sec. 11-1706(c), N.Y.C. Adm. Code) is converted into a New York State personal income tax credit for residents of New York City. (Sec. 606(ggg), Tax Law)

The credit available to married individuals filing joint returns and surviving spouses is $125. For all other taxpayers, the credit is $62.50.

Limitation based on income.—The credit is not available to taxpayers having income of more than $250,000.

Rate reduction credit.—Under the 2017 budget, for taxable years beginning after 2016, a rate reduction credit is also allowed to New York City taxpayers having income not exceeding $500,000. (Sec. 606(ggg)(4-b), Tax Law; Important Notice N-17-5)

For married filing jointly taxpayers with NYC taxable income of $21,600 or less, the credit is 0.171% of city taxable income. If NYC taxable income is over $21,600 (but not over $500,000), the credit is $37 plus 0.228% of the excess over $21,600.

For head of household taxpayers with NYC taxable income of $14,400 or less, the credit is 0.171% of city taxable income. If NYC taxable income is over $14,400 (but not over $500,000), the credit is $25 plus 0.228% of the excess over $14,400.

For single or married filing separate taxpayers with NYC taxable income of $12,000 or less, the credit is 0.171% of city taxable income. If NYC taxable income is over $12,000 (but not over $500,000), the credit is $21 plus 0.228% of the excess over $12,000.

• *Household credit*

This credit was amended, for taxable years beginning on or after January 1, 2007, for families with gross household incomes under $30,000 per year who pay child care expenses for children under age four. The credit can be worth up to $1,000 and will be combined with the already existing state and federal child care tax credits. Families who qualify for the credit, but do not file taxes because they have no income, would receive a $1,000 refund check instead. (Sec. 11-1706(e), N.Y.C. Adm. Code)

For an individual who is not married nor the head of a household nor a surviving spouse, a household credit will be allowed, to be determined according to the following table (Sec. 11-1706(b), N.Y.C. Adm. Code):

For taxable years beginning:	The credit shall be:
in 1998	$ 12
in 1999	$ 30
in 2000	$ 45
in 2001-2005	$ 62.50
after 2005	$ 115

For any husband and wife, head of household or surviving spouse, a household credit will be allowed, to be determined by multiplying the number of exemptions for which the taxpayer is entitled to a deduction for the taxable year as specified below:

For taxable years beginning:	The credit shall be:
in 1998	$ 12
in 1999	$ 35
in 2000	$ 85
in 2001-2005	$ 125
after 2005	$ 230

If a taxpayer changes his status during the taxable year from resident to nonresident, or from nonresident to resident, the household credit will be prorated according to the number of months in the period of residence.

The amount of the credit may not exceed the amount of the tax, reduced by the credit for a trust beneficiary receiving an accumulation distribution.

• *College tuition*

A credit or deduction against New York City personal income tax is phased in for allowable college tuition expenses, up to $10,000 annually for each student. This parallels to the New York state personal income tax credit or deduction.

Allowable college tuition expenses.—Allowable college tuition expenses are the amount of qualified college tuition expenses of eligible students paid by the taxpayer during the taxable year, limited to $10,000 for each student. (Sec. 11-1715(d)(4), N.Y.C. Adm. Code)

Amount of credit.—The amount of the credit is the allowable college tuition expenses, multiplied by the applicable percentage.

The phase-in percentages are as follows:

— After 2003, 100% of such expenses are allowable.

— In 2003, 75% of such expenses were allowable.

— In 2002, 50% of such expenses were allowable.

— In 2001, 25% of such expenses were allowable.

However, no deduction is allowed to a taxpayer who claims the New York state credit or deduction under Sec. 606(t), Tax Law. (Sec. 11-1715(d)(4), N.Y.C. Adm. Code)

[¶516-600]

NYC PERSONAL INCOME TAX WITHHOLDING

[¶516-605] NYC Personal Income Tax Withholding--In General

The New York City provisions relating to the withholding of tax (Sec. 11-1771, N.Y.C. Adm. Code — Sec. 11-1778, N.Y.C. Adm. Code) parallel state law. See ¶16-605 and following.

In view of the joint administration of the state and city taxes, combined New York State and City of New York withholding tax returns are filed with the Commissioner of Taxation and Finance together with payment. The aggregate amount of state and city tax withheld determines whether returns and payment are required quarter-monthly, semimonthly, monthly, semiannually or annually. (Reg. Sec. 291.1; Reg. Sec. 291.2)

Withholding tables are discussed at ¶516-610.

• *Supplemental wages*

The New York City treatment of supplemental wages is covered in Reg. Sec. 291.1(b).

[¶516-610] NYC Withholding Tables

The current New York City withholding tax tables and methods are provided in NYS-50-T-NYC.

Previous withholding publications.—Prior to May 1, 2011, the New York City withholding tables and methods were provided in Publication NYS-50-T.

However, because of a rate increase enacted in 2010 for high income taxpayers, certain parts of NYS-50-T were revised for payrolls made on or after September 1, 2010. The updated information was contained in the following versions of Publication NYS-50-T.2:

Publication NYS-50-T.2, *Revised New York City Withholding Tax Computation Rules* (effective January 1, 2011).

Publication NYS-50-T.2, *Revised New York City Withholding Tax Computation Rules* (effective September 1, 2010).

Additional information concerning New York State and Yonkers was provided in Publication NYS-50-T.1, *Revised New York State and Yonkers Withholding Tax Computation Rules* (effective January 1, 2010).

NEW YORK CITY UNINCORPORATED BUSINESS TAX

[¶519-001]
NYC UNINCORPORATED BUSINESS TAX

[¶519-005] NYC Unincorporated Business Tax—In General

The unincorporated business tax is imposed upon unincorporated business taxable income allocated to New York City, at the rate of 4%. (Sec. 11-503(a), N.Y.C. Adm. Code)

[¶519-100]
NYC UNINCORPORATED BUSINESS TAXPAYERS AND RATES

[¶519-105] NYC Unincorporated Business Taxpayers and Rates--In General

The New York City unincorporated business tax is levied on any individual or unincorporated entity (including a partnership, fiduciary or corporation in liquidation) engaged in any trade, business, profession or occupation wholly or partly carried on within New York City. (Sec. 11-503(a), N.Y.C. Adm. Code) There is also a credit against New York City personal income tax for unincorporated business income tax paid. See ¶516-405.

For the statutory definition of "unincorporated business," see ¶519-110.

For rate of tax, see ¶519-120.

[¶519-110] Unincorporated Business Taxpayers Subject to NYC Tax

An unincorporated business is any trade, business, profession or occupation conducted, engaged in or being liquidated by an individual or unincorporated entity, including a partnership or fiduciary or a corporation in liquidation. (Sec. 11-502(a), N.Y.C. Adm. Code) Except as noted below, entities subject to the New York City business tax on corporations are excluded from the definition of unincorporated business, as are insurance businesses that are members of the New York Insurance Exchange.

For taxable years beginning after 2001, the law specifically provides that the term "unincorporated entity" includes an entity classified as a partnership for federal income tax purposes, regardless of whether the entity is formed as a corporation, joint-stock company, joint-stock association, body corporate, or body politic, or whether the entity is organized under a federal or state statute, or under a statute of a federally recognized Indian tribe, or under a statute of a country other than the United States that describes or refers to the entity as incorporated. (Sec. 11-501(m), N.Y.C. Adm. Code) Thus, an entity classified as a partnership for federal income tax purposes will be subject to the unincorporated business tax, rather than the general corporation tax, even if it is incorporated. (*Finance Memorandum 02-4*)

Unincorporated associations subject to City general corporation tax: Generally, businesses subject to the New York City general corporation tax are excluded from the City unincorporated business tax (Sec. 11-502(a), N.Y.C. Adm. Code).

Effective January 1, 1996, the definition of "corporation" for general corporation tax purposes was amended to include unincorporated associations that are classified as corporations pursuant to IRC Sec. 7701(a)(3) (including limited liability companies that are so classified) and publicly-traded partnerships that are treated as corporations for federal tax purposes pursuant to IRC Sec. 7704. (Sec. 11-602(1), N.Y.C. Adm. Code) However, unincorporated organizations that would be treated as a corporation under this new definition, but were subject to City unincorporated business tax for their 1995 taxable year, may make a one-time election to remain subject to the City unincorporated business tax for taxable years beginning 1996 and thereafter. The election, once made, will remain in effect until revoked by the unincorporated organization.

Vendors of utility services: Generally, an unincorporated business subject to the New York City tax on vendors of utility services is taxable for New York City unincorporated business tax purposes on the percentage of its net income allocable to the city and not attributable to receipts taxed as a vendor of utility services. (Sec. 11-502(a), N.Y.C. Adm. Code)

Generally, an unincorporated entity will be treated as carrying on any business activity in whole or in part in the City by any other unincorporated entity in which the first entity owns an interest. However, the ownership by an unincorporated entity of an interest in another unincorporated entity *not* carrying on any business activity in whole or in part in New York City will not be considered the conduct of an unincorporated business in the City. (Sec. 11-502(a), N.Y.C. Adm. Code)

Caution: The foregoing sentence is not intended to preclude the taxation, where appropriate, of an entity that provides services in whole or in part in New York City to another unincorporated entity located outside the City, nor is it intended to preclude an unincorporated entity from being treated as engaged in an unincorporated business in whole or in part in the City, where appropriate, by reason of activities carried on in the City on its behalf by a partner. (Legislative Memo in Support of Ch. 128, Laws 1996)

For taxable years beginning on or after August 1, 2002, an unincorporated business that is a partner in a partnership subject to tax under a local law imposing a tax on utilities, as defined in Sec. 11-1101(6), N.Y.C. Adm. Code, is not considered to be carrying on the trade, business, profession, or occupation carried on by the partnership. (Sec. 11-502(a), N.Y.C. Adm. Code)

• *Entities carrying on two or more businesses*

If an individual or unincorporated entity carries on in whole or in part two or more businesses in New York City, all of the businesses will be treated as a single business. (Sec. 11-502(a), N.Y.C. Adm. Code)

• *Services as employee*

The performance of services by an individual as an employee or as an officer or director of a corporation, society, association, or political entity, or as a fiduciary, is not deemed to be an unincorporated business, unless such services constitute part of a business regularly carried on by the individual. (Sec. 11-502(b), N.Y.C. Adm. Code)

Real estate salespeople.—The Department of Finance has issued a statement of audit procedure discussing the proper classification of real estate salespeople as employees or independent contractors. (Statement of Audit Procedure UBT-2009-1rev)

• *Purchases and sales of property for own account*

Individuals or other unincorporated entities (other than dealers) will not be deemed to be engaged in an unincorporated business solely by reason of:

(1) the purchase, holding and sale of property or the entry into, assumption, offset, assignment, or other termination of a position in property, or both, for their own accounts;

(2) the acquisition, holding or disposition, other than in the ordinary course of a trade or business, of interests in an unincorporated entity that itself qualifies for the self-trading exemption; or

(3) any combination of the activities described in paragraphs (1) and (2) and any other activity not otherwise constituting the conduct of an unincorporated business. (Sec. 11-502(c), N.Y.C. Adm. Code)

The term "dealer" means an individual or unincorporated entity that (1) holds or disposes of property that is stock in trade of the taxpayer, inventory or is otherwise held for sale to customers in the ordinary course of the taxpayer's trade or business, or (2) regularly offers to enter into, assume, offset, assign or otherwise terminate positions in property with customers in the ordinary course of the taxpayer's trade or business. (Sec. 11-501(l), N.Y.C. Adm. Code) An individual or unincorporated entity will not be treated as a dealer based solely on its ownership of an interest in an entity that is a dealer, nor will an unincorporated entity be treated as a dealer based solely on the ownership by a dealer of an interest in that unincorporated entity.

The term "property" includes stocks and securities as well as notional principal contracts, foreign currencies, publicly-traded commodities and derivative financial instruments (including options, forward or future contracts, and other instruments) in property. (Sec. 11-502(c), N.Y.C. Adm. Code) Certain securities not qualifying as "investment capital," as defined in the rules governing the definition of investment capital for City general corporation tax purposes (see ¶505-460), are excluded, as are all interests in unincorporated entities. Property and positions in property held by dealers in such property or positions in property, respectively, are also excluded.

The receipt by an individual or other unincorporated entity of $25,000 or less of gross receipts during a taxable year (determined without regard to any deductions) from an unincorporated business wholly or partly carried on within New York City by such individual or unincorporated entity will not cause the individual or other unincorporated entity to be treated as not engaged solely in exempt activities.

Investors: If an unincorporated entity is "primarily engaged" in activities qualifying for the self-trading exemption and/or the acquisition, holding or disposition of interests, as an investor, in unincorporated entities carrying on any unincorporated business in the City, the self-trading activities of the taxpayer (including those of a "primarily engaged" entity in which the taxpayer owns an interest that are attributed to the taxpayer), will not be subject to unincorporated business income tax.

An unincorporated entity that qualifies for this partial exemption may exclude from its unincorporated business gross income any income and gains from activity qualifying for the self-trading exemption, including income with respect to securities loans, and other substantially similar income and gains from ordinary and routine trading and investment activity to the extent determined by the Commissioner of Finance. (Sec. 11-506(c)(10), N.Y.C. Adm. Code)

An unincorporated entity will be considered to be "primarily engaged" in the designated activities if at least 90% of the gross value of its assets is represented by assets qualifying for the self-trading exemption, interests in unincorporated entities not carrying on any unincorporated business in the City, or investments in unincorporated entities carrying on any unincorporated business in the City held by the taxpayer as an investor. In determining whether a taxpayer meets the above test, the average gross value of the assets over the year will be taken into account under rules patterned after those applicable to the New York City General Corporation Tax. The Commissioner of Finance is, however, given discretion to use net values or to exclude assets if he or she deems it necessary to properly reflect the primary activities of the taxpayer. In addition, if a taxpayer holds securities purchased on margin or securities hedged by offsetting positions, the Commissioner may use net values in applying the 90% test.

A taxpayer will be treated as owning an interest in an unincorporated entity as an investor if it is not a general partner, is not authorized by the entity's governing instrument to manage or participate in the day-to-day business of the entity, and is not actually managing or participating in the entity's day-to-day business. A taxpayer can also qualify as an investor in an unincorporated entity, regardless of the taxpayer's involvement in management or status as a general partner, if the unincorporated entity itself meets the 90% test, and the taxpayer does not receive a distributive share of the entity's income, gain, loss, deduction, credit and basis from a business carried on in whole or in part in New York City that is materially greater than its distributive share of any other item of income, gain, loss deduction, credit or basis of the entity.

• *Holding, leasing and managing property*

An owner of real property or lessee or fiduciary (except a dealer holding real property primarily for sale to customers in the ordinary course of his or her trade or business) who is carrying on an unincorporated business in whole or in part in New York City (whether or not such business is carried on at or is connected with the property), will not be deemed to be an unincorporated business as a result of the holding, leasing or managing of real property, if, and only to the extent that, the property is held, leased or managed for the purpose of producing rental income or gain upon the property's sale or other disposition. (Sec. 11-502(d), N.Y.C. Adm. Code)

The conduct by the owner, lessee or fiduciary, at the property, of a trade, business, profession or occupation will be deemed to be an incident to the holding, leasing or managing of the property and will not be deemed to be the conduct of an unincorporated business, provided the trade, business, profession or occupation is conducted solely for the benefit of tenants at such real property, as an incidental service to such tenants, and is not open or available to the general public.

Garage, parking or storage services provided to tenants: Generally, where an owner, lessee or fiduciary holds, leases or manages real property and operates at the property a garage, parking lot or other similar facility that is open or available to the general public, the operation of the garage, parking lot or other facility will be considered an unincorporated business subject to tax. However, for taxable years beginning after 1995, the provision by any such owner, lessee or fiduciary of parking, garaging or motor vehicle storage service on a monthly or longer term basis at the facility to tenants in the building as an incidental service to the tenants will *not* be deemed an unincorporated business, even if the garage is open or available to the public. As a result, the income from such tenants received for monthly or longer termparking, garaging or storage service will not be subject to tax, while the income received from monthly or longer term parking service for nontenants and from all other parking, garaging or storage service provided to tenants and nontenants will be subject to tax. Losses and expenses of the garage or parking operation will not be deductible for unincorporated tax purposes to the extent directly or indirectly attributable to the building tenants that are monthly or longer-term parkers.

Taxpayers claiming the partial exemption for parking income from tenants must attach to their unincorporated business tax return such information with regard to the provision of monthly or longer term parking, garaging, or storage services to tenants as the Commissioner of Finance may require. If a taxpayer's UBT return omits in any material respect the required information relating to parking services provided to tenants at a garage, parking lot or similar facility, the provision of all parking, garaging and storage services to tenants at that facility will be taxable as an unincorporated business.

- *Sales representative*

An individual, other than one who maintains an office or who employs one or more assistants or who otherwise regularly carries on a business, is not deemed to be engaged in an unincorporated business solely by reason of selling goods, wares, merchandise or insurance for more than one enterprise. (Sec. 11-502(e), N.Y.C. Adm. Code)

- *Exempt trusts and organizations*

A trust or other unincorporated organization which by reason of its purposes or activities is exempt from federal income tax is not deemed to be an incorporated business. (Sec. 11-502(f), N.Y.C. Adm. Code)

- *Real estate mortgage investment conduits*

An entity that is treated for federal income tax purposes as a real estate mortgage investment conduit (REMIC) is not subject to the unincorporated business tax. (Sec. 11-122, N.Y.C. Adm. Code) The exemption does not apply to holders of regular or residual interests, as defined in IRC Sec. 860G, or on income from such interests.

[¶519-120] Rate of NYC Tax

The tax is imposed at the rate of 4% of unincorporated business taxable income (Sec. 11-503(a), N.Y.C. Adm. Code)

For the definition of unincorporated business taxable income, see ¶519-215.

[¶519-200]
NYC UNINCORPORATED BUSINESS TAX COMPUTATION OF INCOME

[¶519-205] NYC Unincorporated Business Tax Computation of Income--In General

The New York City unincorporated business tax adopts the federal income tax provisions for determination of items of gross income (Sec. 11-506(a), N.Y.C. Adm. Code) and deduction (Sec. 11-507, N.Y.C. Adm. Code), with certain modifications (Sec. 11-506(b) and 11-506(c)), as the basis of computing the unincorporated business income subject to tax.

Business interest deduction limitation.—For information on New York City's treatment of the IRC Sec. 163(j) limitation on deducting business interest expense, see ¶519-225 and *Business Tax Practitioner Newsletter*, Vol. 1, May 2019. See also *Finance Memorandum 18-11* regarding the attribution of interest deductions for taxpayers with IRC Sec. 163(j) limitations.

IRC Sec. 965 Repatriation income.—IRC Sec. 965 income is a component of federal taxable income, and there are no specific statutory modifications under the UBT that exclude this income from City tax computations. Accordingly, for purposes of the UBT, the net IRC Sec. 965 income reported to the IRS must be incorporated into the starting point of City tax calculations. (*Finance Memorandum 18-10*, New York City Department of Finance)

IRC §734 and §743 basis adjustments.—The New York City Department of Finance has issued a statement of audit procedure that explains when adjustments to the basis of partnership assets under IRC §734 and §743 will affect the calculation of New York City unincorporated business taxable income. The statement concludes that distributions of partnership assets and transfers of partnership interests have different potential effects on unincorporated business taxable income, as they trigger different federal income tax consequences under §734 and §743. The statement includes several examples illustrating the unincorporated business tax treatment of basis adjustments. (*Statement of Audit Procedure UBT-2017-1*)

[¶519-210] NYC Unincorporated Business Gross Income Defined

Unincorporated business gross income is defined as the sum of the items of income and gain of the business includable in gross income for the taxable year for federal income tax purposes, including income and gain from any property employed in the business, or from liquidation of the business, or from collection of installment obligations of the business with certain modifications. (Sec. 11-506(a), N.Y.C. Adm. Code)

• *Sales or dispositions of interests in other unincorporated entities*

For taxable years beginning after 1995, unincorporated business income includes income or gain from the sale or other disposition by an unincorporated entity of an interest in another unincorporated entity if and to the extent that the income or gain is attributable to a trade, business, profession or occupation carried on in whole or in part in New York City by the other unincorporated entity. The character of a partner's distributive share of gross income, gains, losses and deductions of an unincorporated entity will be determined as if the gross income, gains, losses and deductions were realized directly by the partner, regardless of how the interest in the unincorporated entity was acquired or whether the distributive share is proportionate to the interest of the partner in the unincorporated entity's capital. (Sec. 11-506(a), N.Y.C. Adm. Code)

CCH CAUTION: The above provision does not apply to payments to a partner treated under IRC Sec. 707 as occurring between a partnership and a nonpartner. In addition, the provision is not intended to affect the treatment of a taxpayer's distributive share of income, gains, losses or deductions from a partnership as qualifying for the self-trading exemption or as taxable income, gain, loss or deduction from an unincorporated business in the taxpayer's hands.

[¶519-215] NYC Unincorporated Business Taxable Income

The New York City taxable income for an unincorporated business is the excess of its unincorporated business gross income, as modified, over its unincorporated business deductions allocated to New York City, less the deductions not subject to allocation and the unincorporated business exemptions. (Sec. 11-505, N.Y.C. Adm. Code)

[¶519-225] NYC Unincorporated Business Gross Income— Additions to Federal Gross Income

The following additions must be made to the federal gross income of an unincorporated business in connection with items attributable to the business (Sec. 11-506(b), N.Y.C. Adm. Code):

(1) Interest on state or local bonds (other than New York);

(2) Interest or dividends on bonds of any federal authority, commission or instrumentality which is exempt from federal income tax but not from state or local income taxes;

(3) The amount of the depreciation for taxpayers exercising the election permitted for liberalized depreciation for research and development property and manufacturing property if the property was sold or otherwise disposed of during the taxable year;

¶519-210

(4) The entire amount allowable as an exclusion or deduction for stock transfer taxes in determining federal gross income but only to the extent that such taxes are incurred and paid in market-making transactions;

(5) The amount allowed as an exclusion or deduction for sales and use taxes imposed but only that amount which is not in excess of the amount of the credit permitted for sales and use taxes paid on certain machinery and equipment (see ¶519-410);

(6) The amount allowed as an exclusion or deduction for rent in determining federal gross income but only the amount which is not in excess of the amount of the real estate tax escalation credit;

(7) The amount allowed as an exclusion or deduction for relocation expenses in determining federal gross income but only the amount which is not in excess of the amount of credit allowed for relocation costs for industrial and commercial employment opportunities;

(8) Except for qualified mass commuting vehicles, the amount which would properly be includable in federal income tax purposes had the taxpayer not made an election under IRC Sec. 168(f)(8) as it was in effect for safe harbor leases agreements entered into prior to January 1, 1984;

(9) Upon disposition of property (except for property subject to the provisions of IRC Sec. 168 placed in service in New York State for taxable years beginning after 1984 and property subject to IRC Sec. 280-F, concerning luxury automobiles), the amount, if any, by which the aggregate of the amounts allowable as a depreciation deduction under IRC Sec. 167 exceeds the aggregate of the amounts allowable as the accelerated cost recovery system deduction under IRC Sec. 168;

(10) The amount allowed as an exclusion or deduction for sales and use taxes in determining federal gross income, but only the amount which is not in excess of the amount of credits allowed with respect to sales and use taxes paid on electricity used in manufacturing, processing or assembling;

(11) In the case of a taxpayer who is an eligible energy user, the amount allowed as an exclusion or deduction for energy charges in determining federal gross income, but only the portion of the exclusion or deduction which is not in excess of the sum of the special rebates allowed to the vendor of energy services (This provision is repealed, effective November 1, 2000.);

(12) In the case of a taxpayer who is a supplier of fuel services, the entire amount allowed as an exclusion or deduction for discounts made by the taxpayer in determining federal gross income (This provision is repealed, effective November 1, 2000.);

(13) The amount allowed as an exclusion or deduction for sales and use taxes imposed by Sec. 1107, Tax Law (or for any interest imposed in connection therewith), in determining federal gross income, but only to the extent of the portion of the exclusion or deduction that is not in excess of the amount of the credit allowed pursuant to Sec. 11-503(k), N.Y.C. Adm. Code;

(14) (*Note:* This provision was repealed in 2005, applicable retroactively to taxable years beginning after 1999) in the event of a stock or asset acquisition during the taxable year or within the three immediately preceding taxable years, 5% of the amount of acquisition-related interest (to the extent deducted in the computation of unincorporated business taxable income). The amount cannot exceed a limitation amount, which is the product of the taxpayer's acquisition-related interest and a fraction. The numerator of the fraction is (1) the taxpayer's total cost of any target corporation acquired in a corporate acquisition or (2) the value of the assets acquired during the taxpayer's taxable year or in the three

852 Guidebook to New York Taxes

immediately preceding taxable years, but only if the acquisition occurred on or after July 1, 1989. The denominator of the fraction is the taxpayer's average total debt for the taxable year;

(15) The amount allowed as an exclusion or deduction in determining federal gross income of any loss, other than as a dealer, from the holding, sale, disposition, assumption, offset or termination of a position in, property, or other substantially similar losses from ordinary and routine trading or investment activity to the extent determined by the Commissioner of Finance, realized in connection with activities described in Sec. 11-502(c)(2), N.Y. Adm. Code, if, and to the extent that, such activities are not deemed an unincorporated business carried on by a taxpayer pursuant to Sec. 11-502(c);

(16) In the case of a taxpayer that is an unincorporated entity described in Sec. 11-502(c)(4)(b), N.Y.C. Adm. Code, the amount allowed as an exclusion or deduction in determining federal gross income of any loss realized from the sale or other disposition of an interest in another unincorporated entity if, and to the extent that, such loss is attributable to activities of such other unincorporated entity not deemed an unincorporated business carried on by the taxpayer pursuant to Sec. 11-502(c);

(17) The amount allowed as an exclusion or deduction in determining federal gross income of any loss realized from the holding, leasing or managing of real property if, and to the extent that, such holding, leasing or managing of real property is not deemed an unincorporated business carried on by the taxpayer pursuant to Sec. 11-502(d), N.Y.C. Adm. Code;

(18) The amount allowed as an exclusion or deduction in determining federal gross income of any loss realized from the provision by an owner, lessee or fiduciary holding, leasing or managing real property of the service of parking, garaging or storing of motor vehicles on a monthly or longer term basis to tenants at such real property if, and to the extent that, the provision of such services to such tenants is not deemed an unincorporated business carried on by the taxpayer pursuant to 11-502(d), N.Y.C. Adm. Code. (Sec. 11-506(b), N.Y.C. Adm. Code); and

(19) The amount of the increase in the federal interest deduction allowed under IRC Sec. 163(j)(10). This relates to the federal CARES Act amendment increasing the cap of the business interest expense limitation and allowing an election to use 2019 adjusted taxable income for 2020. The modification is required for taxable years beginning in 2019 and 2020 (Sec. 11-506(b)(17), N.Y.C. Adm. Code; *Finance Memorandum 20-6*);

(20) For taxable years beginning before 2021, the amount of increase in the federal deduction allowed under any amendment to IRC Sec. 461(l) made after March 1, 2020. This relates to the federal suspension of the excess business loss limitation (Sec. 11-506(b)(18), N.Y.C. Adm. Code; *Finance Memorandum 20-6*); and

(21) The amount of the industrial business zone credit allowed, to the extent that relocation costs were deducted in the current or preceding tax year. (Sec. 11-503(n)(6), N.Y.C. Adm. Code)

• *2003 Budget—Related member expenses*

Under the 2003 budget bill (as amended by the Ch. 686, Laws 2003, technical corrections legislation), New York City requires an addition for certain royalty payments made to a related member. (Sec. 11-506(e), N.Y.C. Adm. Code) These anti-PIC (passive investment company) provisions, also referred to as expense disallowance provisions, are similar to the general corporation tax provisions; see the detailed discussion at ¶505-417.

[¶519-230] NYC Unincorporated Business Gross Income-- Subtractions from Federal Gross Income

The following subtractions are made from the federal gross income of an unincorporated business in connection with items attributable to the business (Sec. 11-506(c), N.Y.C. Adm. Code):

(1) Interest on bonds of the United States and its possessions to the extent includable in federal gross income;

(2) Interest or dividends on bonds of any authority, commission or instrumentality of the United States which is includable in federal gross income, but which is exempt from state or local income taxes by federal statute;

(3) Interest or dividend income exempt by the New York State or New York City law authorizing the issuance of the obligations or securities on which paid, to the extent includable in federal gross income;

(4) 50% of dividends to the extent includible in federal gross income and not otherwise subtracted. No subtraction will be allowed for any portion of a stock dividend with respect to which a dividend deduction would be disallowed by IRC Sec. 246(c) if the unincorporated business were a corporation.

(5) Any tax refund or credit for overpayment of income taxes levied by New York State, New York City or any other taxing jurisdiction of the petroleum business tax imposed by Art. 13-A, Tax Law, to the extent includable in federal gross income;

(6) With respect to gain derived from the sale or other disposition of property acquired prior to January 1, 1966 (except for stock in trade, or accounts and notes receivable acquired in the ordinary course of trade or business for services rendered or from the sale of property which is stock in trade) the difference between (a) the amount of gain reported for federal purposes; and (b) any gain which would be included in federal gross income if the basis of property had been equal to its fair market value on January 1, 1966, as adjusted for federal income tax purposes for the period on or after January 1, 1966, or the fair market value on the date of its sale or other disposition prior to January 1, 1966. The total modification may not exceed the taxpayer's net gain from the sale or other disposition of all such property;

(7) Except for qualified mass commuting vehicles, the amount properly includable in federal gross income solely as a result of safe harbor lease election made under IRC Sec. 168(f)(8) as it was in effect for agreements entered into prior to January 1, 1984;

(8) Upon disposition of property (except for property subject to the provisions of IRC Sec. 168 placed in service in New York State for taxable years beginning after 1984 and property subject to IRC Sec. 280-F, concerning luxury automobiles), the amount, if any, by which the aggregate accelerated cost recovery systems deduction under IRC Sec. 168 exceeds the aggregate of the depreciation deduction under IRC Sec. 167;

(9) the amount of any income or gain (to the extent includible in gross income for federal income tax purposes) realized by an owner of real property, a lessee or a fiduciary from the holding, leasing or managing of real property to the extent that such holding, leasing or managing is not deemed to constitute an unincorporated business carried on by the taxpayer;

(10) the amount of any income or gain (to the extent includible in gross income for federal income tax purposes), including but not limited to, dividends, interest, payments with respect to securities loans, income from notional principal contracts, or income and gains, other than as a dealer, from the holding, sale, disposition, assumption, offset or termination of a position in, property, or other

substantially similar income from ordinary and routine trading or investment activity to the extent determined by the Commissioner of Finance, realized in connection with activities described in Sec. 11-502(c)(2), N.Y.C. Adm. Code, if, and to the extent that, such activities are not deemed an unincorporated business carried on by the taxpayer pursuant Sec. 11-502(c);

(11) in the case of a taxpayer that is an unincorporated entity described in Sec. 11-502(c)(4)(b), N.Y.C. Adm. Code, the amount of any income or gain (to the extent includible in gross income for federal income tax purposes) realized from the sale or other disposition of an interest in another unincorporated entity if, and to the extent that, such income or gain is attributable to activities of the other unincorporated entity not deemed an unincorporated business carried on by the taxpayer pursuant to Sec. 11-502(c); and

(12) the amount of any income or gain (to the extent includible in gross income for federal income tax purposes) realized from the provision by an owner, lessee or fiduciary holding, leasing or managing real property of the service of parking, garaging or storing of motor vehicles on a monthly or longer term basis to tenants at such real property if, and to the extent that, the provision of such services to such tenants is not deemed an unincorporated business pursuant Sec. 11-502(d), N.Y.C. Adm. Code.

[¶519-240] NYC Accounting Periods and Methods

New York City required the taxable year (Sec. 11-513(a), N.Y.C. Adm. Code) and method of accounting (Sec. 11-513(b), N.Y.C. Adm. Code) of the unincorporated business to be the same as those used for federal income tax purposes. If there are any changes in the taxable year or method of accounting for federal income tax purposes, similar changes must be made for purposes of the New York City unincorporated business tax. (Sec. 11-513(c), N.Y.C. Adm. Code)

[¶519-250] NYC Deductions--In General

The deductions that can be taken by an unincorporated business are the items of loss and deduction directly connected with or incurred in the conduct of the business, which are allowable for federal income tax purposes for the taxable year (including losses and deductions connected with any property employed in the business) with certain modifications. (Sec. 11-507, N.Y.C. Adm. Code)

• *Charitable contributions*

A deduction for charitable contributions is allowed to the same extent that the contributions would be deductible for federal income tax purposes if made by a corporation, but the deduction may not exceed 5% of the amount by which the unincorporated business gross income exceeds the sum of (a) unincorporated business deductions (without the charitable contributions deduction) and (b) the deductions for accelerated depreciation and research and development facilities. (Sec. 11-507(1), N.Y.C. Adm. Code)

Personal charitable contributions, or contributions not made by the unincorporated business itself, are not deductible for unincorporated tax purposes if they are of the type which would be deductible for federal income tax purposes if made by a corporation. (Rule Sec. 28-06(b)) To be deductible for unincorporated business tax purposes, the charitable contribution must be directly connected with, or incurred in, the conduct of the unincorporated business, an entity separate and distinct from the owners or operators of the business.

• *Net operating losses*

A deduction is allowed for net operating losses incurred by an unincorporated business, in an amount computed in the same manner as the net operating loss deduction which would be allowed for the taxable year for federal income tax purposes if the unincorporated business were an individual taxpayer (but determined solely by reference to the gross income and deductions, allocated to the city, of the unincorporated business), provided that the net operating loss deduction is determined as if the unincorporated business had elected (pursuant to IRC Sec. 172) to relinquish the entire carryback period with respect to net operating losses, except for the first $10,000 of losses, sustained during taxable years ending after June 30, 1989. (Sec. 11-507(2), N.Y.C. Adm. Code) In the case of a partnership, no net operating loss carryback or carryover to any taxable year will be allowed unless one or more of the partners during the taxable year were persons having a proportionate interest or interests, amounting to at least 80% of all such interests, in the unincorporated business gross income and unincorporated business deductions of the partnership which sustained the loss for which a carryback or carryover is claimed. In such an event, the carryback or carryover allowable on account of the loss may not exceed the percentage of the amount otherwise allowable, determined by dividing the sum of the proportionate interests in the unincorporated business gross income and unincorporated business deductions of the partnership, for the year to which the loss is carried back or carried over, attributable to such partners, by the sum of the proportionate interests owned by all partners for the taxable year.

Note: The law has been amended to provide that, for taxable years beginning before 2021, any amendment to IRC Sec. 172 made after March 1, 2020, does not apply. Accordingly, the New York City unincorporated business tax does not conform to federal CARES Act amendments, including (1) a five-year carryback period for NOLs arising in tax years beginning in 2018, 2019, and 2020, and (2) suspension of the 80% of taxable income limitation for those years. (Sec. 11-507(2)(c), N.Y.C. Adm. Code; *Finance Memorandum 20-6*)

• *Payment to owner or partner*

No deduction is allowed for amounts paid to a proprietor or partner for services or use of capital. (Sec. 11-507(3), N.Y.C. Adm. Code)

Payments to partners for services do not include amounts paid or incurred by an unincorporated business to a partner of the business which reasonably represent the value of services provided the employees of the partner. (Rule Sec. 28-06(d)) The amounts paid or incurred for the employee services must actually be disbursed by the unincorporated business and included in that partner's gross income for federal income tax purposes, and would constitute allowable business deductions in the case of reasonable compensation for the personal services of a proprietor or a partner of the unincorporated business. See ¶ 519-255.

EXAMPLE: Partnership AB, Corporation C and the individual Mr. D form a joint venture called the ABCD Construction Company to construct a building in Staten Island. Each member of the Company contributes an equal amount of capital to the venture. In addition, Mr. A, a partner in Partnership AB will serve as engineering supervisor for the construction. Ms. E, the president of Corporation C, will serve as a work site supervisor. Mr. D, an attorney, will handle all the legal affairs of the Company. The office staff of Partnership AB will provide all the office services needed by the Company. The in-house accounting staff of Corporation C will handle all of the Company's accounting matters. Payments made by the Company for the services of Mr. A, Ms. E and Mr. D are not allowed as deductions in the calculation of the Company's unincorporated business taxable income. Payments made by the Company for the office and accounting services provided by the members of the joint venture will be allowed as deductions if such payments are included in the respective member's gross income for Federal tax purposes.

Payments to partners for use of capital do not include amounts paid or incurred by an unincorporated business to a partner of the business which reasonably represent the value of the use of real or personal property of the partner by the unincorporated business, and would constitute allowable business deductions in the case of reasonable compensation for personal services by a proprietor or a partner. (Rule Sec. 28-06(d)) See ¶519-255. The amounts paid or incurred for such use of property must be actually disbursed by the unincorporated business and included in that partner's gross income for federal income tax purposes.

Example 1: F and G form a partnership to engage in the construction business. F contributes $100,000 in cash to the partnership. G contributes machinery worth $100,000 to the partnership. No deduction will be allowed to the partnership for payments made to G for use of the machinery nor to F for the use of the cash. G has not retained title to the machinery and, therefore, payments to G are not-deductible partnership distributions.

Example 2: Partnership AB maintains an office in a building owned by B, a partner in AB. The partnership pays B a reasonable rental for the use of the office space. Such rental payments will be allowed as a deduction to the partnership.

In *New York Yankees Partnership v. O'Cleireacain & c.,* the New York Court of Appeals rejected the Department of Finance's argument that the characterization of payments received in liquidation of a partner's interest in a partnership for federal income tax purposes was controlling for City unincorporated business tax (UBT) purposes. In *New York Yankees,* the taxpayer claimed a UBT deduction for payments paid to liquidating partners that constituted their shares in player contracts that had been amortized by the partnership in current or prior tax years. The partnership claimed a deduction for the guaranteed payments for unrealized receivables on their federal tax returns, and claimed an identical deduction for City UBT purposes. The City denied the deficiency, claiming that although no portion of the payments were specifically for services rendered to the partnership or interest for use of the liquidating partners' capital, IRC Sec. 736(a)(2), which characterizes payments made liquidation of a partner's interest as a guaranteed payment, and IRC Sec. 707(c), which treats guaranteed payments as payments to a partner for services or the use of capital, was controlling. The Court disagreed, noting that IRC Sec. 707(c) was not intended to define guaranteed payments as payments for services or the use of capital but, rather, was intended merely to implement the "recapture rule" and prevent taxpayers from benefiting from differences in the tax rates between ordinary income and capital gains when the actual depreciation of an asset is less than the amount amortized. Because the Commissioner had acknowledged that the payments were not for services or the use of capital, the payments were deductible.

• *Income taxes*

No deduction is allowed for income taxes imposed by New York City, New York State or any other taxing jurisdiction or the petroleum business tax imposed by Art. 13-A, Tax Law. (Sec. 11-507(4), N.Y.C. Adm. Code)

• *Interest on loans to carry tax-exempt securities—Expenses in connection with nontaxable income—Amortizable premiums on exempt bonds*

No deduction is allowed for (Sec. 11-507(5), N.Y.C. Adm. Code):

(1) interest on indebtedness incurred or continued to purchase or carry obligations or securities the income from which is exempt from the unincorporated business tax;

(2) expenses paid or incurred for the production or collection of such income or the management, conservation or maintenance of property held for the production of such income; or

(3) the amortizable bond premium on any bond the interest income from which is exempt from the unincorporated business tax.

• *Capital gains and losses*

No deduction is allowed in respect to the excess of net long-term capital gain over net short-term capital loss. (Sec. 11-507(6), N.Y.C. Adm. Code) In addition, capital losses incurred in the unincorporated business will be treated as ordinary losses and will be allowed in full.

• *Certain special depreciation and research and development expenditures*

No deduction is allowed for depreciation or expenditures on property for which the taxpayer has exercised the election for liberalized depreciation for research and development property and manufacturing property. (Sec. 11-507(7), N.Y.C. Adm. Code)

• *Interest, expenses and amortizable bond premiums in connection with income taxable by New York City but not for federal purposes*

A deduction is allowed for (Sec. 11-507(8), N.Y.C. Adm. Code):

(1) interest on indebtedness incurred or continued to purchase or carry obligations or securities the income from which is subject to New York City unincorporated business tax but exempt from federal income tax;

(2) ordinary and necessary expenses paid or incurred during the taxable year for the production or collection of such income or the management, conservation or maintenance of property held for the production of such income; and

(3) the amortizable bond premium for the taxable year on any bond the interest on which is subject to the New York City unincorporated business tax but exempt from federal income tax.

• *Expenditures for industrial waste treatment facilities and air pollution control facilities*

Deductions, at the election of the taxpayer, are allowed for expenditures paid or incurred for industrial waste treatment facilities and air pollution control facilities. (Sec. 11-507(9), N.Y.C. Adm. Code).

• *Depletion*

Natural resource depletion cannot be deducted on a percentage basis. (Sec. 11-507(10), N.Y.C. Adm. Code).

• *Federal employment credits adjustment*

A deduction is allowed for the portion of wages and salaries paid or incurred for the taxable year and not allowed as a business expense deduction under IRC Sec. 280C, as a result of taking federal employment credits. (Sec. 11-507(11), N.Y.C. Adm. Code)

• *Safe harbor leases*

Except for qualified mass commuting vehicles, a deduction is allowed for any amount which the taxpayer could have excluded had it not made a safe harbor lease election under IRC Sec. 168(8)(f) for agreements entered into prior to January 1, 1984. (Secs. 11-507(12) and 11-507(13), N.Y.C. Adm. Code) If such an election was made, no deduction is allowed for the amount deductible for federal income tax purposes solely as a result of the election.

• *Federal bonus depreciation—partial decoupling*

With respect to certain provisions enacted by the federal Job Creation and Worker Assistance Act of 2002 (P.L. 107-147) (JCWAA) and the Jobs and Growth Tax Relief Reconciliation Act of 2003 (P.L. 108-27) (JGTRRA), including additional 30%

and 50% depreciation deductions allowed in the first year "qualified property" is placed in service, New York City law has been amended to generally limit the depreciation deduction for qualified property to the deduction that would have been allowed for such property under IRC Sec. 167 had the property been acquired by the taxpayer on September 10, 2001. However, the depreciation deductions for qualified Resurgence Zone property, qualified New York Liberty Zone property, and qualified New York Liberty Zone leasehold improvements, as well as the additional first-year expense deduction under IRC Sec. 179 for qualified New York Liberty Zone property, are the same for New York City unincorporated business tax purposes as for federal tax purposes. (Sec. 11-507(20), (21), and (22), N.Y.C. Adm. Code; *Finance Memorandum 02-3)*

As amended, the New York City law also requires appropriate adjustments to the amount of any gain or loss included in unincorporated business entire net income upon the disposition of any property for which the federal and New York City depreciation deductions differ. (Sec. 11-506(d), N.Y.C. Adm. Code; *Finance Memorandum 02-3)*

For taxable years beginning on or after January 1, 2004, in the case of a passenger motor vehicle or a sport utility vehicle subject to the provisions of Sec. 11-507(24) (see "Sport utility vehicles" below), the limitation under IRC Sec. 280F(a)(1)(A)(i) applicable to the amount allowed as a deduction under Sec. 11-507(21) must be determined as of the date such vehicle was placed in service and not as of September 10, 2001. (Sec. 11-507(21), N.Y.C. Adm. Code)

• *Sport utility vehicles*

For taxable years beginning on or after January 1, 2004, in the case of a taxpayer that is not an eligible farmer, no deduction may be taken for the amounts allowable as a deduction under IRC Sec. 167, IRC Sec. 168, and IRC Sec. 179 with respect to a sport utility vehicle that is not a passenger automobile as defined in IRC Sec. 280F(d)(5). (Sec. 11-507(23), N.Y.C. Adm. Code)

Instead, the deduction must be computed *as if* the sport utility vehicle *were* a passenger automobile as defined in IRC Sec. 280F(d)(5). (Sec. 11-507(24), N.Y.C. Adm. Code)

The Department of Finance has provided schedules setting forth the applicable New York City SUV limits; see *Finance Memorandum 19-1,* March 2, 2020.

Upon the disposition of property to which Sec. 11-507(23) and (24) apply, the amount of any gain or loss includible in unincorporated business gross income must be adjusted to reflect the above modifications attributable to such property. (Sec. 11-506(f), N.Y.C. Adm. Code)

• *Federal accelerated cost recovery system*

Except for property subject to IRC Sec. 280-F (concerning luxury automobiles) and property subject to the provisions of IRC Sec. 168 which is placed in service in New York State for taxable years beginning after December 31, 1984, no deduction is allowed for the amount allowable as the accelerated cost recovery system deduction under IRC Sec. 168. (Sec. 11-507(14), N.Y.C. Adm. Code)

Except for property subject to IRC Sec. 280-F (concerning luxury automobiles) and property subject to the provisions of IRC Sec. 168 which is placed in service in New York State for taxable years beginning after December 31, 1984, and provided a safe harbor lease deduction has not been disallowed, a taxpayer is allowed with respect to property which is subject to IRC Sec. 168, the depreciation deduction allowable under IRC Sec. 167 as the section would have applied to property placed in service on December 31, 1980. (Sec. 11-507(15), N.Y.C. Adm. Code)

- *Expenses related to holding, leasing or managing real property*

No deduction is allowed to an owner of real property, a lessee or a fiduciary for interest, depreciation or any other expense directly or indirectly attributable to the holding, leasing or managing of real property or to income or gain therefrom if and to the extent that the holding, leasing or managing of the property is not deemed to constitute an unincorporated business carried on by the taxpayer. (Sec. 11-507(16), N.Y.C. Adm. Code)

- *Expenses related to holding, purchasing and selling property for own account*

No deduction is allowed for any expenses directly or indirectly attributable to holding, purchasing or selling property for one's own account if and to the extent that such activity is not deemed to be an unincorporated business carried on by the taxpayer. (Sec. 11-507(17), N.Y.C. Adm. Code)

- *Investors*

An unincorporated entity that qualifies as an "investor" for unincorporated business tax purposes (see ¶ 519-110) will not be allowed a deduction for any losses or expenses directly or indirectly attributable to the sale or other disposition of an interest in another unincorporated entity if and to the extent that the losses or expenses are attributable to activities of the other entity that are not deemed to be an unincorporated business carried on by the taxpayer. (Sec. 11-507(18), N.Y.C. Adm. Code)

- *Services related to parking, garaging or storing motor vehicles for tenants on a monthly or longer term basis*

No deduction is allowed for interest, depreciation or other expenses directly or indirectly attributable to holding, leasing or managing real property for parking, garaging or storing motor vehicles on a monthly or longer-term basis to tenants at the property if and to the extent that the provision of such services is not deemed an unincorporated business. (Sec. 11-507(18), N.Y.C. Adm. Code)

[¶519-255] NYC Deduction for Personal Services of Proprietor or of Partner of Unincorporated Business

New York City provides a deduction for reasonable compensation for the personal services of a proprietor or of each partner actively engaged in the unincorporated business. (Sec. 11-509(a), N.Y.C. Adm. Code) The reasonableness of any such deduction is subject to determination by the Commissioner of Finance. (Rule Sec. 28-08(a)) This deduction, which is not subject to allocation, is limited to the lesser of (1) $5,000 for the owner or each active partner, or (2) 20% of the unincorporated business taxable income computed without the benefit of the deduction for compensation for personal services or the unincorporated business exemptions for taxable years beginning before January 1, 2007. The dollar amount of the deduction is increased to a maximum of $10,000 for taxable years beginning on or after January 1, 2007.

> *EXAMPLE 1:* A, an individual, has unincorporated business taxable income (computed without deductions for compensation for his services or the unincorporated business exemptions) of $15,000. He actually drew from the business a salary of $6,000. Assuming the amount drawn would not exceed a reasonable allowance, the allowable deduction for A's services is $3,000 (20% of the $15,000), which in this case is the maximum deduction allowable. The $5,000 limitation is not applicable because it exceeds the 20% of income limitation on the aggregate of allowable deductions for compensation of a proprietor and active partners.

EXAMPLE 2: If, in Example 1 above, A drew no salary, the $3,000 would be allowable as a deduction for his services, assuming such amount would not exceed a reasonable allowance under the circumstances.

[¶519-260] NYC Deductions for Expenditures for Industrial Waste Treatment Facilities and Air Pollution Control Facilities

A taxpayer may elect to deduct expenditures for the construction, erection or improvement of industrial waste and air pollution control facilities. (Sec. 11-507(9), N.Y.C. Adm. Code) The functions of such eligible facilities are specifically defined by statute.

In order to establish eligibility, the facilities must be depreciable under IRC Sec. 167, situated in New York City, used in the taxpayer's trade or business, and certified by the State Commissioner of Environmental Conservation as meeting applicable standards.

If there is a change in the use of the property within ten years after the deduction was taken, the change must be reflected in the return for the year in which it occurs. Should the taxpayer fail to obtain a permanent certificate or has a permanent certificate revoked, such circumstances must also be reported. Upon any such notification, the Commissioner of Finance may recompute the tax for any year affected by the change and may assess an individual tax. Such an assessment may be made within three years from the filing of the required information. (Sec. 11-523(a), N.Y.C. Adm. Code)

If the eligible property is sold or otherwise disposed of, the gain or loss upon such a disposition is the same as for federal tax purposes without regard to the deduction permitted. (Sec. 11-507(9), N.Y.C. Adm. Code)

[¶519-265] NYC Natural Resource Depletion Deduction

No deduction is permitted for natural resource depletion on a *percentage* basis as provided in IRC Sec. 163. A depletion deduction is permitted, however, in an amount allowable under IRC Sec. 611, which permits *cost* depletion. (Sec. 11-507(10), N.Y.C. Adm. Code)

[¶519-300]

NYC UNINCORPORATED BUSINESS TAX EXEMPTIONS

[¶519-305] NYC Unincorporated Business Tax Exemptions—In General

Every unincorporated business is allowed an exemption of $5,000. (Sec. 11-510, N.Y.C. Adm. Code) For taxable years of less than 12 months, the exemption is prorated. The proration will be made on a daily basis at the rate of $13.70 per calendar day unless the return is filed for a period of one or more whole months beginning on the first day and ending on the last day of a calendar month, in which event the proration is to be made on a monthly basis at the rate of $416.67 per month. (Rule Sec. 28-09(a))

The exemption is not subject to allocation even though the unincorporated business is carried on both within and without New York City. Only one specific exemption is allowed to an individual, partnership, or other unincorporated entity, even though the individual or other entity carries on two or more unincorporated businesses.

EXAMPLE 1: Partnership A & B, in existence and doing business on January 1, 1975, is terminated and liquidated on May 31, 1975, by the admission of a new partner, C, and the formation of a new partnership A B C which continues the business from June 1, 1975 through December 15, 1975, at which time it is terminated and completely liquidated. On the unincorporated business tax return of partnership A & B for the period beginning January 1, 1975, and ended May 31, 1975, a prorated exemption of $2,083.35, representing five months at $416.67 per month, will be allowed. The prorated exemption allowable to partnership A B C for the period June 1, 1975, through December 15, 1975, is $2,712.60, or 198 days at $13.70 per day.

EXAMPLE 2: Individual A sold his unincorporated business under a deferred payment agreement on December 31, 1973, and received payments under the agreement in 1974 and in 1975, with the final payment being received on April 15, 1975. A's unincorporated business exemption will be $5,000 for 1974 and $1,438.50 (105 days at $13.70 per day) for 1975.

• *Additional exemption*

Taxable years beginning before July 1, 1994: For taxable years beginning before July 1, 1994, a partner in an unincorporated business that is itself subject to New York City unincorporated business tax or to New York City business tax on corporations is allowed an exemption equal to the amount of the partner's proportionate interest in the excess of unincorporated business gross income over unincorporated business deductions (including the deduction for personal services of owners and active partners). This exemption is limited to the amount that is included in the partner's unincorporated business taxable income allocable to New York City or included in the corporate partner's net income allocable to New York City.

No additional exemption is allowed for amounts distributed to an individual member of a partnership who also carries on his own separate and independent unincorporated business and who is not required or permitted to include his distributive share of partnership income in computing his own separate unincorporated gross income. (Rule Sec. 28-09(b))

Rule Sec. 28-09(b)(4) provides that the additional exemption allowed an unincorporated business with respect to a corporate partner is limited to the corporate partner's net income allocable to New York City, even though the corporate partner does not pay a New York City general corporation tax measured by allocated net income because one of the alternative measures of the general corporation tax produces a higher tax. (Rule Sec. 28-09(b)) However, in *Weil, Gotshal & Manges, & c. v. O'Cleireacain*, the New York Court of Appeals affirmed a lower court decision that held that, to the extent that a corporate partner is subject to tax based on an alternative tax calculation, a corresponding exemption will be allowed under the unincorporated business tax so as to avoid double taxation. The Court further found that the plain language of the statute, and the legislative history that preceded its enactment, further supported the taxpayer's contention that the purpose of the unincorporated business tax was to reach only income not taxed under the general corporation tax and was not intended to tax the same business income twice.

For the text of Weil, *Gotshal & Manges & c. v. O'Cleireacain* in the "N.Y. City— New Matters" division in Volume 7.

Taxable years beginning on or after July 1, 1994: The additional exemption is eliminated for taxable years beginning after June 30, 1994. Instead, partners in unincorporated businesses who are subject to unincorporated business tax and are required to include in unincorporated business taxable income their distributive share of income, gain, loss and deductions of, or guaranteed payments from, the unincorporated business, may claim a tax credit (see ¶519-445).

[¶519-350]

NYC UNINCORPORATED BUSINESS TAX ALLOCATION AND APPORTIONMENT

[¶519-355] NYC Allocation of Income

An unincorporated entity that conducts business both within and without New York City may allocated to the city a fair and equitable portion of the excess of its unincorporated business gross income over its unincorporated business deductions. (Sec. 11-508(a), N.Y.C. Adm. Code)

"Regular place of business" requirement: For taxable years beginning before July 1, 1996, an unincorporated business that did not have a regular place of business outside New York City was required to allocate *all* of its excess unincorporated business gross income to the city. However, for taxable years beginning after June 30, 1996, this "regular place of business" requirement has been eliminated.

• *Methods of allocating income*

The allocation to New York City is by the taxpayer's books (see ¶ 519-360), by formula involving the three factors of property, payroll and gross income (see ¶ 519-365), or by other methods approved by the Commissioner of Finance. (see ¶ 519-370)

For rules concerning the allocation of investment income, see ¶ 519-357.

[¶519-357] NYC Allocation of Investment Income

For taxable years beginning on or after July 1, 1994, investment income of an unincorporated business allocated to New York City is determined by: (1) multiplying the amount of the entity's investment capital invested in each stock, bond or other security (other than governmental securities) during the period covered by its return by its issuer's allocation percentage; (2) adding together the sums obtained; and (3) dividing the result by the total of the entity's investment capital invested during the reporting period in stocks, bonds and other securities. (Sec. 11-508(f), N.Y.C. Adm. Code)

• *Issuer's allocation percentage*

The issuer's allocation percentage of a business subject to New York City general corporation tax or utility tax is the percentage of the appropriate measure that is required to be allocated within New York City on the business' general corporation or utility report for the preceding year. The "appropriate measure" is entire capital in the case of an issuer or obligor subject to City general corporation tax and, in the case of a business subject to City utility tax, gross income.

The issuer's allocation percentage of a business subject to New York City banking corporation tax is determined as follows:

(a) in the case of a banking corporation described in Sec. 11-640(a)(1)—(8), N.Y.C. Adm. Code, that is organized under the laws of the United States, New York or any other state of the United States, the issuer's allocation percentage is its alternative entire net income allocation percentage for the preceding year. The issuer's allocation percentage of a banking corporation whose alternative entire net income for the preceding year is derived exclusively from business carried on within New York City will be 100%.

(b) in the case of a banking corporation described in Sec. 11-640(a)(2), N.Y.C. Adm. Code, that is organized under the laws of a country other than the United States, the issuer's allocation percentage is determined by dividing (1) the taxpayer's receipts from loans (including a taxpayer's portion of a participation in a loan), financing leases within New York City, and all other business receipts within and without the City for the preceding year, by the gross income of the issuer or obligor from all sources within and without the United States for the preceding year, whether or not included in alternative entire net income.

(c) in the case of an issuer or obligor described in Secs. 11-640(a)(9) or 11-640(d)(2), N.Y.C. Adm. Code, the issuer's allocation percentage is determined by dividing the portion of the entire capital of the issuer or obligor allocable to New York City for the preceding year by the entire capital, wherever located, of the issuer or obligor for the preceding year.

Failure to file report: If a report for a preceding year is not filed or, if filed, does not contain adequate information that would permit the determination of the issuer's allocation percentage, then the percentage to be used is, at the discretion of the Commissioner of Finance, either the issuer's allocation percentage derived from the most recently filed report or reports of the issuer or obligor or a percentage calculated by the Commissioner reasonably to indicate the issuer's or obligor's degree of economic presence in the City during the preceding year.

Discretion of Commissioner to adjust percentages: The Commissioner may adjust any investment allocation percentage to properly reflect the activity, business or income of an unincorporated business within New York City. (Sec. 11-508(h), N.Y.C. Adm. Code)

• *Determination of investment capital*

A taxpayer's investment capital is determined by taking the average value of the gross assets included therein (less liabilities deductible therefrom pursuant to Sec. 11-501(h), N.Y.C. Adm. Code). The value of investment capital that consists of marketable securities is the security's fair market value. The value of investment capital other than marketable securities is the value shown on the business' books and records in accordance with generally accepted accounting principles.

[¶519-360] NYC Allocation by Taxpayer's Books

For taxable years beginning before January 1, 2005, the portion allocable to the city could be determined from the books of the business if the methods used in keeping the books were approved by the Commissioner of Finance as fairly and equitably reflecting the income from the city. (Sec. 11-508(b), N.Y.C. Adm. Code; Rule Sec. 28-07(c))

For taxable years beginning after 2004, the books and records method is no longer the preferred allocation method under the unincorporated business tax. Instead, taxpayers are generally required to use the three-factor allocation formula discussed at ¶519-365.

Certain taxpayers that were properly using the books and records method may elect to continue using that method for taxable years beginning before 2012. (Sec. 11-508(b)(2), N.Y.C. Adm. Code)

[¶519-365] NYC Business Allocation Percentage

Income allocable to New York City is generally determined on the basis of a three-factor formula that compares the taxpayer's City property, payroll and gross income to property, payroll and gross income from all sources. (Sec. 11-508(c), N.Y.C. Adm. Code) For tax years beginning before 2005, the books and records method could be used, and certain eligible taxpayers may elect to continue using the books and records method through the 2011 tax year; see ¶519-360.

Beginning in 2009, a single sales factor is being phased in over 10 years. (Sec. 11-508(i), N.Y.C. Adm. Code; Finance Memorandum 09-2)

Specifically, the gross income factor is increased, and the payroll and property factors decreased, as indicated for the taxable years below:

— for 2009, 40% gross income—30% payroll—30% property;

— for 2010, 46%—27%—27%;

— for 2011, 53%—23.5%—23.5%;

— for 2012, 60%—20%—20%;

— for 2013, 67%—16.5%—16.5%;

— for 2014, 73%—13.5%—13.5%;

— for 2015, 80%—10%—10%;

— for 2016, 87%—6.5%—6.5%;

— for 2017, 93%—3.5%—3.5%; and

— after 2017, 100% gross income.

Previously, each factor was weighted equally in determining the taxpayer's business allocation percentage.

For taxable years beginning on or after July 1, 1996, and before 2011, manufacturing businesses may elect to double-weight the gross income factor of their business allocation percentage (see discussion below).

The three factors that comprise the business allocation percentage are:

(1) *Property percentage:* the average value, at the beginning and end of the taxable year, of real property (including real property rented to the business) and tangible personal property connected with the business and located in New York City, divided by the values for all such property located both within and outside New York City (for taxable years beginning after 2004, personal property rented to the taxpayer is also included; real and personal property rented to the taxpayer are valued at eight times the annual rent);

(2) *Payroll percentage:* wages and other compensation paid to employees in connection with business in New York City divided by the total compensation paid to all employees wherever employed; and

(3) *Gross income percentage:* gross sales or service charges within New York City divided by all such sales and charges wherever made. For taxable years beginning before July 1, 1996, receipts from sales of tangible personal property were allocated to New York City if the sales were negotiated or consummated by an employee or agent working out of or connected with a New York City office of the taxpayer. However, for tax years beginning on or after July 1, 1996, sales of tangible personal property are allocated to the City only where the goods are shipped to points within the City. However, see the "Dock sales" discussion below.

Receipts from the performance of services are allocated to the City to the extent that the services are performed in the City. (Sec. 11-508(c)(3), N.Y.C. Adm. Code)

The Commissioner of Finance may prescribe another method of allocating business income upon a determination that the methods described above do not fairly and adequately reflect the business income of a taxpayer.

• *Dock sales*

Taxpayers having receipts from dock sales for tax periods beginning after 1999 may request permission to allocate those receipts in a manner consistent with New York State Reg. Sec. 4-4.2, which was amended to set forth a destination rule with respect to dock sales. Existing New York City tax law requires taxpayers to include in the numerator of the gross income factor any receipts from sales of tangible personal property where shipment is made to a point within the city. Under the amended state regulation, however, receipts from sales of tangible personal property are allocated to New York State under the following circumstances:

(1) where shipment is made to a point within the state;

(2) where possession of the property is transferred to the purchaser or the purchaser's designee within the state, unless the destination of the property is a point outside New York; or

(3) where possession of the property is transferred to the purchaser or designee outside the state but the destination of the property is within the state.

The regulation establishes a presumption that the destination of property is where the possession is transferred, unless the taxpayer provides sufficient evidence to establish the destination.

Prior to filing a return for tax periods beginning after 1999, a New York City taxpayer having dock sales will be allowed to request advance permission to allocate the receipts according to the amended state regulation. The request should contain a statement setting forth the reasons why the taxpayer believes the use of the dock sales rule is necessary to properly reflect the taxpayer's income within and outside the city, a detailed explanation of how the business allocation percentage would be calculated using the dock sales method, and a comparison of the gross income factor calculated using the dock sales rule and using the point of shipment rule. Taxpayers who receive permission to use the dock sales rule must attach a copy of the Department's response when filing the return. (*Statement of Audit Procedure: Audits of Taxpayers Having Receipts from Dock Sales*, New York City Department of Finance, Audit Division, December 28, 2000)

• *Missing factors*

If one of the factors is missing, the other two percentages are added and the sum is divided by two. If two of the factors are missing, the remaining percentage is the allocation percentage. A factor is not missing merely because its numerator is zero, but it is missing if both its numerator and its denominator are zero. (Rule Sec. 28-07(d))

• *Manufacturing businesses*

For taxable years beginning on or after July 1, 1996, and before 2011, a manufacturing business, in determining its business allocation percentage, may elect to double weight its gross income factor. (Sec. 11-508(g), N.Y.C. Adm. Code; Rule Sec. 28-07(d))

The election must be made on a timely filed (determined with regard to extensions granted) original report for the taxable year and, once made, is irrevocable for that year. Separate elections must be made for each taxable year. (Sec. 11-508(g), N.Y.C. Adm. Code; Rule Sec. 28-07(d))

Failure to make the election will preclude the corporation from double weighting its receipts factor, unless the Commissioner of Finance determines that permission should be granted in the interests of fairness and equity due to a change in circumstances resulting from an audit adjustment. (Sec. 11-508(g), N.Y.C. Adm. Code; Rule Sec. 28-07(d))

"Manufacturing business" defined.—The term "manufacturing business" means an unincorporated business primarily engaged in the manufacturing and sale of tangible personal property. The term "manufacturing" includes the process (including the assembly process)

(i) of working raw materials into wares suitable for use or

(ii) that gives new shapes, new qualities or new combinations to matter which already has gone through some artificial process, by the use of machinery, tools, appliances and other similar equipment. (Sec. 11-508(g), N.Y.C. Adm. Code; Rule Sec. 28-07(d))

To qualify as manufacturing, a process must result in a significant change in the raw materials or component parts so that the end product is substantially different in nature or form from the raw materials or component parts. Manufacturing does not include the mere packaging or labeling of goods and includes finishing partially finished goods only if the goods are not usable for their intended purpose in their unfinished state. (Rule Sec. 28-07(d))

Manufacturing may include printing, under certain circumstances, and may also include the design and development of pre-written computer software. However, manufacturing does not include the furnishing of information services subject to sales tax under Sec. 1105(c)(1), Tax Law, regardless of whether the information is provided in tangible form. In addition, a taxpayer that performs services for a customer, including manufacturing services, on property or raw materials belonging to the customer will not be considered a manufacturing business. (Rule Sec. 28-07(d))

A business will be considered to be primarily engaged in manufacturing if more than 50% of its gross receipts for the taxable year are derived from the sale of tangible personal property manufactured by the taxpayer. (Sec. 11-508(g), N.Y.C. Adm. Code; Rule Sec. 28-07(d))

The Department of Finance has issued a rule that sets forth a number of examples illustrating the application of the provisions discussed above. (Rule Sec. 28-07(d))

• *Publishers and broadcasters*

For the allocation of gross sales or charges to subscribers located in the City, there is a special direct allocation provision (based on the mailing or billing address) with respect to taxpayers engaged in the business of publishing newspapers or periodicals, or broadcasting radio or television programs through the public airwaves or by cable, direct or indirect satellite transmission, or any other means of transmission. For newspapers and periodicals, a subscriber is located in the City if the mailing address for the subscription is within the City. For program services, a subscriber is located in the City if the billing address for the subscription is within the City. (Sec. 11-508(e-1), N.Y.C. Adm. Code) See also *Finance Memorandum 02-4.*

• *Management services to investment companies*

For tax years beginning after 2000, in calculating the receipts factor of the business allocation percentage, receipts from management, administrative, or distribution services performed for regulated investment companies are deemed to arise from services performed in New York City in the same proportion as the regulated investment company's shares are held by New York state domiciliaries. (Sec. 11-508(e-2), N.Y.C. Adm. Code)

• *Registered brokers and dealers of securities and commodities*

For taxable years beginning after 2008, various receipts from the services of registered brokers and dealers of securities and commodities must be sourced using the customer's mailing address. (Sec. 11-508(e-3), N.Y.C. Adm. Code; Finance Memorandum 09-2)

See also *Update on Audit Issues: Income Allocation*, November 25, 2016.

[¶519-370] Other NYC Methods of Allocation

The portion allocable to New York City will be determined in accordance with rules and regulations of the Commissioner of Finance if it appears to the Commissioner that the income from the city is not fairly and equitably reflected by either allocation by the taxpayer's books or by allocation by formula. (Sec. 11-508(d), N.Y.C. Adm. Code)

In addition, the Commissioner is specifically authorized to make adjustments to any business allocation percentage to properly reflect the activity, business or income of an unincorporated business within New York City. (Sec. 11-508(h), N.Y.C. Adm. Code)

Request for permission to use an alternative allocation method.—The Department of Finance has announced that, if a taxpayer believes that using the statutory method of allocation does not lead to a result that fairly and equitably reflects New York City income, the taxpayer may obtain the department's consent to use a different allocation method by submitting a written request, separate and apart from the tax return, describing the alternative method. The request, which is applicable only to a single tax year, may be made before or after the filing of the return. Unless consent to use an alternative method is granted prior to the filing of the return, the statutory method for allocation must be used on the return. (*Notice,* New York City Department of Finance, February 2, 2012)

The written request must fully explain the proposed alternative allocation method. The explanation must provide full information regarding the nature and scope of the business activities carried on within and outside New York City and provide complete details of how the proposed method would allocate income on a more equitable basis than the statutory method. The taxpayer must submit calculations of the tax due under both the statutory method and the proposed alternative method. (*Notice,* New York City Department of Finance, February 2, 2012)

Subscribers can view the announcement.

[¶519-375] NYC Real Estate Income and Deductions Not Subject to Allocation

Income and deductions from the rental of real property, and gain and loss from the sale, exchange or other disposition of real property, are not subject to allocation but are considered to be entirely derived from or connected with the state, other than New York State, in which the property is located or, if the property is in New York State, the political subdivision of New York State. Where a building is held partly for occupancy and use by the unincorporated business and partly for the production of rental income, the value of the property should be apportioned on a fair and equitable basis and only the portion of such value attributable to occupancy and use by the unincorporated business should be included in the property percentage of the allocation formula. (Sec. 11-508(e), N.Y.C. Adm. Code; Rule Sec. 28-07(f))

[¶519-400]

NYC UNINCORPORATED BUSINESS TAX CREDITS

[¶519-445] NYC Credit for Partners in Unincorporated Businesses Required to Include Distributive Shares from Partnership in Unincorporated Business Taxable Income

For taxable years beginning on or after July 1, 1994, a credit is allowed to partners in unincorporated businesses who are subject to unincorporated business tax and are required to include in unincorporated business taxable income their distributive share of income, gain, loss and deductions of, or guaranteed payments from, the unincorporated business. The credit must be taken after the fixed dollar credit, but before any other credit. (Sec. 11-503(j), N.Y.C. Adm. Code)

• *Calculation of credit*

The credit is equal to the lesser of the following amounts:

(1) the sum of (a) the unincorporated business tax paid by the unincorporated business for the taxable year ending within or with the taxable year of the partner and (b) the amount of any credit or credits taken by the unincorporated business (other than the fixed dollar tax credit allowed under Sec. 11-503(b), N.Y.C. Adm. Code), for its taxable year ending within or with the taxable year of the partner, to the extent that such credits do not reduce the unincorporated business's tax to an amount below zero, multiplied by a fraction, the numerator of which is the net total of the partner's distributive share of income, gain, loss and deductions of, and guaranteed payments from the unincorporated business, and the denominator of which is the sum of the net total distributive shares of income, gain, loss and deductions of, and guaranteed payments to, all partners in the unincorporated business for whom or which such net total (as separately determined for each partner) is greater than zero, for the taxable year; or

(2) the difference between (a) the tax on the unincorporated business taxable income of the partner, without allowance of any credits, and (b) the tax computed as if the partner had no distributive share or guaranteed payments with respect to the unincorporated business. The amounts so computed are subject to the following modifications:

(i) the amounts are determined without taking into account any carryforward or carryback by the partner of a net operating loss;

(ii) unincorporated business taxable income is treated as zero if, prior to taking into account any distributive share or guaranteed payments from any unincorporated business or any net operating loss carryforward or carryback, the partner's unincorporated business taxable income is less than zero; and

(iii) if the partner's net total distributive share of income, gain, loss and deductions of, and guaranteed payments from, any unincorporated business is less than zero, its net total is treated as zero.

In addition, the amount determined under (2) may not be less than zero.

• *Credit limitations*

The credit (or sum of the credits) that may be taken by a partner for a taxable year with respect to an unincorporated business or businesses in which he, she or it is a partner may not exceed the tax on the partner's unincorporated business taxable income for the year, as reduced by the fixed dollar tax credit.

• *Carryforward of unused credit*

Excess credit may be carried forward and used in any of the succeeding seven taxable years. Credits first arising in a particular year must be taken before any credit carryforwards, and carryforwards attributable to the earliest taxable year must be taken before any credit carryforwards attributable to a subsequent taxable year.

Where a partner is itself a partnership, no credit carryforward will be allowed unless one or more of the partners of the partnership during such year has a proportionate interest or interests, amounting to at least 80% of all interests in the unincorporated business gross income and unincorporated business deductions of the partnership that was allowed the credit for which the carryforward is claimed. The carryforward allowable on account of the credit may not exceed the percentage of the amount otherwise allowable, determined by dividing (1) the sum of the proportionate interests in the unincorporated business gross income and unincorporated business deductions of the partnership, for the year to which the credit is carried forward, attributable to such partners, by (2) the sum of such proportionate interests owned by all partners for the taxable year. The amount by which the carryforward otherwise allowable exceeds the amount allowable pursuant to the preceding sentence may not be carried forward to any other taxable year.

NEW YORK CITY PROPERTY

[¶520-000]

NYC--INTRODUCTION

[¶520-010] NYC Overview

Property taxes in New York City are imposed only on real property (see ¶520-310), unless otherwise exempt, as well as on special franchises in the city. Special franchises are the rights and privileges possessed by certain utilities to lay property across public ways and lands. (see ¶520-330) All real property located in New York City is subject to tax. (see ¶520-110)

The provisions of the Real Property Tax Law, governing property taxation statewide, apply equally within New York City, and certain provisions of the Real Property Tax Law deal specifically with property within New York City. In addition, provisions of the New York City Charter and the New York City Administrative Code amplify or supersede provisions of the Real Property Tax Law, as authorized by the state statute. General property tax provisions of statewide application are discussed in the "Property" division of this Reporter. Discussed below are those provisions that apply specifically to New York City.

• *Classification of property*

Property within New York City is divided into four classes under the Real Property Tax Law: (see ¶520-105)

    (1) class one consists of one-, two-, and three-family homes;

    (2) class two consists of other residential property;

    (3) class three consists of utility property; and

    (4) class four consists of all other property.

• *Persons liable for payment of tax*

Assessment of tax is made against the real property, which is liable to sale for unpaid taxes or special assessments. (Sec. 304(1), Real Property Tax Law) However, owners of property, or of an interest in property, are personally liable for property taxes if they are residents of the city or town in which the property or interest is assessed and if their names are correctly entered on the tax roll. (Sec. 926(1), Real Property Tax Law) See ¶20-245 for a discussion regarding renters' liability for tax.

• *Tax rates*

Tax rates are determined by the City Council, but changes in the relative share of the tax burden of each class may not exceed limitations set by the Real Property Tax Law.

In addition, the increase in assessed valuation of property is limited by the Real Property Tax Law, with a different limit set for each class. Moreover, the New York State Constitution limits the amount of taxes to be raised to $2^1/2\%$ of the average full valuation of the taxable property within the city. However, this limitation may be exceeded under certain circumstances.

For a discussion of New York City tax rates, see ¶520-405.

[¶520-100]

NYC--TAXABILITY OF PROPERTY AND PERSONS

[¶520-105] NYC Classification of Property

Classification of property located in special assessing units is mandatory under the Real Property Tax Law. (Sec. 1802(1), Real Property Tax Law) Special assessing units are assessing units with a population of one million or more, which describes only New York City and Nassau County.

Property in New York City is divided into four classes. Different tax rates are imposed on each class in order to minimize changes in the relative share of the total tax levy paid by each class: (see ¶520-405) NYC Rates of Tax; Sec. 1803-b, Real Property Tax Law

(1) Class 1 property consists of:

(a) all one-, two- and three-family residential real property, other than property held in cooperative or condominium form of ownership, with the exception of condominiums of no more than three dwellings units that were included in Class 1 on a previous assessment roll and bungalow colonies in existence prior to 1940 located on land held in cooperative ownership for the sole purpose of maintaining one-family residences for its members own use;

(b) residential condominiums of no more than three stories in height, no dwelling unit of which was previously on an assessment roll as a dwelling unit in other than condominium form of ownership;

(c) mobile homes or trailers that are owner-occupied and separately assessed; and

(d) vacant land other than land in the borough of Manhattan south of or adjacent to the south side of 110th St., provided the land is (i) zoned residential, or is immediately adjacent to property improved with a residential structure and has been owned by the same owner as the adjacent residential property since January 1, 1989, and has a total area of 10,000 square feet or less, or (ii) located in the borough of Manhattan north of or adjacent to the north side of 110th St., provided the vacant land was classified within this class on the assessment roll with a taxable status date of January 5, 2008 and the owner of the land has entered into a recorded agreement with a governmental entity on or before December 31, 2008 requiring construction of housing affordable to persons or families of low income in accordance with the provisions of the Private Housing Finance Law.

(2) Class 2 property is all residential real property that is not designated as Class 1, except hotels and motels and other commercial properties:

(a) Sub-Class 2a; (4 – 6 unit rental building)

(b) Sub-Class 2b; (7 – 10 unit rental building)

(c) Sub-Class 2c; and (2 – 10 unit cooperative or condominium)

(d) Class 2. (11 units or more)

(*Definitions of Property Assessment Terms*, New York City Department of Finance, http://www.nyc.gov/html/dof/html/property/)

(3) Class 3 consists of utility real property. (see ¶520-330 NYC Utilities)

(4) Class 4 consists of all property not classified as Class 1, 2, or 3.

(Sec. 1802(1), Real Property Tax Law)

¶520-100

[¶520-105] NYC Classification of Property

Classification of property located in special assessing units is mandatory under the Real Property Tax Law. (Sec. 1802(1), Real Property Tax Law, ¶96-878) Special assessing units are assessing units with a population of one million or more, which describes only New York City and Nassau County.

Property in New York City is divided into four classes. Different tax rates are imposed on each class in order to minimize changes in the relative share of the total tax levy paid by each class: (see ¶520-405 NYC Rates of Tax; Sec. 1803-b, Real Property Tax Law)

(1) Class 1 property consists of:

(a) all one-, two- and three-family residential real property, other than property held in cooperative or condominium form of ownership, with the exception of condominiums of no more than three dwellings units that were included in Class 1 on a previous assessment roll and bungalow colonies in existence prior to 1940 located on land held in cooperative ownership for the sole purpose of maintaining one-family residences for its members own use;

(b) residential condominiums of no more than three stories in height, no dwelling unit of which was previously on an assessment roll as a dwelling unit in other than condominium form of ownership;

(c) mobile homes or trailers that are owner-occupied and separately assessed; and

(d) vacant land other than land in the borough of Manhattan south of or adjacent to the south side of 110th St., provided the land is (i) zoned residential, or is immediately adjacent to property improved with a residential structure and has been owned by the same owner as the adjacent residential property since January 1, 1989, and has a total area of 10,000 square feet or less, or (ii) located in the borough of Manhattan north of or adjacent to the north side of 110th St., provided the vacant land was classified within this class on the assessment roll with a taxable status date of January 5, 2008 and the owner of the land has entered into a recorded agreement with a governmental entity on or before December 31, 2008 requiring construction of housing affordable to persons or families of low income in accordance with the provisions of the Private Housing Finance Law.

(2) Class 2 property is all residential real property that is not designated as Class 1, except hotels and motels and other commercial properties:

(a) Sub-Class 2a; (4 – 6 unit rental building)

(b) Sub-Class 2b; (7 – 10 unit rental building)

(c) Sub-Class 2c; and (2 – 10 unit cooperative or condominium)

(d) Class 2. (11 units or more)

(*Definitions of Property Assessment Terms*, New York City Department of Finance, http://www.nyc.gov/html/dof/html/property/)

(3) Class 3 consists of utility real property. (see ¶520-330 NYC Utilities)

(4) Class 4 consists of all property not classified as Class 1, 2, or 3.

(Sec. 1802(1), Real Property Tax Law)

[¶520-110] NYC Taxable Situs of Property and Taxpayers

All real property in New York City is assessed in the City. This is true irrespective of the location of the owner, since all assessments are made against the real property. (Sec. 304(1), Real Property Tax Law)

For a discussion of real property in New York City, see ¶520-310.

[¶520-140] NYC Condominiums, Townhomes, and Cooperatives

Discussed below are property tax rebate and abatement provisions.

CCH COMMENT: Buildings damaged by Superstorm Sandy.—New York City adopted a local law that allows the issuance of property tax rebates for tax lots seriously damaged by Hurricane Sandy on October 29 and 30, 2012. The rebate will be paid to the owner who owned the building on October 30, 2012, and is equal to two-thirds of that portion of the annual tax on an eligible real property that is attributable to the assessed valuation of the improvements on the property. (Sec. 11-240, N.Y.C. Adm. Code; Sec. 467-g, Real Property Tax Law; Rule Sec. 51-01)

Pro-rated rebates are available for eligible cooperative properties and residential real properties consisting of one-family, owner-occupied houses situated on land held in cooperative ownership by owner-occupiers that constituted bungalow colonies in existence prior to 1940. (Sec. 11-240, N.Y.C. Adm. Code; Sec. 467-g, Real Property Tax Law; Rule Sec. 51-01)

Rebates are not allowed for property with no annual tax, or for a property with real property tax arrears in excess of $25.00 for fiscal year 2013 or any prior year. (Sec. 11-240, N.Y.C. Adm. Code; Sec. 467-g, Real Property Tax Law; Rule Sec. 51-01)

A partial property tax abatement is allowed to certain homeowners of residential cooperative and condominium units in class-two multi-family residential properties. The abatement, which was first allowed for the 1996 fiscal year, is determined on the basis of the average assessment per residential unit. (Sec. 467-a(2), Real Property Tax Law; Rule Sec. 50-01) An "applicant" for the abatement means the board of managers of a condominium or the board of directors of a cooperative apartment corporation. In addition, the Commissioner of Finance may by rule designate the owner of a dwelling unit as an applicant. (Sec. 467-a(1), Real Property Tax Law)

The Department of Finance issued a FAQ sheet that details eligibility for the abatement and application procedures. (FAQ - Co-Op/Condo Rev. 07.09.2013)

CCH COMMENT: Cooperative apartments.—For purposes of the abatement, tenant-stockholders of cooperative apartment corporations are deemed to own the dwelling unit that is represented by their shares of stock in the corporation. Any abatements must be credited by the appropriate taxing authority against the tax due on the property as a whole. The reduction in real property taxes received must, in turn, be credited by the cooperative apartment corporation against the amount of the taxes attributable to eligible dwelling units at the time of receipt. A civil penalty of not more than $10,000 may be imposed on each member of a cooperative board of directors who willfully fails to credit fully the abatement. (Sec. 467-a(6), Real Property Tax Law)

- *Eligibility requirements*

Sponsors (including those who succeed to the rights and assume the obligations of the original sponsor) of condominium and cooperative projects are ineligible to claim the abatement. Also ineligible are unit owners or tenant-stockholders who, as of an applicable status date, own more than three dwelling units in any one property held in cooperative or condominium form of ownership. (Sec. 467-a(2), Real Property Tax Law; Rule Sec. 50-03)

The abatement may be granted to a cooperative or condominium dwelling unit held in trust solely for the benefit of a person or persons who would otherwise be eligible to receive a tax abatement if that person or persons legally owned the unit. In addition, the property will not be prohibited from receiving the abatement if the property or certain dwelling units within are receiving benefits pursuant to §425 (School Tax Relief exemption (STAR)) or §459-c (persons with disabilities and limited incomes exemption) of the Real Property Tax Law. (Sec. 467-a(2), Real Property Tax Law)

Property that receives other real property tax exemptions or abatements is generally ineligible to claim the abatement. Property that qualifies for "J-51" abatements (a tax program administered under Sec. 11-243, N.Y.C. Adm. Code, that grants tax exemptions and abatements for improvements to substandard dwellings—see ¶520-215 Housing) or veteran's or senior citizens exemptions, however, is eligible.

- *Determination of abatement*

The partial tax abatement amounts for fiscal years commencing in calendar years 2012 through 2018 are:

Eligible dwelling units in property whose	Amount of Tax Abatement						
average unit assessed value is	2012	2013	2014	2015	2016	2017	2018
$50,000 or less	25%	26.5%	28.1%	28.1%	28.1%	28.1%	28.1%
$50,001 - $55,000	22.5%	23.8%	25.2%	25.2%	25.2%	25.2%	25.2%
$55,001 - $60,000	20%	21.2%	22.5%	22.5%	22.5%	22.5%	22.5%
$60,001 and above	17.5%	17.5%	17.5%	17.5%	17.5%	17.5%	17.5%

(Sec. 467-a(2), Real Property Tax Law)

Tax abatements for fiscal years commencing in calendar years from 1996 through 2011 were determined in accordance with the following table:

Eligible dwelling units in property whose	Amount of Tax Abatement		
average unit assessed value is	1996	1997	1998-2011
Less than or equal to $15,000	4.00%	16.00%	25.0%
Greater than $15,000	2.75%	10.75%	17.5%

(Sec. 467-a(2), Real Property Tax Law)

The abatements are computed on the net real property taxes attributable to or due on eligible dwelling units after deductions for other allowable exemptions or abatements. If the billable assessed value of a property is reduced after the assessment roll becomes final, any abatement previously granted must be adjusted. The difference between the original abatement and the adjusted abatement will be deducted from any credit otherwise due.

- *Denial, termination, or revocation of abatement*

The Commissioner may deny, terminate or revoke an abatement upon a determination that the transfer of a dwelling unit was made primarily for the purpose of receiving an abatement. Upon making such determination, the Commissioner will also deny, terminate or revoke any abatement applied for or granted with respect to any unit owned by the transferor that otherwise would have been eligible for an abatement. In making such determination, the Commissioner may consider, among other factors, the relationship, if any, between the transferor and the transferee and whether the terms of the transfer are consistent with the terms generally found in transfers of comparable dwelling units. (Sec. 467-a(2), Real Property Tax Law)

Phase outs for owners currently receiving the abatement.—The abatement will be phased out if the owner is not using the unit as their primary residence and the owner received the abatement in 2011/2012. (Sec. 467-a(2), Real Property Tax Law)

• *Application for abatement*

Applications for new cooperative and condominium developments must be submitted to the Commissioner of Finance by the board of managers of a condominium or the board of directors of a cooperative apartment corporation for the fiscal years beginning in calendar years 2014-2018 will be established by the commissioner, provided that such date or dates may not be later than the February 15 for such calendar years. (Sec. 467-a(3), Real Property Tax Law)

• *Green roof tax abatement*

A property tax abatement is allowed for the construction of a green roof on a class one, two, or four property in New York City, equal to $4.50 per square foot of green roof space. A green roof is an addition to at least 50% of a roof's space on a eligible building that includes a growth medium and a vegetation layer of drought resistant and hardy plant species that covers at least 80% of the addition. (Sec. 499-bbb, Real Property Law)

Beginning with tax years commencing on or after July 1, 2014, and ending on or before June 30, 2019, the tax abatement is increased from $4.50 per square foot to $5.23 per square foot of a green roof. (Sec. 499-bbb, Real Property Law)

The amount of the tax abatement may not exceed the lesser of $200,000 (prior to December 18, 2013, $100,000) or the tax liability for the eligible building in the tax year for which the tax abatement is taken. The abatement begins on July 1 following the approval of an application for tax abatement by a designated agency and is available for one year. Tax abatement applications must be filed between January 1, 2009, and March 15, 2018. (Sec. 499-bbb, Real Property Law; Sec. 499-ccc, Real Property Law)

The amount that can be spent in any one year on the abatement program is capped at $750,000 in City fiscal year 2015 and $1 million in City fiscal years 2016, 2017, 2018, and 2019. The aggregate amount of abatements will be allocated by the New York City Department of Finance among eligible applicants on a pro rata basis. (Sec. 499-bbb, Real Property Law)

• *Abatement for solar electric generating systems*

A property tax abatement is granted for the construction of a solar electric generating system in connection with a class one, two, or four building in New York City. (Sec. 499-bbbb, Real Property Law) A "solar electric generating system" is a system that uses solar energy to generate electricity. Eligible solar electric generating system expenditures include reasonable expenditures for materials, labor costs properly allocable to on-site preparation, assembly and original installation, architectural and engineering services, and designs and plans directly related to the construction or installation of the solar electric generating system. (Sec. 499-aaaa, Real Property Law)

If the solar electric generating system is placed in service on or after January 1, 2011, and before January 1, 2013, the amount of the tax abatement is equal to the lesser of: 5% of eligible solar electric generating system expenditures; the amount of taxes payable in such tax year; or $62,500. If the solar electric generating system is placed in service on or after January 1, 2013, and before January 1, 2014, the amount of the tax abatement is equal to the lesser of: 2.5% of eligible solar electric generating system expenditures; the amount of taxes payable in such tax year; or $62,500. If the solar electric generating system is placed in service on or after January 1, 2014, and before January 1, 2019, the amount of the tax abatement is the lesser of: 5% of such expenditures; the amount of taxes payable in such tax year; or $62,500. (Sec. 499-bbbb, Real Property Law)

The tax abatement begins on the July 1 following the approval of an application for tax abatement by a designated agency and may not be carried over to any subsequent tax year. (Sec. 499-bbbb, Real Property Law)

[¶520-145] NYC Construction Work in Progress

Except for commercial buildings (see discussion below), buildings under construction are not assessed in a tax year if construction was begun after the preceding January 5 and the building is not ready for occupancy on the following January 5, unless the building is ready for occupancy, or a part of it is occupied, prior to April 15. (Sec. 11-209, N.Y.C. Adm. Code)

For commercial buildings, the duration of the exemption is three years, rather than one year. (Sec. 11-209, N.Y.C. Adm. Code)

[¶520-155] NYC Disabled Persons

A partial real property tax exemption of up to 50% of a property's assessed valuation is allowed for persons with disabilities whose incomes are limited due to such disabilities. (Sec. 11-245.4, N.Y.C. Adm. Code) The exemption applies to real property owned by one or more persons with disabilities and extends to property owned jointly or separately by a husband and wife or by siblings as long as one of them has a disability.

Only real property or the portion of real property used exclusively for residential purposes is entitled to the exemption. (Sec. 11-245.4, N.Y.C. Adm. Code) Further, the disabled person must use and occupy the real property as a legal residence unless the person is absent while occupying a residential health care facility.

For a discussion of disabled veterans for New York City purposes, see ¶520-335 NYC Veterans.

• *Computation of exemption*

For disabled persons with annual incomes less than $50,000, the exemption is equal to 50% of the assessed valuation. For persons with incomes between $50,000 and $58,400, the partial exemption is computed on the basis of the combined income of the owners of the property as follows: (Sec. 11-245.4, N.Y.C. Adm. Code)

Combined Income	Exemption
More than $50,000 but less than $51,000	45%
$51,000 or more but less than $52,000	40%
$52,000 or more but less than $53,000	35%
$53,000 or more but less than $53,900	30%
$53,900 or more but less than $54,800	25%
$54,800 or more but less than $55,700	20%
$55,700 or more but less than $56,600	15%
$56,600 or more but less than $57,500	10%
$57,500 or more but less than $58,400	5%

The combined income amount may be reduced by the amount paid for a disabled person's stay in a residential health care facility.

The exemption is applied after all other applicable partial exemptions have been subtracted from the total amount assessed. (Sec. 11-245.4, N.Y.C. Adm. Code) However, the exemption may not be combined with the New York City real property tax exemption for persons 65 years of age or older.

Proof of eligibility for the exemption is required. (Sec. 11-134, N.Y.C. Adm. Code)

• *Credit for persons with disabilities*

New York City taxpayers who qualify for the exemption for persons with disabilities and limited incomes may claim a credit against their City Fiscal Year (CFY) 2000 real estate tax liability equal to the difference between the amount of tax due for CFY 1999 and the amount of tax that would have been due if the exemption had applied to the assessment roll completed in calendar year 1998. Taxpayers must apply for the credit at the same time they file their application for exemption for CFY 2000, and the amount of the credit shall not exceed the amount of taxes due for CFY 2000. (Ch. 447, Laws 1998)

• *Rent-controlled dwellings*

For a discussion of exemptions and abatements for disabled persons or senior citizens in rent-controlled dwellings, see ¶520-315.

[¶520-165] NYC Energy Systems or Facilities

A full or partial exemption for a 14-year period is available for increases in assessment attributable to reasonable costs of alterations or improvements to multiple dwellings to conserve the use of fuel, electricity or other energy sources (including the installation of meters for the purpose of monitoring the amount of electricity consumed in each dwelling). The alterations or improvements had to begin after January 1, 1980, and generally be completed within 30 months from the date of commencement. The 30-month period for completion may be extended to 60 months for alterations or improvements by housing development fund companies organized pursuant to Article 11, Private Housing Finance Law, carried out with the substantial assistance of federal, state or local grants, loans or subsidies, or alterations or improvements carried out in property transferred from the City of New York that are completed within seven years from the date of transfer. (Sec. 11-243(b), N.Y.C. Adm. Code)

Under New York City's J-51 Program, the exemption includes conversions from a direct electricity metering system to a system that includes a master meter and submeters in any cooperative, condominium, or housing development fund company organized under Article 11 of the Private Housing Finance Law. (Sec. 11-243(b), N.Y.C. Adm. Code)

The Department of Housing Preservation and Development may extend the period of completion for projects carried out with the substantial assistance of federal, state or local grants, loans or subsidies, provided completion occurs within 60 months from the commencement of construction. All conversions, improvements, or alterations must, however, be completed prior to June 30, 2020.

See also ¶520-330 NYC Utilities.

• *Computation of exemption*

Where applicable, whole or partial exemption of increases in assessed valuation are available as follows:

Years	Exemption
1—10	100%
11	80%
12	60%
13	40%
14	20%

(Sec. 11-243(b)(10), N.Y.C. Adm. Code)

The exemption will usually commence with the first tax period immediately following the completion of the alteration or improvement. Exemptions may commence at the beginning of any tax period subsequent to the start of the alteration or improvement if the alterations or improvements are:

— aided by a loan or grant under Articles 8, 8-A, 11, 12, 15 or 22, Private Housing Finance Law, Sec. 696-a, or Sec. 99-h, General Municipal Law, Sec. 312 of the Housing Act of 1964 (42 U.S.C. § 1452b), or the Cranston-Gonzalez National Affordable Housing Act; (42 U.S.C. § 12701 *et seq.*)

— started after July 1, 1983, by a housing development fund company organized under Article 11, Private Housing Finance Law, and carried out with the substantial assistance of federal, state or local grants, loans or subsidies; or

— carried out on property transferred from the City of New York, where the alterations or improvements are completed within seven years from the date of transfer.

(Sec. 11-243(b)(10), N.Y.C. Adm. Code)

• *Additional abatement*

Qualified projects are also eligible for tax abatements for a period of up to 20 years in an amount not greater than 8-1/3% of the reasonable costs of the alterations or improvements. (Sec. 11-243(c)(1), N.Y.C. Adm. Code) The abatement of taxes in any consecutive 12-month period may not exceed the amount of taxes payable for that period. The aggregate abatement may not exceed 90% of the reasonable cost of the improvement or alteration (50%, if the alteration or improvement is done in conjunction with the conversion of a nonresidential building or structure situated in New York County to a Class A multiple dwelling).

The additional abatement will usually commence on the later of July 1, 1978, or the first tax period immediately following the completion of the alteration or improvement. Abatements may commence at the later of the beginning of any tax period subsequent to the start of the alteration or improvement or:

— July 1, 1976, if aided by a loan pursuant to Article 8, Private Housing Finance Law and completed after December 31, 1975;

— July 1, 1977, if aided by a loan pursuant to Article 15, Private Housing Finance Law;

— July 1, 1980, if aided by a loan pursuant to Article 8-A, Private Housing Finance Law or Sec. 312 of the Housing Act of 1964; (42 U.S.C. § 1452b)

— July 1, 1988, if started after that date by a qualified nonprofit corporation pursuant to IRC Sec. 501(c)(3) that has entered into a regulatory agreement with the Local Housing Agency requiring operation of the property as housing for low and moderate income persons and families; or

— July 1, 1992, if started after that date and aided by a loan or grant pursuant to Article 11, 12 or 22, Private Housing Finance Law, Sec. 696-a or Sec. 99-h, General Municipal Law, or the Cranston-Gonzelez National Affordable Housing Act. (42 U.S.C. § 12701 *et seq.*)

(Sec. 11-243(c)(1), N.Y.C. Adm. Code)

[¶520-200] NYC Historic Property

A full or partial exemption for a 14-year period is available for increases in assessment attributable to reasonable costs of alterations or improvements pursuant to permits issued by the Landmarks Commission to the exteriors of designated historic landmark sites or structures. (Sec. 11-243(b), N.Y.C. Adm. Code) Generally, the alterations or improvements must be completed within 36 months from the date of commencement. The 36-month period for completion may be extended to 60 months for alterations or improvements by housing development fund companies organized pursuant to Article 11, Private Housing Finance Law, carried out with the substantial assistance of federal, state or local grants, loans or subsidies, or alterations or improvements carried out in property transferred from the City of New York that are completed within seven years from the date of transfer.

• *Computation of exemption*

Where applicable, whole or partial exemption of increases in assessed valuation are available as follows:

YearsExemption

1—10	100%
11	80%
12	60%
13	40%
14	20%

The exemption will usually commence with the first tax period immediately following the completion of the alteration or improvement. Exemptions may commence at the beginning of any tax period subsequent to the start of the alteration or improvement if the alterations or improvements are:

— aided by a loan or grant under Articles 8, 8-A, 11, 12, 15 or 22, Private Housing Finance Law, Sec. 696-a, or Sec. 99-h, General Municipal Law, Sec. 312 of the Housing Act of 1964 (42 U.S.C. § 1452b), or the Cranston-Gonzelez National Affordable Housing Act; (42 U.S.C. § 12701 et seq.)

— started after July 1, 1983, by a housing development fund company organized under Article 11, Private Housing Finance Law, and are carried out with the substantial assistance of federal, state or local grants, loans or subsidies; or

— carried out on property transferred from the City of New York, where the alterations or improvements are completed within seven years from the date of transfer.

• *Additional abatement*

Qualified projects are also eligible for tax abatements for a period of up to 20 years in an amount not greater than $8^{1}/3\%$ of the reasonable costs of the alterations or improvements. (Sec. 11-243(c), N.Y.C. Adm. Code) The abatement of taxes in any consecutive 12-month period may not exceed the amount of taxes payable for that period. The aggregate abatement may not exceed 90% of the reasonable cost of the improvement or alteration (50%, if the alteration or improvement is done in conjunction with the conversion of a nonresidential building or structure situated in New York County to a Class A multiple dwelling).

The additional abatement will usually commence on the later of July 1, 1978, or the first tax period immediately following the completion of the alteration or improvement. Abatements may commence at the later of beginning of any tax period subsequent to the start of the alteration or improvement or:

— July 1, 1976, if aided by a loan pursuant to Article 8, Private Housing Finance Law and completed after December 31, 1975;

— July 1, 1977, if aided by a loan pursuant to Article 15, Private Housing Finance Law;

— July 1, 1980, if aided by a loan pursuant to Article 8-A, Private Housing Finance Law or Sec. 312 of the Housing Act of 1964; (42 U.S.C. § 1452b)

— July 1, 1988, if started after that date by a qualified nonprofit corporation pursuant to IRC Sec. 501(c)(3) that has entered into a regulatory agreement with the Local Housing Agency requiring operation of the property as housing for low and moderate income persons and families; or

— July 1, 1992, if started after that date and aided by a loan or grant pursuant to Article 11, 12 or 22, Private Housing Finance Law, Sec. 696-a, or Sec. 9-h, General Municipal Law, or the Cranston-Gonzelez National Affordable Housing Act. (42 U.S.C. § 12701 *et seq.*)

[¶520-205] NYC Homestead

New York City has no specific provisions for homestead exemptions, aside from the senior citizen homeowners exemption (SCHE) discussed below. However, residential real property is separately classified and taxed at a preferential rate. (see ¶ 520-105 NYC Classification of Property and ¶ 520-405 NYC Rates of Tax)

CCH COMMENT: Buildings damaged by Superstorm Sandy.—New York City adopted a local law that allows the issuance of property tax rebates for tax lots seriously damaged by Hurricane Sandy on October 29 and 30, 2012. The rebate will be paid to the owner who owned the building on October 30, 2012, and is equal to two-thirds of that portion of the annual tax on an eligible real property that is attributable to the assessed valuation of the improvements on the property. (Sec. 11-240, N.Y.C. Adm. Code; Sec. 467-g, Real Property Tax Law; Sec. 11-240, N.Y.C. Adm. CodeRule Sec. 51-01)

Pro-rated rebates are available for eligible cooperative properties and residential real properties consisting of one-family, owner-occupied houses situated on land held in cooperative ownership by owner-occupiers that constituted bungalow colonies in existence prior to 1940. (Sec. 11-240, N.Y.C. Adm. Code; Sec. 467-g, Real Property Tax Law; Rule Sec. 51-01)

Rebates are not allowed for property with no annual tax, or for a property with real property tax arrears in excess of $25.00 for fiscal year 2013 or any prior year. (Sec. 11-240, N.Y.C. Adm. Code; Sec. 467-g, Real Property Tax Law; Rule Sec. 51-01)

• *Partial abatement for senior citizen homeowners exemption (SCHE)*

Persons age 65 or over, having incomes of less than $58,400 per year, are entitled to a partial abatement of the assessed valuation of a residence that they own and occupy. For persons age 65 or over with annual incomes less than $50,000, the exemption is equal to 50% of the assessed valuation. If title to the property is vested in either the husband or wife, their combined income is used for exemption eligibility and may not exceed this $50,000 limit, unless one of the owners is absent from the property due to divorce, legal separation or abandonment. In this case, the income of the spouse, or ex-spouse, remaining on the property is considered for exemption and subject to the income limit. (Sec. 11-245.3, N.Y.C. Adm. Code)

> **CCH COMMENT: *Application deadline.*—**Applications and deadline information for each year may be accessed on the Department's website. (*New York City Department of Finance*, http://www1.nyc.gov/site/finance/benefits/landlords-sche.page)

See also ¶ 520-315 NYC Senior Citizens.

For persons with annual incomes of more than $50,000 but less than $58,400 as of July 1, 2017, the following exemptions are allowed:

Annual Income . . . . **Percentage of Assessed Valuation Exempt**

Annual Income	Percentage of Assessed Valuation Exempt
More than $50,000 but less than $51,000	45%
$51,000 or more but less than $52,000	40%
$52,000 or more but less than $53,000	35%
$53,000 or more but less than $53,900	30%
$53,900 or more but less than $54,800	25%
$54,800 or more but less than $55,700	20%
$55,700 or more but less than $56,600	15%
$56,600 or more but less than $57,500	10%
$57,500 or more but less than $58,400	5%

In determining income, certain deductions are allowed (e.g., for inheritances, veterans disability compensation, money earned through employment in the federal foster grandparent program, and payments made to individuals because of their status as victims of Nazi persecution; Sec. 11-245.3, N.Y.C. Adm. Code)

The exemption is inapplicable to school taxes if a child residing at the property attends a public elementary or secondary school. (Sec. 11-245.3, N.Y.C. Adm. Code)

The applicant for exemption must have held title to the property for at least 12 consecutive months prior to the date of application. Determination of ownership during the 12-month period for a surviving spouse, who takes the property by devise or descent upon the death of the spouse in whose name the property was vested at the time of death, takes into account the period during which the property was held by the deceased spouse. The ownership period of both spouses is deemed continuous and is deemed the period of ownership of the survivor. (Sec. 11-245.3, N.Y.C. Adm. Code)

Cooperative apartments.—Title to real property owned by a co-op apartment corporation in which a 65 year old or older tenant-stockholder resides and which is represented by his or her share(s) of stock (as determined by its or their proportional relationship to the total outstanding stock, including that owned by the corporation) will be deemed to be vested in the tenant-stockholder. (Sec. 11-245.3, N.Y.C. Adm. Code)

Age and occupancy requirement.—If the owners of the property are husbands and wives, or siblings, one of the owners must be 65 years of age or over. Exemptions are granted only if the property is the legal residence of, or is occupied by, the owners of the property. Exceptions are made to this rule if the property is vacant due to the following two circumstances:

(1) the owner is absent from the property while receiving health-related care as an inpatient of a residential health care facility, provided that any income accruing to that person exceeds the amount paid for the facility's care, and that the property, during the confinement, is not occupied by persons other than the owner's spouse or co-owner; or

(2) if real property is owned by a husband or wife, or an ex-husband or ex-wife, and either is absent from the property due to divorce, legal separation or abandonment, an exemption may be granted if an exemption was previously granted when both owners resided on the property, and the person remaining on the property is 62 years of age or over.

Once granted, an exemption will not be rescinded solely because of the death of the older spouse provided the surviving spouse is at least 62 years of age. (Sec. 11-245.3, N.Y.C. Adm. Code)

Residency requirement.—The exemption applies if the property is used exclusively for residential purposes and is the legal residence and occupied in whole or in part by the owner or all of the owners. Any portion of the property that is not used for residential purposes is subject to tax on a prorated basis. (Sec. 11-245.3, N.Y.C. Adm. Code)

Proof of eligibility for the exemption is required. (Sec. 11-134, N.Y.C. Adm. Code)

• *School Tax Relief Program (STAR)*

The STAR program provides a partial exemption from school property taxes. (See ¶ 20-205 Homesteads for a complete discussion of the STAR program exemptions).

CCH COMMENT: Basic STAR Exemption Registration Program.—The New York City Department of Finance advises all homeowners receiving a Basic STAR property tax exemption to register with the New York State Department of Taxation and Finance in order to receive the exemption in 2014 and subsequent years. The registration period began on August 19, 2013, and will continue through December 31, 2013. Homeowners may register online or by calling (518) 457-2036 Monday through Friday, 8:30 a.m. - 8:00 p.m., or Saturdays, 9:00 a.m. - 1:00 p.m. Additional information may be found on the tax department's website at http://www.tax.ny.gov/pit/property/star13/default.htm. (*Notice,* New York City Department of Finance, September 12, 2013)

NEW DEVELOPMENTS: Beginning with assessment rolls used to levy school district taxes for the 2016-2017 school year, the existing School Tax Relief (STAR) exemption program is closed to new applicants, and a new refundable personal income tax credit is established in its place, Current recipients of STAR exemptions are permitted to keep the exemptions as long as they continue to own their homes, but upon transfer of the property to a new owner, the new owner would only be eligible for the income tax credit program. Current STAR exemption recipients have the option of giving up their STAR exemptions in favor of the personal income tax credit, though it is not required. (Sec. 425(16), Real Property Tax Law)

If the owners of a parcel that is receiving the STAR exemption want to claim the personal income tax credit in lieu of such exemption, they all must renounce that exemption in the manner provided by Sec. 496, Real Property Tax Law, and must pay any required taxes, interest and penalties, on or before December 31 of the taxable year for which they want to claim the credit. Any such renunciation is irrevocable. (Sec. 425(16), Real Property Tax Law)

• *Voluntary STAR exemption renunciation*

A property owner may voluntarily renounce his or her claim to a school tax relief (STAR) exemption. The owner must file an application form authorized by the tax commissioner, together with a $500 application fee, with the commissioner of finance in New York City no later than 10 years after the levy of taxes on the assessment roll. If an applicant is renouncing a STAR exemption in order to qualify for the personal income tax credit authorized by Sec. 606(eee), Tax Law, and no other exemptions are being renounced on the same application, no processing will apply. (Sec. 496, Real Property Tax Law)

The assessed value of the property will be multiplied by the tax rate or rates that were applied to that assessment roll, and interest will be added to the product for each month or portion thereof since the levy of taxes on the assessment roll. (Sec. 496, Real Property Tax Law)

The property owner must pay the total amount due to the county treasurer within 15 days of the mailing of the form. (Sec. 496, Real Property Tax Law)

[¶520-210] NYC Household Goods

New York City has no specific provisions regarding household goods. Since personal property is exempt from property tax (see ¶520-295), such issues generally do not arise. (Sec. 300, Real Property Tax Law)

[¶520-215] NYC Housing

Full or partial exemptions or tax abatements are provided for new or substantially rehabilitated multiple dwellings, conversions of Class B multiple dwellings to Class A multiple dwellings, and for the elimination of substandard living conditions in multiple dwellings.

• *New multiple dwellings (421-a/ Affordable New York Housing Program)*

New multiple dwellings in New York City may be eligible for either a 10-year, 15-year, 20-year, or 25-year partial exemption from tax, if they meet certain requirements. (Sec. 421-a, Real Property Tax Law; Sec. 11-245, N.Y.C. Adm. Code) The 10-year exemption is mandatory under the Real Property Tax Law, while the 15- and 25-year exemptions are authorized by the Real Property Tax Law but subject to adoption by the New York City Department of Housing Preservation and Development. All three exemption provisions may be limited by the city government. The city government has adopted provisions relating to all three.

The 20-year exemption applies under the Real Property Tax Law unless excluded by local law. (Sec. 421-a(2)(a)(iv)(A), Real Property Tax Law)

Any dwelling that is occupied as the residence or home of three or more families living independently of each other is a multiple dwelling for purposes of these exemptions. Hotels are excluded. If specific conditions are met, a new multiple dwelling includes new residential construction and the concurrent conversion, alteration or improvement of a pre-existing building or structure. (Sec. 421-a(1), Real Property Tax Law)

For many Sec. 421-a exemptions, construction must be commenced before December 31, 2015. (Sec. 421-a(2)(a)(iv)(A), Real Property Tax Law; Sec. 421-a(2)(c)(ii), Real Property Tax Law) The project will be exempt for the first three years of construction. A preliminary certificate of eligibility must be obtained in order to qualify for a six-year period of construction, although the project will only be eligible for a maximum of three years of benefits during the construction period. (Sec. 421-a(2)(a)(i), Real Property Tax Law)

Ten-year exemption.—A decreasing 10-year partial tax exemption is granted to new multiple dwellings that meet certain requirements. The land on which they are built must have been vacant or underutilized three years before construction was begun, and the property must meet certain geographic location requirements. During construction, up to a maximum period of three years, and for the first two years after completion, the property is 100% exempt. For the third and fourth years, the exemption is 80%; for the fifth and sixth years, 60%; for the seventh and eighth years, 40%; and for the ninth and tenth years, 20%. Applications for exemption must be filed with the assessors between February 1 and March 15. (Sec. 421-a(2)(a), Real Property Tax Law)

Generally, property is considered underutilized prior to construction only if the building or buildings:

— contained no more than the permissible floor area ratio for nonresidential buildings in the zoning district in question and either (a) had a floor area ratio that was 75% or less of the maximum floor area ratio for residential buildings in the zoning district, or (b) if the land was not zoned to permit residential use on the date 36 months prior to the commencement of construction, had a floor area ratio that was 75% or less of the floor area ratio of the residential building that replaces the nonresidential building;

— had an assessed valuation equal to or less than 75% of the assessed valuation of the land on which the building or buildings were situated; or

— by reason of the configuration of the building or substantial structural defects not brought about by deferred maintenance practices or intentional conduct, could no longer be functionally or economically utilized in the capacity in which it was formerly utilized.

(Sec. 11-245.1(a-3), N.Y.C. Adm. Code)

For properties located south of or adjacent to either side of 110th Street in Manhattan, the 75% figures in the underutilization test, above, are replaced with 50% figures. (Sec. 11-245.1(a-4), N.Y.C. Adm. Code)

15-year exemption.—A 15-year exemption is provided for new multiple dwellings meeting the requirements for the 10-year exemption that are located in areas other than those excluded by local law. Property in Manhattan adjacent to or south of 110th St. must meet additional requirements for the 15-year exemption:

(1) the construction must be carried out with the substantial assistance of grants, loans or subsidies from a federal state or local agency or instrumentalities; or

(2) the local housing agency must have imposed a requirement or have certified that 20% of the units be affordable to low-or moderate-income families.

Eligible property is 100% exempt during construction, up to a maximum of three years, and for the first 11 years after completion of construction. The property is 80% exempt in the 12th year after completion; 60% in the 13th year following completion; 40% in the 14th year following completion; and 50% in the 15th year following completion.

New York property tax abatement provisions for new multiple dwellings are extended to include any buildings that provide a certain percentage of affordable housing units to low- and moderate-income residents in the Greenpoint-Williamsburg section of the Bronx. Existing local residents must have priority for the purchase or rental of 50% of the affordable units. (Sec. 421-a(6), Real Property Tax Law)

20-year exemption.—A decreasing 20-year partial tax exemption is available for certain qualifying new multiple dwellings in Manhattan south of or adjacent to either side of 110th Street. (Sec. 421-a(2)(a)(iv), Real Property Tax Law)

25-year exemption.—A 25-year exemption is granted to new multiple dwellings meeting other applicable requirements that are either eligible for mortgage insurance provided by the rehabilitation mortgage insurance corporation or are located in:

— a neighborhood preservation program area as determined by the local housing agency;

— a neighborhood preservation area as determined by the New York City Planning Commission as of June 1, 1985; or

— an area receiving funding for a neighborhood preservation project pursuant to the neighborhood reinvestment act. (42 U.S.C. § 180 *et seq.*)

Property south of or adjacent to 110th St. in Manhattan is ineligible for the 25-year exemption. Property located in areas excluded by local law is also ineligible.

Property eligible for the 25-year exemption is 100% exempt during construction, up to a maximum of three years, and is 100% exempt for the first 21 years following completion of construction. The property is 80% exempt in the 22nd year following completion, 60% exempt in the 23rd year following completion, 40% exempt in the 24th year following completion, and 20% exempt in the 25th year following completion.

Qualifications.—The following conditions apply:

— the owner of the property must pay taxes annually in an amount equal to the taxes payable on the property immediately prior to the start of construction, without regard to any exemption that may have been applicable, in addition to taxes payable in a year of partial exemption;

— if the land on which the dwelling is built was improved with a residential building or buildings immediately prior to the commencement of new construction and the building or buildings contain more than 20 dwelling units, the new construction must contain at least five dwelling units for every Class A dwelling that is, each dwelling unit ordinarily occupied as a permanent residence (Sec. 4(8)(a), Multiple Dwelling Law) in existence immediately prior to construction;

— land mapped as a public park is ineligible;

— land that has been used for ten or more years prior to October 1, 1971, as a private park open to the public without charge is ineligible; and

— if a local rent stabilization law exists, the units are subject to rent control throughout the exemption period, regardless of the provisions of the local law, unless excluded from the local law due to the condominium or cooperative status of the unit.

For purposes of the New York property tax exemption for new multiple dwellings, a local housing authority may impose a maximum filing fee equal to 0.04% of the total project cost or total project sell-out price. The local housing authority also may charge an additional fee when an applicant submits a defective application that delays processing or causes the local housing authority to expend additional resources to process the application. (Sec. 421-a(4)(b), Real Property Tax Law)

Extension of benefits for new multiple dwellings.—Benefits are extended for certain eligible new multiple dwellings. "Eligible multiple dwelling" means a multiple dwelling or home ownership project containing six or more dwelling units created through new construction or eligible conversion for which the commencement date is after December 31, 2015, and on or before June 15, 2022, and for which the completion date is on or before June 15, 2026. (Sec. 421-a(16), Real Property Tax Law)

Eligible sites, except hotels, will be exempt from real property taxation, other than assessments for local improvements. A rental project that meets all requirements will receive a 35-year benefit and a homeownership project that meets all requirements will receive a 20-year benefit. A "35-year benefit" is defined as (1) for the construction period, a 100% exemption from real property taxation, other than assessments for local improvements; (2) for the first 25 years of the restriction period, a 100% exemption from real property taxation, other than assessments for local improvements; and (3) for the final 10 years of the restriction period, an exemption from real property taxation, other than assessments for local improvements, equal to the affordability percentage, which is the number of affordable housing units in an eligible site divided by the total number of dwelling units in the site. A "20-year benefit" is defined as (1) for the construction period, a 100% exemption from real property taxation, other than assessments for local improvements; (2) for the first 14 years of the restriction period, a 100% exemption from real property taxation, other than assessments for local improvements, provided, however, that no exemption may be given for any portion of a unit's assessed value that exceeds $65,000; and (3) for the final six years of the restriction period, a 25% exemption from real property taxation, other than assessments for local improvements, provided, however, that no exemption may be given for any portion of a unit's assessed value that exceeds $65,000. (Sec. 421-a(16)(a), Real Property Tax Law)

During the restriction period, a rental project must comply with any of the enumerated affordability options. An affordability election must be made in the application and cannot be changed once made. (Sec. 421-a(16)(f), Real Property Tax Law)

A full property tax abatement is authorized for 35 years on new residential projects with 300 or more units in certain enhanced affordability areas of Manhattan, Brooklyn, and Queens if the project creates a specific number of affordable rental units and meets newly established minimum construction wage requirements for each locale. The units must remain affordable for 40 years. For all other affordable developments in New York City, the period of affordability and abatement eligibility are tied to the number of affordable units. (Sec. 421-a(16), Real Property Tax Law)

Benefits for extended affordability properties.—An extended affordability property may be granted an extended benefit, provided, however, that such extended benefit will be available only if all residential tax lots in such extended affordability property operate as rental housing. An "extended affordability property" means a 20-year benefit property or a 25-year benefit property that complies with the rent stabilization or affordable housing provisions. "Extended benefit" means, for any extended affordability property, a 50% exemption from real property taxation, other than assessments for local improvements, for the extended affordability period. An extended affordability period is 15 years after the original expiration for a 20-year benefit property, and 10 years after the original expiration for a 25-year benefit property. (Sec. 421-a(17), Real Property Tax Law)

• *Abatement for rent control or tenant protection buildings*

A real property tax abatement exists for Class Two buildings located in New York City that are subject to either the emergency housing rent control law or the rent and rehabilitation law enacted pursuant to the emergency housing rent control law or to the Emergency Tenant Protection Act of 1974. The amount of the abatement is determined by calculating 50% of the economic loss attributed to the building owner as a result of changes to the amortization period for such buildings, which will be measured by a specified fractional formula. An abatement will commence on July 1 following the approval of an application for tax abatement by the Department of Finance and may not be carried over to any subsequent tax year and may not reduce or be offset by any other tax benefit provided, approved or calculated by the city or the state. (Sec. 467-i, Real Property Tax Law; Uncodified Sec. 65, Ch. 20 (S.B. 6012), Laws 2015)

• *Improvements to substandard dwellings (J-51 program)*

Increases in property tax assessments attributable to the conversion of multiple or private dwellings or the elimination of unhealthy or dangerous conditions may qualify for full or partial property tax exemptions for 14- or 34-year periods. (Sec. 11-243(b), N.Y.C. Adm. Code) Generally, projects must be completed within 30 months from the date of commencement. The 30-month period may be extended to 60 months for projects by housing development fund companies organized pursuant to Article 11, Private Housing Finance Law, that are carried out with the substantial assistance of federal, state or local grants, loans or subsidies, or involve property transferred from the City of New York where the conversion, alteration or improvements are completed within seven years from the date of transfer. The Department of Housing Preservation and Development may also extend the period of completion for projects carried out with the substantial assistance of federal, state or local grants, loans or subsidies, provided completion occurs within 60 months from the commencement of construction. All conversions, improvements or alterations must, however, be completed prior to June 30, 2020.

In order to be eligible for J-51 benefits, a redevelopment company must (1) be organized and operated as a mutual redevelopment company, (2) continue to be organized and operating as a mutual redevelopment company and to own and operate the multiple dwelling receiving such benefits, and (3) enter into a binding and irrevocable agreement with the Commissioner of Housing and Community Renewal, the supervising agency, the New York City housing development corporation, or the New York state housing finance agency prohibiting the dissolution or reconstitution of such redevelopment company, until the earlier of 15 years from the commencement of such benefits or the expiration of any tax exemption granted to such redevelopment company. (Sec. 11-243(d)(3-b), N.Y.C. Adm. Code)

14-year property.—A 14-year full or partial exemption is available for the following improvements, alterations or conversions:

— conversion of Class B multiple dwellings to Class A multiple dwellings;

— conversion of nonresidential buildings or structures located in New York, Bronx, Kings, Queens or Richmond Counties to Class A multiple dwellings;

— alterations or improvements to eliminate existing unhealthy or dangerous conditions or to replace inadequate and obsolete sanitary facilities that represent fire or health hazards, including asbestos abatement that is required by federal, state or local law;

— conversion of residential units registered with the New York City Loft Board as interim multiple dwellings; and

— alterations or improvement to private dwellings, conversion of private dwellings to multiple dwellings or conversion of multiple dwellings to private dwellings as part of a project that has applied for or receives federal state or local benefits, grants, loans or subsidies.

Class A multiple dwellings are multiple dwellings that are ordinarily occupied for permanent residence purposes. (Sec. 4(8)(a), Multiple Dwelling Law) Class B multiple dwellings are multiple dwellings that are ordinarily occupied transiently, as a more or less temporary abode. (Sec. 4(9), Multiple Dwelling Law)

Where applicable, the exemptions from increased valuation are applied as follows:

Years - Exemption Percentage

1—10	100%
11	80%
12	60%
13	40%
14	20%

34-year property.—A 34-year full or partial exemption is available for the following improvements, alterations or conversions:

(1) moderate rehabilitation of substantially occupied Class A multiple dwellings; and

(2) alterations or improvements commenced on or after September 1, 1987, that constitute the substantial rehabilitation of Class A multiple dwellings, or the conversion of buildings or structures into Class A multiple dwellings as part of a program to provide housing for low and moderate income households.

Whole or partial exemptions from the increased valuation are available as follows:

Years - Exemption Percentage

1—30	100%
31	80%
32	60%
33	40%
34	20%

Additional abatement.—Qualified conversions, alterations and improvements may also receive tax abatements for up to 20 years in an amount not greater than 8-1/3% of the reasonable cost of the conversion, alterations or improvements. (Sec. 11-243(c), N.Y.C. Adm. Code) The abatement of taxes in any consecutive 12-month period may not exceed the amount of taxes payable in that period. The Department of Housing Preservation sets dollar limitations on the amount of abatement that may be allowed.

Alterations or improvements that qualify for a 34-year exemption under subparagraph (2), above, may be eligible for an increased 20-year tax abatement. (Sec.

11-243(c)(2) and (3), N.Y.C. Adm. Code) The total abatement of taxes on the property, including the land, may not exceed the lesser of the actual cost of the alterations or improvements or 150% of the certified reasonable cost of the alterations or improvements. The annual abatement of tax is limited to $12^1/2\%$ of the certified reasonable cost. Increased abatements also apply where moderate rehabilitations, without restriction as to location, or other types of rehabilitation within a poverty area, is carried out with substantial financial assistance from governmental agencies or instrumentalities, certain not- for-profit philanthropic organizations, or a Federal Housing Administration neighborhood strategy area program.

Anti-harassment provisions apply to taxpayers applying for or receiving exemptions or tax abatements where the certified reasonable cost per dwelling unit of the conversion or improvement exceeds $7,500. (Sec. 11-243(aa), N.Y.C. Adm. Code) All owners of record of the property must file an affidavit to the effect that, within five years prior to the cut-off date, they have not been found to have harassed or unlawfully evicted tenants by judgment or determination of a court or agency under state or local law. If the affidavits are not filed, or if any person with an interest in the property has been found to have harassed or unlawfully evicted tenants, no exemption or abatement will be permitted.

Exemption for increase in cubic content.—J-51 benefits are extended to alterations, improvements, or conversions for an expansion of cubic content to an existing building or structure. The benefit is available only if at least 50% of the floor area of the completed building consists of the original structure. Additionally, in Manhattan, south of 110th Street and north of lower Manhattan, in a newly created exclusion area, no such J-51 tax benefits may be conferred unless the properties are also aided by a grant, loan, or subsidy from a federal, state, or local agency. (Sec. 11-243(b-1), N.Y.C. Adm. Code)

• *448-a program - Rehabilitation of multiple dwellings*

Under New York City's 488-a program, eligible improvements to certain Class A and Class B multiple dwelling units that are commenced after July 1, 1980, and before December 31, 2011, may qualify for a 32-year tax exemption to the extent of any increase in the property's assessed valuation as a result of the improvement. The exemption applies to:

(1) any Class B multiple dwelling; and

(2) any Class A multiple dwelling used for single room occupancy that contains no more than 25% (40%, in the case of multiple dwellings containing 10 dwelling units or less) Class A dwellings units that contain lawful sanitary and kitchen facilities within the unit.

(Sec. 11-244, N.Y.C. Adm. Code)

Excluded from the exemption are college or school dormitories, club houses, and residences whose occupancy is restricted to an institutional use. (Sec. 11-244, N.Y.C. Adm. Code)

"Eligible improvements" are limited to the following classes of work:

— replacement of a boiler or burner or installation of an entire new heating system;

— replacement or upgrading of the electrical system;

— replacement or upgrading of elevators;

— installation or replacement or upgrading of the plumbing system, including water main and risers;

¶520-215

— replacement or installation of walls, ceilings, floors or trim where necessary;

— replacement or upgrading of doors, installation of security devices and systems;

— installation, replacement or upgrading of smoke detectors, fire alarms, fire escapes, or sprinkler systems;

— replacement or repair of roof, leaders and gutters;

— replacement or installation of bathroom facilities;

— installation of wall and pipe insulation;

— replacement or upgrading of street connections for water or sewer services;

— replacement or installation of windows, or installation of window gates or guards;

— installation or replacement of boiler smoke stack;

— pointing, waterproofing and cleaning of entire building exterior surface;

— improvements designed to conserve the use of fuel, electricity or other energy sources;

— work necessary to effect compliance with all applicable laws including but not limited to the multiple dwelling law, the New York City Housing Maintenance Code and the building code; and

— improvements unique to congregate living facilities, as defined by rules and regulations promulgated by the Department of Housing Preservation and Development.

(Sec. 11-244, N.Y.C. Adm. Code)

Property that qualifies for this exemption is also eligible for abatement of taxes in the amount of 12^1/2% of the reasonable cost of eligible improvements certified by the Department of Housing Preservation and Development. The abatement begins on the first day of the first tax quarter following the commencement of construction of eligible improvements. The abatement may not exceed the amount of taxes otherwise payable in the corresponding year. The abatement is effective for a period of 15 consecutive years from the date the abatement first becomes effective. (Sec. 11-244, N.Y.C. Adm. Code)

Penalty provisions.—Exemption or abatement under these provisions may be revoked or reduced by the Department of Housing Preservation and Development or the Department of Finance under the following conditions:

— the application for benefits contained a false statement or false information as a material matter, or omitted a material matter, in which case the revocation may be retroactive;

— real estate taxes, water, sewer or other municipal charges, or payments in lieu of such taxes or charges, have remained due and owing for more than one year, in which case the revocation may be retroactive to the time the taxes were first due and payable; or

— the eligible real property fails to comply with the requirements for exemption.

(Sec. 11-244, N.Y.C. Adm. Code)

• *New residential construction (421-b exemption)*

A 10-year full or partial decreasing exemption is provided for newly constructed, reconstructed or converted owner-occupied one-and two-family residences in New York City (as discussed below, the exemption has also been extended to certain multiple dwellings). To be eligible, the construction, reconstruction or conversion must have been: (Sec. 421-b(2), Real Property Tax Law)

— begun after July 1, 1978, and before July 1, 1982, and must be completed by April 1, 1984;

— begun after July 1, 1982, and before July 1, 1986, and completed before July 1, 1988;

— begun on or after July 1, 1986, and before July 1, 1990, and completed by July 1, 1992;

— begun after July 1, 1990, and before July 1, 1994, and completed by July 1, 1996;

— begun on or after July 1, 1994, and before July 1, 1998, and completed by July 1, 2000;

— begun on or after July 1, 1998, and before July 1, 2002, and completed by July 1, 2004; or

— begun on or after July 1, 2002, and before July 1, 2006, and completed by July 1, 2011.

Phaseout of exemption.—The exemption is based on the amount of the increased valuation due to the construction, reconstruction, or conversion, and is limited to two years after commencement of renovations. Whole or partial exemptions of the increased valuation are available for subsequent years as follows: (Sec. 421-b(1), Real Property Tax Law)

First two years after the earlier of the completion of the construction, reconstruction, or conversion, or the expiration of the above 2-year period 100%

Third year 75%

Fourth year 62.5%

Fifth year 50%

Sixth year 37.5%

Seventh year 25%

Eighth year 12.5%

Applications for exemptions must be filed with the assessors between February 1 and March 15, and upon certification by the housing agency, the collecting officer will be notified of the exemption amount. The exemption may be revoked if the housing agency finds that the property is not being used for residential purposes after two years of exemption. (Sec. 421-b(3), Real Property Tax Law)

Residential property in the Sec. 421-b program will be assessed as residential, notwithstanding that it was constructed on vacant land originally assessed in a nonresidential (*i.e.,* industrial or commercial) class. (Sec. 421-b(1), Real Property Tax Law)

Demolished property.—If a private dwelling, whether owner occupied or not, is fully demolished and removed on or after September 1, 2004, the tax lot upon which the dwelling was located will not be eligible for exemption for three years following the issuance of the demolition and removal permit. (Sec. 421-b(1), Real Property Tax Law)

Multiple dwellings.—The exemption is expanded to include certain owner occupied multiple dwellings containing no more than four units, provided that the dwellings are developed in a governmentally assisted project and are constructed, reconstructed, or converted on real property that has been acquired by the federal government through the foreclosure of a federally-insured mortgage loan and conveyed to an owner approved by the local housing agency for the purpose of rehabilitation, in accordance with an agreement between the owner and the federal government. (Sec. 421-b, Real Property Tax Law)

• *Low income housing (420-c exemption)*

As a result of legislation enacted in 2004 (Ch. 522 and Ch. 526), an exemption under Real Property Tax Law Sec. 420-c will be governed by special provisions under Sec. 420-c(4) if the application for exemption is approved on or after September 28, 2004. (see "Exemption approved on or after September 28, 2004," below) Exemption applications approved before that date are governed by the provisions discussed immediately below (however, any amendment to a regulatory agreement on or after September 28, 2004), will require a new application for exemption pursuant to Sec. 420-c(4). (Sec. 420-c(3), Real Property Tax Law)

In New York City, real property owned by a corporation, partnership, or limited liability company (LLC) formed for the purpose of providing housing accommodations for persons and families of low income and used for that purpose is exempt from local real property taxation, provided that the corporation, partnership, or LLC:

— is organized as a non-profit housing development fund company, is a non-profit housing corporation that is not incorporated as a housing development fund company, is a wholly-owned subsidiary of such a company, or is a partnership or LLC the controlling interest of which is held by such a company or corporation, by a wholly owned subsidiary of such a company, or by a corporation sponsored or formed by such a company or corporation;

— has received a loan from a municipality, the state of New York, or the housing trust fund corporation;

— enters into a regulatory agreement with the municipality, the state, or the housing trust fund corporation guaranteeing the provision of housing accommodations for persons and families of low income; and

— is a participant in the federal low income housing tax credit program.

(Sec. 420-c, Real Property Tax Law)

Any exemption under this provision will expire upon the expiration or termination of the regulatory agreement.

Exemption approved on or after September 28, 2004.—The New York City low-income housing property tax exemption, which was previously available to certain participants in the federal low-income housing tax credit program, is now applicable with respect to eligible real property that participates in, *or has participated in*, the tax credit program. A regulatory agreement must require that units formerly assisted under the tax credit program be rented in accordance with the income requirements of the program. In addition, the exemption is no longer limited to owners receiving certain governmental loans. (Sec. 420-c(1), Real Property Tax Law)

"Eligible owner" is defined to mean one or more eligible entities holding legal and beneficial title to eligible real property or a legal and beneficial leasehold interest with a term of at least 30 years in eligible real property. "Eligible entity" means a corporation, partnership, or limited liability company at least 50% of the controlling interest of which is held by a charitable organization. The charitable organization must be (or must wholly owned and controlled by) an entity that is formed for purposes including the provision of housing accommodations for low-income persons and families and that has received written recognition of exemption under IRC Sec. 501(c)(3) or IRC Sec. 501(c)(4). (Sec. 420-c(a)(4), Real Property Tax Law)

• *Redevelopment companies*

Property tax exemptions granted by contract to redevelopment companies are covered generally in the New York State property tax discussion at ¶ 20-215 Housing.

In New York City, where the local legislative body has acted to extend the property tax exemption of a mutual redevelopment company for an additional 25 years after the initial tax exemption period has expired, the amount of taxes to be paid by the mutual redevelopment company during the final 11 years of such additional 25-year exemption period must not be less than an amount equal to the greater of (1) 10% of the annual rent or carrying charges of the project minus utilities for the residential portion of the project or (2) the taxes payable by such company for the residential portion of the project in the 14th year of such additional 25-year exemption period.

In addition, the local legislative body may further extend the period of such additional 25-year exemption for up to a total period of 35 years from the date of expiration of the initial tax exemption. However, the amount of taxes to be paid by the mutual redevelopment company during any such extension beyond the additional 25-year exemption period must not be less than an amount equal to the greater of (1) 10% of the annual rent or carrying charges of the project minus utilities for the residential portion of the project or (2) the taxes payable by such company for the residential portion of the project in the 14th year of such additional 25-year exemption period. (Sec. 125, Private Housing Finance Law)

Where a local legislative body has acted to extend the tax exemption of a mutual redevelopment company for the maximum period, an additional tax exemption may be granted for a period of up to 50 years, provided that the amount of taxes to be paid during any such period of tax exemption may be not less than an amount equal to the greater of (1) 10% of the annual rent or carrying charges of the project minus utilities for the residential portion of the project, or (2) the taxes payable by such company for the residential portion of the project during the tax year commencing July 1, 2000, and ending on June 30, 2001. Such grant of an additional tax exemption period will take effect upon the expiration of the maximum period provided for in Sec. 125(1)(a-2), Private Housing Finance Law. (Sec. 125(1)(a-4), Private Housing Finance Law)

Following the expiration of the exemption, the phase-out exemption allowed under the Real Property Tax Law cannot apply in any year where the total period of tax exemption granted would exceed 60 years. (Sec. 423, Real Property Tax Law)

• *City property rebate*

New York City allowed a property tax rebate in the amount of $400 (or the annual tax liability imposed on the property if such amount was less than $400). The rebate was authorized for six consecutive fiscal years, beginning July 1, 2003. (Sec. 11-239(1), N.Y.C. Adm. Code)

[¶520-230] NYC Intangible Property

All intangible property is exempt from New York State and New York City property taxation because *ad valorem* taxation of intangible property is prohibited by the New York State Constitution. (Art. XVI, Sec. 3, N.Y. Const.)

[¶520-255] NYC Low-Income Persons

In New York City, real property owned by a corporation, partnership, or limited liability company (LLC) formed for the purpose of providing housing accommodations for persons and families of low income and used for that purpose is exempt from local real property taxation, provided that certain conditions are met. (Sec. 420-c, Real Property Tax Law) For a complete discussion, see ¶520-215 NYC Housing.

[¶520-265] NYC Manufacturing and Industrial Property

The Industrial and Commercial Abatement Program (ICAP) provides property tax abatements for varying periods of up to 25 years for eligible industrial and commercial buildings that are built, modernized, rehabilitated, expanded, or otherwise physically improved. (Sec. 11-269, N.Y.C. Adm. Code; Sec. 11-268, N.Y.C. Adm. Code; Industrial And Commercial Abatement Program (ICAP), New York City Department of Finance, http://www.nyc.gov/html/dof/html/property/property_tax_reduc_incentive.shtml)

ICAP replaced the Industrial Commercial Exemption Program (ICIP) which ended in 2008. Previously approved ICIP benefits were not affected. See below for information on ICIP.

To be eligible for commercial new construction benefits, applicants may build anywhere in New York City except in Manhattan, south of the centerline of 96th Street and north of Murray, Frankfort, and Dover Streets. To be eligible for commercial renovation benefits, applicants may be expanding, modernizing, or otherwise improving an existing structure anywhere in the City except in Manhattan, between the centerline of 59th Street and the centerline of 96th Street. In Manhattan, benefits are available for renovation in three areas, although the benefits depend on the area in which the project is located: the Garment Center District; an area in lower Manhattan bounded generally by Murray Street, South Street, Battery Place and West Street; and the remainder of Manhattan below 59th Street. (Sec. 11-269, N.Y.C. Adm. Code)

The abatement base used to determine the amount of the abatement is the amount by which the post-completion tax on a building or structure exceeds 115% of the initial tax levied on the building or structure. The initial tax is determined by multiplying the final taxable assessed value, without regard to any exemptions, shown on the assessment roll with a taxable status date immediately preceding the issuance of the first building permit by the initial tax rate. The initial tax rate is the final tax rate applicable to the assessment roll with a taxable status date immediately preceding the issuance of the first building permit. If no permit was required, the initial tax and the initial tax rate will be determined based on the assessment roll with a taxable status date immediately preceding the commencement of construction. (Sec. 11-269, N.Y.C. Adm. Code)

Applicants must make a minimum required expenditure (MRE) equal to at least 30% of the taxable assessed value of the project in the year of the issuance of the building permit or, if no permit is required, the start of construction. The MRE must be made no later than four years from the date of the issuance of the first building permit for the project, or, if no permit is required, the start of construction. ICAP also provides an additional tax abatement benefit for industrial construction projects that meet a higher MRE of 40%.

No tax abatement benefits will be allowed for residential or utility property, which includes all property used by a utility in the ordinary course of business, as well as land and buildings owned by a utility. Benefits are available for commercial construction work or renovation construction work on a building or structure for the property's square footage used to provide lodging and support services for transient guests. A property may be subject to varying abatement schedules, depending on the percentage of the property that is dedicated to retail purposes. (Sec. 11-269, N.Y.C. Adm. Code; Sec. 11-270, N.Y.C. Adm. Code)

ICAP benefits may be suspended if a court or the Environmental Control Board finds that there has been a violation of the New York City construction or building codes that is classified as immediately hazardous, or for the failure to provide a fire protection system or emergency power system, fire safety and evacuation plan, or an emergency action plan, or obstruction of a means of egress at the property. (Sec. 11-271, N.Y.C. Adm. Code)

New peaking electric generating facilities.—The Industrial and Commercial Abatement Program (ICAP) allows tax abatements for certain new peaking electric generating facilities in New York City. The amount of the abatement is 100% of the abatement base for 15 years, with the first year of the abatement beginning in the tax year that is the sooner of the completion of construction or four years from the issuance of the first building permit or, if no permit is required, the commencement of construction. (Sec. 11-269(c)(2-a), N.Y.C. Adm. Code)

For industrial construction work on a peaking unit, the minimum required expenditure is 30% of the property's taxable assessed value in the tax year with a taxable status date immediately preceding the issuance of the first building permit or, if no permit was required, the commencement of construction. Expenditures for residential construction work or construction work on portions of property to be used for restricted activities cannot be included in the minimum required expenditure. The abatement will be adjusted for inflation. (Sec. 11-269, N.Y.C. Adm. Code)

A "peaking unit" includes all real property used in connection with the generation of electricity, and any facilities used to interconnect the peaking unit with the electric transmission or distribution system; it does not include any facilities that are part of the electric transmission or distribution system. The peaking unit is considered industrial property, and it may be comprised of a single turbine and generator or multiple turbines and generators located at the same site. (Sec. 11-268, N.Y.C. Adm. Code)

No benefits will be granted for construction work performed pursuant to a building permit that begins after April 1, 2019. If no building permit is required, no benefits will be granted for construction work that begins after April 1, 2019. (Sec. 11-271, N.Y.C. Adm. Code)

An applicant whose property has been granted benefits for industrial construction work as a peaking unit and who converts the property in any tax year to a use that no longer qualifies it as a peaking unit, or who uses the property in a manner inconsistent with the definition of a peaking unit, will be ineligible for abatement benefits during that tax year, and clawback provisions will apply. (Sec. 11-272, N.Y.C. Adm. Code)

• *ICIP program*

New industrial or commercial construction projects may be entitled to full or partial exemption or to deferral of tax if certified as eligible by the New York City Department of Finance under the Industrial or Commercial Incentive Program (ICIP). Industrial or commercial construction projects that were submitted to the New York City Industrial and Commercial Incentive Board for certification on or before November 4, 1984, and that were certified as eligible, continue to be partially exempt under former provisions.

Applications, as well as detailed information regarding eligible areas and deadlines, may be obtained by calling the Department of Finance ICIP Unit at (212) 361-7167 or by writing to the ICIP Unit at 66 John Street, 13th Floor, New York, NY 10038. (New York City Tax Benefits Guide, New York City Department of Finance, January 1998)

Applications must be received by June 30, 2008. For building permits issued prior to July 1, 2008, benefits will be available for construction work that continues past that date. (Sec. 489-dddd, Real Property Tax Law)

COMPLIANCE NOTE: Renewal applications.—The Industrial and Commercial Incentive Program (ICIP) exemption ended in 2008. However, benefit recipients must complete a renewal application (Certificate of Continuing Use, CCU) to renew the exemption. For the 2014/2015 Tax Year, the Department of Finance launched the online renewal system to make filing a renewal quicker and easier. On September 23, 2013, the department mailed all ICIP recipients letters which contained a User ID and Password to log in to the renewal system. Additional information may be obtained on the department's website. (http://www.nyc.gov/html/dof/html/property/property_tax_reduc_incentive_icip.shtml)

• *Projects certified by the New York City Department of Finance*

Special exemption areas.—Industrial construction work performed in any area of New York City, or commercial construction work performed in a special exemption area, that has been issued a certificate of eligibility from the New York City Department of Finance is granted a 22-year or 25-year decreasing exemption. (Sec. 489-bbbb, Real Property Tax Law; Sec. 11-256(i), N.Y.C. Adm. Code; Sec. 11-257(a), N.Y.C. Adm. Code) The amount of exemption is determined according to the charts below:

Tax year following date of issuance . . . . **Amount of exemption**
of certificate of eligibility:

Tax year	Amount of exemption
1 through 13	Tax on 100% of exemption base
14	Tax on 90% of exemption base
15	Tax on 80% of exemption base
16	Tax on 70% of exemption base
17	Tax on 60% of exemption base
18	Tax on 50% of exemption base
19	Tax on 40% of exemption base
20	Tax on 30% of exemption base
21	Tax on 20% of exemption base
22	Tax on 10% of exemption base

For recipients who filed an application for a certificate of eligibility after June 30, 1995, the following amounts apply:

Tax year following date of issuance . . . . **Amount of exemption**
of certificate of eligibility:

Tax year	Amount of exemption
1 through 16	Tax on 100% of exemption base
17	Tax on 90% of exemption base

18 . . . . Tax on 80% of exemption base

19 . . . . Tax on 70% of exemption base

20 . . . . Tax on 60% of exemption base

21 . . . . Tax on 50% of exemption base

22 . . . . Tax on 40% of exemption base

23 . . . . Tax on 30% of exemption base

24 . . . . Tax on 20% of exemption base

25 . . . . Tax on 10% of exemption base

In addition, industrial projects with a 25% minimum required expenditure (see "Expenditure requirements," below) are eligible to receive an abatement based on the real estate taxes in the year prior to the start of the project. (Sec. 11-257(a)(3), N.Y.C. Adm. Code) The abatement percentage in years one through four is 50%, followed by eight years of abatement declining at 10% every two years.

Regular exemption areas.—Certified commercial construction work performed in a regular exemption area is granted exemption in the following amounts: (Sec. 489-bbbb, Real Property Tax Law; Sec. 11-256(i), N.Y.C. Adm. Code; Sec. 11-257(c), N.Y.C. Adm. Code)

Tax year following date of issuance . . . . **Amount of exemption**
of certificate of eligibility:

1 through 8 . . . . Tax on 100% of exemption base

9 . . . . Tax on 80% of exemption base

10 . . . . Tax on 60% of exemption base

11 . . . . Tax on 40% of exemption base

12 . . . . Tax on 20% of exemption base

For recipients who filed an application for a certificate of eligibility after June 30, 1995, the following amounts apply: (Sec. 11-257(c), N.Y.C. Adm. Code)

Tax year following date of issuance . . . . **Amount of exemption**
of certificate of eligibility:

1 through 11 . . . . Tax on 100% of exemption base

12 . . . . Tax on 80% of exemption base

13 . . . . Tax on 60% of exemption base

14 . . . . Tax on 40% of exemption base

15 . . . . Tax on 20% of exemption base

Deferral areas.—Certified commercial construction work performed in a deferral area is granted the following deferral of tax in accordance with the following chart: (Sec. 11-257(d), N.Y.C. Adm. Code)

Tax year following date of issuance . . . . **Amount of exemption**
of certificate of eligibility:

1 through 3 . . . . Deferral of tax payment on 100% of the exemption base

4 . . . . Deferral of tax payment on 80% of the exemption base

5 . . . . Deferral of tax payment on 60% of the exemption base

6 . . . . Deferral of tax payment on 40% of the exemption base

7 . . . . Deferral of tax payment on 20% of the exemption base

8 through 10 . No tax payments are to be deferred and no deferred tax payments are required to be made

11 through 20 . Payment each year of 10% of total dollar amount of tax payments deferred

Renovation exemption areas.—Certified renovation construction work performed in a renovation exemption area is granted exemption in the following amounts: (Sec. 11-257(e), N.Y.C. Adm. Code)

Tax year following date of issuance . . . . **Amount of exemption**

of certificate of eligibility:

1 through 8 . . . . Tax on 100% of exemption base

9 . . . . Tax on 80% of exemption base

10 . . . . Tax on 60% of exemption base

11 . . . . Tax on 40% of exemption base

12 . . . . Tax on 20% of exemption base

New construction exemption area.—Certified construction of a qualified new building or structure in a new construction area (i.e., specified areas of Manhattan) is granted exemption in the following amounts: (Sec. 11-257(e.1), N.Y.C. Adm. Code)

Tax year following date of issuance . . . . **Amount of exemption**

of certificate of eligibility:

1 through 4 . . . . Tax on 100% of exemption base

5 . . . . Tax on 80% of exemption base

6 . . . . Tax on 60% of exemption base

7 . . . . Tax on 40% of exemption base

8 . . . . Tax on 20% of exemption base

The Temporary Commercial Incentive Area Commission determines the boundaries of special exemption areas, regular exemption areas, excluded areas and deferral areas. (Sec. 11-258(a), N.Y.C. Adm. Code) Areas of the city that lie outside the Borough of Manhattan, as well as areas north of the center line of 96th Street in Manhattan, that are not designated as special exemption areas are regular exemption areas. Areas in Manhattan south of 96th St. are deferral areas unless designated as excluded areas. (Sec. 11-258(c), N.Y.C. Adm. Code)

Qualifying property.—For purposes of the exemption, industrial property is nonresidential property on which after completion of industrial construction work, a building or structure will exist wherein at least 75% of the total net square footage is used or immediately available and held out for use for manufacturing activities involving the assembly of goods or the fabrication or processing of raw materials. (Sec. 11-256(k), N.Y.C. Adm. Code)

Determinations of eligibility for the industrial or commercial exemptions are made in accordance with regulations issued by the Department of Finance, reproduced at ¶523-611 and following.

Expenditure requirements.—To continue to benefit from this exemption or deferral of payment, the taxpayer must present evidence that $1/2$ of the minimum required expenditure has been made on the project no later than 18 months after the effective date of the certificate of eligibility, and must present evidence that the full amount of the minimum required expenditure has been made within 36 months after the effective date. For recipients who filed an application for a certificate of eligibility after June 30, 1995, the minimum required expenditure is generally an amount equal to 10% (previously 20%) of the initial assessed value. The Department of Finance may increase the percentage of initial assessed value required to be expended to an amount up to 50% of the initial assessed value, but such increases will not apply to projects for which preliminary certificates of eligibility have been issued on the effective date of the increase. (Sec. 11-261(d), N.Y.C. Adm. Code; Sec. 11-256(n), N.Y.C. Adm. Code; Rule Sec. 14-10(b))

The Department of Finance may designate restricted activities by regulation. Restricted activities are entertainment activities that the Department determines should not be encouraged through the benefits of the commercial exemption. If any part of a property is to be used for restricted activities, no benefits may be granted for construction work. (Sec. 11-256(t), N.Y.C. Adm. Code)

• *Commercial revitalization areas*

With respect to the ICIP exemptions, certain restrictions have been eliminated for properties that are located in a commercial revitalization area and with respect to which an application for a certificate of eligibility has been filed after June 30, 2000. Specifically, such properties are not subject to the provision that otherwise denies eligibility to a commercial property in which more than 15% of the total net square footage of any building or structure was used for manufacturing activities during the preceding two years. (Sec. 489-aaaa, Real Property Tax Law; Sec. 11-256(f)(3), N.Y.C. Adm. Code; Sec. 11-256(f-1), N.Y.C. Adm. Code)

In addition, ICIP property tax abatements are expanded for taxpayers that file an application for a certificate of eligibility for industrial construction work in a commercial revitalization area after June 30, 2000. Although an industrial property will generally qualify for the abatement only if it has at least 75% of its total net square footage used or immediately available for use in manufacturing activities, properties in a commercial revitalization area may qualify for a pro rata abatement if at least 25% of the space is devoted to manufacturing activities. (Sec. 489-bbbb, Real Property Tax Law; Sec. 11-257(f), N.Y.C. Adm. Code)

• *Projects certified by the Industrial and Commercial Incentive Board*

Industrial and commercial construction projects submitted prior to February 1, 1986, and certified by the New York City Industrial and Commercial Incentive Board, may continue to be granted a partial decreasing exemption. The extent of exemption of increases in value of the property due to the new construction are as follows:

Construction or reconstruction of industrial structures, reconstruction of commercial structures in areas where the exemption applies as of right or reconstruction of specially needed commercial structures - 19 years beginning at 95% and decreasing by 5% annually;

Reconstruction of other commercial structures, construction of commercial structures in areas where the exemption applies as of right or construction of specially needed commercial structures—ten years beginning at 50% and decreasing by 5% each year; and

Construction of other new commercial structures—five years beginning at 50% and decreasing by 10% each year. (Sec. 489-ddd, Real Property Tax Law; Sec. 11-250(a), N.Y.C. Adm. Code)

Definitions.—For purposes of the exemption, "industrial" means property used primarily for the manufacturing or assembling of goods or the processing of raw materials. "Commercial" means any non-residential property used primarily for the buying, selling or otherwise providing of goods or services, provided that the use of the property has not been designated as a restricted commercial use pursuant to Sec. 11-249. (Sec. 489-aaa, Real Property Tax Law; Sec. 11-247(e), N.Y.C. Adm. Code)

The Industrial and Commercial Incentive Board is responsible for making determinations on qualification for the exemption and for issuing certificates of eligibility. The Board also designates areas of the city in which exemptions for commercial construction or reconstruction are granted as of right, areas from which exemptions are excluded, and commercial uses for which the granting of exemptions are restricted. (Sec. 489-ccc, Real Property Tax Law; Sec. 11-249(a), N.Y.C. Adm. Code)

Certificate of use.—The exemption continues each year of the exemption period, provided the taxpayer files a certificate of use annually indicating the continuing use for industrial or commercial purposes. (Sec. 489-ggg, Real Property Tax Law; Sec. 11-253, N.Y.C. Adm. Code)

Applications for certification of projects for exemption under these provisions were accepted between March 1, 1982, and January 31, 1986. (Sec. 11-251, N.Y.C. Adm. Code)

[¶520-295] NYC Personal Property

The New York Real Property Tax Law applies to all real property in the state (except for property that is specifically exempted by statute), including those located in New York City. (Sec. 300, Real Property Tax Law) Personal property, whether tangible or intangible, is not taxed as such.

For a discussion of real property, see ¶520-310.

[¶520-310] NYC Real Property

All real property within New York City is taxable unless specifically exempt. In general, the types of real property subject to taxation elsewhere in the state are also subject to New York City taxation. For a detailed discussion of taxable real property, see ¶20-310.

[¶520-315] NYC Senior Citizens

Under the Senior Citizens Rent Increase Exemption (SCRIE) and Disability Rent Increase Exemption (DRIE) programs, certain low-income senior citizens or disabled persons living in rent-controlled, rent-regulated or publicly aided housing may receive a rent increase exemption order, and the owners of the property within which they live may benefit from a tax abatement. (Sec. 467-c, Real Property Tax Law; Sec. 26-405(m), N.Y.C. Adm. Code)

To be eligible for the SCRIE and DRIE exemptions, heads of households must meet the following requirements: (Sec. 26-405(m)(2), N.Y.C. Adm. Code)

— they must be at least 62 years of age;

— the total annual household income may not exceed $50,000;

— if the head of household does not receive a monthly allowance for shelter under the social services law, the maximum rent must exceed $1/3$ of the aggregate disposable income or the maximum rent after the expected increase must exceed that amount; and

— if the head of the household does receive a monthly allowance for shelter pursuant to the social services law, the maximum rent must exceed the maximum allowance for shelter to which the head of household is entitled or the maximum rent after the expected increase must exceed that amount.

A rent exemption order is valid for two years. The rent exemption order also constitutes the tax abatement certificate, and a copy is given to the owner of the property. (Sec. 26-405(m)(6), N.Y.C. Adm. Code) The rent exemption order provides that the landlord may not collect from a tenant who has been issued the order any rent in excess of ⅓ of the aggregate disposable income, or the maximum collectible rent in effect on December 31 of the year preceding the order, whichever is greater, if the head of household does not receive a monthly allowance for shelter under the social services law. (Sec. 26-405(m)(3), N.Y.C. Adm. Code) If the tenant does receive a monthly allowance, the landlord may not collect rent in excess of either the maximum allowance for shelter that the head of household is entitled to receive, or the maximum collectible rent in effect on December 31 of the year preceding the order, whichever is greater.

Senior citizen heads of household who move from the rent-controlled dwelling to another within the city may retain all or part of the exemption, the amount carried over being the least of the following: (Sec. 26-406, N.Y.C. Adm. Code)

— the amount by which the rent in the new apartment exceeds the rent actually paid in the old apartment, after reductions;

— the amount of the exemption on the old apartment; or

— the amount by which the new rent exceeds one-third of the household income.

The senior citizen must file an application every other year with the New York City Department for the Aging. (Sec. 26-405(m)(5), N.Y.C. Adm. Code)

Surviving members of a household are authorized to apply for a transfer of the head of household's property tax benefit under the Senior Citizens Rent Increase Exemption (SCRIE) and Disability Rent Increase Exemption (DRIE) programs. The option to transfer either benefit is available for a period of six months after the head of household dies or permanently leaves the household, or 90 days after the date of notice from the supervising agency informing the household that the rent increase exemption benefit has expired upon the death of the head of household, whichever is later. (Sec. 467-c(4-a), Real Property Tax Law)

In a city with a population of 1 million or more, anyone granted a rent increase exemption order that is in effect as of January 1, 2015, or that takes effect on or before July 1, 2015, may continue in the programs even if their rent does not meet the ⅓ ratio of rent-to-income requirement.

Individuals who are dropped from the SCRIE and DRIE programs due to a non-recurring item of income are permitted to reapply the next year and be accepted at the previously frozen rent amount. (Sec. 467-b, Real Property Tax Law; Sec. 467-c, Real Property Tax Law)

• *Abatements*

Abatements of real property taxes are provided for buildings containing a rent-controlled or rent-regulated dwelling unit in which a senior citizen or disabled head of household resides. (Sec. 467-b(2), Real Property Tax Law; Sec. 26-406, N.Y.C. Adm. Code) The abatement for each taxpayer is equal to the difference between the sum of the maximum rents collectible under the rent exemption orders, and the amount that would have been collectible if no rent exemption had been granted.

As the incidence of the tax is not on the renter, the tax abatement is awarded to the property owner. (Sec. 26-406, N.Y.C. Adm. Code) The practical effect, however, is to reduce the senior citizen's rent in an amount equal to the tax reduction for the property owner, since the amount of tax abatement is applied to reduce the maximum rent or legal regulated rent.

Applications for the rent exemption order, and consequently the abatement certificate, must be made by the senior citizen head of household to the New York City Department for the Aging. (Sec. 26-405(m)(5), N.Y.C. Adm. Code)

The abatement may not reduce the tax for any year below zero. If the abatement certificate authorizes an amount in excess of a tax installment, the balance may be carried over to subsequent installments until exhausted. (Sec. 26-406(e), N.Y.C. Adm. Code)

• *Homestead exemption*

Persons age 65 or over, having incomes of less than $58,400 per year, are entitled to a partial abatement of the assessed valuation of a residence that they own and occupy. For a complete discussion of this program, see ¶520-205 NYC Homestead.

[¶520-330] NYC Utilities

Real property located within New York City, owned by a water-works corporation subject to the provisions of the Public Service Law, and used exclusively for the sale, furnishing and distribution of water for domestic, commercial and public purposes, is exempt. (Sec. 485-d, Real Property Tax Law; Sec. 11-245.2, N.Y.C. Adm. Code)

[¶520-335] NYC Veterans

The property of war-time veterans, their spouses, or their unremarried surviving spouses or surviving dependents, is eligible for the alternative veterans' exemption if used as their primary residence or if the veteran or unremarried surviving spouse is absent from the property due to medical reasons or institutionalization. (Sec. 458-a, Real Property Tax Law) Property qualifying for the eligible funds or pro-rata veterans' exemptions prior to January 6, 1985, may continue to receive these exemptions. (Sec. 458(6)(a)(ii), Real Property Tax Law)

The eligible funds exemption is applicable to school taxes. (Sec. 11-245.46, N.Y.C. Adm. Code)

CCH COMMENT: *Relocation during the year.*—Property owners receiving the veterans tax exemption are authorized to receive a prorated exemption if they move from one property to another midway through the tax year, ensuring that veterans receive the maximum benefit possible. (Sec. 11-245.9, N.Y.C. Adm. Code)

A veteran who served during a specified period of conflict (Sec. 458-a of the Real Property Tax Law) will receive a 15% exemption of the assessed value of his or her property. The maximum amount of the exemption is $4,140 for Class 1 property and $24,300 for Classes 2 and 4 property. (New York City Department of Finance, http://www.nyc.gov/html/dof/html/property/veterans.shtml)

• *Alternative exemption*

In addition, the City has increased the maximum alternative exemptions provided under state law as authorized by Sec. 458-a of the Real Property Tax Law. The maximum exemption allowable on qualifying residential real property under the

Alternative Veterans Tax Exemption is the lesser of $48,000 or $48,000 multiplied by the latest class ratio for wartime veterans, $32,000 or $32,000 multiplied by the latest class ratio for combat veterans, and $160,000 or $160,000 multiplied by the latest class ratio for veterans with service-connected disabilities. (Sec. 11-245.6, N.Y.C. Adm. Code)

New York City is authorized to extend the alternative veterans' property tax exemption to school taxes. The local legislative body, after public hearings and adoption of a local law, may grant eligible veterans such an exemption from their school taxes. (Sec. 458-a, Real Property Tax Law)

• *Cooperatives*

An exemption is allowed for that proportion of the assessment of such real property owned by a cooperative apartment corporation determined by the relationship of such real property vested in such tenant-stockholder to such real property owned by such cooperative apartment corporation in which such tenant-stockholder resides. (Sec. 11-245.45, N.Y.C. Adm. Code) The exemption also applies to the alternative exemption. (Sec. 11-245.5, N.Y.C. Adm. Code) Any exemption that is granted will be credited by the appropriate taxing authority against the assessed valuation of such real property. The reduction in real property taxes realized thereby will be credited by the cooperative apartment corporation against the amount of such taxes otherwise payable by or chargeable to such tenant-stockholder.

New York City may not reduce the maximum exemption levels for the alternative veteran's exemption below those set for the 1985 assessment rolls.

• *Gold Star parents*

A partial exemption is available for Gold Star Parents (i.e., mothers and fathers of Americans killed while in military service for the United States during wartime). Gold Star Parents are generally entitled to a 15% property tax exemption. Further, Gold Star Parents having a son or daughter who received a commendation are eligible for an additional 10% exemption. (Sec. 11-245.7, N.Y.C. Adm. Code; *Press Release 468-00*, New York City Mayor's Office, December 14, 2000)

[¶520-400]

NYC--RATES

[¶520-405] NYC Rates of Tax

Each year, the New York City Council sets the tax rate for each class of real property. The rate is applied to the property's taxable assessed value to determine the amount of real estate tax due for the year.

Setting the new tax rates often takes place after the New York City Department of Finance has already printed the tax bills for the coming year. When this occurs, the prior year's tax rates are used instead to calculate the amount to be paid. Once the tax bill is determined, the Department of Finance mails a revised bill based on the proper rates to all property owners. Any increase or decrease of taxes due to the new rates will be applied to this bill.

• *Current rates*

Current rates for real property can be accessed on the New York City Department of Finance website at http://www1.nyc.gov/site/finance/taxes/property-tax-rates.page. Old rates can be found there as well.

• *Absentee landlord surcharge*

A surcharge, equal to 25% of net real property taxes, is imposed for fiscal years beginning on or after July 1, 2006. The surcharge applies to class one property, excluding vacant land, that provides rental income and that is not the primary residence of the owner or of the owner's parent or child. (Sec. 11-238, N.Y.C. Adm. Code)

The City may increase the surcharge amount up to 50% of net real property taxes for subsequent fiscal years. (Sec. 307-a, Real Property Tax Law)

[¶520-600]

NYC--VALUATION, ASSESSMENT, AND EQUALIZATION

[¶520-605] NYC Overview

The Commissioner of Finance is responsible for assessing real property within New York City. (Sec. 11-201, N.Y.C. Adm. Code) The taxable status of all real property assessable for taxation in New York City is fixed on January 5 for the succeeding fiscal year. (see ¶520-110; Sec. 1507, N.Y.C. Charter)

The Commissioner is required to fix the valuation of property in New York City at sums that will establish a just and equal relation between the valuations of property in each borough and throughout the entire city. (Sec. 11-212(a), N.Y.C. Adm. Code) For a discussion of valuation procedures, see ¶520-610; for valuation methods in general, see ¶520-615.

Terminology.—The term "assess" is used frequently in tax circles to refer to the fixing of the tax in a delinquency situation; that is, the final determination of the tax. That is not the use of the term in property taxation. A more appropriate term might be "proportionment." Assessment is the application of a statutory percentage to the valuation sum to reach the "assessed valuation." For example, if property is valued at $1,000 and the assessment percentage is 25%, the assessed valuation would be $250. Further confusing is the fact that the term assessment is frequently made to stand for the whole process of valuing property and entering it on the tax rolls. Thus the reader must be alert for the nuances when this particular word is used.

Limitation on increases.—The assessed value of any individual parcel classified in class one (generally, all one-, two- and three-family residential real property) may not increase by more than 6% in any one year, as measured from the assessment on the previous year's assessment roll. (Sec. 1805(1), Real Property Tax Law) In addition, assessments on such property may not increase by more than 20% in any five-year period.

The assessed valuation of class 2 property (all residential real property that is not designated as class one, except hotels and motels and other commercial properties) with fewer than 11 residential units may not be increased by more than 8% in any one year, and may not be increased by more than 30% in any five-year period. (Sec. 1805(2), Real Property Tax Law)

Increases in the assessed valuation of other class 2 property and class 4 property (all real property not classified as class 1 or class 2 residential property or class 3 utility property) are phased in over five years. (Sec. 1805(3), Real Property Tax Law)

[¶520-610] NYC Valuation Procedures

"Value" is not defined in New York statutes or regulations. However, New York courts have generally held that the standard for tax assessment purposes is the value of property in its current use, not its value at a presumed "highest and best use". The assessor's task is to determine the estimated market value of the property.

Assessors begin to assess real property on the first day of July of each year that is not a Saturday, Sunday or legal holiday. (Sec. 1508, N.Y.C. Charter) Assessors are required to determine two valuations for each parcel, one for the parcel as it would be if wholly unimproved, and another for the property as improved. (Sec. 11-207, N.Y.C. Adm. Code) In each case, the valuation must be the sum for which the parcel would sell under ordinary circumstances, in the assessor's judgment.

Notification of increase.—When the assessed valuation of a property is increased, the assessors must notify the owners of property, if on record, of the increase at least 30 days prior to the final date for filing any appeal. (Sec. 1511, N.Y.C. Charter)

Failure to permit entry upon property.—A property owner who refuses to allow an assessor or the Commissioner of Finance to enter upon real property and into buildings and structures at reasonable times to ascertain the character of the property is guilty of a misdemeanor. (Sec. 1521, N.Y.C. Charter) Upon a finding of guilt, the offense is punishable by not more than 30 days imprisonment, a fine of not more than $50, or both.

• *Income and expense statements*

Owners of certain income-producing property are required to submit a statement of income and expenses attributable to the property. (Sec. 11-208.1, N.Y.C. Adm. Code)

The filing date for real property income and expense (RPIE) statements is June 1. For owners whose books and records reflecting the operation of the property are maintained on a fiscal year basis, the RPIE statement will be for the last fiscal year concluded as of May 1. (Sec. 11-208.1, N.Y.C. Adm. Code)

The period for an extension for filing RPIE statements for Class 2 co-operatives/condominiums is 60 days. (Sec. 11-208.1, N.Y.C. Adm. Code)

Exclusion from filing RPIE statements.—The following owners are not required to submit a claim of exclusion:

— property that has an assessed valuation of forty thousand dollars or less;

— residential property containing ten or fewer dwelling units;

— property classified in class one or two as defined in article eighteen of the real property tax law containing six or fewer dwelling units and one retail store; or

— special franchise property that is assessed pursuant to Article 6 of the Real Property Tax Law.

(Sec. 11-208.1(5), N.Y.C. Adm. Code)

Exclusion forms for exemptions from filing RPIE statements must be filed by June 1, and penalty provisions are added for the failure to submit a claim of exclusion, effective for income and expense statements that are required to be filed on or after June 1, 2014. (Sec. 11-208.1(4), N.Y.C. Adm. Code)

Penalty provisions for the failure to file an RPIE statement allow the penalty to become a lien on the property if the failure to file is not cured, effective for income and expense statements that are required to be filed on or after June 1, 2014. These tax liens will be eligible for lien sales if the property has other qualifying charges, such as delinquent property taxes, water charges, or emergency repair charges. (Sec. 11-208.1, N.Y.C. Adm. Code)

Valuation of income producing property.—The New York City Department of Finance, Property Division, has issued a statement of assessment procedure document that discusses the process that the department uses to value property when the owner has not provided income and expense information. The department estimates the value of such properties using comparable rental properties, at times making adjustments. Property owners may forward income and expense statements to the department, and may not request a hearing before the New York City Tax Commission if the information is not provided. However, the department will review the information to determine whether the value on the property should be corrected. (*Statement of Assessment Procedure*, New York City Department of Finance, Property Division, June 8, 2009)

• *Valuation methods*

For a discussion of the valuation methods used in New York City, see ¶520-615.

[¶520-615] NYC Valuation Methods in General

The most commonly used methods, both throughout the country and by New York City, are the cost method, the income method (called the income capitalization method in New York City), and the market data method (called the comparative sales method in New York City). Each method has advantages and disadvantages. A particular method often becomes associated with certain types of properties. These methods are discussed at the following paragraphs:

— cost method;

— income method; and

— market data method.

[¶520-750]

NYC--PAYMENT, COLLECTION OF TAXES

[¶520-756] Payment of Tax

Owners of real property generally are not required to file returns with respect to real property taxes. However, owners of income-producing real property valued at more than $40,000 are generally required to submit an annual statement of income and expenses attributable to the property. This statement must be filed on or before June 1. (Sec. 11-208.1, N.Y.C. Adm. Code; Rule Sec. 33-01)

Due dates.—For property with an assessed value of $250,000 or less, four equal installments are due July 1, October 1, January 1, and April 1. For property with an assessed value of over $250,000, two equal installments are due July 1 and January 1. Discounts are allowed for early quarterly or semiannual payments with the discount amount dependent on the date when the full payment occurs. (Sec. 1519-a, N.Y.C. Charter)

Statements of account.—The New York City Department of Finance replaced annual property tax bills, delinquency and all other property tax billing-related notices with Statements of Account. The statement of account is a summary of all property-related charges, including current property taxes due, and indicates any previous outstanding charges. The Department will automatically apply any pending credits to a taxpayer's current property tax liability and reflect this on the Statement of Account. (*Statement of Account FAQs*, New York City Department of Finance, November 24, 2004)

The statement of account will be mailed to taxpayers four times a year before taxes are due in January, April, July, and October. Taxpayers may make payments online, by sending a check with the attached statement coupon, or by visiting one of the Department's borough business centers. (*Statement of Account FAQs*, New York City Department of Finance, November 24, 2004)

Hurricane Sandy extended due date.—New York City Mayor Michael R. Bloomberg signed Introductory No. 979 that granted property tax relief to taxpayers affected by Hurricane Sandy. The legislation provided an interest-free extension on the next property tax bill for residential properties damaged beyond repair or in need of extensive structural repairs before they could be inhabited. The grace period postponed payments due on January 1, 2013, to April 1, 2013. (Sec. 11-224.1, N.Y.C. Adm. Code; Sec. 1519-a, N.Y.C. Charter)

• *Installment payments*

An owner of any class of property may enter into a payment plan for the satisfaction of delinquent real property taxes, assessments, sewer rents, sewer surcharges, water rents, and any other charges. (Sec. 11-245, N.Y.C. Adm. Code)

• *Payment methods*

The New York City Commissioner of Finance is specifically authorized to accept and require the payment of real property taxes by electronic funds transfer (EFT). The Commissioner requires the payment of real property taxes by EFT for properties with annual real property tax liability equal to or greater than $300,000. (Sec. 11-128, N.Y.C. Adm. Code; Rule Sec. 44-02; *Finance Memorandum 05-2-R*, New York City Department of Finance, April 20, 2005)

EFT payment programs.—Taxpayers required to make real property tax payments by EFT may choose between participating in either of the following programs:

— Taxpayer initiated program. In such a program, taxpayers initiate payment by EFT, including payment by Fed Wire; or

— Automatic debit program (ACH Debit or ACH Credit). In such a program, taxpayers authorize the Department of Finance (or its authorized designee) to debit the taxpayer's account for the amounts due.

(Sec. 11-128(d), N.Y.C. Adm. Code)

NYCe-File system.—The NYCeFile Property Tax Payment Service is a secure and beneficial way to make real estate tax payments via the Internet. (https://www.nyctax.fleet.com)

Timely payment.—Payment of real property taxes by EFT are deemed timely and not subject to interest charges if:

— for taxpayers enrolled in a taxpayer initiated program, (i) the taxpayer properly initiates payment on the statutory due date for such taxes; and (ii) on the date that the tax payment is due, such account contains sufficient funds to enable the successful completion of the EFT; or

— for taxpayers enrolled in an automatic debit program, (i) the Department of Finance has been authorized to debit the taxpayer's account on the last date by which the real property taxes may be paid without the accrual of interest; (ii) such account is properly identified; and (iii) on the date such payment is due, such account contains sufficient funds to enable the successful completion of the EFT.

(Sec. 11-128(g), N.Y.C. Adm. Code)

Monthly property tax payment program.—Property owners can register for the Department of Finance's monthly payment program. Through this option, property owners will authorize DOF to set up automatic monthly payments that will withdraw funds from their checking account and pay property bills prior to their due date. The option gives property owners an easy, convenient tool to help them budget for their property tax payments. (Notice, New York City Department of Finance, January 24, 2020)

Property owners who register before Jan. 30 will have their first monthly payment deducted on Feb. 1. Anyone who registers after Feb. 1 will see their first withdrawal on March 1. Property owners whose deductions start on or after March 1 may need to make additional payments to ensure their property taxes are paid in full by the deadline to avoid interest charges. The next deadline for paying property taxes is April 1 for properties billed quarterly and July 1 for properties billed semiannually. Nearly all individual homeowners pay their property taxes quarterly. Many apartment building and commercial building owners pay their taxes semiannually. Both are eligible for the program. (Notice, New York City Department of Finance, January 24, 2020)

Property owners who receive quarterly bills and who register for the monthly program will have their quarterly bill divided into three monthly payments, while individuals who receive semiannual bills will have their payments divided into six monthly payments.

There is no charge for enrolling in the program, and no interest will be charged to property owners who do not pay each month as long as the total quarterly or semiannual bill is paid by the due date. All New York City property owners are eligible to register for the free program, except for property owners whose taxes are paid by a mortgage company. (Notice, New York City Department of Finance, January 24, 2020)

Hardship exemption.—If a taxpayer is unable to enroll in a required EFT program or becomes unable to make payments by EFT, the taxpayer may seek a waiver by written application to the Department of Finance, setting forth the reasons for such inability. Granting of a waiver is discretionary, and the following criteria may be considered:

— the hardship (whether financial or practical) created for the taxpayer seeking the waiver by participation in the EFT program;

— the length of time for which the waiver is requested; and

— any other relevant factors.

(Sec. 11-128(i), N.Y.C. Adm. Code)

Following application, the Commissioner must issue a written determination within 10 days of the Department's receipt of the waiver request. However, a waiver may not be granted with respect to the payment of any installment of real property taxes that is due within 30 days of the date of the waiver request. (Sec. 11-128(i), N.Y.C. Adm. Code)

[¶520-758] Assessment of Delinquent Tax

Interest is imposed if taxes are not paid on property with an assessed value of $250,000 or less by July 15, October 15, January 15, or April 15. Interest is imposed if taxes are not paid on property with an assessed value over $250,000 by July 1 or January 1. (Sec. 11-224.1, N.Y.C. Adm. Code)

[¶520-770] Penalties

New York City statutes provide civil and criminal penalties for certain actions and inactions.

Failure to file income and expense reports or claims of exclusion.—In the event that an owner of income-producing property fails to timely file an income and expense statement (determined with regard to any extension of time for filing), the owner will be subject to a penalty not to exceed 3% of the assessed value of the income-producing property determined for the current fiscal year. However, if the statement is not filed by December 31, the penalty imposed may not to exceed 4% of the assessed value. (Sec. 11-208.1(d)(1), N.Y.C. Adm. Code; Rule Sec. 33-02; Rule Sec. 33-03)

If, in the year immediately following the year in which an owner fails to file by December 31, the owner again fails to timely file an income and expense statement (determined with regard to any extension of time for filing), the owner will be subject to a penalty not to exceed 5% of the assessed value of the property determined for the current fiscal year. The owner will also be subject to a penalty of up to 5% of the assessed value in any year immediately succeeding a year in which a penalty of up to 5% could have been imposed, if in the succeeding year the owner fails to timely file an income and expense statement (determined with regard to any extension of time for filing). The penalties will be determined by the commissioner after notice and an opportunity to be heard. (Sec. 11-208.1(d)(1), N.Y.C. Adm. Code; Rule Sec. 33-02; Rule Sec. 33-03)

Applicable to income and expense statements that are required to be filed on or after June 1, 2014, in the year immediately following the year in which an owner fails to file by December 31, the owner again fails to timely file an income and expense statement (determined with regard to any extension of time for filing), the owner will be subject to a penalty not to exceed 5% of the assessed value of the property determined for the current fiscal year. The owner will also be subject to a penalty of up to 5% of the assessed value in any year immediately succeeding a year in which a penalty of up to 5% could have been imposed, if in the succeeding year the owner fails to timely file an income and expense statement (determined with regard to any extension of time for filing). The penalties will be determined by the commissioner after notice and an opportunity to be heard, and an opportunity to cure the failure to file. (Sec. 11-208.1(d)(1), N.Y.C. Adm. Code; Rule Sec. 33-02; Rule Sec. 33-03)

Effective October 18, 2014, the rule governing penalties for failure to file income and expense statements is amended by eliminating the percentage penalty and establishing a set penalty amount based on final actual assessed valuation for the property for the calendar year in which such a statement was required to be filed.

Final Actual Assessed Valuation	Penalty Amount
$40,001 to $99,999	$300
$100,000 to $249,999	$750
$250,000 to $499,999	$1,500
$500,000 to $999,999	$3,000
$1 million to $4,999,999	$5,000
$5 million to $9,999,999	$20,000
$10 million to $14,999,999	$40,000
$15 million to $24,999,999	$60,000
$25 million and above	$100,000

Additionally, effective October 18, 2014, the percentage penalty amount for owners who fail to file an income and expense statement by the December 31, and the percentage penalty amount for owners who fail to file an income and expense statement for consecutive years are eliminated. (Rule Sec. 33-03)

Applicable to income and expense statements that are required to be filed on or after June 1, 2014, the penalties will be a lien on the income-producing property and will continue until paid. Such lien shall be a tax lien within the meaning of Sec. 11-319 and Sec. 11-401 and may be collected, sold, enforced or foreclosed. If the penalties are not paid within 30 days from the date of entry, the commissioner will impose interest at the rate of interest applicable to the property for a delinquent tax on real property, to be calculated to the date of payment from the date of entry. The penalties may also be collected in an action brought against the owner of the income-producing property in a court of competent jurisdiction. The institution of any action will not suspend or bar the right to pursue any other remedy for the recovery of such penalties. (Sec. 11-208.1(d)(1), N.Y.C. Adm. Code; Rule Sec. 33-02; Rule Sec. 33-03)

Effective October 5, 2014, owners of income-producing property who are required to submit a claim of exclusion but fail to do so by June 1, or in the event of an extension, by the extended due date, will be subject to a penalty of (1) $100 for failure to submit a claim of exclusion in one year, (2) $500 for failure to submit a claim of exclusion in two consecutive years, and (3) $1,000 for failure to submit a claim of exclusion in three consecutive years or more. The penalty will be a lien on the real property as to which the statement or claim was required to be filed and will continue to be a lien until paid. The lien may be enforced by tax lien sale, in rem foreclosure, or any other means provided by law for enforcement of tax liens. Penalties not paid within 30 days from the date entered in the records of the Department of Finance will accrue interest on the amount of the penalty at the rate applicable to the affected real property for delinquent real property taxes, calculated from the date of entry to the date of payment. Penalties may be waived for innocent purchasers or for good cause. (Rule Sec. 33-03)

Certain industrial and commercial properties.—The department of finance may deny, reduce, suspend, revoke or terminate any exemption from or abatement or deferral of tax payments for the failure to comply with the requirements or making a false application, certificate, report or other document in connection with certain industrial and commercial properties. (Sec. 11-265, N.Y.C. Adm. Code; Sec. 11-276, N.Y.C. Adm. Code)

Failure to pay by EFT.—Any real property taxes that are required to be paid by electronic funds transfer (EFT), but for which an installment payment is not paid by EFT and is paid instead by any other method, including payment by check, the following occurs:

— with respect to the first installment paid by any other method, the Department of Finance will mail a warning notice to the taxpayer setting forth the EFT payment requirements and the penalties for failure to do so; and

— with respect to each subsequent installment paid by any other method, a penalty charge of 1% of the amount of the tax installment that was required to be paid by EFT will be imposed.

(Sec. 11-128(k)(1), N.Y.C. Adm. Code)

Any penalty imposed will be a lien against the real property for which the taxpayer failed to make a payment by EFT, and will accrue interest at the same rate as is imposed on a delinquent tax on real property. (Sec. 11-128(k)(2), N.Y.C. Adm. Code)

• *Criminal penalties*

Failure to permit an assessor or the Commissioner of Finance to enter real property and into buildings and structures at reasonable times to ascertain the character of the property is a misdemeanor, punishable by not more than 30 days imprisonment, a fine of not more than $50, or both. (Sec. 1521, N.Y.C. Charter)

NEW YORK CITY HOTEL OCCUPANCY TAX

[¶531-001]
NYC HOTEL OCCUPANCY TAX

[¶531-005] NYC Hotel Occupancy Tax--In General

The hotel occupancy tax is imposed on every occupancy of each room in a hotel in New York City. The term "hotel" includes an apartment hotel, a motel (including motel efficiency units, boarding house, tourist cabins, bed and breakfasts, guest houses, or club, regardless of whether meals are served). The hotel occupancy tax is based on the amount of money received from the occupant, including service fees. (Sec. 11-2502(a), N.Y.C. Adm. Code; Sec. 11-2501(5), N.Y.C. Adm. Code) For detailed guidance for businesses subject to the New York City hotel occupancy tax, see Finance Memorandum 08-1REV; Finance Memorandum 09-3; and Statement of Audit Procedure HTX-2009-01.

• *"Occupancy" defined*

"Occupancy" is the use or possession, or the right to the use or possession of any room or rooms in a hotel, or the right to the use or possession of the furnishings or to the services and accommodations accompanying the use and possession of the room or rooms. "Right to the use or possession" includes the rights of a room remarketer. (Sec. 11-2501(4), N.Y.C. Adm. Code)

Hotel no shows.—Where a hotel, under its guaranteed reservations policy, holds a room for a person who made the reservation, and bills him for it even though he fails to appear, it must charge and collect the hotel occupancy tax on the "no show" billing because the term "occupancy" includes the right to use or occupy a hotel room. The Department of Finance has issued a statement of audit procedure (SAP) that provides guidance to auditors in connection with audits of hotel operators under the hotel room occupancy tax where such hotel operators bill guests for "no show". (Sec. 11-2501(4), N.Y.C. Adm. Code) (*Statement of Audit Procedure HTX-2008-1*, New York City Department of Finance, Audit Division, March 14, 2008)

Subletting.—Persons subletting hotel rooms are no longer defined as operators. Generally, if a person sublets a room after renting it from an operator, the taxable occupancy is the original occupancy. Under such circumstances, the original hotel operator is required to collect the tax from the original occupant. However, the original operator must collect the tax from the sublessee in cases where the original occupant or any sublessee of the room is directly or indirectly related to the original hotel operator, as follows:

—the original hotel operator owns directly or indirectly a 5% or greater interest in the occupant;

—the occupant owns directly or indirectly a 5% or greater interest in the original hotel operator;

—one or more persons own directly or indirectly 5% or greater interests in both the occupant and the original hotel operator; or

—the occupant is an officer, director, manager (including a manager of an LLC), trustee, fiduciary, or employee of the original hotel operator or is an individual who is a member of the family of an individual original hotel operator. (Rule Sec. 12-01)

The Department of Finance has issued a statement of audit procedure (SAP) concerning the subletting rule changes discussed above, which become effective June 1, 2002. The SAP provides guidance to hotel room occupancy tax auditors in auditing and resolving the tax liabilities of hotel room resellers for periods beginning prior to June 1, 2002, using an accelerated audit procedure. (*Statement of Audit Procedure 01-2-HTX: Audits of Resellers of Hotel Rooms,* New York City Department of Finance, Audit Division, July 24, 2001)

• *"Operator" defined*

An operator is any person operating a hotel in New York City, including, but not limited to, the owner or proprietor of such premises, lessee, sublessee, mortgagee in possession, licensee or any other person otherwise operating such hotel. Any occupant who sublets or otherwise contracts away the right to the use or possession of a room is not an operator. However, a private club that, as an accommodation to its members, makes rooms available to the members in its own buildings will still be considered an operator. (Sec. 11-2501(12), N.Y.C. Adm. Code; Rule Sec. 12-01) (Finance Memorandum 08-1REV)

• *"Room" defined*

The term "room" includes any portion of a hotel, whether used for dwelling, commercial or any other purposes, except:

— a bathroom or lavatory;

— a place of assembly;

— a store, stand or counter to which access is had directly from public thoroughfares or street or mezzanine lobbies; and

— a lobby, public dining room or other public room when employed as such; provided, however, when such lobby, public dining room or other public room is used exclusively for a private purpose, the occupancy thereof is subject to tax (unless the room qualifies as a place of assembly).

(Rule Sec. 12-01) (Finance Memorandum 08-1REV)

Kitchenettes.—The term "room" also includes walk-in kitchenettes enclosed by walls with one or more doorways, archways or other openings, that are supplied with a cooking appliance, including but not limited to a range, microwave, convention oven, or hot plate, and contain at least one item from each of two of the following three categories:

(1) a sink with running water, or dishwasher;

(2) a refrigerator;

(3) a cabinet, counter top, or table.

Example 1: A hotel suite contains a kitchenette with a microwave oven, refrigerator, sink, cabinets and counter top. The kitchenette is a walk-in area with three walls and a wide opening on the fourth side. The kitchenette is a room.

Example 2: Same facts as above, except all items are set into a wall and there is no appurtenant walk-in area. The kitchenette is not a room.

Example 3: Same facts as in Example No. 1, except the microwave is not in the kitchenette but rather is outside the kitchenette. The kitchenette is a room.

The Department of Finance has issued a statement of audit procedure (SAP) that auditors should follow this definition of a room to all tax periods on or after April 1, 1990, which are open for audit, unless they are instructed otherwise by a supervisor. (*Statement of Audit Procedure HTX-2008-2,* New York City Department of Finance, Audit Division, March 14, 2008)

• *Bed and breakfast accommodations*

A bed and breakfast (B&B) that is regularly used and kept open for guests comes within the definition of a "hotel." The occupancy for consideration of multiple rooms in a residential apartment, condominium or house, that are regularly used and kept open for the lodging of guests is subject to tax. (*Statement of Audit Procedure HTX-2008-03*, New York City Department of Finance, March 14, 2008) In determining whether rooms are "regularly used and kept open for the lodging of guests," auditors may consider the following:

— the advertising of the availability of these rooms;

— the listing of the rooms with B&B services in tourist guides or by lodging industry associates;

— the availability of common hotel services (i.e. linen or food services);

— the frequency and regularity with which the rooms are rented;

— the reporting of the income earned from these rentals for federal income tax purposes; and

— the amount and nature of the expenses deducted in connection with the rental of these rooms.

(*Statement of Audit Procedure HTX-2008-03*, New York City Department of Finance, March 14, 2008)

The occupancy by a guest for consideration of one room in a dwelling ordinarily occupied by an individual as his or her own dwelling will not be subject to the hotel room occupancy tax even if the room is regularly used and kept open for the lodging of guests. The renting of just one room in a person's own dwelling place comes within the exception to the definition of a "hotel". This exception is limited to a single room rented in an individual's residence. A single room rented in a dwelling that the individual owner or tenant operating the B&B does not regularly occupy as his or her own residence comes within the definition of a "hotel". The occupancy of such a room for consideration is subject to the hotel room occupancy tax. (*Statement of Audit Procedure HTX-2008-03*, New York City Department of Finance, March 14, 2008)

• *Room remarketers*

The hotel occupancy tax is based on the amount of money received from the occupant, including service fees. Online travel companies will continue to pay the hotel occupancy tax, which will be based on the wholesale rate, to the hotel, which will remit such payment to the Department of Finance. However, online travel companies are required to pay to the department the difference in hotel taxes based on the wholesale rate and the amount actually charged the occupant. Specifically, the following provisions are applicable: booking and service fees are added to the list of terms that could be deemed "consideration" or rent for hotel occupancy; a new term "room remarketer" is defined (online travel Website) to be any person, excluding the hotel operator, that would have the right, through the Internet, or elsewhere, to offer, reserve, book, or distribute, the transfer of hotel room occupancy; the room remarketer is allowed to collect from the occupant, and remit to the hotel, the portion of the tax that is determined on the amount that the remarketer pays to the hotel operator ("net rent"). The hotel operator then remits this tax portion to the department; and the room remarketer is required to charge the occupant the amount of the tax that the remarketer owes to the department based on the amount the occupant pays to the remarkter that is in excess of the amount that the remarketer pays to the hotel operator (now termed "additional rent"). (Sec. 11-2501, N.Y.C. Adm. Code; Sec. 11-2502, N.Y.C. Adm. Code) For additional information regarding additional rent charged by room remarketers, see Finance Memorandum 09-3 and Statement of Audit Procedure HTX-2009-01.

Room remarketers are required to collect the hotel tax on the full amount charged to the occupant and remit the tax collected directly to Finance. Remarketers will then be allowed a refund or credit for any tax paid to the hotel operator or another remarketer for that occupancy. Only remarketers that have registered with

Finance to collect the tax and have collected and remitted the tax for a particular quarterly filing period may apply for the refund or credit. In order to apply for the new credit or refund, room remarketers must include the following in a schedule attached to their quarterly hotel tax filing: (1) the names and New York City hotel tax identification numbers of the hotels and/or room remarketers to whom they paid hotel tax during the quarter; and (2) the amounts paid to each hotel operator or remarketer during that quarter. (Finance Memorandum 10-3) However, effective June 1, 2016, any occupancy conveyed or furnished by a hotel operator to a room remarketer for the purpose of re-selling to an occupant are exempt from the hotel tax. (Finance Memorandum 16-5) The room remarketer is still responsible for collecting and remitting the hotel tax on the sale to the occupant. remarketers are entitled to an exemption from the hotel tax for occupancies they acquire from hotel operators, but they must provide them with a New York State Room Remarketer's Exempt Purchase Certificate in order to claim it. Remarketers still collect tax on the full amount charged to the occupant and remit the tax collected directly to the department. Remarketers are still allowed a refund or credit for any tax paid to a hotel operator for an occupancy conveyed prior to June 1, 2016, or any tax paid to another remarketer for an occupancy. Only remarketers that have registered with the department to collect the hotel tax, and have collected and remitted hotel tax for a particular quarterly filing period, may apply for this refund or credit. The new law also specifies that when occupancy of a hotel room(s) is sold for a single fee with other items or services, unless the rent qualifies for this exemption, the entire amount is considered taxable rent. However, if the operator or room remarketer provides the occupant with a sales slip, invoice, receipt or other statement that separately states a reasonable amount of the total charge as rent for occupancy, only the separately stated amount is subject to the hotel tax. (Finance Memorandum 16-5)

Refunds and credits.—A room remarketer may take a credit on its quarterly hotel tax return for taxes paid to hotel operators or other room remarketers. However, taking the credit at that time is deemed to be part of the application for that credit, is subject to audit and may ultimately not be allowed. In order to apply for a credit or refund, room remarketers must include a schedule attached to their quarterly hotel tax filing with the name, address and amount paid to each hotel operator or room remarketer. In the alternative, a room remarketer may attach a summary schedule and make all details available to the Commissioner of Finance upon request. A credit or refund must be requested in writing within one year of the date the hotel tax was paid by the occupant to the room remarketer. (Finance Memorandum 16-5)

Effective September 1, 2012, the 2012 budget legislation (Ch. 59 (A.B. 9059), Laws 2012) facilitates the compliance of hotel room remarketers with the state and local sales tax collection obligations adopted in 2010 (Ch. 57, Laws 2010). The provisions enacted in the 2012 budget bill do the following:

— provide a method to compute the portion of the bill taxable as rent when an occupancy is sold together with other items for a single price. Specifically, when occupancy is provided for a single consideration with property, services, amusement charges, or any other items, whether or not such other items are taxable, the rent portion of the consideration for such transaction must be computed as follows: either the total consideration received by the room remarketer multiplied by a fraction, the numerator of which is the consideration payable for the occupancy by the room remarketer and the denominator of which is such consideration payable for the occupancy plus the consideration payable by the remarketer for the other items being sold, or by any other method as may be authorized by the Commissioner of Taxation and Finance. If the room remarketer fails to separately state the tax on the rent so computed on a sales slip, invoice, receipt, or other statement given to the occupant or fails to maintain records of the prices of all components of a transaction, the entire consideration shall be treated as rent subject to tax;

— permit room remarketers to provide the information about the amount of the sales tax due on any invoice given to the customer prior to the completion of the occupancy;

— allow room remarketers to report sales of occupancies in the sales tax filing period in which the occupancy ended, rather than in the sales tax period during which they collected the consideration for the occupancy; and

— simply the process by which a room remarketer claims credit for sales tax paid on its acquisition of a hotel room. For instance, in order to qualify for a refund or credit against the amount of tax collected and required to be remitted, a room remarketer can provide the name, business address, telephone number, and the address of the hotel where the occupancy took place if the room remarketer requests the hotel operator's certificate of authority number and is not provided that number.

(Sec. 11-2502, N.Y.C. Adm. Code) (Summary of Tax Provisions in SFY 2012-13 Budget, New York Department of Taxation and Finance, April 2012) (TSB-M-12(8)S)

Forms to file.—The specialized tax return for room remarketers, Form HTX-RR, will no longer be used after the period ending August 31, 2010. Room remarketers must begin filing Form HTX, the hotel tax returns currently used by hotel operators, beginning with the tax quarter that starts on September 1, 2010.

Registration requirements.—Room remarketers offering hotel rooms in New York City must complete and file a Certificate of Registration with the department within three days of the date they begin offering hotel rooms in New York City. The department will then send remarketers a Certificate of Authority to collect hotel tax on the department's behalf. The certificate must be prominently displayed where occupants will see it. In the case of a room remarketer that offers New York City hotel rooms on the Internet, the Certificate of Authority should be scanned and displayed on the room remarketer's website. (Finance Memorandum 16-5)

• *Hotel reward points program*

The Department of Finance has issued a memorandum regarding the New York City hotel room occupancy tax with respect to complimentary rooms and complimentary room upgrades provided by a hotel to members of rewards points programs. Specifically, when a member guest receives a complimentary room upgrade, the hotel must collect tax on the value of the original room, but not on the value of the upgrade. When a member guest redeems points for a room, the hotel is not required to collect tax on the occupancy. According to the Department of Finance, when a member guest receives a complimentary room upgrade. (Finance Memorandum 06-2)

[¶531-010]
NYC HOTEL OCCUPANCY TAX EXEMPTIONS

[¶531-015] NYC Hotel Occupancy Tax Exemptions--In General

The hotel occupancy tax is not imposed upon:

(1) permanent residents (Sec. 11-2502(b), N.Y.C. Adm. Code), defined as persons who have been hotel room occupants for at least 180 consecutive days (Sec. 11-2501(8), N.Y.C. Adm. Code); or

(2) any organization described in Sec. 1116(a), Tax Law to the extent such organization is exempt under Sec. 1105(e), Tax Law. (Sec. 11-2502(c), N.Y.C. Adm. Code)

An exempt occupant must provide the hotel operator with a copy of the state exempt organization certificate showing it is exempt from the state tax to rebut the presumption that the rent is subject to New York City tax. The certificate from the

New York City Commissioner of Finance, certifying the organization is exempt from the City tax, is no longer required.

An occupant who, under the provision of the rent stabilization program, requests a lease after August 31, 1990, will be tentatively accorded the status of permanent resident, regardless of whether the occupant has satisfied the 180-consecutive-day requirement. (Sec. 11-2502(b), N.Y.C. Adm. Code) The hotel operator will not be permitted to collect tax from a permanent resident for any day, commencing with the date the lease is requested, which falls within a period of continuous occupancy. If the occupancy ceases to occupy a room or rooms in the hotel prior to the completion of 180 consecutive days of occupancy, however, the unpaid taxes will immediately become due, and must be collected from the occupant.

For detailed guidance for businesses subject to the New York City hotel occupancy tax, see Finance Memorandum 08-1REV.

• *Exempt occupants*

Occupancies by certain individuals and organizations are exempt from the hotel tax imposed on rent for hotel occupancy. These exempt individuals and organizations include, but are not limited to:

— New York state and any of its agencies, instrumentalities, public corporations and political subdivisions;

— The United States of America and its agencies and instrumentalities;

— the United Nations and any international organizations of which the United States is a member;

— diplomatic missions and diplomats;

— organizations that have qualified for exempt status under the New York state sales tax law, such as qualifying charities and educational institutions, certain posts or organizations consisting of past or present members of the armed forces and certain Indian nations or tribes; and

— organizations that are organized and operated exclusively for religious, charitable, scientific, testing for public safety, literary or educational purposes, or to foster national or international amateur sports competition or for the prevention of cruelty to children or animals.

(Finance Memorandum 08-1REV)

• *Nontaxable occupancies*

Complimentary accommodations. When a hotel furnishes complimentary accommodations to individuals for which there is no rent or other consideration paid, the hotel is not required to collect hotel tax on the normal cost of the room. However, where there is consideration, such as the promise by the occupant of the room to bring future business to the hotel by a tour guide, travel representative or other person, the room is subject to hotel tax based on the normal rental price of the room. (Finance Memorandum 08-1REV)

Lodging furnished to employees for owner's convenience. Lodging furnished by a hotel operator to an employee for the hotel operator's convenience are not subject to the hotel tax provided: (i) the employer receives no cash or other consideration for lodging from the employee; and (ii) the value of the lodging is not income to the employee under federal or New York income tax laws. (Finance Memorandum 08-1REV)

If a hotel operator receives cash or other consideration from an employee for lodging or the value of the lodging is income to the employee for federal or New York income tax purposes, the lodging is subject to the hotel tax. If an employee becomes a permanent resident of the hotel, the hotel operator is no longer required to collect the hotel tax on the charges to the employee for occupancy, and the employee is entitled to a refund of the hotel tax previously paid on charges for occupancy at the hotel. (Finance Memorandum 08-1REV)

Summer camps. A camp for children that provides overnight sleeping accommodations and a program of instructions, training or other organized activities that campers are required to pursue under the supervision of counsellors or other supervisory personnel is not a hotel. However, unless otherwise exempted or excluded from tax, if guest facilities are provided for parents or others, hotel tax is due on the occupancy charges. (Finance Memorandum 08-1REV)

Nursing, rest or convalescent homes. A facility that is registered with or licensed by a New York state governmental agency, whether publicly or privately owned and operated, which accepts persons who require special care on account of age, illness, or mental or physical incapacity, and which provides this special care either by nurses, orderlies or aides, is not a hotel. Accordingly, the charges for occupancy in this type of facility are not subject to the hotel tax. (Finance Memorandum 08-1REV)

• *Subletting*

For purposes of qualifying as a permanent resident, days of consecutive occupancy do not include any day that a person's occupancy of a room has been sublet or otherwise contracted away. In addition, if a person leases two or more rooms in a hotel and sublets them on various days, the person may not aggregate the days on which the different rooms have not been sublet in order to qualify for permanent resident status. (Rule Sec. 12-01)

• *Persons displaced by World Trade Center attack*

The tax did not apply to any person occupying a room in a hotel solely and directly as a result of having been involuntarily displaced from premises by the attack on the World Trade Center on September 11, 2001, provided that such former premises were not subject to the hotel tax or the New York City sales and use tax. (Sec. 11-2502(d), N.Y.C. Adm. Code)

[¶531-020]
NYC HOTEL OCCUPANCY TAX BASIS

[¶531-025] NYC Hotel Occupancy Tax Basis--In General

The hotel occupancy tax is based on the daily rental value of the hotel room occupied. (Sec. 11-2502(a), N.Y.C. Adm. Code) If the rent is paid or charged on a weekly, monthly or other term basis, the daily rental value is determined by dividing the rent for the whole term by the number of days in the term. If the rent is for more than one room, the daily rent per room is calculated by multiplying the daily rent for the particular room, or a similar room, when the room is rented alone with similar bath facilities, and the denominator of which is the total of the daily rent for the individual rooms in the group of rooms, or similar rooms, when such rooms are rented alone with similar bath facilities.

The hotel occupancy tax is based on the amount of money received from the occupant, including service fees. Thus, online travel companies will continue to pay the hotel occupancy tax, which will be based on the wholesale rate, to the hotel, which will remit such payment to the Department of Finance. However, online travel companies are required to pay to the department the difference in hotel taxes based on the wholesale rate and the amount actually charged the occupant. Specifically, the following provisions are applicable: booking and service fees are added to the list of terms that could be deemed "consideration" or rent for hotel occupancy; a new term "room remarketer" is defined (online travel Website) to be any person, excluding the hotel operator, that would have the right, through the Internet, or elsewhere, to offer, reserve, book, or distribute, the transfer of hotel room occupancy; the room remarketer is allowed to collect from the occupant, and remit to the hotel, the portion of the tax that is determined on the amount that the remarketer pays to the hotel operator ("net rent"). The hotel operator then remits this tax portion to the department; and the room remarketer is required to charge the occupant the amount of the tax that the remarkter owes to the department based on the amount the occupant pays to the remarkter that is in excess of the amount that the remarketer pays to the hotel operator (now termed "additional rent"). (Sec. 11-2501, N.Y.C. Adm. Code; Sec. 11-2502, N.Y.C. Adm. Code) (Finance Memorandum 09-3)

Whenever a taxable occupancy is booked by an occupant through a room remarketer, the hotel operator and the room remarketer must each collect a portion of the hotel tax due. Any tax collected by a remarketer must be turned over to Department of Finance. A Statement of Audit Procedure (SAP) discusses the following issues that may arise during the course of a hotel tax audit as a result of this requirement. However, effective June 1, 2016, any occupancy conveyed or furnished by a hotel operator to a room remarketer for the purpose of re-selling to an occupant are exempt from the hotel tax. (Finance Memorandum 16-5)

Remarketers are required to collect the hotel tax on the full amount charged to the occupant and remit the tax collected directly to Finance. Remarketers will then be allowed a refund or credit for any tax paid to the hotel operator or another remarketer for that occupancy. Only remarketers that have registered with Finance to collect the tax and have collected and remitted the tax for a particular quarterly filing period may apply for the refund or credit. In order to apply for the new credit or refund, room remarketers must include the following in a schedule attached to their quarterly hotel tax filing: (1) the names and New York City hotel tax identification numbers of the hotels and/or room remarketers to whom they paid hotel tax during the quarter; and (2) the amounts paid to each hotel operator or remarketer during that quarter. (Finance Memorandum 10-3) However, effective June 1, 2016, any occupancy conveyed or furnished by a hotel operator to a room remarketer for the purpose of re-selling to an occupant are exempt from the hotel tax. (Finance Memorandum 16-5) The room remarketer is still responsible for collecting and remitting the hotel tax on the sale to the occupant. remarketers are entitled to an exemption from the hotel tax for occupancies they acquire from hotel operators, but they must provide them with a New York State Room Remarketer's Exempt Purchase Certificate in order to claim it. Remarketers still collect tax on the full amount charged to the occupant and remit the tax collected directly to the department. Remarketers are still allowed a refund or credit for any tax paid to a hotel operator for an occupancy conveyed prior to June 1, 2016, or any tax paid to another remarketer for an occupancy. Only remarketers that have registered with the department to collect the hotel tax, and have collected and remitted hotel tax for a particular quarterly filing period, may apply for this refund or credit. The new law also specifies that when occupancy of a hotel room(s) is sold for a single fee with other items or services, unless the rent qualifies for this exemption, the entire amount is considered taxable rent. However, if the operator or room remarketer provides the occupant with a sales slip, invoice, receipt or other statement that separately states a reasonable amount of the total charge as rent for occupancy, only the separately stated amount is subject to the hotel tax. (Finance Memorandum 16-5)

A room remarketer may take a credit on its quarterly hotel tax return for taxes paid to hotel operators or other room remarketers. However, taking the credit at that time is deemed to be part of the application for that credit, is subject to audit and may ultimately not be allowed. In order to apply for a credit or refund, room remarketers must include a schedule attached to their quarterly hotel tax filing with the name, address and amount paid to each hotel operator or room remarketer. In the alternative, a room remarketer may attach a summary schedule and make all details available to the Commissioner of Finance upon request. A credit or refund must be requested in writing within one year of the date the hotel tax was paid by the occupant to the room remarketer. (Finance Memorandum 16-5)

For detailed guidance for businesses subject to the New York City hotel occupancy tax, see Finance Memorandum 08-1REV; Finance Memorandum 09-3; Finance Memorandum 16-5; and Statement of Audit Procedure HTX-2009-01.

Advance payment of tax by remarketers: Remarketers generally get paid when a customer reserves a room in advance of the actual occupancy. Remarketers will also collect the hotel tax at that point. However, the hotel tax is a tax upon the occupancy of hotel rooms in New York City, and is not due unless the occupant has the "use or possession, or the right to the use or possession" of a room. Because remarketers may have remitted the hotel tax in the quarter in which the tax was collected, remarketers may need to file refund applications to recover advance payments of hotel tax in the event the reservation is cancelled and the occupancy never takes place. (Statement of Audit Procedure HTX-2009-01)

Cancellations and cancellation fees: The current policy for hotel tax is that cancellation fees are not taxable, but guaranteed no-show payments are taxable because they still give a right to occupy the room. This policy should also be followed for remarketers. (Statement of Audit Procedure HTX-2009-01)

Discounts and coupons: Discounts, whether funded by the remarketer, the hotel, or shared between them, represent actual reductions to the price of a hotel room. The rent taxable under the hotel tax should also be reduced accordingly. (Statement of Audit Procedure HTX-2009-01)

Records: The hotel tax collected must be separated out in the remarketer's books and records using a reasonable method that allows auditors to verify that the net rent amounts and the additional rent amounts used were correct, and that the right amount of hotel tax has been collected and paid. (Statement of Audit Procedure HTX-2009-01)

Service fees: Currently, the definition of rent includes "any service and/or booking fees that are a condition of occupancy." Whether and when a "service fee" is a condition of occupancy will depend on the nature of the fee, i.e. whether it can be tied to a specific, identifiable service provided to a particular occupant other than merely facilitating the right to occupy a room, and on whether it occurs with every occupancy. Fees are presumed to be a condition of occupancy unless a remarketer can demonstrate otherwise. The SAP provides examples of taxable service fees and possible examples of service fees that are not a condition of occupancy. (Statement of Audit Procedure HTX-2009-01)

Unbundling packages: When a remarketer has put together or purchased a package for resale and the remarketer knows the price of the components, a "cost of components" method should be used to determine what part of the package represents taxable additional rent. The taxable additional rent would be based on the ratio of the wholesale cost of the hotel room to the wholesale cost of all the components of the package multiplied by the total mark-up for the package. However, many remarketers buy packages from other remarketers, who may have bought them from others, and so on. They frequently have no idea of the cost of some or all of the components. In that instance, a 15% markup on 70% of the average retail rate of a similar room may be used to compute additional rent. (Statement of Audit Procedure HTX-2009-01)

Multiple remarketer transactions: If a remarketer purchases rooms from a hotel and sells them to a second remarketer that then sells to the occupant, each remarketer is responsible for collecting hotel tax on its own markup, and the hotel is responsible for the hotel tax on the discounted rate it charges the first remarketer. (Statement of Audit Procedure HTX-2009-01)

Promotions: Remarketers do not have additional rent in each and every room transaction. Instead, their various promotional programs contemplate that they may give a room to an occupant for free, yet still pay the hotel at the usual discounted rate, or that they may sell a room to an occupant for less than the usual discounted rate. In either of these situations, the remarketer will generate a loss and no additional hotel tax will be collected and remitted by the remarketer. (Statement of Audit Procedure HTX-2009-01)

For detailed guidance for businesses subject to the New York City hotel occupancy tax, see Finance Memorandum 08-1REV; Finance Memorandum 09-3; and Statement of Audit Procedure HTX-2009-01.

Effective September 1, 2012, the 2012 budget legislation (Ch. 59 (A.B. 9059), Laws 2012) facilitates the compliance of hotel room remarketers with the state and local sales tax collection obligations adopted in 2010 (Ch. 57, Laws 2010). The provisions enacted in the 2012 budget bill do the following:

— provide a method to compute the portion of the bill taxable as rent when an occupancy is sold together with other items for a single price. Specifically, when occupancy is provided for a single consideration with property, services, amusement charges, or any other items, whether or not such other items are taxable, the rent portion of the consideration for such transaction must be computed as follows: either the total consideration received by the room remarketer multiplied by a fraction, the numerator of which is the consideration payable for the occupancy by the room remarketer and the denominator of which is such consideration payable for the occupancy plus the consideration payable by the remarketer for the other items being sold, or by any other method as may be authorized by the Commissioner of Taxation and Finance. If the room remarketer fails to separately state the tax on the rent so computed on a sales slip, invoice, receipt, or other statement given to the occupant or fails to maintain records of the prices of all components of a transaction, the entire consideration shall be treated as rent subject to tax;

— permit room remarketers to provide the information about the amount of the sales tax due on any invoice given to the customer prior to the completion of the occupancy;

— allow room remarketers to report sales of occupancies in the sales tax filing period in which the occupancy ended, rather than in the sales tax period during which they collected the consideration for the occupancy; and

— simply the process by which a room remarketer claims credit for sales tax paid on its acquisition of a hotel room. For instance, in order to qualify for a refund or credit against the amount of tax collected and required to be remitted, a room remarketer can provide the name, business address, telephone number, and the address of the hotel where the occupancy took place if the room remarketer requests the hotel operator's certificate of authority number and is not provided that number.

(Sec. 11-2502, N.Y.C. Adm. Code) (Summary of Tax Provisions in SFY 2012-13 Budget, New York Department of Taxation and Finance, April 2012) (TSB-M-12(8)S)

[¶531-030]
NYC HOTEL OCCUPANCY TAX RATE

[¶531-035] NYC Hotel Occupancy Tax Rate--In General

The rate of the hotel occupancy tax is determined in accordance with the following tax table (Sec. 11-2502(a), N.Y.C. Adm. Code):

Rent Per Day   Tax

Less than $10 . . . . $0

$10 or more, but less than $20 . . . .$0.50

$20 or more, but less than $30 . . . . 1.00

$30 or more, but less than $40 . . . . 1.50

$40 or more 2.00

For detailed guidance for businesses subject to the New York City hotel occupancy tax, see Finance Memorandum 08-1REV.

• *Additional tax*

In addition, a tax is imposed for every occupancy of each room in a hotel in New York City at the rate of 5% of the rent or charge per day for each such room. (Sec. 11-2502(a), N.Y.C. Adm. Code)

• *Online travel companies (room remarketers)*

The hotel occupancy tax is based on the amount of money received from the occupant, including service fees. Online travel companies will continue to pay the hotel occupancy tax, which will be based on the wholesale rate, to the hotel, which will remit such payment to the Department of Finance. However, online travel companies are required to pay to the department the difference in hotel taxes based on the wholesale rate and the amount actually charged the occupant. Specifically, the following provisions are applicable: booking and service fees are added to the list of terms that could be deemed "consideration" or rent for hotel occupancy; a new term "room remarketer" is defined (online travel Website) to be any person, excluding the hotel operator, that would have the right, through the Internet, or elsewhere, to offer, reserve, book, or distribute, the transfer of hotel room occupancy; the room remarketer is allowed to collect from the occupant, and remit to the hotel, the portion of the tax that is determined on the amount that the remarketer pays to the hotel operator ("net rent"). The hotel operator then remits this tax portion to the department; and the room remarketer is required to charge the occupant the amount of the tax that the remarkter owes to the department based on the amount the occupant pays to the remarkter that is in excess of the amount that the remarketer pays to the hotel operator (now termed "additional rent"). (Sec. 11-2501, N.Y.C. Adm. Code; Sec. 11-2502, N.Y.C. Adm. Code) For additional information, see Finance Memorandum 09-3. For audit issues and procedures for audits of hotel tax returns prepared by room remarketers, see Statement of Audit Procedure HTX-2009-01.

Remarketers are required to collect the hotel tax on the full amount charged to the occupant and remit the tax collected directly to Finance. Remarketers will then be allowed a refund or credit for any tax paid to the hotel operator or another remarketer for that occupancy. (Finance Memorandum 10-3)

Effective September 1, 2012, the 2012 budget legislation (Ch. 59 (A.B. 9059), Laws 2012) facilitates the compliance of hotel room remarketers with the state and local sales tax collection obligations adopted in 2010 (Ch. 57, Laws 2010). The provisions enacted in the 2012 budget bill do the following:

— provide a method to compute the portion of the bill taxable as rent when an occupancy is sold together with other items for a single price. Specifically, when occupancy is provided for a single consideration with property, services, amusement charges, or any other items, whether or not such other items are taxable, the rent portion of the consideration for such transaction must be computed as follows: either the total consideration received by the room remarketer multiplied by a fraction, the numerator of which is the consideration payable for the occupancy by the room remarketer and the denominator of which is such consideration payable for the occupancy plus the consideration payable by the remarketer for the other items being sold, or by any other method as may be authorized by the Commissioner of Taxation and Finance. If the room remarketer fails to separately state the tax on the rent so computed on a sales slip, invoice, receipt, or other statement given to the occupant or fails to maintain records of the prices of all components of a transaction, the entire consideration shall be treated as rent subject to tax;

— permit room remarketers to provide the information about the amount of the sales tax due on any invoice given to the customer prior to the completion of the occupancy;

— allow room remarketers to report sales of occupancies in the sales tax filing period in which the occupancy ended, rather than in the sales tax period during which they collected the consideration for the occupancy; and

— simply the process by which a room remarketer claims credit for sales tax paid on its acquisition of a hotel room. For instance, in order to qualify for a refund or credit against the amount of tax collected and required to be remitted, a room remarketer can provide the name, business address, telephone number, and the address of the hotel where the occupancy took place if the room remarketer requests the hotel operator's certificate of authority number and is not provided that number.

(Sec. 11-2502, N.Y.C. Adm. Code) (Summary of Tax Provisions in SFY 2012-13 Budget, New York Department of Taxation and Finance, April 2012) (TSB-M-12(8)S)

[¶531-040]

NYC HOTEL OCCUPANCY TAX LICENSE

[¶531-045] NYC Registration

Every hotel operator or room remarketer must file with the Commissioner of Finance a certificate of registration within three days after commencing business or opening new hotels. Within five days of such registration, the Commissioner of Finance must issue without charge to the operator or room remarketer a certificate of authority, which allows the operator to collect the hotel occupancy tax. The certificate must state the hotel to which it is applicable. (Sec. 11-2514, N.Y.C. Adm. Code)

Such certificates or duplicates must be prominently displayed so that they may be seen by all occupants and persons seeking occupancy. Certificates of authority are nonassignable and nontransferable and must be surrendered immediately to the Commissioner of Finance upon the cessation of business at the hotel named or upon its sale or transfer. (Sec. 11-2514, N.Y.C. Adm. Code)

Remarketers are required to collect the hotel tax on the full amount charged to the occupant and remit the tax collected directly to Finance. Remarketers will then be allowed a refund or credit for any tax paid to the hotel operator or another remarketer for that occupancy. (Finance Memorandum 10-3) Room remarketers offering hotel rooms in New York City must complete and file a Certificate of Registration with Finance within three days of the date they begin offering hotel rooms in New York City. Finance will then send remarketers a Certificate of Authority to collect tax on Finance's behalf. The certificate must be prominently displayed where occupants will see it. In the case of a room remarketer that offers New York City hotel rooms on the Internet, the Certificate of Authority should be scanned and displayed on the room remarketer's web site. (Finance Memorandum 10-3)

Effective September 1, 2012, the 2012 budget legislation (Ch. 59 (A.B. 9059), Laws 2012) facilitates the compliance of hotel room remarketers with the state and local sales tax collection obligations adopted in 2010 (Ch. 57, Laws 2010). The provisions enacted in the 2012 budget bill do the following:

— provide a method to compute the portion of the bill taxable as rent when an occupancy is sold together with other items for a single price. Specifically, when occupancy is provided for a single consideration with property, services, amusement charges, or any other items, whether or not such other items are taxable, the rent portion of the consideration for such transaction must be computed as follows: either the total consideration received by the room remarketer multiplied by a fraction, the numerator of which is the consideration payable for the occupancy by the room remarketer and the denominator of which is such consideration payable for the occupancy plus the consideration payable by the remarketer for the other items being sold, or by any other method as may be authorized by the Commissioner of Taxation and Finance. If the room remarketer fails to separately state the tax on the rent so computed on a sales slip, invoice, receipt, or other statement given to the occupant or fails to maintain records of the prices of all components of a transaction, the entire consideration shall be treated as rent subject to tax;

— permit room remarketers to provide the information about the amount of the sales tax due on any invoice given to the customer prior to the completion of the occupancy;

— allow room remarketers to report sales of occupancies in the sales tax filing period in which the occupancy ended, rather than in the sales tax period during which they collected the consideration for the occupancy; and

— simply the process by which a room remarketer claims credit for sales tax paid on its acquisition of a hotel room. For instance, in order to qualify for a refund or credit against the amount of tax collected and required to be remitted, a room remarketer can provide the name, business address, telephone number, and the address of the hotel where the occupancy took place if the room remarketer requests the hotel operator's certificate of authority number and is not provided that number.

(Sec. 11-2502, N.Y.C. Adm. Code) (Summary of Tax Provisions in SFY 2012-13 Budget, New York Department of Taxation and Finance, April 2012) (TSB-M-12(8)S)

For detailed guidance for businesses subject to the New York City hotel occupancy tax, see Finance Memorandum 10-3; Finance Memorandum 08-1REV; and Finance Memorandum 09-3. For audit issues and procedures for audits of hotel tax returns prepared by room remarketers, see Statement of Audit Procedure HTX-2009-01.

[¶531-050]
NYC HOTEL OCCUPANCY TAX REPORTS

[¶531-053] NYC Records

Hotel operators and room remarketers must keep records of every occupancy and of all rent paid, charged or due and of the tax owed. Records must be available for inspection at any time upon demand by the Commissioner of Finance and must be preserved for three years. Also, the Commissioner may require any person who has elected to maintain records in an electronic format to make such electronic records available and accessible, notwithstanding that they are also maintained in a hard copy format. (Sec. 11-2503, N.Y.C. Adm. Code) Failure to maintain record can result in various penalty provisions, which are discussed at ¶531-076 NYC Penalties.

Effective September 1, 2010, legislation modified the law with respect to the obligations of room remarketers and affects the records that must be kept. Under the law, the remarketers are required to collect the hotel tax on the full amount charged to the occupant and remit the tax collected directly to Finance. Remarketers will then be allowed a refund or credit for any tax paid to the hotel operator or another remarketer for that occupancy. (Finance Memorandum 10-3) Room remarketers offering hotel rooms in New York City must complete and file a Certificate of Registration with Finance within three days of the date they begin offering hotel rooms in New York City. Finance will then send remarketers a Certificate of Authority to collect tax on Finance's behalf. The certificate must be prominently displayed where occupants will see it. In the case of a room remarketer that offers New York City hotel rooms on the Internet, the Certificate of Authority should be scanned and displayed on the room remarketer's website. (Finance Memorandum 10-3)

Effective September 1, 2012, the 2012 budget legislation (Ch. 59 (A.B. 9059), Laws 2012) facilitates the compliance of hotel room remarketers with the state and local sales tax collection obligations adopted in 2010 (Ch. 57, Laws 2010). The provisions enacted in the 2012 budget bill do the following:

— provide a method to compute the portion of the bill taxable as rent when an occupancy is sold together with other items for a single price. Specifically, when occupancy is provided for a single consideration with property, services, amusement charges, or any other items, whether or not such other items are taxable, the rent portion of the consideration for such transaction must be computed as follows: either the total consideration received by the room remarketer multiplied by a fraction, the numerator of which is the consideration payable for the occupancy by the room remarketer and the denominator of which is such consideration payable for the occupancy plus the consideration payable by the remarketer for the other items being sold, or by any other method as may be authorized by the Commissioner of Taxation and Finance. If the room remarketer fails to separately state the tax on the rent so computed on a sales slip, invoice, receipt, or other statement given to the occupant or fails to maintain records of the prices of all components of a transaction, the entire consideration shall be treated as rent subject to tax;

— permit room remarketers to provide the information about the amount of the sales tax due on any invoice given to the customer prior to the completion of the occupancy;

— allow room remarketers to report sales of occupancies in the sales tax filing period in which the occupancy ended, rather than in the sales tax period during which they collected the consideration for the occupancy; and

— simply the process by which a room remarketer claims credit for sales tax paid on its acquisition of a hotel room. For instance, in order to qualify for a refund or credit against the amount of tax collected and required to be remitted, a room remarketer can provide the name, business address, telephone number, and the address of the hotel where the occupancy took place if the room remarketer requests the hotel operator's certificate of authority number and is not provided that number.

(Sec. 11-2502, N.Y.C. Adm. Code) (Summary of Tax Provisions in SFY 2012-13 Budget, New York Department of Taxation and Finance, April 2012) (TSB-M-12(8)S)

[¶531-056] NYC Returns

Every hotel operator and room remarketer must file a return with the Commissioner of Finance showing occupancies, rents and taxes due for the quarterly periods ending on the last day of February, May, August and November of each year. (Sec. 11-2504, N.Y.C. Adm. Code) The returns must be filed within 20 days after the end of the period covered. The Commissioner may, however, permit or require returns to be made on other dates or for shorter periods. Electronic filing of the return may be permitted by the Commissioner. (Rule Sec. 12-07)

Room remarketers are required to collect the hotel tax on the full amount charged to the occupant and remit the tax collected directly to Finance. Remarketers will then be allowed a refund or credit for any tax paid to the hotel operator or another remarketer for that occupancy. (Finance Memorandum 10-3)

The specialized tax return for room remarketers, Form HTX-RR, will no longer be used after the period ending August 31, 2010. Room remarketers must begin filing Form HTX, the hotel tax returns currently used by hotel operators, beginning with the tax quarter that starts on September 1, 2010. (Finance Memorandum 10-3)

Room remarketers offering hotel rooms in New York City must complete and file a Certificate of Registration with Finance within three days of the date they begin offering hotel rooms in New York City. Finance will then send remarketers a Certificate of Authority to collect tax on Finance's behalf. The certificate must be prominently displayed where occupants will see it. In the case of a room remarketer that offers New York City hotel rooms on the Internet, the Certificate of Authority should be scanned and displayed on the room remarketer's web site. (Finance Memorandum 10-3)

Effective September 1, 2012, the 2012 budget legislation (Ch. 59 (A.B. 9059), Laws 2012) facilitates the compliance of hotel room remarketers with the state and local sales tax collection obligations adopted in 2010 (Ch. 57, Laws 2010). The provisions enacted in the 2012 budget bill do the following:

— provide a method to compute the portion of the bill taxable as rent when an occupancy is sold together with other items for a single price. Specifically, when occupancy is provided for a single consideration with property, services, amusement charges, or any other items, whether or not such other items are taxable, the rent portion of the consideration for such transaction must be computed as follows: either the total consideration received by the room remarketer multiplied by a fraction, the numerator of which is the consideration payable for the occupancy by the room remarketer and the denominator of which is such consideration payable for the occupancy plus the consideration payable by the remarketer for the other items being sold, or by any other method as may be authorized by the Commissioner of Taxation and Finance. If the room remarketer fails to separately state the tax on the rent so computed on a sales slip, invoice, receipt, or other statement given to the occupant or fails to maintain records of the prices of all components of a transaction, the entire consideration shall be treated as rent subject to tax;

— permit room remarketers to provide the information about the amount of the sales tax due on any invoice given to the customer prior to the completion of the occupancy;

— allow room remarketers to report sales of occupancies in the sales tax filing period in which the occupancy ended, rather than in the sales tax period during which they collected the consideration for the occupancy; and

— simply the process by which a room remarketer claims credit for sales tax paid on its acquisition of a hotel room. For instance, in order to qualify for a refund or credit against the amount of tax collected and required to be remitted, a room remarketer can provide the name, business address, telephone number, and the address of the hotel where the occupancy took place if the room remarketer requests the hotel operator's certificate of authority number and is not provided that number.

(Sec. 11-2502, N.Y.C. Adm. Code) (Summary of Tax Provisions in SFY 2012-13 Budget, New York Department of Taxation and Finance, April 2012) (TSB-M-12(8)S)

For detailed guidance for businesses subject to the New York City hotel occupancy tax, see Finance Memorandum 10-3; Finance Memorandum 08-1REV and Finance Memorandum 09-3. For audit issues and procedures for audits of hotel tax returns prepared by room remarketers, see Statement of Audit Procedure HTX-2009-01.

[¶531-060]

NYC HOTEL OCCUPANCY TAX COLLECTION

[¶531-063] Payment of NYC Tax

The hotel occupancy tax must be paid at the time of filing the quarterly returns required by the Commissioner of Finance. (Sec. 11-2505, N.Y.C. Adm. Code) Payment of tax is due, however, regardless of whether the return correctly shows the amount of rents collected and taxes owed. Electronic payment of the tax may be permitted by the Commissioner. (Rule Sec. 12-07)

For detailed guidance for businesses subject to the New York City hotel occupancy tax, see Finance Memorandum 08-1REV.

• *Bulk sales*

A purchaser or transferee of the bulk of any part or the whole of an operator's hotel or of the operator's lease, license or other agreement to possess or operate such hotel, or of the equipment, furnishings, fixtures, supplies or stock of merchandise pertaining to the conduct or operation of the hotel may become liable for payment of any taxes due by the seller if the transferee fails to notify the Commissioner of Finance within ten days of the transfer. (Sec. 11-2510(c), N.Y.C. Adm. Code)

Upon failure of a purchaser, transferee or assignee of a bulk sale to give proper notice, or whenever the Commissioner of Finance notifies the purchaser, transferee or assignee that a possible claim for taxes exists, anything transferred becomes liable to a first priority lien for taxes. (Sec. 11-2510(c), N.Y.C. Adm. Code) Failure of the purchaser or transferee to give proper notice renders him liable for tax.

• *Extension of time*

There is no provision for extension of time for payment of tax. (Rule Sec. 12-07) If an extension of time for filing a return is granted, a tentative tax is computed and paid.

• *Jeopardy assessments*

If the Commissioner of Finance, in his discretion, believes that a taxpayer subject to the commercial rent or occupancy tax is about to cease business, leave the state, or remove or dissipate the assets out of which tax or penalties might be satisfied, and that any such tax or penalty will not be paid when due, he or she may declare the tax or penalty to be immediately due and payable. (Sec. 11-2510(a), N.Y.C. Adm. Code)

• *Settlement of liability for small facility operators*

The Department of Finance has offered to settle outstanding hotel occupancy tax liabilities of certain bed and breakfast operators and transient apartment lessors for periods prior to March 1, 2005. The settlement procedures are available to an "eligible operator," which is defined as (1) an operator of a bed and breakfast in which fewer than 10 rooms are offered for occupancy by guests; (2) an operator of any other hotel having fewer than 10 rooms; or (3) an owner or lessee of any number of furnished living units or apartments intended for single-family occupancy that the owner or lessee regularly uses and keeps open for lodging of guests on a transient basis for consideration. (Finance Memorandum 04-1)

[¶531-076] NYC Penalties

If any amount of tax is not paid on or before the last date prescribed for payment, interest on the amount at the rate set by the Commissioner of Finance, or, if no rate is set, at the rate of 6% per year, must be paid for the period from the last date prescribed for payment to the date of payment. (Sec. 11-2515(a), N.Y.C. Adm. Code)

For current interest rates, and rates in effect for prior periods, see ¶589-204.

In the case of a failure to file a return on or before the prescribed date, unless it is shown that the failure is due to reasonable cause and is not due to willful neglect, there will be added to the amount required to be shown as tax on the return 5% of the amount of the tax if the failure is for not more than one month, with an additional 5% for each additional month or fraction thereof during which the failure continues, not exceeding 25% in the aggregate. (Sec. 11-2515(b), N.Y.C. Adm. Code) In the case of a failure to file a return of tax within 60 days of the date prescribed for filing the return, unless it is shown that the failure is due to reasonable cause and not due to willful neglect, the addition to tax will not be less than the lesser of $100 or 100% of the amount required to be shown as tax on the return.

In the case of failure to pay the amount shown as tax on a return on or before the prescribed date, unless it is shown that the failure is due to reasonable cause and not due to willful neglect, there will be added to the amount shown as tax on the return $1/2$ of 1% of the amount of the tax if the failure is not for more than one month, with an additional $1/2$ of 1% for each additional month or fraction thereof during which the failure continues, not exceeding 25% in the aggregate. (Sec. 11-2515(b), N.Y.C. Adm. Code)

If any part of an underpayment of tax is due to negligence or intentional disregard of the tax laws or regulations, a penalty of 5% of the underpayment will be added to the tax. An amount equal to 50% of the interest payable with respect to the portion of the underpayment which is attributable to the negligence or intentional disregard will be added for the period beginning on the last date prescribed by law for payment of the underpayment and ending on the date of the assessment of the tax. (Sec. 11-2515(c), N.Y.C. Adm. Code)

If any part of an underpayment is due to fraud, a penalty equal to 50% of the underpayment will be added to the tax, as well as an amount equal to 50% of the interest payable with respect to the portion of the underpayment which is attributable to the fraud. (Sec. 11-2515(d), N.Y.C. Adm. Code)

• *Additional penalty*

Any person who, with fraudulent intent, fails to pay any tax or to make, render, sign, or certify any return, or to supply any information within the time required, will be liable for an additional penalty of not more than $1,000. (Sec. 11-2515(e), N.Y.C. Adm. Code)

[¶531-080]

NYC HOTEL OCCUPANCY TAXPAYER REMEDIES

[¶531-081] NYC Refunds

The Commissioner of Finance will refund or credit, without interest, any tax, penalty or interest erroneously, illegally, or unconstitutionally collected or paid if application to the Commissioner of Finance for the refund is made within one year from the date of the payment. (Sec. 11-2507, N.Y.C. Adm. Code)

For detailed guidance for businesses subject to the New York City hotel occupancy tax, see Finance Memorandum 08-1REV.

NEW YORK CITY COMMERCIAL RENT OR OCCUPANCY TAX

[¶532-100]
NYC COMMERCIAL RENT OR OCCUPANCY TAX

[¶532-110] NYC Commercial Rent or Occupancy Tax--In General

The commercial rent or occupancy tax is an annual tax imposed on every tenant of taxable premises within New York City whose base rent exceeds certain statutory minimums. (Sec. 11-702(a)(1), N.Y.C. Adm. Code) For exemptions, see ¶532-210.

Geographical boundaries of tax.—As originally enacted, the commercial rent or occupancy tax was imposed on all qualified taxable premises within New York City. Over the course of several years, however, the geographical boundaries of the tax have been increasingly narrowed. The tax is limited to qualified premises located in the Borough of Manhattan south of center line of 96th Street (see ¶532-210).

• *Tenant*

A "tenant" is any person paying or required to pay rent for premises as a lessee, sublessee, licensee or concessionaire. (Sec. 11-701(3), N.Y.C. Adm. Code) Included within the definition of "person" are individuals, partnerships, societies, associations, joint stock companies, corporations, estates, receivers, assignees, trustees or any other persons acting in a fiduciary capacity, whether appointed by a court or otherwise. (Sec. 11-701(1), N.Y.C. Adm. Code)

Owner.—The owner of record of a building, who occupies space therein, is not considered to be a tenant for commercial rent or occupancy tax purposes. (Rule Sec. 7-01)

• *Taxable premises*

The term "taxable premises" means any premises in New York City occupied, used or intended to be occupied or used for the purpose of carrying on or exercising any trade, business, profession, vocation or commercial activity, including any premises so used even though it is used solely for the purpose of renting, or granting the right to occupy or use, the same premises in whole or in part to tenants. (Sec. 11-701(4), N.Y.C. Adm. Code)

Examples of premises occupied or used by a tenant as taxable premises include:

(1) premises occupied or used as leased departments in department stores, as florists, beauty parlors, barber shops, lunchrooms, shoe repairing shops, optometrists, or any other commercial activity;

(2) premises occupied or used in City parks, as restaurants, golf courses, archery ranges, boating concessions, or any other commercial activity;

(3) advertising signs on the tops of buildings or outside of buildings or structures, or located on otherwise unoccupied land;

(4) automobile parking lots and garages, tennis courts, skating rinks, baseball fields and other enterprises;

(5) business of any kind conducted by a tenant in premises used for both residential and business purposes to the extent that such premises is used for business purposes;

(6) safe deposit vaults rented as an incident to a business, such as the leasing of a safe deposit vault by a stockbroker for the safekeeping of securities;

(7) office space and desk space; and

(8) premises occupied or used in ball parks, theatres, race tracks, etc. for the sale of refreshments, programs, or the checking of clothing.

(Sec. 11-703(a), N.Y.C. Adm. Code)

Physical occupancy not necessary.—A tenant is subject to commercial rent or occupancy tax if it has a possessory right to business premises and is required to pay rent, even where physical occupancy of the premises has been terminated (*Letter of Deputy Commissioner of Legal Affairs*). To this effect, the Department of Finance has stated that a tenant whose liability to pay rent continued after the taxable premises were destroyed by fire remained subject to tax. (*New York City Finance Administration Bulletin*) Similarly, the Department has held that rent payments made during a period that taxable premises were being renovated, prior to the tenant's physical occupancy, were subject to tax. (*Department of Finance Bulletin*)

• *Presumption of taxability*

There is a statutory presumption that all premises are taxable premises until the contrary is established. (Rule Sec. 7-06) However, premises not devoted to or intended for use in the conduct of a trade or business are not taxable premises. (Rule Sec. 7-01)

In *Peat Marwick Main & Co. v. New York City Department of Finance*, the New York Supreme Court, Appellate Division, held that an accounting firm's payments for use of a luxury skybox at a sports arena were not subject to tax. While acknowledging that the firm's use of the skybox to entertain guests served a business purpose, the Court noted:

While it is true that entertaining business associates, clients or employees would fall within a broad definition of "commercial activity," that approach would extend the tax to unreasonable lengths; it would, for example, reach the residential apartment where business associates are occasionally entertained. There is no indication in the statute's language or history that the tax was intended to have such a broad reach.

The distinction between taxable commercial activity and nontaxable social activity with business benefits is not easily drawn and we make no attempt here to establish a comprehensive standard to govern future cases. [* * *] At the very least, however, the ordinary meaning of the words used in the statute—"premises * * * occupied or use for the purpose of carrying on or exercising any trade, business, profession, vocation or commercial activity" (Administrative Code Sec. 11-701(5))—suggest that the tax was intended to apply to premises where an integral part of a commercial enterprise is carried out.

Federal tax-exempt organizations.—Organizations that are exempt from federal taxation pursuant to IRC Sec. 501(a) (other than organizations described in IRC Sec. 501(c)(2) or (25)) will be deemed to have rebutted the presumption that the premises occupied or used by them are taxable premises, provided the premises are not used substantially in connection with an unrelated trade or business. (Rule Sec. 7-01) Accordingly, the burden of proving that the premises are taxable premises is on the Commissioner of Finance. However, if such premises are used substantially in connection with an unrelated trade or business, the presumption of taxability remains in effect and the burden of proving the premises are not taxable remains on the organization.

The above listed federal tax-exempt organizations will also be deemed to have rebutted the presumption of taxability of the premises used or occupied by them if the premises are subleased in whole or in part by the organization, provided that the rent received by the organization from the sublease qualifies for exclusion from unrelated business taxable income under IRC Sec. 512(b)(3) (determined without regard to IRC Sec. 512(b)(4) or (13)). In determining whether premises occupied, used or intended to be occupied or used by a nonprofit organization will be considered to be used substantially in connection with an unrelated trade or business, consideration will be given to all of the facts and circumstances of each case, including the following:

(1) the portion of the square footage used in connection with the unrelated trade or business;

(2) the portion of gross receipts derived from unrelated business activities at the premises; and

(3) the number of personnel at the premises engaged in unrelated business activities.

EXAMPLE: X Corp. is a nonprofit organization exempt from federal income tax under Internal Revenue Code section 501(c)(4). As part of its nonprofit activities, X Corp. publishes a magazine on topics related to its exempt purpose that carries advertisements of a general nature. The income from selling advertising space in the magazine is subject to tax as income from an unrelated business. Fifty percent (50%) of the staff located at premises rented by X Corp. in New York City are exclusively engaged in selling advertising space in the magazine. On the basis of the facts of this case, the premises will be considered to be used substantially in connection with an unrelated business and X Corp. will not be deemed to have rebutted the presumption that those premises are taxable premises.

EXAMPLE: Y Corp. is a nonprofit organization exempt from federal income tax under Internal Revenue Code section 501(c)(4). Y Corp. enters into a lease of office space in New York City. Before the commencement of the lease term, Y Corp. determines that it does not require all of the space it leased and, therefore, Y Corp. immediately subleases 60% of the space to another organization exempt from federal income tax under Internal Revenue Code section 501(c)(4). The rent received from the sublease is not subject to federal income tax as income from an unrelated trade or business. Of the remaining 40% of the space, Y Corp. uses one half in connection with an unrelated trade or business and one half in connection with its nonprofit activities. Because 80% (60% plus $1/2$ of 40%) of the total space leased by Y Corp. is not used in connection with an unrelated trade business, Y Corp. will be deemed to have rebutted the presumption that the premises are taxable premises.

• *Base rent*

For a discussion of base rent, see ¶532-320.

[¶532-200]

NYC COMMERCIAL RENT OR OCCUPANCY TAX-- EXEMPTIONS

[¶532-210] NYC Commercial Rent or Occupancy Tax-- Exemptions

Exemptions from the imposition of commercial rent or occupancy taxes may be available based on ownership, use, or location of the property, in addition to other circumstances.

• *Governmental organizations*

The following governmental organizations are exempt from the payment of commercial rent or occupancy tax:

(1) The State of New York, or any public corporation (including a public corporation created pursuant to agreement or compact with another state or the Dominion of Canada), improvement district or other political subdivision of the state;

(2) The United States of America (to the extent that it is immune from taxation); and

(3) The United Nations or other world-wide international organizations of which the United States of America is a member.

(Sec. 11-704(a)(1), (2), (3), N.Y.C. Adm. Code)

• *Religious, charitable, and educational organizations*

Nonprofit corporations, associations, trusts, community chests, funds or foundations that are organized and operated exclusively for religious, charitable, or educational purposes, or for the prevention of cruelty to children or animals, are exempt from payment of commercial rent or occupancy tax, provided: (1) no part of their net earnings inure to the benefit of any private shareholder or individual; and (2) no substantial part of their activities involve the carrying on propaganda or otherwise attempting to influence legislation. (Sec. 11-704(a)(4), N.Y.C. Adm. Code)

An organization operated for the primary purpose of carrying on a trade or business for profit, regardless of whether all of its profits are payable to one or more nonprofit religious, charitable or educational organization, is subject to tax.

• *Tenants with tax aggregating $1 or less*

An exemption from commercial rent and occupancy tax is provided for any tenant who would otherwise be subject to commercial rent or occupancy tax aggregating not more than $1 for a tax year with respect to all taxable premises used by the tenant. (Sec. 11-704(a)(5), N.Y.C. Adm. Code)

> **EXAMPLE:** A tenant has desk space in an office which he is entitled to use for one day each week during the tax year for which he pays $3.25 per month, or $39.00 a year. Since the tax on $39.00 is 98¢ ($2^1/2\%$ × $39.00), which is less than $1.00 for the tax year, the tenant is exempt from the payment of such tax with respect to taxable premises used by him.

• *Tenants located in the World Trade Center area*

An exemption from the commercial rent and occupancy tax is provided for any tenant located in the World Trade Center Area. (Sec. 11-704(a)(6), N.Y.C. Adm. Code)

• *Tenants using premises for less than 14 days per year*

Tenants using premises for no more than 14 days in a tax year (whether or not consecutive) where their agreement with their landlord does not require them to pay rent for a longer period are exempt from the payment of commercial rent or occupancy tax. (Sec. 11-704(b)(1), N.Y.C. Adm. Code)

> **EXAMPLE:** Under an agreement entered into by a tenant with his landlord, the tenant has the right to use office space on the landlord's premises for one day a week for a period of one year, for which he is required to pay rent of $20.00 for each such day. Under the agreement, the tenant has the right to terminate his occupancy at any time before the end of the year without the payment of any additional rent. After the tenth day of occupancy, the tenant terminates his occupancy. Since the total occupancy of the tenant is not more than 14 days, viz., 10 days, and the tenant is not required to pay additional rent for a longer period, he is exempt from paying the tax with respect to the rent paid by him for such premises.

● *Base rent below statutory minimums*

Tenants whose base rents are below the statutory minimums for the periods specified in the following chart are exempt from the payment of commercial rent or occupancy tax: (Sec. 11-704(b)(2), N.Y.C. Adm. Code)

Tax years beginning on or after:	and ending on or before:	Base rent does not exceed:
June 1, 2001		$249,999
December 1, 2000	May 31, 2001	$149,999
June 1, 1997	November 30, 2000	$99,999
June 1, 1996	May 31, 1997	$39,999
June 1, 1995	May 31, 1996	$30,999
June 1, 1994	May 31, 1995	$20,999
June 1, 1985	May 31, 1994	$10,999
June 1, 1984	May 31, 1985	$7,999
June 1, 1981	May 31, 1984	$4,999

Notwithstanding the above chart, a tenant whose annualized base rent, for the tax year beginning June 1, 1995, and ending May 31, 1996, was at least $31,000 per year but did not exceed $39,999, was exempt from tax for the period beginning September 1, 1995, and ending May 31, 1996.

The base rent of a lease for a period of less than one year will be determined as if it had been on an equivalent basis for the entire year.

● *Sublease for residential purposes*

A tenant who uses taxable premises for renting to others for residential purposes to the extent at least 75% of the rentable floor space is exempt from commercial rent or occupancy tax with respect to rent paid for the premises from the time that construction commences. This exemption does not apply to hotels, apartment hotels or lodging houses. (Sec. 11-704(d), N.Y.C. Adm. Code)

EXAMPLE: On June 1, 1963, a builder leases a plot of land for 99 years. Under the terms of the lease, the builder has the right to, and does, construct an apartment house for residential purposes. The builder pays the landlord an annual rent of $100,000. On December 1, the builder commences the construction of the apartment house. When the building is completed, it will contain apartments available for residential purposes to the extent of 80% of the rentable floor space in the building. The builder is required to pay the tax on the rent due the landlord for the period from June 1 to December 1. The builder is exempt from paying the tax with respect to the rent paid for the premises from the time that construction of the building commenced, viz., December 1.

The exemption applies to a tenant of a building erected prior to the time he or she became a tenant, which building is rented to others for residential purposes to the extent of 75% or more of the floor space thereof. (Rule Sec. 7-04)

EXAMPLE: A real estate concern becomes the lessee of an apartment house erected in 1950. The apartment house contains 100,000 square feet of rentable floor space, of which 80,000 square feet are for residential purposes. The real estate concern is exempt from the payment of the tax on the rents paid by it, but, nevertheless, is required to file an information return.

● *Premises used for dramatic, musical arts, or theatrical performances*

A tenant who uses taxable premises for a dramatic or musical arts performance for less than four weeks is exempt from the payment of commercial rent or occupancy tax if, prior to or at the time of commencement of the performance, there was no indication that the performance was intended to continue for less than four weeks. (Sec. 11-704(e), N.Y.C. Adm. Code)

For purposes of the commercial rent or occupancy tax, the term "dramatic or musical arts performance" involves a performance or repetition of a performance in a theatre, opera house or concert hall or a live dramatic performance, whether or not musical in part. The term does not include circuses, ice skating shows or aquashows, performances of any kind in a roof garden, cabaret or other similar place, or radio or television performances, whether or not such performances are prerecorded for later broadcast. (Sec. 11-701(17), N.Y.C. Adm. Code)

> *EXAMPLE:* A producer of a play rents a theatre for the production of the play for a period of twelve weeks. The play is not a success, and the producer closes down the show at the end of three weeks. The producer is exempt from the payment of the tax with respect to the rent paid by it for the use of the theatre.

A tenant who uses taxable premises for the production and performance of a theatrical work is exempt from the payment of commercial rent or occupancy tax with respect to rent paid for the premises for a period not exceeding 52 weeks. The exemption begins on the date that the production of the theatrical work commences, but does not apply where production commenced prior to June 1, 1995. (Sec. 11-704(e), N.Y.C. Adm. Code)

The term "theatrical work" means a performance (or repetition thereof) in a theater of a live dramatic performance (whether or not musical in part) that contains sustained plots or recognizable thematic material, including so-called legitimate theater plays or musicals, dramas, melodramas, comedies, compilations, farces or reviews, provided that the performance is intended to be open to the public for at least two weeks. The term does not include performances of any kind in a roof garden, cabaret or similar place, circuses, ice skating shows, aqua shows, variety shows, magic shows, animal acts, concerts, industrial shows or similar performances, or radio or television performances, whether or not such performances are prerecorded for later broadcast. (Sec. 11-704(e), N.Y.C. Adm. Code)

• *Settlement funds or grantor trusts dealing with claims arising from the Holocaust*

Qualified settlement funds or grantor trusts set up to deal with claims arising from the Holocaust, World War II, and Nazi persecution are exempt from commercial rent tax. (Sec. 13, Tax Law)

• *Taxable premises located in Manhattan north of 96th Street or in the Bronx, Brooklyn, Queens and Staten Island*

An exemption from commercial rent or occupancy tax is allowed with respect to rent from otherwise taxable premises located in the Borough of Manhattan north of the center line of 96th Street or in the Boroughs of the Bronx, Brooklyn, Queens or Staten Island. (Sec. 11-704(h), N.Y.C. Adm. Code)

• *Application for exemption*

There is a statutory presumption that all premises are taxable premises and that all rent paid or required to be paid by a tenant is taxable base rent until the contrary is established. The burden of proving that the presumptive base rent or any portion thereof is not included in the measure of the commercial rent or occupancy tax imposed is on the tenant. (Sec. 11-703(a), N.Y.C. Adm. Code)

Religious charitable and educational organizations claiming exemptions from commercial rent or occupancy tax under Sec. 11-704(a)(4), N.Y.C. Adm. Code, and persons claiming that premises used by nonprofit organizations are not taxable premises may apply to the Commissioner of Finance for a determination of whether such premises are taxable. The Commissioner, if satisfied that the applicant is entitled to the exemption or that the premises in question are not taxable, will issue a letter to that effect to the applicant. (Rule Sec. 7-05)

Affidavit in support of application.—A nonprofit organization claiming an exemption under Sec. 11-704(a)(4), N.Y.C. Adm. Code, or claiming that premises are not taxable premises, must submit an affidavit containing the following information:

(1) the type of organization using the premises;

(2) the purposes for which the organization is organized;

(3) the organization's actual activities;

(4) the source and disposition of the organization's income;

(5) whether any of the organization's income is credited to surplus or may inure to any private stockholder or individual; and

(6) other facts that may affect the organization's right to exemption including, in the case of a claim that certain premises are not taxable premises, a description of the activities carried on at the premises by the organization and a description of any sublease or other arrangement whereby any other person or entity occupies or uses the premises.

The affidavit must be supplemented by:

(1) a copy of the articles and certificate of incorporation (or articles of association), and by-laws;

(2) a financial statement showing the organization's assets and liabilities for the most recent year;

(3) a statement of the organization's receipts and disbursements for the most recent year;

(4) a copy of the organization's federal, state and city income tax returns for the most recent three years; and

(5) a photostatic copy of the letter, if any, from the United States Treasury Department granting the organization exemption from federal income taxation.

[¶532-300]
NYC COMMERCIAL RENT OR OCCUPANCY TAX COMPUTATION

[¶532-310] NYC Commercial Rent or Occupancy Tax Computation--In General

Commercial rent or occupancy tax is computed by applying the tax rate (see ¶532-380) to base rent (see ¶532-320), after applying applicable exclusions and apportionments or allocation. (Sec. 11-702, N.Y.C. Adm. Code)

[¶532-320] NYC Base Rent

Subject to the deductions and reductions listed in the following paragraphs, base rent is the rent paid for taxable premises by a tenant to his or her landlord. (Sec. 11-701(7), N.Y.C. Adm. Code)

"Rent" is the consideration paid or required to be paid by a tenant for the use or occupancy of premises, valued in money, whether received in money or otherwise, including all credits and property or services of any kind and including any payment required to be made by a tenant on behalf of his or her landlord for real estate taxes, water rents or charges, sewer rents or any other expenses (including insurance) normally payable by a landlord who owns the realty other than expenses for the improvement, repair or maintenance to the tenant's premises. (Sec. 11-701(6), N.Y.C. Adm. Code)

In *SIN, Inc. v. Department of Finance of the City of New York*, the New York Court of Appeals rejected the Department's contention that payments for improvements for leased commercial office space were rent for purposes of the commercial rent or occupancy tax. Although the lease specifically incorporated the tenant's obligation to spend approximately $1,000,000 to improve the premises, the Court noted:

Here, the statutory language is unambiguous. Whatever else "rent" may include as defined in the local law, it clearly excludes, without express or implied qualification, "expenses for the *improvement* repair or maintenance of the tenant's premises." Contrary to respondent's contention, this plain language admits no distinction between major and minor improvements, between those primarily made for the benefit of the landlord and those for the tenant, or between those bargained for as consideration under the lease and those initiated at will by the tenant. The term "improvement" commonly refers to a valuable addition or amelioration of real estate, "amounting to more than mere repairs or replacement * * * and intended to enhance its value, beauty or utility," including "any permanent structure or other development" or "expenditure to extend the useful life of an asset [, which is] capitalized as part of the asset's costs." This term, without condition or modification in the statute, should be given its ordinary meaning and significance [* * *].

Statutory presumption: Until the contrary is established, all rent paid or required to be paid by a tenant to a landlord is presumed to be base rent. (Rule Sec. 7-06) The burden of proving that presumptive base rent or any portion thereof is not included in the measure of commercial rent or occupancy tax is on the tenant.

• *Services*

The Department of Finance has issued a Tax Policy Bulletin providing general guidelines to be followed in determining whether a tenant's payment of charges for services provided by a landlord are made for the use or occupancy of the premises, in which case they are rent, or are made for other purposes, in which they are not rent. (*Commercial Rent or Occupancy Tax Policy Bulletin 1083*, February 4, 1983) Although the ultimate decision in each case is dependent upon the facts and circumstances present, the following guidelines apply:

Building services.—Building services are services that contribute to the proper functioning of the business premises as a usable business facility. They include, among others, the providing of heat, air conditioning, window washing, janitorial services, refuse removal, security guard service and like services furnished by a landlord.

Charges for building services that a tenant could not provide on his own, independent of the landlord, such as central heating, central air conditioning or elevator service, are always included in base rent. Charges for those building services which the tenant could provide on his own, but, instead, chooses to obtain from the landlord, such as janitorial services or security guard services, are to be included in base rent only if the charges for the services are paid pursuant to a lease as part of the rent obligation.

Business services.—Where the consideration paid or required to be paid by a tenant is for the use or occupancy of taxable premises and services (for example, stenographic services, answering services or mail services) are furnished by the landlord or lessor, the total consideration paid or required to be paid will be included in the computation of base rent. However, if the agreement between the landlord or sublessor with the tenant separately states the amount of the consideration applicable to the rent for the premises and the amount applicable to the services, only the amount applicable to the rent for the premises will be regarded as base rent.

Utility services.—Charges for separately metered utility services (e.g. electricity, steam, gas, etc.) are excluded from base rent. However, when the utility service is provided by the landlord through submetering, the exclusion from base rent is permitted only to the extent that the charge does not exceed what utilities serving the area charge for the same amount of utility service.

Water and sewer charges as well as non-metered utility charges, or utility charges based on estimates or engineering surveys, are included in base rent.

• *Shareholders of cooperative corporations*

Although shareholders of cooperative corporations are subject to tax if their premises are occupied, used or intended to be occupied or used for the purpose of carrying on or exercising any trade, business, profession, vocation or commercial activity, payments made as an owner are not includable in determining taxable rent. (Rule Sec. 7-01) "Payments made as an owner" include:

(1) the initial purchase price of the shares of stock or other evidence of the ownership of the tenant-owner;

(2) payments made by the tenant-owner as his share on account of the principal amount of any mortgage on the premises or on account of any interest on such mortgage;

(3) payments made by the tenant-owner as his or her share of the cost of capital improvements to the premises;

(4) payments made by the tenant-owner as his or her share of real estate taxes and assessments, and water or sewer rents;

(5) payments made by the tenant-owner as his or her share of the cost of insurance on the premises; and

(6) any other payments made by the tenant-owner that are in the nature of capital expenditures.

The following payments are not considered as "payments made as an owner" and, therefore, are includable as rent:

(1) Payments made by a tenant-owner that are applicable to the operation of the premises, and are necessary for the occupancy and use by the tenant-owner, such as payments made for fuel, gas and electricity;

(2) operating and maintenance expenditures other than those deemed to be in the nature of capital expenditures, such as expenditures for normal repairs, salaries and wages paid to elevator operators and doormen, superintendents and other personnel for the proper functioning and use of the premises by the tenant-owner.

• *Rent measured by gross receipts*

Whenever the rent paid by a tenant for his or her occupancy of taxable premises is measured in whole or in part by the gross receipts from the tenant's sales within the place, the tenant's rent, to the extent paid on the basis of such gross receipts, will be deemed not to exceed 15% of the gross receipts. (Sec. 11-704(g), N.Y.C. Adm. Code)

The 15% limitation applies where the rental agreement provides for a rent based wholly or partly on a percentage of sales receipts and the stated percentage exceeds 15%. (Rule Sec. 7-01) The maximum rent in such cases is the higher of 15% of gross receipts or the fixed rental plus 15% of sales subject to the percentage.

EXAMPLE: A tenant leases a store for an annual rental of 25% of his gross receipts from sales. The gross receipts for the year total $200,000 and the tenant pays his landlord $50,000. The rent subject to tax is $30,000 (15% of $200,000).

EXAMPLE: A tenant leases a store for an annual rental of $50,000 plus 25% of his gross receipts from sales in excess of $200,000. The gross receipts for the year total $300,000 and the tenant pays his landlord $75,000. The rent subject to tax is $65,000 ($50,000 fixed rental plus 15% of sales over $200,000).

• *Theatre rentals*

Where a theatre owner and theatrical producer enter into a "four wall contract" for the rental of a theatre, the amount of rent paid by the producer to the theatre owner constitutes base rent and is subject to the tax. (Rule Sec. 7-01) Under a "four wall contract," a theatre owner, as landlord, merely leases the theatre building to the producer for a fixed rental.

Booking contract.—Where a theatre owner and a theatrical producer enter into an booking contract for the use of a certain theatre, whereby the theatre owner agrees to furnish to the producer a lighted, heated and cleaned theatre, with the scenery and equipment contained therein, the necessary stage hands, carpenters, electricians, property men, janitors, ushers, ticket sellers, doorkeepers, house orchestra, etc. for a percentage of the box office receipts, the portion of the receipts paid by the producer to the theatre owner that is applicable to the use or occupancy of the theatre will be deemed to be base rent subject to commercial rent or occupancy tax. (Rule Sec. 7-01) The burden of establishing the amount of the receipts not applicable to the use or occupancy of the theatre is on the producer.

• *Premises used both for residential purposes and as taxable premises*

If a tenant pays an undivided rent for premises used both for residential purposes and as taxable premises, the tax is applied to the portion of rent that is ascribable to the taxable premises. (Sec. 11-702(c), N.Y.C. Adm. Code) If the rent ascribable to the taxable premises does not exceed $50 per month, the rental may be excluded from the tenant's base rent.

Statutory presumption—Rent ascribed to taxable premises.—There is a conclusive statutory presumption that the rent ascribable to taxable premises is the amount that the tenant deducts as rent for the premises in determining the tenant's federal income tax (as reduced by any disallowance of such deduction which is not being contested) that is fairly attributable to the tax period or tax year. (Sec. 11-703(b), N.Y.C. Adm. Code)

The Commissioner of Finance is specifically authorized to require any tenant who uses premises for both residential purposes and as taxable premises and who pays an undivided rent for the entire premises so used to provide the Commissioner with a signed and notarized request to the U.S. Director of Internal Revenue for photostatic copies of the tenant's income tax return for any year when the Commissioner deems the return necessary to determine rent ascribable to the taxable premises. (Sec. 11-713(6), N.Y.C. Adm. Code) The Commissioner may treat the rent for the entire premises as rent used as taxable premises if a tenant refuses to provide a signed written request.

• *Allocation of single rent for two or more taxable premises*

Where, under the terms of a lease, a tenant pays a single rent to a landlord for two or more taxable premises, at least one of which is taxable premises, the rent applicable to each premises is ascertained by adding together the percentages of the property, wages and salary, and receipts factors and dividing the total by three. (Rule Sec. 7-01) If the numerator and denominator of any factor are both zero, the factor is deemed to be non-existent and is omitted in calculating the average of the percentages. In such event, the total of the remaining percentages is divided by the existing factors. If the numerator alone is zero and the denominator is represented by an amount, the resultant factor (that is, zero) must be included in the calculation of the average of the percentages. The average percentage thus obtained for each taxable premises is then applied to the total single rent paid for all taxable premises to obtain the amount of the rent applicable to each taxable premises.

Property factor.—The property factor is determined by dividing the average value of tangible and personal property employed or used by the tenant in each taxable premises occupied or used during the tax period by the average value of all tangible personal property employed or used by the tenant in all taxable premises occupied or used during the tax period. The term "tangible personal property" means and includes all corporeal personal property, such as furniture, furnishings, machinery, tools, implements, goods, wares and merchandise, and do not mean or include money, deposits in banks, shares of stocks, bonds, notes, credits, or evidences of an interest in property and evidences of debt. The values as at the beginning and the end of each tax period may be averaged to obtain the value of the tangible personal property employed or used in the taxable premises.

Wages and salaries factor.—The wages and salaries factor is determined by dividing the total compensation paid during the tax period to officers and employees who work in, from, or are attached to each taxable premises by the total compensation paid during the tax period to all officers and employees engaged or employed in all of the taxable premises. The wages and salaries factor must include all forms of compensation paid to officers and regular employees. Amounts paid to independent contractor are excluded.

Receipts factor.—The receipts factor is determined by dividing receipts from sales and services during each taxable period applicable to each taxable premises by receipts from sales and services during each taxable period applicable to all taxable premises.

Discretion of Commissioner to use alternate allocation formula.—Upon a determination that the three-factor allocation formula noted above works unfairly or inequitably to a particular taxpayer or class of taxpayers, the Commissioner of Finance may require a different or other method of allocation that is calculated to effect a fair and proper apportionment of rent applicable to each taxable premises.

• *Persons using or occupying two or more locations in the same premises*

Where a tenant occupies or uses two or more locations in the same premises that constitute taxable premises, the aggregate of the rentals paid for all such locations in the same premises are deemed to be rent paid for one taxable premises. (Rule Sec. 7-01)

• *Assignment of parking space*

A tenant operating a garage or parking lot who assigns a specific space to another person for the parking of a motor vehicle used by the assignee in the conduct of a trade, business, profession, vocation or commercial activity, may deduct the amounts received by or due to the operator for the parking space. (Rule Sec. 7-06) The parking lot operator must, at the time that the space is assigned, obtain a Certificate of Assigned Space Use from the assignee.

A deduction will not be allowed where the tenant of the parking space is exempt from tax under Rule Sec. 7-04(f).

[¶532-325] NYC Base Rent Reductions--Subleases

In computing base rent, a tenant may deduct rent received by or due to the tenant from a subtenant of any part of the premises. (Sec. 11-701(7), N.Y.C. Adm. Code; Rule Sec. 7-01)

> *EXAMPLE:* A tenant rents a store for business purposes for a rent of $34,000 per year. He sublets part of the store to a concessionaire for business purposes for a rent of $18,000 per year. The tenant's base rent is $16,000.

No deduction will be permitted if the subtenant is exempt from tax because it uses the premises for no more than 14 days in a tax year, whether or not consecutive, and the subtenant's agreement with the tenant does not require the subtenant to pay rent for a longer period.

EXAMPLE: A tenant rents a store for business purposes for an annual rent of $12,000. During the year he permits the use of a portion of the store for a period of one day each month by a concessionaire who pays rent of $500 for each day's occupancy. The tenant's base rent is $12,000. Since the concessionaire is exempt from tax because he uses the premises for less than 14 days in a tax year, rent paid by the concessionaire is not deductible from the rent paid by the tenant.

A tenant may subtract the amount of rent received for premises that do not constitute taxable premises and that are used by the subtenant as lodging or residential premises (including residential premises in hotels, apartment hotels or lodging houses).

EXAMPLE: The owner of a hotel leases the hotel to an operating company, which pays the owner an agreed rent. The operating company rents rooms in the hotel to residential guests. The operating company's base rent consists of the rent paid by it to the owner, less the amounts received or due to it from the guests.

A tenant may deduct rent received or due from a subtenant who is exempt from tax pursuant to Sec. 11-704(a), N.Y.C. Adm. Code.

EXAMPLE: A lessee of an office building rents office space in the building to commercial tenants and to a charitable organization which uses the office for nonprofit purposes. The lessee, in order to arrive at the amount of his base rent, may deduct from the rent paid by him the rent received by him from the charitable organization, as well as the rent received by him from the commercial tenants.

A tenant may deduct rent received or due from a subtenant for premises that do not constitute taxable premises to the extent that the rent is deductible from the base rent of such tenant by reason of Sec. 11-704(c)(5), N.Y.C. Adm. Code.

A tenant may deduct rent received or due from a subtenant for premises that do not constitute taxable premises, pursuant to a common law relationship of landlord and tenant, except where it is received as rent, whether or not such landlord-tenant relationship exists, for premises which are occupied as or constitute:

(a) a locker, safe deposit box, or beach cabana;

(b) storage space in part of a warehouse or in part of any other structure or area in which goods are stored;

(c) garage space or parking space in any part of a garage, of a parking lot or of a parking area where the entire garage, entire parking lot or entire parking area accommodates more than two motor vehicles;

(d) an occupancy of a type which customarily has not been the subject of such a common law relationship of landlord and tenant.

EXAMPLE: A civic organization enters into a lease with a sublessor of a building for a period of two years. Under the lease, the civic organization agrees to pay the lessor an annual rental of $3,000.

The premises occupied by the civic organization does not constitute taxable premises. Accordingly, the rental paid by the civic organization to the sublessor may be taken as a deduction from the rent paid by the sublessor in determining the sublessor's base rent.

EXAMPLE: The lessee of a public garage rents space in the garage to a private individual for the storage of the latter's automobile which is devoted solely to personal use. The lessee, for the purpose of determining the amount of his base rent, may not deduct from the rent paid by him to his landlord the amounts received by him from the owner of the automobile for storage of the car. If the space were rented for the storage of motor vehicles used in business, such as trucks, the lessee would be permitted to deduct the amounts received by him for the storage of such trucks in arriving at the amount of his base rent unless the subtenant is exempt from tax thereon.

EXAMPLE: A broker holding securities for the account of its customers places such securities in a safe deposit box rented from a bank, for which the broker pays a fixed rental charge. The bank is a tenant of the premises. No common-law relationship exists between the bank and the broker. The rent received by the bank from the broker may be deducted from its rent for the purpose of computing its base rent subject to tax. The broker must report the rent paid by him to the bank as his base rent for the occupancy of the safe deposit box.

[¶532-330] NYC Base Rent Reductions--Reductions Attributable to Taxpayer's Own Use of Property

A taxpayer's base rent may be reduced by the amount of the taxpayer's rent for, or reasonably ascribable to, the taxpayer's own use of the premises (Sec. 11-704(c), N.Y.C. Adm. Code):

(1) as premises used for railroad transportation purposes. The term "premises used for railroad transportation purposes" means the portion of the premises of any person, actually operating a railroad, that are used by such person for normal or necessary railroad transportation purposes. (Sec. 11-701(8), N.Y.C. Adm. Code) "Normal or necessary railroad transportation purposes" does not include any activities that are normally carried on by persons not engaged in furnishing railroad transportation service (such as the operation of retail stores, barber shops, restaurants, theatres, hotels, and newsstands), nor activities that are not deemed transportation purposes under Secs. 489-b and 489-m, Real Property Tax Law;

(2) as premises used for air transportation purposes. The term "premises used for air transportation purposes" means the portion of any premises, located within an airport or within an air transportation terminal shared by more than one air line, of any person actually operating an air line as a common carrier, used by such person for normal or necessary air transportation purposes. (Sec. 11-701(9), N.Y.C. Adm. Code) The words "normal or necessary air transportation purposes" does not include any activities that are normally carried on by persons not engaged in furnishing air transportation services (such as the operation of retail stores, barber shops, restaurants, theatres, hotels and newsstands);

(3) as piers insofar as the premises are used in interstate or foreign commerce;

(4) that are located in, upon, above or under any public street, highway or other public place, and that are defined as "special franchise property" in the Real Property Tax Law;

(5) that are taxed pursuant to Sub. 1, Ch. 22-A, N.Y.C. Admn. Code, or Ch. 20, N.Y.C. Adm. Code, to the extent that the premises are subject to, and during the period that they are subject to, such tax.

(6) that are taxed pursuant to Sec. 11-1005(b) or (c), N.Y.C. Adm. Code;

(7) that are advertising signs, advertising space, vending machines or newsstands within or attached to stations, platforms, stairways, entranceways, passageways, mezzanines or tracks of a rapid transit subway or elevated railroad operated by the New York city transit authority when the rent of the tenant or of the tenant's landlord is payable to such authority; or

(8) as premises used for omnibus transportation purposes. The term "premises used for omnibus transportation purposes" means the portion of any premises located within a passenger terminal of any person actually operating an omnibus line or route as a common carrier, used by such person for normal or necessary omnibus line or route transportation purposes. (Sec. 11-701(18), N.Y.C. Adm. Code) The words "normal or necessary omnibus line or route transportation purposes" does not include any activities, which are normally carried on by persons not engaged in furnishing omnibus line or route transportation services such as the operation of retail stores, barber shops, restaurants, theatres, hotels and newsstands.

[¶532-340] NYC Base Rent Reductions--Property in Manhattan North of 96th Street, or in the Boroughs of the Bronx, Brooklyn, Queens, or Staten Island (Pre-September 1, 1995)

For periods beginning September 1, 1995, and thereafter, tenants of taxable premises located in the Borough of Manhattan north of the center line of 96th Street, or in the Boroughs of the Bronx, Brooklyn, Queens or Staten Island, are exempt from commercial rent or occupancy tax (see ¶532-210).

Base rent reductions for periods between June 1, 1989, through August 31, 1995.— A 30% reduction in base rent was allowed for periods between June 1, 1989, through August 31, 1995, for taxable premises located in the Borough of Manhattan north of the center line of 96th Street, or in the Boroughs of the Bronx, Brooklyn, Queens or Staten Island. (Sec. 11-704(h), N.Y.C. Adm. Code) The reduction was made after all other commercial rent or occupancy tax exemptions and deductions were taken.

[¶532-345] NYC Base Rent Reductions--Property in Manhattan South of 96th Street

The base rent of taxable premises located in the Borough of Manhattan south of the center line of 96th Street may be reduced by 35% for periods beginning September 1, 1998 and thereafter. The reduction must be made after all other commercial rent or occupancy tax exemptions and deductions have been taken. (Sec. 11-704(h), N.Y.C. Adm. Code)

• *Commercial Revitalization Program (CRP)*

The purpose of the Commercial Revitalization Program (CRP) is to increase tenant occupancy in office and retail space in lower Manhattan and in certain other areas of the City, and to reduce building obsolescence by encouraging investment in older commercial space or conversion to residential use. The CRP provides a commercial rent tax special reduction for nonresidential or mixed-use premises built before 1975 and located in designated abatement zones. Applicants are also required to make certain minimum expenditures to improve the eligible premises.

• *Special reduction in base rent*

Tenants of certain commercial premises located in lower Manhattan are allowed a special reduction in determining taxable base rent. (Sec. 11-704(i), N.Y.C. Adm. Code)

[¶532-350] NYC Base Rent Reductions--Relocation and Employment Assistance Program

The law provides for a reduction in base rent with respect to certain eligible businesses that relocate to the "eligible area". (i.e., all areas of New York City excluding the part lying south of the center line of 96th Street in Manhattan) (Sec. 11-704(f), N.Y.C. Adm. Code; Sec. 22-621(f); Sec. 22-622, N.Y.C. Adm. Code)

However, the tax no longer applies to premises in the eligible area (see ¶532-210).

[¶532-380] NYC Rate of Tax

Commercial rent or occupancy tax is imposed at the rate of 6% on base rents exceeding the statutory minimum of $249,999. (Sec. 11-702(a), N.Y.C. Adm. Code)

A credit allowed to tenants having a base rent of at least $250,000 but not more than $300,000 is discussed at ¶532-420. See also ¶532-345 for a discussion of the 35% base rent reduction.

• *Prior periods*

Statutory minimums applicable in prior periods are listed at ¶532-210.

• *Annualized rent*

Rent for a period of less than one year is determined on an annualized basis.

[¶532-400]

NYC COMMERCIAL RENT OR OCCUPANCY TAX CREDITS

[¶532-420] NYC Additional Credits

A credit is allowed to a tenant whose base rent is at least $250,000 but not more than $300,000. The credit is determined by multiplying 3.9% of the base rent by a fraction, the numerator of which is $300,000 minus the amount of base rent, and the denominator of which is $50,000. (Sec. 11-704.3, N.Y.C. Adm. Code)

Small business tax credit. A small business tax credit against the commercial rent and occupancy tax is available for tax years beginning on and after June 1, 2018. (Sec. 11-704.4, N.Y.C. Adm. Code) The credit amount is 100% for taxpayers with incomes of $5 million or less and who pay less than $500,000 per year in rent. A partial sliding scale credit, calculated based on income and rent factors, is available for:

— taxpayers with incomes of $5 million or less who pay between $500,000 and $550,000 per year in rent; and

— taxpayers with incomes between $5 million and $10 million who pay less than $550,000 per year in rent.

[¶532-500]

NYC COMMERCIAL RENT OR OCCUPANCY TAX RETURNS, RECORDS AND PAYMENTS

[¶532-510] NYC Returns

Tenants subject to commercial rent or occupancy tax must file quarterly returns with the Commissioner of Finance for three-month periods ending on the last days of August, November and February of each year. Returns are due within twenty days from the expiration of the period covered thereby. A final return covering the taxes payable for the entire tax year must be filed on or before June 20. (Sec. 11-705(a), N.Y.C. Adm. Code)

A tenant who claims an energy cost savings credit must attach a schedule in support of the credit to the return in which the credit is claimed. The credit will not be allowed until the complete schedule is received by the Commissioner of Finance. (Sec. 11-704.1(5), N.Y.C. Adm. Code)

For tax years beginning on or after September 1, 1995, no return is required with respect to taxable premises located in the Borough of Manhattan north of the center line of 96th Street or in the Boroughs of the Bronx, Brooklyn, Queens or Staten Island.

For tax years beginning on or after June 1, 2001, no final return is due if (1) the tenant's rent, determined without regard to any reduction in rent or base rent otherwise allowed, does not exceed $200,000 for the tax year and (2) the amount of rent received or due from any subtenant of the exempt tenant does not exceed $200,000 for the tax year. For tax years beginning on or after June 1, 1997, and ending before June 1, 2001, no such final return was due if (1) the tenant's rent, determined without regard to any reduction in rent or base rent otherwise allowed, did not exceed $75,000 for the tax year and (2) the amount of rent received or due from any subtenant of the exempt tenant did not exceed $75,000 for the tax year. No final return was required for tax years beginning on or after June 1, 1995, and ending on or before May 31, 1997, if: (1) such tenant's rent, determined without regard to any reduction in rent or base rent otherwise allowed, did not exceed $15,000 for the tax year, and (2) in the case of a tenant who had more than one taxable premises, the aggregate rents for all such premises, determined without regard to any deduction from or reduction in rent or base rent, did not exceed $15,000 for the tax year. (Sec. 11-705(a), N.Y.C. Adm. Code)

• *Information returns*

The Commissioner of Finance may require the filing of information returns and supplemental information returns by landlords and by tenants of taxable premises, whether or not they are required to pay commercial rent or occupancy tax. (Sec. 11-705(b), N.Y.C. Adm. Code)

• *Amended returns*

The Commissioner of Finance may require amended returns or amended information returns to be filed within 20 days after notice. (Sec. 11-705(a), N.Y.C. Adm. Code)

• *Discretion of Commissioner to require returns for other periods*

The Commissioner of Finance may permit or require returns (including final returns) to be made for other periods and upon such dates as the Commissioner may specify to insure the payment of tax. In addition the Commissioner may grant an extension of time not exceeding 90 days within which to file any commercial rent or occupancy tax return. An application for an extension must be made in writing prior to the due date of a return.

Where an extension of time is granted, the taxpayer must file a tentative return on or before the due date of the return. The tentative return must show the estimated tax due that must be paid at the time of filing of the tentative return. A final return must be filed on or before the date of expiration of the period of time granted. (Sec. 11-705(a), N.Y.C. Adm. Code; Sec. 11-713(2), N.Y.C. Adm. Code; Rule Sec. 7-09)

[¶532-530] Payment of NYC Tax

Payment of tax accompanies the filing of the returns (see ¶532-510), which are due on March 20, June 20, September 20 and December 20. (Sec. 11-706, N.Y.C. Adm. Code) The tax paid with the final return (due June 20) must equal the amount by which the actual tax for the tax year exceeds the amounts previously paid.

• *Cessation of business*

If a tenant ceases to do business, commercial rent or occupancy tax, as measured by the tenant's base rent for the prior part of the tax year, becomes due immediately, and the tenant must file a final return within 20 days from the cessation of business.

Normal returns will be required, however, if, notwithstanding the cessation of business, the tenant continues to pay rent for the taxable premises.

•*Discretion of Commissioner to declare tax due immediately*

The Commissioner of Finance may declare tax or penalties to be due and payable immediately if the Commissioner believes that a taxpayer is about to cease business, leave the state or remove or dissipate assets out of which tax or penalties might be satisfied and that such tax or penalties will not be paid when due. (Sec. 11-712(a), N.Y.C. Adm. Code) To enforce the collection of such tax or penalties, the Commissioner may issue a warrant for collection.

•*Refund of overpayment*

If a final return shows that the amount of tax paid for the tax year exceeds the actual tax owed for the year, the Commissioner must refund the excess payment, unless the Commissioner has reason to believe that the final return is inaccurate. (Sec. 11-706, N.Y.C. Adm. Code) The making of a refund does not preclude the Commissioner from making a determination that additional tax is due or from pursuing any other method to recover the full amount of the actual tax due for the tax year.

[¶532-540] NYC Records

Landlords and tenants of taxable premises must keep records of all rents paid and/or received. (Sec. 11-707, N.Y.C. Adm. Code) The records must identify each tenant, the rent required to be paid, the rent paid and received, the location of each premises and the periods of commencement and termination of every occupancy. (Rule Sec. 7-11) Landlords and tenants must also keep copies of all leases or agreements that fix the rents or rights of tenants of taxable premises, plus any other records, receipts and other papers that are relevant to the ascertainment of tax.

Records must be offered for inspection and examination at any time upon demand by the Commissioner of Finance, or the Commissioner's duly authorized agent or employee.

Records must be maintained for a three year period, unless the Commissioner of Finance consents to their destruction within the three-year period or requires that they be kept for a longer time. Leases or agreements that fix the rents or rights of a tenant must be kept for a period of three years after the expiration of the tenancy.

•*Failure to keep records*

Any person who willfully fails to keep or retain any records required to be kept or retained is guilty of a misdemeanor. (Rule Sec. 7-17)

[¶535-100]

NYC ALCOHOLIC BEVERAGE TAX

[¶535-105] Alcoholic Beverages

New York City's Alcoholic Beverage Tax is covered in the New York City Administrative Code, Title 11, Chapter 20, Subchapter 5 (Tax on Beer and Liquor) and Title 11, Chapter 24 (Tax on Retail Licensees of the State Liquor Authority).

The excise tax on distributors and noncommercial importers is imposed at the rates of 12¢ per gallon on beer and 26 4/10¢ per liter on liquor. (Sec. 11-2056(a), N.Y.C. Adm. Code)

The tax on retail licensees is imposed at a rate equal to 25% of the license fees imposed on retailers under the state alcohol beverage control laws. (Sec. 11-2402, N.Y.C. Adm. Code)

Comprehensive coverage of taxation of alcohol, as well as licensing and distribution information is provided in Wolters Kluwer, CCH Liquor Control Law Reporter. For more information go to CCHGroup.com or contact an account representative at 888-CCH-REPS (888-224-7377).

NEW YORK CITY TAXICAB LICENSE TRANSFER TAX

[¶536-001]

NYC TAXICAB LICENSE TRANSFER TAX

[¶536-005] Imposition of NYC Tax

The tax is imposed on the transfer of an interest in or the transfer of an actual taxicab license at a percentage of the consideration given for the license. (Sec. 11-1402(a), N.Y.C. Adm. Code) The transfer of an economic interest in a taxicab license resulting from the transfer of shares of stock in a corporation or the transfer of an interest or interests in a partnership or association which holds the license is treated as a transfer of a license and is subject to tax. (Sec. 11-1402(b), N.Y.C. Adm. Code) When the taxicab and other property are transferred along with the license, the tax is computed on the total consideration paid for both the license and the property, minus the fair market value of the property. (Sec. 11-1402(d), N.Y.C. Adm. Code)

[¶536-100]

NYC TAXICAB LICENSE TRANSFER TAX EXEMPTION

[¶536-105] NYC Taxicab License Transfer Tax Exemption--In General

Transactions by or with the following are exempt from the transfer tax (Sec. 11-1405(a), N.Y.C. Adm. Code):

(1) the state, its agencies, instrumentalities, public corporations or political subdivisions as purchaser, user or consumer;

(2) the United States and any of its agencies and instrumentalities as purchaser or consumer to the extent they are immune from taxation;

(3) the United Nations or any other international organization to which the United States is a member; and

(4) any nonprofit corporation, association, trust, community chest, fund or foundation organized and operated exclusively for religious, charitable, or educational purposes, or for the prevention of cruelty to animals, and not substantially engaged in carrying on propaganda or otherwise attempting to influence legislation. The exemption does not extend to an organization primarily operated for profit, even though the profits go to an exempt organization.

The tax does not apply to the transfer of a license or the interest in the license by a lease, license or other rental arrangement which does not exceed six months. (Sec. 11-1405(b), N.Y.C. Adm. Code)

[¶536-200]

NYC TAXICAB LICENSE TRANSFER TAX RATE AND BASIS

[¶536-205] In General

The tax is imposed at the rate of 5% of the consideration paid for the transfer, through March 20, 2017. Effective March 21, 2017, the rate is reduced to 0.5% of the consideration paid for the transfer. (Sec. 11-1402(a), N.Y.C. Adm. Code) If the taxicab or any other property is included in the transfer, the tax is based on the percentage of the total consideration given for all of the property transferred. (Sec. 11-1402(b), N.Y.C. Adm. Code)

[¶536-300]

NYC TAXICAB LICENSE TRANSFER TAX RETURNS

[¶536-305] Joint Returns

The transferee and the transferor must file a joint return with the Taxi and Limousine Commission containing whatever information the Commissioner of Finance may require. (Sec. 11-1404(a), N.Y.C. Adm. Code) The returns must be filed when the tax is paid, within 30 days of the approval of the transfer. (Sec. 11-1403, N.Y.C. Adm. Code) If the information contained in the returns is not sufficient, the Commissioner of Finance may use other available information to determine the tax due. (Sec. 11-1406, N.Y.C. Adm. Code) The taxpayer may appeal within 90 days after receiving notice of the Commissioner's decision.

[¶536-400]

NYC TAXICAB LICENSE TRANSFER TAX COLLECTION

[¶536-405] Payment of NYC Tax

The tax must be paid by the transferee to the Taxi and Limousine Commission within 30 days of the license transfer. (Sec. 11-1403, N.Y.C. Adm. Code) No transfer of a license or the interest in a license becomes effective until the transfer tax is paid. The person transferring the license may be held liable for the tax if the transferee fails to pay.

[¶550-001]

NYC MOTOR VEHICLES

[¶550-002] NYC Tax on Commercial Motor Vehicles and Motor Vehicles for Transportation of Passengers

The New York City Tax on Commercial Motor Vehicles and Motor Vehicles for the Transportation of Passengers, imposed under Chapter 8 of Title 11 of the New York City Administrative Code, is an annual tax on the use of commercial vehicles and motor vehicles which transport passengers in the City of New York. (Sec. 11-802(a), N.Y.C. Adm. Code) Should this tax be considered invalid solely because it is based on motor vehicle usage in the city, it may also be deemed to be based on the privilege of using the public highways or streets of New York City by such vehicles. (Sec. 11-802(b), N.Y.C. Adm. Code)

The following topics are discussed below:

— motor vehicles and persons subject to tax;

— exemptions;

— basis and rate;

— returns and reports;

— assessment, revision, and appeal;

— payment, collection of tax;

— penalties; and

— refunds and remedies.

• *Motor vehicles and persons subject to tax*

New York City imposes a tax on the use in the city of commercial motor vehicles and on the use in the city of motor vehicles for the transportation of passengers. (Sec. 11-802(a), N.Y.C. Adm. Code) The tax is to be paid by the owners of the vehicles, and is imposed in addition to all other use taxes, including the compensating use tax.

For purposes of the tax, an "owner" is any person owning a commercial motor vehicle or vehicle used for passenger transportation, including a purchaser under a reserve title contract, conditional sales agreement or vendor's lien agreement. (Sec. 11-801(5), N.Y.C. Adm. Code) Also included are licensees, lessees and bailees with exclusive use of such a taxable vehicle for 30 days or more. The term "motor vehicle" refers to a vehicle powered by power other than muscular power that is operated on a public highway or public street.

CCH CAUTION: In the case of a commercial motor vehicle or vehicle for the transportation of passengers under the exclusive use of a lessee, licensee or bailee for a period of less than 30 days, the tax is payable by the owner of the vehicle and not the lessee, licensee or bailee. (Rule Sec. 6-01)

Commercial motor vehicles.—A tax is imposed on the use, in the city, of commercial motor vehicles. (Sec. 11-802(a), N.Y.C. Adm. Code) The tax is imposed on commercial motor vehicles used principally within the city, that is, if most of their mileage during the year is within the city, regardless of whether the business of their owners or operators is principally within the city. The tax is also imposed on commercial motor vehicles used principally in connection with business carried on within the city, regardless of the mileage within or without the city. (Rule Sec. 6-02)

The term "commercial motor vehicle" includes a truck, trailer, semi-trailer or other motor vehicle constructed or specially equipped for the transportation of goods, wares and merchandise (also known as an auto truck and light delivery car), as well as any traction engine, road roller, tractor crane, truck crane, power shovel, road building machine, snow plow, road sweeper, sand spreader, well driller, well servicing equipment or earth-moving equipment. (Sec. 11-801(3), N.Y.C. Adm. Code)

Motor vehicles for the transportation of passengers.—A tax is imposed on the use in the city of vehicles for the transportation of passengers. (Sec. 11-802(a), N.Y.C. Adm. Code) The tax is imposed on motor vehicles for the transportation of passengers which are used regularly even though not principally in the city. (Rule Sec. 6-02) A motor vehicle is deemed to be used regularly if it is used in the city 30 or more days during a tax year.

"Motor vehicles for the transportation of passengers" include:

— motor vehicles licensed as taxicabs or coaches, or motor vehicles not so licensed which carry passengers for compensation, whether the compensation paid is based on mileage, trip, time consumed or any other basis, and

— omnibuses. However, omnibuses that are used regularly in the city and are operated pursuant to certain franchises are not included in this definition.

(Sec. 11-801(4), N.Y.C. Adm. Code)

"Motor vehicles for the transportation of passengers" do *not* include the following:

— motor vehicles used principally for the transportation of children to and from schools and certain day camps;

— motor vehicles used exclusively for the transportation of passengers in connection with funerals;

— motor vehicles for the transportation of passengers where neither the owner of the motor vehicle, nor any of the owner's affiliates are engaged in transporting passengers by motor vehicle for hire, has a place of business and a telephone number, or solicits business or specifically advertises in New York City.

(Sec. 11-801.4.(b), N.Y.C. Adm. Code)

• *Exemptions*

The following entities and organizations are exempt from tax for vehicles which they own, operate or lease for their exclusive use:

— New York State, any public corporation (including a corporation created pursuant to an agreement or compact with another state or Canada), improvement district or political subdivision;

— the United States;

— the United Nations or other world-wide international organization of which the U.S. is a member;

— any corporation, association, trust, community chest, fund or foundation organized and operated exclusively for religious, charitable or educational purposes, or for the prevention of cruelty to children or animals. No part of the net earnings of such organization may inure to the benefit of any private individual or shareholder and no substantial part of the activities of the organization may be the carrying on of propaganda or otherwise attempting to influence legislation;

— any foreign nation or representative thereof is exempt from tax for motor vehicles for which it need not pay a registration fee under the Vehicle and Traffic Law; and

— dealers in new and used motor vehicles are exempt where the use of the vehicle is confined to demonstrations to prospective customers or to delivery by or to the dealer where the vehicle bears the dealer's license plates.

(Sec. 11-803, N.Y.C. Adm. Code)

• *Basis and rate*

The tax is imposed on the use of commercial motor vehicles and motor vehicles for the transportation of passengers for hire upon the public highways of New York City during the tax year. (Sec. 11-802(a), N.Y.C. Adm. Code)

If the first use of a motor vehicle subject to tax occurs on or after December 1 and before March 1, the tax imposed is one-half of the annual rate. If the first use is on or after March 1 in any taxable year, the tax is one-fourth of the annual rate. (Sec. 11-802(c), N.Y.C. Adm. Code) The payment of the tax covers the year from June 1 through May 31. (Sec. 11-801(14), N.Y.C. Adm. Code)

Commercial motor vehicles.—For commercial motor vehicles the tax rate is determined by the maximum gross weight. (Sec. 11-802(a), N.Y.C. Adm. Code) The maximum gross weight is the vehicle's gross weight plus the weight of the load to be carried by the vehicle. (Sec. 11-801(8), N.Y.C. Adm. Code)

For tax years beginning on or after June 1, 1990:

10,000 lbs or less	$40
over 10,000 lbs to 12,500	$200
over 12,500 lbs to 15,000	$275
over 15,000 lbs	$300

Motor vehicles for transportation of passengers.—For tax years beginning on and after June 1, 2019, all motor vehicles for transportation of passengers, including medallion taxicabs, are taxed at a flat rate of $400. Previously, medallion taxicabs were taxed at a rate of $1,000. (Sec. 11-802(a), N.Y.C. Adm. Code)

• *Returns and reports*

Every owner of a motor vehicle subject to tax must file an annual return with the Commissioner of Finance on or before June 20 of the tax year. (Sec. 11-807(a), N.Y.C. Adm Code) The Commissioner may grant an extension of time for the filing of returns, not exceeding 60 days, if good cause exists. (Sec. 11-815, N.Y.C. Adm. Code) The Commissioner may permit or require the filing of returns, supplemental returns or information returns other than those specified in the regulations. (Sec. 11-807(c), N.Y.C. Adm. Code)

A taxpayer who acquires a motor vehicle subject to tax after the commencement of a tax year and who has not filed a return or supplemental return with respect to the motor vehicle, must file a return for the vehicle within two days after its acquisition by the owner. (Sec. 11-807(a), N.Y.C. Adm Code)

• *Assessment, revision, and appeal*

If a return is not filed or, if filed, is incorrect or insufficient, the Commissioner of Finance may determine the amount of tax on the basis of available information, including external indices. (Sec. 11-810, N.Y.C. Adm. Code) Notice of the determination must be given to the person against whom the tax is assessed.

The Commissioner's determination will finally and irrevocably fix the amount of the tax due unless the person against whom it is assessed, within 90 days from the date that the notice is given, serves a petition upon the Commissioner and files a petition with the New York City Tax Appeals Tribunal. If the person has requested a conciliation conference, the petitions must be filed within 90 days from the mailing of the conciliation decision or the date of the Commissioner's discontinuance of the conciliation proceedings.

Decisions of the New York City Tax Appeals Tribunal sitting *en banc* are reviewable under Article 78, Civil Practice Law and Rules, provided an application is made to the Supreme Court within four months from the date of the Tribunal's decision. (Sec. 11-810, N.Y.C. Adm. Code)

Such an appeal cannot be instituted until the amount of the tax in question plus applicable penalties is deposited with the Commissioner of Finance and an undertaking, issued by an approved surety company, is filed for all costs and charges which may accrue in the proceeding, payable if the determination is confirmed or the proceeding dismissed. At the taxpayers option, the undertaking may be an amount sufficient to include the tax, penalties, costs and charges, and, if this option is exercised, the deposit of the tax and penalties will not be required as a condition precedent for the appeal.

• *Payment, collection of tax*

The tax must be paid at the time of the filing of the annual or supplemental return. The tax is due and payable on the last day the return was required to be filed, regardless of whether the return was actually filed. Payment is made to the Commissioner of Finance. (Sec. 11-808(a), N.Y.C. Adm. Code)

Generally, tax is paid by the owner of the vehicle. In the case of a commercial motor vehicle or vehicle for the transportation of passengers under the exclusive use of a lessee, licensee or bailee for a period of less than thirty days, the tax is payable by the owner of the vehicle and not the lessee, licensee or bailee. (Rule Sec. 6-01)

The Commissioner may extend the time for filing returns when good cause exists. (Sec. 11-815, N.Y.C. Adm. Code)

Payment of the tax is indicated by a tax stamp affixed to the motor vehicle. (Rule Sec. 6-09) Such stamps are nontransferable except when a certificate has been obtained.

Replaced or transferred vehicles.—When a vehicle subject to tax is replaced during the tax year, the owner is entitled to have the amount of tax already paid credited toward the tax payable with respect to the replacement vehicle, subject to the approval of the Commissioner. (Sec. 11-808(b), N.Y.C. Adm. Code) No additional tax is payable unless, because of the nature or the maximum gross weight of the vehicle, a higher tax is required.

If a vehicle subject to tax is transferred during the tax year, the new owner is not required to pay tax with respect to the transferred vehicle for the balance of the year if, when the return is submitted, it is accompanied by a certificate signed by the prior owner indicating that the prior owner has not had the tax paid credited toward any replacement vehicle and will not seek such credit in the future.

Medallion taxicabs.—The tax imposed on medallion taxicabs is due and payable in two equal installments. The first installment is due and payable on or before the last day on which the return or supplemental return for the tax year is required to be filed, and the second installment is due on or before the first day of December of the tax year. If, however, a medallion taxicab is acquired after the first day of November in a given tax year, the full amount of the tax imposed for the tax year shall be due and payable on or before the last day on which the supplemental return is required to be filed. (Sec. 11-808(c), N.Y.C. Adm. Code)

• *Penalties*

If any amount of tax is not paid on or before the last date prescribed for payment, interest on the amount due must be paid for the period from the last date prescribed for payment to the actual date of payment. (Sec. 11-817(a), N.Y.C. Adm. Code) The rate of such interest is set by the Commissioner, or, if no rate is set, the rate is to be 7.5% per year.

For current interest rates, and rates in effect for prior periods.

Failure to file return.—In the case of a failure to file a return on or before the prescribed date (including any extension of time to file), unless it is shown that the failure is due to reasonable cause and not willful neglect, there will be added to the amount required to be shown as tax on the return 5% of the amount of the tax if the failure to file is not for more than one month. (Sec. 11-817(b), N.Y.C. Adm. Code) An additional 5% will result for each additional month or fraction thereof for which the failure continues, not to exceed 25% in the aggregate.

In the case of a failure to file a return of tax within 60 days of the date prescribed for filing (including any extension of time to file), unless it is shown that the failure is due to reasonable cause and not willful neglect, the addition to tax will not be less than the lesser of $100 or 100% of the amount required to be shown as tax on such return.

Failure to make payment.—In the case of a failure to pay the amount shown as tax on a return on or before the prescribed date (including any extensions of time to file), unless it is shown that the failure is due to reasonable cause and not willful neglect, there will be added to the amount shown as tax on the return $1/2$ of 1% of the amount of the tax if the failure is not for more than one month, with an additional $1/2$ of 1% for each additional month or fraction thereof during which the failure continues, not to exceed 25% in the aggregate. (Sec. 11-817(b), N.Y.C. Adm. Code)

If any part of an underpayment of tax is due to negligence or intentional disregard of the tax laws or regulations (but without intent to defraud), a penalty of 5% of the underpayment of the underpayment will be added to the tax. (Sec. 11-817(c), N.Y.C. Adm. Code) In addition to this 5% penalty, there will also be added an amount equal to 50% of the interest payable with respect to the portion of the underpayment attributable to negligence or intentional disregard, for the period beginning on the last day prescribed by law for payment of such underpayment (determined without regard to any extension) and ending on the date of the assessment (or the date of the payment, if earlier).

If any part of the underpayment is due to fraud, a penalty equal to 50% of the underpayment will be added to the tax as well as an amount equal to 50% of the interest payable with respect to the portion of the underpayment attributable to fraud. (Sec. 11-817(d), N.Y.C. Adm. Code)

Additional penalty.—Any person who, with fraudulent intent, fails to pay any tax or to make, render, sign or certify any return or to supply any information within the time required, will be liable for an additional penalty of not more than $1,000. (Sec. 11-817(e), N.Y.C. Adm. Code)

• *Refunds and remedies*

A written application for the refund of any tax, penalty or interest erroneously, illegally, or unconstitutionally collected or paid must be filed within one year from the payment thereof. (Sec. 11-811(a), N.Y.C. Adm. Code) The Commissioner may, in lieu of a refund, grant the taxpayer a credit toward other payments of the tax.

A refund application must set forth the grounds upon which the claim is made and must indicate on its face that it has been filed within one year of the payment of the tax and must be accompanied by a canceled check or other evidence of tax payment. (Rule Sec. 6-12)

After receipt of the information and any corresponding evidence, the Commissioner will make a determination and give notice to the applicant. (Sec. 11-811(b), N.Y.C. Adm. Code) An appeal from the determination of the Commissioner of Finance must be instituted under Article 78 of the New York Civil Practice Law and Rules within 90 days of the giving of the notice of determination.

[¶550-005] NYC Tax on Resident Owners of Motor Vehicles

The New York City tax on owners of motor vehicles is imposed by Chapter 22 of Title 11 of the New York City Administrative Code. The tax is collected by the Department of Motor Vehicles at the time of registration. (Sec. 11-2204, N.Y.C. Adm. Code)

• *Persons and vehicles subject to tax*

The tax is imposed on the registration of passenger and suburban vehicles owned by the following:

(1) New York City residents (Sec. 11-2202, N.Y.C. Adm. Code), including both those persons who actually reside in the city and nonresidents who have lived in the city for at least 184 days in the year preceding the registration application (Sec. 11-2201(4), N.Y.C. Adm. Code);

(2) other residents who regularly keep, store, garage or maintain a motor vehicle in the city which is required to be registered (Sec. 11-2202, N.Y.C. Adm. Code) "Other resident" is defined to include persons, firms, copartnerships, trustees, associations and corporations (Sec. 11-2201(6), N.Y.C. Adm. Code); and

(3) owners of leased or rented passenger motor vehicles. (Sec. 11-2202, N.Y.C. Adm. Code)

• *Exemptions*

Owners exempt from the tax include the following:

— owners exempt from New York State registration fees, including municipalities, foreign consulates or diplomats, public authorities and disabled veterans;

— owners for whom the vehicle and traffic law registration requirements are inapplicable;

— the State of New York, its agencies and instrumentalities as well as the other states and their agencies and instrumentalities pursuant to an agreement or compact;

— the United States of America, its agencies and instrumentalities;

— the United Nations or other international organization of which the United States is a member; and

— any corporation or association, trust, community chest, fund or foundation organized and operated exclusively for religious, charitable or educational purposes or for the prevention of cruelty to children or animals. The earnings of such an organization cannot benefit a private individual or shareholder.

(Sec. 11-2203, N.Y.C. Adm. Code)

In addition, residents of New York City who have not lived in the city at least 30 days in the year preceding the application for registration and nonresidents who are members of the United States armed forces are not required to pay the tax since they are not within the definition of "resident". (Sec. 11-2201(4), N.Y.C. Adm. Code)

Any owner claiming an exemption must furnish a "City of New York Vehicle Use Exemption Certificate."

• *Rate*

A tax of $15 is imposed at the time of registration of each taxable passenger or suburban vehicle. (Sec. 11-2202, N.Y.C. Adm. Code)

• *Administration and collection*

The tax is administered by the Commissioner of Finance except that the tax is collected by the New York State Department of Motor Vehicles at the time of registration. (Sec. 11-2204, N.Y.C. Adm. Code)

NEW YORK CITY TOBACCO

[¶555-100]
NYC TOBACCO TAX RATES AND PRODUCTS SUBJECT TO TAX

[¶555-101] Imposition and Rate of NYC Tax

New York City imposes a tax on cigarettes and on other tobacco products.

• *Cigarette tax*

A New York City tax is imposed at the rate of 75¢ for each ten cigarettes or fraction thereof possessed for sale or used in the city, except as otherwise provided ($1.50 on a pack of 20 cigarettes). (Sec. 11-1302(a), N.Y.C. Adm. Code) (*Important Notice N-02-18*, New York Department of Taxation and Finance, June 28, 2002) The tax rate is scheduled to drop to 2¢ per 10 cigarettes after December 31, 2020. (Sec. 11-1302, N.Y.C. Adm. Code)

In addition, a state tax is imposed at the rate of $4.35 per pack. (*Important Notice N-10-4*, New York Department of Taxation and Finance, June 2010)

Although little cigars are taxed at the same rate as cigarettes in the state as of August 1, 2010, little cigars are still considered a "tobacco product" and a "cigar" as defined in Article 20 of the Tax Law. Packs of little cigars are not required to have tax stamps affixed to them. The New York City tax on cigarettes of $1.50 per pack does not apply to little cigars. (*TSB-M-10(4)M*, Office of Tax Policy Analysis, New York Department of Taxation and Finance, July 20, 2010). However, effective June 1, 2018, little cigars are subject to the New York City tax on other tobacco products (see below).

If a pack of cigarettes contains more than 20 cigarettes, the tax on the cigarettes in excess of 20 is imposed at the rate of 38¢ for each five cigarettes or fraction thereof.

To calculate the correct amount of sales tax due on the sale of cigarettes within New York City, the amount of the city excise tax ($15.00 per carton, $1.50 per pack) must be subtracted from the retail selling price of the cigarettes before the sales tax is computed on the resulting amount. (*Important Notice N-02-18*, New York Department of Taxation and Finance, June 28, 2002)

Every package of cigarettes must have stamps of the proper denomination affixed. (Rule Sec. 4-02)

The tax is imposed only once on each package of cigarettes and is in addition to all other taxes. (Sec. 11-1302(a), N.Y.C. Adm. Code) It is presumed that all sales or uses of cigarettes are subject to the tax until it is established otherwise, and the burden of proving that a sale or use is not taxable is on the vendor or purchaser. (Sec. 11-1302(d), N.Y.C. Adm. Code)

Out of city sales.—A tax is not imposed on cigarettes possessed in the city by any agent or wholesale dealer for sale to a dealer outside the city, or for sale and shipment to any person in another state for use in another state. (Rule Sec. 4-20)

The sale of cigarettes shipped to a person outside the city but within the state for use outside of the city is subject to tax. For example, a sale by a New York City agent or wholesale dealer to a dealer in Westchester County is not subject to the tax; however, the sale of cigarettes by a dealer who ships them to an ultimate consumer in Westchester County for use in Westchester is a taxable transaction. The sale of cigarettes from a dealer in the city to an ultimate consumer in New Jersey is not taxable.

• *Tobacco tax*

Effective June 1, 2018, a New York City Tax is imposed at the rate of 10% of the price floor for a package of the specified category of tobacco product, exclusive of sales tax. The rates are set forth below, which are to be consistent with the price floors described in Sec. 17-176.1(d), N.Y.C. Adm. Code:

— cigars, 80¢ per single cigar (cigar packages, 80¢ for first cigar, plus $0.175 for each additional cigar);

— little cigars, $1.09 per pack;

— smokeless tobacco, 80¢ per 1.2 oz. plus an additional 20¢ for each 0.3 oz. or any fraction thereof in excess of 1.2 oz.;

— snus, 80¢ per 0.32 oz. plus an additional 20¢ for each 0.08 oz. or any fraction thereof in excess of 0.32 oz.;

— shisha, $1.70 per 3.5 oz. plus an additional 34¢ for each 0.7 oz, or any fraction thereof in excess of 3.5 oz.; and

— loose tobacco, 25¢ per 1.5 oz. package plus an additional 5¢ for each 0.3 oz. or any fraction thereof in excess of 1.5 oz.

(Sec. 11-1302.1, N.Y.C. Adm. Code)

It is presumed that all sales of other tobacco products are subject to the tax until it is established otherwise, and the burden of proving that a sale or use is not taxable is on the dealer or purchaser. (Sec. 11-1302.1(e), N.Y.C. Adm. Code)

[¶555-102] Definitions (NYC)

Relevant definitions for purposes of the cigarette and/or tobacco tax are provided by statute.

Cigarette.—For purposes of the tax, a cigarette is defined as a roll for smoking made wholly or in part of tobacco or any other substance, irrespective of size or shape, whether or not the tobacco or substance is flavored, adulterated or mixed with any other ingredient, the wrapper or cover of which is made of paper or any other substance or material except tobacco. "Cigarette" does not include a research tobacco product. (Sec. 11-1301(1), N.Y.C. Adm. Code; Sec. 20-201, N.Y.C. Adm. Code)

Cigar.—"Cigar" is defined as any roll of tobacco for smoking that is wrapped in leaf tobacco or in any substance containing tobacco, with or without a tip or mouthpiece, but does not include a little cigar. (Sec. 11-1301(14), N.Y.C. Adm. Code)

Little cigar.—A "little cigar" is any roll of tobacco for smoking that is wrapped in leaf tobacco or in any substance containing tobacco and that weighs no more than four pounds per thousand or has a cellulose acetate or other integrated filter. (Sec. 11-1301(15), N.Y.C. Adm. Code)

Loose tobacco.—"Loose tobacco" includes any product that consists of loose leaves or pieces of tobacco that is intended for use by consumers in a pipe, roll-your-own cigarette, or similar product or device. (Sec. 11-1301(16), N.Y.C. Adm. Code)

Smokeless tobacco.—"Smokeless tobacco" is defined as any tobacco product that consists of cut, ground, powdered, or leaf tobacco and that is intended to be placed in the oral or nasal cavity. (Sec. 11-1301(17), N.Y.C. Adm. Code)

Snus.—"Snus" includes any smokeless tobacco product marketed and sold as snus, and sold in ready-to-use pouches or loose as a moist powder. (Sec. 11-1301(18), N.Y.C. Adm. Code)

Tobacco product.—A "a tobacco product" includes any product which contains tobacco that is intended for human consumption, including any component, part, or accessory of such product. Tobacco products include, but are not limited to, any cigar, little cigar, chewing tobacco, pipe tobacco, roll-your-own tobacco, snus, bidi, snuff, shisha, or dissolvable tobacco product. Tobacco product does not include cigarettes or any product that has been approved by the United States food and drug administration for sale as a tobacco use cessation product or for other medical purposes and that is being marketed and sold solely for such purposes. "Tobacco product" does not include research tobacco products. (Sec. 11-1301(19), N.Y.C. Adm. Code)

Research tobacco product.—A tobacco product or cigarette that is labeled as a research tobacco product, manufactured for use in research for health, scientific, or similar experimental purposes, is exclusively used for such purposes by an accredited college, university or hospital, or a researcher affiliated with an accredited college, university or hospital, and is not offered for sale or sold to consumers for any purpose. (Sec. 11-1301(21), N.Y.C. Adm. Code)

Shisa.—"Shisha" is defined as any product that contains tobacco and is smoked or intended to be smoked in a hookah or water pipe. (Sec. 11-1301(20), N.Y.C. Adm. Code)

Sale or purchase.—The term "sale" or "purchase" is defined as any transfer of title or possession or both, by any exchange or barter, conditional or otherwise, in any manner or by any means whatsoever or any agreement therefor. (Sec. 11-1301(3), N.Y.C. Adm. Code; Sec. 20-201, N.Y.C. Adm. Code)

Agent.—An agent is any person in or out of New York City, including wholesale dealers, authorized by the Commissioner of Finance to affix adhesive or meter stamps used in paying the cigarette tax to packages of cigarettes. (Sec. 11-1301(9), N.Y.C. Adm. Code; Sec. 11-1302(g), N.Y.C. Adm. Code; Sec. 20-201, N.Y.C. Adm. Code)

An agent has the right to appoint a person in his employ to affix the stamps to any cigarettes under the agents control. (Rule Sec. 4-15)

Dealer.—A "dealer" is defined as a wholesale or retail dealer. (Sec. 11-1301(5), N.Y.C. Adm. Code; Sec. 20-201, N.Y.C. Adm. Code)

Wholesale dealer.—A wholesale dealer is defined as any person who sells cigarettes or, effective June 1, 2018, tobacco products, to retail dealers or to other persons for purposes of resale only and as any person who owns, operates or maintains one or more vending machines on premises owned or occupied by another person. (Sec. 11-1301(6), N.Y.C. Adm. Code; Sec. 20-201, N.Y.C. Adm. Code)

Retail dealer.—A retail dealer is any person, other than a wholesale dealer, who is engaged in selling cigarettes or, effective June 1, 2018, tobacco products. (Sec. 11-1301(7), N.Y.C. Adm. Code; Sec. 20-201, N.Y.C. Adm. Code) For purposes of the law, the possession or transportation at any one time of more than 400 cigarettes by any person other than a manufacturer, an agent or a licensed wholesale or retail dealer is presumptive evidence that the person is a retail dealer. Effective June 1, 2018, the possession or transportation at any one time of more than 400 cigarettes or little cigars, or more than 50 cigars, or more than one pound of loose tobacco, smokeless tobacco, snus or shisha, or any combination thereof, by any person other than a manufacturer, an agent, a licensed wholesale dealer or a person delivering cigarettes or tobacco products in the regular course of business for a manufacturer, an agent or a licensed wholesale or retail dealer, is presumptive evidence that such person is a retail dealer. (Sec. 11-1301(7), N.Y.C. Adm. Code)

[¶555-104] Persons Liable for the NYC Tax

For cigarettes, agents or distributors appointed by the Commissioner of Finance pay the tax by purchasing from the Commissioner adhesive stamps which are then affixed to the individual packages of cigarettes. (Rule Sec. 4-15; Rule Sec. 4-04) It is intended, however, that the ultimate liability for the tax be on the consumer, and the agent paying the tax is required to collect it from the consumer by adding the amount of the tax to the purchase price of the cigarettes. (Sec. 11-1302(a), N.Y.C. Adm. Code)

The cigarette tax may also be paid through the use of metering machines (see ¶ 555-802).

In addition, a tax is imposed on tobacco products other than cigarettes (Other Tobacco Products or OTP).

• *Other tobacco products (OTP)*

Effective June 1, 2018, wholesale dealers are liable for the collection and payment of other tobacco products (OTP) taxes to the Commissioner of Finance. Generally, the OTP tax must be paid by wholesale dealers on OTP sold to retail dealers in New York City. Wholesale dealers must file tax returns and pay the tax on a monthly basis on or before the 20th day of the month following the month for which the tax return is required, unless the Commissioner of Finance has exempted the particular wholesale dealer from filing. Retail dealers are required to be able to prove that tax has been paid on tobacco products in their possession. They are also required to pass-on the tax to their customers. (Sec. 11-1302.1(f), N.Y.C. Adm. Code) (Finance Memorandum 18-5)

[¶555-107] NYC Tax on the Use of Cigarettes

The New York City cigarette tax, assessed at the rate discussed at ¶ 555-101, is imposed on the use of all cigarettes in the city, except as otherwise provided. (Sec. 11-1302(a), N.Y.C. Adm. Code)

See ¶ 555-202 for exemptions from the tax.

• *"Use" defined*

For purposes of the tax on the use of cigarettes, the term "use" means the exercise of a right or power, actual or constructive, and includes but is not limited to the receipt, storage, keeping or retention of cigarettes for any length of time. (Sec. 11-1301(4), N.Y.C. Adm. Code) It does not include the possession of cigarettes for sale by a dealer.

[¶555-108] "Drop Shipments" (NYC)

In the case of drop shipments, where an out-of-state manufacturer solicits an order directly from a retail dealer in the City and the billing and payment on account of such sale is made through a wholesale dealer, the sale to the retail dealer is deemed to have been made by the wholesale dealer, and proper stamps must be affixed to the packages of cigarettes prior to delivery to the retail dealer unless the retail dealer is an agent appointed by the Commissioner of Finance. (Rule Sec. 4-21)

[¶555-200]
NYC TOBACCO TAX EXEMPTIONS

[¶555-201] NYC Tobacco Tax Exemptions--In General

The tax on cigarettes possessed for sale is not imposed on the following:

— cigarettes sold to the United States;

— cigarettes sold to or by a voluntary unincorporated organization of the armed forces of the United States operating a place for the sale of goods pursuant to the regulations promulgated by the appropriate executive agency of the United States;

— cigarettes possessed in the city by any agent or wholesale dealer for sale to a dealer outside the city or for sale and shipment to any person in another state for use there, provided such agent or wholesale dealer complies with the applicable regulations;

— cigarettes sold to the State of New York, or any public corporation (including a public corporation created pursuant to an agreement or compact with another state or with Canada); or to an improvement district or other political subdivision of the state where it is the purchaser, user or consumer and does not purchase the cigarettes for resale.

(Sec. 11-1302(b), N.Y.C. Adm. Code; Rule Sec. 4-03)

Effective June 1, 2018, the tax imposed on other tobacco products does not apply to:

— the state of New York, or any public corporation (including a public corporation created pursuant to agreement or compact with another state or the Dominion of Canada), improvement district or other political subdivision of the state where it is the purchaser, user or consumer;

— the United States of America;

— the United Nations or other worldwide international organizations of which the United States of America is a member;

— any corporation, or association, or trust, or community chest, fund or foundation, organized and operated exclusively for religious, charitable, or educational purposes, or for the prevention of cruelty to children or animals, no part of the net earnings of which inures to the benefit of any private shareholder or individual, and no substantial part of the activities of which is carrying on propaganda, or otherwise attempting to influence legislation, excluding organizations operated for the primary purpose of carrying on a trade or business for profit, whether or not all of its profits are payable to one or more organizations described above; and

— tobacco products possessed in the city by any dealer for sale outside the city or for sale and shipment to any person in another state for use there, provided such dealer complies with the applicable regulations.

(Sec. 11-1302.1(b), N.Y.C. Adm. Code)

[¶555-202] NYC Use Tax Exemption

The tax on cigarettes used in New York City does not apply to the use, other than for sale, of 400 cigarettes or fewer brought into the city on or in the possession of any person. (Sec. 11-1302(b), N.Y.C. Adm. Code)

[¶555-500]

NYC TOBACCO TAX LICENSE

[¶555-501] NYC Wholesale and Retail Dealers

Wholesale and retail dealers must be licensed in order to engage in business in New York City. (Sec. 11-1303(a) and (b), N.Y.C. Adm. Code; Sec. 20-202, N.Y.C. Adm. Code) No one may permit any premises under his control to be used by any other person who is not licensed to conduct business. Licenses must be conspicuously displayed at the place for which they are issued. Pharmacies are prohibited from obtaining a license to engage in business as a retail dealer. (Sec. 20-202, N.Y.C. Adm. Code)

[¶555-502] NYC License Applications and Fees

A license application must be filed by every wholesale or retail dealer for each place of business at which cigarettes or tobacco products are to be sold. Retail dealers must obtain their licenses from the Commissioner of Consumer and Worker Protection. (Sec. 11-1303(b), (c) and (g), N.Y.C. Adm. Code; Sec. 20-202, N.Y.C. Adm. Code)

• *Duplicate licenses*

A duplicate license may be issued for a fee of $15 to the holder of a license which has been defaced, destroyed or lost (Sec. 11-1303(b), (c) and (g), N.Y.C. Adm. Code; Sec. 20-204, N.Y.C. Adm. Code)

• *License fees*

The annual fee for a wholesale cigarette or tobacco dealer's license is $600. (Sec. 11-1303(b), (c) and (g), N.Y.C. Adm. Code)

A biennial fee of $200 is imposed for a retail dealer's license. (Sec. 20-202, N.Y.C. Adm. Code)

• *Expiration date*

Wholesale licenses expire on January 31 succeeding the date of issuance, unless previously suspended or revoked. (Sec. 11-1303(b), (c) and (g), N.Y.C. Adm. Code)

For retail dealers, even-numbered licenses expire on December 31 of the even-numbered year, and odd-numbered licenses expire on December 31 of the odd-numbered year, next succeeding the year in which the license is issued. (Sec. 20-202, N.Y.C. Adm. Code)

[¶555-504] NYC Prohibited Sales and Purchases

No agent or dealer may sell cigarettes or tobacco products to an unlicensed wholesale or retail dealer or to a wholesale or retail dealer whose license has been suspended or revoked. (Sec. 11-1303(d), N.Y.C. Adm. Code; Sec. 20-205, N.Y.C. Adm. Code) No dealer may purchase cigarettes or tobacco products from anyone other than a manufacturer or a licensed wholesale dealer.

[¶555-600]

NYC TOBACCO TAX RETURNS

[¶555-601] NYC Tobacco Tax Returns--In General

The Commissioner of Finance is authorized to require the filing of monthly reports by agents or dealers. (Sec. 11-1308, N.Y.C. Adm. Code; Rule Sec. 4-18) Under this power, agents must file reports on or before the 15th day of each month covering the transactions for the preceding calendar month. Wholesale dealers who are not also agents may be required to file reports showing the receipt and disposition of all unstamped cigarettes and any other information that may be required by the Commissioner. (See ¶555-603 for specific reporting requirements)

Agents and wholesale dealers are also required to keep records and invoices of deliveries. (See ¶555-604)

Effective June 1, 2018, wholesale dealers of tobacco products are required to file returns on a monthly basis, due on the 20th day of each month following the end of the month or other interval covered by the return, unless the Commissioner otherwise prescribes a different interval. (Sec. 11-1302.1(g), N.Y.C. Adm. Code)

• *Jenkins Act*

The federal Jenkins Act requires any person selling or transferring cigarettes in interstate commerce to report such shipments to the tobacco tax administrator of the state into which the shipments are made. This requirement applies to cigarettes shipped into New York City.

[¶555-602] NYC Transporters

Whenever cigarettes or tobacco products are shipped into the city, the railroad company, trucking company, express company or carrier must file a copy of the freight bill with the Commissioner of Finance within 10 days after the delivery. (Sec. 11-1307(b), N.Y.C. Adm. Code)

[¶555-603] NYC Agents' and Dealers' Monthly Reports

Agents appointed by the Commissioner of Finance are required to file reports on the 15th day of each month with the Commissioner which show, among other things, the number of unstamped cigarettes (Rule Sec. 4-18):

(1) on hand at the beginning of the month;

(2) purchased or received during the month;

(3) on hand at the end of the month; and

(4) sold or disposed of during the month.

The reports must also show the number of stamps:

(1) on hand at the beginning of the month;

(2) purchased during the month;

(3) on hand at the end of the month;

(4) affixed or otherwise disposed of at the end of the month; and

(5) the number of stamped cigarettes, with New York City stamps and joint New York State-New York City stamps affixed, on hand at the end of the month.

Monthly reports must be filed on or before the 15th day of each month covering the transactions for the preceding calendar month.

Wholesale dealers who are not also agents may also be required to file reports showing the receipts and disposition of all stamped and unstamped cigarettes and any other information the Commissioner may require.

[¶555-604] NYC Records and Invoices

Agents and wholesale dealers must keep records showing every purchase, sale or other disposition of cigarettes and stamps handled. (Rule Sec. 4-17) Agents authorized to keep metering machines must keep a daily record of meter readings on forms approved by the Commissioner of Finance.

Every agent or dealer must keep records of:

(1) cigarettes on which a tax must be paid and those on which no tax is required;

(2) cigarettes returned because they have become unsalable;

(3) stamped or unstamped cigarettes transferred to or from other agents;

(4) cigarettes sold and delivered in New York City; and

(5) cigarettes sold and delivered outside the city, including the quantities sold and the names and addresses of the purchasers.

(Rule Sec. 4-17)

Agents must also keep records showing monthly inventories, at the beginning and the close of each month, of unstamped cigarettes and of the number of stamps on hand. (see ¶555-603)

• *Invoices*

At the time of delivering cigarettes to any person, each agent or wholesale dealer in the city must make a duplicate invoice showing:

(1) the date of delivery;

(2) the number of packages and cigarettes in each shipment delivered; and

(3) the name of the purchaser to whom delivery is made.

Each dealer must retain invoices showing:

(1) the number of packages and cigarettes in each shipment of cigarettes received;

(2) the date the cigarettes were received; and

(3) the name of the shipper.

All invoices and records must be maintained for a period of three years, subject to the use and inspection of the Commissioner. The above invoice requirements are also applicable to tobacco products dealers with respect to tobacco products delivered and received. (Sec. 11-1307(a), N.Y.C. Adm. Code)

[¶555-606] NYC Use Tax Returns

Anyone liable for the tax on the use of cigarettes must file a return together with the amount of tax due within 24 hours after the liability for the tax accrues. (Sec. 11-1302(f), N.Y.C. Adm. Code)

[¶555-800]

NYC TOBACCO TAX COLLECTION

[¶555-801] Payment of NYC Tax

The cigarette tax is advanced and paid to the Commissioner of Finance by appointed agents or distributors who purchase adhesive stamps from the Commissioner. (Sec. 11-1302(a), (e), (g) and (h), N.Y.C. Adm. Code) The tax may also be paid through the use of metering machines. Payment of the tax is shown by affixing or imprinting stamps to packages of cigarettes to be sold in the city.

Effective June 1, 2018, a tax is imposed on tobacco products other than cigarettes (Other Tobacco Products or OTP). Generally, the OTP tax must be paid by wholesale dealers on OTO sold to retail dealers in New York City. (Sec. 11-1302.1(f), N.Y.C. Adm. Code)

• *Tax as part of sales price*

It is the consumer, however, who is ultimately liable for the cigarette tax. (Sec. 11-1302(a), (e), (g) and (h), N.Y.C. Adm. Code) Therefore, the agent, distributor, or dealer paying tax to the Commissioner is to collect it from the consumer by adding the amount of the tax to the sales price of the cigarettes.

• *Other tobacco products (OTP)*

Effective June 1, 2018, wholesale dealers are liable for the collection and payment of other tobacco products (OTP) taxes to the Commissioner of Finance. Generally, the OTP tax must be paid by wholesale dealers on OTP sold to retail dealers in New York City. Wholesale dealers must file tax returns and pay the tax on a monthly basis on or before the 20th day of the month following the month for which the tax return is required, unless the Commissioner of Finance has exempted the particular wholesale dealer from filing. Retail dealers are required to be able to prove that tax has been paid on tobacco products in their possession. They are also required to pass-on the tax to their customers. (Sec. 11-1302.1(f), N.Y.C. Adm. Code) (Finance Memorandum 18-5)

Determination of the OTP tax. The wholesale dealer pays the OTP tax on OTP shipped to retail dealers in New York City. For OTP, other than cigars and little cigars, the wholesale dealer calculates the OTP tax based on the weight of the particular tobacco product sold to the retail dealer in accordance with the schedule provided in Admin. Code Sec. 11-1302.1(a). For little cigars, the wholesale dealer calculates the OTP tax based on the number of packs of 20 little cigars sold to the retail dealer, multiplied by the amount stated on the schedule provided in Sec. 11-1302.1(a). (Finance Memorandum 18-5)

For cigars, the wholesale dealer's calculation of the OTP tax is based on the package sold by the wholesale dealer to the retail dealer in New York City. (For further guidance, please see the instructions to the form that must be filled out by the wholesale dealer.) The tax is always 10% of the price floor calculated for the package sold by the wholesale dealer. (Finance Memorandum 18-5)

Requirements for retail dealers. The retail dealer is liable for tax on all tobacco products in its possession on which tax has not been paid by the wholesale dealer. In order to prove the tax has been paid, the retail dealer is required to produce invoices from licensed wholesale dealers for all tobacco products held by the retail dealer.

Although the price floor is used by the wholesale dealer to calculate the tax, the price floor is actually enforced at the retail level. In determining the total sales price, retail dealers must add the OTP tax amount to the price floor to ensure the passing-on of the OTP tax to the consumer. Sales tax, which is calculated on the basis of the total sales price including the OTP tax, must also be added on at the retail level. (Finance Memorandum 18-5)

Inasmuch as retail dealers can sell individual cigars, as well as cigars in packages that differ in size from the package in which the cigars are purchased, the calculation of the correct OTP tax pass-on to the consumer presents unique problems with regard to cigars. To simplify this problem, the Department of Finance will allow for a safe harbor of 25 cents per cigar. Although the price floor is determined by the packaging in which the retail dealer sells cigars to the consumer, for purposes of the retail safe harbor it does not matter whether cigars are sold individually, by the box or by the sub-package. The safe harbor pass-on amount is always 25 cents per cigar. (Finance Memorandum 18-5)

[¶555-802] NYC Stamps

Provisions governing stamp types, sales, and placement of stamps are discussed below.

• *Credit sales of stamps*

The Finance Commissioner may permit both resident and nonresident agents to pay for stamps within 30 days from the date of sale, consignment or delivery of the stamps, provided a surety bond satisfactory to the Commissioner is filed with him. (Sec. 11-1304(b), N.Y.C. Adm. Code; Rule Sec. 4-15)

Performance bonds.—In addition to the credit bond described above, an agent may be required to file with the Commissioner a surety bond guaranteeing the proper discharge and performance of his duties as an agent. (Rule Sec. 4-15)

Deposit of securities.—In lieu of the performance or credit bonds mentioned above, an agent may deposit with the Finance Commissioner a personal bond together with securities, in amounts approved by the Commissioner. These securities may be sold to recover sums due, but no sale will be held without a hearing or court determination. See Rule Sec. 4-15 for additional information.

• *Adhesive stamps*

The Commissioner of Finance has prescribed stamps in two-cent and four-cent denominations which are on sale at banks designated by the Commissioner as fiscal agents or sub-agents, (Rule Sec. 4-07) Agents authorized to affix stamps are assigned to banks from which they purchase stamps either for cash or on 30 days of credit. Stamps may be purchased over-the-counter or by mail. If purchased by mail, no shipping charge will be made by the bank.

The stamps will be sold in the form of a single stamp for payment of the New York City tax or in the form of a joint stamp prepared and issued by the state and the city for payment of both state and city taxes.

• *Meter stamps*

The use of a metering machine to pay New York City cigarette tax or the use of a joint meter impression showing payment of both state and city cigarette taxes may be permitted by the Commissioner of Finance in lieu of the use of adhesive stamps. (Rule Sec. 4-08)

Payment of the tax must be made either in cash at the time the meter is set or on 30 days of credit on the same terms and conditions as apply to adhesive stamps.

• *Affixing and canceling stamps*

Agents are required to affix stamps evidencing payment of the cigarette tax and to cancel the stamps before the cigarettes are sold or offered for sale and before they are delivered to any dealer in the city. (Sec. 11-1305(a), N.Y.C. Adm. Code; Rule Sec. 4-10) If stamps have been affixed and canceled prior to an agent receiving them, no additional stamps are required.

An agent may appoint an employee to affix the stamps to any cigarettes under the agent's control. (Rule Sec. 4-15)

Placement of stamps.—The stamps must be affixed on each individual package of cigarettes so that they are clearly visible to the purchaser. (Rule Sec. 4-10) When affixed to "rounds" or "flats" of 50 cigarettes or more, they must be placed so that they will be destroyed when the container is opened. Unstamped cigarettes must be kept separate from stamped cigarettes.

Cancellation of stamps.—All adhesive stamps must be canceled in waterproof ink with the number assigned to the agent before the cigarettes to which the stamps are affixed are offered for sale. (Sec. 11-1304(b), N.Y.C. Adm. Code) Meter stamps require no cancellation as they incorporate the identifying number of the agent into their design.

[¶555-806] NYC Receipt of Cigarettes by Dealers

Each dealer who is not also an agent must, immediately upon receipt of any cigarettes, mark in ink on each unopened box, carton or container the word "received" and the year, month, day and hour of such receipt. (Sec. 11-1305(b) and (d), N.Y.C. Adm. Code; Rule Sec. 4-11) The dealer must also sign the unopened containers.

• *Retail dealers*

Retail dealers must, within 24 hours of receipt of any cigarette, open each box, carton or container to determine whether or not the proper stamps have been affixed. (Rule Sec. 4-11) If the cigarettes are unstamped, the retailer must immediately notify the dealer from whom the cigarettes were purchased and arrange for delivery of stamped cigarettes to replace the unstamped cigarettes within 24 hours. The retailer must keep a record of the time at which the arrangements were made and the name of the individual representing the dealer.

• *Presumption of violation*

Whenever cigarettes on which stamps have not been affixed or canceled or which have not been marked as having been received within the preceding 24 hours are found in a dealer's place of business, the presumption is that the cigarettes are kept in violation of the law. (Sec. 11-1305(b) and (d), N.Y.C. Adm. Code)

[¶555-810]
NYC TOBACCO TAX PENALTIES

[¶555-811] Failure to NYC Pay Tax

A penalty equal to 50% of the amount of tax due is imposed on anyone who fails to pay the tax on cigarettes when due. Effective June 1, 2018, a penalty equal to 300% of the amount of the tax due is imposed on anyone who fails to pay the tax on other tobacco products when due. (Sec. 11-1317(a), N.Y.C. Adm. Code; Rule Sec. 4-23)

For current underpayment and overpayment interest rates, and rates in effect for prior periods, see ¶589-204.

[¶555-812] NYC Penalties for Possession of Unstamped, Unlawfully Stamped Cigarettes, or Untaxed Tobacco Products

With some exceptions, any person, other than an agent, who possesses or transports unstamped or unlawfully stamped packages of cigarettes in the city for purposes of sale or who sells or offers such cigarettes for sale, or who willfully attempts to evade payment of the cigarette tax is guilty of a misdemeanor. (Sec. 11-1304(d), N.Y.C. Adm. Code; Rule Sec. 4-23)

Anyone previously convicted two or more times under this section or who, regardless of any prior convictions, willfully possesses or transports for sale 10,000 or more cigarettes in unstamped or unlawfully stamped packages is guilty of a Class E felony. (Sec. 11-4012(a)(2), N.Y.C. Adm. Code; *TSB-M-04(6)M*, New York State Department of Taxation and Finance, December 13, 2004)

Any person who willfully possesses, transports for sale, sells, or offers to sell 30,000 or more cigarettes in unstamped or unlawfully stamped packages is guilty of a Class D felony. (Sec. 11-4012(c), N.Y.C. Adm. Code)

Effective June 1, 2018, any person who willfully attempts to evade or defeat the tax, or conducts any willful act or omission with respect to the tax imposed on other tobacco products will be guilty of a misdemeanor. (Sec. 11-4012.1, N.Y.C. Adm. Code)

• *Presumption of violation*

The possession or transportation by any person other than an agent at any one time of 400 or more cigarettes in unstamped or unlawfully stamped packages is presumptive evidence that the possession or transportation is for purposes of sale. (Rule Sec. 4-23)

• *Exemptions*

Common or contract carriers, warehousemen and public officers lawfully in possession of unstamped cigarettes are not subject to the above penalties. (Sec. 11-1317(c), N.Y.C. Adm. Code; Rule Sec. 4-23)

[¶555-813] NYC Additional Penalties

In addition to any other penalty imposed by the cigarette tax law, any person in the possession or control of more than 1,000 cigarettes in unstamped or unlawfully stamped packages is subject to a penalty of $100 for each 200 cigarettes or fraction thereof in excess of 1,000. A separate penalty applies if a person knowingly possesses or has control of such cigarettes. (Sec. 11-1317(b), N.Y.C. Adm. Code)

• *Authority to seal premises*

The Commissioner of Finance is authorized to order the sealing of the premises operated by a person engaging in sales who does not possess a valid license on at least two occasions within a three-year period. (Sec. 11-4023, N.Y.C. Adm. Code)

• *Sales below listed price or floor price*

The following penalties are imposed for selling cigarettes and tobacco products below the floor price or listed price by using coupons, vouchers, rebates, or similar instruments, or by multi-package discounts:

— $1,000 for the first violation in a five-year period;

— $2,000 for the second violation in a five-year period; and

— $5,000 for the third violation in a five-year period.

(Sec. 17-176.1, N.Y.C. Adm. Code)

NEW YORK CITY REAL PROPERTY TRANSFER TAX

[¶556-100]

NYC PERSONS AND CONVEYANCES--SUBJECT TO TAX

[¶556-105] NYC Persons and Conveyances--Subject to Tax

The real property transfer tax is imposed on each deed at the time of delivery by a grantor to a grantee when the consideration for the real property and any improvement thereon exceeds $25,000, regardless of whether the improvement is included in the same deed. (Sec. 11-2102(a), N.Y.C. Adm. Code) If the real property subject to tax is situated partly within and partly without the boundaries of New York City, the consideration and net consideration subject to tax is that part which is attributable to that portion of the real property situated within New York City or to the interest in such portion.

Ordinarily, the tax will be paid by the grantor. However, if the grantor does not pay or is an exempt person, liability for payment falls upon the grantee. (Rule Sec. 23-03)

An individual condominium unit that is required to be used in whole or part as a hotel room by the contract of sale or other document determining the conditions under which such condominium is transferred is presumed not to be a residential condominium unit and, therefore, is subject to transfer tax. (Rule Sec. 23-03)

The transfer of an equitable title or interest in real property, such as a beneficial interest in a trust or a life estate, is a taxable conveyance and, therefore, is subject to New York City real property transfer tax. (*Update on Audit Issues: Real Property Transfer Tax—Transfer of Equitable Interest*, New York City Department of Finance, June 2008)

Any transfer of a one, two, or three family house, an individual residential condominium unit, or an individual residential cooperative apartment, or any economic interest in any such property, the consideration for the transfer does not include the amount of any amount of any mortgage, lien, or encumbrance on the property that existed before the transfer and remains on the property after the transfer. (Sec. 11-2102(f), N.Y.C. Adm. Code) The exclusion does not apply to transfers to a mortgagee, lienor, or encumbrancer or to qualified real estate investment trust transfers nor to mortgages, liens, or encumbrances placed on the property or increased in amount in connection with or in anticipation of the transfer or by reason of deferred payments of the purchase price. A rule provides guidance as to when a lien is considered to be placed on the property in connection with or in anticipation of the transfer and when a lien on the property following the transfer is considered to be the same as the lien that was on the property prior to the transfer. (Rule Sec. 23-03(k)) The rule also includes numerous examples illustrating its application. A 2003 Tax Appeals Tribunal decision determined that Rule Sec. 23-03(k), amended in 1999, applies retroactively to the 1997 effective date of Sec. 11-2102(f), N.Y.C. Adm. Code.

• *Definitions*

Transfers may be subject to the tax depending on whether certain documents or transfers meet applicable definitions under the law.

Deed.—The word "deed," as used in the real property transfer tax law, is defined to mean any document or writing other than a will, whereby real property or an interest therein is created, vested, granted, bargained, sold, transferred, assigned or otherwise conveyed, including any such document or writing whereby any leasehold interest in real property is granted, assigned or surrendered. (Sec. 11-2101(2), N.Y.C. Adm. Code)

The devise of an interest in real property under a will is not subject to the real property transfer tax; however, a deed given by an executor in connection with the sale of an interest in real property is subject to the tax. (Rule Sec. 23-01)

Consideration.—The term "consideration" refers to the price actually paid or required to be paid for the real property or interest therein, without deduction for mortgages, liens or encumbrance, whether or not expressed in the deed and whether paid or required to be paid. (Sec. 11-2101(9), N.Y.C. Adm. Code) The term includes the cancellation or discharge of an indebtedness or obligation. It also includes the amount of any mortgage, lien or encumbrance, whether or not the underlying indebtedness is assumed.

Where an option to purchase real property or an economic interest therein is exercised, consideration includes the amount paid or required to be paid to the grantor or his designee for the option. (Rule Sec. 23-02)

> *EXAMPLE:* A parcel of real estate is sold for $50,000 cash subject to an existing mortgage of $30,000 which remains on the property after delivery of the deed. The consideration for the transfer is $80,000 and the tax applies to the deed.

> *EXAMPLE:* A parcel of real estate is sold for $30,000. The deed recites that the consideration is $10 and other good and valuable consideration. The consideration for the transfer is $30,000 and the tax applies to the deed.

> *EXAMPLE:* Separate deeds by which each of the tenants-in-common of realty conveys his own interest in the property of a common grantee for a consideration of less than $25,000 for each deed are not subject to tax, even though in total the consideration paid by the grantee is more than $25,000.

> *EXAMPLE:* A owns real property worth $50,000. B owns real property which is also worth $50,000. A and B exchange their real property. The tax applies to the transfer of A's realty and the transfer of B's realty. The consideration in each case is the fair market value of the property received in exchange for the realty conveyed.

> *EXAMPLE:* A owns real property having a fair market value of $50,000, subject to a $30,000 mortgage. B owns unencumbered realty having a fair market value of $20,000. A and B exchange realty. The consideration for the transfer of A's property is the fair market value of the property received ($20,000) plus the amount of the mortgage upon the realty conveyed ($30,000), or $50,000. The consideration for the transfer of B's property is $20,000. Although B receives consideration having a fair market value of $50,000, only $20,000 of this is in exchange for B's property. The balance ($30,000) is deemed to be in exchange for B's taking A's property subject to the $30,000 mortgage. Since the consideration for B's property is less than $25,000, there is no tax on the transfer of B's property.

Net consideration.—The term "net consideration" is defined to mean any consideration, excluding any mortgage or other lien or encumbrance on the real property or interest therein which existed before the delivery of the deed and remains on it after the delivery of the deed. (Sec. 11-2101(10), N.Y.C. Adm. Code) In determining the amount of net consideration, only the amounts reflecting encumbrances on the property existing before the sale and not removed thereby may be deducted. (Rule Sec. 23-02) No deduction is made on account of any encumbrance placed on the property in connection with the sale, or by reason of deferred payments of the purchase price whether represented by notes or otherwise.

EXAMPLE: A parcel of real property is sold for $50,000 subject to an existing mortgage of $35,000 which remains thereon after the deed is delivered. The mortgage is not treated as part of the net consideration for the conveyance. Consequently, the tax computed upon the net consideration viz: $15,000.

EXAMPLE: A parcel of real estate is sold for $50,000, free and clear of mortgages, liens and encumbrances. The purchaser gives a purchase money mortgage to the seller or third party in the amount of $35,000 to secure the payment of a portion of the purchase price. The mortgage was placed on the property as a result of the sale and cannot be deducted in determining the net consideration. Consequently, the tax is to be computed on the consideration of $50,000.

EXAMPLE: A parcel of real property was sold on January 10, 1950, of $60,000 subject to a first mortgage of $30,000. On July 10, 1959, the property is sold for $80,000, subject to the balance of the mortgage remaining unpaid, viz., $10,000. The balance of the purchase price, viz., $70,000 is paid in cash. The tax is to be computed on the net consideration of $70,000.

EXAMPLE: A parcel of real property is sold on July 15, 1959, for $75,000. Under the terms of the contract of sale, the grantor agrees to, and does, pay off an existing mortgage of $20,000, and agrees to take $45,000 in cash and a purchase money mortgage for $30,000. The tax is to be computed on the consideration of $75,000.

Real property.—The term "real property" is defined to mean every estate or right, legal or equitable, present or future, vested or contingent, in lands, tenements or hereditaments, which are located in whole or in part within the City of New York. (Sec. 11-2101(5), N.Y.C. Adm. Code) It does not include a mortgage, a release of mortgage or a leasehold interest in a one-, two-, or three-family house or an individual dwelling unit in a dwelling which is to be occupied or is occupied as the residence or home of four or more families living independently of each other. "Real property" does not include rights to sepulture (burial plots). The term includes an easement and a life estate, but not a license for the use of real property which confers a privilege of use without conveying an interest or estate therein. (Rule Sec. 23-02) The term includes excess zoning rights in connection with zoning lot mergers and development rights relating to landmark designated posts. Furthermore, "real property" includes an ownership interest in a condominium unit.

Grantor.—The person making, executing or delivering the deed is defined as the "grantor" for purposes of the real property transfer tax. (Sec. 11-2101(14), N.Y.C. Adm. Code) The term "grantor" also includes the person or persons who transfer an economic interest in real property.

Grantee.—The term "grantee" refers to the person or persons accepting the deed or obtaining any of the real property which is the subject of the deed or any interest therein. (Sec. 11-2101(15), N.Y.C. Adm. Code) The term "grantee" also includes the person or persons to whom an economic interest in real property is transferred.

• *Presumption of taxability*

All deeds and transfers of economic interests are presumed to be taxable. If the net consideration includes property other than money, it is presumed that the consideration is the value of the real property or interest therein. (Sec. 11-2103, N.Y.C. Adm. Code) These presumptions prevail until the contrary is established, and the burden of proof is on the taxpayer. If a lien or other encumbrance exists on the real property before the deed is delivered, and remains on the property after delivery, the burden of proving the encumbrance and its amount is on the taxpayer.

[¶556-200]

NYC REAL PROPERTY TRANSFER TAX--EXEMPTIONS

[¶556-201] NYC Real Property Transfer Tax--Exemptions

A transaction is exempt from tax if the "consideration" does not exceed $25,000. (Sec. 11-2102(a), N.Y.C. Adm. Code) Mortgages, releases of mortgages, leaseholds for a term of years or part of a year and burial plots (rights to sepulture) are excluded from the statutory definition of "real property". (Sec. 11-2101(5), N.Y.C. Adm. Code) Similarly, real property devised under a will, or transferred by an executor's deed given in accordance with the terms of a will, is not taxable. (Rule Sec. 23-02)

The regulations provide the following examples of situations in which the tax does not apply (Rule Sec. 23-03):

(1) a conveyance of realty without consideration and otherwise than in connection with a sale, including a deed conveying realty as a bona fide gift;

(2) a deed to confirm title already vested in the grantee;

(3) an option for the purchase of real property or a contract for the sale of real property, if the contract does not vest legal or equitable rights;

(4) partition deeds, unless, for a consideration, some of the parties take shares greater in value than their undivided interests;

(5) a deed executed by a debtor conveying real property to an assignee for the benefit of his creditors; however, when the assignee conveys such property to a creditor or sells it to any other person, the deed by him is taxable if the consideration exceeds $25,000;

(6) conveyance to a receiver of realty included in the receivership assets, and reconveyance of such realty upon termination of the receivership;

(7) new stock certificates issued to replace old stock certificates because of a mere change of name; and

(8) transfers made pursuant to a confirmed plan of reorganization.

Foreign governments, persons acting on behalf of such governments, and heads of foreign governments' diplomatic missions are exempt to the extent that the government or person in question is exempt from the payment of tax under the Vienna Convention on Consular Relations or the Vienna Convention on Diplomatic Relations. For the exemption to apply, the property conveyed must be used exclusively for diplomatic or consular purposes or as the residence of the head of the diplomatic mission or consular post. An exemption is also provided for foreign governments, as well as persons acting on their behalf, to the extent that they are exempt from the payment of tax under any treaty or convention to which the United States and the foreign government are parties. (Rule Sec. 23-05)

• *State of New York*

An exemption from the real property transfer tax is provided for the State of New York, its agencies, instrumentalities, public corporations (including a public corporation created pursuant to agreement or compact with another state or Canada) and political subdivisions. (Sec. 11-2106(a)(1), N.Y.C. Adm. Code)

• *United States*

The United States and any of its agencies and instrumentalities, insofar as they are immune from taxation, are exempt from the real property transfer tax. (Sec. 11-2106(a)(2), N.Y.C. Adm. Code) However, this exemption does not relieve a grantee of the United States and its agencies or instrumentalities of the liability for payment of the tax or from filing a return.

- *United Nations or similar organizations*

A deed by or to the United Nations, or other world-wide international organization of which the United States is a member, is not subject to tax. (Sec. 11-2106(b)(1), N.Y.C. Adm. Code)

- *Charitable organizations*

The real property transfer tax does not apply to any deed by or to a corporation, association or trust, community chest, fund or foundation, organized and operated exclusively for religious, charitable or educational purposes, or for the prevention of cruelty to animals and children. (Sec. 11-2106(b)(2), N.Y.C. Adm. Code) No part of the net earnings of the organization may inure to the benefit of any private shareholder or individual, and no substantial part of its activities may constitute carrying on propaganda or otherwise attempting to influence legislation.

The New York City Department of Finance has issued a statement of audit procedure regarding charitable organizations that discusses the examination of a transaction to determine if the transaction should be subject to real property transfer tax. The "step transaction doctrine" will be applied if a series of transactions was entered into pursuant to binding agreements, or evidence exists that the series of transactions was entered into pursuant to a plan, even if there is no binding contract. (*Statement of Audit Procedure RPTT 2008-1*, New York City Department of Finance, February 29, 2008)

The doctrine will be used to prevent the use of a charity as a means to avoid paying transfer tax on an otherwise taxable transfer or series of transfers. If the Department determines that the step transaction doctrine should be applied and the transactions are deemed taxable, this will be treated as evidence that the charitable entity in question is not operating exclusively for religious, charitable or education purposes. (*Statement of Audit Procedure RPTT 2008-1*, New York City Department of Finance, February 29, 2008)

- *Deeds to state and federal governments*

An exemption is available for any deed to the State of New York, its agencies, instrumentalities, public corporations and political subdivisions, or to the United States, its agencies and instrumentalities. (Sec. 11-2106(b)(5), N.Y.C. Adm. Code)

- *Deeds prior to May 1, 1959*

A deed delivered pursuant to a contract made prior to May 1, 1959, is exempt from the real property transfer tax. (Sec. 11-2106(b)(4), N.Y.C. Adm. Code) Additionally, a deed delivered by any governmental body or person which is exempt from payment of the tax as a result of a sale at a public auction held in accordance with a contract made prior to May 1, 1959, is exempt from tax. (Sec. 11-2106(b)(5), N.Y.C. Adm. Code)

- *Deeds given as security for debts*

The realty transfer tax is not imposed upon a deed or instrument given solely as security for, or a transaction the sole purpose of which is to secure, a debt or obligation or a deed or instrument given, or a transaction entered into, solely for the purpose of returning such security. (Sec. 11-2106(b)(6), N.Y.C. Adm. Code)

- *Conveyances between agent, dummy, straw and conduit, or principal*

A deed from a person acting as a mere agent, dummy, straw or conduit to his principal, or from the principal to such a person, is not subject to tax. (Sec. 11-2106(b)(7), N.Y.C. Adm. Code)

• *Cooperative housing corporation transfers*

A real property transfer tax exemption is allowed for certain transfers of interests in cooperative housing corporation stock and appurtenant proprietary leaseholds as a result of actions to enforce liens, security interests or other rights on or in such stock and proprietary leaseholds. (Sec. 11-2106(c), N.Y.C. Adm. Code) Where the stock and the appurtenant leasehold are transferred to the cooperative housing corporation, the corporation's wholly owned subsidiary, a mortgagee of the property owned by the corporation or the mortgagee's wholly owned subsidiary, neither the corporation nor the mortgagee are liable as grantees for the payment of tax.

• *Mere change of identity or form of ownership*

Deeds, instruments or transactions conveying or transferring real property or economic interests in real property that effect a mere change of identity or form of ownership or organization, to the extent that beneficial ownership remains the same (other than conveyances to a cooperative housing corporation of the land and building or buildings comprising the cooperative dwelling or dwellings) are exempt from City real property transfer taxes. (Sec. 11-2106(b)(8), N.Y.C. Adm. Code; Rule Sec. 23-05(b)(8)) The term "cooperative housing corporation" does not include a housing company organized and operating pursuant to the provisions of Articles 2, 4, 5 or 11, Private Housing Finance Law.

The following are types of transfers that may qualify for the mere-change exemption in whole or in part (Instructions, Form NYC-REP Schedule M):

(1) a transfer of property to a new or pre-existing corporation in which the owners of the property prior to the transfer are shareholders;

(2) a transfer of property by one wholly owned subsidiary of a corporation to another wholly owned subsidiary of the same corporation;

(3) a transfer of property to a new or pre-existing partnership in which the owners of the property prior to the transfer are partners;

(4) a transfer of property to a trust in which the owners of the property prior to the transfer have a beneficial interest;

(5) a distribution of property by a corporation or partnership to its shareholders or partners; or

(6) a distribution of property by a trust to a trust beneficiary.

> *EXAMPLE:* A transfer of property owned by three individuals as equal tenants-in-common to a corporation or partnership in which the three individuals are equal shareholders or partners will be fully exempt as a mere change of form of ownership. (Instructions, Form NYC-REP Schedule M)

> *EXAMPLE:* A transfer of a cooperative apartment owned by one individual to a corporation in which the individual is a 25% shareholder will be exempt to the extent that the individual retains a 25% beneficial interest in the coop after the transfer. (Instructions, Form NYC-REP Schedule M)

> *EXAMPLE:* Corporation X is owned 25% by individual A and 75% by individual B. If corporation X distributes property to A and B as equal tenants-in-common, the transfer will be exempt to the extent A retains the same 25% interest in the property and B retains a 50% interest in the property. The transfer will be taxable to the extent of the additional 25% interest in the property transferred to A. (Instructions, Form NYC-REP Schedule M)

Applicable tax rate: When the exemption for a mere change of identity or form of ownership applies, the consideration subject to tax is reduced proportionately to the extent the beneficial ownership remains the same. (Rule Sec. 23-05(b)(8)) However, for transfers occurring after December 31, 1998, the determination of the applicable tax rate (see discussion at ¶556-301) will be made prior to the application of the exemption. Thus, the tax rate applicable to transfers for consideration exceeding $500,000 will apply even though the portion of the consideration taxable after applying the exemption is $500,000 or less.

Controlling interests: For transactions involving economic interests, the determination of whether a controlling economic interest has been transferred is made prior to the application of the exemption. (Rule Sec. 23-05(b)(8)) Thus, the transfer of a controlling economic interest will be taxable to the extent the beneficial ownership does not remain the same, even though the portion of the interest subject to tax represents, in the case of a corporation, less than 50 of the total combined voting power of all classes of stock of the corporation or, in the case of a partnership, association, trust, or other entity, less than 50 of the capital, profits, or beneficial interest in the entity.

EXAMPLE: A and B, two equal tenants-in-common of Parcel 1, transfer their interests in Parcel 1 to X Corporation on January 1, 1995, each receiving 50% of the outstanding stock of X. The transfer is wholly exempt from tax as a mere change in identity or form of ownership or organization because the beneficial ownership of the real property remains the same as before the transfer. (Rule Sec. 23-05(b)(8))

EXAMPLE: A and B are equal partners in AB Partnership. AB Partnership owns two properties. Parcel 1 is unencumbered commercial real property with a fair market value of $1,000,000. Parcel 2 is unencumbered commercial real property with a fair market value of $2,000,000. AB has other assets valued at $1,000,000. On January 1, 1995, AB Partnership distributes all of its assets to A and B in complete liquidation. B receives Parcel 2. A receives Parcel 1 and all the other assets. The tax on the distribution of Parcel 1 to A is measured by the fair market value of Parcel 1 of $1,000,000 reduced by 50% because A had a 50% beneficial interest in the parcel prior to the liquidation and has retained that interest after the distribution. Therefore, $500,000 (50% × $1,000,000) is subject to tax. The tax due on the distribution is $13,125 (2.625% × $500,000). Similarly, the distribution of Parcel 2 to B is exempt from tax as a mere change of identity or form of ownership or organization to the extent of 50% because B owned a 50% beneficial interest in the property prior to the liquidation and has retained that beneficial interest. Therefore, the taxable amount is $1,000,000 (50% × $2,000,000), and the tax due on the distribution of Parcel 2 is $26,250 (2.625% × $1,000,000). (Rule Sec. 23-05(b)(8))

EXAMPLE: T, an individual, owns 20 shares in a cooperative housing corporation attributable to an apartment in the building. The apartment is leased to a tenant for residential use. T transfers the shares attributable to the apartment to Y Corporation, her wholly owned corporation. Because T retains a 100% beneficial ownership of the apartment, the transfer is exempt from tax as a mere change of identity or form of ownership or organization. (Rule Sec. 23-05(b)(8))

EXAMPLE: J owns 70% of the stock of X Corp, whose sole asset is 80% of the stock of Y Corp. Y Corp's sole asset is an unencumbered parcel of commercial real property in New York City with a fair market value of $1,000,000. On February 1, 1999, J transfers all of her stock in X Corp to a newly formed corporation, Z Corp, in return for 60% of Z Corp's stock. (The other 40% of Z Corp's stock is owned by shareholders who have no independent interest in X Corp, Y Corp, or Y Corp's parcel of real property.) J's transfer of the X stock is a transfer of a 56% interest (70% × 80%) in the real property and is, therefore, subject to tax as a transfer of a controlling economic interest. The value of the consideration received in exchange, the Z Corp stock, is $560,000 ($1,000,000 × 56%). The transaction is exempt as a mere change of identity or form of ownership or organization to the extent that A retains a beneficial interest in the property following the merger. In this case, J retains a 33.6% interest in the property (56% × 60%). Therefore, the merger is exempt as a mere change of identity or form of ownership or organization to that extent. The tax is imposed on $224,000 (.224/.56 × $560,000). The tax due is $5,936 ($224,000 × 2.625%). The tax rate is based on the full value of the consideration, $560,000, rather than the amount subject to tax. (Rule Sec. 23-05(b)(8))

Other illustrative examples are set forth in the governing rule. (Rule Sec. 23-05(b)(8))

• *Housing development fund company transfers*

A real property transfer tax exemption is enacted for a qualifying deed, instrument or transaction conveying or transferring real property or an economic interest therein by or to any housing development fund company (HDFC) to an entity the controlling interest of which is held by an HDFC. To qualify, a regulatory agreement must restrict more than 50% of the floor area to residential real property and at least two-thirds of the residential real property to use by persons of low income and families of low income for a term of 30 years or more. The regulatory agreement must be with the state of New York or a municipal corporation or any other public corporation created by or pursuant to any law of the state of New York, and must require mutual consent for revocation or amendment. If the regulatory agreement restricts less than 100% of the current or future floor area to persons of low income, then the transfer is taxable in proportion to the floor area that is not so restricted. (Sec. 11-2106(b)(9), N.Y.C. Adm. Code)

If the regulatory agreement is not in place at the time of the transfer, tax must be calculated and paid without application of the exemption. However, if the property is made subject to a qualifying regulatory agreement within two years of the transfer, the Commissioner of Finance may subsequently issue a refund, determined as if the qualifying regulatory agreement were in place at the time of transfer. The application for refund must be made within 12 months of the qualifying regulatory agreement's effective date. (Sec. 11-2106(b)(9), N.Y.C. Adm. Code)

• *Application for exemption*

A grantor (or a grantee otherwise liable for payment) who claims an exemption from the real property transfer tax must submit an application for exemption to the Commissioner, in the form of an affidavit, together with such information as will enable the Commissioner to rule upon its status. (Rule Sec. 23-06) The affidavit must set forth:

(1) the type of organization;

(2) the purposes for which it is organized;

(3) its actual activities;

(4) the source and disposition of its income;

(5) whether any of its income is credited to surplus or may inure to any private stockholder or individual; and

(6) such other facts as may affect its right to exemption.

In addition, the affidavit must be supplemented by certain exhibits, such as the applicant's certificate of incorporation, or its articles of association, a copy of its bylaws, a financial statement, a current statement of receipts and disbursements, and a copy of the letter from the U.S. Treasury Department granting the applicant an exemption under the Internal Revenue Code. Further information may also be required.

The Commissioner will review the application and, if satisfied, will issue a letter exempting the applicant from the real property transfer tax. A copy of this letter should be attached to any return required to be filed.

[¶556-300]

NYC REAL PROPERTY TRANSFER TAX--RATE AND BASIS

[¶556-301] NYC Real Property Transfer Tax--Rate and Basis--In General

The real property transfer tax is imposed on conveyances of real property within New York City when the consideration exceeds $25,000, and is calculated at the following rates (Sec. 11-2102(a), N.Y.C. Adm. Code):

(1) 1 of the consideration for conveyances (or grants, assignments, or surrenders of leasehold interests) of one-, two-, or three-family houses, individual residential condominium units, or individual dwelling units in a dwelling occupied by four or more families living independently of each other, where the consideration is $500,000 or less; 1.425 where the consideration is more than $500,000;

(2) 1.425 of the consideration for all other conveyances (or grants, assignments, or surrenders of leasehold interest) where the consideration is $500,000 or less;

(3) 2.625 of the consideration for all other conveyances (or grants, assignments, or surrenders of leasehold interest) where the consideration is more than $500,000.

For purposes of any real property transfer tax which New York state has allowed cities with a population of one million or more to impose, the consideration for conveyances or transfers of individual residential property excludes the amount of any mortgage, lien, or encumbrance that existed before the delivery of the deed or transfer and remains after the date of delivery. (Sec. 11-2102(f), N.Y.C. Adm. Code)

• *Real estate investment trust transfers*

Transfers of interests in real property after June 9, 1994, to qualified real estate investment trusts (REITs), or to a partnership or corporation in which a REIT owns a controlling interest immediately following such conveyance, where the conveyance occurs in connection with the initial formation of the REIT, are subject to a real property transfer tax at a rate that is 50 of the general rate. (Sec. 11-2102(e), N.Y.C. Adm. Code) Until September 1, 2020, the reduced rate is also available for certain transfers to *existing* REITs.

For eligibility qualifications, see ¶556-303.

• *Allocation of purchase price between real property and assets*

If a transaction subject to real property transfer tax includes assets in addition to real property or interest therein, an apportionment should be made between the total consideration that is attributable to the sale of the real property (i.e., the land and the building), and the consideration that is attributable to the other assets (e.g., good will, furniture, non-attached fixtures, etc.). (Sec. 11-2102(d), N.Y.C. Adm. Code) Only the consideration that is attributable to the land and building is subject to tax.

If a good faith apportionment is *not* made between the real property and the assets, tax will be imposed on the part of the total consideration that the value of the real property or interest therein bears to the value of all assets (including the real property and interest therein.)

"Good faith" apportionment.—In *Petitions of 761 Hotel Associates, Grantor, and Parc 51 Associates*, the New York City Tax Appeals Tribunal, Administrative Law Judge Division, rejected the City's argument that a good faith allocation of a property's purchase price could be rejected if it did not "accurately reflect the economic realities". Instead, the ALJ held that a good faith allocation made between real property and other assets transferred in a sale must be accepted by the Commissioner of Finance for real property transfer tax purposes even if another allocation would appear to be more appropriate.

Note: A definition of "good faith" is not contained in the New York City Administrative Code or the Department's real property transfer tax regulations. However, in *761 Hotel Associates, supra,* the ALJ stated the test as follows:

[T]he determination of whether the parties acted in good faith is essentially a subjective finding as to the parties' honest intent, which can be determined through an examination of objective criteria. Such criteria includes whether: (1) the allocation is reasonable on its face; (2) the parties had adverse tax interests with respect to the allocation; and (3) the parties negotiated at arms-length. *See 212 Corp. v. Commissioner,* 70 T.C. 788, 800 (1978), and *Black Industries, Inc. v. Commissioner,* 38 T.C.M. 242, 252-253 (1979). Although there is no comparable "good faith" provision under the federal tax law, the Tax Court held, in those cases, that it will not disturb an allocation where the parties dealt with each other at arm's length and there is no reason to question the bona fides of the allocation (footnotes omitted).

• *Vacant land*

The New York City Department of Finance has issued a statement of audit procedure that provides guidance to taxpayers and auditors concerning the real property transfer tax rate that is applicable to transfers of vacant land. In general, the transfer of vacant land is taxed at the higher rate of 1.425% where the consideration is $500,000 or less, or at the rate of 2.625% where the consideration exceeds $500,000. (*Statement of Audit Procedure RPTT 2008-2,* New York City Department of Finance, February 29, 2008)

However, when a vacant lot is transferred with a one, two or three-family house, the lower real property transfer tax rate will apply if all of the following conditions are met:

— the vacant lot is adjacent to a one, two or three-family house;

— the vacant lot is owned by the owner of that house;

— the vacant lot is transferred pursuant to the same contract of sale as the adjacent house;

— the vacant lot is sold to the same buyer as the adjacent house; and

— the vacant lot is conveyed to that buyer as part of the same transfer as the adjacent house, as evidenced by a single deed and/or the simultaneous delivery of deeds.

(*Statement of Audit Procedure RPTT 2008-2,* New York City Department of Finance, February 29, 2008)

• *Transfer recording filing fee*

A transfer recording filing fee of $100 may be required in New York City. (Sec. 333(3), Real Property Law)

[¶556-303] NYC Real Estate Investment Trust Transfers

Transfers of interests in real property after June 9, 1994 to qualified real estate investment trusts (REITs) or to a partnership or corporation in which a REIT owns a controlling interest immediately following such conveyance, where such conveyance is made in connection with the initial formation of the REIT, are subject to a real property transfer tax at a rate that is 50% of the general rate. (Sec. 11-2102(e), N.Y.C. Adm. Code)

CCH CAUTION: The reduced real estate transfer tax rates have been expanded to include transfers between July 13, 1996, and before September 1, 2020, to qualified existing REITS (that is, transfers that do *not* occur in connection with the initial formation of the REIT). For details, see note below.

• *Transfers occurring in connection with the initial formation of the REIT*

To be eligible for the reduced real estate transfer tax rate, transfers after June 9, 1994, made in connection with the initial formation of the REIT must meet the following conditions:

Ownership retention requirement.—The value of the ownership interests in the REIT, or in a partnership or corporation in which the REIT owns a controlling interest, must be equal to an amount not less than 40% of the value of the equity interest in the real property or interest therein conveyed by the grantor to the grantee. Ownership interests must be retained by the grantor (or owners of the grantor) for a period of not less than two years from the date of the conveyance (unless the grantor dies, in which case the two-year retention period will be deemed to be satisfied, notwithstanding any conveyance of the interest as a result of such death).

75% reinvestment requirement.—In addition, 75% or more of the cash proceeds received by the REIT from the sale of ownership interests in the REIT upon its initial formation must be used: (a) to make payments on loans secured by any interest in real property (including an ownership interest in an entity owning real property) that is owned directly or indirectly by such REIT; (b) to pay for capital improvements to real property or any interest therein owned directly or indirectly by such REIT; (c) to pay costs, fees, and expenses (including brokerage fees and commissions, professional fees and payments to or on behalf of a tenant as an inducement to enter into a lease or sublease) incurred in connection with the creation of a leasehold or sublease pertaining to real property or an interest therein owned directly or indirectly by such REIT; (d) to acquire any interest in real property (including an ownership interest in any entity owning real property), apart from any acquisition to which a reduced rate of tax is applicable; or (e) for reserves established for any of the purposes noted in (a), (b) or (c), above. (Sec. 11-2102(e)(2)(D), N.Y.C. Adm. Code)

Fair market value.—For purposes of measuring the consideration from the conveyance, the value of the real property or interest therein is equal to the estimated market value as determined by the commissioner of finance for real property tax purposes as reflected on the most recent notice of assessment issued by such commissioner, or such other value as the taxpayer may establish to the satisfaction of the commissioner. (Sec. 11-2102(e)(3), N.Y.C. Adm. Code)

• *Transfers between July 13, 1996, and September 1, 2020, to existing REITs*

Transfers of property interests to existing REITS between July 13, 1996, and September 1, 2020, will be eligible for the reduced real estate transfer tax rate if the value of the ownership interests in the REIT, or in a partnership or corporation in which the REIT owns a controlling interest, is equal to an amount not less than 50% of the value of the equity interest in the real property or interest therein conveyed by the grantor to the grantee. Ownership interests must be retained by the grantor (or owners of the grantor) for a period of not less than two years from the date of the conveyance (unless the grantor dies, in which case the two-year retention period will be deemed to be satisfied, notwithstanding any conveyance of the interest as a result of such death). (Sec. 11-2102(e)(2)(B), N.Y.C. Adm. Code)

The 75% reinvestment rule discussed above does *not* apply.

[¶556-305] Allocation of Property Partly Within and Partly Without New York City

The real property transfer tax is imposed only on conveyances of real property which is actually within the boundaries of New York City. In the event that the property is partly within and partly without the city, the consideration and net consideration subject to tax is that part of the total consideration and total net consideration attributable to that portion of the real property situated within New York City or attributable to the interest in that portion. (Sec. 11-2102(a), N.Y.C. Adm. Code)

For purposes of determining the net consideration attributable to property situated within New York City, that part of the net consideration subject to tax is the proportion which the assessed valuation of the property situated within the territorial limits of the city bears to the assessed valuation of the entire property conveyed. (Rule Sec. 23-04) The assessed valuations used in the computation are those in effect at the time of the conveyance.

> EXAMPLE: A parcel of land situated partly within Westchester County and partly within Bronx County is conveyed by deed, dated July 15, 1983. The purchase price of the property is $200,000, subject to a first mortgage of $90,000. The assessed valuations of the property in effect at the time of the conveyances are as follows:

Property situated within Bronx County $120,000

Property situated within Westchester County $40,000

The following shows the computation of the consideration subject to tax:

Item

No.

1. Assessed valuation of property partly situated in Westchester County $40,000

2. Assessed valuation of property partly situated in Bronx County . $120,000

3. Total assessed valuation $160,000

4. Ratio of assessed valuation of property partly situated in Bronx County to total assessed valuation of property situated within and without the City of New York ($^{Item\ 2}/_{Item\ 3}$) 75%

5. Total consideration $200,000

6. Total consideration subject to tax ($^{Item\ 5}/_{Item\ 4}$) . . . . $150,000.

[¶556-400]

NYC REAL PROPERTY TRANSFER TAX--RETURNS

[¶556-401] NYC Real Property Transfer Tax--Returns

A joint return is required from both the grantor and the grantee, whether or not a tax is due on the conveyance. (Sec. 11-2105(a), N.Y.C. Adm. Code) Only the United States, the State of New York, its agencies, instrumentalities, public corporations, and political subdivisions are exempt from the filing requirement. (Sec. 11-2106(a), N.Y.C. Adm. Code) As an example, a return would be required even though the consideration for the deed is $25,000 or less and the conveyance is not subject to tax because of the dollar amount exclusion. (Rule Sec. 23-09)

The return must be filed with the Commissioner of Finance. (Sec. 11-2105(a), N.Y.C. Adm. Code) Filing is accomplished by delivering the return to the register for transmittal to the Commissioner of Finance. The return must be signed under oath by both the grantor or his agent and the grantee or his agent. If either the grantor or the grantee has failed to sign the return, it will be accepted as a return, but the party who fails to sign is subject to the penalties applicable to a person who has failed to file a return and the period of limitations for assessment of tax or of additional tax will not apply to that party.

The Commissioner of Finance is authorized to prescribe the form of the return and the information it is required to contain. (Sec. 11-2105(a), N.Y.C. Adm. Code)

LLCs. Limited liability companies (LLCs) are required to disclose the individual members of the company when it files a joint real property transfer tax return for any sale of real residential property that it is named the grantor or grantee in. This only applies to residential property containing one- to four-family dwelling units. The joint tax return must be accompanied with a list identifying all the members, managers, and any other authorized persons. (Sec. 11-2105(h), N.Y.C. Adm. Code)

• *Due date*

The return must be filed with the Commissioner of Finance at the time of payment of any tax or, in the case of a deed not subject to tax, within 30 days after the delivery of the deed by the grantor to the grantee but before the recording of the deed. (Sec. 11-2105(a), N.Y.C. Adm. Code) In the case of the transfer of an economic interest in real property, the return must be filed at the time of payment of tax, or, if the transfer is not subject to tax, within 30 days after the transfer.

Cooperative housing corporations must file an information return by February 15 of each year overing the reporting period beginning on January 6 of the preceding year and ending on January 5 of the year of filing. (Sec. 11-2105(g), N.Y.C. Adm. Code)

Extensions.—The Commissioner is authorized to extend the time for filing a return, upon showing of good cause, for a period not exceeding 30 days. (Sec. 11-2112, N.Y.C. Adm. Code) An application for the extension must be made in writing prior to the due date of the return. (Rule Sec. 23-03) Even if the application is granted, the taxpayer is required to file a tentative return before the due date of the return, showing the estimated tax due and paying the amount as estimated. A final return is then due on or before the date to which the time of filing the return is extended. Payment of the balance due is required with the final return, with interest.

• *Evidence of filing*

Upon filing the real property transfer tax return, evidence of the filing is affixed to the deed by the register. (Sec. 11-2105(a), N.Y.C. Adm. Code) The Commissioner is authorized to provide for the use of stamps as evidence of payment.

• *More than one grantor or grantee*

In the event that a deed has more than one grantor or more than one grantee, the return may be signed by any one grantor and by any one grantee. (Sec. 11-2105(e), N.Y.C. Adm. Code) Those persons not signing, however, are not relieved of liability for the tax imposed.

• *Amended returns*

The Commissioner is empowered to require amended returns to be filed within 20 days after notice, and to include the information specified in the notice sent to the taxpayer. (Sec. 11-2105(c), N.Y.C. Adm. Code)

• *Preservation of returns*

Tax returns submitted under the real property transfer tax are preserved for three years and thereafter until the Commissioner of Finance permits their destruction. (Sec. 11-2105(b), N.Y.C. Adm. Code)

• *Record keeping*

The Commissioner is authorized to require every grantor and grantee to make and keep records and to furnish them upon request. (Sec. 11-2112, N.Y.C. Adm.

Code) By regulation, every grantor and grantee is required to keep complete records of conveyances of real property, including copies of the contract of sale, the title report, if any, the return or affidavit filed, the amount of liens and encumbrances on the realty at the time of delivery of the deed, the closing statement, and the general books of account of a person which would reflect the sale or purchase of real property. (Rule Sec. 23-11)

• *Secrecy of returns*

It is unlawful for the Commissioner, the register or any officer or employee of the Department of Finance or register to divulge or make known in any manner any information contained in or relating to any return provided for by the real property transfer tax. (Sec. 11-2115(a), N.Y.C. Adm. Code) An exception to this prohibition is allowed, however, if the disclosure is in accordance with proper judicial order or is otherwise allowed by law. Included among those persons excepted are the United States or any department thereof, the State of New York or any department thereof, the City of New York or any department thereof, provided the information is requested for official business, the register, the corporation counsel or other legal representative of the city, and the district attorney of any county within the city.

[¶556-600]

NYC REAL PROPERTY TRANSFER TAX--COLLECTION

[¶556-601] NYC Real Property Transfer Tax--Collection

Generally, the real property transfer tax will be calculated by the taxpayer and collected from the grantor by the grantee at the time of closing the title. The tax will then be paid by the grantee or by the title company, as his representative, to the register at the time of recording the deed.

• *Payment of tax*

The tax must be paid to the Commissioner of Finance at the office of the register in the county where the deed is or would be recorded within 30 days after the delivery of the deed by the grantor to the grantee but before the recording of the deed, or, in the case of a tax on the transfer of an economic interest in real property, at such place as the Commissioner of Finance designates, within 30 days after the transfer. (Sec. 11-2104, N.Y.C. Adm. Code)

• *Suits and warrants for collection*

Whenever a grantor or grantee fails to pay any tax, penalty or interest imposed by the real property transfer tax, the Commissioner is authorized to request the Corporation Counsel for New York City to bring an action for the enforcement of payment of the tax on behalf of the city, in any court of the State of New York, or of any other state, or of the United States. (Sec. 11-2111(a), N.Y.C. Adm. Code)

The Commissioner has at his disposal an additional or alternate remedy for the collection of tax: the issuance of a warrant to the grantor, grantee or other person liable for the tax which may be found in the city, for the payment of the tax together with any penalty or interest, and the cost of executing the warrant. (Sec. 11-2111(b), N.Y.C. Adm. Code) The sheriff files the warrant with the county clerk who enters the warrant in the judgment docket.

• *Liens*

Once the county clerk receives the warrant from the sheriff and enters it upon the judgment docket, the warrant so docketed becomes a lien on the real and personal property of the person against whom it was issued. (Sec. 11-2111(b), N.Y.C. Adm. Code) If a warrant is returned not satisfied in full, the Commissioner of Finance may issue new warrants and seek remedies as though the city recovered judgment and execution had been returned unsatisfied.

• *Penalties*

If any amount of realty transfer tax is not paid on or before the last date prescribed for payment, interest on the amount at the rate set by the Commissioner of Finance, or, if no rate is set, at the rate of 7.5% per year, must be paid for the period from the last date prescribed for payment to the date of payment. (Sec. 11-2114(a), N.Y.C. Adm. Code)

For current interest rates, and rates in effect for prior periods, see ¶589-204.

In the case of a failure to file a real estate transfer tax return on or before the prescribed date, unless it is shown that the failure is due to reasonable cause and not due to willful neglect, there will be added to the amount required to be shown as tax on the return 5% of the amount of the tax if the failure is for not more than one month, with an additional 5% for each additional month or fraction thereof during which the failure continues, not exceeding 25% in the aggregate. (Sec. 11-2114(b), N.Y.C. Adm. Code) In the case of a failure to file a return of tax within 60 days of the date prescribed for filing the return, unless it is shown that the failure is due to reasonable cause and not due to willful neglect, the addition to tax will not be less than the lesser of $100 or 100% of the amount required to be shown as tax on the return.

In the case of failure to pay the amount shown as tax on a return on or before the prescribed date, unless it is shown that the failure is due to reasonable case and not due to willful neglect, there will be added to the amount shown as tax on the return $1/2$ of 1% of the amount of the tax if the failure is not for more than one month, with an additional $1/2$ of 1% for each additional month or fraction thereof during which the failure continues, not exceeding 25% in the aggregate.

If any part of an underpayment of realty transfer tax is due to negligence or intentional disregard of the tax laws or regulations, a penalty of 5% of the underpayment will be added to the tax. (Sec. 11-2114(c), N.Y.C. Adm. Code) An amount equal to 50% of the interest payable with respect to the portion of the underpayment which is attributable to the negligence or intentional disregard will be added for the period beginning on the last date prescribed by law for payment of the underpayment and ending on the date of the assessment of the tax.

If any part of an underpayment is due to fraud, a penalty equal to 50% of the underpayment will be added to the tax, as well as an amount equal to 50% of the interest payable with respect to the portion of the underpayment which is attributable to the fraud. (Sec. 11-2114(d), N.Y.C. Adm. Code)

If a cooperative housing corporation fails to timely file an information return, a $100 penalty is imposed. (Sec. 11-2114(i), N.Y.C. Adm. Code)

Additional penalty.—Any person who, with fraudulent intent, fails to pay any tax or to make, render, sign, or certify any return, or to supply any information within the time required, will be liable for an additional penalty of not more than $1,000. (Sec. 11-2114(e), N.Y.C. Adm. Code)

NEW YORK CITY MORTGAGE RECORDING TAX

[¶557-001]

NYC MORTGAGE RECORDING TAX

[¶557-005] Description of NYC Tax

The mortgage recording tax is imposed on the recording of a mortgage on real property situated within the City of New York. (Sec. 11-2601(a), N.Y.C. Adm. Code) The tax is in addition to the state tax on mortgages. (Sec. 11-2604, N.Y.C. Adm. Code) Supplemental instruments and additional mortgages may also be taxed. (Sec. 11-2601(e), N.Y.C. Adm. Code)

[¶557-100]

NYC TAXPAYER AND RATES

[¶557-105] NYC Taxpayers

The tax is payable by either the mortgagor or the mortgagee at the time of recording of the mortgage, which may not be recorded without payment of the tax. (Sec. 11-2602, N.Y.C. Adm. Code) The tax is paid to the recording officer of the county in which the real property or any part of the property is situated. In cases where the real property is situated within and without the city, the recording officer of the county in which the mortgage is first recorded collects the recording tax.

[¶557-110] Rate of NYC Tax

The tax is imposed at the following rates (Sec. 11-2601(d), N.Y.C. Adm. Code):

(1) $1 for each $100 or major fraction thereof with respect to real property securing a principal debt or obligation of less than $500,000;

(2) $1.125 for each $100 or major fraction thereof with respect to one-, two-, or three-family houses, and individual residential condominium units securing a principal debt or obligation of $500,000 or more; and

(3) $1.75 for each $100 or major fraction thereof with respect to all other property.

For mortgages recorded prior to August 1, 1990, the tax rates were as follows:

(1) 50¢ for each $100 or major fraction thereof with respect to one-, two-, or three-family houses, individual cooperative apartments, individual residential condominium units, and real property securing a principal debt of less than $500,000 (Sec. 11-2601(b), N.Y.C. Adm. Code);

(2) 62.5¢ for each $100 or major fraction thereof with respect to one-, two-, or three-family houses, individual cooperative apartments, and individual residential condominium units securing a principal debt or obligation of $500,000 or more (Sec. 11-2601(c), N.Y.C. Adm. Code); and

(3) $1.25 for each $100 or major fraction thereof with respect to all other real property securing a principal debt or obligation of $500,000 or more.

[¶557-150]

NYC MORTGAGE RECORDING TAX COMPUTATION

[¶557-151] NYC Mortgage Recording Tax Computation--In General

The tax is levied on each $100 or principal fraction thereof of the amount of the principal debt or obligation secured by a mortgage on real property situated within the City of New York. (Sec. 11-2601(a), N.Y.C. Adm. Code) Apportionment applies to property lying both within and outside of the city. (Sec. 11-2602, N.Y.C. Adm. Code) Mortgages that form part of the same or related transactions and have the same or related mortgages may be treated as a single mortgage for purposed of determining the applicable rate of tax. (Sec. 11-2601(e), N.Y.C. Adm. Code)

NEW YORK CITY SALES AND USE

[¶560-000]
NYC SALES AND USE TAXES

[¶560-001] NYC Sales and Use Taxes—Introduction

The New York City sales and use tax is generally imposed at the rate of 4.5%.

The New York City sales and use tax is imposed in addition to the general 4% New York state tax and the revenues therefrom are paid to the Municipal Assistance Corporation. (Sec. 1107(a), Tax Law) (ST-03-8, New York State Department of Taxation and Finance) Therefore, the combined state and local tax rate imposed in New York City includes the 4% state tax, the Metropolitan Commuter Transportation District tax (MCTD) (see ¶60-110), and the 4.5% city tax. (ST-05-3, New York State Department of Taxation and Finance, April 2005) For a list of combined state and local rates, see ¶61-735 Local Rates.

New York City, however, does not impose a tax on the furnishing of an entertainment or information service by means of telephony or telegraphy. In addition, the New York City tax on parking is imposed at the rate of 6%. (Sec. 1107(a), Tax Law; Sec. 11-2002(g), N.Y.C. Adm. Code) There is an additional 8% tax imposed on parking in Manhattan. (Sec. 11-2049, N.Y.C. Adm. Code)

New York City had also enacted separate taxes at the rate of 4.5% on certain services, such as barbering, health salons and credit rating and reporting services. (Sec. 11-2002(h), N.Y.C. Adm. Code; Sec. 11-2040(a)1, N.Y.C. Adm. Code)

Moreover, New York City has imposed separate taxes on coin-operated amusement devices, hotel occupancies (see ¶531-005), alcoholic beverages (see ¶535-105), and tobacco.

[¶560-005] Persons and Sales Subject to NYC Tax

New York City imposes the sales and use tax on generally the same sales and services as those on which the statewide sales and use tax is imposed. (Sec. 11-2002, N.Y.C. Adm. Code; Sec. 1210(a)(1), Tax Law) However, New York City does not impose a tax on the furnishing of an entertainment or information service by means of telephony or telegraphy. Furthermore, New York City taxes certain services (such as barbering, health salons and credit rating and reporting services) not subject to the statewide sales and use tax.

For a discussion of miscellaneous personal services and related sales in New York City, see TB-ST-575.

• *General sales and use tax*

The New York City sales tax is imposed on receipts from the following categories of items or services:

- retail sales (including rentals) of tangible personal property;

- gas, electricity, refrigeration and steam, and telephone and telegraph services;

- enumerated services, which include—(a) information services, (b) processing and printing services, (c) installation, repair and maintenance services performed upon tangible personal property, (d) storage and safe deposit rental, and (e) real estate maintenance, service or repair;

- food and drink sold by restaurants and caterers;

- hotel room occupancy;

- admission charges, social or athletic club dues, and roof garden or cabaret charges;

- parking, garaging or storing of motor vehicles (except receipts paid to a homeowner's association by its members for such services); and

- beauty, barbering, hair restoring, manicuring, pedicuring, electrolysis, massage services and other similar services, as well as services by weight control salons, health salons, gymnasiums, Turkish and sauna baths or similar establishments and charges for the use of such facilities (whether or not any tangible personal property is transferred in connection with the service) (the tax is imposed through November 30, 2023). However, services rendered by certain health care professions (such as physicians, osteopaths, dentists, nurses, physiotherapists, chiropractors, podiatrists, optometrists, ophthalmic dispensers and other licensed persons performing similar services) and services performed on pets and other animals are excluded from tax.

(Sec. 11-2002, N.Y.C. Adm. Code) (TB-ST-329)

Wages, salaries and other compensation paid by an employer to an employee for performing, in such capacity, any of the above-mentioned services are not subject to tax.

Motor vehicle parking, storing or garaging services are not subject to the temporary municipal assistance tax. (Sec. 1107(b)(8), Tax Law)

For a discussion of the application of New York City sales tax to health and fitness clubs, see TB-ST-329.

For a discussion of the New York City sales tax exemption for clothing and footwear, see ¶560-010.

• *Sales tax on certain services*

In addition, New York City also imposes a sales and use tax on the following services:

- protective and detective services, excluding such services performed by port watchmen;

- real property interior cleaning and maintenance services performed on a regular contractual basis for a term of 30 days or more, including such services provided by a contractor to a landlord, managing agent or tenant or by a landlord or managing agent to a tenant; and

- credit rating and credit reporting services, including services provided by mercantile and consumer credit rating or reporting bureaus or agencies, rendered in written or oral form or in any other manner.

(Sec. 11-2040, N.Y.C. Adm. Code)

Wages, salaries and other compensation paid by an employer to an employee for performing, in such capacity, any of the above-mentioned services are not subject to tax. (Sec. 11-2040, N.Y.C. Adm. Code)

Organizations exempt from tax are the same as those exempt under the basic sales and use provisions. (Sec. 11-2042, Sec. 11-2040, N.Y.C. Adm. Code)

A refund or credit of the temporary municipal assistance tax paid on the sale or use of tangible personal property which is later used by the purchaser in performing a service subject to the separate New York City tax will be allowed against the New York City tax on services if the property has become a physical component of the property on which the service is performed or has been transferred to the purchaser of the service in connection with its performance. (Sec. 11-2043, N.Y.C. Adm. Code) Such refund or credit, however, does not include interest.

Protective and detective services, interior decorating and designing services, and interior cleaning and maintenance services, performed on a regular contractual basis for a term of 30-days or more, are not subject to the temporary municipal assistance tax to the extent that a city tax is already imposed on such services. (Sec. 1107(b)(8), Tax Law)

Credit rating services.—New York City imposes a local sales tax on credit rating services. The Department of Taxation and Finance has concluded that the best method of determining the delivery location of a credit rating service subject to New York City's local sales tax is the address to which the invoice for the service is sent. Therefore, a credit rating service that is invoiced to an address within New York City will be subject to the City's local sales tax. No sales tax is due to either the State or New York City if the credit rating service is invoiced to an address outside of New York City. This rule applies to all taxable sales of credit rating services originally invoiced to an address within New York City on or after September 1, 2015. Additionally, this rule supersedes the conclusion in Advisory Opinion TSB-A-13(27)S that delivery of a credit rating service occurs at the location of the representative of a client who signs an engagement letter, but that opinion remains valid in all other respects. (TSB-M-15(4)S)

Interior decorating and designing services—Interior design and decorating services delivered in New York City are subject to tax at the rate of $4^3/_8\%$ (the 4% state tax and the Metropolitan Commuter Transportation District tax). When interior decorating and design services are sold in conjunction with other taxable services or property, the charge for the decorating and design services delivered in New York City must be separately stated on the bill given to the customer. If the charges are not separately stated, the entire charge (including the decorating and design charges) will be subject to tax at the combined state and local rate. Interior decorating services that are performed in conjunction with the sale of tangible personal property by the decorator to the customer will be subject to tax if the tangible personal property associated with the decorating service is transferred or delivered to the customer (or the customer's designee) in New York State. In New York City, the portion of the bill that represents the sale of tangible personal property is subject to the combined state and local sales tax. However, if the interior decorating and design services are separately stated, contracted for, and separately itemized on the bill or invoice given to the customer, the interior design and decorating services are subject only to the state and Metropolitan Commuter Transportation District tax. (TSB-M-95(13)S)

Transportation services provided by affiliated livery vehicle.—Charges for transportation services provided by affiliated livery vehicles wholly within New York City are excluded from the state and local sales taxes on transportation services. Therefore, businesses collecting tax on services provided wholly within New York City may stop collecting sales tax on those services. Sales tax collected but not yet remitted to the department must either be returned to the customer or remitted to the department. The business may not keep sales tax money collected from customers on behalf of the department. (Sec. 1101(b)(34), Tax Law) (TSB-M-10(15)S) The exclusion applies only to charges for transportation services that are performed by an affiliated livery vehicle wholly within New York City. Therefore, only charges for trips that begin and end in New York City are not subject to sales tax. Charges for services provided by an affiliated livery vehicle for trips that begin in New York City and end in a New York locality outside New York City, or that begin in a New York locality outside New York City but end in New York City, remain subject to sales tax. For purposes of the local sales tax imposed on transportation service, the sales tax is computed by using the tax rate for the jurisdiction where the service commenced. (TSB-M-10(15)S)

A business whose only service is using an affiliated livery vehicle(s) to provide transportation services wholly within New York City is no longer required to be registered for sales tax purposes solely for providing that service. If that is the only service the business provides, it may file a final sales tax return and surrender its Certificate of Authority. In addition, the business must remit any sales tax collected and not previously remitted with the final sales tax return, unless it can prove that it returned the sales tax collected to the customer. A business that uses an affiliated livery vehicle(s) to provide transportation services that remain subject to sales tax as described above must continue to be registered and must collect sales tax on these services. (TSB-M-10(15)S)

If a business was registered for sales tax purposes and remitted sales tax that was collected on its charges for livery service provided using an affiliated livery vehicle wholly within New York City after June 1, 2009, the business may be eligible for a credit or refund of sales tax previously remitted to the department. However, the business must be able to prove that it paid the tax to the department with its sales tax return and that it has returned to the customer the sales tax it collected from the customer. To apply for a credit or refund, the business would file Form AU-11, Application for Credit or Refund of Sales and Use Tax, together with proof of repayment of tax to its customer. Businesses must keep detailed records of their charges, tax collected on those charges, and refunds (if any) of tax to their customers. Customers who paid tax to a livery service provider for service wholly within New York City on or after June 1, 2009, may apply to the livery company or to the department using Form AU-11 for a refund of tax paid. Customers that apply to the department for refunds must be able to prove that they paid the tax to a service provider, such as by submitting a receipt showing the date of the service, the amount paid, and the amount of tax collected by the service provider. (TSB-M-10(15)S)

However, effective March 1, 2013, the Department of Taxation and Finance has reconsidered its interpretation so that the exclusion will also apply to charges for transportation services provided by affiliated livery vehicles for trips that either begin or end in New York City. For example, under this new interpretation, charges for transportation services provided by affiliated livery vehicles for trips that begin in New York City and end in Nassau County are now excluded from sales tax. Similarly, charges for transportation services that begin in Nassau County and end in New York City are also excluded from sales tax. In addition, the exclusion from sales tax for trips that both begin and end in New York City remains in effect. The revised policy is effective for charges for transportation services provided by affiliated livery vehicles on or after March 1, 2013. Taxpayers are not eligible to apply for a refund of any sales tax that was properly collected and remitted based on the policy that was in effect before March 1, 2013. (TSB-M-13(2)S)

For purposes of this new exclusion, "affiliated livery vehicle" means a for-hire motor vehicle with a seating capacity of up to six persons, including the driver, other than a black car or luxury limousine, that is authorized and licensed by the taxi and limousine commission of a city of one million or more to be dispatched by a livery base station located in such a city and regulated by such taxi and limousine commission. In addition, the charges for service provided by an affiliated livery vehicle must be on the basis of flat rate, time, mileage, or zones and not on a garage-to-garage basis. As used in this new provision, the term "luxury limousine" has the same meaning as limousine. (Sec. 1101(b)(34), Tax Law) (TSB-M-10(15)S)

• *Yoga facilities in New York City*

Charges for yoga classes by facilities in New York City that offer only instruction in various yoga disciplines are not considered to be weight control salons, health salons, or gymnasiums. As a result, charges by these facilities for yoga classes are not subject to New York City local sales tax. Charges for yoga instruction by a facility that otherwise qualifies as a weight control salon, health salon, or gymnasium (i.e., a facility that also offers its customers access to exercise equipment, Pilates or aerobics classes) are subject to the New York City local sales tax. Charges to customers for the use of any tangible personal property (i.e., yoga mats) are subject to both state and local sales taxes. Charges to rent mats are also subject to state and local sales taxes. (TB-ST-329)

• *Transportation and delivery of gas or electricity*

All receipts from the sale of the services of transporting, transmitting, distributing, or delivering gas or electricity are subject to the full New York City local sales tax, even if purchased from someone other than the vendor of the gas or electricity. The commodities of gas and electricity themselves are already subject to New York City sales tax. (Important Notice N-09-12)

[¶560-010] NYC Exemptions

In general, the same exemptions that apply to the statewide sales and use tax are applicable to the New York City sales and use tax. (Sec. 1107(b), Tax Law)

• *Clothing and footwear*

Clothing and footwear costing less than $110, including items used to make or repair clothing and footwear and that becomes a physical component part of it, is exempt from New York City's sales and compensating use taxes. Clothing and footwear costing $110 or more is subject to New York City sales and use tax (previously, all clothing and footwear was exempt from New York City sales and use tax). (Sec. 1107(b)(10), Tax Law; Sec. 1210(a)(4)) (Important Notice N-09-12)

The New York City exemption for clothing, footwear, and items used to make exempt clothing also applies to the Metropolitan Commuter Transportation District (MCTD) taxes. (Sec. 1109(g)(9), Tax Law) (TSB-M-06(6)S)

For special transitional provisions relating to sales in New York City of clothing and footwear costing $110 or more, see Important Notice N-09-12.

For a discussion of the state tax treatment of clothing and footwear, see ¶60-290 Clothing.

• *Machinery and equipment used in production*

An exemption from New York City sales and use tax is also provided for machinery and equipment used or consumed in manufacturing, processing, or production. (Sec. 1107(a), Tax Law)

The production exemption from city sales and use tax imposed in New York City includes purchases of the following parts, tools, supplies and services that are delivered in New York City:

— parts with a useful life of one year or less, tools or supplies for use or consumption directly and predominantly in the production process;

— parts with a useful life of one year or less, tools or supplies for use directly and predominantly in or on exempt telephone central office equipment or station apparatus, or comparable telegraph equipment; and

— the services of installing, repairing, maintaining or servicing exempt machinery, equipment, apparatus, parts, tools and supplies.

(Sec. 1105-B(d), Tax Law) (TSB-M-96(5)S)

This expanded exemption applies to any qualifying purchase in which delivery or transfer of possession of the parts, tools, supplies or services is made on or after September 1, 1996. This is so even if the purchase is made under a contract that was entered into before September 1, 1996.

Thus, on and after September 1, 1996, the New York City production exemption applies to:

(1) production machinery and equipment (which includes parts with a useful life of more than one year);

(2) qualifying telephone central office equipment or station apparatus, or comparable telegraph equipment (including parts with a useful life of more than one year);

(3) the parts, tools or supplies used directly and predominantly in or on such qualifying machinery, equipment or apparatus; and

(4) the services of installing, repairing, maintaining or servicing the exempt machinery, equipment, apparatus, parts, tools or supplies.

Purchases of these items and services are exempt from the combined sales or use tax rate when delivered in New York City on or after September 1, 1996.

> **CCH CAUTION:** The exemption does *not* apply to the services that are subject to tax under Sec. 1105(c)2, Tax Law. These services include producing, fabricating, processing, printing and imprinting performed on tangible personal property furnished by the customer.
>
> To claim the exemption, the purchaser should give the seller of the property or services a properly completed Form ST-121, *Exempt Use Certificate*.

• *Property used in live dramatic or musical productions*

Property used or consumed in the production of live dramatic or musical performances in a theater or other similar place of assembly in New York City is exempt from New York City sales and use taxes. The theater or other similar place of assembly must have a seating capacity of 100 or more rigidly anchored chairs; however, roof gardens, cabarets, or similar venues do not qualify. A "place of assembly" must have a stage in which scenery and scenic elements are used and an approved seating plan. At the time the tangible personal property is purchased, performances must be intended to be presented to the public on a regular basis of at least five per week for a period of at least two consecutive weeks. The content of each performance must be the same and admission must be charged. (Secs. 1107(d) and 1210(a)(5), Tax Law)

> **CCH CAUTION:** Services that are rendered with respect to exempt property and that are described in Sec. 1105(c)(2) and (3), Tax Laws, are also exempt. These services include producing, fabricating, processing, printing, and imprinting performed on tangible personal property furnished by the customer and installing, maintaining, servicing, or repairing tangible personal property not held for sale in the regular course of business. The exemption, however, does *not* apply to tangible personal property which is permanently affixed to or becomes an integral part of a structure, building, or real property.

• *Lower Manhattan exemptions*

Two sales and use tax exemptions exist for certain purchases of tangible personal property and services related to new commercial office space leases (as opposed to ground leases) of 10 years or more commencing on or after September 1, 2005. The exemptions differ based on the location of the leased premises in two specific eligible areas. The first area (Eligible Area A) consists of a broad area of lower Manhattan below City Hall. The second area (Eligible Area B) consists of the World Trade Center site, the World Financial Center, and the Battery Park City area. (Sec. 1115(ee), Tax Law) (TSB-M-05(12)S) The date by which a qualifying commercial lease must commence in Eligible Area A is September 1, 2020 and the exemption for Eligible Area A will expire on December 1, 2021. The date by which a qualifying commercial lease must commence in Eligible Area B is September 1, 2022 and the exemption for Eligible Area B will expire on December 1, 2023. (Sec. 1115(ee), Tax Law) (TSB-M-09(14)S; TSB-M-14(10)S) For additional information, see ¶60-460 Lease and Rentals.

• *Marine container terminals*

For a discussion of the state tax exemption in New York City for marine container terminals, see ¶60-740 Transportation.

• *Residential energy sources*

New York City may exempt or impose reduced rates on retail sales and uses of certain residential energy sources. (Sec. 1210(a)(3)(i), Tax Law) For a list of local sales and use tax rates on sales and installations of residential solar energy systems equipment, see Publication 718-S.

[¶560-015] NYC Tax Rates

The New York City sales and use tax is generally imposed at the rate of 4.5%. (Sec. 1107, Tax Law; Sec. 1210, Tax Law) (Important Notice N-09-12) Therefore, the combined state and local tax rate imposed in New York City is 8.875% This includes the 4% state tax, the Metropolitan Commuter Transportation District (MCTD) tax (see ¶60-110 Rates of Tax), and the 4.5% city tax.

• *Parking*

The New York City tax on parking is imposed at the rate of 6%. (Sec. 11-2002(g), N.Y.C. Adm. Code) In addition, there is an additional 8% tax imposed on parking in Manhattan (see ¶560-030). (Sec. 11-2049, N.Y.C. Adm. Code)

• *Services*

The separate New York City tax on certain services, such as barbering, health salons, manicuring, pedicuring, and credit rating and reporting services is also imposed at the rate of 4.5%. The tax on such services can be imposed through November 30, 2023. (Sec. 1107, Tax Law; Sec. 11-2002(h), N.Y.C. Adm. Code; Sec. 11-2040(a), N.Y.C. Adm. Code)

• *Residential energy sources*

New York City may exempt or impose reduced rates on retail sales and uses of certain residential energy sources. (Sec. 1210(a)(3)(i), Tax Law) For a list of local sales and use tax rates on sales and installations of residential solar energy systems equipment, see Publication 718-S, ¶65-914.

[¶560-020] NYC Registration

All persons required to collect the tax, or purchasing tangible personal property for resale, must be registered with the Department of Taxation and Finance. (Sec. 1134, Tax Law, Sec. 11-2017, N.Y.C. Adm. Code) Certificates of Registration and Certificates of Authority to collect tax are for both the statewide and local taxes.

See Reg. 525.3 relating to joint administration of state and local taxes.

[¶560-025] Returns and Payment of NYC Tax

Returns are filed with, and taxes are paid to, the Department of Taxation and Finance. Beginning with the March-May 2012 quarterly sales tax returns (due June 20, 2012) and the annual returns for sales tax years beginning March 1, 2012, sales of the following services in New York City are no longer reported on Part 3 of Schedule N, Taxes on Selected Sales and Services in New York City Only (quarterly ST-100.5, ST-810.5, annual ST-101.5): interior cleaning and maintenance services (regardless of the length of the contract); protective and detective services; and interior decorating and design services. The listed services must now be reported on the main sales tax return (quarterly ST-100 or ST-810, annual ST-101). The sales tax rates on these services are not affected by this change. (Important Notice N-12-3)

[¶560-030] New York City Parking Tax

The New York City parking tax is imposed at the rate of 6% on receipts from services providing parking, garaging or storing of motor vehicles. (Sec. 1107(c), Tax Law; Sec. 11-2002, N.Y.C. Adm. Code) For the corresponding state parking tax, see ¶60-665. The services of parking, garaging and storing motor vehicles within New York City are subject to the state tax, the New York City local tax, and the Metropolitan Commuter Transportation District (MCTD) tax. The borough of Manhattan has an additional 8% parking tax that applies unless the purchaser is a certified exempt resident. (TB-ST-679)

Receipts for parking, garaging, or storing motor vehicles paid to a homeowner's association by its members are not subject to tax. The exemption includes parking charges paid by members of a homeowner's association to a person leasing a parking facility from the homeowner's association. For the exemption to apply, the association's membership must consist exclusively of owners or residents of residential dwelling units and the association must own or operate the facility in which the services are provided or performed. (Sec. 11-2002, N.Y.C. Adm. Code) (TSB-M-01(3)S)

Manhattan parking tax.—An additional 8% tax is imposed on parking, garaging or storing of motor vehicles in New York County (Manhattan). Receipts for parking, garaging, or storing motor vehicles paid to a homeowner's association by its members are not subject to the tax. The exemption also applies to parking charges paid by members of a homeowner's association to a person leasing a parking facility from the homeowner's association. (Sec. 11-2049, N.Y.C. Adm. Code) (TSB-M-01(3)S)

New York County residents who park, garage or store motor vehicles that they own or lease (for a term of one year or more) on a monthly or longer-term basis are exempt from the 8% additional parking tax if they obtain exemption certificates, valid for up to two years, from the New York City Department of Finance. For the exemption to apply, the county resident must be a natural person who maintains his or her primary residence in New York County and registers the motor vehicle at such primary residence. A lease will not be regarded as a "lease for a term of one year or more" if it extends beyond a one-year period as a result of the right to exercise an option to renew or other like provision. (Sec. 11-2051, N.Y.C. Adm. Code; Rule Sec. 19-02; Rule Sec. 19-03)

In addition, facilities owned and operated by a city (or an agency or instrumentality of a city) or a public corporation, the majority of whose members are appointed by the city's chief executive officer, its legislative body, or both, are also exempt from tax. (Sec. 1107(c), Tax Law)

• *Record-keeping requirements*

Taxpayers who provide motor vehicle parking, garaging or storage services in New York City and who are required to pay state sales and use taxes, New York City temporary municipal assistance sales and use tax, and New York City sales and use tax on parking services in Manhattan are subject to special record-keeping requirements. (Sec. 1142-A, Tax Law; Reg. Part 538) (TSB-M-05(7)S) Organizations specified under Sec. 1116, Tax Law, are exempt from these provisions.

Each parking facility operator in Manhattan is required to furnish a ticket or other documentation to each purchaser of parking services, except as described below. The parking facility operator must keep the original ticket or a true copy of it. Each ticket issued must indicate the parking facility operator's name and the address of the parking facility. (TB-ST-679) The ticket must also indicate the date and time of entry of the purchaser's motor vehicle, and the date and time of exit, unless:

— the purchaser is charged a flat fee for the service based on time elapsed;

— the price indicated on the ticket is specified as a flat fee; and

— it is not the facility operator's practice to stamp the date and time on flat-fee tickets when the purchaser pays for the parking.

(TB-ST-679)

Tickets issued by a parking facility operator must be: consecutively numbered, or issued by a computer in a manner approved by the department. The parking facility operator must submit the proposed numbering scheme or the computer issuance procedure to the department at least 20 days prior to its use. A parking facility operator does not have to get prior approval if the operator: uses only one form and type of ticket at a facility, and the consecutive numbers of the tickets do not repeat for that facility in a calendar year. (TB-ST-679)

If a ticket is issued to a purchaser that allows parking for a period of a month or more, the ticket must indicate either the purchaser's name and signature, or the identification number assigned to the purchaser by the parking facility operator. However, persons who sell parking services on a monthly or longer-term basis, and who issue a computer access card or a pre-numbered decal or tag to a purchaser of the services, are not required to give a ticket to the purchaser or to keep copies of the ticket. For monthly or longer-term services, the parking facility operator must keep a list of the name, address, and signature of each purchaser of monthly or longer-term parking services, the valid period of the services, and the number of authorized vehicles entitled to the services. (TB-ST-679)

All persons required to collect tax on parking services in New York City (including parking facility operators in Manhattan) must report information regarding the location of each facility in New York City, as well as additional information for each facility located in Manhattan, when filing their sales and use tax returns. (TB-ST-679) They must report the:

— total weekday receipts for each month;

— total weekend receipts for each month;

— total monthly receipts for nonresident parking purchased on a monthly (or longer-term) basis for each month;

— total monthly receipts for Manhattan resident parking for each month; and

— quarterly or annual totals for each of the above categories.

(TB-ST-679)

Exemption from special recordkeeping requirements.—A Manhattan parking facility operator may apply to the department for an exemption from some or all of the additional recordkeeping requirements if the facility operator demonstrates that: the facility operator has limited annual liability (under $25,000 in annual sales and use tax in any twelve-month period); and the rules create undue hardship for the operator. The department will specify the period of time that an exemption is granted, and the exemption may be terminated or modified under certain conditions. (TB-ST-679)

Parking facility walkabouts.—An authorized employee of the department has the right to conduct a walkabout observation of a parking facility in Manhattan in a manner that does not unreasonably interfere with the operation of the parking facility or the parking facility operator. The person conducting the walkabout is not required to give advance notice of his or her intent to enter the premises for the purpose of conducting the walkabout. If the parking facility operator fails to keep and make records available or does not cooperate with the authorized employee conducting the walkabout, the department may estimate the amount of tax due. (TB-ST-679)

Returns.—In addition, taxpayers must file reports or schedules, or make separate entries on the return, for each separate place of business providing motor vehicle parking, garaging or storage services. The return must identify the specific location, address and licensed capacity of each place of business, include applicable license numbers and schedules of information prescribed by the Commissioner of Taxation and Finance and accompany the state and state-administered local sales and use tax returns. Taxpayers may be exempt from these requirements provided the annual limited liability incurred under Article 28, Tax Law, creates undue hardship.

Penalties.—In addition to other civil and criminal penalties, parking facility operators may also be subject to the following:

— Failure to keep any of the additional records required will subject the operator to a penalty of up to $500 per month or part of a month;

— An additional penalty may be imposed on any parking facility operator who fails to consent to a walkabout or who interferes with the conduct of the walkabout. The penalty for failure to consent or for interference is an amount of up to $500 for the first day of such failure to consent or interference, and up to $1,000 for each subsequent day of noncompliance. The total of these amounts may not exceed $10,000; and

— Any parking facility operator who willfully fails to include all of the information required on the ticket or other documentation will be guilty of a misdemeanor.

(Sec. 1145(g), Tax Law) (TB-ST-679)

For further discussion of motor vehicle parking, garaging and storage services and record-keeping requirements, see ¶60-570, ¶60-665, and ¶61-220 in the New York state "Sales and Use" division.

[¶560-040]
NYC SALES AND USE TAXES PENALTIES

[¶560-043] Criminal Penalties--Misdemeanors (NYC)

In addition to other penalties, any person who commits any of the following offenses is guilty of a misdemeanor:

(1) refusal to testify or to produce books or records in a material matter pending before the Tax Commission (Sec. 11-2026(c), N.Y.C. Adm. Code);

(2) failure to file a return (Sec. 11-2028(b), N.Y.C. Adm. Code);

(3) failure to make, cause to be made, give or cause to be given a willfully false return, certificate, affidavit, representation, information, testimony or statement required to be made;

(4) failure to file a required registration certificate;

(5) failure to display or surrender a certificate of authority;

(6) assignment or transferal of a certificate of authority without authority;

(7) willful failure to state tax separately on a bill, statement, memorandum or receipt upon which tax is required to be stated separately;

(8) willful failure to collect tax from a customer;

(9) failure to maintain required records.

• *Penalties upon conviction*

Any person convicted of any of the offenses listed above is subject to a maximum fine of $1,000, a maximum imprisonment term of one year, or both.

[¶580-100]
UTILITIES SUBJECT TO TAX

[¶580-102] "Utility" Defined

The term "utility" is defined as every person subject to the supervision of the Department of Public Service. (Sec. 11-1101(6), N.Y.C. Adm. Code)

In addition, for taxable periods beginning on or after August 1, 2002, if 80% or more of a taxpayer's gross receipts consist of charges for the provision of mobile telecommunications services to customers, the taxpayer is included under the definition of "utility" regardless of whether the taxpayer is supervised by the Department of Public Service. For purposes of this provision, the gross receipts of a taxpayer do not include the gross receipts of any other related or unrelated person. (Sec. 11-1101(6), N.Y.C. Adm. Code)

[¶580-103] Vendors of Utility Services

Every vendor of utility services in New York City is required to pay an excise tax to the Commissioner of Finance for the privilege of exercising its franchise or franchises, holding property or doing business in the city. (Sec. 11-1102(a), N.Y.C. Adm. Code)

For exemptions from the N.Y.C. utility excise tax see ¶580-201.

See ¶580-302 for exclusions from "gross income".

[¶580-104] "Vendor of Utility Services" Defined (NYC)

The term "vendor of utility services" is defined as every person that is not subject to the supervision of the Department of Public Service, and not otherwise a utility as defined in Sec. 11-1101(6), N.Y.C. Adm. Code, who (1) furnishes or sells gas, electricity, steam, water, or refrigeration, (2) furnishes or sells gas, electric, steam, water, refrigeration, or telecommunications services, or (3) operates omnibuses (whether or not such operation is on the public streets). (Sec. 11-1101(7), N.Y.C. Adm. Code) A person will be deemed a vendor of utility services regardless of whether the furnishing, selling, or operating of the utility product or service constitutes the main activity of the person or is merely incidental.

•*Landlord furnishing electricity to tenants*

Included within the definition of "vendors of utility services" are landlords who furnish or sell electricity to their tenants. In *Sage Realty Corp. v. O'Cleiracain*, the New York Supreme Court, Appellate Division, upheld the right of the City to include non-metered electricity in "income" subject to utility taxes, and held that including non-metered electricity as an element of rent for commercial rent tax purposes and in gross operating income for purposes of the utility tax was consistent with the intent of both statutes and did not result in impermissible double taxation. However, the legislature has subsequently enacted a provision permitting landlords to exclude from the measure of tax the gross operating income from certain sales of commodities or services to tenants (see ¶580-303).

For the text of *Sage Realty Corp. v. O'Cleiracain.*

[¶580-105] "Telecommunications Services" Defined (NYC)

The term "telecommunications services" is defined to mean telephony or telegraphy, or telephone or telegraph service, including, but not limited to, any transmission of voice, image, data, information, and paging, through the use of wire, cable, fiber-optic, laser, microwave, radio wave, satellite, or similar media, or any combination thereof. (Sec. 11-1101(9), N.Y.C. Adm. Code) The term also includes services that are ancillary to the provision of telephone service (such as, but not limited to, dial tone, basic service, directory information, call forwarding, caller-identification, and call waiting and the like), plus any equipment and services provided therewith.

The term does not include (1) services that alter the substantive content of the message received by the recipient from that sent, if the charges for those services are separately stated, (2) cable television services, or (3) qualified air safety and navigation services. (Sec. 11-1101(9), N.Y.C. Adm. Code)

For a discussion of bundled services and VoIP telephone service, see Finance Memorandum 07-1.

New York City's enhanced 911 emergency telephone system surcharge and wireless communications service surcharge are discussed at ¶580-310.

[¶580-200]

NYC UTILITIES TAX EXEMPTIONS

[¶580-201] NYC Utilities--Exclusions From Gross Income

For purposes of computing the utility excise tax, an exclusion from gross income is allowed for amounts received by railroads from the transportation of freight, and income received from the operation of hotels, multiple dwellings or office buildings by persons in the business of operating or leasing sleeping or parlor railroad cars, or of operating railroads other than street surface, rapid transit, subway or elevated railroads. (Sec. 11-1101(4), N.Y.C. Adm. Code)

For further information regarding the full extent of the exclusions from gross income, see ¶580-302.

[¶580-202] NYC Sales for Resale

An exemption from the excise tax is provided for the gross income of a utility that is derived from sales for resale to vendors of utility services who are validly subject to the New York City excise tax, except to the extent that the gross income is derived from sales of gas, electricity, steam, water, or refrigeration, or gas, electric, steam, water, or refrigeration service to a landlord for resale to its tenants as an incident to the landlord's activity of renting premises to the tenants. (Sec. 11-1102(b), N.Y.C. Adm. Code)

[¶580-300]

NYC UTILITIES TAX RATE AND BASIS

[¶580-301] NYC Utilities--In General

For the privilege of exercising a franchise or franchises, holding property or doing business in New York City, an excise tax is levied on the gross income or gross operating income of utilities, as the case may be, for the calendar month preceding each monthly return. The tax is imposed at the rate of 2.35% on the gross income of utilities which are subject to the supervision of the Department of Public Service (other than certain omnibus operators, discussed below). (Sec. 11-1102(a), N.Y.C. Adm. Code) Vendors of utility services (other than certain omnibus operators, discussed below) are subject to tax on their gross operating income at the rate of 2.35%. See ¶580-104 for the definition of "vendor of utility services"

•*Omnibus operators*

Persons subject to the jurisdiction of the Department of Public Service who are engaged in the operation of omnibuses that have a carrying capacity of more than seven persons (other than limited fare omnibuses) are taxed at the rate of 1.17% on the basis of their gross income. (Sec. 11-1102(a), N.Y.C. Adm. Code)

Operators of omnibuses that have a carrying capacity of more than seven persons but which are not subject to the supervision of the Department of Public Service are taxed at the rate of 1.17% on the basis of their gross operating income.

Omnibuses operated under contracts made pursuant to provisions of the education law, and not subject to the jurisdiction of the Department of Public Service, that are used exclusively for transporting children to and from schools are also subject to the excise tax at the rate of 1.17%.

For the tax applicable to certain school buses and vans.

Limited fare omnibus companies are subject to tax at the rate of one-tenth of 1% on gross income received from commuter service. Gross income received from all other sources by limited fare omnibus companies is taxed at the 1.17% rate. (Sec. 11-1102(d), N.Y.C. Adm. Code)

•*Railroads*

Common carriers subject to the supervision of the Department of Public Service, such as street surface, rapid transit, subway and elevated railroads, are taxed on the basis of gross income at the rate of 2.35%. (Sec. 11-1102(a), N.Y.C. Adm. Code)

Persons engaged in the business of operating or leasing sleeping and parlor railroad cars, or operating railroads other than street surface, rapid transit, subway or elevated railroads are subject to tax at the rate of 3.52% of gross income.

•*Partnerships*

If a partnership is subject to the utility tax as a utility or a vendor of utility services, no partner in the partnership is subject to the utility tax on the partner's distributive share of the partnership's gross income or gross operating income. If the partner is separately subject to the supervision of the Department of Public Service or is a utility or vendor of utility services based on activities exclusive of the partnership's activities, then that partner is subject to the utility tax only on its separate gross income or separate gross operating income. (Sec. 11-1102(f), N.Y.C. Adm. Code)

•*Ambulettes*

The driver of an omnibus or ambulette is not included in determining the carrying capacity of the vehicle. Omnibuses and ambulettes with a carrying capacity of seven or less passengers are not subject to the tax. (*Statement of Audit Procedure UTX – 2008-01*, New York City Department of Finance, March 21, 2008)

[¶580-302] "Gross Income" Defined (NYC)

The term "gross income" is defined as all receipts from sales made or services rendered in New York City. (Sec. 11-1101(4), N.Y.C. Adm. Code) Gross income includes receipts from the sale of residuals and by-products (except sale of real property), cash, credits and property of any kind or nature (whether or not the sale or service is rendered for profit), without any deduction on account of the cost of the property sold, the cost of material used, labor or services, delivery costs, any other costs, interest or discount paid, or any other expense.

Gross income also includes profits from the sale of securities, profits from the sale of real property growing out of the ownership, use of, or interest in the property, and profits from the sale of personal property (other than property of a kind which would be properly included in the inventory of the taxpayer if on hand at the close of the taxable period for which a return is made). Receipts from interest, dividends and royalties (without any deductions for any expense incurred in connection with the receipt), and gains or profits realized from any other source are also included in gross income.

• *Exclusions from gross income*

The following amounts received by a utility from sales made or services rendered are not included in taxable gross income (Sec. 11-1101(4), N.Y.C. Adm. Code):

(a) amounts received by railroads from the transportation of freight;

(b) receipts received from the operation of hotels, multiple dwellings or office buildings by persons in the business of operating or leasing sleeping or parlor railroad cars, or of operating railroads other than street surface, rapid transit, subway and elevated railroads;

(c) interest or dividends received from a corporation by persons in the business of operating or leasing sleeping or parlor railroad cars, or who operate railroads other than street surface, rapid transit, subway and elevated railroads;

(d) interest or dividends received from a corporation by persons who are subject to tax under the provisions of Sec. 186-a of the Tax Law;

(e) receipts from rents or rentals (except for rents or rentals derived from facilities which are used in the public service). However, rents and rental fees which are derived from other utilities with respect to the operation of terminal facilities (and received by persons in the business of operating railroads other than street surface, rapid transit, subways and elevated railroads) will not be included in gross income, except that amounts received which are in excess of a user proportion of New York City real property and special franchise taxes and expenses of maintenance and operation is deemed to be gross income subject to tax.

• *Mobile telecommunications services*

Gross income includes 84% of charges for the provision of mobile telecommunications services where the place of primary use of the services is within the territorial limits of the City. (Sec. 11-1101(4), N.Y.C. Adm. Code)

[¶580-303] "Gross Operating Income" Defined (NYC)

The term "gross operating income" is defined as receipts from sales made or services rendered in New York City by vendors of utility services. (Sec. 11-1101(5), N.Y.C. Adm. Code) Gross operating income includes cash, credits and property of any kind or nature (whether or not the sale made or service rendered is for profit), without any deduction on account of the cost of the property sold, the cost of the materials used, labor or other services, delivery costs, interest, discount paid or any other costs or expenses.

Vendors of utility services are taxed on their gross operating income. (Sec. 11-1102(a), N.Y.C. Adm. Code)

• *Landlord furnishing electricity to tenants*

Included within the definition of "vendors of utility services" are landlords who furnish or sell electricity to their tenants. In *Sage Realty Corp. v. O'Cleiracain* (see "N.Y. City—New Matters" division in Volume 7), the New York Supreme Court, Appellate Division, upheld the right of the City to include non-metered electricity in "income" subject to utility taxes, and held that including non-metered electricity as an element of rent for commercial rent tax purposes and in gross operating income for purposes of the utility tax was consistent with the intent of both statutes and did not result in impermissible double taxation. However, the legislature has subsequently enacted a provision permitting landlords to exclude from the measure of tax the gross operating income from certain sales of commodities or services to tenants.

Applicable retroactively to January 1, 1998, the gross operating income of a landlord may be excluded from the measure of tax to the extent the income is derived from sales to its tenants of gas, electricity, steam, water, or refrigeration, or gas, electric, steam, water, or refrigeration service, as an incident to its activity of renting premises to the tenants; provided, however, that with regard to its sales of gas, electricity, or steam, or gas, electric, or steam services, the exclusion applies only to the extent that the tax has been validly paid or accrued with respect to a prior sale of the commodities or services. (Sec. 11-1102(e), N.Y.C. Adm. Code) If the landlord purchases the commodities or services in a transaction the receipts from which are not subject to tax, and if the gross operating income from the landlord's resale of the commodities or services to tenants as an incident to renting premises to the tenants is subject to tax, then the gross operating income derived from the resale is conclusively presumed to be equal to the landlord's cost of the commodities or services. (Sec. 11-1101(5), N.Y.C. Adm. Code)

• *Mobile telecommunications services*

Gross operating income includes 84% of charges for the provision of mobile telecommunications services where the place of primary use of the services is within the territorial limits of the City. (Sec. 11-1101(5), N.Y.C. Adm. Code)

[¶580-310] NYC E-911 and Wireless Communications Surcharges

New York City imposes a monthly 911 surcharge of $1 per telephone access line on the customers of every telephone service supplier within the City. (Sec. 303, County Law; Sec. 11-2323, N.Y.C. Adm. Code) (*Important Notice NYC-02-2*)

In addition, through December 31, 2017, the City imposes a 911 wireless communications service surcharge of 30¢ per month. The surcharge is imposed on each wireless communications device, and it must be reflected on bills rendered for wireless communications service provided to a customer whose place of primary use is within the five boroughs of New York City. (Sec. 308-a, County Law; Sec. 11-2343, N.Y.C. Adm. Code) (*Important Notice NYC-02-2*)

The *place of primary use* is the primary business or residential street address of the customer, within the licensed service area of the wireless communications service provider. A customer's address under a service contract in effect on July 28, 2002 may, for the remainder of the contract term (excluding any extension or renewal), be treated as that customer's place of primary use for purposes of determining the wireless tax jurisdiction. (*Important Notice NYC-02-2*)

• *Wireless communications surcharges*

Effective December 1, 2017, pursuant to authorization in Sec. 186-g, Tax Law, a surcharge on wireless communications service is imposed at a rate of 30¢ per month on each wireless communications device in service during any part of the month, in addition to a surcharge on prepaid wireless communications service at a rate of 30¢ per retail sale. Wireless communications service suppliers are directed to add the surcharge to the billings of customers, and prepaid wireless communications sellers are directed to collect the surcharge from customers, beginning December 1, 2017. (Sec. 11-2351, N.Y.C. Adm. Code; Sec. 11-2352, N.Y.C. Adm. Code)

• *Voice over Internet Protocol (VoIP) service*

The monthly 911 surcharge of $1 per telephone access line, or equivalent, is imposed on Voice over Internet Protocol (VoIP) service. The surcharge must be added to bills by September 5, 2010. (Sec. 11-2323, N.Y.C. Adm. Code)

• *Telecommunications service suppliers*

All service suppliers (1) must separately state and add 911 surcharges to every customer's bill; (2) must provide an accounting to the City of the amounts billed and collected using Form NYC-E-911; and (3) are entitled to retain an administrative fee equal to 2% of its surcharge collections. (*Important Notice NYC-02-2*)

[¶580-500]

NYC UTILITIES TAX CREDITS

[¶580-502] Credit for NYC Sales and Use Tax Paid on Machinery and Equipment

In determining the gross income or gross operating income of public utilities, a taxpayer is allowed a credit against the amount of sales and compensating use taxes due with respect to the purchase or use by the taxpayer of machinery and equipment for use or consumption directly and predominantly in the production of steam for sale, by means of manufacturing, processing, generating, assembling, refining, mining, or extracting. The credit is also allowed with respect to the purchase by the taxpayer of telephone central office equipment, station apparatus, or comparable telegraph equipment for use directly and predominantly in receiving at destination, or initiating and switching, telephone or telegraph communication. The credit is not allowed for purchases of parts with a useful life of one year or less, or tools or supplies that are used in connection with the machinery, equipment, or apparatus referred to above. (Sec. 11-1105(b)(1), N.Y.C. Adm. Code)

The amount of credit will be limited to the amount of the sales and compensating use taxes paid during the taxable period covered by the return on which the credit is taken, less the amount of any credit or refund of the sales and compensating use taxes during that taxable period. If the credit exceeds the amount of tax payable for the taxable period in question, the excess amount will be refunded or credited. However, the excess amount will not be refunded or credited for vendors of utility services who are entitled to a credit and/or refund for sales and compensating use taxes under Chapters 5 and 6 ("Business Income Tax" and "City Business Tax") of the New York City Administrative Code. (Sec. 11-1105(b)(2), N.Y.C. Adm. Code)

Where the taxpayer receives a refund or credit of any tax imposed under Sec. 1107, Tax Law, for which the taxpayer has claimed a credit in a prior taxable period, the amount of the refund or credit will be added to the New York City utilities tax of the taxable period in which the refund or credit of tax under Sec. 1107 is received. (Sec. 11-1105(b)(3), N.Y.C. Adm. Code)

[¶580-503] Credit for Amount of Rebates and Discounts Issued to Nonresidential Energy Users and Energy Redistributors in Revitalization Areas (NYC)

A credit against the utility tax is allowed for the amount of special rebates and discounts which are required to be made by utilities to qualified nonresidential energy users on purchases of electricity or natural gas by the nonresidential users and to eligible redistributors of energy in revitalization areas. (Sec. 11-1105.1, N.Y.C. Adm. Code)

The credits must be claimed for the taxable period immediately succeeding the taxable period in which the rebates or discounts are made. If the credit exceeds the amount of tax payable for a particular taxable period, the excess amount will be refunded and considered to be an erroneous payment of tax. (Sec. 11-1105.1, N.Y.C. Adm. Code)

NEW YORK CITY INSURANCE

[¶585-100]
NYC INSURANCE TAXPAYERS AND RATES

[¶585-101] NYC Insurance Taxpayers and Rates--In General

The fire department tax is based on gross direct premiums from fire insurance less return premiums (Sec. 11-903, N.Y.C. Adm. Code).

[¶585-105] NYC Taxpayers

The fire department tax is imposed on every foreign and alien fire insurance corporation, association or individual which insures property against loss or damage by fire. (Sec. 11-903, N.Y.C. Adm. Code) A foreign insurer is any insurer, other than a mutual insurance company, which is incorporated or organized under the laws of any state other than New York. (Sec. 11-901, N.Y.C. Adm. Code) An alien insurer is any insurer incorporated or organized under the laws of any foreign nation, or of any province or territory not included under the definition of a foreign insurer.

[¶585-150] NYC Tax Rates

The fire department tax is levied at the rate of 2% of all gross direct premiums less return premiums. (Sec. 11-903, N.Y.C. Adm. Code)

[¶585-200]
NYC INSURANCE TAX COMPUTATION

[¶585-201] NYC Insurance Tax Computation--In General

The fire department tax is based on all gross direct fire insurance premiums, less return premiums, received during the preceding calendar year for insurance against property loss or damage by fire in New York City. (Sec. 11-903, N.Y.C. Adm. Code)

NEW YORK CITY PRACTICE AND PROCEDURE

[¶589-050]

NYC ADMINISTRATION OF TAXES

[¶589-064] NYC Administrative Documents

The New York City Department of Finance issues a number of administrative documents. They are discussed in the paragraphs below.

• *Letter rulings*

Taxpayers and other persons concerned with the relevance of statutory or administrative regulatory provisions administered by the New York City Department of Finance may request a letter ruling from the Office of Legal Affairs. (Rule Sec. 16-01) Letter rulings express the view of the Department of Finance concerning the applicability of city laws, regulations or other precedential material to the facts specified in the request. (Rule Sec. 16-05) Rulings are binding upon the Department of Finance only with respect to the person requesting the ruling, provided that the facts are the same as those stated in the request.

Rulings permitted.—Letter rulings may be requested with respect to substantive or procedural questions that may arise in response to a specified set of facts, including questions arising during an audit, examination of a tax return (see ¶589-102), or a claim for credit or refund. (see ¶589-224) Rulings will not be issued, however, with respect to the following:

— issues or facts regarding which a notice of determination or a notice of disallowance of a claim for refund or credit has been issued;

— issues or facts regarding which a taxpayer has been granted leave to appeal or where the Department of Finance is seeking or has been granted leave to appeal an adverse decision;

— issues that are clearly and adequately addressed by statutes, regulations, published rulings, or other official pronouncements of the Department of Finance;

— issues that, in accordance with a public pronouncement, are under study by the Department of Finance; or

— issues that require factual determinations.

(Rule Sec. 16-01)

Taxes administered by New York state.—Letter rulings will not be issued on questions pertaining to the following taxes that are administered by the New York State Department of Taxation and Finance on behalf of the City:

— the New York City personal income tax on residents;

— the New York City earnings tax on nonresidents;

— the New York City mortgage recording tax;

— the New York City leaded motor fuel tax; and

— New York City alcoholic beverage taxes.

Hypothetical facts.—The Department of Finance reserves the right not to issue rulings based on hypothetical facts.

Form of request.—Requests for letter rulings must be made on forms prescribed by the Department of Finance and accompanied by a non-refundable processing fee of $250. (Rule Sec. 16-02) Requests should contain the following information:

— the name, address, and identification number (social security or federal employer identification number) of the person requesting the ruling;

— the specific set of facts to which the request relates;

— the exact issue to be resolved;

— the names of all parties relative to the request; and

— copies of all relevant documents (i.e. deeds, contracts).

The taxpayer must state whether the request relates to a matter currently under audit or for which a notice of determination, or a notice of disallowance of claim for credit or refund has been issued, or for which there is a pending claim for credit or refund.

The request for a ruling must be submitted to the Office of Legal Affairs, Department of Finance, 345 Adams Street, 3rd Floor, Brooklyn, N.Y. 11201.

Withdrawal of request.—A taxpayer may withdraw a request for a ruling at any time within 30 days from the date of acknowledgment of the receipt of the request by the Department of Finance. After such 30-day period, a request may only be withdrawn with the written approval of the Office of Legal Affairs.

Time limitations.—Rulings will be mailed within 90 days of the receipt of a complete request; the 90-day period may be extended by the Commissioner for a period of up to 30 additional days. (Rule Sec. 16-06) Additional extensions of time will be permitted if agreed to in writing by the taxpayer and the Office of Legal Affairs.

Effect of ruling.—A ruling binds the Department of Finance only with respect to the person to whom the ruling is issued, so a taxpayer cannot rely on a ruling issued to another taxpayer. The conclusions of a ruling must be followed, however, by all the operating units of the Department where the factual situations are essentially the same. (Rule Sec. 16-05(a))

Revocation or modification of ruling.—Letter rulings may be revoked or modified at any time. Such revocation or modification will apply to all years open under relevant statutes, unless the Commissioner or the Commissioner's delegate limits the retroactive effect of the revocation or modification. (Rule Sec. 16-05) The revocation or modification will not usually be applied retroactively to the person requesting the ruling or to a taxpayer whose tax liability was directly involved in the ruling, provided:

— there has been no misstatement or omission of material facts;

— facts subsequently developed are not materially different from the facts on which the ruling was based;

— there has been no change in the applicable law;

— the ruling was originally issued with respect to a prospective or proposed transaction;

— the taxpayer directly involved in the ruling acted in good faith in reliance upon the ruling; and

— retroactive revocation would be to the taxpayer's detriment.

• *Exemption rulings*

Taxpayers claiming exemption from one or more income, excise, or property taxes must apply for an exemption ruling. The New York City income, excise, and property tax laws contain specific provisions exempting persons and property from tax

Organizations or persons exempt from federal or New York state taxes often qualify for exemption under the city's income or excise tax laws; however, exemption from federal or state taxes does not automatically result in a city exemption, and exemption from city real estate taxes does not automatically carry over to exempt a person from other city taxes. Thus, a not-for-profit membership corporation was held subject to the city's general corporation tax and commercial rent tax, notwithstanding its federal income tax exemption. (*Pan Am Athletic & Social Club, Inc. v. Commissioner of Finance*, 94 AD2d 606, 461 NYS2d 1017 (1st Dept. 1983))

> **CCH PLANNING NOTE:** *Having a federal income tax exemption letter helpful.*—Having a federal income tax exemption letter may expedite the city's ruling on exempt status for income and excise tax purposes.

A person or organization claiming exemption from a city tax is required to apply for it by submitting to the Office of Legal Affairs such information as will enable the Commissioner of Finance to rule on the applicant's claim. A corporation or other entity claiming exemption as a nonprofit organization is generally required to submit an affidavit setting forth:

— the type of organization;

— the purposes for which it was organized;

— its activities;

— the source and disposition of its income;

— whether any income or profit inures to the benefit of any private shareholder or individual; and

— any other facts that may affect its right to exemption.

Along with the affidavit, the following documents should also be submitted:

— a copy of the organization's bylaws;

— a copy of the certificate of incorporation;

— a balance sheet and statement of receipts and disbursements for the most recent year; and

— copies of any letters from the IRS or New York State Department of Taxation and Finance granting the organization exemption from federal or state taxes. Any prior exemption letters from New York City should also be included.

(Rule Sec. 7-05)

• *Policy bulletins*

The Commissioner of Finance issues policy bulletins, binding on taxpayers and the Department, which are intended to be used as a guide on the treatment of a particular item or issue.

• *Finance memoranda*

The Department of Finance issues finance memoranda to advise taxpayers and tax professionals of the Department's current position and/or procedures with respect to specific issues. The memoranda are merely advisory and explanatory in nature. They are not declaratory rulings or rules of the Department. They do not have legal force or effect, do not set precedent, and are not binding on taxpayers.

• *Statements of audit procedure*

The Audit Division of the Department of Finance makes statements of audit procedure available to the public.

[¶589-066] NYC Conformance to Federal Tax Law

Generally, the definition of any term under the federal income tax law is adopted when the same term is used, in a comparable context, in the New York City business tax laws. (Sec. 11-601, N.Y.C. Adm. Code)

[¶589-100]

NYC RETURN FILING AND PAYMENT OF TAX

[¶589-102] NYC Returns and Payments in General

The return filing and payment requirements for various taxes imposed by New York City are summarized in the paragraphs below. See also ¶589-104 (estimated tax payments), ¶589-106 (electronic filing), and ¶589-108 (payment methods).

• *Business corporation tax*

Generally, returns of calendar-year corporations are due by March 15 (April 15, for tax years beginning on or after January 1, 2016) following the taxable year. Similarly, fiscal-year corporations must file within $2^{1}/_{2}$ months ($3^{1}/_{2}$ months, for tax years beginning on or after January 1, 2016) after the end of the fiscal year. (Sec. 11-653(1)(a), N.Y.C. Adm. Code; Sec. 11-655, N.Y.C. Adm. Code)

The return is filed using Form NYC-2. (Instructions, Form NYC-2)

Extensions.—The Commissioner may grant a reasonable extension of time for filing returns and for payment of the tax. In the case of an annual return, an automatic six-month extension will be granted if an application is filed as prescribed, and a properly estimated tax is paid. (Sec. 11-655, N.Y.C. Adm. Code)

Tax will be deemed to be properly estimated if the amount paid is either:

—not less than 90% of the tax finally determined; or

—not less than the tax shown on the taxpayer's report for the preceding taxable year (provided the preceding year was a full 12-month year). (Sec. 11-656, N.Y.C. Adm. Code; Rule Sec. 11-89)

The Commissioner may grant up to two additional three-month extensions of time, provided good cause is shown. Applications for extension must be made prior to the expiration of the prior extension. (Rule Sec. 11-89)

Federal or New York State changes.—The Department of Finance has issued a memo explaining how to report federal and New York State changes; see Finance Memorandum 17-5.

• *Banking corporation tax*

Returns are required to be filed annually on or before the 15th day of the third month following the close of the taxable year (March 15 for calendar-year taxpayers). (Sec. 11-646(a), N.Y.C. Adm. Code; Rule Sec. 3-05)

The balance of any tax due is payable at the time of filing the return. (Sec. 11-647(a), N.Y.C. Adm. Code; Rule Sec. 3-06)

Extensions.—The Commissioner of Finance may grant a reasonable extension of time for filing returns whenever good cause exists. An automatic six-month extension of time is granted where the application for extension is filed with the Commissioner of Finance on or before the due date and is accompanied by the amount properly estimated as the tax due, provided that such amount is either not less than 90% of the actual tax liability or not less than the preceding taxable year's (12-month) liability. Further extensions of time not exceeding three months in the aggregate may be granted. (Sec. 11-646(c), N.Y.C. Adm. Code; Sec. 11-647(b), N.Y.C. Adm. Code; Rule Sec. 3-05)

Federal or New York State changes.—The Department of Finance has issued a memo explaining how to report federal and New York State changes; see Finance Memorandum 17-5.

• *Personal income, sales and use taxes*

The New York City personal income and sales and use taxes are administered by the New York State Department of Taxation and Finance and are reported as part of the state returns. See ¶ 89-102.

• *Unincorporated business tax*

On or before the 15th day of the fourth month (the third month, for taxpayers classified as partnerships for federal income tax purposes, applicable to tax years beginning after 2015) following the close of a taxable year, an unincorporated business income tax return must be made and filed by any unincorporated business having unincorporated business gross income, without any deduction for the cost of goods sold or services performed, of more than $95,000. (Sec. 11-514(a), N.Y.C. Adm. Code)

The balance of any tax shown on the face of the return, not previously paid as an installment of estimated tax, must be paid at the time of filing the return. (Sec. 11-514(a), N.Y.C. Adm. Code)

Extensions.—The Commissioner of Finance may grant a reasonable extension of time for filing any return, declaration, statement or other required document up to a period of six months. (Sec. 11-517, N.Y.C. Adm. Code)

Federal or New York State changes.—The Department of Finance has issued a memo explaining how to report federal and New York State changes; see Finance Memorandum 17-5.

• *Hotel occupancy tax*

Hotel operators must file a return with the Commissioner of Finance showing occupancies, rents, and taxes due for the quarterly periods ending on the last day of February, May, August, and November of each year. The returns, along with payment of the tax due, must be filed within 20 days after the end of the period covered. (Sec. 11-2504, N.Y.C. Adm. Code; Sec. 11-2505, N.Y.C. Adm. Code; Rule Sec. 12-07)

• *Commercial rent or occupancy tax*

Payment of tax accompanies the filing of quarterly returns, which are due on March 20, June 20, September 20, and December 20. The tax paid with the final return (June 20) must equal the amount by which the actual tax for the year exceeds the amounts previously paid. (Sec. 11-705, N.Y.C. Adm. Code; Sec. 11-706, N.Y.C. Adm. Code)

• *Tobacco tax*

Cigarette tax reports must be filed on or before the 15th day of each month covering the transactions for the preceding calendar month. (Sec. 11-1308, N.Y.C. Adm. Code; Rule Sec. 4-18) Wholesale dealers of other tobacco products are required to file returns on a monthly basis, due on the 20th day of each month following the end of the month or other interval covered by the return, unless the Commissioner otherwise prescribes a different interval. (Sec. 11-1302.1(g), N.Y.C. Adm. Code)

• *Utility tax*

Taxpayers subject to the New York City utility tax generally must file a return with the Commissioner of Finance on or before the 25th day of each month. However, a taxpayer whose city utility tax liability in the preceding calendar year was $100,000 or less is permitted to file returns semi-annually, rather than monthly, on the 25th day of the month following each taxable period. Payment of the tax must accompany the return. (Sec. 11-1104, N.Y.C. Adm. Code; Sec. 11-1105, N.Y.C. Adm. Code)

[¶589-104] NYC Estimated Payments and Returns

The estimated tax payments required for certain New York City taxes are summarized below.

• *Business corporation tax*

If a taxpayer's estimated tax can reasonably be expected to be more than $1,000 for the current taxable period, a declaration of estimated tax is required. The declaration is generally due June 15 for calendar-year taxpayers. As discussed below, however, later dates may be used by taxpayers that do not meet the estimated tax requirements until later in the calendar year. (Sec. 11-657, N.Y.C. Adm. Code)

Due dates.—Declarations are generally due on or before June 15 for calendar-year taxpayers. However, if the requirements (that is, expected tax liability exceeding $1,000) are first met after May 31 and before September 1, the declaration is due on or before September 15; if requirements are first met after September 1, the declaration is due on or before December 15. Instead of the declaration due on December 15, the taxpayer may elect to file a completed report, with payment of any unpaid balance of tax by February 15 of the succeeding year. (Sec. 11-657, N.Y.C. Adm. Code)

Corresponding dates apply to fiscal-year taxpayers. (Sec. 11-657(6), N.Y.C. Adm. Code)

Payments.—If the tax liability for the preceding tax year (the *second* preceding tax year, for amounts due on or after March 15, 2017) is more than $1,000, the first installment of estimated tax for the current year is 25% of the preceding year's tax (the *second* preceding year's tax, for amounts due on or after March 15, 2017), regardless of the taxpayer's income forecasts for the current year. (Sec. 11-658, N.Y.C. Adm. Code)

This advance payment may be used to offset estimated tax payments if they are required (see further discussion below). If not, the payment is credited against the tax due with the next annual report. Any overpayment of tax resulting from payment of the first installment is refunded with interest. (Sec. 11-658(5), N.Y.C. Adm. Code)

For calendar-year taxpayers filing declarations on or before June 15, the amount of estimated tax is paid in three equal installments (after deducting the amount of any first installment based on the preceding year's tax liability) on June 15, September 15, and the following December 15. If the declaration is first required to be filed by September 15, any estimated tax due (after deducting the amount of the first installment) is paid in two equal installments on September 15 and December 15. If the declaration is not required to be filed before September 15, any estimated tax due (after deducting the first installment) is paid at the time of filing the declaration. Corresponding dates apply to fiscal-year taxpayers. (Sec. 11-658, N.Y.C. Adm. Code)

- *Banking corporation tax*

For banking corporations, the requirements for estimated tax declarations and payments parallel those described above for the general corporation tax. (Sec. 11-644, N.Y.C. Adm. Code; Sec. 11-645, N.Y.C. Adm. Code; Rule Sec. 3-06)

- *Unincorporated business tax*

An unincorporated business must make a declaration of estimated tax if its estimated tax can reasonably be expected to exceed $3,400. (Sec. 11-511(a), N.Y.C. Adm. Code)

The due dates for the filing of declarations of estimated unincorporated business tax are as follows:

(1) if the unincorporated business first meets the requirements for filing a declaration of estimated tax on or before April 1, the declaration must be filed by April 15;

(2) if the requirements are met after April 1 and before June 2, the declaration must be filed by June 15;

(3) if the requirements are met after June 1 and before September 2, the declaration must be filed by September 15; and

(4) if the requirements are met after September 1, the declaration must be filed by January 15 of the succeeding year.

(Sec. 11-511(c), N.Y.C. Adm. Code)

For fiscal year taxpayers, the corresponding months of the fiscal year are substituted. (Sec. 11-511(g), N.Y.C. Adm. Code)

A final return accompanied by full payment of the amount of tax due may be filed by February 15 in lieu of a declaration otherwise due by January 15. (Sec. 11-511(f), N.Y.C. Adm. Code)

Payment deadlines.—The dates for payment of New York City unincorporated business estimated taxes are as follows:

(1) if the declaration is filed by April 15, estimated tax is payable in four equal installments, the first one with the declaration and the remaining three by June 15, September 15 and January 15;

(2) if the declaration is filed after April 15 and not after June 15, the tax is payable in three equal installments, the first with the declaration, and the others by September 15 and January 15;

(3) if the declaration is filed after June 15 and not after September 15, the tax is payable in two equal installments, one with the declaration and the other by January 15; and

(4) if the declaration is filed after September 15, the tax is payable in full with the declaration.

(Sec. 11-512(a), N.Y.C. Adm. Code)

Fiscal year taxpayers substitute the corresponding months of the fiscal year. (Sec. 11-512(d), N.Y.C. Adm. Code)

[¶589-106] NYC Electronic Filing

New York City personal income tax is reported and paid in conjunction with a taxpayer's state personal income tax, and both are administered by the New York State Department of Taxation and Finance. The state's program for electronic filing of personal income taxes is discussed at ¶89-106.

For purposes of various New York City taxes, including the business corporation tax and the unincorporated business tax, the New York City Commissioner of Finance is authorized to establish programs or systems whereby taxpayers may elect to file and sign designated returns, reports, or other forms electronically. (Rule Sec. 17-03)

Specific electronic filing programs implemented by the New York City Department of Finance are discussed below.

• *New York City business tax electronic filing programs*

New York City hotel room occupancy tax returns may be filed by telephone or computer using the Department of Finance's Telefile or PCAccess program. (Rule Sec. 12-07; Rule Sec. 17-03) Tax payments may be made in conjunction with such returns through authorized electronic debits. Forms, instructions, and the downloadable PCAccess program are available at the following Internet address: www.ci.nyc.ny.us/html/dof/html/hoteltax.html.

Business Tax e-File (BTeF). The Department of Finance participates in four of the IRS Fed/State Modernized e-File programs allowing New York City corporations, businesses, and individuals to electronically file their federal and NYC business tax returns together: 1120, 1065, 1040 and 1041. (Business Tax e-File (BTeF))

In addition, the following forms must be filed electronically: NYC-202, NYC-202S, NYC-202EIN, NYC-2, NYC-2A, NYC-3A, NYC-3L, NYC-4S, NYC-4SEZ, NYC-204, NYC-204EZ, and NYC-EXT (for corporations and partnerships). (FAQs for Mandated E-Filing)

The mandate applies to:

(1) tax preparers who have prepared more than 100 documents and used tax software to prepare corporate and partnership tax documents. The 100 documents (or more) should consist of all documents completed by the members/employees of a company (including all locations). The count should include extensions, amended and prior year returns, and estimated tax payments.

(2) corporations or partnerships that do not use a tax preparer and use software approved by the NYC Department of Finance to file returns and/or extensions.

Tax preparers who meet the mandate criteria cannot opt out of the electronic filing mandate. Taxpayers wanting to opt out can request a hardship waiver. (FAQs for Mandated E-Filing)

Authorization to e-file. To become authorized to file NYC business tax returns electronically, a tax preparer must (1) use software that has been approved for e-file by the Department of Finance, and (2) be authorized to e-file corporation, partnership, or individual tax returns by the IRS.

For taxpayers, the taxpayer must: use software that has been approved for e-file by the Department of Finance; and be authorized to e-file corporation or partnership tax returns by the IRS; or use a tax preparer who is an IRS authorized e-file provider. (BTeF FAQs)

Additional FAQs. For additional information, see the following Department of Finance sites:

http://www1.nyc.gov/site/finance/taxes/tax-professionals-business-tax-e-file.page

http://www1.nyc.gov/assets/finance/downloads/pdf/10pdf/mandatory_efile.pdf

http://www1.nyc.gov/site/finance/taxes/tax-btef-faq.page

[¶589-108] NYC Payment Methods

The New York City Commissioner of Finance is authorized to establish programs whereby taxpayers and other persons required to collect and pay over any tax may do so by electronic means. (Rule Sec. 17-03(b))

Under existing electronic filing programs, certain New York City business tax payments may be made electronically in conjunction with the electronic filing of forms. (see ¶589-106)

• *Sales and use, motor fuel, and petroleum business taxes*

The Department of Taxation and Finance has implemented a program requiring tax payments by electronic fund transfers (EFT) or certified check by state and local taxpayers whose sales and use taxes, prepaid sales and use taxes on motor fuel and diesel motor fuel, or petroleum business taxes exceed certain statutory thresholds. (Sec. 10, Tax Law) The EFT payment provisions for these New York City taxes are the same as the state provisions. (see ¶89-108)

• *Personal income tax*

All taxpayers (other than health care providers) who are required to deduct and withhold an aggregate of $35,000 or more of New York state personal income tax, New York City personal income tax, New York City income tax surcharge, City of Yonkers income tax, or nonresident city earnings tax (repealed effective July 1, 1999) must pay the tax by electronic funds transfer (EFT) on or before the due date to a bank, banking house, or trust company designated by the Commissioner of Taxation and Finance. (Sec. 9(b), Tax Law) The EFT payment provisions for these New York City taxes are the same as the state provisions. (see ¶89-108)

[¶589-110] NYC Mailing Rules and Legal Holidays

Timely mailing is treated as timely filing. This means that if a tax return, payment, claim, notice, petition or other document is deposited in the mail, postage prepaid and properly addressed, the U.S. Postal Service postmark date stamped on the envelope is deemed the date of delivery, i.e., if the Department of Finance receives the item after the due date, it is timely filed or paid if the date stamped by the U.S. Postal Service is not later than the due date. (Sec. 11-531(a), N.Y.C. Adm. Code; Sec. 11-682(1), N.Y.C. Adm. Code; Sec. 11-717(d), N.Y.C. Adm. Code; Sec. 11-819(d), N.Y.C. Adm. Code; Sec. 11-1115(d), N.Y.C. Adm. Code; Sec. 11-1215(d), N.Y.C. Adm. Code; Sec. 11-1315(d), N.Y.C. Adm. Code; Sec. 11-1415(a), N.Y.C. Adm. Code; Sec. 11-1517(d), N.Y.C. Adm. Code; Sec. 11-2116(d), N.Y.C. Adm. Code; Sec. 11-2216(d), N.Y.C. Adm. Code; Sec. 11-2416(d), N.Y.C. Adm. Code; Sec. 11-2517(d), N.Y.C. Adm. Code)

A similar rule applies to postmarks not made by the U.S. Postal Service (i.e., office-metered mail) if the item is received within five days of the postmarked date. If the item is received after five days, it is considered timely filed only if the sender establishes that the delay was the fault of the post office. For petitions or other documents required to be filed with the New York City Tax Appeals Tribunal, however, the five-day rule does not apply. Instead, a document bearing a postmark not made by the U.S. Postal Service that is received after the due date is timely only if it is received within the time ordinarily required for a U.S. postmarked item to reach its destination. Where an envelope has both a U.S. and private postmark, the private postmark is disregarded and the U.S. postmark controls the date of mailing. (Rule Sec. 17-01(b); Rule Sec. 1-17(b))

If any document is sent by registered mail, the date of registration is deemed the date of delivery. Similarly, if the document is sent by certified mail, the date postmarked on the sender's receipt is deemed the date of delivery. (Rule Sec. 17-01(c); Rule Sec. 1-17(c)) If a document is sent by certified mail but without an officially dated sender's receipt, the date of the postmark on the envelope is controlling. (*Matter of Liebman*)

• *Private delivery services*

A document delivered by a designated private delivery service is deemed to be filed on the date recorded or marked by the private delivery service. Accordingly, for City tax purposes, deliveries by designated private delivery services are comparable to deliveries by the United States Post Office. (Sec. 11-531(a), N.Y.C. Adm. Code; Sec. 11-682(1), N.Y.C. Adm. Code; Sec. 11-717(f), N.Y.C. Adm. Code; Sec. 11-819(f), N.Y.C. Adm. Code; Sec. 11-1115(f), N.Y.C. Adm. Code; Sec. 11-1215(f), N.Y.C. Adm. Code; Sec. 11-1315(f), N.Y.C. Adm. Code; Sec. 11-1415(f), N.Y.C. Adm. Code; Sec. 11-2116(f), N.Y.C. Adm. Code; Sec. 11-2416(f), N.Y.C. Adm. Code; Sec. 11-2517(f), N.Y.C. Adm. Code)

See also Finance Memorandum 02-4.

• *Department mailing*

Notices from the Department of Finance may be mailed to the taxpayer at the address given in the last return filed, unless the taxpayer has given notice of a change of address. (Sec. 11-531(b), N.Y.C. Adm. Code; Sec. 11-682(2), N.Y.C. Adm. Code; Sec. 11-717(a), N.Y.C. Adm. Code; Sec. 11-819(a), N.Y.C. Adm. Code; Sec. 11-1115(a), N.Y.C. Adm. Code; Sec. 11-1215(a), N.Y.C. Adm. Code; Sec. 11-1315(a), N.Y.C. Adm. Code; Sec. 11-1415(a), N.Y.C. Adm. Code; Sec. 11-1517(a), N.Y.C. Adm. Code; Sec. 11-2116(a), N.Y.C. Adm. Code; Sec. 11-2216(a), N.Y.C. Adm. Code; Sec. 11-2416(a), N.Y.C. Adm. Code; Sec. 11-2517(a), N.Y.C. Adm. Code) Mailing to the last known address is presumptive evidence of receipt by the person to whom the item is addressed. Evidence of mailing is often provided by the Form 3877 mail manifold maintained by the Department of Finance.

Any period of time that is determined by the giving of notice begins to run from the date of mailing. For example, the period of time in which to file a petition for hearing or judicial review runs from the date of mailing by the Department, not the date of receipt by the taxpayer. (Sec. 11-680(2), N.Y.C. Adm. Code; Sec. 11-681(1), N.Y.C. Adm. Code)

• *Saturday, Sunday, or legal holiday*

When the last day prescribed for performing any act falls on a Saturday, Sunday, or legal holiday in New York state, the performance of the act (including mailing) is timely if done on the next succeeding day that is not a Saturday, Sunday, or legal holiday. (Sec. 11-531(c), N.Y.C. Adm. Code; Sec. 11-682(3), N.Y.C. Adm. Code; Sec. 11-717(e), N.Y.C. Adm. Code; Sec. 11-819(e), N.Y.C. Adm. Code; Sec. 11-1115(e), N.Y.C. Adm. Code; Sec. 11-1215(e), N.Y.C. Adm. Code; Sec. 11-1315(e), N.Y.C. Adm. Code; Sec. 11-1415(e), N.Y.C. Adm. Code; Sec. 11-1517(e), N.Y.C. Adm. Code; Sec. 11-2116(e), N.Y.C. Adm. Code; Sec. 11-2216(e), N.Y.C. Adm. Code; Sec. 11-2416(e), N.Y.C. Adm. Code; Sec. 11-2517(e), N.Y.C. Adm. Code)

[¶589-130]

NYC AUDITS

[¶589-142] NYC Record Maintenance and Production

The New York City Department of Finance has issued some general rules regarding the creation and retention of books and records for purposes of the corporate business taxes, unincorporated business tax, hotel occupancy tax, commercial rent tax, cigarette tax, utility tax, and insurance tax. (Rule Sec. 26-01; Rule Sec. 26-02; Rule Sec. 26-03; Rule Sec. 26-04; Rule Sec. 26-05; Rule Sec. 26-06; Rule Sec. 26-07)

• *General requirements*

Taxpayers are required to maintain all records that are necessary to a determination of the correct tax liability, and all such records must be made available on request by the Department of Finance. The records must include permanent books of account or record (including inventories where applicable) as are sufficient to establish the amount of gross income, deductions, credits, and other matters required to be shown on any tax return. (Rule Sec. 26-03)

If a taxpayer retains records in both machine-sensible and hard copy formats, the taxpayer must make the records available to the Department in machine-sensible format upon the Department's request. However, the Department may request hard copy printouts instead of retained machine-sensible records at the time of examination. (Rule Sec. 26-03)

These rules do not prohibit a taxpayer from demonstrating tax compliance with traditional hard copy documents or reproductions thereof. In addition, taxpayers are not required to construct machine-sensible records other than those created in the ordinary course of business. A taxpayer that does not create the electronic equivalent of a traditional paper document in the ordinary course of business is not required to construct such a record for tax purposes. Computer printouts that are created for validation, control, or other temporary purposes need not be retained. (Rule Sec. 26-03; Rule Sec. 26-04)

These rules do not relieve taxpayers of the responsibility to retain hard copy records that are created or received in the ordinary course of business as required by existing law and regulations. In addition, taxpayers should make periodic checks on all records being retained for use by the Department. If any required records are subsequently lost, destroyed, damaged, or found to be incomplete or materially inaccurate, the taxpayer must recreate the files within a reasonable period of time. (Rule Sec. 26-03)

A taxpayer may contract with a third-party to provide custodial or management services with respect to the records. However, the contract will not relieve the taxpayer of its responsibilities under these rules. (Rule Sec. 26-05)

• *Machine-sensible record requirements*

Machine-sensible records used to establish tax compliance must contain sufficient transaction-level information so that the details underlying the records can be identified and made available to the Department upon request. At the time of examination, the retained records must be capable of being retrieved and converted to a standard record format as specified by the Department. (Rule Sec. 26-04)

When a taxpayer uses electronic data interchange processes and technology, the level of record detail, in combination with other records related to the transaction, must be equivalent to that contained in an acceptable paper record. The retained records should contain such information as vendor name, invoice date, product description, quantity purchased, price, amount of tax, and indication of tax status, where applicable. Codes may be used to identify some or all of the data elements, as long as the taxpayer provides a method allowing the Department to interpret the coded information.

Specific documentation for all retained files must be kept, and any change to a data processing system that affects the accounting system must be documented in order to preserve an accurate chronological record. The record should include any changes to software or systems and any changes to the formats of files. (Rule Sec. 26-04)

In conjunction with meeting the above requirements, a taxpayer may create files solely for the Department's use. For example, a taxpayer may create a file that contains the transaction-level detail from the database management system. The taxpayer should document the process that created the separate file to show the relationship between the file and the original records. (Rule Sec. 26-05)

• *Alternative storage for hard copy documents*

Taxpayers may convert hard copy documents received or produced in the normal course of business to microfilm, microfiche, or another storage-only imaging system and may discard the original hard copy documents. All data stored on a such a system must be maintained and arranged in a manner that permits the location of any particular record. In addition, upon request by the Department, the taxpayer must provide facilities and equipment for reading, locating, and reproducing such documents. (Rule Sec. 26-06)

• *Tax-specific provisions*

In addition to the general rules discussed above, specific recordkeeping requirements are prescribed by statute and rule for various New York City taxes, as discussed below.

Unincorporated business tax.—Taxpayers must keep permanent books of account or records, including inventories, sufficient to establish the amount of gross income, deductions, credits, and other matters required to be shown on any return. Taxpayers must use a system of accounting that will enable the Commissioner to ascertain whether liability for tax is incurred and, if so, the correct amounts required to be reported. Books and records must be retained so long as their contents may become material in the administration of the unincorporated business tax, and they must be kept at locations accessible to representatives from the Department of Finance. (Rule Sec. 28-19)

Hotel occupancy tax.—Hotel operators must keep records of every occupancy, of all rent paid, charged, or due thereon, and of the tax payable. The records must be available for inspection at any time upon demand by the Commissioner and generally must be preserved for three years. However, the Commissioner may require that the records be kept longer or may consent to their destruction before the end of the three-year period. (Sec. 11-2503, N.Y.C. Adm. Code; Rule Sec. 12-14)

Commercial rent tax.—Landlords and tenants of taxable premises must keep records identifying the tenant, the rent required to be paid, the rent paid and received, the location of the premises, and the periods of commencement and termination of every occupancy. The records must be available for inspection at any time upon demand by the Commissioner and must be preserved for three years, except that leases or agreements that fix the rents or rights of a tenant must be kept for a period of three years after the expiration of the tenancy thereunder. In addition, the Commissioner may require that the records be kept longer or may consent to their destruction before the end of the three-year period. (Sec. 11-707, N.Y.C. Adm. Code; Rule Sec. 7-11)

Tobacco tax.—All invoices and records must be maintained for a period of three years, subject to the use and inspection of the Commissioner. (Sec. 11-1307, N.Y.C. Adm. Code) Additional record maintenance requirements with respect to the tobacco tax are discussed at ¶ 555-604.

Real property transfer tax.—Grantors and grantees are required to keep complete records of conveyances of real property or economic interests therein, including copies of the contract of sale, the title report, and the closing statement. The records must be available for inspection at any time upon demand by the Commissioner and generally must be preserved for three years. However, the Commissioner may require that the records be kept longer or may consent to their destruction before the end of the three-year period. (Rule Sec. 23-11)

Utility tax.—Business records must be maintained and offered for inspection at any time upon demand by the Commissioner. Such records generally must be preserved for three years. However, the Commissioner may require that the records be kept longer or may consent to their destruction before the end of the three-year period. (Sec. 11-1103, N.Y.C. Adm. Code)

[¶589-160]

NYC COLLECTION OF TAX

[¶589-164] NYC Assessment of Delinquent Tax

Before collection and enforcement actions can be begin, the taxpayer's liability for tax (i.e. the amount properly owed) must be determined. The assessment process fixes that liability.

Typically, the taxpayer's liability is assessed by the filing of a tax return reporting the tax owed. (see ¶ 589-102) Subject to audit and review, the amount of tax that a return shows due, or what would have been due except for a mathematical error, is deemed assessed on the date of filing the return.

If a taxpayer fails to file a return, or if the Commissioner of Finance considers the return to be incorrect or insufficient, and determines that there is a deficiency of tax, the Department of Finance mails a notice of the claimed deficiency to the taxpayer. The Department uses the term "notice of determination" to describe the statutory notice for all income and excise taxes.

Deficiency defined.—A deficiency is defined as the amount of tax imposed (the correct tax) less the amount shown as tax on the taxpayer's returns, and less any amounts previously assessed (or collected without assessment) as a deficiency, plus the amount of any rebates. (Sec. 11-521(g), N.Y.C. Adm. Code; Sec. 11-672(8), N.Y.C. Adm. Code)

> **CCH EXAMPLE:** *Calculation of deficiency.*—If the tax imposed is $1,200 and the tax shown on a taxpayer's return is $900, the deficiency would be $300.

Rebate defined.—The term rebate means an abatement, credit, refund, or other repayment made on the grounds that the tax was less than the amount shown due on the return. (Sec. 11-521(g), N.Y.C. Adm. Code; Sec. 11-672(8), N.Y.C. Adm. Code)

> **CCH EXAMPLE:** *Calculation of rebate.*—The amount of a general corporation tax shown due on the return is $900, and the amount paid as estimated taxes for the year is $1,200. A $300 refund is made. This refund is not a rebate because it is not made on the grounds that the tax imposed is less than the amount shown

due on the return. If, however, the Commissioner of Finance determines that the tax imposed is $800 and refunds $400, $100 of the refund is a rebate since it is made on the grounds that the tax imposed ($800) is less than the tax shown on the return ($900). This rebate is taken into account in arriving at the amount of any deficiency subsequently determined.

• *Notice of deficiency*

Notice of the deficiency (known as a notice of determination) must be sent to the taxpayer. The corporate and unincorporated business tax laws require that the notice be mailed by certified or registered mail to the taxpayer's last known address. If the Commissioner of Finance has received notice that a person is acting for the taxpayer in a fiduciary capacity, a copy of the notice must also be mailed to the fiduciary. (Sec. 11-521(a), N.Y.C. Adm. Code; Sec. 11-672(1), N.Y.C. Adm. Code) For a discussion of mailing rules and legal holidays, see ¶589-110.

The notice of determination becomes an assessment, fixing the amount owed, unless the taxpayer challenges the liability by timely filing a request for conciliation (which suspends the running of the period of limitations for the filing of a petition) (see ¶589-230) or a petition for hearing. The petition generally must be filed within 90 days from the mailing date of the notice of determination, the mailing date of the conciliation decision or the date of the Commissioner's confirmation of the discontinuance of the conciliation proceeding. For the corporate business taxes (i.e., general corporation and banking corporation) and the unincorporated business tax, if the notice of determination or conciliation decision is addressed to a person outside of the United States, the period is 150 days instead of 90 days. (Sec. 11-521(b), N.Y.C. Adm. Code; Sec. 11-672(2), N.Y.C. Adm. Code; Sec. 11-708, N.Y.C. Adm. Code; Sec. 11-810, N.Y.C. Adm. Code; Sec. 11-906, N.Y.C. Adm. Code; Sec. 11-1206, N.Y.C. Adm. Code; Sec. 11-1310, N.Y.C. Adm. Code; Sec. 11-1406, N.Y.C. Adm. Code; Sec. 11-2107, N.Y.C. Adm. Code; Sec. 11-2206, N.Y.C. Adm. Code; Sec. 11-2407, N.Y.C. Adm. Code; Sec. 11-2506, N.Y.C. Adm. Code) Failure to timely file a petition for hearing makes the amount asserted in the notice of determination a final and irrevocable assessment (with certain exceptions).

No assessment can be made and, therefore, no levy or collection action can commence (except in jeopardy situations) until:

(1) a notice of determination has been mailed to the taxpayer and the time for filing a petition has expired;

(2) the decision of the New York City Tax Appeals Tribunal after hearing on a timely filed petition has become final (i.e., the decision is issued and the time to appeal to the courts has expired); or

(3) the taxpayer has waived the restrictions on assessment and collection of the deficiency, in whole or in part, by a signed notice in writing filed with the Commissioner.

(Sec. 11-521, N.Y.C. Adm. Code; Sec. 11-672, N.Y.C. Adm. Code)

The New York City Department of Finance has issued a statement of audit procedure that provides guidance to its auditors and employees on how to satisfy notification requirements for all taxes due or additional taxes due using the Professional Audit Support System (PASS) and the FAIRTAX computer system. (*Statement of Audit Procedure PP-2008-06*, New York City Department of Finance, March 13, 2008)

• *Limitations period*

The various city income and excise tax laws contain specific provisions governing the time within which the Commissioner of Finance must act to assess a deficiency of tax. Any deficiency assessed and collected after the pertinent period of limitations is recoverable as an overpayment. (Sec. 11-526(d), N.Y.C. Adm. Code; Sec. 11-677(4), N.Y.C. Adm. Code)

The general rule is that assessment of a deficiency must be made within three years from the filing date of the return for the tax year to which the deficiency relates. (Sec. 11-523(a), N.Y.C. Adm. Code; Sec. 11-674(1), N.Y.C. Adm. Code; Sec. 11-717(b), N.Y.C. Adm. Code; Sec. 11-819(b), N.Y.C. Adm. Code; Sec. 11-906(a), N.Y.C. Adm. Code; Sec. 11-1115(b), N.Y.C. Adm. Code; Sec. 11-1215(b), N.Y.C. Adm. Code; Sec. 11-1315(b), N.Y.C. Adm. Code; Sec. 11-1415(b), N.Y.C. Adm. Code; Sec. 11-2116(b), N.Y.C. Adm. Code; Sec. 11-2416(b), N.Y.C. Adm. Code; Sec. 11-2517(b), N.Y.C. Adm. Code) For corporate and unincorporated business tax purposes, where the return was filed before the statutory due date, the assessment must be made within three years of the due date. (Sec. 11-523(b), N.Y.C. Adm. Code; Sec. 11-674(2), N.Y.C. Adm. Code)

CCH EXAMPLE: Determining period of assessment.—Corporation A files its general corporation tax return for the calendar year 1992 (due date March 15, 1993) on March 3, 1993. The period for assessment expires on March 15, 1996. If the corporation had an extension of time to file until June 15, 1993, and filed its return on June 2, 1993, the period within which an assessment may be made expires on June 2, 1996.

No return or fraudulent return.—An assessment may be made at any time if no return is filed, or if the taxpayer files a willfully false or fraudulent return with intent to evade tax. For a discussion of civil penalties and criminal penalties, see ¶589-206 and ¶589-208, respectively. Filing a correct amended return does not start the three-year period of limitations if the original return was false or fraudulent.

Extensions.—The taxpayer and the Commissioner of Finance may extend the time for making an assessment by written agreement executed before the time expires, and the extended period may be further extended by subsequent written agreements made before the end of the period previously agreed on. (Sec. 11-523(c)(2), N.Y.C. Adm. Code; Sec. 11-674(3)(b), N.Y.C. Adm. Code; Sec. 11-1115(c), N.Y.C. Adm. Code; Sec. 11-1215(c), N.Y.C. Adm. Code; Sec. 11-1315(c), N.Y.C. Adm. Code; Sec. 11-1415(c), N.Y.C. Adm. Code; Sec. 11-2116(c), N.Y.C. Adm. Code; Sec. 11-2416(c), N.Y.C. Adm. Code; Sec. 11-2517(c), N.Y.C. Adm. Code)

CCH PLANNING NOTE: Consolidation of a number of years into one audit.—Extension agreements allow the consolidation of a number of years into one audit examination, saving both the Department of Finance and taxpayer time, effort, and money. Extension agreements also give the parties additional time to resolve disputes without the issuance of a statutory notice of deficiency. They also forestall the issuance of estimated assessments that may greatly exaggerate taxpayer's liability.

• *Suspension of running of period*

After a notice of determination is mailed, the running of the period of limitations on assessment or collection of tax is suspended for the time during which assessment or collection of the tax by levy is prohibited. (Sec. 11-523(e), N.Y.C. Adm. Code; Sec. 11-674(5), N.Y.C. Adm. Code) This is the time during which the taxpayer can file a petition for hearing (e.g., 90 days; see ¶589-234), and if a petition is filed, the taxpayer will have an additional four months starting from the date of mailing of the N.Y.C. Tax Appeals Tribunal's decision. During this four-month period, the taxpayer can apply for judicial review of the decision. (Sec. 11-521(c), N.Y.C. Adm. Code; Sec. 11-672(3), N.Y.C. Adm. Code) (See ¶589-236)

> *CCH EXAMPLE: Determining suspension of running of period.*—Corporation A files its general corporation tax return for 1991 on March 15, 1992. The Department of Finance issues a notice of determination for that tax year on February 14, 1995. Taxpayer timely petitions for a hearing and subsequently a decision affirming the deficiency stated in the notice is mailed to the taxpayer, by certified or registered mail, on July 28, 1996. The taxpayer chooses not to file an appeal to the courts so the decision becomes final on November 28, 1996. The assessment made on November 28, 1996, is timely even though made more than three years after the filing of the tax return for 1991.

If a jeopardy assessment was issued and then abated because the Commissioner of Finance found that no jeopardy exists, the period of limitations on assessment of a deficiency is suspended from the date of the jeopardy assessment until expiration of the 10th day after the date the jeopardy assessment was abated. (Sec. 11-534(g), N.Y.C. Adm. Code; Sec. 11-685(7), N.Y.C. Adm. Code)

> *CCH EXAMPLE: Determining suspension of running of period for wrongly issued jeopardy assessment.*—The Department is auditing corporation A's tax return for 1991, filed March 15, 1992. Information is obtained that causes the Commissioner to issue a jeopardy assessment on February 14, 1995. At the hearing held to determine whether the issuance of a jeopardy assessment was reasonable, taxpayer satisfies the Commissioner that a jeopardy situation does not exist and the Commissioner abates the jeopardy assessment on March 10, 1995. The Commissioner may thereafter issue a notice of determination for the tax year 1991 until March 20, 1995, 10 days after the abatement of the jeopardy, even though it would be more than three years from the filing of the return.

[¶589-178] NYC Requirement to Post Bond or Security

Article 78 petitions for judicial review of the following taxes generally will not be permitted unless the amount of the tax sought to be reviewed, with penalties and interest, is deposited and a surety is filed with the Commissioner of Finance to the effect that the taxpayer will be responsible for all costs or charges that may accrue if the proceeding is dismissed or the tax confirmed: commercial rent or occupancy (Sec. 11-708, N.Y.C. Adm. Code); commercial vehicles (Sec. 11-810, N.Y.C. Adm. Code); insurers (Sec. 11-906, N.Y.C. Adm. Code); utilities (Sec. 11-1106, N.Y.C. Adm. Code); horse race admissions (Sec. 11-1206, N.Y.C. Adm. Code); tobacco products (Sec. 11-1310, N.Y.C. Adm. Code); taxicab license transfers (Sec. 11-1406, N.Y.C. Adm. Code); real property transfer (Sec. 11-2107, N.Y.C. Adm. Code); owners of motor vehicles (Sec. 11-2206, N.Y.C. Adm. Code); liquor authority licenses (Sec. 11-2407, N.Y.C. Adm. Code); and hotel room occupancies (Sec. 11-2506, N.Y.C. Adm. Code). Alternatively, however (except for appeals involving tobacco product taxes), a deposit of tax, penalties, and interest is not required if the surety is in an amount sufficient, in addition to the costs and charges that may accrue, to cover the tax, penalties, and interest.

The filing of a surety and/or deposit of tax, penalties, and interest with the Commissioner is not a jurisdictional requirement of an Article 78 petition to review New York City general corporation or unincorporated business income taxes. However, the payment of tax, deposit of deficiency, or filing of a bond and surety will preclude the Commissioner's authority to institute collection proceedings with respect to the tax, penalty, or interest that is subject to Article 78 judicial review. (Sec. 11-530(c); Sec. 11-681(3), N.Y.C. Adm. Code)

[¶589-186] NYC Agreements in Compromise of Tax Due

The Department of Finance is authorized to settle and adjust excise and non-property tax claims in favor of or against the city and, except with respect to cases within the jurisdiction of the Tax Appeals Tribunal, make determinations in contested cases. (Sec. 1504(2), N.Y.C. Charter)

In addition, under the Taxpayer Assistance Act of 2002 (Ch. 513), the Department of Finance is authorized to compromise City-administered excise and nonproperty taxes. The provisions are similar to those applicable at the state level. (see ¶89-186) (Sec. 1504(2), N.Y.C. Charter; *Finance Memorandum 02-4*)

Rules adopted by the Department of Finance establish procedures for offers-in-compromise. (Rule Sec. 34-01, *et seq.*) Fixed and final matters may be compromised only on the basis of doubt as to collectibility. Nonfinal matters may be compromised only on one or both of the following grounds: (1) doubt as to collectibility and (2) doubt as to liability. "Doubt as to collectibility" means the taxpayer has been discharged in bankruptcy or can be shown to be insolvent. "Doubt as to liability" means there is some doubt as to the taxpayer's liability and whether the Department could prevail against the taxpayer in administrative or judicial proceedings. (Rule Sec. 34-01; Rule Sec. 34-02)

An offer-in-compromise must be filed on forms prescribed by the department. The offer-in-compromise must contain, among other things, the tax liabilities included in the offer; the total amount the taxpayer is offering to pay; a brief indication of the grounds for the offer; and the taxpayer's agreement to comply with the department's general conditions for accepting the offer. (Rule Sec. 34-03)

An offer-in-compromise based in whole or in part on doubt as to collectibility requires a showing that the taxpayer has been discharged in bankruptcy or is insolvent. An offer-in-compromise based in whole or in part on doubt as to liability must be supported by appropriate facts, evidentiary documents, and legal arguments submitted in writing by the taxpayer. (Rule Sec. 34-03)

No offer-in-compromise will be accepted unless the taxpayer agrees to several conditions regarding payment and other matters. (Rule Sec. 34-04) Reasons for rejection of an offer-in-compromise include failure to meet the statutory requirements, making a frivolous offer or filing an offer for the purpose of delaying the collection of tax liabilities, and failure to make full financial disclosure. (Rule Sec. 34-05) The Commissioner must notify the taxpayer in writing of the decision to accept the offer-in-compromise. Generally, within 60 days of notification of acceptance, the taxpayer must make full payment of the compromise amount. (Rule Sec. 34-06)

For a discussion of the Voluntary Disclosure and Compliance Program, see Tax Amnesty.

[¶589-188] NYC Installment Payments

Under the New York City Taxpayer Bill of Rights, taxpayers are entitled, in cases of hardship, to enter into installment agreements at the discretion of the Department of Finance in order to facilitate the collection of payments due. The Department may require financial statements prior to and during the administration of such agreements and may cancel any such agreement in the event of default or a change in the taxpayer's financial condition.

[¶589-192] NYC Tax Amnesty

A voluntary disclosure and compliance program is available for taxes administered by the New York City Department of Finance. (*Business Tax Practitioner Newsletter*, Vol. 1, May 2019)

Eligible for participation in the program are taxpayers that are not currently under audit by the department, are disclosing tax liabilities that the department has not already determined or identified at the time of the disclosure, are not currently a party to a criminal investigation by the state or a one of its political subdivisions, and are not seeking to disclose participation in a tax avoidance transaction that is a federal or state reportable transaction. (Sec. 11-131, N.Y.C. Admin. Code)

Upon the execution of an agreement between the taxpayer and the department, the department will waive penalties for failure to pay the tax liability, failure to file a return or report for such tax liability, and failure to pay estimated tax. (Sec. 11-131, N.Y.C. Admin. Code)

The New York City Department of Finance has issued a revised statement of audit procedure (SAP) that discusses the Unified Program associated with the Voluntary Disclosure and Compliance Program (VDCP), which allows tax amnesty for all taxes under certain conditions. The unified program allows a delinquent taxpayer to make one request to participate in both the state and city VDCPs without making separate requests to each jurisdiction. As part of the unified program, New York City will conform to state procedures, including those requiring taxpayers to identify themselves on their application. The taxpayer receives one agreement detailing the terms of both jurisdictions, and an authorized employee from each jurisdiction will sign the agreement. All requests to participate in the unified program must be made with the New York State Department of Taxation and Finance. (*Statement of Audit Procedure PP-2009-1rev.*, New York City Department of Finance, August 5, 2009)

• *Prior amnesty periods*

The New York State 2005 budget legislation established a voluntary compliance initiative that was in effect from October 1, 2005, until March 1, 2006. The New York City Department of Finance also established certain settlement procedures and provided guidance to taxpayers electing to participate in the state's VCI. (*Finance Memorandum 05-7*)

The 2003 budget bill (A.B. 8388, Laws 2003), created a temporary three-month tax amnesty program that was effective during New York City's fiscal year beginning July 1, 2003. (Sec. 11-127, N.Y.C. Adm. Code) The Department of Finance accepted applications for amnesty from October 20, 2003, through January 23, 2004. The amnesty program was available for a limited category of taxes (i.e., those taxes administered by the City) and applied to tax liabilities for taxable periods ending, or transactions occurring, on or before December 31, 2001.

The amnesty program authorized the waiver of certain penalties and interest with respect to the payment of certain overdue tax liabilities and barred any civil, administrative, or criminal action or proceeding. (Sec. 11-127, N.Y.C. Adm. Code) However, failure to pay all designated taxes plus interest required by the amnesty program invalidated any amnesty granted. (Sec. 11-127, N.Y.C. Adm. Code)

Amnesty was not available to any taxpayers that received a benefit under any previous amnesty program. (See Sec. 11-125, N.Y.C. Adm. Code; Ch. 765, Laws 1985) Likewise, amnesty was not granted to any taxpayer that was the subject of any criminal investigation or criminal proceedings, or that had been convicted of a crime related to a designated tax. (Sec. 11-127(e), N.Y.C. Adm. Code)

The Department of Finance promulgated rules implementing the amnesty program. (Rule Sec. 1-19 through Rule Sec. 1-26)

A three-month amnesty program (from September 1, 1994, through November 30, 1994) was available to certain taxpayers having commercial rent or occupancy tax liabilities for tax periods ending on or before May 31, 1993, utility tax liabilities for tax periods ending on or before March 31, 1994, real property transfer tax liabilities with respect to taxable events occurring before April 1, 1994, and hotel room occupancy tax liabilities for tax periods ending on or before February 28, 1994. (Sec. 11-125, N.Y.C. Adm. Code; Rule Sec. 1-11)

[¶589-200]

NYC INTEREST AND PENALTIES

[¶589-204] NYC Interest Rates

The interest rate applicable to underpayments and overpayments of tax is set by the Commissioner of Finance on a quarterly basis. The underpayment rate is the sum of the federal short-term rate determined by the U.S. Secretary of Treasury rounded to the nearest full percent plus seven percentage points. The overpayment (refund) rate, where applicable, is the rounded federal short-term rate plus two percentage points. If the commissioner does not set an interest rate, the rate is deemed to be set at 7.5% (interest rates for underpayment of City unincorporated business tax and the tax on foreign and alien insurers cannot be less than 7.5%). (Sec. 11-537(f)(1), N.Y.C. Adm. Code; Sec. 11-687(5)(a), N.Y.C. Adm. Code; Sec. 11-715(h)(1), N.Y.C. Adm. Code; Sec. 11-817(g)(1), N.Y.C. Adm. Code; Sec. 11-905(g)(1), N.Y.C. Adm. Code; Sec. 11-1114(g)(1), N.Y.C. Adm. Code; Sec. 11-1213(g)(1), N.Y.C. Adm. Code; Sec. 11-1317(d)(2), N.Y.C. Adm. Code; Sec. 11-1413(g)(1), N.Y.C. Adm. Code; Sec. 11-1515(g)(1), N.Y.C. Adm. Code; Sec. 11-2114(g)(1), N.Y.C. Adm. Code; Sec. 11-2414(g)(1), N.Y.C. Adm. Code; Sec. 11-2515(g)(1), N.Y.C. Adm. Code; Sec. 11-2714(g)(1), N.Y.C. Adm. Code)

• *Underpayment rate—current period*

For the period October 1 through December 31, 2020, the underpayment rate of interest is 7.5% for the following taxes (the rate was the same for the period July 1 through September 30, 2020) (see http://www1.nyc.gov/site/finance/taxes/business-interest-rates.page):

- unincorporated business income tax;
- general corporation tax (business tax);
- banking corporation tax (business tax);
- commercial rent or occupancy tax;
- tax on commercial motor vehicles and motor vehicles for transportation of passengers;
- tax upon foreign and alien insurers;
- utility tax;
- horse race admissions tax;
- cigarette tax;
- tax on transfer of taxicab licenses;
- real property transfer tax;
- tax on retail licensees of the State Liquor Authority; and
- hotel rooms occupancy tax.

• *Overpayment (refund) rate—current period*

For the period October 1 through December 31, 2020, the overpayment rate of interest is 2% for the following taxes (the rate was the same for the period July 1 through September 30, 2020) (see http://www1.nyc.gov/site/finance/taxes/business-interest-rates.page):

- general corporation tax (business tax);

- banking corporation tax (business tax);

- unincorporated business income tax; and

- tax on foreign and alien insurers.

[¶589-206] NYC Civil Penalties

Civil penalties are generally administered under specific provisions of the New York City Administrative Code that cover procedures to be followed in cases of failure to file a return or pay tax, tax deficiencies due to negligence or fraud, underpayment of estimated tax, and other situations warranting the imposition of penalties.

• *Failure to timely file*

If a taxpayer fails to file a tax return when due, including any extensions of time for filing, the penalty is 5% of the tax due for each month or part of a month that the return is late. However, the penalty is not imposed if the failure was due to reasonable cause and not willful neglect; and in any event, it may not exceed 25% in the aggregate. For this purpose, the tax due is the tax liability shown on the return, less credits and timely payments, and plus any deficiencies later assessed. Thus, the penalty is imposed only on the net amount of the tax properly payable with the return, and a late-filing taxpayer who owes no tax or is entitled to a refund incurs no penalty. (Sec. 11-525(a), N.Y.C. Adm. Code; Sec. 11-676(1), N.Y.C. Adm. Code; Sec. 11-715(c), N.Y.C. Adm. Code; Sec. 11-817(b), N.Y.C. Adm. Code; Sec. 11-905(b), N.Y.C. Adm. Code; Sec. 11-1114(b), N.Y.C. Adm. Code; Sec. 11-1213(b), N.Y.C. Adm. Code; Sec. 11-1413(b), N.Y.C. Adm. Code; Sec. 11-1515(b), N.Y.C. Adm. Code; Sec. 11-2114(b), N.Y.C. Adm. Code; Sec. 11-2414(b), N.Y.C. Adm. Code; Sec. 11-2515(b), N.Y.C. Adm. Code)

A minimum penalty of the lesser of $100 or 100% of the tax due is imposed when no return is filed within 60 days of the date prescribed. (Sec. 11-525(a)(1)(B), N.Y.C. Adm. Code; Sec. 11-676(1)(a), N.Y.C. Adm. Code; Sec. 11-715(c)(1)(B), N.Y.C. Adm. Code; Sec. 11-817(b)(1)(B), N.Y.C. Adm. Code; Sec. 11-905(b)(1)(B), N.Y.C. Adm. Code; Sec. 11-1114(b)(1)(B), N.Y.C. Adm. Code; Sec. 11-1213(b)(1)(B), N.Y.C. Adm. Code; Sec. 11-1413(b)(1)(B), N.Y.C. Adm. Code; Sec. 11-1515(b)(1)(B), N.Y.C. Adm. Code; Sec. 11-2114(b)(1)(B), N.Y.C. Adm. Code; Sec. 11-2414(b)(1)(B), N.Y.C. Adm. Code; Sec. 11-2515(b)(1)(B), N.Y.C. Adm. Code)

• *Failure to timely pay*

If a taxpayer fails to pay a tax when due (including any extensions of time for payment), the penalty is 0.5% of the amount of the tax for each month or fraction thereof for which the failure continues, up to an aggregate of 25%, unless the failure is shown to be due to reasonable cause and not willful neglect. Where the penalty relates to the net amount due with a return, it runs from the due date of the payment. Where the penalty relates to a deficiency, it begins to run on the 11th day after notice and demand for payment. The penalty is imposed only on the net amount of tax due, so that a partial payment on or before the beginning of a month reduces the penalty for that month. (Sec. 11-525(a)(2), N.Y.C. Adm. Code; Sec. 11-676(1), N.Y.C. Adm. Code; Sec. 11-715(c), N.Y.C. Adm. Code; Sec. 11-817(b), N.Y.C. Adm. Code; Sec. 11-905(b), N.Y.C. Adm. Code; Sec. 11-1114(b), N.Y.C. Adm. Code; Sec. 11-1213(b), N.Y.C. Adm. Code; Sec. 11-1413(b), N.Y.C. Adm. Code; Sec. 11-1515(b), N.Y.C. Adm. Code; Sec. 11-2114(b), N.Y.C. Adm. Code; Sec. 11-2414(b), N.Y.C. Adm. Code; Sec. 11-2515(b), N.Y.C. Adm. Code)

• *Negligence penalties*

An additional penalty of 5% of a deficiency is assessable if any part of a deficiency is due to the taxpayer's negligence or intentional disregard of the law, rules or regulations, but without intent to defraud. (Sec. 11-525(b)(1), N.Y.C. Adm. Code; Sec. 11-676(2)(a), N.Y.C. Adm. Code; Sec. 11-715(d)(1), N.Y.C. Adm. Code; Sec. 11-817(c)(1), N.Y.C. Adm. Code; Sec. 11-905(c)(1), N.Y.C. Adm. Code; Sec. 11-1114(c)(1), N.Y.C. Adm. Code; Sec. 11-1213(c)(1), N.Y.C. Adm. Code; Sec. 11-1413(c)(1), N.Y.C. Adm. Code; Sec. 11-1515(c)(1), N.Y.C. Adm. Code; Sec. 11-2114(c)(1), N.Y.C. Adm. Code; Sec. 11-2414(c)(1), N.Y.C. Adm. Code; Sec. 11-2515(c)(1), N.Y.C. Adm. Code)

A negligence surcharge equal to 50% of the interest due on the part of the underpayment attributable to negligence is also imposed. (Sec. 11-525(b)(2), N.Y.C. Adm. Code; Sec. 11-676(2)(b), N.Y.C. Adm. Code; Sec. 11-715(d)(2), N.Y.C. Adm. Code; Sec. 11-817(c)(2), N.Y.C. Adm. Code; Sec. 11-905(c)(2), N.Y.C. Adm. Code; Sec. 11-1114(c)(2), N.Y.C. Adm. Code; Sec. 11-1213(c)(2), N.Y.C. Adm. Code; Sec. 11-1413(c)(2), N.Y.C. Adm. Code; Sec. 11-1515(c)(2), N.Y.C. Adm. Code; Sec. 11-2114(c)(2), N.Y.C. Adm. Code; Sec. 11-2414(c)(2), N.Y.C. Adm. Code; Sec. 11-2515(c)(2), N.Y.C. Adm. Code)

Negligence generally means carelessness, indifference, or inattention, while intentional disregard of the law or regulations occurs where a taxpayer knowingly fails to compute his or her tax in accordance with the law or regulations. Negligence or intentional disregard exists, for example, where a taxpayer's failure to keep accurate or adequate records results in a substantial understatement of income or the taxpayer claims a deduction two years after payment of the amount deducted. On the other hand, an honest mistake by a taxpayer, especially if based on the advice of a competent tax advisor, will not give rise to the penalty. In all cases, the taxpayer has the burden of showing that he or she used due care.

Under the unincorporated business tax and the general corporation tax, failure by a payee to include any amounts of dividends, patronage dividends, or interest covered by an information return in the payee's gross income is treated as negligence in the absence of clear and convincing evidence to the contrary. The penalty imposed in such cases, however, is only 5% of the portion of the deficiency that is attributable to the failure, rather than 5% of the entire deficiency, as is the general rule when any part of a deficiency is due to negligence. (Sec. 11-525(b)(3), N.Y.C. Adm. Code; Sec. 11-676(2)(c), N.Y.C. Adm. Code)

• *Tax fraud acts*

A tax fraud act is willfully engaging in an act or causing another to engage in an act during which a person:

— fails to make, sign, or file any tax return or report;

— knows that a return, report, or other document contains false or fraudulent information;

— knowingly supplies or submits false or fraudulent information;

— engages in any schemes to defraud the city or state;

— fails to remit collected taxes;

— fails to collect required taxes;

— fails to pay any tax with the intent to evade that tax; or

— issues a false, fraudulent, or counterfeit exemption, interdistributor sales, or resale certificate.

(Sec. 11-4002, N.Y.C. Adm. Code)

• *Fraud penalties*

If any part of a deficiency is due to fraud, a penalty is added to the amount of the underpayment of tax equal to two times the deficiency. In addition, a fraud surcharge applies. It is equal to 50% of the interest due on the part of the underpayment attributable to fraud. The fraud penalty is in lieu of and not in addition to the late filing, late payment, and negligence penalties discussed above. (Sec. 11-525(f), N.Y.C. Adm. Code; Sec. 11-676(6), N.Y.C. Adm. Code; Sec. 11-715(e), N.Y.C. Adm. Code; Sec. 11-817(d), N.Y.C. Adm. Code; Sec. 11-905(d), N.Y.C. Adm. Code; Sec. 11-1114(d), N.Y.C. Adm. Code; Sec. 11-1213(d), N.Y.C. Adm. Code; Sec. 11-1413(d), N.Y.C. Adm. Code; Sec. 11-1515(d), N.Y.C. Adm. Code; Sec. 11-2114(d), N.Y.C. Adm. Code; Sec. 11-2414(d), N.Y.C. Adm. Code; Sec. 11-2515(d), N.Y.C. Adm. Code) Assertion of the fraud penalty, however, does not pose double jeopardy when the taxpayer has been previously punished under a criminal plea for failure to report the same income, because the penalty is remedial in nature. (*Matter of Intercity Electrical Contracting Corp.*)

False or fraudulent documents.—The submission of false or fraudulent documents to the department will result in a penalty of $100 per document submitted or $500 per tax return submitted. This penalty is in addition to any other penalties or additions provided by law. (Sec. 11-525(l), N.Y.C. Adm. Code)

The failure to make, maintain, or make available any unincorporated business tax, general corporation tax, bank tax, or utilities tax records will result in a maximum penalty of $1,000 for the first quarterly period, and a maximum penalty of $5,000 for each additional quarterly period for which the failure occurs. For tax deficiencies due to fraud, the penalty imposed is equal to two times the deficiency. (Sec. 11-525(f), N.Y.C. Adm. Code; Sec. 11-676(15), N.Y.C. Adm. Code; Sec. 11-1114(l), N.Y.C. Adm. Code)

• *Underpayment of estimated taxes*

Under the corporate and unincorporated business tax laws, a taxpayer may be required to file a declaration of estimated taxes and make installment payments of estimated tax. (See ¶589-104) If a taxpayer fails to pay all or any part of an installment of estimated tax, he or she is deemed to have made an underpayment of estimated tax. (Sec. 11-525(c), N.Y.C. Adm. Code; Sec. 11-676(3), N.Y.C. Adm. Code)

The amount of the penalty is computed by applying to the underpayment the interest rate or rates in effect for the period (see ¶589-204), but not beyond the due date of the return (including extensions). (Sec. 11-525(c), N.Y.C. Adm. Code; Sec. 11-676(3), N.Y.C. Adm. Code) Compound interest rates do not apply in computing this underpayment penalty. (Sec. 11-537(g), N.Y.C. Adm. Code; Sec. 11-687(6), N.Y.C. Adm. Code)

CCH PLANNING NOTE: *File appropriate form to determine penalty.*—In general, the fastest way to determine the penalty amount, or if there is an underpayment of exception, is simply to fill out the applicable form (*Form NYC-221* for unincorporated businesses and *Form NYC-222* for corporations).

• *Substantial understatement penalties*

Additional civil penalties are imposed for substantial understatement of the following taxes.

Business taxes.—For purposes of the corporate business taxes (i.e., general corporation and banking corporation) and unincorporated business tax, a 10% penalty is imposed against taxpayers making a substantial understatement of tax liability. A substantial understatement is an omission of tax on the report or return for the tax year equal to at least 10% of the correct tax or $10,000 ($5,000 for S corporations and unincorporated businesses), whichever is greater. (Sec. 11-525(j), N.Y.C. Adm. Code; Sec. 11-676(11), N.Y.C. Adm. Code)

> *CCH EXAMPLE: Determining substantial underpayment.*—A corporation whose correct liability for the tax year is $110,000 reports its tax owed as $75,000. The underpayment of $35,000 exceeds both 10% of the tax and $10,000 and therefore is substantial.

> *CCH EXAMPLE: Determining substantial underpayment.*—A corporation whose correct tax for the year is $20,000 reports and pays $17,000. Though the underpayment is more than 10% of the correct liability, it is less than the $10,000 minimum and therefore is not substantial.

If a substantial underpayment exists, a penalty equal to 10% of the understatement is imposed unless one of the following three exceptions applies:

> (1) there is substantial authority for the taxpayer's treatment of the item to which the underpayment is attributed;

> (2) there is an adequate disclosure on the return (or in a statement attached to the return) of the facts affecting the treatment of the item; or

> (3) the Commissioner of Finance waives the penalty on the taxpayer's showing of good faith and reasonable cause for the understatement.

(Sec. 11-525(j), N.Y.C. Adm. Code; Sec. 11-676(11), N.Y.C. Adm. Code)

Commercial rent and utility taxes.—A substantial understatement of tax penalty applies to the commercial rent and utility taxes. The penalty is 10% of the amount of any underpayment attributable to the understatement. For this purpose, a substantial understatement is defined as an understatement exceeding the greater of 10% of the tax required to be shown on the year's final return or $5,000. (Sec. 11-715(j), N.Y.C. Adm. Code; Sec. 11-1114(i), N.Y.C. Adm. Code)

• *Fraudulent failure to perform required act*

In addition to any other penalties, the Commissioner of Finance may impose a penalty of up to $1,000 against any person who, with fraudulent intent, fails to pay the tax due or fails to make, sign or certify any return or supply information within the time required. The Commissioner can, in his discretion, waive, reduce or compromise this penalty. (Sec. 11-525(g), N.Y.C. Adm. Code; Sec. 11-676(7), N.Y.C. Adm. Code; Sec. 11-715(f), N.Y.C. Adm. Code; Sec. 11-817(e), N.Y.C. Adm. Code; Sec. 11-905(e), N.Y.C. Adm. Code; Sec. 11-1114(e), N.Y.C. Adm. Code; Sec. 11-1213(e), N.Y.C. Adm. Code; Sec. 11-1413(e), N.Y.C. Adm. Code; Sec. 11-1515(e), N.Y.C. Adm. Code; Sec. 11-2114(e), N.Y.C. Adm. Code; Sec. 11-2414(e), N.Y.C. Adm. Code; Sec. 11-2515(e), N.Y.C. Adm. Code) The corporate business tax law defines person, for purposes of this penalty provision, to include an individual, corporation, or partnership, or an officer or employee of any corporation, or a member or employee of any partnership, who as such an officer, employee or member is under a duty to perform the act in respect of which the violation occurs. (Sec. 11-676(10), N.Y.C. Adm. Code)

• *Aiding or assisting in filing of fraudulent returns*

Any person who, for compensation, aids, assists in, or procures the filing of fraudulent returns with the intent to evade tax is subject to a penalty not exceeding $10,000. The penalty for aiding or assisting in the filing of a fraudulent tax return applies whether or not the person required to present the return has knowledge of, or consents to, the falsity or fraud. This penalty, which is in addition to any other penalty provided by law, applies to the general corporation, unincorporated business, commercial rent and utility taxes. (Sec. 11-525(k), N.Y.C. Adm. Code; Sec. 11-676(12), N.Y.C. Adm. Code; Sec. 11-715(k), N.Y.C. Adm. Code; Sec. 11-1114(j), N.Y.C. Adm. Code)

The penalty is broadly worded to apply to anyone who aids, assists in, procures, counsels or advises the preparation or presentation of any return, report, declaration, statement or other document that is false or fraudulent as to any material matter. A person who orders (or procures) a subordinate to participate in the preparation of the false or fraudulent return is subject to the penalty. Persons who merely provide typing, reproducing, or other mechanical assistance are not treated as having aided or assisted in the preparation of the fraudulent document. (Sec. 11-525(k), N.Y.C. Adm. Code; Sec. 11-676(12), N.Y.C. Adm. Code; Sec. 11-715(k), N.Y.C. Adm. Code; Sec. 11-1114(j), N.Y.C. Adm. Code)

• *Failure to provide identification*

The Commissioner of Finance may impose a penalty of up to $1,000 for failure of any person to provide the Department of Finance with an identifying number within 30 days of a written demand. The Commissioner may extend the time for compliance upon a showing of good cause. (Sec. 11-102.1, N.Y.C. Adm. Code)

• *Failure to file information returns relating to certain interest payments*

Under the general corporation tax, a corporation that fails to file information returns relating to interest payments to majority shareholders is subject to a penalty of $500 unless it is shown that the failure is due to reasonable cause and not due to willful neglect. (Sec. 11-676(13), N.Y.C. Adm. Code)

[¶589-208] NYC Criminal Penalties

New York City Administrative Code Title 11, Chapter 40, contains criminal penalties, imposed in addition to civil penalties, for offenses against the city tax laws. These penalties consist of fines or imprisonment, or both. In addition, tax offenses may be prosecuted as felonies under New York Penal Law.

• *Felonies*

Any person who, with intent to evade city business tax or utility tax, commits any of the following offenses, is guilty of a class E felony:

• failure to file a city business tax return or report for three consecutive taxable years with respect to any city business taxes (other than declarations of estimated tax); or

• failure to file a return for 36 consecutive calendar months in the case of city personal income tax.

(Sec. 11-4003, N.Y.C. Adm. Code)

Penalties upon conviction.—Upon conviction of the offenses noted above, the applicable sentencing and disposition provisions of the Penal Law apply, subject to the limitations that the maximum fine that a court may impose is $50,000 ($250,000 in the case of a corporation). (Sec. 11-4001(c), N.Y.C. Adm. Code)

City business, unincorporated business income, utility taxes—false or fraudulent returns.—Any person who, with intent to evade city business, unincorporated business income, or utility tax, files a false or fraudulent return or report and substantially understates his or her tax liability is guilty of a class E felony. (Sec. 11-4004(b), N.Y.C. Adm. Code)

"Substantially understated" defined.—A tax is substantially understated if the amount required to be shown on a return or report exceeds the amount shown by at least $1,500 and the taxpayer, without reasonable cause for belief that his or her conduct is lawful, intended to evade at least the amount of the excess. (Sec. 11-4004(c), N.Y.C. Adm. Code)

City business, unincorporated business income, utility taxes—aiding or assisting filing of false or fraudulent returns.—Any person who, with intent to evade city business, unincorporated business income or utility tax, aids or assists, for compensation, in the preparation of a fraudulent or false return or report (other than declarations of estimated tax) that results in the understatement of tax liability by more than $1,500 is guilty of a class E felony. (Sec. 11-4005, N.Y.C. Adm. Code)

• *Misdemeanors*

Any person who commits any of the offenses listed below is guilty of a misdemeanor. Upon conviction, the applicable sentencing and disposition provisions of the Penal Law apply, subject to the limitation that the maximum fine that a court may impose for a class A misdemeanor is $10,000 ($20,000, in case of a corporation). (Sec. 11-4001(c), N.Y.C. Adm. Code)

(1) failure to make, sign, certify or file a city business, unincorporated business income or utility tax return or report, or to supply required information, with intent to evade tax; (Sec. 11-4002, N.Y.C. Adm. Code)

(2) providing false or fraudulent information, with intent to evade the payment of city business, unincorporated business income or utility tax; (Sec. 11-4002, N.Y.C. Adm. Code)

(3) making, signing, certifying or filing a false or fraudulent city business, unincorporated business income or utility tax return or report (other than an estimated tax return), with intent to evade tax; (Sec. 11-4004(a), N.Y.C. Adm. Code)

(4) aiding or assisting in the preparation or presentation of fraudulent city business, unincorporated business or utility tax returns, reports, statements or other documents (other than an estimated tax return) (see ¶ 589-104) for a fee or other compensation. (Sec. 11-4005(a), N.Y.C. Adm. Code) It is not a defense that the falsity or fraud was with the knowledge or consent of the person authorized or required to present the return, report, declaration, statement or other document;

(5) failure to pay city business, unincorporated business income or utility taxes, with intent to evade the payment of tax; (Sec. 11-4006, N.Y.C. Adm. Code)

(6) failure to comply with the terms of a subpoena or, after reasonable notice, to produce material books, papers and documents, in the person's possession or under his or her control in matters involving city business, commercial rent or occupancy, commercial motor vehicle, insurance, utility, horse race admissions, cigarettes, taxicab licenses, coin-operated amusement devices, real property transfers, motor vehicles, state liquor license, hotel room occupancy taxes, or annual vault charges, who testifies falsely in any material matter pending before the Commissioner of Finance; (Sec. 11-4007, N.Y.C. Adm. Code)

(7) willful failure to pay tax or file a commercial rent or occupancy, commercial motor vehicle, foreign or alien insurance, horse race admission, cigarette, taxicab license transfer, coin-operated amusement device, real property transfers, motor vehicle ownership, state liquor authority licensee, or annual vault charge return or report within the time required; (Sec. 11-4008, N.Y.C. Adm. Code)

(8) willfully making or subscribing a commercial rent or occupancy, commercial motor vehicle, foreign or alien insurance, horse race admission, cigarette, taxicab license transfer, coin-operated amusement device, real property transfer, motor vehicle, state liquor authority licensee, hotel room occupancy, or annual vault charge return, report or other document that the person does not believe to be true and correct as to all material matters. (Sec. 11-4009, N.Y.C. Adm. Code) Any person who willfully delivers or discloses any document that is known to be fraudulent or false as to any material matter is also guilty of a misdemeanor; the omission of a material matter with intent to deceive will constitute the delivery or disclosure of a document known to be false;

(9) willful failure to collect horse race admission or hotel room occupancy taxes; (Sec. 11-4010, N.Y.C. Adm. Code)

(10) willful failure to file a required bond; (see ¶589-178) (Sec. 11-4011, N.Y.C. Adm. Code)

(11) willful attempt to evade, defeat, or not pay city cigarette tax; (Sec. 11-4012, N.Y.C. Adm. Code) A third conviction of attempting to evade, defeat or not pay tax is a class E felony;

(12) possession or transportation for the purpose of sale of unstamped or unlawfully stamped packages of cigarettes subject to tax, or sale or offering for sale unstamped or unlawfully stamped packages of cigarettes by a person other than an authorized agent. (Sec. 11-4012, N.Y.C. Adm. Code) The possession or transportation within New York City of 5,000 or more cigarettes at any one time in unstamped or unlawfully stamped packages is presumptive evidence that the cigarettes are possessed or transported for the purpose of sale and are subject to tax. Similarly, the possession within New York City of more than 400 cigarettes at any one time in unstamped or unlawfully stamped packages is presumptive evidence that the cigarettes are subject to tax.

The misdemeanor provisions do not apply to common or contract carriers or warehousemen engaged in lawfully transporting or storing unstamped packages of cigarettes as merchandise; employees of such carrier or warehouseman acting within the scope of their employment; public officers or employees in the performance of official duties requiring possession or control of unstamped or unlawfully stamped packages of cigarettes; temporary incidental possession by employees or agents of persons lawfully entitled to possession; or to persons whose possession is for the purpose of aiding police officers in the performance of their duties;

(13) willful attempt to evade or defeat the tax on other tobacco products, or conducting any willful act or omission with respect to the tax imposed on other tobacco products; (Sec. 11-4012.1, N.Y.C. Adm. Code)

(14) counterfeiting, forging, causing or procuring to be counterfeited or forged, or aiding or assisting in counterfeiting or forging commercial motor vehicle stamps, indicia of payment or indicia that no tax is payable. (Sec. 11-4014, N.Y.C. Adm. Code) A person who knowingly acquires, possesses, disposes or uses a counterfeited or forged stamp or document, or who transfers a stamp or document without authorization is also guilty of a misdemeanor;

(15) failure to exhibit a commercial motor vehicle stamp or other document to the Commissioner of Finance, the Commissioner's authorized agent or employee, or a state or city police officer; (Sec. 11-4014, N.Y.C. Adm. Code)

(16) counterfeiting, forging, causing or procuring to be counterfeited or forged, or aiding or assisting in counterfeiting or forging any receipt or document evidencing payment or exemption from the tax on owners of motor vehicles. (Sec. 11-4015, N.Y.C. Adm. Code) A person who knowingly acquires, possesses, disposes or uses counterfeited or forged documents is also guilty of a misdemeanor;

(17) willful failure to make a hotel room occupancy tax return or report; (Sec. 11-4016, N.Y.C. Adm. Code)

(18) willful failure to pay over hotel room occupancy tax; (Sec. 11-4016, N.Y.C. Adm. Code)

(19) willful failure to file a registration certificate required under hotel room occupancy tax provisions; (Sec. 11-4016, N.Y.C. Adm. Code)

(20) willful failure to display or surrender a certificate of authority required under hotel room occupancy tax provisions. (Sec. 11-4016, N.Y.C. Adm. Code) A person who willfully assigns or transfers a certificate of authority in violation of applicable provisions of the hotel occupancy tax is also guilty of a misdemeanor;

(21) willful failure to charge hotel occupancy tax separately on a bill, statement, memorandum or receipt; (Sec. 11-4016, N.Y.C. Adm. Code)

(22) violation of secrecy provisions of the New York City Administrative Code; (Sec. 11-4017, N.Y.C. Adm. Code)

(23) willful failure to keep or retain commercial rent or occupancy, horse race admission, taxicab license transfer, real property transfer, motor vehicle, state liquor authority license tax or annual vault charge records required to be kept or retained; (Sec. 11-4018(a), N.Y.C. Adm. Code)

(24) willful simulation, alteration, defacing, destruction or removal of evidence of the filing of a real property transfer tax return or the payment of tax; (Sec. 11-4018(b), N.Y.C. Adm. Code)

(25) failure to file a commercial motor vehicle certificate of registration or information registration certificate; (Sec. 11-4018(c), N.Y.C. Adm. Code) or

(26) refusal to permit personnel authorized by the Commissioner to inspect vaults or premises subject to annual vault charges. (Sec. 11-4018(d), N.Y.C. Adm. Code)

[¶589-220]

NYC TAXPAYER RIGHTS AND REMEDIES

[¶589-224] NYC Refunds

If a tax liability has been overpaid, the taxpayer may seek a refund or credit of the overpayment by filing a claim or application for refund or credit within the period of limitations prescribed by law.

Overpayment of a liability can arise in several ways, including the following:

(1) an overpayment exists when a tax, penalty or interest charge has been erroneously, illegally, or unconstitutionally collected or paid; (Sec. 11-709(a), N.Y.C. Adm. Code)

(2) the payment of an amount as tax for a tax period in which there is no tax liability is considered an overpayment; (Sec. 11-526(c), N.Y.C. Adm. Code; Sec. 11-677(3), N.Y.C. Adm. Code)

(3) taxes collected or paid after the period of limitations on assessment or collection has expired are considered overpayments; (Sec. 11-526(d), N.Y.C. Adm. Code; Sec. 11-677(4), N.Y.C. Adm. Code)

(4) the application of certain statutory credits (sales tax credits, stock transfer credit, relocation credits against the general corporation and unincorporated business taxes) is considered an overpayment to be credited and refunded if greater than the tax owed.

A refund or credit can be obtained whether the overpayment was made by the taxpayer with the filing of his return or pursuant to a deficiency assessment. In either case, there is no requirement that the taxes be recorded as having been paid under protest or duress in order for the taxpayer to obtain a refund or credit.

[¶589-230] NYC Taxpayer Conferences

The Commissioner of Finance has established conciliation conference procedures to settle contested tax determinations, denials of refunds or tax credits, and charges imposed under Ch. 5 (unincorporated business tax), Ch. 6 (city business taxes), Ch. 7 (commercial rent or occupancy taxes), Ch. 8 (motor vehicles), Ch. 9 (foreign or alien insurers), Ch. 11 (utilities), Ch. 12 (horse race admissions), Ch. 13 (cigarettes), Ch. 14 (transfer of taxicab licenses), Ch. 21 (real property transfers), Ch. 22 (tax on owners of motor vehicles), Ch. 24 (state liquor authority licenses), or Ch. 25 (hotel room occupancies), Title 11, New York City Administrative Code, or to resolve disputes arising from the notification of the refusal to grant, the suspension of, or the revocation of cigarette licenses issued pursuant to Ch. 13. (Sec. 11-124, N.Y.C. Adm. Code)

Conciliation conferences seek to resolve taxpayer disputes in a quick and inexpensive manner without resorting to a formal hearing. (Sec. 11-124, N.Y.C. Adm. Code)

• *Request for conference*

Conciliation conferences usually begin with the filing of an original and copy of a written request with the Bureau of Conciliation, New York City Department of Finance, 345 Adams Street, Brooklyn, New York 11201. (Rule Sec. 38-04)

Form of request.—The request should contain the following information:

(1) the name, address and taxpayer identification number (employer identification number or social security number) of the taxpayer and, if applicable, the taxpayer's representative;

(2) the taxable years or periods involved and the type of the tax in question;

(3) the action or actions of the operating division that are protested;

(4) the facts, law or reasons that the requestor asserts are relevant to the controversy;

(5) a signed acknowledgment by the requestor that the request is made with knowledge that a willfully false representation is a misdemeanor punishable under Sec. 11-4004, New York City Administrative Codes;

(6) a legible copy of the statutory notice being protested; and

(7) if applicable, the original or a legible copy of the power of attorney.

The Bureau of Conciliation may request additional information in order to process the request for a conference and to resolve outstanding issues. (Rule Sec. 38-04)

• *Time limitations*

Requests for conciliation must be filed within the statutory time limitations for filing a petition. (Rule Sec. 38-04) A timely request for a conference suspends the running of the period of limitations for the filing of a petition for hearing with the Tax Appeals Tribunal. (Sec. 11-124, N.Y.C. Adm. Code) It does not, however, suspend the accrual of any amount due as additions to tax, interest or penalties.

Referral of petition by Tax Appeals Tribunal.—Where a conciliation conference has not been conducted, the Tax Appeals Tribunal may, at the request of the taxpayer and consent of the Commissioner, refer a tax appeal to the Bureau of Conciliation. (Rule Sec. 38-04)

• *Hearing procedures*

The Bureau of Conciliation will acknowledge and review requests for conferences. Where a request is not filed in a timely manner, a conciliation order will be issued dismissing the request; such dismissal will not constitute a conciliation order giving the requestor 90 days in which to file a petition with the City Tax Appeals Tribunal. (Rule Sec. 38-05)

Where the request for conciliation is timely filed, parties will be given 30 days written notice of the time and place of the first conciliation conference. Notices of adjourned or continued conferences must be mailed to the parties at least 10 days before the scheduled date of the continued or adjourned conference.

• *Conciliation orders*

After reviewing the statements, documents and comments submitted during the conference, the conciliator will serve a proposed resolution upon the requestor, incorporating a consent and waiver. (Rule Sec. 38-03) If the proposal is acceptable, the requestor has 15 days in which to execute the consent and waive any right to a petition for a hearing on resolved issues. If the taxpayer does not agree with the proposed consent and does not execute it within 15 days, the proposed resolution will be withdrawn and a conciliation decision will be issued discontinuing conciliation. The service of the decision discontinuing conciliation will start the running of the 90-day period for filing a petition, or reinstate any previously filed petition, with respect to any issues not resolved at conciliation.

Discontinuance of conciliation.—At any time prior to the issuance of the conciliation order the requestor may discontinue the conciliation conference by serving a written request for a discontinuance. (Rule Sec. 38-06)

• *Precedential effect*

Conciliation orders are not considered precedent, nor are they given any force or effect in any subsequent conciliation conference with regard to the requestor or any other person. (Rule Sec. 38-05)

• *Representation of parties*

A taxpayer who requests a conciliation conference may appear personally or be represented by a spouse, parent, or child. (Rule Sec. 38-03) A minor under 18 years of age may be represented by his or her adult spouse, parent, guardian or by the person who prepared the minor's return. An emancipated minor may request a conciliation conference and appear on his or her own behalf.

A court-appointed representative may request a conciliation proceeding or appear on behalf of a taxpayer who is mentally or physically incapable of filing a petition or appearing on his or her own behalf.

A partnership may act through a general partner. A corporation may be represented by any officer.

Where a power of attorney is executed and filed with the Bureau, a taxpayer may be represented by any of the following:

> (1) an attorney-at-law licensed to practice in any jurisdiction of the United States;

> (2) a public accountant or certified public accountant duly qualified to practice in any jurisdiction of the United States;

> (3) on behalf of a corporation, an employee who is not an officer; or

> (4) an enrolled agent enrolled to practice before the IRS.

Representation by permission of Director.—Any other person may appear and represent a taxpayer for a particular matter by special permission of the Director of the Bureau of Conciliation.

[¶589-232] NYC Small Claims Hearings

A petitioner may elect to have a hearing held in the Small Claims Unit of the New York City Tax Appeals Tribunal if the amount in controversy does not exceed $10,000, excluding penalties and interest. (Rule Sec. 1-11) Small claims hearings are informal hearings conducted by impartial presiding officers. Formal rules of evidence are relaxed to allow the officer to consider anything that the officer believes to be necessary or desirable for a just and equitable determination.

• *Representation of parties*

A petitioner may be represented in a small claims hearing by any person authorized to appear on his or her behalf before the Tax Appeals Tribunal. (Rule Sec. 1-03) In addition, a petitioner may be represented by his or her spouse, domestic partner, child or parent; representation by other parties will be permitted only if approved by the Tribunal.

• *Discontinuance of hearing*

At any time before the conclusion of a small claims hearing, a petitioner may, by written notice to the president of the Tribunal, discontinue the proceeding and request transfer to a formal hearing before an Administrative Law Judge. (Sec. 169(e), N.Y.C. Charter; Rule Sec. 1-11) The transfer will be without prejudice to the rights of either party with respect to subsequent proceedings before the Administrative Law Judge. Once transferred, the matter cannot be transferred back to the small claims unit.

• *Effect of final determination*

Determinations of presiding officers are conclusive on all parties and must be rendered within three months after completion of the hearing or the submission of briefs, whichever is later. (Rule Sec. 1-11) Determinations are regarded as final decisions of the Tribunal and are not subject to *en banc* review by the Tribunal or judicial review. (Sec. 169(e), N.Y.C. Charter) The Tribunal may, however, order a rehearing upon proof or allegation of misconduct by the presiding officer.

Determinations of presiding officers are not considered precedent, nor are they given any force or effect in other proceedings in the Tribunal.

[¶589-234] NYC Administrative Appeals

Taxpayers seeking administrative review of disputes involving city-administered taxes may request a formal hearing with the New York City Tax Appeals Tribunal (prior to October 1, 1992, the Tribunal was authorized to consider only appeals involving City-administered excise taxes). (Rule Sec. 1-04) The Tribunal, which is composed of three Tribunal commissioners, the Administrative Law Judge Unit and the Small Claims Unit (see ¶589-232), is part of the Department of Finance, but its powers, functions, duties, and obligations are separate from and independent of the authority of the Commissioner of Finance.

Where the amount in controversy does not exceed $10,000, excluding penalties or interest, the petitioner may elect to have the proceeding conducted in the Small Claims Unit. (see ¶589-232) (Rule Sec. 1-11) Otherwise, the matter will initially be assigned to an Administrative Law Judge (ALJ).

• *Stay of proceedings*

The filing of a petition with the Tax Appeals Tribunal will stay both the collection of any taxes and the payment of any refund of taxes (including penalties and interest) that are the subject of the petition, unless the Commissioner determines that the assessment or collection of the tax, charge, penalty or interest will be jeopardized by delay. (Sec. 170(c), N.Y.C. Charter)

• *Petition for hearing*

Proceedings in the New York City Tax Appeals Tribunal are commenced by the filing of a petition containing the following information:

(1) the name, address and telephone number of the petitioner and, if applicable, the petitioner's representative;

(2) an identifying number or numbers prescribed by the Commissioner of Finance (for example, social security numbers, employer identification numbers or other numeric designations suitable for proper identification of the petitioner), to be used for administrative purposes only;

(3) the date of the statutory notice and the tax or annual vault charge involved, identifying the relevant sections, chapter and title of the Administrative Code;

(4) the taxable years or periods involved, or the date of the transaction;

(5) the amount in controversy (identifying the principal, interest and penalty, if any, separately);

(6) separately numbered paragraphs stating each error of fact or law that the petitioner alleges has been made, together with a statement of the facts or law relied upon by the petitioner to establish the alleged error;

(7) the relief sought by the petitioner;

(8) if the amount in controversy is less than $10,000, whether the petitioner wants the proceeding to be conducted as a small claims proceeding; (see ¶589-232)

(9) if the right to an expedited hearing exists, whether the petitioner waives such right;

(10) a legible copy of the statutory notice being protested; and

(11) a power of attorney, if applicable.

(Rule Sec. 1-04)

¶589-234

The petition must be signed by the petitioner, or the petitioner's representative, and contain an acknowledgement that the petition is made with knowledge that a willfully false representation is a misdemeanor punishable under Sec. 210.45, Penal Law. (For a discussion of civil penalties, see ¶589-206, and for criminal penalties, see ¶589-208)

The original and two conformed copies of the petition, plus proof of service of a copy of the petition on the Commissioner of Finance, must be filed with the New York City Tax Appeals Tribunal, One Centre Street, Suite 2400, New York, New York 10007.

Time limitations.—Petitions for administrative review must be filed within certain statutory time limitations. For a discussion of the limitations, see ¶589-240.

Review of petition.—Petitions for hearings are acknowledged and reviewed by the Chief Administrative Law Judge. (Rule Sec. 1-04) If the petition is not in the correct form, it will be returned with a statement indicating the requirements with which it does not comply; the taxpayer will be extended an additional 30 days in which to file a corrected petition. Failure to file a corrected petition within the 30-day period may result in the entry of a determination dismissing the petition.

Answer.—Once the petition is properly filed, the Chief Administrative Law Judge will provide the petitioner with a written, dated acknowledgement and forward the petition and a copy of the acknowledgement to the Commissioner of Finance for the preparation of the answer. The answer must be filed within 60 days from the date that the Chief Administrative Law Judge acknowledges receipt of a petition in the proper form.

If the Commissioner fails to file the answer within the 60-day period, the petitioner may make a motion, on notice to the Commissioner, for a determination of default.

CCH PLANNING NOTE: *Determination of default not mandatory.*—The New York City Tax Appeals Tribunal, Administrative Law Judge Division, has held the requirement for filing a timely answer as being directory rather than mandatory. (*Heller Financial, Inc. & Combined Affiliates*) Thus, a taxpayer seeking a determination of default should claim and be able to demonstrate prejudice due to the late answer.

Reply.—Within 20 days from the service of the answer, the petitioner may file a reply.

Once a reply has been filed, or after the expiration of 20 days from the service of the answer, the controversy will be deemed to be at issue and scheduled for a pre-hearing conference.

• *Hearing procedures*

Once an issue is joined, the Chief Administrative Law Judge will schedule a conference. Parties must be given at least 30 days' notice of the first hearing date, and at least 10 days' notice of any adjourned or continued hearing date. Requests by either party for a preference in scheduling will be honored to the extent possible. (Rule Sec. 1-12)

Conduct of hearing.—Hearings before administrative law judges are conducted formally. The parties may call and examine witnesses, introduce exhibits, cross-examine opposing witnesses on any relevant matters, impeach the credibility of witnesses, and rebut the evidence against them. Technical rules of evidence will, however, be disregarded to the extent permitted by the decisions of New York courts, provided the evidence offered appears to be relevant and material to the issues. (Rule Sec. 1-12)

- *Burden of proof*

Generally, the burden of proof in a proceeding before the Tax Appeals Tribunal is on the petitioner. In proceedings involving City business or unincorporated business taxes, however, the burden is on the Commissioner to establish the following:

(1) whether a petitioner has been guilty of fraud with intent to evade tax;

(2) whether a petitioner is liable as the transferee of property of a taxpayer (but not to show that the taxpayer was liable for the tax);

(3) whether a petitioner is liable for any increase in a deficiency where the increase was assessed after the initial notice of deficiency was mailed and a petition filed (unless the increase in the deficiency was the result of a change or correction of federal or state taxable income required to be reported, of which the Commissioner has no knowledge at the time that the notice of deficiency was mailed); and

(4) whether a person is liable for penalties under Sec. 11-525(k) or Sec. 11-676, New York City Administrative Code.

(Sec. 11-529(e), N.Y.C. Adm. Code; Sec. 11-680(5), N.Y.C. Adm. Code)

- *Determinations*

The ALJ must render a determination within six months after completion of a hearing or the submission of briefs, whichever is later. (Sec. 171(a), N.Y.C. Charter; Rule Sec. 1-12) The six-month period may be extended, for good cause shown, for an additional three months.

The determination of the ALJ is a final determination of any matters in controversy unless a party takes exception by timely requesting review by the New York City Tax Appeals Tribunal (see below). (Rule Sec. 1-12) Determinations of administrative law judges are not considered precedent, nor are they given any force or effect in other proceedings within the Tribunal.

- *Review by Tax Appeals Tribunal*

Administrative law judge determinations are reviewable by the Tax Appeals Tribunal sitting en banc if either party, within 30 days after the giving of notice of the determination, files an exception and three conformed copies with the President of the Tribunal. (Rule Sec. 1-13) Exceptions must be filed either personally or by certified or registered mail. The 30-day period may be extended if good cause for the extension is shown. Copies of the exception must be served on the other party. Either party may request oral argument.

Tribunal Review.—The Tribunal will review the record and may, to the extent necessary or desirable, exercise all of the powers that it could have exercised if it had made the earlier determination. (Rule Sec. 1-13) However, the Tribunal must follow as precedent its prior precedential decisions (excluding decisions of small claims presiding officers) and decisions of the New York State Tax Appeals Tribunal or of any federal or New York state court or the U.S. Supreme Court insofar as those decisions pertain to substantive legal issues before the tribunal. (Sec. 170(d), N.Y.C. Charter) A decision affirming, reversing, modifying, or remanding the ALJ's determination must be issued within six months from the date that the exception was filed, the briefs were submitted, or oral argument was concluded, whichever is later.

• *Judicial review*

An *en banc* decision of the Tribunal that is not subject to further administrative review will irrevocably decide all the issues raised in the proceeding unless, within four months after the issuance of the tribunal's decision, the petitioner applies for judicial review pursuant to Article 78, Civil Practice Law and Rules. (Sec. 171(b), N.Y.C. Charter; Rule Sec. 1-18) A Tribunal order that does not finally decide all matters and issues contained in the petition will not, however, be deemed final for purposes of Article 78 review until the Tribunal renders a decision on the remaining matters and issues.

For a discussion of judicial appeals, see ¶ 589-236.

[¶589-236] NYC Judicial Appeals and Remedies

New York City Tax Appeals Tribunal decisions that are not subject to further administrative review irrevocably decide all issues that were raised in the proceeding unless, within four months after notice of the decision is served on all parties, the taxpayer applies for judicial review pursuant to a special proceeding under Article 78, Civil Practice Law and Rules. (Sec. 11-530(a), N.Y.C. Adm. Code; Sec. 11-708, N.Y.C. Adm. Code; Sec. 11-810, N.Y.C. Adm. Code; Sec. 11-906, N.Y.C. Adm. Code; Sec. 11-1106, N.Y.C. Adm. Code; Sec. 11-1206, N.Y.C. Adm. Code; Sec. 11-1310, N.Y.C. Adm. Code; Sec. 11-1406, N.Y.C. Adm. Code; Sec. 11-1508, N.Y.C. Adm. Code; Sec. 11-1943, N.Y.C. Adm. Code; Sec. 11-2021, N.Y.C. Adm. Code; Sec. 11-2107, N.Y.C. Adm. Code; Sec. 11-2206, N.Y.C. Adm. Code; Sec. 11-2407, N.Y.C. Adm. Code; Sec. 11-2506, N.Y.C. Adm. Code; Sec. 11-2707, N.Y.C. Adm. Code; Rule Sec. 1-18)

However, effective June 1, 2018, for decisions regarding the tax on other tobacco products, proceedings must be instituted by the person against whom the tax was assessed within 30 days after the giving of the notice of decision. (Sec. 11-1310, N.Y.C. Adm. Code)

• *Venue*

Appeals from the New York City Tax Appeals Tribunal are commenced in the Supreme Court, Appellate Division, First Department. (Sec. 506, Civil Practice Law and Rules)

• *Procedures*

A proceeding for relief under Article 78 is initiated by the service of a notice of petition or of an order to show cause. (Sec. 7804, Civil Practice Law and Rules) If the order to show cause is granted by the court, the order will specify the time and manner of service; otherwise the notice of petition, together with the petition and any affidavits specified in the notice, must be served at least 20 days before the time the petition is noticed to be heard.

A description of the petition and other pleadings and the times for service thereof is found in the statute.

• *Deposit of tax*

Article 78 petitions for judicial review of certain taxes will not be permitted unless the amount of the tax sought to be reviewed, with penalties and interest, is deposited and a surety is filed with the Commissioner of Finance to the effect that the taxpayer will be responsible for all costs or charges that may accrue if the proceeding is dismissed or the tax confirmed.

For a discussion of the requirement to post bond or security, see ¶ 589-178.

• *Federal court actions*

An assessment may be appealed to a federal court if there is a question involving the U.S. Constitution or a federal statute. However, the right to bring a federal suit is limited by the Tax Injunction Act and the fundamental principle of comity. The Tax Injunction Act prohibits injunctions in federal district courts against the assessment, levy, or collection of any state tax when there is a "plain, speedy, and efficient remedy" in state courts. (28 U.S.C. § 1341) Because this federal provision has been the subject of considerable litigation, the case law interpreting this provision should be researched if a federal action is contemplated.

In addition, any appeal of a state tax case to a federal court would be subject to established principles of federal jurisdiction and abstention. Federal constitutional provisions are discussed at ¶ 589-052.

[¶589-240] NYC Limitations Period for Appeals

Petitions for administrative review must be filed within the following statutory time limitations:

(1) appeal from a notice of deficiency involving New York City unincorporated business income (Sec. 11-521(b), N.Y.C. Adm. Code) or corporate income (Sec. 11-672(2), N.Y.C. Adm. Code) taxes, 90 days (150 days if addressed to a taxpayer whose last known address is outside the U.S.);

(2) appeal from a notice of determination of taxes on commercial rent or occupancy (Sec. 11-708, N.Y.C. Adm. Code), commercial vehicles (Sec. 11-810, N.Y.C. Adm. Code), insurers (Sec. 11-906, N.Y.C. Adm. Code), utilities (Sec. 11-1106, N.Y.C. Adm. Code), horse race admissions (Sec. 11-1206, N.Y.C. Adm. Code), cigarettes (including the licensing of wholesale and retail dealers) (Sec. 11-1310, N.Y.C. Adm. Code), taxicab licenses (Sec. 11-1406, N.Y.C. Adm. Code), real property transfers (Sec. 11-2107, N.Y.C. Adm. Code), motor vehicle owners (Sec. 11-2206, N.Y.C. Adm. Code), alcoholic beverage licenses (Sec. 11-2407, N.Y.C. Adm. Code), and hotel room occupancies (Sec. 11-2506, N.Y.C. Adm. Code), 90 days.

The limitation periods noted above may not be extended. (Sec. 170(a), N.Y.C. Charter) The periods are, however, suspended during the period a timely request for a conciliation conference is pending.

TOPICAL INDEX

»»→ References are to paragraph (¶) numbers.

A

Abatement of tax
. property taxes 20-810

Administration of taxes
. administrative remedies 61-620
. New York City 515-020; 589-064

Admissions, entertainment, and dues
. sales and use taxes 60-230

Advertising
. sales and use taxes 60-240

Agriculture
. property taxes 20-115
. sales and use taxes 60-250

Air pollution control facilities
. corporation tax
. . New York City 505-440

Aircraft
. sales and use taxes 60-740

Alcoholic beverages
. alcoholic beverage tax 37-001
. . New York City 535-105
. sales and use taxes 60-260

Alimony 16-012; 16-207

Allocation and apportionment
. corporation tax 11-505; 11-510; 11-515
. . apportionment formulas 11-520
. . payroll factor 11-535
. . property factor 11-530
. . sales factor 11-525
. . specific industries 11-540
. New York City—see specific New York City tax headings
. pass-through entities 11-515
. personal income tax
. . business income 16-515

Appeals
. administrative appeals 89-234
. . limitations period 89-240
. property taxes 20-906

Assessment of property
. property taxes 20-610
. . appeals 20-906
. . New York City 520-605; 520-610
. . valuation methods 20-615

Assessment of tax
. administrative appeals 89-234
. . limitations period 89-240
. delinquent tax 89-164
. limitations period 89-144

Audits
. conciliation conferences 89-230
. limitations period 89-144

Aviation fuel taxes 40-005

B

Banking institutions
. abandoned savings accounts and checks 37-351
. corporation tax 10-340
. New York City—see New York City banking corporation tax

Boats and vessels
. sales and use taxes 60-740

Business entities
. corporations 10-210
. exempt organizations 10-245
. limited liability companies (LLCs) 10-240
. partnerships
. . general partnerships 10-220
. . limited liability partnerships 10-225
. . limited partnerships 10-225
. S corporations 10-215

Business income
. allocation and apportionment
. . corporations 11-510; 11-515; 11-520
. . nonresidents 16-515
. . pass-through entities 11-520

C

Charitable organizations
. property taxes 20-285

Cigarette tax 55-001
. audits
. . limitations period 89-144
. New York City—see New York City cigarette and tobacco
. . . . products taxes

Claim of right adjustment
. personal income tax 16-225

Classification of property
. property taxes 20-105
. . New York City 520-105

Clothing
. sales and use taxes 60-290

Collection of tax
. administrative appeals 89-234
. . limitations period 89-240
. conciliation conferences 89-230
. delinquent tax 89-164
. New York City—see under New York City
. offers in compromise 89-186

College Savings Program 16-255

Computation of tax
. corporation tax 10-505; 10-510
. . modifications to federal taxable income . . . 10-600; 10-800
. . New York City—see New York City business corporation tax
. personal income tax 15-505; 15-510
. . modifications to federal AGI 16-005 16-205
. . New York City 515-405

Computers and software
. property taxes 20-135
. sales and use taxes 60-310

Conformity to federal law
. corporation tax 10-515
. New York City taxes 589-066
. personal income tax 15-515

Congestion surcharge 35-326

Construction materials and services
. sales and use taxes 60-330

Corporations
. allocation and apportionment—see Allocation and
. . . . apportionment
. audits
. . limitations period 89-144
. banking institutions 10-340
. bonus depreciation deduction 10-670; 10-900
. capital contributions 10-911
. credits available 12-001
. dividends received deduction 10-630
. domestic production activities deduction 10-660
. environmental remediation insurance credit 10-701
. farm donations to food pantries credit 10-701
. federal and state provisions, interaction 10-210
. foreign dividends 10-810
. foreign source income 10-695
. gains and losses 10-640
. . capital loss carryovers 10-635
. . subsidiary capital 10-825
. insurance companies 10-335
. interest expense 10-645
. interest income
. . federally exempt 10-610
. . subsidiary capital 10-815
. net operating loss 10-805
. New York City—see specific New York City tax headings
. related-party transactions
. . royalty payments 10-620; 10-835

Corporations—continued
. returns 89-102
. . electronic filing 89-106
. . estimated tax 89-104
. S corporations—see S corporations
. targeted business activities 10-845
. tax addbacks 10-615
. tax rates 10-380
. tax refunds 10-840
. taxable income 10-505; 10-510
. . additions 10-600
. . federal conformity 10-515
. . prior law 10-530
. . subtractions 10-800
. . wages
. . . federal employment credit 10-855

Credits against tax
. corporation tax 12-001
. personal income tax 16-805
. . New York City 516-405
. sales and use taxes 61-270

D

Death benefits
. personal income tax 16-240

Deferred compensation
. Sec. 457 plans 16-345

Depletion
. personal income tax 16-037; 16-243

Depreciation
. corporation tax 10-670; 10-900
. . New York City 505-416; 505-431; 505-450
. personal income tax 16-040; 16-245

Diesel fuel taxes 40-003

Disability benefits 16-247

Dividends
. corporation tax 10-810
. . dividends received deduction 10-630
. . New York City 505-413; 505-428
. personal income tax
. . government obligations 16-250
. . nonresidents 16-530

Document recording tax
. mortgages 37-052
. real property transfers 37-051
. stock transfers 37-053

Doing business in New York 10-075

Doing business in New York City 505-215

Domestic production activities deduction
. corporation tax 10-660
. personal income tax 16-085

Drop shipments
. sales and use taxes 60-340

Due dates
. returns 89-102
. . sales and use taxes 61-220

E

Education expenses
. college savings plans 16-255
. . excess distributions 16-050

Educational organizations
. property taxes 20-285
. sales and use taxes 60-580

Electricity
. sales and use taxes 60-750

Electronic filing
. returns and payments 89-106
. . New York City 589-106
. sales and use taxes 61-220

Electronic funds transfers 89-108
. New York City 589-108

Employer compensation expense tax (ECET) 10-380

Energy systems or facilities
. property taxes 20-165
. . New York City 520-165

Enterprise zones
. relocation assistance
. . New York City 507-005; 507-006
. sales and use taxes 60-360

Environmental taxes and fees 37-151

Estates and trusts
. computation of tax 15-215
. residency 15-205
. . New York City 515-215
. . nonresidents 15-215
. returns 89-102
. . electronic filing 89-106

Estimated tax 89-104
. New York City 589-104

Executive Mansion Trust Fund contributions
. personal income tax 16-220

Exempt organizations 10-245
. property taxes 20-285
. returns 89-102
. sales and use taxes 60-580
. unrelated business income 32-225
. . allocation 32-255
. . exempt entities 32-235
. . federal conformity 32-241
. . net operating losses 32-243
. . tax rate 32-265
. . taxable period 32-247

Exemptions
. personal income tax 15-535
. property taxes 20-505
. sales and use taxes
. . exemption certificates 61-020
. withholding of tax 16-660

F

Farming
. property taxes 20-115
. sales and use taxes 60-250

Federal adjusted gross income (AGI), New York
. . modifications 16-005; 16-205
. alimony 16-012; 16-207
. basis adjustments 16-215
. claim of right adjustment 16-225
. college savings plans 16-255
. . excess distributions 16-050
. death benefits 16-240
. depletion 16-037; 16-243
. depreciation 16-040; 16-245
. disability income 16-247
. domestic production activities deduction 16-085
. exempt interest 16-075
. flexible benefit program deferrals 16-065
. interest on federal and state obligations 16-250; 16-280
. investment expenses 16-080; 16-285
. military pay 16-308
. net operating loss 16-105
. new business investments 16-270
. organ donors 16-307
. previously taxed income 16-320
. retirement benefits 16-135; 16-345
. royalty payments
. . related parties 16-125; 16-330
. S corporation shareholders 16-113; 16-317
. state credit items 16-090
. state income taxes 16-145
. . refunds 16-360
. targeted business activities 16-350
. wages paid deduction 16-290

Federal conformity
. corporation tax 10-515
. New York City taxes 589-066
. personal income tax 15-515

Federal taxable income, New York modifications
. corporation tax 10-600; 10-800

Federal taxable income, New York City modifications
. banking institutions 510-401
. . additions to federal base 510-420
. . double depreciation 510-438
. . gain or loss adjustments 510-440
. . international banking facilities 510-433
. . subtractions from federal base 510-430
. corporation tax 505-401; 505-405
. . additions to federal base 505-422
. . subtractions from federal base 505-447

Federal/state issues
. comparison of federal and New York law
. . corporation tax 10-055
. . personal income tax 15-055
. doing business in another state
. . allocation and apportionment 11-505
. doing business in New York 10-075

Filing status 15-305

Financial institutions
. abandoned savings accounts and checks 37-351
. corporation tax 10-340; 10-525

Fishing
. sales and use taxes 60-250

Food products
. sales and use taxes 60-390

G

Gains and losses
. corporation tax
. . capital loss carryovers 10-635
. . emerging technology investments 10-640
. . mortgage recording tax credit 10-640
. . New York City 505-425
. . subsidiary capital 10-825
. personal income tax
. . new business investments 16-270
. . nonresidents 16-555

Gaming and wagering taxes 35-301

Gasoline taxes 40-001

Government transactions
. sales and use taxes 60-420

H

Hazardous waste fees 37-151

Health care facilities
. health facility tax 35-001
. property taxes 20-195

Homestead exemption
. property taxes 20-205

Housing redevelopment
. property taxes 20-215

I

Industrial business zones
. relocation assistance
. . New York City 507-006

Industrial property
. property taxes 20-265
. . New York City 520-265

Insurance companies 10-335; 10-525; 88-010
. basis of tax 88-020
. deductions 88-025
. exemption from tax 88-015
. fire insurance
. . New York City 585-101
. tax rates 88-030

Intangible property
. property taxes 20-230
. . New York City 520-230

Interest and penalties—see Penalties and interest

Interest expense
. corporation tax 10-645
. . New York City 505-413; 505-419

Interest income
. corporation tax 10-610; 10-815
. . New York City 505-413
. personal income tax
. . government obligations 16-075; 16-250; 16-280
. . nonresidents 16-530

Internet/electronic commerce
. sales and use taxes 60-445

Interstate transactions
. sales and use taxes
. . nexus 60-025

Investment expenses
. personal income tax 16-080; 16-285

Itemized deductions 15-545
. high-income limitation
. . New York City 515-405

L

Leases and rentals
. commercial rent or occupancy
. . New York City—see New York City commercial rent or
      occupancy tax
. property taxes 20-245
. real property transfer tax 37-051
. sales and use taxes 60-460
. . lodging 60-480
. . motor vehicles 60-570

Limited liability companies (LLCs) 10-240

Limited liability partnerships (LLPs) 10-225

Limited partnerships 10-225

Lodging
. hotel occupancy
. . New York City—see New York City hotel occupancy tax
. sales and use taxes 60-480

M

Mailing rules
. New York City taxes 589-110

Manufacturers and processors
. sales and use taxes 60-510

Medical supplies and drugs
. medical marijuana tax 35-251
. sales and use taxes 60-520

**Metropolitan Commuter Transportation District (MCTD)
   surcharge**
. corporation tax 10-380
. sales and use taxes 60-110
. telecommunication services 80-440
. transportation and transmission companies 80-040
. utilities 80-240

**Metropolitan Transportation Authority (MTA) payroll
   tax** 10-380

Military
. military pay 16-308
. residency 15-175

Mortgage recording tax 37-052
. New York City 557-005; 557-105

Motor fuel taxes 40-001
. audits
. . limitations period 89-144
. aviation fuel taxes 40-005
. diesel fuel taxes 40-003
. gasoline taxes 40-001
. sales and use taxes 60-560

Motor vehicles
. commercial and passenger transportation motor
      vehicle tax
. . New York City 550-002
. property taxes 20-275
. sales and use taxes 60-570

Motor vehicles—continued
. tax on resident owners
. . New York City 550-005

N

Natural gas
. sales and use taxes 60-750

Nazi persecution victims
. reparation payments 16-335

Net operating loss
. corporation tax 10-805
. . New York City 505-437
. personal income tax 16-105

New York City
. administration of taxes 515-020
. . administrative documents 589-064
. . conformity to federal law 589-066
. alcoholic beverage tax 535-105
. appeals
. . administrative appeals 589-234; 589-240
. . judicial appeals 589-236
. banking institutions—see New York City banking corporation
. . . tax
. cigarette and tobacco products taxes— see New York City
. . . cigarette and tobacco products taxes
. collection of tax
. . delinquent tax 589-164
. . installment payments 589-188
. . offers in compromise 589-186
. . surety requirement 589-178
. . voluntary disclosure program 589-192
. corporation tax—see New York City business corporation tax;
. . . New York City general corporation tax (prior law)
. insurance companies
. . fire department tax—see New York City fire department tax
. leases and rentals
. . commercial rentals—see New York City commercial rent or
. . . occupancy tax
. . hotel occupancy—see New York City hotel occupancy tax
. mortgage recording tax—see New York City mortgage
. . . recording tax
. motor vehicle taxes
. . commercial and passenger transportation motor
. . . vehicles 550-002
. . resident owners 550-005
. parking tax 560-030
. payment of tax 589-102
. . estimated tax 589-104
. . installment payments 589-188
. . mailing rules 589-110
. . payment methods 589-108
. penalties and interest
. . civil penalties 589-206
. . criminal penalties 589-208
. . interest rates 589-204
. personal income tax—see specific headings
. real property
. . property taxes—see New York City property taxes
. . transfer tax—see New York City real property transfer tax
. records maintenance 589-142
. refunds of tax 589-224
. returns 589-102
. . electronic filing 589-106
. . failure to file or pay tax 589-206
. . mailing rules 589-110
. rights of taxpayers
. . administrative appeals 589-234; 589-240
. . conciliation conferences 589-230
. . judicial appeals 589-236
. . refunds 589-224
. . small claims hearings 589-232
. sales and use taxes—see New York City sales and use taxes
. tax amnesty 589-192
. taxicabs—see New York City taxicab license transfer tax
. unincorporated businesses—see New York City
. . . unincorporated business tax
. utilities—see New York City utility tax

New York City banking corporation tax 510-201
. allocation and apportionment 510-601
. . allocation percentage 510-601
. . alternative entire net income 510-606

New York City banking corporation tax—continued
. allocation and apportionment—continued
. . Commissioner adjustment 510-608
. . deposits factor 510-604
. . international banking facilities 510-605
. . payroll factor 510-602
. . receipts factor 510-603
. . taxable assets 510-607
. double depreciation 510-438
. estimated tax 589-104
. exempt corporations 510-225
. federal base 510-401; 510-410
. . additions 510-420; 510-422
. . subtractions 510-430; 510-432
. gain or loss adjustments 510-440
. interest and dividends 510-422
. international banking facilities 510-433
. . allocation 510-605
. partner in unincorporated business 510-825
. relocation assistance 510-820
. returns 589-102
. tax rates 510-250

New York City business corporation tax 505-205
. air pollution control facilities 505-440
. allocation and apportionment 506-501
. . business allocation percentage 506-515
. . combined reports 506-503
. . discretionary allocation 506-540
. . investment allocation percentage 506-525
. . payroll factor 506-518
. . property factor 506-516
. . receipts factor 506-517
. . single receipts factor 506-505
. beer production credit 507-018
. biotechnology business credit 507-032
. capital gains, pre-1966 505-444
. depreciation 505-416; 505-431; 505-450
. dividends and interest 505-413; 505-428
. estimated tax 589-104
. exempt corporations 505-220
. machinery and equipment
. . sales and use tax credit 507-020; 507-030
. net operating loss 505-437
. nexus 505-215
. partner in unincorporated business 507-025
. pre-reform general corporation tax— see New York City
. . . general corporation tax (prior law)
. relocation assistance 507-005; 507-006; 507-015
. . real estate taxes 507-010
. research and development property 505-450
. returns 589-102
. royalties 505-417; 505-432
. subsidiary capital and income . . 505-419; 505-425; 505-490
. tax addbacks 505-410
. tax base 505-401; 505-405; 505-422
. . business capital tax base 505-460
. . income-plus-compensation tax base 505-470
. tax credits 507-001
. tax rates 505-251
. wages paid deduction 505-434

New York City cigarette and tobacco products taxes 555-101
. definitions 555-102
. drop shipments 555-108
. exemptions 555-201; 555-202
. liability for taxes 555-104
. monthly reports 555-603
. payment of tax 555-801
. penalties 555-811; 555-812; 555-813
. prohibited sales and purchases 555-504
. records and invoices 555-604
. returns 555-601; 555-606; 589-102
. stamps 555-802
. transporters 555-602
. use of cigarettes defined 555-107
. wholesale and retail dealers 555-501
. . license application and fees 555-502
. . receipt of cigarettes 555-806

New York City commercial rent or occupancy tax . . 532-110
. base rent 532-320
. own use of property 532-330
. properties in certain boroughs 532-340; 532-345
. relocation of business 532-350

New York City commercial rent or occupancy tax—continued
. base rent—continued
.. subleases 532-325
. computation of tax 532-310
. exemptions 532-210
. payment of tax 532-530
. records maintenance 532-540
. returns 532-510; 589-102
. tax credits 532-420
. tax rate 532-380

New York City fire department tax 585-101; 585-105
. computation of tax 585-201
. tax rate 585-150

New York City general corporation tax (prior law) . 505-205;
  505-410; 505-447
. air pollution control facilities 505-440
. allocation and apportionment 506-505
.. business allocation percentage 506-515
.. discretionary allocation 506-540
.. investment allocation percentage 506-525
.. payroll factor 506-518
.. property factor 506-516
.. receipts factor 506-517
. beer production credit 507-018
. biotechnology business credit 507-032
. business capital tax base 505-460
. combined reports 506-503
. depreciation 505-416; 505-431
. dividends 505-413; 505-428
. income-plus-compensation tax base 505-470
. interest 505-413
. machinery and equipment
.. sales and use tax credit 507-020; 507-030
. net operating loss 505-437
. nexus 505-215
. partner in unincorporated business 507-025
. relocation assistance 507-005; 507-006; 507-015
.. real estate taxes 507-010
. royalties 505-417; 505-432
. subsidiary capital 505-419; 505-425; 505-490
. tax addbacks 505-410
. tax base 505-405; 505-422
. tax credits 507-001
. tax rates 505-251
. wages paid deduction 505-434

New York City hotel occupancy tax 531-005
. basis of tax 531-025
. exemptions 531-015
. payment of tax 531-063
.. penalties 531-076
. records maintenance 531-053
. refunds of tax 531-081
. registration 531-045
. returns 531-056; 589-102
. tax rate 531-035

New York City mortgage recording tax . . . 557-005; 557-105
. computation of tax 557-151
. tax rates 557-110

New York City personal income tax— see specific headings

New York City property taxes 520-010
. assessment 520-605
.. valuation procedures 520-610
. classification of property 20-105; 520-105
. condominiums and cooperatives 520-140
. construction work in progress 520-145
. delinquent taxes 520-758
. disabled persons 520-155
. energy systems or facilities 520-165
. historic property 520-200
. homestead exemption 520-205
. household goods 520-210
. housing rehabilitation 520-215
. industrial property 520-265
. intangible property 520-230
. low-income housing 520-255
. payment of tax 520-756
.. penalties 520-770
. personal property 520-295
. real property 520-310
. senior citizens 520-205; 520-315
. situs of property 520-110

New York City property taxes—continued
. tax rates 520-405
. valuation methods 520-615
. valuation procedures 520-610
. veterans 520-335
. water works corporation 520-330

New York City real property transfer tax 556-105
. allocation 556-305
. basis of tax 556-301
. exemptions 556-201
. payment of tax 556-601
. real estate investment trusts 556-303
. returns 556-401
. tax rate 556-301

New York City sales and use taxes 560-001; 560-005
. exemptions 560-010
. parking tax 560-030
. payment of tax 560-025
. penalties 560-043
. registration 560-020
. returns 560-025; 589-102
. tax rates 560-015

New York City taxicab license transfer tax 536-005
. exemptions 536-105
. joint returns 536-305
. payment of tax 536-405
. tax rate 536-205

New York City unincorporated business tax 519-005;
  519-105
. accounting methods 519-240
. allocation of income 519-355
.. alternative methods 519-370
.. books and records method 519-360
.. business allocation percentage 519-365
.. investment income 519-357
.. real estate income and deductions 519-375
. beer production credit 507-018
. computation of income 519-205
. deductions 519-250
.. depletion 519-265
.. industrial waste and air pollution facilities 519-260
.. reasonable compensation 519-255
. estimated tax 589-104
. exemptions 519-305
. gross income 519-210
.. additions to federal gross income 519-225
.. subtractions from federal gross income 519-230
. partner's distributive share 519-445
. returns 589-102
. tax rate 519-120
. tax year 519-240
. taxable income 519-215
. unincorporated business defined 519-110

New York City utility tax
. gross income defined 580-302
. gross operating income defined 580-303
. machinery and equipment 580-502
. nonresidential energy user and energy redistributor
    rebates 580-503
. railroad income exclusion 580-201
. returns 589-102
. sales for resale 580-202
. tax rates 580-301
. telecommunications services 580-105
. utility defined 580-102
. vendors 580-103; 580-104
. wireless and emergency 911 surcharges 580-310

New York state militia
. payment for active service 16-308

Nexus
. corporation tax 10-075
.. New York City 505-215
. sales and use taxes 60-025

Nonprofit organizations—see Exempt organizations

Nonresidents 15-105
. business income 16-515
. estates and trusts 15-215
. filing thresholds 15-265
. gains and losses 16-555
. income from intangibles 16-530

Nonresidents—continued
. New York source income 16-505
. partners 16-565
. personal services compensation 16-570
. retirement income 16-545
. S corporation shareholders 16-565
. withholding of tax 16-615

Notice of deficiency 89-164
. New York City 589-164

O

Offers in compromise 89-186
. New York City 589-186

Opioid excise tax 35-276

Organ donors 16-307

P

Part-year residents 15-105
. business income 16-515
. New York source income 16-505

Partnerships
. allocation and apportionment 11-515; 11-520
. general partnerships 10-220
. limited liability partnerships 10-225
. limited partnerships 10-225
. partner's distributive share 15-185
.. nonresidents 16-565
. returns 89-102
.. electronic filing 89-106

Pass-through entities
. allocation and apportionment 11-515; 11-520
. distributive share taxation 15-185
. returns 89-102
.. estimated tax 89-104

Payment of tax
. electronic filing 89-106
. electronic funds transfer 89-108
. estimated tax 89-104
. New York City—see under New York City
. payment methods 89-108
. penalties and interest—see Penalties and interest
. property taxes 20-756
. refunds 89-224
.. New York City 589-224
. sales and use taxes 61-220

Penalties and interest 89-202
. abatement 89-210
. civil penalties 89-206
.. New York City 589-206
. criminal penalties
.. New York City 589-208
. interest rates 89-204
.. New York City 589-204
. property taxes 20-752; 20-770

Pensions and annuities 16-345

Personal exemptions 15-535

Personal income tax—see specific headings

Personal property
. property taxes 20-295; 20-645
.. New York City 520-295

Personal services
. nonresidents 16-570
. sales and use taxes 60-665

Property taxes
. abatement 20-810
. agriculture 20-115
. assessment
.. appeals 20-906
.. valuation procedures 20-610
. classification of property 20-105
. computers and software 20-135
. construction work in progress 20-145
. energy systems or devices 20-165
. exemptions 20-205; 20-505

Property taxes—continued
. health care facilities 20-195
. homestead exemption 20-205
. housing organizations 20-215
. industrial property 20-265
. intangible property 20-230
. motor vehicles 20-275
. multiple dwelling units 20-215
. New York City—see New York City property taxes
. nonprofit organizations 20-285
. payment of tax 20-756; 20-758
.. interest 20-752
.. penalties 20-770
. personal property 20-295; 20-645
. real property defined 20-310
. renter liability 20-245
. storm or flood damage 20-640
. tax rates 20-405
. utility property 20-330
. valuation methods 20-615
. valuation procedures 20-610; 20-640

Public Law 86-272 10-075
. New York City 505-215

Public utilities—see Utilities

Q

Qualified subchapter S subsidiaries (QSSSs) 10-215

R

Railroads
. sales and use taxes 60-740

Rates of tax—see Tax rates

Real estate investments trusts (REITs) 10-525

Real property
. mortgage recording tax 37-052
.. New York City 557-005
. property taxes—see Property taxes
. transfer tax 37-051
.. New York City 556-105

Refunds of tax 89-224
. corporation tax
.. subtraction from federal taxable income 10-840
. New York City 589-224
. personal income tax
.. state and local taxes 16-360
. sales and use taxes 61-610

Regulated industries
. banks and financial institutions 10-340
. insurance companies 10-335

Regulated investment companies (RICs) 10-525

Related parties
. combined reports 11-550
. interest expense
.. New York City 505-419
. royalty payments
.. corporation tax 10-620; 10-835
.. New York City 505-417; 505-432
.. personal income tax 16-125; 16-330
. subsidiary capital income
.. New York City 505-425

Religious organizations
. property taxes 20-285
. sales and use taxes 60-580

Relocation and employment assistance
. banking institutions 510-820
. corporation tax
.. New York City 507-005; 507-006; 507-010; 507-015

Reparation payments 16-335

Resales
. sales and use taxes 60-650

Research and development property
. corporation tax
.. New York City 505-450

Residency 15-105; 15-260

Residency—continued
. estates and trusts 15-205
. . New York City 515-215
. resident defined 15-110
. . New York City 515-210

Retaliatory tax
. insurance companies 88-010

Retirement benefits 16-345
. employer contributions 16-135
. lump-sum distributions 15-355
. . New York City 515-220
. nonresidents 16-545

Returns 89-102
. aviation fuel taxes 40-005
. cigarette tax 55-001
. . New York City 555-606
. combined reports 11-550
. . New York City 506-503
. corporation tax 89-102
. diesel fuel taxes 40-003
. due dates 89-102
. electronic filing 89-106
. . New York City 589-106
. estates and trusts 89-102
. estimated tax 89-104
. exempt organizations 89-102
. filing status 15-305
. filing thresholds 15-260
. motor fuel taxes 40-001
. New York City 589-102
. nonresidents and part-year residents 15-105; 15-265
. partnerships 89-102
. penalties 89-206
. . abatement 89-210
. personal income tax 89-102
. real property transfer tax
. . New York City 556-401
. return preparers
. . penalties 89-206
. S corporations 89-102
. sales and use taxes 61-220
. tobacco products tax 55-005
. . New York City 555-606
. withholding of tax 89-102

Rights of taxpayers
. administrative appeals 89-234
. . limitations period 89-240
. conciliation conferences 89-230
. New York City—see under New York City

Royalty payments
. related parties
. . corporation tax 10-620; 10-835
. . New York City 505-417; 505-432
. . personal income tax 16-125; 16-330

S

S corporations 10-215; 10-525
. allocation and apportionment 11-515; 11-520
. New York City—see New York City general corporation tax
   (prior law)
. returns 89-102
. shareholders 15-185
. . distributive share reporting 16-113
. . modification to federal AGI 16-317
. . nonresidents 16-565
. tax rates 10-380

Sales and use taxes 60-020
. administrative remedies 61-620
. admissions, entertainment and dues 60-230
. advertising 60-240
. agriculture 60-250
. aircraft 60-740
. alcoholic beverages 60-260
. audits
. . limitations period 89-144
. basis of tax 61-110
. boats and vessels 60-740
. clothing and footwear 60-290
. computers and software 60-310
. construction materials and services 60-330

Sales and use taxes—continued
. drop shipments 60-340
. enterprise zones 60-360
. exemption certificates 61-020
. food products and grocery items 60-390
. government transactions 60-420
. internet/electronic commerce 60-445
. leases and rentals 60-460
. local tax rates 61-735
. lodging 60-480
. manufacturers, processors or refiners 60-510
. medical supplies and drugs 60-520
. motor fuels 60-560
. motor vehicles 60-570
. New York City—see New York City sales and use taxes
. nexus 60-025
. nonprofit organizations 60-580
. payment of tax 61-220
. refunds or credits 61-610
. returns 61-220; 89-102
. . electronic filing 89-106
. sales for resale 60-650
. sales tax transactions 60-020
. services 60-665
. tax credits 61-270
. tax rate 60-110
. taxes paid to another state 61-270
. transportation equipment and services 60-740
. use tax transactions 60-020
. vendor registration 61-240

Savings and loan associations 10-340

School tax relief (STAR) program
. property taxes 20-205

Senior citizens
. property taxes
. . New York City 520-205; 520-315

September 11 Victim Compensation Fund
. exemption of payments 16-335

Social security benefits 16-345

Sport utility vehicles
. depreciation 16-040

Standard deduction 15-540

START-UP NY program
. sales and use taxes 60-580

Stock transfer tax 37-053

Surplus lines tax
. insurance companies 88-010

T

Tax credits—see Credits against tax

Tax incentives
. sales and use taxes 60-360

Tax liens—see Liens for taxes

Tax payments—see Payment of tax

Tax rates
. aviation fuel taxes 40-005
. cigarette tax 55-001
. . New York City 555-101
. corporate income tax 10-380
. . New York City 505-251
. diesel fuel taxes 40-003
. insurance companies 88-030
. mortgage recording tax
. . New York City 557-110
. motor fuel taxes 40-001
. personal income tax 15-355; 515-300
. . New York City 515-301; 515-315; 515-320
. property taxes 20-405
. . New York City 520-405
. real property transfer tax
. . New York City 556-301
. sales and use taxes 60-110
. . local rates 61-735
. . New York City 560-015
. tobacco products tax 55-005
. . New York City 555-101

Taxicabs and for-hire vehicles
. congestion surcharge 35-326
. taxicab license transfer tax
. . New York City—see New York City taxicab license transfer
tax
. taxicab trip tax 35-051

Taxpayer rights and remedies—see Rights of taxpayers

Telecommunication services 80-410
. exclusions from tax 80-420
. interstate private service providers 80-435
. MCTD surcharge 80-440
. refunds and credits 80-450
. tax rate 80-430
. telecommunication services defined 80-410
. . New York City 580-105
. wireless and emergency 911 surcharges . . 80-445; 80-530
. . New York City 580-310

Telecommuting employees
. personal services compensation 16-570

Third-party sales
. sales and use taxes 60-340

Tobacco products tax 55-005
. New York City—see New York City cigarette and tobacco
products taxes

Transportation and transmission companies 80-010
. exemption from tax 80-020
. gross earnings tax 80-035
. issued capital stock tax 80-030
. MCTD surcharge 80-040

Transportation equipment and services
. congestion surcharge 35-326
. sales and use taxes 60-740
. transportation network company fee 35-351

Trucks and trailers
. sales and use taxes 60-740

U

Unclaimed property 37-351

Unincorporated businesses
. New York City—see New York City unincorporated business
tax

Unitary business group
. corporation tax 11-550
. . New York City 506-503

Unrelated business income 32-225
. allocation 32-255
. exempt entities 32-235
. exempt organizations 10-245
. federal conformity 32-241
. net operating losses 32-243
. tax rate 32-265
. taxable period 32-247

Use tax 60-020

Utilities
. local taxes 80-501
. . cable television systems 80-510
. . emergency telephone system surcharge 80-530

Utilities—continued
. local taxes—continued
. . Erie County surcharge 80-540
. . MCTD surcharge 80-240
. New York City—see New York City utility tax
. property taxes 20-330
. sales and use taxes 60-750
. telecommunication services 80-410
. . exclusions from tax 80-420
. . interstate private service providers 80-435
. . MCTD surcharge 80-440
. . refunds and credits 80-450
. . tax rate 80-430
. . wireless services surcharge 80-445
. utility defined 80-210
. utility services 80-210
. . exemption from tax 80-220
. . tax rate 80-230

V

Valuation of property
. assessment procedures 20-610
. . New York City 520-610
. real property 20-640
. valuation methods 20-615
. . New York City 520-615

Vendor registration
. sales and use taxes 61-240

Veterans
. property taxes
. . New York City 520-335

Voluntary disclosure program
. New York City 589-192

W

Wage income
. nonresidents 16-570
. withholding of tax 16-615

Waterfront Commission payroll tax 35-101

Withholding of tax 16-605
. New York City 516-605
. nonwage income 16-655
. penalties 89-206
. returns 89-102
. tax tables 16-620
. . New York City 516-610
. wages 16-615
. withholding exemptions 16-660

Work in progress, construction
. property taxes 20-145
. . New York City 520-145

Y

Yonkers
. nonresident earnings tax 35-201
. resident income tax surcharge 35-151